THE OFFICIAL ACT® PREP GUIDE

THE OFFICIAL ACT® PREP GUIDE

The **ONLY** Official Prep Guide
from the Makers of the ACT

ACT®

WILEY

ACT endorses the *Code of Fair Testing Practices in Education* and the *Code of Professional Responsibilities in Educational Measurement*, guides to the conduct of those involved in educational testing. ACT is committed to ensuring that each of its testing programs upholds the guidelines in each *Code*. A copy of each *Code* may be obtained free of charge from ACT Customer Services. (70), P.O. Box 1008, Iowa City, IA 52243-1008, 319-337-1429.

ACT Publications
P.O. Box 168
Iowa City, Iowa 52243-0168

ISBN 978-1-394-19650-0
ePub 978-1-394-19651-7

Cover design: Wiley
Printed in the United States of America
PB Printing   SKY10040057_031523

Contents

Preface

You want to do your best on the ACT® test, and this book can help. It supplements our free booklet, *Preparing for the ACT,* and our *ACT Online Prep*™ (a web-based preparation program for the ACT). This book features six actual ACT tests—all of which include the optional writing test—which you can use for practice, and it gives detailed explanatory answers to every question to help you review.

Using this book will help you become familiar with the following:

- The content of the ACT
- The procedures you'll follow when you're actually taking the ACT
- The types of questions you can expect to find on the ACT
- Suggestions on how to approach the questions
- General test-taking strategies

This book is intended to help you **know what to expect** when you take the ACT so you can relax and concentrate on doing your best. The more you know about what to expect on any test you take, the more likely it is that your performance on that test will accurately reflect your overall preparation and achievement in the areas it measures. Knowing what to expect can help reduce any nervousness you may feel as you approach the test.

The ACT measures your understanding of what you've been taught in core high school courses that you should have completed by the time you finish high school. Because it has taken you years to learn all this material, it might take you some time to review for the ACT. You can't expect to cram for the ACT in a night or two. However, any review should be helpful to you, even if it just makes you more comfortable when you actually sit down to take the ACT. We hope this book helps you to gauge how much reviewing you feel you need to do and identify subject areas on which to focus your efforts.

Your purchase of *The Official ACT® Prep Guide* includes access to eight full-length, digital practice tests via the Wiley Online Platform. Use these assets to simulate the test day experience or customize your practice using the pool of questions available. Detailed rationales and official explanations are provided for every question from the makers of the ACT® test.

Terms of Use: The PIN code included with this book offers access to the companion online course for 12 months from the date of activation for the original purchaser only. ACT and Wiley are not responsible for delivering PIN codes to customers who borrow or purchase used copies of this study guide. The unique PIN code included with this book grants access only to the companion online course and not to other Wiley or ACT-owned password protected websites.

Online course access is subject to limitations and may not be available indefinitely. Continuity of service may be affected by various factors such as maintenance, upgrades, technical difficulties, or a change in market demand. To maximize use of all online prep materials included with your book, it is recommended that you activate your one-time PIN as soon as you begin your prep journey for your upcoming ACT test.

How This Book Is Arranged

This book is divided into five parts:

Part One: **Getting Acquainted with the ACT.** Chapters in this part introduce the ACT, explain how to prepare, and present general test-taking techniques and strategies for you to consider.

Part Two: **Taking and Evaluating Your First Practice Test.** This part includes a practice test along with guidance on how to use the test to identify areas where you may need to invest more time and effort.

Part Three: **Improving Your Score.** Chapters in this part present test-taking strategies tailored for each subject test—English, math, reading, and science—along with suggestions for taking the optional writing test.

Part Four: **Taking Additional Practice Tests.** In this part, you have the opportunity to take five additional practice tests, see the results, and interpret your scores to determine how well prepared you are to take the ACT.

Part Five: **Moving Forward to Test Day.** This part prepares you for test day by explaining how to register for the ACT and describing what to expect on the day of the test, so you show up on time with everything you need.

The parts are identified by bars on the edge of their right-hand pages.

Before You Begin

There is no standardized way to prepare for the ACT. Everyone learns and prepares differently. Some people prepare best when they are by themselves. Others need to work with fellow students to do their best. Still others function best in a structured class with a teacher leading them through their work. Use whatever method works best for you. Keep in mind, though, that when you actually take the ACT, it will be just you and the test.

As you use this book to prepare for the ACT, consider working in 1-hour segments (except when you're taking the timed practice tests, of course). If you want to invest more than 1 hour a day, that's fine, but take breaks to stretch and give your mind a chance to absorb the material. Toiling to the point of burnout is counterproductive.

Part One:
Getting Acquainted with the ACT Test

In This Part

This part introduces you to the ACT, the five tests that it is composed of (English, mathematics, reading, science, and the optional writing test), and testing procedures. It also features test-taking strategies and skills that apply to all of the component tests. Specifically, you will do the following:

Find out what is covered on the tests.

Determine when you can use a calculator and the types of calculators you are permitted to use and prohibited from using.

Get a preview of what you can expect on test day.

Obtain guidance on how to prepare for test day.

Learn test-taking strategies that may improve your scores on all of the tests.

Chapter 1:
About the ACT

The ACT® measures your achievement in core academic areas important for your college and career success: English, math, reading, science, and (optionally) writing. It isn't an IQ test—it doesn't measure your basic intelligence. It's an achievement test that's been carefully designed—using surveys of classroom teachers, reviews of curriculum guides for schools all over the country, and advice from curriculum specialists and college faculty members—to be one of several effective tools for evaluating your college and career readiness.

The individual tests that make up the ACT consist of questions that measure your knowledge and skills. You're not required to memorize facts or vocabulary to do well on the ACT. Of course, all the terms, formulas, and other information you learned in your classes will be useful to you when you take the ACT. However, last-minute cramming (such as memorizing 5,000 vocabulary words or the entire periodic table of elements) won't directly improve your performance on the ACT.

Description of the Full ACT Test

The full ACT consists of four multiple-choice tests—English, mathematics, reading, and science—and an optional writing test. Topics covered on these five tests correspond very closely to topics covered in typical high school classes. Table 1.1 gives you a snapshot of all five tests.

Table 1.1: ACT Tests			
Test	**Questions**	**Time**	**Content Covered**
English	75 questions	45 minutes	Measures standard written English knowledge and skills along with English language conventions
Mathematics	60 questions	60 minutes	Measures mathematical skills students have typically acquired in courses taken up to the beginning of grade 12
Reading	40 questions	35 minutes	Measures reading comprehension
Science	40 questions	35 minutes	Measures the interpretation, analysis, evaluation, reasoning, and problem-solving skills required in the natural sciences
Writing (optional)	1 prompt	40 minutes	Measures writing skills emphasized in high school English classes and in entry-level college composition courses

Questions on the tests are intended to help assess college and career readiness. The following sections provide an overview of what you should know to perform well on each test. For additional details, check out the ACT College and Career Readiness Standards presented in chapter 12.

English Test

75 questions, 45 minutes

The English test consists of five essays or passages, each of which is accompanied by a sequence of multiple-choice test questions. Different passage types are employed to provide a variety of rhetorical situations. Passages are chosen not only for their appropriateness in assessing writing skills but also to reflect students' interests and experiences.

You will receive four scores for the ACT English test: a total test score based on all 75 questions and three reporting category scores based on the following:

- Production of Writing

- Knowledge of Language

- Conventions of Standard English

Production of Writing

Production of Writing questions test knowledge and skills in two areas of English composition:

- Topic development in terms of purpose and focus

- Organization, unity, and cohesion

Topic Development in Terms of Purpose and Focus

Examples of knowledge and skills tested include the following:

- Determine the relevance of material to the topic or the focus of the passage or paragraph.

- Identify the purpose of a word or phrase (for example, to identify a person, to define a term, or to help describe an object).

- Determine whether a passage has met a specific goal.

- Use a word, phrase, or sentence to accomplish a specific purpose, such as to convey a feeling or attitude or to illustrate a given statement.

Organization, Unity, and Cohesion

Examples of knowledge and skills tested include the following:

- Determine the need for transition words or phrases to define relationships in terms of time or logic.

- Determine the most logical place for a sentence in a paragraph or in the passage as a whole.

- Provide a suitable conclusion for a paragraph or passage.

- Provide a suitable introduction for a paragraph or passage.

- Rearrange sentences in a paragraph or rearrange paragraphs in a passage to establish a logical flow.

- Determine the most logical place to divide a paragraph to achieve a stated goal.

Knowledge of Language

Knowledge of Language questions test your ability to clearly and succinctly express yourself in written English. Knowledge and skills tested include the following:

- Revise unclear, clumsy, and confusing writing.

- Delete redundant and wordy material.

- Revise an expression to make it conform to the style and tone used throughout the passage.

- Determine logical connections between clauses.

- Choose the most appropriate word or phrase in terms of the sentence content.

Conventions of Standard English

Conventions of Standard English questions test knowledge and skills such as the following:

- Determine the need for punctuation or conjunctions to join clauses or to correct awkward-sounding fragments, fused sentences, and faulty subordination and coordination of clauses.

- Recognize and correct inappropriate shifts in verb tense.

- Recognize and correct disturbances in sentence structure, such as faulty placement of adjectives, participial phrase fragments, missing or incorrect relative pronouns, dangling or misplaced modifiers, faulty parallelism, and run-on sentences.

- Maintain consistent and logical verb tense and voice and pronoun person within a paragraph or passage.

Note: Spelling and the rote recall of grammar rules are not tested.

Mathematics Test

60 questions, 60 minutes

The mathematics test presents multiple-choice questions that require you to use reasoning skills to solve practical math problems. The material covered on the test emphasizes the major content areas that are prerequisites to successful performance in entry-level courses in college mathematics. Some questions may belong to a set of several questions (for example, several questions about the same graph or chart).

Conceptual knowledge and computational skills are assumed as background for the problems, but recall of complex formulas and extensive computation is not required.

Nine scores are reported for the ACT mathematics test: a total test score based on all 60 questions and eight reporting category scores based on specific mathematical knowledge and skills. The reporting categories are:

- Preparing for Higher Mathematics, which includes separate scores for Number and Quantity, Algebra, Functions, Geometry, and Statistics and Probability

- Integrating Essential Skills

- Modeling

Preparing for Higher Mathematics

This category captures the more recent mathematics that students are learning, starting when they begin using algebra as a general way of expressing and solving equations. This category is divided into the following five subcategories:

- Number and Quantity
- Algebra
- Functions
- Geometry
- Statistics and Probability

Number and Quantity

Math questions in this category test your knowledge of numbers and fundamental math concepts and operations, including the following:

- Perform calculations on whole numbers and decimals.
- Recognize equivalent fractions and fractions in lowest terms.
- Locate rational numbers (whole numbers, fractions, decimals, and mixed numbers) on the number line.
- Recognize single-digit factors of a number.
- Identify a digit's place value.
- Demonstrate knowledge of elementary number concepts, including rounding, ordering of decimals, pattern identification, primes, and greatest common factor.
- Write powers of 10 using exponents.
- Comprehend the concept of length on the number line, and find the distance between two points.
- Understand absolute value in terms of distance.
- Find the distance between two points with the same x-coordinate or y-coordinate in the coordinate plane.
- Add, subtract, and multiply matrices (tables of numbers).
- Order fractions.
- Find and use the least common multiple.
- Demonstrate knowledge of complex numbers and multiply two complex numbers.

- Comprehend the concept of irrational numbers, such as π.

- Apply properties of rational exponents.

- Use relations involving addition, subtraction, and scalar multiplication of vectors and matrices.

- Analyze and draw conclusions based on number concepts.

Algebra and Functions

The mathematics test contains questions that require knowledge of and skills in algebra, functions, or both. *Algebra* involves formulas and equations in which letters and other symbols are used to represent unknown or unspecified values. A *function* is a rule, equation, or expression that produces exactly one output for any given input; for example, $2x$ is a function in that any input used for x results in an output that is twice the input's value.

Algebra

Algebra knowledge and skills tested include the following:

- Demonstrate knowledge of basic expressions, such as $b + g$ to identify a total.

- Solve equations in the form $x + a = b$, where a and b are whole numbers or decimals.

- Use substitution to evaluate mathematical expressions.

- Combine like terms, such as $2x + 5x$.

- Add and subtract algebraic expressions.

- Multiply two binomials.

- Match inequalities with their graphs on the number line.

- Demonstrate knowledge of slope.

- Solve real-world problems by using first-degree equations.

- Solve inequalities.

- Match linear or compound inequalities with their graphs on the number line.

- Add, subtract, and multiply polynomials.

- Solve quadratic equations.

- Factor quadratics.

- Work with squares/square roots and cubes/cube roots of numbers.

- Work with scientific notation.

- Solve problems involving positive integer exponents.

- Determine the slope of a line from an equation.

- Solve linear inequalities when the method involves reversing the inequality sign.

- Solve systems of two linear equations.

- Solve absolute value equations and inequalities.

- Match quadratic inequalities with their graphs on the number line.

Functions

Questions that involve functions test your ability to do the following:

- Understand the concept of a function having a well-defined output value at each valid input value.

- Extend a given pattern by a few terms for patterns that have a constant increase or decrease between terms or that have a constant factor between terms.

- Evaluate linear, quadratic, and polynomial functions expressed in function notation at the integer level.

- Interpret statements that use function notation in terms of their context.

- Find the domain of polynomial functions and rational functions.

- Find the range of polynomial functions.

- Find where a rational function's graph has a vertical asymptote.

- Use function notation for simple functions of two variables.

- Relate a graph to a situation described qualitatively in terms of faster change or slower change.

- Build functions for relations that are inversely proportional or exponential.

- Find a recursive expression for the general term in a sequence described recursively.

- Evaluate composite functions of integer values.

- Compare actual values and the values of a modeling function to judge model fit and compare models.

- Demonstrate knowledge of geometric sequences.

- Demonstrate knowledge of unit circle trigonometry.

- Match graphs of basic trigonometric functions with their equations.

- Use trigonometric concepts and basic identities to solve problems.

- Demonstrate knowledge of logarithms.

- Write an expression for the composite of two simple functions.

Algebra and Functions

Questions that involve both algebra and functions test your ability to do the following:

- Solve problems using whole numbers and decimals in the context of money.

- Solve one- or two-step arithmetic problems using positive rational numbers, such as percent.

- Relate a graph to a situation described quantitatively.

- Solve two- or three-step arithmetic problems involving concepts such as rate and proportion, sales tax, percentage off, and estimation.

- Perform word-to-symbol translations.

- Solve multistep arithmetic problems that involve planning or converting units of measure (for example, feet per second to miles per hour).

- Build functions and write expressions, equations, or inequalities with a single variable for common pre-algebra settings, such as rate and distance problems and problems that involve proportions.

- Match linear equations with their graphs in the coordinate plane.

- Solve word problems containing several rates, proportions, or percentages.

- Build functions and write expressions, equations, and inequalities for common algebra settings.

- Interpret and use information from graphs in the coordinate plane.

- Solve complex math problems involving percent of increase or decrease or requiring integration of several concepts.

- Build functions and write expressions, equations, and inequalities when the process requires planning and/or strategic manipulation.

- Analyze and draw conclusions based on properties of algebra and/or functions.

- Analyze and draw conclusions based on information from graphs in the coordinate plane.

- Identify characteristics of graphs based on a set of conditions or on a general equation, such as $y = ax^2 + c$.

- Given an equation or function, find an equation or function whose graph is a translation by specified amounts up or down.

Geometry

Geometry questions are based primarily on the mathematical properties and relationships of points, lines, angles, two-dimensional shapes, and three-dimensional objects. Knowledge and skills tested include the following:

- Estimate the length of a line segment based on other lengths in a geometric figure.

- Calculate the length of a line segment based on the lengths of other line segments that go in the same direction (for example, overlapping line segments and parallel sides of polygons with only right angles).

- Perform common conversions of money and of length, weight, mass, and time within a measurement system (for example, inches to feet and hours to minutes).

- Compute the area and perimeter of triangles, rectangles, and other polygons.

- Use properties of parallel lines to find the measure of an angle.

- Exhibit knowledge of basic angle properties and special sums of angle measures (for example, 90°, 180°, and 360°).

- Use geometric formulas when all necessary information is given.

- Locate points in the coordinate plane.

- Translate points up, down, left, and right in the coordinate plane.

- Use several angle properties to find an unknown angle measure.

- Count the number of lines of symmetry of a geometric figure.

- Use symmetry of isosceles triangles to find unknown side lengths or angle measures.

- Recognize that real-world measurements are typically imprecise and that an appropriate level of precision is related to the measuring device and procedure.

- Compute the perimeter of composite geometric figures with unknown side lengths.

- Compute the area and circumference of circles.

- Given the length of two sides of a right triangle, find the length of the third side.

- Express the sine, cosine, and tangent of an angle in a right triangle as a ratio of given side lengths.

- Determine the slope of a line from points or a graph.

- Find the midpoint of a line segment.

- Find the coordinates of a point rotated 180° around a given center point.

- Use relationships involving area, perimeter, and volume of geometric figures to compute another measure (for example, surface area for a cube of a given volume and simple geometric probability).

- Use the Pythagorean theorem.

- Apply properties of 30°–60°–90°, 45°–45°–90°, similar, and congruent triangles.

- Apply basic trigonometric ratios to solve right-triangle problems.

- Use the distance formula.

- Use properties of parallel and perpendicular lines to determine an equation of a line or coordinates of a point.

- Find the coordinates of a point reflected across a vertical or horizontal line or across $y = x$.

- Find the coordinates of a point rotated 90° across a vertical.

- Recognize special characteristics of parabolas and circles (for example, the vertex of a parabola and the center or radius of a circle).

- Use relationships among angles, arcs, and distances in a circle.

- Compute the area of composite geometric figures when planning and/or visualization is required.

- Use scale factors to determine the magnitude of a size change.

- Analyze and draw conclusions based on a set of conditions.

- Solve multistep geometry problems that involve integrating concepts, planning, and/or visualization.

Statistics and Probability

Statistics is a branch of mathematics that involves the collection and analysis of large quantities of numerical data. *Probability* is a branch of mathematics that involves calculating the likelihood of an event occurring or a condition existing. Statistics and Probability questions test your ability to do the following:

- Calculate averages.

- Read and extract relevant data from a basic table or chart, and use the data in a computation.

- Use the relationship between the probability of an event and the probability of its complement.

- Calculate the missing data value given the average and all other data values.

- Translate from one representation of data to another (for example, from a bar graph to a circle graph).

- Compute probabilities.

- Describe events as combinations of other events (for example, using *and*, *or*, and *not*).

- Demonstrate knowledge of and apply counting techniques.

- Calculate the average given the frequency counts of all the data values.

- Manipulate data from tables and charts.

- Use Venn diagrams in counting.

- Recognize that when data summaries are reported in the real world, results are often rounded and must be interpreted as having appropriate precision.

- Recognize that when a statistical model is used, model values typically differ from actual values.

- Calculate or use a weighted average.

- Interpret and use information from tables and charts, including two-way frequency tables.

- Recognize the concepts of conditional and joint probability and of independence expressed in real-world contexts.

- Distinguish among mean, median, and mode for a list of numbers.

- Analyze and draw conclusions based on information from tables and charts, including two-way frequency tables.

- Understand the role of randomization in surveys, experiments, and observational studies.

- Demonstrate knowledge of conditional and joint probability.

- Recognize that part of the power of statistical modeling comes from looking at regularity in the differences between actual values and model values.

Integrating Essential Skills

Students learn some of the most useful mathematics before grade 8: rates and percentages; proportional relationships; area, surface area, and volume; average and median; expressing numbers in different ways; using expressions to represent quantities and equations to capture relationships; and other topics. Each year, students should grow in what they can accomplish using learning from prior years. Students should be able to solve problems of increasing complexity, combine skills in longer chains of steps, apply skills in more varied contexts, understand more connections, and increase fluency. In order to assess whether students have had appropriate growth, all questions in this reporting category focus on the higher-level cognitive skills, such as making decisions on how to approach a problem, comparing, reasoning, planning, applying algebra strategically, drawing conclusions, solving novel problems, and the like.

Modeling

Modeling uses mathematics to represent with a model an analysis of an actual, empirical situation. Models often help us predict or understand the actual. However, sometimes knowledge of the actual helps us understand the model, such as when addition is introduced to students as a model of combining two groups. The Modeling reporting category represents all questions that involve producing, interpreting, understanding, evaluating, and improving models. Each modeling question is also counted in the other appropriate reporting categories previously identified. Thus, the Modeling reporting category is an overall measure of how well a student uses modeling skills across mathematical topics.

Reading Test

40 questions, 35 minutes

The reading test comprises four sections, each containing one long or two shorter prose passages that are representative of the level and kinds of text commonly encountered in first-year college curricula. Passages include literary narratives and informational texts from the humanities, natural sciences, and social sciences. One informational passage may include a mixed-information format—visual and quantitative elements (like graphs, diagrams, tables) that acccompany the passage and contain additional information related to the passage topic. The passages vary in terms of how challenging and complex they are.

Four scores are reported for the ACT reading test: a total test score based on all 40 questions, and three reporting category scores based on specific knowledge and skills. You will also see an Understanding Complex Texts indicator.

The reading test measures your reading comprehension in three general areas:

- Key Ideas and Details
- Craft and Structure
- Integration of Knowledge and Ideas

Key Ideas and Details

These questions focus primarily on identifying key details in the passage and grasping the overall meaning of the passage. Reading skills tested fall into these categories:

- Close reading
- Central ideas, themes, and summaries

Close Reading

Close-reading skills involve your ability to do the following:

- Locate and interpret facts or details in a passage.
- Draw logical conclusions.

- Paraphrase statements.

- Identify the sequence of events or place events in their correct sequence.

- Identify stated or implied cause-effect relationships.

- Identify stated or implied comparative relationships.

Central Ideas, Themes, and Summaries

Questions that focus on central ideas, themes, and summaries challenge your ability to do the following:

- Identify or infer the main idea of a paragraph.

- Identify or infer the central idea or theme of a passage.

- Differentiate key ideas from secondary ideas.

- Summarize key ideas and information.

Craft and Structure

Some reading questions go beyond the meaning of the passage to challenge your understanding of how the author crafted and structured the passage. Reading skills tested in this area are divided into three categories:

- Word meanings and word choice

- Text structure

- Purpose and point of view

Word Meanings and Word Choice

Reading questions may focus on the meaning or impact of a word or phrase, challenging your ability to do the following:

- Use context to determine the meaning of a word or phrase, including determining technical, academic, and connotative meanings.

- Understand the implication of a word or phrase and of descriptive language.

- Determine the meaning of figurative language in context.

Text Structure

Text-structure questions ask you to analyze how various structural elements function to serve a specific purpose in the passage. To answer such questions, you may need to do one of the following:

- Analyze the overall structure of a passage.

- Analyze how one or more sentences in a passage relate to the whole passage.

- Identify or infer the function of one or more paragraphs in a passage.

- Determine the function or effect of specific words or phrases in a passage.

Purpose and Point of View

The reading test may include questions that challenge your ability to do the following:

- Identify or infer the author's or narrator's purpose or intent.

- Determine how an author's or narrator's purpose or intent shapes the content and style of the passage.

- Recognize an author's or narrator's point of view.

Integration of Knowledge and Ideas

Reading questions may require that you go beyond simply reading and understanding a passage. Some questions will require analyzing two passages. Others may ask you to integrate information from different formats (like graphs, diagrams, and tables). Reading skills tested in the area of Integration of Knowledge and Ideas are divided into three categories:

- Arguments

- Multiple texts

- Mixed-information format

Arguments

Questions in this category may test your ability to do the following:

- Identify or infer the central claim being presented in the passage.

- Analyze how one or more sentences offer reasons for or support the claim.

- Differentiate between fact and opinion.

- Recognize errors in reasoning or identify information that would strengthen or weaken a claim in the passage.

Multiple Texts

Multiple-text questions involve reading two passages and may test your ability to do the following:

- Make connections between people, relationships, and ideas across the two passages.

- Draw logical conclusions using information from the two passages.

- Compare text structure, purpose, and perspective in the two passages.

Mixed-Information Format

Though these questions are not as common as questions about arguments and multiple texts, you may also encounter questions that ask you to understand mixed-information formats. These questions test your ability to do the following:

- Identify and interpret information represented in quantitative or graphic formats (e.g., graphs, diagrams, tables).

- Draw conclusions and compare information across a passage and graphic element.

Science Test

40 questions, 35 minutes

The science test measures the interpretation, analysis, evaluation, reasoning, and problem-solving skills required in the natural sciences: life science/biology; physical science/chemistry, physics; and earth and space science.

The test assumes that students are in the process of taking the core science course of study (three years or more) that will prepare them for college-level work and have completed a course in earth science and/or physical science and a course in biology. The test presents several sets of scientific information, each followed by a number of multiple-choice test questions. The scientific information is conveyed in the form of reading passages and graphic representations—graphs (charts), tables, and illustrations.

Four scores are reported for the ACT science test: a total test score based on all 40 questions and three reporting category scores based on scientific knowledge, skills, and practices. The reporting categories are:

- Interpretation of Data

- Scientific Investigation

- Evaluation of Models, Inferences, and Experimental Results

Interpretation of Data

Interpretation of Data involves the following skills:

- Select data from a data presentation (for example, a food web diagram, a graph, a table, or a phase diagram).

- Identify features of a table, graph, or diagram (for example, units of measurement).

- Find information in text that describes a data presentation.

- Understand scientific terminology.

- Determine how the values of variables change as the value of another variable changes in a data presentation.

- Compare or combine data from one or more data presentations (for example, order or sum data from a table).

- Translate information into a table, graph, or diagram.

- Perform an interpolation or extrapolation using data in a table or graph (for example, categorize data from a table using a scale from another table).

- Determine and/or use a mathematical relationship that exists between data.

- Analyze presented information when given new information.

Scientific Investigation

Questions that apply to scientific investigation are typically related to experiments and other research. Such questions challenge your ability to do the following:

- Find information in text that describes an experiment.

- Understand the tools and functions of tools used in an experiment.

- Understand the methods used in an experiment.

- Understand experimental design.

- Identify a control in an experiment.

- Identify similarities and differences between experiments.

- Determine which experiments use a given tool, method, or aspect of design.

- Predict the results of an additional trial or measurement in an experiment.

- Determine the experimental conditions that would produce specified results.

- Determine the hypothesis for an experiment.

- Determine an alternate method for testing a hypothesis.

- Understand precision and accuracy issues.

- Predict the effects of modifying the design or methods of an experiment.

- Determine which additional trial or experiment could be performed to enhance or evaluate experimental results.

Evaluation of Models, Inferences, and Experimental Results

Some questions on the science test challenge your ability to evaluate models, inferences, and experimental results. (A *model* is a description of an object or phenomenon intended to explain and predict its behavior.) To answer such questions, you must be able to do the following:

- Find basic information in a model.

- Identify implications in a model.

- Determine which models present certain information.

- Determine which hypothesis, prediction, or conclusion is, or is not, consistent with one or more data presentations, models, or pieces of information in text.

- Identify key assumptions in a model.

- Identify similarities and differences between models.

- Determine whether presented information or new information supports or contradicts (or weakens) a hypothesis or conclusion and why.

- Identify the strengths and weaknesses of models.

- Determine which models are supported or weakened by new information.

- Determine which experimental results or models support or contradict a hypothesis, prediction, or conclusion.

- Use new information to make a prediction based on a model.

Writing Test (Optional)

1 prompt, 40 minutes

The writing test is a 40-minute essay test that measures your writing skills—specifically those writing skills emphasized in high school English classes and in entry-level college composition courses.

The test asks you to produce an essay in response to a contemporary issue. You will be given a prompt that presents the issue and provides three different perspectives on it. Your task is to write an essay in which you develop a perspective on the issue, providing a convincing rationale through discussion of your perspective's strengths and weaknesses, and explore how it relates to at least one other perspective, recognizing relationships between or among conflicting views.

Trained readers will evaluate your essay for the evidence it provides of a number of core writing skills. You will receive a total of five scores for this test: four domain scores (provided by two readers) based on an analytic scoring rubric and a single subject-level writing score reported on a scale of 2–12 (reflecting a rounded average of the four domain scores). The four domain scores are

- Ideas and Analysis

- Development and Support

- Organization

- Language Use and Conventions

Ideas and Analysis

Effective writing depends on effective ideas. It is important to think carefully about the issue in the prompt and compose an argument that addresses the issue meaningfully, allowing any reader to understand why your argument is worth considering. In evaluating the ideas and analysis in your essay, readers will look for your ability to do the following:

- Generate a clear main idea that establishes your perspective on the issue and the thesis that will direct your essay.

- Engage with multiple perspectives on the issue by analyzing the relationship between your perspective and at least one other perspective.

- Clarify your understanding of the issue and differing perspectives on it by providing a relevant context for discussion, describing the circumstances surrounding the issue and connecting the specific issue in the prompt to a broader situation.

- Analyze critical elements such as implications (potential effects of decisions) and complexities (factors that complicate an issue or challenge a perspective).

Development and Support

No single idea should be left to speak for itself. Even the best ideas must be developed and supported to be effective in a written argument. By explaining and illustrating your points, you help the reader understand your thinking. In evaluating this dimension of your essay, readers will look for your ability to do the following:

- Clarify your ideas by explaining your reasoning.

- Bolster your claims with persuasive examples.

- Convey the significance of your perspective by exploring reasons why your ideas are worth considering; address why your argument might be more compelling than another.

- Extend your argument by considering qualifications, exceptions, counterarguments, and complicating factors. Convey your understanding of the limitations of your argument, demonstrating to the reader that you have considered its potential weaknesses.

Organization

Organizational choices are essential to effective writing. Guide the reader through your discussion by arranging your ideas according to the logic of your argument, making sure that the connections among ideas are clear. As readers evaluate the organization of your essay, they will look for your ability to do the following:

- Unify your essay by making strategic use of a controlling idea, ensuring all ideas are working in service of the thesis, and employing other organizational techniques (e.g., theme or motif).

- Group ideas clearly, with each paragraph limited to the discussion of related ideas while still linked to the argument as a whole.

- Produce a sequence of ideas that follows a clear logic, both in terms of the argument's overall structure (e.g., introduction, body, conclusion) and within the argument itself, with each point following logically from the last.

- Use transitions to connect ideas, both within paragraphs (e.g., relating claims to support) and across paragraphs (e.g., moving from discussion of one point to that of another).

Language Use and Conventions

Skillful language use enhances argumentative writing. Strategic choices in the vocabulary you use and the style you employ can make your essay more effective. To evaluate your use of language, readers will look for your ability to do the following:

- Make precise word choices that communicate your ideas with clarity. Use specific rather than vague terms that enhance understanding (e.g., "a lot of free music is available today" vs. "the endless volumes of free music available today can be overwhelming").

- Demonstrate control over a variety of sentence structures. Use a mixture of simple and complex sentences, exhibiting as much grammatical control over longer sentences as shorter ones.

- Match the style of your writing to the audience and purpose (e.g., more evocative language to convey emotional appeals versus a more neutral voice to convey an argument based on reason).

- Accurately apply the conventions of grammar, word usage, syntax, and mechanics.

The Fifth Test

ACT is dedicated to meeting professional testing standards. To accomplish this, ACT includes additional questions on the test that do not count toward your score. This practice ensures that ACT develops questions that are fair and of the highest possible quality.

If you are taking the full ACT test, you should expect to take a 20-minute fifth test that includes additional questions.

ACT Test Formats: Paper and Online

The ACT is available as a paper test and as an online test in certain states and educational districts. Some sections may look slightly different online than they do on paper. For example, English items may be indicated by highlighted text instead of underlining, or you may see highlighted asterisks in brackets in the essay instead of numbers in boxes. Likewise, reading items may refer to highlighting in the passage instead of containing line references. Regardless of format, what is most important is the knowledge and skills you have developed over your course of study. If you know the material, whether you choose answers by marking them on paper or clicking an option on a computer screen will likely make little difference.

Using a Calculator

You may use a permitted calculator only on the mathematics test, but you are not required to do so. All math problems on the test can be solved without a calculator, and you may be able to perform some of the math more quickly in your head or on scratch paper.

Note: You may use any four-function, scientific, or graphing calculator as long as it is a permitted calculator modified, if necessary, as described in the following. For additional details and ACT's most current calculator policy, visit www.act.org/the-act/testday.

Certain types of calculators, including the following, are prohibited:

- Calculators with built-in or downloaded computer algebra system (CAS) functionality, including the TI-89, TI-92, TI-Nspire CAS, HP Prime, HP 48GII, HP 40G, HP 49G, HP 50G, fx-ClassPad 400, ClassPad 300, ClassPad 330, and all Casio models that start with CFX-9970G. (Using the TI-89 is the most common reason students are dismissed from the ACT for prohibited calculator use.)

- Handheld, tablet, or laptop computers, including PDAs.

- Electronic writing pads or pen-input devices (the Sharp EL 9600 is permitted).

- Calculators built into cell phones or any other electronic communication devices.

- Calculators with a typewriter keypad (letter keys in QWERTY format). This does not apply to calculators that are provided in a secure test delivery platform. Letter keys not in QWERTY format are permitted.

The following types of calculators are permitted but only after they are modified as noted:

- Calculators that can hold programs or documents (remove all documents and all programs that have CAS functionality).

- Calculators with paper tape (remove the tape).

- Calculators that make noise (mute the device).

- Calculators with an infrared data port (completely cover the infrared data port with heavy opaque material, such as duct tape or electrician's tape). These calculators include the Hewlett-Packard HP 38G series, HP 39G series, and HP 48G.

- Calculators that have power cords (remove all power and electrical cords).

- Accessible calculators (such as audio-talking or braille calculators) may be allowed under the accessibility policies for the ACT test. (Visit www.act.org for details.)

If you choose to use a calculator during the mathematics test, follow these guidelines:

- Use a calculator you are accustomed to using. A more powerful, but unfamiliar, calculator may be a disadvantage. If you are unaccustomed to using a calculator, practice using it when you take the practice tests in this book, so you are comfortable with using it in a test situation.

- Sharing calculators during the test is not permitted.

- Make sure your calculator works properly. If your calculator uses batteries, the batteries should be strong enough to last throughout the testing session.

- Bring a spare calculator and/or extra batteries.

In a computer-based testing environment:

- An on-screen calculator may be available.

- Calculators may not be connected in any way to the computer or device being used for testing.

Taking the Test

Knowing what to expect on test day can alleviate any anxiety you may feel. The following list describes the steps you will take through the testing day:

1. You must report to the test center by the reporting time.

    - If you are testing on a *national test* date and are taking the full ACT test, the reporting time is 8:00 AM.

        ○   You will need to bring the following:

        – A printed copy of your ACT admission ticket, which contains important match information that cannot be found anywhere else. Failure to bring your admission ticket will delay your scores.

        – Acceptable photo ID; if you do not bring acceptable photo ID, you will not be allowed to take the test.

        – Sharpened no. 2 soft-lead pencils with good erasers (no mechanical pencils or ink pens).

        – A permitted calculator, if you would like to use one.

- If you are testing during the week day at your school through *state and district* testing, the reporting time will be at the same time you usually report for school.

  ○   You will need to bring the following:

  –   Acceptable photo ID

  –   Sharpened no. 2 soft-lead pencils with good erasers (no mechanical pencils or ink pens)

  –   A permitted calculator, if you would like to use one

(**Note:** You will *not* be admitted to test if you are late or if your ID does not meet ACT's requirements.)

2. When all examinees present at the reporting time are checked in and seated, wait until you are notified to start the test.

3. A short break is scheduled after the first two tests. You are prohibited from using a cell phone or any electronic device during the break, and you may not eat or drink anything in the test room. (If you take the ACT with writing, you will have time before the writing test to relax and sharpen your pencils.)

4. When time has expired, paper tests are collected. Online tests must be submitted prior to your dismissal.

Note: If you do not complete all your tests for any reason, tell a member of the testing staff whether or not you want your answer document or online test to be scored before you leave the test center. If you do not, all tests attempted will be scored.

Summary

This book should help you to understand how to get ready to take the ACT. Knowing the basics should get you started. By now, you should have a fair idea of what to expect at the test center and know where to find more information: on ACT's website at www.act.org. Now that you know the basic information, you should be ready to start preparing for the ACT.

Prep Online!

Want even more ways to prep? Go to act.wiley.com to access our online platform or use our companion app. Take online practice tests and track your progress, create your own question sets, and use flash cards to practice. Flag difficult or confusing questions for review. To get started, go to act.wiley.com, and register with the PIN on the back of the front cover of this book. Once registered, you can also use our companion app if you prefer to study from your mobile device.

Chapter 2: Preparation, Skills, and Strategies

Performance on the ACT is largely influenced by two factors: the knowledge and skills you acquire over your many years of formal education and your familiarity with the test format and questions.

The best preparation for the ACT is taking rigorous high school classes. If you've taken challenging courses, paid attention in class, and completed your assignments satisfactorily, you've already done much of the preparation required to do well on the ACT.

Your familiarity with the test format and questions and your comfort and confidence in tackling the ACT also play an important role in how well you do on the test. Of course, no test-taking strategy can help you choose the correct answer when you don't understand the question or don't have the knowledge and skills to answer it, but certain strategies and skills can help you avoid common mistakes that will lower your score, such as misreading an answer choice or spending too much time on any given question.

The suggestions in this chapter are designed to help you build on the preparation that you have already completed. They're taken from advice gathered over years—from education specialists, testing specialists, and people who, similar to you, have taken lots of tests. Read the advice, try it out, and see whether it helps. Realize that you can choose how you will take the ACT. Then make intelligent choices about what will work for you.

Mental Preparation

The best mental preparation for the ACT is rigorous course work, but mental preparation also involves confidence and clear thinking. The following tips will help make you feel calmer and more confident so that you'll do your very best on the ACT.

Identify Strengths and Address Areas of Improvement

One of the best ways to prepare mentally for the test is to identify your strengths and areas of improvement, then work toward addressing the areas that may hamper your performance on the test. For example, if time expires before you have a chance to answer all of the questions on a practice test, you need to work on pacing. If you struggle to comprehend word problems in math, you need to practice solving more word problems. However, if you breeze through reading comprehension questions, you might not need to spend time improving your reading comprehension skills.

The following sections explain how to identify strengths and areas of improvement and address issues that may hamper your performance on the test.

Take the First Practice Test

To evaluate your ACT readiness take the first practice test in chapter 3 and analyze the results, as instructed in chapter 4. The test-taking experience and the results will help reveal your strengths and areas of improvement. If you do well on the first practice test, you can be confident that you know the material and are comfortable with the test format. You may decide to take additional practice tests for confirmation or review the test-taking skills in this chapter and in chapters 5 through 9 to see whether they can help you do even better.

If your performance on the first practice test falls short of your goal, you may need to do additional course work in certain subject areas or invest additional time and effort developing effective test-taking strategies and skills. Do not be discouraged if you do not meet your goal on the practice test. Be thankful that your areas for improvement were identified prior to test day and that you now have the information you need to formulate your improvement plan.

Identify Subject Areas to Review

Some students do better in certain subjects than in others. The practice tests in this book will help you identify your stronger and weaker subjects. As you take and score the practice tests, create a list of the subject areas and types of questions you struggle to answer. For example, if you had trouble answering math questions about angles in a triangle, the circumference of a circle, the volume of a cube, the relationships among parallel and perpendicular lines, and so forth, you may need a refresher course in plane geometry.

When taking practice tests on the online platform (act.wiley.com), you can flag questions that you found difficult or confusing. Then, on the Metrics tab, you can click on any assessment to view a list of flagged questions. Use this list to look for patterns and prioritize subjects to review and practice.

Chapter 1 includes a list of subject areas covered on each portion of the ACT to help you categorize the questions you answered incorrectly and identify subject areas you need to study or review.

Plan Your Practice and Study Time

To stay on track leading up to test day, set up a reasonable schedule to practice and study for the ACT. **Set aside small amounts of time** for studying over an extended period—days, weeks, or even months—so you won't feel the need to cram in the days leading up to the test.

Make your schedule flexible enough to allow for a surprise homework assignment or some unexpected fun. And find a way to reward yourself as you get the work done, even if it's just a checklist you can mark to show your progress. A flexible schedule with regular rewards will prevent burnout while keeping you motivated.

Develop a Positive Mental Attitude

Approach the ACT confident that you will do your best. Although confidence alone obviously isn't enough to ensure good performance on a test, doubt and fear can hurt your performance. Be confident in your ability to do well on the ACT. **You will do well!** You just need to be prepared.

Some small changes can make a surprising difference. For example, how you imagine yourself taking the exam may affect how well you actually do. Negative thoughts have a way of generating negative results. So **practice positive thinking;** imagine yourself meeting the challenge of the exam with ease. The day of the test, tell yourself you intend to do your best, and believe it.

Keep the Test in Perspective

Remembering that the ACT is only one part of the process of your education and training will help you keep it in perspective. So will remembering that the ACT and tests similar to it are designed to provide you with feedback and direction. Your scores can help make decisions about your future education and career choices. Think of the test as an opportunity to get to know more about yourself, not as a potential barrier to your future plans.

Another way to keep the ACT in perspective is to use the test as an opportunity to identify careers that match your interests, abilities, and values; explore suitable college majors; and start choosing high school courses that align with your future education and career goals.

General Test-Taking Strategies and Skills

How you approach the ACT and various types of questions, how well you manage your time, whether you change answers, and other factors may affect how well you do on the ACT. The following sections present a few test-taking strategies and skills to help you perform to the best of your ability.

Remain Calm

When you're under pressure during a test, an unexpected question or a minor incident such as breaking a pencil can be very upsetting. For many students, the natural tendency at such times is to panic. Panic detracts from test performance by causing students to become confused and discouraged and to have trouble recalling information they know.

It's a good idea to have a strategy ready for dealing with incidents that might rattle your nerves. One effective strategy is to take a brief time out to center yourself. Take slow, deep breaths and let yourself relax. Put the test temporarily out of mind. Close your eyes if you want. Visualize yourself confidently resuming work on the test, turning in a completed answer document, and leaving the room with a feeling of having done your best work. Allow 20 to 30 seconds for your time out, which is probably all you'll need to regain your composure.

Pace Yourself

The ACT, similar to many tests, must be completed within a specific and limited amount of time. Working quickly and efficiently is one of the skills necessary for conveying how much you've learned in the subject area being tested.

To develop an effective, efficient pace, time yourself as you take the practice tests. If time expires before you have a chance to answer all the questions, you know that you need to work faster next time. If you rushed through the test, had time remaining at the end, and made careless mistakes, you know that you will need to work at a more relaxed pace and be more careful in answering questions.

Warning: Don't try to push yourself to work so fast that you make errors. Answering 50 questions carefully and correctly and leaving 10 unanswered is better than answering 60 questions too quickly and missing 20 because of mistakes.

Although you won't want to lose time by being distracted, you shouldn't obsess about time either. Use all of the time available so you can do your very best on the test.

Some people suggest more formal methods for pacing yourself by allocating a certain amount of time per question or set of questions, as in the following examples:

- **Divide the available time by the number of questions.** For example, on the mathematics test, divide 60 minutes by 60 questions, and you know you have 1 minute per question.

- **Divide the available time into different stages of the writing process.** If you're taking the optional writing test, you may want to allocate the time to planning, writing, and revising/editing your essay. Keep in mind that you probably won't have enough time to fully draft, revise, and then recopy your essay, so spending a few minutes planning your essay before you start writing it is usually wise.

Keep in mind that these strategies are not foolproof, that some questions will take you longer to answer than others, and that doing the math to calculate your time allocations takes time. You may be better off developing a feel for the time and occasionally checking the clock to make sure you're on track to finish, perhaps with a few minutes remaining at the end to check answers you were unsure of. If you want to keep track of your pace while taking the ACT, bring a watch. Not all testing centers have wall clocks.

Know the Directions Ahead of Time

You can save yourself precious moments on the ACT by being familiar with the directions ahead of time. Then, when taking the test, you can read the directions to refresh your memory instead of having to spend time and mind power processing those directions. For example, the ACT English, reading, and science tests ask for the "best" answer, and the mathematics test asks for the "correct" answer. This simple difference in the instructions signals an important distinction to keep in mind as you're working through those tests. Because only one answer is "correct" in the mathematics test, you'll want to be sure your understanding of the question and your calculations are precise—so that your answer matches one, and only one, of the possible answers. In the other tests, more than one of the possible answers may be correct to some degree, and you'll need to be careful to select the "best" answer among those potentially "correct" ones. You'll find the directions for each test in the practice ACT tests in this book.

The directions for the writing test are also very important, because they spell out the aspects of writing that will be evaluated. They also tell you where in the test booklet you can plan your essay and where you should write your final version. The directions for the writing test and a sample answer document appear in the practice ACT tests in this book.

Before you take the ACT, become familiar with the answer document. Knowing in advance how to use the answer document will save you time and prevent worry when you take the actual ACT.

Read Carefully and Thoroughly

Just as it's important to read and understand the directions for a test, it's also important to read and understand each question and answer choice on the test. As you've probably discovered somewhere along the line, you can miss even the simplest test question by reading carelessly and overlooking an important word or detail. Some questions on the ACT, for instance, require more than one step, and the answer to each preliminary step may be included as an answer choice. If you read these questions too quickly, you can easily make the mistake of choosing a plausible answer that relates to a preliminary step but is the incorrect answer to the question.

Take the time to read each question carefully and thoroughly before choosing your answer. Make sure you understand exactly what the question asks and what you are to do to answer it. You may want to underline or circle key words in the test booklet (see the later section "Write Notes in Your Test Booklet"). Reread the item if you are confused.

Watch the question's wording. Look for words such as *not* or *least,* especially when they are not clearly set off with underlining, capital letters, or bold type. Don't make careless errors because you only skimmed the question or the answer choices. Pay close attention to qualifying words such as *all, most, some, none; always, usually, seldom, sometimes, never; best, worst; highest, lowest; smaller, larger.* (There are many other qualifying words; these are only a few examples of related groups.) When you find a qualifier in one of the responses to a question, a good way to determine whether or not the response is the best answer is to substitute related qualifiers and see which makes the best statement. For example, if a response says, "Tests are always difficult," you might test the truth of the word *always* by substituting *sometimes* and the other words related to *always.*

If any of the words other than the one in the answer makes the best statement, then the response is not the best answer.

Pay close attention to modifying or limiting phrases in the statement. For instance, a question in the reading test might have the following as a possible answer: "Lewis and Clark, the great British explorers, began their historic trip to the West Coast by traveling up the Mississippi." The answer is incorrect because Lewis and Clark were not British but were US citizens. (You would not be expected to know from memory that Lewis and Clark were US citizens; that information would be included in the passage.)

Read all the answer choices before selecting one. Questions on the ACT often include answer choices that seem plausible but aren't quite correct. Even though the first answer choice may appeal to you, the correct or best answer may be farther down the list.

When taking the writing test, read the writing prompt carefully. Before you start to plan your essay, make sure you understand the writing prompt and the specific issue it asks you to respond to.

Choose Strategies for Answering Easier and More Difficult Questions

A strategy for taking the ACT is to answer the easy questions first and skip the questions you find difficult. After answering all of the easy questions, go back and answer the more difficult questions, as time permits. When you skip a question, mark it in the test booklet (but not on the answer document), so you can quickly flip back to it later. Also, make absolutely sure that on the answer document, you skip the set of answer choices that correspond to the question you skipped.

Use Logic on More Difficult Questions

When you return to more difficult questions, use logic to eliminate incorrect answer choices. Compare the remaining answer choices and note how they differ. Such differences may provide clues as to what the question requires. Eliminate as many incorrect answer choices as you can, then make an educated selection from the remaining choices. See the next section for additional guidance.

Choose a Strategy for Guessing on Multiple-Choice Questions

On some standardized tests, you're penalized for each incorrect answer. On the ACT multiple-choice tests, however, your raw score is based on the number of questions you answer correctly—nothing is deducted for wrong answers.

Because you're not penalized for guessing on the ACT, answering every question is advantageous. Here's a good way to proceed:

1.   If a question stumps you, try to eliminate wrong choices. Narrowing your choices increases your odds of guessing the correct answer.

2.   If you still aren't sure about the answer, take your best guess.

You don't need a perfect reason to eliminate one answer and choose another. Sometimes an intelligent guess is based on a hunch—on something you may know but don't have time to consciously recognize in a timed-test situation.

Maybe you've heard some advice about how to answer questions when you don't know the correct answer, such as "When in doubt, choose 'C,'" or "When in doubt, select the longest (or shortest) alternative," or "If 'none of the above' (or a similar response) is among the answer choices, select it." Although these bits of advice may hold true now and then, the questions on the ACT have been carefully written to make these strategies ineffective.

Choose a Strategy for Changing Answers

You think you marked the wrong answer choice on a certain question. Do you go with your original answer or change it to the new answer? Some people advise always going with your first response. And surely everyone has had the experience of agonizing over a response, trying to decide whether to change it, then doing so only to find out later that the first answer was the correct one.

However, some research by education and testing specialists suggests that you should change your answer when you change your mind. If you're like the test-takers in the study, your second answer is more likely to be the correct one.

So, how can you decide what to do? Before you change an answer, think about how you approached the question in the first place. Give some weight to the reasons why you now believe another answer is better. Don't mechanically follow an arbitrary rule just because it works for somebody else. Know yourself; then trust yourself to make intelligent, informed decisions.

Write Notes in Your Test Booklet

You're allowed to write in the test booklet, so feel free to write notes in the test booklet to flag key details or to work out a problem on paper.

Mark Your Answers Carefully

Only answers marked on the answer document during the time allowed for a particular test will count. Carefully mark your answers on the answer document as you work through the questions on each test.

Remember that during an actual test you may not fill in answers or alter answers on your answer document after "stop" is called.

For the writing test, writing (or printing) legibly in English in the correct place in the test booklet is vital. If readers cannot read what you have written, they will be unable to score your essay. You are allowed to write in cursive or print your essay, but you must do so clearly. Keep in mind, you must write your essay **using a soft-lead pencil (not a mechanical pencil).** You must write on the lined pages in the answer folder. If you make corrections, do so thoroughly. You may write corrections or additions neatly between the lines of your essay, but you may not write in the margins.

Plan to Check Your Answers

When you reach the end of one of the ACT tests with several minutes to spare, you may feel you've done quite enough. Resist the temptation to rest. Use the remaining time to check your work, as follows:

- For the multiple-choice tests, be sure you've marked all your answers in the proper section on the answer document.

- Be certain you've answered all the questions on your answer document, even the ones you weren't sure about. (Of course, you must be very careful to stop marking ovals when time is called.)

- When you reach the end of the mathematics test, check your calculations. You may check your calculations using the test booklet or scratch paper, or using a permitted calculator (see chapter 1).

- Check your answer document for stray pencil marks that may be misread by the scoring machine. Erase any such marks cleanly and completely.

- Be sure you've marked only one answer on your answer document for each question.

- If there are too many questions for you to check all of your answers, be sure to check those that you feel most uncertain about first, then any others that you have time for on that test.

- At the end of the writing test, take a few minutes to read over your essay. Correct any mistakes in spelling, grammar, usage, or punctuation. If you see any words that are difficult to read, rewrite them so they're legible. Make any revisions neatly between the lines (but do not write in the margins).

Learn Strategies for Specific Tests

In addition to the general test-taking strategies presented in the preceding sections there are specific strategies for each of the ACT tests. For example, on the mathematics test, if a question includes an illustration, you may want to write dimensions given in the question on the illustration to help you visualize what the question is asking. In part 3 of this book, the chapters provide test-taking tips for each of the ACT tests along with additional information that reveals the types of questions you can expect to encounter on each test.

Summary

All the strategies outlined in this chapter are merely suggestions intended to give you ideas about good preparation habits and strategies for getting through the ACT in the best, most efficient manner possible. Some of the strategies will work for you, others won't. Feel free to pick and choose from among all the strategies in this chapter, as well as the more specific strategies in part 3, so that you have a test-taking plan that works best for you.

Prep Online!

Want even more ways to prep? Go to act.wiley.com to access our online platform or use our companion app. Take online practice tests and track your progress, create your own question sets, and use flash cards to practice. Flag difficult or confusing questions for review. To get started, go to act.wiley.com, and register with the PIN on the back of the front cover of this book. Once registered, you can also use our companion app if you prefer to study from your mobile device.

NOTES

2

Part Two:
Taking and Evaluating Your First Practice Test

In This Part

In this part, you have the opportunity to take, score, and evaluate your first practice test. This exercise enables you to identify your strengths and weaknesses, so you can develop an efficient study plan that focuses on areas where you need the most improvement. In this part, you will do the following:

Simulate testing conditions, so you become acclimated to the conditions you will experience on test day.

Take a complete practice test comprising all five ACT tests—English, mathematics, reading, science, and the optional writing test.

Score your test to gauge your overall performance.

Review explanatory answers to understand why you answered each question correctly or incorrectly.

Determine whether you need to work more on subject matter or on test-taking strategies and skills.

Analyze your performance on each test to gain better insight on the knowledge and skills in greatest need of improvement.

3

Chapter 3:
Taking and Scoring Your First ACT Practice Test

In this chapter, you take the first of the six practice tests in this book, score the test, and review the answers with explanations. We encourage you to take the test under conditions similar to those you will encounter on test day and to try your very best.

After you take and score the test and review the answers, you will be well poised to analyze your performance in chapter 4. The results of this first practice test will help you identify subject areas you may need to review and test-taking strategies, such as pacing, that you may want to work on prior to test day.

Simulating Testing Conditions

Taking the practice tests can help you become familiar with the ACT. We recommend that you take the tests under conditions that are as similar as possible to those you will experience on the actual test day. The following tips will help you make the most of the practice tests:

- The four multiple-choice tests require a total of 2 hours and 55 minutes. Try an entire practice test in one sitting, with a

10-minute break between the mathematics test and the reading test. (If you are taking the writing test, you may also take a break of roughly 5 minutes after the science test.)

- Sit at a desk with good lighting. You will need sharpened no. 2 pencils with good erasers. You may not use mechanical pencils or highlight pens. Remove all books and other aids from your desk. On test day, you will not be allowed to use references or notes. Scratch paper is not needed as each page of the mathematics test has a blank column that you can use for scratch work. In some circumstances you are not permitted to write in your test booklet. In those circumstances, you'll be given scratch paper, and you can use it to jot down the numbers of the questions you skip.

- If you plan to use a calculator on the mathematics test, review the details about permissible calculators on ACT's website, www.act.org. Use a calculator with which you are familiar for both the practice test and on the test day. You may use any four-function, scientific, or graphing calculator on the mathematics test, except as specified on ACT's website and in chapter 1.

- Use a digital timer or clock to time yourself on each test. Set your timer for 5 minutes less than the allotted time for each test so you can get used to the 5-minute warning. (Students approved for self-paced extended time should set a timer for 60-minute warnings up to the total time allowed—5 hours for the multiple-choice tests. If you take the optional writing test, you will then have an additional hour to complete that test.)

Did you know? Our online platform practice tests time you automatically! Go to act.wiley.com to prep online or use our companion app.

- Allow yourself only the time permitted for each test.

- Detach and use one sample multiple-choice answer document.

- Read the general test directions on the first page of the practice test. After reading the directions, start your timer and begin with the English test. Continue through the science test, taking a short break between the mathematics test and the reading test. If you do not plan to take the ACT writing test, score your multiple-choice tests using the information beginning on page 101.

- If you plan to take the writing test, take a short break after the science test. Detach (or photocopy) the writing test answer document that follows the writing test planning pages. Then read the test directions on the first page of the practice ACT writing test. After reading the directions, start your timer, then carefully read the prompt. After you have considered what the prompt is asking you to do, use the pages provided to plan your essay, and then write your essay on the answer document. After you have finished, score your essay using the information beginning on page 108.

The ACT® *Sample Answer Document*

EXAMINEE STATEMENTS, CERTIFICATION, AND SIGNATURE

1. **Statements**: I understand that by registering for, launching, starting, or submitting answer documents for an ACT® test, I am agreeing to comply with and be bound by the *Terms and Conditions: Testing Rules and Policies for the ACT® Test* ("Terms").

   I UNDERSTAND AND AGREE THAT THE TERMS PERMIT ACT TO CANCEL MY SCORES IN CERTAIN CIRCUMSTANCES. THE TERMS ALSO LIMIT DAMAGES AVAILABLE TO ME AND REQUIRE ARBITRATION OF CERTAIN DISPUTES. BY AGREEING TO ARBITRATION, ACT AND I BOTH WAIVE THE RIGHT TO HAVE THOSE DISPUTES HEARD BY A JUDGE OR JURY.

   I understand that ACT owns the test questions and responses, and I will not share them with anyone by any form of communication before, during, or after the test administration. I understand that taking the test for someone else may violate the law and subject me to legal penalties. I consent to the collection and processing of personally identifying information I provide, and its subsequent use and disclosure, as described in the ACT Privacy Policy (www.act.org/privacy.html). I also permit ACT to transfer my personally identifying information to the United States, to ACT, or to a third-party service provider, where it will be subject to use and disclosure under the laws of the United States, including being accessible to law enforcement or national security authorities.

2. **Certification**: Copy the italicized certification below, then sign and date in the spaces provided.

   *I agree to the **Statements** above and certify that I am the person whose information appears on this form.*

   _____

   _____

   _____

   Your Signature _____ Today's Date _____

Do NOT mark in this shaded area.	**USE A NO. 2 PENCIL ONLY.** (Do NOT use a mechanical pencil, ink, ballpoint, correction fluid, or felt-tip pen.)

A NAME, MAILING ADDRESS, AND TELEPHONE (Please print.)

Last Name _____ First Name _____ MI (Middle Initial) _____

House Number & Street (Apt. No.); or PO Box & No.; or RR & No. _____

City _____ State/Province _____ ZIP/Postal Code _____

Area Code _____ Number _____ Country _____

ACT, Inc.—Confidential Restricted when data present

ALL examinees must complete block A – please print.

Blocks B, C, and D are required for all examinees. Find the MATCHING INFORMATION on your ticket. Enter it EXACTLY the same way, even if any of the information is missing or incorrect. Fill in the corresponding ovals. If you do not complete these blocks to match your previous information EXACTLY, your scores will be **delayed up to 8 weeks**.

ACT®
PO BOX 168, IOWA CITY, IA 52243-0168

B MATCH NAME
(First 5 letters of last name)

Ovals A through Z for each of the 5 letter positions.

C MATCH NUMBER

Number ovals 1 through 9 and 0 for each position.

D DATE OF BIRTH

Month	Day	Year
○ January		
○ February		
○ March	1 1	1 1
○ April	2 2	2 2
○ May	3 3	3 3
○ June	4 4	4
○ July	5 5	5
○ August	6 6	6
○ September	7 7	7
○ October	8 8	8
○ November	9 9	9
○ December	0 0	0 0

01121523W   (A)203023-001:654321   ISD36401   Printed in the US.

Your First Practice Test

PAGE 2

Marking Directions: Mark only **one** oval for each question. Fill in response completely. Erase errors cleanly without smudging.

Correct mark: ◯ ⬤ ◯ ◯

- -

Do NOT use these *incorrect* **or** *bad* **marks.**

Incorrect marks: ⊘ ⊗ ⬭ ⊙
Overlapping mark: ◯ ◯ ⬭◯
Cross-out mark: ◯ ⬤ ◯
Smudged erasure: ◯ ◯ ◑ ◯
Mark is too light: ◐◯ ◯ ◯

BOOKLET NUMBER

Print your 5-character **Test Form** in the boxes at the right <u>and</u> fill in the corresponding ovals.

FORM

TEST 1: ENGLISH

1 Ⓐ Ⓑ Ⓒ Ⓓ	14 Ⓕ Ⓖ Ⓗ Ⓙ	27 Ⓐ Ⓑ Ⓒ Ⓓ	40 Ⓕ Ⓖ Ⓗ Ⓙ	53 Ⓐ Ⓑ Ⓒ Ⓓ	66 Ⓕ Ⓖ Ⓗ Ⓙ
2 Ⓕ Ⓖ Ⓗ Ⓙ	15 Ⓐ Ⓑ Ⓒ Ⓓ	28 Ⓕ Ⓖ Ⓗ Ⓙ	41 Ⓐ Ⓑ Ⓒ Ⓓ	54 Ⓕ Ⓖ Ⓗ Ⓙ	67 Ⓐ Ⓑ Ⓒ Ⓓ
3 Ⓐ Ⓑ Ⓒ Ⓓ	16 Ⓕ Ⓖ Ⓗ Ⓙ	29 Ⓐ Ⓑ Ⓒ Ⓓ	42 Ⓕ Ⓖ Ⓗ Ⓙ	55 Ⓐ Ⓑ Ⓒ Ⓓ	68 Ⓕ Ⓖ Ⓗ Ⓙ
4 Ⓕ Ⓖ Ⓗ Ⓙ	17 Ⓐ Ⓑ Ⓒ Ⓓ	30 Ⓕ Ⓖ Ⓗ Ⓙ	43 Ⓐ Ⓑ Ⓒ Ⓓ	56 Ⓕ Ⓖ Ⓗ Ⓙ	69 Ⓐ Ⓑ Ⓒ Ⓓ
5 Ⓐ Ⓑ Ⓒ Ⓓ	18 Ⓕ Ⓖ Ⓗ Ⓙ	31 Ⓐ Ⓑ Ⓒ Ⓓ	44 Ⓕ Ⓖ Ⓗ Ⓙ	57 Ⓐ Ⓑ Ⓒ Ⓓ	70 Ⓕ Ⓖ Ⓗ Ⓙ
6 Ⓕ Ⓖ Ⓗ Ⓙ	19 Ⓐ Ⓑ Ⓒ Ⓓ	32 Ⓕ Ⓖ Ⓗ Ⓙ	45 Ⓐ Ⓑ Ⓒ Ⓓ	58 Ⓕ Ⓖ Ⓗ Ⓙ	71 Ⓐ Ⓑ Ⓒ Ⓓ
7 Ⓐ Ⓑ Ⓒ Ⓓ	20 Ⓕ Ⓖ Ⓗ Ⓙ	33 Ⓐ Ⓑ Ⓒ Ⓓ	46 Ⓕ Ⓖ Ⓗ Ⓙ	59 Ⓐ Ⓑ Ⓒ Ⓓ	72 Ⓕ Ⓖ Ⓗ Ⓙ
8 Ⓕ Ⓖ Ⓗ Ⓙ	21 Ⓐ Ⓑ Ⓒ Ⓓ	34 Ⓕ Ⓖ Ⓗ Ⓙ	47 Ⓐ Ⓑ Ⓒ Ⓓ	60 Ⓕ Ⓖ Ⓗ Ⓙ	73 Ⓐ Ⓑ Ⓒ Ⓓ
9 Ⓐ Ⓑ Ⓒ Ⓓ	22 Ⓕ Ⓖ Ⓗ Ⓙ	35 Ⓐ Ⓑ Ⓒ Ⓓ	48 Ⓕ Ⓖ Ⓗ Ⓙ	61 Ⓐ Ⓑ Ⓒ Ⓓ	74 Ⓕ Ⓖ Ⓗ Ⓙ
10 Ⓐ Ⓑ Ⓒ Ⓓ	23 Ⓐ Ⓑ Ⓒ Ⓓ	36 Ⓕ Ⓖ Ⓗ Ⓙ	49 Ⓐ Ⓑ Ⓒ Ⓓ	62 Ⓕ Ⓖ Ⓗ Ⓙ	75 Ⓐ Ⓑ Ⓒ Ⓓ
11 Ⓐ Ⓑ Ⓒ Ⓓ	24 Ⓕ Ⓖ Ⓗ Ⓙ	37 Ⓐ Ⓑ Ⓒ Ⓓ	50 Ⓕ Ⓖ Ⓗ Ⓙ	63 Ⓐ Ⓑ Ⓒ Ⓓ	
12 Ⓕ Ⓖ Ⓗ Ⓙ	25 Ⓐ Ⓑ Ⓒ Ⓓ	38 Ⓕ Ⓖ Ⓗ Ⓙ	51 Ⓐ Ⓑ Ⓒ Ⓓ	64 Ⓕ Ⓖ Ⓗ Ⓙ	
13 Ⓐ Ⓑ Ⓒ Ⓓ	26 Ⓕ Ⓖ Ⓗ Ⓙ	39 Ⓐ Ⓑ Ⓒ Ⓓ	52 Ⓕ Ⓖ Ⓗ Ⓙ	65 Ⓐ Ⓑ Ⓒ Ⓓ	

TEST 2: MATHEMATICS

1 Ⓐ Ⓑ Ⓒ Ⓓ Ⓔ	11 Ⓐ Ⓑ Ⓒ Ⓓ Ⓔ	21 Ⓐ Ⓑ Ⓒ Ⓓ Ⓔ	31 Ⓐ Ⓑ Ⓒ Ⓓ Ⓔ	41 Ⓐ Ⓑ Ⓒ Ⓓ Ⓔ	51 Ⓐ Ⓑ Ⓒ Ⓓ Ⓔ
2 Ⓕ Ⓖ Ⓗ Ⓙ Ⓚ	12 Ⓕ Ⓖ Ⓗ Ⓙ Ⓚ	22 Ⓕ Ⓖ Ⓗ Ⓙ Ⓚ	32 Ⓕ Ⓖ Ⓗ Ⓙ Ⓚ	42 Ⓕ Ⓖ Ⓗ Ⓙ Ⓚ	52 Ⓕ Ⓖ Ⓗ Ⓙ Ⓚ
3 Ⓐ Ⓑ Ⓒ Ⓓ Ⓔ	13 Ⓐ Ⓑ Ⓒ Ⓓ Ⓔ	23 Ⓐ Ⓑ Ⓒ Ⓓ Ⓔ	33 Ⓐ Ⓑ Ⓒ Ⓓ Ⓔ	43 Ⓐ Ⓑ Ⓒ Ⓓ Ⓔ	53 Ⓐ Ⓑ Ⓒ Ⓓ Ⓔ
4 Ⓕ Ⓖ Ⓗ Ⓙ Ⓚ	14 Ⓕ Ⓖ Ⓗ Ⓙ Ⓚ	24 Ⓕ Ⓖ Ⓗ Ⓙ Ⓚ	34 Ⓕ Ⓖ Ⓗ Ⓙ Ⓚ	44 Ⓕ Ⓖ Ⓗ Ⓙ Ⓚ	54 Ⓕ Ⓖ Ⓗ Ⓙ Ⓚ
5 Ⓐ Ⓑ Ⓒ Ⓓ Ⓔ	15 Ⓐ Ⓑ Ⓒ Ⓓ Ⓔ	25 Ⓐ Ⓑ Ⓒ Ⓓ Ⓔ	35 Ⓐ Ⓑ Ⓒ Ⓓ Ⓔ	45 Ⓐ Ⓑ Ⓒ Ⓓ Ⓔ	55 Ⓐ Ⓑ Ⓒ Ⓓ Ⓔ
6 Ⓕ Ⓖ Ⓗ Ⓙ Ⓚ	16 Ⓕ Ⓖ Ⓗ Ⓙ Ⓚ	26 Ⓕ Ⓖ Ⓗ Ⓙ Ⓚ	36 Ⓕ Ⓖ Ⓗ Ⓙ Ⓚ	46 Ⓕ Ⓖ Ⓗ Ⓙ Ⓚ	56 Ⓕ Ⓖ Ⓗ Ⓙ Ⓚ
7 Ⓐ Ⓑ Ⓒ Ⓓ Ⓔ	17 Ⓐ Ⓑ Ⓒ Ⓓ Ⓔ	27 Ⓐ Ⓑ Ⓒ Ⓓ Ⓔ	37 Ⓐ Ⓑ Ⓒ Ⓓ Ⓔ	47 Ⓐ Ⓑ Ⓒ Ⓓ Ⓔ	57 Ⓐ Ⓑ Ⓒ Ⓓ Ⓔ
8 Ⓕ Ⓖ Ⓗ Ⓙ Ⓚ	18 Ⓕ Ⓖ Ⓗ Ⓙ Ⓚ	28 Ⓕ Ⓖ Ⓗ Ⓙ Ⓚ	38 Ⓕ Ⓖ Ⓗ Ⓙ Ⓚ	48 Ⓕ Ⓖ Ⓗ Ⓙ Ⓚ	58 Ⓕ Ⓖ Ⓗ Ⓙ Ⓚ
9 Ⓐ Ⓑ Ⓒ Ⓓ Ⓔ	19 Ⓐ Ⓑ Ⓒ Ⓓ Ⓔ	29 Ⓐ Ⓑ Ⓒ Ⓓ Ⓔ	39 Ⓐ Ⓑ Ⓒ Ⓓ Ⓔ	49 Ⓐ Ⓑ Ⓒ Ⓓ Ⓔ	59 Ⓐ Ⓑ Ⓒ Ⓓ Ⓔ
10 Ⓕ Ⓖ Ⓗ Ⓙ Ⓚ	20 Ⓕ Ⓖ Ⓗ Ⓙ Ⓚ	30 Ⓕ Ⓖ Ⓗ Ⓙ Ⓚ	40 Ⓕ Ⓖ Ⓗ Ⓙ Ⓚ	50 Ⓕ Ⓖ Ⓗ Ⓙ Ⓚ	60 Ⓕ Ⓖ Ⓗ Ⓙ Ⓚ

TEST 3: READING

1 Ⓐ Ⓑ Ⓒ Ⓓ	8 Ⓕ Ⓖ Ⓗ Ⓙ	15 Ⓐ Ⓑ Ⓒ Ⓓ	22 Ⓕ Ⓖ Ⓗ Ⓙ	29 Ⓐ Ⓑ Ⓒ Ⓓ	36 Ⓕ Ⓖ Ⓗ Ⓙ
2 Ⓕ Ⓖ Ⓗ Ⓙ	9 Ⓐ Ⓑ Ⓒ Ⓓ	16 Ⓕ Ⓖ Ⓗ Ⓙ	23 Ⓐ Ⓑ Ⓒ Ⓓ	30 Ⓕ Ⓖ Ⓗ Ⓙ	37 Ⓐ Ⓑ Ⓒ Ⓓ
3 Ⓐ Ⓑ Ⓒ Ⓓ	10 Ⓕ Ⓖ Ⓗ Ⓙ	17 Ⓐ Ⓑ Ⓒ Ⓓ	24 Ⓕ Ⓖ Ⓗ Ⓙ	31 Ⓐ Ⓑ Ⓒ Ⓓ	38 Ⓕ Ⓖ Ⓗ Ⓙ
4 Ⓕ Ⓖ Ⓗ Ⓙ	11 Ⓐ Ⓑ Ⓒ Ⓓ	18 Ⓕ Ⓖ Ⓗ Ⓙ	25 Ⓐ Ⓑ Ⓒ Ⓓ	32 Ⓕ Ⓖ Ⓗ Ⓙ	39 Ⓐ Ⓑ Ⓒ Ⓓ
5 Ⓐ Ⓑ Ⓒ Ⓓ	12 Ⓕ Ⓖ Ⓗ Ⓙ	19 Ⓐ Ⓑ Ⓒ Ⓓ	26 Ⓕ Ⓖ Ⓗ Ⓙ	33 Ⓐ Ⓑ Ⓒ Ⓓ	40 Ⓕ Ⓖ Ⓗ Ⓙ
6 Ⓕ Ⓖ Ⓗ Ⓙ	13 Ⓐ Ⓑ Ⓒ Ⓓ	20 Ⓕ Ⓖ Ⓗ Ⓙ	27 Ⓐ Ⓑ Ⓒ Ⓓ	34 Ⓕ Ⓖ Ⓗ Ⓙ	
7 Ⓐ Ⓑ Ⓒ Ⓓ	14 Ⓕ Ⓖ Ⓗ Ⓙ	21 Ⓐ Ⓑ Ⓒ Ⓓ	28 Ⓕ Ⓖ Ⓗ Ⓙ	35 Ⓐ Ⓑ Ⓒ Ⓓ	

TEST 4: SCIENCE

1 Ⓐ Ⓑ Ⓒ Ⓓ	8 Ⓕ Ⓖ Ⓗ Ⓙ	15 Ⓐ Ⓑ Ⓒ Ⓓ	22 Ⓕ Ⓖ Ⓗ Ⓙ	29 Ⓐ Ⓑ Ⓒ Ⓓ	36 Ⓕ Ⓖ Ⓗ Ⓙ
2 Ⓕ Ⓖ Ⓗ Ⓙ	9 Ⓐ Ⓑ Ⓒ Ⓓ	16 Ⓕ Ⓖ Ⓗ Ⓙ	23 Ⓐ Ⓑ Ⓒ Ⓓ	30 Ⓕ Ⓖ Ⓗ Ⓙ	37 Ⓐ Ⓑ Ⓒ Ⓓ
3 Ⓐ Ⓑ Ⓒ Ⓓ	10 Ⓕ Ⓖ Ⓗ Ⓙ	17 Ⓐ Ⓑ Ⓒ Ⓓ	24 Ⓕ Ⓖ Ⓗ Ⓙ	31 Ⓐ Ⓑ Ⓒ Ⓓ	38 Ⓕ Ⓖ Ⓗ Ⓙ
4 Ⓕ Ⓖ Ⓗ Ⓙ	11 Ⓐ Ⓑ Ⓒ Ⓓ	18 Ⓕ Ⓖ Ⓗ Ⓙ	25 Ⓐ Ⓑ Ⓒ Ⓓ	32 Ⓕ Ⓖ Ⓗ Ⓙ	39 Ⓐ Ⓑ Ⓒ Ⓓ
5 Ⓐ Ⓑ Ⓒ Ⓓ	12 Ⓕ Ⓖ Ⓗ Ⓙ	19 Ⓐ Ⓑ Ⓒ Ⓓ	26 Ⓕ Ⓖ Ⓗ Ⓙ	33 Ⓐ Ⓑ Ⓒ Ⓓ	40 Ⓕ Ⓖ Ⓗ Ⓙ
6 Ⓕ Ⓖ Ⓗ Ⓙ	13 Ⓐ Ⓑ Ⓒ Ⓓ	20 Ⓕ Ⓖ Ⓗ Ⓙ	27 Ⓐ Ⓑ Ⓒ Ⓓ	34 Ⓕ Ⓖ Ⓗ Ⓙ	
7 Ⓐ Ⓑ Ⓒ Ⓓ	14 Ⓕ Ⓖ Ⓗ Ⓙ	21 Ⓐ Ⓑ Ⓒ Ⓓ	28 Ⓕ Ⓖ Ⓗ Ⓙ	35 Ⓐ Ⓑ Ⓒ Ⓓ	

The ACT® *Sample Answer Document*

EXAMINEE STATEMENTS, CERTIFICATION, AND SIGNATURE

1. **Statements**: I understand that by registering for, launching, starting, or submitting answer documents for an ACT® test, I am agreeing to comply with and be bound by the *Terms and Conditions: Testing Rules and Policies for the ACT® Test* ("Terms").

   I UNDERSTAND AND AGREE THAT THE TERMS PERMIT ACT TO CANCEL MY SCORES IN CERTAIN CIRCUMSTANCES. THE TERMS ALSO LIMIT DAMAGES AVAILABLE TO ME AND REQUIRE ARBITRATION OF CERTAIN DISPUTES. BY AGREEING TO ARBITRATION, ACT AND I BOTH WAIVE THE RIGHT TO HAVE THOSE DISPUTES HEARD BY A JUDGE OR JURY.

   I understand that ACT owns the test questions and responses, and I will not share them with anyone by any form of communication before, during, or after the test administration. I understand that taking the test for someone else may violate the law and subject me to legal penalties. I consent to the collection and processing of personally identifying information I provide, and its subsequent use and disclosure, as described in the ACT Privacy Policy (www.act.org/privacy.html). I also permit ACT to transfer my personally identifying information to the United States, to ACT, or to a third-party service provider, where it will be subject to use and disclosure under the laws of the United States, including being accessible to law enforcement or national security authorities.

2. **Certification**: Copy the italicized certification below, then sign and date in the spaces provided.

*I agree to the **Statements** above and certify that I am the person whose information appears on this form.*

_____

_____

_____   _____
Your Signature   Today's Date

Do NOT mark in this shaded area.

USE A NO. 2 PENCIL ONLY.
(Do NOT use a mechanical pencil, ink, ballpoint, correction fluid, or felt-tip pen.)

A **NAME, MAILING ADDRESS, AND TELEPHONE**
(Please print.)

Last Name   First Name   MI (Middle Initial)

House Number & Street (Apt. No.); or PO Box & No.; or RR & No.

City   State/Province   ZIP/Postal Code

Area Code   Number   Country

ACT, Inc.—Confidential Restricted when data present

ALL examinees must complete block A – please print.

Blocks B, C, and D are required for all examinees. Find the MATCHING INFORMATION on your ticket. Enter it EXACTLY the same way, even if any of the information is missing or incorrect. Fill in the corresponding ovals. If you do not complete these blocks to match your previous information EXACTLY, your scores will be **delayed up to 8 weeks**.

ACT®
PO BOX 168, IOWA CITY, IA 52243-0168

01121523W   (A)203023-001:654321   ISD36401   Printed in the US.

B MATCH NAME (First 5 letters of last name)

C MATCH NUMBER

D DATE OF BIRTH

Month	Day	Year
○ January		
○ February		
○ March		
○ April		
○ May		
○ June		
○ July		
○ August		
○ September		
○ October		
○ November		
○ December		

PAGE 2

Marking Directions: Mark only **one** oval for each question. Fill in response completely. Erase errors cleanly without smudging.

Correct mark: ○ ● ○ ○

Do NOT use these *incorrect* or *bad* **marks.**

Incorrect marks: ⊘ ⊗ ⊜ ⊙
Overlapping mark: ○ ○ ⊗
Cross-out mark: ○ ⊗ ○ ○
Smudged erasure: ○ ○ ⊙ ○
Mark is too light: ◍ ○ ○ ○

BOOKLET NUMBER

Columns of ovals numbered 1 2 3 4 5 6 7 8 9 0 (ten columns)

Print your 5-character **Test Form** in the boxes at the right <u>and</u> fill in the corresponding ovals.

FORM

① ① Ⓜ Ⓒ ①
② ② ②
③ ③
④ ④
⑤ ⑤
⑥ ⑥
⑦ ⑦
⑧ ⑧
⑨ ⑨
⓪ ⓪

TEST 1: ENGLISH

1 Ⓐ Ⓑ Ⓒ Ⓓ	14 Ⓕ Ⓖ Ⓗ Ⓙ	27 Ⓐ Ⓑ Ⓒ Ⓓ	40 Ⓕ Ⓖ Ⓗ Ⓙ	53 Ⓐ Ⓑ Ⓒ Ⓓ	66 Ⓕ Ⓖ Ⓗ Ⓙ
2 Ⓕ Ⓖ Ⓗ Ⓙ	15 Ⓐ Ⓑ Ⓒ Ⓓ	28 Ⓕ Ⓖ Ⓗ Ⓙ	41 Ⓐ Ⓑ Ⓒ Ⓓ	54 Ⓕ Ⓖ Ⓗ Ⓙ	67 Ⓐ Ⓑ Ⓒ Ⓓ
3 Ⓐ Ⓑ Ⓒ Ⓓ	16 Ⓕ Ⓖ Ⓗ Ⓙ	29 Ⓐ Ⓑ Ⓒ Ⓓ	42 Ⓕ Ⓖ Ⓗ Ⓙ	55 Ⓐ Ⓑ Ⓒ Ⓓ	68 Ⓕ Ⓖ Ⓗ Ⓙ
4 Ⓕ Ⓖ Ⓗ Ⓙ	17 Ⓐ Ⓑ Ⓒ Ⓓ	30 Ⓕ Ⓖ Ⓗ Ⓙ	43 Ⓐ Ⓑ Ⓒ Ⓓ	56 Ⓕ Ⓖ Ⓗ Ⓙ	69 Ⓐ Ⓑ Ⓒ Ⓓ
5 Ⓐ Ⓑ Ⓒ Ⓓ	18 Ⓕ Ⓖ Ⓗ Ⓙ	31 Ⓐ Ⓑ Ⓒ Ⓓ	44 Ⓕ Ⓖ Ⓗ Ⓙ	57 Ⓐ Ⓑ Ⓒ Ⓓ	70 Ⓕ Ⓖ Ⓗ Ⓙ
6 Ⓕ Ⓖ Ⓗ Ⓙ	19 Ⓐ Ⓑ Ⓒ Ⓓ	32 Ⓕ Ⓖ Ⓗ Ⓙ	45 Ⓐ Ⓑ Ⓒ Ⓓ	58 Ⓕ Ⓖ Ⓗ Ⓙ	71 Ⓐ Ⓑ Ⓒ Ⓓ
7 Ⓐ Ⓑ Ⓒ Ⓓ	20 Ⓕ Ⓖ Ⓗ Ⓙ	33 Ⓐ Ⓑ Ⓒ Ⓓ	46 Ⓕ Ⓖ Ⓗ Ⓙ	59 Ⓐ Ⓑ Ⓒ Ⓓ	72 Ⓕ Ⓖ Ⓗ Ⓙ
8 Ⓕ Ⓖ Ⓗ Ⓙ	21 Ⓐ Ⓑ Ⓒ Ⓓ	34 Ⓕ Ⓖ Ⓗ Ⓙ	47 Ⓐ Ⓑ Ⓒ Ⓓ	60 Ⓕ Ⓖ Ⓗ Ⓙ	73 Ⓐ Ⓑ Ⓒ Ⓓ
9 Ⓐ Ⓑ Ⓒ Ⓓ	22 Ⓕ Ⓖ Ⓗ Ⓙ	35 Ⓐ Ⓑ Ⓒ Ⓓ	48 Ⓕ Ⓖ Ⓗ Ⓙ	61 Ⓐ Ⓑ Ⓒ Ⓓ	74 Ⓕ Ⓖ Ⓗ Ⓙ
10 Ⓕ Ⓖ Ⓗ Ⓙ	23 Ⓐ Ⓑ Ⓒ Ⓓ	36 Ⓕ Ⓖ Ⓗ Ⓙ	49 Ⓐ Ⓑ Ⓒ Ⓓ	62 Ⓕ Ⓖ Ⓗ Ⓙ	75 Ⓐ Ⓑ Ⓒ Ⓓ
11 Ⓐ Ⓑ Ⓒ Ⓓ	24 Ⓕ Ⓖ Ⓗ Ⓙ	37 Ⓐ Ⓑ Ⓒ Ⓓ	50 Ⓕ Ⓖ Ⓗ Ⓙ	63 Ⓐ Ⓑ Ⓒ Ⓓ	
12 Ⓕ Ⓖ Ⓗ Ⓙ	25 Ⓐ Ⓑ Ⓒ Ⓓ	38 Ⓕ Ⓖ Ⓗ Ⓙ	51 Ⓐ Ⓑ Ⓒ Ⓓ	64 Ⓕ Ⓖ Ⓗ Ⓙ	
13 Ⓐ Ⓑ Ⓒ Ⓓ	26 Ⓕ Ⓖ Ⓗ Ⓙ	39 Ⓐ Ⓑ Ⓒ Ⓓ	52 Ⓕ Ⓖ Ⓗ Ⓙ	65 Ⓐ Ⓑ Ⓒ Ⓓ	

TEST 2: MATHEMATICS

1 Ⓐ Ⓑ Ⓒ Ⓓ Ⓔ	11 Ⓐ Ⓑ Ⓒ Ⓓ Ⓔ	21 Ⓐ Ⓑ Ⓒ Ⓓ Ⓔ	31 Ⓐ Ⓑ Ⓒ Ⓓ Ⓔ	41 Ⓐ Ⓑ Ⓒ Ⓓ Ⓔ	51 Ⓐ Ⓑ Ⓒ Ⓓ Ⓔ
2 Ⓕ Ⓖ Ⓗ Ⓙ Ⓚ	12 Ⓕ Ⓖ Ⓗ Ⓙ Ⓚ	22 Ⓕ Ⓖ Ⓗ Ⓙ Ⓚ	32 Ⓕ Ⓖ Ⓗ Ⓙ Ⓚ	42 Ⓕ Ⓖ Ⓗ Ⓙ Ⓚ	52 Ⓕ Ⓖ Ⓗ Ⓙ Ⓚ
3 Ⓐ Ⓑ Ⓒ Ⓓ Ⓔ	13 Ⓐ Ⓑ Ⓒ Ⓓ Ⓔ	23 Ⓐ Ⓑ Ⓒ Ⓓ Ⓔ	33 Ⓐ Ⓑ Ⓒ Ⓓ Ⓔ	43 Ⓐ Ⓑ Ⓒ Ⓓ Ⓔ	53 Ⓐ Ⓑ Ⓒ Ⓓ Ⓔ
4 Ⓕ Ⓖ Ⓗ Ⓙ Ⓚ	14 Ⓕ Ⓖ Ⓗ Ⓙ Ⓚ	24 Ⓕ Ⓖ Ⓗ Ⓙ Ⓚ	34 Ⓕ Ⓖ Ⓗ Ⓙ Ⓚ	44 Ⓕ Ⓖ Ⓗ Ⓙ Ⓚ	54 Ⓕ Ⓖ Ⓗ Ⓙ Ⓚ
5 Ⓐ Ⓑ Ⓒ Ⓓ Ⓔ	15 Ⓐ Ⓑ Ⓒ Ⓓ Ⓔ	25 Ⓐ Ⓑ Ⓒ Ⓓ Ⓔ	35 Ⓐ Ⓑ Ⓒ Ⓓ Ⓔ	45 Ⓐ Ⓑ Ⓒ Ⓓ Ⓔ	55 Ⓐ Ⓑ Ⓒ Ⓓ Ⓔ
6 Ⓕ Ⓖ Ⓗ Ⓙ Ⓚ	16 Ⓕ Ⓖ Ⓗ Ⓙ Ⓚ	26 Ⓕ Ⓖ Ⓗ Ⓙ Ⓚ	36 Ⓕ Ⓖ Ⓗ Ⓙ Ⓚ	46 Ⓕ Ⓖ Ⓗ Ⓙ Ⓚ	56 Ⓕ Ⓖ Ⓗ Ⓙ Ⓚ
7 Ⓐ Ⓑ Ⓒ Ⓓ Ⓔ	17 Ⓐ Ⓑ Ⓒ Ⓓ Ⓔ	27 Ⓐ Ⓑ Ⓒ Ⓓ Ⓔ	37 Ⓐ Ⓑ Ⓒ Ⓓ Ⓔ	47 Ⓐ Ⓑ Ⓒ Ⓓ Ⓔ	57 Ⓐ Ⓑ Ⓒ Ⓓ Ⓔ
8 Ⓕ Ⓖ Ⓗ Ⓙ Ⓚ	18 Ⓕ Ⓖ Ⓗ Ⓙ Ⓚ	28 Ⓕ Ⓖ Ⓗ Ⓙ Ⓚ	38 Ⓕ Ⓖ Ⓗ Ⓙ Ⓚ	48 Ⓕ Ⓖ Ⓗ Ⓙ Ⓚ	58 Ⓕ Ⓖ Ⓗ Ⓙ Ⓚ
9 Ⓐ Ⓑ Ⓒ Ⓓ Ⓔ	19 Ⓐ Ⓑ Ⓒ Ⓓ Ⓔ	29 Ⓐ Ⓑ Ⓒ Ⓓ Ⓔ	39 Ⓐ Ⓑ Ⓒ Ⓓ Ⓔ	49 Ⓐ Ⓑ Ⓒ Ⓓ Ⓔ	59 Ⓐ Ⓑ Ⓒ Ⓓ Ⓔ
10 Ⓕ Ⓖ Ⓗ Ⓙ Ⓚ	20 Ⓕ Ⓖ Ⓗ Ⓙ Ⓚ	30 Ⓕ Ⓖ Ⓗ Ⓙ Ⓚ	40 Ⓕ Ⓖ Ⓗ Ⓙ Ⓚ	50 Ⓕ Ⓖ Ⓗ Ⓙ Ⓚ	60 Ⓕ Ⓖ Ⓗ Ⓙ Ⓚ

TEST 3: READING

1 Ⓐ Ⓑ Ⓒ Ⓓ	8 Ⓕ Ⓖ Ⓗ Ⓙ	15 Ⓐ Ⓑ Ⓒ Ⓓ	22 Ⓕ Ⓖ Ⓗ Ⓙ	29 Ⓐ Ⓑ Ⓒ Ⓓ	36 Ⓕ Ⓖ Ⓗ Ⓙ
2 Ⓕ Ⓖ Ⓗ Ⓙ	9 Ⓐ Ⓑ Ⓒ Ⓓ	16 Ⓕ Ⓖ Ⓗ Ⓙ	23 Ⓐ Ⓑ Ⓒ Ⓓ	30 Ⓕ Ⓖ Ⓗ Ⓙ	37 Ⓐ Ⓑ Ⓒ Ⓓ
3 Ⓐ Ⓑ Ⓒ Ⓓ	10 Ⓕ Ⓖ Ⓗ Ⓙ	17 Ⓐ Ⓑ Ⓒ Ⓓ	24 Ⓕ Ⓖ Ⓗ Ⓙ	31 Ⓐ Ⓑ Ⓒ Ⓓ	38 Ⓕ Ⓖ Ⓗ Ⓙ
4 Ⓕ Ⓖ Ⓗ Ⓙ	11 Ⓐ Ⓑ Ⓒ Ⓓ	18 Ⓕ Ⓖ Ⓗ Ⓙ	25 Ⓐ Ⓑ Ⓒ Ⓓ	32 Ⓕ Ⓖ Ⓗ Ⓙ	39 Ⓐ Ⓑ Ⓒ Ⓓ
5 Ⓐ Ⓑ Ⓒ Ⓓ	12 Ⓕ Ⓖ Ⓗ Ⓙ	19 Ⓐ Ⓑ Ⓒ Ⓓ	26 Ⓕ Ⓖ Ⓗ Ⓙ	33 Ⓐ Ⓑ Ⓒ Ⓓ	40 Ⓕ Ⓖ Ⓗ Ⓙ
6 Ⓕ Ⓖ Ⓗ Ⓙ	13 Ⓐ Ⓑ Ⓒ Ⓓ	20 Ⓕ Ⓖ Ⓗ Ⓙ	27 Ⓐ Ⓑ Ⓒ Ⓓ	34 Ⓕ Ⓖ Ⓗ Ⓙ	
7 Ⓐ Ⓑ Ⓒ Ⓓ	14 Ⓕ Ⓖ Ⓗ Ⓙ	21 Ⓐ Ⓑ Ⓒ Ⓓ	28 Ⓕ Ⓖ Ⓗ Ⓙ	35 Ⓐ Ⓑ Ⓒ Ⓓ	

TEST 4: SCIENCE

1 Ⓐ Ⓑ Ⓒ Ⓓ	8 Ⓕ Ⓖ Ⓗ Ⓙ	15 Ⓐ Ⓑ Ⓒ Ⓓ	22 Ⓕ Ⓖ Ⓗ Ⓙ	29 Ⓐ Ⓑ Ⓒ Ⓓ	36 Ⓕ Ⓖ Ⓗ Ⓙ
2 Ⓕ Ⓖ Ⓗ Ⓙ	9 Ⓐ Ⓑ Ⓒ Ⓓ	16 Ⓕ Ⓖ Ⓗ Ⓙ	23 Ⓐ Ⓑ Ⓒ Ⓓ	30 Ⓕ Ⓖ Ⓗ Ⓙ	37 Ⓐ Ⓑ Ⓒ Ⓓ
3 Ⓐ Ⓑ Ⓒ Ⓓ	10 Ⓕ Ⓖ Ⓗ Ⓙ	17 Ⓐ Ⓑ Ⓒ Ⓓ	24 Ⓕ Ⓖ Ⓗ Ⓙ	31 Ⓐ Ⓑ Ⓒ Ⓓ	38 Ⓕ Ⓖ Ⓗ Ⓙ
4 Ⓕ Ⓖ Ⓗ Ⓙ	11 Ⓐ Ⓑ Ⓒ Ⓓ	18 Ⓕ Ⓖ Ⓗ Ⓙ	25 Ⓐ Ⓑ Ⓒ Ⓓ	32 Ⓕ Ⓖ Ⓗ Ⓙ	39 Ⓐ Ⓑ Ⓒ Ⓓ
5 Ⓐ Ⓑ Ⓒ Ⓓ	12 Ⓕ Ⓖ Ⓗ Ⓙ	19 Ⓐ Ⓑ Ⓒ Ⓓ	26 Ⓕ Ⓖ Ⓗ Ⓙ	33 Ⓐ Ⓑ Ⓒ Ⓓ	40 Ⓕ Ⓖ Ⓗ Ⓙ
6 Ⓕ Ⓖ Ⓗ Ⓙ	13 Ⓐ Ⓑ Ⓒ Ⓓ	20 Ⓕ Ⓖ Ⓗ Ⓙ	27 Ⓐ Ⓑ Ⓒ Ⓓ	34 Ⓕ Ⓖ Ⓗ Ⓙ	
7 Ⓐ Ⓑ Ⓒ Ⓓ	14 Ⓕ Ⓖ Ⓗ Ⓙ	21 Ⓐ Ⓑ Ⓒ Ⓓ	28 Ⓕ Ⓖ Ⓗ Ⓙ	35 Ⓐ Ⓑ Ⓒ Ⓓ	

Practice Test 1

EXAMINEE STATEMENTS, CERTIFICATION, AND SIGNATURE

1. Statements: I understand that by registering for, launching, starting, or submitting answer documents for an ACT® test, I am agreeing to comply with and be bound by the *Terms and Conditions: Testing Rules and Policies for the ACT® Test* ("Terms").

I UNDERSTAND AND AGREE THAT THE TERMS PERMIT ACT TO CANCEL MY SCORES IN CERTAIN CIRCUMSTANCES. THE TERMS ALSO LIMIT DAMAGES AVAILABLE TO ME AND REQUIRE ARBITRATION OF CERTAIN DISPUTES. BY AGREEING TO ARBITRATION, ACT AND I BOTH WAIVE THE RIGHT TO HAVE THOSE DISPUTES HEARD BY A JUDGE OR JURY.

I understand that ACT owns the test questions and responses, and I will not share them with anyone by any form of communication before, during, or after the test administration. I understand that taking the test for someone else may violate the law and subject me to legal penalties.

I consent to the collection and processing of personally identifying information I provide, and its subsequent use and disclosure, as described in the ACT Privacy Policy (www.act.org/privacy.html). I also permit ACT to transfer my personally identifying information to the United States, to ACT, or to a third-party service provider, where it will be subject to use and disclosure under the laws of the United States, including being accessible to law enforcement or national security authorities.

2. Certification: Copy the italicized certification below, then sign, date, and print your name in the spaces provided.

*I agree to the **Statements** above and certify that I am the person whose information appears on this form.*

_____

_____

Your Signature   Today's Date   Print Your Name

Form 23MC1

2023 | 2024

Directions

This booklet contains tests in English, mathematics, reading, and science. These tests measure skills and abilities highly related to high school course work and success in college. **Calculators may be used on the mathematics test only.**

The questions in each test are numbered, and the suggested answers for each question are lettered. On the answer document, the rows of ovals are numbered to match the questions, and the ovals in each row are lettered to correspond to the suggested answers.

For each question, first decide which answer is best. Next, locate on the answer document the row of ovals numbered the same as the question. Then, locate the oval in that row lettered the same as your answer. Finally, fill in the oval completely. Use a soft lead pencil and make your marks heavy and black. **Do not use ink or a mechanical pencil.**

Mark only one answer to each question. If you change your mind about an answer, erase your first mark thoroughly before marking your new answer. For each question, make certain that you mark in the row of ovals with the same number as the question.

Only responses marked on your answer document will be scored. Your score on each test will be based only on the number of questions you answer correctly during the time allowed for that test. You will **not** be penalized for guessing. **It is to your advantage to answer every question even if you must guess.**

You may work on each test **only** when the testing staff tells you to do so. If you finish a test before time is called for that test, you should use the time remaining to reconsider questions you are uncertain about in that test. You may **not** look back to a test on which time has already been called, and you may **not** go ahead to another test. To do so will disqualify you from the examination.

Lay your pencil down immediately when time is called at the end of each test. You may **not** for any reason fill in or alter ovals for a test after time is called for that test. To do so will disqualify you from the examination.

Do not fold or tear the pages of your test booklet.

**DO NOT OPEN THIS BOOKLET
UNTIL TOLD TO DO SO.**

The ONLY Official Prep Guide from the Makers of the ACT

1 ■ ■ ■ ■ ■ ■ ■ ■ 1

ENGLISH TEST
45 Minutes—75 Questions

DIRECTIONS: In the five passages that follow, certain words and phrases are underlined and numbered. In the right-hand column, you will find alternatives for the underlined part. In most cases, you are to choose the one that best expresses the idea, makes the statement appropriate for standard written English, or is worded most consistently with the style and tone of the passage as a whole. If you think the original version is best, choose "NO CHANGE." In some cases, you will find in the right-hand column a question about the underlined part. You are to choose the best answer to the question.

You will also find questions about a section of the passage, or about the passage as a whole. These questions do not refer to an underlined portion of the passage, but rather are identified by a number or numbers in a box.

For each question, choose the alternative you consider best and fill in the corresponding oval on your answer document. Read each passage through once before you begin to answer the questions that accompany it. For many of the questions, you must read several sentences beyond the question to determine the answer. Be sure that you have read far enough ahead each time you choose an alternative.

PASSAGE I

NASA's Inaugural Artist in Residence

[1]

For over forty years, Laurie Anderson has appropriated electronics, video, and sound, to create art that defies categorization. In 1972,
₁

Anderson ignited her career; by conducting
₂
a symphony using only car horns. [A] Five years

later, she invented a violin that clones as an audiotape
₃
player. Anderson went on to stage technology-enhanced

performance art, direct music videos, and invent tools
₄
to manipulate sound. [B] In 2002, Anderson's fascination

with technology contributed to her being named the first

artist in residence at NASA, where she was given free

rein to explore the facilities in search of inspiration. [C]

[2]

She found her inspiration in how technology

has developed over time. When Anderson was

growing up in the 1950s, space travel and artificial

intelligence existed only in science fiction stories.

1. **A.** NO CHANGE
   B. sound, to create,
   C. sound to create,
   D. sound to create

2. **F.** NO CHANGE
   G. Anderson, to ignite her career,
   H. Anderson igniting her career
   J. Anderson ignited her career

3. **A.** NO CHANGE
   B. duplicates
   C. doubles
   D. copies

4. **F.** NO CHANGE
   G. the invention of
   H. inventing
   J. to invent

GO ON TO THE NEXT PAGE.

A half century later, at NASA, Anderson witnessed the
realization of both. During a visit to a virtual airport
    5

control center, Anderson viewed panoramic images of
                                        6

the red planet, courtesy from a video feed provided of
                                7
the Mars Global Surveyor satellite. At the Jet Propulsion

Laboratory in Pasadena, California, she was introduced

to robots that function autonomously through control-

and-sensor-processing software. [D]

[3]

Drawing on her NASA experiences, Anderson

wrote and produced a ninety-minute performance

art piece titled *The End of the Moon*. The performance

features Anderson on a candlelit stage, standing
                                        8

in front of an image of the moon's surface. 9

5. Which choice provides the most effective transition
   from the first two sentences of the paragraph to the rest
   of the paragraph?
   A. NO CHANGE
   B. In fact, science fiction masters like Ray Bradbury
      and Isaac Asimov received much acclaim for their
      work at this time.
   C. Anderson, who grew up in Chicago, studied classi-
      cal violin as a child.
   D. NASA has grown considerably since it was estab-
      lished in 1958.

6. F. NO CHANGE
   G. eyeballed all-encompassing snapshots
   H. beheld wide-ranging pictorial images
   J. ogled comprehensive photographs

7. A. NO CHANGE
   B. from a video feed provided by
   C. of a video feed provided by
   D. by a video feed provided of

8. Which of the following alternatives to the underlined
   portion would NOT be acceptable?
   F. stage, where she stands
   G. stage as she stands
   H. stage. She stands
   J. stage; standing

9. At this point, the writer is considering adding the following true sentence:

   Neil Armstrong was the first man to be photographed walking on the moon's surface.

   Should the writer make this addition?
   A. Yes, because the sentence contributes to the para-
      graph's discussion of how Anderson uses photog-
      raphy in her performance art.
   B. Yes, because the sentence contributes to the para-
      graph's discussion of how and why *The End of the
      Moon* is a reimagining of NASA's first moon
      landing.
   C. No, because the sentence is not relevant to the
      paragraph's description and interpretation of *The
      End of the Moon*.
   D. No, because the sentence is not relevant to the
      paragraph's critique of Anderson's struggle to
      make performance art commercially viable.

GO ON TO THE NEXT PAGE.

1 ■ ■ ■ ■ ■ ■ ■ ■ ■ 1

Anderson begins the show by referencing the technology to which she was privy at NASA.
—————10—————
Anderson then complements these references by

subtly demonstrating its impact on music. While
—————11

sweeping the bow over the strings of a viola, Anderson
—————————————12—————————————
manipulates the music via a laptop computer. The string

music that transforms into electronic sounds, which then
—————13—————
reverberate into futuristic, otherworldly music. The result

is surreal and stimulating exactly what you might expect
—————————14—————————
from NASA's inaugural artist in residence.

10. **F.** NO CHANGE
    G. to, which she was privy,
    H. to which, she was privy,
    J. to which she was privy,

11. **A.** NO CHANGE
    B. technology's
    C. one's
    D. this

12. Which choice provides the most vivid description of Anderson's action?
    F. NO CHANGE
    G. moving a bow over a stringed instrument,
    H. producing music by playing a viola,
    J. rubbing an instrument with a bow,

13. **A.** NO CHANGE
    B. music is transformed
    C. music, transforming
    D. music transforming

14. **F.** NO CHANGE
    G. stimulating: and
    H. stimulating—
    J. stimulating;

> Question 15 asks about the preceding passage as a whole.

15. The writer is considering adding the following sentence to the essay:

    > Her "talking stick," for instance, was a six-foot-long baton that could record and replicate sounds.

    If the writer were to add this sentence, it would most logically be placed at:

    A. Point A in Paragraph 1.
    B. Point B in Paragraph 1.
    C. Point C in Paragraph 1.
    D. Point D in Paragraph 2.

PASSAGE II

Zebra ID: Biological Bar Codes

[1]

Even though every zebra has a unique pattern of bold stripes on its coat, the animals look remarkably alike.
Zebras are willful animals. When in a herd, they become
—————————16—————————
a mass of blended stripes and similar features that confuses a lion on the hunt. One zebra resembling another is not

16. Which choice most effectively leads the reader from the first sentence of this paragraph to the information that follows in the rest of the paragraph?
    F. NO CHANGE
    G. Observing zebras in a small group, rather than in a herd, might not make a difference.
    H. Researchers don't celebrate this about zebras.
    J. This is helpful to zebras.

GO ON TO THE NEXT PAGE.

beneficial to researchers, though. Biologists trying to monitor individual zebras sometimes joke that finding one in the wild typically is <u>easy</u> it's finding the same

17

one twice that's hard.

[2]

<u>Working together,</u> scientists at the University of

18

Illinois and Princeton University developed a software program called StripeSpotter, which catalogs and identifies zebras. StripeSpotter translates the pattern of stripes on a zebra's <u>side, into an identifier,</u> similar to a bar code, that

19

can be compared to other zebra stripe-pattern identifiers

that have been stored in a database. [20]

[3]

The process begins when a researcher uploads a still photograph of a zebra to StripeSpotter. [A] The researcher then crops a rectangular section of the photograph, making sure to <u>capture</u> the stripes on the zebra's side.

21

[B] StripeSpotter converts that section into <u>a stark black-</u>

22

<u>and-white image composed of parallel, vertical lines.</u>

22

17. A. NO CHANGE
B. easy for them
C. easy;
D. easy,

18. Which choice most effectively leads the reader from the preceding paragraph into the rest of the essay?
F. NO CHANGE
G. Thinking about how computer science could play a role,
H. Aware that biologists enjoy the joke,
J. To solve this problem,

19. A. NO CHANGE
B. side into an identifier,
C. side, into an identifier
D. side into an identifier

20. At this point, the writer is considering adding the following true sentence:

Some researchers believe that the stripes on zebras help the animals identify one another in a herd.

Should the writer make this addition here?
F. Yes, because it makes clear that zebras have always been able to do what StripeSpotter can do.
G. Yes, because it shifts the essay back to its main topic, interpreting the stripes on zebras.
H. No, because it isn't relevant to the explanation of what StripeSpotter is and how it works.
J. No, because it doesn't specify why it is important that zebras are able to identify one another.

21. A. NO CHANGE
B. apprehend
C. acquire
D. take

22. The writer is considering revising the underlined portion to the following:

an image of even, black-and-white lines.

Given that the information is accurate, should the writer make this revision?
F. Yes, because the revision reveals that StripeSpotter can be used to make line art based on a zebra's stripes.
G. Yes, because unlike the original wording, the revision highlights that a zebra identification code is made up of parallel lines.
H. No, because the revision lacks the clarity and specificity of the description in the original wording.
J. No, because the revision suggests that the means through which StripeSpotter creates images are largely unscientific.

GO ON TO THE NEXT PAGE.

1 ■ ■ ■ ■ ■ ■ ■ ■ ■ **1**

The widths of the lines <u>correspond</u> perfectly to the widths
           ₂₃

of the zebra's stripes. <u>Providing</u> the zebra's "StripeCode,"
           ₂₄

unique to each animal in much the same way a fingerprint

is unique to each person. The StripeCode is logged in the

database, where a researcher uploading a new photograph

of a zebra can scan the stored codes to find a potential

match.

[4]

    [C] StripeSpotter has proved so useful that

<u>it's developers</u> plan to design similar programs
  ₂₅

for identifying other <u>animals.</u> Any pattern
            ₂₆

<u>present</u> over an animal's life could be translated
₂₇

into an identification code—spots on a leopard's

<u>hide, the wrinkled trunk of an elephant,</u> rings on
             ₂₈

a tortoise's shell. So far, StripeSpotter has helped

researchers <u>thoroughly</u> monitor the social interactions
         ₂₉

and migration patterns of endangered zebra species

in Kenya. [D]

---

23. A. NO CHANGE
   B. has corresponded
   C. is corresponding
   D. corresponds

24. F. NO CHANGE
   G. Resulting in
   H. This is
   J. As

25. A. NO CHANGE
   B. its' developers
   C. its developers'
   D. its developers

26. F. NO CHANGE
   G. animals, though these programs have not yet been created.
   H. animals through a comparable means.
   J. animals that are not zebras.

27. The writer is considering revising the underlined portion to the following:

     that stays relatively constant

Should the writer make this revision?

   A. Yes, because the revision more clearly indicates that some animal patterns are more precise than a zebra's stripes when used for identification.
   B. Yes, because the revision more clearly explains the key characteristic an animal pattern must have to be useful as the basis of an identification code.
   C. No, because the revision provides less support for the essay's earlier claim that a zebra's stripes can be translated into an identification code with ease.
   D. No, because the revision offers a less clear explanation of how researchers decide which animal patterns can be used for identification.

28. Which choice is most consistent with the word pattern used in the other two examples in this sentence?
   F. NO CHANGE
   G. an elephant's trunk that has wrinkles,
   H. wrinkles on the trunk of an elephant,
   J. wrinkles on an elephant's trunk,

29. Which choice most strongly emphasizes that one benefit of StripeSpotter is that it allows researchers to monitor the activities of zebras without causing the animals harm or distress?
   A. NO CHANGE
   B. conveniently
   C. inventively
   D. humanely

GO ON TO THE NEXT PAGE.

Question 30 asks about the preceding passage as a whole.

30. The writer is considering adding the following sentence to the essay:

> He or she has to be sure not to include any grass, foliage, or other surrounding objects or animals in the cropped area.

If the writer were to add this sentence, it would most logically be placed at:

F. Point A in Paragraph 3.
G. Point B in Paragraph 3.
H. Point C in Paragraph 4.
J. Point D in Paragraph 4.

PASSAGE III

Celadon Remnants

[1] At the Broadway Station of the Long Island
Rail Road in Flushing, Queens, commuters ponder a
mural spanning over three hundred square feet on
the station's south wall. [2] But as they come closer,
commuters notice the silhouettes are also mosaics,
constructed entirely of ceramic shards. [3] From afar,
the mural appears as a series of aquamarine, vase-shaped
silhouettes against a white tile background. 32

The mural, titled *Celadon Remnants*, is
artist Jean Shin's homage on the Korean American
community in Flushing. When she was commissioned
by the Metropolitan Transportation Authority of
New York City to spawn a site-specific artwork,

visually representing her dual identity was a means
sought by Shin as an American and a Korean. She
chose to use traditional celadon pottery, albeit in
a new way.

31. A. NO CHANGE
B. Station, of the Long Island Rail Road,
C. Station of, the Long Island Rail Road,
D. Station, of the Long Island Rail Road

32. Which sequence of sentences makes this paragraph most logical?
F. NO CHANGE
G. 1, 3, 2
H. 2, 1, 3
J. 3, 1, 2

33. A. NO CHANGE
B. about
C. to
D. of

34. F. NO CHANGE
G. accomplish
H. perform
J. produce

35. A. NO CHANGE
B. sought by Shin was a means of visually representing her dual identity
C. a means of visually representing her dual identity was sought by Shin
D. Shin sought a means of visually representing her dual identity

GO ON TO THE NEXT PAGE.

1 ■ ■ ■ ■ ■ ■ ■ ■ ■ 1

Celadon is a ceramic ware named for its'
aquamarine glaze. Originally from China, celadon was
further developed in the tenth and eleventh centuries in
Korea, in which inlaid designs and decorative elements

were added. Over the centuries, celadon became a cultural
treasure in Korea. Today, South Korean ceramicists will
accept nothing less than perfection in creating their art. In
fact, if the ceramicist deems a piece imperfect, he or she
will often scrap it entirely.

Shin decided that these scraps, or shards,
would be an ideal medium for her mural. In 2008, she
contacted ceramicists in the South Korean city of Icheon
for celadon shards and arranged to be shipped to Queens.
The ceramicists sent Shin over six thousand shards.

Using the shards—many of whose are adorned with

alphabetic symbols and assorted patterns—Shin
constructed her mural.

For Shin, the shards themselves took on
significance: they represented her feeling of

being broken off or "fractured" from their birthplace

of Seoul, South Korea. In Queens, Shin's use of
the fragments to construct an artwork that
celebrated a Korean tradition. The result is sublime.

---

36. **F.** NO CHANGE
   G. it is
   H. it's
   J. its

37. **A.** NO CHANGE
   B. whereas
   C. where
   D. past

38. Given that all the choices are true, which one most effectively leads the reader from the first two sentences of the paragraph to the rest of the paragraph?
   F. NO CHANGE
   G. The celadon's color is a result of iron oxide's transformation from ferric to ferrous iron during the firing process.
   H. It has been theorized that the name "celadon" derives from the Sanskrit words for *green* and *stone.*
   J. Shin Sang-ho, one of Korea's most celebrated modern ceramicists, began his career re-creating traditional celadon.

39. The best placement for the underlined portion would be:
   A. where it is now.
   B. after the word *ceramicists.*
   C. after the word *city.*
   D. after the word *arranged.*

40. **F.** NO CHANGE
   G. which
   H. whom
   J. that

41. Which choice provides the most specific description of the adornments on the shards of celadon?
   A. NO CHANGE
   B. Korean characters and labyrinthine patterns—
   C. different letters and a plethora of patterns—
   D. numerous symbols and various designs—

42. **F.** NO CHANGE
   G. significance: and
   H. significance,
   J. significance

43. **A.** NO CHANGE
   B. they're
   C. her
   D. its

44. **F.** NO CHANGE
   G. Shin used
   H. using
   J. DELETE the underlined portion.

GO ON TO THE NEXT PAGE.

The silhouettes merge Shin's past and present, creating
an exquisite meditation on Korean American identity.
₄₅

45. Which of the following alternatives to the underlined portion would NOT be acceptable?
   A. present to create
   B. present and they create
   C. present. They create
   D. present; they create

PASSAGE IV

Captain Charles Young's Road to the Giant Sequoias

Able to grow as tall as a twenty-six-story building and as wide as a city street, Earth has the largest living things, which are giant sequoia trees. Sequoia National Park in California's Sierra Nevada mountain range
₄₆

contains 275 known caves. Yet until 1903, few visitors
₄₇
could gain access to the trees in the park's Giant

Forest: there was no completed road.
₄₈

The US Army—which from 1891 to 1913 was
₄₉
responsible for improving national parks during the summer months—had managed to complete only about six miles to the road of the Giant Forest. Army Captain
₅₀
Charles Young, however, was not deterred. The first black superintendent of a national park and a revered leader of the army's all-black 9th and 10th Cavalries, Young had the
₅₁
experience needed to direct the completion of the project.

46. F. NO CHANGE
   G. it is known that the largest living things on Earth are giant sequoia trees.
   H. on Earth are the largest living things—giant sequoia trees.
   J. giant sequoia trees are the largest living things on Earth.

47. Given that all the choices are accurate, which one provides the most effective transition between the first sentence of this paragraph and the last sentence of this paragraph?
   A. NO CHANGE
   B. harbors endangered species like the bighorn sheep and the California condor.
   C. boasts the greatest concentration of giant sequoia groves in the world.
   D. is approximately 84% wilderness.

48. F. NO CHANGE
   G. Forest: because there was
   H. Forest; because there was
   J. Forest;

49. A. NO CHANGE
   B. Army, which—
   C. Army, which
   D. Army which,

50. F. NO CHANGE
   G. to the road from
   H. from the road to
   J. of the road to

51. A. NO CHANGE
   B. Cavalries, Young having
   C. Cavalries; Young had
   D. Cavalries. Young had

GO ON TO THE NEXT PAGE.

1 ■ ■ ■ ■ ■ ■ ■ ■ **1**

In June 1903, under Young's command, the soldiers began work on the road. Soon the eleven-mile route was complete. By the middle of August, vehicles could enter the park. Young and his troops had succeeded where no one else had; they enabled visitors to get to the giant sequoias more easily.

Because he had his troops
    52

send most of their efforts into the road,
    53
Young was just as concerned with maintaining the park's natural features. His troops guarded the grounds against illegal grazing, poaching, and logging. Nevertheless, since tourist foot traffic tended to damage
    54
some of the giant sequoias, Young had his soldiers place fences around the most damaged trees to protect them from future bad stuff.
    55

Over one hundred years later, the contributions Young made possible has been counted among the
    56

most significant in the park's history. ｜57｜ In 2003, the National Park Service decided to formally recognize the efforts of Captain Young (who

being promoted to lieutenant colonel in 1916).
    58

52. **F.** NO CHANGE
    G. Although
    H. Unless
    J. If

53. **A.** NO CHANGE
    B. channel
    C. convey
    D. shape

54. **F.** NO CHANGE
    G. Additionally,
    H. Thus,
    J. Still,

55. **A.** NO CHANGE
    B. further harm in the future.
    C. further harm.
    D. bad stuff.

56. **F.** NO CHANGE
    G. was
    H. are
    J. is

57. At this point, the writer is considering adding the following true statement:

    Park enthusiast George Palmer was the one who petitioned the National Park Service to recognize Young's contributions.

    Should the writer make this addition here?

    A. Yes, because it explains why it took so long for the National Park Service to formally recognize Young's accomplishments.
    B. Yes, because it provides information about how Palmer inspired Young's actions at the park.
    C. No, because it suggests that other people besides Palmer had already petitioned the National Park Service on Young's behalf.
    D. No, because it provides information that is only loosely related to the main subject of the essay.

58. **F.** NO CHANGE
    G. having been
    H. had been
    J. DELETE the underlined portion.

GO ON TO THE NEXT PAGE.

Today, those who visit the park use Young's road to reach the Giant Forest, which is home to General Sherman, the
<u>59</u>
world's largest tree.
<u>59</u>

59. Which of the following choices best concludes the sentence and the essay?
   A. NO CHANGE
   B. where, among the trees dedicated to and named for US generals and presidents, the Colonel Young Tree also stands.
   C. where, even beneath the cover of nightfall, people can enjoy park-sponsored activities such as lantern tours.
   D. which is a popular place to visit.

Question 60 asks about the preceding passage as a whole.

---

60. Suppose the writer's primary purpose had been to provide an overview of the history of Sequoia National Park. Would this essay accomplish that purpose?
   F. Yes, because it explains how the construction of roads through the park has led to broadscale changes from the park's establishment to today.
   G. Yes, because it describes how Young's contributions led to a historic surge in annual visits to the park.
   H. No, because it focuses on Young's military career rather than on the history of the park.
   J. No, because it instead chronicles one significant part of the park's history.

PASSAGE V

The Curious Case of *Turritopsis Dohrnii*

For decades, the diminutive jellyfish *Turritopsis dohrnii*—mere millimeters wide as an adult—did not unveil much notice from scientists. But in 1988,
<u>61</u>

61. A. NO CHANGE
   B. disclose
   C. reveal
   D. elicit

marine biology student Christian Sommer observed
<u>62</u>

62. F. NO CHANGE
   G. marine, biology student, Christian Sommer,
   H. marine biology student, Christian Sommer,
   J. marine biology student Christian Sommer,

T. dohrnii doing something astonishing. Reverting
<u>63</u>
from mature jellyfish to hydroid colonies, an earlier

63. A. NO CHANGE
   B. astonishing: reverting
   C. astonishing; reverting
   D. astonishing reverting

GO ON TO THE NEXT PAGE.

1 ■ ■ ■ ■ ■ ■ ■ ■ ■ **1**

life stage. In a sense, they grew younger.
                    —64—

T. dohrnii has no brain or heart. After fertilization,
                  —65—
a T. dohrnii egg develops into a free-swimming, ovoid

larva. In time, the larva settles on the ocean floor and

transforms into a mound of cells—a hydroid colony.

Buds grow on the colony and develop into young jellyfish

with the familiar bell-like shape and tentacles. These

jellyfish then detach from the colony, and drift away
                              —66—
reaching maturity in a few weeks.

After Sommer's discovery, studies confirmed that

T. dohrnii's life cycle is not a one-way street. An adult

T. dohrnii, if stressed—by injury, disease, or even just
   —67—
old age, has the ability to revert to a hydroid colony. That

colony can then create new jellyfish, which in turn can

also revert to hydroid colonies. There's no apparent limit

to these perpetual cycles of metamorphic transformation.
                    —68—

In the 1990s, journalists nicknamed T. dohrnii the
                        —69—

"immortal jellyfish." It is true that scientists have
                                    —70—
replicated all stages of T. dohrnii's life cycle, but
                —70—
each individual T. dohrnii isn't immortal. Although

the cells of the adult are essentially recycled during

its transformation, all the new jellyfish grow into

separate organisms—albeit genetically equivalent ones.

64. If the writer were to delete the underlined sentence, the paragraph would primarily lose:

   F. information explaining that *T. dohrnii* had been observed reverting from maturity to an earlier life stage.

   G. a statement that helps clarify the previous details about *T. dohrnii*'s reversion to hydroid colonies.

   H. an alternate perspective that contradicts Sommer's conclusions about *T. dohrnii*.

   J. evidence that Sommer continued to observe *T. dohrnii* over time.

65. Given that all the choices are accurate, which one best helps the sentence introduce the main focus of the paragraph?

   A. NO CHANGE

   B. been found primarily in the Mediterranean Sea and in waters near Japan.

   C. only eight tentacles as a young jellyfish but over eighty as an adult.

   D. a multistage life cycle.

66. **F.** NO CHANGE

   G. colony and, drift away

   H. colony and drift away,

   J. colony and drift away

67. **A.** NO CHANGE

   B. *T. dohrnii*, if stressed

   C. *T. dohrnii* if stressed,

   D. *T. dohrnii* if stressed

68. **F.** NO CHANGE

   G. endlessly recurring cycles of transformation.

   H. transformative cycles of metamorphosis.

   J. cycles of transformation.

69. Which of the following alternatives to the underlined portion would NOT be acceptable?

   A. journalists invented a nickname for *T. dohrnii*:

   B. journalists nicknamed *T. dohrnii*, calling it the

   C. journalists' nickname for *T. dohrnii*: the

   D. journalists began calling *T. dohrnii* the

70. Given that all the choices are accurate, which one provides the most relevant information at this point in the essay?

   F. NO CHANGE

   G. the cells and genes of *T. dohrnii* can, theoretically, live indefinitely,

   H. an adult *T. dohrnii* is about as big as a trimmed pinkie nail,

   J. *T. dohrnii* has spread throughout many oceans of the world,

GO ON TO THE NEXT PAGE.

In a way, the new jellyfish are clones <u>amidst the</u>
                                              71
originating adult.

     Scientists are still studying how *T. dohrnii* achieves

<u>its</u> transformations. At the cellular level, what the jellyfish
 72

<u>does, which is</u> called transdifferentiation, wherein one
        73

type of cell becomes another type. 74 Understanding

the mechanisms of *T. dohrnii*'s particular kind of

transdifferentiation <u>may yield insights into aging</u>
                                              75
<u>and disease in all animals, including humans.</u>
                      75

71. A. NO CHANGE
    B. with
    C. of
    D. to

72. F. NO CHANGE
    G. all of their
    H. all of it's
    J. their

73. A. NO CHANGE
    B. does to transform,
    C. does is
    D. does,

74. At this point, the writer is considering adding the following true statement:

    T. dohrnii's abilities, however, can't save it from lethal encounters with, say, boat propellers or ravenous sea slugs.

Should the writer make this addition here?

    F. Yes, because it adds details about the environmental dangers that *T. dohrnii* may face.
    G. Yes, because it reveals that individual *T. dohrnii* aren't actually immortal.
    H. No, because it suggests that boat propellers and sea slugs are the only true dangers for *T. dohrnii*.
    J. No, because it interrupts the discussion of *T. dohrnii*'s cellular transdifferentiation.

75. Given that all the choices are accurate, which one would best conclude the essay by emphasizing specific benefits of *T. dohrnii* research?

    A. NO CHANGE
    B. is the life's work of Shin Kubota, who studies the only thriving captive population of *T. dohrnii*.
    C. is really important, although there are few experts devoted to the study of this fascinating creature.
    D. will require much diligence, since *T. dohrnii* only produces offspring under very specific conditions.

END OF TEST 1

STOP! DO NOT TURN THE PAGE UNTIL TOLD TO DO SO.

Your First Practice Test

2    **2**

MATHEMATICS TEST
60 Minutes—60 Questions

DIRECTIONS: Solve each problem, choose the correct answer, and then fill in the corresponding oval on your answer document.

Do not linger over problems that take too much time. Solve as many as you can; then return to the others in the time you have left for this test.

You are permitted to use a calculator on this test. You may use your calculator for any problems you choose,

but some of the problems may best be done without using a calculator.

Note: Unless otherwise stated, all of the following should be assumed.

1. Illustrative figures are NOT necessarily drawn to scale.
2. Geometric figures lie in a plane.
3. The word *line* indicates a straight line.
4. The word *average* indicates arithmetic mean.

---

1. For all nonzero values of x and y, which of the following expressions is equivalent to $-\dfrac{35x^5y^4}{5xy}$?

   A. $-7x^4y^3$
   B. $-7x^5y^4$
   C. $-7x^6y^5$
   D. $-30x^4y^3$
   E. $-40x^4y^3$

2. The degree measures of the 3 angles of the triangle below are expressed in terms of x. What is the value of x ?

   F. 10
   G. 12
   H. 24
   J. 30
   K. 36

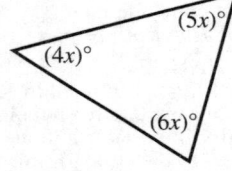

$(5x)°$
$(4x)°$
$(6x)°$

3. A 48.5-ounce batch of cologne will be used to fill empty bottles. Each full bottle will contain 0.35 ounces of cologne. This batch of cologne will fill at most how many bottles full of cologne?

   A. 13
   B. 14
   C. 122
   D. 138
   E. 139

4. Of the 200 parking spaces in a parking lot, 6% of the spaces are reserved for handicapped parking. Of those parking spaces NOT reserved for handicapped parking, 20 are suitable for compact cars only. How many spaces that are NOT reserved for handicapped parking are suitable for noncompact cars?

   F. 160
   G. 168
   H. 174
   J. 180
   K. 188

DO YOUR FIGURING HERE.

GO ON TO THE NEXT PAGE.

2 △ △ △ △ △ △ △ △ △ **2**

5. What is the value of $2|2 - 9| - 3(5 + 2)$?

    A. -35
    B. -27
    C. -18
    D. $\;\;-8$
    E. $\;\;-7$

DO YOUR FIGURING HERE.

6. Ricardo started a savings account for his daughter Ruth by depositing $500 into the account for her 1st birthday. For each successive birthday, Ricardo deposits $200 more than the amount deposited for the previous birthday. This is the only money deposited into the account. What is the total amount of money Ricardo will have deposited into the account for Ruth up to and including her 6th birthday?

    F. $4,000
    G. $4,200
    H. $4,700
    J. $4,900
    K. $6,000

7. Tawanna bought a used car. She made an initial payment of $700.00. She then made 36 equal monthly payments. The total amount Tawanna paid for the car was $7,000.00. What was the amount of each of her monthly payments?

    A. $\;\;$19.44
    B. $175.00
    C. $194.44
    D. $213.89
    E. $360.00

8. Which of the following matrices is equal to

$\begin{bmatrix} 9 & 2 \\ -4 & 1 \end{bmatrix} + \begin{bmatrix} -6 & 8 \\ 7 & 6 \end{bmatrix}$?

    F. $\begin{bmatrix} -40 & 84 \\ 31 & -26 \end{bmatrix}$

    G. $\begin{bmatrix} 3 & 10 \\ 11 & 7 \end{bmatrix}$

    H. $\begin{bmatrix} 3 & 10 \\ 3 & 7 \end{bmatrix}$

    J. $\begin{bmatrix} 11 & 2 \\ -3 & 13 \end{bmatrix}$

    K. $\begin{bmatrix} 15 & 10 \\ 11 & 7 \end{bmatrix}$

GO ON TO THE NEXT PAGE.

2 △ △ △ △ △ △ △ △ △ **2**

DO YOUR FIGURING HERE.

9. Lyle and Ming are painting an art room. They started with 4 gallons of paint. On the first day, Lyle used $\frac{1}{2}$ gallon of paint and Ming used $1\frac{1}{4}$ gallons of paint. How many gallons of paint were left when they completed their first day of painting?

A. $1\frac{3}{4}$

B. $2\frac{1}{4}$

C. $2\frac{3}{4}$

D. $3\frac{1}{4}$

E. $3\frac{1}{2}$

10. In the standard (x,y) coordinate plane, what is the slope of the line through $(-3,1)$ and $(5,6)$?

F. $-\frac{5}{2}$

G. $-\frac{5}{8}$

H. $\frac{5}{8}$

J. $\frac{5}{2}$

K. $\frac{7}{2}$

11. The lengths of corresponding sides of 2 similar right triangles are in the ratio 4:5. The hypotenuse of the smaller triangle is 24 inches long. How many inches long is the hypotenuse of the larger triangle?

A. 1.25
B. 9
C. 20
D. 25
E. 30

12. The lengths of the 3 sides of right triangle $\triangle ABC$ shown below are given in meters. What is sin A ?

F. $\frac{8}{17}$

G. $\frac{8}{15}$

H. $\frac{15}{17}$

J. $\frac{17}{15}$

K. $\frac{17}{8}$

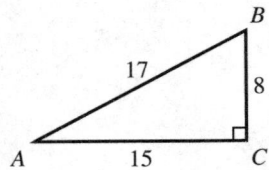

GO ON TO THE NEXT PAGE.

2 △ △ △ △ △ △ △ △ △ **2**

13. In the figure shown below, C is on the segment with endpoints A and D. The distance between A and B is 2,000 km, between A and C is 1,600 km, between A and D is 2,500 km, and between B and C is 1,200 km. What is the distance, in kilometers, between B and D ?

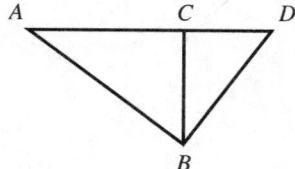

DO YOUR FIGURING HERE.

- **A.** $100\sqrt{481}$
- **B.** $300\sqrt{7}$
- **C.** 900
- **D.** 1,200
- **E.** 1,500

14. What is the sum of the 2 solutions of the equation $x^2 - 4x - 45 = 0$?

- **F.** −45
- **G.** −5
- **H.** 0
- **J.** 4
- **K.** 9

15. In the figure shown below, all angles are right angles, and the side lengths given are in inches. What is the area, in square inches, of the figure?

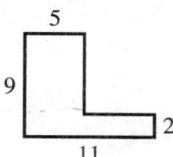

- **A.** 42
- **B.** 57
- **C.** 67
- **D.** 89
- **E.** 99

16. Quadrant I of the standard (x,y) coordinate plane is shown on a large computer screen. A blinking dot is positioned at (2,3). The dot makes exactly 2 moves: first, horizontally in the positive x direction for 4 seconds at a speed of 0.5 coordinate units per second; then, vertically in the positive y direction for 2 seconds at the same speed. At what point is the dot located after these 2 moves?

- **F.** (2,6)
- **G.** (3,5)
- **H.** (4,4)
- **J.** (5,3)
- **K.** (6,5)

GO ON TO THE NEXT PAGE.

2 △ △ △ △ △ △ △ △ △ **2**

DO YOUR FIGURING HERE.

Use the following information to answer questions 17–19.

A weeklong summer camp is held in June for children in Grades 3–6. Parents and guardians who enrolled their children for camp by May 15 received a 20% discount off the regular enrollment fee for each child enrolled. For each grade, the table below gives the number of children enrolled by May 15 as well as the *regular* enrollment fee per child. The grade of any child is that child's grade in school as of May 15.

Grade	Enrollment by May 15	Regular enrollment fee
3	20	$350
4	15	$400
5	28	$450
6	18	$500

17. By May 15, Mr. Ramirez had enrolled his 2 children for camp. One child was in Grade 4, and the other was in Grade 6. What was the total amount Mr. Ramirez paid to enroll his 2 children?

    A. $720
    B. $800
    C. $820
    D. $860
    E. $880

18. Which of the following equations gives a true relationship between the *regular* enrollment fee, f, and the grade, g, of any child enrolled in the camp?

    F. $f = g + 50$
    G. $f = 50g$
    H. $f = 50g + 200$
    J. $f = 50g + 300$
    K. $f = 300g + 50$

19. By May 15, Ms. Chen had enrolled her 2 children for camp. One child was in Grade 3, and the other was in Grade 4. For each grade, the names of all the children enrolled by May 15 will be entered into a drawing for a free T-shirt. For each grade, 1 name will be randomly drawn. What is the probability that the names of both of Ms. Chen's children will be drawn?

    A. $\dfrac{7}{60}$

    B. $\dfrac{2}{81}$

    C. $\dfrac{1}{300}$

    D. $\dfrac{100}{2,187}$

    E. $\dfrac{1}{3,240}$

GO ON TO THE NEXT PAGE.

2 △ △ △ △ △ △ △ △ △ **2**

DO YOUR FIGURING HERE.

20. You drove 18 miles in 20 minutes at a constant speed and did NOT exceed the speed limit, given in miles per hour. Among the following, which is the *lowest* that the speed limit could have been?

F. 45
G. 50
H. 55
J. 60
K. 65

21. What value of x makes the equation $-\frac{1}{81} = -3^x$ true?

A. -4

B. 4

C. 27

D. $-\frac{1}{4}$

E. $\frac{1}{243}$

22. The equation $R = \frac{P}{I^2}$ gives the resistance, R, in terms of the power, P, and the current, I, of an electrical system. Which of the following expressions gives I in terms of P and R ?

F. $\sqrt{\frac{R}{P}}$

G. $\sqrt{\frac{P}{R}}$

H. $\frac{P}{R}$

J. $\frac{R}{P}$

K. PR

23. One welcome sign flashes every 8 seconds, and another welcome sign flashes every 12 seconds. At a certain instant, the 2 signs flash at the same time. How many seconds elapse until the 2 signs next flash at the same time?

A. 4
B. 10
C. 20
D. 24
E. 96

GO ON TO THE NEXT PAGE.

2 △ △ △ △ △ △ △ △ △ **2**

24. The area of a certain square is 900 square inches. What is the perimeter of this square, in inches?

- **F.** 30
- **G.** 60
- **H.** 120
- **J.** 225
- **K.** 450

25. The Department of Natural Resources (DNR) is estimating the deer population in Twin Pines County. Several months ago, DNR rangers captured, tagged, and then released 108 deer. Recently, DNR rangers captured 54 deer in the county and found that 36 of them had been tagged in the earlier capture. The DNR estimates the deer population in the county using the proportion below. What is the DNR estimate of the deer population in the county?

$$\frac{\text{tagged deer in capture 1}}{\text{deer population}} = \frac{\text{tagged deer in capture 2}}{\text{deer in capture 2}}$$

- **A.** 108
- **B.** 126
- **C.** 144
- **D.** 162
- **E.** 198

26. In an arithmetic sequence, the 10th term (a_{10}) is 30 and the common difference is 2. What is the 1st term (a_1) ?

- **F.** −28
- **G.** 6
- **H.** 11
- **J.** 12
- **K.** 15

27. A *pedometer* records the number of steps a person takes as he or she walks. When a pedometer records 3,898 steps taken by a person who covers a distance of 2.25 feet per step, how much distance, to the nearest 0.1 mile, did the person cover?

(Note: 1 mile = 5,280 feet)

- **A.** 0.3
- **B.** 0.6
- **C.** 1.4
- **D.** 1.7
- **E.** 3.0

28. Among a group of 20 students, 13 students are members of the Math Club, 11 students are members of the Drama Club, and 9 students are members of both clubs. How many of the 20 students are NOT members of either club?

- **F.** 4
- **G.** 5
- **H.** 6
- **J.** 11
- **K.** 13

DO YOUR FIGURING HERE.

GO ON TO THE NEXT PAGE.

2 △ △ △ △ △ △ △ △ △ **2**

29. To increase the mean of 7 numbers by 4, by how much would the sum of the 7 numbers have to increase?

   A.   4
   B.   7
   C. 11
   D. 28
   E. 56

DO YOUR FIGURING HERE.

30. Which of the following is an equation of the circle in the standard (x,y) coordinate plane whose center is at $(4,-3)$ and whose radius is 5 coordinate units long?

   F. $(x - 4)^2 + (y + 3)^2 = 5$
   G. $(x - 4)^2 + (y + 3)^2 = 25$
   H. $(x - 3)^2 + (y + 4)^2 = 25$
   J. $(x + 3)^2 + (y - 4)^2 = 5$
   K. $(x + 4)^2 + (y - 3)^2 = 25$

31. All 25 students in a chemistry class took a test. Each student earned a test score that was an integer number of points, and no 2 students earned the same test score. The median test score was 80 points. How many students earned a test score that was greater than 80 points?

   A.   5
   B. 12
   C. 13
   D. 14
   E. 20

32. Shefali goes to a farmers' market every Saturday. Two Saturdays ago, Shefali purchased 3 apples and 4 oranges for a total of $3.47. Last Saturday, she purchased 12 oranges, but no apples, and spent $6.36. Today, she only has one $10 bill. Given that none of the prices have changed over the last 3 weeks, what is the maximum number of apples she can purchase today?

   (Note: No sales tax is charged at this farmers' market.)

   F. 18
   G. 19
   H. 21
   J. 22
   K. 23

GO ON TO THE NEXT PAGE.

2 △ △ △ △ △ △ △ △ △ **2**

Use the following information to answer questions 33–36.

Fletcher purchased 5 items at Hippity-Bippity Toy Store for a total of $18.55, which included sales tax. When he arrived home, he discovered that his receipt was torn and did not show the price of the bag of balloons or the 6% sales tax applied to the sum of the 5 prices. The partial receipt is shown below.

Hippity-Bippity Toy Store

Date: 12-20-2014
Time: 2:30 p.m.

Item	Price
Bag of marbles	$2.00
Doll	$6.00
Car	$3.00
Jump rope	$4.00
Bag of balloo	

33. Fletcher left his home 1 hour 15 minutes before he entered the store. He spent 25 minutes in the store before he made his purchase. What time did Fletcher leave his home?

   A.   12:50 p.m.
   B.   1:10 p.m.
   C.   1:20 p.m.
   D.   1:30 p.m.
   E.   1:40 p.m.

34. To the nearest $0.10, what was the price of the bag of balloons?

   F. $1.10
   G. $2.40
   H. $2.50
   J. $2.70
   K. $3.50

35. The price of the doll was how much greater than the mean of the 4 prices shown on the partial receipt?

   A. $1.50
   B. $2.00
   C. $2.25
   D. $2.50
   E. $3.00

GO ON TO THE NEXT PAGE.

2 △ △ △ △ △ △ △ △ △ **2**

36. Malik will spend a total of $30.00 before sales tax on *x* bags of marbles and *y* cars purchased at the prices shown on the partial receipt. One of the following line segments graphed in the standard (*x*,*y*) coordinate plane contains points for all possible combinations of *x* and *y*. Which one?

DO YOUR FIGURING HERE.

F.
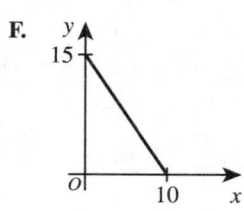

J.
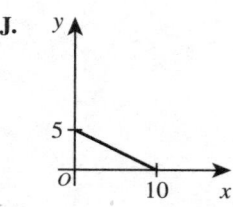

G.
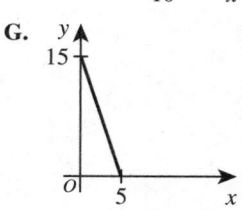

K.
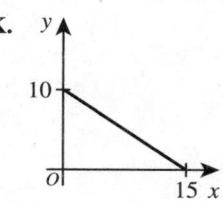

H.
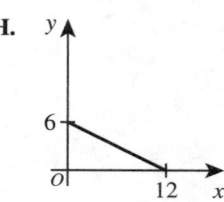

37. In △*DEF*, shown in the figure below, $\overline{EG}$ is an altitude, ∠*DEF* is a right angle, *EF* = 20 centimeters, and the measure of ∠*EDF* is 30°. What is *EG*, in centimeters?

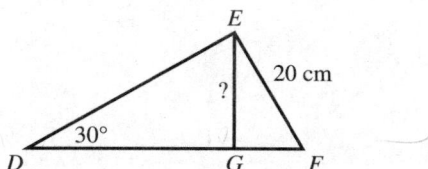

A. 10
B. 10√3
C. 20
D. 20√3
E. 40

GO ON TO THE NEXT PAGE.

2 △ △ △ △ △ △ △ △ △ **2**

38. Let the polynomial functions f and g be defined as $f(x) = x^2 + 7x - 3$ and $g(x) = x^2 - 4x + 5$.   Let $h(x) = f(x) - g(x)$. What is $h(2)$?

   F. -16
   G. 8
   H. 14
   J. 22
   K. 24

39. A student is using a protractor, as shown below, to find the measures of the interior angles of $\triangle ABC$. Which of the following is closest to the degree measure of $\angle C$?

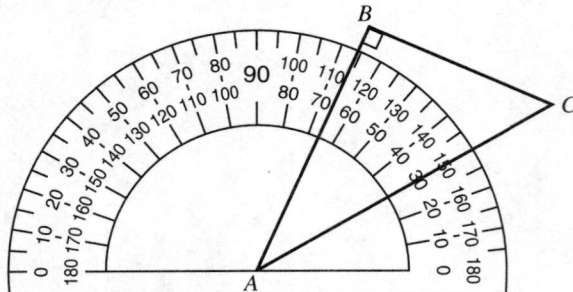

   A. $36°$
   B. $44°$
   C. $46°$
   D. $54°$
   E. $66°$

40. For real numbers x and y such that $0 \le x \le 5$ and $y \ge 9$, the expression $\dfrac{x+y}{y}$ can have which of the following values?

   F. 0

   G. $\dfrac{10}{9}$

   H. $\dfrac{14}{5}$

   J. 5

   K. 6

41. Given the functions $f(x) = x^2 + 1$ and $g(x) = x - 3$, which of the following expressions is $f(g(x))$?

   A. $x^2 - 8$
   B. $x^2 - 6x + 10$
   C. $x^2 + x - 2$
   D. $x^3 + x - 3$
   E. $x^3 - 3x^2 + x - 3$

GO ON TO THE NEXT PAGE.

2 △ △ △ △ △ △ △ △ △ 2

42. Given that the equation $\frac{4x - y}{x + y} = \frac{5}{2}$ is true, what is the value of $\frac{x}{y}$?

F. $\frac{2}{3}$

G. $\frac{5}{2}$

H. $\frac{7}{3}$

J. $\frac{7}{5}$

K. $\frac{7}{18}$

DO YOUR FIGURING HERE.

43. Juro traveled to 3 locations during a workday. Juro remained at each location a whole number of hours. The graph below shows the relationship between time, in hours, into his workday and total distance, in kilometers, traveled. Which of the following values is closest to Juro's average speed, in kilometers per hour, for the parts of the workday when he was traveling?

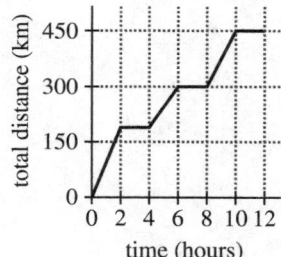

A. 45
B. 57
C. 60
D. 75
E. 94

44. What is the amplitude of the function $y = 3 \sin x$?

F. 1

G. 3

H. 6

J. $\frac{1}{3}$

K. $\frac{3}{2}$

GO ON TO THE NEXT PAGE.

2   **2**

45. For all nonzero values of w, which of the following expressions is equivalent to $\frac{4}{w} + \frac{2}{w^2}$?

A. $\frac{2w+1}{w^2}$

B. $\frac{4w+2}{w^2}$

C. $\frac{6}{w+w^2}$

D. $\frac{6}{w^2}$

E. $\frac{6}{w^3}$

DO YOUR FIGURING HERE.

46. Let A, B, and C represent the digits in the hundreds, tens, and ones places, respectively, of a certain 3-digit whole number. Let D, E, and F represent the digits in the hundreds, tens, and ones places, respectively, of a different 3-digit whole number. The positive difference between the 2 numbers is greater than 100. Which of the following inequalities *must* be true?

F. $|A - D| \geq 1$

G. $|B - E| \geq 1$

H. $|C - F| \geq 1$

J. $A - D \geq 1$

K. $B - E \geq 1$

47. A number line graph includes the points at real numbers a and b, as shown below. Which of the following inequalities expresses an interval that must include the product ab ?

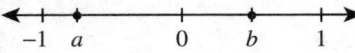

A. $-1 < ab < a$
B. $a < ab < 0$
C. $0 < ab < b$
D. $b < ab < 1$
E. $1 < ab < 2$

48. Sani's course grade in his chemistry class is based on 3 tests and 1 final exam. Each of the 3 test scores is weighted as 20% of the course grade, and the final exam score is weighted as 40% of the course grade. Sani's 3 test scores are 78, 86, and 82, respectively. What is the minimum score that Sani will have to earn on the final exam in order to receive a course grade of at least 86 ?

F. 82
G. 84
H. 90
J. 92
K. 98

GO ON TO THE NEXT PAGE.

2 △ △ △ △ △ △ △ △ △ **2**

49. The triangle below has vertices $A(-1,-2)$, $B(2,2)$, and $C(-1,4)$. What is the area of $\triangle ABC$, in square coordinate units?

DO YOUR FIGURING HERE.

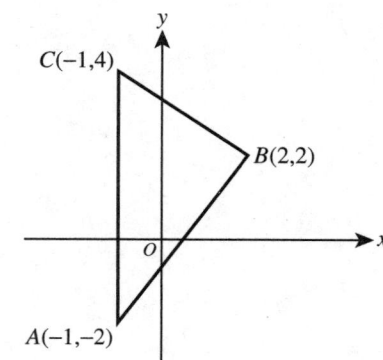

   A. 9

   B. 15

   C. 18

   D. $\frac{5}{2}\sqrt{13}$

   E. $3\sqrt{13}$

50. For some real number x, $\sqrt{x^2} \neq x$. Therefore x is:

   F. zero.
   G. greater than π.
   H. irrational.
   J. negative.
   K. undefined.

51. In the standard (x,y) coordinate plane below, point A has coordinates $(2,-4)$, and point $B(8,-1)$ divides $\overline{AC}$ so that the ratio $AB:BC$ is 1:3. What are the coordinates of point C ?

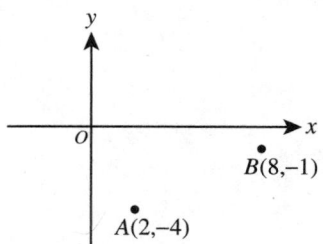

   A. $(-16,-13)$
   B. $(\ 10,\ \ 0)$
   C. $(\ 14,\ \ 2)$
   D. $(\ 26,\ \ 8)$
   E. $(\ 32,\ 11)$

52. A wire binds 4 identical posts together as shown below. Each post has a 3-inch radius. What is the length, to the nearest inch, of the shortest wire that will go around the 4 posts without overlap?

   F. 21
   G. 31
   H. 33
   J. 43
   K. 52

GO ON TO THE NEXT PAGE.

2 △ △ △ △ △ △ △ △ △ 2

53. Given that b is rational and $i = \sqrt{-1}$, the product of the expression $(3 + bi)$ and which of the following expressions must be a rational number?

   A. i
   B. bi
   C. $3bi$
   D. $3 + bi$
   E. $3 - bi$

DO YOUR FIGURING HERE.

54. For positive integers x and y where $x < 8$, $\log_x 8 = y$. What is the value of y ?

   F. 1
   G. 2
   H. 3
   J. 4
   K. 8

55. The right triangle shown below is 8 squares high and 10 squares long. One of the following values is the ratio of the shaded area to the unshaded area. Which one?

   A. $\frac{3}{7}$

   B. $\frac{3}{10}$

   C. $\frac{7}{13}$

   D. $\frac{7}{20}$

   E. $\frac{15}{28}$

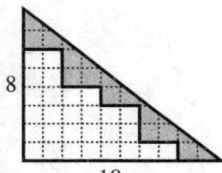

56. For all positive integers x, which of the following expressions is equivalent to $x^{\frac{1}{4}} \cdot x^{\frac{1}{6}}$?

   F. $\sqrt{x^{24}}$

   G. $\sqrt[5]{x}$

   H. $\sqrt[5]{x^{12}}$

   J. $\sqrt[12]{x^5}$

   K. $\sqrt[24]{x}$

GO ON TO THE NEXT PAGE.

2 △ △ △ △ △ △ △ △ △ **2**

57. One day on the New York Currency Exchange, 1 British pound (£1) could be exchanged for $2.75 in U.S. currency, and 1 Canadian dollar ($1) could be exchanged for $0.92 in U.S. currency. On that day, how much Canadian currency, rounded to the nearest Canadian cent, could be exchanged for £2 ?

A. $0.41
B. $1.84
C. $2.07
D. $5.06
E. $5.98

58. The sides of an acute triangle measure 17 cm, 16 cm, and 15 cm, respectively. The measure of the smallest angle of the triangle is a solution for A to which of the following equations?

F. $17^2 = 15^2 + 16^2 - 2(15)(16)\sin A$

G. $17^2 = 15^2 + 16^2 - 2(15)(16)\cos A$

H. $16^2 = 15^2 + 17^2 - 2(15)(17)\cos A$

J. $15^2 = 16^2 + 17^2 - 2(16)(17)\sin A$

K. $15^2 = 16^2 + 17^2 - 2(16)(17)\cos A$

59. Set A and Set B each consist of 5 distinct numbers. The 2 sets contain identical numbers with the exception of the number with the least value in each set. The number with the least value in Set B is greater than the number with the least value in Set A. The value of which of the following measures *must* be greater for Set B than for Set A ?

A. Mean only
B. Median only
C. Range only
D. Mean and range only
E. Mean, median, and range

60. Of the 16 cars on a rental-car lot, 6 are minivans, 7 are sedans, and 3 are hatchbacks. Thalia will rent 3 of these cars, chosen at random, for business associates. What is the probability that Thalia will rent 1 of each of the 3 types of cars?

F. $\dfrac{1}{3}$

G. $\dfrac{1}{16}$

H. $\dfrac{3}{16}$

J. $\dfrac{9}{40}$

K. $\dfrac{9}{80}$

END OF TEST 2

STOP! DO NOT TURN THE PAGE UNTIL TOLD TO DO SO.

DO NOT RETURN TO THE PREVIOUS TEST.

3 ▬▬▬▬▬▬▬▬▬▬▬▬▬▬ **3**

READING TEST

35 Minutes—40 Questions

DIRECTIONS: There are several passages in this test. Each passage is accompanied by several questions. After reading a passage, choose the best answer to each question and fill in the corresponding oval on your answer document. You may refer to the passages as often as necessary.

Passage I

LITERARY NARRATIVE: Passage A is adapted from the autobiography *A Peculiar Treasure* by Edna Ferber (©1960 by Morris L. Ernst, et al., Trustees). Passage B is adapted from the memoir *Pull Me Up: A Memoir* by Dan Barry (©2004 by Dan Barry).

Passage A by Edna Ferber

The printing shop and pressroom were separated from the front office only by a doorway, and the door never was closed. There were the type forms and tables, the linotype machine (a new and fearsome invention to
5 me), the small press, the big newspaper press, the boiler plate, the trays of type, all the paraphernalia that goes to make up the heart of a small-town newspaper. The front room is its head, but without the back room it could not function or even live. The linotype and the
10 small press went all day, for there the advertising was set up and printed, as well as handbills, programs, all the odds and ends classified as job printing. Mac, who ruled this domain, was the perfect example of the fictional printer. He had come in years before, his brown
15 hair curled over a mild brow, his limp shirt seemed perennial. But his eye was infallible, and few if any shrdlus and etaoins marred the fair sequence of Mac's copy. His voice was soft, gentle, drawling, but he was boss of the print shop from the cat to the linotype oper-
20 ator. Mac seldom talked but sometimes—rarely—he appeared in the front office, a drooping figure, with a piece of news by which he had come in some devious way. Standing at the side of the city editor's desk he would deliver himself of this information, looking mild
25 and limply romantic. It always proved to be a bombshell.

Such was the make-up of the Appleton, Wisconsin, Daily Crescent office.

In the past thirty years all sorts of ex-newspaper
30 men from Richard Harding Davis to Vincent Sheean and John Gunther have written about the lure of the reporter's life, the smell of printer's ink, the adventure of reporting. It all sounds slightly sentimental and silly, but it's true—or it was, at least, in my newspaper expe-
35 rience. To this day I can't smell the scent of white paper, wet ink, oil, hot lead, mucilage and cats that goes to make up the peculiar odor of any newspaper plant, be

it Appleton, Wisconsin, or Cairo, Egypt, that I don't get a pang of nostalgia for the old reporting days. "I was
40 once a newspaper man myself" has come to be a fun phrase. But practically everyone seems to have been, or to have wanted to be, a newspaper reporter.

Passage B by Dan Barry

Ink. The building smelled of ink, spilled and bled. It was a tart and chemical smell, the kind that weaves
45 into the fabric of your clothes and then under your skin, the kind that comes home with you, sits with you at the dinner table, tells you constantly what it is you do. Car mechanics know their smell, as do fishermen and hair stylists, nurses and short-order cooks. You are a man
50 who chases halibut, a woman who perms hair. You smell of it.

I waded into that invisible veil of ink, inhaled it deeply, allowed it to wash over me. It smelled of words and phrases, rants and ideas, sports scores and felony
55 arrests, announcements of marriage and notices of death. Maybe the chemical-like aroma was inducing hallucination, but I doubted it. In a squat concrete building, no different from all the others in a drab Connecticut industrial park, I was experiencing a moment
60 of revelation—an epiphany, really, at the age of twenty-five.

This is what I do.

Pinned like a manifesto to a bulletin board in the center of this ink-perfumed building was a typewritten
65 note from my new employer, announcing that on this day, October 17, 1983, I would begin working as a reporter for a daily newspaper. The note formalized my calling in life with a splash of perspective that would stay with me forever:

70 *Dan is a former intern at the* Daily News *in New York and a graduate assistant for the journalism department at New York University. His writing has appeared in the* Daily News, *the* New York Times *and the* Rocky Mountain News. *Soon it will appear in*
75 *trashcans throughout north-central Connecticut. Please make him feel relevant.*

Reading the note, I thought, I'm home.

GO ON TO THE NEXT PAGE.

3 ▐███████████████████████████████████▌ **3**

Finding my way had not been easy. The internship at the *Daily News* had ended, the graduate degree from
80 NYU had been shoved in a drawer, and I had returned to living beside the sump pump in my parents' basement. I spent my days splitting sod for a lawn and sprinkling company alongside Eddie, who had taken to calling me "Professor," and my nights typing out pro-
85 fessional love letters to the *New London Day*, the *Asbury Park Press*, the *Poughkeepsie Journal*, the *Stamford Advocate*, the *Anywhere Clarion-Bugle-Star-Record-Sentinel*, and every other Northeastern newspaper that I had never read.

Questions 1–4 ask about Passage A.

---

1. It can reasonably be inferred that Passage A is narrated from the point of view of someone who:

   A. once worked in the newspaper business.
   B. recently started a career in the newspaper business.
   C. is outside the newspaper business and is evaluating the inner workings of various news offices.
   D. is outside the newspaper business and longs to be a reporter.

2. Based on Passage A, the narrator believes that, compared to what goes on in the front office, what goes on in the printing shop and pressroom is:

   F. more tedious.
   G. equally critical.
   H. equally chaotic.
   J. less regulated.

3. The narrator of Passage A most nearly characterizes Mac as both:

   A. innately talented and professionally incompetent.
   B. innately talented and professionally inexperienced.
   C. temperamentally unimposing and professionally inexperienced.
   D. temperamentally unimposing and professionally invaluable.

4. According to the narrator of Passage A, Mac would occasionally appear in the front office in order to:

   F. set up and print the advertising.
   G. supervise the linotype operator.
   H. chastise the reporters for having too many errors in their copy.
   J. share newsworthy information with the city editor.

Questions 5–7 ask about Passage B.

---

5. What is the epiphany the narrator of Passage B experienced at the age of twenty-five?

   A. He couldn't live in his parents' basement forever.
   B. His dream of being a reporter had finally been realized.
   C. He would rather write news stories than work for a lawn company.
   D. His success as a reporter would depend on his work ethic.

6. Based on Passage B, the note that the narrator's employer wrote can best be described as:

   F. mildly sarcastic.
   G. overtly solemn.
   H. blatantly apologetic.
   J. particularly optimistic.

7. The last sentence of Passage B mainly serves to indicate that the narrator:

   A. had disdain for most northeastern newspapers.
   B. was familiar with the newspapers published around the area.
   C. was desperate to find a newswriting job.
   D. had extensive newswriting experience.

Questions 8–10 ask about both passages.

---

8. Compared to the description of the newspaper office mentioned in Passage A, the description of the newspaper office mentioned in Passage B provides less information about the:

   F. types of machines used to print the newspaper.
   G. outside appearance of the office building.
   H. number of people who work in the office.
   J. types of stories being written and printed for the newspaper.

9. Compared to Passage A, the style of Passage B is more strongly characterized by its use of:

   A. technical jargon.
   B. dialogue.
   C. formal diction.
   D. figurative language.

10. Based on the passages, who would be most likely to associate the smell of ink with pleasant memories?

    F. The narrator of Passage A only
    G. The narrator of Passage B only
    H. Both narrators
    J. Neither narrator

GO ON TO THE NEXT PAGE.

3   3

Passage II

SOCIAL SCIENCE: This passage is adapted from the book *Lost Discoveries: The Ancient Roots of Modern Science—from the Babylonians to the Maya* by Dick Teresi (©2002 by Dick Teresi).

"In the history of culture," wrote mathematician Tobias Dantzig in 1930, "the discovery of zero will always stand out as one of the greatest single achievements of the human race." Zero, he said, marked a
5 "turning point" in math, science, and industry. He also noted that the zero was invented not in the West but by the Indians in the early centuries after Christ. Negative numbers followed soon thereafter. The Maya invented zero in the New World at approximately the same time.
10 Europe, says Dantzig, did not accept zero as a number until the twelfth or thirteenth century.

There are many "biographies of zero," and Dantzig's concise and spirited account of the birth of a number is adequate for most of us. He sees zero's
15 invention appearing on an Indian's counting board in, say, the first or second century A.D. The Indian counting board had columns for the ones, tens, hundreds, thousands, and so on. To "write" 302, for instance, a mathematician would put a 2 in the first (right) column
20 and a 3 in the third, leaving the second column empty. On one fateful day, as Dantzig sees it, an unknown Indian drew an oval in the second column. He called it *sunya*, for "empty" or "blank." *Sunyata*, an important concept in Buddhism, is often translated as "emptiness"
25 or "void."

The Arabs turned *sunya* into *sifr* ("empty" in Arabic), which became *zephirum* in Italy, and eventually zero. In Germany and elsewhere, *sifr* became *cifra*, and then, in English, *cipher*. In other words, it took
30 over a thousand years for Western civilization to accept a number for "nothing." Dantzig blames the Greeks. "The concrete mind of the ancient Greeks could not conceive the void as a number, let alone endow the void with a symbol."

35 That's the short version, and not a bad one. You don't want to hear the long version, so let's suffice with a medium-sized tale.

Zero lay rustling in the weeds for many centuries before that Indian drew it on a counting board. It was
40 an unnamed, unwritten force. It took many more centuries after the Indians and the Maya dared speak its name before zero was promoted to a full-fledged number.

The U.S. Library of Congress defends our calendar
45 and its missing zero. "There has never been a system of recording reigns, dynasties, or eras," the library states, "that did not designate its first year as the year 1." In fact, the Maya had both years 0 and days 0.

The Babylonians had no zero, but they knew some-
50 thing was wrong. If they numbered the first year of

each king's reign as year 1, then added up the number of years of each separate reign, they'd end up with too many years unless each king died just before midnight on New Year's Eve and his successor took the throne
55 after midnight. Thus, the Babylonians called a king's first year the *accession year*. The following year was year 1. The accession year was a kind of year 0. The Babylonians, so far as we know, never articulated zero, but seemed aware that there was a missing number in
60 their system.

The contemporary mathematician who has conducted the most rigorous research on nothing is Robert Kaplan, the author of *The Nothing That Is: A Natural History of Zero*. Zero turns up throughout history in dif-
65 ferent cultures as a series of dots and circles, and Kaplan writes of following "the swarm of dots we find in writings from a host of languages, across great spans of time, and on topics mathematical and otherwise."

Kaplan traces the roots of zero to Sumer and
70 Babylonia. The Sumerians counted by tens and sixties, a system adopted by the Babylonians, who eclipsed them in Mesopotamia. The Babylonians, far ahead of the Romans and Greeks to come, imposed a positional notation on the old Sumerian sexagesimal system. Writ-
75 ing their numbers on clay, the Babylonians needed a symbol to put in the "empty" columns, just as we today use zero to differentiate between 302 and 32.

Somewhere between the sixth and third centuries B.C., the Babylonians began using two slanted tacklike
80 symbols to insert in the empty columns. They borrowed the slanty tacks from their language, where they were used as periods, among other things. However, the Babylonians used their "zero" only in the middle of numbers, never at the end. Clearly, this was not a full-
85 fledged zero.

Kaplan argues that when Alexander invaded the Babylonian empire in 331 B.C., he hauled off zero along with the gold. Shortly thereafter we find the symbol 0 for zero in the papyri of Greek astronomers, but the
90 mathematicians never pursued the concept.

11. According to the passage, the Babylonian and Indian civilizations were similar in that they both:

A. wrote zero using tacklike symbols.

B. referred to their rulers' first year in power as the *accession year*.

C. derived their names for zero from their respective religions.

D. used a symbol for zero in the middle of numbers.

GO ON TO THE NEXT PAGE.

3 ▮▮▮▮▮▮▮▮▮▮▮▮▮▮▮▮▮▮▮▮▮▮▮▮▮▮▮▮▮▮▮ **3**

12. As it is presented in the second paragraph (lines 12–25), the story of an unknown person drawing an oval on a counting board is best described as:

F. a factual account from a document Dantzig discovered.
G. a factual account from ancient Indian writings.
H. Dantzig's theory of how a historic invention occurred.
J. Kaplan's theory of how a historic invention occurred.

13. According to the passage, the Maya invented zero at about the same time as:

A. the Indians invented zero.
B. the Sumerians invented zero.
C. Alexander invaded Babylonia.
D. Europe accepted zero as a number.

14. As it is used in line 21, the phrase *fateful day* most nearly refers to a day that was:

F. unfortunate.
G. momentous.
H. ominous.
J. foretold.

15. According to the passage, in Germany, the word for zero became:

A. *sunya*.
B. *zephirum*.
C. *sifr*.
D. *cifra*.

16. In the passage, Dantzig criticizes the ancient Greeks because he thinks they:

F. lacked the abstract thinking necessary to think of the void as a number.
G. attempted to use zero in their mathematics before they understood it fully.
H. were unwilling to share their knowledge of zero with other European countries.
J. focused so much on negative numbers that they couldn't imagine a number for the void.

17. The passage author most clearly indicates that he thinks his readers wouldn't be interested in hearing:

A. the story of how the Maya conceived of zero.
B. what Dantzig contributed to mathematics.
C. the long version of the story of zero.
D. who drew the oval on the counting board in India.

18. The statement "Zero lay rustling in the weeds for many centuries" (line 38) most nearly means that the concept of zero:

F. had far-reaching effects on mathematics.
G. existed long before it was articulated.
H. had been developed and then forgotten.
J. was initially rejected by mathematicians.

19. The passage author responds to the US Library of Congress's statement that there has never been a system of dates with a year 0 by:

A. arguing that undiscovered civilizations may have had years 0.
B. citing an expert who disagrees with the statement.
C. suggesting that the Library of Congress's research is authoritative.
D. providing an example that contradicts the statement.

20. The passage author most clearly indicates that compared to other contemporary mathematicians' research on zero, Kaplan's research is more:

F. interesting.
G. speculative.
H. thorough.
J. admired.

GO ON TO THE NEXT PAGE.

3

3

Passage III

HUMANITIES: This passage is adapted from *I'll Take You There: Mavis Staples, The Staples Singers, and the March Up Freedom's Highway* by Greg Kot (©2014 by Greg Kot).

To fans of the Staples Singers in the '60s, the relative anonymity of Mavis Staples was puzzling. With an improbably deep voice bursting out of a diminutive five-foot frame, she projected the deepest commitment
5 to whatever she was singing, losing herself in every word as though reliving a critical moment in her personal story.

And yet she still wasn't a marquee name like Aretha Franklin, Gladys Knight, Diana Ross, and Dusty
10 Springfield. Part of this was by design—Mavis enjoyed singing with her family and preferred to melt into the group. Even when her father brought her out front to sing lead after her brother Pervis's voice changed in the '50s, she did so reluctantly. "I loved singing those bari-
15 tone harmonies, I always thought that was the best job you could have," Mavis said. She also felt a certain comfort being guided by her father, who had essentially taught her how and what to sing. Little had changed in the decades since, even as it was apparent that Mavis
20 had star power. "Mavis was and is a quartet singer," says Anthony Heilbut. "From a very early age she grew up singing harmony or singing lead in a group with four voices and her father's guitar. She was trained to sing with the guitar, whereas Aretha sang with the piano. It's
25 a very different approach."

Not only that, Pops's idiosyncratic guitar style made it difficult for Mavis to easily adapt to a different context. So, too, was the unspoken communication between Mavis and her siblings, the way they harmo-
30 nized with her, even the way they clapped hands together, a high-speed ripple that approximated an entire percussion section by itself. "I've been singing a long time," Mavis says, "and I could never find anyone to clap like Pervis and Cleedi."

35 But Al Bell never forgot the day in Arkansas when the teenage Mavis's voice bowled him over and left him in tears in what was essentially a solo performance of "On My Way to Heaven" during a Staples Singers show.

40 "In signing the Staples Singers, I thought of it as signing three acts in one," Bell says. "I wanted to record Pops and Mavis as solo artists. I knew it would add more to them from a personal appearance standpoint, bring them a broader, more diverse audience. I
45 would hear Pops sitting around and just playing his guitar at Stax Records and I thought, 'I've got to get this man down on tape.' His singing, I knew there was a lot more songs that could have been done with Pops as a vocalist, because he was so distinctive. With Mavis I
50 saw no boundaries at all—I saw her walking past all of them."

Steve Cropper had already won the Staples family's trust while recording *Soul Folk in Action*, so Bell had him produce what would be Mavis's self-titled
55 debut album.

"The attitude at Stax was that she's a superstar who nobody really knows about, and we have to figure out how to get her out there," Cropper recalls. "But it wasn't easy, because she puts limits on herself. There
60 were only certain songs she would try. Her upbringing, her feeling about what songs would or wouldn't go down with Pops, gave me the impression she didn't want to go too far too fast. So I approached the whole thing with kid gloves. I didn't want to lose her trust or
65 do something damaging."

Cropper found Pops a thoughtful and willing collaborator in the studio, but there was no question his word still counted more than anyone else's in the family, even though his children were well into adult-
70 hood. "Every now and then, Mavis would reference Pops in terms of putting his foot down about dating," Cropper says. "There were lines he didn't want to cross when it came to his family's well-being, and that included what kind of songs they would sing, what
75 message they would put out."

The guitarist knew he was running a risk presenting Mavis with a set of secular songs that didn't have any of the gospel or message-oriented underpinnings favored by Pops and the Staples Singers. Whereas her
80 first attempt at cutting a solo single, a cover of "Crying in the Chapel" for Epic Records, had some tenuous religious imagery, the tracks chosen for the *Mavis Staples* solo album were the sort of pop-oriented love and relationship songs that Pops typically shunned.

85 But Mavis was hardly insulated from the pop world as a fan and listener. She swooned over Sam Cooke's "You Send Me" the first time she heard it, and her cover of it on her debut album sounds wistful, as if she were singing both to a newfound love and Cooke's
90 memory.

21. The main purpose of the passage is to:
   A. introduce Bell as an important figure in the career of the Staples Singers.
   B. compare Mavis Staples to other famous female singers like Ross and Franklin.
   C. present a theory that Pops Staples was the driving force behind Mavis Staples's success as a singer.
   D. describe Mavis Staples's transition from a quartet singer to a solo artist.

GO ON TO THE NEXT PAGE.

3   3

22. It can most reasonably be inferred from the passage that Mavis Staples's relative anonymity in the '60s was puzzling to her fans mainly because she had a:

F. more distinct voice than her brother, who became more famous than she did.

G. greater vocal range than many other artists of the time.

H. voice that reminded fans of singers whose names were on the marquee.

J. powerful voice and a personal approach to her performances.

23. In the context of the passage, what does the author most nearly mean when he states, "Part of this was by design" (line 10)?

A. The Staples Singers had perfected their harmonies.

B. Mavis Staples did not initially desire a solo career.

C. Female singers in the '60s usually performed solo.

D. Mavis Staples had planned her career trajectory at a young age.

24. The main purpose of the third paragraph (lines 26–34) is to:

F. clarify how each member of the Staples Singers contributed to creating the group's unique sound.

G. show that change was difficult for Mavis Staples because of her musical connection with her family.

H. explain that Pops Staples chose the songs his family sang during concerts.

J. describe the performance style of the Staples Singers.

25. The main idea of the seventh paragraph (lines 56–65) is that:

A. Cropper brought the Staples Singers success by pushing them to try genres outside of their usual repertoire.

B. Cropper was careful about how he encouraged Mavis Staples to explore new opportunities with her music.

C. Stax Records was innovative because they took risks by signing unknown singers.

D. Mavis Staples was initially unwilling to perform without backup singers.

26. Based on the passage, regarding his family, Pops Staples's attitude can best be described as:

F. tolerant.

G. resentful.

H. protective.

J. ambivalent.

27. As it is used in line 5, the phrase *losing herself* most nearly refers to the way Mavis Staples:

A. sang as if the song lyrics evoked poignant episodes from her past.

B. clapped her hands along with a song.

C. transitioned to a new song when she felt moved by her siblings' harmonies.

D. danced on stage when her father or brother sang.

28. According to the passage, what event led directly to Mavis Staples becoming the lead singer of the Staples Singers?

F. Pops Staples leaving the group

G. Cleedi Staples learning the guitar

H. Pervis Staples's voice changing

J. Mavis Staples's voice becoming deeper

29. Based on the passage, Bell's reaction to hearing Mavis Staples's performance of "On My Way to Heaven" can most nearly be described as one of:

A. utter dismay.

B. reluctant acceptance.

C. mild amusement.

D. deep admiration.

30. The passage indicates that, compared to the songs traditionally chosen by the Staples Singers, the songs chosen for Mavis Staples's first solo album were:

F. more serious; they focused on global issues.

G. more pop oriented; they focused on love and relationships.

H. less personal; they were not originally written for her.

J. less upbeat; they were not meant to be played on a dance floor.

GO ON TO THE NEXT PAGE.

Passage IV

NATURAL SCIENCE: This passage is adapted from the book *Mycophilia: Revelations from the Weird World of Mushrooms* by Eugenia Bone (©2011 by Eugenia Bone).

There are a number of fungi that live in mutualist relationships in which a balance of interests occurs between two organisms. Lichen has a mutualistic relationship with photosynthesizing algae and bacteria.
5 And there are also commensal relationships, where the fungus may not be doing the host any good or any harm, either—the raison d'être of some yeasts in our body, for example, is unknown and may be commensal. But mycorrhizal fungi are the princes of mutualism.
10 "Fungi can't make their own food," said Gary Lincoff. "So they made a strategic choice to team up with plants."

Ninety percent of natural land plants are thought to have mycorrhizal fungi partners. It's a masterpiece of
15 evolution: Mycorrhizal fungi break down nutrients like phosphorus, carbon, water, and nitrogen into a readily assimilative form and deliver them to the plant in return for sugar produced by the plant via photosynthesis. The fungus needs sugar for energy and to launch its spores,
20 and the tree needs nutrients because (despite what I learned in school) tree roots don't do the job adequately. Tree roots primarily anchor the tree in the soil. While tree roots will absorb moisture if watered and nutrients if fertilized, it is the mycorrhizal fungus *grow-*
25 *ing on and in the tree roots* that provides the tree with the lion's share of its nutrition and water. Mycorrhizal fungi significantly expand the reach of plant roots, and by extending the root system, increase the tree's nutrient and water uptake.

30 In the wild, mycorrhizal fungi are key to not just the health of single trees but to healthy forest ecosystems. A single fungal genotype or clone can colonize the roots and maintain the nutritional requirements of many trees at once. And multiple fungi can colonize the
35 roots of all or most of the trees in a forest. The hyphae, those threadlike strings of cells that are the fungus, function as pathways for shuttling nutrients, water, and organic compounds around the forest. The mycologist Paul Stamets believes that mycorrhizal fungi function
40 as a giant communications network between multiple trees in a forest—he calls it "nature's Internet." Others have described this linkage as the "architecture of the wood-wide web."

Weaker plants are able to tap into this network,
45 too, like hitchhikers on a nutritional superhighway. Young seedlings struggling to grow in the shadow of established trees tap into the larger, older tree's fungal network to improve their nutritional uptake. This network exists to benefit not only established trees and
50 seedlings of the same species but also trees from different species, and at different stages of development. So one multitasking fungus, its hyphae attached to the roots of multiple trees in the forest, can simultaneously provide a different nutritional load as needed to differ-
55 ent trees. It's a couture service.

The old trees in a forest function as hubs for these mycelial networks. "Like spokes of a wheel," said Suzanne Simard, a professor of forestry at the University of British Columbia who studies mycorrhizae. Rhi-
60 zomorphs (ropes of hyphae) connect the foundation tree with other trees—like an express stop on a subway system where lots of local trains come through—and the bigger the tree, the larger the hub. That's because the largest trees have the greatest root system, and the
65 more roots there are, the more real estate there is for the fungus to colonize. "In one forest, we found 47 trees linked by two species of fungi composed of 12 individuals," said Simard. (By individuals, she means two genetically distinct fungal entities.) "Talk about two
70 degrees of separation!" Even nonphotosynthesizing plants take advantage of "the hub." Parasites like the Indian pipe depend totally on mycorrhizal fungi for its nutritive needs. It taps into the nutrients and water provided by the mycorrhizae and connects via the mycor-
75 rhizae to a photosynthesizing plant for sugar.

Despite the fact that fungi are microscopic organisms, the functions they perform are often on an ecosystem or landscape scale. If you could take an x-ray look at the soil, you'd see that underneath the forest duff
80 there is a layer of mycorrhizal mycelium running between, on, and in the roots of plants. It's like a stratum of life between the duff and the soil that holds water and nutrients in the ground. And when that stratum is disrupted, or not present, plants suffer. In fact,
85 ecosystems with inadequate mycorrhizal fungi can experience catastrophic losses of plant biomass.

31. The main purpose of the passage is to:

   A. contrast mutualist relationships with commensal relationships and contend that mycorrhizal fungi have a commensal relationship with plants.
   B. describe mycorrhizal fungi's relationship with plants and explain how this relationship plays an integral role in ecosystems.
   C. summarize how the Internet was inspired by networks of mycorrhizal fungi and clarify how the Internet and mycorrhizal networks are similar.
   D. establish that mycorrhizal fungi pose a threat to forests and suggest a way of curbing their influence on ecosystems.

32. According to the passage, compared to the typical amount of water a tree's roots provide the tree, the typical amount of water mycorrhizal fungi provide the tree is:

   F. about the same.
   G. much larger.
   H. much smaller.
   J. somewhat smaller.

GO ON TO THE NEXT PAGE.

3 ━━━━━━━━━━━━━━━━━━━━━━━━━━━━━━━ **3**

33. The main idea of the fourth paragraph (lines 44–55) is that:
    A. networks of fungi benefit different species of trees at various levels of development.
    B. young seedlings typically tap into the roots of trees that are the same species as the seedlings.
    C. established trees genetically alter fungal networks to benefit different species of trees.
    D. different species of trees can be identified based on their nutritional uptake.

34. The author uses the metaphor of an express stop in a subway system in order to:
    F. explain why parasites are harmful to larger trees.
    G. contrast two distinct mycelial networks.
    H. clarify how larger trees function in a mycelial network.
    J. illustrate how different species of fungi grow to be different sizes.

35. In the passage, the relationship between yeast and the human body is cited as an example of a:
    A. definite commensal relationship.
    B. possible commensal relationship.
    C. definite mutualist relationship.
    D. possible mutualist relationship.

36. The author most likely includes the quote from Lincoff (lines 10–12) to:
    F. suggest that mycorrhizal fungi have a commensal relationship with plants.
    G. contend that mycorrhizal fungi serve the same function as some yeasts in the human body.
    H. indicate why mycorrhizal fungi have a mutualist relationship with plants.
    J. explain why mycorrhizal fungi cannot make their own food.

37. As it is used in line 44, the phrase *tap into* most nearly means:
    A. endorse.
    B. finish.
    C. lift.
    D. use.

38. Based on the passage, young seedlings are often dependent on fungal networks because the seedlings are:
    F. struggling to grow in an established tree's shadow.
    G. trying to defend themselves against parasites.
    H. in need of a specific nutrient that is unused by established trees.
    J. susceptible to a wider range of diseases than established trees are.

39. Based on the passage, the author would most likely agree that Indian pipe's level of dependency on mycorrhizal fungi is:
    A. absolute.
    B. about the same as its dependence on nonphotosynthesizing plants.
    C. less than its dependence on nonphotosynthesizing plants.
    D. uncertain.

40. Which of the following statements, if true, would most WEAKEN the claim made by the author in lines 83–86 of the passage?
    F. Over a three-year span, two forests with different tree types increase the amount of mycorrhizal mycelium at the same rate.
    G. Over a three-year span, two forests with the same amount of mycorrhizal mycelium both lost the majority of their plant biomass.
    H. During a given year, after the majority of mycorrhizal mycelium dies in a forest, the plants in the forests flourish.
    J. During a given year, after the majority of mycorrhizal mycelium dies in a forest, the plants in the forests suffer.

Your First Practice Test

END OF TEST 3

STOP! DO NOT TURN THE PAGE UNTIL TOLD TO DO SO.

DO NOT RETURN TO A PREVIOUS TEST.

SCIENCE TEST
35 Minutes—40 Questions

DIRECTIONS: There are several passages in this test. Each passage is followed by several questions. After reading a passage, choose the best answer to each question and fill in the corresponding oval on your answer document. You may refer to the passages as often as necessary.

You are NOT permitted to use a calculator on this test.

Passage I

The freezing point of an aqueous solution (T_f), in °C, can be calculated using the equation

$$T_f = -1.86 \times m \times i$$

where m is the concentration of the solute in moles of solute per kilogram of H_2O (mol/kg H_2O) and i is the average number of particles produced by 1 formula unit of the solute when the formula unit dissolves in H_2O. The *theoretical i value* of a solute is the total number of particles produced when 1 formula unit of the solute dissolves in H_2O. Table 1 gives, for 4 ionic compounds, the chemical formula and the theoretical i value. Table 2 shows how the *observed i value* at 25°C for these compounds changes with solute concentration.

	Table 1	
Name	Chemical formula	Theoretical i value
Sodium chloride	$NaCl$	2
Potassium chloride	KCl	2
Magnesium chloride	$MgCl_2$	3
Ammonium sulfate	$(NH_4)_2SO_4$	3

Table 2				
Concentration of aqueous solution (mol/kg H_2O)	Observed i value at 25°C for:			
	NaCl	KCl	$MgCl_2$	$(NH_4)_2SO_4$
0.1	1.87	1.85	2.58	2.30
0.2	1.85	1.83	2.63	2.19
0.3	1.84	1.81	2.68	2.12
0.4	1.84	1.80	2.76	2.07
0.5	1.84	1.80	2.84	2.03
0.6	1.85	1.80	2.92	2.00
0.7	1.85	1.79	3.01	1.97
0.8	1.86	1.79	3.11	1.96
0.9	1.86	1.79	3.21	1.94
1.0	1.87	1.80	3.32	1.92
2.0	1.97	1.83	4.57	1.87

Table 2 adapted from B. A. Kunkel, "Comments on 'A Generalized Equation for the Solution Effect in Droplet Growth.'" ©1969 by American Meteorological Society.

GO ON TO THE NEXT PAGE.

4 ○ ○ ○ ○ ○ ○ ○ ○ ○ **4**

1. Based on Table 2, what is the observed i value for a 0.6 mol/kg H_2O solution of $(NH_4)_2SO_4$?

    A. 1.97
    B. 2.00
    C. 2.03
    D. 2.92

2. According to Table 2, which compounds have observed i values less than 2.50 at all the concentrations listed?

    F. NaCl, KCl, and $MgCl_2$ only
    G. NaCl, KCl, and $(NH_4)_2SO_4$ only
    H. KCl, $MgCl_2$, and $(NH_4)_2SO_4$ only
    J. NaCl, KCl, $MgCl_2$, and $(NH_4)_2SO_4$

3. According to Table 2, at which of the following concentrations is the observed i value for KCl the *lowest* ?

    A. 0.3 mol/kg H_2O
    B. 0.6 mol/kg H_2O
    C. 0.9 mol/kg H_2O
    D. 2.0 mol/kg H_2O

4. Based on Tables 1 and 2, which ionic compound has the largest deviation from its theoretical i value at a concentration of 2.0 mol/kg H_2O ?

    F. NaCl
    G. KCl
    H. $MgCl_2$
    J. $(NH_4)_2SO_4$

5. Consider the following substances: sodium chloride, potassium chloride, magnesium chloride, ammonium sulfate, and water. Which of these substances would be classified as a solvent in the solutions represented in Table 2 ?

    A. Ammonium sulfate only
    B. Water only
    C. Sodium chloride, potassium chloride, and magnesium chloride only
    D. Water, sodium chloride, potassium chloride, magnesium chloride, and ammonium sulfate

6. Sucrose $(C_{12}H_{22}O_{11})$ is a molecular compound and remains intact when it dissolves in water. Based on this information and the passage, would the theoretical i value for $C_{12}H_{22}O_{11}$ more likely be less than that of KCl or greater than that of KCl ?

    F. Less; the theoretical i value for $C_{12}H_{22}O_{11}$ is most likely 1.
    G. Less; the theoretical i value for $C_{12}H_{22}O_{11}$ is most likely 4 or greater.
    H. Greater; the theoretical i value for $C_{12}H_{22}O_{11}$ is most likely 1.
    J. Greater; the theoretical i value for $C_{12}H_{22}O_{11}$ is most likely 4 or greater.

Your First Practice Test

GO ON TO THE NEXT PAGE.

4   **4**

Passage II

Some mutations in *Escherichia coli* allow the bacteria to survive exposure to an antibiotic. These antibiotic-resistant bacteria may have a different *relative fitness* (a measure of survival and reproductive success) than *E. coli* without mutations. Scientists conducted a study to determine the relative fitness of 5 *E. coli* strains—1 nonmutated (Strain U) and 4 mutated (Strains W, X, Y, and Z)—when the strains were exposed for 24 hr to each of 5 different concentrations of the antibiotic *streptomycin* (see Table 1). The effect of the mutation in each of Strains W–Z is listed in Table 2.

Table 1					
	Relative fitness of *E. coli* exposed for 24 hr to a streptomycin concentration (in μg/mL*) of:				
Strain	0	2	4	6	8
U	1.0	0.5	0.0	0.0	0.0
W	1.2	0.3	0.1	0.0	0.0
X	0.9	0.8	0.5	0.2	0.0
Y	0.7	0.8	0.7	0.5	0.3
Z	1.0	0.1	0.9	0.8	1.5

*micrograms per milliliter

Note: A relative fitness of 0.0 indicates no surviving bacteria.

Table 1 adapted from Viktória Lázár et al., "Bacterial Evolution of Antibiotic Hypersensitivity." ©2013 by EMBO and Macmillan Publishers Limited.

Table 2	
Strain	Effect of mutation
W	Increased rate of cell division
X	Increased rate of streptomycin removal from the cell
Y	Decreased rate of streptomycin entry into the cell
Z	Decreased rate of DNA damage repair

7. Based on Table 1, as streptomycin concentration increased, the relative fitness of Strain Y:

   A. increased only.
   B. decreased only.
   C. increased and then decreased.
   D. decreased and then increased.

8. Based on Table 1, if Strain X had been exposed for 24 hr to a streptomycin concentration of 3 μg/mL, its relative fitness would most likely have been:

   F. less than 0.5.
   G. between 0.5 and 0.8.
   H. between 0.8 and 0.9.
   J. greater than 0.9.

9. According to Table 2, which of the following statements best describes the effect of the mutation in Strain X cells? Compared to nonmutated *E. coli* cells, Strain X cells move streptomycin:

   A. into the cell at a decreased rate.
   B. into the cell at an increased rate.
   C. out of the cell at a decreased rate.
   D. out of the cell at an increased rate.

10. Suppose an equal number of Strain W cells and Strain X cells were exposed for 24 hr to a streptomycin concentration of 2 μg/mL. Based on Table 1, which of Strain W or Strain X would more likely have the greater number of cells survive and reproduce?

   F. Strain W; Strain W had a relative fitness of 0.3, and Strain X had a relative fitness of 0.8.
   G. Strain W; Strain W had a relative fitness of 1.2, and Strain X had a relative fitness of 0.9.
   H. Strain X; Strain X had a relative fitness of 0.8, and Strain W had a relative fitness of 0.3.
   J. Strain X; Strain X had a relative fitness of 0.9, and Strain W had a relative fitness of 1.2.

GO ON TO THE NEXT PAGE.

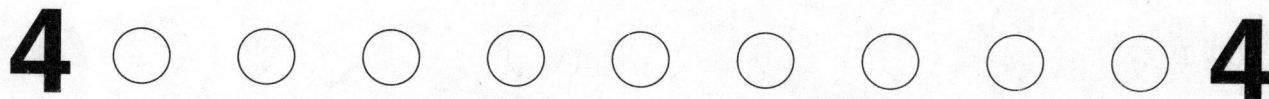

11. Consider the mutated strain with an increased rate of cell division. According to Table 1, what was the relative fitness of this strain when it was exposed for 24 hr to a streptomycin concentration of 4 µg/mL ?

    A. 0.0
    B. 0.1
    C. 0.5
    D. 0.7

12. In the study, the relative fitness of a nonmutated strain that was grown for 24 hr in the absence of an antibiotic was set to 1.0. Was this strain more likely Strain U or Strain Z, and was this strain grown for 24 hr at a streptomycin concentration of 0 µg/mL or at a streptomycin concentration of 8 µg/mL ?

    F. Strain U; 0 µg/mL
    G. Strain U; 8 µg/mL
    H. Strain Z; 0 µg/mL
    J. Strain Z; 8 µg/mL

Your First Practice Test

GO ON TO THE NEXT PAGE.

4 ○ ○ ○ ○ ○ ○ ○ ○ ○ **4**

Passage III

Antimony trioxide (Sb_2O_3) is a chemical compound that is used as a flame retardant in manufacturing plastic bottles made of *polyethylene terephthalate* (PET). PET bottles can retain some Sb_2O_3 after manufacturing, and small amounts of the antimony ion (Sb^{3+}) can be absorbed out of the plastic by water stored in those bottles. Two experiments were performed to study the absorption of Sb^{3+} by water stored in clear plastic bottles made of PET.

Experiment 1

The following steps were performed:

1. An unused PET bottle was filled with 2.0 L of pure water and sealed.

2. The bottle was placed into a box that was maintained at 10°C. An ultraviolet (UV) lightbulb was mounted inside the box (see diagram); only UV light was shone upon the bottle for 16 hr.

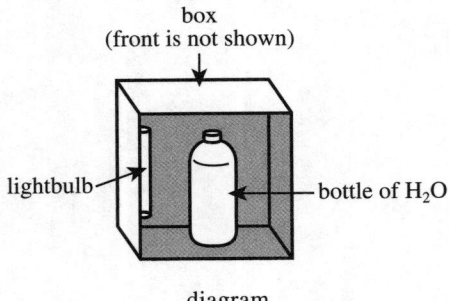

diagram

3. The bottle was then removed from the box, opened, and a 2.0 mL sample of water was removed. The concentration of Sb^{3+} in the sample of water, in nanograms per liter (ng/L; $1 \text{ ng} = 10^{-9} \text{ g}$), was determined.

4. The bottle was emptied, cleaned, and air-dried.

5. The same bottle was then refilled with 2.0 L of pure water and sealed.

6. Steps 2–5 were repeated until the bottle had been reused 28 times at the temperature of 10°C.

Steps 1–6 were repeated 2 more times, except that the box was maintained at temperatures of 30°C and 50°C, respectively. The results for each of the 3 temperatures are shown in Figure 1.

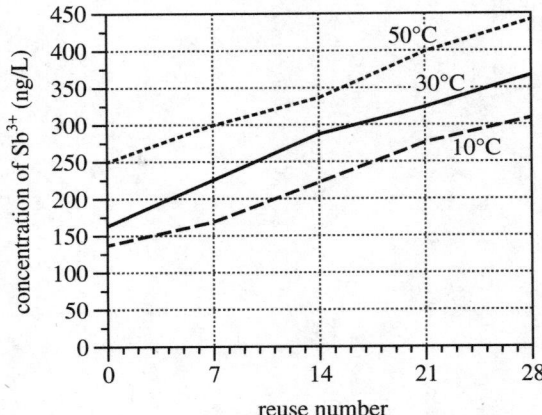

Figure 1

Experiment 2

The procedure in Experiment 1 was repeated, except that in Step 2, the lightbulb inside the box was one that emitted only visible light. The results for each of the 3 temperatures are shown in Figure 2.

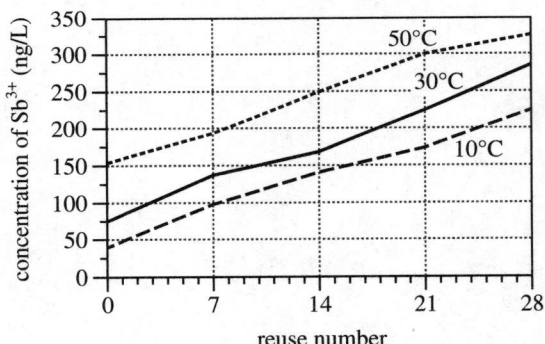

Figure 2

Figures adapted from S. S. Andra, K. C. Makris, and J. P. Shine, "Frequency of Use Controls Chemical Leaching from Drinking-water Containers Subject to Disinfection." ©2011 by Elsevier, B. V.

GO ON TO THE NEXT PAGE.

4 ○ ○ ○ ○ ○ ○ ○ ○ **4**

13. How many times in Experiment 2 was a bottle placed into the box when the box was maintained at 10°C ?

   A. 7
   B. 14
   C. 29
   D. 58

14. Suppose that in Experiment 2 the bottle containing water stored at 50°C had been reused 35 times. At that reuse number, the approximate concentration of Sb^{3+} in the water would have been:

   F. less than 270 ng/L.
   G. between 270 ng/L and 300 ng/L.
   H. between 300 ng/L and 330 ng/L.
   J. greater than 330 ng/L.

15. Assume that the maximum acceptable concentration of Sb^{3+} in drinking water is 6,000 ng/L. This concentration of Sb^{3+} is how many times as great as the concentration of Sb^{3+} in water stored at 50°C in a bottle that was reused 21 times in Experiment 2 ?

   A. 2
   B. 3
   C. 20
   D. 30

16. Which set of experimental conditions resulted in an Sb^{3+} concentration of 140 ng/L in water stored in a bottle that had been reused 14 times?

   F. 10°C, UV light
   G. 10°C, visible light
   H. 30°C, UV light
   J. 30°C, visible light

17. The substance composing the bottles tested in the experiments is best classified as which of the following?

   A. Alloy
   B. Polymer
   C. Element
   D. Salt

18. Suppose that in Experiment 1 a temperature of 20°C had been tested. At a reuse number of 21, the Sb^{3+} concentration would most likely have been between:

   F. 125 ng/L and 175 ng/L.
   G. 175 ng/L and 225 ng/L.
   H. 225 ng/L and 275 ng/L.
   J. 275 ng/L and 325 ng/L.

19. Did Experiment 1 and Experiment 2, respectively, take more than 1 day or less than 1 day to complete?

	Experiment 1	Experiment 2
A.	more	more
B.	more	less
C.	less	more
D.	less	less

GO ON TO THE NEXT PAGE.

Your First Practice Test

4 ○ ○ ○ ○ ○ ○ ○ ○ 4

Passage IV

Introduction

During the *early Earth period* (the first 2 billion years after Earth formed), the Sun produced only about 70% of the light and heat that it does today. Consequently, if early Earth's atmosphere had been identical to Earth's atmosphere today, the average surface temperature would have been well below the freezing point of water. However, geologic evidence indicates that a large amount of liquid water was present on the surface. Two hypotheses were proposed to explain how 3 heat-absorbing greenhouse gases—carbon dioxide (CO_2), ammonia (NH_3), and methane (CH_4)—in early Earth's atmosphere contributed to the presence of liquid water on the surface.

Hypothesis 1

During the early Earth period, volcanic eruptions released both CO_2 and NH_3 into the atmosphere. In addition, microbes produced CH_4 by metabolizing hydrogen (H_2) gas. Compared with atmospheric greenhouse gas concentrations at present day, those on early Earth were considerably greater: the CO_2 concentration was about 100 times as great, the NH_3 concentration was about 20 times as great, and the CH_4 concentration was about 1,000 times as great. These higher-than-present atmospheric concentrations of CO_2, NH_3, and CH_4 absorbed enough heat to maintain an average surface temperature that allowed for liquid water.

Hypothesis 2

The only source of atmospheric CO_2, NH_3, and CH_4 on early Earth was volcanic eruptions. Compared with atmospheric CO_2 and NH_3 concentrations at present day, those on early Earth were somewhat greater: the CO_2 concentration was about 40 times as great and the NH_3 concentration was about 10 times as great. The CH_4 concentration was about the same as its present value. At those concentrations, the 3 gases by themselves would not have absorbed enough heat to raise the average surface temperature above freezing. However, atmospheric concentrations of both nitrogen (N_2) and H_2 were approximately twice what they are today. These higher-than-present concentrations of N_2 and H_2 greatly enhanced the heat-absorbing effects of the 3 greenhouse gases, maintaining an average surface temperature that allowed for liquid water.

20. A supporter of Hypothesis 1 and a supporter of Hypothesis 2 would be likely to agree that, during the early Earth period, magma from beneath Earth's crust contained:

F.   carbon compounds but not nitrogen compounds.
G.   nitrogen compounds but not carbon compounds.
H.   both carbon compounds and nitrogen compounds.
J.   neither carbon compounds nor nitrogen compounds.

21. Suppose that the current atmospheric CO_2 concentration on Earth is approximately 395 parts per million (ppm). Based on Hypothesis 2, the atmospheric CO_2 concentration on early Earth was most likely closest to which of the following values?

A.   395 ppm
B.   15,800 ppm
C.   39,500 ppm
D.   197,500 ppm

22. Which of the hypotheses, if either, indicated that 2 additional gases were necessary for CO_2, NH_3, and CH_4 to absorb enough heat for liquid water to exist on early Earth's surface?

F.   Hypothesis 1 only
G.   Hypothesis 2 only
H.   Both Hypothesis 1 and Hypothesis 2
J.   Neither Hypothesis 1 nor Hypothesis 2

23. In regard to the source of CH_4 in early Earth's atmosphere, which of the following statements describes a difference between Hypothesis 1 and Hypothesis 2 ? According to Hypothesis 1, CH_4 was:

A.   released from volcanic eruptions, whereas according to Hypothesis 2, CH_4 was produced by microbial metabolism.
B.   released from volcanic eruptions, whereas according to Hypothesis 2, CH_4 was produced by chemical reactions between CO_2 and H_2O.
C.   produced by microbial metabolism, whereas according to Hypothesis 2, CH_4 was released from volcanic eruptions.
D.   produced by microbial metabolism, whereas according to Hypothesis 2, CH_4 was produced by chemical reactions between CO_2 and H_2O.

GO ON TO THE NEXT PAGE.

4 ○ ○ ○ ○ ○ ○ ○ ○ **4**

24. The metabolism of the microbes referred to in Hypothesis 1 is most likely represented by which of the following balanced chemical equations?

   F. $CO_2 + 4H_2 \rightarrow CH_4 + 2H_2O$

   G. $CO_2 + 2H_2O \rightarrow CH_4 + 2O_2$

   H. $CH_4 + 2O_2 \rightarrow CO_2 + 2H_2O$

   J. $CH_4 + 2H_2O \rightarrow CO_2 + 4H_2$

25. Hypothesis 1 would be best supported by which of the following findings involving CO_2 or CH_4 ?

   A. Evidence that 4 billion years ago the concentration of CO_2 was 20 times the present concentration

   B. Evidence that 4 billion years ago the concentration of CH_4 was 20 times the present concentration

   C. 3.5-billion-year-old rock samples containing evidence of CO_2 produced by microbes

   D. 3.5-billion-year-old rock samples containing evidence of CH_4 produced by microbes

26. Suppose that if Earth's atmospheric N_2 concentration were increased from its present value, the atmosphere would scatter a higher percentage of incoming sunlight, resulting in cooler surface temperatures. This information would *weaken* which of the hypotheses, if either?

   F. Hypothesis 1 only

   G. Hypothesis 2 only

   H. Both Hypothesis 1 and Hypothesis 2

   J. Neither Hypothesis 1 nor Hypothesis 2

GO ON TO THE NEXT PAGE.

4    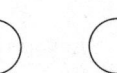   **4**

Passage V

Viscous fluid flow occurs when various parts of a fluid interact with each other to produce forces that inhibit flow and generate heat. Students performed 3 studies of viscous fluid flow using the experimental setup shown in Figure 1 below.

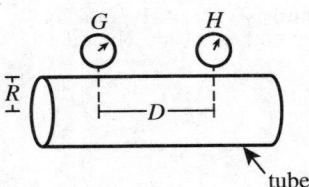

Figure 1

In each trial of the studies, the students sent a fluid through a tube such that the fluid completely filled the tube. The fluid had a viscosity η; the tube had a radius R and was fitted with 2 pressure gauges, Gauge G and Gauge H, that were a distance D apart. The pressure of the fluid at Gauge G minus the pressure of the fluid at Gauge H always equaled 5 kilopascals. (A *kilopascal*, kPa, is a unit of pressure, which is defined as force per unit area.) Using a flow meter, the students measured the fluid's flow rate through the tube, F, in milliliters per second (mL/sec).

Study 1

The students measured F for various fluids, each having a different η, that flowed, one at a time, through a tube having an R of 5.00 mm and a D of 1.00 m (see Table 1).

Table 1	
η (10^{-3} Pa·sec*)	F (mL/sec)
1.00	1,230
2.00	615
3.00	410
4.00	307
5.00	246
*pascal second	

Study 2

The students measured F for a fluid having an η of 1.0×10^{-3} Pa·sec that flowed through each of various tubes having the same D, 1.00 m, but different R (see Table 2).

Table 2	
R (mm)	F (mL/sec)
1.00	1.97
2.00	31.5
3.00	159
4.00	504
5.00	1,230

Study 3

The students measured F for a fluid having an η of 1.0×10^{-3} Pa·sec that flowed through each of various tubes having the same R, 5.00 mm, but different D (see Table 3).

Table 3	
D (m)	F (mL/sec)
0.50	2,460
1.00	1,230
1.50	820
2.00	615
2.50	492

27. Suppose that a sixth trial had been performed in Study 1 for which the fluid's flow rate had equaled 920 mL/sec. In that trial, the viscosity of the fluid would most likely have been:

   A. less than 1.00×10^{-3} Pa·sec.
   B. between 1.00×10^{-3} Pa·sec and 2.00×10^{-3} Pa·sec.
   C. between 2.00×10^{-3} Pa·sec and 3.00×10^{-3} Pa·sec.
   D. greater than 3.00×10^{-3} Pa·sec.

GO ON TO THE NEXT PAGE.

4 **4**

28. In Study 2, which variables were held constant?

   F. R and F
   G. F and η
   H. η and D
   J. R and D

29. Based on the information given, if the pressure at Gauge G was 105 kPa, what was the pressure at Gauge H ?

   A.   95 kPa
   B. 100 kPa
   C. 105 kPa
   D. 110 kPa

30. Based on the information given, in what direction was the fluid flowing?

   F. From Gauge G toward Gauge H, because the pressure at Gauge G was greater than the pressure at Gauge H.
   G. From Gauge G toward Gauge H, because the pressure at Gauge G was less than the pressure at Gauge H.
   H. From Gauge H toward Gauge G, because the pressure at Gauge H was greater than the pressure at Gauge G.
   J. From Gauge H toward Gauge G, because the pressure at Gauge H was less than the pressure at Gauge G.

31. The viscosity of each fluid investigated in the studies resulted from which of the following types of interaction between parts of the fluid?

   A. Friction
   B. Combustion
   C. Magnetism
   D. Gravity

32. In Study 3, when D was equal to 2.50 m, approximately what volume of fluid flowed past either gauge in 1 *minute* ?

   F. 25,000 mL
   G. 30,000 mL
   H. 37,000 mL
   J. 49,000 mL

33. The *pressure gradient* between any 2 points lying on a horizontal line inside a tube equaled the absolute value of the difference in pressure between the 2 points divided by the distance between the 2 points. What was the pressure gradient between Gauges G and H during Study 1 ?

   A. 5 kPa/m
   B. 1 kPa/m
   C. 5 kPa/mm
   D. 1 kPa/mm

Your First Practice Test

GO ON TO THE NEXT PAGE.

4 ○ ○ ○ ○ ○ ○ ○ ○ ○ **4**

Passage VI

Wheat growth is negatively affected by higher-than-normal salt (NaCl) concentrations in the soil. Scientists investigated whether the negative effects are countered by adding to the soil either a species of bacteria (Species R) or a mixture of proteins from marine algae (PMA).

Study 1

First, 240 identical 2 L pots were each filled with 1.5 kg of a certain soil. Next, 5 wheat seeds were planted in each pot, and the pots were divided equally into 4 groups (Groups 1–4). Then, all the pots in each group received 1 of 4 treatments (see Table 1).

Table 1

Group	Treatment
1	0.5 L of H_2O
2	0.5 L of H_2O containing 9.3 g/L of NaCl
3	0.5 L of H_2O containing Species R and 9.3 g/L of NaCl
4	0.5 L of H_2O containing PMA and 9.3 g/L of NaCl

Note: The addition of 9.3 g/L of NaCl to the pots in Groups 2–4 resulted in a higher-than-normal NaCl concentration in the soil in those pots.

After treatment, each pot was irrigated once every 3 days with either 0.5 L of H_2O only (Group 1) or 0.5 L of H_2O containing 9.3 g/L of NaCl (Groups 2–4). The average number of seeds germinated per pot was then determined for each group at 3, 5, 7, and 9 days after treatment (see Table 2).

Table 2

Days after treatment	Average number of seeds germinated per pot			
	Group 1	Group 2	Group 3	Group 4
3	4.8	0.0	1.1	2.8
5	5.0	0.0	4.3	4.0
7	5.0	0.2	5.0	4.6
9	5.0	0.4	5.0	4.8

Study 2

An additional 240 of the 2 L pots were prepared, treated, and irrigated as in Study 1. Nine days after treatment, all but 1 seedling were removed from each of the pots that had multiple seedlings. Each pot was then irrigated as in Study 1 for an additional 75 days. The average plant height was then determined for each group (see Figure 1).

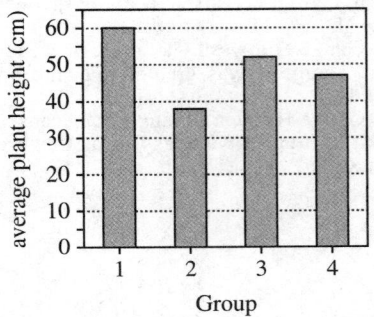

Figure 1

Table 2 and Figure 1 adapted from Elhafid Nabti et al., "Restoration of Growth of Durum Wheat (*Triticum durum* var. waha) Under Saline Conditions Due to Inoculation with the Rhizosphere Bacterium *Azospirillum brasilense* NH and Extracts of the Marine Alga *Ulva lactuca*." ©2010 by Springer Science and Business Media, LLC.

GO ON TO THE NEXT PAGE.

34. According to the results of Study 1, from 3 days after treatment through 9 days after treatment, the average number of seeds that had germinated per pot for Group 4:

  F. increased only.
  G. decreased only.
  H. increased and then remained constant.
  J. decreased and then remained constant.

35. Based on the results of Study 2, how many of the groups had an average plant height greater than 1 *meter* ?

  A. 0
  B. 1
  C. 3
  D. 4

36. The presence of more than 1 plant in a pot can negatively affect the growth of all the plants in the pot, due to competition among the plants. What action was taken in Study 2 to prevent competition among the plants?

  F. Only one seed was planted per pot.
  G. Only one seedling was planted per pot.
  H. After an initial period of growth, all seeds except one were removed from each pot that had multiple seeds.
  J. After an initial period of growth, all seedlings except one were removed from each pot that had multiple seedlings.

37. Consider the claim "The average height of the plants in a group was affected by the number of days that the pots in that group were irrigated." Can this claim be evaluated on the basis of the results of Study 2 ?

  A. Yes, because the number of days of irrigation was the same for all the groups.
  B. Yes, because the number of days of irrigation was different for each group.
  C. No, because the number of days of irrigation was the same for all the groups.
  D. No, because the number of days of irrigation was different for each group.

38. Consider the statement "Treatment with Species R was more effective at promoting seed germination in soil with a higher-than-normal NaCl concentration than was treatment with PMA." Are the results of Study 1 for 5, 7, and 9 days after treatment consistent with this statement?

  F. Yes; on each of those days, the average number of seeds germinated per pot was greater for Group 3 than for Group 4.
  G. Yes; on each of those days, the average number of seeds germinated per pot was greater for Group 4 than for Group 3.
  H. No; on each of those days, the average number of seeds germinated per pot was greater for Group 3 than for Group 4.
  J. No; on each of those days, the average number of seeds germinated per pot was greater for Group 4 than for Group 3.

39. Let x represent the number of days after treatment until germination was first observed among the Group 2 pots in Study 1. Based on the results of Study 1, x is given by which of the following expressions?

  A. $x < 3$
  B. $3 \leq x < 5$
  C. $5 < x \leq 7$
  D. $x > 7$

40. Consider the statement "On average, plant height was greater for the plants treated with H_2O containing PMA and NaCl than it was for the plants treated with either H_2O containing NaCl only or H_2O containing Species R and NaCl." Do the results of Study 2 support this statement?

  F. Yes; the average plant height in Group 3 was greater than the average plant height in Groups 2 and 4.
  G. Yes; the average plant height in Group 4 was greater than the average plant height in Groups 2 and 3.
  H. No; the average plant height in Group 3 was greater than that in Group 2 but less than that in Group 4.
  J. No; the average plant height in Group 4 was greater than that in Group 2 but less than that in Group 3.

END OF TEST 4

STOP! DO NOT RETURN TO ANY OTHER TEST.

Your First Practice Test

You may wish to photocopy these sample answer document pages to respond to the practice ACT Writing Test.

Please enter the information at the right before beginning the writing test.

Use a No. 2 pencil only. Do NOT use a mechanical pencil, ink, ballpoint, or felt-tip pen.

WRITING TEST BOOKLET NUMBER

Print your 9-digit **Booklet Number** in the boxes at the right.

WRITING TEST FORM

Print your 5-character **Test Form** in the boxes at the right and fill in the corresponding ovals.

Begin WRITING TEST here.

If you need more space, please continue on the following page.

WRITING TEST

If you need more space, please continue on the following page.

2

WRITING TEST

_____

_____

_____

_____

_____

_____

_____

_____

_____

_____

_____

_____

_____

_____

_____

_____

_____

_____

_____

_____

_____

_____

_____

_____

_____

If you need more space, please continue on the following page.

3

WRITING TEST

_____

_____

_____

_____

_____

_____

_____

_____

_____

_____

_____

_____

_____

_____

_____

_____

_____

_____

_____

_____

STOP here with the writing test.

4

Practice Writing Test Prompt 1

Your Signature: _____
(Do not print.)

Print Your Name Here: _____

Your Date of Birth:

	–		–		

Month   Day   Year

Form 23WT2

 WRITING TEST
BOOKLET

You must take the multiple-choice tests before you take the writing test.

Directions

This is a test of your writing skills. You will have **forty** (40) minutes to read the prompt, plan your response, and write an essay in English. Before you begin working, read all material in this test booklet carefully to understand exactly what you are being asked to do.

You will write your essay on the lined pages in the **answer document** provided. Your writing on those pages will be scored. You may use the unlined pages in this test booklet to plan your essay. Your work on these pages will not be scored.

Your essay will be evaluated based on the evidence it provides of your ability to:

- clearly state your own perspective on a complex issue and analyze the relationship between your perspective and at least one other perspective
- develop and support your ideas with reasoning and examples
- organize your ideas clearly and logically
- communicate your ideas effectively in standard written English

Lay your pencil down immediately when time is called.

DO NOT OPEN THIS BOOKLET UNTIL TOLD TO DO SO.

   PO Box 168
Iowa City, IA 52243-0168

The ONLY Official Prep Guide from the Makers of the ACT

Spirit Week

Spirit Week, whether centered on homecoming or simply celebrating the school and its student body, is common in US high schools. Students participate in a wide range of activities, including assemblies, costume or dress-up days, games and competitions, and parades. But all these activities take a lot of time, and all the commotion can be distracting. Such an environment makes it easier for students to turn their attention away from academics and toward social and athletic events. Should schools continue the practice of Spirit Week?

Read and carefully consider these perspectives. Each suggests a particular way of thinking about the question above.

Perspective One	Perspective Two	Perspective Three
Academics should be the highest priority of every school. Events such as Spirit Week send the message that putting fun before work is acceptable.	Team spirit and goodwill are essential to the survival of any community. Spirit events bring students closer together and create a friendly, harmonious environment.	Many students have interests other than those represented by Spirit Week. Such events force those students to engage in a type of activity they would rather avoid.

Essay Task

Write a unified, coherent essay in which you address the question of whether schools should continue the practice of Spirit Week. In your essay, be sure to:

- clearly state your own perspective and analyze the relationship between your perspective and at least one other perspective
- develop and support your ideas with reasoning and examples
- organize your ideas clearly and logically
- communicate your ideas effectively in standard written English

Your perspective may be in full agreement with any of those given, in partial agreement, or completely different.

Planning Your Essay

Your work on these prewriting pages will not be scored.

Use the space below and on the back cover to generate ideas and plan your essay. You may wish to consider the following as you think critically about the task:

Strengths and weaknesses of different perspectives on the issue
- What insights do they offer, and what do they fail to consider?
- Why might they be persuasive to others, or why might they fail to persuade?

Your own knowledge, experience, and values
- What is your perspective on this issue, and what are its strengths and weaknesses?
- How will you support your perspective in your essay?

If you need more space to plan, please continue on the back of this page.

Planning Your Essay

Use this page to continue planning your essay. Your work on this page will not be scored.

Scoring Your Practice Test

After taking your first ACT practice test, you are ready to score the test to see how you did overall. In this chapter, you learn how to determine your raw score, convert raw scores to scale scores, compute your Composite score, determine your estimated percentile ranks for each of your scale scores, and score your practice writing test.

Prep Online!

Practice tests taken on the online platform are scored automatically, allowing you to review your performance and see important areas to focus on right away.

When scoring each practice test and reviewing your scores, remember that your scores on the practice tests are only estimates of the scores that you will obtain on the ACT. If your score isn't as high as you expected, it could mean a number of things. Maybe you need to review important content and skills. Maybe you should work a little faster when taking the test. Perhaps you simply weren't doing your best work on the test. Or maybe you need to take more challenging courses to be better prepared. Keep in mind that a test score is just one indicator of your level of academic knowledge and skills. You know your own strengths and weaknesses better than anyone else, so keep them in mind as you evaluate your performance.

On each of the four multiple-choice tests (English, mathematics, reading, and science), the number of questions you answer correctly is called a *raw score*. To figure out your raw scores for the practice tests in this book, count all your correct answers for each test using the scoring keys provided in the next section, "Scoring Your Multiple-Choice Practice Tests." Then you can convert your raw scores into *scale* scores.

A raw score is converted to a scale score to enhance score interpretation and allow comparability across different forms. Scale scores are the scores that ACT reports to students, high schools, colleges, and scholarship agencies. One of the reasons ACT uses scale scores is to adjust for small differences among different forms of the ACT. After you've converted your raw scores for the practice tests to scale scores, you'll want to convert your scale scores to percentile ranks. Percentile ranks, which are explained in the following pages, are useful for interpreting your scores relative to the scores of others who have taken the ACT.

If you took the optional practice writing test, the later section "Scoring Your Practice Writing Test Essay" includes an analytic rubric for evaluating your essay and estimating your writing test score. Although it is difficult to be objective about one's own work, it is to your advantage to read your own writing critically. Becoming your own editor helps you grow as a writer and as a reader, so it makes sense for you to evaluate your own practice essay. However, it likely will be helpful for you to give your practice essay to another reader to get another perspective: perhaps that of a classmate, a parent, or an English teacher, for example. To rate your essay, you and your reader should read the analytic rubric on pages 109–110 and the examples on pages 299–324, and then assign your practice essay a score of 1 (low) through 6 (high) in each of the four writing domains (Ideas and Analysis, Development and Support, Organization, and Language Use and Conventions).

Your writing test domain scores are based on the analytic rubric used to score the essays, whereas the overall score is calculated from the four domain scores.

Finally, convert your writing test score to percentile ranks using the procedures described. Percentile ranks enable you to compare your writing test score to those of others who have taken the writing test.

Scoring Your Multiple-Choice Practice Tests

To score your multiple-choice practice tests, follow these eight steps:

STEP 1. Write a "1" in the blank for each English test question that you answered correctly. An example is provided in the box below:

	Key		Your answer was
1.	A		Incorrect
2.	J	1	Correct
3.	B	1	Correct
4.	G	___	Incorrect

English ■ Scoring Key ■ Practice Test 1

	Key			Key			Key	
1.	D	_____	26.	F	_____	51.	A	_____
2.	J	_____	27.	B	_____	52.	G	_____
3.	C	_____	28.	J	_____	53.	B	_____
4.	F	_____	29.	D	_____	54.	G	_____
5.	A	_____	30.	G	_____	55.	C	_____
6.	F	_____	31.	A	_____	56.	H	_____
7.	C	_____	32.	G	_____	57.	D	_____
8.	J	_____	33.	C	_____	58.	H	_____
9.	C	_____	34.	J	_____	59.	B	_____
10.	F	_____	35.	D	_____	60.	J	_____
11.	B	_____	36.	J	_____	61.	D	_____
12.	F	_____	37.	C	_____	62.	F	_____
13.	B	_____	38.	F	_____	63.	B	_____
14.	H	_____	39.	D	_____	64.	G	_____
15.	B	_____	40.	G	_____	65.	D	_____
16.	J	_____	41.	B	_____	66.	H	_____
17.	C	_____	42.	F	_____	67.	B	_____
18.	J	_____	43.	C	_____	68.	J	_____
19.	B	_____	44.	G	_____	69.	C	_____
20.	H	_____	45.	B	_____	70.	G	_____
21.	A	_____	46.	J	_____	71.	C	_____
22.	H	_____	47.	C	_____	72.	F	_____
23.	A	_____	48.	F	_____	73.	C	_____
24.	H	_____	49.	A	_____	74.	J	_____
25.	D	_____	50.	J	_____	75.	A	_____

STEP 2. Compute your total number correct for the English test by adding the numbers you entered in Step 1. Write this total in the blank in the shaded box below. This is your raw score.

Number Correct (Raw Score) for:

Total Number Correct for English Test (75 questions)   _____

STEP 3. Repeat Steps 1 and 2 for the ACT mathematics, reading, and science tests using the scoring keys on this page and the following page,

Mathematics ■ Scoring Key ■ Practice Test 1

	Key			Key			Key	
1.	A	_____	21.	A	_____	41.	B	_____
2.	G	_____	22.	G	_____	42.	H	_____
3.	D	_____	23.	D	_____	43.	D	_____
4.	G	_____	24.	H	_____	44.	G	_____
5.	E	_____	25.	D	_____	45.	B	_____
6.	K	_____	26.	J	_____	46.	F	_____
7.	B	_____	27.	D	_____	47.	B	_____
8.	H	_____	28.	G	_____	48.	J	_____
9.	B	_____	29.	D	_____	49.	A	_____
10.	H	_____	30.	G	_____	50.	J	_____
11.	E	_____	31.	B	_____	51.	D	_____
12.	F	_____	32.	J	_____	52.	J	_____
13.	E	_____	33.	A	_____	53.	E	_____
14.	J	_____	34.	H	_____	54.	H	_____
15.	B	_____	35.	C	_____	55.	A	_____
16.	H	_____	36.	K	_____	56.	J	_____
17.	A	_____	37.	B	_____	57.	E	_____
18.	H	_____	38.	H	_____	58.	K	_____
19.	C	_____	39.	D	_____	59.	A	_____
20.	H	_____	40.	G	_____	60.	J	_____

Number Correct (Raw Score) for:

Total Number Correct for Math Test (60 questions)   _____

Reading ■ Scoring Key ■ Practice Test 1

	Key			Key			Key	
1.	A	_____	15.	D	_____	29.	D	_____
2.	G	_____	16.	F	_____	30.	G	_____
3.	D	_____	17.	C	_____	31.	B	_____
4.	J	_____	18.	G	_____	32.	G	_____
5.	B	_____	19.	D	_____	33.	A	_____
6.	F	_____	20.	H	_____	34.	H	_____
7.	C	_____	21.	D	_____	35.	B	_____
8.	F	_____	22.	J	_____	36.	H	_____
9.	D	_____	23.	B	_____	37.	D	_____
10.	H	_____	24.	G	_____	38.	F	_____
11.	D	_____	25.	B	_____	39.	A	_____
12.	H	_____	26.	H	_____	40.	H	_____
13.	A	_____	27.	A	_____			
14.	G	_____	28.	H	_____			

Number Correct (Raw Score) for:

Total Number Correct for Reading Test (40 questions)   _____

Science ■ Scoring Key ■ Practice Test 1

	Key			Key			Key	
1.	B	_____	15.	C	_____	29.	B	_____
2.	G	_____	16.	G	_____	30.	F	_____
3.	C	_____	17.	B	_____	31.	A	_____
4.	H	_____	18.	J	_____	32.	G	_____
5.	B	_____	19.	A	_____	33.	A	_____
6.	F	_____	20.	H	_____	34.	F	_____
7.	C	_____	21.	B	_____	35.	A	_____
8.	G	_____	22.	G	_____	36.	J	_____
9.	D	_____	23.	C	_____	37.	C	_____
10.	H	_____	24.	F	_____	38.	F	_____
11.	B	_____	25.	D	_____	39.	C	_____
12.	F	_____	26.	G	_____	40.	J	_____
13.	C	_____	27.	B	_____			
14.	J	_____	28.	H	_____			

Number Correct (Raw Score) for:

Total Number Correct for Science Test (40 questions)   _____

STEP 4. On each of the four tests, the total number of correct responses yields a raw score. Use the conversion table on the following page to convert your raw scores to scale scores. For each of the four tests, locate and circle your raw score or the range of raw scores that includes it in the conversion table. Then, read across to either outside column of the table and circle the scale score that corresponds to that raw score. As you determine your scale scores, enter them in the blanks provided below. The highest possible scale score for each test is 36. The lowest possible scale score for any of the four tests is 1.

	Your Scale Scores
English	_____
Mathematics	_____
Reading	_____
Science	_____
Sum of Scores	_____

STEP 5. Compute your Composite score by averaging the four scale scores. To do this, add your four scale scores and divide the sum by 4. If the resulting number ends in a fraction, round it off to the nearest whole number. (Round down any fraction less than one-half; round up any fraction that is one-half or more.) Enter this number in the appropriate blank below. This is your Composite score. The highest possible Composite score is 36. The lowest possible Composite score is 1.

	Your Scale Scores
English	_____
Mathematics	_____
Reading	_____
Science	_____
Sum of Scores	_____
Composite Score (sum ÷ 4)	_____

Scale Score Conversion Table: Practice Test 1

Scale Score	Raw Score				Scale Score
	English	Mathematics	Reading	Science	
36	73–75	59–60	39–40	39–40	36
35	70–72	57–58	38	38	35
34	68–69	55–56	37	–	34
33	67	54	36	37	33
32	66	53	35	36	32
31	65	51–52	34	35	31
30	63–64	49–50	33	34	30
29	62	47–48	32	–	29
28	60–61	45–46	31	33	28
27	59	42–44	30	32	27
26	57–58	39–41	–	30–31	26
25	55–56	37–38	29	28–29	25
24	52–54	35–36	27–28	26–27	24
23	49–51	32–34	26	24–25	23
22	46–48	30–31	24–25	22–23	22
21	43–45	29	23	21	21
20	40–42	27–28	21–22	19–20	20
19	38–39	25–26	20	18	19
18	36–37	22–24	19	16–17	18
17	34–35	19–21	17–18	15	17
16	32–33	15–18	16	13–14	16
15	28–31	12–14	14–15	12	15
14	26–27	9–11	13	11	14
13	25	7–8	11–12	10	13
12	23–24	6	9–10	9	12
11	19–22	5	8	8	11
10	16–18	4	7	7	10
9	14–15	3	6	6	9
8	12–13	–	5	5	8
7	10–11	2	4	4	7
6	8–9	–	–	3	6
5	6–7	1	3	–	5
4	5	–	2	2	4
3	3–4	–	–	1	3
2	2	–	1	–	2
1	0–1	0	0	0	1

STEP 6. Use the table on the following page to determine your estimated percentile ranks (percent at or below) for each of your scale scores. In the far left column of the table, circle your scale score for the English test (from the preceding page). Then read across to the percentile rank column for that test; circle or put a checkmark beside the corresponding percentile rank. Use the same procedure for the other three tests (from the preceding page). Using the right-hand column of scale scores for your science test and Composite scores may be easier. As you mark your percentile ranks, enter them in the blanks provided. You may also find it helpful to compare your performance with the national mean (average) score for each of the four tests and the Composite as shown at the bottom of the table.

National Norms for ACT Test Scores
Reported During the 2022–2023 Reporting Year

Score	English	Math	Reading	Science	Composite	STEM	Score
36	100	100	100	100	100	100	36
35	99	99	98	99	99	99	35
34	96	99	96	98	99	99	34
33	94	98	94	97	98	98	33
32	93	97	91	96	96	97	32
31	91	96	89	95	95	96	31
30	90	95	87	93	93	94	30
29	89	93	84	92	91	93	29
28	87	91	82	90	89	90	28
27	85	89	80	88	86	88	27
26	83	85	77	86	83	85	26
25	81	81	75	83	80	81	25
24	77	77	72	78	76	77	24
23	73	73	68	72	72	72	23
22	68	68	63	65	67	68	22
21	64	65	57	60	62	63	21
20	58	62	52	54	56	57	20
19	52	58	46	48	50	51	19
18	48	53	41	41	45	45	18
17	44	47	36	34	38	37	17
16	40	38	32	28	32	29	16
15	35	25	27	22	26	21	15
14	29	14	23	17	19	13	14
13	23	6	17	12	13	7	13
12	19	2	12	8	7	3	12
11	14	1	7	5	2	1	11
10	9	1	3	3	1	1	10
9	4	1	2	1	1	1	9
8	2	1	1	1	1	1	8
7	1	1	1	1	1	1	7
6	1	1	1	1	1	1	6
5	1	1	1	1	1	1	5
4	1	1	1	1	1	1	4
3	1	1	1	1	1	1	3
2	1	1	1	1	1	1	2
1	1	1	1	1	1	1	1
Mean:	19.5	19.9	20.9	20.3	20.3	20.3	
SD:	7.2	5.7	7.1	5.9	6.0	5.5	

Note: These ranks are reported as "US Rank" on ACT score reports during the 2022–2023 reporting year (September 2022 through August 2023). The ranks are based on ACT-tested high school graduates of 2020, 2021, and 2022 (n=4,315,490).

Scoring Your Practice Writing Test Essay

To score your practice writing test essay, follow these steps:

STEP 1. Use the analytic rubric on the following two pages to score your essay. Because many essays do not fit the exact description at each score point, read each description and try to determine which paragraph in the rubric best describes most of the characteristics of your essay.

Critiquing your own writing can be difficult. If possible, ask a trusted source to help you use the rubric and determine your score. If you must evaluate your essay on your own, try to be as objective as you can and remember that any reader of your essay would understand only what you wrote, not what you meant to write. In either case, you may find it useful to consult chapters 4 and 9 for additional information regarding the rubric and sample essays to which you can compare your own.

The ACT Writing Test Analytic Rubric

	Ideas and Analysis	Development and Support	Organization	Language Use and Conventions
Score 6: **Responses at this scorepoint demonstrate effective skill in writing an argumentative essay.**	The writer generates an argument that critically engages with multiple perspectives on the given issue. The argument's thesis reflects nuance and precision in thought and purpose. The argument establishes and employs an insightful context for analysis of the issue and its perspectives. The analysis examines implications, complexities and tensions, and/or underlying values and assumptions.	Development of ideas and support for claims deepen insight and broaden context. An integrated line of skillful reasoning and illustration effectively conveys the significance of the argument. Qualifications and complications enrich and bolster ideas and analysis.	The response exhibits a skillful organizational strategy. The response is unified by a controlling idea or purpose, and a logical progression of ideas increases the effectiveness of the writer's argument. Transitions between and within paragraphs strengthen the relationships among ideas.	The use of language enhances the argument. Word choice is skillful and precise. Sentence structures are consistently varied and clear. Stylistic and register choices, including voice and tone, are strategic and effective. While a few minor errors in grammar, usage, and mechanics may be present, they do not impede understanding.
Score 5: **Responses at this scorepoint demonstrate well-developed skill in writing an argumentative essay.**	The writer generates an argument that productively engages with multiple perspectives on the given issue. The argument's thesis reflects precision in thought and purpose. The argument establishes and employs a thoughtful context for analysis of the issue and its perspectives. The analysis addresses implications, complexities and tensions, and/or underlying values and assumptions.	Development of ideas and support for claims deepen understanding. A mostly integrated line of purposeful reasoning and illustration capably conveys the significance of the argument. Qualifications and complications enrich ideas and analysis.	The response exhibits a productive organizational strategy. The response is mostly unified by a controlling idea or purpose, and a logical sequencing of ideas contributes to the effectiveness of the argument. Transitions between and within paragraphs consistently clarify the relationships among ideas.	The use of language works in service of the argument. Word choice is precise. Sentence structures are clear and varied often. Stylistic and register choices, including voice and tone, are purposeful and productive. While minor errors in grammar, usage, and mechanics may be present, they do not impede understanding.
Score 4: **Responses at this scorepoint demonstrate adequate skill in writing an argumentative essay.**	The writer generates an argument that engages with multiple perspectives on the given issue. The argument's thesis reflects clarity in thought and purpose. The argument establishes and employs a relevant context for analysis of the issue and its perspectives. The analysis recognizes implications, complexities and tensions, and/or underlying values and assumptions.	Development of ideas and support for claims clarify meaning and purpose. Lines of clear reasoning and illustration adequately convey the significance of the argument. Qualifications and complications extend ideas and analysis.	The response exhibits a clear organizational strategy. The overall shape of the response reflects an emergent controlling idea or purpose. Ideas are logically grouped and sequenced. Transitions between and within paragraphs clarify the relationships among ideas.	The use of language conveys the argument with clarity. Word choice is adequate and sometimes precise. Sentence structures are clear and demonstrate some variety. Stylistic and register choices, including voice and tone, are appropriate for the rhetorical purpose. While errors in grammar, usage, and mechanics are present, they rarely impede understanding.
Score 3: **Responses at this scorepoint demonstrate some developing skill in writing an argumentative essay.**	The writer generates an argument that responds to multiple perspectives on the given issue. The argument's thesis reflects some clarity in thought and purpose. The argument establishes a limited or tangential context for analysis of the issue and its perspectives. Analysis is simplistic or somewhat unclear.	Development of ideas and support for claims are mostly relevant but are overly general or simplistic. Reasoning and illustration largely clarify the argument but may be somewhat repetitive or imprecise.	The response exhibits a basic organizational structure. The response largely coheres, with most ideas logically grouped. Transitions between and within paragraphs sometimes clarify the relationships among ideas.	The use of language is basic and only somewhat clear. Word choice is general and occasionally imprecise. Sentence structures are usually clear but show little variety. Stylistic and register choices, including voice and tone, are not always appropriate for the rhetorical purpose. Distracting errors in grammar, usage, and mechanics may be present, but they generally do not impede understanding.

(continued)

Your First Practice Test

The ACT Writing Test Analytic Rubric

	Ideas and Analysis	*Development and Support*	*Organization*	*Language Use and Conventions*
Score 2: **Responses at this scorepoint demonstrate weak or inconsistent skill in writing an argumentative essay.**	The writer generates an argument that weakly responds to multiple perspectives on the given issue. The argument's thesis, if evident, reflects little clarity in thought and purpose. Attempts at analysis are incomplete, largely irrelevant, or consist primarily of restatement of the issue and its perspectives.	Development of ideas and support for claims are weak, confused, or disjointed. Reasoning and illustration are inadequate, illogical, or circular, and fail to fully clarify the argument.	The response exhibits a rudimentary organizational structure. Grouping of ideas is inconsistent and often unclear. Transitions between and within paragraphs are misleading or poorly formed.	The use of language is inconsistent and often unclear. Word choice is rudimentary and frequently imprecise. Sentence structures are sometimes unclear. Stylistic and register choices, including voice and tone, are inconsistent and are not always appropriate for the rhetorical purpose. Distracting errors in grammar, usage, and mechanics are present, and they sometimes impede understanding.
Score 1: **Responses at this scorepoint demonstrate little or no skill in writing an argumentative essay.**	The writer fails to generate an argument that responds intelligibly to the task. The writer's intentions are difficult to discern. Attempts at analysis are unclear or irrelevant.	Ideas lack development, and claims lack support. Reasoning and illustration are unclear, incoherent, or largely absent.	The response does not exhibit an organizational structure. There is little grouping of ideas. When present, transitional devices fail to connect ideas.	The use of language fails to demonstrate skill in responding to the task. Word choice is imprecise and often difficult to comprehend. Sentence structures are often unclear. Stylistic and register choices are difficult to identify. Errors in grammar, usage, and mechanics are pervasive and often impede understanding.

STEP 2. Because your writing test domain scores are the sum of two readers' ratings of your essay, multiply your own 1–6 rating from step 1 by 2. Or, have both you and someone else read and score your practice essay, add those ratings together, and record the total in the Domain Score column in step 3.

STEP 3. Enter your writing test domain scores in the following box.

		Domain Score
Ideas and Analysis	_____ × 2 =	_____
Development and Support	_____ × 2 =	_____
Organization	_____ × 2 =	_____
Language Use and Conventions	_____ × 2 =	_____

STEP 4. Enter the sum of the second-column scores here _____.

STEP 5. Divide sum by 4[†] (range 2–12). This is your writing test score.

[†]Round value to the nearest whole number. Round down any fraction less than one-half; round up any fraction that is one-half or more.

STEP 6. Use the table on the following page to determine your estimated percentile rank (percent at or below) for your writing test score.

National Norms for ACT Writing Scores
Reported During the 2022–2023 Reporting Year

	ACT Score National Ranks	
Score	ELA	Writing
36	100	
35	99	
34	99	
33	99	
32	99	
31	97	
30	95	
29	93	
28	91	
27	88	
26	86	
25	83	
24	80	
23	76	
22	72	
21	67	
20	62	
19	57	
18	52	
17	46	
16	40	
15	34	
14	28	
13	22	
12	17	100
11	12	99
10	8	99
9	5	96
8	3	91
7	1	69
6	1	56
5	1	31
4	1	17
3	1	6
2	1	2
1	1	
Mean:	18.8	6.3
SD:	6.3	1.8

Note: These ranks are reported as "US Rank" on ACT score reports during the 2022–2023 reporting year (September 2022 through August 2023). The ranks are based on ACT-tested high school graduates of 2020, 2021, and 2022 who took the ACT Writing test (n=1,475,833).

Reviewing Explanatory Answers

After scoring your test, review the questions and answers to gain a better understanding of why each correct answer is correct and why the other choices for each question are wrong. We encourage you to review the explanatory answers for all questions, not just those you missed. As you read through the explanations, note any subject matter or concepts you don't fully understand, such as subject-verb agreement on the English test or how to calculate the volume of three-dimensional objects on the mathematics test.

> When taking practice tests on the online platform (act.wiley.com), you can flag questions that you found difficult or confusing. By clicking on each question, you can review the explanation, and you can even add notes to help you keep track of what you have learned and where you need to focus.

The following sections give the correct answers for each question along with an explanation of why each correct answer is correct, why each of the other choices is wrong, and (in some cases) insight into why certain wrong answers may have been tempting choices. For more guidance on how to identify subject areas or skills you may need to work on, turn to chapter 4.

ENGLISH • PRACTICE TEST 1 • EXPLANATORY ANSWERS

Passage I

Question 1. The best answer is **D** because it does not include any unnecessary punctuation.

The best answer is NOT:

A because it has an unnecessary comma after *sound*.

B because it has two unnecessary commas that incorrectly set off "to create" from the rest of the sentence.

C because it has an unnecessary comma after *create*.

Question 2. The best answer is **J** because it is the only option that is structurally sound and avoids creating a sentence fragment. It uses the preposition *by* at the beginning of the dependent clause to link it to the independent clause "Anderson ignited her career," which creates a complete sentence.

The best answer is NOT:

F because it inserts a semicolon after *career*. This creates a sentence fragment, because the phrase after the semicolon lacks a subject and a main verb.

G because it creates a sentence fragment after the semicolon. The phrase after the semicolon lacks a subject and a main verb.

H because the sentence features two consecutive dependent clauses, which creates a sentence fragment.

Question 3. The best answer is **C** because *doubles* is precise and appropriately conveys how the violin can be used both as a violin and as an audiotape player.

The best answer is NOT:

A because *clones* is illogical and imprecise in the context of the sentence.

B because, like A, *duplicates* is illogical and imprecise in the context of the sentence.

D because, like A and B, *copies* is illogical and imprecise in the context of the sentence.

Question 4. The best answer is **F** because it is structurally sound and the verb *invent* is parallel in structure to the verbs in the surrounding phrases.

The best answer is NOT:

G because the phrase "the invention of" disrupts the parallel structure of the series of phrases and creates an ambiguous meaning.

H because the word *inventing* disrupts the parallel structure of the series of phrases and creates an ambiguous meaning.

J because the phrase "to invent" disrupts the parallel structure of the series of phrases and creates an ambiguous meaning.

Question 5. The best answer is **A** because it provides the most effective transition between Anderson's childhood interests and her witnessing of major achievements in space travel and artificial intelligence later in life.

The best answer is NOT:

B because commentary about science fiction writers Ray Bradbury and Isaac Asimov provides a weak transition in context, with little relation to the sentences that follow in the paragraph.

C because the reference to Anderson's childhood music study provides an illogical transition in context, having no relation to the other sentences in the paragraph.

D because the statement about NASA's growth provides a weak transition in context and has little relation to the other sentences in the paragraph.

Question 6. The best answer is **F** because it maintains the overall style and tone of the essay.

The best answer is NOT:

G because with *eyeballed* and *snapshots*, the phrasing introduces an informal tone that is not consistent with the rest of the essay.

H because with *beheld* and "pictorial images," the phrasing introduces an elevated, formal tone that is not consistent with the rest of the essay.

J because *ogled* introduces an informal tone that is not consistent with the rest of the essay.

Question 7. The best answer is **C** because *of* and *by* are the most idiomatically correct prepositions in context and give the clearest and most precise description of how the video feed was provided by the satellite.

   The best answer is NOT:

   A because *from* and *of* are idiomatically incorrect prepositions in context, and they create an unclear sentence.

   B because *from* is an idiomatically incorrect preposition in context, and it creates an unclear sentence.

   D because *by* and *of* are idiomatically incorrect prepositions in context, and they create an unclear sentence.

Question 8. The best answer is **J** because it inserts a semicolon after *stage* and creates a sentence fragment. What comes after the semicolon is a participial phrase that lacks a subject and main verb. This makes **J** the only alternative that is NOT acceptable.

   The best answer is NOT:

   F because an independent clause with a subject and a main verb is followed by a comma and a dependent clause, which creates a complete and structurally sound sentence.

   G because it creates a complete and structurally sound sentence with a subject and a main verb.

   H because it creates two complete and structurally sound sentences that each have a subject and a main verb.

Question 9. The best answer is **C** because it clearly and correctly explains why the new sentence should not be added. The suggested addition's information about Neil Armstrong is not directly relevant to the paragraph's description of Anderson's performance art piece.

   The best answer is NOT:

   A because the suggested addition does not contribute information that is directly relevant to the paragraph's description of Anderson's performance art piece. The paragraph does not discuss how Anderson uses photography in her performance art.

   B because the suggested addition does not contribute information that is directly relevant to the paragraph's description of Anderson's performance art piece. The paragraph does not directly claim that the piece was a reimagining of the first moon landing.

   D because it provides an incorrect reason for not adding the sentence. The paragraph does not relate any information about whether Anderson's art was commercially viable.

Question 10. The best answer is **F** because it does not include any unnecessary punctuation.

> **The best answer is NOT:**

G because it has two unnecessary commas that set off the phrase "which she was privy" from the rest of the sentence.

H because it has two unnecessary commas that set off the phrase "she was privy" from the rest of the sentence.

J because it has an unnecessary comma after *privy*.

Question 11. The best answer is **B** because it is the only option that is clear and avoids using a vague or ambiguous pronoun.

> **The best answer is NOT:**

A because the possessive pronoun *its* is ambiguous and lacks a clear antecedent.

C because the possessive pronoun *one's* is ambiguous and lacks a clear antecedent.

D because the pronoun *this* is ambiguous and lacks a clear antecedent.

Question 12. The best answer is **F** because it provides the clearest and most vivid information about the action ("sweeping the bow over the strings") and the instrument used by Anderson ("a viola").

> **The best answer is NOT:**

G because the phrase does not specify the instrument in use, which makes it less vivid than the description in F.

H because the phrase "producing music" does not vividly describe Anderson's action while playing a viola.

J because the word *rubbing* makes it unclear how or where the bow moves, and the phrase "an instrument" does not indicate what kind of instrument is involved in Anderson's action.

Question 13. **The best answer is B** because it is the only option that has correct sentence structure. It creates a complete sentence, with an independent clause that has a subject and a main verb, followed by a comma and a dependent clause.

The best answer is NOT:

A because it adds the relative pronoun *that* before the verb, creating a sentence with two dependent clauses that lack a main verb, which is a sentence fragment.

C because it creates a long dependent clause that lacks a main verb, which is a sentence fragment.

D because, like C, it creates a long dependent clause that lacks a main verb, which is a sentence fragment.

Question 14. **The best answer is H** because the dash provides the appropriate punctuation to signal a sharp break in thought and to set off the nonessential phrase that follows in the rest of the sentence.

The best answer is NOT:

F because punctuation is needed to set off the nonessential phrase that follows from the rest of the sentence.

G because a colon should not be combined with *and* when introducing a nonessential phrase.

J because a semicolon is not used to set off a nonessential phrase that lacks a subject and main verb.

Question 15. **The best answer is B** because Anderson's talking stick provides a clear and relevant example that supports the claim that Anderson invented tools that manipulated sound.

The best answer is NOT:

A because placing the sentence at Point A would interrupt the chronological sequence established by "in 1972" and "five years later." The reference "five years later" would be unclear with this sentence placement. Additionally, in contrast to the symphony and violin mentioned in the second and third sentences, it is unclear whether the talking stick qualifies as "art that defies categorization."

C because placing the sentence at Point C would undermine the logic of the paragraph. The sentence does not indicate whether Anderson created the talking stick while at NASA, and so it is unclear whether this sentence would provide an example relevant to the sentence that precedes Point C.

D because placing the sentence at Point D weakens the logic of the paragraph, which focuses on describing technological innovations that Anderson witnessed and was inspired by.

Passage II

Question 16. The best answer is **J** because it is the only option that provides a logical transition from the first sentence, which is about how zebras look alike, to the next sentence, which discusses how having similar stripes confuses predators.

The best answer is NOT:

F because the willfulness of zebras does not provide an effective transition at this point in the paragraph.

G because the question of observing zebras in a small group or large herd does not provide an effective transition at this point in the paragraph.

H because the idea that researchers don't celebrate how similar zebras look does not provide an effective transition at this point in the paragraph.

Question 17. The best answer is **C** because it is the only option that has correct sentence structure. It uses a semicolon to connect the first independent clause to the independent clause that follows.

The best answer is NOT:

A because it has no punctuation between two independent clauses, which creates a run-on sentence.

B because it also has no punctuation between two independent clauses, which creates a run-on sentence.

D because the comma after *easy* is separating two independent clauses, which creates a run-on sentence.

Question 18. The best answer is **J** because it is the only option that provides a logical transition to the information presented in the paragraph it introduces. The preceding paragraph introduces the problem of identifying the same zebra more than once, and this paragraph discusses one solution to that problem: StripeSpotter.

The best answer is NOT:

F because although the scientists did work together, it doesn't provide an effective transition at this point in the essay.

G because although computer science is important in the rest of the essay, this phrase doesn't effectively connect with the first paragraph.

H because biologists' enjoyment of the joke isn't an effective transition at this point in the essay and has little relation to the other sentences in the paragraph.

Question 19. The best answer is **B** because it inserts a comma before the nonessential phrase "similar to a bar code," effectively setting off that phrase from the sentence.

The best answer is NOT:

A because it inserts an unnecessary comma after *side*.

C because it inserts an unnecessary comma after *side* and omits the necessary comma after *identifier* that sets that phrase off from the sentence.

D because it fails to include the necessary comma after *identifier*.

Question 20. The best answer is **H** because it clearly explains why the new sentence should not be added. The information about how zebras might use stripes to identify one another is not relevant to the paragraph's discussion of StripeSpotter and how it works.

The best answer is NOT:

F because the information about whether zebras can do what StripeSpotter can do isn't relevant at this point in the essay, and the sentence should not be added.

G because the essay hasn't shifted away from its focus on interpreting stripes on zebras, so this reason to add the sentence is inaccurate.

J because although the sentence should not be added, the issue of whether zebras can identify one another is not a sufficient reason to add the irrelevant sentence here.

Question 21. The best answer is **A** because *capture* is precise and appropriately conveys what the researcher is doing while cropping the photograph.

The best answer is NOT:

B because *apprehend* is illogical and imprecise in the context of the sentence.

C because *acquire* is illogical and imprecise in the context of the sentence.

D because *take* is illogical and imprecise in the context of the sentence.

Question 22. The best answer is **H** because it clearly explains why the revision should not be made. The original phrase is clearer and includes more details about the image than the proposed revision does.

The best answer is NOT:

F because the proposed revision does not indicate that StripeSpotter can be used to make line art.

G because the original wording more clearly conveys that the image is composed of parallel lines, so the statement in G is false.

J because although it correctly indicates that the revision should not be made, the proposed revision does not imply that the way StripeSpotter creates images is unscientific.

Question 23. The best answer is **A** because it is the only option with correct subject-verb agreement. The plural subject *widths* must have a plural verb.

The best answer is NOT:

B because "has corresponded" is a singular verb, and the subject of the sentence is plural.

C because "is corresponding" is a singular verb, and the subject of the sentence is plural.

D because *corresponds* is a singular verb, and the subject of the sentence is plural.

Question 24. The best answer is **H** because it is the only option that has correct sentence structure. It creates a complete sentence with a subject and a main verb.

The best answer is NOT:

F because it begins the sentence with the progressive-tense verb "providing." The resulting sentence lacks a subject, which creates a sentence fragment.

G because it begins the sentence with the phrase "resulting in." Like F, the resulting sentence lacks a subject, which creates a sentence fragment.

J because it begins the sentence with the preposition *as*. The resulting sentence lacks a subject and main verb, which creates a sentence fragment.

Question 25. The best answer is **D** because it is the only choice that uses the correct form of the possessive pronoun *its*.

The best answer is NOT:

A because *it's* is a contraction for "it is," not the possessive pronoun that is needed here.

B because *its'* is an incorrect form of the possessive pronoun *its*.

C because *developers* is not possessive in this sentence and does not need an apostrophe.

Question 26. **The best answer is F** because it has the clearest, most concise wording.

The best answer is NOT:

G because it is redundant; the sentence already says that the programs have been planned, which means that they have not yet been created.

H because it is redundant; "similar programs" and "comparable means" have the same meaning.

J because it is redundant; "other animals" and "that are not zebras" have the same meaning.

Question 27. **The best answer is B** because it explains why the revision should be made. The information about the pattern needing to stay relatively constant is the most important characteristic for the researchers involved in the project, and it is more specific than the original wording.

The best answer is NOT:

A because although the revision should be made, it does not indicate that some animal patterns are more precise than a zebra's stripes.

C because the revision does not provide less support for the idea that zebra stripes can be translated into an identification code.

D because the revision provides a better explanation, not a worse one, about which animal patterns might be useful for identification.

Question 28. **The best answer is J** because it maintains the stylistic word pattern the writer has established in the other two examples in the sentence. The pattern in the other examples is to name the feature first and then to use a prepositional phrase to state where the feature is located on the animal.

The best answer is NOT:

F because it does not maintain the word pattern the writer has established in the other two examples in the sentence.

G because, like F, it does not maintain the word pattern the writer has established in the other two examples in the sentence.

H because, like F and G, it does not maintain the word pattern the writer has established in the other two examples in the sentence.

Question 29. The best answer is **D** because *humanely* best emphasizes the idea that StripeSpotter allows the researchers to monitor the zebras with compassion and without causing harm.

The best answer is NOT:

A because *thoroughly* does not indicate that researchers could monitor the zebras without harming them.

B because *conveniently* does not indicate that researchers could monitor the zebras without harming them.

C because *inventively* also does not indicate that researchers could monitor the zebras without harming them.

Question 30. The best answer is **G** because Point B in Paragraph 3 is the most logical place to add information about what a person must be sure not to include in the cropped portion of a photograph. The sentence before discusses cropping a photo while using StripeSpotter, so adding the information here would contribute to the overall explanation of the process.

The best answer is NOT:

F because placing the sentence at Point A would insert information about cropping the photograph before the essay mentions that the photograph is cropped, which is illogical.

H because placing the sentence at Point C illogically inserts information about cropping a photograph into a paragraph that is focused on other uses for StripeSpotter and how the program has helped researchers.

J because placing the sentence at Point D illogically places information about cropping a photograph right after a sentence about how StripeSpotter has helped researchers.

Passage III

Question 31. The best answer is **A** because it does not include any unnecessary punctuation.

The best answer is NOT:

B because it uses two unnecessary commas around the phrase "of the Long Island Rail Road."

C because it uses two unnecessary commas around the phrase "the Long Island Rail Road."

D because it has an unnecessary comma after *Station*.

Question 32. The best answer is **G** because it places the sentences and ideas in logical order. Sentence 1 introduces the idea of the mural. Sentence 3 describes what the mural looks like from afar. Sentence 2 contrasts that with what the mural looks like up close.

The best answer is NOT:

F because it has the sentences in illogical order. The sentence that contrasts what the mural looks like up close appears before the description of what the mural looks like from afar, which doesn't make sense in context.

H because it has the sentences in illogical order. It begins the essay with a sentence that contrasts the appearance of the mosaics up close, but the essay hasn't mentioned the mosaics yet.

J because it has the sentences in illogical order. It begins the essay by describing what the mural looks like from a distance, but the essay hasn't explained which mural is being discussed yet.

Question 33. The best answer is **C** because it is the only option that creates a standard English idiom ("homage to").

The best answer is NOT:

A because the phrase "homage on" is not an idiomatically sound expression in standard English.

B because the phrase "homage about" is an idiomatic expression that does not make sense in the context of this sentence.

D because the phrase "homage of" is not an idiomatically sound expression in standard English.

Question 34. The best answer is **J** because *produce* is precise and appropriately explains what Shin was asked to do.

The best answer is NOT:

F because *spawn* is illogical and imprecise in the context of creating a work of art.

G because *accomplish* is imprecise because it doesn't convey what exactly Shin is doing.

H because *perform* is illogical and imprecise in the context of creating a visual work of art.

Question 35. The best answer is **D** because it creates a logical sentence with correctly placed modifiers. The introductory dependent clause is meant to modify *Shin*, and option D correctly places Shin's name right after the introductory clause, making the meaning of the sentence clear.

> **The best answer is NOT:**
>
> **A** because the introductory clause incorrectly modifies "visually representing," creating an illogical sentence.
>
> **B** because the introductory clause incorrectly modifies *sought*, creating an illogical sentence.
>
> **C** because the introductory clause incorrectly modifies "a means," creating an illogical sentence.

Question 36. The best answer is **J** because it is the only choice that uses the correct form of the possessive pronoun *its*.

> **The best answer is NOT:**
>
> **F** because *its'* is an incorrect form of the possessive pronoun *its*.
>
> **G** because the phrase "it is" is ungrammatical and not the possessive pronoun needed here.
>
> **H** because *it's* is a contraction for "it is," not the possessive pronoun *its*.

Question 37. The best answer is **C** because it is the only option that has correct sentence structure. It correctly uses the subordinating conjunction *where* to connect the independent clause before the comma to the dependent clause that follows the comma.

> **The best answer is NOT:**
>
> **A** because it illogically uses the phrase "in which" to join the clauses.
>
> **B** because it illogically uses the subordinating conjunction *whereas* to join the clauses.
>
> **D** because it joins two independent clauses using only a comma, which creates a run-on sentence.

Question 38. The best answer is **F** because it is the only option that provides a logical transition from the first two sentences, which lay out the origins of celadon, to the next two sentences, which focus on celadon ceramicists in South Korea today.

The best answer is NOT:

G because the information about why celadon changes color is not an effective transition here.

H because the origin of the word *celadon* is not an effective transition here.

J because the information about Shin Sang-ho is not an effective transition here.

Question 39. The best answer is **D** because it creates a logical sentence with correctly placed modifiers. The phrase "for celadon shards" must be placed after *arranged*; otherwise, the sentence says that Shin arranged for herself to be shipped to Queens.

The best answer is NOT:

A because the phrase "for celadon shards" is incorrectly placed so that it appears to modify *Icheon*, creating an illogical sentence.

B because the phrase "for celadon shards" is incorrectly placed so that it appears to modify *ceramicists*, creating an illogical sentence.

C because the phrase "for celadon shards" is incorrectly placed so that it appears to modify *city*, creating an illogical sentence.

Question 40. The best answer is **G** because the relative pronoun which is appropriate in the context and agrees with its antecedent, *shards*.

The best answer is NOT:

F because the relative pronoun *whose* refers to people, not objects, such as shards.

H because the pronoun *whom* refers to people, not objects, such as shards.

J because the demonstrative pronoun *that* in the phrase "of that" refers to one thing, and the antecedent in the sentence (*shards*) is plural.

Question 41. The best answer is B because it provides the most specific information about what is on the shards, specifying that the characters on the shards are in Korean and that the designs are labyrinthine.

>   The best answer is NOT:

>   **A** because "alphabetic symbols and assorted patterns" is not as specific as B is.

>   **C** because "different letters and a plethora of patterns" is a vague description, not a specific one.

>   **D** because "numerous symbols and various designs" is also a vague description.

Question 42. The best answer is F because it correctly uses a colon to mark a sharp break in the sentence. By using a colon after *significance*, the writer is showing that the clause following the colon explains the shards' significance.

>   The best answer is NOT:

>   **G** because it incorrectly inserts the conjunction *and* before the clause that follows the colon.

>   **H** because it uses a comma to indicate a sharp break in thought, which is incorrect. Moreover, it creates a run-on sentence.

>   **J** because it fails to use punctuation to indicate a sharp break in thought, which is incorrect.

Question 43. The best answer is C because it is the only option with correct pronoun-antecedent agreement. The pronoun *her* agrees with the antecedent *Shin*, whom the essay has identified as female.

>   The best answer is NOT:

>   **A** because it uses the pronoun *their* to refer to Shin, whom the essay has identified as female.

>   **B** because it uses the contraction *they're*, which does not agree in number with the antecedent and is not a possessive pronoun.

>   **D** because it incorrectly uses the pronoun *its* to refer to Shin.

Question 44. The best answer is **G** because it is the only option that has correct sentence structure. It creates a grammatically correct sentence by including a subject and main verb.

The best answer is NOT:

F because the phrase "Shin's use of" lacks a main verb, which creates a sentence fragment.

H because the verb *using* lacks a subject, which creates a sentence fragment.

J because deleting the phrase results in a sentence that lacks a subject and main verb, which creates a sentence fragment.

Question 45. The best answer is **B** because it is the only option that does not have correct sentence structure. There is no punctuation between the two independent clauses, which creates a run-on sentence. This makes **B** the only alternative that is NOT acceptable.

The best answer is NOT:

A because it has correct sentence structure. The verb "to create" makes what follows it a direct object.

C because it has correct sentence structure. The period after the first independent clause creates two complete sentences.

D because it has correct sentence structure. It uses a semicolon to separate two independent clauses.

Passage IV

Question 46. The best answer is **J** because it is the only option that has correct sentence structure. The sentence's introductory phrase correctly modifies "giant sequoia trees," because the trees are able to grow "as tall as a twenty-six-story building and as wide as a city street."

The best answer is NOT:

F because the introductory phrase incorrectly modifies *Earth*, as if the planet is able to grow "as tall as a twenty-six-story building and as wide as a city street."

G because the introductory phrase incorrectly modifies the vague pronoun *it* as if it is able to grow "as tall as a twenty-six-story building and as wide as a city street."

H because the introductory phrase is too far from *things* and "giant sequoia trees" to modify them clearly.

Question 47. The best answer is C because it provides the most logical transition in context. To facilitate the transition from the previous sentence's description of giant sequoia trees generally to the following sentence's details about the lack of road access to the Giant Forest, it is logical to focus this sentence on the giant sequoia groves in Sequoia National Park.

The best answer is NOT:

A because the number of caves in the park provides no logical transition from the description of giant sequoia trees generally to the details about the lack of road access to the Giant Forest.

B because the information about the endangered species provides no logical transition from the description of giant sequoia trees generally to the details about the lack of road access to the Giant Forest.

D because the park's percentage of wilderness provides no logical transition from the description of giant sequoia trees generally to the details about the lack of road access to the Giant Forest.

Question 48. The best answer is F because it is the only option that has correct sentence structure. It correctly uses a colon to introduce an independent clause.

The best answer is NOT:

G because it incorrectly uses a colon to introduce a dependent clause, which creates a sentence fragment.

H because it incorrectly uses a semicolon to introduce a dependent clause, which creates a sentence fragment.

J because it incorrectly uses a semicolon to introduce a phrase, which creates a sentence fragment.

Question 49. The best answer is A because the parenthetical information about the Army being responsible for improving national parks needs to be set off from the main structure of the sentence with appropriate punctuation. The punctuation used to set off a parenthetical element must match. Because the parenthetical ends with a dash after *months*, it must be introduced by a parallel dash after *Army*.

The best answer is NOT:

B because it does not clearly or appropriately set off a logical parenthetical element with matching punctuation.

C because in this sentence the parenthetical information ends with a dash, so it cannot be introduced by a comma.

D because it does not clearly or appropriately set off a logical parenthetical element with matching punctuation.

Question 50. The best answer is **J** because "of the road to" supplies the correct idiomatic prepositional phrases needed to make this sentence most understandable.

The best answer is NOT:

F because it uses prepositional phrases that create a confusing and unclear sentence.

G because it uses prepositional phrases that create a confusing and unclear sentence.

H because it also uses prepositional phrases that create a confusing and unclear sentence.

Question 51. The best answer is **A** because it is the only option that has correct sentence structure. It correctly supplies the sentence's subject and verb.

The best answer is NOT:

B because it is a sentence fragment. It does not provide a main verb to accompany the subject, *Young*.

C because it is a sentence fragment. The semicolon incorrectly isolates the phrases before it from the main structure of the sentence.

D because it creates a sentence fragment. What precedes the period is not an independent clause.

Question 52. The best answer is **G** because it provides the most logical conjunction to frame the ideas presented in this sentence. *Although* pairs logically with "Young was just as concerned" in the sentence.

The best answer is NOT:

F because the conjunction *because* is illogical in context.

H because the conjunction *unless* is illogical in context.

J because the conjunction *if* is also illogical in context.

Question 53. The best answer is **B** because *channel* is precise and appropriately expresses that the troops were focusing their efforts on the road.

The best answer is NOT:

A because the meaning of *send* is illogical and imprecise in the context of describing the troops' efforts.

C because the meaning of *convey* is illogical and imprecise in the context of describing the troops' efforts.

D because the meaning of *shape* is illogical and imprecise in the context of describing the troops' efforts.

Question 54. **The best answer is G** because the transition word *additionally* signals clearly and logically that this sentence is related to and building upon the previous sentence's idea of the troops guarding the park's grounds.

The best answer is NOT:

F because the adverb *nevertheless* suggests that the idea in this sentence is in opposition to the idea in the preceding sentence, which is illogical.

H because the adverb *thus* suggests a cause-and-effect relationship with the idea in the preceding sentence, which is illogical.

J because the adverb *still* suggests that the actions described in this sentence happened in spite of the actions described in the previous sentence, which is illogical.

Question 55. **The best answer is C** because it maintains the overall style and tone of the essay. The language here is neither overly informal nor too formal.

The best answer is NOT:

A because the wording is too informal compared to the rest of the essay.

B because although the wording maintains the overall style and tone of the essay, the wording itself is redundant. The phrase "further harm" already expresses the idea of protecting the trees in the future, making "in the future" redundant.

D because the wording is too informal compared to the rest of the essay.

Question 56. **The best answer is H** because it is the only option with correct subject-verb agreement. The plural subject *contributions* must have a plural verb.

The best answer is NOT:

F because "has been counted" is a singular verb, and the subject of the sentence is plural.

G because "was counted" is a singular verb, and the subject of the sentence is plural.

J because "is counted" is a singular verb, and the subject of the sentence is plural.

Your First Practice Test

Question 57. The best answer is D because it clearly explains why the new sentence should not be added. The information about who petitioned for the National Park Service to recognize Captain Young is not directly relevant within the context of the paragraph and the essay.

The best answer is NOT:

A because the proposed addition does not explain why it took so long for the National Park Service to recognize Captain Young, and the sentence should not be added.

B because there is no information to indicate that Palmer inspired Young's actions, and the context would suggest that Palmer petitioned the National Park Service sometime after Young completed his work there. Also, the sentence should not be added.

C because although the sentence should not be added, the suggested addition does not suggest that other people had already petitioned the National Park Service to recognize Young.

Question 58. The best answer is H because it is the only option that has correct sentence structure. It creates a complete clause with *who* as a subject and "had been" as a verb.

The best answer is NOT:

F because *being* is a present participle, not a main verb, and this creates a sentence with incorrect subordination.

G because the phrase "having been" results in a clause that lacks a main verb, which creates a sentence with incorrect subordination.

J because although *promoted* is a verb, it lacks a necessary helping verb, which creates a sentence with incorrect subordination.

Question 59. The best answer is B because the information that there is a tree named after Young alongside other trees named after prominent people is the best conclusion in the context of this paragraph's discussion of the National Park Service recognizing Young's efforts. This choice resonates with the essay's overall appreciative description of Young's work in Sequoia National Park.

The best answer is NOT:

A because the detail about the world's largest tree isn't closely related to the essay's focus on Young's work in Sequoia National Park. Therefore, it is not a fitting conclusion to the sentence and the essay.

C because the details about present-day activities in the Giant Forest isn't closely related to the essay's focus on Young's work in Sequoia National Park. Therefore, it is not a fitting conclusion to the sentence and the essay.

D because the claim that the Giant Forest is a popular spot to visit isn't closely related to the essay's focus on Young's work in Sequoia National Park. Therefore, it too is not a fitting conclusion to the sentence and the essay.

Question 60. **The best answer is J** because this option clearly indicates why the essay does not meet the writer's primary purpose. The essay focuses on the vital road project—completed under the leadership of Captain Young—that opened Sequoia National Park's Giant Forest to visitors.

The best answer is NOT:

F because the essay does not describe changes that roads have brought about from the park's establishment to present day.

G because the essay does not develop the idea that Young's actions created a surge in visitors to the park.

H because the essay does not describe Young's military career as a whole, but rather his specific role in the construction of the road to Giant Forest.

Passage V

Question 61. **The best answer is D** because *elicit* is precise and appropriately expresses the idea that the jellyfish had not attracted significant attention from scientists.

The best answer is NOT:

A because *unveil* is illogical and imprecise in the context of describing the amount of attention the jellyfish attracted from scientists.

B because *disclose* is illogical and imprecise in the context of describing the amount of attention the jellyfish attracted from scientists.

C because *reveal* is illogical and imprecise in the context of describing the amount of attention the jellyfish attracted from scientists.

Question 62. **The best answer is F** because the name "Christian Sommer" is an essential element and should not be set off by commas in the sentence. If Sommer's name were set off from the rest of the sentence, that would indicate that the identity of the marine biology student is clear without having to provide a name, which isn't the case.

The best answer is NOT:

G because the name "Christian Sommer" is an essential element and should not be set off with commas. It also adds an unnecessary comma after *marine*.

H because the name "Christian Sommer" is an essential element and should not be set off with commas.

J because the name "Christian Sommer" is an essential element and should not be set off with a comma.

Question 63. The best answer is **B** because it correctly uses a colon to mark a sharp break in the sentence. By using a colon after *astonishing*, the writer introduces a phrase specifying what Christian Sommer observed.

The best answer is NOT:

A because it uses a period to mark a sharp break in thought, which creates a sentence fragment beginning with *reverting*.

C because it uses a semicolon to mark a sharp break in thought, which creates a sentence fragment beginning with *reverting*.

D because it fails to use punctuation to mark a sharp break in thought, which creates an ambiguous and unclear sentence.

Question 64. The best answer is **G** because this option clearly indicates what would be lost if the sentence were deleted. The sentence expresses, in plain language, that the jellyfish were essentially growing younger, an idea that clarifies information presented earlier in the paragraph.

The best answer is NOT:

F because the paragraph makes clear that the jellyfish revert to an earlier life stage in the preceding sentence, so deleting this sentence would not remove the information from the paragraph.

H because this sentence does not present a different perspective or contradict anything Sommer concluded.

J because this sentence does not suggest that Sommer continued to observe the jellyfish.

Question 65. The best answer is **D** because it is the only option that provides a logical introduction to the paragraph's focus on the jellyfish's life stages.

The best answer is NOT:

A because the details about the jellyfish's anatomy do not logically introduce the information in the rest of the paragraph.

B because the details about where the jellyfish lives do not logically introduce the information in the rest of the paragraph.

C because the details about the jellyfish's anatomy do not logically introduce the information in the rest of the paragraph.

Question 66. **The best answer is H** because it appropriately uses a comma to set off the participial phrase that starts with *reaching*.

The best answer is NOT:

F because it has an unnecessary comma after *colony* and lacks the necessary comma setting off the phrase that starts with *reaching*.

G because it has an unnecessary comma after *and* and lacks the necessary comma setting off the phrase that starts with *reaching*.

J because it lacks the necessary comma setting off the phrase that starts with *reaching*.

Question 67. **The best answer is B** because it uses a comma to set off the nonessential phrase introduced by the subordinating conjunction *if*. This phrase is closed by a matching comma after *age*.

The best answer is NOT:

A because it has an unnecessary dash that interrupts the phrase introduced by *if*.

C because it lacks punctuation setting off the phrase introduced by *if* and includes an unnecessary comma after *stressed*.

D because it lacks punctuation setting off the phrase introduced by *if*.

Question 68. **The best answer is J** because it provides the clearest, most concise wording.

The best answer is NOT:

F because it is redundant; "no apparent limit" and "perpetual cycles" have similar meanings, and "metamorphic transformation" is itself redundant.

G because it is redundant; "no apparent limit" and "endlessly recurring" have similar meanings, and *transformative* and *metamorphosis* have essentially the same meaning.

H because it is redundant; *transformative* and *metamorphosis* have essentially the same meaning.

Question 69. The best answer is **C** because it has incorrect sentence structure. The sentence lacks a main verb, which creates a sentence fragment. This makes **C** the only alternative that is NOT acceptable.

The best answer is NOT:

A because it uses a colon to signal a sharp break in thought and introduce the nickname for *T. dohrnii*, which creates a complete and structurally sound sentence.

B because it uses a comma to set off the participial phrase beginning with *calling*, which creates a complete and structurally sound sentence.

D because it creates a simple sentence that is complete and structurally sound.

Question 70. The best answer is **G** because at this point the essay is considering whether the jellyfish can accurately be described as immortal. Therefore, the details about the lifespans of the jellyfish's cells and genes are the most relevant option.

The best answer is NOT:

F because the information about scientists replicating the jellyfish's life stages is not relevant in the context of considering whether the jellyfish can accurately be described as immortal.

H because the detail about the jellyfish's size is not relevant in the context of considering whether the jellyfish can accurately be described as immortal.

J because the detail about the jellyfish's spread through many oceans is not relevant in the context of considering whether the jellyfish can accurately be described as immortal.

Question 71. The best answer is **C** because *of* is the correct idiomatic preposition needed to make this sentence understandable.

The best answer is NOT:

A because the phrase "clones amidst" is not an idiomatically sound expression in standard English, and it creates an unclear sentence.

B because the phrase "clones with" creates an unclear sentence.

D because the phrase "clones to" is not an idiomatically sound expression in standard English, and it creates an unclear sentence.

Question 72. The best answer is **F** because it has the correct pronoun-antecedent agreement and uses the correct possessive form of *it*. The verb *achieves* indicates that the jellyfish is being referred to in the singular. Therefore, the singular pronoun *its* is correct.

The best answer is NOT:

G because it uses the plural pronoun *their* when the verb *achieves* indicates that the jellyfish is being referred to in the singular.

H because it uses the contraction *it's*, meaning "it is," instead of the singular possessive pronoun *its*.

J because it uses the plural pronoun *their* when the verb *achieves* indicates that the jellyfish is being referred to in the singular.

Question 73. The best answer is **C** because it is the only option that has correct sentence structure. It creates a complete sentence with a subject and main verb.

The best answer is NOT:

A because it is a sentence fragment. It does not provide a main verb to accompany the subject, *what*.

B because it is a sentence fragment. Like A, it does not provide a main verb to accompany the subject, *what*.

D because it is a sentence fragment. Like A and B, it does not provide a main verb to accompany the subject, *what*.

Question 74. The best answer is **J** because it clearly explains why the sentence should not be added. The information about lethal encounters is not relevant to the paragraph's discussion of ongoing research into the jellyfish's cellular transformations.

The best answer is NOT:

F because the sentence is irrelevant and should not be added, and the suggested addition doesn't add details about environmental dangers.

G because the sentence is irrelevant and should not be added, and the suggested addition is not the first indication in the essay that the jellyfish aren't truly immortal.

H because the suggested addition does not state or imply that these are the only dangers facing the jellyfish.

Your First Practice Test

Question 75. **The best answer is A** because it provides the most effective conclusion to the essay while providing specific information about the benefits of *T. dohrnii* research, indicating that research into the jellyfish may inform us about aging and disease.

The best answer is NOT:

B because the details about Shin Kubota do not provide a fitting conclusion or indicate any benefits of research into the jellyfish.

C because it is vague and does not provide a fitting conclusion or indicate any benefits of research into the jellyfish.

D because the focus on the jellyfish producing offspring in specific conditions does not provide a fitting conclusion or indicate any benefits of research into the jellyfish.

Question 1. The correct answer is A. First divide the constants to get $-\frac{35}{5}$, or -7, and then apply the exponent rule for division to get $x^{5-1}y^{4-1}$, or $x^4 y^3$. By combining the constant and the variable expression, the fraction is equivalent to $-7x^4 y^3$. If you answered **B**, you may have correctly calculated the constant as -7, and then you may have thought the exponents in the denominator of the fraction were both 0 and applied the exponent rule for division to get $x^{5-0}y^{4-0}$, or $x^5 y^4$, thus obtaining $-7x^5 y^4$. If you answered **C**, you may have correctly calculated the constant as -7, and then, you may have incorrectly applied the exponent rule for division and added exponents to get $x^{5+1}y^{4+1}$, or $x^6 y^5$, thus obtaining $-7x^6 y^5$. If you answered **D**, you may have subtracted the constants, $-(35-5)=-30$, and correctly applied the exponent rule for division to get $-30x^4 y^3$. If you answered **E**, you may have added the constants, $-(35+5)=-40$, and correctly applied the exponent rule for division to get $-40x^4 y^3$.

Question 2. The correct answer is G. The sum of the measures of the interior angles of any triangle is $180°$. To find the value of x, solve the equation $4x+5x+6x=180$. Thus, $15x=180 \Leftrightarrow x=12$. If you answered **F**, you may have thought adjacent angles are complementary (or sum to $90°$) and solved $4x+5x=90$ to get $9x=90 \Leftrightarrow x=10$. If you answered **H**, you may have thought the sum of the measures of the interior angles was $360°$ and solved $4x+5x+6x=360$ to get $15x=360 \Leftrightarrow x=24$. If you answered **J**, you may have thought only one of the interior angles was needed and solved $6x=180$ to get $x=30$. Similarly, for **K**, you may have solved $5x=180$ to get $x=36$.

Question 3. The correct answer is D. First, divide the total volume of the batch of cologne by the volume of cologne that will be contained in each full bottle to get $\frac{48.5\,\text{oz}}{0.35\,\text{oz/bottle}} \approx 138.57$ bottles. Because the approximate 0.57 represents a partially filled bottle, round down to the nearest whole number of bottles, 138. If you answered **A** or **B**, you may have computed $\frac{48.5}{3.5} \approx 13.86$ and then either rounded down to get 13 or rounded up to get 14. If you answered **C**, you may have rounded up before dividing, $\frac{49}{0.4}=122.5$, and then rounded down to get 122. If you answered **E**, you may have divided correctly but then incorrectly rounded 138.57 up to 139.

Question 4. The correct answer is G. The number of spaces reserved for accessible parking is equal to $200(0.06)=12$. So, there are $200-12=188$ spaces NOT reserved for accessible parking. Of these 188 spaces, 20 are suitable for compact cars only. Thus, the remaining $188-20=168$ spaces are suitable for noncompact cars. If you answered **F**, you may have subtracted 20% of the number of spaces in the parking lot from the total, $200-200(0.20)=200-40=160$. If you answered **H**, you may have correctly subtracted the 20 spaces that are suitable for compact cars from the total but subtracted 6 instead of 6% for the number of accessible parking spaces, $200-6-20=174$. If you answered **J**, you may have subtracted only the 20 spaces that are suitable for compact cars from the total, $200-20=180$. If you answered **K**, you may have subtracted only the 6% of spaces that are reserved for accessible parking from the total, $200-200(0.06)=200-12=188$.

Question 5. The correct answer is E. Simplify using the order of operations. The first step is to simplify within the grouping symbols: $2|2-9|-3(5+2)=2|-7|-3(7)=2(7)-3(7)$. Next, moving from left to right, multiply terms, before subtracting: $2(7)-3(7)=14-21=-7$. If you answered **A**, you may not have simplified the absolute value: $2|-7|-3(7) \Rightarrow 2(-7)-3(7)$. So, $-14-21=-35$. If you answered **B**, you may have (1) not simplified the absolute value and (2) incorrectly distributed to the first term only in the parentheses: $2|2-9|-3(5+2) \Rightarrow 2(-7)-3(5)+2$. So, $-14-15+2=-27$. If you answered **C**, you may have (1) incorrectly treated the absolute value like parentheses and (2) incorrectly distributed to the first term only in each grouping symbol: $2|2-9|-3(5+2) \Rightarrow 2(2)-9-3(5)+2$. So, $4-9-15+2=-18$. If you answered **D**, you may have (1) incorrectly treated the absolute value bars like parentheses and (2) incorrectly distributed to the first term only in the absolute value bars: $2|2-9|-3(5+2) \Rightarrow 2|2|+|-9|-3(7)$. So, $4+9-21=-8$.

Question 6. The correct answer is K. Every year Ricardo will put in at least $500, and on years 2, 3, 4, 5, and 6 he will put in $200 more than the previous year. So, there will be 5 birthdays when the additional $200 will need to be accounted for. The equation to compute the total is $\$500(6)+\$200(1+2+3+4+5)$, which yields a total of $6,000. If you chose **F**, you may have forgotten to increase the amount by $200 for each successive birthday: $\$500(6)+\$200(6-1)$. If you chose **G**, you may have just added the dollar amounts and multiplied by the number of years: $(\$500+\$200)(6)$. If you chose **H**, you may have computed $\$500(6+1)+\$200(6)$. If you chose **J**, you may have added the dollar amounts and multiplied by an extra birthday: $(\$500+\$200)(6+1)$.

Question 7. The correct answer is B. First, subtract the initial payment from the total amount: $\$7,000.00-\$700.00=\$6,300.00$. Then, take that amount and divide it by the 36 payments: $\$6,300.00 \div 36=\$175.00$. If you chose **A**, you may have mistakenly divided the initial $700.00 payment by 36. If you chose **C**, you may have forgotten to subtract the initial payment and computed $\$7,000.00 \div 36$. If you chose **D**, you may have added the initial payment instead of subtracting and then divided: $(\$7,000.00+\$700.00) \div 36$. If you chose **E**, you may have thought you should divide by the initial payment and multiply by the number of monthly payments: $(\$7,000.00 \div \$700.00)(36)$.

Question 8. The correct answer is H. To add matrices, add elements in the same position to each other: $\begin{bmatrix} 9 & 2 \\ -4 & 1 \end{bmatrix} + \begin{bmatrix} -6 & 8 \\ 7 & 6 \end{bmatrix} = \begin{bmatrix} 9+(-6) & 2+8 \\ (-4)+7 & 1+6 \end{bmatrix} = \begin{bmatrix} 3 & 10 \\ 3 & 7 \end{bmatrix}$. If you chose **F**, you may have multiplied the matrices instead of adding: $\begin{bmatrix} 9 & 2 \\ -4 & 1 \end{bmatrix}\begin{bmatrix} -6 & 8 \\ 7 & 6 \end{bmatrix} = \begin{bmatrix} 9(-6)+2(7) & 9(8)+2(6) \\ -4(-6)+1(7) & -4(8)+1(6) \end{bmatrix}$. If you chose **G**, you may have added 4 instead of -4 to 7 in the 2nd row 1st column: $\begin{bmatrix} 9+(-6) & 2+8 \\ 4+7 & 1+6 \end{bmatrix}$. If you chose **J**, you may have added elements from the same matrix to each other: $\begin{bmatrix} 9+2 & -6+8 \\ (-4)+1 & 7+6 \end{bmatrix}$. If you chose **K**, you may have computed with only positive values instead of using -6 and -4: $\begin{bmatrix} 9+6 & 2+8 \\ 4+7 & 1+6 \end{bmatrix}$.

Question 9. The correct answer is B. Subtract the amount that both Lyle and Ming used from the starting amount: $4 - \left(\frac{1}{2} + 1\frac{1}{4}\right) = 4 - 1\frac{3}{4} = 2\frac{1}{4}$. There were $2\frac{1}{4}$ gallons of paint left. If you chose **A**, you may have added the amounts that Lyle and Ming used: $\frac{1}{2} + 1\frac{1}{4}$. If you chose **C**, you may have only subtracted the amount that Ming used: $4 - 1\frac{1}{4}$. If you chose **D**, you may have forgotten to use 1 when combining or subtracting the amounts: $(4) - \left(\frac{1}{2} + 1\frac{1}{4}\right) \rightarrow 4 - \left(\frac{3}{4}\right)$. If you chose **E**, you may have only subtracted the amount Lyle used: $4 - \frac{1}{2}$.

Question 10. The correct answer is H. The formula for the slope of a line, m, is $m = \frac{y_2 - y_1}{x_2 - x_1}$. Substituting into the formula yields $m = \frac{6-1}{5-(-3)} = \frac{5}{8}$. If you chose **F**, you may have switched the numerator values and made a sign error in the denominator: $\frac{1-6}{5-3}$. If you chose **G**, you may have switched the values in the denominator: $\frac{6-1}{-3-5}$. If you chose **J**, you may have made an error with the negative value in the denominator and computed $\frac{6-1}{5-3}$. If you chose **K**, you may have thought you should add the values in the slope formula: $\frac{6+1}{5+(-3)}$.

Question 11. The correct answer is E. Let x be the length, in inches, of the larger triangle's hypotenuse. The hypotenuse length of the smaller triangle corresponds to the hypotenuse length of the larger triangle so the ratio of the side lengths is $24:x$. Because the ratios of corresponding side lengths are equal, $24:x$ is equivalent to $4:5$. Write each ratio as a fraction and set the ratios equal: $\frac{24}{x} = \frac{4}{5}$. Solve for x by cross multiplying and dividing: $4x = 5 \cdot 24 \rightarrow x = \frac{5 \cdot 24}{4} = 30$. If you chose **A**, you may have thought the length of the larger triangle's hypotenuse is the ratio of the greater lengths to the shorter lengths expressed as a decimal: $\frac{5}{4} = 1.25$. If you chose **B**, you may have thought the solution is the values in the given ratio added together: $4 + 5$. If you chose **C**, you may have thought the solution is the values in the given ratio multiplied together: $4 \cdot 5$. If you chose **D**, you may have thought the solution is the difference of the ratio values added to the shorter hypotenuse length: $24 + (5 - 4)$.

Question 12. The correct answer is F. In a right triangle, the sine of an angle measure is equal to the ratio of the opposite side to the hypotenuse. The hypotenuse is the longest side in a right triangle. So, $\sin A = \frac{8}{17}$. If you chose **G**, you may have thought it was the ratio of the opposite side to the adjacent side. If you chose **H**, you may have thought it was the ratio of the adjacent side to the hypotenuse. If you chose **J**, you may have thought it was the ratio of the hypotenuse to the adjacent side. If you chose **K**, you may have thought it was the ratio of the hypotenuse to the opposite side.

Question 13. The correct answer is E. The Pythagorean theorem states that the sum of the squares of the legs (a and b) of a right triangle is equal to the square of the hypotenuse (c). The formula is $a^2 + b^2 = c^2$. Notice that $1,600^2 + 1,200^2 = 2,000^2$. Because $AC^2 + BC^2 = AB^2$, $\triangle ABC$ is a right triangle with hypotenuse $\overline{AB}$ and $m\angle ACB = 90°$. The measure of $\angle BCD$ is also $90°$ because $\angle ACB$ and $\angle BCD$ form a straight angle. This makes $\triangle BCD$ a right triangle. BD can be found by computing $AD - AC = 2,500 - 1,600 = 900$ km. Applying the Pythagorean theorem and substituting yields $BC^2 + CD^2 = BD^2 \rightarrow 1,200^2 + 900^2 = BD^2$. Therefore, $BD = \sqrt{1,200^2 + 900^2} = 1,500$ km. If you chose **A**, you may have thought $\overline{BD}$ and $\overline{BC}$ were legs in a right triangle with hypotenuse $\overline{AD}$: $BD^2 + 1,200^2 = 2,500^2$. If you chose **B**, you may have mixed up BD and $1,200$ in your equation: $BD^2 + 900^2 = 1,200^2$. If you chose **C**, you may have thought CD and BD were equal: $2,500 - 1,600$. If you chose **D**, you may have thought BC and BD were equal.

Question 14. The correct answer is J. First, factor the equation: $(x-9)(x+5) = 0$. Then, set each factor equal to zero: $x - 9 = 0$ and $x + 5 = 0$. Next, solve for x by adding 9 to both sides and subtracting 5 from both sides, respectively. This yields $x = 9$ and $x = -5$. Finally, add the solutions: $9 + (-5) = 4$. If you chose **F**, then you may have thought the constant term in the equation is the sum of the solutions. If you chose **G**, you may have found one of the solutions and stopped. If you chose **H**, you may have thought since the equation is equal to zero that the sum of the solutions is zero. If you chose **K**, you may have thought the solutions were 4 and 5.

Question 15. The correct answer is B. Divide the figure into 2 rectangles such that you have a 9-inch by 5-inch rectangle and a 2-inch by 6-inch rectangle. Note, the 6 comes from taking the longest horizontal side length and subtracting the top horizontal side length to find the unknown horizontal side length: $11 - 5 = 6$. Next, find the area, in square inches, of each rectangle by multiplying the length times the width: $(9)(5) = 45$ and $(2)(6) = 12$. Finally, add the areas together to get the total area of the figure in square inches: $45 + 12 = 57$. If you chose **A**, you may have computed the area, in square inches, of the gap to the right of the figure and computed $(9-2)(11-5)$. If you chose **C**, you may have overestimated the area, in square inches, by counting part of the figure twice: $(2)(11) + (5)(9)$. If you chose **D**, you may have thought the area could be computed by subtracting the area of a 5-inch by 2-inch rectangle from the area of a 9-inch by 11-inch rectangle: $(9)(11) - (5)(2)$. If you chose **E**, you may have overestimated by finding the area of a 9-inch by 11-inch rectangle: $(9)(11)$.

Question 16. The correct answer is H. To find the new coordinates, you add the distance traveled to the starting coordinate values since the dot is moving in the positive direction for both x and y. The distance traveled is the speed multiplied by the time. Perform 2 separate calculations for the x-coordinate and y-coordinate since the horizontal and vertical moves use different times: $(2+(0.5)(4), 3+(0.5)(2)) \rightarrow (2+2, 3+1) \rightarrow (4, 4)$. The dot's final location is at $(4, 4)$. If you chose **F**, you may have combined the times for the horizontal and vertical moves and added the distance traveled to just the y-coordinate: $(2, 3+(0.5)(4+2))$. If you chose **G**, you may have switched the times for the horizontal and vertical moves: $(2+(0.5)(2), 3+(0.5)(4))$. If you chose **J**, you may have combined the times for the horizontal and vertical moves and added the distance traveled to just the x-coordinate: $(2+(0.5)(4+2), 3)$. If you chose **K**, you may have just added the times to the coordinates: $(2+4, 3+2)$.

Question 17. The correct answer is A. The regular enrollment fee for a Grade 4 and Grade 6 child is $400 and $500, respectively. Mr. Ramirez enrolled his children early so he only has to pay 80% of the regular fee. To find the amount he paid, add the fees for each grade and then reduce that amount by 20% by multiplying the total by 80% expressed as a decimal: $(1-0.2)(400+500) = (0.8)(900) = 720$. Mr. Ramirez paid $720. If you chose **B**, you may have only reduced the Grade 6 fee: $(1-0.2)(500)+400$. If you chose **C**, you may have only reduced the Grade 4 fee: $(1-0.2)(400)+500$. If you chose **D**, you may have thought a 20% discount meant you should reduce each fee by $20 and computed $400+500-20-20$. If you chose **E**, you may have thought a 20% discount meant you should reduce the total fee amount by $20 and computed $400+500-20$.

Question 18. The correct answer is H. The general equation for a line is $y = mx + b$ or $f = mg + b$ for this situation. The regular enrollment fees range from $350 for Grade 3 to $500 for Grade 6. Notice the fees increase by $50 as the grade increases by 1. This is the rate of change or slope (m) of the equation. The fixed cost, b, which is also called the y-intercept, can be found by substituting values from the table. For example, $(g, f) \rightarrow (3, 350)$. Substitute and solve for b: $350 = 50(3) + b \rightarrow b = 350 - 150 = 200$. Therefore, the equation is $f = 50g + 200$. If you chose **F**, you may have thought you needed to add the increase in price for each grade to the grade. If you chose **G**, you may have calculated the rate of change correctly, but not taken into account the fixed cost. If you chose **J**, you may have calculated the rate of change correctly, but thought the fixed cost was the enrollment fee of Grade 3 minus the rate of change: $f = 50g + (350 - 50)$. If you chose **K**, you may have thought $m = 50$ and $b = 350 - 50$ and then mixed up the substituting of the m and b values in the equation.

Question 19. The correct answer is C. For the child in Grade 3, there is a $\frac{1}{20}$ chance of being drawn because there are 20 children in Grade 3. For the child in Grade 4, there is a $\frac{1}{15}$ chance of being drawn because there are 15 children in Grade 4. Since each grade's drawing is independent, you need to multiply the chances of each of Ms. Chen's children being drawn times each other to get the probability of both children being drawn: $\frac{1}{20} \cdot \frac{1}{15} = \frac{1}{300}$. Therefore, there is a $\frac{1}{300}$ chance of both of Ms. Chen's children getting drawn for the free tshirt. If you chose **A**, you may have thought the chances for each child being drawn needed to be added and computed: $\frac{1}{20} + \frac{1}{15}$. If you chose **B**, you may have not thought each grade was independent and instead thought the chances were 2 out of the total number of children: $\frac{2}{20 + 15 + 28 + 18}$. If you chose **D**, you may have used the number of children in each of Grades 3 and 4 and divided by the total number of children. Then, you may have multiplied those chances: $\frac{20}{20 + 15 + 28 + 18} \cdot \frac{15}{20 + 15 + 28 + 18}$. If you chose **E**, you may have thought Ms. Chen's 2 children were being randomly drawn one at a time from all the children enrolled and computed $\frac{2}{20 + 15 + 28 + 18} \cdot \frac{1}{20 + 15 + 28 + 18 - 1}$.

Question 20. The correct answer is H. Convert to miles per hour so you can compare with the speed limits in the choices. There are 60 minutes in an hour, so driving 18 miles in 20 minutes can be converted by multiplying by 60: $\frac{18 \text{ miles}}{20 \text{ min}} \cdot \frac{60 \text{ min}}{1 \text{ hr}} = \frac{54 \text{ miles}}{1 \text{ hr}}$. Your speed was 54 miles per hour. You did not exceed the speed limit, so the lowest speed limit that is greater than or equal to 54 miles per hour is 55 miles per hour. If you chose **F** or **G**, you may have underestimated or picked a common speed limit because you were not sure how to do the calculations. If you chose **J**, you may have estimated that 18 miles in 20 minutes is about a minute per mile, which is 60 miles per hour. If you chose **K**, you may have used $\frac{20}{18}$ as the rate in miles per minute and rounded $\frac{20}{18} \cdot 60$ to the nearest multiple of 5.

Question 21. The correct answer is A. The left side of the equation can be rewritten using exponents: $-\frac{1}{81} = -\frac{1}{3^4} = -3^{-4}$. Therefore, $-3^{-4} = -3^x$. Since the bases are equal, the exponents are equal. This means $x = -4$. If you chose **B**, you may have solved $-81 = -3^x$, not knowing that the exponent should be negative to put 81 in the denominator. If you chose **C**, you may have divided -81 by -3. If you chose **D**, you may have rewritten the equation as $\frac{1}{81} = 3^x$ and known that $3^4 = 81$ but thought the answer should be the negative reciprocal of 4 instead of just -4. If you chose **E**, you may have divided both sides of the equation by -3: $x = -\frac{1}{81} \div -3 = \frac{1}{243}$.

Question 22. The correct answer is G. First, multiply both sides of the equation by I^2 to get $I^2 R = P$. Then, divide by R to get $I^2 = \frac{P}{R}$. Finally, cancel the exponent by taking the square root to get $I = \sqrt{\frac{P}{R}}$. If you chose **F**, you may have thought dividing both sides by P results in $\frac{R}{P} = I^2$ instead of $\frac{R}{P} = \frac{1}{I^2}$. If you chose **H**, you may have forgotten to take the square root. If you chose **J**, you may have thought dividing both sides by P results in $\frac{R}{P} = I^2$ and forgotten to take the square root. If you chose **K**, you may have computed the product of the variables that are not I.

Question 23. The correct answer is D. The time between the lights flashing at the same time is the least common multiple of 8 and 12. Multiples for 8 are 8, 16, 24, 32, 40, $\cdots$. Now, list multiples for 12 until one number matches the other multiples: 12, 24, $\cdots$. Because 24 is the least number in both lists, the answer is 24 seconds. If you chose **A**, you may have calculated the difference of the times: $12 - 8 = 4$. If you chose **B**, you may have calculated the average of the times: $\frac{8 + 12}{2} = 10$. If you chose **C**, you may have calculated the sum of the times: $8 + 12$. If you chose **E**, you may have calculated the product of the times: $8 \cdot 12 = 96$.

Question 24. The correct answer is H. First, take the square root of the area, A, to find the side length, s, because $A = s^2$. So, $s = \sqrt{900} = 30$ inches. Then, multiply by 4 to find the perimeter, P, because $P = 4s$. Therefore, $P = 4 \cdot 30 = 120$ inches. If you chose **F**, you may have only found the side length: $\sqrt{900} = 30$. If you chose **G**, you may have multiplied the side length by 2 instead of 4 giving half the perimeter: $2\sqrt{900} = 60$. If you chose **J**, you may have divided the area by 4: $\frac{900}{4} = 225$. If you chose **K**, you may have have divided the area by 2: $\frac{900}{2} = 450$.

Question 25. The correct answer is D. Substitute the given values into the proportion and solve by cross multiplying and dividing to find x, the deer population: $\frac{108}{x} = \frac{36}{54} \rightarrow 36x = 54(108) \rightarrow x = \frac{54(108)}{36} = 162$. If you chose **A**, you may have thought 108 is the population since it is the greatest given value. If you chose **B**, you may have added and subtracted instead of multiplying and dividing: $108 + 54 - 36 = 126$. If you chose **C**, you may have added the counts of tagged deer from both captures: $108 + 36 = 144$. If you chose **E**, you may have found the sum of all the given numbers: $108 + 54 + 36$.

Question 26. The correct answer is J. The formula for an arithmetic sequence is $a_n = a_1 + (n-1)d$, where a_n is the nth term, a_1 is the first term, and d is the common difference. Substitute and solve for a_1: $30 = a_1 + (10-1)2 \rightarrow 30 = a_1 + 18 \rightarrow a_1 = 30 - 18 = 12$. If you chose **F**, you may have substituted 30 instead of 10 for n, the term number: $30 = a_1 + (30-1)2 \rightarrow 30 = a_1 + 58 \rightarrow a_1 = 30 - 58 = -28$. If you chose **G**, you may have substituted correctly, but then attempted to divide both sides of the equation by 2 (incorrectly ignoring a_1), and then subtracted 9: $30 = a_1 + (10-1)2 \rightarrow \frac{30}{2} = a_1 + 9 \rightarrow a_1 = 15 - 9 = 6$. If you chose **H**, you may have substituted correctly, but failed to distribute 2 to both the 10 and 1 inside the parenthesis: $30 = a_1 + (10-1)2 \rightarrow 30 = a_1 + 20 - 1 \rightarrow 30 = a_1 + 19 \rightarrow a_1 = 30 - 19 = 11$. If you chose **K**, you may have divided the 30, the 10th term, by 2, the common difference: $30 \div 2 = 15$.

Question 27. The correct answer is D. Convert from steps to miles using conversion factors making sure the labels of *feet* and *steps* cancel and the label *mile* remains in the numerator: $3,898 \text{ steps} \cdot \frac{2.25 \text{ ft}}{1 \text{ step}} \cdot \frac{1 \text{ mile}}{5,280 \text{ ft}} = \frac{3,898 \cdot 2.25}{5,280}$ miles ≈ 1.7 miles. If you chose **A**, you may have divided by 2.25 instead of multiplying: $\frac{3,898}{5,280 \cdot 2.25}$. If you chose **B**, you may have set up the conversion fractions where feet and steps canceled, but the label of *miles* was in the denominator, thus giving the reciprocal of the correct answer: $\frac{5,280}{2.25 \cdot 3,898}$. If you chose **C**, you may have computed $\frac{5,280}{3,898}$. If you chose **E**, you may have computed $\frac{5,280 \cdot 2.25}{3,898}$.

Question 28. The correct answer is G. First, find the total number of members in the clubs. Keep in mind that 9 students are in both clubs, which means you will have to subtract so that you don't count some students twice: $13 + 11 - 9 = 15$. Then, subtract the number of members from the total number of students: $20 - 15 = 5$. Therefore, there are 5 students that are not members of either club. If you chose **F**, you may have ignored the intersection of 9 and computed $13 + 11 - 20$. If you chose **H**, you may have ignored the total of 20 and computed $13 + 11 - 2(9)$. If you chose **J**, you may have ignored the club counts of 13 and 11 and computed $20 - 9$. If you chose **K**, you may have computed $13 + 11 + 9 - 20$.

Question 29. The correct answer is D. The mean is the sum of all the values divided by the number of values. To increase the mean of 7 numbers by 4, you must increase the sum by 4(7), or 28, because the total sum will be divided by 7. If you chose **A**, you may have increased the sum by 4 forgetting to account for the division in the formula. If you chose **B**, you may have increased the sum by the number in the group. If you chose **C**, you may have added the given numbers: $4 + 7$. If you chose **E**, you may have thought the sum would have to increase by twice as much as necessary: $2(4)(7)$.

Question 30. The correct answer is G. The equation of a circle with center (h, k) and a radius length of r is $(x - h)^2 + (y - k)^2 = r^2$. Substituting the given values into the equation yields $(x - 4)^2 + (y - (-3))^2 = 5^2$, which simplifies to $(x - 4)^2 + (y + 3)^2 = 25$. If you chose **F**, you may have forgotten to square the radius. If you chose **H**, you may have switched the center's (x, y) coordinates. If you chose **J**, you may have switched the (x, y) coordinates and forgotten to square the radius. If you chose **K**, you may have thought the coordinates are added to x and y instead of subtracted.

Question 31. The correct answer is B. The median is the middle term in a set of terms ordered from least to greatest. The middle term in a set of 25 terms is the 13th term because $\frac{25}{2} = 12.5$. Since $25 - 13 = 12$, there are 12 students that earned a test score greater than 80 points. If you chose **A**, you may have computed $(1 - 0.8)(25)$, which is 20% of the total number of students. If you chose **C**, you may have computed $\frac{25}{2}$ and rounded up, thinking 13 students earned a score greater than 80 points. If you chose **D**, you may have computed $\frac{25}{2} + 1$ and rounded up, thinking 14 students earned a score greater than 80 points. If you chose **E**, you may have computed 0.8(25), which is 80% of the total number of students.

Question 32. The correct answer is J. Let x be the cost of apples and y be the cost of oranges in dollars. Next, set up the system of equations: $3x + 4y = 3.47$ and $12y = 6.36$. Solve for y in the second equation by dividing by 12: $y = \frac{6.36}{12} = 0.53$. Then, substitute the cost of oranges in the first equation and solve for the cost of apples: $3x + 4(0.53) = 3.47 \rightarrow 3x + 2.12 = 3.47 \rightarrow x = \frac{3.47 - 2.12}{3} = 0.45$. Finally, divide the \$10 by the cost of apples and round down: $\frac{10}{x} = \frac{10}{0.45} \approx 22$. Therefore, 22 apples is the maximum number Shefali can purchase. If you chose **F**, you may have computed $\frac{10}{y} = \frac{10}{0.53}$ and rounded down. If you chose **G**, you may have computed $\frac{10}{y} = \frac{10}{0.53}$ and rounded up. If you chose **H**, you may have confused the number of apples and oranges: $4x + 3y = 3.47$. So, $x = \frac{3.47 - 3(0.53)}{4} = 0.47$ and $\frac{10}{0.47} \approx 21$. If you chose **K**, you may have computed $\frac{10}{x} = \frac{10}{0.45}$ and rounded up.

Question 33. The correct answer is A. The receipt shows the time of purchase was 2:30 p.m., and Fletcher was in the store for 25 minutes before the purchase. Subtracting 25 minutes from 2:30 p.m. yields 2:05 p.m., which is when he entered the store. He left his home 1 hour and 15 minutes before he entered the store. Subtracting an hour would be 1:05 p.m., and subtracting an additional 15 minutes would make the time he left 12:50 p.m. If you chose **B**, you may have computed $2:30 - 0:25 = 2:05 \rightarrow 2:05 - 1:15 \rightarrow (2-1):(15-5) = 1:10$. If you chose **C**, you may have subtracted 1:00 and subtracted 0:25, but mistakenly added 0:15 instead of subtracting. If you chose **D**, you may have subtracted 1:00, but not known to also subtract 0:25 and 0:15. If you chose **E**, you may have subtracted 1:15 but mistakenly added 0:25.

Question 34. The correct answer is H. The total with 6% sales tax is \$18.55, which means the total before tax, x, can be found with the equation $x + 0.06x = 18.55$. Solving for x yields $1.06x = 18.55 \rightarrow x = \frac{18.55}{1.06} = 17.50$. Next, subtract the 4 known prices to get the price of the bag of balloons: $\$17.50 - (\$2 + \$6 + \$3 + \$4) = \$17.50 - \$15 = \$2.50$. If you chose **F**, you may have rounded $18.55(0.06)$. If you chose **G**, you may have rounded $(18.55 - 15) - 0.06(18.55)$. If you chose **J**, you may have rounded $(18.55 - 15) - 0.06(15)$. If you chose **K**, you may have rounded $(18.55 - 15) - 0.06$.

Question 35. The correct answer is C. First, find the mean of the 4 items: $\frac{\$2 + \$6 + \$3 + \$4}{4} = \$3.75$. Then, subtract the mean from the price of the doll: $\$6.00 - \$3.75 = \$2.25$. If you chose **A**, you may have computed $\frac{\$2 + \$6 + \$3 + \$4}{2} - \$6$. If you chose **B**, you may have subtracted the range of the 4 prices from the price of the doll instead of the mean: $\$6 - (\$6 - \$2)$. If you chose **D**, you may have subtracted the median from the price of the doll: $\$6 - \frac{\$3 + \$4}{2}$. If you chose **E**, you may have computed the mean without using the price of the doll: $\$6 - \frac{\$2 + \$3 + \$4}{3}$.

Question 36. The correct answer is K. The price for a bag of marbles is $2. The price for a car is $3, so the equation for spending $30 on x bags of marbles and y cars is $2x + 3y = 30$. Substituting $y = 0$ into the equation and solving for x yields the x-intercept: $2x + 3(0) = 30 \rightarrow x = \frac{30}{2} = 15$. Similarly, the y-intercept can be found by substituting $x = 0$ and solving: $2(0) + 3y = 30 \rightarrow y = \frac{30}{3} = 10$. Therefore, the graph is the line segment that contains the points $(15, 0)$ and $(0, 10)$. If you chose **F**, you may have confused the x-intercept and the y-intercept or thought the equation is $3x + 2y = 30$. If you chose **G**, you may have mixed up the price of the car with the price of the doll and confused the x-intercept and the y-intercept: $6x + 2y = 30$. If you chose **H**, you may have calculated $\frac{30}{2+3}$ to get a y-intercept of 6 and then $\frac{30-6}{2}$ to get an x-intercept of 12. If you chose **J**, you may have mistakenly chosen the price of the car for the coefficient of x and the price of the doll as the coefficient of y: $3x + 6y = 30$.

Question 37. The correct answer is B. Triangle $\triangle DEF$ is a right triangle, so $m\angle F = 180° - 90° - 30° = 60°$. Triangle $\triangle EFG$ is a right triangle because $\overline{EG}$ is an altitude, so $m\angle EGF = 90°$. In right triangle trigonometry, the sine of an angle measure is equal to the length of the opposite side divided by the length of the hypotenuse (SOH). Therefore, $\sin(\angle F) = \frac{EG}{EF}$. Substituting $EF = 20$ and $m\angle F = 60°$ into that equation and then solving for EG yields $\sin(60°) = \frac{EG}{20} \rightarrow EG = 20 \cdot \sin(60°) = 20 \cdot \frac{\sqrt{3}}{2} = 10\sqrt{3}$. If you chose **A**, you may have thought $\sin(60°)$ is $\frac{1}{2}$ instead of $\frac{\sqrt{3}}{2}$. If you chose **C**, you may have thought EF and EG are equal. If you chose **D**, you may have computed $20\tan(60°)$ instead of $20\sin(60°)$. If you chose **E**, you may have computed $20 \cdot 2$.

Question 38. The correct answer is H. First, write function h by subtracting the other functions: $h(x) = [x^2 + 7x - 3] - [x^2 - 4x + 5] = x^2 + 7x - 3 - x^2 + 4x - 5 = 11x - 8$. Then, substitute 2 for x and simplify: $h(2) = 11(2) - 8 = 22 - 8 = 14$. If you chose **F**, you may have computed $-x^2 - 7x + 3 - x^2 + 4x - 5 \rightarrow -2(2^2) - 3(2) - 2$. If you chose **G**, you may have computed $x^2 + 7x - 3 - x^2 - 4x + 5 \rightarrow 3(2) + 2$. If you chose **J**, you may have computed $x^2 + 7x - 3 + x^2 + 4x - 5 \rightarrow 2(2^2) + 11(2) - 8$. If you chose **K**, you may have computed $x^2 + 7x - 3 - x^2 + 4x + 5 \rightarrow 11(2) + 2$.

Question 39. The correct answer is D. The interior angle measures of a triangle total $180°$. The measure of $\angle B$ is $90°$. The protractor can be used to estimate the measure of $\angle A: 66° - 30° = 36°$ or $150° - 114° = 36°$. Subtract the sum of the measures of $\angle A$ and $\angle B$ from $180°$ to estimate the measure of $\angle C: 180° - [90° + 36°] = 54°$. If you chose **A**, you may have stopped at estimating the measure of $\angle A: 66° - 30°$. If you chose **B**, you may have computed $74° - 30°$. If you chose **C**, you may have computed $180° - [90° + (74° - 30°)]$. If you chose **E**, you may have computed $180° - [90° + (150° - 126°)]$.

Question 40. The correct answer is G. Substituting $x = 1$ and $y = 9$ into the expression yields $\frac{x+y}{y} = \frac{1+9}{9} = \frac{10}{9}$. If you chose **F**, you may have substituted $x = 0$ and $y = 0$ and thought the y-values could cancel: $\frac{x + \cancel{y}}{\cancel{y}} = \frac{0 + \cancel{0}}{\cancel{0}}$. If you chose **H**, you may have switched the range of values for x and y and substituted $x = 9$ and $y = 5$: $\frac{x+y}{y} = \frac{9+5}{5}$. If you chose **J**, you may have substituted $x = 5$ and $y = 9$ and thought the y-values could cancel: $\frac{x + \cancel{y}}{\cancel{y}} = \frac{5 + \cancel{9}}{\cancel{9}}$. If you chose **K**, you may have substituted $x = 5$ and $y = 9$ and made a simplification error: $\frac{x+y}{y} = \frac{5+9}{9} \rightarrow 5 + \frac{9}{9} = 5 + 1$.

Question 41. The correct answer is B. First, substitute function g into function f: $f(g(x)) = (x-3)^2 + 1$. Then, simplify the exponent by multiplying the binomial times itself: $(x-3)(x-3) + 1 = x^2 - 3x - 3x + 9 + 1$. Finally, combine the like terms: $x^2 - 6x + 10$. If you chose **A**, you may have made a mistake with the exponent: $x^2 - 3^2 + 1$. If you chose **C**, you may have added the functions: $x^2 + 1 + x - 3$. If you chose **D**, you may have multiplied the first term of g by f, then subtracted the second term without multiplying: $(x^2 + 1)x - 3$. If you chose **E**, you may have multiplied the functions: $(x^2 + 1)(x - 3)$.

Question 42. The correct answer is H. Rearrange the given equation by cross multiplying: $\frac{4x - y}{x + y} = \frac{5}{2} \rightarrow 2(4x - y) = 5(x + y) \rightarrow 8x - 2y = 5x + 5y$. Then, isolate the variables on opposite sides of the equal sign: $8x - 5x = 5y + 2y \rightarrow 3x = 7y$. Finally, get the constants on one side of the equal sign and the variables on the other by dividing by 3 and $y : \frac{x}{y} = \frac{7}{3}$. If you chose **F**, you may have distributed incorrectly: $2(4x - y) = 5(x + y) \rightarrow 8x - y = 5x + y$. If you chose **G**, you may have thought the answer was the fraction given in the equation. If you chose **J**, you may have set the numerators and denominators equal to each other, added the equations, and solved for $x : 4x - y = 5$ and $x + y = 2 \rightarrow 5x = 7 \rightarrow x = \frac{7}{5}$ If you chose **K**, you may have set up the incorrect equations $4x - y = 2$ and $x + y = 5$, then solved and calculated $x = \frac{7}{5}$ and $y = \frac{18}{5}$, which makes $\frac{x}{y} = \frac{\frac{7}{5}}{\frac{18}{5}}$.

Question 43. The correct answer is D. The graph shows a total distance traveled of 450 km since it stops at a vertical height of 450. The horizontal axis shows 12 hours of data; however, the 3 flat parts (horizontal line segments) of the graph represent when Juro was NOT traveling. Each flat part of the graph is 2 hours. Subtracting those times from the 12 hour total $(12 - (3)(2))$ yields the actual travel time of 6 hours. To find the average speed for the parts of the workday when Juro was traveling, divide the distance traveled by the travel time: $\frac{450}{6} = 75$ km per hour. If you chose **A**, you may have calculated $\frac{450}{10}$. If you chose **B**, you may have calculated $\frac{450}{10 - 2(1)}$. If you chose **C**, you may have calculated $\frac{300}{6-1}$. If you chose **E**, you may have calculated $\frac{188}{2}$.

Question 44. The correct answer is G. The amplitude of a sine function is half the distance between the greatest and the least values of the curve. In the equation $y = A \sin(x)$, the value of $|A|$ is the amplitude. Therefore, the amplitude of $y = 3 \sin x$ is 3. If you chose **F**, you may have calculated $\frac{3}{3}$. If you chose **H**, you may have calculated the distance between the greatest and least value of the curve: $3(2)$. If you chose **J**, you may have calculated 3^{-1}. If you chose **K**, you may have thought the value in the equation should be halved.

Question 45. The correct answer is B. Get a common denominator by multiplying the first term by $\frac{w}{w}$, which yields $\frac{4w}{w^2} + \frac{2}{w^2}$. Then, add the numerators: $\frac{4w+2}{w^2}$. If you chose **A**, you may have canceled a 2: $\frac{\cancel{4}w + \cancel{2}}{w^2} \to \frac{2w+1}{w^2}$. If you chose **C**, you may have just added the numerators and denominators: $\frac{4+2}{w+w^2}$. If you chose **D**, you may have just added the numerators and not gotten a common denominator correctly: $\frac{4}{w^2} + \frac{2}{w^2}$. If you chose **E**, you may have calculated $\frac{4+2}{w(w^2)}$.

Question 46. The correct answer is F. For ABC and DEF to be 3-digit whole numbers, they must be integers in the range $[100, 999]$. If $A = D$ (so $|A - D| = 0$), then the positive difference between ABC and DEF will be less than 100, since the difference between any two numbers within the ranges $[100, 199], [200, 299], \ldots, [900, 999]$ is less than 100. Therefore, since the positive difference between ABC and DEF is greater than 100, it must be true that $|A - D| \neq 0$, or $|A - D| \geq 1$. Choices **G**, **H**, **J**, and **K** may be disproved by the following counterexample. Consider $A = 2$, $B = 0$, $C = 0$, $D = 4$, $E = 0$, and $F = 0$, so that $ABC = 200$ and $DEF = 400$. These are both 3-digit whole numbers, and since $400 - 200 = 200 > 100$, these two numbers satisfy the condition that the positive difference between the two numbers is greater than 100. Since $B = C = E = F = 0$, the three values $|B - E|$, $|C - F|$, and $B - E$ will all be equal to 0, which is less than 1. The value $A - D = 2 - 4 = -2$ is also less than 1. Therefore, the only value that is greater than or equal to 1 in this example is $|A - D| = |2 - 4| = |-2| = 2$.

Question 47. The correct answer is B. The number line shows that a is located to the left of 0, so the value of a is negative, or $a < 0$. Similarly, b is located between 0 and 1, so $0 < b < 1$. The multiplication property of inequality states that multiplying an inequality by a negative value will change the direction of the inequality symbol. Multiplying $0 < b < 1$ by a therefore yields $0(a) > b(a) > 1(a)$, or $a < ab < 0$. If you chose **A**, you may have forgotten to change the direction of the inequality symbols when multiplying by a and used the fact that $-1 < 0$ to get $0(a) < b(a) < 1(a) \to 0 < ab < a \to -1 < ab < a$. If you chose **C**, **D**, or **E**, you may not have realized that the inequalities $0 < ab, 1 < ab$, and $b < ab$, respectively, must be false, since the inequalities $ab < 0$ and $b > 0$ are true.

Question 48. The correct answer is J. Let the final exam grade be represented by f. Since Sani's test scores of 78, 86, and 82 are each worth 20% of the course grade, and the final exam score is worth 40% of the course grade, Sani's course grade can be calculated as $0.2(78) + 0.2(86) + 0.2(82) + 0.4f = 49.2 + 0.4f$. For Sani's course grade to be at least 86, the final exam score, f, must satisfy the inequality $49.2 + 0.4f \geq 86$. Subtracting 49.2 from each side of the inequality and then dividing each side by 0.4 yields $f \geq 92$. Therefore, Sani will have to earn a minimum score of 92 on the final exam to receive a course grade of at least 86. If you chose **F**, you may have calculated the average of Sani's 3 test scores: $\frac{78 + 86 + 82}{3} = \frac{246}{3} = 82$. If you chose **G**, you may have calculated the average of Sani's highest two test scores: $\frac{86 + 82}{2} = \frac{168}{2} = 84$. If you chose **H**, you may have tried to minimize the score too early by rounding $86 - 49.2 = 36.8$ down to 36 on the right-hand side of the inequality and then divided by 0.4 to get $f \geq 90$. If you chose **K**, you may have weighted all the exams equally and solved the inequality $\frac{78 + 86 + 82 + f}{4} \geq 86$ to get $246 + f \geq 86(4)$, or $f \geq 98$.

Question 49. The correct answer is A. The area of any triangle is $\frac{1}{2}bh$, where b is the length of the base of the triangle and h is the length of the height of the triangle. In this triangle, the base is the vertical line segment $\overline{AC}$. Since $A(-1, -2)$ and $C(-1, 4)$ share an x-coordinate, the length of the base $\overline{AC}$ can be found by subtracting the y-coordinates of the two points: $AC = 4 - (-2) = 4 + 2 = 6$. The base and the height must be perpendicular, so the length of the height of the triangle is the horizontal distance from the point $B(2, 2)$ to the point $D(-1, 2)$ that lies on $\overline{AC}$. Since $B(2, 2)$ and $D(-1, 2)$ share a y-coordinate, this distance can be found by subtracting the x-coordinates of the two points: $BD = 2 - (-1) = 2 + 1 = 3$. Therefore, the area of $\triangle ABC$, in square coordinate units, is $\frac{1}{2}(AC)(BD) = \frac{1}{2}(6)(3) = 9$. If you chose **B**, you may have used side $\overline{AB}$ as the base of the triangle and used the distance formula to calculate $AB = \sqrt{(2 - (-2))^2 + (2 - (-1))^2} = \sqrt{16 + 9} = 5$, so that $\frac{1}{2}(5)(6) = 15$. If you chose **C**, you may have forgotten to include the factor of $\frac{1}{2}$ in the area equation. If you chose **D**, you may have used side $\overline{BC}$ as the height of the triangle and side $\overline{AB}$ as the base of the triangle. In this case, $AB = 5$ and $BC = \sqrt{(2 - 4)^2 + (2 - (-1))^2} = \sqrt{4 + 9} = \sqrt{13}$, so that $\frac{1}{2}(5)(\sqrt{13}) = \frac{5}{2}\sqrt{13}$. If you chose **E**, you may have used side $\overline{BC}$ as the height of the triangle, so that $\frac{1}{2}(6)(\sqrt{13}) = 3\sqrt{13}$.

Question 50. The correct answer is J. For all real numbers, $\sqrt{x^2} = |x|$, so the statement $\sqrt{x^2} \neq x$ is equivalent to $|x| \neq x$. This is only true if x is negative. If you chose **F**, you may have thought $\sqrt{0}$ was undefined, but $\sqrt{0^2} = |0| = 0$. If you chose **G**, **H**, or **K**, you may have been unable to find a counterexample. Consider $x = -2$, which is less than π, rational, and defined. In this example, $\sqrt{(-2)^2} = \sqrt{4} = 2$, but $2 \neq -2$. Thus, $\sqrt{x^2} \neq x$.

Question 51. The correct answer is D. The change in the x-coordinate from point A to point B is $\Delta x = 8 - 2 = 6$. The change in the y-coordinate from point A to point B is $\Delta y = -1 - (-4) = -1 + 4 = 3$. For the ratio $AB:BC$ to be equal to $1:3$, the change in the x-coordinate from point B to point C must be $3(\Delta x) = 3(6) = 18$, and the change in the y-coordinate from point B to point C must be $3(\Delta y) = 3(3) = 9$. Therefore, point C has coordinates $(8+18, -1+9) = (26, 8)$. If you chose **A**, you may have subtracted $3(\Delta x)$ and $3(\Delta y)$ from the x- and y-coordinates of point A to get $(2 - 3(6), -4 - 3(3)) = (2 - 18, -4 - 9)$. If you chose **B**, you may have thought the ratio $AB:BC$ was $3:1$ and then divided Δx and Δy by 3 before adding to the respective coordinates of point B, resulting in $\left(8 + \frac{6}{3}, -1 + \frac{3}{3}\right)$. If you chose **C**, you may have forgotten to multiply Δx and Δy by 3 before adding to the respective coordinates of point B, resulting in $(8+6, -1+3)$. If you chose **E**, you may have multiplied Δx and Δy by $1+3 = 4$ before adding to the respective coordinates of point B, resulting in $(8 + 4(6), -1 + 4(3))$.

Question 52. The correct answer is J. By drawing a vertical diameter and a horizontal diameter through each post, we see that the wire will touch each of the 4 circular posts on $\frac{1}{4}$ of the post's circumference. Each circular post has a circumference of $(2\pi)(3) = 6\pi$, so the total length of wire needed to span $\frac{1}{4}$ of each post's circumference is $4\left(\frac{1}{4}\right)(6\pi) = 6\pi$ inches.

The wire will also span the distance between the centers of two adjacent posts 4 times. The distance between the centers of adjacent circles is twice the radius length, or $2(3) = 6$ inches, so the total length of wire needed to span this distance four times is $4(6) = 24$ inches. Therefore, the length of the shortest wire that will go around the 4 posts without overlap is $24 + 6\pi \approx 43$ inches. If you chose **F**, you may have calculated only half the length of wire needed, $\frac{1}{2}(24 + 6\pi) \approx 21$ inches. If you chose **G**, you may have calculated the correct amount of wire that touches each post, but only half of the amount needed between posts, $\frac{1}{2}(24) + 6\pi \approx 31$ inches. If you chose **H**, you may have calculated the correct amount of wire needed between posts, but only half the amount of wire that touches each post, $24 + \frac{1}{2}(6\pi) = 24 + 3\pi \approx 33$ inches. If you chose **K**, you may have used the cross-sectional area of the circular posts, instead of the circumference, in your calculations, $24 + (3)^2\pi = 24 + 9\pi \approx 52$ inches.

Question 53. The correct answer is E. Multiplying any imaginary number of the form $a+bi$, where a and b are rational numbers, by its conjugate, $a-bi$, will always result in a rational number. Using $i^2 = (\sqrt{-1})^2 = -1$, we have $(3+bi)(3-bi) = 9 + 3bi - 3bi - b^2i^2 = 9 - b^2(-1) = 9 + b^2$. Because b is a rational number, b^2 is also a rational number, so $9 + b^2$ is a rational number. If you chose **A**, you may have thought the conjugate of any complex number is i, but $(3+bi)(i) = 3i + bi^2 = 3i - b$, which is not rational because $3i$ is imaginary. If you chose **B**, you may have thought the conjugate of any complex number is its imaginary part, bi, but $(3+bi)(bi) = 3bi + b^2i^2 = 3bi - b^2$, which is not rational because $3bi$ is imaginary. If you chose **C**, you may have thought the conjugate of any complex number is the product of its real and imaginary parts, but $(3+bi)(3bi) = 9bi + 3b^2i^2 = 9bi - 3b^2$, which is not rational because $9bi$ is imaginary. If you chose **D**, you may have thought the square of any complex number was rational, but $(3+bi)(3+bi) = 9 + 3bi + 3bi + b^2i^2 = 9 + 6bi - b^2$, which is not rational because $6bi$ is imaginary.

Question 54. The correct answer is H. Start by converting the logarithmic equation $\log_x(8) = y$ to its equivalent exponential equation, $x^y = 8$. The only two ways to write 8 in the form x^y where x and y are positive integers are 8^1 and 2^3. The only one of these expressions that fits the requirement that the base (x) is strictly less than 8 is 2^3. Therefore, $y = 3$. If you chose **F**, you may have thought x could be 8. If you chose **G**, you may have thought $4^2 = 8$. If you chose **J**, you may have thought $2^4 = 8$. If you chose **K**, you may have thought $1^8 = 8$.

Question 55. The correct answer is A. The area of any triangle with a base of length b and height of length h is $\frac{1}{2}bh$; so, the area of this triangle is $\frac{1}{2}(10)(8) = 40$ square units. The unshaded area can be found by adding up all the unit squares within the unshaded region, 28 square units. The shaded area can be found by subtracting the unshaded area from the total area of the triangle, $40 - 28 = 12$ square units. Finally, the ratio of the shaded area to the unshaded area is $\frac{12}{28} = \frac{3}{7}$. If you chose **B**, you may have calculated the ratio of the unshaded area to the whole area, $\frac{12}{40} = \frac{3}{10}$. If you chose **C**, you may have tried to calculate the ratio of the unshaded area to the shaded area, but used bh for the whole area, $\frac{28}{(10)(8)-28} = \frac{28}{52} = \frac{7}{13}$. If you chose **D**, you may have tried to calculate the ratio of the unshaded area to the whole area but used bh for the whole area, $\frac{28}{(10)(8)} = \frac{7}{20}$. If you chose **E**, you may have estimated the shaded area as 5 triangles, each with an area of approximately 3 square units, $\frac{3(5)}{28} = \frac{15}{28}$.

Question 56. **The correct answer is J.** To multiply exponential expressions that have the same base, we apply the product rule, $x^m \cdot x^n = x^{m+n}$. Thus, $x^{\frac{1}{4}} \cdot x^{\frac{1}{6}} = x^{\frac{1}{4}+\frac{1}{6}}$. Next, to simplify the sum in the exponent, we find the least common denominator, use it to rewrite each fraction, and then add: $x^{\frac{1}{4}+\frac{1}{6}} = x^{\frac{3}{12}+\frac{2}{12}} = x^{\frac{5}{12}}$. Finally, to rewrite the expression $x^{\frac{5}{12}}$ as a radical expression, we use the fractional exponent rule $x^{\frac{m}{n}} = \sqrt[n]{x^m}$, where the numerator m gives the power on the base x and the denominator n gives the root in the radical symbol. Therefore, $x^{\frac{5}{12}} = \sqrt[12]{x^5}$. If you answered **F**, you may have incorrectly multiplied the exponents instead of adding to get $x^{\left(\frac{1}{4}\right)\left(\frac{1}{6}\right)} \Rightarrow x^{\frac{1}{24}}$, and then incorrectly applied the fractional exponent rule and used 24 as the power on x under a square root: $\sqrt{x^{24}}$. If you answered **G**, you may have correctly applied the product rule for exponents to get $x^{\frac{1}{4}+\frac{1}{6}}$, but then incorrectly added the sum in the exponent by adding together both numerators and both denominators: $x^{\frac{1}{4}+\frac{1}{6}} \Rightarrow x^{\frac{1+1}{4+6}} \Rightarrow x^{\frac{2}{10}} \Rightarrow x^{\frac{1}{5}} \Rightarrow \sqrt[5]{x}$. If you answered **H**, you may have correctly applied the product rule for exponents and simplified to get $x^{\frac{5}{12}}$, but then incorrectly applied the fractional exponent rule and used 5 as the root and 12 as the power on x : $\sqrt[5]{x^{12}}$. If you answered **K**, you may have incorrectly multiplied the exponents instead of adding: $x^{\left(\frac{1}{4}\right)\left(\frac{1}{6}\right)} \Rightarrow x^{\frac{1}{24}} \Rightarrow \sqrt[24]{x}$.

Question 57. **The correct answer is E.** First, convert the British currency into U.S. currency: £2 $\times \frac{\$2.75 \text{ (U.S.)}}{£1} = \$5.50$ in U.S. currency. Next, convert this amount into Canadian currency: $\$5.50 \times \frac{\$1.00 \text{ (CAN)}}{\$0.92} \approx \$5.98$ in Canadian currency. If you answered **A**, you may have incorrectly divided the U.S. equivalent of $1 (CAN) by the British currency, $\frac{0.92}{2} = 0.41$. If you answered **B**, you may have incorrectly multiplied the British currency by the U.S. equivalent of $1 (CAN), $2(0.92) = 1.84$. If you answered **C**, you may have incorrectly divided the British currency by the U.S. equivalent of $1 (CAN), $\frac{2}{0.92} \approx 2.17$, and then incorrectly subtracted 0.10 to round down to the nearest cent, $2.17 - 0.10 = 2.07$. If you answered **D**, you may have incorrectly multiplied the amount to be converted by the 2 conversion values, $2(2.75)(0.92) = 5.06$.

Question 58. The correct answer is K. In any triangle, the shortest side is always opposite the smallest interior angle. Thus, the shortest side in the given triangle, 15 cm, is opposite angle A. Now, let $a = 15$ cm, $b = 16$ cm, and $c = 17$ cm be the lengths of the legs of the triangle opposite angles A, B, and C, respectively. The law of cosines states that $a^2 = b^2 + c^2 - 2bc \cos A$. Substituting the values for a, b, and c into the law of cosines, we get $15^2 = 16^2 + 17^2 - 2(16)(17)\cos A$. Solving this equation for A gives the measure of the smallest angle of the triangle. If you answered **F**, you picked an equation with the sides incorrectly substituted and with an incorrect trigonometric function of the angle. If you answered **G** or **H**, you picked an equation with the sides incorrectly substituted. If you answered **J**, you picked an equation with the sides correctly substituted, but with an incorrect trigonometric function of the angle.

Question 59. The correct answer is A. Let Set A be represented by $A = \{a, w, x, y, z\}$, where $a < w < x < y < z$. Then, Set B may be represented by $B = \{b, w, x, y, z\}$, where $a < b$. The mean of Set A is equal to $\frac{a+w+x+y+z}{5}$, and the mean of Set B is equal to $\frac{b+w+x+y+z}{5}$. Because $a < b$, $\frac{a+w+x+y+z}{5} < \frac{b+w+x+y+z}{5}$. If you answered **B** or **E**, you may not have noted that both sets have the same median, x, the middle value of the ordered data. If you answered **C** or **D**, you may not have noted that the range of Set B, $z - b$, must be less than the range of Set A, $z - a$. That is, $a < b \Leftrightarrow z + a < z + b$, and subtracting both a and b from both sides, we get $(z+a) - a - b < (z+b) - a - b$ or $z - b < z - a$.

Question 60. The correct answer is J. In total, there are $16 \cdot 15 \cdot 14 = 3{,}360$ different ways that 3 cars may be chosen from 16 cars: 16 choices for the first pick, 15 choices for the second pick, and 14 choices for the third pick. Let $M =$ minivan, $S =$ sedan, and $H =$ hatchback. The set of possible outcomes for the random choice of 1 of each of the 3 types of cars may be represented by the set $\{MSH, MHS, SMH, SHM, HMS, HSM\}$. Each of the 6 outcomes in the set is equally likely and has a probability that is equal to $\frac{6 \cdot 7 \cdot 3}{16 \cdot 15 \cdot 14}$. Therefore, the probability that Thalia will rent 1 of each of the 3 types of cars is equal to $6 \cdot \left(\frac{6 \cdot 7 \cdot 3}{16 \cdot 15 \cdot 14}\right) = \frac{756}{3{,}360} = \frac{9}{40}$. If you answered **F**, you picked the probability of choosing 1 specific car type out of the 3 car types available. If you answered **G**, you picked the probability of choosing 1 specific car out of the 16 cars available. If you answered **H**, you picked the proportion of the 16 cars that will be chosen, $\frac{3}{16}$. If you answered **K**, you may have thought there were only 3 possible outcomes instead of 6 and computed $3 \cdot \left(\frac{6 \cdot 7 \cdot 3}{16 \cdot 15 \cdot 14}\right) = \frac{9}{80}$.

Passage I

Question 1. The best answer is A because the narrator of Passage A describes the inner workings of a newspaper office and print shop in detail in the first paragraph (lines 1–26), which suggests that she witnessed and participated in daily operations there. In the context of a discussion of "the lure of the reporter's life" (lines 31–32), the narrator directly refers to her experiences in the newspaper business: "It all sounds slightly sentimental and silly, but it's true—or it was, at least, in my newspaper experience" (lines 33–35). She also recalls the scents that cause her to feel "a pang of nostalgia for the old reporting days" (line 39).

The best answer is NOT:

B because the narrator of Passage A refers to being reminded of the newsroom "to this day" (line 35) with "a pang of nostalgia" (line 39), suggesting a former career in the newspaper business, not a recently started one.

C because the narrator of Passage A reveals that the Appleton, Wisconsin, *Daily Crescent* office (lines 27–28) is the news office she describes in the first paragraph (lines 1–26), an office with which she seems very familiar; the narrator does not evaluate the inner workings of various news offices.

D because the narrator of Passage A demonstrates knowledge of the newspaper business in the first paragraph (lines 1–26), and in lines 33–39 she refers to her past newspaper experiences. The narrator does not suggest that she longs to be a reporter; in fact, it would be more reasonable to conclude from Passage A that she used to be one.

Question 2. The best answer is G because the narrator of Passage A suggests that the back room was made up of the printing shop and pressroom, which "were separated from the front office only by a doorway, and the door never was closed" (lines 1–3). The narrator emphasizes that the front office and the back room are equally critical to the newspaper. Lines 7–9: "The front room is its head, but without the back room it could not function or even live."

The best answer is NOT:

F because the narrator of Passage A does not characterize what goes on in the printing shop and pressroom as more tedious than what goes on in the front office. In fact, the narrator describes the linotype machine in the back room as "a new and fearsome invention" (line 4), which suggests some excitement.

H because the narrator of Passage A does not suggest that what goes on in either the front office or the printing shop and pressroom is chaotic. The first paragraph (lines 1–26) suggests a robust but steady daily routine at the newspaper.

J because the printing shop and the pressroom are portrayed by the narrator of Passage A as being regulated, and no less regulated than the front office; for instance, "the linotype and the small press went all day" (lines 9–10), overseen by Mac. Without the steady operations in the back room, the newspaper "could not function or even live" (line 9).

Question 3. **The best answer is D** because the narrator of Passage A describes Mac's voice as "soft, gentle, drawling" (line 18) and states that he "seldom talked" (line 20), and when he did stop by the front office, he did so without imposition. He was "a drooping figure" (line 21) with a newsworthy story to share. Yet, Mac was also an invaluable resource to the newspaper whose "eye was infallible" (line 16) and who did not let errors interfere with "the fair sequence" (line 17) of his copy.

The best answer is NOT:

A because Mac is portrayed as being both innately talented and professionally competent in lines 16–26: Mac is described as having an "infallible" (line 16) eye for errors and a talent for discovering news that "always proved to be a bombshell" (lines 25–26).

B because although Mac's innate talent is suggested in lines 16–26, Mac is described as someone who "had come in years before, his brown hair curled over a mild brow, his limp shirt seemed perennial" (lines 14–16), which suggests that he is professionally experienced.

C because although Mac is characterized as being temperamentally unimposing in lines 18–23, he is portrayed as professionally experienced in lines 14–16.

Question 4. **The best answer is J** because the narrator of Passage A states that on the rare moments when Mac would appear in the front office, he would do so "with a piece of news" (lines 21–22), his purpose to share his newsworthy find with the city editor. Lines 23–25: "Standing at the side of the city editor's desk he would deliver himself of this information, looking mild and limply romantic."

The best answer is NOT:

F because although the narrator of Passage A states that "the linotype and the small press went all day, for there the advertising was set up and printed" (lines 9–11), the narrator does not specify that Mac would appear in the front office to set up and print the advertising.

G because although the narrator of Passage A states that Mac "was boss of the print shop from the cat to the linotype operator" (lines 18–20), the narrator does not make clear that Mac would appear in the front office to supervise the linotype operator.

H because although the narrator of Passage A states that Mac's "eye was infallible" (line 16), the narrator also points out that Mac's voice was "soft, gentle, drawling" (line 18) and that he "seldom talked" (line 20). The narrator does not indicate that Mac would appear in the front office to chastise reporters.

Question 5. The best answer is **B** because the narrator of Passage B experiences the epiphany that "this is what I do" (line 62) at the age of twenty-five, as he "waded into that invisible veil of ink" (line 52) at his first newswriting job, realizing that he was finally living his dream of being a reporter.

The best answer is NOT:

A because the narrator of Passage B does not directly connect the epiphany he describes in lines 59–62 to how long he might continue to live in his parents' basement.

C because the narrator of Passage B already knows that he would rather write news stories than work for a lawn company, which is why he was trying to find a newswriting job (lines 82–89).

D because the narrator of Passage B does not directly discuss his work ethic or how it might relate to his success as a reporter.

Question 6. The best answer is **F** because the note written by the employer of the narrator of Passage B (lines 70–76) lists publications in which the narrator's writing has appeared, before stating that his writing soon "will appear in trashcans throughout north-central Connecticut" (lines 74–75), lightly mocking the narrator's new job as a reporter. The office bulletin board note, conveyed in a serious tone, is a workplace introduction and welcome to the narrator, and yet it ends sarcastically with the request for others in the office to "please make him feel relevant" (lines 75–76).

The best answer is NOT:

G because although the note appears to be formal and serious in tone and approach, it can't accurately be described as overtly solemn due to its sarcastic humor regarding the relevance of the writing of the narrator of Passage B.

H because the note is not obviously apologetic, even regarding the mocking suggestion that the writing of the narrator of Passage B will end up in trashcans (lines 74–75).

J because the note does not convey optimism but rather teasingly suggests that the new career of the narrator of Passage B might prove not to be impressive or influential.

Question 7. **The best answer is C** because the last sentence of Passage B (lines 82–89) describes the narrator working at a job unrelated to newswriting but, at night, "typing out professional love letters" (lines 84–85) to various northeastern newspapers that he admits he "had never read" (line 89), showing that he was desperate to find a newswriting job. The name of one newspaper listed, the seemingly fictitious *Anywhere Clarion-Bugle-Star-Record-Sentinel*, strongly conveys that the narrator was willing to work at just about any newspaper in the region.

The best answer is NOT:

A because although the sentence conveys that the narrator of Passage B had never read most northeastern newspapers, the sentence does not show that he had disdain for them.

B because although the sentence makes clear that the narrator of Passage B is familiar with the newspapers published in the area, the sentence mainly serves to portray the narrator as reaching out to any newspaper that might offer him a job.

D because the sentence does not refer to the newswriting experience of the narrator of Passage B at all; instead, the sentence conveys that the narrator is working for a lawn company as he contacts several newspapers to find a job.

Question 8. **The best answer is F** because Passage A includes detailed information about the types of machines used to print the newspaper (lines 3–12) as part of its description of the office, whereas Passage B does not provide such information.

The best answer is NOT:

G because Passage B provides information about the outside appearance of the office building, whereas Passage A does not. The office in Passage B is in "a squat concrete building, no different from all the others in a drab Connecticut industrial park" (lines 57–59).

H because neither Passage A nor Passage B provides information about the number of people who work in the office.

J because neither Passage A nor Passage B provides information about the stories being written and printed for the newspaper. Passage B, though, does allude to the newspaper's printed "rants and ideas, sports scores and felony arrests, announcements of marriage and notices of death" (lines 54–56).

Your First Practice Test

Question 9. **The best answer is D** because the use of figurative language is central to the storytelling style of Passage B. The smell of ink is personified in lines 44–47. As the narrator began his new job, he "waded into that invisible veil of ink" (line 52), a metaphor. The narrator exaggerates with the statement that "maybe the chemical-like aroma was inducing hallucination" (lines 56–57), and the bulletin board note is "pinned like a manifesto" (line 63), figurative language in the form of a simile. Although Passage A uses some figurative language, its overall writing style is not as strongly characterized by figurative language as the style of Passage B is.

The best answer is NOT:

A because Passage B does not use technical jargon at length, whereas Passage A refers to technical names of machines and materials (lines 3–6) and technical jargon and terms such as "shrdlus and etaoins" (line 17) and "mucilage" (line 36).

B because although Passage A and Passage B both contain quoted material, neither passage uses dialogue.

C because the style of Passage A, not Passage B, is more strongly characterized by its use of formal diction, with more straightforward descriptions and slightly elevated word choices overall, whereas Passage B is more casual in its approach to storytelling. It begins with a sentence fragment (line 43), includes second person narration (lines 49–51), and has moments of humor, especially in lines 70–89.

Question 10. **The best answer is H** because the passages support that both narrators associate the smell of ink with pleasant memories. The narrator of Passage A connects other writers' reflections regarding "the smell of printer's ink" (line 32) to her own experiences: "To this day I can't smell the scent of white paper, wet ink, oil, hot lead, mucilage and cats that goes to make up the peculiar odor of any newspaper plant, be it Appleton, Wisconsin, or Cairo, Egypt, that I don't get a pang of nostalgia for the old reporting days" (lines 35–39). The narrator of Passage B recalls, "I waded into that invisible veil of ink, inhaled it deeply, allowing it to wash over me" (lines 52–53), and later describes the building in which he worked as "ink-perfumed" (line 64).

The best answer is NOT:

F because the narrator of Passage B also associates the smell of ink with pleasant memories, as conveyed in details and descriptions in lines 43–67.

G because the narrator of Passage A also associates the smell of ink with pleasant memories, as conveyed in details and descriptions in lines 29–39.

J because both narrators associate the smell of ink with pleasant memories, as conveyed in details and descriptions in lines 29–39 of Passage A and lines 43–67 of Passage B.

Passage II

Question 11. **The best answer is D** because the passage explains Dantzig's theory that zero was first represented as an oval on an Indian counting board. The oval, a symbol, was drawn in the empty space that served as a placeholder in a middle of columns of numbers (lines 14–25). Later, the passage states that when writing numbers in clay, "the Babylonians began using two slanted tacklike symbols to insert in the empty columns" (lines 79–80) and specifies that "the Babylonians used their 'zero' only in the middle of numbers, never at the end" (lines 82–84).

The best answer is NOT:

A because the passage states that the Babylonians used tacklike symbols in the empty columns between numbers to write zero (lines 79–80), but the passage does not indicate that Indian civilizations did so.

B because the passage states that "the Babylonians called a king's first year the *accession year*" (lines 55–56), but the passage does not indicate that Indian civilizations did so.

C because although the passage connects the name *sunya* for the oval drawn on an Indian counting board to "*Sunyata*, an important concept in Buddhism" (lines 23–24), the passage does not indicate that the Babylonians had a name for zero that was derived from their religion. "The Babylonians, so far as we know, never articulated zero" (lines 57–58).

Question 12. **The best answer is H** because the paragraph begins with a reference to "Dantzig's concise and spirited account" (line 13) of the invention of zero and describes how Dantzig "sees zero's invention" (lines 14–15) occurring on a counting board. The story of an unknown person drawing an oval on a counting board is presented as Dantzig's theory with the phrase, "as Dantzig sees it" (line 21).

The best answer is NOT:

F because the paragraph does not provide information that suggests Dantzig discovered a document that offers a factual account of the story.

G because the paragraph does not refer to particular ancient Indian writings from which a factual account of the story has been drawn.

J because the paragraph does not connect the story to Kaplan or mention any of Kaplan's theories directly.

Question 13. The best answer is A because the passage states that, according to Dantzig, "the zero was invented not in the West but by the Indians in the early centuries after Christ" (lines 6–7). The passage then indicates that "the Maya invented zero in the New World at approximately the same time" (lines 8–9).

The best answer is NOT:

B because the passage discusses the Sumerian roots of zero (lines 69–74), not the Sumerians' invention of zero. Based on the historical context provided in the last three paragraphs of the passage (lines 69–90), the Sumerian contributions to zero occurred long before the Maya invented zero.

C because the passage states that Alexander invaded the Babylonian empire in 331 BC (lines 86–87), much earlier than when the Maya invented zero, which was around the same time the Indians did, according to Dantzig (lines 5–9). Dantzig speculates the time frame for the invention of zero as the first or second century AD (lines 14–16).

D because the passage indicates that, according to Dantzig, Europe "did not accept zero as a number until the twelfth or thirteenth century" (lines 10–11), much later than when the Maya invented zero.

Question 14. The best answer is G because the passage begins with Dantzig's ideas that the invention of zero "will always stand out as one of the greatest single achievements of the human race" (lines 2–4) and "marked a 'turning point' in math, science, and industry" (lines 4–5). Lines 14–25 describe Dantzig's account of zero's first appearance on a counting board as a day best characterized as "momentous," based on the context of the passage.

The best answer is NOT:

F because the passage characterizes the invention of zero as groundbreaking and transformative (lines 1–5). Therefore, to describe the day on which zero was first drawn as "unfortunate," which suggests that regrettable outcomes followed, does not make sense in the context of the passage.

H because the passage suggests that the invention of zero revolutionized math, science, and industry (lines 4–5). Therefore, to describe the day that zero was first drawn as "ominous," which suggests a threat or danger to come, does not make sense in the context of the passage.

J because the passage presents the invention of zero as occurring on a random day, naturally and unplanned, as a person worked on a counting board (lines 14–25). Therefore, to describe the day that zero was first drawn as "foretold," which suggests that the events of the day were prophesied or predicted, does not make sense in the context of the passage.

Question 15. The best answer is **D** because the passage states that "the Arabs turned *sunya* into *sifr* ('empty' in Arabic), which became *zephirum* in Italy, and eventually zero. In Germany and elsewhere, *sifr* became *cifra*" (lines 26–28).

The best answer is NOT:

A because the passage indicates that *sunya* was a word given to zero in Indian civilizations (lines 21–23), likely in the first or second century AD (lines 14–16).

B because the passage indicates that *zephirum* became the word for zero in Italy (line 27).

C because the passage indicates that "the Arabs turned *sunya* into *sifr*" (line 26).

Question 16. The best answer is **F** because the passage states that Dantzig "blames the Greeks" (line 31) for Western civilization taking over a thousand years to accept a number that represents a void. Dantzig explains, "The concrete mind of the ancient Greeks could not conceive the void as a number, let alone endow the void with a symbol" (lines 32–34).

The best answer is NOT:

G because although the last paragraph (lines 86–90) states that we find the symbol "0" for zero in the papyri of Greek astronomers shortly after 331 BC, "the mathematicians never pursued the concept" (lines 89–90).

H because the passage does not indicate that the ancient Greeks were unwilling to share their knowledge of zero with other European countries.

J because the passage does not support that a focus on negative numbers is the reason the ancient Greeks could not imagine a number for the void. The passage simply mentions that negative numbers soon followed the invention of zero (lines 7–8).

Question 17. The best answer is **C** because the passage author directly addresses the reader to point out that "you don't want to hear the long version" (lines 35–36) of the story of zero.

The best answer is NOT:

A because the passage author does not indicate that he thinks readers wouldn't be interested in hearing the story of how the Maya conceived of zero. Instead, he provides details about the concept and use of zero by the Maya in lines 8–9, 40–43, and 47–48.

B because the passage author does not indicate that he thinks readers wouldn't be interested in hearing what Dantzig contributed to mathematics, a topic that is not central to the passage.

D because the passage author does not indicate that he thinks readers wouldn't be interested in hearing about who drew the oval on the counting board. He does make clear, though, that the exact identity of the person is unknown (lines 21–22).

Question 18. The best answer is **G** because it offers an accurate, literal meaning of the figurative statement "Zero lay rustling in the weeds for many centuries" (line 38) in the context of the passage. The phrase "lay rustling in the weeds" suggests something present that has not yet been fully realized. This is reflected in part in the idea that "the Babylonians had no zero, but they knew something was wrong" (lines 49–50); their knowledge of zero was emerging but not yet fully shaped.

The best answer is NOT:

F because the far-reaching effects of the concept of zero on mathematics are long-established and clearly present (lines 4–5), lacking the suggestion of something subtle and undiscovered, as the phrase "lay rustling in the weeds for many centuries" implies in context.

H because if the concept of zero "had been developed and then forgotten," the concept could not accurately be described as "rustling in the weeds." This figurative phrase suggests steady but nearly imperceptible activity that is difficult to draw out.

J because for the concept of zero to have been rejected, it would need to have been openly known and articulated, which would require an interpretation of the phrase "lay rustling in the weeds for centuries" that does not make sense in context.

Question 19. The best answer is **D** because the passage author provides an example that directly contradicts the US Library of Congress's statement that there has never been a system of dates with a year 0 when he states, "In fact, the Maya had both years 0 and days 0" (lines 47–48).

The best answer is NOT:

A because the passage author does not respond to the US Library of Congress's statement by arguing that undiscovered civilizations may have had years 0.

B because the passage author does not cite an expert in response to the statement from the US Library of Congress; instead, he offers a direct but uncited response in lines 47–48.

C because instead of suggesting that the US Library of Congress's research is authoritative, the passage author offers a direct refutation of the US Library of Congress's statement in his example in lines 47–48.

Question 20. The best answer is **H** because the passage author directly states that "the contemporary mathematician who has conducted the most rigorous research on nothing is Robert Kaplan, the author of *The Nothing That Is: A Natural History of Zero*" (lines 61–64).

The best answer is NOT:

F because the passage author does not directly make the point that Kaplan's research on zero is more interesting than that of other contemporary mathematicians.

G because the passage author does not offer the idea that Kaplan's research is more speculative than that of other contemporary mathematicians. In fact, by stating that Kaplan's research on zero is "the most rigorous" (line 62), the passage author suggests that it is less speculative than others' research.

J because although the passage author presents Kaplan's research as valuable, he does not directly mention that it is more admired than other contemporary mathematicians' research.

Passage III

Question 21. The best answer is D because the passage describes both Mavis Staples's experience as a quartet singer with her family as well as details about the production of her first solo album. Lines 8–25 demonstrate how Mavis Staples's identity was shaped by her early experience as a quartet singer, and the passage proceeds to relate Bell's efforts to record Mavis Staples as a solo artist (lines 41–42), and Cropper's production of "what would be Mavis's self-titled debut album" (lines 54–55).

The best answer is NOT:

A because although the fourth and fifth paragraphs (lines 35–51) describe Bell's work with Mavis Staples, this information contributes to the passage's overall focus on Mavis Staples and the trajectory of her career.

B because Franklin and Ross are only briefly mentioned in lines 8–10, and the comparison mainly serves to introduce how Mavis Staples's experience singing in the family quartet shaped her outlook as a performer.

C because although the passage author indicates that Pops Staples was an influential figure in Mavis Staples's career, he does not directly attribute her success to his influence.

Question 22. The best answer is J because the passage describes how "fans of the Staples Singers" (line 1) witnessed how Mavis Staples performed with "an improbably deep voice" (line 3) and with "the deepest commitment to whatever she was singing" (lines 4–5). Her voice and personal style of singing put her on par with talents such as Franklin, Knight, Ross, and Springfield even as she experienced "relative anonymity" (lines 1–2) as a singer. It can be inferred that the contrast between her great talent and her anonymity is what puzzled her fans.

The best answer is NOT:

F because although details in the first paragraph (lines 1–7) relate that Mavis Staples's voice was "improbably deep" (line 3), the passage does not indicate that her brother became more famous than Mavis Staples did.

G because the passage does not provide details about Mavis Staples's vocal range or how it compared to that of other artists of the time. Instead, it is stated that only that she "loved singing those baritone harmonies" (lines 14–15).

H because the passage author does not directly compare Mavis Staples's voice to that of any other artists of the time. Rather, he notes a contrast between Mavis Staples's lack of celebrity and the popularity of other artists of the time (lines 8–10).

Question 23. The best answer is B because the passage author makes clear that Mavis Staples did not initially want to become a "marquee name" (line 8) by singing solo. He describes Mavis Staples's preference to instead sing as a member of the Staples Singers. Lines 10–12 note that "Mavis enjoyed singing with her family and preferred to melt into the group." As further evidence of Mavis Staples's desire to blend in with the group, the passage author states that when she was brought forward to be the group's lead singer, "she did so reluctantly" (line 14).

The best answer is NOT:

A because the quotation from the passage refers to Mavis Staples's preference as an individual performer, not to the priorities of the Staples Singers as a group.

C because the quotation from the passage refers to Mavis Staples's preference as an individual performer, not to the preferences of popular female singers of the 1960s.

D because although the passage indicates that Mavis Staples was trained to sing at a young age, it does not indicate that she had mapped out a specific plan for her singing career.

Question 24. The best answer is G because the paragraph mainly provides examples indicating what may have made it "difficult for Mavis to easily adapt to a different context" (lines 27–28). The passage author notes Pops Staples's guitar style and Mavis Staples's innate musical connection with Pervis and Cleedi as factors that made it more challenging for Mavis Staples to move on from the quartet.

The best answer is NOT:

F because although the paragraph mentions Pops Staples's distinctive way of playing guitar, it does not describe the individual contributions of the other members of the group.

H because the paragraph does not contain a reference to Pops Staples making the song choices, nor does the paragraph focus on the songs the Staples Singers sang in concert.

J because although the paragraph makes clear that the Staples Singers' performances included guitar, harmonization, and clapping, it does not characterize a particular performance style.

Question 25. The best answer is **B** because the paragraph relates Cropper's perspective as he worked "to figure out how to get her out there" (lines 57–58). Mindful that "she didn't want to go too far too fast" (lines 62–63), Cropper acted carefully. As he states, "I didn't want to lose her trust or do something damaging" (lines 64–65).

The best answer is NOT:

A because the paragraph primarily focuses on Cropper's work with Mavis Staples as a solo performer. The paragraph does not include detailed information about his work with the Staples Singers.

C because the paragraph primarily focuses on Cropper's work with Mavis Staples. The paragraph does not include information about the overall strategy at Stax Records for working with unknown singers.

D because the paragraph provides no information that suggests that Mavis Staples was unwilling to perform without backup singers.

Question 26. The best answer is **H** because, as Cropper reflects on Pops Staples's guiding involvement with the family quartet, he states that "there were lines he didn't want to cross when it came to his family's well-being" (lines 72–73), which suggests that protecting his family was a priority for Pops Staples.

The best answer is NOT:

F because Pops Staples is characterized as someone who would put "his foot down" (line 71) about things like dating. The passage also indicates that there were certain songs that "wouldn't go down with Pops" (lines 61–62), suggesting that there were certain things he was not tolerant of when it came to his family.

G because the passage provides no characterization of Pops Staples as being resentful, and he is described as a "thoughtful and willing contributor in the studio" (lines 66–67).

J because the passage provides no information that suggests that Pops Staples was uncertain or wavering in his decisions about his family. The description of Pops Staples "putting his foot down about dating" (lines 71) suggests that his decisions were final and not negotiable.

Question 27. The best answer is **A** because the passage author indicates that Mavis Staples's way of "losing herself in every word" (lines 5–6) derived from her "deepest commitment to whatever she was singing" (lines 4–5). He further clarifies that Mavis Staples sang "as though reliving a critical moment in her personal history" (lines 6–7).

The best answer is NOT:

B because the passage states that Mavis Staples committed herself totally "to whatever she was singing" (line 5) and does not indicate whether clapping contributed as a factor.

C because the passage does not provide any information about how Mavis Staples may have led her siblings in a transition to a new song.

D because the passage does not provide any information that indicates whether Mavis Staples may have danced while other members of the quartet sang.

Question 28. The best answer is **H** because, as the passage states, Mavis Staples's "father brought her out front to sing lead after her brother Pervis's voice changed in the '50s" (lines 12–14).

The best answer is NOT:

F because the passage does not provide any information indicating that Pops Staples left the Staples Singers.

G because although the passage indicates that Pops Staples played the guitar (line 26), it does not provide information that indicates that Cleedi also played guitar.

J because although the passage author does describe Mavis Staples's voice as "deep" (line 3), he directly attributes Pervis's voice change as the reason for her father's decision to have her sing lead (lines 12–14).

Question 29. The best answer is **D** because the passage states that Mavis Staples's performance of "On My Way to Heaven" "bowled [Bell] over and left him in tears" (lines 36–37). It can be inferred that Bell's admiration was deep and persistent because he "never forgot the day" (line 35) when he witnessed this performance.

The best answer is NOT:

A because "dismay" connotes a negative reaction to Mavis Staples's singing while the passage clearly characterizes Bell's reaction as very positive.

B because "reluctant acceptance" indicates that Bell didn't really want to like Mavis Staples's performance while the passage makes clear that Bell responded positively to the performance without reservation.

C because there is no indication in the passage that Bell found Mavis Staples's performance amusing or humorous.

Question 30. The best answer is G because the passage makes clear that the songs chosen for Mavis Staples's first solo album were "secular songs" (line 77) that lacked the "gospel or message-oriented underpinnings" (line 78) that Pops Staples chose for the Staples Singers. Instead, her solo album featured "the sort of pop-oriented love and relationship songs that Pops typically shunned" (lines 83–84).

The best answer is NOT:

F because the passage indicates that the songs were primarily focused on love and relationships.

H because the passage does not specify who wrote the songs that Mavis Staples sang on her solo album or whether they were written specifically for her.

J because the passage provides no information about the upbeat tone or danceability of the music of the Staples Singers or the songs on Mavis Staples's solo album.

Passage IV

Question 31. The best answer is B because the passage primarily focuses on describing mycorrhizal fungi and explaining how it helps plants thrive. Describing its impact on plants, the passage author states that "mycorrhizal fungi break down nutrients like phosphorous, carbon, water, and nitrogen into a readily assimilative form and deliver them to the plant" (lines 15–17) and describes how the fungi "increase the tree's nutrient and water uptake" (lines 28–29). She goes on to explain how the fungi play a key role in ecosystems, noting that, "In the wild, mycorrhizal fungi are key to not just the health of single trees but to healthy forest ecosystems" (lines 30–32) and "the functions they perform are often on an ecosystem or landscape scale" (lines 77–78).

The best answer is NOT:

A because although the first paragraph (lines 1–12) briefly compares mutualist and commensal relationships, the passage focuses on the mutualistic relationship between mycorrhizal fungi and forest plants.

C because although the passage describes mycorrhizal fungi functioning as a "giant communications network" (line 40) that has been referred to as "nature's Internet" (line 41), the passage's purpose is to describe the mycorrhizal fungi's network and its relationship to plants, not to discuss the invention of the Internet.

D because the passage instead explores the beneficial effects of mycorrhizal fungi on plants.

Question 32. **The best answer is G** because the passage author indicates that while tree roots may absorb some water and nutrients (lines 23–24) mycorrhizal fungus delivers most of the tree's water. She states that fungus on tree roots "provides the tree with the lion's share of its nutrition and water" (lines 25–26).

The best answer is NOT:

F because the passage author states that mycorrhizal fungus "provides the tree with the lion's share of its nutrition and water" (lines 25–26), not the same amount of water.

H because the passage author states that mycorrhizal fungus "provides the tree with the lion's share of its nutrition and water" (lines 25–26), not a smaller amount of water.

J because the passage author states that mycorrhizal fungus "provides the tree with the lion's share of its nutrition and water" (lines 25–26), not a smaller amount of water.

Question 33. **The best answer is A** because the overall focus of the paragraph is to describe how fungal networks benefit all different types of plants, from weaker plants to young seedlings to established trees. Lines 48–51: "This network exists to benefit not only established trees and seedlings of the same species but also trees from different species, and at different stages of development."

The best answer is NOT:

B because although the paragraph mentions young seedlings tapping into the roots of trees that are of the same species (lines 46–48), the main point of the paragraph is that the fungal network benefits many different types of plants at many different stages.

C because the paragraph does not indicate that established trees or any type of plant can genetically alter fungal networks for further benefit. Rather, the paragraph makes clear that it's the network itself that benefits the trees.

D because although the paragraph mentions that nutritional uptake can differ among different trees (lines 54–55), the main point of the paragraph is not about how these trees are identified. Rather, the paragraph focuses on describing how the fungal network benefits many different types of plants at many different stages.

Question 34. **The best answer is H** because the metaphor serves to further illustrate the passage author's statement that "The old trees in a forest function as hubs for these mycelial networks" (lines 56–57). Just as express stops on a subway are connected to numerous train lines, large foundational trees host numerous connections to other trees with the help of mycelial networks.

The best answer is NOT:

F because neither the metaphor mentioned nor the surrounding text describes the Indian pipe parasite as being damaging to trees.

G because neither the metaphor mentioned nor the surrounding text discusses two distinct mycelial networks.

J because neither the metaphor mentioned nor the surrounding text suggests that different species of fungi grow to be different sizes.

Question 35. **The best answer is B** because the passage author states that the purpose of "some yeasts in our body, for example, is unknown and may be commensal" (lines 7–8). "Unknown" and "may be" indicate that it is possible, but not definite, that the relationship is commensal.

The best answer is NOT:

A because the words "unknown" and "may be" in lines 7–8 indicate that such a relationship is possible but not definite.

C because there is no indication in the passage that the relationship between some yeasts and the human body is mutualistic. The passage only mentions the possibility of a commensal relationship.

D because there is no indication in the passage that the relationship between some yeasts and the human body is mutualistic. The passage only mentions the possibility of a commensal relationship.

Question 36. **The best answer is H** because Lincoff's quotation helps define mycorrhizal fungi's relationship with plants as mutualistic. The passage author states that mutualistic relationships are ones "in which a balance of interests occurs between two organisms" (lines 1–3). Lincoff's quotation explains how the relationship is beneficial to fungi: fungi can't make their own food but obtain food through their mutually beneficial partnership with plants.

The best answer is NOT:

F because the passage author states just before the quote from Lincoff that "mycorrhizal fungi are the princes of mutualism" (line 9). There is no indication in the passage that the fungi have a commensal relationship with plants.

G because earlier in the passage, it is made clear that some yeasts may have commensal relationships with the human body (lines 5–8), and, as the passage author states just before the quote from Lincoff, "mycorrhizal fungi are the princes of mutualism" (line 9). Based on these details, mycorrhizal fungi cannot serve the same function as do yeasts in the human body.

J because although the quote from Lincoff states that mycorrhizal fungi are unable to produce their own food, it does not provide a reason or explanation as to why this is the case.

Question 37. **The best answer is D** because the sentences that follow describe how the fungal network can benefit trees and other plants. Lines 46–48: "Young seedlings struggling to grow in the shadow of established trees tap into the larger, older tree's fungal network to improve their nutritional uptake." Using the information in this quotation as well as information in lines 44–45, it can be inferred that "tap into" means "use."

The best answer is NOT:

A because the word "endorse" would indicate that the weaker plants approve or recommend the fungi network, which does not make sense in this context. The paragraph makes clear that weaker plants use the fungal network to obtain nutrition.

B because the word "finish" would indicate that the weaker plants cause the fungal network to cease to exist, which does not make sense in this context. The paragraph makes clear that weaker plants use the fungal network to obtain nutrition.

C because the word "lift" would indicate that the weaker plants cause the fungal network to be shifted to a higher elevation, which does not make sense in this context. The paragraph makes clear that weaker plants use the fungal network to obtain nutrition.

Question 38. **The best answer is F** because the passage states that "Young seedlings struggling to grow in the shadow of established trees tap into the larger, older tree's fungal network to improve their nutritional uptake" (lines 46–48).

The best answer is NOT:

G because the passage does not indicate that young seedlings utilize an older tree's fungal network to defend themselves against parasites.

H because the passage does not indicate that young seedlings need a specific nutrient from an older tree's fungal network. Instead, it indicates that they improve their overall nutritional uptake (lines 46–48).

J because the passage does not indicate that young seedlings are susceptible to a wider range of diseases. Instead, the passage indicates that the fungal network supports "young seedlings struggling to grow in the shadow of established trees" (lines 45–46).

Question 39. **The best answer is A** because the passage states that "Indian pipe depend totally on mycorrhizal fungi for its nutritive needs" (lines 71–73). Total dependency is synonymous with "absolute."

The best answer is NOT:

B because the passage states that Indian pipe is a nonphotosynthesizing plant that is "totally" (line 72) dependent on mycorrhizal fungi, and it does not further indicate that Indian pipe is also dependent on other nonphotosynthesizing plants. Therefore, this comparison is inaccurate.

C because the passage states that Indian pipe is a nonphotosynthesizing plant that is "totally" (line 72) dependent on mycorrhizal fungi, and it does not further indicate that Indian pipe is also dependent on other nonphotosynthesizing plants. Therefore, this comparison is inaccurate.

D because the passage establishes that the Indian pipe depends "totally" (line 72) on mycorrhizal fungi for its needs. The relationship between the Indian pipe and the network is clear and absolute, not uncertain.

Question 40. **The best answer is H** because the statement provided claims that plants in the forests flourished after the death of most of its mycorrhizal mycelium. This directly contradicts the passage's claim that a lack of adequate mycorrhizal fungi will correlate with "catastrophic losses of plant biomass" (line 86). If the statement in H is assumed to be true, it would weaken the passage's point about the effects of low mycorrhizal fungi in an ecosystem.

The best answer is NOT:

F because the statement provided does not challenge the passage's statement in lines 83–86. It mentions an increase in the amount of mycorrhizal mycelium, but it does not mention the effects of this increase on the forest ecosystem.

G because the statement provided does not challenge the passage's statement in lines 83–86. It mentions that two forests with the same amount of mycorrhizal mycelium lost most of their plant biomass, but it doesn't mention whether the forests had an adequate amount of fungi to begin with.

J because the statement provided corroborates rather than challenges the passage's statement in lines 83–86 by stating that a loss of mycorrhizal mycelium would correlate with negative effects on the forest's plants.

Passage I

Question 1. The best answer is B. According to Table 2, the observed i value for a 0.6 mol/kg H_2O solution of $(NH_4)_2SO_4$ is 2.00. Therefore, **B** is correct. **A**, **C**, and **D** are each incorrect; they are each inconsistent with the data in Table 2.

Question 2. The best answer is G. According to Table 2, the observed i values for each of NaCl, KCl, and $(NH_4)_2SO_4$ are less than 2.50 at all listed concentrations. According to Table 2, the observed i values for $MgCl_2$ are greater than 2.50 at all listed concentrations. Therefore, the compounds with observed i values less than 2.50 at all concentrations listed are NaCl, KCl, and $(NH_4)_2SO_4$ only; **G** is correct. **F** is incorrect because it both includes $MgCl_2$ and does not include $(NH_4)_2SO_4$. **H** is incorrect because it both includes $MgCl_2$ and does not include NaCl. **J** is incorrect because it includes $MgCl_2$.

Question 3. The best answer is C. According to Table 2, the lowest observed i value for KCl is 1.79, which occurs at concentrations of 0.7, 0.8, and 0.9 mol/kg H_2O. Therefore, **C** is correct. **A** is incorrect because the observed i value for KCl at a concentration of 0.3 mol/kg H_2O is 1.81, which is not the lowest observed i value. **B** is incorrect because the observed i value for KCl at a concentration of 0.6 mol/kg H_2O is 1.80, which is not the lowest observed i value. **D** is incorrect because the observed i value for KCl at a concentration of 2.0 mol/kg H_2O is 1.83, which is not the lowest observed i value.

Question 4. The best answer is H. Table 1 lists the theoretical i value for each of the 4 compounds, whereas Table 2 lists the observed i value at a concentration of 2.0 mol/kg H_2O for each of the 4 compounds. The compound's deviation from its theoretical i value is the difference between the corresponding values from each table. For NaCl, the difference is 0.03. For KCl, the difference is 0.17. For $MgCl_2$, the difference is 1.57. For $(NH_4)_2SO_4$, the difference is 1.13. The difference for $MgCl_2$ is the greatest. Therefore, $MgCl_2$ has the largest deviation from its theoretical i value at a concentration of 2.0 mol/kg H_2O; **H** is correct. **F**, **G**, and **J** are each incorrect because the difference for each compound is not the greatest.

Question 5. The best answer is B. The passage states that the solutions represented in Table 2 are all aqueous solutions. An aqueous solution is a solution in which the solvent is water. The passage also states that each of the solutes are dissolved in H_2O, which is the chemical formula for water. A solvent of a solution is the substance that is used to dissolve the solute. Therefore, water is the only solvent for all the solutions represented in Table 2; **B** is correct. **A** is incorrect because ammonium sulfate is not a solvent in the data presented. **C** is incorrect because sodium chloride, potassium chloride, and magnesium chloride are not solvents in the data presented. **D** is incorrect because sodium chloride, potassium chloride, magnesium chloride, and ammonium sulfate are not solvents in the data presented.

Question 6. The best answer is F. The passage describes the theoretical i value as the total number of particles produced when 1 formula unit of the solute dissolves in water. Because a sucrose molecule remains intact when it dissolves in water, 1 formula unit of sucrose would produce 1 particle when dissolved in water. Therefore, the theoretical i value for sucrose is most likely 1. According to Table 1, the theoretical i value for KCl is 2. Therefore, the theoretical i value for sucrose would more likely be less than that of KCl; **F** is correct. **G** is incorrect; the theoretical i value of sucrose is most likely 1. **H** is incorrect; the theoretical i value of sucrose would more likely be less than that of KCl. **J** is incorrect; the theoretical i value of sucrose would more likely be less than that of KCl, and the value is most likely 1.

Passage II

Question 7. The best answer is C. According to Table 1, as the streptomycin concentration increased from 0 µg/mL to 2 µg/mL, the relative fitness of Strain Y increased, and as the streptomycin concentration increased from 2 µg/mL to 8 µg/mL, the relative fitness of Strain Y decreased. Therefore, **C** is correct. **A**, **B**, and **D** are each incorrect; they are each inconsistent with the data trend in Table 1.

Question 8. The best answer is G. According to Table 1, as the streptomycin concentration increased, the relative fitness of Strain X decreased only. Due to this constant trend, the relative fitness for Strain X at streptomycin concentrations not directly shown in Table 1 can be estimated. According to Table 1, at a streptomycin concentration of 2 µg/mL, the relative fitness for Strain X was 0.8, and at a streptomycin concentration of 4 µg/mL, the relative fitness of Strain X was 0.5. Therefore, at a streptomycin concentration of 3 µg/mL, the relative fitness of Strain X would most likely have been between 0.5 and 0.8, so **G** is correct. **F** is incorrect; the relative fitness would most likely have been less than 0.5 at streptomycin concentrations greater than 4 µg/mL, not at 3 µg/mL. **H** is incorrect; the relative fitness would most likely have been between 0.8 and 0.9 at streptomycin concentrations between 0 µg/mL and 2 µg/mL. **J** is incorrect; the relative fitness would most likely never have been greater than 0.9.

Question 9. The best answer is D. Table 2 states that the effect of the mutation present in Strain X is an increased rate of streptomycin removal from the cell. This implies that each Strain X cell moves streptomycin out of the cell faster than a nonmutated cell does, so **D** is correct. **A**, **B**, and **C** are each incorrect; they are each inconsistent with the effect of mutation for Strain X given in Table 1.

Question 10. The best answer is H. According to the passage, relative fitness is a measure of survival and reproductive success, and according to the note within Table 1, a relative fitness of 0.0 indicates no surviving bacteria. This implies that the greater the relative fitness, the greater the cell survival and reproductive success. According to Table 1, at a streptomycin concentration of 2 µg/mL, the relative fitness of Strain W was 0.3 and the relative fitness of Strain X was 0.8, so **H** is correct. **F** is incorrect; Strain W would more likely not have had a greater number of cells survive and reproduce. **G** is incorrect; Strain W would more likely not have had a greater number of cells survive and reproduce, and the relative fitness values of Strain W and Strain X are inconsistent with the data in Table 1. **J** is incorrect; the relative fitness values of Strain W and Strain X are inconsistent with the data in Table 1.

Question 11. The best answer is B. According to Table 2, the strain with an increased rate of cell division was Strain W. According to Table 1, at a streptomycin concentration of 4 µg/mL, the relative fitness of Strain W was 0.1, so **B** is correct. **A**, **C**, and **D** are each incorrect; each of the relative fitness values is for a strain other than Strain W at a streptomycin concentration of 4 µg/mL.

Question 12. The best answer is F. According to the passage, the study contained 1 nonmutated strain, Strain U. According to Table 1, Strain U had a relative fitness of 1.0 at a streptomycin concentration of 0 µg/mL and a relative fitness of 0.0 at a streptomycin concentration of 8 µg/mL. Therefore, **F** is correct. **G** is incorrect; at a streptomycin concentration of 8 µg/mL, Strain U did not survive. **H** and **J** are each incorrect; Strain Z was a mutated strain according to the passage and Table 2.

Passage III

Question 13. The best answer is C. The passage states that the procedure in Experiment 1 was repeated for Experiment 2. The procedure in Experiment 1 indicates that Steps 2–5 were repeated for a given temperature until the bottle was reused 28 times. Thus, the total number of times in Experiment 1 that a bottle was placed in a box maintained at 10°C was 29: 1 use plus 28 reuses. This was therefore also the case for 10°C in Experiment 2. Therefore, **C** is correct. **A** and **B** are each incorrect; a bottle was placed into a box at 10°C more than 7 or 14 times in Experiment 2. **D** is incorrect; 58 is the number of times across both experiments that a bottle was placed in a box maintained at 10°C.

Question 14. The best answer is J. Figure 2 indicates that, for a temperature of 50°C, as the reuse number increased from 0 through 28, the concentration of Sb^{3+} increased only. Further, at reuse number 28 (the highest reuse number tested in the experiments), the Sb^{3+} concentration in the water was approximately 330 ng/L. It is reasonable to conclude based on the trend in the data that if the reuse number were increased beyond 28, the Sb^{3+} concentration in the water would likely continue to increase beyond 330 ng/L. Therefore, **J** is correct. **F**, **G**, and **H** are each incorrect; the trend indicates that as the reuse number increases, the Sb^{3+} concentration increases only.

Question 15. The best answer is **C.** Figure 2 indicates that water stored at 50°C in a bottle that was reused 21 times had an Sb^{3+} concentration of approximately 300 ng/L. A value of 6,000 ng/L is 20 times as great as 300 ng/L. Therefore, **C** is correct. **A** is incorrect, because a factor of 10 is missing from the division. **B** is incorrect, because a factor of 10 is missing from the division and a neighboring data point (30°C) was used. **D** is incorrect because a neighboring data point (30°C) was used.

Question 16. The best answer is **G.** Figures 1 and 2 indicate that, at a reuse number of 14, all the results in both experiments were greater than 140 ng/L except for 10°C in Experiment 2. The description of Experiment 2 indicates that the lightbulb used emitted visible light only. Therefore, **G** is correct. **F** is incorrect; the lightbulb used in Experiment 2 emitted visible light only. **H** and **J** are each incorrect; at a reuse number of 14, the results in both experiments at 30°C were greater than 140 ng/L.

Question 17. The best answer is **B.** The passage states that the bottles used in the experiments were made of plastic. Plastics are examples of materials called polymers. Therefore, **B** is correct. **A** is incorrect; plastics are not examples of alloys. **C** is incorrect; plastics are not single elements. **D** is incorrect; plastics are not examples of salts.

Question 18. The best answer is **J.** Figure 1 indicates that, at reuse number 21, the Sb^{3+} concentration was approximately 275 ng/L at 10°C, approximately 325 ng/L at 30°C, and approximately 400 ng/L at 50°C. Thus, it is reasonable to conclude that as temperature increases at a constant reuse number, the Sb^{3+} concentration increases only. So, if a temperature of 20°C had been tested, the resulting Sb^{3+} concentration at reuse number 21 would most likely be greater than the result for 10°C and less than the result for 30°C. Therefore, **J** is correct. **F**, **G**, and **H** are each incorrect; the result at reuse number 21 and 20°C would most likely be greater than 275 ng/L and less than 325 ng/L.

Question 19. The best answer is **A.** The description of Experiment 1 indicates that Step 2 of the procedure required 16 hr to complete. Moreover, Step 2 was repeated multiple times for the same bottle, making it impossible to complete Experiment 1 within the span of a single day (24 hr). Since the procedure of Experiment 1 was repeated for Experiment 2 (with a different type of lightbulb), neither experiment could have been completed in a single day. Therefore, **A** is correct. **B**, **C**, and **D** are each incorrect; both experiments must have required more than 1 day to complete.

Passage IV

Question 20. The best answer is **H.** Both Hypothesis 1 and Hypothesis 2 state that, on early Earth, volcanic eruptions released CO_2 and NH_3 into the atmosphere. In addition to what is stated in each hypothesis, to answer this item correctly, one must know that the C in CO_2 represents carbon, the N in NH_3 represents nitrogen, and magma from beneath the Earth's crust is released as lava during volcanic eruptions. Therefore, **H** is the correct answer. **F**, **G**, and **J** are each incorrect; each is inconsistent with both Hypothesis 1 and Hypothesis 2.

Question 21. The best answer is B. According to Hypothesis 2, compared to present day, the CO_2 concentration on early Earth was about 40 times as great. If the current CO_2 concentration is 395 ppm, 40 times 395 ppm is equal to 15,800 ppm. Therefore, **B** is correct. **A**, **C**, and **D** are each incorrect; each is inconsistent with Hypothesis 2.

Question 22. The best answer is G. According to Hypothesis 1, on early Earth, the higher-than-present concentrations of CO_2, NH_3, and CH_4 absorbed enough heat to allow for liquid water. According to Hypothesis 2, on early Earth, the concentrations of CO_2, NH_3, and CH_4 alone would not have absorbed enough heat to allow for liquid water. However, the higher-than-present concentrations of N_2 and H_2 in the atmosphere enhanced the heat-absorbing effects of CO_2, NH_3, and CH_4 and allowed liquid water to exist. Therefore, **G** is correct. **F**, **H**, and **J** are each incorrect; each is inconsistent with the question asked.

Question 23. The best answer is C. According to Hypothesis 1, on early Earth, volcanoes released only CO_2 and NH_3 into the atmosphere, and microbes produced CH_4 by metabolizing H_2. In contrast, Hypothesis 2 stated that, on early Earth, the only source of atmospheric CO_2, NH_3, and CH_4 was volcanic eruptions. Therefore, **C** is correct. **A**, **B**, and **D** are incorrect; each is inconsistent with at least one hypothesis.

Question 24. The best answer is F. Hypothesis 1 states that microbes produced CH_4 by metabolizing H_2. Therefore, in a balanced chemical equation that represented microbial metabolism, CH_4 would be a product, and H_2 would be a reactant. So, **F** is correct. **G** is incorrect; H_2 is not metabolized in the reaction. **H** and **J** are each incorrect; in each equation, H_2 is not metabolized, and CH_4 is not produced as a product.

Question 25. The best answer is D. Hypothesis 1 states that on early Earth, microbes produced CH_4, so evidence of CH_4 producing microbes supports Hypothesis 1. Therefore, **D** is correct. **A** is incorrect; Hypothesis 1 states that on early Earth the CO_2 concentration was 100 times the present concentration. **B** is incorrect; Hypothesis 1 states that on early Earth the CH_4 concentration was 1,000 times the present concentration. **C** is incorrect; Hypothesis 1 states that CO_2 was produced by volcanic eruptions.

Question 26. The best answer is G. Hypothesis 1 does not mention N_2. Hypothesis 2 states that on early Earth the concentration of N_2 was approximately twice what it is today, and that the higher-than-present concentration of N_2 contributed to an increase in the heat-absorbing effects of greenhouse gases, maintaining a surface temperature that allowed for liquid water. The supposition that an increase in N_2 concentration from its present value would result in cooler surface temperatures would weaken Hypothesis 2. Therefore, **G** is correct. **F**, **H**, and **J** are each incorrect; each is inconsistent with the question asked.

Passage V

Question 27. The best answer is B. The results of Study 1 indicate that as η increased, F decreased only. Further, when η was 1.00×10^{-3} Pa·sec, F was 1,230 mL/s; and when η was 2.00×10^{-3} Pa·sec, F was 615 mL/s. Therefore, if F were 920 mL/s, that would most likely result from testing a viscosity greater than 1.00×10^{-3} Pa·sec and less than 2.00×10^{-3} Pa·sec. So, **B** is correct. **A**, **C**, and **D** are each incorrect, because each is inconsistent with the data trend in Table 1.

Question 28. The best answer is H. The description of Study 2 indicates that each trial was performed with η $= 1.0 \times 10^{-3}$ Pa·sec and $D = 1.00$ m. Further, Table 2 indicates that both R and F varied from trial to trial. So, **H** is correct. **F** is incorrect because neither R nor F was held constant. **G** is incorrect because F was not held constant. **J** is incorrect because R was not held constant.

Question 29. The best answer is B. The description of the apparatus shown in Figure 1 indicates that:

(fluid pressure at Gauge G) − (fluid pressure at Gauge H) = 5 kPa

Therefore, if the pressure at Gauge G was 105 kPa, the pressure at Gauge H would have to be 100 kPa. So, **B** is correct. **A**, **C**, and **D** are each incorrect because each is inconsistent with the information provided about the gauges.

Question 30. The best answer is F. To answer this item correctly, one must understand that fluids flow from regions of high pressure to regions of low pressure. The description of the apparatus shown in Figure 1 indicates that the pressure at Gauge G was always 5 kPa greater than the pressure at Gauge H. Therefore, **F** is correct. **G** is incorrect because it is contrary to the fact that fluids flow from regions of high pressure to regions of low pressure. **H** is incorrect because it is inconsistent with the description of the apparatus. **J** is incorrect because it is both inconsistent with the description of the apparatus and contrary to the fact that fluids flow from regions of high pressure to regions of low pressure.

Question 31. The best answer is A. To answer this item correctly, one must know that viscosity in a fluid is a result of frictional forces within the fluid. So, **A** is correct. **B** is incorrect because combustion is an example of a chemical reaction, and no chemical reactions were involved in the studies. **C** is incorrect because viscosity is not a magnetic phenomenon. **D** is incorrect because viscosity is not dependent upon, or affected by, gravity.

Question 32. The best answer is G. According to the results of Study 3, when D was 2.50 m, F was 492 mL/s. So, each second the fluid was flowing, 492 mL of fluid flowed past either gauge. Therefore, the volume of fluid that flowed past either gauge in 1 min was (492 mL/s) × (60 s) = 29,250 mL, which is approximately 30,000 mL. So, **G** is correct. **F** is incorrect; 25,000 mL is too low an estimate. **H** and **J** are each incorrect; each is too high an estimate.

Question 33. The best answer is **A.** The description of Study 1 indicates that D was 1.00 m in each trial. Further, the description of the apparatus shown in Figure 1 indicates that the fluid pressure at Gauge G was always 5 kPa greater than the fluid pressure at Gauge H. Thus, the absolute value of the pressure difference between the gauges was 5 kPa, and the distance between them was 1 m. Therefore, the pressure gradient between the gauges during Study 1 was (5 kPa) ÷ (1 m) = 5 kPa/m. So, **A** is correct. **B** is incorrect; it mistakenly involves the value of R. **C** is incorrect; it mistakenly involves the units of measure for R. **D** is incorrect; it mistakenly involves both the value of R and the units of measure for R.

Passage VI

Question 34. The best answer is **F.** According to the results of Study 1, as the number of days after treatment increased from 3 to 5 to 7 to 9, the average number of seeds germinated per pot in Group 4 increased from 2.8 to 4.0 to 4.6 to 4.8. Thus, as one variable increased, the other increased only. So, **F** is correct. **G, H,** and **J** are each incorrect; they are each inconsistent with the data trend in Table 2.

Question 35. The best answer is **A.** According to the results of Study 2, the greatest average plant height was approximately 60 cm, which is only 0.6 m. Thus, no group had an average plant height greater than 1 m. So, **A** is correct. **B, C,** and **D** are each incorrect; they are each inconsistent with the data in Figure 1.

Question 36. The best answer is **J.** The description of Study 2 indicates that the procedures of Study 1 were repeated with an additional 240 pots. However, nine days after treatment, all but 1 of the seedlings were removed from pots that had multiple seedlings. This helped to ensure there would be only 1 seedling per pot during the 75-day growing period that followed. So, **J** is correct. **F** is incorrect; the pots in Study 2 were prepared in the same manner as in Study 1, so 5 seeds were planted in each pot. **G** is incorrect; seeds were planted, not seedlings. **H** is incorrect; at no time were seeds removed from any pot.

Question 37. The best answer is **C.** The description of Study 2 indicates that the procedures of Study 1 were repeated for an additional 240 pots. This implies that all 240 pots in Study 2 were irrigated over a period of 9 days. The description of Study 2 goes on to indicate that after those procedures had been completed, each pot was then irrigated as in Study 1 over a period of 75 additional days. Thus, the number of irrigation days was the same for each pot, regardless of which group it was assigned to. Therefore, it is not possible to determine whether average plant height was or was not affected by the number of irrigation days. So, **C** is correct. **A, B,** and **D** are each incorrect because the number of irrigation days was not varied among groups, so the claim cannot be evaluated based on Study 2.

Question 38. The best answer is F. Table 1 indicates that Group 3 was treated with Species R, Group 4 was treated with PMA, and both were treated with higher-than-normal NaCl concentrations. At 5 days after treatment, the average number of germinated seeds per pot was higher for Group 3 (4.3) than for Group 4 (4.0). At 7 days after treatment, the result for Group 3 (5.0) was also higher than that for Group 4 (4.6). And the results were similar for 9 days after treatment. Therefore, the results indicate that treatment with Species R resulted in more germinated seeds on average than did treatment with PMA on each of those days. So, F is correct. G is incorrect; on those days, the average number of seeds germinated per pot was greater for Group 3 than for Group 4. H and J are each incorrect; the results of the study are consistent with the statement.

Question 39. The best answer is C. The results of Study 1 indicate that the average number of seeds germinated per pot in Group 2 was 0.0 at both 3 and 5 days after treatment, 0.2 at 7 days after treatment, and 0.4 at 9 days after treatment. This implies that the first observations of seed germination could not have occurred earlier than 5 days after treatment and must have occurred no later than 7 days after treatment. So, C is correct. A and B are each incorrect; the results indicate that no seed germination was observed earlier than 5 days after treatment. D is incorrect; the results indicate that seed germination must have been observed no later than 7 days after treatment.

Question 40. The best answer is J. According to Table 1, Group 2 was treated with H_2O containing NaCl only, Group 3 was treated with H_2O containing Species R and NaCl, and Group 4 was treated with H_2O containing PMA and NaCl. So, if the statement were supported, the average plant height would be greater for Group 4 than for either Group 2 or 3. However, the results of Study 2 show that the average plant height for Group 4 was less than that for Group 3 and greater than that for Group 2. So, J is correct. F and G are each incorrect; the results of Study 2 do not support the statement. H is incorrect; the average plant height for Group 4 was less than that for Group 3.

Chapter 4:
Identifying Areas for Improvement

Your practice test scores alone provide very little insight into what you need to do to improve your score. For example, you may have missed a certain math question because you haven't yet taken trigonometry or because you misread the question or the answer choices or because you were anxious about finishing the test on time.

When evaluating your performance on any of the practice tests in this book or elsewhere, examine not only *whether* you answered a question correctly or incorrectly but also *why* you answered it correctly or incorrectly. Recognizing why you chose the correct or incorrect answer sheds light on what you need to do to improve your score on future practice tests and on the ACT. Perhaps you need to review certain subjects, take a particular course, develop a better sense of how much time to spend on each question, or read questions and answer choices more carefully.

In this chapter, we offer guidance on how to evaluate your performance on ACT Practice Test 1 in order to identify subject areas and test-taking strategies and skills that you may need to work on. Take a similar approach to evaluate your performance on subsequent practice tests.

Reviewing Your Overall Performance

After you have determined your scores, consider the following questions as you evaluate how you did on the practice tests. Keep in mind that many of these questions require you to make judgment calls based on what you were thinking or the steps you took to decide on the answer choice you selected. The answer explanations in chapter 4 may help you make these determinations, but ultimately you are the only one who can determine why or how you chose the correct or incorrect answer.

Did you run out of time before you completed a test?

If so, read the sections in this book on pacing yourself. See chapter 2 for general advice that applies to all tests, and see chapters 5 through 9 for advice specific to each test. Perhaps you need to adjust the way you use your time in responding to the questions. Remember, there is no penalty for guessing, so try to answer all questions, even if you have to make an educated guess.

Did you spend too much time trying to understand the directions to the tests?

Make sure you understand them now, so you won't have to spend too much time reading them when you take the test.

Did you rush through the test and make mistakes?

People tend to make mistakes when they are in a hurry. If you had plenty of time remaining at the end of the test but made mistakes, you probably hurried through the test and made errors such as these:

- Misreading a passage
- Misreading a question
- Not reading or considering all answer choices
- Selecting a response that was an incomplete answer
- Selecting an answer that did not directly respond to the question

Did a particular type of question confuse you?

Use the explanatory answers following each practice test to help you identify any mistakes you may have made regarding certain question types or answer choices. The explanatory answers can help you understand why you may have chosen the incorrect answer and avoid making that same mistake again.

After taking a practice test on the online platform, you can go to the Metrics tab, click on the bar graph of any assessment, and then navigate to a list of right and wrong answers. This can help you find the right explanations and determine areas to focus on. If you flagged questions that you found difficult or confusing, you can also see them listed here.

Highlighting Strengths and Areas for Improvement on the English Test

The process of scoring your English practice test and reviewing the answer explanations should reveal the reason you chose the correct or incorrect answer for each question. If you struggled to answer questions on the test because you have not yet acquired certain English language knowledge and skills, review the questions and your answers closely to determine more specifically what you need to work on.

The English test requires knowledge and skills in several areas. The best way to raise your score is to improve your English language skills, which you can accomplish in the following ways:

- Take an English composition course. Such a course will help you write more clearly, logically, and concisely while developing a better understanding of English punctuation, grammar, and usage conventions.

- Practice your writing skills in other courses. In most courses, including English literature, social science, speech, and perhaps even science, you have opportunities to practice your writing skills and receive feedback.

- Read well-written publications in the form of books, magazine articles, and online content from reputable sources—material that has been professionally edited. As you read, pay attention to punctuation, grammar, usage, sentence structure, writing strategy, organization, and style to see how a variety of writers express themselves while adhering to the same conventions.

- Practice writing and having your writing edited by an English teacher or someone else who is qualified to provide feedback.

Test-Taking Errors

A low test score does not necessarily mean that you lack the English language knowledge and skills required to do well on the test. It may indicate that you rushed through the test and made mistakes, spent too much time on certain questions that you didn't finish, or committed some other test-taking error(s). As you evaluate your answers to determine *why* you missed certain questions, consider your test-taking strategies and skills. Place a checkmark next to each of the following common test-taking errors you think you need to work on eliminating:

Worked too slowly: You may need to improve your reading speed and comprehension or try answering the easy questions first and then returning to the harder questions if time remains.

Rushed through the test: If you finished with plenty of time remaining but made mistakes, you may need to spend more time reading and understanding the passages, reading the questions, or carefully considering all of the answer choices.

Misread passages: If you missed questions because of misreading or misinterpreting passages, work on your reading comprehension. Try reading more carefully and rereading when you do not fully understand a passage.

Misread questions: Every question points to the correct answer, so read questions carefully and make sure you understand what a question is asking before you choose your answer.

Did not consider all answer choices: If you tend to select the first answer choice that seems to be correct, try considering all answer choices before making your final selection. A good way to double-check an answer is to find reasons to eliminate the other three choices.

Did not consider the writing style: The entire passage conveys the author's overall writing style, which you may need to consider when answering certain style-related questions.

Did not consider a question's context: Writing strategy and organization questions often require consideration of surrounding text. You may need to skim the passage first before answering these questions or read one or two sentences before or after the sentence in question.

Did not account for a word's connotations: Many words have a *denotation* (a literal meaning or dictionary definition) and a *connotation* (a thought or emotion that the word evokes from the reader or listener). To answer some usage questions, you must consider what the word means in the context in which it is used.

Did not connect an underlined portion of text with its corresponding question: The underlined portion of the text and the corresponding question work together to point to the correct answer choice, so be sure to consider them both when selecting your answer.

Overlooked differences in the answer choices: Answer choices may differ so subtly that you overlook the differences, so be sure to recognize what's different about each choice before selecting your answer.

Chose an answer that introduced a new error: Some answer choices correct the error in the underlined text but introduce a new error. Do not choose an answer that creates a new error.

Did not choose the best answer: Two or more answers may be correct, but the English test requires that you choose the *best* answer. Again, consider all answer choices before selecting an answer.

Did not reread the sentence using the selected answer: A great way to double-check an answer is to insert it in place of the underlined text and then reread the sentence to make sure it makes sense.

Missed a two-part question: With a two-part question, each of the answer choices typically starts with "yes" or "no" followed by a reason, so you must determine first whether the answer is yes or no and then why. Carefully compare and consider the reasons before making your selection.

Did not consider interrelated questions: A question may be easier to answer after you have answered the next question, so consider skipping back to a question if you feel that answering the current question has given you new insight.

See chapter 5 for in-depth coverage of test-taking strategies and skills that may help to raise your English test score.

Highlighting Strengths and Areas for Improvement on the Mathematics Test

The process of scoring your mathematics practice test and reviewing the answer explanations should reveal your strengths and any areas for improvement. You may discover that you are a whiz at algebra and geometry but are in dire need of a refresher course in trigonometry. Or, you may find that your math knowledge and skills are sound in all areas but you need to work on test-taking strategies to ensure that your test results accurately reflect your knowledge and skills.

Use the checklists in the following sections to flag subject areas and test-taking skills you may need to focus on.

Math Subject Areas

If you struggled to answer questions on the test because you have not yet acquired the requisite math language knowledge and skills, review the questions and your answers closely to determine more specifically what you need to work on.

Your performance on the ACT mathematics test may be affected by your ability to handle certain types of questions. For example, you may breeze through straightforward, basic math questions but get tripped up by word problems. As you evaluate your performance on mathematics in Practice Test 1, try to identify the types of questions you struggle with most:

Basic math: These questions are straightforward with very little text. You just need to do the math.

Basic math in settings: These are word problems that challenge your ability to translate the problem into one or more mathematical equations and then solve those equations.

Very challenging math problems: These can be basic math or basic math in settings questions that challenge your ability to reason mathematically and perhaps draw from your knowledge of more than one math subject area to solve them. In addition to the differences in how math problems are presented, you may encounter *question sets*—two or more sequential math problems related to the same information.

Test-Taking Errors

Incorrect or unanswered questions on the practice test may be less of a reflection of your math knowledge and skills and more a reflection of your test-taking strategies and skills. As you review your scores and answers, try to determine whether you committed any of the following common test-taking errors:

Worked too slowly: If you answered questions correctly but your score suffered from unanswered questions because you ran out of time, you may simply need more practice to improve your speed.

Rushed through the test: If you finished with plenty of time remaining but made mistakes, you may need to spend more time reading and understanding the questions and doing the math before selecting an answer.

Got stuck on a very challenging question: Answering the easy questions first and then returning to the harder questions later may help you address this issue.

Misread the question: The question contains all information you need to answer it. Misreading the question may cause you to extract and use the wrong information in your calculations or calculate an answer for something other than what the question directed.

Overlooked information in the answer choices: Answer choices often provide clues as to what form the answer is in. A glance at the answer choices can often clarify what the question is asking for.

Overlooked or misinterpreted information in an image: Many math questions include an image, table, or graph that provides key information. Misreading an image will lead you to select the wrong answer choice.

Did not use logic to solve a problem: Math questions, especially the very challenging ones, often test your ability to reason through problems.

Not doing the math: Although you are not required to show your work on the test, consider writing out your calculations to double-check your reasoning and avoid mental errors. Also, when a question includes an image, consider writing any dimensions provided in the question on to the image so that the image contains all of the measurements you have to work with.

Not double-checking your answers: For many questions, you can insert the answer you think is correct into the equation provided and do the math to double-check the answer choice. Take the opportunity to double-check answers when given the opportunity.

For math test strategies and tips, turn to chapter 6.

Highlighting Strengths and Areas for Improvement on the Reading Test

The process of scoring the reading practice test and reviewing the answer explanations should reveal the reason you chose the correct or incorrect answer for each question. Reasons for choosing wrong answers or struggling with certain questions can be classified in three categories:

Subject matter

The type of passage—literary narrative or informational—may affect your ability to read and comprehend the passage and answer questions about it. For example, you may have no trouble answering questions about fact-based passages in social science and natural science but struggle reading and understanding literary narratives.

Reading skills

The reading test is designed to evaluate numerous skills, including the ability to identify details in the text, draw generalizations about those details, and understand the meaning of a word or phrase based on how it is used in a sentence. In addition, each passage challenges you to read quickly and with understanding.

Test-taking strategies and skills

Not reading the entire passage, misreading the question or answer choices, and not verifying an answer choice with the passage can all lead to careless mistakes.

Use the checklists in the following sections to flag the types of reading passages, reading skills, and test-taking strategies and skills you may need to focus on.

Types of Reading Passages

Your ability to comprehend reading passages and answer questions about them may vary based on the type of passage. For example, if you are accustomed to reading science books and articles, you are probably familiar with many of the concepts and vocabulary in the science passages on the test; therefore, you might expect to have no trouble reading, comprehending, and answering questions about such passages. However, if you have read very little fiction, you may find it challenging to identify the plot (sequence of events), draw conclusions about characters, or sense the mood that a passage is intended to evoke. In short, you may struggle more with certain types of reading passages than with others.

As you score your reading test and review the answer explanations, use the following checklist to flag any types of reading passages you found particularly challenging:

Literary narrative: Passages from short stories, novels, and memoirs

Social science: Informational passages that cover topics such as anthropology, archaeology, biography, business, economics, education, geography, history, political science, psychology, and sociology

Humanities: Informational passages about topics including architecture, art, dance, ethics, film, language, literary criticism, music, philosophy, radio, television, and theater

Natural science: Informational passages related to subjects such as anatomy, astronomy, biology, botany, chemistry, ecology, geology, medicine, meteorology, microbiology, natural history, physiology, physics, technology, and zoology

Reading Skills Tested

The ability to read, comprehend, and answer questions about passages involves numerous skills. Questions on the test are written specifically to evaluate these skills. As you review the answer explanations, place a checkmark next to any of the following skills you think you need to develop more fully:

Identify and interpret details: Nearly all questions require an ability to identify and interpret details from the passage that support whichever answer choice you select.

Many questions specifically state, "According to the passage …" This skill is essential for performing well on the reading test.

Determine the main idea of a paragraph(s) or passage: A few questions may require an ability to recognize the general meaning or point of one or more paragraphs.

Understand comparative relationships (comparison and contrast): Questions may ask about comparisons and contrasts made in the passage.

Understand cause-effect relationships: Some reading passages explore cause-effect relationships. Others are accompanied by questions that more subtly test your ability to identify cause-effect relationships.

Make generalizations: To answer many reading questions, you must be able to draw conclusions from or make generalizations about details provided in the passage.

Determine the meaning of words or phrases from context: You are likely to encounter several questions on the ACT reading test that challenge you to determine the meaning of a word or phrase based on the context in which it is used.

Understand sequences of events: A few reading test questions may require an ability to read and comprehend a series of events.

Draw conclusions about the author's purpose and method: You may be asked to get into the mind of the author and figure out what their attitude, purpose, or method is.

Understand arguments: Some items may ask you to identify an argument being made in a passage or to examine support for an argument.

For more about reading skills tested, including examples of the types of questions used to evaluate these skills, turn to chapter 7.

Test-Taking Errors

Even if your reading speed and comprehension are solid, you may miss questions by committing one or more of the following common test-taking errors. Place a checkmark next to each error you think you may be susceptible to making:

Read too slowly or too quickly: By reading too slowly, you may not have sufficient time to read all passages and answer all questions. However, reading too quickly may result in errors or having to return to a passage several times to locate the evidence needed to decide which answer choice is correct.

Did not read the entire passage: Skim-reading a passage is useful for understanding what a passage is about, but it often results in overlooking the details required to answer specific questions. Read the entire passage word for word.

Misread the question: Questions, especially those that contain the word *NOT*, can be tricky. Make sure you understand what a question is asking as you evaluate the various answer choices.

Misread or overlooked an answer choice: Misreading an answer choice or not considering all answer choices can result in mistakes. Consider all answer choices and read them carefully.

Did not verify an answer choice with the passage: If time allows, try to verify every answer choice by locating details in the passage that support it. Use the same technique to rule out other answer choices when necessary.

For additional reading test strategies and tips, turn to chapter 7.

Highlighting Strengths and Areas for Improvement on the Science Test

The process of scoring the science practice test and reviewing the answer explanations should reveal the reason you chose the correct or incorrect answer for each question. Reasons for choosing wrong answers or struggling with certain questions can be classified into three categories:

Subject matter

The science test does not require in-depth knowledge of biology, chemistry, earth science, space science, or physics. Nor does it require you to memorize formulas or solve complex math problems. However, questions are presented in the context of these subject areas, and you may need some knowledge of scientific terms or concepts to answer some of the questions.

Passage type

Science passages are presented in three different formats: Data Representation (graphs, tables, illustrations); Research Summaries (from experiments); and Conflicting Viewpoints (alternative theories and hypotheses). You may struggle more with the items presented in one type of passage than in the others.

Test-taking strategies and skills

The science test evaluates your ability to extract and use information presented in a variety of formats to solve problems and answer questions. Even if you are highly skilled and knowledgeable in all science subject areas, your score will suffer if you make careless mistakes or are so careful that you run out of time before answering all of the questions.

Use the checklists in the following sections to flag the subject areas, passage types, and test-taking strategies and skills you may need to focus on.

Science Subject Areas

You may benefit from identifying subject areas in which you struggle. Use the following checklist to flag subject matter you may need to review:

Biology: Cell biology, botany, zoology, microbiology, ecology, biochemistry, genetics, and evolution

Chemistry: Properties of matter, acids and bases, kinetics and equilibria, thermo-chemistry, organic chemistry, and nuclear chemistry

Earth and Space sciences: Geology, meteorology, oceanography, environmental science, stars, planets, galaxies, and the universe.

Physics: Mechanics, gravitation, thermodynamics, electromagnetism, fluids, solids, and optics

Types of Science Passages

As you review answer explanations and evaluate your performance on the science test, check to see whether you had more trouble with items in certain types of science passages than others. Place a checkmark next to any passage types that you found particularly challenging:

Data Representation passages focus primarily on assessing your ability to understand, evaluate, and interpret information presented in graphs, tables, and illustrations.

Research Summary passages focus primarily on assessing your ability to understand, analyze, and evaluate the design, execution, and results of one or more experiments.

Conflicting Viewpoints passages focus primarily on assessing your ability to compare and evaluate alternative theories, hypotheses, or viewpoints on a specific observable phenomenon.

For more about these different passage types and guidance on how to approach the items in them effectively, turn to chapter 8.

Test-Taking Errors

As mentioned previously, the science test does not require in-depth scientific knowledge. It relies more on your ability to understand and identify detailed information presented in a variety of formats—text, graphs, tables, and diagrams. If your science test score is lower than you had hoped, you may have committed one or more test-taking errors. Place a checkmark next to each of the following test-taking errors that you think you need to work on avoiding:

Worked too slowly: If time expired before you had a chance to answer all 40 questions, you need to pick up the pace.

Worked too quickly: If you finished with plenty of time remaining but made mistakes, you need to practice slowing down and reading the science passages, questions, and answer choices more carefully.

Misread or misinterpreted text: If you missed questions because you misread a passage, question, or answer choice, check this box.

Misread or misinterpreted a graph or table: Graphs, tables, and images contain much of the information required to answer the science test questions.

Misread or misinterpreted a research summary: You may need to develop a better understanding of the scientific method for designing and conducting experiments.

Did not use reason effectively to find the answer: Most of the questions on the science test challenge your ability to think and reason. If you struggled to understand questions,

Your First Practice Test

check this box. You may be able to improve your score by adopting a problem-solving strategy that steps you through the question, as discussed in chapter 8.

For science test-taking strategies that will help you avoid these common mistakes and others, turn to chapter 8.

Highlighting Strengths and Areas for Improvement on the Writing Test

The optional writing test is designed to evaluate your ability to write at a level expected of students entering first-year college English composition courses. A solid essay demonstrates your ability to clearly state your perspective on a complex issue and analyze the relationship between your perspective and at least one other perspective, develop and support your ideas with reasoning and examples, organize your ideas clearly and logically, and communicate your ideas effectively in standard written English.

As noted in chapter 3, we strongly recommend consulting others to help you evaluate your writing practice test. Self-assessment is an invaluable skill, but others often see what we cannot. If you must work independently, read your essay with the most critical eye you can, asking yourself whether a reader who came to it with no knowledge of the prompt or what you meant to say would understand your argument. After scoring your writing practice test, use the checklists in the following sections (organized by domain) to highlight writing skills you may need to develop more fully and to avoid errors related to writing strategy and process.

Writing Skills Tested

As you evaluate your writing practice test, consider which skills contributed to your scores. In chapter 9, a full set of sample essays is included. Though the prompt there is different than the one in chapter 3, the quality of writing in each of the essays is similar to that of essays for any topic. Comparing your own work to those samples will help you evaluate the skill displayed in your practice test. You may be able to improve your scores significantly by more fully developing only one or two of the following skills. Place a checkmark next to each skill you think you need to work on:

Clearly state your own perspective on a complex issue and analyze the relationship between your perspective and at least one other perspective: If another reader cannot easily identify a clear perspective, practice formulating thesis statements. Whenever you write an essay, practice stating your thesis in the first few sentences of the essay. By presenting your perspective in the introduction, you not only state your main idea clearly but also give your essay a focal point.

If you had trouble analyzing the relationship between your perspective and at least one other perspective, practice writing counterarguments. Pick a debatable issue and choose a stance. Now, imagine what someone who disagrees with you might say, and practice writing paragraphs that first present the other person's side of the issue. Then offer your response. Next, imagine a perspective that is in general agreement with yours but differs in some important ways. How do you respond to this perspective? As you think and write, ask yourself: What accounts for the similarities and differences among your perspective and others you can imagine? Where are the strengths and weaknesses in these other perspectives, and where are the strengths and weaknesses in your own? Most importantly, ask yourself how engaging with another view—whether it generally agrees or disagrees with your own—can help you advance an argument. Considering these questions as you practice can help you learn to analyze and engage with different perspectives.

Develop and support your ideas with reasoning and examples: Failure to support your assertions can result in a lower score. Remember that every claim you make should be backed up with good supporting evidence. Ask yourself whether the reasoning or evidence you provided sufficiently explains your thinking, or whether another sentence or two would help clarify your meaning. As you explain the reasoning behind your argument, remember that logical fallacies, including overgeneralization and moral equivalence (associating minor offenses with moral atrocities), can weaken your ideas. Additionally, the assumption that a reader shares or inherently understands your viewpoint can lead to underdevelopment of ideas.

Organize your ideas clearly and logically: An essay should flow directly from point A to point B and not repeat itself or wander off track. Consider the extent to which the ideas in the body paragraphs are focused on arguing the thesis: are there ideas present that are not obviously connected to your main point? Are the ideas clearly related to one another? How might transitions be improved? Similarly, think about the order in which your ideas are presented: does the arrangement add meaning (e.g., opening with a metaphor that describes the issue in the prompt, refuting counterarguments before building your own, or concluding with an example that illustrates the argument) or are the ideas essentially listed? Do the ideas build upon one another or do they function in isolation? Thinking about questions such as these can help you learn to write a more cohesive essay. (Prewriting, discussed in the next section, can help ensure that your essay is well organized.)

Communicate your ideas effectively in standard written English: If your essay contains several errors in grammar, usage, and mechanics, it would be beneficial to review rules and practice a variety of exercises associated with those. Equally important, however, are word choice, sentence structure, and style. If your essay does not include much variety of either vocabulary or sentence type, you might practice constructing the same sentences in different ways, experimenting with synonyms and fluctuating between simple and complex sentences. Pay close attention to the voice and tone: how might a reader interpret your attitude about the issue? How much personality belongs in the argument, and how can it be conveyed through word choice? Answering these sorts of questions can help you with evaluating your writing and improving your use of language to reach an audience.

You can develop all of these skills in high school English classes and other classes that require you to write essays and where you receive feedback that targets these skills. For more about improving your writing test score, along with sample essays that demonstrate the differences between high-scoring and lower-scoring essays, turn to chapter 9.

Writing Strategy or Process Errors

When scoring an essay, the focus is on the product, but the score may be a reflection of the process used to produce that essay. For example, prewriting (planning) can help you think of good ideas, ensure that your ideas are presented logically, and remind you to provide evidence to support your ideas. After scoring your practice essay, think back on your process, including planning, and how it impacted your essay and place a checkmark next to any of these writing strategy or process errors you may have committed:

Poor pacing: Composing too quickly may result in careless errors, whereas working too slowly may result in an incomplete essay or insufficient time to review and correct errors.

Insufficient prewriting (planning): It is difficult to write an effective essay, especially in timed conditions, if you have not spent time thinking about how to approach the task, considering what you might want to say and how to say it most constructively. If you had trouble generating and developing ideas or engaging with multiple perspectives, consider using the guided prewriting section found in the test booklet. The questions presented in this section are intended to help you produce a perspective and analyze its relationships with other points of view. They are also useful as you think about how you will support your ideas. Because it can be difficult to organize your ideas as you write, you may want to consider using the prewriting space to write an outline or draw a diagram. You do not need a detailed outline, but starting with a thesis and mapping a structure to support it can help you define the logic of your argument before you begin to write it. This can be particularly helpful when writing in timed conditions.

Not reviewing or editing: If you completed your essay with time to spare, did not review or edit it, and your essay has errors related to grammar, usage, sentence structure, or style, check this box. Practice with reading and editing while you write, even just with sentences and paragraphs, will help you get better at this.

Insufficient practice: Producing well-written essays requires practice and feedback, which you often receive only in a formal English composition course. The practice writing tests in this book provide additional opportunities, but we strongly recommend that you have your practice writing tests evaluated by a qualified third party—perhaps an English teacher or a fellow student who is a strong writer.

For additional tips on improving your writing test score, turn to chapter 9.

3

Part Three:
Improving Your Score

In This Part

This part features various ways to improve your scores on the English, mathematics, reading, science, and optional writing tests. Here, you get a preview of the types of questions you can expect on each test, along with test-taking strategies and skills that apply specifically to each test:

- **English:** Find out more about test content, look at sample questions, and develop strategies for choosing the best answer.

- **Mathematics:** Learn about the subject areas covered on the test, the types of math problems you will encounter, and strategies for improving your speed and accuracy in answering questions.

- **Reading:** Discover the types of reading passages you will encounter on the test, the types of questions you will need to answer, and strategies for improving your reading speed and comprehension.

- **Science:** Identify the areas of science covered on the test, the types of questions you will encounter, and test-taking strategies and skills for extracting information from passages and using it to reason your way to the correct answers.

- **Writing:** Check out a sample writing prompt, find out what the people scoring your essay will be looking for, read sample scored essays from poor to excellent, and pick up a few strategies that may help to raise your writing score.

Chapter 5:
Improving Your English Score

On the ACT English test, you have 45 minutes to read five passages, or essays, and answer 75 multiple-choice questions about them—an average of 15 questions per essay. The essays on the English test cover a variety of subjects; the sample passages that follow this discussion range from a personal essay about the different ways of figuring one's age to an informative essay about the legal history of school dress codes.

Content of the ACT English Test

The ACT English test is designed to measure your ability to make the wide variety of decisions involved in revising and editing a given piece of writing. The test measures your understanding of the Conventions of Standard English (punctuation, usage, and sentence structure); Production of Writing (topic development, organization, unity, and cohesion); and Knowledge of Language (word choice, style, and tone). Although you may use more informal or conversational language in your own writing, the test emphasizes the standard written English that is taught in schools around the country.

Different passage types are used to provide a variety of rhetorical situations. Passages are chosen not only for their appropriateness in assessing writing skills but also to reflect students' interests and experiences.

Questions on the English test fall into three categories:

- **Production of Writing** (topic development, organization, unity, and cohesion)

- **Knowledge of Language** (precision and concision in word choice, consistency in style and tone)

- **Conventions of Standard English** (sentence structure and formation, punctuation, and usage)

You will receive four scores for the ACT English test: a total test score based on all 75 questions and three reporting category scores based on specific knowledge and skills in the categories previously described. If you choose to take the writing test, you will also receive an English Language Arts (ELA) score based on an average of your English, reading, and writing test scores.

You will **not** be tested on spelling, vocabulary, or rote recall of the rules of grammar. Grammar and usage are tested only within the context of the essay, not by questions such as "Must an appositive always be set off by commas?" Likewise, you won't be tested directly on your vocabulary, although the better your vocabulary is, the better equipped you'll be to comprehend the reading passages and answer questions that involve choosing the most appropriate word.

The English test doesn't require you to memorize what you read. The questions and essays are side-by-side for easy reference. This is **not** a memorization test.

The questions discussed on the following pages are taken from the sample passages and questions that follow on pages 217–223. If you prefer, you can work through the sample passages and questions before you read the rest of this discussion. However, to better understand the English test, you may want to first read the discussion, then work through the sample passages and questions.

Types of Questions on the ACT English Test

Many questions refer to an underlined portion of the essay. (As noted in Chapter 1, items taken online will be marked by highlighting instead of underlining. In the examples that follow, which show items as they would appear on paper, we'll stick to underlining.) You must decide on the best alternative for that underlined portion. Usually, your options include NO CHANGE, which means that the essay is best as it's written. Sometimes, you'll also have the option of deleting the underlined portion. For example, the following question (from Sample Passage II on pages 219–221) offers you the option of removing the word *to* from the sentence.

Otherwise, this difference points
₂₁
to significant underlying cultural values.
₂₂

22. **F.** NO CHANGE
    G. on
    H. at
    J. DELETE the underlined portion.

In this example, the best answer is not to delete the underlined portion but to leave it as it is (**F**).

Other questions on the English test may ask about a section of the essay or an aspect of the essay as a whole. For example, in the following question (from Sample Passage I on pages 217–219), you're given a sentence to be added to the essay, and then you're asked to decide the most logical place in the essay to add that sentence.

---

15. The writer wants to add the following accurate sentence to the essay:

> Those same German influences helped spawn a similar musical form in northern Mexico known as *norteño*.

The sentence would most logically be placed at:

A. Point A in Paragraph 1.
B. Point B in Paragraph 2.
C. Point C in Paragraph 3.
D. Point D in Paragraph 4.

In this example, the best answer is **C**, because Paragraph 3 focuses on the European musical influences on the O'odham people of Arizona, and the last sentence of the paragraph specifically refers to the musical influences of German immigrants.

Let's look at some additional examples of the kinds of questions you're likely to find on the ACT English test. If you want to know what an individual question looks like in the context of the passage in which it appears, turn to the pages indicated. You can also use those sample passages and questions for practice, either before or after reading this discussion.

Conventions of Standard English

Conventions of Standard English questions focus on the conventions of punctuation, grammar and usage, and sentence structure and formation.

Punctuation questions involve identifying and correcting the following misplaced, missing, or unnecessary punctuation marks:

- Commas
- Apostrophes
- Colons, semicolons, and dashes
- Periods, question marks, and exclamation points

These questions address not only the rules of punctuation but also the use of punctuation to express ideas clearly. For example, you should be prepared to show how punctuation can be used to indicate possession or to set off a parenthetical element.

In many punctuation questions, the words in every choice will be identical, but the commas or other punctuation marks will vary. It's important to read the choices carefully in order to notice the presence or absence of commas, semicolons, colons, periods, and other punctuation. The following example of a punctuation question comes from Sample Passage I on pages 217–219.

Around this time the polka music and button

accordion played by German immigrant rail-

road <u>workers; left</u> their mark on waila.
      14

14. F. NO CHANGE
    G. workers
    H. workers:
    J. workers,

It may help you to read through this sentence without paying attention to the punctuation so you can identify its grammatical construction. The subject of this sentence is "the polka music and button accordion." What follows that subject might seem like the predicate verb of the sentence, but it's not. The phrase "played by German immigrant railroad workers" is a participial phrase (a phrase formed with the past participle "played"). This participial phrase functions as an adjective because it modifies the nouns it follows ("the polka music and button accordion").

After the participial phrase is the predicate verb of the main clause, "left." Then comes a phrase that explains what was left (the direct object "their mark") and a prepositional phrase that explains where it was left ("on waila").

Now we can deal with the question about what kind of punctuation should follow that participial phrase. Sometimes, these phrases are set off from the main clause with commas to indicate that the phrase is parenthetical or provides information not essential to the meaning of the sentence. That's not the case here for two reasons. First, there's no comma at the beginning of the participial phrase. Second, the phrase is essential to the sentence; the sentence is not referring to just any polka music and button accordion but to the music and accordion played by those German immigrant railroad workers (presumably, not while they were working on the railroad).

Ignoring the participial phrase for a minute, we need to ask ourselves what kind of punctuation we would usually place between the subject "the polka music and button accordion" and the verb "left." Our answer should be no punctuation at all, making **G** the best answer. Of course, you could answer this question without this rather tedious analysis of the parts of the sentence. You might simply decide that because the sentence contains no other punctuation, you would never insert a single punctuation mark between the subject and the predicate of the main clause. Or you might just plug in each of the four punctuation choices—semicolon, no punctuation, colon, comma—and choose the one that looks or sounds best to you.

Grammar and usage questions involve choosing the best word or words in a sentence based on grammar and usage conventions. Some examples of poor and better phrases are given in the following.

- Grammatical agreement

  (Subject and verb)

  "The owner of the bicycles *are* going to sell them."
  should be:
  "The owner of the bicycles *is* going to sell them."

  * * *

  (Pronoun and antecedent)

  "Susan and Mary left *her* briefcases in the office."
  should be:
  "Susan and Mary left *their* briefcases in the office."

  * * *

- Pronoun forms and cases

  "Seymour and Svetlana annoyed *there* parents all the time."
  should be:
  "Seymour and Svetlana annoyed *their* parents all the time."

  * * *

- Idioms

  "The definition of a word can be looked *down* in the dictionary."
  should be:
  "The definition of a word can be looked *up* in the dictionary."

Questions dealing with pronouns often have to do with using the proper form and case of the pronoun. Sometimes they address a pronoun's agreement with its antecedent, or referent. In such cases, consider the entire sentence, and sometimes the preceding sentence, to make sure you know what the antecedent is. Consider the following question (from Sample Passage I on pages 217–219).

As the dancers step to
the music, they <u>were also stepping</u> in time to a
8
sound that embodies <u>their</u> unique history and
9
suggests the influence of outside cultures on
their music.

9. **A.** NO CHANGE
    B. they're
    C. it's
    D. its'

Here, the possessive pronoun in question refers back to the subject of the main clause ("they"), which in turn refers back to the subject of the introductory subordinate clause ("the dancers"). Thus, the best answer is the third-person plural possessive pronoun ("their," **A**). Choice **B** might seem like a possibility because *they're* sounds like *their* (that is, they're homonyms). However, *they're* is a contraction for *they are*. We can rule out **C** and **D** because of the pronoun-antecedent agreement problem and also because *it's* is not a possessive pronoun but a contraction for *it is,* and *its'* is not even a word.

Sentence structure questions involve the effective formation of sentences, including dealing with relationships between and among clauses, placement of modifiers, and shifts in construction. Following are some examples:

- Subordinate or dependent clauses and participial phrases

  "These hamsters are excellent pets *because providing* hours of cheap entertainment."

  This sentence could be rewritten as:

  "These hamsters are excellent pets, providing hours of cheap entertainment." (participial phrase)

  It could also be revised as:

  "These hamsters are excellent pets because they provide hours of cheap entertainment." (subordinate/dependent clause)

- Run-on or fused sentences

  "We discovered that all of our friends had already seen the *movie they* thought it was terrible.

  This sentence should actually be two:

  "We discovered that all of our friends had already seen the *movie. They* thought it was terrible.

- Comma splices

    "The anteaters had terrible *manners, they* just ate and ran."

    This sentence could be rewritten as:

    "The anteaters had terrible *manners. They* just ate and ran."

    Because a semicolon can serve as a "soft" period, the sentence could also be rewritten as:

    "The anteaters had terrible *manners; they* just ate and ran."

- Sentence fragments

    "*When he* burned his lunch."

    This needs a subject to let us know who "he" is and what he did:

    "*Julio didn't lose his temper when he* burned his lunch."

- Misplaced modifiers

    "*Snarling and snapping, Juanita* attempted to control her pet turtle."

    Unless Juanita was doing the snarling and snapping, the sentence should be rewritten:

    "*Snarling and snapping, the pet turtle* resisted Juanita's attempt to control it." It could also be rewritten this way:

    "Juanita attempted to control her *pet turtle, which snarled and snapped.*"

- Shifts in pronoun person or number

    "Hamsters should work at the most efficient pace that *one* can."

    This should be rewritten as:

    "Hamsters should work at the most efficient pace that *they* can."

Many questions about sentence structure and formation will ask you about how clauses and phrases are linked. This means that you may have to consider punctuation or the lack of punctuation, which can create problems such as comma splices, run-on sentences, or sentence fragments. You also may have to consider various words that can be used to link clauses and phrases: conjunctions such as *and, but, because,* and *when,* and pronouns such as *who, whose, which,* and *that.* The following question (from Sample Passage I on pages 217–219) is a good example of a sentence structure question.

It is a social

music that performed at weddings, birthday
————————————
4

parties, and feasts.

4.　F.　NO CHANGE
　　 G.　music in which it is performed
　　 H.　music, performing
　　 J.　music, performed

What would be the best way to link the clause "It is a social music" and the phrase "performed [or performing] at weddings, birthday parties, and feasts"? Relative pronouns such as *that* and *which* stand in for the noun that the relative clause modifies. (They relate the clause to the noun.) One way to try out choices such as **F** and **G** is to replace the relative pronoun with the noun and then decide if the resulting statement makes sense:

> Social music performed at weddings, birthday parties, and feasts. (**F**)

This does not make sense. Musicians perform, but the music itself does not. Music *is* performed.

> In social music it is performed at weddings, birthday parties, and feasts. (**G**)

This also seems nonsensical. What does *it* refer to—social music?

The other two choices offer a different approach to connecting information in a sentence. The phrases "performing at weddings, birthday parties, and feasts" (**H**) and "performed at weddings, birthday parties, and feasts" (**J**) are participial phrases. Similar to adjective clauses, these phrases modify a noun. We can rule out **H** for the same reason that we rejected **F**: it doesn't make sense to think of "social music" as "performing." However, it sounds fine to refer to "social music" as "performed" (**J**).

Production of Writing

Production of Writing questions focus on writing strategy and organization.

Topic development questions focus on the choices made and strategies used by a writer in the act of composing or revising an essay. These questions may ask you to make decisions concerning the appropriateness of a sentence or essay in relation to purpose, audience, unity, or focus, or the effect of adding, revising, or deleting supporting material.

The following question (from Sample Passage I on pages 217–219) is a fairly typical example of the kinds of writing decisions that strategy questions ask you to make.

In the early 1900s the O'odham became acquainted with marching bands and wood-wind instruments (which explains the presence of saxophones in waila).
₁₃

13. Given that all of the choices are accurate, which one provides the most relevant information at this point in the essay?
   A. NO CHANGE
   B. (although fiddles were once widely used in waila bands).
   C. (even though they're now often constructed of metal).
   D. (which are frequently found in jazz bands also).

It's important to read these questions carefully and, sometimes, to reread the essay or parts of the essay. This question is fairly clear-cut, but it does suggest that you need a pretty good sense of what Paragraph 3 is about. A quick review of the paragraph indicates that it is focused on how the O'odham and their music were influenced by other musical styles and instrumentation they encountered.

Which of these parenthetical statements is most relevant to that focus? Choice **D**, which states that woodwind instruments are frequently found in jazz bands, is not. Likewise, choice **C**, which indicates that woodwind instruments are now often constructed of metal, strays from the paragraph's topic. Choice **B**, which points out that fiddles were once widely used in waila bands, is getting closer, but this too seems a diversion, unconnected to the other information in this paragraph. Guitars, woodwinds, and button accordions are mentioned but not fiddles or violins.

Choice **A**, however, provides an appropriate and relevant elaboration. It draws the connection between the O'odhams' introduction to marching bands and woodwinds in the early 1900s and the eventual inclusion of saxophones in a typical waila band.

Organization questions deal with the order and coherence of ideas in an essay and the effective choice of opening, transitional, and closing statements. For example, you may be asked about the organization of ideas (the most logical order for sentences within a paragraph or paragraphs within an essay) or about the most logical transitional phrase or statement.

The following question (from Sample Passage II on pages 219–221) is a good example of the kind of organization question you might encounter.

Today, after many birthdays and
New Year's Days, I now find meaningful the
difference I once found confusing. Otherwise,
                                    21
this difference points to significant underlying
                                    22
cultural values.

21. **A.** NO CHANGE
    B. Though,
    C. In fact,
    D. Then,

The choices in this question are sometimes referred to as conjunctive adverbs or transitional words or phrases because their main job is to connect or link the statement in one sentence with the statement in a preceding sentence. These are often little words—*so, thus, soon, yet, also*—that do a lot of work to make an essay logical.

In order to answer such questions correctly, it helps to think about the logical relationship between the sentences, as well as the logical relationships expressed by the choices. The main statement of the opening sentence of this paragraph is "I now find meaningful the difference [in computing one's age] I once found confusing." The second sentence states, "This difference points to significant underlying cultural values." The writer then goes on to explain those cultural values.

Which of these four choices enables readers to move most easily from the opening sentence into the rest of this paragraph? Choice **A** suggests that the second statement contrasts with the first statement. A typical dictionary definition for *otherwise* is "in different circumstances." Similarly, choice **B**, *though,* suggests that the statement to follow is contrary to or in opposition to the preceding statement. Neither of those adverbs works well here. Nor does *then* (choice **D**), which usually expresses a time relationship—meaning "next" or "soon after in time."

The best choice here is **C**. The phrase *in fact* is often used to introduce a statement that builds on the preceding statement. We can pare down these opening sentences to their bare essentials to show that the phrase works well here: "I now find the difference in computing one's age meaningful. In fact, the difference points to important cultural values about life experience and longevity."

Knowledge of Language

These questions involve effective word choices in terms of writing style, tone, clarity, and economy. Sometimes, a phrase or sentence that isn't technically ungrammatical is nevertheless confusing because it's poorly written. Sometimes, a word or phrase clashes with the tone of the essay. Good writing also involves eliminating excessively wordy or redundant material and vague or awkward expressions.

Similar to most writing strategy and organization questions, style questions require a general understanding of the essay as a whole. The following style question (from Sample Passage III on pages 221–223) focuses on the issues of economy and consistency of tone.

> The school board members believed that wearing "play clothes" to school made the students <u>inefficient toward</u> their [32] school work, while more formal attire estab-lished a positive educational climate.
>
> 32. **F.** NO CHANGE
>   **G.** lazy and bored to tears with
>   **H.** blow off
>   **J.** lax and indifferent toward

You will be better able to recognize the appropriateness of choice **J** if you know that *lax* means "lacking necessary strictness, severity, or precision" and *indifferent* means "lacking interest, enthusiasm, or concern." These terms touch on two related but distinct concerns—academic laziness and apathy. One could imagine school board members using these very words in their meetings. And the words are consistent with the overall style and tone of this straightforward, informative essay about a legal case.

Choices **G** and **H** are fairly easy to rule out if you think about the generally formal tone of the essay. It's not that one should never use slang phrases such as "bored to tears" or "blow off" in one's writing; it's just that this particular essay is not the place to use them. When we consider that this statement is describing the school board members' belief, these phrases are even more inappropriate.

It seems more in character for school board members to be concerned about student inefficiency, but **F** is a weak choice because the phrase "inefficient toward their school work" sounds odd or awkward. Perhaps it's the preposition that trips us up. The word *toward* works fine in **J** when describing attitudes ("lax," "indifferent") toward school work, but the word *inefficient* is describing an ability or skill.

* * *

The questions provided here are a small sample of the kinds of questions that might be on the test. The previous question, for example, is only one kind of style question; it doesn't cover all the elements of style that might be addressed on the test. The sample passages and questions at the end of this section have all the examples referred to in this chapter as they would appear in a test. These sample passages and questions and the later practice tests will provide you with a thorough understanding of the ACT English test.

Strategies for Taking the ACT English Test

Pace Yourself

The ACT English test contains 75 questions to be completed in 45 minutes, which works out to exactly 36 seconds per question. Spending $1\frac{1}{2}$ minutes skimming through each essay leaves you about 30 seconds to respond to each question. If you spend less time than that on each question, you can use the remaining time allowed for this test to review your work and to return to the questions that were most difficult for you. Another way to think of it is that you have 45 minutes to read and answer the questions for five essays, giving you a maximum of 9 minutes for each essay and its questions.

Be Aware of the Writing Style Used in the Essay

The five essays cover a variety of topics and are written in a variety of styles. It's important that you take into account the writing style used in each essay as you respond to the questions.

Some of the essays will be anecdotes or narratives written from an informal, first-person point of view. Others will be more formal essays, scholarly or informative in nature, often written in the third person. Some questions will ask you to choose the best answer based not on its grammatical correctness but on its consistency with the style and tone of the essay as a whole. For example, an expression that's too breezy for an essay on the life of President Herbert Hoover might be just right for a personal narrative about a writer's attempt at learning to skateboard.

Consider a Question's Context before Choosing an Answer

Some people find it helpful to skim an essay before trying to answer the associated questions. Having a general sense of the essay in mind before you begin to answer questions involving writing strategy or style can help. If you encounter questions about the order of sentences within a paragraph, or the order of paragraphs within an essay, or where to add a sentence in an essay, you may want to answer those questions first to make sure that the major elements of the essay are arranged logically. Understanding the order of the passage may make it easier for you to answer some of the other questions.

As you're answering each question, be sure to read at least a sentence or two beyond the sentence containing the portion being questioned. You may need to read even more than that to understand what the writer is trying to say.

Be Aware of the Connotations of Words

Vocabulary isn't tested in an isolated way on the ACT English test. Nevertheless, a good vocabulary and an awareness of not only the dictionary definitions of words but also the connotations (feelings and associations) suggested by those words will help you do well on the test.

The following question (from Sample Passage II on pages 219–221) asks you to think about how certain words and their connotations can function in terms of the rest of the essay.

Many people might be surprised to learn that the American way of computing a person's age differs from the traditional Korean way. In Korean tradition, a person is considered to be already one year old at the time of his or her birth.

As a child growing up in two cultures, I found this <u>contest</u> a bit confusing.
16

16. **F.** NO CHANGE
G. change
H. dispute
J. difference

Which word best captures or summarizes what has been described in the preceding paragraph? The word *contest* (**F**) doesn't seem right because it suggests a competition between opposing sides or teams. In a similar vein, the word *dispute* (**H**) doesn't fit here because it generally refers to a verbal debate or argument. The word *change* (**G**) is a little off because it expresses the idea of transformation, making something or someone different, which doesn't accurately summarize that opening paragraph. The word *difference* (**J**), however, seems just right. It echoes the verb in the first sentence of the preceding paragraph, but more importantly, it accurately reflects the writer's perspective up to this point in the essay that the American way and the Korean way of computing a person's age are not competing or arguing with each other. They are simply unlike each other (and because of that mismatch, a bit confusing).

In questions such as this one, you have to focus on what the words mean and what associations the words have for the typical reader.

Look for a Stated Question

Before responding to a question identified by an underlined portion, check for a stated question preceding the options. If there is one, it will provide you with some guidelines for deciding on the best choice. Some questions will ask you to choose the alternative to the underlined portion that is NOT or LEAST acceptable. Here's an example from Sample Passage I on pages 217–219.

The music is

mainly instrumental—the bands generally con-
                          3
sist of guitar, bass guitar, saxophones, accor-

dion, and drums.

3. Which of the following alternatives to the underlined portion would NOT be acceptable?

   A. instrumental; in general, the bands
   B. instrumental, the bands generally
   C. instrumental. The bands generally
   D. instrumental; the bands generally

For these types of questions, look closely at the underlined portion, because the question has told you that it *is* acceptable. Likewise, three of the alternative choices are acceptable. The best answer, in this case, is the one that is *not* acceptable. In the underlined portion, a dash is used between two independent clauses: "The music is mainly instrumental" and "the bands generally consist of guitar, bass guitar, saxophones, accordion, and drums." The dash is sometimes thought of as a less formal type of punctuation, but it can work quite well to provide emphasis or to signal that an explanation will follow.

Placing a period (**C**) or a semicolon (**D**) between these two independent clauses would also be acceptable. Likewise, choice **A** is acceptable because it too places a semicolon between the two clauses, using the phrase "in general" rather than the adverb "generally." Choice **B** is not acceptable and is, therefore, the best answer. A comma is not usually a strong enough punctuation mark between two independent clauses not joined by a conjunction. Notice that this sentence has other commas, used to distinguish nouns in a series. How would a reader know that the comma between the clauses is a much stronger break than those other commas?

Whether a stated question is presented or not, you should carefully examine what is underlined in the essay. Consider the features of writing that are included in the underlined portion. The options for each question will contain changes in one or more aspects of writing.

Note the Differences in the Answer Choices

Many of the questions that refer to underlined portions will involve more than one aspect of writing. Examine each choice and note how it differs from the others. Consider all the features of writing that are included in each option.

Avoid Making New Mistakes

Beware of correcting mistakes in the essay and, in your haste, picking a response that creates a new mistake. Be observant, especially in questions where the responses have similar wording. One comma or apostrophe can make all the difference, as the following question (from Sample Passage III on pages 221–223) illustrates.

His challenge

initiated a <u>review, of students' rights</u> and admin-
                          43

istrative responsibility <u>in public education.</u>
                                44

43. **A.** NO CHANGE
    B. review, of students' rights,
    C. review of students' rights
    D. review of students' rights,

Perhaps you took only a moment to reject choice **A** because of the unnecessary comma between the noun *review* and the prepositional phrase "of students' rights." And if you were able to make that call, you may have ruled out choice **B** for the same reason. It is probably more difficult to recognize that the comma between the noun *rights* and the conjunction *and* (**D**) is unnecessary and misleading. Because you were thinking about how the underlined portion should be punctuated, you may also have wondered about the plural apostrophe in the word *students'* but then realize that the apostrophe is in the same place in all four choices. (The best answer is **C**.)

Determine the Best Answer

There are at least two approaches you can take to determine the best answer to a question about an underlined portion. One approach is to reread the sentence or sentences containing this portion, substitute each of the answer choices in turn, and decide which is best. Another approach is to decide how the underlined portion might best be phrased and then look for your phrasing among the choices offered. If the underlined portion is correct as it is, select the NO CHANGE option.

If you can't decide which option is best, you may want to mark the question in your test booklet so you can return to it later. Remember: you're not penalized for guessing, so after you've eliminated as many options as you can, take your best guess.

Reread the Sentence Using Your Selected Answer

After you have selected the answer you feel is best, reread the corresponding sentence or sentences in the essay, substituting the answer you've selected for the underlined portion or for the boxed numeral. Sometimes an answer that sounds fine out of context doesn't fit within the sentence or essay. Be sure to keep in mind both the punctuation marks and words in each possible response; sometimes just the omission of a comma can make an important difference.

Watch for Questions about the Entire Essay or a Section of the Essay

Some questions ask about a section of the essay. They are identified by a question number in a box at the appropriate point in the essay, rather than by an underlined portion. (If you're taking the test online, you will see highlighted asterisks in brackets instead of numbers in boxes.) Here's an example from Sample Passage II on pages 219–221.

Perhaps the celebration of New
Year's Day in Korean culture is <u>heightened</u>
                                              19
because it is thought of as everyone's birthday
party. [20]

20. If the writer were to delete the preceding sentence, the paragraph would primarily lose:

F. a comment on the added significance of the Korean New Year celebration.
G. a repetitive reminder of what happens every birthday.
H. a defense of the case for celebrating every birthday.
J. an illustration of the Korean counting system.

This question asks you to think about the role this sentence plays in terms of the paragraph as a whole. If the sentence were deleted, the paragraph would lose the elaboration on the point that Korean tradition indicates that everyone becomes a year older on New Year's Day, regardless of when they were actually born. Without the sentence, the point about the "added significance of the Korean New Year celebration" (**F**) would have been unstated.

Some other questions ask about an aspect of the essay as a whole. If you are taking the test on paper, these questions are placed at the end of the essay, following boxed instructions like these:

Question 15 asks about the
preceding passage as a whole.

If you are testing online, similar instructions will appear above the individual items at the end of the item set. You may want to read any questions that ask about the essay as a whole first so you can keep them in mind while you're reading through the essay. For questions about a section of the essay or the essay as a whole, you must decide the best answer on the basis of the particular writing or revision problem presented in the question.

Be Careful with Two-Part Questions

Some questions require extra thought because you must decide not only which option is best but also which supporting reason for an option is most appropriate or convincing. The following question occurs at the end of Sample Passage III on pages 221–223. Each option begins with either a yes or no response, followed by a supporting reason for that response.

> Question 45 asks about the preceding passage as a whole.

45. Suppose the writer's primary purpose had been to write a persuasive essay urging students to exercise their constitutional rights. Would this essay accomplish that purpose?

    A. Yes, because the essay focuses on how Kevin encouraged other students to exercise their constitutional rights.

    B. Yes, because the essay focuses on various types of clothing historically worn by students as a freedom of expression.

    C. No, because the essay suggests that the right to wear blue jeans was not a substantial constitutional right in the 1970s.

    D. No, because the essay objectively reports on one case of a student exercising a particular constitutional right.

Once you decide whether the essay would or would not fulfill the writer's goal, as described in the question, you need to decide which reason or explanation provides the most appropriate support for the answer and is most accurate in terms of the essay. Sometimes, the supporting reason does not accurately reflect the essay (the explanations in **B** and **C**, for example). Sometimes, the reason accurately reflects the essay but doesn't logically support the answer to the question. And sometimes, the reason might logically support the question (that is, the writer's goal) but that reason overstates the focus of the essay. It may be fair to say that Kevin Bannister's case led to a review of student rights, but this essay does not at any point describe Kevin encouraging other students to exercise their rights, as **A** states. The best answer is **D**; this essay is more an objective reporting on a legal case about student rights (and that case's historical significance) than it is a persuasive argument or call to students to exercise those rights.

Watch for Interrelated Questions

As pointed out previously, you'll sometimes find that the best way to answer questions about a passage is not necessarily in their numbered order. Occasionally, answering a question after you've answered the one that follows it is easier. Or you might find two questions about different elements of the same sentence, in which case considering them both together may be helpful.

In the following example (from Sample Passage III on pages 221–223), considering questions 40 and 41 together may be helpful, because they're contained in the same sentence. First, answer the question that seems easier to you. Once you've solved that problem in the sentence, turn to the other question.

The court remained unconvinced, <u>therefore,</u> that
₄₀

40. F. NO CHANGE
    G. thus,
    H. moreover,
    J. however,

<u>when wearing</u> jeans would actually impair the
₄₁
learning process of Kevin or of his fellow class-

mates.

41. A. NO CHANGE
    B. by wearing
    C. wearing
    D. having worn

Questions 40 and 41 deal with different kinds of writing problems. Question 40 is about choosing the most logical transitional word, and question 41 is about the correct use in this sentence of the gerund (a verb form with an -*ing* ending that's used as a noun). You might find that answering question 41 helps you to figure out the answer to question 40. The best answer to question 41 is C—the noun phrase "wearing jeans" works as the subject of the dependent clause "that wearing jeans would actually impair the learning process of Kevin or of his fellow classmates." Try penciling in your answer choice for 41 (that is, edit the essay) so that you can more easily read the sentence while responding to question 40. Does this approach make it easier for you to decide that the most logical answer to question 40 is J ("however")?

* * *

Remember that this section is only an overview of the English test. Directly or indirectly, a question may test you in more than one of the areas mentioned, so do not become overly concerned with categorizing a question before you answer it. And, although awareness of the types of questions can help you be a more critical and strategic test-taker, just remember: the type of question you're answering isn't important. Most importantly, focus on what the question asks and do your best to pick the best answer based on evidence provided in the passage.

SAMPLE PASSAGE I

The Music of the O'odham

[1]

For some people, traditional American Indian music is associated and connected with high penetrating vocals accompanied by a steady drumbeat. In tribal communities in the southwestern United States, however, one is likely to hear something similar to the polka-influenced dance music of northern Mexico. The music is called "waila." Among the O'odham tribes of Arizona, waila has been popular for more than a century. The music is mainly

instrumental—the bands generally consist of guitar, bass guitar, saxophones, accordion, and drums. [A]

[2]

Unlike some traditional tribal music, waila does not serve a religious or spiritual purpose. It is a social music that performed at weddings, birthday parties,

and feasts. The word itself comes from the Spanish

word for dance, *baile*. Check to cheek, the dance is performed to the relaxed two-step tempo, and the bands

often play long past midnight. As the dancers step to the

music, they were also stepping in time to a sound that

1. A. NO CHANGE
   B. connected by some of them
   C. linked by association
   D. associated

2. F. NO CHANGE
   G. popular, one might say, for
   H. really quite popular for
   J. popular for the duration of

3. Which of the following alternatives to the underlined portion would NOT be acceptable?
   A. instrumental; in general, the bands
   B. instrumental, the bands generally
   C. instrumental. The bands generally
   D. instrumental; the bands generally

4. F. NO CHANGE
   G. music in which it is performed
   H. music, performing
   J. music, performed

5. A. NO CHANGE
   B. word, itself,
   C. word, itself
   D. word itself.

6. F. NO CHANGE
   G. Couples dance cheek to cheek to the relaxed two-step tempo,
   H. A relaxed two-step tempo, the couples dance cheek to cheek,
   J. Cheek to cheek, the two-step tempo relaxes dancing couples,

7. A. NO CHANGE
   B. play long, past,
   C. play, long past,
   D. play, long past

8. F. NO CHANGE
   G. are also stepping
   H. have also stepped
   J. will also step

embodies <u>their</u> unique history and suggests the influence
₉

of outside cultures on their music. ⊡10 [B]

[3]

The O'odham <u>in the 1700s</u> first encountered the
₁₁

guitars of Spanish missionaries. In the 1850s the O'odham

<u>have borrowed</u> from the waltzes and mazurkas of
₁₂

people of European descent on their way to California.

In the early 1900s the O'odham became acquainted

with marching bands and woodwind instruments

<u>(which explains the presence of saxophones in waila).</u>
₁₃

Around this time the polka music and button accordion

played by German immigrant railroad <u>workers;</u> left their
₁₄

mark on waila. [C]

---

9. **A.** NO CHANGE
   B. they're
   C. it's
   D. its'

10. At this point, the writer is considering adding the following true statement:

    > The agricultural practices of the O'odham are similar to those of the Maya.

    Should the writer make this addition here?

    F. Yes, because the sentence establishes that the O'odham often borrowed ideas from other groups.
    G. Yes, because the sentence provides important information about the O'odham people.
    H. No, because the sentence is not supported by evidence of a connection between the O'odham and the Maya.
    J. No, because the sentence distracts from the paragraph's focus on waila's uses and influences.

11. All of the following would be acceptable placements for the underlined portion EXCEPT:

    A. where it is now.
    B. at the beginning of the sentence (revising the capitalization accordingly).
    C. after the word *guitars*.
    D. after the word *missionaries* (ending the sentence with a period).

12. **F.** NO CHANGE
    G. have been borrowing
    H. were borrowed
    J. borrowed

13. Given that all of the choices are accurate, which one provides the most relevant information at this point in the essay?

    A. NO CHANGE
    B. (although fiddles were once widely used in waila bands).
    C. (even though they're now often constructed of metal).
    D. (which are frequently found in jazz bands also).

14. **F.** NO CHANGE
    G. workers
    H. workers:
    J. workers,

[4]

It should be no surprise that musicians these days are adding touches of rock, country, and reggae to waila. Some listeners fear that an American musical form may soon be lost. But the O'odham are playing waila with as much energy and devotion as ever. A unique blend of traditions, waila will probably continue changing for as long as the O'odham use it to express their own sense of harmony and tempo. [D]

> Question 15 asks about the preceding passage as a whole.

15. The writer wants to add the following accurate sentence to the essay:

> Those same German influences helped spawn a similar musical form in northern Mexico known as *norteño*.

This sentence would most logically be placed at:

A. Point A in Paragraph 1.
B. Point B in Paragraph 2.
C. Point C in Paragraph 3.
D. Point D in Paragraph 4.

SAMPLE PASSAGE II

How Old Am I?

Many people might be surprised to learn that the American way of computing a person's age differs from the traditional Korean way. In Korean tradition, a person is considered to be already one year old at the time of his or her birth.

As a child growing up in two cultures, I found this <u>contest</u> a bit confusing. When I was in the fifth grade, was I ten or eleven years old? To add to the confusion, every New Year's Day a <u>person according</u> to this Korean counting system, becomes a year older, regardless of his or her actual birthday. <u>Birthdays are important throughout the world.</u> A person who is sixteen years old on his or her birthday in March would become seventeen years old on the following New Year's Day, even though he or she isn't expected to turn seventeen (in "American" years) until that next birthday in March. Perhaps the celebration of New Year's Day in Korean culture is <u>heightened</u> because it is thought of as

16. F. NO CHANGE
    G. change
    H. dispute
    J. difference

17. A. NO CHANGE
    B. person,
    C. person;
    D. person who,

18. F. NO CHANGE
    G. Most cultures celebrate birthdays.
    H. Birthdays focus attention on a culture's youth.
    J. DELETE the underlined portion.

19. A. NO CHANGE
    B. raised
    C. lifted
    D. lighted

everyone's birthday party. ☐20

Today, after many birthdays and New Year's Days, I now find meaningful the difference I once found confusing. <u>Otherwise,</u> this difference points
21

<u>to</u> significant underlying cultural values. The practice of
22

advancing a <u>person's age</u> seems to me to reflect the value a
23

society places on life experience and longevity. <u>Their</u> idea
24

was demonstrated often <u>when</u> my elderly relatives, who
25
took pride in reminding younger folk of their "Korean

age." <u>With great enthusiasm,</u> they added on a year every
26
New Year's Day. By contrast American society has often

been described as one <u>that</u> values the vibrant energy of
27

youth over the wisdom and experience gained with age. ☐28

After a certain age, many Americans I know would

<u>balk, refuse, and hesitate</u> at the idea of adding a year or
29
two to what they regard as their actual age.

20. If the writer were to delete the preceding sentence, the paragraph would primarily lose:
   F. a comment on the added significance of the Korean New Year celebration.
   G. a repetitive reminder of what happens every birthday.
   H. a defense of the case for celebrating every birthday.
   J. an illustration of the Korean counting system.

21. A. NO CHANGE
   B. Though,
   C. In fact,
   D. Then,

22. F. NO CHANGE
   G. on
   H. at
   J. DELETE the underlined portion.

23. A. NO CHANGE
   B. persons' age
   C. persons age
   D. person's age,

24. F. NO CHANGE
   G. One's
   H. Its
   J. This

25. A. NO CHANGE
   B. by
   C. while
   D. as if

26. Which choice would most clearly communicate the elderly relatives' positive attitude toward this practice?
   F. NO CHANGE
   G. Duplicating an accepted practice,
   H. Living with two birthdays themselves,
   J. Obligingly,

27. A. NO CHANGE
   B. whose
   C. this
   D. whom

28. If the writer were to delete the phrases "the vibrant energy of" and "the wisdom and experience gained with" from the preceding sentence, the sentence would primarily lose:
   F. its personal and reflective tone.
   G. an element of humor.
   H. details that illustrate the contrast.
   J. the preference expressed by the writer.

29. A. NO CHANGE
   B. balk and hesitate
   C. refuse and balk
   D. balk

Even something as <u>visibly</u> simple or natural as
₃₀
computing a person's age can prove to be not so clear-cut.
Traditions like celebrating birthdays reveal how deeply we
are affected by the culture we live in.

30. **F.** NO CHANGE
   G. apparently
   H. entirely
   J. fully

SAMPLE PASSAGE III

Wearing Jeans in School

In 1970, the school board in Pittsfield,
New Hampshire, approved a dress code that
prohibited students from wearing certain types
of <u>clothing.</u> The school board members believed that
₃₁
wearing "play clothes" to school made the students

<u>inefficient toward</u> their school work, while more formal
₃₂
attire established a positive educational climate. When
twelve-year-old Kevin Bannister wore a pair of blue jeans
to school, he was sent home for violating the dress code.

<u>Kevin and his parents believed that his constitutional</u>
₃₃
<u>rights had been violated.</u> The United States District
₃₃

<u>Court of New Hampshire;</u> agreed to hear Kevin's case.
₃₄
His claim was based on the notion of personal liberty—the
right of every individual to the control of his or her own

31. Given that all the choices are accurate, which one would best illustrate the term *dress code* as it is used in this sentence?

   A. NO CHANGE
   B. clothing that was inappropriate.
   C. clothing, including sandals, bell-bottom pants, and "dungarees" (blue jeans).
   D. clothing that is permitted in some schools today.

32. **F.** NO CHANGE
   G. lazy and bored to tears with
   H. blow off
   J. lax and indifferent toward

33. Given that all the choices are accurate, which one would most effectively introduce the main idea of this paragraph?

   A. NO CHANGE
   B. The principal said dungarees and blue jeans were the same thing, so Kevin should have known better.
   C. If Kevin's jeans had been dirty and torn, the principal might have been justified in expelling him.
   D. These events occurred in a time of social unrest, and emotions were running high.

34. **F.** NO CHANGE
   G. Court, of New Hampshire
   H. Court of New Hampshire
   J. Court of New Hampshire,

person—protected by the Constitution's Fourteenth
Amendment. The court agreed with Kevin that a person's
right <u>for wearing</u> clothing of his or her own choosing is,
in fact, protected by the Fourteenth Amendment.

The <u>court noted, however</u> that restrictions may be justified
in some circumstances, such as in the school setting.

So did Kevin have a right to wear blue jeans to
school? The court determined that the school board had
failed to show that wearing jeans actually inhibited the
educational <u>process, which is guided by authority figures.</u>

Furthermore, the board offered no evidence to back up <u>it's</u>

claim <u>that</u> such clothing created a negative educational
environment. Certainly the school board would
be justified in prohibiting students from wearing
clothing that was unsanitary, revealing, or obscene.
The court remained unconvinced, <u>therefore,</u> that

<u>when wearing</u> jeans would actually impair the learning
process of Kevin or of his fellow classmates.

<u>Kevin Bannister's case was significant in that it</u>
<u>was the first in the United States to address clothing</u>
<u>prohibitions of a school dress code.</u> His challenge

35. A. NO CHANGE
B. of wearing
C. to wear
D. wearing

36. F. NO CHANGE
G. court noted, however,
H. court, noted however,
J. court noted however,

37. A. NO CHANGE
B. process, which has undergone changes since the 1970s.
C. process, a process we all know well.
D. process.

38. F. NO CHANGE
G. they're
H. its
J. ones

39. A. NO CHANGE
B. where
C. which
D. in which

40. F. NO CHANGE
G. thus,
H. moreover,
J. however,

41. A. NO CHANGE
B. by wearing
C. wearing
D. having worn

42. Which choice would most effectively begin this paragraph and convey the importance of this case?
F. NO CHANGE
G. Therefore, Kevin's case reminds us that you should stand up for your rights, no matter how old you are.
H. The case for personal liberty means the right to speak up must be taken seriously by the courts.
J. All in all, clothing is an important part of our identity.

initiated a <u>review, of students' rights</u> and administrative
₄₃

responsibility <u>in</u> public education.
₄₄

43. **A.** NO CHANGE
    B. review, of students' rights,
    C. review of students' rights
    D. review of students' rights,

44. **F.** NO CHANGE
    G. on
    H. with
    J. about

> Question 45 asks about the preceding passage as a whole.

45. Suppose the writer's primary purpose had been to write a persuasive essay urging students to exercise their constitutional rights. Would this essay accomplish that purpose?

    A. Yes, because the essay focuses on how Kevin encouraged other students to exercise their constitutional rights.
    B. Yes, because the essay focuses on various types of clothing historically worn by students as a freedom of expression.
    C. No, because the essay suggests that the right to wear blue jeans was not a substantial constitutional right in the 1970s.
    D. No, because the essay objectively reports on one case of a student exercising a particular constitutional right.

Improving Your Score

Answer Key for English Test Sample Questions

1.	D	16.	J	31.	C
2.	F	17.	B	32.	J
3.	B	18.	J	33.	A
4.	J	19.	A	34.	H
5.	A	20.	F	35.	C
6.	G	21.	C	36.	G
7.	A	22.	F	37.	D
8.	G	23.	A	38.	H
9.	A	24.	J	39.	A
10.	J	25.	B	40.	J
11.	C	26.	F	41.	C
12.	J	27.	A	42.	F
13.	A	28.	H	43.	C
14.	G	29.	D	44.	F
15.	C	30.	G	45.	D

Prep Online!

Want even more ways to prep? Go to act.wiley.com to access our online platform or use our companion app. Take online practice tests and track your progress, create your own question sets, and use flash cards to practice. Flag difficult or confusing questions for review. To get started, go to act.wiley.com, and register with the PIN on the back of the front cover of this book. Once registered, you can also use our companion app if you prefer to study from your mobile device.

Chapter 6: Improving Your Math Score

The ACT mathematics test asks you to answer 60 multiple-choice questions in 60 minutes. The questions are designed to measure your mathematical achievement—the knowledge, skills, and reasoning techniques that are taught in mathematics courses through the beginning of grade 12 and that are prerequisites for college mathematics courses. Therefore, the questions cover a wide variety of concepts, techniques, and procedures. Naturally, some questions will require computation, but you are allowed to use a calculator on the mathematics test. You'll need to understand basic mathematical terminology and to recall some basic mathematical principles and formulas. However, the questions on the test are designed to emphasize your ability to reason mathematically, not to focus on your computation ability or your ability to recall definitions, theorems, or formulas.

Content of the ACT Mathematics Test

The ACT mathematics test emphasizes the major content areas that are prerequisites to successful performance in entry-level courses in college mathematics.

Nine scores are reported for the ACT mathematics test: a total test score based on all 60 questions and eight reporting category scores based on specific mathematical knowledge and skills. The reporting categories are Preparing for Higher Mathematics (which includes separate scores for Number and Quantity, Algebra, Functions, Geometry, and Statistics and Probability); Integrating Essential Skills; and Modeling. Descriptions follow.

Preparing for Higher Math

This category captures the more recent mathematics that students are learning, starting when they begin using algebra as a general way of expressing and solving equations. This category is divided into the following five subcategories:

- **Number and Quantity:** Demonstrate knowledge of real and complex number systems. You will understand and reason with numerical quantities in many forms, including integer and rational exponents, and vectors and matrices.

- **Algebra:** Solve, graph, and model multiple types of expressions. You will employ many different kinds of equations, including but not limited to linear, polynomial, radical, and exponential relationships. You will find solutions to systems of equations, even when represented by simple matrices, and apply your knowledge to applications.

- **Functions:** The questions in this category test knowledge of function definition, notation, representation, and application. Questions may include, but are not limited to, linear, radical, piecewise, polynomial, and logarithmic functions. You will manipulate and translate functions, as well as find and apply important features of graphs.

- **Geometry:** Define and apply knowledge of shapes and solids, such as congruence and similarity relationships or surface area and volume measurements. Understand composition of objects and solve for missing values in triangles, circles, and other figures, including using trigonometric ratios and equations of conic sections.

- **Statistics and Probability:** Describe center and spread of distributions, apply and analyze data collection methods, understand and model relationships in bivariate data, and calculate probabilities, including the related sample spaces.

Integrating Essential Skills

These questions address concepts typically learned before grade 8, such as rates and percentages; proportional relationships; area, surface area, and volume; average and median; and expressing numbers in different ways. You will solve problems of increasing complexity, combine skills in longer chains of steps, apply skills in more varied contexts, understand more connections, and become more fluent.

Modeling

This category represents all questions that involve producing, interpreting, understanding, evaluating, and improving models. Each question is also counted in the other previously identified appropriate reporting categories. This category is an overall measure of how well you use modeling skills across mathematical topics.

Types of Questions on the ACT Mathematics Test

The questions on the ACT mathematics test differ in terms of content and complexity. The rest of this section gives you examples of questions—of various types and complexities from all content areas. All of the questions used in the examples are from actual ACT mathematics tests that have been taken by students from across the country. A solution strategy is given for each question. As you read and work through each example, please keep in mind that the strategy given is just one way to solve the problem. Other strategies may work even better for you.

Basic Math Problems

The type of question you're probably the most familiar with (and probably find the easiest) is the stripped-down, bare-bones, basic math problem. Problems of this type are simple and straightforward. They test readily identifiable skills in the content areas, usually have very few words and no extra information, ask the very question you'd expect them to ask, and usually have a numeric answer.

Question 1 is a good example of a basic math problem.

---

1. What is 4% of 1,100?

    A.   4
    B.   4.4
    C. 40
    D. 44
    E. 440

This problem has very few words, asks a direct question, and has a numeric answer. The solution is simple: Convert 4% to a decimal and multiply by 1,100 to get $(0.04)(1,100) = 44$, choice **D**. You probably wouldn't need your calculator on this problem, but remember that you may use it if you wish. If you chose answer **B** or **E**, you may have used rules about moving decimal points and moved the wrong number of places.

Question 2 is a basic algebra problem.

---

2. For all x, $(x + 4)(x - 5) = ?$

   F. $x^2 - 20$

   G. $x^2 - x - 20$

   H. $2x - 1$

   J. $2x^2 - 1$

   K. $2x^2 - x + 20$

You should know what to do to answer the question the instant you read the problem—use the distributive property (FOIL—first, outside, inside, last) and get
$x(x - 5) + 4(x - 5) = x^2 - 5x + 4x + 4(-5) = x^2 - x - 20$, choice **G**. On this problem, you probably wouldn't use your calculator. If you chose **F**, you probably just multiplied the first terms and the last terms. Check your answer by substituting a number (try 6) into the original expression and into your answer. If the results are not equal, then the expressions cannot be equivalent.

Question 3 is an example of a basic problem from algebra.

---

3. If $x + y = 1$, and $x - y = 1$, then $y = ?$

   A. -1

   B. 0

   C. $\dfrac{1}{2}$

   D. 1

   E. 2

This problem gives you a system of linear equations with unknowns x and y and asks for the value of y. You might be able to solve this problem intuitively—the only number that can be added to and subtracted from another number and give the same result for the problem ($x + y$ and $x - y$ both give 1) is 0, so y must be 0, choice **B**. Or, you could use algebra and reason that, because $x + y$ and $x - y$ both equal 1, they equal each other, and $x + y = x - y$ gives $2y = 0$, so $y = 0$. Although some calculators have graphing or matrix functions for solving problems of this type, using a calculator on this problem would probably take most students longer than solving it with one of the strategies given here. If you chose answer **D**, you probably found the value of x rather than the value of y.

Question 4 is an example of a basic problem in geometry.

---

4. What is the slope of the line containing the points $(-2,7)$ and $(3,-3)$?

   F.   4

   G. $\dfrac{1}{4}$

   H.   0

   J. $-\dfrac{1}{2}$

   K. -2

This problem has a few more words than some of the other examples of basic problems you've seen so far, but the most important word is *slope*. Seeing that you are given two points, you would probably think of the formula that defines the slope of a line through two points:

$$\frac{y_1 - y_2}{x_1 - x_2}.$$

Applying the formula gives $\frac{7 - (-3)}{-2 - 3} = \frac{10}{-5} = -2$, choice **K**. If you chose answer **J**, you probably got the expression for slope upside down. The change in y goes on top.

Here is another basic geometry problem from the ACT mathematics test.

---

5. If the measure of an angle is $37\frac{1}{2}°$, what is the measure of its supplement, shown in the figure below?

   A. $52\frac{1}{2}°$

   B. $62\frac{1}{2}°$

   C. $127\frac{1}{2}°$

   D. $142\frac{1}{2}°$

   E.   Cannot be determined from the given information

Similar to many geometry problems, this problem has a figure. The figure tells you what you are given (an angle of $37\frac{1}{2}°$) and what you're asked to find (its supplement, marked by "?"). You need not mark anything on the figure, because all the important information is already there. If you know that the sum of the measure of an angle and the measure of its supplement equals 180°, a simple subtraction gives the correct answer ($180° - 37\frac{1}{2}° = 142\frac{1}{2}°$), choice **D**. If you chose **A**, you found the complement, not the supplement.

A word of caution is in order here. You probably noticed that "Cannot be determined from the given information" is one of the options for question 5. Statistics gathered over the years for the ACT mathematics test show that many students choose "Cannot be determined from the given information" even when the answer can be determined. You should not think that whenever "Cannot be determined from the given information" is an option, it is automatically the correct answer. It isn't, as question 5 demonstrates. Later in this section is a question for which the correct answer is "Cannot be determined from the given information." Be sure to think carefully about problems with this answer choice.

You'll also find basic geometry problems, such as question 6, on the ACT mathematics test.

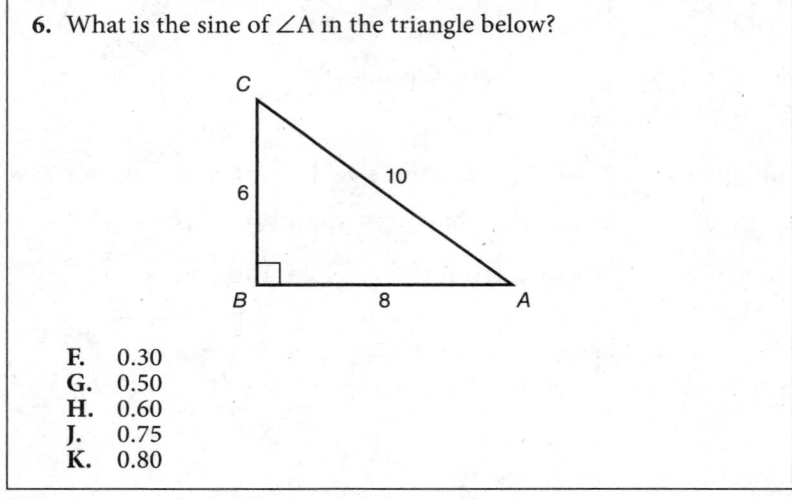

6. What is the sine of ∠A in the triangle below?

F.   0.30
G.   0.50
H.   0.60
J.   0.75
K.   0.80

This question asks you to find the sine of ∠A in the triangle shown in the figure. If you have studied trigonometry, you've seen questions similar to this before. The lengths of all three sides of the triangle are given on the figure, even though only two are actually needed for finding sin ∠A. The extra information is there not to confuse you but rather to test your ability to sort out the information you need from the information you are given. Picking 6 (the length of the side opposite ∠A) and 10 (the length of the hypotenuse) and forming the ratio gives the correct answer, 0.60, choice **H**. The cosine and the tangent of ∠A are also present in the answer choices. In order to do well on problems such as this one, you need to be able to tell which trigonometric function is which.

Basic Math Problems in Settings

Basic math problems in settings are what people often call *word problems* or *story problems*. They typically describe situations from everyday life in which you need to apply mathematics in order to answer a real-life question. The major difference between this type of problem and the basic math problems that you've seen in the examples so far is that the problem isn't set up for you—you have to set it up yourself. Most people find this to be the most difficult part of word problems. The key steps are reading the problem carefully, deciding what you're trying to find, sorting out what you really need from what's given, and then devising a strategy for finding the answer. Once the problem is set up, finding the answer is not much different from solving a basic math problem.

You can find basic math problems in settings in all of the content areas. Question 7 is an example.

---

7. What is the total cost of 2.5 pounds of bananas at $0.34 per pound and 2.5 pounds of tomatoes at $0.66 per pound?

   A. $1.00
   B. $2.40
   C. $2.50
   D. $3.50
   E. $5.00

Here, you're asked to find the total cost of some bananas and tomatoes. The important information is that the total cost includes 2.5 pounds of bananas at $0.34 per pound and 2.5 pounds of tomatoes at $0.66 per pound. A straightforward solution strategy would be to multiply to find the cost of the bananas and the cost of the tomatoes and then add to find the total cost. Now, the problem you're left with is very basic—calculating 2.5(0.34) + 2.5(0.66). Using your calculator might save time and avoid computation errors, but if you see that 2.5(0.34) + 2.5(0.66) = 2.5 (0.34 + 0.66) = 2.5(1.00) = 2.50, answer **C**, you might be able to do the computation more quickly in your head.

Basic algebra problems also can be in settings. Question 8 is an example.

---

8. The relationship between temperature expressed in degrees Fahrenheit (*F*) and degrees Celsius (*C*) is given by the formula

$$F = \frac{9}{5}C + 32$$

If the temperature is 14 degrees Fahrenheit, what is it in degrees Celsius?

   F. $-10°$
   G. $-12°$
   H. $-14°$
   J. $-16°$
   K. $-18°$

In this problem, you're given a relationship (in the form of an equation) between temperatures expressed in degrees Fahrenheit (F) and degrees Celsius (C). You're also given a temperature of 14 degrees Fahrenheit and asked what the corresponding temperature would be in degrees Celsius. Your strategy would probably be to substitute 14 into the equation in place of the variable F. This leaves you with a basic algebra problem—solving the equation $14 = \frac{9}{5}C + 32$ for C. Before going on to the next problem, checking your answer would probably be a good idea. If you chose $-10°$ (answer choice **F**), substitute -10 for C, multiply by $\frac{9}{5}$, and add 32 to see if the result is $14°F$ and confirm that your answer choice was indeed correct. Checking doesn't take long, and you might catch an error.

Question 9 is an example of an algebra problem in a setting.

---

9. Amy drove the 200 miles to New Orleans at an average speed 10 miles per hour faster than her usual average speed. If she completed the trip in 1 hour less than usual, what is her usual driving speed, in miles per hour?

    A. 20
    B. 30
    C. 40
    D. 50
    E. 60

After reading the problem, you know that it is about travel and that the basic formula "distance equals the rate multiplied by the time" ($D = rt$) or one of its variations $\left(r = \frac{D}{t} \text{ or } t = \frac{D}{r}\right)$ will probably be useful. For travel problems, a table is often an efficient way to organize the information. Because the problem asks for Amy's usual speed (rate), it would probably be wise to let the variable r represent her usual speed in miles per hour (mph). You might organize your table like this:

	Distance (miles)	Rate (mph)	Time (hours)
Usual trip	200	r	$\dfrac{200}{r}$
This trip	200	$r + 10$	$\dfrac{200}{(r+10)}$

Then, because the time for this trip $\left(\frac{200}{(r+10)}\right)$ is 1 hour less than the time for the usual trip $\left(\frac{200}{r}\right)$, solving $\frac{200}{(r+10)} = \frac{200}{r} - 1$ will give the answer. Solving this equation is a matter of using routine algebra skills and procedures. The solution, $r = 40$, choice **C,** answers the question, "What is her usual driving speed?" A quick check shows that driving 200 miles at 40 mph takes 5 hours and that driving 200 miles at 50 mph (which is 10 mph faster) takes 4 hours (which is 1 hour less). This quick check should convince you that your answer is correct.

Geometry problems can be in settings, too. Question 10 is an example.

---

10. A map is laid out in the standard (x,y) coordinate plane. How long, in units, is an airplane's path on the map as the airplane flies along a straight line from City A located at (20,14) to City B located at (5,10)?

    F. $\sqrt{1,201}$

    G. $\sqrt{241}$

    H. $\sqrt{209}$

    J. 7

    K. $\sqrt{19}$

In this problem, you're told that you will be working with the standard (x,y) coordinate plane and that you will need to find a distance. The distance formula should immediately come to mind. All you need is two points, and those are given. The problem now becomes a basic math problem—applying the distance formula:

$$\sqrt{\left(x_1-x_2\right)^2+\left(y_1-y_2\right)^2} = \sqrt{(20-5)^2+(14-10)^2} = \sqrt{241}\,(\mathbf{G}).$$

Your calculator might be useful in finding $(20-5)^2 + (14-10)^2$, but you should not press the square root key because most of the answer choices are in radical form.

A geometry problem in a setting is illustrated by question 11.

---

11. A person 2 meters tall casts a shadow 3 meters long. At the same time, a telephone pole casts a shadow 12 meters long. How many meters tall is the pole?

    A. 4

    B. 6

    C. 8

    D. 11

    E. 18

Question 11 has no figure, which is sometimes the case with geometry problems. It might be wise to draw your own figure and label it with the appropriate numbers from the problem. "A person 2 meters tall casts a shadow 3 meters long" is a pretty good clue that you should draw a right triangle with the vertical leg labeled 2 and the horizontal leg labeled 3. And, "a telephone pole casts a shadow 12 meters long" suggests that you should draw another right triangle with the horizontal leg labeled 12. Finding the height of the pole amounts to finding the length of the other leg of your second triangle, which you would label with a variable, say h. Your figure would be similar to this:

Improving Your Score

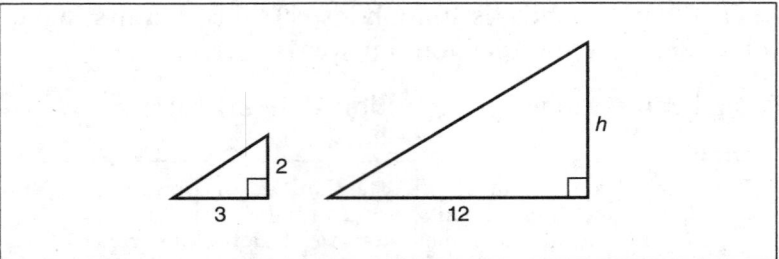

The triangles are similar (they're both right triangles and the angle that the sun's rays make with the ground is the same for both because the shadows were measured at the same time), so finding the height of the pole amounts to setting up and solving a proportion between corresponding sides of the triangles—a basic math problem. Your proportion might be $\frac{3}{12}=\frac{2}{h}$. Cross multiply—that is, multiply the numerator of each (or one) side by the denominator of the other side—to get $3(h) = 12(2)$, or $3h = 24$, and solve to get $h = 8$, choice **C.** Because the numbers are quite simple to work with, you probably wouldn't use your calculator on this problem.

Last (but not least) of the basic math questions, question 12 shows an example of a trigonometry problem in a setting.

12. The hiking path to the top of a mountain makes, at the steepest place, an angle of 20° with the horizontal, and it maintains this constant slope for 500 meters, as illustrated below. Which of the following is the closest approximation to the change in elevation, in meters, over this 500-meter section?

(Note: You may use the following values, which are correct to 2 decimal places:
cos 20° ≈ 0.94; sin 20° ≈ 0.34; tan 20° ≈ 0.36)

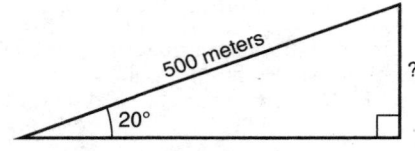

F. 20
G. 170
H. 180
J. 250
K. 470

This problem has a figure, and the figure is labeled with all the necessary information, including a question mark to tell you what you need to find. To set up the problem, you need to decide which of the trigonometric ratios involves the hypotenuse and the side opposite the given angle of a right triangle. Once you decide that the sine ratio is appropriate, you have only a basic trigonometry problem to solve: $\sin 20° = \frac{h}{500}$, or $500 \sin 20° = h$. Then, using the approximation for sin 20° given in the note, calculate $h \approx 500(0.34) = 170$, choice **G**. You may want to use your calculator to avoid computation errors. If you chose **K**, then you probably used the value for cosine rather than sine. Answer **H** comes from using tangent rather than sine.

Very Challenging Problems

The ACT mathematics test emphasizes reasoning ability, so it naturally has problems that can be very challenging. Because these problems are designed to test your understanding of mathematical concepts and your ability to pull together what you have learned in your math classes, they will probably be unlike problems you usually see. Some will be in settings, and some won't. Some will have figures, and some won't. Some will have extra information that you should ignore, and some won't have enough information, so the correct answer will be "Cannot be determined from the given information." Some will have numeric answers, some will have answers that are expressions or equations that you have to set up, and some will have answers that are statements for you to interpret and judge. On some questions your calculator will be helpful, and on others it will be better not to use it. All of the questions will share one important characteristic, however—they will challenge you to think hard and plan a strategy before you start to solve them.

Question 13 is a challenging problem.

13. If 537^{102} were calculated, it would have 279 digits. What would the digit farthest to the right be (the ones digit)?

  A. 1
  B. 3
  C. 4
  D. 7
  E. 9

You certainly wouldn't want to calculate 537^{102} by hand, and your calculator doesn't display enough digits for you to be able to read off the ones digit for this very large number, so you have to figure out another way to see the ones digit. A good place to start might be to look at the ones digit for powers of 7 because 7 is the ones digit of 537. Maybe there will be a pattern: $7^0 = 1$, $7^1 = 7$, $7^2 = 49$, $7^3 = 343$, $7^4 = 2,401$, $7^5 = 16,807$, $7^6 = 117,649$, $7^7 = 823,543$. It looks like the pattern of the ones digits is 1, 7, 9, 3, 1, 7, 9, 3, . . ., with the sequence of these 4 digits repeating over and over. Now, if you can decide where in this pattern the ones digit of 537^{102} falls, you'll have the problem solved. You might organize a chart like this:

Ones digit	1	7	9	3
Power of 7	0	1	2	3
	4	5	6	7

The next row would read "8 9 10 11" to show that the ones digits of 7^8, 7^9, 7^{10}, and 7^{11}, respectively, are 1, 7, 9, and 3. You could continue the chart row after row until you got up to 102, but that would take a lot of time. Instead, think about where 102 would fall. The numbers in the first column are the multiples of 4, so 100 would fall there because it is a multiple of 4. Then 101 would be in the second column, and 102 would fall in the third column. Therefore, the ones digit of 537^{102} is 9, choice **E**.

Question 14 is an algebra problem designed to challenge your ability to think mathematically and use what you've learned.

---

14. If $a < -1$, which of the following best describes a general relationship between a^3 and a^2?

   F. $a^3 > a^2$

   G. $a^3 < a^2$

   H. $a^3 = a^2$

   J. $a^3 = -a^2$

   K. $a^3 = \dfrac{1}{a^2}$

Here you are told that $a < -1$. Then you are asked for the relationship between a^3 and a^2. By stopping to think for a moment before trying to manipulate the given inequality or experimenting with numbers plugged into the answer choices, you might realize that if $a < -1$, then a is a negative number, so its cube is a negative number. Squaring a negative number, however, gives a positive number. Every negative number is less than every positive number, so the correct relationship between a^3 and a^2 is $a^3 < a^2$, choice **G**. Of course, there are other ways to approach the problem.

For another very challenging algebra problem, look at question 15.

---

15. If $\left(\dfrac{4}{5}\right)^n = \sqrt{\left(\dfrac{5}{4}\right)^3}$, then $n = ?$

   A. $-\dfrac{3}{2}$

   B. -1

   C. $-\dfrac{2}{3}$

   D. $\dfrac{2}{3}$

   E. $\dfrac{3}{2}$

In this problem, you're asked to find the value of a variable, but the variable is in the exponent. After some thought you might decide to try to rewrite $\sqrt{\left(\frac{5}{4}\right)^3}$ so that it is $\frac{5}{4}$ raised to a power. You should remember that the square root is the same as the $\frac{1}{2}$ power, so, after using some properties of exponents, $\sqrt{\left(\sqrt{\frac{5}{4}}\right)^3} = \left(\left(\sqrt{\frac{5}{4}}\right)^3\right)^{\frac{1}{2}} = \left(\frac{5}{4}\right)^{\frac{3}{2}}$. Now at least the left side and the right side of the equation have the same form, but the bases of the two expressions aren't the same—they're reciprocals. In thinking about the connection between reciprocals and exponents, it is good to realize that taking the opposite of the exponent (that is, making it have the opposite sign) will flip the base, because $a^{-k} = \frac{1}{a^k}$. That means $\left(\frac{5}{4}\right)^{\frac{3}{2}} = \left(\frac{4}{5}\right)^{-\frac{3}{2}}$. So now, with $\left(\frac{4}{5}\right)^n = \left(\frac{4}{5}\right)^{-\frac{3}{2}}$, $n = -\frac{3}{2}$, choice **A**.

Geometry problems can also be very challenging. Question 16 is an example.

---

16. In the standard (x,y) coordinate plane, the triangle with vertices at $(0,0)$, $(0,k)$, and $(2,m)$, where m is constant, changes shape as k changes. What happens to the triangle's area, expressed in square coordinate units, as k increases starting from 2?

    F. The area increases as k increases.
    G. The area decreases as k increases.
    H. The area always equals 2.
    J. The area always equals m.
    K. The area always equals $2m$.

This problem might seem confusing at first because it contains two different variables and no figure to clarify. You're told that m is a constant but k changes. So, to get started, you could pick a value for m, say $m = 1$. Then, at least you can start sketching a figure. The point $(0,k)$ is on the y-axis and k increases starting with 2, so you could start by drawing a figure similar to this:

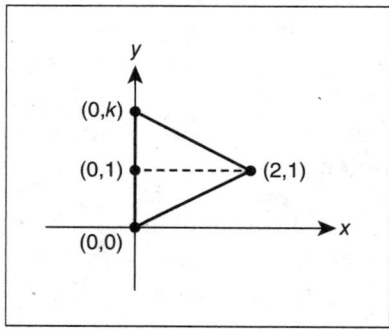

You can see the triangle that the problem mentions. If you think of the line segment from $(0,0)$ to $(0,k)$ as the base and the line segment from $(2,1)$ to $(0,1)$ as the height, you can see that as k increases, the base of the triangle gets longer but the height remains the same. From geometry, you know that the area of a triangle is given by $\frac{1}{2}$(base)(height). Therefore, the area will increase as the base gets longer. So, the area will increase as k increases, choice **F**. You should be able to reason that for any value of *m*, the result would have been the same, and you can feel confident that the correct answer is the first answer choice.

Question 17 is an example of a very challenging geometry problem.

17. In the figure below, $\overline{AB} \cong \overline{AC}$ and $\overline{BC}$ is 10 units long. What is the area, in square inches, of $\triangle ABC$?

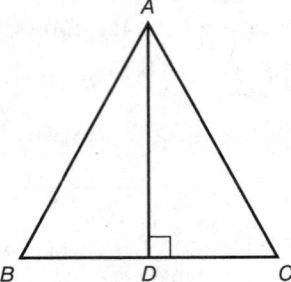

A. 12.5

B. 25

C. $25\sqrt{2}$

D. 50

E. Cannot be determined from the given information

This problem has a figure, but none of the information given is marked on the figure. A wise move is to mark the figure yourself to indicate which sides are congruent and which side is 10 units long. You need to find the area of $\triangle ABC$, and you know that the base $\overline{BC}$ is 10 units long. You need the measure of the height $\overline{AD}$ before you can apply the formula for the area of a triangle. You might ask yourself, "Is there any way to get the height?" If you were given the measure of one of the angles or the measure of one of the congruent sides, you might be able to find the height, but no other information is given. With a little more thought, you should realize that the height can be any positive number because there are infinitely many isosceles triangles with bases 10 units long. You conclude that not enough information is given to solve this problem, and the correct answer choice is **E**: "Cannot be determined from the given information."

This is the example that was mentioned earlier when "Cannot be determined from the given information" is the correct answer. Remember not to jump to a hasty conclusion when "Cannot be determined from the given information" is an answer choice. Sometimes it is the right answer, but sometimes it isn't.

Very challenging problems can be in settings, too. Question 18 is an example.

---

18. A bag of pennies could be divided among 6 children, or 7 children, or 8 children, with each getting the same number, and with 1 penny left over in each case. What is the smallest number of pennies that could be in the bag?

F. 22
G. 43
H. 57
J. 169
K. 337

In this problem, whenever the pennies in the bag (which contains an unknown number of pennies) are divided evenly among 6 children, 7 children, or 8 children, 1 penny is always left over. This means that if you take the extra penny out of the bag, then the number of pennies left in the bag will be divisible (with no remainder) by 6, 7, and 8. You should ask yourself, "What is the smallest number that is divisible by 6, 7, and 8?" In mathematical terminology, you're looking for the least common multiple of 6, 7, and 8. One way to find the least common multiple is to use the prime factorizations of the three numbers and to find the product of the highest power of each prime that occurs in one or more of the three numbers. This process will yield $2^3 \cdot 3 \cdot 7 = 168$. (As a check: $168 \div 6 = 28$, $168 \div 7 = 24$, and $168 \div 8 = 21$.) But wait! You're not quite finished. Remember to add back in the penny that you took out of the bag originally to make the divisions come out even. Thus, your answer is 169, choice **J**.

Question 19 is an example of an algebra word problem that is very challenging.

---

19. There are n students in a class. If, among those students, $p\%$ play at least 1 musical instrument, which of the following general expressions represents the number of students who play NO musical instrument?

A. np

B. $.01np$

C. $\dfrac{(100 - p)n}{100}$

D. $\dfrac{(1 - p)n}{.01}$

E. $100(1 - p)n$

This is an example of a problem that has a mathematical expression as its answer. Finding an expression to answer a question usually makes you think more than finding a numerical answer because the variables require you to think abstractly. In this problem, you are told that out of a class of n students, $p\%$ play 1 or more musical instruments. Finding the percent of students who play no musical instrument is simple: $(100 - p)\%$. To find the number of students who play no musical instrument, you'd probably want to convert $(100 - p)\%$ to a decimal and multiply by n. If $100 - p$ were a number you'd automatically move the decimal point two places to the left. But, because there's no decimal point to move in 100 − p, you have to think about what you need to do to convert (100 − p)% to a decimal. Moving the decimal point two places to the left is the same as dividing by 100, so (100 − p)% as a decimal is $\frac{100-p}{100}$, and the number of students who play no musical instrument is $\frac{(100-p)n}{100}$, choice **C**.

Question 20 is an example of a very challenging geometry problem in a setting.

20. Starting at her doorstep, Ramona walked down the sidewalk at 1.5 feet per second for 4 seconds. Then she stopped for 4 seconds, realizing that she had forgotten something. Next she returned to her doorstep along the same route at 1.5 feet per second. The graph of Ramona's distance (d) from her doorstep as a function of time (t) would most resemble which of the following?

F.
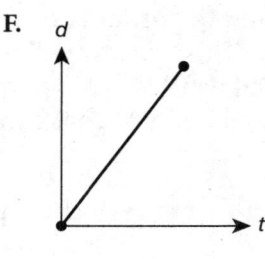

J.
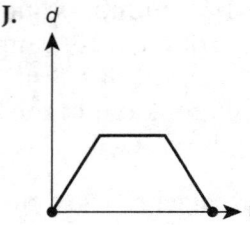

G.
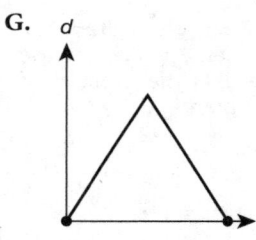

K.
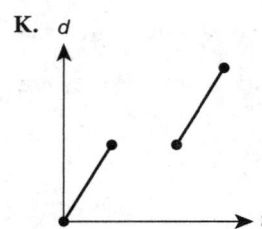

H.
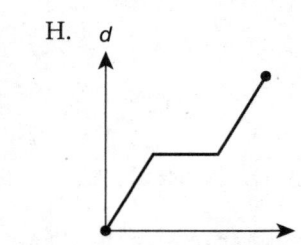

This problem is different from any of the problems you've seen so far because its answer is a graph. And, instead of giving you an equation and asking you to identify the equation's graph, this problem describes a situation and asks you to decide which graph represents the situation. You need to think about what the description of each of Ramona's activities says in terms of distance as a function of time and what each activity would translate into graphically. For example, at first, Ramona walked at a constant rate down the sidewalk. Therefore, she moved farther away from her doorstep as time elapsed, and her distance from her doorstep increased at a constant rate as time increased. So, the first part of the graph should be a line segment with a positive slope. Unfortunately, all five graphs start out this way, so none of the options can be eliminated at this point. The next thing Ramona did was stop for 4 seconds. If she stood still, her distance from her doorstep would not change even though time was still elapsing. This part of the graph should then reflect a constant value for d as time increases. It should be a horizontal line segment. This information allows you to eliminate options **F**, **G**, and **K**, because they do not have a horizontal line segment. Ramona's next activity helps you decide between **H** and **J**. Ramona walked back home at the same rate along the same route as before. On her way back home, her distance from her doorstep decreased at a constant rate as elapsed time increased. This would be graphed as a line segment with a negative slope, and therefore **J** is the correct graph.

Another word problem that challenges you to think mathematically is question 21.

---

21. An object detected on radar is 5 miles to the east, 4 miles to the north, and 1 mile above the tracking station. Among the following, which is the closest approximation to the distance, in miles, that the object is from the tracking station?

A. 6.5
B. 7.2
C. 8.3
D. 9.0
E. 10.0

This problem is about computing a distance, but it's a distance in three-dimensional space without a picture to help you. For this problem, drawing a sketch of the situation might help. Your sketch might be a "box" such as this:

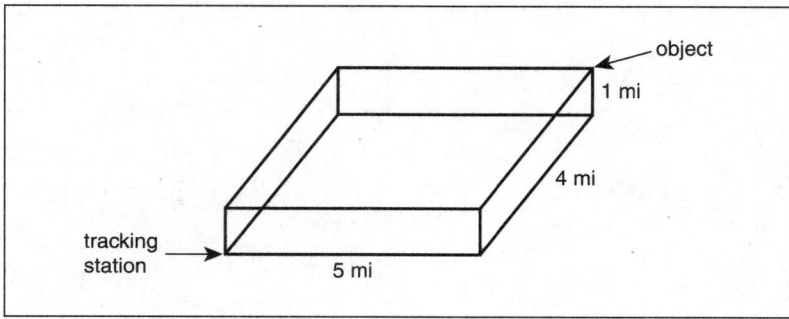

You need to find the length of the diagonal from the lower left corner of the front of the box to the top right corner of the back of the box. This is the hypotenuse of a right triangle ($\triangle OBT$ on the following redrawn figure) that has its right angle at B. One leg of this triangle has length 1, but the other leg is $\overline{BT}$, and you don't know the length of $\overline{BT}$.

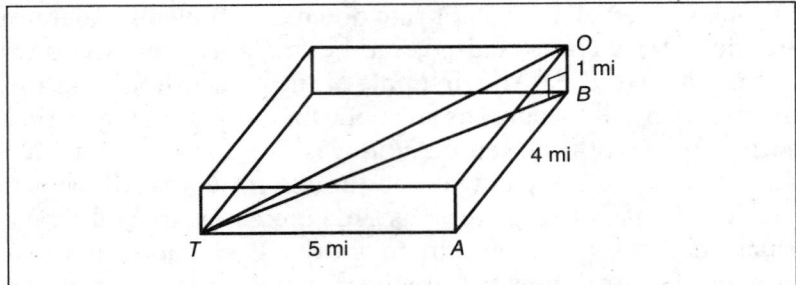

A closer look shows that $\overline{BT}$ is the hypotenuse of $\triangle TAB$, which has its right angle at A and legs that measure 5 and 4. Using the Pythagorean theorem gives $BT = \sqrt{5^2 + 4^2} = \sqrt{41}$.

Now you can use the Pythagorean theorem again to get $OT = \sqrt{BT^2 + OB^2} = \sqrt{\left(\sqrt{41}\right)^2 + 1^2} = \sqrt{42}$ which is about 6.5, choice **A**.

Question Sets

The mathematics test often contains sets of questions that all relate to the same information. Questions 22–24 illustrate a question set that relates to information from a paragraph and a graph. The mathematics test sometimes contains two question sets with two to four questions per set.

Use the following information to answer questions 22–24.

At both Quick Car Rental and Speedy Car Rental, the cost, in dollars, of renting a full-size car depends on a fixed daily rental fee and a fixed charge per mile that the car is driven. However, the daily rental fee and the charge per mile are not the same for the 2 companies. In the graph below, line Q represents the total cost for Quick Car Rental and line S represents the total cost for Speedy Car Rental.

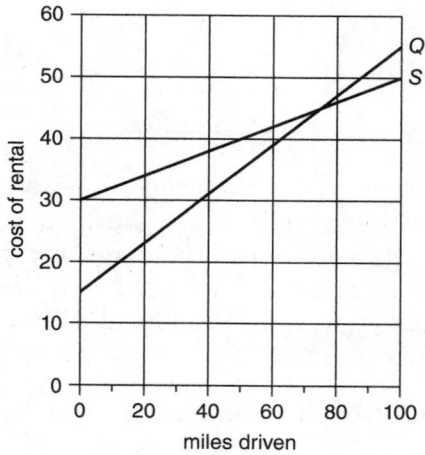

22. Robert plans to rent a full-size car for 1 day and drive only 50 miles. If his only consideration is to incur the least cost, which company should he choose?

    F. Quick Car Rental, because the cost is $5.00 less.
    G. Quick Car Rental, because the cost is $15.00 less.
    H. Either company, because the costs are equal.
    J. Speedy Car Rental, because the cost is $5.00 less.
    K. Speedy Car Rental, because the cost is $15.00 less.

Improving Your Score

23. If you rent a full-size car from Quick Car Rental for 1 day, how much more would the total rental cost be if you drove the car 78 miles than if you drove it 77 miles?

    A. $0.10
    B. $0.15
    C. $0.20
    D. $0.40
    E. $0.55

24. What would be the total cost of renting a full-size car from Speedy Car Rental for 1 day and driving the car 150 miles?

    F. $ 60
    G. $ 75
    H. $ 85
    J. $ 90
    K. $120

Once you've looked at the information given for a group of questions, you can use the same sorts of strategies to answer the questions that you would use on any question on the ACT mathematics test. Question 22 requires you to read the graph and compare the costs of renting a car from the two companies, assuming that the car is going to be driven 50 miles. From the graph, the cost for Speedy Car Rental appears to be about $40, and the cost of Quick Car Rental appears to be about $35. These points are marked on the graph that is redrawn below.

So Robert will incur the least cost if he rents from Quick Car Rental because that cost is $5 less, choice **F**.

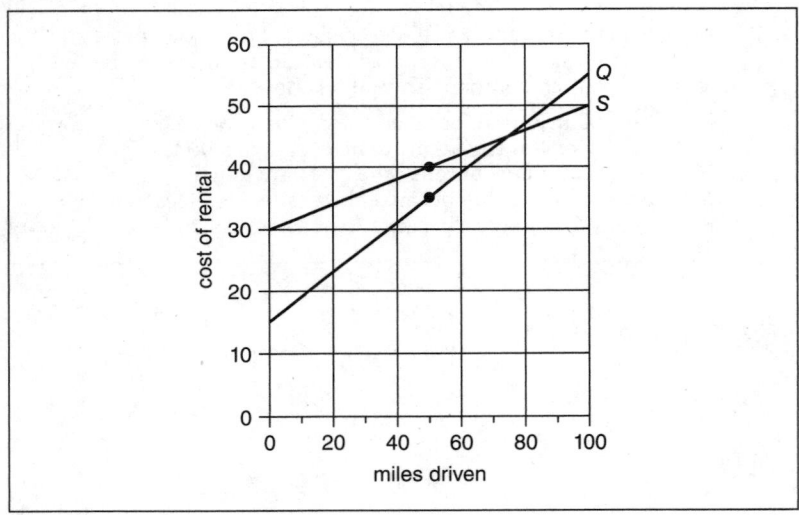

Question 23 requires you to determine how much more Robert would pay if he rented a car from Quick Car Rental and drove 78 miles than if he drove 77 miles. Using mathematical concepts might be a better approach than trying to read the graph, because you might not be able to read the graph accurately enough. You know from coordinate geometry that, in the standard (x,y) coordinate plane, the slope of a line gives the rate of change in y per unit change in x, which is exactly what you want to find in this problem—how much the cost at Quick Car Rental changes when the car is driven 1 more mile.

The formula to determine the slope of a line is $m = \dfrac{(y_2 - y_1)}{(x_2 - x_1)}$, where m is the slope, (x_1, y_1) are the coordinates of one point, and (x_2, y_2) are the coordinates of the other. Two points that are easy to read accurately off the graph are $(0,15)$ and $(50,35)$, labeled on the following redrawn graph. Plug the coordinates into the equation to get $m = \dfrac{(\$35 - \$15)}{(50 \text{ miles} - 0 \text{ miles})} = \dfrac{(\$20)}{(50 \text{ miles})} = \$0.40$ per mile. So, the difference for driving 78 miles instead of 77 miles (that is, for driving 1 more mile) is $0.40, choice **D**.

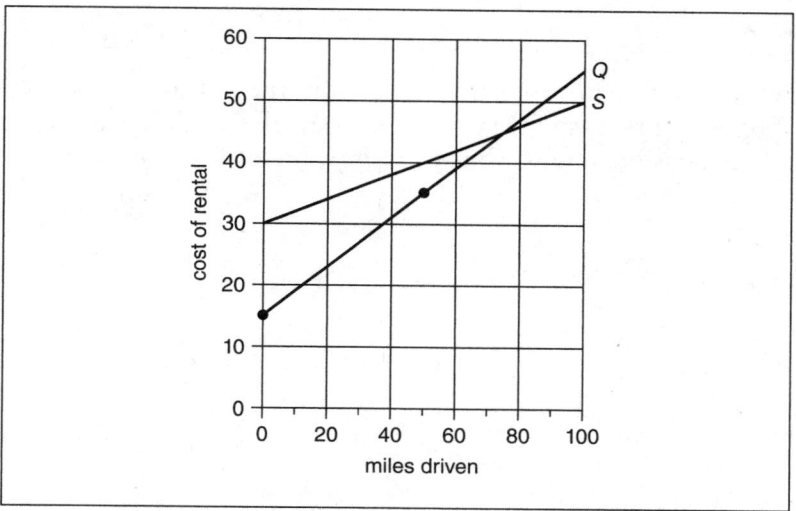

In question 24, you are asked for the cost of renting a car from Speedy Car Rental and driving it 150 miles. You can't simply read the cost off the graph, because 150 isn't on the graph, but you can find an equation of the line for Speedy Car Rental and then plug 150 into the equation. Recall that a line is determined by any two points on the line—call them (x_1, y_1) and (x_2, y_2)—and that one way of finding an equation of the line is by first finding slope with $m = \dfrac{y_2 - y_1}{x_2 - x_1}$ and then using the two-point form of the equation of a line, $(y - y_1) = m(x - x_1)$. Here, you can use two points that are easy to read off the graph for Speedy Car Rental, such as $(0,30)$ and $(100,50)$, shown on the redrawn graph on the next page. The slope through any two points on this line is $m = \dfrac{50 - 30}{100 - 0} = \dfrac{20}{100} = 0.2$, and the equation $(y - 30) = 0.2(x - 0)$ fits all of the points on the line. This equation can be rewritten as $(y - 30) = 0.2x$. So, when $x = 150$, that means $(y - 30) = 0.2(150)$ and then $y - 30 = 30$ and then $y = 60$. The cost is $60, choice **F**.

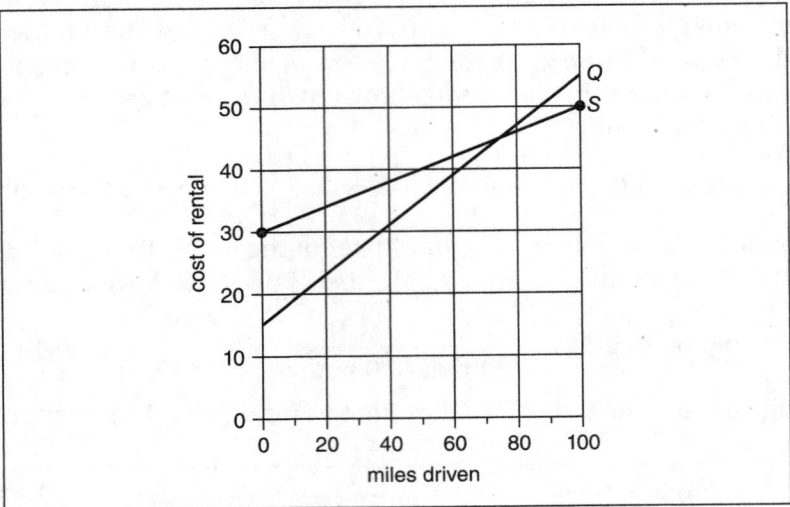

As you have seen in the sample questions in this section, the mathematics test includes many types of questions. Some will be easy for you, and some will be hard. They all will require you to demonstrate as much as possible about what you know and can do in mathematics.

	Answer Key for Mathematics Test Sample Questions				
1.	D	9.	C	17.	E
2.	G	10.	G	18.	J
3.	B	11.	C	19.	C
4.	K	12.	G	20.	J
5.	D	13.	E	21.	A
6.	H	14.	G	22.	F
7.	C	15.	A	23.	D
8.	F	16.	F	24.	F

Strategies for Taking the ACT Mathematics Test

Pace Yourself

You have 60 minutes to answer 60 questions, which gives you an average of 1 minute per problem. Some problems will take you less than 1 minute, and some will take you more. Don't spend too much time on any one question. You should keep a close eye on your watch to make sure you work at a pace that will enable you to finish the test in the 60 minutes allotted. When determining your pace, be aware that the questions are arranged approximately in order of difficulty: easier questions first and hardest last.

Answer All Questions

Answer all questions even if you have no idea how to solve some of them. If you're stumped and have time, eliminate as many of the options as you can and then guess from among the remaining choices. If time is running out and you don't have time to eliminate any of the options, guess anyway. Even a wild guess has a 20% chance of being correct, but a blank has no chance of being correct. Remember, your score is based solely on the number of questions you answer correctly—there is no penalty for guessing and no penalty for wrong answers. Scores are most comparable if everyone answers every question.

Answer All the Easy Questions First, Then Go Back to Answer the Hard Ones

Easy and *hard* are relative terms. What might be easy for one student might be hard for another. You know which math topics are easy for you and which are hard. Answer all the questions that are easy for you and then go back to the hard ones. Remember that you don't get more points for answering hard questions. All questions, no matter how easy or hard, count equally toward your mathematics total score. If you don't see a way to solve a problem, or if the method you're using seems to be taking a lot of time, take your best guess (as explained in the previous section) or skip the question and move on to questions that you can answer more easily. If you skip the question, don't forget to mark in the test booklet (never on the answer document) all those questions that you skip so that you can easily return to them later.

Note: In some circumstances you are not permitted to write in your test booklet. In those circumstances, you'll be given scratch paper, and you can use it to jot down the numbers of the questions you skip.

Read Each Problem Carefully

Read carefully enough so you know what you're trying to find before you start looking for it and so you know what you have to work with to help you find it. Remember that questions may contain extraneous details you will need to ignore or insufficient information to solve the problem. Think twice before choosing "Cannot be determined from the given information," because test-takers often choose this option when the answer, in fact, can be determined from the information given. Make sure you are not overlooking a key piece of information provided or an alternate strategy for solving the problem.

Look for Information in the Answer Choices

Sometimes looking at the answer choices provides valuable information about the form of the answer. For example, you might be able to judge whether your answer should be left in radical form or converted to a decimal approximation, whether your polynomial answer should be left in factored form or multiplied out, or whether you should spend time reducing a probability to lowest terms. For some problems, you have to analyze the options as part of your solution strategy. For example, when a question asks, "Which of the following statements is true?" and the statements are the five options, you probably need to examine each option in turn. Sometimes, using the options gives you an alternate way to solve a problem. For example, suppose you're trying to solve a quadratic equation and you can't get the quadratic expression to factor and can't remember the quadratic formula. You might be able to get the correct answer by substituting the options, in turn, into the equation until one works. This strategy should be used very sparingly, however, because it can be more time-consuming than other strategies.

Use Illustrations Wisely and Whenever You Can

The old saying "A picture is worth a thousand words" holds true on the mathematics test:

- Refer to illustrations whenever they are provided.

- If no illustration is provided and one might be useful, draw your own illustration in the test booklet. This can be especially helpful in solving word problems.

- Transfer information from the question to the illustration, if you think it might be helpful. For example, you might write dimensions on the figure that are given in the question but aren't shown on the figure or that you calculate in the process of solving the problem, or you might add marks to show congruences or draw auxiliary lines such as perpendiculars and diagonals.

Note: In some circumstances you are not permitted to write in your test booklet. In those circumstances, you'll be given scratch paper to use.

Use Your Calculator Wisely

Each problem on the mathematics test can be solved in a reasonable amount of time without a calculator. A calculator is most helpful if you are very familiar with the one you bring to the test and you use it wisely during the test. Experimenting with the capabilities of a new calculator during the testing session or using a calculator in situations when a non-calculator approach would be better can cost you precious time. Bring the calculator that you are most familiar with—the one you use in your math classes or at home—but make sure it is an ACT-permitted calculator (visit www.actstudent.org for details). Don't worry that other students have more sophisticated calculators than yours; the type of calculator that students use should not make a difference in their scores. Use your calculator wisely; remember that a non-calculator strategy is often better than a calculator strategy. And don't believe everything your calculator tells you. Make sure the numbers it gives you are reasonable and make sense.

Think!

Your head is by far a more powerful and efficient problem-solving tool than a pencil or a calculator. Think before you plunge in and begin working on a problem. Don't panic if you suddenly can't remember a formula or all of the steps of a procedure you've been taught. You can often find another way to do a problem that will work just as well. For example, you don't have to write and solve an equation for every algebra word problem. You might be able to reason through such a problem and get the correct answer without an equation. Sometimes the best option is to let your common sense about numbers take over.

Show Your Work

You have certainly heard this before—probably in every math class you've ever taken. Of course, you're not going to have time during the test to write down every step for every problem the way you might on a homework assignment, but writing down at least some of what you are thinking and doing as you solve a problem will be worth the time it takes. If you're using a calculator, you can write down the numbers that you plug into it and the intermediate results it gives you, to keep a running record of what you did. If you don't write anything down and your answer for a problem doesn't match any of the answer choices, your only alternative is to start over. But, if you have at least something written down, you may be able to go back over your work and find your mistake. Also, if you have time at the end of the test to go back and check your answers, having something written down will enable you to check your work more quickly.

Check Your Answers

Before you leave a question, make sure your answer makes sense. Don't believe everything your calculator tells you; make sure that the answer your calculator displays makes sense to you and that your answer actually answers the question. For example, if a problem about oranges and apples asks for the number of apples, make sure your answer doesn't give the number of oranges, or if a problem asks for the altitude of a triangle, make sure your answer isn't the hypotenuse. Remember, if you have time remaining after answering all of the questions, use it wisely and go back and check your work. That's a skill that will help you in college and career, too.

Prep Online!

Want even more ways to prep? Go to act.wiley.com to access our online platform or use our companion app. Take online practice tests and track your progress, create your own question sets, and use flash cards to practice. Flag difficult or confusing questions for review. To get started, go to act.wiley.com, and register with the PIN on the back of the front cover of this book. Once registered, you can also use our companion app if you prefer to study from your mobile device.

Chapter 7: Improving Your Reading Score

Designed to measure your reading comprehension, the ACT reading test comprises four sections, three of which contain one long prose passage and one that contains two shorter prose passages. One of the sections may include a mixed-information format—visual and quantitative elements (like graphs, diagrams, and tables) that accompany the passage and contain information relevant to the passage topic. Each passage or passage set is followed by 9–11 multiple-choice questions, for a total of 40 questions. You are given 35 minutes to complete the test. The passages on the reading test come from published materials, such as books and magazines, written at a level that a first-year college student can expect to read for a class.

Content of the ACT Reading Test

The ACT reading test contains a mix of passages from the following categories:

- **Literary narrative** (literary passages from short stories, novels, and memoirs)

- **Humanities** (informational passages on architecture, art, dance, ethics, film, language, literary criticism, music, philosophy, radio, television, and theater)

- **Social science** (informational passages on anthropology, archaeology, biography, business, economics, education, environmentalism, geography, history, political science, psychology, and sociology)

- **Natural science** (informational passages on anatomy, astronomy, biology, botany, chemistry, ecology, geology, medicine, meteorology, microbiology, natural history, physiology, physics, technology, and zoology)

Each passage is preceded by a heading that identifies what type of passage it is ("Informational" or "Literary Narrative"), names the author, and may include a brief note that helps in understanding the passage. Each section contains a set of multiple-choice test questions. These questions do not test the rote recall of facts from outside the passage, isolated vocabulary terms, or rules of formal logic. In sections that contain two short passages, some of the questions involve both of the passages in the section. In sections that contain an element like a graph, figure, or table, some of the questions will involve the graphic or quantitative element.

You will receive four scores for the ACT reading test: a total test score based on all 40 questions and three reporting category scores based on the following specific knowledge and skills. You will also see an Understanding Complex Texts indicator, which is meant to indicate your level of proficiency in understanding the central meaning in complex texts.

Key Ideas and Details

Read texts closely to determine central ideas and themes. Summarize information and ideas accurately. Read closely to understand relationships and draw logical inferences and conclusions including understanding sequential, comparative, and cause-effect relationships.

Craft and Structure

Determine word and phrase meanings, analyze an author's word choice, analyze text structure, understand authorial purpose and perspective, and analyze characters' points of view. You will interpret authorial decisions and differentiate between various perspectives and sources of information.

Integration of Knowledge and Ideas

Understand authors' claims, differentiate between facts and opinions, and make connections between different texts. Some questions will require you to analyze how authors construct arguments, evaluating reasoning and evidence from various sources; others will require you to piece together information from multiple texts or from different formats (e.g., graphs, diagrams, or tables).

If you choose to take the writing test, you will also receive an English Language Arts (ELA) score based on an average of your English, reading, and writing test scores.

Types of Questions on the ACT Reading Test

On the reading test, the questions fall into one of the three reporting categories previously described. You shouldn't worry about these categories while you're taking the reading test. It's most important that you focus on the questions themselves and on what they ask you about a given passage. Because each passage is different, the kinds of questions will vary from passage to passage. Still, there are some general types of questions you're likely to encounter. Most questions will ask you to do one of the following:

- Identify and interpret details.
- Determine the main idea of a paragraph, paragraphs, or a passage.
- Understand comparative relationships (comparisons and contrasts).
- Understand cause-effect relationships.
- Make generalizations.
- Determine the meaning of words from context.
- Understand sequences of events.
- Analyze the author's purpose and method.
- Understand and analyze arguments.
- Understand information across multiple texts.

Sometimes the reading test contains other types of questions, but don't worry. Just make sure you read each passage and its questions carefully. You'll find that the information you need to determine the best answer for a question is always available in the passage. Questions that illustrate some common types of questions on the reading test follow.

Representative ACT Reading Test Questions

Details. Some test questions ask you to locate or understand a key detail from a passage. A detail can be something as seemingly simple as a characteristic of a person, place, or thing, or a particular date. Other questions of this type require you to do a bit more interpreting of minor or subtly stated details. The question below was taken from a literary narrative about a violin lesson, which is found on page 265.

1. Allegra states that Mr. Kaplan will know she hasn't practiced the concerto if:

   A. she isn't ready for the shift on the second page.
   B. the dynamics in her playing are unacceptable.
   C. she has trouble playing the first movement's cadenza fast enough.
   D. her tape doesn't sound good enough.

You'll have to look around the passage for the information you need—not unusual for this kind of question. Choice **A** is the best answer. In the fifth paragraph (lines 17–27), Allegra is getting ready to play for Mr. Kaplan. She notes that "he was going to know the instant I got to the top of the second page that I hadn't been practicing the Mozart. At that spot there's a fast shift from first finger to fourth finger on the G string, and you have to get ready for it. You can't let a shift like that take you by surprise" (lines 22–27). It is clear from these lines that Allegra thinks Mr. Kaplan will know she hasn't practiced if she isn't ready for this shift. Mr. Kaplan mentions the dynamics of Allegra's playing, but this is after she has played the piece for him (**B**). Likewise, the cadenza and Allegra's tape are mentioned in the passage, but neither is mentioned in relation to Mr. Kaplan knowing that Allegra hasn't practiced. In the sixth paragraph (lines 28–33), Allegra notes that there are three cadenzas in the concerto, but she doesn't state that she's worried about playing the first movement's fast enough (**C**). In lines 59–62, it's clear that the tape was made before this particular lesson (**D**).

Main Ideas. To answer this kind of question, you need to be able to determine the focus of a passage or of a paragraph or paragraphs in a passage. You shouldn't count on finding this information summed up in the first paragraph of a passage or in the first sentence of a paragraph. You may have been advised to make the first sentence of each paragraph the topic sentence in your own writing, but not every writer does that. You'll need to figure out what the author's main point is in one or more paragraphs or in an entire passage by reading the paragraph(s) or passage carefully.

Main idea questions can be fairly straightforward. The following question, based on a social science passage about the development of perceptual abilities (page 268), is pretty direct:

---

2. The main point of the passage is that:

   F.   during the first four to seven months of life, babies learn at an accelerated pace.
   G.   organisms deprived of critical life experiences may or may not develop normal sensory performance.
   H.   the development of perceptual abilities is the result of the interaction between nature and experience.
   J.   research concerned with physical skills and abilities adds little to our knowledge of the growth of the mind.

The idea that the interaction between nature and experience shapes the development of perceptual abilities (**H**) is the clear focus of the entire passage. In the first paragraph, the author states that "the ancient central question of psychology" is "how much is due to nature and how much to nurture (or, in developmental terms, to maturation and to learning)" (lines 5–8). The second through eighth paragraphs (lines 9–85) describe research designed to help answer this question as it relates to the development of perceptual abilities in children. The last paragraph sums up the passage by saying that this research helps us "catch the first glimpse of how mind is constructed out of matter by experience" (lines 88–89). Though in lines 50–53 the author describes the rapid development of infants between four and seven months old, this is only a minor part of the passage, so **F** is incorrect. The seventh paragraph (lines 61–73) does mention that organisms can be permanently harmed if they miss critical life experiences, but this, also, isn't the main point of the passage, making **G** incorrect. Choice **J** is just plain wrong: the whole passage deals with how research on physical skills and abilities has added to our knowledge of the growth of the mind.

As that example shows, you may have to rule out answer choices that either are supporting (rather than main) ideas or simply misstate what the passage says. Both types of wrong answers appear in this next example, based on the natural science passage about lightning and fire (page 270):

3. One of the main points of the third paragraph (lines 41–61) is that:

    A. Arizona researchers record tree mortality by volume.
    B. tree mortality rates fail to capture the true extent of lightning-inflicted damage.
    C. ponderosa pine trees are resistant to secondary diseases.
    D. pine tree forests draw fewer lightning strikes than many other habitat types in Arizona.

Choice **B** is the best answer here. Tree mortality rates "describe only direct injury" to trees (line 56), but lightning can also kill trees indirectly by making them vulnerable to insects, wind, and mistletoe and by causing fires. Although **A** is true, according to lines 54–56, the fact that Arizona researchers record tree mortality by volume is a minor point. The paragraph never claims that ponderosa pine trees are resistant to secondary diseases or that pine tree forests draw fewer lightning strikes than do many other habitat types in Arizona, so both **C** and **D** are incorrect.

Some questions for literary narrative passages will use phrases such as *main conflict* or *main theme* instead of *main idea*, but you should approach the questions in the same way as you would other main idea questions. Here's an example based on a literary narrative passage about a young woman, Cally Roy (page 266):

4. The main conflict in this passage could best be described as the:

    F. tension between the narrator's mother and Frank.
    G. hostility expressed between the narrator and her mother.
    H. narrator's efforts to break her ties to her mother and grandmothers.
    J. narrator's internal struggle to connect with her past and find her future.

You have to read the whole passage carefully to sort out what the main conflict is because there's at least some truth to all of the answer choices. Choice **J** turns out to be the best of the four choices because the main conflict is within the narrator herself. She journeys away from home and "into the city's bloody heart" (lines 18–19), she wonders "about the meaning of [her] spirit name" (line 22), she feels out of place in her "Frankenstein body" (line 76), and she ends the passage torn between her "city corner" and her life "back home" (lines 82–83). The narrator says her mother loves Frank "too much to live with" him (lines 36–37) and also that Frank "can't drag himself away from the magnetic field of mother's voice" (lines 68–69), but the tension between the narrator's mother and Frank isn't the main conflict of the passage, making **F** wrong. There could be some hostility between the narrator and her mother because the narrator doesn't seem to want to go to the tribal college like her mother wants her to (see lines 79–82), but the narrator also wants to "curl next to her and be a small girl again" (lines 74–75), so mother-daughter hostility isn't the main conflict, either, ruling out **G**. Choice **H** misses the mark because although the narrator has left her home and her mother, her grandmothers are only briefly talked about in the passage (see lines 24–33), so the main conflict can't revolve around them.

Comparative Relationships. You're likely to find questions asking you to make comparisons and contrasts in passages that contain a lot of information or that feature multiple characters or points of view. This kind of test question can make you process a lot of information—you may be asked to weigh one concept against another and identify a significant difference between the two. But comparison and contrast questions aren't always overly complicated. In the following example, based on a humanities passage about the artist Pieter Saenredam (page 269), the comparison is directly made in a few lines in the passage:

---

5. According to the passage, Saenredam and Vermeer were similar in their:

    A. weak draftsmanship despite their careful observation of subjects.
    B. principles of design and spatial dimension.
    C. use of shadow and religious subjects.
    D. limited production and their desire for perfection.

Lines 16–17 state, "Like Vermeer, Saenredam was a perfectionist and his output was fairly small." Thus, **D** is the best answer. It speaks to both parts of the similarity—their output being fairly small and the idea that they were both perfectionists. The passage states that Saenredam was an "outstanding draftsman" (lines 17–18), so **A** cannot be true. The passage does not give us information about Vermeer's principles of design and spatial dimension (**B**), nor does it indicate that Vermeer used shadows and religious subjects in a way similar to Saenredam (**C**).

Cause-Effect Relationships. Cause-effect questions can arise in passages when it is important to understand the cause or result of specific actions, events, or ideas. In a literary narrative passage, perhaps one character's actions caused another character to act a certain way. In an informational passage, it might be important to understand the consequences of a specific decision or policy. Sometimes the answer to a cause-effect question is stated in the passage; sometimes you have to piece together the information you've read and work out the answer on your own.

Here's an example of a fairly direct cause-effect question, based on the literary narrative passage about Cally Roy (page 266):

---

6. The narrator implies that losing her indis has caused her to:

    F. cling to her family.
    G. leave her home.
    H. remember its every detail.
    J. fight with her family.

The information needed to answer this question is in the first paragraph: once the narrator lost her indis, she says, she "began to wander from home, first in my thoughts, then my feet took after" (lines 11–13). Choice **G** is therefore the best answer. Choice **F** is pretty much the opposite of the truth, in the sense that the narrator decided to leave home. Although the narrator claims she "remember[s] every detail" of her indis (line 5), this isn't because she lost it but because "the turtle hung near my crib, then off my belt, and was my very first play toy" (lines 5–7). So **H** can't be the best answer. Choice **J** is incorrect because the narrator never really implies that losing her indis has caused her to fight with her family. Although her mother was "in a panic" (line 27) over the narrator's decision to leave, this seems more out of concern for the narrator than the result of a fight.

Following is an example of a somewhat more complex cause-effect question, this time based on the natural science passage on lightning and fire (page 270):

---

7. The third paragraph (lines 41–61) suggests that if lightning did not fix atmospheric nitrogen, then:
    A. rain could not fall to Earth, leaving nitrogen in the atmosphere.
    B. less nitrogen would be found on Earth.
    C. electrical current could not be conducted by air.
    D. lightning bolts would strike the earth with less frequency.

Although the question lets you know to look in the third paragraph, the wording of that paragraph is subtle and requires close reading. The relevant information is in lines 45–46: "Lightning helps to fix atmospheric nitrogen into a form that rain can bring to Earth." This matches nicely with **B**, which says that less nitrogen would be found on Earth. Although nitrogen would remain in the atmosphere if lightning didn't fix it, the paragraph never suggests that rain wouldn't fall to Earth, making **A** tempting but wrong. The paragraph doesn't suggest that if lightning didn't fix atmospheric nitrogen, electrical current couldn't be conducted by air or that lightning bolts would strike the earth with less frequency, making **C** and **D** incorrect.

Generalizations. This type of question usually asks you to take a lot of information—sometimes the whole passage—and boil it down into a more concise form. A generalization question may involve interpreting mood, tone, or character, or it may ask you to make some kind of general observation or draw a conclusion about the nature of an argument the author is making. The following example, based on the literary narrative about Allegra's violin lesson (page 265), focuses on personality or character:

---

8. Based on the passage, Allegra's attitude toward Mr. Kaplan is best described as one of:
    F. low-key ridicule.
    G. good-natured respect.
    H. resentful obedience.
    J. close friendship.

This question requires you to sum up Allegra's attitude toward Mr. Kaplan based on the passage as a whole. The best answer is **G**. Though there is no one specific moment that establishes this good-natured respect, their interactions and conversation most strongly suggest Allegra's attitude toward her teacher. Allegra clearly wants to perform well for Mr. Kaplan, which shows her respect for him. We can see this in the way Allegra practices the shift without making any noise (lines 46–47) and in the fact that she had worked so hard on her tape for the Bloch Competition. And there are lighthearted moments throughout that speak to this respect being good-natured. Allegra loves her lessons ("In the summer I get to have morning lessons twice a week, and I love it" [lines 14–15]); she notes with affection the way Mr. Kaplan looks (lines 41–42); and she and Mr. Kaplan smile or laugh at moments during practice (lines 76, 88, 90). There is no indication in the passage that Allegra views Mr. Kaplan with an attitude of ridicule (**F**). There are moments that could be misread as ridicule, like when Allegra notes that Mr. Kaplan's "ears stick out in a funny way" (line 41), but it's important to read those moments in the larger context of the passage. Allegra goes on to say, "I love the way he looks" (lines 41–42), which speaks to her fondness for Mr. Kaplan. There's also nothing in the passage to point to a general attitude of resentful obedience (**H**). Allegra takes direction from Mr. Kaplan, but she doesn't display any resentment. And while Allegra and Mr. Kaplan are comfortable with each other, it goes too far to say that Allegra's attitude toward Mr. Kaplan is one of close friendship (**J**). They have a good working relationship, but there's nothing in the passage to suggest that Allegra considers Mr. Kaplan a close friend. At one point Allegra compares Mr. Kaplan to her softball coach when she says, "My softball coach and my violin teacher were overlapping each other" (5–6). This suggests that Allegra views Mr. Kaplan as another adult in a role of authority rather than a close friend.

Meanings of Words. Questions about meanings of words ask you to determine from context what a particular word, phrase, or statement most nearly means. In some cases, the word or words will probably be unfamiliar to you, but even when familiar words are tested, you'll have to look at the context in which they appear to determine the closest synonym or paraphrase. Sometimes looking at a single sentence of the passage is enough to figure this out, but other times you'll have to look at sentences before or after the given word, phrase, or statement in order to determine the closest meaning.

Many meanings-of-words questions will focus on a single word or a short phrase. The answer choices will include synonyms for the word or phrase that you might find in a dictionary or thesaurus, but only one of the choices will truly reflect how the word or phrase is used in this particular case. Look at the following example, based on the humanities passage about Pieter Saenredam (page 269):

---

9. As it is used in line 71, the word *fixes* most nearly means:
   A. establishes.
   B. corrects.
   C. repairs.
   D. hardens.

All of the answer choices could be synonyms for *fixes* depending on context. Only Choice **A**, though, makes sense here. The passage tells us that certain drawings contain such detailed information that we can place the artist at a specific time and place. Thus, the ink-wash shadow in this drawing establishes (fixes) a time. It would not make sense to say that the shadow corrects (**B**), repairs (**C**), or hardens (**D**) the time.

Sequence of Events. In some passages, the order, or sequence, in which events happen is important. Sequence-of-events questions may ask you to determine when, for example, a character in a literary narrative passage did something or to figure out the order in which the researchers described in an informational passage performed certain steps in a biology experiment.

Sequence questions will often require you to take in information from the whole passage or from large sections of the passage in order to determine a correct order of events. This is true of the question below, based on a natural science passage about the small-comet theory (page 271):

---

10. Which of the following events mentioned in the passage occurred first chronologically?

   F. Frank and Sigwarth presented new evidence that leaves little doubt Earth is being bombarded by something.
   G. Frank and Sigwarth first put forth the small-comet theory.
   H. Frank and Sigwarth analyzed photos of the electrical phenomena that accompany sunspots.
   J. Frank and Sigwarth had difficulty getting the scientific community to accept their ideas.

The passage details how Frank and Sigwarth came up with the small-comet theory, the scientific community's reaction to the theory, and new developments since the theory was first presented. Because the timeline skips around in the passage, it's important to read carefully to understand the sequence of events. The best answer is **H**. In the sixth paragraph (lines 41–50), we're told that the small-comet theory first started to take shape when Sigwarth was Frank's graduate student. As they analyzed photos, they noticed dark specks appearing in images from a NASA satellite. Lines 59–62 state: "Based on their images, the Iowa scientists estimated 20 comets an hour . . . were bombarding the Earth." Thus, the analysis of the images eventually led to the small-comet theory. Choice **F** cannot be correct because this new evidence was presented after the small-comet theory had been put forth (lines 15–19). This choice may be tempting because it appears in the passage before Choice **H**. The same is true of Choice **G**. But since the photo analysis eventually led to the small-comet theory, it would be incorrect to state that the theory was put forth first (**G**). The passage also makes clear that Frank and Sigwarth's theory was not well received by the scientific community when it was first put forth, so Choice **J** has to come after Choices **G** and **H**.

Author's Purpose and Method. Questions about the author's purpose or method focus on the craft of writing—the main purpose of a passage, what role parts of a passage (such as a paragraph) play in the whole work, and so on.

An example should help clear up what this category is about. Taken from a social science passage on the Erie Canal (page 267), this question asks you to consider the function of a paragraph in the passage:

11. In the context of the passage, the sixth paragraph (lines 39–52) primarily functions to:

   A. outline the obstacles Clinton faced in getting public approval for the Erie Canal.
   B. explain how Clinton's plan won over a reluctant state legislature when the federal government refused to help.
   C. detail how the Erie Canal gamble paid off in the economic advancement of New York.
   D. describe the vast logistical and financial concerns of the Erie Canal project.

In the fifth paragraph, we're told that the idea of a canal connecting the Hudson with the Great Lakes "had been around for many years but always dismissed as hopelessly impracticable" (lines 28–29). The sixth paragraph builds on this by describing the major issues involved in the construction of the Erie Canal. Therefore, the best answer is Choice **D**. The first sentence of this paragraph states, "One can understand the reluctance, for the project was huge by the standards of the day" (lines 39–40). The paragraph then details what made the project so daunting: the canal would be the longest in the world, it would require moving 11.4 million cubic yards of earth and rock, and its expense was equal to 1 percent of the entire country's gross domestic product. Choice **A** is incorrect because these are not obstacles Clinton himself had to face to gain public support; in fact, the passage notes only that Clinton built public support (line 37) and doesn't indicate that there were obstacles to this at all. Choice **B** is incorrect because there's no information in the paragraph about how the plan won over the reluctant state legislature. Choice **C** is incorrect because although the paragraph notes that the Erie Canal "put the Empire in the Empire State" (lines 51–52), it doesn't *detail how*; this is explored in the rest of the passage.

Arguments. Some questions deal with the arguments and claims made in passages. These questions may ask you to identify an argument or to examine support for a statement made in the passage. They may also ask you to identify the difference between fact and opinion, or to understand how an author might try to persuade readers. The examples below will help you understand what kinds of questions you might see in this category. The first is taken from the humanities passage about Pieter Saenredam (page 269) and asks you to identify a main claim from the passage:

12. One of the passage's central claims is that:

   F. Saenredam's detailed drawings provide deep insights into his paintings and his life.
   G. Saenredam was an outstanding draftsman, though he produced relatively little of importance.
   H. Vermeer, Rembrandt, and Saenredam all incorporated fiction into their art in some degree.
   J. taken together, the work of Vermeer, Rembrandt, and Saenredam represents the Golden Age of Dutch art.

Choice **F** is the correct answer because it identifies one of the passage's central claims. In the second paragraph of the passage, we're told that many of Saenredam's drawings survive, and that "they offer intimate insights into his art and life" (line 20). The passage author then spends a significant portion of the passage exploring what those insights are. We can see this in lines 39–80, which detail the different aspects of Saenredam's life and art that can be gleaned from his drawings. Since so much of the passage is spent exploring this idea, we can call this a central claim of the passage. Choice **G** might be tempting because we're told that Saenredam was an outstanding draftsman and that "his output was fairly small" (line 17). But Choice **G** goes a step beyond this in asserting that Saenredam produced little of importance. While we know that he doesn't enjoy the same level of fame as Vermeer or Rembrandt, the passage does not assert that his work is of little importance; rather, the author notes that many connoisseurs consider Saenredam an equal of these more famous artists and that Saenredam produced works "among the supreme masterpieces of Dutch art" (lines 51–52). Choice **H** is incorrect because it is a detail in the last paragraph of the passage (lines 81–89) rather than a central claim. Choice **J** is incorrect because this is not a statement made in the passage. In the first line of the passage we're told that "thanks to Vermeer and Rembrandt, art of the 17th-century Dutch Golden Age is box-office magic" (lines 1–2), but this is not further explored or explained in the passage.

The next example is from the social science passage about the Erie Canal (page 267). It focuses on a specific statement in the passage and asks you to determine how the author supports that statement:

---

13. What evidence does the author provide to support the claim that "New York became the greatest boomtown the world has ever known" (lines 70–72)?

    A. A quotation from Holmes regarding New York's status after the Eric Canal opened
    B. The percentage of American exports passing through the port of New York in 1800
    C. Statistics that show New York's population from 1790 to 1860
    D. Details about other projects undertaken in New York after the Erie Canal was completed

---

The answer to this question can be found in the ninth paragraph (lines 70–78), right after the claim in lines 70–72. Questions that ask for supporting evidence will not always be this straightforward and will often require that you look at the wider passage to find the answer, but in this case the answer can be found in the same paragraph as the claim. The best answer is **C** because this paragraph follows up the claim by providing statistics to show how the population of New York increased after the Erie Canal opened. Earlier in the passage we're told that the Erie Canal was finished in 1825. According to population statistics provided in the ninth paragraph, the population of New York had been increasing at a rate of roughly 30,000 every decade before the Erie Canal opened. After the canal's opening, the population increased at a much faster pace: by more than 100,000 from 1830 to 1840, more than 200,000 from 1840 to 1850, and almost 300,000 from 1850 to 1860. Choice **A** is incorrect because the quotation from Holmes in lines 66–67 mainly helps show how much produce flowed eastward after the canal opened; it points to prosperity but doesn't provide specific support for the claim. Choice **B** is incorrect because the canal had not been finished in 1800. The 9 percent of American exports passing through New York in 1800 is low; in 1860, after the canal had been open for several decades, that percentage was much higher. Choice **D** is incorrect because the passage doesn't describe other projects undertaken in New York after the canal was completed. "Megaprojects" are mentioned in lines 90–92, but they are not specific to New York, and they are provided as examples to show how the success of the Erie Canal encouraged big thinking.

Answer Key for Reading Test Sample Questions

1. A	6. G	11. D
2. H	7. B	12. F
3. B	8. G	13. C
4. J	9. A	
5. D	10. H	

Strategies for Taking the ACT Reading Test

Performance on the ACT reading test relies not only on reading speed and comprehension but also on test-taking strategies and skills. The following sections describe strategies and skills specifically for improving your ACT reading test score.

Pace Yourself

Before you read the first passage of the reading test, you may want to take a quick look through the entire reading test. If you choose to do this, flip through the pages and look at each of the passages and their questions. (Note that the passages begin on the pages to your left, and the questions follow.) You don't need to memorize anything—you can look at any of the reading test passages and questions during the time allotted for that test.

Some readers find that looking quickly at the questions first gives them a better idea of what to look for as they're reading the passage. It you're a slow reader, though, this may not be a good strategy. If you do decide to preview the questions, don't spend too much time on them—just scan for a few key words or ideas that you can watch for when you read the passage. To see what approach works best for you, you might want to try alternating between previewing the questions and not previewing the questions as you work through the practice tests in this book. Remember that when you take the ACT for real, a clock will be running. Plan your approach for the reading test before you take the actual ACT.

Use the Time Allotted

You have 35 minutes to read four passages and answer 40 questions. You'll want to pace yourself so you don't spend too much time on any one passage or question. If you take 2 to 3 minutes to read each passage, you'll have about 35 seconds to answer each question associated with the passage. Some of the questions will take less time, which will allow you more time for the more challenging ones.

Because time is limited, you should be very careful in deciding whether to skip more difficult questions. If you skip the difficult questions from the first passage until you work through the entire reading test, for example, you may find that you've forgotten so much of the first passage that you have to reread it before you can answer the questions that puzzled you the first time through. It may work better for you to think of the test as four separate units, giving yourself time to finish every passage and item set (approximately 8 minutes and 30 seconds each). Then you can try to complete all the questions for a passage within its allotted time. Answer all the questions; you're not penalized for guessing.

Think of an Overall Strategy That Works for You

Are you the kind of person who likes to get the big picture first, then carefully go over your work? Do you like to answer the questions you're sure of right away and then go back and puzzle out the tougher ones? Or are you something of a perfectionist? (Do you find it hard to concentrate on a question until you know you got the one before it right?) There isn't any right way or wrong way to approach the reading test—just make sure the way you choose is the way that works best for you.

Keep the Passage as a Whole in Mind

Your initial look at the whole reading test should give you some ideas about how to approach each passage. Notice the subject heading and short paragraph before each passage. These "advance organizers" tell you whether the passage is literary narrative or informational, where the passage comes from, who wrote it, and sometimes a little information about the passage. Occasionally an advance organizer will define a difficult word, explain a concept, or provide background information. Reading the advance organizers carefully should help you be more prepared as you approach each passage.

Always remember that the reading test asks you to refer to and reason on the basis of the passage. You may know a lot about the subject of some of the passages you read, but try not to let what you already know influence the way you answer the questions, because the author's perspective may differ from yours. There's a reason why many questions begin with "According to the passage" or "It can reasonably be inferred from the passage." If you read and understand the passage well, your reasoning ability will help you to figure out the correct answer. During the reading test, you can refer back to the passages as often as you like.

Find a Strategy for Approaching Each Question

First, read each question carefully so you know what it asks. Look for the best answer, but read and consider all the options, even though you may feel you've identified the best one. Ask yourself whether you can justify your choice as the best answer.

Some people find it useful to answer the easy questions first and skip the difficult ones (being careful, of course, to mark the answer document correctly and to mark in the test booklet the

Improving Your Score

questions they skipped). Then they go back and consider the difficult questions. When you're working on a test question and aren't certain about the answer, try to eliminate choices you're sure are incorrect. If you can rule out a couple of choices, you'll improve your chances of selecting the correct answer. Keep referring back to the passage for information.

Reading Strategies Summary

The sample passages used as examples in this section can be found on the following pages. They come from ACT tests that thousands of students have already taken. Remember, the passages and items in this section don't represent every type you're likely to see, but they should give you a good idea of some of the kinds of questions you'll encounter when you take the ACT reading test. For a more complete picture of what the ACT reading test will look like, six complete reading tests are included in the six practice ACT tests in chapters 3 and 10. And remember that the best way to do well on the ACT reading test is to have a solid understanding of each passage—so read quickly but carefully.

Prep Online!

Want even more ways to prep? Go to act.wiley.com to access our online platform or use our companion app. Create your own question sets to practice. Use highlighting and notes to analyze each passage. To get started, go to act.wiley.com, and register with the PIN on the back of the front cover of this book.

Sample Passage I

LITERARY NARRATIVE: This passage is adapted from the novel *The Mozart Season* by Virginia Euwer Wolff (©1991 by Virginia Euwer Wolff).

The hair on a violin bow is the part of the bow, traditionally made of horsehair, that makes contact with the strings when the violin is played.

"Now that you're warmed up, let's revisit Mr. Mozart," said Mr. Kaplan.

It was a gorgeous June morning and in my mind I heard another voice: "Now that you're warmed up, let's
5 demolish those Vikings." My softball coach and my violin teacher were overlapping each other.

With my softball coach, it was stairsteps and laps and endless batting practice. With Mr. Kaplan it was eight repetitions of very fast B-major scales and five
10 minutes of octaves. Two weeks after being the shortstop on the team that had lost in the second round of the district play-offs, I was at my lesson, looking for the Mozart concerto.

In the summer I get to have morning lessons twice
15 a week, and I love it. I work best in the mornings. Things haven't had time to get so cluttered yet.

I put the music on the stand and got ready. With Mr. Kaplan you don't whine or mutter. It doesn't help. "We want right notes, not excuses" is what all music
20 teachers say, I guess. He doesn't have to say it very many times; you learn it fast. Mr. Kaplan and I'd been together for seven years, and he was going to know the instant I got to the top of the second page that I hadn't been practicing the Mozart. At that spot there's a fast
25 shift from first finger to fourth finger on the G string, and you have to get ready for it. You can't let a shift like that take you by surprise.

"Straight through. Right, Allegra? Including cadenzas." A cadenza is the part where the violin plays
30 alone; it's harder than the rest of the piece, and it gets the audience all excited when you do it in a concert. There are three cadenzas in this concerto, one in each movement.

"Right."

35 The introduction is forty-one measures long. This time, instead of playing just the last two measures of it on the piano, Mr. Kaplan played the whole thing. He wears half-glasses, and he has a balding head with some blondish-gray hair on the back, and a mostly gray
40 short beard, and he's a little bit slumped over when he sits at the piano. His ears stick out in a funny way. I love the way he looks. The introduction to the first movement, the part the orchestra would play, mostly announces what the solo violin will play when it
45 begins. That way you get to listen to it twice.

While he was doing it, I practiced the G-string shift without making any noise, sliding my hand up and down the fingerboard.

I love this concerto. Mozart only wrote five of
50 them for the violin. The year before, Mr. Kaplan had let me choose which one to learn, the third one or this one, and I'd taken them both home and spun my bow the way you spin a tennis racquet. If it landed with the hair toward me, I'd learn the third, in G; and if it landed
55 with the hair away from me, I'd learn this one. When Mr. Kaplan and my parents found out I'd treated my bow With Such Astonishing Disrespect, they got very alarmed about it.

I'd worked very hard on it for several months, and
60 in February, we'd made a tape of it to send to a contest. I'd worried and fretted and trembled, but we'd gotten the tape made. After that, I'd sort of neglected it. In softball season I'd practically stopped being a violinist.

Mr. Kaplan, who was having fun playing the intro-
65 duction, got to the BUM-*pum-pa-pum* part that comes right before the violin begins. I was ready. It starts on a high D and goes on up from there.

I got through the first movement all right, and I made some genuine messes of the beautiful double-
70 stops near the end of the second-movement cadenza. Double-stops are two notes at once, on separate strings. And I was sure the last-movement cadenza was making it Abundantly Clear to Mr. Kaplan that I hadn't even seen it for a long time. But the end was fine. The *Blip-
75 te-de-bip-bip-bip* came out very, very soft and nice.

Mr. Kaplan leaned back, smiling and saying a kind of "ah." Then he turned sideways on the bench. "Isn't this a beautiful song, Allegra?"

"Yep." It is. Mr. Kaplan calls overtures and
80 symphonies and concertos "songs" sometimes. I waited for him to say the rest.

He leaned forward and flipped the pages. "Hmmm. I'm concerned about the articulation in spots, and some of the dynamics aren't at all what they should be
85 and . . . Hmmm." Then he turned sideways on the bench again, straddling it. "Are you willing to play this concerto a thousand times by September?"

I laughed. That would be more times than I'd brush my teeth by then. He watched me thinking. He
90 started to smile, then he got up and walked across the studio, away from me. Then he turned around. "Your tape was accepted," he said. "For the Bloch Competition. The finals are on Labor Day."

Sample Passage II

LITERARY NARRATIVE: This passage is adapted from *The Antelope Wife* by Louise Erdrich (©1998 by Louise Erdrich).

My mother sewed my birth cord, with dry sage and sweet grass, into a turtle holder of soft white buckskin. She beaded that little turtle using precious old cobalts and yellows and Cheyenne pinks and greens in a careful
5 design. I remember every detail of it, me, because the turtle hung near my crib, then off my belt, and was my very first play toy. I was supposed to have it on me all my life, bury it with me on reservation land, but one day I came in from playing and my indis was gone.
10 I thought nothing of it, at first and for many years, but slowly over time the absence . . . it will tell. I began to wander from home, first in my thoughts, then my feet took after, so at last at the age of eighteen, I walked the road that led from the front of our place to the wider
15 spaces and then the country beyond that, where that one road widened into two lanes, then four, then six, past the farms and service islands, into the dead wall of the suburbs and still past that, finally, into the city's bloody heart.

20 My name is Cally Roy. Ozhawashkwamashko-deykway is what the spirits call me. All my life so far I've wondered about the meaning of my spirit name but nobody's told it, seen it, got ahold of my history flying past. Mama has asked, she has offered tobacco, even
25 blankets, but my grandmas Mrs. Zosie Roy and Mary Shawano only nod at her, holding their tongues as they let their eyes wander. In a panic, once she knew I was setting out, not staying home, Mama tried to call up my grandmas and ask if I could live at their apartment in
30 the city. But once they get down to the city, it turns out they never stop moving. They are out, and out again. Impossible to track down. It's true, they are extremely busy women.

So my mom sends me to Frank.

35 Frank Shawano. Famous Indian bakery chef. My Mama's eternal darling, the man she loves too much to live with.

I'm weary and dirty and sore when I get to Frank's bakery shop, but right away, walking in and the bell
40 dinging with a cheerful alertness, I smell those good bakery smells of yeasty bread and airy sugar. Behind the counter, lemony light falls on Frank. He is big, strong, pale brown like a loaf of light rye left to rise underneath a towel. His voice is muffled and weak, like
45 it is squeezed out of the clogged end of a pastry tube. He greets me with gentle pleasure.

"Just as I'm closing." His smile is very quiet. He cleans his hands on a towel and beckons me into the back of the bakery shop, between swinging steel doors.
50 I remember him as a funny man, teasing and playing games and rolling his eyes at us, making his pink sugar-cookie dogs bark and elephants trumpet. But now he is serious, and frowns slightly as I follow him up the back

stairs and into the big top-floor apartment with the
55 creaky floors, the groaning pipes, odd windows that view the yard. My little back room, no bigger than a closet, overlooks this space.

I'm so beat, though, I just want to crawl into my corner and sleep.

60 "Not too small, this place?" He sounds anxious.

I shake my head. The room seems okay, the mattress on the floor, the blankets, and the shelves for my things.

"Call your mom?" Frank gives orders in the form
65 of a question. He acts all purposeful, as though he is going back downstairs to close up the store, but as I dial the number on the kitchen wall phone he lingers. He can't drag himself away from the magnetic field of my mother's voice, muffled, far off, but on the other
70 end of the receiver. He stands in the doorway with that same towel he brought from downstairs, folding and refolding it in his hands.

"Mama," I say, and her voice on the phone suddenly hurts. I want to curl next to her and be a small
75 girl again. My body feels too big, electric, like a Frankenstein body enclosing a tiny child's soul.

We laugh at some corny joke and Frank darts a glance at me, then stares at his feet and frowns. Reading between my Mama's pauses on the phone, I
80 know she is hoping I'll miss the real land, and her, come back and resume my brilliant future at the tribal college. In spite of how I want to curl up in my city corner, I picture everything back home. On the wall of my room up north, there hang a bundle of sage and
85 Grandma Roy's singing drum. On the opposite wall, I taped up posters and photos. Ever since I was little, I slept with a worn bear and a new brown dog. And my real dog, too, curled at my feet sometimes, if Mama didn't catch us. I never liked dolls. I made good scores
90 in math. I get to missing my room and my dog and I lose track of Mama's voice.

Sample Passage III

INFORMATIONAL: This passage is adapted from the article "10 Moments that Made American Business" by John Steele Gordon (©2007 by American Heritage Publishing).

The cost of overland transportation had been a limiting factor in the world economy since time immemorial. Any material with a low value-to-weight ratio, such as foodstuffs, that couldn't be transported to
5 distant markets by water couldn't be sold in those markets at a price anyone would pay. This meant that national economies were fragmented into an infinity of local ones.

Until the Industrial Revolution, there was only one
10 way to reduce these transportation costs: build artificial rivers. By the end of the eighteenth century England was well laced with canals, greatly facilitating industrialization as factories could sell their goods profitably throughout the entire country.

15 But the new United States was 10 times the size of England and far less developed. And a considerable mountain range divided the more developed eastern seaboard from the fertile, resource-rich, and rapidly growing West. Settlers west of the Appalachians had no
20 choice but to send their crops down the Mississippi to market.

Along the whole great chain of mountains that stretched from Maine to Alabama, there was only a single gap—where the Mohawk River tumbles into the
25 Hudson near Albany—at which a canal was even theoretically possible.

The idea of building a canal to connect the Hudson with the Great Lakes there had been around for many years but always dismissed as hopelessly impracticable.
30 Even Thomas Jefferson thought the idea "little short of madness." DeWitt Clinton, however, did not. Born into a prominent New York family (his uncle had been governor of New York and then Vice President under James Madison), Clinton would be the mayor of New York
35 City and governor of the state for most of the first quarter of the nineteenth century. A shrewd politician, he built public support for the canal and pushed it through a reluctant state legislature.

One can understand the reluctance, for the project
40 was huge by the standards of the day. At 363 miles the Erie would be by far the longest canal in the world. It would require moving, largely by hand, 11.4 million cubic yards of earth and rock—well over three times the volume of the Great Pyramid of Egypt—and build-
45 ing 83 locks in what was still a semiwilderness. The budget, seven million dollars, was about equal to one percent of the gross domestic product of the entire country. Nonetheless, when the federal government refused to help, New York decided to go it alone. It was
50 a gigantic roll of the economic dice, but one that paid off beyond even Clinton's dreams. The Erie Canal put the Empire in the Empire State.

The canal was a success even before it fully opened, as traffic burgeoned on the completed parts,
55 helping fund continuing construction. When it was finished in 1825, ahead of schedule and under budget, traffic was tremendous from the start. It is not hard to understand why. Before, it had taken three weeks and cost $120 to ship a ton of flour from Buffalo to New
60 York City. With the canal, it took eight days and cost $6.

Produce that had gone down the Mississippi to New Orleans now began to flow eastward. In a few years the Boston poet and physician Oliver Wendell
65 Holmes (father of the Supreme Court justice) described New York as "that tongue that is licking up the cream of commerce and finance of a continent." In 1800 about 9 percent of American exports passed through the port of New York. By 1860 it was 62 percent.

70 With the opening of the Erie Canal, New York became the greatest boomtown the world has ever known. The population of New York had been increasing by about 30,000 every decade since 1790, with 123,000 inhabitants in 1820. By 1830, however, New
75 York's population had reached 202,000; by 1840, 313,000. It was 516,000 in 1850 and 814,000 in 1860. Development roared up Manhattan Island, at the astonishing rate of about two blocks a year.

Thanks to the Erie Canal, by the 1840s New
80 York's financial market was the largest in the country. In that decade the telegraph began to spread quickly, allowing more and more people to trade in the New York market, which has dominated American financial activity ever since.

85 Even so, perhaps the greatest consequence of the Erie Canal was that its success made the country far more receptive to other projects of unprecedented scale and scope and encouraged its entrepreneurs and politicians to think big. The result was a still-continuing
90 string of megaprojects—the Atlantic cable, the Brooklyn Bridge, the Panama Canal, Hoover Dam, the interstate highway system, the Apollo missions—that have marked the economic history of the United States and shaped the national character.

Sample Passage IV

INFORMATIONAL: This passage is adapted from Morton Hunt's *The Story of Psychology* (© 1993 by Morton Hunt).

In the passage, the term *maturation* refers to the process of growth and development, and the term *perceptual ability* refers to the capacity to recognize something through the senses (sight, smell, touch, etc.).

Much maturation research is concerned with physical skills and physical attributes, and adds little to our knowledge of the growth of the mind. But research on the development of perceptual abilities begins to pro-
5 vide solid factual answers to the ancient central question of psychology: How much is due to nature and how much to nurture (or, in developmental terms, to maturation and to learning)?

The work has been focused on early infancy, when
10 perceptual abilities evolve rapidly; its aim is to discover when each new ability first appears, the assumption being that at its first appearance, the new ability arises not from learning but from maturation of the optic nervous structures and especially of that part of
15 the brain cortex where visual signals are received and interpreted.

Much has been learned by simply watching infants. What, exactly, do very young infants see? Since we cannot ask them what they see, how can we
20 find out?

In 1961, the psychologist Robert Fantz devised an ingenious method of doing so. He designed a stand in which, on the bottom level, the baby lies on her back, looking up. A few feet above is a display area where
25 the experimenter puts two large cards, each containing a design—a white circle, a yellow circle, a bull's-eye, a simple sketch of a face. The researcher, peering down through a tiny peephole, can watch the movement of the baby's eyes and time how long they are directed at
30 one or the other of each pair of patterns. Fantz found that at two months babies looked twice as long at a bull's-eye as at a circle of solid color, and twice as long at a sketch of a face as at a bull's-eye. Evidently, even a two-month-old can distinguish major differences and
35 direct her gaze toward what she finds more interesting.

Using this technique, developmental psychologists have learned a great deal about what infants see and when they begin to see it. In the first week infants distinguish light and dark patterns; during the first month
40 they begin to track slowly moving objects; by the second month they begin to have depth perception, coordinate the movement of the eyes, and differentiate among hues and levels of brightness; by three months they can glance from one object to another, and can dis-
45 tinguish among family members; by four months they focus at varying distances, make increasingly fine distinctions, and begin to recognize the meaning of what they see (they look longer at a normal sketch of a face than at one in which the features have been scrambled);
50 and from four to seven months they achieve stereopsis, recognize that a shape held at different angles is still the same shape, and gain near-adult ability to focus at varying distances.

Exactly how maturation and experience interact in
55 the brain tissues to produce such developmental changes is becoming clear from neuroscience research. Microscopic examination of the brains of infants shows that as the brain triples in size during the first two years of life, a profusion of dendrites (branches) grow from
60 its neurons and make contact with one another.

By the time a human is twelve, the brain has an estimated hundred trillion synapses (connections between nerve cells). Those connections are the wiring plan that establishes the brain's capabilities. Some of
65 the synaptic connections are made automatically by chemical guidance, but others are made by the stimulus of experience during the period of rapid dendrite growth. Lacking such stimulus, the dendrites wither away without forming the needed synapses. Mice
70 reared in the dark develop fewer dendritic spines and synaptic connections in the visual cortex than mice reared in the light, and even when exposed to light never attain normal vision.

Why should nature have done that? Why should
75 perceptual development be possible only at a critical period and not later? It does not make evolutionary sense for the organism to be permanently impaired in sensory performance just because it fails to have the proper experiences at specific times in its development.
80 But some brain researchers say that there is an offsetting advantage: the essential experiences are almost always available at the right time, and they fine-tune the brain structure so as to provide far more specific perceptual powers than could result from genetic con-
85 trol of synapse formation.

With that, the vague old terms nature and nurture take on precise new meaning. Now, after so many centuries of speculation, we catch the first glimpse of how mind is constructed out of matter by experience.

Sample Passage V

INFORMATIONAL: This passage is adapted from the article "Sublime Architecture: Sacred Interiors Aglow" by Holland Cotter (©2002 by The New York Times Company).

Thanks to Vermeer and Rembrandt, art of the 17th-century Dutch Golden Age is box-office magic. One reason is obvious: both artists are charismatic stylists and humane thinkers. The same is true of Pieter
5 Saenredam (1597–1665), their contemporary and, in the view of many connoisseurs, their equal, but who doesn't enjoy their popular fame. While they painted people, he painted buildings: church interiors in which the human figure was insignificant or absent. In fact,
10 Saenredam is often referred to as an architectural portraitist, whose exacting eye for measurement, light and detail gives his pictures the accuracy of scientific photographs. But are they really so true to life? Or are they, like photographs, a mix of fact, error and wishful
15 illusion?

Like Vermeer, Saenredam was a perfectionist and his output was fairly small. He was also an outstanding draftsman and—this is not true of Vermeer—many of his drawings survive. All directly related to the paint-
20 ings, they offer intimate insights into his art and life.

About that life we know both a little and a lot. He was born in Assendelft. After his father died when he was 10, the family moved to Haarlem, where Saenredam stayed for the rest of his life. He studied art
25 but, being financially independent, never had to make a living from it. At 30 he decided to devote himself to architectural subjects, or perspectives, as they were called. When he died he was buried in the Church of St. Bavo, which he had often painted.

30 Saenredam's fascination with Dutch churches was real, and intense enough to take him on occasional trips away from Haarlem. The longest was to Utrecht, where he stayed from June to October 1636. His long stay in Utrecht may have been forced by a plague outbreak that
35 hit Haarlem soon after he left. In any event, his time in Utrecht was the most fruitful of his career, when he produced some of his greatest images and a visual record of his activities.

Through his drawings we can trace his where-
40 abouts. We learn that he worked in seven different churches, five of which still exist. A soaring Gothic cathedral, called the Dom, was leveled in 1674; his drawings and paintings are the only documentation of its original appearance. The smaller, older Mariakerk—
45 *kerk* is Dutch for church—was derelict when he visited and was pulled down in the 19th century. He spent six weeks there, more time than anywhere else, and in his many views of its interior and exterior, he captured its beauties and eccentricities, as if he were portraying a
50 friend, newly met but instantly beloved. It inspired three paintings of its exterior, which are among the supreme masterpieces of Dutch art.

His work routine was the same for each church. First, he made highly detailed on-the-spot sketches of a
55 building, including close-ups of specific features. Later, in the studio, he converted these studies into more polished drawings, adjusting perspective and scale. Still later—in some cases a quarter century later—he turned these drawings into paintings.

60 Few buildings, at least before photography, were observed with more passionate care. In his on-site drawings, Saenredam seems intent on getting every last little thing down, with epic results. Whole architectural histories can be read in the structural particulars he
65 drew, civic histories in tomb inscriptions he transcribed, histories of religion and fashion in the ornaments he rendered.

Personal and professional stories also come across. Through certain drawings, we can place the artist at a
70 particular church on a particular day, say June 30, 1636. An ink-wash shadow fixes the time: 8 a.m. Another shadow to the left has a different angle: 9 a.m. So we see him moving systematically across the page. Over weeks, we see him succeeding and failing, making bril-
75 liant decisions or botching a job. Some on-site drawings are awesomely exact; others wildly misjudge spatial dimensions or cram surreal amounts of data into a single image. Certain errors of judgment can be corrected later; others are disastrous, resulting in paintings
80 that are architectural fictions.

But fiction is built into this art, just as it is into the portraits of Rembrandt and Vermeer. Reality is deliberately adjusted, edited, dramatized, simplified. A church interior cluttered with the unruly stuff of life—benches,
85 gravestones, water-stained stones—is jotted down on paper, then refined into a network of lines and grids, finally into a painted solid, a container of light, golden-brown or dove gray: a utopian vision with one foot on earth and one foot beyond.

Sample Passage VI

INFORMATIONAL: This passage is adapted from *Fire in America: A Cultural History of Wildland and Rural Fire* by Stephen J. Pyne (©1982 by Princeton University Press).

Lightning affects electrical equilibrium on the earth. Air is a poor conductor, but some electricity constantly leaks to the atmosphere, creating an electrical potential. Electricity moves back according to the gra-
5 dient [change in potential with distance]. During a thunderstorm, the gradient becomes very steep, and the electrical potential discharges as lightning. The discharge may move between any oppositely charged regions—from cloud to earth, from earth to cloud, or
10 from cloud to cloud. It was calculated as early as 1887 that the earth would lose almost all its charge in less than an hour unless the supply were replenished; that is, on a global scale, lightning will discharge to the earth every hour a quantity of electricity equal to the earth's
15 entire charge. Thunderstorms are thus an electromagnetic as well as a thermodynamic necessity. It has been reckoned that the earth experiences some 1,800 storms per hour, or 44,000 per day. Collectively, these storms produce 100 cloud-to-ground discharges per second, or
20 better than 8 million per day globally. And these estimates are probably low. The total energy in lightning bolts varies greatly, but about 250 kilowatt hours of electricity are packed into each stroke. Almost 75 percent of this total energy is lost to heat during discharge.

25 Two types of discharge patterns are commonly identified: the cold stroke, whose main return [ground-to-cloud] stroke is of intense current but of short duration, and the hot stroke, involving lesser currents of longer duration. Cold lightning, with its high voltage,
30 generally has mechanical or explosive effects; hot lightning is more apt to start fires. Studies in the Northern Rockies suggest that about one stroke in 25 has the electrical characteristics needed to start a fire. Whether it does or not depends strongly on the object it
35 strikes, the fuel properties of the object, and the local weather. Ignition requires both heat and kindling. Lightning supplies the one with its current and occasionally finds the other among the fine fuels of rotten wood, needles, grass, or dustlike debris blown from a
40 tree by the explosive shock of the bolt itself.

The consequences of lightning are complex. Any natural force of this magnitude will influence the biological no less than the geophysical environment, and the secondary effects of lightning are significant to life.
45 Lightning helps to fix atmospheric nitrogen into a form that rain can bring to earth. In areas of heavy thunderstorm activity, lightning can function as a major predator on trees, either through direct injury or by physiological damage. In the ponderosa pine forests of
50 Arizona, for example, one forester has estimated that lightning mortality runs between 0.7 and 1.0 percent per year. Other researchers have placed mortality as high as 25—33 percent. For southern pines, the figure may be even steeper. A study in Arkansas calculated
55 that 70 percent of mortality, by volume, was due to

lightning. These figures describe only direct injury, primarily the mechanical destruction of branches and bole; the other major causes of mortality—insects, wind, and mistletoe—are likely secondary effects brought about
60 in trees weakened by lightning. All of these effects, in turn, may be camouflaged by fire induced by lightning.

The process of "electrocution" is increasingly recognized. Lightning scorch areas of between 0.25 and 25 acres have been identified. Nor is the process lim-
65 ited to trees: it has been documented for grasses, tomatoes, potatoes, cabbages, tea, and other crops. Long attributed to inscrutable "die-offs" or to infestation by insects or diseases (often a secondary effect), such sites are now recognized worldwide as a product of physio-
70 logical trauma caused by lightning.

The most spectacular product of lightning is fire. Except in tropical rain forests and on ice-mantled land masses, lightning fire has occurred in every terrestrial environment on the globe, contributing to a natural
75 mosaic of vegetation types. Even in tropical landscapes lightning bombardment by itself may frequently be severe enough to produce a mosaic pattern similar to that resulting from lightning fire. Lightning fires have ignited desert grasslands, tundra, chaparral, swamp-
80 lands, marshes, grasslands, and, of course, forests. Though the intensity and frequency of these fires vary by region, their existence is undeniable.

Sample Passage VII

INFORMATIONAL: This passage is adapted from "Publish and Punish: Science's Snowball Effect" by Jon Van (©1997 by The Chicago Tribune Company).

It's a scientific finding so fundamental that it certainly will make the history books and maybe snag a Nobel Prize if it pans out, but the notion that cosmic snowballs are constantly pelting Earth is something
5 Louis Frank just as soon would have ducked.

Frank is the University of Iowa physicist whose research led him to declare more than a decade ago that Earth is being bombarded by hundreds of house-sized comets day after day that rain water on our planet and
10 are the reason we have oceans. That weather report caused the widely respected scientist to acquire a certain reputation among his colleagues as a bit unstable, an otherwise estimable fellow whose hard work may have pushed him over the edge.

15 Frank and his associate, John Sigwarth, probably went a way toward salvaging their reputations when they presented new evidence that leaves little doubt Earth is indeed being bombarded by *something* in a manner consistent with Frank's small-comet theory.
20 Rather than gloating or anticipating glory, Frank seemed relieved that part of a long ordeal was ending. "I knew we'd be in for it when we first put forth the small-comet theory," Frank conceded, "but I was naive about just how bad it would be. We were outvoted by
25 about 10,000 to 1 by our colleagues. I thought it would have been more like 1,000 to 1."

To the non-scientist this may seem a bit strange. After all, the point of science is to discover information and insights about how nature works. Shouldn't every
30 scientist be eager to overturn existing ideas and replace them with his or her own? In theory, that is the case, but in practice, scientists are almost as loath to embrace radically new ideas as the rest of us.

"Being a scientist puts you into a constant schizo-
35 phrenic existence," contends Richard Zare, chairman of the National Science Board. "You have to believe and yet question beliefs at the same time. If you are a complete cynic and believe nothing, you do nothing and get nowhere, but if you believe too much, you fool your-
40 self."

It was in the early 1980s when the small-comet theory started to haunt Frank and Sigwarth, who was Frank's graduate student studying charged particles called plasmas, which erupt from the sun and cause the
45 aurora borealis (northern lights). As they analyzed photos of the electrical phenomena that accompany sunspots, they noted dark specks appearing in several images from NASA's Dynamics Explorer 1 satellite. They assumed these were caused by static in the trans-
50 mission.

After a while their curiosity about the dark spots grew into a preoccupation, then bordered on obsession.

Try as they did, the scientists couldn't find any plausible explanation of the pattern of dark spots that
55 appeared on their images. The notion that the equipment was picking up small amounts of water entering Earth's upper atmosphere kept presenting itself as the most likely answer.

Based on their images, the Iowa scientists esti-
60 mated 20 comets an hour—each about 30 feet or so across and carrying 100 tons of water—were bombarding the Earth. At that rate, they would produce water vapor that would add about an inch of water to the planet every 10,000 years, Frank concluded. That may
65 not seem like much, but when talking about a planet billions of years old, it adds up.

Such intimate interaction between Earth and space suggests a fundamentally different picture of human evolution—which depends on water—than is com-
70 monly presented by scientists. Frank had great difficulty getting his ideas into a physics journal 11 years ago and was almost hooted from the room when he presented his theory at scientific meetings. Despite the derision, colleagues continued to respect Frank's main-
75 stream work on electrically charged particles in space and the imaging cameras he designed that were taken aboard recent NASA spacecraft to explore Earth's polar regions.

Unbeknown to most, in addition to gathering
80 information on the northern lights, Frank and Sigwarth designed the equipment to be able to snatch better views of any small comets the spacecraft might happen upon. It was those images from the latest flights that caused even harsh critics of the small-comet theory to
85 concede that some water-bearing objects appear to be entering Earth's atmosphere with regularity.

To be sure, it has not been proved that they are comets, let alone that they have anything to do with the oceans. But Frank's evidence opens the matter up to
90 study. Had he been a researcher of lesser standing, his theory probably would have died long ago.

Improving Your Score

Chapter 8:
Improving Your Science Score

The ACT science test asks you to answer 40 multiple-choice questions in 35 minutes. The questions measure the interpretation, analysis, evaluation, and problem-solving skills associated with science. The science test is made up of several passages, each of which is followed by multiple-choice questions.

Content of the ACT Science Test

The content areas of the ACT science test parallel the content of courses commonly taught in grades 7 through 12 and in entry-level college courses. Passages on the test represent the following content areas (examples of subjects included in each content area are given in parentheses):

- **Biology** (cell biology, botany, zoology, microbiology, ecology, biochemistry, genetics, and evolution)

- **Chemistry** (properties of matter, acids and bases, kinetics and equilibria, thermo-chemistry, organic chemistry, and nuclear chemistry)

- **Earth and Space sciences** (geology, meteorology, oceanography, environmental science, stars, planets, galaxies, and the universe)

- **Physics** (mechanics, gravitation, thermodynamics, electromagnetism, fluids, solids, and optics)

Advanced knowledge in these areas is not required, but background knowledge acquired in general, introductory science courses may be needed to correctly respond to some of the items.

The science test stresses science skills and practices over recall of scientific content, complex mathematics skills, and reading ability. The science skills and practices fall into three reporting categories. A brief description of each reporting category is as follows.

- **Interpretation of Data:** Manipulate and analyze scientific data presented in tables, graphs, and diagrams (e.g., recognize trends in data, translate tabular data into graphs, interpolate and extrapolate, and reason mathematically).

- **Scientific Investigation:** Understand experimental tools, procedures, and design (e.g., identify variables and controls) and compare, extend, and modify experiments (e.g., predict the results of additional trials).

- **Evaluation of Models, Inferences, and Experimental Results:** Judge the validity of scientific information and formulate conclusions and predictions based on that information (e.g., determine which explanation for a scientific phenomenon is supported by new findings).

The use of calculators is not permitted on the science test but should also not be needed.

Format of the ACT Science Test

The scientific information presented in each passage of the ACT science test is conveyed in one of three different formats:

- The **Data Representation** format requires you to understand, evaluate, and interpret information presented in graphic or tabular form.

- The **Research Summaries** format requires you to understand, evaluate, analyze, and interpret the design, execution, and results of one or more experiments.

- The **Conflicting Viewpoints** format requires you to evaluate several alternative theories, hypotheses, or viewpoints on a specific observable phenomenon.

You'll find examples of the kinds of passages that you're likely to find in each of the formats in the pages that follow.

The sample ACT science test passages and questions in this section are representative of those you'll encounter in the actual ACT. The following chart illustrates the content area, format, and topic covered by each sample passage given in the remainder of this section:

Passage	Content area	Format	Topic of passage
I	Chemistry	Data Representation	Calorimetry
II	Physics	Research Summaries	Illuminance
III	Biology	Conflicting Viewpoints	Conjugation

Data Representation Format

This type of passage presents scientific information in charts, tables, graphs, and diagrams similar to those found in science journals and texts. Examples of tables used in an actual Data Representation passage administered to students are found in Sample Passage I that follows.

The questions you'll find in the Data Representation format ask you to interpret charts and tables, read graphs, evaluate scatterplots, and analyze information presented in diagrams. There are five sample questions presented with the sample Data Representation passage.

Sample Passage I

A *bomb calorimeter* is used to determine the amount of heat released when a substance is burned in oxygen (Figure 1). The heat, measured in kilojoules (kJ), is calculated from the change in temperature of the water in the bomb calorimeter. Table 1 shows the amounts of heat released when different foods were burned in a bomb calorimeter. Table 2 shows the amounts of heat released when different amounts of sucrose (table sugar) were burned. Table 3 shows the amounts of heat released when various chemical compounds were burned.

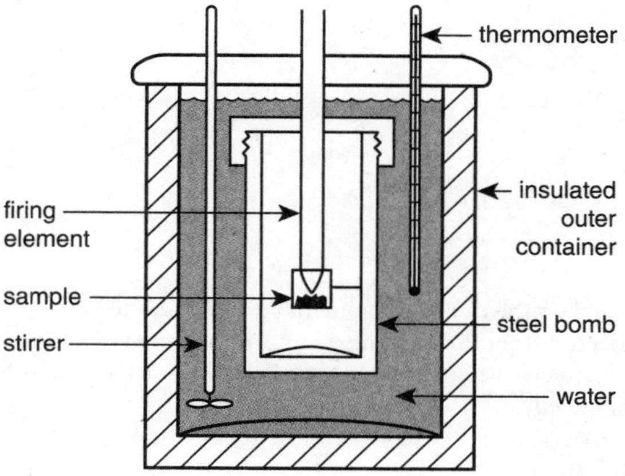

Table 2	
Amount of sucrose (g)	Heat released (kJ)
0.1	1.6
0.5	8.0
1.0	16.0
2.0	32.1
4.0	64.0

Table 3			
Chemical compound	Molecular formula	Mass (g)	Heat released (kJ)
Methanol	CH_3OH	0.5	11.4
Ethanol	C_2H_5OH	0.5	14.9
Benzene	C_6H_6	0.5	21.0
Octane	C_8H_{18}	0.5	23.9

Figure 1

Figure 1 adapted from Antony C. Wilbraham, Dennis D. Staley, and Michael S. Matta, *Chemistry*. ©1995 by Addison-Wesley Publishing Company, Inc.

Table 1			
Food	Mass (g)	Change in water temperature (°C)	Heat released (kJ)
Bread	1.0	8.3	10.0
Cheese	1.0	14.1	17.0
Egg	1.0	5.6	6.7
Potato	1.0	2.7	3.2

Table 1 adapted from American Chemical Society, *ChemCom: Chemistry in the Community.* ©1993 by American Chemical Society.

1. According to Tables 1 and 2, as the mass of successive sucrose samples increased, the change in the water temperature produced when the sample was burned most likely:

   A. increased only.
   B. decreased only.
   C. increased, then decreased.
   D. remained the same.

2. Which of the following graphs best illustrates the relationship between the heat released by the foods listed in Table 1 and the change in water temperature?

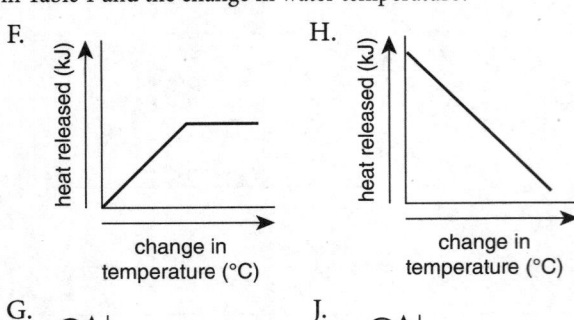

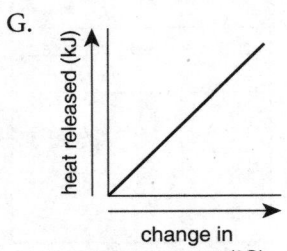

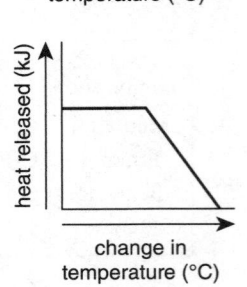

4. Which of the following lists the foods from Tables 1 and 2 in increasing order of the amount of heat released per gram of food?
    F. Potato, egg, bread, sucrose, cheese
    G. Sucrose, cheese, bread, egg, potato
    H. Bread, cheese, egg, potato, sucrose
    J. Sucrose, potato, egg, bread, cheese

3. Based on the data in Table 2, one can conclude that when the mass of sucrose is decreased by one-half, the amount of heat released when it is burned in a bomb calorimeter will:
    A. increase by one-half.
    B. decrease by one-half.
    C. increase by one-fourth.
    D. decrease by one-fourth.

5. Based on the information in Tables 1 and 2, the heat released from the burning of 5.0 g of potato in a bomb calorimeter would most likely be closest to which of the following?
    A. 5 kJ
    B. 10 kJ
    C. 15 kJ
    D. 20 kJ

Discussion of Sample Passage I (Data Representation)

According to this Data Representation passage, the amount of heat generated when a material is burned in oxygen can be determined using a *bomb calorimeter*. The bomb calorimeter has an outer shell made of an insulating material. Inside this shell is a *bomb* (steel casing) immersed in a fixed amount of water. When a material is burned inside the bomb, the water absorbs heat generated by the combustion, causing the temperature of the water to increase. The amount of the increase in water temperature depends on the amount of heat absorbed by the water. So, if we measure the increase in water temperature, we can calculate the amount of heat released when a material is burned inside the bomb.

Note that the passage contains three tables. Table 1 lists the temperature change of the water and the amount of heat generated when 1 g of each of four foods is burned in the calorimeter. Table 2 lists the amounts of heat released when various quantities of the sugar sucrose are burned. Table 3 lists several chemical compounds and their chemical formulas, as well as the amount of heat released for each compound when 0.5 g of the compound is burned in the calorimeter.

1. According to Tables 1 and 2, as the mass of successive sucrose samples increased, the change in the water temperature produced when the sample was burned most likely:
   A. increased only.
   B. decreased only.
   C. increased, then decreased.
   D. remained the same.

Question 1 asks you to determine how the change in water temperature varied as the amount of sucrose burned increased, based on the data in Tables 1 and 2. Notice that the change in water temperature and the amount of heat released are listed in Table 1 for each material burned. In Table 2, the amount of sucrose burned and the amount of heat released are listed, but the change in water temperature is not listed. Let us assume that the relationship between the amount of heat released and the change in water temperature for sucrose is the same as the relationship between the amount of heat released and the change in water temperature for the materials listed in Table 1. According to Table 2, as the amount of sucrose burned increased, the amount of heat released steadily increased. According to Table 1, as the amount of heat released increased, the magnitude of the change in water temperature steadily increased. Therefore, as the amount of sucrose burned increased, the magnitude of the change in the water temperature steadily increased. The best answer is **A**.

2. Which of the following graphs best illustrates the relationship between the heat released by the foods listed in Table 1 and the change in water temperature?

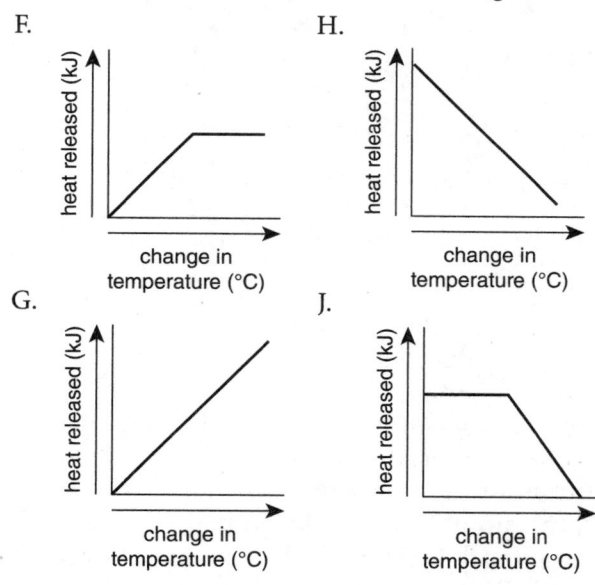

Question 2 asks you to choose a graph that best illustrates the relationship between the amount of heat released and the change in water temperature for the four substances listed in Table 1. According to the data in Table 1, as the change in water temperature increased, the amount of heat released steadily increased. No data in Table 1 supports the conclusion that as the change in water temperature increased the amount of heat released decreased or remained constant. Therefore, **G** is the best answer.

---

3. Based on the data in Table 2, one can conclude that when the mass of sucrose is decreased by one-half, the amount of heat released when it is burned in a bomb calorimeter will:

   A. increase by one-half.
   B. decrease by one-half.
   C. increase by one-fourth.
   D. decrease by one-fourth.

Question 3 asks you to predict, based on the data in Table 2, the fractional change in the amount of heat released by sucrose when the amount of sucrose burned is decreased by half. An examination of the data in Table 2 shows that when the amount of sucrose burned was decreased by half, the amount of heat released decreased by half. For example, when the amount of sucrose burned was decreased from 4.0 g to 2.0 g, the amount of heat released decreased from 64.0 kJ to 32.1 kJ; that is, the amount of heat released also decreased by half. (The amount of heat released actually decreased by 31.9 kJ, which is not exactly half of 64.0 kJ, but the 0.1 kJ difference between 31.9 kJ and 32.0 kJ can be attributed to limitations in the precision of the measurements [the amount of heat released is rounded off to the nearest 0.1 kJ] and can be ignored.) The amount of heat released was also decreased by half when the amount of sucrose burned was decreased from 2.0 g to 1.0 g and again when the amount of sucrose burned was decreased from 1.0 g to 0.5 g. Therefore, one can conclude that when the amount of sucrose burned is decreased by half, the amount of heat released during the burning of sucrose is decreased by half, so **B** is the best answer.

---

4. Which of the following lists the foods from Tables 1 and 2 in increasing order of the amount of heat released per gram of food?

   F. Potato, egg, bread, sucrose, cheese
   G. Sucrose, cheese, bread, egg, potato
   H. Bread, cheese, egg, potato, sucrose
   J. Sucrose, potato, egg, bread, cheese

Question 4 asks you to list the foods from Tables 1 and 2 in increasing order, from the food that releases the least amount of heat per gram of food to the food that releases the greatest amount of heat per gram of food. According to Table 1, the amount of heat released was determined for 1 g samples of each of the foods listed. Therefore, the amount of heat listed in Table 1 for each food item is the amount of heat released per gram of food. In Table 2, the amount of heat released is given for various masses of sucrose. To get the amount of heat released per gram of sucrose we can divide the amount of heat released by the mass of sucrose that was burned. However, an easier method is to notice that a trial was conducted using 1.0 g of sucrose, and during that trial, the amount of heat released was 16.0 kJ. Therefore, the amount of heat released per g of sucrose was 16.0 kJ/g. An inspection of the heat released by the combustion of the foods in Table 1 shows that the potato sample released the least amount of heat (3.2 kJ/g), followed by the egg sample (6.7 kJ/g), the bread sample (10.0 kJ/g), and the cheese sample (17.0 kJ/g). The amount of heat per g released by sucrose, 16.0 kJ/g, places sucrose between the cheese sample and the bread sample. Therefore, the correct order is potato, egg, bread, sucrose, cheese. The best answer is **F**.

---

5. Based on the information in Tables 1 and 2, the heat released from the burning of 5.0 g of potato in a bomb calorimeter would be closest to which of the following?
   A.   5 kJ
   B.   10 kJ
   C.   15 kJ
   D.   20 kJ

Question 5 asks you to use Tables 1 and 2 to estimate the amount of heat released when 5.0 g of potato is burned. Notice that Table 1 provides you with the amount of heat released (3.2 kJ) when 1.0 g of potato is burned. You might guess that burning 5.0 g of potato in the calorimeter would cause the release of five times the amount of heat released when 1.0 g of potato is burned. Do you have any evidence to support this guess? Table 1 only lists the amount of heat released when 1.0 g of potato is burned. Table 2 provides the amount of heat released from various amounts of sucrose, but not potatoes. In the absence of information to the contrary, you can assume that the relationship between the amount of potato burned and the amount of heat released is similar to the relationship between the amount of sucrose burned and the amount of heat released. According to Table 2, the heat released in kJ equals 16 times the mass of sucrose burned in grams. Note that this relationship holds whether 0.1 g of sucrose is burned or 4.0 g of sucrose is burned. For example, if 0.1 g of sucrose is burned, 0.1 g × 16 kJ released per g of sucrose = 1.6 kJ of heat released. If 4.0 g of sucrose is burned, 4.0 g × 16 kJ released per g of sucrose = 64 kJ of heat released. This relationship is a linear relationship. If the relationship between the amount of potato burned and the amount of heat released is also linear, then burning five times the amount of potato will release five times the amount of heat. Because 3.2 kJ of heat was released when 1.0 g of potato was burned, 5 × 3.2 kJ = 16 kJ will be released when 5.0 g of potato is burned. The answer closest to 16 kJ is 15 kJ, choice **C**.

Research Summaries Format

This type of passage provides descriptions of one or more related experiments or studies similar to those conducted by researchers or science students. The descriptions typically include the design, procedures, and results of the experiments or studies. The results are often depicted in graphs or tables. Sample Passage II provides an example of the Research Summaries format that shows the results of two different experiments with light bulbs. The questions you'll find in the Research Summaries format ask you to understand, evaluate, and interpret the design and procedures of the experiments or studies and to analyze the results. There are five sample questions presented with this sample Research Summaries passage.

Sample Passage II

A student studied illumination using the following equipment:

- 6 identical light bulbs (Bulbs A–F)
- Fixture 1, light fixture for Bulbs A–E
- Fixture 2, light fixture for Bulb F
- 2 identical paraffin blocks
- A sheet of aluminum foil having the same length and width as a paraffin block
- A meterstick

Light could pass through each paraffin block, and each block glowed when light passed through it. The aluminum foil was placed between the 2 blocks. The light fixtures, light bulbs, blocks, foil, and the meterstick were arranged as shown in Figure 1.

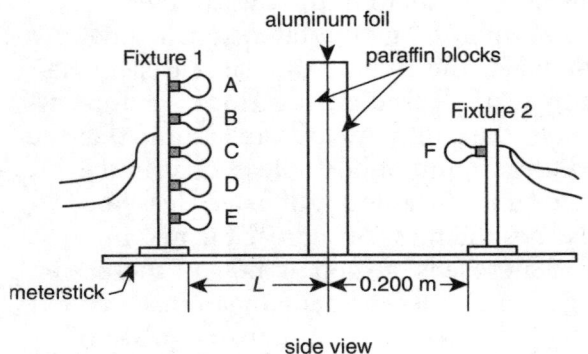

side view

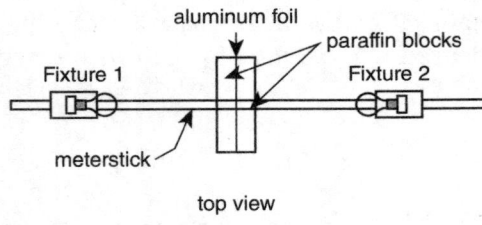

top view

Figure 1

In the following experiments, the base of Fixture 2 was always 0.200 m from the aluminum foil, and L was the distance from the base of Fixture 1 to the aluminum foil. The distance between adjacent bulbs in Fixture 1 was the same for all of the bulbs.

Bulb F was always lit.

Experiment 1

The student turned the room lights off, lit Bulb A, and varied L until the 2 blocks looked equally bright. This process was repeated using Bulbs B–E. The results are shown in Table 1.

Table 1	
Bulb lit (in addition to Bulb F)	L (m) when the blocks looked equally bright
A	0.198
B	0.203
C	0.205
D	0.195
E	0.199

Experiment 2

The procedure from Experiment 1 was repeated using various combinations of Bulbs A–E. The results are shown in Table 2.

Table 2	
Bulb lit (in addition to Bulb F)	L (m) when the blocks looked equally bright
A and B	0.281
A, B, and C	0.347
A, B, C, and D	0.400
A, B, C, D, and E	0.446

Discussion of Sample Passage II (Research Summaries)

This Research Summaries passage describes two experiments in which a student uses two identical paraffin blocks to compare the brightness of the light from one source (Fixture 1) with the brightness of the light from another source (Fixture 2). Fixture 1 contains five light bulbs, Bulbs A through E, and Fixture 2 contains only one light bulb, Bulb F (see Figure 1 in the passage). The two paraffin blocks are set between the fixtures. The two blocks are separated by a sheet of aluminum foil, so that the block on the left is illuminated only by bulbs in Fixture 1, and the block on the right is illuminated only by Bulb F in Fixture 2. The distance, L, between Fixture 1 and the aluminum foil can be varied, but the distance between Fixture 2 and the foil, 0.200 m, is fixed.

In Experiment 1, one bulb at a time is lit in Fixture 1, and Bulb F is lit in Fixture 2. For each combination of lit bulbs, L is varied until the two blocks glow equally brightly. This value of L is recorded in Table 1 along with the combination of lit bulbs used to obtain this value of L. In Experiment 2, two or more bulbs at a time are lit in Fixture 1, and Bulb F is lit in Fixture 2. For each combination of lit bulbs, L is varied until the two blocks glow equally brightly. This value of L is recorded in Table 2 along with the combination of lit bulbs.

---

6. Which of the following best explains why the student turned off the room lights?
   F. To ensure that only the light from Bulbs A–F illuminated the 2 paraffin blocks
   G. To ensure that light from outside the room illuminated the 2 paraffin blocks unequally
   H. To keep the 2 paraffin blocks from casting shadows, because shadows would make the meterstick harder to read
   J. To keep the 2 light fixtures from casting shadows, because shadows would make the meterstick harder to read

---

Question 6 asks you why the student turned off the room lights before measuring L. Recall that the student was to compare the brightness of the light produced by Fixture 1 to the brightness of the light produced by Fixture 2 under a variety of conditions. The presence of light sources other than Fixtures 1 and 2 could have introduced error into the measurements of L by making one fixture or the other seem brighter than it really was. The overhead lights were turned off so that all of the light on the blocks came from the light bulbs in Fixtures 1 and 2. Thus, **F** is the best answer.

---

7. During Experiment 2, suppose the student replaced Fixture 1 with a new fixture. The new fixture held 6 light bulbs, each bulb identical to Bulb F. When all 6 bulbs in the new fixture were lit and the paraffin blocks looked equally bright, L would probably have been closest to:
   A. 0.262 m.
   B. 0.331 m.
   C. 0.415 m.
   D. 0.490 m.

Question 7 proposes that Fixture 1 be replaced by a different fixture holding six light bulbs instead of five. Each of the light bulbs in the new fixture is identical to Bulb F. The question asks you to estimate L for the case that all six light bulbs in the new fixture, as well as Bulb F, are lit. According to Table 2, as the number of lit bulbs in Fixture 1 increased from two to five, L increased. So if the new fixture is used, increasing the number of lit bulbs from five to six, one would expect L to be greater than the value of L given in Table 2 for five lit bulbs in Fixture 1, 0.446 m. Only **D** contains a value for L exceeding 0.446 m, so **D** is the best answer.

---

8. The main purpose of Experiment 1 was to:
  F. calibrate the meterstick.
  G. determine the relationship between L and the number of lit bulbs.
  H. determine if L depended on a lit bulb's position in Fixture 1.
  J. find the brightness of Bulb F.

Question 8 asks you to determine the main purpose of Experiment 1. In Experiment 1, one bulb at a time was lit in Fixture 1, but the location of the lit bulb in Fixture 1 was varied. Thus, the main purpose of Experiment 1 must have been to determine the effect, if any, that the location of the lit bulb had on the value of L. Only **H** states that the purpose of Experiment 1 was to determine if the position of the lit bulb within Fixture 1 affected L, so **H** must be the best answer.

---

9. Suppose that all of the light bulbs in Fixture 1 were replaced with a single bulb. Based on Experiments 1 and 2, if the 2 paraffin blocks looked equally bright when Fixture 2 was 0.200 m from the aluminum foil and $L = 0.446$ m, the brightness of the new light bulb was most likely:
  A. $\frac{1}{6}$ the brightness of one of the original bulbs.
  B. $\frac{1}{5}$ the brightness of one of the original bulbs.
  C. 5 times the brightness of one of the original bulbs.
  D. 6 times the brightness of one of the original bulbs.

Question 9 proposes that the five light bulbs in Fixture 1 be replaced with a single light bulb, and that when the new bulb and Bulb F are lit, for the two blocks to glow equally brightly, L must equal 0.446 m. You are asked to compare the brightness of the new bulb to the brightness of one of the original bulbs in Fixture 1. According to Table 2, the two paraffin blocks glowed equally brightly when all five bulbs in Fixture 1 were lit and L was 0.446 m, the same as the L obtained with the new bulb. Thus, the brightness of the new bulb would have to equal the sum of the brightness of the five original bulbs. Because each of the five original bulbs had the same brightness, the new bulb would have to be five times as bright as one of the original bulbs. Only **C** is consistent with this conclusion, so the best answer is **C**.

10. In Experiment 2, suppose the student had replaced Bulb F with a much brighter light bulb, Bulb G. Compared to L when Bulb F was used, L when Bulb G was used would have been:

   F. greater for every combination of lit bulbs.

   G. smaller for every combination of lit bulbs.

   H. smaller when Bulbs A–E were simultaneously lit and greater when other combinations of light bulbs were lit.

   J. greater when both Bulbs A and B were simultaneously lit and smaller when other combinations of light bulbs were lit.

Question 10 proposes that in Experiment 2, Bulb F be replaced by a much brighter bulb, Bulb G. For each combination of lit bulbs in Fixture 1 and Bulb G lit in Fixture 2, when the two paraffin blocks are equally bright, how would the value of L compare to that obtained when Bulb F was used in Fixture 2? Because Bulb G is brighter than Bulb F and would be the same distance (0.200 m) away from the aluminum foil as Bulb F, the paraffin block closer to Bulb G would glow more brightly than it glowed when Bulb F was used. Thus, for each combination of lit bulbs in Fixture 1, to make the two blocks glow with equal brightness, Fixture 1 would have to be closer to the blocks than when Bulb F was used. That is, when Bulb G was used, L for each combination of lit bulbs in Fixture 1 would have to be less than when Bulb F was used for the two blocks to glow with equal brightness. Only choice **G** is consistent with this conclusion. The best answer is **G**.

Conflicting Viewpoints Format

This type of passage provides several alternative theories, hypotheses, or viewpoints on a specific observable phenomenon. These conflicting viewpoints are based on differing premises or on incomplete data and are inconsistent with one another. Sample Passage III, a biology passage on gene replication, is an example of the Conflicting Viewpoints format. Notice that this passage presents the theories of four different students.

The questions you'll find in Conflicting Viewpoints passages ask you to understand, analyze, evaluate, and compare several competing theories, hypotheses, or viewpoints. Five sample questions are presented with this sample Conflicting Viewpoints passage.

Sample Passage III

Many bacteria contain *plasmids* (small, circular DNA molecules). Plasmids can be transferred from 1 bacterium to another. For this to occur, the plasmid *replicates* (produces a linear copy of itself). The relative position of the genes is the same on the original plasmid and on the linear copy, except that the 2 ends of the linear copy do not immediately connect.

While replication is occurring, 1 end of the linear copy leaves the donor bacterium and enters the recipient bacterium. Thus, the order in which the genes are replicated is the same as the order in which they are transferred. Unless this process is interrupted, the entire plasmid is transferred, and its 2 ends connect in the recipient bacterium.

Four students studied the way in which 6 genes (F, X, R, S, A, and G) on a specific plasmid were donated by a type of bacterium (see the figure). The students determined that the entire plasmid is transferred in 90 min and that the rate of transfer is constant. They also determined that the genes are evenly spaced around the plasmid, so 1 gene is transferred every 15 min. They disagreed, however, about the order in which the genes are replicated and thus transferred. Four models are presented.

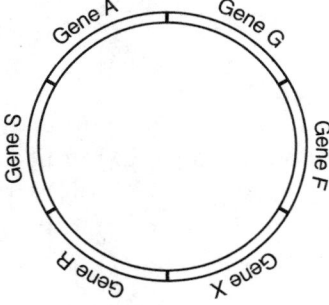

Student 1

Replication always begins between Gene F and Gene X. Gene X is replicated first and Gene F is replicated last.

Student 2

Replication always begins between Gene F and Gene X. However, the direction of replication varies. If Gene F is replicated first, Gene X is replicated last. Conversely, if Gene X is replicated first, Gene F is replicated last.

Student 3

Replication can begin between any 2 genes. Replication then proceeds around the plasmid in a clockwise direction (with respect to the figure). Thus, if Gene S is replicated first, Gene A is replicated second, and Gene R is replicated last.

Student 4

Replication can begin between any 2 genes. Likewise, replication can proceed in either direction. So the order of replication varies.

11. Based on the information presented, if the transfer of the linear copy was interrupted 50 min after transfer began, how many complete genes would have been transferred to the recipient bacterium?

    A. 2
    B. 3
    C. 4
    D. 5

12. Based on the model presented by Student 3, if all 6 genes are replicated and the first gene replicated is Gene G, the third gene replicated would be:

    F. Gene F.
    G. Gene A.
    H. Gene S.
    J. Gene X.

13. Which students believe that any of the 6 genes on the plasmid can be the first gene transferred to a recipient bacterium?

    A. Students 2 and 3
    B. Students 2 and 4
    C. Students 3 and 4
    D. Students 2, 3, and 4.

14. Suppose that Student 2's model is correct and that the transfer of genes between 2 bacteria was interrupted after 30 min. Under these conditions, which of the following genes would definitely NOT be transferred from the donor bacterium to the recipient bacterium?

    F. Gene A
    G. Gene R
    H. Gene G
    J. Gene X

15. Suppose that the transfer of genes between 2 bacteria was interrupted, that the last gene transferred was Gene A, and that no incomplete copies of a gene were transferred. Based on this information, Student 1 would say that transfer was most likely interrupted how many minutes after the transfer began?

    A. 15
    B. 30
    C. 45
    D. 60

Discussion of Sample Passage III (Conflicting Viewpoints)

According to this Conflicting Viewpoints passage, plasmids (small DNA molecules, each molecule consisting of genes arranged in a circle) are found in bacteria. While a plasmid is replicating (producing an identical copy of itself) in one bacterium, the gene copies are being transferred to a second bacterium, the recipient bacterium, eventually forming a complete copy of the plasmid in the recipient bacterium.

Notice the diagram of a plasmid in the passage. The plasmid in the diagram contains six genes. The passage tells us that when the plasmid replicates, it produces a linear copy of itself; that is, the six genes in the copy are arranged in the same order as in the original plasmid, but the genes in the copy are first arranged in a row rather than in a circle. The plasmid copies one gene at a time, and, according to the passage, the gene copies are transferred to the recipient bacterium one at a time in the order in which the copies are produced. For example, if the plasmid copies Gene F, followed by Gene X, Gene F will be transferred to the recipient bacterium first, followed by Gene X. Once all of the genes of the original plasmid have been copied and transferred to a recipient bacterium, the two ends of the linear plasmid copy connect to each other, forming a circle just like the one in the passage.

Four students agree that the rate of gene transfer between bacteria is constant and occurs at the rate of one gene every 15 minutes, so a complete plasmid is transferred between the bacteria in $6 \times 15 = 90$ minutes. However, the identity of the first gene to be replicated and the direction (clockwise or counterclockwise around the circle) in which replication proceeds are subjects of disagreement among the four students.

- According to Student 1, Gene X is always replicated and transferred first, and Gene F is always replicated and transferred last. That is, replication always starts with Gene X and proceeds in a clockwise direction around the plasmid.

- According to Student 2, replication always begins with either Gene F or Gene X. If Gene F is first, then Gene X is last; that is, if replication begins with Gene F, then replication proceeds in a counterclockwise direction around the plasmid. If Gene X is first, then Gene F is last; that is, if replication begins with Gene X, then replication proceeds in a clockwise direction around the plasmid.

- According to Student 3, replication can start with any gene but always proceeds in a clockwise direction around the plasmid.

- According to Student 4, replication can start with any gene and can proceed in either direction around the plasmid.

11. Based on the information presented, if the transfer of the linear copy was interrupted 50 min after transfer began, how many complete genes would have been transferred to the recipient bacterium?

    A. 2
    B. 3
    C. 4
    D. 5

Question 11 asks you to predict how many complete genes would have been transferred to the recipient bacterium if gene transfer had been interrupted 50 minutes after transfer had begun. According to the passage, one gene was transferred every 15 minutes. Therefore, three genes would have been transferred in $3 \times 15 = 45$ minutes. A partial gene transfer would have occurred in the remaining 5 minutes, but the question asks about complete gene transfers, so you can ignore the partial gene transfer. The answer is three genes. Therefore, the best choice is **B**.

12. Based on the model presented by Student 3, if all 6 genes are replicated and the first gene replicated is Gene G, the third gene replicated would be:

    F. Gene F.
    G. Gene A.
    H. Gene S.
    J. Gene X.

Question 12 asks you to suppose that all six genes in a plasmid are replicated and that Gene G is the first gene replicated. You are asked to predict the third gene replicated, assuming that Student 3's model is correct. According to Student 3's model, replication can start with any gene but always proceeds around the plasmid in a clockwise direction. Therefore, starting with Gene G and proceeding in a clockwise direction, Gene F would be the second gene replicated and Gene X would be the third gene replicated. The best answer is **J**.

13. Which students believe that any of the 6 genes on the plasmid can be the first gene transferred to a recipient bacterium?

    A. Students 2 and 3
    B. Students 2 and 4
    C. Students 3 and 4
    D. Students 2, 3, and 4

Question 13 asks which students believe that any of the six genes on the plasmid can be the first gene transferred to a recipient bacterium. According to the passage, the order in which genes are transferred is the same as the order in which genes are replicated. Student 1 asserts that replication always begins with Gene X, so Student 1 would *disagree* with the statement that any of the six genes on the plasmid can be the first gene transferred. Student 2 asserts that replication always begins with either Gene X or Gene F, so Student 2 would *disagree* with the statement that any of the six genes on the plasmid can be the first gene transferred.

According to Students 3 and 4, replication can begin between any two genes on the plasmid, so they *agree* that any of the six genes on the plasmid can be the first gene transferred to a recipient bacterium. Because only Students 3 and 4 agree that any gene on the plasmid can be the first gene transferred, the best answer is **C**.

---

14. Suppose that Student 2's model is correct and that the transfer of genes between 2 bacteria was interrupted after 30 min. Under these conditions, which of the following genes would definitely NOT be transferred from the donor bacterium to the recipient bacterium?

- **F.** Gene A
- **G.** Gene R
- **H.** Gene G
- **J.** Gene X

Question 14 asks you to suppose that the transfer of genes between two bacteria was interrupted 30 minutes after the transfer began. You are asked to select from among a list of genes (A, R, G, and X) the gene that could NOT have been transferred to the recipient bacterium within the allotted 30 minutes, assuming that Student 2's model is correct. According to the passage, one complete gene transfer occurs every 15 minutes. Therefore, two complete gene transfers would have occurred after $2 \times 15 = 30$ minutes. Based on Student 2's model, gene transfer can start with Gene X and proceed around the plasmid in a clockwise direction, or transfer can start with Gene F and proceed around the plasmid in a counterclockwise direction. If transfer had started with Gene X, Gene R would have been the second gene transferred. If transfer had started with Gene F, Gene G would have been the second gene transferred. Therefore, we conclude Genes X, R, F, and G could have been transferred. The only gene in the list that could not have been transferred is Gene A. Based on Student 2's model, if Gene X had been the first gene transferred, then $4 \times 15 = 60$ minutes would have been required for Gene A to be transferred, because Gene A is the fourth gene in the clockwise direction from Gene X. If Gene F had been the first gene transferred, $3 \times 15 = 45$ minutes would have been required for Gene A to be transferred, because Gene A is the third gene in the counterclockwise direction from Gene F. The best answer is **F**.

---

15. Suppose that the transfer of genes between 2 bacteria was interrupted, that the last gene transferred was Gene A, and that no incomplete copies of a gene were transferred. Based on this information, Student 1 would say that transfer was most likely interrupted how many minutes after the transfer began?

- **A.** 15
- **B.** 30
- **C.** 45
- **D.** 60

Question 15 asks you to suppose that the transfer of genes between two bacteria was interrupted after the transfer of Gene A had been completed, and that no incomplete transfer of a gene occurred after the transfer of Gene A. You are asked to determine the number of minutes between the time that gene transfer began and the time at which gene transfer was interrupted, assuming that Student 1's model is correct. According to Student 1, Gene X is always transferred first, and Gene F is always transferred last. That is, transfer always starts with Gene X and proceeds in a clockwise direction around the plasmid. If we count genes in the clockwise direction, starting with Gene X, we find that Gene A is the fourth gene, so Gene A would have been the fourth gene transferred. According to the passage, each complete transfer of a gene requires 15 minutes. Thus, the number of minutes between the time at which the transfer of Gene X began and the time at which the transfer of Gene A was completed would have been $4 \times 15 = 60$ minutes. The best answer is **D**.

Answer Key for Science Test Sample Questions					
1.	A	6.	F	11.	B
2.	G	7.	D	12.	J
3.	B	8.	H	13.	C
4.	F	9.	C	14.	F
5.	C	10.	G	15.	D

Strategies for Taking the ACT Science Test

Performance on the ACT science test relies mainly on the ability to understand and process scientific information presented in various formats but can also be affected by problem-solving strategies and skills. The following sections describe strategies and skills specifically for improving your ACT science score.

Develop a Problem-Solving Method

Because you have only a limited time in which to take the science test, you may find it helpful to work out a general problem-solving method that you can use for all or most of the questions. The method described here is certainly not the only way to solve the problems, but it is one that works for most science problems. Whether you see a way to adapt this method, or you work out your own approach, use the method that works best for you.

One approach to solving problems is to break the process into a series of smaller steps, such as these:

1. Restate the problem in your own words.

2. Decide what information is needed to solve the problem.

3. Extract the needed information from the passage. Information may include data, concepts, or even conclusions you've been able to draw from the information provided.

4.   Consider any additional scientific knowledge (terms or concepts) you may have.

5.   Organize the information and use reason to arrive at the answer.

6.   Compare your answer to the answer choices and choose the option you think is correct.

Take Notes

As you read a question, take notes in the test booklet or on scratch paper to record what the question is asking and what information you have at your disposal to answer the question. (In some circumstances you are not permitted to write in your test booklet. In those circumstances, you'll be given scratch paper to use.) Sometimes, the process of writing down or reviewing notes reveals the answer or helps you develop an effective approach to finding the answer.

Pace Yourself

Remember, you have 35 minutes to read several passages and their accompanying questions (40 questions altogether). That's about 5 minutes for each passage and the accompanying questions. You can think of it as 40 questions in 35 minutes, or a little less than a minute per question. If you're like most people, you'll find some of the passages more familiar and probably easier than some of the others, so it's a good idea to try to work fast enough to allow yourself time to come back to any questions you have trouble answering the first time.

Practice Interpreting Graphs, Tables, and Diagrams

Much of the information you need to answer the science test questions is presented graphically in the form of graphs, tables, and diagrams. Practice interpreting tables and different types of graphs, including pie charts, line charts, bar or column charts, and scatter charts, especially those included in science articles. Examine graphs and tables closely until you understand the data and can pick out specific pieces of data.

Tip: Pay attention to any and all text in graphs, tables, or diagrams, because any of this text is likely present to serve as instruction for how to interpret the data:

Graphs

Read the axis labels and the labels for any lines (curves) present. Typically, the y-axis indicates what is being measured (the dependent variable) and the x-axis most often indicates what is being manipulated (the independent variable). Some graphs may have a legend (labeled *Key*) that identifies line styles and the quantities they represent. Graphs may also have notes at the bottom of the graph to supply additional information.

Tables

Look at the column and row headings, which will identify quantities and their units of measure. Often (but not always) manipulated variables (independent variables) will be on the left side of the graph and the measured quantity (the dependent variable) will be to the right of the graph. Some tables will have notes at the bottom that provide vital information for interpreting the data.

Diagrams

Diagrams often contain labeled parts and could represent everything from a food web to a laboratory setup or show the cross-section of an object, such as the layers of Earth or of Earth's atmosphere. Diagrams generally contain more text than numbers. Look for a title (above the diagram) or a caption (below the diagram) and for labels on the diagram itself. The diagram may not have a title, but parts of it may be labeled, as in a diagram of a laboratory setup that sheds light on how an experiment works.

Give yourself some time to figure out what the graph, table, or diagram is showing you in general. You can always look at these graphic representations more closely when answering questions, but having a general idea of what they show may shed light on what the questions are asking.

Make the Most of the Information in Graphs

Graphs illustrate data in ways that can be very useful if you follow a few rules. First, it's important to identify what is being displayed in the graph (e.g., mass, volume, velocity). What unit or units of measurement is (are) used (e.g., grams, liters, kilometers per hour)? Graphs usually have axis labels that provide this information and some will have a key or legend or other short explanation of the information presented. Many graphs consist of two axes (horizontal and vertical), both of which will be labeled, and some may have dual axes with more than one curve. Remember, the first thing to find out about any graph is exactly what the numbers represent.

Once you've identified what is being presented in a graph, you can begin to look for trends in the data. The main reason for using a graph is to show how one characteristic of the data tends to influence other characteristics.

For a coordinate graph, notice how a change on the horizontal axis (or x-axis) relates to the position of the variable on the vertical axis (or y-axis). If the curve shows angles upward from lower left to upper right (as in Figure 1a), then, as the variable shown on the x-axis increases, so does the variable on the y-axis (a *direct relationship*). An example of a direct relationship is that a person's weight increases as his or her height increases. If the curve goes from the upper left to the lower right (as in Figure 1b), then, as the variable on the x-axis increases, the variable on the y-axis decreases (an *inverse relationship*). An example of an inverse relationship is that the more players there are on a soccer team, the less time each of them gets to play (assuming everyone gets equal playing time). If the graph shows a vertical or horizontal line (as in Figure 1c), the variables are probably unrelated.

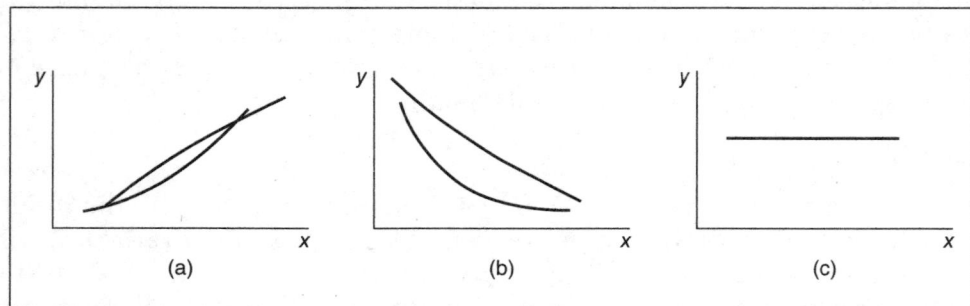

Figure 1

Sometimes, a question will ask you to estimate a value for one characteristic based on a given value of another characteristic that is beyond the limits of the curve shown on the graph. In this case, the solution will require you to *extrapolate,* or extend, the graph. If the curve is a relatively straight line, just use your pencil to extend that line far enough for the value called for to be included. If the graphed line is a curve, use your best judgment to extend the line to follow the apparent pattern. Figure 2 shows how to extend both types of graphs.

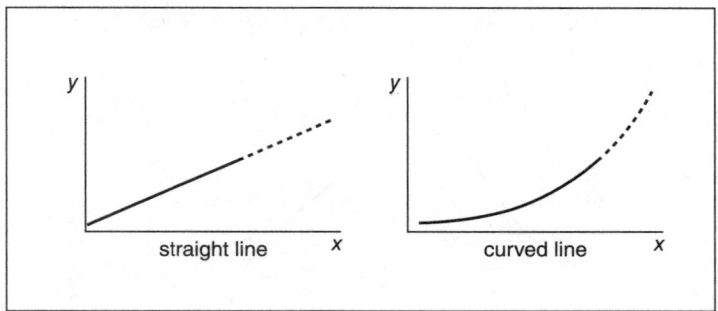

Figure 2

Another type of graph problem asks you to estimate a value that falls between two known values on a curve. This process is called *interpolation.* If the curve is shown, it amounts to finding a point on the curve that corresponds to a given value for one characteristic and reading the value for the other characteristic. (For example, "For a given x, find y.") If only scattered points are shown on the graph, draw a "best-fit line," a line that comes close to all of the points. Use this line to estimate the middle value. Figure 3 shows a best-fit line.

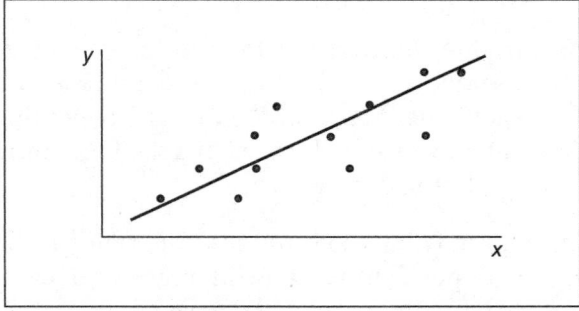

Figure 3

One very useful kind of graph shows more than one curve on the same pair of axes. Such a graph might be used when the results of a number of experiments are compared or when an experiment involves more than two variables. Analysis of this sort of graph requires that you determine the relationship shown by each curve and then determine how the curves are related to one another. Figure 4 shows a graph with multiple curves.

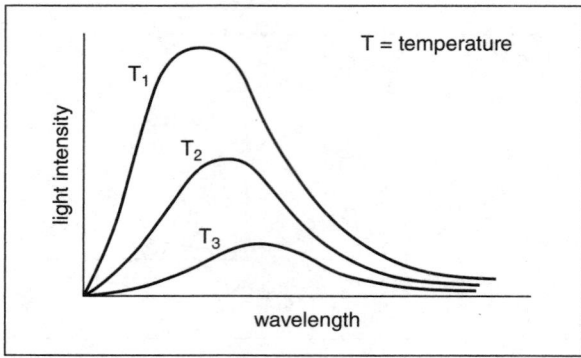

Figure 4

Make the Most of the Information in Tables

To understand what a table is showing you, you need to identify the information or data presented. You need to know two things about the information or data: the purpose it serves in the experiment and the unit (or units) of measurement used to quantify it. Generally, experiments intentionally vary one characteristic (the independent variable) to see how it affects another (the dependent variable). Tables may report results for either or both.

Once you have identified the variables, it might be helpful to sketch a graph to illustrate the relationship between them. You might sketch an x-axis and a y-axis next to the table and decide which variable to represent on each axis. Mark off the axes with evenly spaced intervals that enable all of the numbers for a category to fit along each axis. Plot some points. Again, draw a best-fit line and characterize the relationship shown.

As with graphs and diagrams, you may be asked to look for trends in the data. For example, do the numbers representing the dependent variable increase or decrease as the numbers representing the independent variable increase or decrease? If no pattern is clear, you may want to sketch a rough graph as discussed above. You may also need to make predictions about values of quantities between the data points shown (interpolation) or beyond the limits of those shown on the table (extrapolation). Another type of problem may require you to compare data from multiple columns of a table or between two or more graphs or tables. A simple examination of the numbers may be enough to see a relationship, but you may find it helpful to sketch a graph containing a curve for each category. The curves may be compared as described previously in "Make the Most of the Information in Graphs."

Develop an Understanding of Scientific Investigations

When working with a Research Summaries passage, you should be able to understand scientific processes. This includes identifying the designs of experiments, identifying assumptions and hypotheses underlying the experiments, identifying controls and variables, determining the effects of altering the experiments, identifying similarities and differences between the experiments, identifying the strengths and weaknesses of the experiments, developing other experiments that will test the same hypothesis, making hypotheses or predictions from research results, and creating models from research results.

Carefully Analyze Conflicting Viewpoints

When reading a Conflicting Viewpoints passage, first read the introductory information. This describes the phenomena about which the viewpoints will differ. It may also present a graph, table, or diagram, as well as discuss aspects that all of the viewpoints share. Then, read each viewpoint closely and note what is the same and different in each. Note each viewpoint's strengths and weaknesses. Use your own scientific knowledge and common sense to draw conclusions about each viewpoint. Which viewpoint sounds most credible? Which has the most evidence to back it up? With an understanding of and opinion about each viewpoint, you are better equipped to understand and answer questions about them.

Prep Online!

Want even more ways to prep? Go to act.wiley.com to access our online platform or use our companion app. Take online practice tests and track your progress, create your own question sets, and use flash cards to practice. Flag difficult or confusing questions for review. To get started, go to act.wiley.com, and register with the PIN on the back of the front cover of this book. Once registered, you can also use our companion app if you prefer to study from your mobile device.

Improving Your Score

Chapter 9:
Improving Your Score on the Optional Writing Test

On the ACT writing test, you have 40 minutes to read a prompt and to plan and write an essay in response to it. The prompts on the writing test cover a variety of subjects intended to reflect engaging conversations about contemporary issues, and they are designed to be appropriate for response in a 40-minute timed test.

The writing test is an optional test on the ACT. Should you decide to take the writing test, it will be administered after the multiple-choice tests. Taking the writing test will not affect your scores on any of the multiple-choice tests or the Composite score. Rather, *in addition* to your scores from the multiple-choice tests and your Composite score, you will receive a writing score and may receive an English Language Arts (ELA) score.

You will have a short break between the end of the last multiple-choice test and the beginning of the writing test.

Content of the ACT Writing Test

The test consists of one writing prompt that describes a complex issue and provides three different perspectives on the issue. You are asked to read the prompt and write an essay in which you develop your own perspective on the issue. Your essay must analyze the relationship between your perspective and one or more perspectives. You may adopt one of the perspectives given in the prompt as your own, or you may introduce one that is completely different from those given. The test offers guidance and structure for planning and prewriting, but planning and prewriting are optional and do not count toward the score. Your score will also not be affected by the perspective you take on the issue. Your essay will be evaluated based on the evidence that it provides of your ability to do the following:

- Clearly state your own perspective on a complex issue and analyze the relationship between your perspective and at least one other perspective.

- Develop and support your ideas with reasoning and examples.

- Organize your ideas clearly and logically.

- Communicate your ideas effectively in standard written English.

How Your Essay Will Be Scored

Your essay will be scored analytically using a rubric with four domains that correspond to different writing skills (turn to chapter 3 for a copy of the actual analytic rubric for the ACT writing test). Two trained readers will separately score your essay, giving it a rating from 1 (low) to 6 (high) in each of the following four domains: Ideas and Analysis, Development and Support, Organization, and Language Use and Conventions. Each domain score represents the sum of the two readers' scores using the ACT Writing Test Analytic Rubric in chapter 3. If the readers' ratings differ by more than one point, a third reader will evaluate the essay and resolve the discrepancy. Your writing score is calculated from your domain scores and is reported on a scale of 2 to 12.

The readers take into account that you had merely 40 minutes to compose and write your essay. Within that time limit, polish your essay as best as you can. Make sure that all words are legible; handwriting is not scored, but readers must be able to decipher the essay. With careful planning, you should have time to briefly review and edit your essay after you have finished writing it. Keep in mind that you probably will not have time to rewrite or even recopy your essay. Instead, you should take a few minutes to think through your essay and jot preliminary notes on the planning pages in the scoring booklet before you begin to write. Prewriting (planning) helps you organize your ideas, manage your time, and keep you on track as you compose your essay.

Sample Prompt and Essays

In preparation for the ACT writing test, examine the sample writing prompt, essays, and scoring explanations in the following sections. The sample prompt shows what you can expect to encounter on test day; the sample essays serve as models of low-, medium-, and high-scoring essays; and the scoring explanations provide insight into the criteria the readers will use to score your essay.

Sample ACT Writing Test Prompt

Writing test prompts are similar to the following example. The standard directions in the Essay Task section are a part of all prompts used in the writing test. You might want to practice by planning for and writing in response to this prompt for 40 minutes before you look ahead to the sample responses from other writers. If you took the practice test in chapter 3 and choose not to respond to this sample prompt, you may want to compare your essay to the sample essays that follow. Although the topics are different, evaluating the quality of the writing is a similar process.

Online Instruction

Traditional classroom instruction has a number of benefits. Teachers and students often build better relationships when education happens in a face-to-face environment, which can promote personalized instruction and deeper learning. But recent years have seen the rise of online education, where instruction is carried out through videos, web streams, and discussion boards. Learners are increasingly turning to these options for everything from high school and college coursework to technical training and workforce certification. Given the benefits of classroom instructions, how beneficial is this trend toward online education?

Read and carefully consider these perspectives. Each suggests a particular way of thinking about the question above.

Perspective One	Perspective Two	Perspective Three
Traditional education has never served all learners well. Online options ensure that more people have access to an education that meets their needs.	The purpose of education is to learn as much as you can, and the best way to learn is in a classroom with the teacher. The trend toward online education offers little benefit for people who wish to be truly educated.	The most important factor in education is the quality of instruction. Learners can benefit more from a great teacher online than a poor one in the classroom.

Improving Your Score

Essay Task

Write a unified, coherent essay in which you address the question of whether the trend of online instruction is beneficial. In your essay, be sure to:

- clearly state your own perspective and analyze the relationship between your perspective and at least one other perspective
- develop and support your ideas with reasoning and examples
- organize your ideas clearly and logically
- communicate your ideas effectively in standard written English

Your perspective may be in full agreement with any of those given, in partial agreement, or completely different.

Planning Your Essay

Your work on these prewriting pages will not be scored.

Use the space below to generate ideas and plan your essay. You may wish to consider the following as you think critically about the task:

Strengths and weaknesses of different perspectives on the issue

- What insights do they offer, and what do they fail to consider?
- Why might they be persuasive to others, or why might they fail to persuade?

Your own knowledge, experience, and values

- What is your perspective on this issue, and what are its strengths and weaknesses?
- How will you support your perspective in your essay?

Sample Essay Responses

The essays that follow are sample essays produced in response to the given writing prompt. The essays and the accompanying scoring explanations illustrate how writing at different levels is evaluated and scored for the ACT writing test. The essays in no way represent a full range of ideas, approaches, or styles that could be used. Although we all can learn from reading other people's writing, you are encouraged to bring your own distinct voice and writing skills to the test. You want to produce your own best essay for the writing test—not an imitation of someone else's essay writing.

The following essays have been evaluated using the analytic rubric for the ACT writing test (see chapter 3). This same rubric will be used to score the response that you write for the ACT writing test. Each essay is followed by a scoring explanation that comments on the essay.

Improving Your Score

Sample Essay 1

From my perspective I agree with the first perspective because eventhough traditional learning has served learners well dont mean that everyone that was taught had gotten caught on to everything. Also I agree to where online education has the access to meet others needs because sometimes traditional education isnt meant for some people, Others my like to learn in other ways and that may be not in a class room with a teacher.

Sample Essay 1 (Score: 1111)

Score Explanation

The attempt to take a position by agreeing with one of the perspectives does not demonstrate skill in writing an argumentative essay.

Ideas and Analysis (1): Limited evaluation of the issue is confusing. Though the writer claims agreement with a position, the analysis results in a contradiction ("even though traditional learning has served learners well [that doesn't] mean that . . . [everyone understood] everything"). A thesis is absent, and the writer's intentions are difficult to discern.

Development and Support (1): An attempt to relay ideas provided in the prompt's first perspective is present, but the effort lacks development and support. Reasoning is largely absent, as it consists of a single, unsupported assertion ("others [may] like to learn in other ways and that may not be in a class room with a teacher"), and no illustration is provided.

Organization (1): This response does not exhibit an organizational structure, in part because there are very few ideas to organize. There is little evidence of grouped ideas, and a lone transition word ("also") is misused, failing to connect one sentence to the other ("caught on to everything. Also I agree . . .").

Language Use and Conventions (1): The response indicates little ability to use language to support an argument. Word choice is imprecise and often difficult to comprehend, even when words from the prompt are incorporated. Sentence structures are unclear, stylistic and register choices are difficult to identify, and errors in grammar, usage, and mechanics are pervasive ("I agree to where online education has the access to meet others needs").

Sample Essay 2

Online instruction

Online Instruction. Could be good for certain people. People that just wanna know whats going on. and only want a grade. I disagree with perspective #1 because only a teacher that is face to face with the student can answer their questions. In an online course students who may have question probably wont be able to be answered and left with questions because it's only a video. which could lead to bad grades. Either the student won't do the work or get the answers wrong without reason. Online work is so boxed in and the world isn't boxed in. It's better for students to go to class with other students. You'll need help one day and your parents won't be able to help so you'll use family and friends. Same with school. If yur teacher can't help your classmate will. Online schools are all one on one without help. I think Online Instruction is bad for people.

And it should be made differently. But some
People do better alone which is why
I don't think it should be tooken away.

Sample Essay 2 (Score: 2222)

Score Explanation

The writer acknowledges that there are multiple perspectives but limits an imprecise discussion to only one.

Ideas and Analysis (2): There is some confusion around the thesis—the response recognizes that online instruction is good for some students and bad for others ("Online Instruction could be good for certain people."), but focuses an incomplete discussion on the idea that online instruction is not beneficial ("In an online course . . . [questions cannot be answered]," "Online work is so boxed in," "I think Online Instruction is bad for people"). The argument consists primarily of the repeated claim that the traditional classroom environment is better for students' educational experiences; attempts to consider a different perspective are presented without any discussion ("I think Online Instruction is bad for people, And it should be made differently"), making them seem irrelevant to the argument.

Development and Support (2): The response neglects exploration of how online instruction may be beneficial. Insubstantial discussion of the detriments of online instruction leads to weak development. The idea that students would be left with questions is based on an unconsidered assumption that online instruction is limited to videos and that there would be no avenue for students to seek clarification (such as a discussion board or message to the instructor). Additionally, the idea that students need peers for help essentially repeats that assumption. While the response has the appearance of moving toward additional support, the repetition fails to push the argument forward.

Organization (2): The response does attempt to organize an argument, but it exhibits a rudimentary organizational structure. Introductory and concluding statements are included but weakly frame the writer's argument; as noted above, inattention to a second perspective (benefits of online instruction) and repetition in support inhibit coherence around a central idea. Transitions throughout the single paragraph are largely absent and relationships among ideas are not clear ("get the answers wrong without reason. Online work is so boxed in . . .").

Language Use and Conventions (2): Like the other domains, the use of language to convey an argument is dominated by imprecision. For example, what exactly does it mean that students might "just wanna know what's going on" or "only want a grade"? Similarly, "parents" and "family" are used as if they are distinct from one another. Errors in sentence construction and punctuation influence meaning and stylistic choices, including the casual tone, are not appropriate for the rhetorical purpose. In combination, these issues weaken the argument.

Sample Essay 3

In recent years more citizens have been using online classes instead of entering a classroom with teachers by your side. While a teacher right by your side could be nice, would it be better to learn by teachers in videos?

When learning pupils normally want to feel like they are in a safe environment or even be comfortable. Learning online gives the oppertunity to learn in your own home or somewhere that makes you feel relaxed and safe. Most pupils will say they learn better in an environment that they enjoy, with online they can have the best environment they desire. While being in a classroom with others might keep learners company, it could also be a distraction. Learning while other pupils are talking or horseplaying makes it extreamly difficult.

Nobody likes taking classes that they wont use with their major, with online classes there is a wide variety of classes to take that will boost the learners knowlage and assist them with their work life. Also with normally schooling a decent teacher isn't always provided. Imagine being in a class that won't provide any knowlage for your job and the teacher doesn't teach well; so you're in a class getting horendous grades for a class you may never use again.

In some asspects being face to face with a teach would be nice theres also reasons why it wouldn't. With videos you can rewind if you dont understand, teachers on the other hand would be getting annoyed if they were requested to repeat the samething till you understood the concept. Also with online classes the program normally doesn't go on till you understand the concept, so you can go at your own pace.

In recent year online learning has became an option for learners. While having a teacher face to face may be helpful they wouldn't always stop and wait for you to understand. In upcoming years online schooling may be the new form of education.

Sample Essay 3 (Score: 3333)

Score Explanation

The writer generates an argument that recognizes multiple perspectives, but is simplistic in its analysis.

Ideas and Analysis (3): The response offers a clear position that online instruction is more beneficial than the traditional classroom method, but the analysis does not explore the issue with any depth. The idea that "using online classes" is on the rise allows the writer to contextualize the issue (suggesting we should consider the issue because the phenomenon is common), but the discussion remains superficial and repetitious. An alternative perspective (that traditional classroom instruction "could be nice") is shared at several points, but in what ways this may be true is never addressed.

Development and Support (3): The argument offers more in the way of claims than support for those claims. The points made to support the main idea that online instruction is more beneficial than traditional instruction are repetitious or left to speak for themselves (rather than clarifying for the reader why the point is worth considering). For example, the first body paragraph offers support for the idea that students need a safe environment, but feeling "relaxed and safe" and having "the best environment they desire" repeat rather than elaborate the point. An attempt to introduce complexity (that students are distracted by peers) receives the same superficial treatment. The second body paragraph follows a similar pattern and the third body paragraph introduces two new ideas that go largely unattended.

Organization (3): A basic organizational structure allows for most ideas to be logically grouped (e.g., the first body paragraph discusses the learning environment, while the second discusses availability and utility of classes). In this way, the response largely coheres around evaluation of the benefits of online learning. Transitions between and within paragraphs sometimes clarify the relationships among ideas ("When learning," "While being in a classroom with others might," "Also with normally schooling," "With videos you can"), though an occasional misstep forces the reader to make assumptions. For instance, the transition to the third body paragraph, "In some asspects being face to face with a teach would be nice," suggests these positive aspects will be discussed, but the reader must use the entire paragraph to determine that its topic is pace.

Language Use and Conventions (3): The use of language is basic. Word choice is general and occasionally imprecise ("more citizens," "have the best environment they desire," "classes that they wont use with their major," "would be nice"). Sentence structures are usually clear but show little variety. The writer's ability to make appropriate stylistic and register choices is hindered at times by general language and errors, even as the errors generally do not impede understanding ("In some asspects being face to face with a teach would be nice theres also reasons why it wouldnt," "learn by teachers in videos," "the learners knowlage," "Also with normally schooling").

Sample Essay 4

The growing trend of online education is both beneficial and unbeneficial to learning students. Students need to have face-to-face interactions with other students and instructors in order to get the most out of their learning experience, yet online classes offer courses that certain schools might not offer. Online education provides a disadvantage to students in social relations, doesn't allow for deeper understanding achieved in the classroom setting, yet does provide opportunity for advanced courses.

If students were to attend online schooling alone without face-to-face interactions, the student may lack in social situations. The traditional classroom settings allow students to practice public speaking skills and daily social interactions. When entering the workforce this is extremely important. for example; Someone hoping to be hired as a doctor will

will likely be a better candidate if thay have strong social relationship skills, because communication is a major part of the job.

The traditional classroom setting also allows opportunity for students to ask insightful questions and engage in meaningful discussions. These interactions are the basis from which deeper understanding grows. A deeper understanding is very important in learning. Memorization of information and answers is a good skill, but does not test critical thinking or real-life scenarios. Having a deeper understanding and knowledge will better your problem solving skills. In real-life situations, knowing the facts will get you nowhere unless you know how to apply them.

Online education has many drawbacks, but also has some benefits. Many small schools do not offer particular classes. If students wish to take that class, online opportunities will allow that. Students will have opportunities to expand their knowledge and take advanced courses with the option of online education.

My perspective is much different than the perspectives provided. I believe that online education can be beneficial in particular situations and to a certain extent, but the traditional classroom setting will offer critical-life-skills that an online education cannot provide. finding a balance between traditional and online education can be beneficial. Taking online classes to expand knowledge while still participating in traditional learning settings to better social relationships can be the perfect combination to maximize your learning experience.

Sample Essay 4 (Score: 4444)

Score Explanation

Despite the limited extent to which it conveys the significance of the issue, the argument engages with multiple perspectives, comparing the benefits of traditional and online education.

Ideas and Analysis (4): This argument recognizes the complexity of the issue: the question under examination does not have a simple answer and because there are benefits to both methods of instruction, the best opportunities for students to maximize their learning will come from a balance between the two. The response maintains clear focus on this purpose throughout, making it easy for the reader to follow the analysis. The societal value of education is not explicitly stated, but the discussion of benefits and drawbacks implies that education is a priority. The writer understands that there are merits to more than one side of this issue—recognizing them contributes to analysis and developing them contributes to supporting that analysis.

Development and Support (4): The clear focus of this response contributes to its development. For each point intended to support the thesis, ideas are extended through elaboration rather than repetition, occasionally pointing toward implications (that "public speaking skills and daily social interactions" will be relevant when joining the workforce supports the claim that face-to-face interactions are important). Though it continues to illustrate adequately, the second body paragraph lacks some clarity around why students cannot ask meaningful questions in an online environment and neglects to explain why online instruction is limited to "memorization of information." Importantly, acknowledging that online education can offer more advanced courses and help students expand their knowledge complicates an argument that is otherwise focused on the positive implications of traditional education. Considering qualifications and complications is one key distinction between the upper and lower halves of the rubric.

Organization (4): The response exhibits a clear, common organizational strategy. The structure provides clarity in grouped ideas, though it does not support synthesis of ideas. Although somewhat abrupt from paragraph to paragraph, clear transitions help move the reader from one idea to the next and understand the relationships among ideas ("If students were to attend online schooling alone . . .," "The traditional classroom setting also allows . . ."). Within paragraphs, movement from one idea to another is solid ("meaningful discussions. These interactions . . . deeper understanding. A deeper understanding . . ."). The overall shape of the response reflects an emergent controlling purpose: exploring each of the three supporting points to build support for the thesis, which is fully expressed in the conclusion. The ideas flow logically from a statement that a balanced approach is most appropriate to evaluation of the strongest method to consideration of benefits of the alternative to a concluding statement that emphasizes the thesis.

Language Use and Conventions (4): The use of language in this response conveys the argument with clarity. Despite some instances of awkward phrasing ("provides a disadvantage to students in social relations," "the student may lack in social situations") and some repetition (e.g., interactions), overall word choice is adequate and sometimes precise ("likely be a better candidate," "insightful questions," "engage in meaningful discussions"). Varied sentence structures ("If students were to attend . . .," "The traditional classroom settings allow . . .," "for example; someone hoping . . .") contribute to clarity in organization and analysis, serving as transitions and development of the argument. Stylistic and register choices, including a practical and contemplative tone, are appropriate for an argument that advocates for a balance of both types of learning methods. Errors in grammar, usage, and mechanics are present, but they rarely impede understanding.

Sample Essay 5

When it comes to choosing between traditional classroom instruction and online learning, people are gradually giving up the former and adopting the latter for the reason that it provides convenience; but as far as I am concerned, traditional classroom teaching can be more beneficial and has more advantages. In fact, there are certainly many more benefits to interacting with your teacher directly.

First of all, when people learn from others face-to-face, the most critical advantage is the ability to communicate if there are some problems or confusion. Teachers will give answers to clarify confusing topics and offer help to find solutions when there are issues. What the student needs can be taken into consideration and result in an answer tailored to those needs, which improves efficiency in learning and comprehension. Perspective one claims that traditional education doesn't provide a good fit for everybody, but online options ensure that people will meet their needs due to the various options available on the internet. If one doesn't want to learn deeply about a topic, the online platform may be sufficient.

However, people who want to learn about a specific topic in depth may need a teacher fact-to-face to truly absorb the material and come to a competent understanding of it. For example, I once studied a math topic that was very difficult to comprehend. I first looked on the Internet for online courses. I was happy to find a lot of study materials, but as I got further through them, I became confused on certain points that I didn't get from the courses. I felt that the online instructors talked too fast and weren't always easy to follow. But I could not stop a video to ask questions, so my mom got me a tutor to help with the ideas that I was struggling with. That was really a better experience compared to learning online on my own. When I didn't understand things, I called on my tutor to help me, and I talked to him about my thought process, from which he could assess where I went astray. Learning what I did wrong at first helped me when I moved to more difficult levels of the math subject later on. It would be very difficult to learn a complicated subject, where you have to build an understanding step by step, if you couldn't address confusion as it comes up.

If people want to get further on what they learn, the best way is to listen to teachers directly. Scientists work together fact-to-face so that they can collaborate on projects by communicating. If they were working apart, only communicating through the Internet, they wouldn't quickly understand each other, if at all. So when ideas and processes rise to a certain level of complexity, the ability to interact in person is crucial to comprehending what one wants to learn.

From what has been mentioned above there are many benefits that people gain from classroom learning, for the reason that it provides a more efficient, high quality education and results a greater understanding between learners and instructors. Therefore, students should choose to learn with a teacher in the classroom because it will have a greater outcome for them.

Sample Essay 5 (Score: 5555)

Score Explanation

The writer uses a detailed personal example to analyze multiple perspectives on the issue, addressing implications and critiquing underlying values.

Ideas and Analysis (5): The argument productively engages with multiple perspectives. The detailed example allows the writer to elaborate on and support Perspective Two while evaluating the limitations of Perspective One. The thesis—face-to-face communication is more beneficial because "it provides a more efficient, high quality education and results [in] a greater understanding between learners and instructors"—addresses the idea that there are layers to the educational experience, which reflects precision in thought and purpose. Analysis involves consideration of underlying values (e.g., efficiency, quality) and challenges the assumption that online instruction could provide a student with complete understanding, even when concepts rise to a certain level of complexity ("If one doesn't want to learn deeply about a topic, the online platform may be sufficient."). Analysis also addresses complexities of online communication by discussing that not all online instruction is equal in its ability to instruct ("It would be very difficult to learn a complicated subject, where you have to build an understanding step by step, if you couldn't address confusion as it comes up."; "If they were working apart, only communicating through the internet, they wouldn't quickly understand each other, if at all.").

Development and Support (5): Development of ideas and support deepen the reader's understanding of the argument. The writer recognizes that online instruction may be sufficient in some circumstances, but not if one hopes to achieve a higher level of understanding; this qualification enriches the thesis that traditional classroom instruction is more advantageous to a student's educational experience. While the example of collaboration among scientists is underdeveloped, the brief discussion illustrates the importance of communication when working with complex problems—reasoning that supports the thesis. The detailed example exhibits purposeful reasoning and illustration and is well integrated—the focus is entirely on elaborating the point that interacting with teachers face-to-face is most beneficial for learning deeply. The account capably conveys the significance of the argument.

Organization (5): The chronological order of the personal example contributes to a productive organizational strategy. The response is focused on the thesis throughout, reflecting an argument that maintains a controlling idea. A logical sequencing of ideas contributes to the effectiveness of the argument as it first establishes that direct interaction with teachers has more benefits than online instruction, then complicates the assumption that online instruction can meet all needs of all students, before exploring drawbacks of online education, and ultimately leads to a conclusion that reaffirms the thesis. Though the transition to scientists is not smooth or effective, most of the movement from idea to idea throughout the response consistently clarifies relationships ("If one doesn't want to learn deeply about a topic, the online platform may be sufficient. However, people who want to learn about a specific topic in depth may need a teacher . . .").

Language Use and Conventions (5): Advanced sentence structures ("It would be very difficult to learn a complicated subject, where you have to build an understanding step by step, if you couldn't address confusion as it comes up.") contribute to clarity and convey ideas with precision, while the stylistic choice to describe a personal experience particularly suited to discussing the issue is purposeful and productive. Though vocabulary choices are not elevated, word choices are specific and suit the purpose of explaining the argument ("critical advantage," "confused on certain points," "greater understanding between learners and instructors"). Due to the precision and clarity throughout the essay, occasional imprecision is largely unnoticeable.

Sample Essay 6

The contemporary classroom is the result of several improvements made by each subsequent generation in order to achieve the highest quality and efficiency of teaching possible. Of these changes in more recent times, online support and even entirely internet based courses have been adopted to further improve the modern learning environment. However, the question of whether or not these drastic changes truly have a beneficial impact has been raised. While both physical and online institutions present harms and benefits, I believe the use of both in tandem accomplishes the shared goal of education: to equip students with the tools to succeed in their futures.

To begin, the traditional classroom has its perks over the sole use of online instruction. A hands on education bestows on students so much more than information about particular subjects. For example, open-ended discussion and other group activities encourage and develop cooperation, collaboration, and overall social skills. It would be exceedingly difficult to synthesize these critical skills within a digital platform. Additionally, classroom instruction benefits students through organization and regimentation that online courses can only hope to achieve. Deadlines embody this juxtaposition, because

While most online courses allow students to put off their work to an end-of-course deadline, a traditional classroom a teacher guides students through their workload by requiring proof of progress day-to-day. Students can further benefit from teamwork and guidance as they further develop in-person relationships with instructors and peers, especially if they choose tak an active role in their education by reaching out to teachers and classmates when help is needed.

This, however, does not mean that the traditional classroom is superior in all aspects. In every physical classroom there exists a "back row," often populated by less engaged students who are less encouraged to participate. While social skills may be better learned in person, engagment is necessary to learn at all. Online courses usually require participation in discussion forums that provide a platform in which to consider all contributions equally. Engagement is also better promoted in online instruction through a broad range of subjects, offering greater access to courses that interest an individual student. Beyond more subjects, online instruction may also provide a richer context for understanding. Traditional instruction can be limited in scope of subject matter, as well as restricted to the knowledge and opinions of the school— or even classroom— and then further restricted to the knowledge and opinions of those ready to speak up. This is evidenced across many university campuses where one dominant political or social view tends to dictate the discussions and even sentiments of a student body. While a tradional classroo may be a better environment to equip students with social skills, an online

Improving Your Score

environment may allow for greater diversity of thought.

The thing is, developing the skills to socially interact with a narrow segment of the population is about as useful as developing the ability to consider many perspectives in forming your own opinion, but not the skills to contribute to a larger discussion: not at all. After weighing both sides, it is difficult to decide that one is superior to the other. That is why I advocate for compromise. A system that utilizes the strengths of both education platforms will eradicate the weaknesses of both as well. If it is truly the quality and efficiency of education that we most value, then students should be offered the best, most engaging instruction regardless of platform.

Sample Essay 6 (Score: 6666)

Score Explanation

This argument critically examines each instructional method, ultimately framing the issue as a matter of individual contribution to larger conversations.

Ideas and Analysis (6): The precise thesis acknowledges the nuances of traditional and online education. Analysis of the value of each method on its own and in comparison to the other concludes that compromise is a necessity and not just a way to appease everyone ("A system that utilizes the strengths of both education platforms will eradicate the weaknesses of both as well."). An examination of the complexities of student engagement leads to an exploration of how online instruction can serve those students who remain unengaged by traditional instruction. The factors that keep each method from fully serving all students are situated in the context of educational trends across time, always with the goals to "achieve the highest quality and efficiency of teaching" and "to equip students with the tools to succeed in their future."

Development and Support (6): Having established the historical context of continuous efforts to improve education, the writer develops an argument that the "contemporary classroom" has the power to provide the highest quality of education by integrating traditional and online methods. Critical evaluation emerges in the comparisons between the two methods, and qualifications and complications enrich and bolster ideas and analysis. For example, the truism that traditional classrooms provide socialization is complicated by such observations as students develop only limited social skills in the physical classroom ("skills to socially interact with a narrow segment of the population") and "an online environment may allow for greater diversity of thought." This bolsters the analysis that, in both social skills and subject matter, a combination of traditional and online instruction provides the education students need to prepare for the future.

Organization (6): The response exhibits a skillful organizational strategy which is unified by the controlling idea that using physical and online instruction in tandem eliminates the limitations and increases the benefits of both. The precise thesis brings unity and cohesion to this argument. The thesis guides a logical progression of ideas: The piece begins by introducing the main idea but uses the development of supporting ideas to build toward the clarity of that main idea ("the use of both in tandem accomplishes the shared goal of education"), and then restates the thesis more forcefully in the conclusion ("A system that utilizes the strengths of both education platforms will eradicate the weaknesses of both as well."). Transitions between and within paragraphs are extremely effective at unifying the essay. The clarity with which the writer moves back and forth between instructional methods and advantages and disadvantages strengthens relationships among ideas ("open-ended discussion and other group activities encourage and develop cooperation, collaboration, and overall social skills. It would be exceedingly difficult to synthesize these critical skills within a digital platform.").

Language Use and Conventions (6): The use of language enhances the argument. Skillful and precise word choice creates distinctions which add depth to ideas ("In every physical classroom there exists a 'back row,' often populated by less engaged students who are less encouraged to participate."). Sentence structures are consistently varied and clear, and help convey complex relationships among ideas ("If it is truly the quality and efficiency of education that we most value, then students should be offered the best, most engaging instruction regardless of platform."). Stylistic and register choices, including notes of caution that convey the high stakes of the argument, are strategic and effective in advocating for a compromise to best equip students for their futures ("one dominant . . . view tends to dictate . . . discussions and even sentiments"). A few minor errors in grammar, usage, and mechanics have no impact on the clarity of the argument.

Strategies for Taking the ACT Writing Test

Although your writing score reflects the quality of the product (the essay) you write, the writing process you follow can have a major impact on your score. For example, if you do not spend a few minutes prewriting (planning) before you start writing, you could "paint yourself into a corner" by following a line of logic that leads to an illogical conclusion and have no time left to start over.

The following sections present a few writing, prewriting, and postwriting strategies to improve the process you follow when writing your essay. Of course, no writing process can make up for a lack of knowledge and skill, which take years of study and practice to develop. If you need to sharpen your writing skills, we recommend that you take a course in English composition and practice writing and studying others' writing frequently.

Prewrite

Some writers like to plunge right in, but this is seldom a good way to do well on a timed essay. Prewriting gets you acquainted with the issue, suggests patterns for presenting your thoughts, and gives you a little breathing room to come up with interesting ideas for introducing and concluding your essay. Before writing, then, carefully consider the prompt and make sure you understand it—reread it if you aren't sure. Decide how you want to answer the question in the prompt. Then jot down your ideas on the topic: identify your own position and list reasons and/ or examples that you will use to explain your point of view on the issue. Write down what you think someone might say in opposition to your point of view, and think about how you would refute their argument. Consider the broader context: what economic, social, historical, cultural, political, etc. circumstances surround it, and how do the specifics of your argument connect to that bigger picture? Try creating an outline or drawing a diagram to help you determine how best to organize the ideas in your essay. You should do your prewriting on the pages provided in your writing test booklet. You can refer back to these notes as you write the essay itself on the lined pages in your answer document.

Write

When you're ready to write your essay, proceed with the confidence that you have prepared well and that you will have attentive and receptive readers who are interested in your ideas. At the beginning of your essay, make sure readers will see that you understand the issue. Explain your point of view in a clear and logical way. If possible, discuss the issue in a broader context and evaluate the implications or complications of the issue. Address other perspectives presented in the prompt. Also consider what others might say to refute your point of view and present a counterargument to those potential objections. Employ logical reasoning and use specific examples to explain and illustrate what you're saying. Vary the structure of your sentences, and choose varied and precise words. Make logical relationships clear by using transitional words and phrases. Don't wander off the topic. End with a strong conclusion that summarizes or reinforces your position.

Is it advisable to organize the essay by using a formula, such as the five-paragraph essay? Points are neither awarded nor deducted for following familiar formulas, so feel free to use one or not as best suits your preference. Some writers find formulas stifling, other writers find them a solid basis on which to build a strong argument, and still other writers just keep them handy to use when needed. The exact numbers of words and paragraphs in your essay are less important than the clarity and development of your ideas. Writers who have something to say usually find that their ideas have a way of sorting themselves out at reasonable length and in an appropriate number of paragraphs.

Review Your Essay

Aim to allow for a few minutes at the end of the testing session to read over your essay. Correct any mistakes in grammar, usage, punctuation, and spelling. If you find any words that are hard to read, recopy them so your readers can read them easily. Make any corrections and revisions neatly, between the lines (but not in the margins). Your readers take into account that you had merely 40 minutes to compose and write your essay. Within that time limit, try to make your essay as polished as you can.

Practice

There are many ways to prepare for the ACT writing test. You may be surprised that these include reading newspapers and magazines, listening to news analysis on television or radio, and participating in discussions and debates about issues and problems. These activities help you become more familiar with current issues, with different perspectives on those issues, and with strategies that skilled writers and speakers use to present their points of view and respond to a range of viewpoints.

Of course, one of the best ways to prepare for the ACT writing test is to practice writing. Practice writing different kinds of texts, for different purposes, with different audiences in mind. The writing you do in your English classes will help you, as will independent practice in writing essays, stories, poems, plays, editorials, reports, letters to the editor, a personal journal, or other kinds of writing that you do on your own. Strive to consider the quality of your writing from someone else's perspective: would a reader see it as well developed and well organized, and having precise, clear, and concise language? Because the ACT writing test asks you to explain your perspective on an issue in a convincing way, engaging in exercises related to persuasive and argumentative writing (such as editorials or essays discussing controversial issues) is especially helpful. However, since many writing skills are transferable from one genre to another, practicing a variety of different kinds of writing will help make you a versatile writer able to adjust to different writing occasions and assignments. Additionally, analyzing others' writing will help you strengthen and evaluate your own. Practice writing critiques of arguments in which you assess clarity of thought, logical reasoning and evidence used to support the thesis, organization of ideas, and the effects of language choices.

Share your writing with others and get feedback. Feedback helps you anticipate how readers might interpret your writing and what types of questions they might have. It will also help you identify your strengths and weaknesses as a writer. Also, keep in mind what the ACT readers will be looking for as they score your essay by examining the analytic rubric for the ACT writing test (in chapter 3). Consult with others (teachers, peers, etc.) to make sure your writing meets the criteria described for the high-scoring essays.

You should also get some practice writing within a time limit. This will help build skills that are important in college and career. Taking the practice ACT writing tests in this book will give you a good idea of what timed writing is like and how much additional practice you may need.

Part Four:
Taking Additional Practice Tests

In This Part

This part features five additional practice tests. Here, you take and score the tests and look at your scores from a number of different perspectives, so you can use the results more effectively in your educational and career planning. Specifically, this part gives you the opportunity to do the following:

Take five additional practice tests.

Score your practice tests to determine your raw score, scaled scores (similar to the scores the ACT reports), and your estimated percentage rank (how well you did compared to other students who took the tests).

Evaluate your ACT scores from different perspectives to gain insight into what your scores mean in terms of college and career planning.

10

Chapter 10: Taking Additional Practice Tests

In this chapter, you'll find five additional practice ACT tests, copies of real answer documents for recording your answers, and explanatory answers for the questions on all of the multiple-choice tests.

Each practice test features the contents of the tests in the same order as they will be on the ACT: the English test, the mathematics test, the reading test, the science test, and the optional writing test. Following each complete practice test, you will find the explanatory answers for the multiple-choice questions on that test in the same pattern as the individual tests (English, mathematics, reading, and science).

Prep Online!

Want even more ways to prep? Go to act.wiley.com to access our online platform or use our companion app. Access all practice tests and track your progress.

Two copies of the answer documents that you can tear out and use to record your answers for the multiple-choice tests precede each practice test. (Two copies of these answer documents have been provided in case you make errors or if you would like to retake a practice test. When you take the actual ACT test, however, only one answer document will be provided.) One copy of the writing test answer document, which you can tear out (or photocopy) and use to write your essay, is provided for each practice writing test.

Simulating Testing Conditions

We recommend that you take all practice tests under conditions similar to those you will experience on test day. See chapter 3 for instructions.

The ACT® Sample Answer Document

EXAMINEE STATEMENTS, CERTIFICATION, AND SIGNATURE

1. **Statements**: I understand that by registering for, launching, starting, or submitting answer documents for an ACT® test, I am agreeing to comply with and be bound by the *Terms and Conditions: Testing Rules and Policies for the ACT® Test* ("Terms").

   I UNDERSTAND AND AGREE THAT THE TERMS PERMIT ACT TO CANCEL MY SCORES IN CERTAIN CIRCUMSTANCES. THE TERMS ALSO LIMIT DAMAGES AVAILABLE TO ME AND REQUIRE ARBITRATION OF CERTAIN DISPUTES. BY AGREEING TO ARBITRATION, ACT AND I BOTH WAIVE THE RIGHT TO HAVE THOSE DISPUTES HEARD BY A JUDGE OR JURY.

   I understand that ACT owns the test questions and responses, and I will not share them with anyone by any form of communication before, during, or after the test administration. I understand that taking the test for someone else may violate the law and subject me to legal penalties. I consent to the collection and processing of personally identifying information I provide, and its subsequent use and disclosure, as described in the ACT Privacy Policy (www.act.org/privacy.html). I also permit ACT to transfer my personally identifying information to the United States, to ACT, or to a third-party service provider, where it will be subject to use and disclosure under the laws of the United States, including being accessible to law enforcement or national security authorities.

2. **Certification**: Copy the italicized certification below, then sign and date in the spaces provided.

   I agree to the **Statements** *above and certify that I am the person whose information appears on this form.*

   _____

   _____

   _____

   Your Signature _____   Today's Date _____

Do NOT mark in this shaded area.

USE A NO. 2 PENCIL ONLY.
(Do NOT use a mechanical pencil, ink, ballpoint, correction fluid, or felt-tip pen.)

A

NAME, MAILING ADDRESS, AND TELEPHONE
(Please print.)

Last Name | First Name | MI (Middle Initial)

House Number & Street (Apt. No.); or PO Box & No.; or RR & No.

City | State/Province | ZIP/Postal Code

Area Code | Number | Country

ACT, Inc.—Confidential Restricted when data present

ALL examinees must complete block A – please print.

Blocks B, C, and D are required for all examinees. Find the MATCHING INFORMATION on your ticket. Enter it EXACTLY the same way, even if any of the information is missing or incorrect. Fill in the corresponding ovals. If you do not complete these blocks to match your previous information EXACTLY, your scores will be **delayed up to 8 weeks.**

ACT®
PO BOX 168, IOWA CITY, IA 52243-0168

B MATCH NAME
(First 5 letters of last name)

C MATCH NUMBER

D DATE OF BIRTH

Month	Day	Year
January		
February		
March		
April		
May		
June		
July		
August		
September		
October		
November		
December		

01121523W   (A)203023-001:654321   ISD36401   Printed in the US.

Taking Additional Practice Tests

PAGE 2

BOOKLET NUMBER

Print your 5-character **Test Form** in the boxes at the right and fill in the corresponding ovals.

FORM

TEST 1: ENGLISH

1 Ⓐ Ⓑ Ⓒ Ⓓ	14 Ⓕ Ⓖ Ⓗ Ⓙ	27 Ⓐ Ⓑ Ⓒ Ⓓ	40 Ⓕ Ⓖ Ⓗ Ⓙ	53 Ⓐ Ⓑ Ⓒ Ⓓ	66 Ⓕ Ⓖ Ⓗ Ⓙ
2 Ⓕ Ⓖ Ⓗ Ⓙ	15 Ⓐ Ⓑ Ⓒ Ⓓ	28 Ⓕ Ⓖ Ⓗ Ⓙ	41 Ⓐ Ⓑ Ⓒ Ⓓ	54 Ⓕ Ⓖ Ⓗ Ⓙ	67 Ⓐ Ⓑ Ⓒ Ⓓ
3 Ⓐ Ⓑ Ⓒ Ⓓ	16 Ⓕ Ⓖ Ⓗ Ⓙ	29 Ⓐ Ⓑ Ⓒ Ⓓ	42 Ⓕ Ⓖ Ⓗ Ⓙ	55 Ⓐ Ⓑ Ⓒ Ⓓ	68 Ⓕ Ⓖ Ⓗ Ⓙ
4 Ⓕ Ⓖ Ⓗ Ⓙ	17 Ⓐ Ⓑ Ⓒ Ⓓ	30 Ⓕ Ⓖ Ⓗ Ⓙ	43 Ⓐ Ⓑ Ⓒ Ⓓ	56 Ⓕ Ⓖ Ⓗ Ⓙ	69 Ⓐ Ⓑ Ⓒ Ⓓ
5 Ⓐ Ⓑ Ⓒ Ⓓ	18 Ⓕ Ⓖ Ⓗ Ⓙ	31 Ⓐ Ⓑ Ⓒ Ⓓ	44 Ⓕ Ⓖ Ⓗ Ⓙ	57 Ⓐ Ⓑ Ⓒ Ⓓ	70 Ⓕ Ⓖ Ⓗ Ⓙ
6 Ⓕ Ⓖ Ⓗ Ⓙ	19 Ⓐ Ⓑ Ⓒ Ⓓ	32 Ⓕ Ⓖ Ⓗ Ⓙ	45 Ⓐ Ⓑ Ⓒ Ⓓ	58 Ⓕ Ⓖ Ⓗ Ⓙ	71 Ⓐ Ⓑ Ⓒ Ⓓ
7 Ⓐ Ⓑ Ⓒ Ⓓ	20 Ⓕ Ⓖ Ⓗ Ⓙ	33 Ⓐ Ⓑ Ⓒ Ⓓ	46 Ⓕ Ⓖ Ⓗ Ⓙ	59 Ⓐ Ⓑ Ⓒ Ⓓ	72 Ⓕ Ⓖ Ⓗ Ⓙ
8 Ⓕ Ⓖ Ⓗ Ⓙ	21 Ⓐ Ⓑ Ⓒ Ⓓ	34 Ⓕ Ⓖ Ⓗ Ⓙ	47 Ⓐ Ⓑ Ⓒ Ⓓ	60 Ⓕ Ⓖ Ⓗ Ⓙ	73 Ⓐ Ⓑ Ⓒ Ⓓ
9 Ⓐ Ⓑ Ⓒ Ⓓ	22 Ⓕ Ⓖ Ⓗ Ⓙ	35 Ⓐ Ⓑ Ⓒ Ⓓ	48 Ⓕ Ⓖ Ⓗ Ⓙ	61 Ⓐ Ⓑ Ⓒ Ⓓ	74 Ⓕ Ⓖ Ⓗ Ⓙ
10 Ⓕ Ⓖ Ⓗ Ⓙ	23 Ⓐ Ⓑ Ⓒ Ⓓ	36 Ⓕ Ⓖ Ⓗ Ⓙ	49 Ⓐ Ⓑ Ⓒ Ⓓ	62 Ⓕ Ⓖ Ⓗ Ⓙ	75 Ⓐ Ⓑ Ⓒ Ⓓ
11 Ⓐ Ⓑ Ⓒ Ⓓ	24 Ⓕ Ⓖ Ⓗ Ⓙ	37 Ⓐ Ⓑ Ⓒ Ⓓ	50 Ⓕ Ⓖ Ⓗ Ⓙ	63 Ⓐ Ⓑ Ⓒ Ⓓ	
12 Ⓕ Ⓖ Ⓗ Ⓙ	25 Ⓐ Ⓑ Ⓒ Ⓓ	38 Ⓕ Ⓖ Ⓗ Ⓙ	51 Ⓐ Ⓑ Ⓒ Ⓓ	64 Ⓕ Ⓖ Ⓗ Ⓙ	
13 Ⓐ Ⓑ Ⓒ Ⓓ	26 Ⓕ Ⓖ Ⓗ Ⓙ	39 Ⓐ Ⓑ Ⓒ Ⓓ	52 Ⓕ Ⓖ Ⓗ Ⓙ	65 Ⓐ Ⓑ Ⓒ Ⓓ	

TEST 2: MATHEMATICS

1 Ⓐ Ⓑ Ⓒ Ⓓ Ⓔ	11 Ⓐ Ⓑ Ⓒ Ⓓ Ⓔ	21 Ⓐ Ⓑ Ⓒ Ⓓ Ⓔ	31 Ⓐ Ⓑ Ⓒ Ⓓ Ⓔ	41 Ⓐ Ⓑ Ⓒ Ⓓ Ⓔ	51 Ⓐ Ⓑ Ⓒ Ⓓ Ⓔ
2 Ⓕ Ⓖ Ⓗ Ⓙ Ⓚ	12 Ⓕ Ⓖ Ⓗ Ⓙ Ⓚ	22 Ⓕ Ⓖ Ⓗ Ⓙ Ⓚ	32 Ⓕ Ⓖ Ⓗ Ⓙ Ⓚ	42 Ⓕ Ⓖ Ⓗ Ⓙ Ⓚ	52 Ⓕ Ⓖ Ⓗ Ⓙ Ⓚ
3 Ⓐ Ⓑ Ⓒ Ⓓ Ⓔ	13 Ⓐ Ⓑ Ⓒ Ⓓ Ⓔ	23 Ⓐ Ⓑ Ⓒ Ⓓ Ⓔ	33 Ⓐ Ⓑ Ⓒ Ⓓ Ⓔ	43 Ⓐ Ⓑ Ⓒ Ⓓ Ⓔ	53 Ⓐ Ⓑ Ⓒ Ⓓ Ⓔ
4 Ⓕ Ⓖ Ⓗ Ⓙ Ⓚ	14 Ⓕ Ⓖ Ⓗ Ⓙ Ⓚ	24 Ⓕ Ⓖ Ⓗ Ⓙ Ⓚ	34 Ⓕ Ⓖ Ⓗ Ⓙ Ⓚ	44 Ⓕ Ⓖ Ⓗ Ⓙ Ⓚ	54 Ⓕ Ⓖ Ⓗ Ⓙ Ⓚ
5 Ⓐ Ⓑ Ⓒ Ⓓ Ⓔ	15 Ⓐ Ⓑ Ⓒ Ⓓ Ⓔ	25 Ⓐ Ⓑ Ⓒ Ⓓ Ⓔ	35 Ⓐ Ⓑ Ⓒ Ⓓ Ⓔ	45 Ⓐ Ⓑ Ⓒ Ⓓ Ⓔ	55 Ⓐ Ⓑ Ⓒ Ⓓ Ⓔ
6 Ⓕ Ⓖ Ⓗ Ⓙ Ⓚ	16 Ⓕ Ⓖ Ⓗ Ⓙ Ⓚ	26 Ⓕ Ⓖ Ⓗ Ⓙ Ⓚ	36 Ⓕ Ⓖ Ⓗ Ⓙ Ⓚ	46 Ⓕ Ⓖ Ⓗ Ⓙ Ⓚ	56 Ⓕ Ⓖ Ⓗ Ⓙ Ⓚ
7 Ⓐ Ⓑ Ⓒ Ⓓ Ⓔ	17 Ⓐ Ⓑ Ⓒ Ⓓ Ⓔ	27 Ⓐ Ⓑ Ⓒ Ⓓ Ⓔ	37 Ⓐ Ⓑ Ⓒ Ⓓ Ⓔ	47 Ⓐ Ⓑ Ⓒ Ⓓ Ⓔ	57 Ⓐ Ⓑ Ⓒ Ⓓ Ⓔ
8 Ⓕ Ⓖ Ⓗ Ⓙ Ⓚ	18 Ⓕ Ⓖ Ⓗ Ⓙ Ⓚ	28 Ⓕ Ⓖ Ⓗ Ⓙ Ⓚ	38 Ⓕ Ⓖ Ⓗ Ⓙ Ⓚ	48 Ⓕ Ⓖ Ⓗ Ⓙ Ⓚ	58 Ⓕ Ⓖ Ⓗ Ⓙ Ⓚ
9 Ⓐ Ⓑ Ⓒ Ⓓ Ⓔ	19 Ⓐ Ⓑ Ⓒ Ⓓ Ⓔ	29 Ⓐ Ⓑ Ⓒ Ⓓ Ⓔ	39 Ⓐ Ⓑ Ⓒ Ⓓ Ⓔ	49 Ⓐ Ⓑ Ⓒ Ⓓ Ⓔ	59 Ⓐ Ⓑ Ⓒ Ⓓ Ⓔ
10 Ⓕ Ⓖ Ⓗ Ⓙ Ⓚ	20 Ⓕ Ⓖ Ⓗ Ⓙ Ⓚ	30 Ⓕ Ⓖ Ⓗ Ⓙ Ⓚ	40 Ⓕ Ⓖ Ⓗ Ⓙ Ⓚ	50 Ⓕ Ⓖ Ⓗ Ⓙ Ⓚ	60 Ⓕ Ⓖ Ⓗ Ⓙ Ⓚ

TEST 3: READING

1 Ⓐ Ⓑ Ⓒ Ⓓ	8 Ⓕ Ⓖ Ⓗ Ⓙ	15 Ⓐ Ⓑ Ⓒ Ⓓ	22 Ⓕ Ⓖ Ⓗ Ⓙ	29 Ⓐ Ⓑ Ⓒ Ⓓ	36 Ⓕ Ⓖ Ⓗ Ⓙ
2 Ⓕ Ⓖ Ⓗ Ⓙ	9 Ⓐ Ⓑ Ⓒ Ⓓ	16 Ⓕ Ⓖ Ⓗ Ⓙ	23 Ⓐ Ⓑ Ⓒ Ⓓ	30 Ⓕ Ⓖ Ⓗ Ⓙ	37 Ⓐ Ⓑ Ⓒ Ⓓ
3 Ⓐ Ⓑ Ⓒ Ⓓ	10 Ⓕ Ⓖ Ⓗ Ⓙ	17 Ⓐ Ⓑ Ⓒ Ⓓ	24 Ⓕ Ⓖ Ⓗ Ⓙ	31 Ⓐ Ⓑ Ⓒ Ⓓ	38 Ⓕ Ⓖ Ⓗ Ⓙ
4 Ⓕ Ⓖ Ⓗ Ⓙ	11 Ⓐ Ⓑ Ⓒ Ⓓ	18 Ⓕ Ⓖ Ⓗ Ⓙ	25 Ⓐ Ⓑ Ⓒ Ⓓ	32 Ⓕ Ⓖ Ⓗ Ⓙ	39 Ⓐ Ⓑ Ⓒ Ⓓ
5 Ⓐ Ⓑ Ⓒ Ⓓ	12 Ⓕ Ⓖ Ⓗ Ⓙ	19 Ⓐ Ⓑ Ⓒ Ⓓ	26 Ⓕ Ⓖ Ⓗ Ⓙ	33 Ⓐ Ⓑ Ⓒ Ⓓ	40 Ⓕ Ⓖ Ⓗ Ⓙ
6 Ⓕ Ⓖ Ⓗ Ⓙ	13 Ⓐ Ⓑ Ⓒ Ⓓ	20 Ⓕ Ⓖ Ⓗ Ⓙ	27 Ⓐ Ⓑ Ⓒ Ⓓ	34 Ⓕ Ⓖ Ⓗ Ⓙ	
7 Ⓐ Ⓑ Ⓒ Ⓓ	14 Ⓕ Ⓖ Ⓗ Ⓙ	21 Ⓐ Ⓑ Ⓒ Ⓓ	28 Ⓕ Ⓖ Ⓗ Ⓙ	35 Ⓐ Ⓑ Ⓒ Ⓓ	

TEST 4: SCIENCE

1 Ⓐ Ⓑ Ⓒ Ⓓ	8 Ⓕ Ⓖ Ⓗ Ⓙ	15 Ⓐ Ⓑ Ⓒ Ⓓ	22 Ⓕ Ⓖ Ⓗ Ⓙ	29 Ⓐ Ⓑ Ⓒ Ⓓ	36 Ⓕ Ⓖ Ⓗ Ⓙ
2 Ⓕ Ⓖ Ⓗ Ⓙ	9 Ⓐ Ⓑ Ⓒ Ⓓ	16 Ⓕ Ⓖ Ⓗ Ⓙ	23 Ⓐ Ⓑ Ⓒ Ⓓ	30 Ⓕ Ⓖ Ⓗ Ⓙ	37 Ⓐ Ⓑ Ⓒ Ⓓ
3 Ⓐ Ⓑ Ⓒ Ⓓ	10 Ⓕ Ⓖ Ⓗ Ⓙ	17 Ⓐ Ⓑ Ⓒ Ⓓ	24 Ⓕ Ⓖ Ⓗ Ⓙ	31 Ⓐ Ⓑ Ⓒ Ⓓ	38 Ⓕ Ⓖ Ⓗ Ⓙ
4 Ⓕ Ⓖ Ⓗ Ⓙ	11 Ⓐ Ⓑ Ⓒ Ⓓ	18 Ⓕ Ⓖ Ⓗ Ⓙ	25 Ⓐ Ⓑ Ⓒ Ⓓ	32 Ⓕ Ⓖ Ⓗ Ⓙ	39 Ⓐ Ⓑ Ⓒ Ⓓ
5 Ⓐ Ⓑ Ⓒ Ⓓ	12 Ⓕ Ⓖ Ⓗ Ⓙ	19 Ⓐ Ⓑ Ⓒ Ⓓ	26 Ⓕ Ⓖ Ⓗ Ⓙ	33 Ⓐ Ⓑ Ⓒ Ⓓ	40 Ⓕ Ⓖ Ⓗ Ⓙ
6 Ⓕ Ⓖ Ⓗ Ⓙ	13 Ⓐ Ⓑ Ⓒ Ⓓ	20 Ⓕ Ⓖ Ⓗ Ⓙ	27 Ⓐ Ⓑ Ⓒ Ⓓ	34 Ⓕ Ⓖ Ⓗ Ⓙ	
7 Ⓐ Ⓑ Ⓒ Ⓓ	14 Ⓕ Ⓖ Ⓗ Ⓙ	21 Ⓐ Ⓑ Ⓒ Ⓓ	28 Ⓕ Ⓖ Ⓗ Ⓙ	35 Ⓐ Ⓑ Ⓒ Ⓓ	

The ACT® *Sample Answer Document*

EXAMINEE STATEMENTS, CERTIFICATION, AND SIGNATURE

1. **Statements**: I understand that by registering for, launching, starting, or submitting answer documents for an ACT® test, I am agreeing to comply with and be bound by the *Terms and Conditions: Testing Rules and Policies for the ACT® Test* ("Terms").

   I UNDERSTAND AND AGREE THAT THE TERMS PERMIT ACT TO CANCEL MY SCORES IN CERTAIN CIRCUMSTANCES. THE TERMS ALSO LIMIT DAMAGES AVAILABLE TO ME AND REQUIRE ARBITRATION OF CERTAIN DISPUTES. BY AGREEING TO ARBITRATION, ACT AND I BOTH WAIVE THE RIGHT TO HAVE THOSE DISPUTES HEARD BY A JUDGE OR JURY.

   I understand that ACT owns the test questions and responses, and I will not share them with anyone by any form of communication before, during, or after the test administration. I understand that taking the test for someone else may violate the law and subject me to legal penalties. I consent to the collection and processing of personally identifying information I provide, and its subsequent use and disclosure, as described in the ACT Privacy Policy (www.act.org/privacy.html). I also permit ACT to transfer my personally identifying information to the United States, to ACT, or to a third-party service provider, where it will be subject to use and disclosure under the laws of the United States, including being accessible to law enforcement or national security authorities.

2. **Certification**: Copy the italicized certification below, then sign and date in the spaces provided.

   *I agree to the **Statements** above and certify that I am the person whose information appears on this form.*

   _____

   _____

   _____   _____
   Your Signature   Today's Date

Do NOT mark in this shaded area.

USE A NO. 2 PENCIL ONLY.
(Do NOT use a mechanical pencil, ink, ballpoint, correction fluid, or felt-tip pen.)

A — NAME, MAILING ADDRESS, AND TELEPHONE
(Please print.)

Last Name   First Name   MI (Middle Initial)

House Number & Street (Apt. No.); or PO Box & No.; or RR & No.

City   State/Province   ZIP/Postal Code

Area Code   Number   Country

ACT, Inc.—Confidential Restricted when data present

ALL examinees must complete block A – please print.

Blocks B, C, and D are required for all examinees. Find the MATCHING INFORMATION on your ticket. Enter it EXACTLY the same way, even if any of the information is missing or incorrect. Fill in the corresponding ovals. If you do not complete these blocks to match your previous information EXACTLY, your scores will be **delayed up to 8 weeks**.

ACT
PO BOX 168, IOWA CITY, IA 52243-0168

B MATCH NAME
(First 5 letters of last name)

C MATCH NUMBER

D DATE OF BIRTH

Month	Day	Year
January		
February		
March		
April		
May		
June		
July		
August		
September		
October		
November		
December		

01121523W   (A)203023-001:654321   ISD36401   Printed in the US.

PAGE 2

Marking Directions: Mark only **one** oval for each question. Fill in response completely. Erase errors cleanly without smudging.

Correct mark: ○ ● ○ ○

Do NOT use these *incorrect* or *bad* marks.

Incorrect marks: ⊘ ⊗ ◐ ⊖
Overlapping mark: ○ ○ ⊗
Cross-out mark: ○ ⊗
Smudged erasure: ○ ○ ◐ ○
Mark is too light: ◐ ○ ○ ○

BOOKLET NUMBER

(1)(1)(1)(1)(1)(1)(1)(1)(1)
(2)(2)(2)(2)(2)(2)(2)(2)(2)
(3)(3)(3)(3)(3)(3)(3)(3)(3)
(4)(4)(4)(4)(4)(4)(4)(4)(4)
(5)(5)(5)(5)(5)(5)(5)(5)(5)
(6)(6)(6)(6)(6)(6)(6)(6)(6)
(7)(7)(7)(7)(7)(7)(7)(7)(7)
(8)(8)(8)(8)(8)(8)(8)(8)(8)
(9)(9)(9)(9)(9)(9)(9)(9)(9)
(0)(0)(0)(0)(0)(0)(0)(0)(0)

Print your 5-character **Test Form** in the boxes at the right and fill in the corresponding ovals.

FORM

(1)(1)(M)(C)(1)
(2)(2)   (2)
        (3)(3)
        (4)(4)
        (5)(5)
        (6)(6)
        (7)(7)
        (8)(8)
        (9)(9)
        (0)(0)

TEST 1: ENGLISH

1 Ⓐ Ⓑ Ⓒ Ⓓ	14 Ⓕ Ⓖ Ⓗ Ⓙ	27 Ⓐ Ⓑ Ⓒ Ⓓ	40 Ⓕ Ⓖ Ⓗ Ⓙ	53 Ⓐ Ⓑ Ⓒ Ⓓ	66 Ⓕ Ⓖ Ⓗ Ⓙ
2 Ⓕ Ⓖ Ⓗ Ⓙ	15 Ⓐ Ⓑ Ⓒ Ⓓ	28 Ⓕ Ⓖ Ⓗ Ⓙ	41 Ⓐ Ⓑ Ⓒ Ⓓ	54 Ⓕ Ⓖ Ⓗ Ⓙ	67 Ⓐ Ⓑ Ⓒ Ⓓ
3 Ⓐ Ⓑ Ⓒ Ⓓ	16 Ⓕ Ⓖ Ⓗ Ⓙ	29 Ⓐ Ⓑ Ⓒ Ⓓ	42 Ⓕ Ⓖ Ⓗ Ⓙ	55 Ⓐ Ⓑ Ⓒ Ⓓ	68 Ⓕ Ⓖ Ⓗ Ⓙ
4 Ⓕ Ⓖ Ⓗ Ⓙ	17 Ⓐ Ⓑ Ⓒ Ⓓ	30 Ⓕ Ⓖ Ⓗ Ⓙ	43 Ⓐ Ⓑ Ⓒ Ⓓ	56 Ⓕ Ⓖ Ⓗ Ⓙ	69 Ⓐ Ⓑ Ⓒ Ⓓ
5 Ⓐ Ⓑ Ⓒ Ⓓ	18 Ⓕ Ⓖ Ⓗ Ⓙ	31 Ⓐ Ⓑ Ⓒ Ⓓ	44 Ⓕ Ⓖ Ⓗ Ⓙ	57 Ⓐ Ⓑ Ⓒ Ⓓ	70 Ⓕ Ⓖ Ⓗ Ⓙ
6 Ⓕ Ⓖ Ⓗ Ⓙ	19 Ⓐ Ⓑ Ⓒ Ⓓ	32 Ⓕ Ⓖ Ⓗ Ⓙ	45 Ⓐ Ⓑ Ⓒ Ⓓ	58 Ⓕ Ⓖ Ⓗ Ⓙ	71 Ⓐ Ⓑ Ⓒ Ⓓ
7 Ⓐ Ⓑ Ⓒ Ⓓ	20 Ⓕ Ⓖ Ⓗ Ⓙ	33 Ⓐ Ⓑ Ⓒ Ⓓ	46 Ⓕ Ⓖ Ⓗ Ⓙ	59 Ⓐ Ⓑ Ⓒ Ⓓ	72 Ⓕ Ⓖ Ⓗ Ⓙ
8 Ⓕ Ⓖ Ⓗ Ⓙ	21 Ⓐ Ⓑ Ⓒ Ⓓ	34 Ⓕ Ⓖ Ⓗ Ⓙ	47 Ⓐ Ⓑ Ⓒ Ⓓ	60 Ⓕ Ⓖ Ⓗ Ⓙ	73 Ⓐ Ⓑ Ⓒ Ⓓ
9 Ⓐ Ⓑ Ⓒ Ⓓ	22 Ⓕ Ⓖ Ⓗ Ⓙ	35 Ⓐ Ⓑ Ⓒ Ⓓ	48 Ⓕ Ⓖ Ⓗ Ⓙ	61 Ⓐ Ⓑ Ⓒ Ⓓ	74 Ⓕ Ⓖ Ⓗ Ⓙ
10 Ⓕ Ⓖ Ⓗ Ⓙ	23 Ⓐ Ⓑ Ⓒ Ⓓ	36 Ⓕ Ⓖ Ⓗ Ⓙ	49 Ⓐ Ⓑ Ⓒ Ⓓ	62 Ⓕ Ⓖ Ⓗ Ⓙ	75 Ⓐ Ⓑ Ⓒ Ⓓ
11 Ⓐ Ⓑ Ⓒ Ⓓ	24 Ⓕ Ⓖ Ⓗ Ⓙ	37 Ⓐ Ⓑ Ⓒ Ⓓ	50 Ⓕ Ⓖ Ⓗ Ⓙ	63 Ⓐ Ⓑ Ⓒ Ⓓ	
12 Ⓕ Ⓖ Ⓗ Ⓙ	25 Ⓐ Ⓑ Ⓒ Ⓓ	38 Ⓕ Ⓖ Ⓗ Ⓙ	51 Ⓐ Ⓑ Ⓒ Ⓓ	64 Ⓕ Ⓖ Ⓗ Ⓙ	
13 Ⓐ Ⓑ Ⓒ Ⓓ	26 Ⓕ Ⓖ Ⓗ Ⓙ	39 Ⓐ Ⓑ Ⓒ Ⓓ	52 Ⓕ Ⓖ Ⓗ Ⓙ	65 Ⓐ Ⓑ Ⓒ Ⓓ	

TEST 2: MATHEMATICS

1 Ⓐ Ⓑ Ⓒ Ⓓ Ⓔ	11 Ⓐ Ⓑ Ⓒ Ⓓ Ⓔ	21 Ⓐ Ⓑ Ⓒ Ⓓ Ⓔ	31 Ⓐ Ⓑ Ⓒ Ⓓ Ⓔ	41 Ⓐ Ⓑ Ⓒ Ⓓ Ⓔ	51 Ⓐ Ⓑ Ⓒ Ⓓ Ⓔ
2 Ⓕ Ⓖ Ⓗ Ⓙ Ⓚ	12 Ⓕ Ⓖ Ⓗ Ⓙ Ⓚ	22 Ⓕ Ⓖ Ⓗ Ⓙ Ⓚ	32 Ⓕ Ⓖ Ⓗ Ⓙ Ⓚ	42 Ⓕ Ⓖ Ⓗ Ⓙ Ⓚ	52 Ⓕ Ⓖ Ⓗ Ⓙ Ⓚ
3 Ⓐ Ⓑ Ⓒ Ⓓ Ⓔ	13 Ⓐ Ⓑ Ⓒ Ⓓ Ⓔ	23 Ⓐ Ⓑ Ⓒ Ⓓ Ⓔ	33 Ⓐ Ⓑ Ⓒ Ⓓ Ⓔ	43 Ⓐ Ⓑ Ⓒ Ⓓ Ⓔ	53 Ⓐ Ⓑ Ⓒ Ⓓ Ⓔ
4 Ⓕ Ⓖ Ⓗ Ⓙ Ⓚ	14 Ⓕ Ⓖ Ⓗ Ⓙ Ⓚ	24 Ⓕ Ⓖ Ⓗ Ⓙ Ⓚ	34 Ⓕ Ⓖ Ⓗ Ⓙ Ⓚ	44 Ⓕ Ⓖ Ⓗ Ⓙ Ⓚ	54 Ⓕ Ⓖ Ⓗ Ⓙ Ⓚ
5 Ⓐ Ⓑ Ⓒ Ⓓ Ⓔ	15 Ⓐ Ⓑ Ⓒ Ⓓ Ⓔ	25 Ⓐ Ⓑ Ⓒ Ⓓ Ⓔ	35 Ⓐ Ⓑ Ⓒ Ⓓ Ⓔ	45 Ⓐ Ⓑ Ⓒ Ⓓ Ⓔ	55 Ⓐ Ⓑ Ⓒ Ⓓ Ⓔ
6 Ⓕ Ⓖ Ⓗ Ⓙ Ⓚ	16 Ⓕ Ⓖ Ⓗ Ⓙ Ⓚ	26 Ⓕ Ⓖ Ⓗ Ⓙ Ⓚ	36 Ⓕ Ⓖ Ⓗ Ⓙ Ⓚ	46 Ⓕ Ⓖ Ⓗ Ⓙ Ⓚ	56 Ⓕ Ⓖ Ⓗ Ⓙ Ⓚ
7 Ⓐ Ⓑ Ⓒ Ⓓ Ⓔ	17 Ⓐ Ⓑ Ⓒ Ⓓ Ⓔ	27 Ⓐ Ⓑ Ⓒ Ⓓ Ⓔ	37 Ⓐ Ⓑ Ⓒ Ⓓ Ⓔ	47 Ⓐ Ⓑ Ⓒ Ⓓ Ⓔ	57 Ⓐ Ⓑ Ⓒ Ⓓ Ⓔ
8 Ⓕ Ⓖ Ⓗ Ⓙ Ⓚ	18 Ⓕ Ⓖ Ⓗ Ⓙ Ⓚ	28 Ⓕ Ⓖ Ⓗ Ⓙ Ⓚ	38 Ⓕ Ⓖ Ⓗ Ⓙ Ⓚ	48 Ⓕ Ⓖ Ⓗ Ⓙ Ⓚ	58 Ⓕ Ⓖ Ⓗ Ⓙ Ⓚ
9 Ⓐ Ⓑ Ⓒ Ⓓ Ⓔ	19 Ⓐ Ⓑ Ⓒ Ⓓ Ⓔ	29 Ⓐ Ⓑ Ⓒ Ⓓ Ⓔ	39 Ⓐ Ⓑ Ⓒ Ⓓ Ⓔ	49 Ⓐ Ⓑ Ⓒ Ⓓ Ⓔ	59 Ⓐ Ⓑ Ⓒ Ⓓ Ⓔ
10 Ⓕ Ⓖ Ⓗ Ⓙ Ⓚ	20 Ⓕ Ⓖ Ⓗ Ⓙ Ⓚ	30 Ⓕ Ⓖ Ⓗ Ⓙ Ⓚ	40 Ⓕ Ⓖ Ⓗ Ⓙ Ⓚ	50 Ⓕ Ⓖ Ⓗ Ⓙ Ⓚ	60 Ⓕ Ⓖ Ⓗ Ⓙ Ⓚ

TEST 3: READING

1 Ⓐ Ⓑ Ⓒ Ⓓ	8 Ⓕ Ⓖ Ⓗ Ⓙ	15 Ⓐ Ⓑ Ⓒ Ⓓ	22 Ⓕ Ⓖ Ⓗ Ⓙ	29 Ⓐ Ⓑ Ⓒ Ⓓ	36 Ⓕ Ⓖ Ⓗ Ⓙ
2 Ⓕ Ⓖ Ⓗ Ⓙ	9 Ⓐ Ⓑ Ⓒ Ⓓ	16 Ⓕ Ⓖ Ⓗ Ⓙ	23 Ⓐ Ⓑ Ⓒ Ⓓ	30 Ⓕ Ⓖ Ⓗ Ⓙ	37 Ⓐ Ⓑ Ⓒ Ⓓ
3 Ⓐ Ⓑ Ⓒ Ⓓ	10 Ⓕ Ⓖ Ⓗ Ⓙ	17 Ⓐ Ⓑ Ⓒ Ⓓ	24 Ⓕ Ⓖ Ⓗ Ⓙ	31 Ⓐ Ⓑ Ⓒ Ⓓ	38 Ⓕ Ⓖ Ⓗ Ⓙ
4 Ⓕ Ⓖ Ⓗ Ⓙ	11 Ⓐ Ⓑ Ⓒ Ⓓ	18 Ⓕ Ⓖ Ⓗ Ⓙ	25 Ⓐ Ⓑ Ⓒ Ⓓ	32 Ⓕ Ⓖ Ⓗ Ⓙ	39 Ⓐ Ⓑ Ⓒ Ⓓ
5 Ⓐ Ⓑ Ⓒ Ⓓ	12 Ⓕ Ⓖ Ⓗ Ⓙ	19 Ⓐ Ⓑ Ⓒ Ⓓ	26 Ⓕ Ⓖ Ⓗ Ⓙ	33 Ⓐ Ⓑ Ⓒ Ⓓ	40 Ⓕ Ⓖ Ⓗ Ⓙ
6 Ⓕ Ⓖ Ⓗ Ⓙ	13 Ⓐ Ⓑ Ⓒ Ⓓ	20 Ⓕ Ⓖ Ⓗ Ⓙ	27 Ⓐ Ⓑ Ⓒ Ⓓ	34 Ⓕ Ⓖ Ⓗ Ⓙ	
7 Ⓐ Ⓑ Ⓒ Ⓓ	14 Ⓕ Ⓖ Ⓗ Ⓙ	21 Ⓐ Ⓑ Ⓒ Ⓓ	28 Ⓕ Ⓖ Ⓗ Ⓙ	35 Ⓐ Ⓑ Ⓒ Ⓓ	

TEST 4: SCIENCE

1 Ⓐ Ⓑ Ⓒ Ⓓ	8 Ⓕ Ⓖ Ⓗ Ⓙ	15 Ⓐ Ⓑ Ⓒ Ⓓ	22 Ⓕ Ⓖ Ⓗ Ⓙ	29 Ⓐ Ⓑ Ⓒ Ⓓ	36 Ⓕ Ⓖ Ⓗ Ⓙ
2 Ⓕ Ⓖ Ⓗ Ⓙ	9 Ⓐ Ⓑ Ⓒ Ⓓ	16 Ⓕ Ⓖ Ⓗ Ⓙ	23 Ⓐ Ⓑ Ⓒ Ⓓ	30 Ⓕ Ⓖ Ⓗ Ⓙ	37 Ⓐ Ⓑ Ⓒ Ⓓ
3 Ⓐ Ⓑ Ⓒ Ⓓ	10 Ⓕ Ⓖ Ⓗ Ⓙ	17 Ⓐ Ⓑ Ⓒ Ⓓ	24 Ⓕ Ⓖ Ⓗ Ⓙ	31 Ⓐ Ⓑ Ⓒ Ⓓ	38 Ⓕ Ⓖ Ⓗ Ⓙ
4 Ⓕ Ⓖ Ⓗ Ⓙ	11 Ⓐ Ⓑ Ⓒ Ⓓ	18 Ⓕ Ⓖ Ⓗ Ⓙ	25 Ⓐ Ⓑ Ⓒ Ⓓ	32 Ⓕ Ⓖ Ⓗ Ⓙ	39 Ⓐ Ⓑ Ⓒ Ⓓ
5 Ⓐ Ⓑ Ⓒ Ⓓ	12 Ⓕ Ⓖ Ⓗ Ⓙ	19 Ⓐ Ⓑ Ⓒ Ⓓ	26 Ⓕ Ⓖ Ⓗ Ⓙ	33 Ⓐ Ⓑ Ⓒ Ⓓ	40 Ⓕ Ⓖ Ⓗ Ⓙ
6 Ⓕ Ⓖ Ⓗ Ⓙ	13 Ⓐ Ⓑ Ⓒ Ⓓ	20 Ⓕ Ⓖ Ⓗ Ⓙ	27 Ⓐ Ⓑ Ⓒ Ⓓ	34 Ⓕ Ⓖ Ⓗ Ⓙ	
7 Ⓐ Ⓑ Ⓒ Ⓓ	14 Ⓕ Ⓖ Ⓗ Ⓙ	21 Ⓐ Ⓑ Ⓒ Ⓓ	28 Ⓕ Ⓖ Ⓗ Ⓙ	35 Ⓐ Ⓑ Ⓒ Ⓓ	

Practice Test 2

EXAMINEE STATEMENTS, CERTIFICATION, AND SIGNATURE

1. **Statements:** I understand that by registering for, launching, starting, or submitting answer documents for an ACT® test, I am agreeing to comply with and be bound by the *Terms and Conditions: Testing Rules and Policies for the ACT® Test* ("Terms").

   I UNDERSTAND AND AGREE THAT THE TERMS PERMIT ACT TO CANCEL MY SCORES IN CERTAIN CIRCUMSTANCES. THE TERMS ALSO LIMIT DAMAGES AVAILABLE TO ME AND REQUIRE ARBITRATION OF CERTAIN DISPUTES. BY AGREEING TO ARBITRATION, ACT AND I BOTH WAIVE THE RIGHT TO HAVE THOSE DISPUTES HEARD BY A JUDGE OR JURY.

   I understand that ACT owns the test questions and responses, and I will not share them with anyone by any form of communication before, during, or after the test administration. I understand that taking the test for someone else may violate the law and subject me to legal penalties.

   I consent to the collection and processing of personally identifying information I provide, and its subsequent use and disclosure, as described in the ACT Privacy Policy (www.act.org/privacy.html). I also permit ACT to transfer my personally identifying information to the United States, to ACT, or to a third-party service provider, where it will be subject to use and disclosure under the laws of the United States, including being accessible to law enforcement or national security authorities.

2. **Certification:** Copy the italicized certification below, then sign, date, and print your name in the spaces provided.

   *I agree to the **Statements** above and certify that I am the person whose information appears on this form.*

_____

_____

Your Signature _____   Today's Date _____   Print Your Name _____

The **ACT**®   **Form 18MC4**
2023 | 2024

Directions

This booklet contains tests in English, mathematics, reading, and science. These tests measure skills and abilities highly related to high school course work and success in college. **Calculators may be used on the mathematics test only.**

The questions in each test are numbered, and the suggested answers for each question are lettered. On the answer document, the rows of ovals are numbered to match the questions, and the ovals in each row are lettered to correspond to the suggested answers.

For each question, first decide which answer is best. Next, locate on the answer document the row of ovals numbered the same as the question. Then, locate the oval in that row lettered the same as your answer. Finally, fill in the oval completely. Use a soft lead pencil and make your marks heavy and black. **Do not use ink or a mechanical pencil.**

Mark only one answer to each question. If you change your mind about an answer, erase your first mark thoroughly before marking your new answer. For each question, make certain that you mark in the row of ovals with the same number as the question.

Only responses marked on your answer document will be scored. Your score on each test will be based only on the number of questions you answer correctly during the time allowed for that test. You will **not** be penalized for guessing. **It is to your advantage to answer every question even if you must guess.**

You may work on each test **only** when the testing staff tells you to do so. If you finish a test before time is called for that test, you should use the time remaining to reconsider questions you are uncertain about in that test. You may **not** look back to a test on which time has already been called, and you may **not** go ahead to another test. To do so will disqualify you from the examination.

Lay your pencil down immediately when time is called at the end of each test. You may **not** for any reason fill in or alter ovals for a test after time is called for that test. To do so will disqualify you from the examination.

Do not fold or tear the pages of your test booklet.

**DO NOT OPEN THIS BOOKLET
UNTIL TOLD TO DO SO.**

The ONLY Official Prep Guide from the Makers of the ACT

ENGLISH TEST
45 Minutes—75 Questions

DIRECTIONS: In the five passages that follow, certain words and phrases are underlined and numbered. In the right-hand column, you will find alternatives for the underlined part. In most cases, you are to choose the one that best expresses the idea, makes the statement appropriate for standard written English, or is worded most consistently with the style and tone of the passage as a whole. If you think the original version is best, choose "NO CHANGE." In some cases, you will find in the right-hand column a question about the underlined part. You are to choose the best answer to the question.

You will also find questions about a section of the passage, or about the passage as a whole. These questions do not refer to an underlined portion of the passage, but rather are identified by a number or numbers in a box.

For each question, choose the alternative you consider best and fill in the corresponding oval on your answer document. Read each passage through once before you begin to answer the questions that accompany it. For many of the questions, you must read several sentences beyond the question to determine the answer. Be sure that you have read far enough ahead each time you choose an alternative.

PASSAGE I

The Object of Love

[1]

[A] I was waiting at the veterinarian's office recently with my cat when a young woman came in. After she sat down next to me, she asked if I would mind if she took her pet iguana out of its carrier. It was just a baby, she said, and it liked being held. [B]

1. **A.** NO CHANGE
   B. into the veterinarian's office where I was.
   C. in, and there I was, waiting in the office.
   D. in while I was waiting there.

[2]

Now, I'm not fond of iguanas. [C] They're strange, unpredictable creatures that belong deep in a rain forest, walking on the ground or resting
                                      2

2. Which choice provides the most vivid description of iguanas on the floor of a rain forest?
   F. NO CHANGE
   G. scuttling through dank undergrowth
   H. living underneath the treetops
   J. moving about down low

high in the trees, which are hidden in the canopy.
                3

3. **A.** NO CHANGE
   B. trees, they are
   C. trees,
   D. trees;

GO ON TO THE NEXT PAGE.

The ONLY Official Prep Guide from the Makers of the ACT

Wishing to be polite, but with reluctance in my voice,
I told the woman that I didn't mind. She thanked me
as she popped open the plastic carrier and pulled the
iguana out, onto her lap.

[3]

I guardedly examined the animal: A dinosaur-like
thing, it was the size of a cat but armored in gray-green
scales, with a black-striped, whiplike tail two feet long,
It had a spine with tiny spikes, and its muscular limbs
ended with what resembled crinkly leather gloves drawn
tightly over fine-boned human hands. When I looked more
closely, I saw a tiny claw at the tip of each slender finger.

[4]

The woman began to pet the iguana under its
chin, and the little dragon arched its neck and closed
its eyes. The reptile's calmness amazed me, as did the
caress that was given tenderly from the woman to her pet
and watched it peacefully rest. With a twinge of pity, I
thought how sad it was for us to lavish so much affection
on something that couldn't love her back.

[5]

At that moment, the iguana slowly opened its eyes,
which shone large and bright, from its scaly face. [D]

Head slightly cocked, it regarded me, steadily and

fixedly, like a judge delivering a verdict.

4. The writer is considering deleting the underlined portion. Should the underlined portion be kept or deleted?
   F. Kept, because it suggests that the narrator had previously sat next to an iguana, out of its carrier, at the veterinarian's office.
   G. Kept, because it emphasizes the narrator's feelings about the iguana being taken out of its carrier.
   H. Deleted, because it characterizes the narrator in a manner that's inconsistent with how the narrator is characterized in the rest of the essay.
   J. Deleted, because it detracts from the paragraph's purpose of providing background information about iguanas.

5. Given that all the choices are accurate, which one provides the most precise description of the pattern of spikes on the iguana's spine?
   A. NO CHANGE
   B. I saw spikes that looked like they were just beginning to develop,
   C. There were small spikes on its armored back,
   D. Rows of budding spikes lined its spine,

6. F. NO CHANGE
   G. tenderness with which the woman caressed her pet
   H. woman caressing her pet tenderly
   J. tenderness the woman showed

7. A. NO CHANGE
   B. the woman
   C. people
   D. you

8. F. NO CHANGE
   G. large and bright from,
   H. large, and bright from
   J. large and bright from

9. Which of the following alternatives to the underlined portion would NOT be acceptable?
   A. scrutinized
   B. supposed
   C. appraised
   D. considered

10. F. NO CHANGE
    G. having a delivery of
    H. in deliverance with
    J. deliver

GO ON TO THE NEXT PAGE.

1 ■ ■ ■ ■ ■ ■ ■ ■ ■ 1

[6]

"Who are you," it seemed to ask me, "to name

the proper object of love?"

[7]

The veterinary assistant called for my

cat, and me from the hallway that leads to the
                    _____
                         11

examination area. A bit unsettled, I rose and picked

up my cat carrier. As I walked from the waiting room

into the hall, I glanced back and saw the iguana snuggle

down into the young woman's lap, looking as content
                                  _____
                                    12

as a kitten, and close its eyes again.

11. A. NO CHANGE
B. cat, and me from the hallway,
C. cat and me from the hallway,
D. cat and me from the hallway

12. F. NO CHANGE
G. like as if it was giving off the impression of being
H. appearing something like
J. sort of like it was

Questions 13 and 14 ask about the preceding passage as a whole.

---

13. Upon reviewing the essay and finding that some information has been left out, the writer composes the following sentence incorporating that information:

> She told me that her iguana especially liked attention when it was in unfamiliar surroundings, and that this was its first trip to the veterinarian.

If the writer were to add this sentence to the essay, it would most logically be placed at:

A. Point A in Paragraph 1.
B. Point B in Paragraph 1.
C. Point C in Paragraph 2.
D. Point D in Paragraph 5.

14. Suppose the writer's primary purpose had been to describe a moment in which a person notices something unexpected while observing his or her surroundings. Would this essay accomplish that purpose?

F. Yes, because it describes what the narrator, while waiting at the vet, perceived to be a surprising bond between a woman and her pet iguana.
G. Yes, because it recounts a moment when the narrator, while waiting at the vet, realized people often don't know when they're being impolite.
H. No, because it instead tells the story of why the narrator doesn't like iguanas.
J. No, because it instead focuses on providing information about the physical characteristics of iguanas and their habitat.

GO ON TO THE NEXT PAGE.

1

PASSAGE II

Billy Mills Takes the Gold

[1] Runner Billy Mills qualified to run in the 10,000-meter race in the 1964 Tokyo Olympics, but he was a long shot. [2] In Tokyo, however, Mills became the first
_____
15

to win an Olympic gold medal for the United States in this
_____
16

event. [3] His qualifying entry time lagged almost a full minute above the world-record time held by Australian
_____
17

Ron Clarke. [18]

Mills, an Oglala Lakota, spent his childhood on
_____
19

the Pine Ridge Reservation in South Dakota. He started long-distance running while attending boarding school in Kansas. Initially, running was part of his training regimen for boxing, his first love. Mills had dreamed of being a
_____
20

boxer since he was a child.
_____
20

Mills broke numerous high school track records, earning himself an athletic scholarship to the University of Kansas. With Mills as a star runner, Kansas won the 1959 and 1960 NCAA Outdoor Track and Field Championships. After graduation, he became an officer in the Marines and assumed the duties of military life. However, Mills was soon drawn back to the track, and, while still in the Marines, races became part of his life again.
_____
21

15. **A.** NO CHANGE
    B. nonetheless,
    C. in fact,
    D. DELETE the underlined portion.

16. **F.** NO CHANGE
    G. Olympic gold medal,
    H. Olympic gold, medal,
    J. Olympic, gold medal

17. **A.** NO CHANGE
    B. around
    C. behind
    D. from

18. Which of the following sequences of sentences makes this paragraph most logical?
    F. NO CHANGE
    G. 1, 3, 2
    H. 2, 1, 3
    J. 2, 3, 1

19. **A.** NO CHANGE
    B. Mills an Oglala Lakota
    C. Mills an Oglala Lakota,
    D. Mills, an Oglala Lakota

20. Given that all the choices are true, which one most effectively concludes this paragraph and provides a transition to the following paragraph?
    F. NO CHANGE
    G. Yet Mills didn't quite make it as a boxer.
    H. Mills soon realized that he had greater potential as a runner than as a boxer.
    J. Mills also tried playing basketball and football, although he didn't excel at them.

21. **A.** NO CHANGE
    B. his talent raced back to him
    C. he began racing
    D. racing was in his life

GO ON TO THE NEXT PAGE.

Taking Additional Practice Tests

1 ■ ■ ■ ■ ■ ■ ■ ■ ■ 1

At an important point in his training, Mills wrote the
    ‾‾‾‾‾‾‾‾‾‾‾‾‾‾‾‾‾‾‾‾‾‾‾‾‾‾‾‾‾
                                22

words "Gold Medal" in his journal. He was determined to

win, despite being rather unknown as an athlete. |23|

Because of his unremarkable qualifying time, the US

Olympic shoe sponsor didn't even send him running

shoes for the race. Luckily, Mills borrowed a pair and
                    ‾‾‾‾‾‾‾
                      24

was ready to run when he hit the starting line. |25|

All eyes were on the overseers, Mohamed Gammoudi
                        ‾‾‾‾‾‾‾‾
                          26

of Tunisia and Ron Clarke, as they began the last lap of the

race. Suddenly, Mills, who had been in third place, broke
              ‾‾‾‾‾‾‾‾‾‾‾‾‾‾‾‾‾‾‾‾‾‾‾‾‾‾
                        27

from the pack, sprinted ahead, and won the race. Before a

22. Given that all the choices are accurate, which one most effectively introduces the paragraph by returning to the topic of the essay's opening paragraph?
   F. NO CHANGE
   G. A future inductee into the US Track and Field Hall of Fame,
   H. Three weeks before the 1964 Olympics,
   J. Committed to success,

23. If the writer were to delete the word *rather* from the preceding sentence, the sentence would primarily lose a word that:
   A. implies that some people were already aware of Mills's talent.
   B. helps describe Mills's approach to motivating himself for a race.
   C. explains why Mills decided to take on the challenge of running in the Olympics.
   D. emphasizes that Mills needed more training before he could win the race.

24. Which choice best emphasizes Mills's commitment to winning the gold medal?
   F. NO CHANGE
   G. Eventually,
   H. Undeterred,
   J. Concentrating,

25. At this point, the writer is considering adding the following true statement:

   > Bob Hayes, another US runner in the Tokyo Olympics, ran with a borrowed shoe after realizing he only had one of his two shoes with him; he then won the 100-meter race.

   Should the writer make this addition here?
   A. Yes, because it adds important details about two US track and field gold medalists in 1964.
   B. Yes, because it reveals that two runners used other people's shoes to win their races.
   C. No, because it shifts the essay's focus from the US track team members to their shoes.
   D. No, because it interrupts the essay's discussion of Mills preparing for and running the 10,000-meter race.

26. F. NO CHANGE
    G. rulers,
    H. authorities,
    J. leaders,

27. A. NO CHANGE
    B. Mills who had been in third place,
    C. Mills, who had been in third place
    D. Mills who had been in third place

GO ON TO THE NEXT PAGE.

stunned crowd, Mills had run the 10,000 meters 45 seconds
      28
faster than his qualifying time. He set an Olympic record

of 28 minutes 24 seconds, finishing ahead of Mohamed
                         29
Gammoudi and Ron Clarke. As of 2014, he remained the
     29
only US runner to have won an Olympic gold medal in

the 10,000-meter race.

28. **F.** NO CHANGE
    G. has ran
    H. has run
    J. had ran

29. The writer is considering deleting the underlined portion (adjusting the punctuation as needed). Should the underlined portion be kept or deleted?

    A. Kept, because it effectively connects the closing paragraph to the essay's opening paragraph.
    B. Kept, because it adds a detail to the essay's retelling of Mills's victory.
    C. Deleted, because it repeats a point already made clear by the paragraph.
    D. Deleted, because it strays from the main point of the paragraph.

PASSAGE III

Hearing Is Believing

The movie scene unfolds, a boy out exploring trudges
                30
across the snow and arrives at a boarded-up house. As the

lad knocks on the door, it slowly opens. Inside, dim light

from a cracked and dusty window reveals an old man

descending a staircase. Part of what draws an audience

into scenes like this, with that in mind, is the sounds that
             31
accompany the images. The crunch, the knock, the squeak,

the creak.

In most films, such sounds are recorded after the

cameras have stopped rolling, a practice named for Jack

Foley, who was working in Hollywood in the late 1920s

when "talkies" swept silent movies off the screen. It was
                32

Foley whom figured out that squeezing a sock full of
      33

cornstarch, a sound like that of footsteps in the snow. He
     34
put an old rocking chair to work to create the creaking of

30. **F.** NO CHANGE
    G. unfolds a boy,
    H. unfolds. A boy
    J. unfolds a boy

31. **A.** NO CHANGE
    B. this, for the time being,
    C. this, nevertheless,
    D. this

32. Which choice best suggests that talkies swiftly and dramatically put an end to the silent-movie era?

    F. NO CHANGE
    G. invited the beginning of what would one day become a new era in the film industry.
    H. stirred up the movie industry and delighted the general public.
    J. began their entrance onto the screens of Hollywood.

33. **A.** NO CHANGE
    B. himself whom
    C. who
    D. he

34. **F.** NO CHANGE
    G. cornstarch, which makes
    H. cornstarch produces
    J. cornstarch to get

GO ON TO THE NEXT PAGE.

Taking Additional Practice Tests

1 ■ ■ ■ ■ ■ ■ ■ ■ ■ 1

stairs. When a scene called for the sound of more

than one person walking, Foley grabbed a cane to

generate the allusion of many people on foot.
          ‾‾‾‾‾‾‾‾‾‾
               35

Low-budget solutions to big problems that eventually
                                        ‾‾‾‾‾‾‾‾‾‾‾‾‾
                                             36
earned him the status of a Hollywood legend.

Movies with sound were in their infancy at the time.
‾‾
                        37

        The need for "Foley" arises from the sound
                            ‾‾‾‾‾‾‾‾‾‾‾
                                 38
clutter of real life. The job of the sound technician

(whose role is distinct from that of the "Foley artist")
‾‾‾
                          39
is to record dialogue without capturing all the distracting

background noise. An airplane flying overhead. A phone

ringing. A door. Then, while viewing the film in a Foley
         ‾‾‾‾‾‾‾
           40

studio: a small room with a screen, a microphone, and
‾‾‾‾‾‾‾
   41
countless props—the Foley artist re-creates the sounds

of the actors' actions. It was Jack Foley who pioneered

this process.

        Directors adored him. To re-create the

audible ruckus of Caesar's army for the movie

Spartacus, Foley jangled a set of keys in front of

the microphone. That simple act, a Jack Foley classic,

cut the movie's budget by untold thousands of dollars.
                          ‾‾‾‾‾‾
                            42

35. **A.** NO CHANGE
  B. produce the elusion
  C. create the illusion
  D. make the allusion

36. **F.** NO CHANGE
  G. about which they eventually
  H. that eventually even so
  J. eventually

37. **A.** NO CHANGE
  B. A cane was one of the props Foley used to achieve the desired sound effects.
  C. The process he pioneered is one that takes place after the actors have been filmed for the movie.
  D. DELETE the underlined portion.

38. **F.** NO CHANGE
  G. aroused from
  H. arises
  J. arise

39. If the writer were to delete the underlined portion, the essay would primarily lose information that:
  A. establishes what the role of a sound technician is in making a movie.
  B. clarifies the origin of the term "Foley artist."
  C. indicates that various occupations were highly influenced by the work of Jack Foley.
  D. reduces the chance of confusion about whether "sound technician" means "Foley artist."

40. **F.** NO CHANGE
  G. The slamming door, which is not part of the scene.
  H. The sound of a door.
  J. A door slamming.

41. **A.** NO CHANGE
  B. studio—
  C. studio,
  D. studio

42. **F.** NO CHANGE
  G. unspeakable
  H. speechless
  J. endless

GO ON TO THE NEXT PAGE.

The director had planned to ship actors and horses, an

army's <u>worth headed to</u> a battlefield overseas to get an

₄₃

authentic sound recording. Instead, they all stayed home,

and the audience never knew the difference. <u>44</u>

43. **A.** NO CHANGE
    B. worth, were headed to
    C. worth, to
    D. worth

44. The writer is considering deleting the preceding sentence. Should the sentence be kept or deleted?
    F. Kept, because it suggests that audiences eventually came to know about Foley's work.
    G. Kept, because it ends the essay with a detail that suggests the impact of Foley's work on both the makers and viewers of movies.
    H. Deleted, because it shifts the focus of the paragraph from Foley to the movie's director, making a weak ending to an essay about Foley.
    J. Deleted, because it suggests that Foley's work was insignificant to the public.

PASSAGE IV

Talking Bacteria

In her lab at Princeton

<u>University, molecular biologist, Bonnie Bassler</u>

                  ₄₅

leans over a collection of petri <u>dishes; her face</u>

                          ₄₆

illuminated by an aquamarine glow. The glow,

caused by a particular <u>species, of bacteria</u> is confirmation

                             ₄₇

of a phenomenon Bassler has been investigating for years.

Bacteria, the simplest forms of life, have the ability to

communicate with each other.

As a student in graduate school, Bassler became

intrigued with other <u>researchers' and their</u> discoveries

                        ₄₈

involving <u>Vibrio *fischeri*; a</u> luminescent marine bacteria.

                          ₄₉

Researchers found that these bacteria only begin to glow

once they have formed a group. A series of experiments

revealed that each bacterial cell releases an autoinducer,

45. **A.** NO CHANGE
    B. University, molecular biologist Bonnie Bassler,
    C. University, molecular biologist Bonnie Bassler
    D. University molecular biologist Bonnie Bassler

46. **F.** NO CHANGE
    G. dishes and her face is
    H. dishes, her face is
    J. dishes, her face

47. **A.** NO CHANGE
    B. species, of bacteria,
    C. species of bacteria,
    D. species of bacteria

48. **F.** NO CHANGE
    G. researcher's and their
    H. researchers'
    J. researchers

49. **A.** NO CHANGE
    B. *fischeri* which is
    C. *fischeri,*
    D. *fischeri*

Taking Additional Practice Tests

GO ON TO THE NEXT PAGE.

1 ⬛ ⬛ ⬛ ⬛ ⬛ ⬛ ⬛ ⬛ ⬛ **1**

a type of chemical signal. A sensory protein allowed
_____
50

other bacteria to "hear" this molecular message.

Once the bacteria have released a high enough

concentration of autoinducer, they assemble and
_____
51

begin to glow. This "quorum sensing" enables

the bacteria to coordinate their actions and

perform their specific function.

On the contrary, in her own lab,
_____
52

Bassler found evidence of quorum sensing in a

related bacterial species called *Vibrio harveyi*. She also
_____
53

discovered that *V. harveyi* release a second autoinducer,

or AI-2. This AI-2, which Bassler has described as a

chemical "trade language," makes it possible for bacteria

to communicate with other species of bacteria in the

same neck of the woods. She found that each of the
_____
54

species she studied, including ones that live in
____
55

humans, releases AI-2.

After her 2002 discovery, Bassler began

using information from her quorum-sensing

studies to understand how virulent strains of

bacteria found in humans communicate. These
_____
56

disease-spreading bacteria rely on quorum sensing
_____
57

to spread disease. Bassler is hopeful that her ongoing

studies of AI-2 will enable she and her team to disrupt
_____
58

50. F. NO CHANGE
G. would have allowed
H. has allowed
J. allows

51. A. NO CHANGE
B. autoinducer—they
C. autoinducer. They
D. autoinducer they

52. F. NO CHANGE
G. Eventually,
H. Ordinarily,
J. Namely,

53. A. NO CHANGE
B. related, bacterial species, called
C. related, bacterial species called
D. related bacterial species called,

54. F. NO CHANGE
G. neighboring proximity.
H. surrounding locale.
J. vicinity.

55. Which of the following alternatives to the underlined portion would NOT be acceptable?
A. the kinds
B. species
C. those
D. them

56. F. NO CHANGE
G. has been communicating.
H. is communicating.
J. communicates.

57. A. NO CHANGE
B. bacteria that Bassler has studied
C. bacteria that live in humans
D. bacteria

58. F. NO CHANGE
G. her and her team
H. herself and them
J. her and them

GO ON TO THE NEXT PAGE.

quorum sensing 59 .

59. At this point, the writer is considering adding the following information:

> and ultimately develop new methods for treating bacterial infections

Given that the information is accurate, should the writer make this addition here?

A. Yes, because it clarifies that Bassler and her team are focusing their research on bacteria that live in humans.

B. Yes, because it specifies how Bassler's research could directly affect humans.

C. No, because it fails to specify which strains of bacteria are prone to attacking humans' immune systems.

D. No, because it fails to explain how Bassler and her team plan to disrupt quorum sensing.

PASSAGE V

Mapping the London Underground

[1]

Soon after the London Underground subway lines were introduced in the late 1800s, a system for mapping these vicinities creeping beneath was needed so that
60
travelers could navigate this new mode of transportation.

As a result, early maps relied on a geographically accurate
61
scale that simply superimposed the twisting subway lines over standard maps of the city streets above. [A] These maps clearly depicted the few subway lines that extended into suburban London, but they compressed and obscured the compact, heavily trafficked routes
62

60. F. NO CHANGE
   G. subterranean routes
   H. submerged zones
   J. low-down alleys

61. A. NO CHANGE
   B. To provide an example, early
   C. Secondly, early
   D. Early

62. Which choice is clearest and suggests the highest degree of failure of early maps to legibly depict the subway routes directly under central London?
   F. NO CHANGE
   G. in general were disappointing about
   H. made indecipherable
   J. didn't fully capture

GO ON TO THE NEXT PAGE.

Taking Additional Practice Tests

that converged directly under central London. [63]

[2]

In the 1930s, electrical engineer Harry Beck

proposed a solution that would eliminate the need for

geographical accuracy. He created a map that was a

scaled-down linear diagram of the subway lines.

More a stylistic outline of the routes besides a
                                        ‾‾‾‾‾‾‾
                                          64

true-to-life sketch; it did not represent actual
              ‾‾‾‾‾‾
                65
distances between points. [B] Beck's map, modeled

after electrical wiring diagrams, had a clean, grid-like

structure having also color-coded routes. Focusing
          ‾‾‾‾‾‾‾‾‾‾‾
               66

on creating the simplest possible schema to show
                                          ‾‾‾‾‾‾‾
                                            67
travelers how to get from one station to another, he

did away with all references to city streets above.
‾‾‾
                    68
[3]

[1] The London Passenger Transport Board,

which represented the subway lines, initially resisted

Beck's map. [2] Still, willing to try anything to

rise subway ridership and therefore revenues,
‾‾‾
 69

a limited number of copies were printed.
‾‾‾‾‾‾‾‾‾‾‾‾‾‾‾‾‾‾‾‾‾‾‾‾‾‾‾‾‾‾‾‾‾‾‾‾‾‾‾
                   70
[3] Beck's map became a huge success.

63. At this point, the writer is considering adding the following true statement:

> Today, the Tube, as the London Underground subway is called, covers approximately 250 miles of trackway.

Should the writer make this addition here?

A. Yes, because it provides details about the London Underground that explain the significance of the subway's modern name.
B. Yes, because it suggests the need for clear, accurate maps of the expansive London Underground.
C. No, because it is only loosely related to the information about the London Underground that is provided in the first paragraph.
D. No, because it blurs the focus of the first paragraph, which is about the most recent maps of the London Underground.

64. F. NO CHANGE
    G. than
    H. instead
    J. into

65. A. NO CHANGE
    B. sketch, and it
    C. sketch, it
    D. sketch. It

66. F. NO CHANGE
    G. additionally included
    H. and featuring
    J. and

67. A. NO CHANGE
    B. would show
    C. had shown
    D. showed

68. Given that all the choices are accurate, which one gives the clearest example of how Beck created the "simplest possible schema" in his map for subway passengers?
    F. NO CHANGE
    G. had been irritated with the curving lines on early maps of the London Underground.
    H. knew that if his map were to become popular, it had to be easy to use.
    J. created a map that has iconic status today.

69. A. NO CHANGE
    B. increase
    C. enlarge
    D. upend

70. F. NO CHANGE
    G. the board printed a limited number of copies.
    H. copies in a limited number were printed.
    J. copies printed in a limited number.

GO ON TO THE NEXT PAGE.

1 ⬛ ⬛ ⬛ ⬛ ⬛ ⬛ ⬛ ⬛ ⬛ 1

[4] Over a million copies were in circulation within six months. [5] Board members felt that not showing relative distances between stations was too radical. 71

[4]

For most of his life, Beck continued to make small refinements to "the diagram," as he called his map, but he retained it's basic elements. [C] His deceptively simple
                    72

diagrammatic approach to mapping, remains standard in
              73
the field of information design not only in London but also around the world. From Sydney, Australia, to Chicago, Illinois, urban transit maps continue to model this to
                                                    74
navigate the spaces below. [D]

71. For the sake of logic and cohesion, Sentence 5 should be placed:
    A. where it is now.
    B. after Sentence 1.
    C. after Sentence 2.
    D. after Sentence 3.

72. F. NO CHANGE
    G. their
    H. its
    J. its'

73. A. NO CHANGE
    B. diagrammatic, approach to mapping,
    C. diagrammatic approach to mapping
    D. diagrammatic approach, to mapping,

74. F. NO CHANGE
    G. this means Beck created, which remains standard in the field,
    H. Beck's deceptively simple approach to mapping
    J. Beck's innovative method

> Question 75 asks about the preceding passage as a whole.

75. The writer is considering adding the following sentence to the essay:

    Actual distances shouldn't matter to subway passengers, he believed, because they didn't have to make navigational decisions, such as choosing when to turn.

    If the writer were to add this sentence, it would most logically be placed at:
    A. Point A in Paragraph 1.
    B. Point B in Paragraph 2.
    C. Point C in Paragraph 4.
    D. Point D in Paragraph 4.

END OF TEST 1

STOP! DO NOT TURN THE PAGE UNTIL TOLD TO DO SO.

Taking Additional Practice Tests

2 △ △ △ △ △ △ △ △ △ **2**

MATHEMATICS TEST

60 Minutes—60 Questions

DIRECTIONS: Solve each problem, choose the correct answer, and then fill in the corresponding oval on your answer document.

Do not linger over problems that take too much time. Solve as many as you can; then return to the others in the time you have left for this test.

You are permitted to use a calculator on this test. You may use your calculator for any problems you choose, but some of the problems may best be done without using a calculator.

Note: Unless otherwise stated, all of the following should be assumed.

1. Illustrative figures are NOT necessarily drawn to scale.
2. Geometric figures lie in a plane.
3. The word *line* indicates a straight line.
4. The word *average* indicates arithmetic mean.

---

1. The top surface of a rectangular table has an area of 100 square feet and a width of 5 feet. What is the length, in feet, of the surface?

   A. 10
   B. 15
   C. 20
   D. 95
   E. 500

2. A wallet containing 2 five-dollar bills, 9 ten-dollar bills, and 5 twenty-dollar bills is found and returned to its owner. The wallet's owner will reward the finder with 1 bill drawn randomly from the wallet. What is the probability that the bill drawn will be a twenty-dollar bill?

   F. $\frac{1}{16}$

   G. $\frac{1}{10}$

   H. $\frac{1}{5}$

   J. $\frac{5}{16}$

   K. $\frac{5}{11}$

3. In his costume supplies, Elmo the clown has 4 noses, 3 pairs of lips, and 2 wigs. A clown costume consists of 1 nose, 1 pair of lips, and 1 wig. How many different clown costumes can Elmo make?

   A. 3
   B. 9
   C. 12
   D. 14
   E. 24

DO YOUR FIGURING HERE.

GO ON TO THE NEXT PAGE.

2 △ △ △ △ △ △ △ △ △ **2**

4. Esteban and his family are making care packages to send to children at summer camp. Each complete care package contains 5 pens, 2 notebooks, 3 envelopes, 12 cookies, and 5 candy bars. Esteban and his family have already made 7 complete care packages and the following materials remain:

3 boxes of pens (10 pens per box)

4 boxes of notebooks (5 notebooks per box)

2 boxes of envelopes (12 envelopes per box)

84 cookies

$4\frac{1}{2}$ boxes of candy bars (10 candy bars per box)

How many additional complete care packages can Esteban and his family make with the remaining materials?

F.   6
G.   7
H.   8
J.   10
K.   15

5. A formula for the volume of a right circular cone is $V = \frac{1}{3}\pi r^2 h$, where r is the radius of the base and h is the height of the cone. Using $\frac{22}{7}$ as an approximate value for π, which of the following values is closest to the volume, in cubic inches, of a cone with height 28 inches and radius 6 inches?

A.   264
B.   352
C.   1,056
D.   4,224
E.   4,928

6. In △ACD below, B is on $\overline{AC}$, E is on $\overline{AD}$, the measure of ∠CAD is 28°, and $\overline{AD}$ is perpendicular to both $\overline{BE}$ and $\overline{CD}$. What is the measure of ∠CBE ?

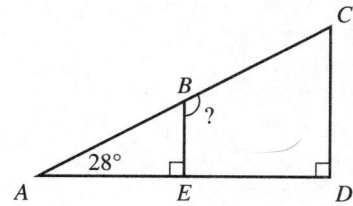

F.   104°
G.   118°
H.   124°
J.   146°
K.   152°

GO ON TO THE NEXT PAGE.

2   **2**

DO YOUR FIGURING HERE.

7. What is the sum of $0.1x^2 + 3x + 80$ and $0.5x^2 - 2x + 60$ for all x ?

   A. $-0.4x^2 + 5x + 20$
   B. $0.6x^2 + x + 140$
   C. $0.6x^2 + 5x + 140$
   D. $x^2 + 5x + 140$
   E. $5.6x^2 + 140$

8. Students studying motion observed a cart rolling at a constant rate along a straight line. The table below gives the distance, d feet, the cart was from a reference point at 1-second intervals from $t = 0$ seconds to $t = 5$ seconds.

t	0	1	2	3	4	5
d	15	18	21	24	27	30

   Which of the following equations represents this relationship between d and t ?

   F. $d = t + 15$
   G. $d = 3t + 12$
   H. $d = 3t + 15$
   J. $d = 15t + 3$
   K. $d = 33t$

9. Dmitry bought a pair of pants at the discounted price of $30. The original price of the pants was $40. What was the percent of the discount?

   A. 4%

   B. 10%

   C. 25%

   D. $33\frac{1}{3}\%$

   E. 75%

10. What is the value of $|-6| - |7 - 41|$?

    F. -40
    G. -28
    H. 28
    J. 40
    K. 54

11. Samantha, Nyla, and Jerry own shares of stock in the Triumph Hotels company. The shares of stock that they own have a combined value of $6,880. Samantha owns 70 shares, Nyla owns 50 shares, and Jerry owns 40 shares. What is the value of the shares Samantha owns?

    A. $ 98
    B. $ 301
    C. $3,010
    D. $4,816
    E. $5,351

GO ON TO THE NEXT PAGE.

2 △ △ △ △ △ △ △ △ △ **2**

12. A new club wants to attract customers who are at least 18 but less than 30 years of age. One of the number lines below illustrates the range of ages, in years, of the customers the club wants to attract. Which number line is it?

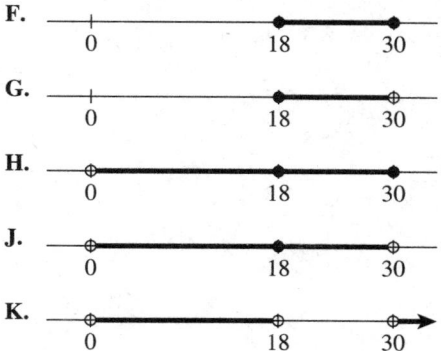

DO YOUR FIGURING HERE.

13. In the figure shown below, E and G lie on $\overline{AC}$, D and F lie on $\overline{AB}$, $\overline{DE}$ and $\overline{FG}$ are parallel to $\overline{BC}$, and the given lengths are in feet. What is the length of $\overline{AC}$, in feet?

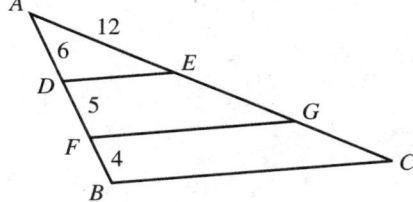

A. 9
B. 18
C. 21
D. 30
E. 36

14. Which of the following integers is closest to $\dfrac{\sqrt{50}}{2}$?

F. 3
G. 4
H. 5
J. 13
K. 14

15. The ratio of Jane's age to her daughter's age is 9:2. The sum of their ages is 44. How old is Jane?

A. 22
B. 33
C. 35
D. 36
E. 40

GO ON TO THE NEXT PAGE.

2   **2**

16. For the next school year, a college will use $\frac{1}{9}$ of the money in its operating budget for library books and $\frac{1}{6}$ of the money in its operating budget for scholarships. What fraction of the operating budget remains for other uses?

 F. $\frac{1}{18}$

 G. $\frac{5}{18}$

 H. $\frac{13}{18}$

 J. $\frac{20}{27}$

 K. $\frac{8}{9}$

DO YOUR FIGURING HERE.

17. What value of x makes the proportion below true?

$$\frac{10}{10+x} = \frac{35}{42}$$

 A.   2
 B.   7
 C. 12
 D. 17
 E. 32

18. The rectangle shown in the figure below is partitioned into 3 triangles, 2 of which are shaded. What is the total area, in square inches, of the 2 shaded regions?

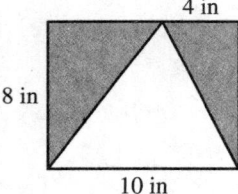

4 in

8 in

10 in

 F. 20
 G. 24
 H. 32
 J. 40
 K. 80

19. Which of the following ordered pairs in the standard (x,y) coordinate plane satisfies the system of inequalities below?

$$x > 2$$
$$y > 0$$
$$x + y < 5$$

 A. (1,3)
 B. (2,2)
 C. (3,1)
 D. (3,2)
 E. (4,0)

GO ON TO THE NEXT PAGE.

2 △ △ △ △ △ △ △ △ △ **2**

20. The graph of $y = 3 - 5\sin(x - \pi)$ is shown in the standard (x,y) coordinate plane below. What is the range of y ?

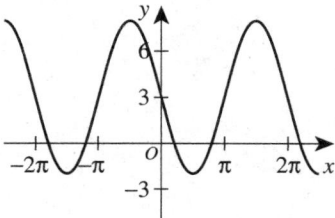

F. $-5 \le y \le 5$
G. $-2 \le y \le 2$
H. $-2 \le y \le 8$
J. $3 \le y \le 8$
K. $3 \le y \le 10$

21. Given functions $f(x) = 2x + 1$ and $g(x) = x^2 - 4$, what is the value of $f\big(g(-3)\big)$?

A. -29
B. -25
C. -19
D. 11
E. 21

22. A fabric store sells flannel and calico fabrics. Joan pays $25 for 3 yards of flannel and 4 yards of calico. Chris pays $11 for 1 yard of flannel and 2 yards of calico. What is the price of 1 yard of calico?

F. $3
G. $4
H. $5
J. $6
K. $7

23. The scores given below were earned by 10 students on a recent biology test. What is the median score?

71, 94, 86, 77, 88, 94, 88, 80, 78, 94

A. 85
B. 86
C. 87
D. 88
E. 91

24. A parallelogram has a perimeter of 84 inches, and 1 of its sides measures 16 inches. If it can be determined, what are the lengths, in inches, of the other 3 sides?

F. 16, 16, 36
G. 16, 18, 18
H. 16, 26, 26
J. 16, 34, 34
K. Cannot be determined from the given information

DO YOUR FIGURING HERE.

GO ON TO THE NEXT PAGE.

2   **2**

DO YOUR FIGURING HERE.

25. In the figure below, all of the small squares are equal in area, and the area of rectangle $ABCD$ is 1 square unit. Which of the following expressions represents the area, in square units, of the shaded region?

A. $\frac{1}{6} \cdot \frac{1}{4}$

B. $\frac{1}{6} \cdot \frac{3}{4}$

C. $\frac{1}{6} \cdot \frac{5}{6}$

D. $\frac{5}{6} \cdot \frac{1}{4}$

E. $\frac{5}{6} \cdot \frac{3}{4}$

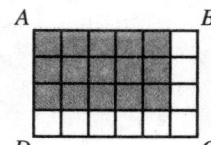

26. A bag contains 16 red marbles, 7 yellow marbles, and 19 green marbles. How many additional red marbles must be added to the 42 marbles already in the bag so that the probability of randomly drawing a red marble is $\frac{3}{5}$?

F. 18
G. 23
H. 37
J. 42
K. 52

27. For all $a > 0$, which of the following expressions is equal to a^{-2} ?

A. $-2a$

B. $-a^2$

C. $\frac{1}{2a}$

D. $\frac{1}{\sqrt{a}}$

E. $\frac{1}{a^2}$

28. Jamie claims, "If a triangle is in Set A, then it is not isosceles." Later, Jamie discovers that $\triangle MNP$ is a counterexample proving this claim false. Which of the following statements *must* be true about $\triangle MNP$?

F. It is isosceles and in Set A.
G. It is scalene and in Set A.
H. It is obtuse and not in Set A.
J. It is scalene and not in Set A.
K. It is isosceles and not in Set A.

GO ON TO THE NEXT PAGE.

2 △ △ △ △ △ △ △ △ △ **2**

Use the following information to answer
questions 29–32.

DO YOUR FIGURING HERE.

Parallelogram $ABCD$ is graphed in the standard (x,y) coordinate plane below. Sides $\overline{AB}$ and $\overline{CD}$ are each $\sqrt{10}$ coordinate units long. Sides $\overline{AD}$ and $\overline{BC}$ are each 5 coordinate units long. The distance between $\overline{AD}$ and $\overline{BC}$ is 3 coordinate units.

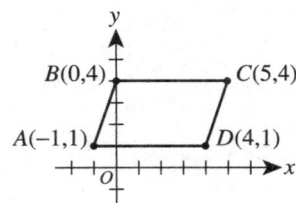

29. What is the area, in square coordinate units, of $ABCD$?

    A.   5
    B.   7.5
    C.   10
    D.   15
    E.   20

30. What is the distance, in coordinate units, from B to D ?

    F.   3
    G.   4
    H.   5
    J.   7
    K.   8

31. What is the slope of $\overleftrightarrow{BC}$?

    A.   0
    B.   1
    C.   4
    D.   5
    E.   Undefined

32. Parallelogram $ABCD$ will be reflected over the y-axis. What will be the coordinates of the image of A ?

    F. $(-4,\ 1)$
    G. $(-1,-1)$
    H. $(\ 1,-1)$
    J. $(\ 1,\ 1)$
    K. $(\ 4,-1)$

33. Which of the following is equivalent to $8^2 \cdot 4^{0.5}$?

    A. 2^7
    B. $4^{4.5}$
    C. $8^{2.5}$
    D. 16^2
    E.   32

GO ON TO THE NEXT PAGE.

2   **2**

34. A school admissions office accepts 2 out of every 7 applicants. Given that the school accepted 630 students, how many applicants were NOT accepted?

- **F.** 140
- **G.** 180
- **H.** 490
- **J.** 1,260
- **K.** 1,575

DO YOUR FIGURING HERE.

35. What is the value of $\log_2 \sqrt{8}$?

- **A.** $\frac{1}{2}$
- **B.** $\frac{3}{2}$
- **C.** $\sqrt{2}$
- **D.** 1
- **E.** 3

36. Jie asked 90 students to choose 1 favorite fruit from 4 options. Jie has begun to represent the results in the circle graph below. Peaches were chosen as the favorite of 15 students. Apples, bananas, and strawberries were each chosen as favorites by an equal number of the remaining students. What must be the measure of the central angle in the circle graph for bananas?

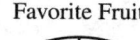

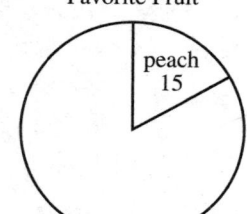

- **F.** 100°
- **G.** 102°
- **H.** 105°
- **J.** 112.5°
- **K.** 115°

37. For all real numbers x such that $x \neq 0$, $\frac{4}{5} + \frac{7}{x} = ?$

- **A.** $\frac{11}{5x}$
- **B.** $\frac{28}{5x}$
- **C.** $\frac{11}{5+x}$
- **D.** $\frac{7x+20}{5+x}$
- **E.** $\frac{4x+35}{5x}$

GO ON TO THE NEXT PAGE.

2 △ △ △ △ △ △ △ △ △ 2

Use the following information to answer questions 38–40.

The Harrisburg Recreation Center recently changed its hours to open 1 hour later and close 3 hours later than it had previously. Residents of Harrisburg age 16 or older were given a survey, and 560 residents replied. The survey asked each resident his or her student status (high school, college, or nonstudent) and what he or she thought about the change in hours (approve, disapprove, or no opinion). The results are summarized in the table below.

Student status	Approve	Disapprove	No opinion
High school	30	4	11
College	14	10	6
Nonstudent	85	353	47
Total	129	367	64

38. What fraction of these nonstudent residents replied that they disapproved of the change in hours?

F. $\frac{1}{3}$

G. $\frac{4}{45}$

H. $\frac{14}{75}$

J. $\frac{353}{367}$

K. $\frac{353}{485}$

39. Suppose a person will be chosen at random from these 560 residents. Which of the following values is closest to the probability that the person chosen will NOT be a high school student and will NOT have replied with no opinion?

A. 0.06
B. 0.09
C. 0.44
D. 0.83
E. 0.98

40. After constructing the table, it was discovered that the student status of 15 residents who replied that they approved had been incorrectly classified as nonstudents. After correcting the errors, exactly 60% of the college students had replied that they approved. To the nearest 1%, what percent of high school students replied that they approved?

F. 60%
G. 67%
H. 70%
J. 75%
K. 82%

GO ON TO THE NEXT PAGE.

2 △ △ △ △ △ △ △ △ △ **2**

41. Set A and Set B each consist of 5 distinct numbers. The 2 sets contain identical numbers with the exception of the number with the least value in each set. The number with the least value in Set B is greater than the number with the least value in Set A. The value of which of the following measures *must* be greater for Set B than for Set A ?

A. Mean only
B. Median only
C. Mode only
D. Mean and median only
E. Mean, median, and mode

42. For all x such that $0 \leq x \leq 90$, which of the following expressions is NOT equal to $\sin x°$?

F. $-\sin(-x°)$

G. $\sin(-x°)$

H. $\cos(90 - x)°$

J. $\cos(x - 90)°$

K. $\sqrt{1 - (\cos x°)^2}$

43. A 3-inch-tall rectangular box with a square base is constructed to hold a circular pie that has a diameter of 8 inches. Both are shown below. What is the volume, in cubic inches, of the smallest such box that can hold this pie?

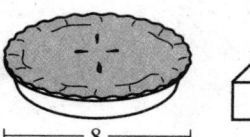 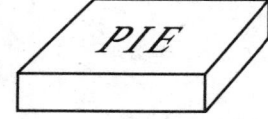

A. 24
B. 64
C. 72
D. 192
E. 512

44. Quadrilateral *ABCD* is shown in the figure below with the lengths of the 4 sides given in meters. The measure of ∠C is 90°. What is tan *A* ?

F. $\frac{4}{12}$

G. $\frac{5}{12}$

H. $\frac{4}{13}$

J. $\frac{5}{13}$

K. $\frac{12}{13}$

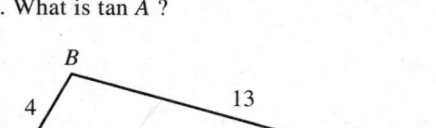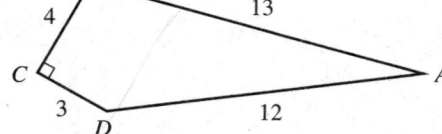

GO ON TO THE NEXT PAGE.

2 △ △ △ △ △ △ △ △ △ 2

45. Given today is Tuesday, what day of the week was it 200 days ago?

 A. Monday
 B. Tuesday
 C. Wednesday
 D. Friday
 E. Saturday

DO YOUR FIGURING HERE.

46. In the figure below, line *m* is perpendicular to line *n*, and both lines intersect line *q* at the same point. The measure of ∠1 is $(3x - 10)°$, and the measure of ∠2 is $(2x + 10)°$. What is the measure of ∠3 ?

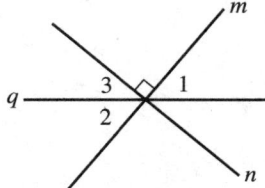

 F. 36°
 G. 40°
 H. 44°
 J. 45°
 K. 54°

47. The greatest common factor of 2 whole numbers is 10. The least common multiple of these same 2 numbers is 120. What are the 2 numbers?

 A.   6 and 20
 B. 10 and 12
 C. 10 and 20
 D. 20 and 60
 E. 30 and 40

48. The side lengths of a certain triangle are 4, 5, and 7 centimeters. Which of the following descriptions best classifies this triangle?

 F. Scalene acute
 G. Scalene right
 H. Scalene obtuse
 J. Isosceles obtuse
 K. Isosceles right

49. A professional baseball team will play 1 game Saturday and 1 game Sunday. A sportswriter estimates the team has a 60% chance of winning on Saturday but only a 35% chance of winning on Sunday. Using the sportswriter's estimates, what is the probability that the team will *lose* both games?

(Note: Neither game can result in a tie.)

 A. 14%
 B. 21%
 C. 25%
 D. 26%
 E. 39%

GO ON TO THE NEXT PAGE.

2   **2**

50. The graph of $f(x) = \dfrac{x-3}{x^2-2x-3}$ is shown below. What is the domain of $f(x)$?

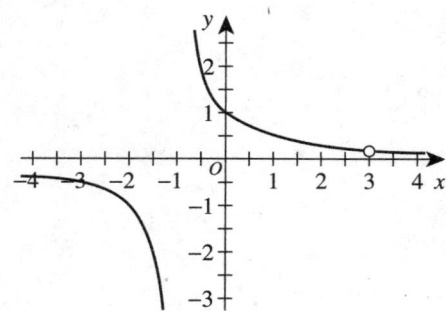

DO YOUR FIGURING HERE.

F. $\{x \mid x \neq -1\}$
G. $\{x \mid x \neq 2\}$
H. $\{x \mid x \neq 3\}$
J. $\{x \mid x \neq -1 \text{ and } x \neq 3\}$
K. $\{x \mid x \neq 0 \text{ and } x \neq 2\}$

51. Get-A-Great-Read Books is adding a new phone line. The phone company says that the first 3 digits of the phone number must be 555, but the remaining 4 digits, where each digit is a digit from 0 through 9, can be chosen by Get-A-Great-Read Books. How many phone numbers are possible?

A. $5(9^4)$
B. $5^3(9^4)$
C. $5^3(10^4)$
D. 9^4
E. 10^4

52. In the standard (x,y) coordinate plane, the circle centered at $(1,3)$ that passes through $(4,7)$ is the set of all points that are:

F. 5 coordinate units from $(1,3)$.
G. 5 coordinate units from both $(1,3)$ and $(4,7)$.
H. 5 coordinate units from the line segment with endpoints $(1,3)$ and $(4,7)$.
J. equidistant from $(1,3)$ and $(4,7)$.
K. equidistant from the line segment with endpoints $(1,3)$ and $(4,7)$.

53. Which of the following values is the x-coordinate of the point in the standard (x,y) coordinate plane where the graph of the line $y = 7$ intersects the graph of the function $y = \ln(x-2) + 3$?

A. 6
B. $e^4 + 2$
C. $4e + 2$
D. $\ln(4) + 2$
E. $\ln(5) + 3$

GO ON TO THE NEXT PAGE.

2 △ △ △ △ △ △ △ △ △ **2**

54. Three copy machines—A, B, and C—copy at the same rate and will all be used to make copies of a report. At 8:00 a.m., all 3 machines begin copying. Machine A breaks down at 10:00 a.m. and is back in service at 1:00 p.m. Machine B breaks down at 12:00 p.m. (noon) and begins copying again at 3:00 p.m. All 3 machines finish copying at 5:00 p.m. when the copying of the report is complete. One of the following graphs shows n, the number of copies made, as a function of t, the time at any given point during the copying. Which graph is it?

DO YOUR FIGURING HERE.

F.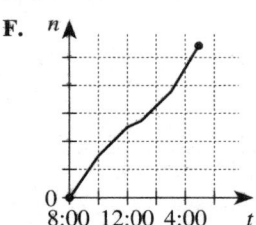

J.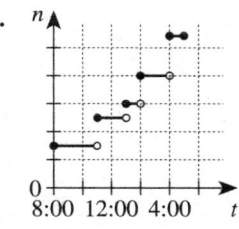

G.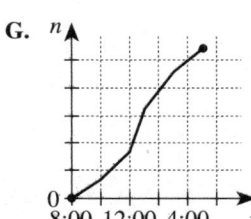

K.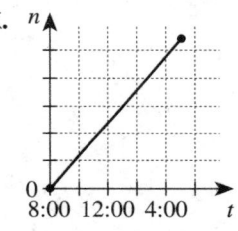

H.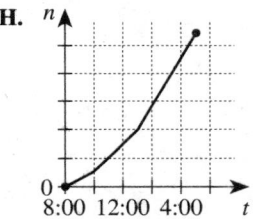

55. A sporting-goods store sells baseball caps for $22 each. At this price, 40 caps are sold per week. For every $1 decrease in price, the store will sell 4 more caps per week. The store will adjust the price to maximize revenue. What will be the maximum possible revenue for 1 week?

(Note: The revenue equals the number of caps sold times the price per cap.)

A. $ 880
B. $ 882
C. $ 924
D. $ 960
E. $1,024

GO ON TO THE NEXT PAGE.

Taking Additional Practice Tests

2   **2**

56. Each of the following graphs in the standard (x,y) coordinate plane has the same scale on both axes. One graph is the graph of $ax + by \le c$, where $0 < a < b < c$. Which one is it?

DO YOUR FIGURING HERE.

F.
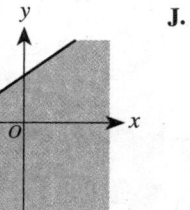

J.
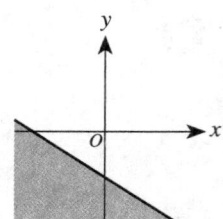

G.
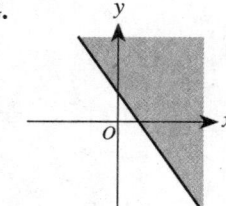

K.
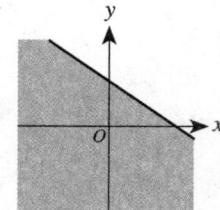

H.
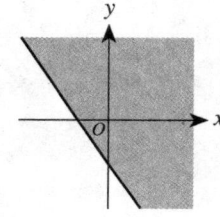

57. The art club designed and made banners of the school colors, blue and white, for their fund-raiser. Each banner required $\frac{1}{4}$ yard of blue material and $\frac{3}{8}$ yard of white material. The club originally planned to purchase exactly enough material to make 500 banners, but found the material to be cheaper if purchased in full bolts—the blue material in 10-yard bolts and the white material in 12-yard bolts. How many extra banners was the club able to make if they purchased enough full bolts to make at least 500 banners?

A. 12
B. 13
C. 15
D. 16
E. 20

GO ON TO THE NEXT PAGE.

2   **2**

58. For all real numbers x and the imaginary number i, which of the following expressions is equivalent to $(x - 3i)^3$?

DO YOUR FIGURING HERE.

- **F.** $x^3 - 9x^2i - 27x + 27i$
- **G.** $x^3 + 9x^2i - 27x - 27i$
- **H.** $x^3 + 3x^2i - 9x - 27i$
- **J.** $x^3 - 3x^2i - 9x + 27i$
- **K.** $x^3 + 27i$

59. The graph in the standard (x,y) coordinate plane below is the graph of one of the following functions. Which one?

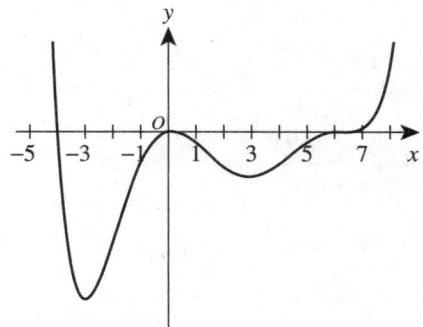

- **A.** $g(x) = x(x - 6)(x + 4)$
- **B.** $h(x) = x^2(x + 6)(x - 4)$
- **C.** $n(x) = x^2(x + 6)^3(x - 4)$
- **D.** $p(x) = x^2(x - 6)^3(x + 4)$
- **E.** $q(x) = x^3(x - 6)^2(x + 4)$

60. The table below shows the numbers of rows and columns in each of 5 matrices.

Matrix	Number of rows	Number of columns
A	m	n
B	m	m
C	k	n
D	m	k
E	n	m

For distinct values of k, m, and n, which of the following matrix products is NOT possible?

- **F.** ED
- **G.** DC
- **H.** CE
- **J.** AE
- **K.** AC

END OF TEST 2

STOP! DO NOT TURN THE PAGE UNTIL TOLD TO DO SO.

DO NOT RETURN TO THE PREVIOUS TEST.

Taking Additional Practice Tests

3 ━━━━━━━━━━━━━━ 3

READING TEST
35 Minutes—40 Questions

DIRECTIONS: There are several passages in this test. Each passage is accompanied by several questions. After reading a passage, choose the best answer to each question and fill in the corresponding oval on your answer document. You may refer to the passages as often as necessary.

Passage I

LITERARY NARRATIVE: Passage A is adapted from the short story "Leaving Memphis" by Lauren Birden (©2008 by Narrative Magazine, Inc.). Passage B is adapted from the short story "Mandarins" by Ryunosuke Akutagawa (©2006 by Fiction, Inc.).

Passage A by Lauren Birden

You see her first in the Memphis bus station on a two-hour layover. You pretend you haven't because she looks ready to talk. "Stonewashed jeans," you think, watching her tap her platform sandals at the front of the
5　boarding line. When she catches you staring, you pull your lips tight and stare at the floor in front of her. She starts toward you anyway. She plops down in the hard plastic seat next to you, moving her purse to her lap. You motion to your open novel and shrug as if to say,
10　"Can't stop now," but she asks, "Where you from?" and now you can't shake her.

You're not a bad person. You just wish Greyhound assigned seating. It's not the straw-blond hair teased up around her face, not even the sad, neglected teeth that
15　make you want to turn off the overhead reading lamp and smile at her in the dark. "I have a sneaking suspicion that we're the same person," she says, and you say, "That's funny," because you know you've been inventing yourself this whole time. She smiles and waits for
20　you to agree how similar the two of you are.

She tells you about the man she's taking the bus to see. "Left for a construction job in Palm Beach. Says my eyes are as blue as the Atlantic Ocean, and he can't bear to look at the thing but one more time if I'm not
25　there with him. You can't trust a man with a gun or a heart, but he swears he loves me." She waits for you to tell her of a better love. You can't think of a story to compare.

She says, "We're the same person." She's waiting
30　for you to tell her yes, that you both have had the same heartache and know about scars and love the same. But you're thinking at the window again as a radio tower passes that reminds you of the Eiffel Tower.

Firefly porch lights are perched, fat and throbbing,
35　outside every occasional home you pass. You say, "You know, you're so very right," and then, nothing more. The woman resigns herself to turning away in the quiet. You're telling the truth for once.

Passage B by Ryunosuke Akutagawa

Evening was falling one cloud-covered winter's
40　day, as I boarded a Tokyo-bound train departing from Yokosuka. I found a seat in the corner, sat down, and leaned my head back against the window frame, half-consciously watching for the station to recede slowly into the distance. But then I heard coming from the
45　ticket-gate the clattering of dry-weather clogs, followed immediately by the cursing of the conductor. The door of the second-class carriage was flung open, and a 13- or 14-year-old girl came bursting in.

At that moment, with a shudder, the train began to
50　lumber slowly forward. I raised my eyes to look for the first time at the girl seated now on the opposite side. She wore her lusterless hair drawn up into a bun, in the traditional shape of a gingko leaf. Apparently from constant rubbing of her nose and mouth with the back of
55　her hand, her cheeks were chapped and red. A grimy woolen scarf of yellowish green hung loosely down to her knees, on which she held a large bundle wrapped in cloth. To blot her existence, I took out my newspaper, and began to read.

60　The girl feverishly endeavored to open the window, the glass apparently proving to be too heavy for her. Gazing coldly at her desperate struggle as she fought with chilled hands, I hoped that she would fail, and at that very moment, the window at last came down
65　with a thud. I would surely have barked at this unknown girl to reclose the window, had it not been for the outside view, which was now growing ever brighter, and for the smell, borne in on the cold air, of earth, dry grass, and water.

70　Just then I saw standing behind the barrier of a desolate crossing three red-cheeked boys. Looking up to see the train as it passed, they raised their hands as one and let out with all the strength of their young voices a high pitched cheer. And at that instant the girl,
75　the full upper half of her body leaning out of the window, abruptly extended her hands and began moving them briskly left and right. Five or six mandarin oranges, radiating the color of the warm sun and filling my heart with sudden joy, descended on the
80　children standing there to greet the passing train.

I knew immediately the meaning of it all. This girl, perhaps leaving home now to go into service as a

GO ON TO THE NEXT PAGE.

3 ███████████████████████████████████████ **3**

maid or an apprentice, had been carrying in her bundle these oranges and tossed them to her younger brothers
85 as a token of gratitude for coming to see her off.

Elated, I raised my head and gazed at the girl with very different eyes. For the first time I was able to forget, at least for a moment, my unspeakable fatigue and this tedious life.

1. Which of the following questions is specifically answered in Passage A?

   A. Why is the character referred to as "you" leaving Memphis?
   B. Why is the blond woman traveling to Palm Beach?
   C. What is the blond woman thinking about at the end of the passage?
   D. Where is the blond woman from originally?

2. As they are used in line 24, what do the words *the thing* refer to?

   F. A construction job
   G. The blond woman's eyes
   H. The Atlantic Ocean
   J. A bus

3. As it is used in line 35, the phrase "every occasional home" most nearly suggests that on the bus trip, the main characters of Passage A are passing through an area in which:

   A. the porches of some homes intermittently glow from the light of fireflies.
   B. most homes do not have a porch light on.
   C. particularly large and bright fireflies swarm around a few of the homes.
   D. the few homes built there are situated far apart.

4. Throughout Passage B, the girl's reaction to the narrator is to:

   F. pay no attention to him.
   G. engage him in conversation.
   H. view him as an annoying intruder.
   J. express surprise to discover she's not alone.

5. The narrator of Passage B hopes that the girl will fail at opening the window. Based on Passage B as a whole, this hope most strongly captures the:

   A. girl's helplessness and her uncertain future.
   B. narrator's typical foul mood and dark state of mind.
   C. three young boys' pleasure in seeing their sister off.
   D. train conductor's impatience with the girl's behavior.

6. It can most reasonably be inferred from Passage B that the girl frantically tries to open the window because she needs to:

   F. be able to throw oranges to her brothers.
   G. prove to herself that she would be able to open the heavy window in an emergency.
   H. create space between herself and the narrator.
   J. freshen the stagnant air in the train with a cool breeze.

7. In Passage B, which of the following pairs of actions most clearly cues the narrator that someone is about to board the train at the last minute?

   A. The cursing of the conductor and the screech of the train's brakes
   B. The bursting open of the second-class-carriage door and the rustle of paper parcels
   C. The clattering of clogs and the cursing of the conductor
   D. The shouting of a young girl and the clattering of clogs

8. Which of the following elements is most clearly similar in the two passages?

   F. The occasional use of the second person point of view
   G. The time period in which each passage is set
   H. The inclusion of key bits of dialogue between characters
   J. The situational premise of the plot

9. Among the characters in both passages, which one is portrayed as being most interested in having a conversation?

   A. "You"
   B. The 13- or 14-year-old girl
   C. The narrator of Passage B
   D. The blond woman

10. Which of the following statements best describes how both "you" of Passage A and the narrator of Passage B react when they first see the blond woman and the young girl, respectively?

    F. They consider the other character to be somewhat pitiful looking.
    G. They are angry that the other character has delayed their departure.
    H. They are surprised by the other character's reason for traveling.
    J. They believe the other character is enviable because life seems so easy for her.

GO ON TO THE NEXT PAGE.

3

3

Passage II

SOCIAL SCIENCE: This passage is adapted from the article "Travels with R.L.S." by James Campbell (©2000 by The New York Times Company).

Robert Louis Stevenson (1850–1894) preferred to circumnavigate civilization, with its increasing reliance on contraptions, and steer toward the rougher fringes. He self-consciously turned his back on the Victorian
5 idol, progress. In similar spirit, he chose the past more often than the present as a setting for fiction. His most popular novels—*Treasure Island*, *Kidnapped*, *The Master of Ballantrae*—are set in a semimythical realm, where the fire of adventure catches on every page.
10 Stevenson loved the sound of clashing swords; he didn't want them getting tangled up in telephone wires overhead.

Stevenson, though, was destined to be a modern man. He was born into a Scottish family of civil engi-
15 neers, esteemed for its technological genius. His grandfather, also Robert, was Britain's greatest builder of lighthouses, and his graceful towers continue to guide sailors today. Three of Robert's sons followed him into the profession, including Robert Louis Stevenson's
20 father, Thomas, who made his own mark in the field of optics—his louvre-boarded screens for the protection of thermometers are still in use today.

It was expected that Robert Louis would enter the family business in turn, and a great wringing of hands
25 greeted his announcement to the contrary. He told his father that he wanted to be a writer, which Thomas Stevenson regarded as no profession at all. We can imagine the consternation when Stevenson's letters arrived bearing pleas such as "Take me as I am . . . I
30 *must* be a bit of a vagabond." And a vagabond was precisely what he set out to be: longhaired, careless about food, walking through France or planning an epic ocean voyage, a far cry from the offices of D. & T. Stevenson, Engineers. He was forging the template for generations
35 of college-educated adventurers to come. "I travel not to go anywhere, but to go," he wrote in *Travels With a Donkey* (1879). "I travel for travel's sake. The great affair is to move."

Stevenson would not be an engineer, but he left his
40 own lights, in Scotland and across the world, by which it is possible to trace his unceasing movement. No other writer, surely, is as much memorialized by the words "lived here" as he is. There are five houses with Stevenson associations in Edinburgh alone, not to men-
45 tion the little schoolhouse he attended as a child and the lavish gardens opposite the family home in Heriot Row, where he played and, the fanciful will have you believe, first acted out the quest for Treasure Island. I have shadowed Stevenson up to the northeast of Scotland,
50 where he tried his hand at being an apprentice engineer, back down to the Hawes Inn at South Queensferry, where David Balfour is tricked into going to sea in *Kidnapped*. There are landmarks in Switzerland, France and on the Pacific Islands where the adventure of his
55 final years took place.

Recently, I stumbled across Abernethy House where Stevenson lived briefly in London when he was 23. It stands in a secluded corner of Hampstead, high up on a hill, and separated from foggy London by farms
60 and heath. It was while standing on Hampstead Hill one night that he gazed down on London and imagined a technological miracle of the future, "when in a moment, in the twinkling of an eye, the design of the monstrous city flashes into vision—a glittering hieroglyph." He is
65 anticipating the effects of electricity and a time when the streetlamps would be lighted "not one by one" by the faithful old lamplighter, but all at once, by the touch of a button. Not for him improvements in optics; give him the flickering gas lamp and the "skirts of
70 civilization" any day.

Lamps occur frequently in Stevenson's writing. There are the essays "A Plea for Gas Lamps" and "The Lantern Bearers," and his poem for children, "The Lamplighter," which celebrates an old custom: "For we
75 are very lucky, with a lamp before the door, / And Leerie stops to light it as he lights so many more." Then there is his memoir in which he describes how, when a child and sick, his nurse would take him to the window, "whence I might look forth into the blue night
80 starred with street lamps, and see where the gas still burned behind the windows of other sickrooms." And the lights shine again, with a subdued glow, in the obituary he wrote of his father. Thomas Stevenson's name may not have been widely known, yet "all the time, his
85 lights were in every part of the world, guiding the mariner."

A year later, Stevenson chartered a schooner and became a mariner himself, sailing circuitously through the South Seas. He had, in a sense, entered the family
90 business at last.

11. As it is used in line 3, the phrase "the rougher fringes" most nearly means the same as which of the following phrases?

A. "The fire of adventure" (line 9)
B. "An epic ocean voyage" (lines 32–33)
C. "A glittering hieroglyph" (line 64)
D. "Skirts of civilization" (lines 69–70)

12. It can reasonably be concluded that the passage author is a credible source of biographical information about Stevenson because the passage author:

F. traveled to several towns and countries where Stevenson lived and worked to research him.
G. has read Stevenson's two most popular novels, *Kidnapped* and *Treasure Island*.
H. worked for a time in the offices of D. & T. Stevenson, Engineers, as Stevenson had.
J. comes from Edinburgh, where the adventure of Stevenson's final years took place.

GO ON TO THE NEXT PAGE.

3 3

13. The main idea of the second paragraph (lines 13–22) is that:

A. Stevenson's grandfather insisted his sons become educated in civil engineering.

B. Stevenson was a modern man whose engineering talents were suppressed by his desire to be a writer.

C. Stevenson's father earned greater esteem for his louvre-boarded screens than Stevenson's grandfather did for his lighthouses.

D. Stevenson was the grandson, son, and nephew of men respected for their technological genius.

14. The main idea of the fifth paragraph (lines 56–70) is that:

F. the plot of one of Stevenson's books was inspired by his vision of electric lights in London.

G. Stevenson envisioned the use of electric street-lights in London before they became reality.

H. Stevenson longed for a time when electricity would replace flickering gas lamps.

J. Stevenson realized that his father's improvements in optics would become the "technological miracle of the future."

15. According to the passage, which of the professions listed below did Stevenson enter into?

I. Apprentice engineer
II. Lamplighter
III. Mariner
IV. Writer
V. Builder

A. IV only

B. I, II, and IV only

C. I, III, and IV only

D. III, IV, and V only

16. The passage author most likely uses the description in lines 10–12 in order to:

F. emphasize how little technological progress had taken place during Stevenson's lifetime.

G. stress that Stevenson was increasingly dependent on modern inventions.

H. create a visual image that helps make Stevenson's opinion about progress more vivid.

J. illustrate that Stevenson was an avid sword fighter.

17. As it is used in line 24, the phrase "a great wringing of hands" most nearly refers to the Stevenson family's:

A. dismay over Stevenson's announcement that he wasn't joining the family business.

B. disapproval of Stevenson's slovenly appearance and poor diet.

C. humiliation at Stevenson publicly renouncing the family business in favor of traveling.

D. consternation at receiving Stevenson's letters pleading to have his family accept his choice.

18. It can most reasonably be inferred from the passage that as a traveler, Stevenson:

F. thought reaching the destination was what made the trip worthwhile.

G. encouraged other young men to take up traveling rather than pursue an education.

H. was searching for a model for the character David Balfour in *Kidnapped*.

J. was happiest when he was on an adventure with no itinerary.

19. As it is used in line 56, the phrase *stumbled across* most nearly means:

A. found by accident.

B. staggered toward.

C. unearthed.

D. tripped over.

20. According to the passage, at the time of his death, Thomas Stevenson was:

F. estranged from Robert Louis, who had refused to join the family business.

G. unaware that his name would become associated with lighthouses.

H. more famous than his son, who was by that time a popular author.

J. not widely known himself, but the results of his work were familiar the world over.

GO ON TO THE NEXT PAGE.

3

3

Passage III

HUMANITIES: This passage is adapted from the article "Proceed with Caution: Using Native American Folktales in the Classroom" by Debbie Reese (©2007 by the National Council of Teachers of English).

Traditional stories include myths, legends, and folktales rooted in the oral storytelling traditions of a given people. Through story, people pass their religious beliefs, customs, history, lifestyle, language, values,
5 and the places they hold sacred from one generation to the next. As such, stories and their telling are more than simple entertainment. They matter—in significant ways—to the well-being of the communities from which they originate. Acclaimed Laguna Pueblo writer
10 Leslie Marmon Silko writes that the oral narrative, or story, was the medium by which the Pueblo people transmitted "an entire culture, a worldview complete with proven strategies for survival." In her discussion of hunting stories, she says:

15 These accounts contained information of critical importance about the behavior and migration patterns of mule deer. Hunting stories carefully described key landmarks and locations of fresh water. Thus, a deer-hunt story
20 might also serve as a map. Lost travelers and lost piñon-nut gatherers have been saved by sighting a rock formation they recognize only because they once heard a hunting story describing this rock formation.

25 Similarly, children's book author Joseph Bruchac writes,

. . . rather than being 'mere myths,' with 'myth' being used in the pejorative sense of 'untruth,' those ancient traditional tales were a
30 distillation of the deep knowledge held by the many Native American nations about the workings of the world around them.

Thus, storytelling is a means of passing along information, but it does not mean there is only one cor-
35 rect version of any given story. During a telling, listeners can speak up if they feel an important fact or detail was omitted, or want to offer a different version of the story. In this way, the people seek or arrive at a communal truth rather than an absolute truth. A storyteller may
40 revise a story according to his or her own interpretation, or according to the knowledge of the audience, but in order for it to be acceptable to the group from which the story originated, it should remain true to the spirit and content of the original.

45 Traditional stories originate from a specific people, and we expect them to accurately reflect those people, but do they? As a Pueblo Indian woman, I wonder, what do our stories look like when they are retold outside our communities, in picture book format,
50 and marketed as "Native American folktales" for children? Are our religious, cultural, and social values presented accurately? Are children who read these folktales learning anything useful about us?

Much of what I bring to bear on my research
55 emanates from my cultural lens and identity as a Pueblo Indian woman from Nambe Pueblo. I was born at the Indian hospital in Santa Fe, New Mexico, and raised on our reservation. As a Pueblo Indian child, I was given a Tewa (our language) name and taught to dance. I went
60 to religious ceremonies and gatherings, and I learned how to do a range of things that we do as Pueblo people. This childhood provided me with "cultural intuition." Cultural intuition is that body of knowledge anyone acquires based upon their lived experiences in a
65 specific place. As a scholar in American Indian studies, I know there are great distinctions between and across American Indian tribal nations. For instance, my home pueblo is very different from the other pueblos in New Mexico, among which there are several different lan-
70 guage groups.

I draw upon both my cultural intuition and knowledge when reading a book about Pueblo Indians. For example, when I read Gerald McDermott's *Arrow to the Sun: A Pueblo Indian Tale* (1974), I wondered what
75 Pueblo the book is about. There are 19 different Pueblos in New Mexico, and more in Arizona. In which Pueblo did this story originate? That information is not included anywhere in the book, and there are other problems as well. In the climax of the story, the boy
80 must prove himself by passing through "the Kiva of Lions, the Kiva of Serpents, the Kiva of Bees, and the Kiva of Lightning" where he fights those elements. McDermott's kivas are frightening places of trial and battle, but I know kivas are safe places of worship and
85 instruction.

Depictions that are culturally acceptable at one Pueblo are not necessarily acceptable at a different Pueblo. As such, elders at one Pueblo would say the book could be used with their children, while elders at
90 another Pueblo would disagree. This is not a question of cultural authenticity; it is one of appropriateness in teaching, given a specific audience.

21. The passage author's reaction to which of the following experiences best exemplifies the point that she brings her own cultural intuition to her reading and research?

A. Learning about Bruchac's perspective on ancient traditional tales
B. Reading a portrayal of kivas in a Pueblo book
C. Presenting her research to a Pueblo community other than her own
D. Discussing the oral narrative with Silko

GO ON TO THE NEXT PAGE.

3

22. The main purpose of the first paragraph (lines 1–24) is to:

F. explain how traditional stories change as they are passed from one generation to the next.
G. discuss the value of traditional stories and their functions within a community.
H. contrast the purposes of folktales with those of myths and legends.
J. demonstrate that folktales measure how a culture's worldview has changed over time.

23. The passage author most strongly suggests that a particular group would deem one of its own stories to be unacceptable if, during a telling, the storyteller:

A. incorporated new details into the story.
B. used his or her own experiences to interpret one event in the story.
C. agreed with an audience member's adding a detail to the story.
D. significantly changed the spirit of the story.

24. One function of the passage author's statement that her home pueblo is very different from the other pueblos in New Mexico is to:

F. describe the culture and traditions of her home pueblo.
G. help support her later analysis and critique of McDermott's book.
H. directly compare the stories of several American Indian tribal nations to those of her tribe.
J. list the criteria she uses to evaluate books marketed as "Native American folktales."

25. The passage author most strongly implies that whether Pueblo elders will approve a book for the children of their community depends on the book's:

A. entertainment value compared to similar books.
B. popularity among other tribal members.
C. appropriateness and relevance to that community's cultural values.
D. successful representation of the worldview of many cultural groups.

26. As she is presented in the passage, Silko indicates that one purpose of Laguna Pueblo hunting stories was to help hunters:

F. locate and rescue lost hunters from other tribes.
G. document the number of successful hunts from one season to the next.
H. identify the behavior and migration patterns of game.
J. find caches of food by following trails made by piñon-nut gatherers.

27. The passage author most directly connects her knowledge of the distinctions between and across American Indian tribal nations to her experiences as:

A. a scholar in American Indian studies.
B. a friend of McDermott.
C. an editor of picture books marketed as "Native American folktales."
D. an elder in her Nambe Pueblo community.

28. As it is used in line 66, the word *great* most nearly means:

F. excessive.
G. significant.
H. exuberant.
J. splendid.

29. Which of the following characteristics among the several Pueblo communities in New Mexico does the passage author most directly use as evidence of their diversity?

A. Their vast geographic differences
B. Their disparity in resources
C. Their varied approaches to parenting
D. Their several different language groups

30. The passage author states that kivas are places she associates with:

F. fear and trial.
G. mystery and excitement.
H. rest and healing from illness.
J. worship and instruction.

GO ON TO THE NEXT PAGE.

3 ███████████████████████████ **3**

Passage IV

NATURAL SCIENCE: This passage is adapted from the article "The Asphalt Jungle" by Peter Del Tredici (©2010 by Natural History Magazine, Inc.).

The ecology of the city is defined not only by the cultivated plants that require maintenance and the protected remnants of natural landscapes, but also by the spontaneous vegetation that dominates the neglected
5 interstices. Greenery fills the vacant spaces between our roads, homes, and businesses; lines ditches and chain-link fences; sprouts in sidewalk cracks and atop neglected rooftops. Some of those plants, such as box elder, quaking aspen, and riverside grape, are native
10 species present before humans drastically altered the land. Others, including chicory, Japanese knotweed, and Norway maple, were brought in intentionally or unintentionally by people. And still others—among them common ragweed, path rush (*Juncus tenuis*), and
15 tufted lovegrass (*Eragrostis pectinacea*)—arrived on their own, dispersed by wind, water, or wild animals. Such species grow and reproduce in many American cities without being planted or cared for. They can provide important ecological services at very little cost to
20 taxpayers, and if left undisturbed long enough they may even develop into mature woodlands.

There is no denying that most people consider many such plants to be "weeds." From a utilitarian perspective, a weed is any plant that grows on its own
25 where people do not want it to grow. From the biological perspective, weeds are opportunistic plants that are adapted to disturbance in all its myriad forms, from bulldozers to acid rain. Their pervasiveness in the urban environment is simply a reflection of the continual dis-
30 ruption that characterizes that habitat—they are not its cause. In an agricultural context, the competition of weeds with economic crops is the primary reason for controlling them. In an urban area, a weed is any plant growing where people are trying to cultivate something
35 else, or keep clear of vegetation altogether. The complaints of city dwellers are usually based on aesthetics (the plants are perceived as ugly, or as signs of blight and neglect) or on security concerns (they shield human activity or provide habitat for vermin).

40 From a plant's perspective, it is not the density of the human population that defines the urban environment, but the abundance of paving (affecting access to soil and moisture) and prevalence of disturbance. In other words, a sidewalk crack is a sidewalk crack
45 whether it is in a city or a suburb. Urbanization is a process, not a place—a process that tends to leave the soil in a compacted, impoverished, and often contaminated state.

The plants that grow and survive in derelict urban
50 wastelands are famous (or infamous) for their ability to grow under extremely harsh conditions. Through a quirk of evolutionary fate, they developed traits in their native habitats that seem to have "preadapted" them to flourish in cities. One study, by biologist Jeremy T.

55 Lundholm of St. Mary's University in Halifax, Nova Scotia, and his then student Ashley Marlin, concluded that many successful urban plants are native to exposed cliffs, disturbed rock outcrops, or dry grasslands, all of which are characterized by soils with a relatively high
60 pH. Cities, with their tall, granite-faced buildings and concrete foundations, are in a sense the equivalent of the natural limestone cliff habitats where those species originated. Similarly, as the British ecologist and "lichen hunter" Oliver L. Gilbert noted in his classic
65 book *The Ecology of Urban Habitats*, the increased use of deicing salts on our roads and highways has resulted in the development of microhabitats along their margins that are typically colonized by calcium-loving grassland species adapted to limestone soils or by salt-loving
70 plants from coastal habitats.

In general, the successful urban plant needs to be *flexible* in all aspects of its life history, from seed germination through flowering and fruiting; *opportunistic* in its ability to take advantage of locally abundant
75 resources that may be available for only a short time; and *tolerant* of the stressful growing conditions caused by an abundance of pavement and a paucity of soil. The plants that grow in our cities managed to survive the transition from one land use to another as cities devel-
80 oped. The sequence starts with native species adapted to ecological conditions before the city was built. Those are followed, more or less in order, by species preadapted to agriculture and pasturage, to pavement and compacted soil, to lawns and landscaping, to infra-
85 structure edges and environmental pollution—and ultimately to vacant lots and rubble.

31. The passage as a whole can best be described as:

   A. an argument for eradicating weeds in urban areas.
   B. a discussion of the factors that contribute to the survival of weeds in urban environments.
   C. a report on the need for increased vegetation in cities and suburbs.
   D. a discussion of how environmentalists are changing their attitudes toward so-called weeds.

32. Based on how the following four perspectives are outlined in the second paragraph (lines 22–39), which one would the author most likely share?

   F. A utilitarian perspective
   G. An agricultural perspective
   H. A biological perspective
   J. A city dweller's perspective

33. It is reasonable to infer that, in the author's opinion, *spontaneous vegetation* (line 4) is most unlike which of the following types of plants mentioned in the passage?

   A. Common ragweed (line 14)
   B. Economic crops (line 32)
   C. Urban plants (line 57)
   D. Calcium-loving grassland species (lines 68–69)

GO ON TO THE NEXT PAGE.

3 ━━━━━━━━━━━━━━━━━━━━━━━━━━━━━━ **3**

34. Which of the following opinions regarding weeds adapting to rather than causing a changing habitat is most clearly implied by the passage?

    F. Removing weeds from places they are considered undesirable is simpler than people realize.

    G. Weeds have wrongly been blamed for contributing to certain kinds of deterioration in urban areas.

    H. Changing people's minds about weeds has caused a pervasive acceptance of them in urban areas.

    J. City vegetation reflects that the life cycle of weeds is simpler than that of cultivated plants.

35. As it is used in line 5, the word *greenery* most nearly refers to:

    A. cultivated plants.

    B. protected natural landscapes.

    C. weeds.

    D. crops.

36. Based on the passage, in comparison to Gilbert's observation in his book, the scientific study by Lundholm and Marlin can best be described as:

    F. complementary; Gilbert reached a conclusion similar to the one reached by Lundholm and Marlin.

    G. contrasting; Lundholm and Marlin conducted a more recent study that questions the note in Gilbert's book.

    H. interdependent; Lundholm and Marlin used Gilbert's book as a foundation for their study.

    J. irrelevant; Gilbert was studying the ecology of urban habitats, while Lundholm and Marlin studied natural environments with high pH soils.

37. The last paragraph most strongly suggests that the author's attitude toward so-called weeds in urban areas is one of:

    A. alarm due to the threat they pose to native plants.

    B. concern as he fears they will not survive in their new habitat.

    C. annoyance over the manner in which they contribute to urban decay.

    D. respect for their ability to adapt to a wide array of challenging conditions.

38. According to the passage, Norway maple was first brought into the urban environment by:

    F. people.

    G. wind.

    H. water.

    J. birds.

39. As it is used in lines 15–16, the phrase *on their own* most nearly means:

    A. one at a time.

    B. without human aid.

    C. in a self-propelled fashion.

    D. voluntarily.

40. According to the passage, if people stopped disturbing weeds in an urban environment, eventually the weeds might:

    F. compete for space and start to die out.

    G. enhance landscaped gardens.

    H. dry out the soil.

    J. develop into woodlands.

END OF TEST 3

STOP! DO NOT TURN THE PAGE UNTIL TOLD TO DO SO.

DO NOT RETURN TO A PREVIOUS TEST.

Taking Additional Practice Tests

SCIENCE TEST

35 Minutes—40 Questions

DIRECTIONS: There are several passages in this test. Each passage is followed by several questions. After reading a passage, choose the best answer to each question and fill in the corresponding oval on your answer document. You may refer to the passages as often as necessary.

You are NOT permitted to use a calculator on this test.

Passage I

A teacher asked each of 4 students to describe the *molecular shape* (the geometrical arrangement of the atoms in a molecule) of each of 4 molecules: arsenic trifluoride (AsF_3), arsenic trichloride ($AsCl_3$), arsenic tribromide ($AsBr_3$), and arsenic triiodide (AsI_3).

Student 1

An AsF_3 molecule is *T-shaped*, with the As atom in the center. All the atoms in AsF_3 lie in the same plane, and there are 2 unique angles—90° and 180°—between adjacent As–F bonds (see Figure 1).

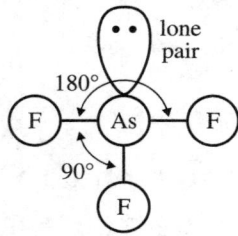

Figure 1

The As atom has a *lone pair* (an outer pair of electrons not involved in chemical bonding) that lies in the same plane as the As and F atoms. These electrons strongly repel the 3 As–F bonds, resulting in the 2 unique bond angles of 90° and 180°.

$AsCl_3$, $AsBr_3$, and AsI_3 are also T-shaped.

Student 2

The shape of an AsF_3 molecule is *trigonal planar*, with the As atom in the center. All the atoms in AsF_3 lie in the same plane, and there is only 1 unique angle—120°—between adjacent As–F bonds (see Figure 2).

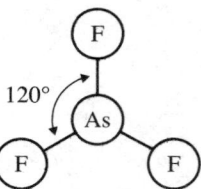

Figure 2

The As atom does not have a lone pair. The 3 As–F bonds repel each other equally, resulting in the 1 unique bond angle of 120°.

$AsCl_3$, $AsBr_3$, and AsI_3 are also trigonal planar.

Student 3

The shape of an AsF_3 molecule is *trigonal pyramidal*, with the As atom in the center. All the atoms in AsF_3 do not lie in the same plane, and there is only 1 unique angle—109°—between adjacent As–F bonds (see Figure 3).

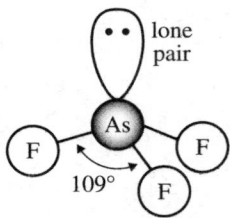

Figure 3

The As atom has a lone pair. The lone pair and the 3 As–F bonds repel each other equally, resulting in the 1 unique bond angle of 109°.

$AsCl_3$, $AsBr_3$, and AsI_3 are also trigonal pyramidal.

GO ON TO THE NEXT PAGE.

Student 4

Student 3 is correct that, due to the lone pair, AsF_3, $AsCl_3$, $AsBr_3$, and AsI_3 molecules are all trigonal pyramidal. AsF_3, $AsCl_3$, $AsBr_3$, and AsI_3 each have only 1 unique bond angle, but that bond angle is different for each of the 4 molecules. The bond angle depends on the size of the atom that is bound to the As atom: the larger the atom that is bound to the As atom, the larger the bond angle. The atoms bound to the As atom, listed by size from smallest to largest, are F, Cl, Br, and I.

After the 4 descriptions were offered, the teacher used a computer program that (1) determined that in each of the 4 molecules, there is only 1 unique bond angle and (2) calculated the bond angle for each molecule (see Table 1).

Table 1	
Molecule	Calculated bond angle
AsF_3	100°
$AsCl_3$	101°
$AsBr_3$	103°
AsI_3	111°

Table adapted from Ian J. McNaught, "Testing and Extending VSEPR with WebMO and MOPAC or GAMESS." ©2011 by Division of Chemical Education, Inc., American Chemical Society.

1. The table below gives the atomic mass (in atomic mass units, amu) of the elements F, Cl, Br, and I.

Element	Atomic mass (amu)
F	19.00
Cl	35.45
Br	79.90
I	126.9

Based on Student 4's description, among the elements listed in the table, as atomic mass increases, *atomic radius*:

A. increases only.
B. decreases only.
C. increases, then decreases.
D. decreases, then increases.

2. Which of the students claimed that the As atom in an AsF_3 molecule has a lone pair?

F. Students 1 and 2 only
G. Students 3 and 4 only
H. Students 1, 3, and 4 only
J. Students 2, 3, and 4 only

3. Which of the students would be likely to agree with the statement "All 4 atoms in an AsF_3 molecule lie in the same plane"?

A. Student 1 only
B. Student 3 only
C. Students 1 and 2 only
D. Students 3 and 4 only

4. Consider the claim that there are 3 unique bond angles in an AsF_3 molecule. This claim is consistent with the description(s) given by which student(s), if any?

F. Student 2 only
G. Students 1 and 2 only
H. Students 3 and 4 only
J. None of the students

5. Based on the descriptions given by Students 1, 2, and 3, which of these students would be likely to agree that the sum of the 3 bond angles in an AsI_3 molecule is equal to 360° ?

A. Students 1 and 2 only
B. Students 1 and 3 only
C. Students 2 and 3 only
D. Students 1, 2, and 3

6. A molecule of ammonia (NH_3) has only 1 unique bond angle, and that bond angle is 107°. The N atom also has a lone pair that strongly repels the 3 N–H bonds. Based on the descriptions given by Students 2 and 3, is the molecular shape of NH_3 more likely trigonal planar or trigonal pyramidal?

F. Trigonal planar; the bond angle is more consistent with Student 2's description.
G. Trigonal planar; the bond angle is more consistent with Student 3's description.
H. Trigonal pyramidal; the bond angle is more consistent with Student 2's description.
J. Trigonal pyramidal; the bond angle is more consistent with Student 3's description.

7. The data in Table 1 are most consistent with the description given by which student?

A. Student 1
B. Student 2
C. Student 3
D. Student 4

GO ON TO THE NEXT PAGE.

4 ○ ○ ○ ○ ○ ○ ○ ○ ○ **4**

Passage II

Each dog in a particular population has a black, brown, or yellow coat. In this population, coat color is determined by 2 unlinked genes: Gene B and Gene E. Gene B has 2 alleles: *B* and *b*. Gene E also has 2 alleles: *E* and *e*. Table 1 shows the possible genotypes for Gene B and Gene E and the resulting coat color phenotypes.

Table 1	
Genotype	Coat color
BBEE	black
BBEe	black
BBee	yellow
BbEE	black
BbEe	black
Bbee	yellow
bbEE	brown
bbEe	brown
bbee	yellow

Two of the dogs with black coats were crossed 3 times (Crosses 1–3). The coat colors of the offspring produced in each cross are shown in Table 2.

Table 2			
	Number of offspring with a:		
Cross	black coat	brown coat	yellow coat
1	8	0	0
2	6	1	2
3	2	2	2

8. After Cross 1 but before Cross 2, a student hypothesized that each of the parents in Cross 1 had the genotype *BBEE*. Was this hypothesis consistent with the results of Cross 1 ?

   F. Yes, because all the offspring of Cross 1 had black coats.
   G. Yes, because all the offspring of Cross 1 had yellow coats.
   H. No, because all the offspring of Cross 1 had black coats.
   J. No, because all the offspring of Cross 1 had yellow coats.

9. What was the Gene B and Gene E genotype of the offspring of Cross 2 that had a brown coat?

   A. *bbee*
   B. *BBEE*
   C. *BbEE* or *BbEe*
   D. *bbEE* or *bbEe*

10. Based on Tables 1 and 2, what fraction of the offspring of Cross 3 had 1 or more copies of the *E* allele of Gene E ?

    F. $\frac{1}{4}$

    G. $\frac{1}{3}$

    H. $\frac{2}{3}$

    J. $\frac{15}{16}$

GO ON TO THE NEXT PAGE.

4 ○ ○ ○ ○ ○ ○ ○ ○ ○ **4**

11. Consider the offspring of each of the 3 crosses. Based on Tables 1 and 2, some of the offspring of which of the crosses, if any, could have had only recessive alleles of Gene B and Gene E ?

   A. Cross 1 only
   B. Crosses 2 and 3 only
   C. Crosses 1, 2, and 3
   D. None of the crosses

12. Suppose 2 of the offspring from Cross 3 with yellow coats are crossed. What percent of the resulting offspring will have yellow coats?

   F.   0%
   G.   25%
   H.   50%
   J. 100%

13. Approximately what percent of the normal gametes produced by a dog with the genotype *BbEE* will contain the *B* allele?

   A.   0%
   B.   25%
   C.   50%
   D. 100%

GO ON TO THE NEXT PAGE.

Taking Additional Practice Tests

4 **4**

Passage III

The *tensile strength* of a paper towel (PT) is the force per unit width required to break the PT when it is clamped and stretched (see diagram).

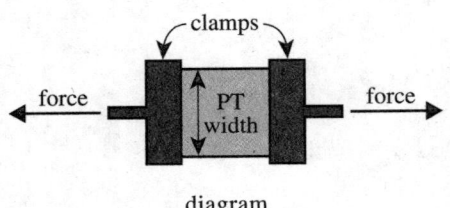

diagram

Dry strength is the tensile strength of a dry PT, and *wet strength* is the tensile strength of a PT that has been submerged in water. The wet strength can be increased by treating the PT with certain chemicals.

Students conducted 2 experiments to study the wet strengths of identical PTs, each 20 cm × 20 cm, treated with glutaraldehyde (GLA) or with GLA and zinc nitrate.

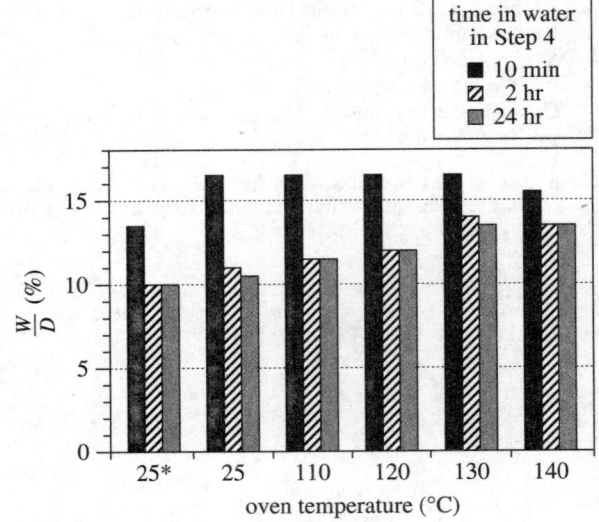

*controls

Figure 1

Experiment 2

Steps 1–5 were repeated with 100 other PTs, except that the test solution contained both GLA and zinc nitrate (see Figure 2).

Experiment 1

First, the dry strengths of 5 PTs were measured, in newtons per meter (N/m), and the average of the measurements, D, was calculated. Then, Steps 1–5 were performed on each of 100 other PTs:

1. A PT was submerged for 30 sec in water (if the PT was to be a control) or in a test solution containing GLA.

2. The PT was dried on a hot plate at 85°C for 4 min.

3. The PT was heated in an oven for 3 min at a certain temperature—25°C for a control PT and 25°C, 110°C, 120°C, 130°C, or 140°C for a treated PT.

4. The PT was submerged in water for 10 min, 2 hr, or 24 hr.

5. The wet strength of the PT was measured in N/m.

The wet strengths of PTs that had been subjected to identical conditions were averaged. Each average wet strength, W, was divided by D and then multiplied by 100. The resulting $\frac{W}{D}$ values are shown in Figure 1.

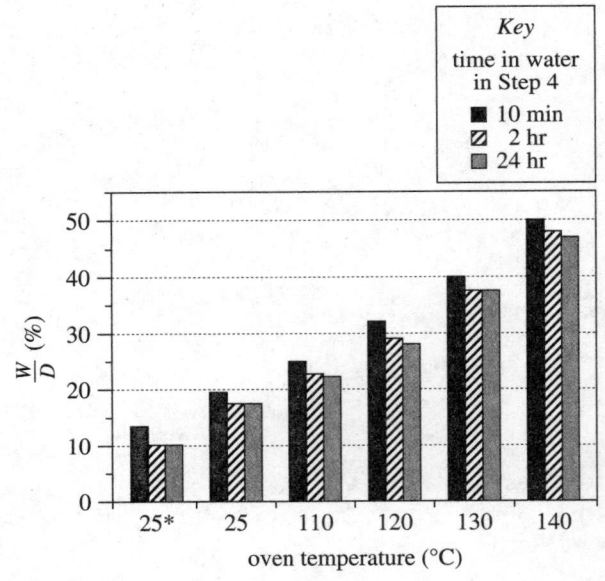

*controls

Figure 2

GO ON TO THE NEXT PAGE.

4 ○ ○ ○ ○ ○ ○ ○ ○ ○ **4**

Figures 1 and 2 adapted from Gordon Guozhong Xu, Charles Qixiang Yang, and Yulin Deng, "Applications of Bifunctional Aldehydes to Improve Paper Wet Strength." ©2002 by John Wiley & Sons, Inc.

14. In Experiment 2, the greatest average wet strength was observed for the PTs that were submerged in water for 10 min after having been heated in an oven at what temperature?

    F.   110°C
    G.   120°C
    H.   130°C
    J.   140°C

15. In Experiment 2, for PTs that were submerged in water for 2 hr, as the oven temperature increased from 110°C through 140°C, the $\frac{W}{D}$ value:

    A.   increased only.
    B.   decreased only.
    C.   remained the same.
    D.   varied, but with no general trend.

16. In Step 1 of Experiment 1, the PTs that would become controls were submerged in what liquid, and in Step 3 of Experiment 1, these control PTs were heated in an oven at what temperature?

	liquid	temperature
F.	water	25°C
G.	water	85°C
H.	GLA solution	25°C
J.	GLA solution	85°C

17. In which of Experiments 1 and 2, if either, did the students measure the wet strengths of PTs that had been submerged in water for a total of 18 hr ?

    A.   Experiment 1 only
    B.   Experiment 2 only
    C.   Both Experiment 1 and Experiment 2
    D.   Neither Experiment 1 nor Experiment 2

18. Which of the following statements comparing the $\frac{W}{D}$ value of the PTs that were submerged in water for 2 hr with the $\frac{W}{D}$ value of the PTs that were submerged in water for 10 min is supported by the results of Experiment 1 ?

    F.   For all the oven temperatures, the $\frac{W}{D}$ value at 2 hr was greater than the $\frac{W}{D}$ value at 10 min.

    G.   For all the oven temperatures, the $\frac{W}{D}$ value at 2 hr was less than the $\frac{W}{D}$ value at 10 min.

    H.   For all the oven temperatures, the $\frac{W}{D}$ value at 2 hr was the same as the $\frac{W}{D}$ value at 10 min.

    J.   For some of the oven temperatures, the $\frac{W}{D}$ value at 2 hr was greater than the $\frac{W}{D}$ value at 10 min; at the other oven temperatures, the $\frac{W}{D}$ value at 2 hr was less than the $\frac{W}{D}$ value at 10 min.

19. One of the students predicted that the wet strengths of PTs would NOT increase after treating the PTs with a solution containing both GLA and zinc nitrate. The results of which experiment better refute or support this prediction? The results of:

    A.   Experiment 1 better refute this prediction.
    B.   Experiment 1 better support this prediction.
    C.   Experiment 2 better refute this prediction.
    D.   Experiment 2 better support this prediction.

20. Based on the results of the experiments, is the dry strength of a paper towel greater than or less than the wet strength of the paper towel?

    F.   Greater; each average wet strength, W, was greater than 100% of D.
    G.   Greater; each average wet strength, W, was less than 100% of D.
    H.   Less; each average wet strength, W, was greater than 100% of D.
    J.   Less; each average wet strength, W, was less than 100% of D.

GO ON TO THE NEXT PAGE.

4   **4**

Passage IV

The tiger frog, *Rana rugulosa*, is a species of frog that is commercially farmed. A farmer conducted 2 experiments to help determine the optimum diet for the growth of *R. rugulosa*.

Prior to the experiments, 10 diets (Diets 1–10) were prepared. The diets differed in the percent by mass of protein, the number of calories per gram (cal/g), or both (see Table 1).

Table 1

Diet	Percent by mass of protein	Calories per gram (cal/g)
1	30.0	5,300
2	32.5	5,300
3	35.0	5,300
4	37.5	5,300
5	40.0	5,300
6	37.0	4,500
7	37.0	4,700
8	37.0	4,900
9	37.0	5,300
10	37.0	5,700

Experiment 1

Each of 5 identical outdoor 1 m³ tanks was prepared as follows: First, the tank was filled with water to a depth of 20 cm. Next, 30 adult *R. rugulosa*, each with a mass of 3.3 g, were placed into the tank. Then the tank was covered with a fine wire mesh.

Each tank of frogs was assigned a different diet: Diet 1, Diet 2, Diet 3, Diet 4, or Diet 5. Each frog was fed 1,000 mg of its assigned diet, twice per day, for the next 12 weeks. At the end of 12 weeks, the average final mass of the frogs was determined for each diet (see Table 2).

Table 2

Diet	Average final mass (g)
1	54.0
2	69.3
3	80.1
4	86.2
5	90.4

Experiment 2

Five more of the outdoor 1 m³ tanks were prepared as in Experiment 1, except that each of the *R. rugulosa* had an initial mass of 7.9 g instead of 3.3 g. Each tank of frogs was assigned a different diet: Diet 6, Diet 7, Diet 8, Diet 9, or Diet 10. Each frog was fed 2,000 mg of its assigned diet, once per day, for the next 12 weeks. At the end of 12 weeks, the average final mass of the frogs was determined for each diet (see Table 3).

Table 3

Diet	Average final mass (g)
6	126.9
7	135.1
8	143.0
9	132.0
10	129.5

Tables adapted from P. Somsueb and M. Boonyaratpalin, "Optimum Protein and Energy Levels for the Thai Native Frog, *Rana rugulosa* Weigmann." ©2001 by Blackwell Science Ltd.

21. The values that were averaged to obtain the data in Tables 2 and 3 were most likely read from which of the following instruments?

   A. Graduated cylinder
   B. Electronic balance
   C. Metric ruler
   D. Calorimeter

22. In Experiment 1, as the percent by mass of protein increased, the average final mass of the frogs:

   F. increased only.
   G. decreased only.
   H. increased, then decreased.
   J. decreased, then increased.

GO ON TO THE NEXT PAGE.

4

23. The fine wire mesh was most likely intended to function in which of the ways described below?

    I. To prevent predators of frogs from entering each tank
    II. To place the frogs into each tank
    III. To keep the frogs from leaving each tank

  A. I and II only
  B. I and III only
  C. II and III only
  D. I, II, and III

24. In Experiment 2, as the number of calories per gram increased, the average final mass of the frogs:

  F. increased only.
  G. decreased only.
  H. increased, then decreased.
  J. decreased, then increased.

25. Which of the statements about the frogs involved in the experiments given below, if either, is(are) consistent with the information in the passage?

    I. All the frogs belonged to the same genus.
    II. All the frogs belonged to the same species.

  A. I only
  B. II only
  C. Both I and II
  D. Neither I nor II

26. Experiment 2 differed from Experiment 1 in which of the following ways?

  F. The initial mass of each frog was greater in Experiment 1 than in Experiment 2.
  G. The initial mass of each frog was greater in Experiment 2 than in Experiment 1.
  H. The quantity of food that each frog was fed per day was greater in Experiment 1 than in Experiment 2.
  J. The quantity of food that each frog was fed per day was greater in Experiment 2 than in Experiment 1.

27. To determine whether the number of calories per gram in the diet of *R. rugulosa* affects the growth of *R. rugulosa*, would the farmer more likely have compared the results of Diets 1–5 or the results of Diets 6–10 ?

  A. Diets 1–5, because those diets varied in the percent by mass of protein but not in the number of calories per gram.
  B. Diets 1–5, because those diets varied in the number of calories per gram but not in the percent by mass of protein.
  C. Diets 6–10, because those diets varied in the percent by mass of protein but not in the number of calories per gram.
  D. Diets 6–10, because those diets varied in the number of calories per gram but not in the percent by mass of protein.

GO ON TO THE NEXT PAGE.

4 ○ ○ ○ ○ ○ ○ ○ ○ **4**

Passage V

In soil, CO_2 is produced through 2 processes—respiration in plant roots and bacterial decomposition of organic matter. A study was done in an oak forest to examine the CO_2 content of soil gas as well as the water content of the soil. The study was done during an 8-week period that began just as the growing season ended.

Study

On October 12, 5 evenly spaced locations in the forest were marked along a 120 m long straight line, starting at one end. At each location, 5 sets of 2 instruments each—a *diffusion well* and a *moisture sensor*—were positioned so that soil gas could be collected and soil water content could be measured at each of 5 soil depths: 10 cm, 30 cm, 60 cm, 100 cm, and 140 cm. The slots near one end of the steel pipe of the diffusion well allowed only soil gas to enter the pipe. The soil gas could be sampled by inserting the needle of a syringe through the airtight seal on the aboveground end of the pipe. See Figure 1.

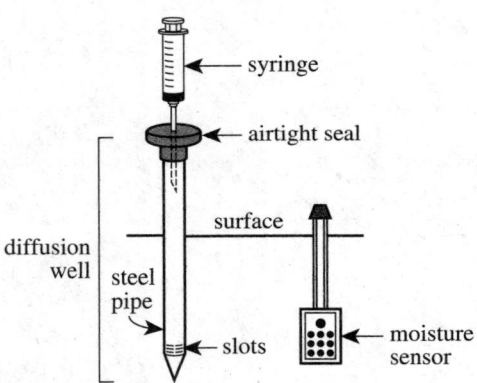

Note: Drawing is not to scale.

Figure 1

At noon on each of 4 dates—October 26, November 9, November 23, and December 7—a 0.5 mL sample of soil gas was collected from each diffusion well and the water content of the soil was read from each moisture sensor. Each soil gas sample was analyzed to determine its CO_2 content. Figure 2 shows the averaged results for CO_2 content of the soil gas, expressed in percent by volume, and Figure 3 shows the averaged results for water content of the soil, expressed in percent by mass.

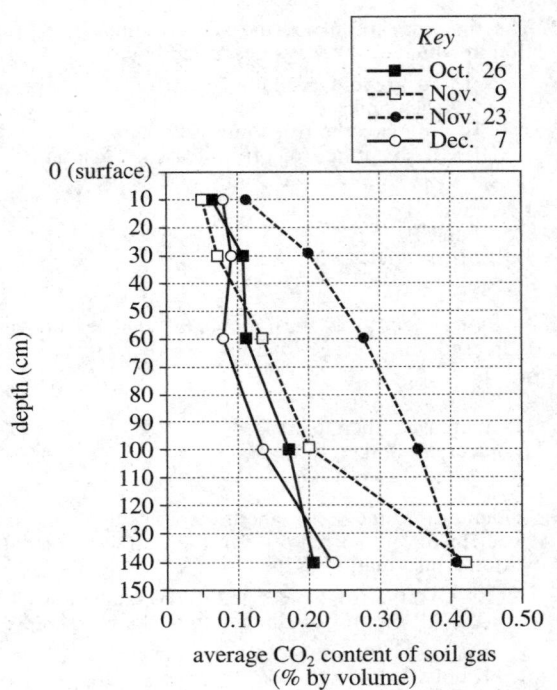

Figure 2

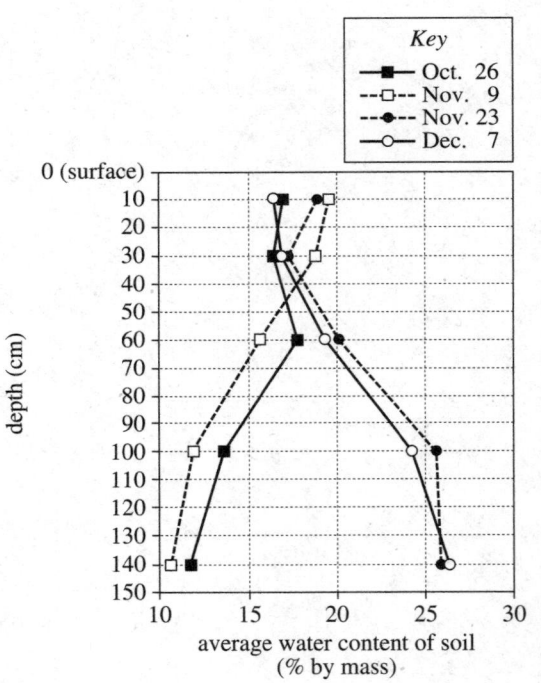

Figure 3

GO ON TO THE NEXT PAGE.

4 ◯ ◯ ◯ ◯ ◯ ◯ ◯ ◯ ◯ **4**

Figures adapted from James M. Dyer and George A. Brook, "Spatial and Temporal Variations in Temperate Forest Soil Carbon Dioxide during the Non-Growing Season." ©1991 by John Wiley & Sons, Ltd.

28. According to Figure 3, at what depth were the average water content values for the 4 dates closest in value?

F. 30 cm
G. 60 cm
H. 100 cm
J. 140 cm

29. The slots at the bottom of a diffusion well's pipe were designed to allow the passage of:

A. soil gas but not soil or water.
B. soil and water but not soil gas.
C. water but not soil or soil gas.
D. soil gas as well as soil and water.

30. What percent of the CO_2 in each soil gas sample was due to bacterial decomposition of organic matter and not due to respiration in plant roots?

F. 10%
G. 25%
H. 50%
J. Cannot be determined from the given information

31. In the study, one step in the determination of CO_2 content was to divide a volume of CO_2 by another volume. That other volume was the volume of a:

A. sample of soil.
B. sample of soil gas.
C. sample of water.
D. steel pipe of a diffusion well.

32. Which of the following statements describing how the average water content generally varied over the 140 cm of soil depth is consistent with Figure 3 ?

F. On each of the 4 dates, the average water content generally increased with depth.
G. On each of the 4 dates, the average water content generally decreased with depth.
H. On October 26 and November 9, the average water content generally increased with depth, whereas on November 23 and December 7, the average water content generally decreased with depth.
J. On October 26 and November 9, the average water content generally decreased with depth, whereas on November 23 and December 7, the average water content generally increased with depth.

33. Suppose that at each of the 5 locations a diffusion well had been positioned at a depth of 145 cm. Based on Figure 2, on November 23, the average CO_2 content of the soil gas at that depth would most likely have been determined to be:

A. less than 0.30% by volume.
B. between 0.30% by volume and 0.35% by volume.
C. between 0.35% by volume and 0.40% by volume.
D. greater than 0.40% by volume.

34. Suppose that a 10 g sample of soil had been collected on November 23 at a depth of 60 cm. Based on Figure 3, what mass of water would most likely have been present in the sample?

F. 1 g
G. 2 g
H. 5 g
J. 10 g

GO ON TO THE NEXT PAGE.

4       **4**

Passage VI

An object falling through a liquid has 3 forces acting on it: gravity, a buoyant force, and *drag* (a force that opposes motion). If the net upward force on the object is equal in magnitude to the net downward force on the object, then the object will fall at *terminal speed*.

A steel ball was dropped from rest into a column of motor oil and into a column of glycerin. Figures 1 and 2 show how the speed of the ball and the drag on the ball varied with time as the ball fell through the oil and through the glycerin, respectively. Figure 3 shows how the depth of the ball varied with time for each case.

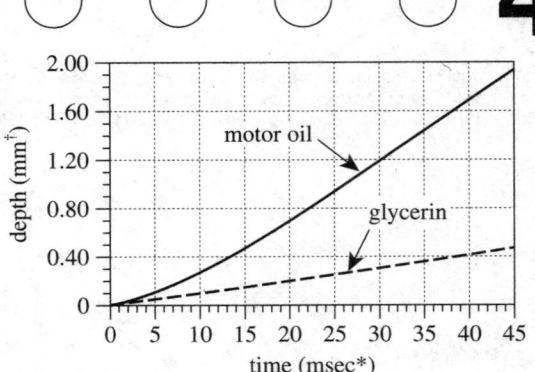

*milliseconds
†millimeters

Figure 3

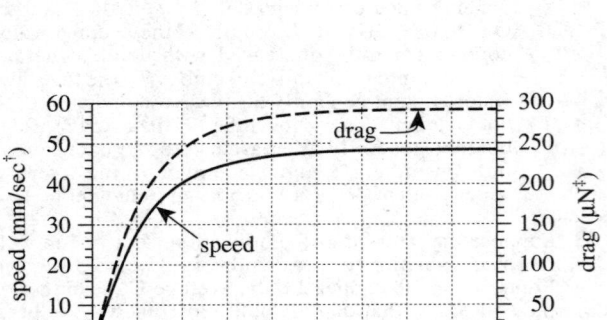

*milliseconds
†millimeters per second
‡micronewtons

Figure 1

35. Based on Figure 3, the depth of the steel ball in the motor oil at time = 50 msec would most likely have been closest to which of the following?

A. 0.50 mm
B. 0.60 mm
C. 1.90 mm
D. 2.10 mm

36. Which of the following diagrams best represents the 3 forces that acted on the steel ball—gravity (*G*), the buoyant force (*B*), and drag (*D*)—as it moved through either liquid?

(Note: Assume that down is toward the bottom of the page.)

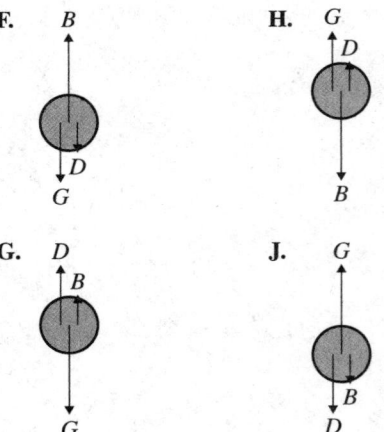

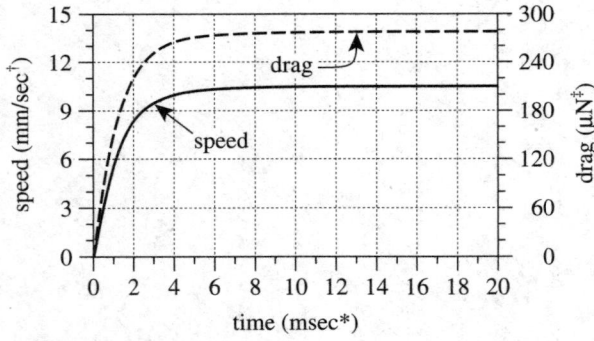

*milliseconds
†millimeters per second
‡micronewtons

Figure 2

GO ON TO THE NEXT PAGE.

4 ○ ○ ○ ○ ○ ○ ○ ○ ○ 4

37. The steel ball required *less* time to reach terminal speed in which liquid?

   A. Motor oil; the ball took less than 10 msec in motor oil but more than 25 msec in glycerin to reach terminal speed.
   B. Motor oil; the ball took more than 25 msec in motor oil but less than 10 msec in glycerin to reach terminal speed.
   C. Glycerin; the ball took less than 10 msec in glycerin but more than 25 msec in motor oil to reach terminal speed.
   D. Glycerin; the ball took more than 25 msec in glycerin but less than 10 msec in motor oil to reach terminal speed.

38. According to Figures 1 and 2, the steel ball's terminal speed was greater in which liquid?

   F. Motor oil; the terminal speed was about 48 mm/sec in motor oil and about 10.5 mm/sec in glycerin.
   G. Motor oil; the terminal speed was about 240 mm/sec in motor oil and about 210 mm/sec in glycerin.
   H. Glycerin; the terminal speed was about 48 mm/sec in glycerin and about 10.5 mm/sec in motor oil.
   J. Glycerin; the terminal speed was about 240 mm/sec in glycerin and about 210 mm/sec in motor oil.

39. Based on Figures 1, 2, and 3, is it reasonable to conclude that the drag on the steel ball was directly proportional to the depth of the ball?

   A. Yes; both the depth and the drag increased only.
   B. Yes; both the depth and the drag increased and then gradually approached a constant value.
   C. No; the depth increased only, whereas the drag increased and then approached a constant value.
   D. No; the depth increased and then approached a constant value, whereas the drag increased only.

40. Based on Figures 1 and 3, at a depth of 0.50 mm in the motor oil, what was the approximate drag exerted on the steel ball?

   F. 230 μN
   G. 250 μN
   H. 270 μN
   J. 290 μN

END OF TEST 4

STOP! DO NOT RETURN TO ANY OTHER TEST.

You may wish to photocopy these sample answer document pages to respond to the practice ACT Writing Test.

Please enter the information at the right before beginning the writing test.

Use a No. 2 pencil only. Do NOT use a mechanical pencil, ink, ballpoint, or felt-tip pen.

WRITING TEST BOOKLET NUMBER

Print your 9-digit **Booklet Number** in the boxes at the right.

WRITING TEST FORM

Print your 5-character **Test Form** in the boxes at the right and fill in the corresponding ovals.

①	①	W	T	A
②	②		④	①
	③			②
	④			③
	⑤			④
	⑥			⑤
	⑦			⑥
	⑧			⑦
	⑨			⑧
	⓪			⑨

Begin WRITING TEST here.

If you need more space, please continue on the following page.

1

Taking Additional Practice Tests

WRITING TEST

_____

_____

_____

_____

_____

_____

_____

_____

_____

_____

_____

_____

_____

_____

_____

_____

_____

_____

_____

_____

_____

_____

If you need more space, please continue on the following page.

2

WRITING TEST

_____

_____

_____

_____

_____

_____

_____

_____

_____

_____

_____

_____

_____

_____

_____

_____

_____

_____

_____

_____

_____

_____

_____

_____

_____

_____

_____

_____

_____

If you need more space, please continue on the following page.

3

Taking Additional Practice Tests

WRITING TEST

_____

_____

_____

_____

_____

_____

_____

_____

_____

_____

_____

_____

_____

_____

_____

_____

_____

_____

_____

_____

_____

_____

_____

_____

_____

STOP here with the writing test.

4

Practice Writing Test Prompt 2

Your Signature: _____
(Do not print.)

Print Your Name Here: _____

Your Date of Birth:

		–			–				
Month			Day			Year			

Form 18W4A

The ACT® WRITING TEST BOOKLET

You must take the multiple-choice tests before you take the writing test.

Directions

This is a test of your writing skills. You will have **forty** (40) minutes to read the prompt, plan your response, and write an essay in English. Before you begin working, read all material in this test booklet carefully to understand exactly what you are being asked to do.

You will write your essay on the lined pages in the **answer document** provided. Your writing on those pages will be scored. You may use the unlined pages in this test booklet to plan your essay. Your work on these pages will not be scored.

Your essay will be evaluated based on the evidence it provides of your ability to:

- clearly state your own perspective on a complex issue and analyze the relationship between your perspective and at least one other perspective
- develop and support your ideas with reasoning and examples
- organize your ideas clearly and logically
- communicate your ideas effectively in standard written English

Lay your pencil down immediately when time is called.

DO NOT OPEN THIS BOOKLET UNTIL TOLD TO DO SO.

PO Box 168
Iowa City, IA 52243-0168

The ONLY Official Prep Guide from the Makers of the ACT

Celebrities and Privacy

Many people believe that celebrities must give up some of their privacy in exchange for the wealth and fame that celebrity status affords. After all, to become a celebrity, one must seek public attention and recognition, and a loss of privacy, some say, is an unavoidable trade-off. But should being a celebrity mean having no right to privacy? Should people who are well known for their work or skill be expected to share details about their home life, family, and loved ones? In a culture that lavishes attention on celebrities, it is worth examining celebrities' right to privacy.

Read and carefully consider these perspectives. Each suggests a particular way of thinking about celebrities' right to privacy.

Perspective One	Perspective Two	Perspective Three
Our belief that celebrities must lose their right to privacy is the product of jealousy and envy. We resent celebrities for their wealth and fame, and so we punish them by intruding into their private lives.	Celebrities do give up some of their rights to privacy when they pursue a career that makes them famous. They can't expect to maintain a private life when the only way to become famous is to capture the imagination of the public.	Most people claim that privacy is important, but these days everyone with a social media account has given up some privacy for the sake of attention. We're not doing anything to celebrities that we aren't already doing to ourselves.

Essay Task

Write a unified, coherent essay about celebrities' right to privacy. In your essay, be sure to:

- clearly state your own perspective on the issue and analyze the relationship between your perspective and at least one other perspective
- develop and support your ideas with reasoning and examples
- organize your ideas clearly and logically
- communicate your ideas effectively in standard written English

Your perspective may be in full agreement with any of those given, in partial agreement, or completely different.

Planning Your Essay

Your work on these prewriting pages will not be scored.

Use the space below and on the back cover to generate ideas and plan your essay. You may wish to consider the following as you think critically about the task:

Strengths and weaknesses of different perspectives on the issue
- What insights do they offer, and what do they fail to consider?
- Why might they be persuasive to others, or why might they fail to persuade?

Your own knowledge, experience, and values
- What is your perspective on this issue, and what are its strengths and weaknesses?
- How will you support your perspective in your essay?

If you need more space to plan, please continue on the following page.

The ONLY Official Prep Guide from the Makers of the ACT

Planning Your Essay

Use this page to continue planning your essay. Your work on this page will not be scored.

Passage I

Question 1. The best answer is A because it clearly and succinctly indicates that the young woman arrived at the same location where the narrator was waiting.

The best answer is NOT:

B because it unnecessarily repeats the first part of the sentence, explaining again that the narrator is waiting in a veterinarian's office.

C because it unnecessarily repeats that the narrator is waiting in the office. This information has already been established in the first part of the sentence, "I was waiting in the veterinarian's office."

D because it unnecessarily repeats that the narrator is there in the office. This information is already established in the first part of the sentence, "I was waiting in the veterinarian's office."

Question 2. The best answer is G because the verb *scuttling* provides a vivid description of the iguana's movement. This choice also provides a description of the iguana's rain forest environment, "dank undergrowth."

The best answer is NOT:

F because "walking on the ground" does not satisfy the requirement in the question that the choice be a vivid description. "Walking on the ground" indicates what the iguana does but is not a vivid description of the iguana's action or environment.

H because "living underneath the treetops" states an obvious point about iguanas and nearly restates the next part of the sentence, "resting high in the trees." No vivid modifiers or verbs are used.

J because the words "down low" are repetitive and the expression "moving about down low" is vague and imprecise.

Question 3. The best answer is C because the comma after *trees* indicates that the iguanas, not the canopy itself, are hidden in the trees.

The best answer is NOT:

A because it is nonsensical given the context of the sentence. The comma after *trees* followed by "which are hidden in the canopy" indicates that the trees themselves are hidden in the canopy.

B because it is a comma splice. "They're . . . trees" is an independent clause. "They are hidden in the canopy" is another independent clause. Two independent clauses cannot be joined using only a comma.

D because the semicolon is incorrectly placed between an independent clause and an explanatory phrase in a simple sentence. Semicolons are used to join two independent clauses.

Question 4. The best answer is G because the contrast between the narrator's desire to be polite and the narrator's reluctance emphasizes the narrator's feelings toward the iguana. If the phrase were removed, the following sentence would suggest the narrator is ambivalent about the iguana's presence, which contrasts with the beginning of the third paragraph when the narrator "guardedly" examines the iguana. The phrase is critical to establishing the narrator's negative feelings toward the iguana.

The best answer is NOT:

F because "wishing to be polite, but with reluctance in my voice" describes an action taking place at the time the woman asked permission to take the iguana out of its carrier. This does not offer any suggestion that the narrator had a previous experience with iguanas out of their carriers at veterinary offices.

H because the narrator's overall attitude toward the iguana is negative. She "guardedly" examines the iguana. She is amazed that the woman "tenderly caresses" the animal and initially feels pity for the woman who gives love to an animal the narrator initially feels can't love the woman back. The phrase "with reluctance in my voice" is consistent with this negative attitude.

J because the purpose of the paragraph is not to provide background information on iguanas in general; it is a continuation of the narrative about the narrator's encounter with an iguana at the veterinarian's office.

Question 5. The best answer is D because the *rows* specified in the response indicate the pattern of spikes that appear on the reptile. The word *lined* also indicates the position and pattern of the spikes.

The best answer is NOT:

A because "it had a spine with tiny spikes" indicates the size of the spikes but not the pattern of the spikes.

B because the spikes "just beginning to develop again" indicates the potential size of the spikes and their development but not the arrangement or pattern of the spikes as stipulated in the stem.

C because "there were small spikes on its armored back" indicates the size of the spikes and provides a visual description of the appearance and texture of the reptile's back but does not indicate the pattern of the spikes.

Question 6. The best answer is G because it creates a clear, logical, and parallel sentence (the verbs *caressed* and *watched* are parallel in form). The pronoun *it* later in the sentence also has a clear and logical antecedent, *pet*.

The best answer is NOT:

F because it is overly wordy and does not fit with the rest of the sentence. The underlined text is not parallel with the phrase "and watched it" later in the sentence, and the pronoun *it* has no clear antecedent.

H because the verb *caressing* is in the ongoing present tense, which is inconsistent with the past tense *watched* later in the sentence. This creates a confusing sequence of time when part of the action is an ongoing present action, *caressing,* and part of the action occurred in the past, *watched.*

J because it results in an illogical and ungrammatical transition to the rest of the sentence. The pronoun *it* in the remaining sentence also has no clear antecedent.

Question 7. **The best answer is B** because the word *woman* clarifies the meaning of the sentence by indicating who is lavishing attention on the iguana and serves as a clear antecedent to the pronoun *her* used later in the sentence.

The best answer is NOT:

A because there is an incorrect shift in pronouns from *us* to *her* in the same sentence. There is also no antecedent for the word *us* in this sentence or the preceding sentence (the narrator does not join the young woman in lavishing affection on the iguana).

C because the plural noun *people* is not a logical antecedent for the singular pronoun *her*. There is no mention in the sentence or in the rest of the essay of a wider audience lavishing attention on the iguana.

D because the pronoun *you* is an incorrect pronoun shift. The essay is a narrative written in the first person, and there aren't any logical or stylistic reasons for the narrator to shift to the second person *you* at this point. *You* does not serve as a logical antecedent for the pronoun *her* used later in the sentence.

Question 8. **The best answer is J** because no comma is needed to separate the modifiers describing the iguana's eyes and how they shone and the prepositional phrase.

The best answer is NOT:

F because there is an unnecessary comma between a modifier and a prepositional phrase. No comma is needed to set off the prepositional phrase "from its scaly face."

G because there is an unnecessary comma between a preposition (*from*) and its object ("its scaly face").

H because there is an unnecessary comma between modifiers joined by the conjunction *and*. No comma is needed here because *and* is joining two adjectives, not two independent clauses.

Question 9. **The best answer is B** because the word *supposed* means to assume. This word does not match the context of the iguana staring steadily and fixedly like a judge, nor is it a reasonable alternative for the word *regarded*. *Supposed* also does not track with the object, *me*, and creates the nonsensical idea that the iguana is assessing the narrator like a judge.

The best answer is NOT:

A because the word *scrutinized* means to study closely. This word matches the context of the rest of the sentence, which compares the iguana to a judge delivering a verdict.

C because the word *appraised* means to survey and evaluate. This word matches the context of the rest of the sentence, which compares the iguana to a judge delivering a verdict.

D because the word *considered* means to look attentively at someone or something. This word matches the context of the rest of the sentence, which states the iguana stares "steadily and fixedly" at the narrator.

Question 10. **The best answer is F** because it clearly indicates that the narrator is comparing the iguana's actions to a judge delivering (or giving) the verdict.

The best answer is NOT:

G because the phrase "having a delivery of a verdict" is awkward and wordy, and it does not make sense in the given context. Without an explanation, it's hard to imagine how an iguana's actions could be like a judge *having* a delivery of a verdict.

H because the phrase "in deliverance with a verdict" does not make sense in this context (a judge delivers a verdict; she does not deliver the verdict with the verdict). The intended meaning of this action is unclear, especially when likened to the actions of the iguana.

J because the plural verb form *deliver* does not agree with the singular noun *judge*.

Question 11. The best answer is D because the sentence is complex (containing an independent and a dependent clause), so commas aren't needed to separate two independent clauses. There also isn't any nonessential information in the portion that needs to be set apart by punctuation.

The best answer is NOT:

A because there is an unnecessary comma between *cat* and the conjunction *and*. The phrase "cat and me" functions as a compound object in this sentence and should not be interrupted by a comma.

B because there are unnecessary commas around words that are essential to the meaning of the sentence ("and me from the hallway"). Setting these words apart with commas indicates that they are not crucial to understanding the sentence, but without them the sentence would state that the cat, not the hallway, leads to the examination room.

C because there is an unnecessary comma between the independent clause ending with *hallway* and the dependent clause beginning with *that*.

Question 12. The best answer is F because the word *looking* offers a concise and effective choice to indicate the comparison between the appearance of the iguana and the appearance of a kitten.

The best answer is NOT:

G because the phrase "like as if it was" offers a wordy and repetitive description of the iguana. This repetition is distracting and unnecessary. It is also overly informal given the style and tone of the rest of the essay.

H because the phrase "appearing something like" is wordy and vague. The phrase also does a poor job of setting up the comparison in the sentence "appearing something like as content as a kitten, and close its eyes again." The meaning here is unclear.

J because the phrase "sort of like it was" is wordy and vague, which makes the comparison in the sentence less clear. The phrase is also overly informal for the style and tone of the essay.

Question 13. **The best answer is B** because placing the sentence at Point B further explains the young woman's statement that the iguana liked being held. The sentence is a logical extension of the preceding sentence.

The best answer is NOT:

A because neither the woman nor her pet iguana have entered the office yet, so placing the sentence at Point A is incorrect. The pronoun *she* in the added sentence would have no antecedent, so it would be unclear who is speaking.

C because placing the sentence at Point C interrupts the logical flow between the narrator's statement that she dislikes iguanas and her reasons for disliking the creatures.

D because placing the sentence at Point D interrupts the narrative flow between the iguana opening its eyes and it staring at the narrator.

Question 14. **The best answer is F** because the essay focuses on the narrator's surprise that the iguana is pampered and loved by its owner. The iguana is lovingly caressed by its owner, which the narrator finds both amazing and unsettling.

The best answer is NOT:

G because there is no indication in the essay that the narrator believes the woman is impolite. The woman politely asks the narrator if she can let the reptile out of its carrier, and the narrator gives her approval. The narrator's guarded response comes from her awe at the relationship between owner and pet, not from annoyance.

H because the essay makes it clear that the narrator does not like iguanas, but it does not tell the story of why the narrator dislikes the creatures. The essay is primarily about the narrator's observation of a bond between the iguana and its owner on a particular day at the veterinary clinic.

J because the essay focuses on the narrator's observations of one iguana in a veterinary clinic. Only a brief mention is given to where iguanas live. Any physical descriptions in the essay focus on one pet iguana, not iguanas in general or as a species.

Taking Additional Practice Tests

Passage II

Question 15. The best answer is A because the conjunction *but* contrasts the achievement of qualifying for the Olympics with the fact that Mills was not expected to do well. This choice also correctly coordinates two independent clauses by joining them with a comma and a coordinating conjunction.

The best answer is NOT:

B because the conjunctive adverb *nonetheless* introduces a second independent clause. Using a comma and no coordinating conjunction between the independent clause ending with *Olympics* and *nevertheless* creates a comma splice. A semicolon after the word *Olympics* would be one option for making this construction correct.

C because it introduces an illogical transition. The fact that Mills qualified but was a long shot establishes a contrast, not an intensification of the first action as "in fact" implies. Furthermore, this option introduces a comma splice by joining two independent clauses with a comma. A semicolon is needed after the word *Olympics* to make this construction correct.

D because it creates a comma splice by joining two independent clauses with a comma. This choice also provides no transitional word indicating a contrast between the ideas that Mills qualified and that he was a long shot.

Question 16. The best answer is F because no comma is needed between the object, *medal,* and the prepositional phrase "for the United States in the event."

The best answer is NOT:

G because no comma is needed between the object, *medal,* and the prepositional phrase that follows.

H because *gold* and *medal* are not coordinating adjectives that require a comma between them. Placing a comma between them indicates that the order of the adjectives can be reversed, but logically, gold must come before medal. Also, no comma is needed between the object, *medal,* and the prepositional phrase that follows.

J because *Olympic* and *gold* are not coordinating adjectives that require a comma between them.

Question 17. **The best answer is C** because the verb *lagged* earlier in the sentence indicates that the qualifying time was slower than that of Ron Clarke. The word *behind* is the only choice that is idiomatic in this context ("lagged behind"), and it also creates the most logical sentence.

The best answer is NOT:

A because the verb *lagged* earlier in the sentence indicates that the qualifying time was slower than that of Ron Clarke. The word *above* does not fit logically with *lagging* (describing Mills's time as both "falling behind" and *above* is confusing). The phrase "lag above" is also not idiomatic.

B because the adverb *around* does not fit logically with the verb *lagged* earlier in the sentence. It is not clear what "lagged around" would mean in this context. "Lagged around" is also not idiomatic.

D because the preposition *from* does not pair logically with the verb *lagged*. The phrase "lagged from" is also not idiomatic.

Question 18. **The best answer is G** because placing Sentence 3 before Sentence 2 presents events in a logical, chronological order. For example, Sentence 3, which describes Mills as having a qualifying time that was one minute slower than the world record holder's, explains Sentence 2's assertion that Mills was a "long shot."

The best answer is NOT:

F because the information about the qualifying times of the runners is interrupted by the result of the Olympic race itself. The sentences create an unnecessary shift in time and are out of chronological order.

H because placing Sentence 2 before Sentence 1 presents a statement that purposefully contrasts with the information that Mills was a "long shot" before the essay has even established that Mills was unlikely to win. The transition word *however* would be unexplained if Sentence 2 were to start the paragraph.

J because this order places the information about Mills winning the gold medal before information about Mills qualifying for the race. Also, this order does not clearly establish up front who Mills is and what race is being discussed.

Question 19. The best answer is **A** because it correctly places commas around the appositive "an Oglala Lakota," which further identifies Mills.

The best answer is NOT:

B because commas are needed to separate the subject of the sentence, *Mills,* from the appositive, which further identifies the subject ("an Oglala Lakota").

C because it does not correctly set off the appositive "an Oglala Lakota" from the rest of the sentence.

D because it does not correctly set off the appositive "an Oglala Lakota" from the rest of the sentence.

Question 20. The best answer is **H** because it follows logically from the information given about Mills's desire to be a boxer and transitions to information that follows about Mills pursuing running.

The best answer is NOT:

F because despite extending the idea from the previous sentence, it does not transition to the next paragraph in the essay, which describes Mills's accomplishments as a runner.

G because despite extending the idea from the previous sentence, it does not transition to the next paragraph in the essay, which describes Mills's accomplishments as a runner. This choice also says that Mills did not make it as a boxer but leaves the reader wondering why.

J because it gives the reader more information about the various sports Mills tried, which doesn't connect with the information about boxing and running in the paragraph. It also doesn't connect well with the information in the next paragraph about Mills as a runner.

Question 21. The best answer is **C** because it clearly establishes that while in the Marines, Mills, rather than his talent, began racing again.

The best answer is NOT:

A because the phrase "races became part of his life again" is a misplaced modifier. This construction indicates that it's the races that are in the Marines, not Mills.

B because the phrase "his talent raced back to him" is a misplaced modifier. In this construction, it's Mills's talent that is in the Marines, which is illogical. Also, the idea that Mill's talent raced back to him is an awkward use of personification that's inconsistent with the tone of the rest of the essay.

D because the phrase "racing was in his life again" is a misplaced modifier. In this construction, it's *racing* that is in the Marines, which is illogical.

Question 22. The best answer is **H** because it refers directly to the 1964 Olympics, the time and place that were established in the first paragraph. It also refers to Mills's training before the Olympics, which effectively introduces the paragraph's focus on Mills's preparations.

The best answer is NOT:

F because it is vague and therefore a weak introduction to the paragraph. It also doesn't reference the topic of the first paragraph.

G because although it hints at Mills's success after the Olympics, it does not effectively introduce the paragraph, which focuses on Mills's preparations and the fact that Mills was a long shot.

J because it is vague and therefore a weak introduction. It also doesn't reference the topic of the first paragraph.

Question 23. The best answer is **A** because in the phrase "rather unknown," *rather* indicates that at least some people knew of Mills's talent before the 1964 Olympics.

The best answer is NOT:

B because the word *rather* in the sentence qualifies *unknown* by indicating that at least some people knew Mills was talented. Removing *rather* indicates Mills was completely unknown, but it does not lose a description of the approach Mills used to motivate himself.

C because removing the word *rather* in the sentence and stating that Mills was entirely unknown does not explain why Mills decided to run in the Olympics. The sentence merely states that Mills was determined to win after qualifying.

D because there is no indication in the sentence that Mills required more training because he was unknown or "rather unknown."

Question 24. **The best answer is H** because the word *undeterred* indicates that Mills did not allow the fact that the Olympic shoe sponsor did not send him shoes to prevent him from racing. Mills borrowed shoes so he can compete.

The best answer is NOT:

F because the word *luckily* implies that it was simple chance that Mills was able to borrow a pair of shoes, not that it was the result of Mills's commitment to winning.

G because the word *eventually* implies that at a later time Mills was able to borrow a pair of shoes. No indication of the role of commitment is indicated here. The word *eventually* is an indication of when, not how.

J because the word *concentrating* here is vague. The reader doesn't know if Mills is concentrating on the race or on borrowing the shoes. There is no suggestion of commitment on Mills's part to borrowing the shoes, merely the suggestion that he is concentrating on an unknown objective.

Question 25. **The best answer is D** because adding the sentence would interrupt the transition between Mills being ready to hit the starting line and the description of the actual race in the following paragraph.

The best answer is NOT:

A because the sentence adds information about only one gold medalist in the 1964 Olympics. Also, this statement is only tangentially related to the topic of the essay and interrupts the transition between Mills being ready to hit the starting line and the description of the actual race in the following paragraph.

B because the sentence is only tangentially related to the topic of the essay and interrupts the transition between Mills being ready to hit the starting line and the actual race described in the following paragraph.

C because it implies that the essay is focused on the US track team. The essay is focused only on one member of the US track team, Mills. Furthermore, only two US runners' shoes are mentioned, not the shoes of all the members as implied in this choice.

Question 26. The best answer is J because it is clear from the context of the essay that the people mentioned in the sentence are in first place and second place at the start of the last lap. Referring to Gammoudi and Clarke as *leaders* is the most logical, idiomatic choice given the sentence.

The best answer is NOT:

F because an *overseer* is one who has authority over others. It is clear from the context of the essay that the people mentioned in the sentence are on their last lap of a race. Therefore, they are runners in the race and not overseers who have authority over the other racers.

G because a *ruler* is one who has authority over others. It is clear from the context of the essay that the people mentioned in the sentence are on their last lap of a race. Therefore, they are runners in the race and not rulers who have authority over the other racers.

H because it is clear from the context of the essay that the people mentioned in the sentence are on their last lap of a race. Therefore, they are runners in the race rather than authorities who may be outside of the race itself.

Question 27. The best answer is A because "who had been in third place" is a clause that adds nonessential information to the main idea of the sentence. Interrupters or nonessential clauses are set off with commas.

The best answer is NOT:

B because two commas are needed to set off a nonessential clause from the rest of the sentence.

C because two commas are needed to set off a nonessential clause from the main sentence. Using one comma creates confusion here because it looks as if Mills is being directly addressed, and there is no antecedent for the pronoun *who*.

D because "who had been in third place" is nonessential information. It is a nonessential clause that needs to be set apart from the main idea of the sentence.

Question 28. The best answer is F because the use of the auxiliary verb *had* requires the use of the participle *run*.

The best answer is NOT:

G because the use of the auxiliary verb *has* requires the use of the participle *run*, not the past tense *ran*. The present *has* also is not appropriate here in the context. The race was completed.

H because the race is completed, requiring the use of the past tense. Using present tense here shifts the verb tense in the paragraph from past to present and creates an illogical sequence of time.

J because the use of the auxiliary verb *had* requires the use of the participle *run*, not the past tense *ran*.

Question 29. **The best answer is C** because **it has already been stated that Mills won the race, beating Gammoudi and Clarke, in the same paragraph as the underlined portion. The information is not needed for emphasis and is therefore unnecessarily repetitious.**

The best answer is NOT:

A because who Mills finished ahead of is not mentioned in the opening paragraph of the essay. Therefore, the underlined portion does not connect in a meaningful way to the opening paragraph of the essay.

B because it has already been stated that Mills won (and therefore beat the former leaders in the race). It merely repeats the fact unnecessarily, without adding additional details.

D because the information is repetitious and not needed, not because it strays from the main point.

Passage III

Question 30. **The best answer is H** because placing a period after the word *unfolds* separates the two independent clauses into two complete sentences.

The best answer is NOT:

F because placing a comma after the word *unfolds* creates a comma splice between two independent clauses.

G because placing a comma after the word *boy* indicates that the movie scene unfolds a boy, which doesn't make sense. It also could be read that the scene, not the boy, is out exploring.

J because a semicolon or a period is needed to separate the independent clauses. Without punctuation, the sentence becomes a run-on, and the logic of the sentence is hard to follow.

Question 31. **The best answer is D** because the sentence clearly introduces information about what draws an audience into a movie scene, which sets up the examples in the next sentence and introduces the topic of the essay.

The best answer is NOT:

A because the pronoun *that* has no clear antecedent, and the expression does not work logically with the rest of the sentence.

B because the expression "for the time being" provides a vague sense of how long the audience might be drawn into a scene by sound, but this information is irrelevant to the rest of the sentence and the essay.

C because *nevertheless* indicates that the information provided in this sentence contrasts with information provided earlier in the essay. This sentence does not, however, provide a contrast; it introduces new information about what draws audience members into scenes like this.

Question 32. **The best answer is F** because the verb *swept* implies that the action was swift and dramatic.

The best answer is NOT:

G because it suggests that silent movies had a gradual exit. Talkies "invited the beginning of what would one day . . ." implies that the transition from silent movies occurred over time, not swiftly or dramatically.

H because it does not mention silent movies or the role that talkies played in their demise.

J because it does not mention silent movies or the role that talkies played in their demise.

Question 33. **The best answer is C** because the pronoun *who* correctly functions as the subject of the verb *figured* (*who* refers to the predicate noun *Foley*).

The best answer is NOT:

A because *whom* functions as the object of a verb or a preposition (the person or thing that receives the action of the verb). Because the action "figured out" in this sentence is done *by* Foley, not *to* Foley, the subject pronoun *who* is required, not the objective pronoun *whom*.

B because *whom* functions as the object of a verb or a preposition (the person or thing that receives the action of the verb). Because the action "figured out" in this sentence is done *by* Foley, not *to* Foley, the subject pronoun *who* is required, not the objective pronoun *whom*. The reflexive pronoun *himself* becomes part of the noun that *who* refers to (Foley himself).

D because the pronoun *he* creates a run-on sentence (two independent clauses are joined without punctuation).

Question 34. The best answer is H because it completes the sentence by clearly and grammatically connecting the act of squeezing a sock of cornstarch with its result ("produces a sound like that of footsteps in the snow").

The best answer is NOT:

F because the phrase "a sound like that of . . ." dangles in the sentence, seeming to describe cornstarch as the sound of footsteps in the snow. The sentence is also incomplete; it doesn't state what Foley figured out about squeezing a bag full of cornstarch.

G because the comma after cornstarch and the pronoun *which* indicates that "which makes a sound like that of footsteps in the snow" is an appositive that describes cornstarch itself, not the act of squeezing a sock full of cornstarch. This results in an incomplete sentence.

J because although "to get" connects the phrase "a sound like that of footsteps in the snow" to the act of squeezing a sock full of cornstarch, the sentence as constructed does not represent a complete thought. (*What* did Foley figure out about squeezing a sock full of cornstarch to get a sound like walking in the snow?)

Question 35. The best answer is C because an *illusion* is perceiving something in a way that misinterprets the thing's true nature. Foley is misleading the audience into perceiving the sound of the cane as many people walking.

The best answer is NOT:

A because an *allusion* is a reference to a historical event in literature or a reference to something in passing. Foley is not creating a reference to history here or a reference to something in passing. The context of the sentence indicates that Foley wants to create the impression that people are walking on foot.

B because *elude* means to evade. Foley is using a cane to create the impression that people are walking on foot, not to avoid people on foot.

D because an *allusion* is a reference to a historical event in literature or a reference to something in passing. Foley is not creating a reference to history here or a reference to something in passing. The context of the sentence indicates that Foley wants to create the impression that people are walking on foot.

Question 36. The best answer is **J** because it results in a clear, logical sentence. *Eventually* functions as an adverb modifying the verb *earned*. This indicates when Foley earned the status of Hollywood legend.

The best answer is NOT:

F because the use of the word *that* in the underlined portion creates an incomplete sentence that lacks a clear subject and verb.

G because it creates an incoherent sentence that lacks a clear subject and verb. It is also unnecessarily wordy.

H because it creates an incoherent sentence that lacks a clear subject and a clear connection between the subject and verb. The phrase "that eventually even so" is also vague and unnecessarily wordy.

Question 37. The best answer is **D** because **ending the sentence with information about Foley's status as a "Hollywood legend" creates a logical transition to the next paragraph, which further explains the process Foley pioneered.**

The best answer is NOT:

A because this information is not directly related to the discussion of Foley's contributions, and it unnecessarily states a fact that has already been clearly established (movies with sound had not been around for long).

B because it unnecessarily repeats information provided earlier about how Foley used a cane as a prop.

C because the fact that sound editing takes place after the action has been filmed has already been explained in the first sentence of the paragraph, "sounds are recorded after the cameras have stopped rolling."

Question 38. The best answer is **F** because "arises from" means to originate from a source or to begin to occur or exist. The Foley process was created in response to the need for absolute quiet when capturing dialogue. (Foley artists add in the "sound clutter of real life" later.)

The best answer is NOT:

G because "aroused from" means to evoke or awaken. "The need for 'Foley'" was not evoked or awakened by the sound clutter of real life; the need didn't even exist until sound was introduced in movies.

H because without the preposition *from*, the sentence suggests that Foley was the source of the "sound clutter of real life," which is illogical.

J because the singular subject "The need for 'Foley'" requires the singular verb *arises*. The form *arise* is used with plural words. The sentence is also lacking the preposition *from* between *arise* and "the sound."

Question 39. **The best answer is D** because the underlined portion draws a distinction between a Foley artist and a sound artist. This reduces the chance that a reader will assume that the terms "sound technician" and "Foley artist" refer to the same role.

The best answer is NOT:

A because the underlined portion indicates that there is a distinction between a Foley artist and a sound artist without explaining the role of either occupation.

B because the underlined portion indicates that there is a distinction between a Foley artist and a sound artist without explaining the origin of the term "Foley artist." The origin of the term is explained in the first sentence of the second paragraph of the essay.

C because the underlined portion indicates that there is a distinction between a Foley artist and a sound artist without indicating the degree to which a sound technician is influenced by the work of John Foley.

Question 40. **The best answer is J** because it continues the subject-verb pattern established in the paragraph: "An airplane flying, a phone ringing, a door slamming."

The best answer is NOT:

F because it breaks the subject-verb pattern established in the paragraph. Only a subject is provided: "An airplane flying, a phone ringing, a door _____?"

G because the clause, "which is not part of the scene," is wordy and unnecessary. This choice also breaks the subject-verb pattern by using the word *slamming* as an adjective, not a verb.

H because it breaks the subject-verb pattern established in the paragraph. Only a subject is provided: "An airplane flying, a phone ringing, a sound of a door."

Question 41. **The best answer is B** because it uses two dashes to correctly set off a nonessential phrase.

The best answer is NOT:

A because it incorrectly sets off a nonessential phrase with a colon and a dash.

C because it incorrectly sets off a nonessential phrase with a comma and a dash.

D because the phrase "a small room with a screen, a microphone, and countless props" interrupts the main clause in the sentence and must be set off with a pair of commas or dashes.

Question 42. The best answer is F because *untold* means too many to count or measure. Here, the amount of money being saved is emphasized. It is so much that the actual amount is unknown.

The best answer is NOT:

G because the sentence implies that the movie's budget was cut drastically, which was positive. The word *unspeakable* suggests that the cut was something negative, which is illogical given the context of the essay.

H because it adds an illogical personification to the essay. To describe the money itself as *speechless* implies that at other times the money spoke.

J because the movie's budget was cut by thousands of dollars, a limited sum. *Endless* implies that the amount that was cut from the movie was infinite.

Question 43. The best answer is C because "an army's worth" is nonessential and therefore needs to be set off with commas. The commas clarify that "an army's worth" refers to the actors and horses.

The best answer is NOT:

A because "an army's worth" is nonessential and needs to be set off with punctuation. Without punctuation, it's difficult to determine who would be headed overseas.

B because it results in a comma splice between two independent clauses.

D because "an army's worth" is nonessential and needs to be set off with punctuation. Without punctuation, the sentence is ungrammatical and illogical.

Question 44. The best answer is G because the sentence emphasizes how Foley's work impacted on both the filmmakers and the audience. It reveals that the actors and horses were able to stay home rather than embark on an expensive journey and that the audience didn't know the difference between the actual sounds of a battlefield and the sounds created using Foley's techniques.

The best answer is NOT:

F because the sentence does not indicate that the audience ever learned about Foley's work.

H because the sentence does not mention the movie's director; therefore, there's no shift in focus from Foley to the director.

J because the sentence does not argue that his work was insignificant to the public; it just states the audience wasn't aware that the sounds were not the actual sounds of a battlefield.

Passage IV

Question 45. The best answer is C because **the comma after the word University correctly separates the introductory clause "in her lab at Princeton University" from the sentence's main clause.**

The best answer is NOT:

A because if the description "molecular biologist" is treated as nonessential and set aside by commas, it is unclear whether it describes Princeton University or Bonnie Bassler.

B because it incorrectly separates with a comma the subject "Bonnie Bassler" from the verb *leans.*

D because a comma is needed after the word *University* in order to separate the introductory clause "in her lab at Princeton University" from the sentence's main clause.

Question 46. The best answer is J because **it correctly uses a comma to separate the main idea of the sentence from an aside that provides additional details.**

The best answer is NOT:

F because a semicolon is used to combine two independent clauses. "Her face illuminated by an aquamarine glow" is not an independent clause.

G because the coordinating conjunction *and* must be preceded by a comma in order to correctly join the two independent clauses.

H because the comma between *dishes* and "her face" must be followed by a coordinating conjunction such as *and* in order to avoid a comma splice.

Question 47. The best answer is C because the comma after *bacteria* paired with the comma after *glow* accurately signals that the nonessential phrase "caused by a particular species of bacteria" describes "the glow."

The best answer is NOT:

A because the prepositional phrase "of bacteria" modifies the word *species.* Prepositional phrases cannot be separated from what they modify by a comma.

B because the prepositional phrase "of bacteria" is essential to the meaning of the sentence and should not be set aside with commas, nor should "of bacteria" be separated from the noun it modifies, *species.*

D because a comma is needed after *bacteria* in order to enclose the entire nonessential phrase "caused by a particular species of bacteria" in commas, signaling that this phrase describes "the glow."

Question 48. The best answer is **H** because it correctly uses the plural possessive form of *researcher*, resulting in a sentence that is both understandable and grammatical.

The best answer is NOT:

F because the text "and their discoveries" requires the noun *researchers* to be nonpossessive. As worded, this sentence describes Bassler as being intrigued not only with the researchers' inventions but also with the researchers themselves.

G because the wording in this option requires *researcher* to be nonpossessive. Also, the singular possessive form *researcher's* does not agree in number with the plural pronoun *their*.

J because as worded, the sentence requires a possessive form of *researcher*. Note that the words "and their," found in two of the other choices, have been removed. The sentence now states that Bassler was intrigued only by the researchers' discoveries, not by the researchers themselves. Only a possessive form of *researcher* in this context would be grammatical.

Question 49. The best answer is **C** because **the phrase "a luminescent marine bacteria" is an appositive renaming *Vibrio fischeri*. This phrase is nonessential and must be set off with a comma.**

The best answer is NOT:

A because it incorrectly uses a semicolon to separate the main part of an independent clause from an appositive phrase. A semicolon is used to join independent clauses.

B because the phrase that follows "a luminescent marine bacteria" is nonessential to the sentence and must be set off with a comma. The words "which is" are also unnecessarily wordy.

D because the phrase "a luminescent marine bacteria" is an appositive renaming *Vibrio fischeri*. This phrase is nonessential and must be set off with a comma.

ENGLISH • PRACTICE TEST 2 • EXPLANATORY ANSWERS

Question 50. The best answer is J because **the present tense** *allows* **is consistent with the use of the present tense in this paragraph.**

The best answer is NOT:

F because it shifts the established verb tense in the paragraph from present to past. The sentence uses present tense verbs to describe the actions of the bacteria: they *assemble, begin,* and *release.* The use of the past tense *allowed* here would create an illogical pattern, with one step in the process of glowing inexplicably happening in the past.

G because the use of the past conditional tense in this series of present tense descriptions suggests an essential step in the glowing may or may not have occurred in the past. The bacteria must, however, *hear* the message to release a high concentration of autoinducer.

H because the shift from the present to the present perfect tense results in an ambiguous, confusing sequence of events.

Question 51. The best answer is A because **a comma is needed to separate the dependent clause from the independent clause in the sentence.**

The best answer is NOT:

B because dashes are used to indicate an abrupt break in thought. There is not an abrupt change in thought between the dependent clause and the independent clause in this sentence; the clauses express a sequence of events that are closely related.

C because it creates a sentence fragment. The words "once the bacteria have released a high enough concentration of autoinducer" create a dependent clause that must be attached to an independent clause to make a complete sentence.

D because it creates a run-on sentence by not using a comma between the dependent clause that begins the sentence and the independent clause that follows.

Question 52. The best answer is G because **it logically indicates that after some time, Bassler discovered a similar process of glowing occurring in a related species of bacteria.**

The best answer is NOT:

F because "On the contrary" signals a contrast. There is no contrast between the discovery of the process of glowing in one species of bacteria and the discovery of a similar process in another species of bacteria.

H because the fact that Bassler made an important scientific discovery suggests that this is a significant event. *Ordinarily* suggests that the discovery was common and ongoing. This *ongoing* discovery does not work with the simple past tense verb *found,* which indicates that the discovery was a one-time event.

J because the word *namely* is used to introduce a specific example of or specific, detailed information about something that has already been discussed. Bassler's *discovery* of the process of glowing in another species of bacteria has not yet been mentioned in the essay; therefore, the use of this transition word is not logical.

Question 53. The best answer is A because **the words "related bacterial species" in the underlined portion are essential to the meaning of the sentence and should not be set off by commas.**

The best answer is NOT:

B because the words *related* and *bacterial* are not coordinating adjectives. A comma between the words indicates they are coordinating and can be reversed without affecting the meaning, but if these two words were reversed the sentence would not make sense. Also, the words "bacterial species" are essential to the sentence and should not be set off by commas.

C because the words *related* and *bacterial* are not coordinating adjectives. The order of the words cannot be reversed, and a comma between the words would incorrectly indicate that they can be.

D because no comma is needed between the word *called* and *Vibrio harveyi.* In this case, there is no need for a comma between a verb and its object.

Question 54. The best answer is J because **it conveys that bacteria can communicate with other bacteria nearby. This choice is not repetitive and does not create an odd or informal image of bacteria within the paragraph.**

The best answer is NOT:

F because it is overly informal for the academic tone of the essay.

G because it is unnecessarily repetitive. Both *neighboring* and *proximity* mean "nearby."

H because it is unnecessarily repetitive. *Locale* means "in the area." To say "surrounding locale" is to repeat the concept of "in the area."

Question 55. The best answer is D because *them* is an object pronoun, a pronoun that refers to a person or thing that receives the action of a verb. A demonstrative pronoun, a pronoun that points to a specific thing, is needed in this part of the sentence to refer back to the word *species*.

The best answer is NOT:

A because "the kinds" refers back to the bacteria that live in humans.

B because *species* clearly refers to a type of bacteria that live in humans.

C because *those* has a clear antecedent in the sentence: *species*.

Question 56. The best answer is F because **the verb form *communicate* correctly agrees with the plural subject "virulent strains" in the sentence.**

The best answer is NOT:

G because *has* is a singular verb, which does not agree with the plural subject "virulent strains."

H because in this sentence *is* is a singular verb, which does not agree with the plural subject "virulent strains."

J because in this sentence *communicates* is a singular verb, which does not agree with the plural subject "virulent strains."

Question 57. The best answer is D because **the words "these bacteria" help the reader understand that the bacteria in the preceding sentence are the bacteria being discussed in this sentence. "These bacteria" also establishes the subject without being redundant.**

The best answer is NOT:

A because it unnecessarily repeats the idea that the bacteria are "disease spreading." The reader has already been told that the bacteria are *virulent,* and this idea is further established later in this sentence with "spreading disease."

B because it has already been established in the paragraph and in the essay that Bassler has studied the bacteria. To repeat the idea here is unnecessary and redundant.

C because it has already been established at the end of the preceding sentence that the bacteria are found in humans. To repeat the idea here is unnecessary and redundant.

Question 58. The best answer is G because **it correctly uses the object pronoun** *her* **as the object of the verb** *enable.* **The words "her team" also clearly refer to the other scientists with whom Bassler is working.**

The best answer is NOT:

F because an object pronoun is required to receive the action of the verb *enable.* The pronoun *she* functions as a subject, not an object.

H because *herself* is a reflexive pronoun, which is ungrammatical in this sentence. The context calls for an object pronoun (*her*). Also, the pronoun *them* has no clear antecedent.

J because the pronoun *them* has no clear antecedent.

Question 59. The best answer is B because **the information would clearly communicate why Bassler and her team study bacteria and what they hope the result of disrupting quorum sensing will be for humans.**

The best answer is NOT:

A because the paragraph has already clearly established that Bassler is working to understand "bacteria found in humans." The proposed information would not serve this function.

C because it is not important to the meaning of the sentence for the reader to know which particular strains of the bacteria attack humans' immune systems.

D because the focus of the essay was on Bassler's discovery of the fact that bacteria in humans use quorum processing, not on how Bassler and her team plan to disrupt that processing. This information would be an inappropriate conclusion because it would require more explanation.

Passage V

Question 60. The best answer is G because *subterranean* refers to something below the surface of the earth, and *routes* refers to different lines the subway system runs. This is a logical and precise choice of words given the context.

The best answer is NOT:

F because it suggests the subway is *creeping* beneath the ground, which doesn't make sense on either a literal or a metaphorical level. The word *vicinity,* meaning "nearby," is also an odd word choice; the system doesn't exist nearby but within the city limits.

H because the word *submerged* typically refers to something pushed below the surface of water. The London subway is not located entirely beneath water, nor does the passage suggest that it is. This description introduces an inaccuracy.

J because the subway is described in the essay as being below the city streets, rather than in alleys that are "low down," which is a vague and confusing description.

Question 61. The best answer is D because **the essay begins by establishing that a system of mapping was needed after the subway system was built. It follows logically that the next sentence would be about the early mapping system, so no transition word is needed.**

The best answer is NOT:

A because the words "as a result" are not logical here. Building the subway did not require the early maps to "superimpose the subway lines over standard maps of London." This is just the technique these maps happened to use.

B because the information that this word introduces is *not* one example of many different types of early maps that were developed; it is the only type that the passage discusses. Therefore, "to provide an example" is incorrect.

C because *secondly* indicates that what follows is the second event, idea, or step in a process or series. However, the information provided in the paragraph is not framed as a series (there is no *firstly*). The transition word *secondly* creates a logical inconsistency.

Question 62. The best answer is H because *indecipherable* indicates that the maps were **not able to be read at all, suggesting the highest degree of failure for a map—it was unusable.**

The best answer is NOT:

F because *obscured* suggests that the routes were difficult, but not impossible, to read. It does not eliminate the possibility that the map could be read and used by subway riders.

G because *disappointing* does not suggest the "highest degree of failure." It indicates that the maps did not live up to expectations but does not say they were not able to serve their function.

J because "didn't fully capture" the subway indicates that the maps at least partially captured the routes.

Question 63. The best answer is C because **this information is only tangentially related to the information in the paragraph. The focus of the first paragraph is on the method of mapping the subway that was devised in the 1800s. Details about the modern subway system distract from the focus on these early maps.**

The best answer is NOT:

A because providing details about the modern subway is not essential information in a paragraph that focuses on early subway mapping systems. Adding the sentence would also interrupt the transition from a discussion of the first attempts to map the subway to the discussion of a later (more effective) method of mapping.

B because the modern name of the subway does not suggest the need for a clear, accurate map. Such a map already exists, according to the essay (thanks to Beck).

D because the first paragraph does not focus on recent maps of the London Underground; it is about the mapping of the Underground in the 1800s.

Question 64. The best answer is G because **the stylistic outline is being compared to the sketch. The construction "more . . . than" works syntactically and creates a clear, precise comparison.**

The best answer is NOT:

F because *besides* means "other than" or "in addition to," neither of which makes sense within the sentence. The "more a" at the beginning of the sentence does not connect logically with *besides*.

H because *instead* creates a sentence with faulty syntax. The construction "more . . . instead" does suggest a comparison, but the preposition *of* would be needed after *instead* to avoid faulty sentence structure. A "more . . . than" construction captures the main idea more precisely.

J because *into* here suggests a transformation from one thing to another. The words "more . . . than" at the beginning of the sentence signal that the sentence will make a comparison, not describe a transformation.

Question 65. The best answer is C because **the beginning of the sentence contains an introductory phrase that requires a comma between it and the main part of the sentence.**

The best answer is NOT:

A because the phrase before the semicolon lacks a verb and therefore is not an independent clause. Semicolons are used to separate independent clauses; a semicolon is not needed and is incorrect.

B because the conjunction *and* suggests that two ideas are being coordinated. Here, there is no coordination between two independent clauses. The beginning of the sentence is an introductory phrase that sets up a comparison to follow.

D because it creates a fragment by placing a period after the introductory phrase that begins the sentence. This phrase lacks a verb and cannot be an independent clause.

Question 66. The best answer is J because **it correctly combines the two adjective phrases "grid-like structure" and "color-coded routes" with the conjunction *and*, making it clear that these were both features of Beck's map.**

The best answer is NOT:

F because it creates an ambiguity that makes the meaning of the sentence unclear: Did the map have a color-coded route, or was it the grid-like structures that had a color-coded route? In the context of the sentence, the phrase "having also" creates a faulty construction.

G because it creates an ambiguity that makes the meaning of the sentence unclear: Did the map have a color-coded route, or was it the grid-like structures that had a color-coded route? It also creates a structurally faulty sentence.

H because it creates an ambiguity that makes the meaning of the sentence unclear: Did the map have a color-coded route, or was it the grid-like structures that had a color-coded route? It also creates a structurally faulty sentence.

Question 67. The best answer is A because "to show" makes the first clause in this sentence a dependent introductory clause, which creates a sentence with grammatically appropriate subordination.

The best answer is NOT:

B because "would show" creates a comma splice by making the introductory phrase at the beginning of the sentence an independent clause.

C because "had shown" creates a comma splice by transforming an introductory phrase into an independent clause.

D because *showed* creates a comma splice by making the introductory phrase at the beginning of the sentence an independent clause.

Question 68. The best answer is F because **it provides a specific example of how Beck simplified the map by deleting the references to the city streets that had obscured some of the Underground routes.**

The best answer is NOT:

G because it merely indicates Beck's annoyance at the curving lines on the map. It does not provide an example of how Beck simplified the existing maps for subway passengers.

H because it indicates that Beck knew the maps had to be simple, but it does not give an example of how Beck created his "simplest possible schema."

J because it indicates the map's iconic status, but it does not provide an example of the map's simple schema.

Question 69. The best answer is B because to *increase* means to become larger or greater in size, amount, or number. This is the correct word given the context, because it's the number of riders (ridership) the Transport Board hoped to increase.

The best answer is NOT:

A because *rise* is an intransitive verb that means to move upward. The subway ridership itself would not literally move upward; rather, the number of riders would increase.

C because *enlarge* means to increase in size rather than number. The subway ridership would not increase in physical size; rather, the number of riders would increase.

D because *upend* means to cause something to be upside down or to fall down. The number of subway riders is increasing; the group is not being turned upside down or caused to fall down.

Question 70. The best answer is G because **"the board" makes it clear that it was the Transport Board that was desperate to increase subway ridership and revenues.**

The best answer is NOT:

F because as written, the sentence indicates it was the limited number of copies that were "willing to try anything to increase subway ridership and therefore revenues." The sentence fails to name "the board" as the group that is printing the copies, which makes this misreading possible.

H because as written, the sentence indicates it was the copies that were "willing to try anything to increase subway ridership and therefore revenues." The sentence fails to name "the board" as the group that is printing the copies, which makes this misreading possible.

J because as written, the sentence indicates it was the copies that were "willing to try anything to increase subway ridership and therefore revenues." The sentence fails to name "the board" as the group that is printing the copies, which makes this misreading possible. In addition, the lack of a verb in this phrase creates a sentence fragment.

Question 71. The best answer is B because Sentence 1 discusses the fact that the Transport Board initially resisted the map, and Sentence 5 explains why the board resisted the map. This is a logical way to present this information and provides a smooth transition to the rest of the paragraph.

The best answer is NOT:

A because Sentence 5, which explains why the Transport Board resisted Beck's map, is out of place in the middle of a discussion about the map's success.

C because placing Sentence 5 after Sentence 2 breaks the logical progression from the board's resistance to the map to the reasons for the resistance. This placement is also not logical because it mentions the creation of copies of the map before mention of the board's initial resistance to the idea.

D because placing Sentence 5 after Sentence 3 breaks the logical progression from the board's resistance to the map to the reasons for the resistance. This placement is also not logical because it explains the board's resistance to the map after mentioning the later copying of the map and the map's success.

Question 72. The best answer is H because *its* is a singular possessive pronoun referring to the word *map*. Because map is singular, the pronoun and antecedent agree in number. Also, a possessive is needed because the sentence is referring to the basic elements that are features of the map.

The best answer is NOT:

F because *it's* is a contraction for "it is." Saying that "he retained it is basic elements" creates a nonsensical, ungrammatical sentence. At this point, the sentence also requires a possessive pronoun to refer back to the map. The contraction *it's* is not possessive.

G because *their* is a plural possessive pronoun. The antecedent of the pronoun in the sentence is *map*, which is singular. A pronoun and its antecedent must agree in number.

J because *its'* is not the correct possessive form of *it*. The correct possessive for it is *its*, without an apostrophe.

Question 73. The best answer is C because **a comma should not separate any of the elements in the noun phrase "approach to mapping," nor should there be a comma between the noun phrase and the verb remains.**

The best answer is NOT:

A because a comma should not separate the noun phrase "approach to mapping" from the verb *remains.*

B because a comma should not separate the adjective *diagrammatic* from the noun phrase "approach to mapping." The comma separating this phrase from the verb *remains* is also incorrect.

D because the comma separates the prepositional phrase "to mapping" from the noun *approach,* which incorrectly breaks up the noun phrase that serves as the subject of the sentence: "[Beck's] approach to mapping."

Question 74. The best answer is J because **it clearly and concisely identifies Beck's mapping method as what other urban transit maps model. This also works as a suitable conclusion for the sentence and the essay because it is a fitting description of Beck's approach as described in the essay.**

The best answer is NOT:

F because the use of the pronoun *this* creates an ambiguous pronoun reference. *This* could refer to the approach, to the field of information, to the map's basic elements, to the world, and so on, which makes the meaning of the sentence unclear.

G because "this means" creates an ambiguous pronoun reference. This option is also redundant because it has already been stated that Beck's approach is "standard in the field."

H because this option is redundant; it has already been stated that Beck's approach is "deceptively simple."

Question 75. The best answer is B because it places the added sentence, which explains why Beck left out the actual distances between points, immediately after the sentence that reveals Beck left out the distances. This creates a logical progression from Beck's decision to the reasoning behind his decision.

The best answer is NOT:

A because Point A occurs during a discussion of early versions of subway maps. The added sentence refers to Beck's maps, which have not been introduced yet. The sentence does not make sense without the information about Beck and his mapping that are provided in Paragraph 2.

C because the sentence immediately before Point C refers to the refinements that Beck made to his map after it had already become a success. The essay makes it clear that even Beck's first maps left out actual distances; therefore, leaving out the distances was not a refinement but part of the original diagram. The added sentence does not logically fit at Point C because this placement suggests Beck's reasons for not including the distances are related to later refinements to the map.

D because the sentence immediately before Point D discusses how Beck's approach to mapping has been widely adopted. The added sentence, however, explains a specific statement made about the map's features in Paragraph 2. This placement for the added sentence not only puts the sentence too far away from the point it is meant to explain but also it interferes with the last paragraph's attempt to describe the broader impact Beck's map has had on the world.

MATHEMATICS • PRACTICE TEST 2 • EXPLANATORY ANSWERS

Question 1. The correct answer is **C.** The area of a rectangle is equal to the product of its width and length, $A = WL$. Because the top surface of the rectangular table has an area of 100 square feet and a width of 5 feet, $100 = 5L$ and $20 = L$. If you chose **E**, you may have set up the equation incorrectly and calculated the area for a length of 100 feet and a width of 5 feet.

Question 2. The correct answer is **J.** The number of possible outcomes (that is, the total number of bills in the wallet) is $2 + 9 + 5 = 16$, and the number of favorable outcomes (choosing a twenty-dollar bill) is 5. The probability of a favorable outcome is equal to $\frac{\text{the number of favorable outcomes}}{\text{the number of possible outcomes}}$. So, the probability of a twenty-dollar bill being randomly selected from the wallet is $\frac{5}{16}$. If you chose **F**, you could have overlooked how many possible favorable outcomes there are.

Question 3. The correct answer is **E.** In order to determine how many combinations of clown costumes Elmo can make, multiply the number of items in each category that makes up a complete costume (noses, pairs of lips, and wigs), $4 \cdot 3 \cdot 2 = 24$. If you chose **B**, you may have added the number of items Elmo has in each category to find the total number of items rather than the number of combinations of items that make a complete costume.

Question 4. The correct answer is **F.** The remaining materials for care packages are 30 pens (3 boxes with 10 pens each, $3 \cdot 10 = 30$), which can fill 6 care packages at 5 pens each ($\frac{30}{5} = 6$); 20 notebooks (4 boxes with 5 notebooks each, $4 \cdot 5 = 20$), which can fill 10 care packages at 2 notebooks each ($\frac{20}{2} = 10$); 24 envelopes (2 boxes with 12 envelopes each, $2 \cdot 12 = 24$), which can fill 8 care packages at 3 envelopes each ($\frac{24}{3} = 8$); 84 cookies, which can fill 7 care packages at 12 cookies each ($\frac{84}{12} = 7$); and 45 bars of candy (4.5 boxes with 10 candy bars each, $4.5 \cdot 10 = 45$), which can fill 9 care packages at 5 candy bars each ($\frac{45}{5} = 9$). Because the remaining pens can create the least number of care packages, 6, that is the additional number of complete care packages Esteban and his family can make with the remaining materials. If you chose **J**, you may have failed to realize that every care package must be complete.

Question 5. The correct answer is **C.** A right circular cone with a height of 28 inches and a radius of 6 inches would have an approximate volume of 1,056 cubic inches: $V = \frac{1}{3}\pi r^2 h = \frac{1}{3}\left(\frac{22}{7}\right)(6^2)(28) = 1{,}056$.

Question 6. The correct answer is **G.** Because $\overline{AD}$ is perpendicular to $\overline{BE}$, the measure of $\angle BEA$ is 90°. The measure of $\angle ABE$ is 62° because the sum of the measures of the angles in a triangle is 180°, and $180° - 28° - 90° = 62°$. Because $\angle ABE$ and $\angle CBE$ create a straight line, the measure of $\angle CBE$ is 118° because $180° - 62° = 118°$.

MATHEMATICS • PRACTICE TEST 2 • EXPLANATORY ANSWERS

Question 7. **The correct answer is B.** The sum of the two expressions can be found algebraically by combining like terms, $(0.1x^2 + 3x + 80) + (0.5x^2 - 2x + 60) = (0.1x^2 + 0.5x^2) + (3x - 2x) + (80 + 60) = 0.6x^2 + x + 140$. If you chose **A**, you may have calculated the difference of the expressions.

Question 8. **The correct answer is H.** The slope-intercept form, $y = mx + b$ where m is the slope and b is the y-intercept, can be used to write the equation of a line that represents the relationship between y and x. The slope of the line that represents the relationship between d and t is the rate at which the cart is rolling, which is $\frac{\text{the change in distance}}{\text{the change in time}} = \frac{30-15}{5-0} = 3$. When you substitute the value of the slope into the slope-intercept form and use d and t in place of y and x, you get $d = 3t + b$. To determine b, the d-intercept of the line, substitute a given ordered pair in the table for d and t in the equation and solve for b. $15 = 3(0) + b \Leftrightarrow 15 = b$. Therefore the equation that represents the relationship between d and t is $d = 3t + 15$. If you chose **J**, you could have mixed up the values of the slope and d-intercept in the equation.

Question 9. **The correct answer is C.** The original price of the pants was $40 but Dmitry bought them at the discounted price of $30 which is $10 less than the original price because $40 - $30 = $10. The percent of the discount is $\left(\frac{10}{40}\right)(100) = 25\%$ of the original price. If you chose **E**, you could have calculated the percent the discounted price is of the original price.

Question 10. **The correct answer is G.** The absolute value of a number is its magnitude. The magnitude of -6 is 6 and the magnitude of $(7 - 41)$ is 34. Therefore, $|-6| - |7 - 41| = 6 - 34 = -28$. If you chose **J**, you may have added 6 and 34.

Question 11. **The correct answer is C.** The total number of shares of stock owned by Samantha, Nyla, and Jerry is $70 + 50 + 40 = 160$. The value of each single share of stock is $\frac{\text{combined value of the shares of stock}}{\text{total number of the shares of stock}} = \frac{\$6,880}{160 \text{ shares}} = \$43$ per share. Therefore, the value of the shares of stock that Samantha owns is $\$43 \times 70 = \$3,010$. If you chose **A**, you may have divided the combined value of the shares of stock by the number of shares of stock owned by Samantha only and rounded to the nearest dollar: $\frac{6,880}{70} \approx 98$. If you chose **B**, you may have erroneously computed $43 \times 7 = 301$. If you chose **D**, you may have thought the value of the shares of stock that Samantha owns is 70% of the combined value of the shares of stock or $0.70(6,880) = 4,816$. If you chose **E**, you may divided the combined value of the shares of stock by the number of shares of stock owned by Nyla and Jerry and then multiplied by the value of the shares of stock that Samantha owns: $\frac{6,880}{50+40} \cdot 70 \approx 5,351$.

Question 12. The correct answer is G. Customers who are at least 18 years of age are represented on the number line by a closed dot on 18 to indicate 18 is part of the solution and shading of the number line to the right of 18. Customers who are less than 30 years of age are represented on the number line by an open dot on 30 to indicate 30 is NOT part of the solution and shading of the number line to the left of 30. As a result, the number line that illustrates the required age range of at least 18 but less than 30 years of age has a line segment with a closed dot on18, shading between 18 and 30, and an open dot on 30. If you chose **F**, you chose the number line that represents customers who were between 18 and 30 years of age, inclusive. If you chose **H**, you chose the number line that represents customers who were 30 years of age or younger. If you chose **J**, you chose the number line that represents customers who were younger than 30 years of age. If you chose **K**, you chose the number line that represents customers who were younger than 18 years of age or older than 30 years of age.

Question 13. The correct answer is D. The Triangle Proportionality Theorem states that if a line parallel to one side of a triangle intersects the other two sides of the triangle, then the line divides these two sides proportionally. Therefore, because $\overline{DE} \cdot \overline{FG}$, then $\frac{AD}{DF} = \frac{AE}{EG} \Leftrightarrow \frac{6}{5} = \frac{12}{EG} \Leftrightarrow 6(EG) = 5(12) \Leftrightarrow 6(EG) = 60 \Leftrightarrow EG = 10$. Similarly, because $\overline{FG} \cdot \overline{BC}$, then $\frac{AF}{FB} = \frac{AG}{GC} \Leftrightarrow \frac{6+5}{4} = \frac{12+10}{GC} \Leftrightarrow \frac{11}{4} = \frac{22}{GC} \Leftrightarrow 11(GC) = 4(22) \Leftrightarrow 11(GC) = 88 \Leftrightarrow GC = 8$. Thus, $AC = AE + EG + GC = 12 + 10 + 8 = 30$. If you chose **B**, you may have found the sum of EG and GC only: $10 + 8 = 18$. If you chose **A**, you may have multiplied the sum of EG and GC by $\frac{AD}{AE}$: $18\left(\frac{6}{12}\right) = 9$. If you chose **E**, you may have multiplied the sum of EG and GC by $\frac{AE}{AD}$: $18\left(\frac{12}{6}\right) = 36$. If you chose **C**, you may have added AE, DF and FB: $12 + 5 + 4 = 21$.

Question 14. The correct answer is G. First, set up an inequality with the closest perfect square integer values below and above the integer 50: $49 < 50 < 64$. Next, take the square root of all three parts: $\sqrt{49} < \sqrt{50} < \sqrt{64} \Leftrightarrow 7 < \sqrt{50} < 8$. Finally, divide all three parts by 2: $\frac{7}{2} < \frac{\sqrt{50}}{2} < \frac{8}{2} \Leftrightarrow 3.5 < \frac{\sqrt{50}}{2} < 4$. Now, $\frac{\sqrt{50}}{2}$ is greater than 3.5 and less than 4, which makes 4 the closest integer to $\frac{\sqrt{50}}{2}$. If you chose **F**, you may have used 36 as the closest perfect square integer value below 50 and neglected to find the closest perfect square integer value above 50: $36 < 50 \Leftrightarrow \frac{\sqrt{36}}{2} < \frac{\sqrt{50}}{2} \Leftrightarrow \frac{6}{2} < \frac{\sqrt{50}}{2} \Leftrightarrow 3 < \frac{\sqrt{50}}{2}$. Similarly, if you chose **H**, you may have used 100 as the closest perfect square integer value above 50 and neglected to find the closest perfect square integer value below 50: $50 < 100 \Leftrightarrow \frac{\sqrt{50}}{2} < \frac{\sqrt{100}}{2} \Leftrightarrow \frac{\sqrt{50}}{2} < \frac{10}{2} \Leftrightarrow \frac{\sqrt{50}}{2} < 5$. If you chose **K**, you may have found that $\sqrt{49} < \sqrt{50} \Leftrightarrow 7 < \sqrt{50}$ and then doubled the value on the left.

Question 15. The correct answer is D. Let x represent a factor of the sum of Jane's age and her daughter's age. Then, we have $9x + 2x = 44 \Leftrightarrow 11x = 44 \Leftrightarrow x = 4$. Therefore, Jane's age is $9(x) = 9(4) = 36$. If you chose **A**, you may have multiplied 4 by the average of the 9 and $2 : 4 \cdot \frac{9+2}{2} = 4 \cdot \frac{11}{2} = 22$. If you chose **B**, you may have subtracted 9 and 2 from the sum of their ages: $44 - 9 - 2 = 33$. If you chose **C**, you may have subtracted 9 from the sum of their ages: $44 - 9 = 35$. If you chose **E**, you may have subtracted 4 from the sum of their ages: $44 - 4 = 40$.

Question 16. The correct answer is H. First, we compute the fraction of the operating budget that is allocated to library books and scholarships. This is the sum of the fractions for each allocation: $\frac{1}{9} + \frac{1}{6} = \frac{2}{18} + \frac{3}{18} = \frac{5}{18}$. To compute the fraction of the operating budget that remains for other uses, we subtract the previous sum from the whole of the operating budget: $1 - \frac{5}{18} = \frac{18}{18} - \frac{5}{18} = \frac{13}{18}$. If you chose **F**, you may have subtracted the fraction of the operating budget that is allocated to library books from the fraction of the operating budget that is allocated to scholarships. If you chose **G**, you selected the fraction of the operating budget that is allocated to library books and scholarships only. If you chose **K**, you selected the fraction of the operating budget that is NOT allocated to library books.

Question 17. The correct answer is A. The second fraction in the proportion may be simplified to $\frac{5}{6}$, so that we have $\frac{10}{10 + x} = \frac{5}{6}$. We may use the multiplication property of equality to solve the proportion. We multiply both sides of the equation by the product $6(10 + x)$:

$$\left(\frac{10}{10 + x} \right) \cdot 6(10 + x) = \left(\frac{5}{6} \right) \cdot 6(10 + x) \Leftrightarrow 10(6) = 5(10 + x) \Leftrightarrow 60 = 50 + 5x$$

Next, we solve the resulting linear equation for $x : 60 = 50 + 5x \Leftrightarrow 10 = 5x \Leftrightarrow x = 2$.

If you chose **B**, you may have subtracted the numerator of the second fraction from the denominator of the second fraction. If you chose **C**, you selected the value of $10 + x$, which is $10 + 2 = 12$. If you chose **D**, you may have subtracted the numerator of the second fraction from the denominator of the second fraction and then added $10 : 42 - 35 + 10 = 17$. If you chose **E**, you selected the value of x for which the denominator of the first fraction will be equal to the denominator of the second fraction. However, $\frac{10}{10 + 32} = \frac{10}{42} \neq \frac{35}{42}$.

Question 18. The correct answer is J. The total area of the 2 shaded triangles can be found by subtracting the area of the unshaded triangle from the area of the rectangle. The area of the rectangle is $8(10) = 80$ square inches. The area of the unshaded triangle is $\frac{1}{2}(10)(8) = 40$ square inches. Thus, the total area of the 2 shaded triangles is $80 - 40 = 40$ square inches. If you chose **F**, you may have thought that the total area of the 2 shaded triangles is $\frac{1}{2}$ the area of the unshaded triangle. If you chose **H**, you may have subtracted 2 times the area of the larger shaded triangle from the area of the rectangle: $80 - 2\left(\frac{1}{2}\right)(6)(8) = 80 - 48 = 32$. If you chose **K**, you may have found the area of the rectangle only.

Question 19. The correct answer is C. We need to find the ordered pair that satisfies all three of the inequalities in the given system. Therefore, the x-coordinate of the ordered pair must be greater than 2, the y-coordinate of the ordered pair must be greater than 0, and the sum of the x-coordinate and the y-coordinate of the ordered pair must be less than 5. The only ordered pair that satisfies all three of the inequalities is $(3,1)$. If you chose **A**, you may have chosen $(1,3)$ because it satisfies the second and third inequalities; however, it does not satisfy the first inequality. Similarly, if you chose **B**, you may have chosen $(2,2)$ because it satisfies the second and third inequalities; however, it does not satisfy the first inequality. If you chose **D**, you may have chosen $(3,2)$ because it satisfies the first and second inequalities; however, it does not satisfy the third inequality. If you chose **E**, you may have chosen $(4,0)$ because it satisfies the first and third inequalities; however, it does not satisfy the second inequality.

Question 20. The correct answer is H. For real numbers b and c, the range of any sine function of the form $y = \sin(bx + c)$ is $-1 \le y \le 1$. Thus, the range of the function $y = \sin(x - \pi)$ is $-1 \le y \le 1$. It follows that $y = 3 - 5\sin(x - \pi)$ will have y-values such that $3 - 5(1) \le y \le 3 + 5(1)$. Thus, the range of $y = 3 - 5\sin(x - \pi)$ is $-2 \le y \le 8$. If you chose **F**, you may have ignored the 3 in the given function and instead found the range of the function $y = -5\sin(x - \pi) : -5(1) \le y \le 5(1) \Leftrightarrow -5 \le y \le 5$. If you chose **G**, you may have computed the range as $3 - 5(1) \le y \le 5(1) - 3 \Leftrightarrow -2 \le y \le 2$. If you chose **J**, you may have thought $0 \le y \le 1$ was the range of the function $y = \sin(x - \pi)$, and then found the range of the function $y = 3 - 5\sin(x - \pi)$ to be $3 - 5(0) \le y \le 3 + 5(1) \Leftrightarrow 3 \le y \le 8$.

Question 21. The correct answer is D. In the composition $f(g(-3))$, first replace each x found in $g(x)$, the inside function, with the input -3. Next, replace each x found in $f(x)$ with the value $g(-3)$. First of all, $g(x) = x^2 - 4$, so $g(-3) = (-3)^2 - 4 = 9 - 4 = 5$. Accordingly, $f(x) = 2x + 1$, so $f(g(-3)) = f(5) = 2(5) + 1 = 10 + 1 = 11$. If you chose **A**, you may have thought $(-5)^2 = -25$ and attempted to compute $g(f(-3))$: $f(-3) = 2(-3) + 1 = -5$, and so $g(f(-3)) = g(-5) = (-5)^2 - 4 \Rightarrow -25 - 4 = -29$. If you chose **B**, you may have thought $(-3)^2 = -9$, so that $g(-3) = -9 - 4 = -13$, and $f(g(-3)) = f(-13) = 2(-13) + 1 = -25$. If you chose **C**, you may have attempted to compute $f(-3) + g(-3)$. However, you may have dropped the constant from the function $f(x) = 2x + 1$, so that $f(-3) = -2(3) = -6$. In addition, you may have thought $(-3)^2 = -9$, so that $g(-3) = -9 - 4 = -13$. Then $f(-3) + g(-3) = -19$. If you chose **E**, you may have found $(f(-3))$: $f(-3) = 2(-3) + 1 = -5$, and so $g(f(-3)) = g(-5) = (-5)^2 - 4 = 21$.

Question 22. The correct answer is G. We may set up a system of two equations in two variables to model the dollar amounts that Joan and Chris each paid for the fabrics. Let x be the price, in dollars, of 1 yard of flannel fabric. Let y be the price, in dollars, of 1 yard of calico fabric. Then we have $\begin{matrix} 3x+4y=25\,(\text{Joan}) \\ x+2y=11\,(\text{Chris}) \end{matrix}$. To solve this system, multiply the second equation by -3, and add it to the first equation. $\begin{matrix} 3x+4y=25 \\ -3(x+2y=11) \end{matrix} \Leftrightarrow \begin{matrix} 3x+4y=25 \\ -3x-6y=-33 \end{matrix} \Leftrightarrow -2y=-8$.

Then, solve for y: $-2y=-8 \Leftrightarrow y=4$. The price, in dollars, of 1 yard of calico fabric is \$4. If you chose **F**, you may have solved the system for x, the price, in dollars, of 1 yard of flannel fabric. If you chose **H**, you may have divided the total number of yards of fabric bought by Joan and Chris in half: $\frac{3+4+1+2}{2}=\frac{10}{2}=5$. If you chose **J**, you may have divided the sum of the dollar amounts that Joan and Chris each paid by the total number of yards of calico fabric bought: $\frac{25+11}{4+2}=\frac{36}{6}=6$. If you chose **K**, you may have found how much more Joan paid and then divided it by how much more calico fabric she bought: $\frac{25-11}{4-2}=\frac{14}{2}=7$.

Question 23. The correct answer is C. To find the median of a data set, arrange the data values in order from least to greatest. The median is the value separating the upper half of the data from the lower half. When a data set has an odd number of values, the median is the exact middle value. When a data set has an even number of values, there are two middlemost values. Average them to find the median. In order from least to greatest, the scores in this data set are $71, 77, 78, 80, 86, 88, 88, 94, 94, 94$. The two middlemost scores are 86 and 88, which makes the key $\frac{86+88}{2}=87$. If you chose **A**, you may have found the mean of the ten scores: $\frac{sum\ of\ the\ scores}{number\ of\ scores}=\frac{850}{210}=85$. If you chose **B**, you selected the average of the mean and the median: $\frac{85+87}{2}=86$. If you chose **D**, you may have chosen the least of the two middlemost scores of the unordered ten scores: $\min\{88,94\}=88$. If you chose **E**, you may have found the mean of the two middlemost scores of the unordered ten scores: $\frac{88+94}{2}=91$.

Question 24. The correct answer is H. Opposite sides of a parallelogram are congruent. Thus, the side of the parallelogram that measures 16 inches has a side opposite to it that also measures 16 inches. It follows that the sum of the measures of the parallelogram's remaining two sides is equal to $84-2(16)=84-32=52$ inches. Therefore, each of the two sides must measure $\frac{52}{2}=26$ inches. If you chose **F**, you may have subtracted the given side from the perimeter and then selected three side lengths whose sum was the value of that difference: $84-16=68$ and $16+16+36=68$. However, sides of length $16, 16, 16,$ and 36 inches do not form a parallelogram. If you chose **G**, you have selected a parallelogram with a perimeter of $16+16+18+18=68$ inches. If you chose **J**, you may have subtracted the given side from the perimeter before dividing by 2: $\frac{84-16}{2}=34$. However, the perimeter of the parallelogram would then be $16+16+34+34=100$ inches.

Question 25. The correct answer is E. First, note that the shaded region is also a rectangle and that each of its dimensions is a fraction of the corresponding dimension of rectangle $ABCD$. Now, let the area of rectangle $ABCD$ be given by $A = LW$, where L is the length and W is the width. Each row in rectangle $ABCD$ has 6 squares, and each row in the shaded region has 5 squares. Thus, the length of the shaded region is $\frac{5}{6}L$. Each column in rectangle $ABCD$ has 4 squares, and each column in the shaded region has 3 squares. Thus, the width of the shaded region is $\frac{3}{4}W$. It follows that the area, in square units, of the shaded region is $\left(\frac{5}{6}L\right)\left(\frac{3}{4}W\right) = \frac{5}{6} \cdot \frac{3}{4}LW = \frac{5}{6} \cdot \frac{3}{4} \cdot (1) = \frac{5}{6} \cdot \frac{3}{4}$. If you chose **A**, you may have computed the area of a single small square only, neglecting the fact that there are 5 small squares in a row and 3 small squares in a column. If you chose **B**, you may have first computed the area of a single small square and also noticed that there are 3 small squares in a column, but you neglected the fact that there are 5 small squares in a row. If you chose **C**, you may have found that the length of the shaded rectangle is $\frac{5}{6}$ the length of rectangle $ABCD$. As a result, you may have multiplied this fraction by the length of a single small square. If you chose **D**, you may have first computed the area of a single small square and also noticed that there are 5 small squares in a row, but you neglected the fact that there are 3 small squares in a column.

Question 26. The correct answer is G. We can set up a proportion where each side represents the probability of randomly drawing a red marble; that is, $\frac{number\ of\ red\ marbles}{total\ marbles}$. Let x be the number of additional red marbles added to the 42 marbles. It follows that $\frac{3}{5} = \frac{16+x}{42+x}$. We can use the multiplication property of equality to solve the proportion. We multiply both sides of the equation by the product $5(42+x)$: $5(42+x)\left(\frac{3}{5}\right) = 5(42+x)\left(\frac{16+x}{42+x}\right) \Leftrightarrow 3(42+x) = 5(16+x) \Leftrightarrow 126+3x = 80+5x$. Next, we solve the resulting linear equation for x: $126+3x = 80+5x \Leftrightarrow 46 = 2x \Leftrightarrow x = 23$. If you chose **F**, you may have computed $\frac{3(42)}{5(16)} + 16 = 17.575$ and rounded up. If you chose **K**, you may have solved the proportion $\frac{3}{5} = \frac{x}{16} \Leftrightarrow x = 9.6$, rounded the solution up to the nearest integer, and added to 42.

Question 27. The correct answer is E. Negative exponents signify multiplicative inverses and thus are the reciprocal of positive exponents. This means that a base raised to a negative exponent is equivalent to 1 divided by the base raised to the positive of the exponent. Therefore, $a^{-2} = \frac{1}{a^2}$. If you chose **A**, you may have multiplied the exponent by the base. If you chose **D**, you may have used the reciprocal of the positive of the exponent in the denominator: $a^{-2} \Rightarrow \frac{1}{\frac{1}{a^2}} \Rightarrow \frac{1}{\sqrt{a}}$.

Question 28. The correct answer is F. Jamie's claim is a conditional statement in the form of a hypothesis followed by a conclusion. The hypothesis of Jamie's claim is "a triangle is in set A," and the conclusion of the claim is "it is not isosceles." Now, the only way for a conditional statement to be false is for the hypothesis to be true and the conclusion to be false. Because $\triangle MNP$ is a counterexample that proves Jamie's claim is false, it must be true that $\triangle MNP$ is a triangle in set A and that $\triangle MNP$ is isosceles. If you chose **G**, you selected the statement for which the hypothesis is true and the conclusion is true. If you chose **H**, you neglected the fact that obtuse triangles may be isosceles or scalene, so you selected the statement for which the hypothesis is false and the conclusion may be true or false. If you chose **J**, you selected the statement for which the hypothesis is false and the conclusion is true. If you chose **K**, you selected the statement for which the hypothesis is false and the conclusion is false.

Question 29. The correct answer is D. The area of a parallelogram is given by the formula $A = bh$ where b is the base and h is the height of the parallelogram. Side $\overline{AD}$ is a base of parallelogram $ABCD$, and the height of parallelogram $ABCD$ is equal to the distance between $\overline{AD}$ and $\overline{BC}$. Therefore, the area, in square coordinate units, of parallelogram $ABCD$ is given by $A = bh = 5(3) = 15$. If you chose **B**, you may have used the formula for the area of a triangle: $A = \frac{1}{2}bh = \frac{1}{2}(5)(3)$. If you chose **E**, you may have used the formula for the perimeter of a square: $A = 4s = 4(5)$.

Question 30. The correct answer is H. To find the distance between two points (x_1, y_1) and (x_2, y_2), we can use the distance formula, $d = \sqrt{(x_2 - x_1)^2 + (y_2 - y_1)^2}$. It follows that the distance between $B(0,4)$ and $D(4,1)$ is given y $d = \sqrt{(4-1)^2 + (0-4)^2} = \sqrt{(3)^2 + (-4)^2} = \sqrt{9+16} = \sqrt{25} = 5$ coordinate units. If you chose **F**, you may have switched the plus and minus signs in the distance formula: $\sqrt{(4+1)^2 - (0+4)^2} \Rightarrow \sqrt{25-16} \Rightarrow \sqrt{9} \Rightarrow 3$. If you chose **J**, you may have incorrectly computed the distance as $\left| (4-1)^2 - (0-4)^2 \right| \Rightarrow \left| 9 - 16 \right| \Rightarrow 7$.

Question 31. The correct answer is A. To find the slope of a line containing two points (x_1, y_1) and (x_2, y_2), use the slope formula $m = \frac{y_2 - y_1}{x_2 - x_1}$. Line $\overleftrightarrow{BC}$ contains the points $B(0,4)$ and $C(5,4)$. It follows that the slope of $\overleftrightarrow{BC}$ is given by $m = \frac{y_2 - y_1}{x_2 - x_1} = \frac{4-4}{5-0} = 0$. If you chose **B**, you may have computed the difference in the x-coordinate and y-coordinate of point $C(5,4)$: $5 - 4 = 1$. If you chose **D**, you may have computed the difference in the x-coordinates of $B(0,4)$ and $C(5,4)$: $5 - 0 = 5$. If you chose **E**, you may have computed the slope as $\frac{run}{rise} = \frac{change\ in\ x}{change\ in\ y}$.

Question 32. The correct answer is J. When we reflect a point over the y-axis, the y-coordinate remains the same, but the x-coordinate is transformed into its opposite (its sign is changed). Therefore, the coordinates of the image of $A(-1,1)$ after reflection over the y-axis are $(1,1)$. If you chose **F**, you selected the image of point $D(4,1)$ after reflection over the y-axis. If you chose **G**, you selected the image of point $A(-1,1)$ after reflection over the x-axis, where the x-coordinate remains the same, but the y-coordinate is transformed into its opposite. If you chose **H**, you selected the image of point $A(-1,1)$ after reflection over the origin $(0,0)$, where both the x- and y-coordinates are transformed into their opposites. If you chose **K**, you selected the image of point $D(4,1)$ after reflection over the x-axis.

Question 33. The correct answer is A. First, rewrite the product $8^2 \cdot 4^{0.5}$ so that each factor has the same base: $(2^3)^2 \cdot (2^2)^{0.5}$. Next, apply the power rule for exponents, $(a^m)^n = a^{mn}$, to each factor. Therefore, we have $(2^3)^2 \cdot (2^2)^{0.5} = 2^{3(2)} \cdot 2^{2(0.5)} = 2^6 \cdot 2^1$. Finally, apply the product rule for exponents, $a^m \cdot a^n = a^{m+n}$, to combine the 2 factors. Thus, we have $2^6 \cdot 2^1 = 2^{6+1} = 2^7$. If you chose **B**, you may have rewritten the base of the first factor as $4 \cdot 2$ and then incorrectly applied the power rule for exponents: $8^2 \cdot 4^{0.5} \Rightarrow (4 \cdot 2)^2 \cdot (4)^{0.5} \Rightarrow (4)^{2(2)} \cdot (4)^{0.5} \Rightarrow 4^{4+0.5}$. If you chose **C**, you may have used the greater of the bases together with the sum of the exponents: $8^2 \cdot 4^{0.5} \Rightarrow 8^{2+0.5} \Rightarrow 8^{2.5}$. If you chose **D**, you may have simplified the second factor and then multiplied it by the base of the first factor: $8^2 \cdot 4^{0.5} \Rightarrow 8^2 \cdot 2 \Rightarrow (8 \cdot 2)^2 \Rightarrow 16^2$. If you chose **E**, you may have multiplied the bases and multiplied the exponents: $8^2 \cdot 4^{0.5} \Rightarrow (8 \cdot 4)^{2 \cdot 0.5} \Rightarrow 32^1$.

Question 34. The correct answer is K. The school admissions office accepts 2 of every 7 applicants. That means that 5 of every 7 applicants are NOT accepted. Let x be the number of applicants that were not accepted. We may set up a proportion where each side represents the ratio $\frac{\text{number of applicants NOT accepted}}{\text{total number of applicants}}$. It follows that $\frac{5}{7} = \frac{x}{x+630}$. We may use the multiplication property of equality to solve the proportion. We multiply both sides of the equation by the product $7(x+630)$: $7(x+630) \cdot \left(\frac{5}{7}\right) = 7(x+630) \cdot \left(\frac{x}{x+630}\right) \Leftrightarrow 5(x+630) = 7x \Leftrightarrow 5x+3,150 = 7x$. Then, we solve the linear equation for x: $5x+3,150 = 7x \Leftrightarrow 2x = 3,150 \Leftrightarrow x = 1,575$. If you chose **F**, you may have divided the total number of applicants into $2+7 = 9$ parts and then computed $\frac{2}{9}(630) = 140$. If you chose **G**, you may have solved the proportion $\frac{2}{7} = \frac{x}{630} \Leftrightarrow x = 180$. If you chose **H**, you may have divided the total number of applicants into 9 parts and then computed $\frac{7}{9}(630) = 490$. If you chose **J**, you may have doubled the number of applicants that were accepted: $2(630) = 1,260$.

Question 35. The correct answer is B. First, note that by the properties of exponents, $\sqrt{8}=\sqrt{2^3}=\left(2^3\right)^{1/2}=2^{3/2}$. Next, note that because the functions $y=\log_2 x$ and $y=2^x$ are inverse functions, then $\log_2\left(2^x\right)=x$. It follows that $\log_2\sqrt{8}=\log_2 2^{3/2}=\frac{3}{2}$. If you chose **A**, you may have simplified the radical but then incorrectly applied the product property of logarithms:

$$\log_2\sqrt{8}=\log_2 2\sqrt{2}\Rightarrow\left(\log_2 2\right)\left(\log_2\sqrt{2}\right)\Rightarrow(1)\left(\log_2 2^{1/2}\right)\Rightarrow\frac{1}{2}.$$ If you chose **C**, you may have simplified the radical but then incorrectly applied the inverse property, $\log_2\left(2^x\right)=x$, and thought that $\log_2\sqrt{8}=\log_2 2\sqrt{2}\Rightarrow\sqrt{2}$. If you chose **E**, you may have dropped the square root when simplifying: $\log_2\sqrt{8}=\log_2 2^3\Rightarrow 3$.

Question 36. The correct answer is F. In a circle graph, each different sector represents a proportion of a total. Moreover, the measure of each central angle of a circle graph is proportional to the quantity it represents. Because there are $360°$ in a circle, Jie must represent each part of the data as a proportion of 360. First, we note that apples, bananas, and strawberries were each chosen as favorites by an equal number of the $90-15=75$ remaining students. Thus, bananas were chosen as the favorite fruit of $\frac{75}{3}=25$ students out of the 90 students in the survey. It follows that Jie will represent bananas on the circle graph as a sector with a central angle that measures $\frac{25}{90}\cdot 360°=100°$. If you chose **G**, you may have thought the central angle in the circle for the 15 students who chose peaches represented 15% and computed $\frac{360-0.15(360)}{3}=\frac{306}{3}=102°$. If you chose **H**, you may have thought the central angle in the circle for the 15 students who chose peaches was $\frac{90}{2}=45$ and computed $\frac{360-45}{3}=\frac{315}{3}=105°$. If you chose **J**, you may have thought the central angle in the circle for the 15 students who chose peaches was $\frac{90}{4}=22.5$ and computed $\frac{360-22.5}{3}=\frac{337.5}{3}=112.5°$. If you chose **K**, you may have thought the central angle in the circle for the 15 students who chose peaches measured $15°$ and computed $\frac{360-15}{3}=\frac{345}{3}=115°$.

Question 37. The correct answer is E. The denominators of the two fractions are unlike. We may rewrite each fraction with a new denominator that is equal to the least common multiple of their denominators: $5x$. We do this by multiplying each of the two fractions by additional fractions that are equivalent to 1. Then we may finally add the numerators of the rewritten fractions. Thus, we have $\frac{x}{x}\cdot\frac{4}{5}+\frac{5}{5}\cdot\frac{7}{x}=\frac{4x}{5x}+\frac{35}{5x}=\frac{4x+35}{5x}$. If you chose **A**, you may have placed the sum of the numerators over the product of the denominators: $\frac{4}{5}+\frac{7}{x}\Rightarrow\frac{4+7}{5x}$. If you chose **B**, you may have placed the product of the numerators over the product of the denominators: $\frac{4}{5}+\frac{7}{x}\Rightarrow\frac{4(7)}{5x}$. If you chose **C**, you may have added the numerators and added the denominators: $\frac{4}{5}+\frac{7}{x}\Rightarrow\frac{4+7}{5+x}$. If you chose **D**, you may have multiplied the numerator and denominator of each fraction and put the sum over the sum of the denominators: $\frac{4}{5}+\frac{7}{x}\Rightarrow\frac{4(5)+7(x)}{5+x}$.

Question 38. The correct answer is K. The total number of nonstudent residents who replied to the survey was $85 + 353 + 47 = 485$. The number of nonstudent residents who replied that they disapproved of the change in hours was 353. Thus, $\frac{353}{485}$ of the nonstudent residents replied that they disapproved of the change in hours. If you chose **F**, you selected the fraction of college students who replied that they disapproved: $\frac{10}{14+10+6}$. If you chose **G**, you selected the fraction of high school students who replied that they disapproved: $\frac{4}{30+4+11}$. If you chose **H**, you selected the fraction of high school and college students who replied that they disapproved: $\frac{4+10}{30+45}$. If you chose **J**, you selected the fraction for which the denominator is the total number of residents who replied with disapproval, including high school and college students, and not the total number of nonstudent residents: $\frac{353}{367}$.

Question 39. The correct answer is D. The total number of college student and nonstudent residents who replied either approve or disapprove is $14 + 10 + 85 + 353 = 462$ residents. This is the total number of residents who were NOT high school students and did NOT reply with no opinion. It follows that the probability that the person chosen will NOT be a high school student and will NOT have replied with no opinion is $\frac{462}{560} = 0.825 \approx 0.83$. If you chose **A**, you may have computed the probability that the person chosen will be a high school student who replied either approve or disapprove: $\frac{30+4}{560} \approx 0.06$. If you chose **B**, you may have computed the probability that the person chosen will be a college student or a nonstudent who replied with no opinion: $\frac{6+47}{560} \approx 0.09$. If you chose **C**, you may have attempted to compute the probability that the person chosen will be a nonstudent who replied approve. However, you may have divided by the total number of residents who replied either approve or with no opinion: $\frac{85}{129+64} = \frac{85}{193} \approx 0.44$. If you chose **E**, you may have computed the probability that the person chosen will NOT be a high school student who replied with no opinion: $1 - \frac{11}{560} \approx 0.98$.

Question 40. The correct answer is H. Of the 15 incorrectly classified residents, some are college students who approved, and some are high school students who approved. We may first set up a linear equation involving the 60% of the college students who approved. Let x be the number of incorrectly classified college students who approved. We know that there are 14 correctly classified college students who approved. Thus, $14 + x = 0.60(14 + 10 + 6 + x)$, or $14 + x = 0.60(30 + x)$. Now we solve for x. We distribute on the right-hand side to get $14 + x = 18 + 0.60x$. Next we subtract the constant term 14 from both sides: $x = 4 + 0.60x$. Then we subtract the variable term $0.60x$ from both sides: $0.40x = 4$. After dividing, we have $x = 10$ college students. This means that the remaining 5 incorrectly classified residents are high school students. Finally, the percent of high school students who replied that they approved is $\frac{30+5}{30+4+11+5} = \frac{35}{50} = 0.70$, or 70%. If you chose **F**, you may have used the table values to find 60% of the total number of college students: $0.60(30) = 18$. Next, you may have computed $\frac{30-(18-15)}{45} = \frac{27}{45} = 0.60$, or 60%. If you chose **G**, you may have used the table values to find the percentage of high school students who replied that they approved: $\frac{30}{45} \approx 0.67$, or 67%. If you chose **J**, you may have used the table values and added 15 to the total number of high school students who replied that they approved: $\frac{30+15}{45+15} = \frac{45}{60} = 0.75$, or 75%. If you chose **K**, you may have used the table values to find the percentage of high school students who replied that they approved and then added 15%. Thus, $\frac{30}{45} \approx 0.67$, and so $67\% + 15\% = 82\%$.

Question 41. The correct answer is A. Let Set A be the set of $\{a,b,c,d,e\}$ where $a < b < c < d < e$. Set B is then $\{x,b,c,d,e\}$ where $a < x < b$. The mean of Set A is $\frac{a+b+c+d+e}{5}$, and the mean of Set B is $\frac{x+b+c+d+e}{5}$. Because $x > a$, $\frac{x+b+c+d+e}{5} > \frac{a+b+c+d+e}{5}$. Thus, the mean of Set B is greater than the mean of Set A. The median of both Set A and Set B is c; thus **B**, **D**, and **E** are not correct answers. Set A and Set B each consists of 5 distinct numbers, so there is no mode for either set. This means that **C** and **E** are not correct answers.

Question 42. The correct answer is G. Because the function $f(x) = \sin x$ is an odd function, $\sin(-x) = -\sin x$. For example, $\sin 30° = \frac{1}{2}$, and $\sin(-30°) = -\frac{1}{2}$. Thus, $\sin(-x°) \neq \sin x°$, so **G** is the correct answer. It is true that $-\sin(-x°) = -(-\sin x°) = \sin x°$, so **F** is not the correct answer. By the cofunction identity, $\cos(90 - x)° = \sin x°$, so **H** is not the correct answer. If you picked **J**, you might not have remembered $\cos(x - 90)° = \cos(-(90 - x)°)$. Because the function $g(\theta) = \cos \theta$ is even, $\cos(-\theta) = \cos(\theta)$. This means that $\cos(x - 90)° = \cos(-(90 - x)°) = \cos(90 - x)° = \sin x°$. Thus, **J** is not the correct answer. If you chose **K**, you might have forgotten the identity, $\sin^2 x + \cos^2 x = 1$. Solving for $\sin x$ gives $\sin x = \pm\sqrt{1 - \cos^2 x}$. Because $0 \leq x \leq 90$, $\sin x° \geq 0$. Thus, $\sin x° = \sqrt{1 - (\cos x°)^2}$, so **K** is not the correct answer.

Question 43. The correct answer is D. The smallest square that will fit a circle with a diameter of 8 inches is a square with side lengths 8 inches. The box will thus have a base that is a square with side length 8 inches. Because the height of the box is 3 inches, the volume is $3(8^2)$, or 192 cubic inches. If you selected **A**, you might have multiplied the side length of the base by the height of the box, 3(8), instead of multiplying the area of the base by the height of the box. If you selected **B**, you might have found the area of the base, instead of the volume of the box. If you selected **C**, you might have confused the height of the box with the side length of the base and found $8(3^2)$ instead of $3(8^2)$. If you selected **E**, you might have found the volume of a cube with side length 8.

Question 44. The correct answer is G. Draw diagonal $\overline{DB}$. Triangle $\triangle BCD$ is a right triangle with $BC = 4$ and $CD = 3$, so $BD^2 = 3^2 + 4^2 = 5^2$. Because $5^2 + 12^2 = 13^2$, $BD^2 + AD^2 = AB^2$, and $\triangle BDA$ is a right triangle with right angle D. The tangent of an angle in a right triangle, is the ratio of the lengths of the side opposite the angle and the side adjacent to the angle. Thus, $\tan A$ is $\dfrac{BD}{AD} = \dfrac{5}{12}$. If you chose **F**, you might have found $\dfrac{BC}{AD}$. If you chose **H**, you might have found $\dfrac{BC}{AB}$. If you chose **J**, you might have found $\sin A = \dfrac{BD}{AB}$. If you chose **K**, you might have found $\cos A = \dfrac{AD}{AB}$.

Question 45. The correct answer is D. There are 7 days in a week. Because $28(7) = 196$, 196 days ago it was Tuesday. This means that 197 days ago was a Monday, 198 days ago was a Sunday, 199 days ago was a Saturday, and 200 days ago was a Friday. If you picked an answer other than **D**, you might have not realized that the remainder when 200 is divided by 7 is equal to 4, or you might not have known to count back 4 days from Tuesday.

Question 46. The correct answer is G. Because $\angle 1$ and $\angle 2$ are vertical angles, they are congruent. This means that $3x - 10 = 2x + 10 \rightarrow x = 20$. Substituting $x = 20$ back into the equation tells us $m\angle 2 = (2(20) + 10)° = 50°$. Because line m is perpendicular to line n, $m\angle 2 + m\angle 3 = 90°$. Because $m\angle 2 = 50°$, $50° + m\angle 3 = 90° \rightarrow m\angle 3 = 40°$. If you selected **F**, you might have thought that $\angle 1$ and $\angle 2$ were supplementary and found the value of x in the equation $3x - 10 + 2x + 10 = 180$. If you selected **H**, you might have estimated from the diagram that $m\angle 3$ was slightly less than $m\angle 2$ but didn't know how to calculate the value exactly. If you selected **J**, you might have thought that line q bisected the angle, making $\angle 2$ and $\angle 3$ congruent. If you selected **K**, you might have found the value of x in the equation $3x - 10 + 2x + 10 = 180$. You might have thought that $m\angle 2 = x° = 36°$ and then found the angle complementary to $36°$: $(90 - 36)°$.

MATHEMATICS • PRACTICE TEST 2 • EXPLANATORY ANSWERS

Question 47. The correct answer is E. Because $30 = 2(3)(5)$ and $40 = 2^3(5)$, the greatest common factor (GCF) of 30 and 40 is $2(5) = 10$, and the least common multiple (LCM) is $2^3(3)(5) = 120$. If you selected **A**, you may not have realized that the GCF of 6 and 20 is 2 and the LCM is 60. If you selected **B**, you may not have realized that the GCF of 10 and 12 is 2 and the LCM is 60. If you selected **C**, you may not have realized that the LCM of 10 and 20 is 20. If you selected **D**, you may not have realized that the GCF of 20 and 60 is 20 and the LCM is 60.

Question 48. The correct answer is H. Because all the sides are different lengths, the triangle is scalene. Because the length of the longest side squared is greater than the sum of the squares of the lengths of the other two sides ($7^2 > 4^2 + 5^2$), the triangle is obtuse. If you selected **F**, you may not have known that in an acute triangle, the length of the longest side squared is less than the sum of the squares of the lengths of the other two sides: $c^2 < a^2 + b^2$. If you selected **G**, you may not have known that in a right triangle, the length of the hypotenuse squared is equal to the sum of the squares of the lengths of the other two sides: $c^2 = a^2 + b^2$. If you selected **J** or **K**, you may not have known that an isosceles triangle has at least two congruent sides.

Question 49. The correct answer is D. Because the team has a 60% chance of winning on Saturday, the probability that they will lose on Saturday is $1 - 0.6 = 0.4$. Because the team has a 35% chance of winning on Sunday, the probability that they will lose on Sunday is $1 - 0.35 = 0.65$. The probability of them losing both games is thus $0.4(0.65) = 0.26$ or 26%. If you selected **A**, you may have found the probability that they will lose on Saturday but win on Sunday: $0.4(0.35) = 0.14$. If you selected **B**, you may have found the probability that they will win both games: $0.6(0.35) = 0.21$. If you selected **C**, you may have found the difference between the given probabilities: $0.6 - 0.35 = 0.25$. If you selected **E**, you may have found the probability that they will win on Saturday but lose on Sunday: $0.6(0.65) = 0.39$.

Question 50. The correct answer is J. The domain of a rational function, like f, excludes any x-values that make the denominator 0. This includes both removable points of discontinuity (holes) and nonremovable points of discontinuity (vertical asymptotes). Solving $0 = x^2 - 2x - 3 = (x-3)(x+1)$ gives us solutions $x = 3$ and $x = -1$. The domain of f is thus $\{x \mid x \neq -1 \text{ and } x \neq 3\}$. If you selected **F**, you might not have known that removable points of discontinuity (like 3 for f) are also domain restrictions. If you selected **G**, you might have incorrectly factored $0 = x^2 - 2x - 3 \to (x-2)(x-3)$ and then found only the nonremovable points of discontinuity for the incorrect function: $f(x) = \dfrac{x-3}{(x-2)(x-3)}$. If you selected **H**, you might not have known that nonremovable points of discontinuity (like −1 for f) are also domain restrictions. If you selected **K**, you might have incorrectly simplified f by canceling the 3s: $f(x) = \dfrac{x-3}{x^2-2x-3} \to \dfrac{x}{x^2-2x}$. You might have then found the domain restrictions of the incorrect function.

Question 51. The correct answer is E. The first three numbers are set and do NOT affect the number of possible phone numbers. The choices for possible phone numbers have the form 555-XXXX. We note that each X in a phone number may be any of the 10 digits allowed (0 through 9). Therefore, we have $10 \cdot 10 \cdot 10 \cdot 10 = 10^4$ possible phone numbers. If you chose **C**, you selected the case where each of the first three digits of a phone number has 5 choices: $5 \cdot 5 \cdot 5 \cdot 10 \cdot 10 \cdot 10 \cdot 10 = 5^3 \left(10^4\right)$. If you chose **D**, you may not have included 0 in the number of digits allowed: $9 \cdot 9 \cdot 9 \cdot 9 = 9^4$. If you chose **A**, you selected the case where only 1 of the first 3 digits of a phone number has 5 choices, $5 \cdot 1 \cdot 1$ or $1 \cdot 5 \cdot 1$ or $1 \cdot 1 \cdot 5$, and each of the last 4 digits of the phone number has 9 choices, 9^4. Thus, $5\left(9^4\right)$.

Question 52. The correct answer is F. A circle is the set of all points whose distance from the center is equal to the radius. Therefore, the measure of the radius of the given circle is equal to the distance between the center, (1,3) and the given point on the circle,(4,7). The distance between any two points $\left(x_1, y_1\right)$ and $\left(x_2, y_2\right)$ is given by $\sqrt{\left(x_2 - x_1\right)^2 + \left(y_2 - y_1\right)^2}$. It follows that the radius of the given circle has a measure of $\sqrt{\left(4-1\right)^2 + \left(7-3\right)^2} = \sqrt{3^2 + 4^2} = \sqrt{9+16} = \sqrt{25} = 5$ coordinate units. Thus, the given circle is the set of all points that are 5 coordinate units from the center (1,3). If you chose **G**, you selected the intersection of circles with radii of 5 coordinate units centered at (1,3) and (4,7). If you chose **H**, you selected the parallel line segments above and below the line segment from (1,3) to (4,7). If you chose **J**, you selected the perpendicular bisector of the line segment with endpoints (1,3) and (4,7). If you chose **K**, you selected the closed region composed of a rectangle whose endpoints are capped off with semicircles. The length of the rectangle is formed by two parallel line segments above and below the line segment from (1,3) to (4,7), and the two semicircles are centered at each of the endpoints (1,3) and (4,7).

Question 53. The correct answer is B. To find the x-coordinate of the point of intersection of the two graphs, we set the right-hand side of the two equations equal to each other and solve for x. First, we have $7 = \ln(x-2) + 3$. Next, we subtract 3 from both sides to get $4 = \ln(x-2)$. Now, we note that the exponent property of logarithms states that $e^{lnx} = e^{\log_e x} = x$. It follows from this property that if we have $e^4 = e^{\ln(x-2)}$, then we will have $e^4 = x-2$. Thus, $x = e^4 + 2$. If you chose **A**, you may have dropped the *ln* and solved the equation $7 = (x-2) + 3$. If you chose **C**, you may have moved the exponent down from the expression e^4 and to the front as multiplication: $e^4 = e^{\ln(x-2)} \Rightarrow 4e = x-2$. If you chose **D**, you may have incorrectly thought $\ln(\ln x) = x$ and attempted to solve using this erroneous property: $\ln(4) = \ln(\ln(x-2)) \Rightarrow \ln(4) = x-2$.

Question 54. The correct answer is F. The three machines copy at the same rate. Thus, as long as they are running together, the number of copies will increase at the same rate, r. When a machine breaks down the rate is reduced by $\frac{1}{3}r$. A rate will correspond to the slope of a line segment on the graph of n versus t. There will be 5 connected line segments on the graph due to the machine break downs. From 8:00 a.m. to 10:00 a.m., the first line segment has slope r. From 10:00 a.m. to 12:00 p.m., the breakdown of Machine A makes the second line segment have slope $\frac{2}{3}r$. From 12:00 p.m. to 1:00 p.m., the intersection of the breakdowns of Machines A and B makes the third line segment have slope $\frac{1}{3}r$. From 1:00 p.m. to 3:00 p.m., the breakdown of Machine B makes the fourthline segment have slope $\frac{2}{3}r$. Finally, from 3:00 p.m. to 5:00 p.m., the slope of the fifth line segment is r. The graph that matches these conditions has the first and fifth line segments with equal and greatest incline, followed by the second and fourth line segments with equal slope, and last, by the third line segment with the least incline. If you chose **G**, you selected the graph for which the number of copies will increase at the greatest rate between 12:00 p.m. and 1:00 p.m.; however, the breakdowns of Machines A and B during this time frame make this impossible. If you chose **H**, you selected the graph for which there are only three connected line segments, which does not match the scenario. If you chose **K**, you selected the graph for which the number of copies will increase at the same rate.

Question 55. The correct answer is E. Let p be the number of $1 decreases in the price of the caps. If $p = 0$, there are 40 caps sold per week. For each $1 decrease in p, 4 more caps are sold. It follows that the number of caps sold for 1 week will be $40 + 4p$. Moreover, the price per cap for 1 week will be $22 - p$. Now, from the given note we know that the revenue, R, for 1 week is $R = (22 - p)(40 + 4p)$. After multiplying the two binomials, we have $R = -4p^2 + 48p + 880$, which is a quadratic function in terms of p. Therefore, the maximum value of R will occur at the vertex. For a given quadratic function $y = ax^2 + bx + c$, the vertex is found by computing $x = -\dfrac{b}{2a}$ and then evaluating y at $x = -\dfrac{b}{2a}$ to find the maximum value. It follows that for $R = -4p^2 + 48p + 880$, $p = -\dfrac{b}{2a} = -\dfrac{48}{2(-4)} = 6$. Then, evaluating at $p = 6$, we find that $R = (22 - 6)(40 + 4(6)) = 16(64) = \$1,024$. If you chose **A**, you may have thought the maximum revenue equals the given number of caps sold times the given price per cap: $40(22) = \$880$. If you chose **C**, you may have thought the maximum revenue equals 4 more than the given number of caps sold times $1 less than the given price per cap: $(40 + 4)(22 - 1) = 44(21) = \$924$. If you chose **D**, you may have thought the maximum revenue equals 8 more than the given number of caps sold times $2 less than the given price per cap: $(40 + 8)(22 - 2) = 48(20) = \$960$.

MATHEMATICS • PRACTICE TEST 2 • EXPLANATORY ANSWERS

Question 56. The correct answer is K. First, we may write the linear inequality in slope-intercept form $y \le -\dfrac{a}{b}x + \dfrac{c}{b}$. From the condition $0 < a < b < c$, we know that the boundary line has a negative slope, $m = -\dfrac{a}{b}$. Moreover, we know that the boundary line has a y-intercept, $\left(0, \dfrac{c}{b}\right)$, located on the positive y-axis. Finally, $y \le -\dfrac{a}{b}x + \dfrac{c}{b}$ indicates that all the (x,y) coordinates on the boundary line and in the half-pane below the boundary line satisfy the inequality. If you chose **F**, you have selected a graph that has a boundary line with a positive slope. If you chose **G**, you have selected a graph that has (x,y) coordinates in the half-plane above the boundary line for which the inequality is NOT true. If you chose **H** or **J**, you have selected a graph that has a boundary line with a y-intercept $\left(0, \dfrac{c}{b}\right)$ located on the negative y-axis.

Question 57. The correct answer is A. First, we note that to make the 500 banners, the club needed to purchase a minimum of $500\left(\dfrac{1}{4}\right) = 125$ yards of blue material and a minimum of $500\left(\dfrac{3}{8}\right) = 187\dfrac{1}{2}$ yards of white material. Next, we note that each 10-yard bolt of blue material can be used to make $\dfrac{10}{1/4} = 40$ banners, and each 12-yard bolt of white material can be used to make $\dfrac{12}{3/8} = 32$ banners. Moreover, $10(13) = 130$ is the closest multiple of 10 that is greater than 125, and $12(16) = 192$ is the closest multiple of 12 that is greater than $187\dfrac{1}{2}$. It follows that the club purchased 130 yards of blue material and 192 yards of white material. The 130 yards of blue material could make $\dfrac{130}{1/4} = 520$ banners, and the 192 yards of white material could make $\dfrac{192}{3/8} = 512$ banners. Therefore, the club was able to make a total of $min(520, 512) = 512$ banners, which included 12 extra banners. If you chose **B**, you may have divided the 130 yards of blue material by the number of yards in a bolt of blue material: $\dfrac{130}{10} = 13$. If you chose **C**, you may have divided the total number of yards of each material that was purchased by the sum of the yards of material needed to make each banner: $\dfrac{130 + 192}{\frac{1}{4} + \frac{3}{8}} = \dfrac{322}{0.625} = 515.2 \Rightarrow 515 - 500 = 15$. If you chose **D**, you may have divided the 192 yards of white material by the number of yards in a bolt of white material: $\dfrac{160}{10} = 16$. If you chose **E**, you may have calculated the overage from the blue material only: $\dfrac{130}{1/4} = 520$ banners with 20 extra banners possible.

Question 58. The correct answer is F. We note that to find the expanded form of $(x-3i)^3$, we may use the cube of a binomial formula: $(a-b)^3 = a^3 - 3a^2b + 3ab^2 - b^3$. There are four terms in the result. The exponents of a decrease in each term, while the exponents of b increase in each term. The middle terms contain a factor of 3, and the second and fourth terms are negative. For the case of $(x-3i)^3$, we have $(x-3i)^3 = (x)^3 - 3(x)^2(3i) + 3(x)(3i)^2 - (3i)^3 = x^3 - 9x^2i + 27xi^2 - 27i^3$. Now, for the imaginary number $i, i^2 = -1$. It follows that $(x-3i)^3 = x^3 - 9x^2i - 27x + 27i$. If you chose **G**, you may have computed $+(3i)^3$ for the last term: $+(3i)^3 = 27(i)^2 i = -27i$. If you chose **J**, you have selected the expression where the middle terms do NOT contain a factor of 3. If you chose **K**, you have selected the expression where the two middle terms are missing.

Question 59. The correct answer is D. First, we note that the graph rises to the left and rises to the right, or $f(x) \to +\infty$, as $x \to -\infty$, and $f(x) \to +\infty$, as $x \to +\infty$. Thus, the degree of the function is even, and the leading coefficient is positive. The graph of the function has zeros located at $x = -4$, $x = 0$, and $x = 6$. These correspond to the polynomial factors $(x+4)$, x, and $(x-6)$. Next, we find the multiplicity of each zero, that is, how many times a particular number is a zero for a given polynomial function. We note that the sign of $f(x)$ does NOT change from one side of $x = 0$ to the other side because the graph touches the x-axis at 0 and turns around. This means that a zero of even multiplicity occurs at $x = 0$. We also note that the sign of $f(x)$ changes from one side of $x = -4$ to the other side and the sign of $f(x)$ changes from one side of $x = 6$ to the other side. That is, the graph crosses the x-axis at −4 and 6. This means that the zero at $x = -4$ and the zero at $x = 6$ are of odd multiplicity. Therefore, the only function that satisfies all the above conditions is $p(x) = x^2(x-6)^3(x+4)$. If you chose **A**, you have selected a function with an odd degree. If you chose **B** or **C**, you have selected a function that has zeros located at $x = -6$, $x = 0$, and $x = 4$. If you chose **E**, you have selected a function that has a zero of odd multiplicity at $x = 0$ and a zero of even multiplicity at $x = 6$.

Question 60. The correct answer is K. We can only multiply two matrices if the number of columns in the first matrix is the same as the number of rows in the second matrix. Matrix A has n columns, and Matrix C has k rows. Therefore, the matrix product AC is NOT possible. If you chose **F**, Matrix E has m columns, and Matrix D has m rows, so the matrix product ED is possible. If you chose **G**, Matrix D has k columns, and Matrix C has k rows, so the matrix product DC is possible. If you chose **H**, Matrix C has n columns, and Matrix E has n rows, so the matrix product CE is possible. If you chose **J**, Matrix A has n columns, and Matrix E has n rows, so the matrix product AE is possible.

Passage I

Question 1. The best answer is **B** because lines 21–22 clearly state why the blond woman is traveling to Palm Beach: "she's taking the bus to see" a man who "left for a construction job" there.

The best answer is NOT:

A because the passage does not address why the character "you" is leaving Memphis.

C because the blond woman turns away from the character "you" at the end of the passage, so there is no indication of what she is thinking.

D because the passage does not address where the blond woman is from originally.

Question 2. The best answer is **H** because lines 22–25 state that the man in Palm Beach thinks the blond woman's eyes are "as blue as" the Atlantic Ocean, and he cannot bear to look at "the thing" (the Atlantic Ocean) one more time if the blond woman isn't there with him.

The best answer is NOT:

F because the man in Palm Beach works in a construction job; it is not the thing he cannot bear to look at.

G because the blond woman's blue eyes are mentioned as a point of comparison with the Atlantic Ocean; they are not the thing the man in Palm Beach cannot bear to look at.

J because a bus is the setting where the scene in the passage takes place; it is not the thing the man in Palm Beach cannot bear to look at.

Question 3. The best answer is **D** because the word *occasional* is modifying *home*, not porch lights or fireflies. The "you" character is watching homes as the bus moves along, and those homes are not close together.

The best answer is NOT:

A because Lines 34–35 state that the porch lights are "perched, fat and throbbing" outside *every* home.

B because Lines 34–35 state that the porch lights are "perched, fat and throbbing" outside *every* home.

C because firefly porch lights are described; actual fireflies are not mentioned.

Question 4. The best answer is **F** because the girl does not acknowledge the narrator in any way.

The best answer is NOT:

G because the girl never speaks.

H because the passage provides no indication of how the girl perceives the narrator or whether she even notices his presence on the train.

J because the girl does not express any reaction to the narrator's presence.

Question 5. The best answer is B because lines 88–89 reveal that the narrator had been in a dark frame of mind before he watched the girl toss the oranges to her brothers, so when he wants her to fail at opening the window, he is feeling "unspeakable fatigue" with his "tedious life."

The best answer is NOT:

A because the passage never suggests that the girl is helpless or has an uncertain future; she struggles with the window but eventually opens it.

C because the narrator doesn't notice the boys until after the window is open.

D because the train conductor is not around when the girl attempts to open the window.

Question 6. The best answer is F because lines 84–85 indicate that the girl needed to open the window to toss oranges "to her younger brothers as a token of gratitude."

The best answer is NOT:

G because there is no evidence in the passage that suggests the girl had to prove anything.

H because the girl never acknowledges the narrator, so there is no support for her needing to create space between the two of them.

J because there is no evidence in the passage that suggests the girl feels a need to freshen the air in the train.

Question 7. The best answer is C because lines 44–46 state that the narrator heard the conductor cursing and the "clattering of dry-weather clogs" coming from the ticket gate. These sounds and the direction from which they emanate provide strong cues that someone is about to board the train at the last minute.

The best answer is NOT:

A because the passage does not reference the screech of the train's brakes.

B because the passage does not reference the rustle of paper parcels.

D because the young girl in the passage does not shout.

Question 8. The best answer is J because the situation described in both passages involves an encounter between two characters traveling in close quarters. In both passages, the encounter has a strong impact on the main character, whose state of mind is shifted by the second character's words or actions.

The best answer is NOT:

F because only Passage A uses the second person point of view.

G because the time period in which these passages are set is never clearly indicated.

H because there is no dialogue in Passage B.

Question 9. The best answer is **D** because the only character in either passage who shows interest in having a conversation is the blond woman in Passage A. The first paragraph in Passage A clearly shows that the "you" character does not want to talk, and neither character in Passage B shows any interest in conversing.

The best answer is NOT:

A because the "you" character's actions in lines 5–11 (pulling lips tight, staring at the floor, motioning to an open novel) are all clear indications that this character has no interest in communicating with the blond woman.

B because the girl is intent on opening the window and shows no interest in communicating with the narrator.

C because lines 52–59 reveal that the narrator is repelled by the girl and even attempts to "blot her existence."

Question 10. The best answer is **F** because in Passage A, the "you" character describes the blond woman as having teased hair and "sad, neglected teeth" (lines 13–14). In Passage B, the narrator describes the girl as having "lusterless hair"; chapped, red cheeks; and "a grimy woolen scarf" (lines 52–56).

The best answer is NOT:

G because Passage A does not suggest that the blond woman delayed the bus's departure.

H because when the "you" character in Passage A and the narrator of Passage B first see the blond woman and the young girl, respectively, neither knows the reason the other character is traveling.

J because both the "you" character in Passage A and the narrator of Passage B use disparaging language to describe the blond woman and the young girl, respectively. There is no evidence in either passage to support the idea that the blond woman and the young girl are envied or that life seems easy to them.

Passage II

Question 11. The best answer is **D** because lines 3–5 make it clear that Stevenson "turned his back on the Victorian idol, progress," and instead steered toward the "rougher fringes." The phrase "skirts of civilization" in lines 69–70 conveys the same idea: Stevenson preferred the gas lamp over any "technological miracle of the future" (line 62).

The best answer is NOT:

A because the phrase "fire of adventure" describes the theme of Stevenson's novels, which is not directly related to his reluctance to embrace progress.

B because the phrase "an epic ocean voyage" refers to a literal sea journey; it is not synonymous with the "rougher fringes" of civilization.

C because the phrase "a glittering hieroglyph" refers to electric lights, which represent progress, something Stevenson objects to.

Question 12. The best answer is **F** because lines 48–60 describe the places the author visited in order to gather information about Stevenson.

The best answer is NOT:

G because there is no evidence in the passage to suggest that Stevenson's novels contain biographical information about Stevenson.

H because the passage contains no evidence to support the idea that the author worked for D. & T. Stevenson, Engineers.

J because where the author "comes from" is not addressed in the passage.

Question 13. The best answer is **D** because the paragraph's focus is on Stevenson's family; lines 14–15 state that Stevenson was "born into a Scottish family of civil engineers, esteemed for its technological genius."

The best answer is NOT:

A because the paragraph never mentions that Stevenson's grandfather insisted on anything.

B because Stevenson's desire to be a writer is not mentioned in the second paragraph.

C because the paragraph does not include a comparison between Stevenson's grandfather's lighthouses and his father's screens.

Question 14. The best answer is **G** because lines 60–64 capture the main idea of the fifth paragraph with the author's description of Stevenson imagining a future London flashing with electric lights.

The best answer is NOT:

F because the paragraph does not mention the plot of any of Stevenson's books.

H because the opposite is true: Stevenson preferred the gas lamps, which is evidenced by the statement "Not for him improvements in optics" (line 68).

J because the main focus of the paragraph is Stevenson's prediction and not his father's engineering feats.

Question 15. The best answer is **C** because line 50 ("he tried his hand at being an apprentice engineer"), lines 87–88 ("Stevenson . . . became a mariner himself"), and lines 6–8 ("his most popular novels . . .") provide evidence that Stevenson was an engineer, a mariner, and a writer.

The best answer is NOT:

A because the passage provides evidence that Stevenson had also been an engineer and a mariner.

B because the passage provides no evidence that Stevenson was a lamplighter.

D because the passage provides no evidence that Stevenson was a builder.

Question 16. **The best answer is H** because the image of telephone wires in line 11 suggests progress, which Stevenson was not interested in; he preferred "the sound of clashing swords" (line 10), which, in the context of the paragraph, represents the opposite of progress.

The best answer is NOT:

F because lines 15–22 provide evidence that technological progress did, in fact, occur in Stevenson's lifetime.

G because lines 1–3 provide evidence that, in fact, Stevenson preferred to avoid civilization's "increasing reliance on contraptions."

J because the passage provides no evidence that Stevenson was a sword fighter.

Question 17. **The best answer is A** because lines 23–25 state that Stevenson had been expected to join the family business. The phrase "a great wringing of hands" is used to describe the family's implied dismay at Stevenson's announcement that he would not, in fact, be following their expectations.

The best answer is NOT:

B because the passage provides no evidence that the family criticized Stevenson's diet.

C because the passage provides no evidence that the family was humiliated; rather, they were greatly disappointed.

D because the family's consternation in line 28 is presented as a possible result of the pleas Stevenson makes in his letters for his family to accept him as he is; it happens later, *after* the wringing of hands over Stevenson's announcement about not joining the family business.

Question 18. **The best answer is J** because lines 35–36 provide a quote from Stevenson revealing that he preferred to travel without a set itinerary: "I travel not to go anywhere, but to go." Lines 37–38 suggest that Stevenson found happiness in open-ended travel: "I travel for travel's sake. The great affair is to move."

The best answer is NOT:

F because Stevenson's own words in lines 35–38 indicate that the destination was not important to him.

G because lines 34–35 indicate that Stevenson provided "the template for generations of college-educated adventurers"; they do not say that traveling should replace education.

H because the only mention of the character David Balfour is in line 52, and there is no indication that Stevenson's travels were a model for Balfour.

Question 19. The best answer is **A** because the meaning of the idiomatic phrase "stumbled across" is "found by accident," and this is the only option that logically fits the context of the sentence. The narrator found Abernethy House by accident.

The best answer is NOT:

B because the passage provides no evidence that the author staggered.

C because the passage provides no evidence that the author "unearthed" a building.

D because the passage provides no evidence that the author "tripped over" a building.

Question 20. The best answer is **J** because lines 83–85 directly state that "Thomas Stevenson's name may not have been widely known," but "his lights were in every part of the world."

The best answer is NOT:

F because the passage provides no evidence that Robert Louis Stevenson and his father, Thomas, were estranged.

G because lines 15–20 explain how Thomas Stevenson's father was "Britain's greatest builder of lighthouses" and how Thomas "followed him into the profession." Clearly, Thomas Stevenson would not have been unaware that his name would become associated with lighthouses.

H because the passage provides no evidence that Thomas was more famous than his son, Robert.

Passage III

Question 21. The best answer is **B** because lines 71–85 suggest that the author's cultural intuition, which she acquired on her reservation, gives her the knowledge to know that "kivas are safe places" and not the "frightening places" described in Gerald McDermott's book. In lines 71–72, the author directly states that she draws upon her cultural intuition when reading a book about Pueblo Indians.

The best answer is NOT:

A because the reference to Bruchac is about storytelling, not about the author's cultural intuition.

C because the passage does not mention where the author has presented her research.

D because the passage provides no evidence that the author and Silko discussed anything.

Question 22. The best answer is **G** because lines 1–13 explain the value and functions of traditional stories: to pass "religious beliefs, customs, history, lifestyle, language, [and] values" from one generation to another and to transmit "an entire culture, a worldview complete with strategies for survival."

The best answer is NOT:

F because there is no mention of stories changing as they are passed from one generation to the next.

H because the paragraph states that traditional stories *include* folktales, myths, and legends; these are not compared or contrasted.

J because there is no mention of a culture's worldview changing over time.

Question 23. The best answer is **D** because lines 41–44 directly state that "in order for it to be acceptable . . . [the story] should remain true to the spirit and content of the original."

The best answer is NOT:

A because lines 33–41 make it clear that it is acceptable for storytellers to add and change details in the stories they are telling.

B because lines 39–40 state that "a storyteller may revise a story according to his or her own interpretation."

C because lines 35–38 suggest that it is acceptable for audience members to offer new details.

Question 24. The best answer is **G** because the author's statement that her home pueblo is different from other pueblos (lines 67–69) precedes her discussion of McDermott's book and provides support for her critique that his book fails to show the differences among the many pueblos in New Mexico (lines 74–78).

The best answer is NOT:

F because the culture and traditions of her home pueblo are not specifically described in the passage; rather, the author discusses the traditions of the Pueblo people as a whole.

H because the author never compares her tribe's stories with the stories of other tribal nations.

J because the passage does not contain a list of criteria the author uses when evaluating books marketed as "Native American folktales."

Question 25. The best answer is **C** because lines 86–88 clearly state that "depictions that are culturally acceptable at one Pueblo are not necessarily acceptable at a different Pueblo." Elders take the cultural values of their *specific* community (or *audience,* line 92) into account when determining whether books are culturally acceptable for children of that community.

The best answer is NOT:

A because the passage does not address the entertainment value of books, comparatively or otherwise.

B because the passage does not address the popularity of books among tribal members.

D because elders are concerned with the appropriateness of books for their *specific communities* (lines 86–92); there is no mention of elders being concerned with the way books represent the worldviews of many groups.

Question 26. The best answer is **H** because lines 16–17 state that the hunting stories contain information "about the behavior and migration patterns of mule deer."

The best answer is NOT:

F because Silko never mentions rescuing hunters from other tribes.

G because there is no mention of documenting the number of successful hunts.

J because Silko mentions locations of fresh water and lost piñon-nut gatherers, but she does not state that hunting stories help people find caches of food.

Question 27. The best answer is **A** because lines 65–67 directly state this: "As a scholar in American Indian studies, I know there are great distinctions between and across American Indian tribal nations."

The best answer is NOT:

B because there is no evidence to suggest that the author and McDermott were friends.

C because there is no evidence to suggest that the author is an editor for picture books.

D because there is no evidence to suggest that the author is an elder.

Question 28. The best answer is **G** because in lines 66–67 the author is making the point that there are "great distinctions" between and across American Indian tribal nations. In this context, *great* is synonymous with *significant*.

> The best answer is NOT:
>
> **F** because *excessive* does not logically fit the context of the paragraph.
>
> **H** because *exuberant* does not logically fit the context of the paragraph.
>
> **J** because *splendid* does not logically fit the context of the paragraph.

Question 29. The best answer is **D** because lines 67–70 directly state that one of the differences among the pueblos in New Mexico is that "there are several different language groups."

> The best answer is NOT:
>
> **A** because the Pueblo communities mentioned are all in New Mexico, so the geographic differences cannot be *vast*.
>
> **B** because a disparity of resources is never discussed.
>
> **C** because approaches to parenting are not discussed.

Question 30. The best answer is **J** because lines 84–85 directly state that the author knows kivas as "safe places of worship and instruction."

> The best answer is NOT:
>
> **F** because the author says that for her, kivas are "safe places," not places of fear and trial.
>
> **G** because kivas are never described by the author as mysterious or exciting.
>
> **H** because kivas are not mentioned in relation to rest or healing.

Passage IV

Question 31. The best answer is **B** because the passage begins with a discussion of "the spontaneous vegetation that dominates the neglected interstices" (lines 3–5), goes on to define weeds (lines 24–25), and then discusses how weeds "survive in derelict urban wastelands" and are "famous (or infamous) for their ability to grow under extremely harsh conditions" (lines 49–51).

> The best answer is NOT:
>
> **A** because the passage never presents an argument for eradicating weeds.
>
> **C** because the passage is not a *report*, and it does not mention a need for more vegetation in urban environments.
>
> **D** because the passage does not mention the work or opinions of environmentalists.

Question 32. The best answer is H because the author's perspective throughout the passage best fits the biological one described in the second paragraph: "weeds are opportunistic plants that are adapted to disturbance" (lines 26–27). Support for this perspective is found in a number of places in the passage: "The plants that grow and survive in derelict urban wastelands are famous . . . for their ability to grow under extremely harsh conditions" (lines 49–51); a successful urban plant is "*opportunistic* in its ability to take advantage of locally abundant resources" (lines 73–75); urban plants are "*tolerant* of the stressful growing conditions" (line 76).

The best answer is NOT:

F because the idea that weeds grow in places where people don't want them is only summarized; it is not developed enough to represent the author's own perspective.

G because the problem of weeds in agriculture is only summarized; it is not developed enough to represent the author's own perspective.

J because the city dweller's notion that weeds are "perceived as ugly" or a potential security hazard is only summarized; it is not developed enough to represent the author's own perspective.

Question 33. The best answer is B because based on lines 31–33, economic crops are agricultural plants, which compete with "spontaneous vegetation," or weeds.

The best answer is NOT:

A because ragweed is a type of "spontaneous vegetation," or weed.

C because urban plants are described as spontaneous plants in the first paragraph.

D because calcium-loving grasses are described as an example of urban weeds (lines 63–70).

Question 34. The best answer is G because lines 28–31 state that weed "pervasiveness in the urban environment is simply a reflection of the continual disruption that characterizes that habitat—they are not its cause."

The best answer is NOT:

F because the process of removing weeds is not discussed in the passage.

H because there is no evidence in the passage to suggest that there is a pervasive acceptance of weeds in urban areas.

J because the passage does not provide a comparison of the life cycle of weeds with the life cycle of other plants.

Question 35. The best answer is C because the word *greenery* refers to the "spontaneous vegetation," or weeds, introduced in lines 4–5 and further defined and discussed throughout the first paragraph.

The best answer is NOT:

A because in the context of the paragraph, *greenery* refers to "spontaneous vegetation," not to cultivated plants.

B because in the context of the paragraph, *greenery* refers to "spontaneous vegetation," not to landscapes that are protected.

D because in the context of the paragraph, *greenery* refers to "spontaneous vegetation," not to crops.

Question 36. The best answer is F because both sources cite specific examples that support the passage author's statement that weeds, "through a quirk of evolutionary fate, . . . developed traits in their native habitats that . . . 'preadapted' them to flourish in cities" (lines 51–54). The transitional word *similarly* (line 63) further establishes the complementary relationship between the study and the book.

The best answer is NOT:

G because the conclusions are similar, so they could not be contrasting.

H because the passage provides no evidence to suggest that Lundholm used Gilbert's book.

J because the paragraph clearly establishes that Lundholm and Marlin's study and Gilbert's book are *not* irrelevant to each other: both sources drew similar conclusions about weeds that originated in limestone-rich habitats.

Question 37. The best answer is D because lines 78–80 state that so-called weeds "managed to survive the transition from one land use to another as cities developed." This statement, and especially the author's use of the word *managed,* makes it clear that the author is appreciative and respectful of urban plants' adaptability and resilience.

The best answer is NOT:

A because the paragraph provides no suggestion of alarm.

B because the paragraph provides no indication that the author fears for weeds' survival; rather, he is impressed by their ability to survive.

C because the paragraph provides no evidence to suggest that the author is ever annoyed about anything.

Question 38. The best answer is **F** because lines 11–13 directly state that Norway maple was among the plants "brought in intentionally or unintentionally by people."

The best answer is NOT:

G because the passage does not indicate that the Norway maple was brought by wind.

H because the passage does not indicate that the Norway maple was brought by water.

J because the passage does not indicate that the Norway maple was brought by birds.

Question 39. The best answer is **B** because lines 15–16 make it clear that "on their own" refers to "dispersed by wind, water, or wild animals," which indicates people were not involved.

The best answer is NOT:

A because the passage provides no evidence that any of the plants being discussed were brought to urban environments one at a time.

C because the passage directly states that the plants were brought by "wind, water, or wild animals"; they were, therefore, not self-propelled.

D because the word *voluntarily* suggests that the plants had a choice, which would be impossible given that plants do not have the ability to choose whether they are relocated or not.

Question 40. The best answer is **J** because lines 20–21 directly state that "if left undisturbed long enough," weeds "may even develop into mature woodlands."

The best answer is NOT:

F because the passage provides no evidence to suggest that weeds would eventually compete for space and die out.

G because the passage provides no evidence to suggest that weeds might eventually enhance landscaped gardens.

H because the passage provides no evidence to suggest that weeds might eventually dry out the soil.

SCIENCE • PRACTICE TEST 2 • EXPLANATORY ANSWERS

Passage I

1. **The best answer is A.** According to Student 4, the atoms from smallest to largest are F, Cl, Br, and I. The table shows that the atoms from smallest to largest atomic mass are F, Cl, Br, and I. As atomic mass increases, atomic radius also increases. **A** is correct. **B, C,** and **D** are incorrect: as atomic mass increases, atomic radius increases.

2. **The best answer is H.** According to the passage, only Student 2 states that As does not have a lone pair. Students 1, 3, and 4 all state that As has a lone pair. **F, G,** and **J** are incorrect: Students 1, 3, and 4 state that As has a lone pair. **H** is correct.

3. **The best answer is C.** Students 1 and 2 both propose planar structures for AsF_3 in which all the atoms lie in the same plane. Students 3 and 4 both propose pyramidal structures in which the As lies above the plane of the three F. Only Students 1 and 2 would agree with the statement. **A, B,** and **D** are incorrect: Students 3 and 4 propose structures for AsF_3 that are not planar, and therefore they are not likely to agree with the statement. **C** is correct.

4. **The best answer is J.** Student 1 claims that there are 2 unique angles in the AsF_3 molecule, and Students 2, 3, and 4 claim that there is only 1 unique angle in the AsF_3 molecule. None of the students would agree that there are 3 unique bond angles in the molecule. **F, G,** and **H** are incorrect: none of the students would agree with the claim. **J** is correct.

5. **The best answer is A.** According to the passage, the sum of the angles in Student 1's model is $180 + 90 + 90 = 360$. The sum of the angles in Student 2's model is $120 + 120 + 120 = 360$. The sum of the angles in Student 3's model is $109 + 109 + 109 = 327$. The sum of the angles in Student 4's model ranges from $100 + 100 + 100 = 300$ to $111 + 111 + 111 = 333$. Only Students 1 and 2 are likely to agree that the sum of the bond angles is equal to 360°. **A** is correct. **B, C,** and **D** are incorrect: only Students 1 and 2 would agree that the sum of the bond angles is 360°.

6. **The best answer is J.** According to the passage, Student 2 claims that As has no lone pair and the molecule is trigonal planar. Student 3 claims that As has a lone pair and, because of this, the molecule is trigonal pyramidal. Because N has a lone pair, it is more likely that it will adopt the trigonal pyramid conformation. **F** and **G** are incorrect: because of the lone pair, it is not likely that the ammonia molecule will adopt a trigonal planar conformation. **H** is incorrect: the bond angle is more consistent with Student 3's description. **J** is correct.

7. **The best answer is D.** According to Table 1, the bond angles vary depending on the type of atom bonded to As. Only Student 4 claimed that the bond angles would vary, and therefore the data is most consistent with Student 4's description. **A, B,** and **C** are incorrect: Students 1, 2, and 3 all claimed that the bond angles would be the same for the different molecules. **D** is correct.

Passage II

8. **The best answer is F.** According to Table 2, all the offspring from Cross 1 had a black coat. If both of the parents were *BBEE,* then all the offspring would have also been *BBEE.* According to Table 1, the genotype *BBEE* corresponds to a black coat. The hypothesis is consistent with the results of Cross 1. **F** is correct. **G** is incorrect: the offspring of Cross 1 had black coats. **H** and **J** are incorrect: the hypothesis is consistent with the results of Cross 1.

9. **The best answer is D.** According to Table 2, the genotypes *bbEE* and *bbEe* resulted in brown coats. The offspring from Cross 2 with a brown coat must have been either *bbEE* or *bbEe.* **A** is incorrect: *bbee* would have a yellow coat. **B** is incorrect: *BBEE* would have a black coat. **C** is incorrect: *BbEE* or *BbEe* would have a black coat. **D** is correct: both *bbEE* and *bbEe* would have a brown coat.

10. **The best answer is H.** According to Table 1, offspring with one or more copies of the *E* allele of Gene E would have a black coat or a brown coat. Table 2 shows that 2 of the Cross 3 offspring had a black coat, and 2 of the offspring had a brown coat. There were 6 offspring total. Four out of 6, or 2/3, of the offspring had one or more copies of the *E* allele of Gene E. **F, G,** and **J** are incorrect: 2/3 of the offspring had one or more copies of the *E* allele of Gene E. **H** is correct.

11. **The best answer is B.** To answer this item, the examinee must be familiar with dominant-recessive gene nomenclature. Capital letter for dominant and lowercase letter for recessive. According to Table 1, the genotype *bbee* with all recessive alleles corresponds to a yellow coat. According to Table 2, only Crosses 2 and 3 had offspring with a yellow coat, and therefore only Crosses 2 and 3 could have had only recessive alleles of Gene B and Gene E. **A** is incorrect: Cross 1 had no offspring with yellow coats. **B** is correct. **C** is incorrect: Cross 1 had no offspring with yellow coats. **D** is incorrect: Crosses 2 and 3 both had offspring with yellow coats that could have had the genotype *bbee.*

12. **The best answer is J.** According to Table 1, the *EE* genotype results in a black or brown coat color, and the *ee* genotype results in a yellow coat color. The observation that the *ee* genotype always corresponds to a yellow coat color indicates that the Gene E phenotypic expression is not affected by Gene B. **F** and **G** are incorrect: the data are not consistent with the hypothesis. **H** is incorrect: *EE* does not always result in a black coat. **J** is correct.

13. **The best answer is C.** To answer this item, the examinee must understand the segregation of chromosomes into gametes. For a dog with the genotype *BbEE,* half of the gametes will contain the *B* allele and the other half will contain the *b* allele. **A, B,** and **D** are incorrect: 50% will contain the *B* allele. **C** is correct.

Passage III

14. **The best answer is J.** According to Figure 2, the highest $\frac{W}{D}$%, corresponding to the greatest average wet strength, was observed for the PTs submerged in water for 10 min and heated in the 140°C oven with a $\frac{W}{D} = 50\%$. **F** is incorrect: the PTs heated in the 110°C oven had a $\frac{W}{D}$ value less than 25%. **G** is incorrect: the PTs heated in the 120°C oven had a $\frac{W}{D}$ value less than 35%. **H** is incorrect: the PTs heated in the 130°C oven had a $\frac{W}{D}$ value of 40%. **J** is correct.

15. **The best answer is A.** According to Figure 2, as the oven temperature increased from 110°C to 140°C, the $\frac{W}{D}$ value for PTs submerged in water for 2 hr increased from approximately 23% to 48%. **A** is correct. **B, C,** and **D** are incorrect: the $\frac{W}{D}$ value increased steadily as the temperature increased.

16. **The best answer is F.** According to the passage, in Step 1 the control PTs were submerged in water, and in Step 3 the control PTs were heated in an oven at 25°C. **F** is correct. **G** is incorrect: the oven temperature was 25°C. **H** and **J** are incorrect: the PTs were submerged in water.

17. **The best answer is D.** According to the passage, the PTs in both Experiments 1 and 2 were soaked in water for 10 min, 2 hr, or 24 hr. None of the PTs was soaked in water for 18 hr. **A, B,** and **C** are incorrect: PTs were not soaked for 18 hr in either experiment. **D** is correct.

18. **The best answer is G.** According to Figure 1, the PTs submerged in water for 10 min had a higher $\frac{W}{D}$ value at all oven temperatures than did the PTs submerged in water for 2 hr. **F** is incorrect: the $\frac{W}{D}$ value at 2 hr was less than the $\frac{W}{D}$ value at 10 min. **G** is correct. **H** is incorrect: the $\frac{W}{D}$ values were not the same. **J** is incorrect: the $\frac{W}{D}$ value at 10 min was always greater than the $\frac{W}{D}$ value at 2 hr.

19. **The best answer is C.** The results of Experiment 2 show that wet strength of PTs treated with both GLA and zinc nitrate was greater than the wet strength of PTs treated with water. Because the results show that treatment with GLA and zinc nitrate did increase the wet strength of the PTS, the results of Experiment 2 refute the prediction. **A** and **B** are incorrect: Experiment 1 did not investigate the effect of treating the PTs with GLA and zinc nitrate. **C** is correct. **D** is incorrect: Experiment 2 does not support the prediction.

20. **The best answer is G.** In both experiments, the wet strength of the PTs is expressed as a percentage of the dry strength. Because this percentage is less than 100%, the dry strength is greater than the wet strength. **F** is incorrect: the wet strength was less than 100% of the dry strength. **G** is correct. **H** and **J** are incorrect: the dry strength was greater than the wet strength.

Passage IV

21. **The best answer is B.** To answer this item, the examinee must be familiar with basic scientific instruments and know that an electronic balance is used to measure mass. Tables 2 and 3 list the average final mass of the adult frogs that would have been measured with an electronic balance. **A** is incorrect: a graduated cylinder is used to measure volume. **C** is incorrect: a metric ruler is used to measure length. **D** is incorrect: a calorimeter is used to measure changes in heat during a chemical reaction or process. **B** is correct: an electronic balance is used to measure mass.

22. **The best answer is F.** According to Table 1, the percent by mass of protein increased in Diets 1–5. Table 2 shows that the average final mass of the frogs also increased for the frogs fed Diets 1–5. **F** is correct. **G, H,** and **J** are incorrect: as the percent by mass of protein increased, the average final mass of the frogs also increased.

23. **The best answer is B.** According to the passage, the frogs were placed in outdoor tanks. It is most likely that the wire mesh was used to keep the frogs in the tanks and to keep predators out of the tanks. The tanks were covered after the frogs were placed in the tanks, so the mesh was not used to place the frogs in the tanks. **A, C,** and **D** are incorrect: the mesh was used to prevent predators from entering the tanks and keep the frogs from leaving the tanks. **B** is correct.

24. **The best answer is H.** According to Table 1, the number of calories per gram increased in Diets 6–10. Table 3 shows that the average final mass of the frogs increased as the frogs were fed Diets 6–8, but then decreased for the frogs fed Diets 8–10. **F, G,** and **J** are incorrect: the average final mass of the frogs increased and then decreased. **H** is correct.

25. **The best answer is C.** To answer this item, the examinee must know that organisms that belong to the same species also belong to the same genus. According to the passage, the species *Rana rugulosa* was studied. All the frogs were the same species and genus. **A, B,** and **D** are incorrect: the frogs belonged to the same genus and the same species. **C** is correct.

26. **The best answer is G.** According to the passage, in Experiment 1 the starting mass of the frogs was 3.3 g, and each frog was fed 1,000 mg of food twice a day for a total of 2,000 mg. In Experiment 2, the starting mass of the frogs was 7.9 g, and each frog was fed 2,000 mg of food once a day. **F** is incorrect: the initial mass of each frog was less in Experiment 1 than in Experiment 2. **G** is correct: the initial mass of each frog in Experiment 2 was 7.9 g, and the initial mass of each frog in Experiment 1 was 3.3 g. **H** and **J** are incorrect: the frogs in both experiments were fed 2,000 mg of food per day.

27. **The best answer is D.** According to Table 1, Diets 1–5 all contained the same number of calories per gram, and the number of calories per gram was varied in Diets 6–10. To determine whether the number of calories per gram in the diet affected the growth, the farmer should have compared the results of Diets 6–10. **A** and **B** are incorrect: the percent by mass of protein was varied in Diets 1–5, and this would give no information about the effect of the number of calories per gram in the diet. **C** is incorrect: Diets 6–10 varied in the number of calories per gram. The percent by mass of protein was held constant. **D** is correct.

Passage V

28. **The best answer is F.** According to Figure 3, the average water content of soil values for the 4 dates were closest to one another, differing by less than 5%, at a depth of 30 cm. F is correct. **G** is incorrect: the values were slightly more spread out at a depth of 60 cm. **H** is incorrect: the values had a range that was greater than 10% at a depth of 100 cm. **J** is incorrect: the values had a range of approximately 15% at a depth of 140 cm.

29. **The best answer is A.** According to the passage, the slots near the end of the steel pipe allowed only soil gas to enter the pipe. **A** is correct. **B, C,** and **D** are incorrect: only soil gas entered the pipe.

30. **The best answer is J.** According to the passage, CO_2 is produced through 2 processes, but the experimental procedure does not provide any way of determining how much of the gas is produced by either process. **F, G,** and **H** are incorrect. **J** is correct: there is no way of knowing what percentage of the gas is produced by respiration in plant roots and how much is produced through decomposition of organic matter in this experiment.

31. **The best answer is B.** According to Figure 2, the percentage recorded is the average CO_2 content of soil gas by volume. To calculate this amount, one would divide the volume of CO_2 by the total volume of the gas sample. **A** is incorrect: to determine the percentage of CO_2 in the gas, one would have to divide by the volume of the gas sample. **B** is correct. **C** is incorrect: the percentage of CO_2 in the gas sample is being calculated, not the percentage of CO_2 in the water sample. **D** is incorrect: not all the gas collected in the steel pipe was analyzed for its CO_2 content, and therefore only the volume of the gas removed from the steel pipe via the syringe should be used in the percentage calculation.

32. **The best answer is J.** According to Figure 3, the average water content of the soil increased for the samples collected on November 23 and December 7, and the average water content decreased for the samples collected on October 26 and November 9. **F** is incorrect: the average water content increased only on November 23 and December 7. **G** is incorrect: the average water content decreased only on October 26 and November 9. **H** is incorrect: the average water content increased on November 23 and December 7 and decreased on October 26 and November 9. **J** is correct.

33. **The best answer is D.** According to Figure 2, for the samples collected on November 23, as the depth increased, the average CO_2 content also increased. At a depth of 140 cm, the average CO_2 content was approximately 0.41% by volume. If another diffusion well was positioned at a depth of 145 cm, then the average CO_2 content of the soil gas would have been greater than 0.40% by volume. **A, B,** and **C** are incorrect: the CO_2 content would have been greater than 0.40%. **D** is correct.

34. **The best answer is G.** According to Figure 3, on November 23 at a depth of 60 cm, the soil had an average water content of 20% by mass. A 10 g sample of soil would have contained 2 g of water (20% of 10 g = 2 g). **F** is incorrect: the mass of water would be 1 g if the average water content was 10% by mass. **G** is correct. **H** is incorrect: the mass of water would be 5 g if the average water content was 50% by mass. **J** is incorrect: if 10 g of water was in the sample, then the sample was 100% water and contained no soil.

Passage VI

35. **The best answer is D.** According to Figure 3, as time increased, the depth in motor oil also increased. At a time of 45 msec, the depth of the steel ball in motor oil was approximately 1.9 mm. The depth at time = 50 msec would most likely have been slightly greater than 1.9 mm. **A, B,** and **C** are incorrect: the depth would have been greater than 1.9 mm. **D** is correct.

36. **The best answer is G.** To answer this item, the examinee must know that buoyant forces are always directed upward and the gravitational force is directed downward. According to the passage, drag is a force that opposes motion. Because the ball is moving downward, drag is an upward force. **F** is incorrect: *D* should be an upward force. **G** is correct. **H** and **J** are incorrect: *G* is a downward force and *B* is an upward force.

37. **The best answer is C.** According to Figure 1, the steel ball in motor oil reaches terminal speed, where the speed remains constant, after approximately 25 msec. Figure 2 shows that the steel ball in glycerin reaches terminal speed after approximately 10 msec. It required less time for the steel ball to reach terminal speed in glycerin. **A** and **B** are incorrect: it took more time to reach terminal speed in motor oil. **C** is correct. **D** is incorrect: it took approximately 25 msec in motor oil and only 10 msec in glycerin.

38. **The best answer is F.** According to Figure 1, the terminal speed of the steel ball in motor oil was approximately 48 mm/sec. Figure 2 shows that the terminal speed of the steel ball in glycerin was approximately 10 mm/sec. The terminal speed was greater in motor oil. **F** is correct. **G** is incorrect: the terminal speed was approximately 48 mm/sec in motor oil and 10 mm/sec in glycerin. **H** and **J** are incorrect: the steel ball's terminal speed was greater in motor oil.

39. **The best answer is C.** According to Figure 3, in both motor oil and glycerin, the depth of the steel ball increased over time. According to Figures 2 and 3, over time the draw increased and then leveled off. The drag on the steel ball was not proportional to the depth of the ball because as the depth increased, the drag increased and then remained roughly constant. **A** and **B** are incorrect: it is not reasonable to conclude that the drag on the steel ball was directly proportional to the depth of the ball. **C** is correct. **D** is incorrect: the drag increased and then remained roughly constant.

40. **The best answer is H.** According to Figure 3, the steel ball reached a depth of 0.50 mm in motor oil after approximately 16 msec. Figure 1 shows that, after 16 msec in motor oil, the drag on the steel ball was approximately 270 μN. **F** is incorrect: the drag reached 230 μN after approximately 9 msec, and at this time the steel ball was at a depth of only about 0.20 mm. **G** is incorrect: the drag reached 250 μN after approximately 11 msec, and at this time the steel ball was at a depth of only about 0.25 mm. **H** is correct: the drag reached 270 μN after approximately 14 msec, and the steel ball at this time was at a depth of about 0.50 mm. **J** is incorrect: the drag reached 290 μN after approximately 30 msec, and the steel ball at this time was at a depth of about 1.20 mm.

The ACT® *Sample Answer Document*

EXAMINEE STATEMENTS, CERTIFICATION, AND SIGNATURE

1. **Statements**: I understand that by registering for, launching, starting, or submitting answer documents for an ACT® test, I am agreeing to comply with and be bound by the *Terms and Conditions: Testing Rules and Policies for the ACT® Test* ("Terms").

   I UNDERSTAND AND AGREE THAT THE TERMS PERMIT ACT TO CANCEL MY SCORES IN CERTAIN CIRCUMSTANCES. THE TERMS ALSO LIMIT DAMAGES AVAILABLE TO ME AND REQUIRE ARBITRATION OF CERTAIN DISPUTES. BY AGREEING TO ARBITRATION, ACT AND I BOTH WAIVE THE RIGHT TO HAVE THOSE DISPUTES HEARD BY A JUDGE OR JURY.

   I understand that ACT owns the test questions and responses, and I will not share them with anyone by any form of communication before, during, or after the test administration. I understand that taking the test for someone else may violate the law and subject me to legal penalties. I consent to the collection and processing of personally identifying information I provide, and its subsequent use and disclosure, as described in the ACT Privacy Policy (www.act.org/privacy.html). I also permit ACT to transfer my personally identifying information to the United States, to ACT, or to a third-party service provider, where it will be subject to use and disclosure under the laws of the United States, including being accessible to law enforcement or national security authorities.

2. **Certification**: Copy the italicized certification below, then sign and date in the spaces provided.

   I agree to the **Statements** *above and certify that I am the person whose information appears on this form.*

   _____

   _____

   _____   _____
   Your Signature   Today's Date

Do NOT mark in this shaded area.

USE A NO. 2 PENCIL ONLY.
(Do NOT use a mechanical pencil, ink, ballpoint, correction fluid, or felt-tip pen.)

A   NAME, MAILING ADDRESS, AND TELEPHONE
(Please print.)

Last Name   First Name   MI (Middle Initial)

House Number & Street (Apt. No.); or PO Box & No.; or RR & No.

City   State/Province   ZIP/Postal Code

Area Code   Number   Country

ACT, Inc.—Confidential Restricted when data present

ALL examinees must complete block A – please print.

Blocks B, C, and D are required for all examinees. Find the MATCHING INFORMATION on your ticket. Enter it EXACTLY the same way, even if any of the information is missing or incorrect. Fill in the corresponding ovals. If you do not complete these blocks to match your previous information EXACTLY, your scores will be **delayed up to 8 weeks**.

ACT®
PO BOX 168, IOWA CITY, IA 52243-0168

B   MATCH NAME
(First 5 letters of last name)

A B C D E F G H I J K L M N O P Q R S T U V W X Y Z

C   MATCH NUMBER

0 1 2 3 4 5 6 7 8 9

D   DATE OF BIRTH

Month	Day	Year
January		
February		
March	1	1
April	2	2
May	3	3
June	4	4
July	5	5
August	6	6
September	7	7
October	8	8
November	9	9
December	0	0

The ONLY Official Prep Guide from the Makers of the ACT

PAGE 2

Marking Directions: Mark only **one** oval for each question. Fill in response completely. Erase errors cleanly without smudging.

Correct mark: ○ ● ○ ○

Do NOT use these *incorrect* **or** *bad* **marks.**

Incorrect marks: ⊘ ⊗ ⊖ ⊙
Overlapping mark: ○ ○ ◖◗
Cross-out mark: ○ ◉ ○ ○
Smudged erasure: ○ ○ ◍ ○
Mark is too light: ◌ ○ ○ ○

BOOKLET NUMBER

FORM

Print your 5-character **Test Form** in the boxes at the right and fill in the corresponding ovals.

TEST 1: ENGLISH

1 Ⓐ Ⓑ Ⓒ Ⓓ	14 Ⓕ Ⓖ Ⓗ Ⓙ	27 Ⓐ Ⓑ Ⓒ Ⓓ	40 Ⓕ Ⓖ Ⓗ Ⓙ	53 Ⓐ Ⓑ Ⓒ Ⓓ	66 Ⓕ Ⓖ Ⓗ Ⓙ
2 Ⓕ Ⓖ Ⓗ Ⓙ	15 Ⓐ Ⓑ Ⓒ Ⓓ	28 Ⓕ Ⓖ Ⓗ Ⓙ	41 Ⓐ Ⓑ Ⓒ Ⓓ	54 Ⓕ Ⓖ Ⓗ Ⓙ	67 Ⓐ Ⓑ Ⓒ Ⓓ
3 Ⓐ Ⓑ Ⓒ Ⓓ	16 Ⓕ Ⓖ Ⓗ Ⓙ	29 Ⓐ Ⓑ Ⓒ Ⓓ	42 Ⓕ Ⓖ Ⓗ Ⓙ	55 Ⓐ Ⓑ Ⓒ Ⓓ	68 Ⓕ Ⓖ Ⓗ Ⓙ
4 Ⓕ Ⓖ Ⓗ Ⓙ	17 Ⓐ Ⓑ Ⓒ Ⓓ	30 Ⓕ Ⓖ Ⓗ Ⓙ	43 Ⓐ Ⓑ Ⓒ Ⓓ	56 Ⓕ Ⓖ Ⓗ Ⓙ	69 Ⓐ Ⓑ Ⓒ Ⓓ
5 Ⓐ Ⓑ Ⓒ Ⓓ	18 Ⓕ Ⓖ Ⓗ Ⓙ	31 Ⓐ Ⓑ Ⓒ Ⓓ	44 Ⓕ Ⓖ Ⓗ Ⓙ	57 Ⓐ Ⓑ Ⓒ Ⓓ	70 Ⓕ Ⓖ Ⓗ Ⓙ
6 Ⓕ Ⓖ Ⓗ Ⓙ	19 Ⓐ Ⓑ Ⓒ Ⓓ	32 Ⓕ Ⓖ Ⓗ Ⓙ	45 Ⓐ Ⓑ Ⓒ Ⓓ	58 Ⓕ Ⓖ Ⓗ Ⓙ	71 Ⓐ Ⓑ Ⓒ Ⓓ
7 Ⓐ Ⓑ Ⓒ Ⓓ	20 Ⓕ Ⓖ Ⓗ Ⓙ	33 Ⓐ Ⓑ Ⓒ Ⓓ	46 Ⓕ Ⓖ Ⓗ Ⓙ	59 Ⓐ Ⓑ Ⓒ Ⓓ	72 Ⓕ Ⓖ Ⓗ Ⓙ
8 Ⓕ Ⓖ Ⓗ Ⓙ	21 Ⓐ Ⓑ Ⓒ Ⓓ	34 Ⓕ Ⓖ Ⓗ Ⓙ	47 Ⓐ Ⓑ Ⓒ Ⓓ	60 Ⓕ Ⓖ Ⓗ Ⓙ	73 Ⓐ Ⓑ Ⓒ Ⓓ
9 Ⓐ Ⓑ Ⓒ Ⓓ	22 Ⓕ Ⓖ Ⓗ Ⓙ	35 Ⓐ Ⓑ Ⓒ Ⓓ	48 Ⓕ Ⓖ Ⓗ Ⓙ	61 Ⓐ Ⓑ Ⓒ Ⓓ	74 Ⓕ Ⓖ Ⓗ Ⓙ
10 Ⓕ Ⓖ Ⓗ Ⓙ	23 Ⓐ Ⓑ Ⓒ Ⓓ	36 Ⓕ Ⓖ Ⓗ Ⓙ	49 Ⓐ Ⓑ Ⓒ Ⓓ	62 Ⓕ Ⓖ Ⓗ Ⓙ	75 Ⓐ Ⓑ Ⓒ Ⓓ
11 Ⓐ Ⓑ Ⓒ Ⓓ	24 Ⓕ Ⓖ Ⓗ Ⓙ	37 Ⓐ Ⓑ Ⓒ Ⓓ	50 Ⓕ Ⓖ Ⓗ Ⓙ	63 Ⓐ Ⓑ Ⓒ Ⓓ	
12 Ⓕ Ⓖ Ⓗ Ⓙ	25 Ⓐ Ⓑ Ⓒ Ⓓ	38 Ⓕ Ⓖ Ⓗ Ⓙ	51 Ⓐ Ⓑ Ⓒ Ⓓ	64 Ⓕ Ⓖ Ⓗ Ⓙ	
13 Ⓐ Ⓑ Ⓒ Ⓓ	26 Ⓕ Ⓖ Ⓗ Ⓙ	39 Ⓐ Ⓑ Ⓒ Ⓓ	52 Ⓕ Ⓖ Ⓗ Ⓙ	65 Ⓐ Ⓑ Ⓒ Ⓓ	

TEST 2: MATHEMATICS

1 Ⓐ Ⓑ Ⓒ Ⓓ Ⓔ	11 Ⓐ Ⓑ Ⓒ Ⓓ Ⓔ	21 Ⓐ Ⓑ Ⓒ Ⓓ Ⓔ	31 Ⓐ Ⓑ Ⓒ Ⓓ Ⓔ	41 Ⓐ Ⓑ Ⓒ Ⓓ Ⓔ	51 Ⓐ Ⓑ Ⓒ Ⓓ Ⓔ
2 Ⓕ Ⓖ Ⓗ Ⓙ Ⓚ	12 Ⓕ Ⓖ Ⓗ Ⓙ Ⓚ	22 Ⓕ Ⓖ Ⓗ Ⓙ Ⓚ	32 Ⓕ Ⓖ Ⓗ Ⓙ Ⓚ	42 Ⓕ Ⓖ Ⓗ Ⓙ Ⓚ	52 Ⓕ Ⓖ Ⓗ Ⓙ Ⓚ
3 Ⓐ Ⓑ Ⓒ Ⓓ Ⓔ	13 Ⓐ Ⓑ Ⓒ Ⓓ Ⓔ	23 Ⓐ Ⓑ Ⓒ Ⓓ Ⓔ	33 Ⓐ Ⓑ Ⓒ Ⓓ Ⓔ	43 Ⓐ Ⓑ Ⓒ Ⓓ Ⓔ	53 Ⓐ Ⓑ Ⓒ Ⓓ Ⓔ
4 Ⓕ Ⓖ Ⓗ Ⓙ Ⓚ	14 Ⓕ Ⓖ Ⓗ Ⓙ Ⓚ	24 Ⓕ Ⓖ Ⓗ Ⓙ Ⓚ	34 Ⓕ Ⓖ Ⓗ Ⓙ Ⓚ	44 Ⓕ Ⓖ Ⓗ Ⓙ Ⓚ	54 Ⓕ Ⓖ Ⓗ Ⓙ Ⓚ
5 Ⓐ Ⓑ Ⓒ Ⓓ Ⓔ	15 Ⓐ Ⓑ Ⓒ Ⓓ Ⓔ	25 Ⓐ Ⓑ Ⓒ Ⓓ Ⓔ	35 Ⓐ Ⓑ Ⓒ Ⓓ Ⓔ	45 Ⓐ Ⓑ Ⓒ Ⓓ Ⓔ	55 Ⓐ Ⓑ Ⓒ Ⓓ Ⓔ
6 Ⓕ Ⓖ Ⓗ Ⓙ Ⓚ	16 Ⓕ Ⓖ Ⓗ Ⓙ Ⓚ	26 Ⓕ Ⓖ Ⓗ Ⓙ Ⓚ	36 Ⓕ Ⓖ Ⓗ Ⓙ Ⓚ	46 Ⓕ Ⓖ Ⓗ Ⓙ Ⓚ	56 Ⓕ Ⓖ Ⓗ Ⓙ Ⓚ
7 Ⓐ Ⓑ Ⓒ Ⓓ Ⓔ	17 Ⓐ Ⓑ Ⓒ Ⓓ Ⓔ	27 Ⓐ Ⓑ Ⓒ Ⓓ Ⓔ	37 Ⓐ Ⓑ Ⓒ Ⓓ Ⓔ	47 Ⓐ Ⓑ Ⓒ Ⓓ Ⓔ	57 Ⓐ Ⓑ Ⓒ Ⓓ Ⓔ
8 Ⓕ Ⓖ Ⓗ Ⓙ Ⓚ	18 Ⓕ Ⓖ Ⓗ Ⓙ Ⓚ	28 Ⓕ Ⓖ Ⓗ Ⓙ Ⓚ	38 Ⓕ Ⓖ Ⓗ Ⓙ Ⓚ	48 Ⓕ Ⓖ Ⓗ Ⓙ Ⓚ	58 Ⓕ Ⓖ Ⓗ Ⓙ Ⓚ
9 Ⓐ Ⓑ Ⓒ Ⓓ Ⓔ	19 Ⓐ Ⓑ Ⓒ Ⓓ Ⓔ	29 Ⓐ Ⓑ Ⓒ Ⓓ Ⓔ	39 Ⓐ Ⓑ Ⓒ Ⓓ Ⓔ	49 Ⓐ Ⓑ Ⓒ Ⓓ Ⓔ	59 Ⓐ Ⓑ Ⓒ Ⓓ Ⓔ
10 Ⓕ Ⓖ Ⓗ Ⓙ Ⓚ	20 Ⓕ Ⓖ Ⓗ Ⓙ Ⓚ	30 Ⓕ Ⓖ Ⓗ Ⓙ Ⓚ	40 Ⓕ Ⓖ Ⓗ Ⓙ Ⓚ	50 Ⓕ Ⓖ Ⓗ Ⓙ Ⓚ	60 Ⓕ Ⓖ Ⓗ Ⓙ Ⓚ

TEST 3: READING

1 Ⓐ Ⓑ Ⓒ Ⓓ	8 Ⓕ Ⓖ Ⓗ Ⓙ	15 Ⓐ Ⓑ Ⓒ Ⓓ	22 Ⓕ Ⓖ Ⓗ Ⓙ	29 Ⓐ Ⓑ Ⓒ Ⓓ	36 Ⓕ Ⓖ Ⓗ Ⓙ
2 Ⓕ Ⓖ Ⓗ Ⓙ	9 Ⓐ Ⓑ Ⓒ Ⓓ	16 Ⓕ Ⓖ Ⓗ Ⓙ	23 Ⓐ Ⓑ Ⓒ Ⓓ	30 Ⓕ Ⓖ Ⓗ Ⓙ	37 Ⓐ Ⓑ Ⓒ Ⓓ
3 Ⓐ Ⓑ Ⓒ Ⓓ	10 Ⓕ Ⓖ Ⓗ Ⓙ	17 Ⓐ Ⓑ Ⓒ Ⓓ	24 Ⓕ Ⓖ Ⓗ Ⓙ	31 Ⓐ Ⓑ Ⓒ Ⓓ	38 Ⓕ Ⓖ Ⓗ Ⓙ
4 Ⓕ Ⓖ Ⓗ Ⓙ	11 Ⓐ Ⓑ Ⓒ Ⓓ	18 Ⓕ Ⓖ Ⓗ Ⓙ	25 Ⓐ Ⓑ Ⓒ Ⓓ	32 Ⓕ Ⓖ Ⓗ Ⓙ	39 Ⓐ Ⓑ Ⓒ Ⓓ
5 Ⓐ Ⓑ Ⓒ Ⓓ	12 Ⓕ Ⓖ Ⓗ Ⓙ	19 Ⓐ Ⓑ Ⓒ Ⓓ	26 Ⓕ Ⓖ Ⓗ Ⓙ	33 Ⓐ Ⓑ Ⓒ Ⓓ	40 Ⓕ Ⓖ Ⓗ Ⓙ
6 Ⓕ Ⓖ Ⓗ Ⓙ	13 Ⓐ Ⓑ Ⓒ Ⓓ	20 Ⓕ Ⓖ Ⓗ Ⓙ	27 Ⓐ Ⓑ Ⓒ Ⓓ	34 Ⓕ Ⓖ Ⓗ Ⓙ	
7 Ⓐ Ⓑ Ⓒ Ⓓ	14 Ⓕ Ⓖ Ⓗ Ⓙ	21 Ⓐ Ⓑ Ⓒ Ⓓ	28 Ⓕ Ⓖ Ⓗ Ⓙ	35 Ⓐ Ⓑ Ⓒ Ⓓ	

TEST 4: SCIENCE

1 Ⓐ Ⓑ Ⓒ Ⓓ	8 Ⓕ Ⓖ Ⓗ Ⓙ	15 Ⓐ Ⓑ Ⓒ Ⓓ	22 Ⓕ Ⓖ Ⓗ Ⓙ	29 Ⓐ Ⓑ Ⓒ Ⓓ	36 Ⓕ Ⓖ Ⓗ Ⓙ
2 Ⓕ Ⓖ Ⓗ Ⓙ	9 Ⓐ Ⓑ Ⓒ Ⓓ	16 Ⓕ Ⓖ Ⓗ Ⓙ	23 Ⓐ Ⓑ Ⓒ Ⓓ	30 Ⓕ Ⓖ Ⓗ Ⓙ	37 Ⓐ Ⓑ Ⓒ Ⓓ
3 Ⓐ Ⓑ Ⓒ Ⓓ	10 Ⓕ Ⓖ Ⓗ Ⓙ	17 Ⓐ Ⓑ Ⓒ Ⓓ	24 Ⓕ Ⓖ Ⓗ Ⓙ	31 Ⓐ Ⓑ Ⓒ Ⓓ	38 Ⓕ Ⓖ Ⓗ Ⓙ
4 Ⓕ Ⓖ Ⓗ Ⓙ	11 Ⓐ Ⓑ Ⓒ Ⓓ	18 Ⓕ Ⓖ Ⓗ Ⓙ	25 Ⓐ Ⓑ Ⓒ Ⓓ	32 Ⓕ Ⓖ Ⓗ Ⓙ	39 Ⓐ Ⓑ Ⓒ Ⓓ
5 Ⓐ Ⓑ Ⓒ Ⓓ	12 Ⓕ Ⓖ Ⓗ Ⓙ	19 Ⓐ Ⓑ Ⓒ Ⓓ	26 Ⓕ Ⓖ Ⓗ Ⓙ	33 Ⓐ Ⓑ Ⓒ Ⓓ	40 Ⓕ Ⓖ Ⓗ Ⓙ
6 Ⓕ Ⓖ Ⓗ Ⓙ	13 Ⓐ Ⓑ Ⓒ Ⓓ	20 Ⓕ Ⓖ Ⓗ Ⓙ	27 Ⓐ Ⓑ Ⓒ Ⓓ	34 Ⓕ Ⓖ Ⓗ Ⓙ	
7 Ⓐ Ⓑ Ⓒ Ⓓ	14 Ⓕ Ⓖ Ⓗ Ⓙ	21 Ⓐ Ⓑ Ⓒ Ⓓ	28 Ⓕ Ⓖ Ⓗ Ⓙ	35 Ⓐ Ⓑ Ⓒ Ⓓ	

The ACT® *Sample Answer Document*

EXAMINEE STATEMENTS, CERTIFICATION, AND SIGNATURE

1. **Statements**: I understand that by registering for, launching, starting, or submitting answer documents for an ACT® test, I am agreeing to comply with and be bound by the *Terms and Conditions: Testing Rules and Policies for the ACT® Test* ("Terms").

I UNDERSTAND AND AGREE THAT THE TERMS PERMIT ACT TO CANCEL MY SCORES IN CERTAIN CIRCUMSTANCES. THE TERMS ALSO LIMIT DAMAGES AVAILABLE TO ME AND REQUIRE ARBITRATION OF CERTAIN DISPUTES. BY AGREEING TO ARBITRATION, ACT AND I BOTH WAIVE THE RIGHT TO HAVE THOSE DISPUTES HEARD BY A JUDGE OR JURY.

I understand that ACT owns the test questions and responses, and I will not share them with anyone by any form of communication before, during, or after the test administration. I understand that taking the test for someone else may violate the law and subject me to legal penalties. I consent to the collection and processing of personally identifying information I provide, and its subsequent use and disclosure, as described in the ACT Privacy Policy (www.act.org/privacy.html). I also permit ACT to transfer my personally identifying information to the United States, to ACT, or to a third-party service provider, where it will be subject to use and disclosure under the laws of the United States, including being accessible to law enforcement or national security authorities.

2. **Certification**: Copy the italicized certification below, then sign and date in the spaces provided.

*I agree to the **Statements** above and certify that I am the person whose information appears on this form.*

_____

_____

_____   _____
Your Signature   Today's Date

Do NOT mark in this shaded area.

USE A NO. 2 PENCIL ONLY.
(Do NOT use a mechanical pencil, ink, ballpoint, correction fluid, or felt-tip pen.)

A NAME, MAILING ADDRESS, AND TELEPHONE (Please print.)

Last Name   First Name   MI (Middle Initial)

House Number & Street (Apt. No.); or PO Box & No.; or RR & No.

City   State/Province   ZIP/Postal Code

Area Code   Number   Country

ACT, Inc.—Confidential Restricted when data present

ALL examinees must complete block A – please print.

Blocks B, C, and D are required for all examinees. Find the MATCHING INFORMATION on your ticket. Enter it EXACTLY the same way, even if any of the information is missing or incorrect. Fill in the corresponding ovals. If you do not complete these blocks to match your previous information EXACTLY, your scores will be **delayed up to 8 weeks**.

ACT®
PO BOX 168, IOWA CITY, IA 52243-0168

B MATCH NAME (First 5 letters of last name)

C MATCH NUMBER

D DATE OF BIRTH

Month	Day	Year
January		
February		
March		
April		
May		
June		
July		
August		
September		
October		
November		
December		

01121523W   (A)203023-001:654321 ISD36401   Printed in the US.

PAGE 2

Marking Directions: Mark only **one** oval for each question. Fill in response completely. Erase errors cleanly without smudging.

Correct mark: ○ ● ○ ○

Do **NOT** use these *incorrect* or *bad* **marks.**

Incorrect marks: ⊘ ⊗ ◑ ⊖
Overlapping mark: ○ ○ ◑⊗
Cross-out mark: ○ ◉ ◑
Smudged erasure: ○ ○ ◑ ○
Mark is too light: ◐ ○ ○ ○

BOOKLET NUMBER

FORM

Print your 5-character **Test Form** in the boxes at the right and fill in the corresponding ovals.

TEST 1: ENGLISH

1 Ⓐ Ⓑ Ⓒ Ⓓ	14 Ⓕ Ⓖ Ⓗ Ⓙ	27 Ⓐ Ⓑ Ⓒ Ⓓ	40 Ⓕ Ⓖ Ⓗ Ⓙ	53 Ⓐ Ⓑ Ⓒ Ⓓ	66 Ⓕ Ⓖ Ⓗ Ⓙ
2 Ⓕ Ⓖ Ⓗ Ⓙ	15 Ⓐ Ⓑ Ⓒ Ⓓ	28 Ⓕ Ⓖ Ⓗ Ⓙ	41 Ⓐ Ⓑ Ⓒ Ⓓ	54 Ⓕ Ⓖ Ⓗ Ⓙ	67 Ⓐ Ⓑ Ⓒ Ⓓ
3 Ⓐ Ⓑ Ⓒ Ⓓ	16 Ⓕ Ⓖ Ⓗ Ⓙ	29 Ⓐ Ⓑ Ⓒ Ⓓ	42 Ⓕ Ⓖ Ⓗ Ⓙ	55 Ⓐ Ⓑ Ⓒ Ⓓ	68 Ⓕ Ⓖ Ⓗ Ⓙ
4 Ⓕ Ⓖ Ⓗ Ⓙ	17 Ⓐ Ⓑ Ⓒ Ⓓ	30 Ⓕ Ⓖ Ⓗ Ⓙ	43 Ⓐ Ⓑ Ⓒ Ⓓ	56 Ⓕ Ⓖ Ⓗ Ⓙ	69 Ⓐ Ⓑ Ⓒ Ⓓ
5 Ⓐ Ⓑ Ⓒ Ⓓ	18 Ⓕ Ⓖ Ⓗ Ⓙ	31 Ⓐ Ⓑ Ⓒ Ⓓ	44 Ⓕ Ⓖ Ⓗ Ⓙ	57 Ⓐ Ⓑ Ⓒ Ⓓ	70 Ⓕ Ⓖ Ⓗ Ⓙ
6 Ⓕ Ⓖ Ⓗ Ⓙ	19 Ⓐ Ⓑ Ⓒ Ⓓ	32 Ⓕ Ⓖ Ⓗ Ⓙ	45 Ⓐ Ⓑ Ⓒ Ⓓ	58 Ⓕ Ⓖ Ⓗ Ⓙ	71 Ⓐ Ⓑ Ⓒ Ⓓ
7 Ⓐ Ⓑ Ⓒ Ⓓ	20 Ⓕ Ⓖ Ⓗ Ⓙ	33 Ⓐ Ⓑ Ⓒ Ⓓ	46 Ⓕ Ⓖ Ⓗ Ⓙ	59 Ⓐ Ⓑ Ⓒ Ⓓ	72 Ⓕ Ⓖ Ⓗ Ⓙ
8 Ⓕ Ⓖ Ⓗ Ⓙ	21 Ⓐ Ⓑ Ⓒ Ⓓ	34 Ⓕ Ⓖ Ⓗ Ⓙ	47 Ⓐ Ⓑ Ⓒ Ⓓ	60 Ⓕ Ⓖ Ⓗ Ⓙ	73 Ⓐ Ⓑ Ⓒ Ⓓ
9 Ⓐ Ⓑ Ⓒ Ⓓ	22 Ⓕ Ⓖ Ⓗ Ⓙ	35 Ⓐ Ⓑ Ⓒ Ⓓ	48 Ⓕ Ⓖ Ⓗ Ⓙ	61 Ⓐ Ⓑ Ⓒ Ⓓ	74 Ⓕ Ⓖ Ⓗ Ⓙ
10 Ⓕ Ⓖ Ⓗ Ⓙ	23 Ⓐ Ⓑ Ⓒ Ⓓ	36 Ⓕ Ⓖ Ⓗ Ⓙ	49 Ⓐ Ⓑ Ⓒ Ⓓ	62 Ⓕ Ⓖ Ⓗ Ⓙ	75 Ⓐ Ⓑ Ⓒ Ⓓ
11 Ⓐ Ⓑ Ⓒ Ⓓ	24 Ⓕ Ⓖ Ⓗ Ⓙ	37 Ⓐ Ⓑ Ⓒ Ⓓ	50 Ⓕ Ⓖ Ⓗ Ⓙ	63 Ⓐ Ⓑ Ⓒ Ⓓ	
12 Ⓕ Ⓖ Ⓗ Ⓙ	25 Ⓐ Ⓑ Ⓒ Ⓓ	38 Ⓕ Ⓖ Ⓗ Ⓙ	51 Ⓐ Ⓑ Ⓒ Ⓓ	64 Ⓕ Ⓖ Ⓗ Ⓙ	
13 Ⓐ Ⓑ Ⓒ Ⓓ	26 Ⓕ Ⓖ Ⓗ Ⓙ	39 Ⓐ Ⓑ Ⓒ Ⓓ	52 Ⓕ Ⓖ Ⓗ Ⓙ	65 Ⓐ Ⓑ Ⓒ Ⓓ	

TEST 2: MATHEMATICS

1 Ⓐ Ⓑ Ⓒ Ⓓ Ⓔ	11 Ⓐ Ⓑ Ⓒ Ⓓ Ⓔ	21 Ⓐ Ⓑ Ⓒ Ⓓ Ⓔ	31 Ⓐ Ⓑ Ⓒ Ⓓ Ⓔ	41 Ⓐ Ⓑ Ⓒ Ⓓ Ⓔ	51 Ⓐ Ⓑ Ⓒ Ⓓ Ⓔ
2 Ⓕ Ⓖ Ⓗ Ⓙ Ⓚ	12 Ⓕ Ⓖ Ⓗ Ⓙ Ⓚ	22 Ⓕ Ⓖ Ⓗ Ⓙ Ⓚ	32 Ⓕ Ⓖ Ⓗ Ⓙ Ⓚ	42 Ⓕ Ⓖ Ⓗ Ⓙ Ⓚ	52 Ⓕ Ⓖ Ⓗ Ⓙ Ⓚ
3 Ⓐ Ⓑ Ⓒ Ⓓ Ⓔ	13 Ⓐ Ⓑ Ⓒ Ⓓ Ⓔ	23 Ⓐ Ⓑ Ⓒ Ⓓ Ⓔ	33 Ⓐ Ⓑ Ⓒ Ⓓ Ⓔ	43 Ⓐ Ⓑ Ⓒ Ⓓ Ⓔ	53 Ⓐ Ⓑ Ⓒ Ⓓ Ⓔ
4 Ⓕ Ⓖ Ⓗ Ⓙ Ⓚ	14 Ⓕ Ⓖ Ⓗ Ⓙ Ⓚ	24 Ⓕ Ⓖ Ⓗ Ⓙ Ⓚ	34 Ⓕ Ⓖ Ⓗ Ⓙ Ⓚ	44 Ⓕ Ⓖ Ⓗ Ⓙ Ⓚ	54 Ⓕ Ⓖ Ⓗ Ⓙ Ⓚ
5 Ⓐ Ⓑ Ⓒ Ⓓ Ⓔ	15 Ⓐ Ⓑ Ⓒ Ⓓ Ⓔ	25 Ⓐ Ⓑ Ⓒ Ⓓ Ⓔ	35 Ⓐ Ⓑ Ⓒ Ⓓ Ⓔ	45 Ⓐ Ⓑ Ⓒ Ⓓ Ⓔ	55 Ⓐ Ⓑ Ⓒ Ⓓ Ⓔ
6 Ⓕ Ⓖ Ⓗ Ⓙ Ⓚ	16 Ⓕ Ⓖ Ⓗ Ⓙ Ⓚ	26 Ⓕ Ⓖ Ⓗ Ⓙ Ⓚ	36 Ⓕ Ⓖ Ⓗ Ⓙ Ⓚ	46 Ⓕ Ⓖ Ⓗ Ⓙ Ⓚ	56 Ⓕ Ⓖ Ⓗ Ⓙ Ⓚ
7 Ⓐ Ⓑ Ⓒ Ⓓ Ⓔ	17 Ⓐ Ⓑ Ⓒ Ⓓ Ⓔ	27 Ⓐ Ⓑ Ⓒ Ⓓ Ⓔ	37 Ⓐ Ⓑ Ⓒ Ⓓ Ⓔ	47 Ⓐ Ⓑ Ⓒ Ⓓ Ⓔ	57 Ⓐ Ⓑ Ⓒ Ⓓ Ⓔ
8 Ⓕ Ⓖ Ⓗ Ⓙ Ⓚ	18 Ⓕ Ⓖ Ⓗ Ⓙ Ⓚ	28 Ⓕ Ⓖ Ⓗ Ⓙ Ⓚ	38 Ⓕ Ⓖ Ⓗ Ⓙ Ⓚ	48 Ⓕ Ⓖ Ⓗ Ⓙ Ⓚ	58 Ⓕ Ⓖ Ⓗ Ⓙ Ⓚ
9 Ⓐ Ⓑ Ⓒ Ⓓ Ⓔ	19 Ⓐ Ⓑ Ⓒ Ⓓ Ⓔ	29 Ⓐ Ⓑ Ⓒ Ⓓ Ⓔ	39 Ⓐ Ⓑ Ⓒ Ⓓ Ⓔ	49 Ⓐ Ⓑ Ⓒ Ⓓ Ⓔ	59 Ⓐ Ⓑ Ⓒ Ⓓ Ⓔ
10 Ⓕ Ⓖ Ⓗ Ⓙ Ⓚ	20 Ⓕ Ⓖ Ⓗ Ⓙ Ⓚ	30 Ⓕ Ⓖ Ⓗ Ⓙ Ⓚ	40 Ⓕ Ⓖ Ⓗ Ⓙ Ⓚ	50 Ⓕ Ⓖ Ⓗ Ⓙ Ⓚ	60 Ⓕ Ⓖ Ⓗ Ⓙ Ⓚ

TEST 3: READING

1 Ⓐ Ⓑ Ⓒ Ⓓ	8 Ⓕ Ⓖ Ⓗ Ⓙ	15 Ⓐ Ⓑ Ⓒ Ⓓ	22 Ⓕ Ⓖ Ⓗ Ⓙ	29 Ⓐ Ⓑ Ⓒ Ⓓ	36 Ⓕ Ⓖ Ⓗ Ⓙ
2 Ⓕ Ⓖ Ⓗ Ⓙ	9 Ⓐ Ⓑ Ⓒ Ⓓ	16 Ⓕ Ⓖ Ⓗ Ⓙ	23 Ⓐ Ⓑ Ⓒ Ⓓ	30 Ⓕ Ⓖ Ⓗ Ⓙ	37 Ⓐ Ⓑ Ⓒ Ⓓ
3 Ⓐ Ⓑ Ⓒ Ⓓ	10 Ⓕ Ⓖ Ⓗ Ⓙ	17 Ⓐ Ⓑ Ⓒ Ⓓ	24 Ⓕ Ⓖ Ⓗ Ⓙ	31 Ⓐ Ⓑ Ⓒ Ⓓ	38 Ⓕ Ⓖ Ⓗ Ⓙ
4 Ⓕ Ⓖ Ⓗ Ⓙ	11 Ⓐ Ⓑ Ⓒ Ⓓ	18 Ⓕ Ⓖ Ⓗ Ⓙ	25 Ⓐ Ⓑ Ⓒ Ⓓ	32 Ⓕ Ⓖ Ⓗ Ⓙ	39 Ⓐ Ⓑ Ⓒ Ⓓ
5 Ⓐ Ⓑ Ⓒ Ⓓ	12 Ⓕ Ⓖ Ⓗ Ⓙ	19 Ⓐ Ⓑ Ⓒ Ⓓ	26 Ⓕ Ⓖ Ⓗ Ⓙ	33 Ⓐ Ⓑ Ⓒ Ⓓ	40 Ⓕ Ⓖ Ⓗ Ⓙ
6 Ⓕ Ⓖ Ⓗ Ⓙ	13 Ⓐ Ⓑ Ⓒ Ⓓ	20 Ⓕ Ⓖ Ⓗ Ⓙ	27 Ⓐ Ⓑ Ⓒ Ⓓ	34 Ⓕ Ⓖ Ⓗ Ⓙ	
7 Ⓐ Ⓑ Ⓒ Ⓓ	14 Ⓕ Ⓖ Ⓗ Ⓙ	21 Ⓐ Ⓑ Ⓒ Ⓓ	28 Ⓕ Ⓖ Ⓗ Ⓙ	35 Ⓐ Ⓑ Ⓒ Ⓓ	

TEST 4: SCIENCE

1 Ⓐ Ⓑ Ⓒ Ⓓ	8 Ⓕ Ⓖ Ⓗ Ⓙ	15 Ⓐ Ⓑ Ⓒ Ⓓ	22 Ⓕ Ⓖ Ⓗ Ⓙ	29 Ⓐ Ⓑ Ⓒ Ⓓ	36 Ⓕ Ⓖ Ⓗ Ⓙ
2 Ⓕ Ⓖ Ⓗ Ⓙ	9 Ⓐ Ⓑ Ⓒ Ⓓ	16 Ⓕ Ⓖ Ⓗ Ⓙ	23 Ⓐ Ⓑ Ⓒ Ⓓ	30 Ⓕ Ⓖ Ⓗ Ⓙ	37 Ⓐ Ⓑ Ⓒ Ⓓ
3 Ⓐ Ⓑ Ⓒ Ⓓ	10 Ⓕ Ⓖ Ⓗ Ⓙ	17 Ⓐ Ⓑ Ⓒ Ⓓ	24 Ⓕ Ⓖ Ⓗ Ⓙ	31 Ⓐ Ⓑ Ⓒ Ⓓ	38 Ⓕ Ⓖ Ⓗ Ⓙ
4 Ⓕ Ⓖ Ⓗ Ⓙ	11 Ⓐ Ⓑ Ⓒ Ⓓ	18 Ⓕ Ⓖ Ⓗ Ⓙ	25 Ⓐ Ⓑ Ⓒ Ⓓ	32 Ⓕ Ⓖ Ⓗ Ⓙ	39 Ⓐ Ⓑ Ⓒ Ⓓ
5 Ⓐ Ⓑ Ⓒ Ⓓ	12 Ⓕ Ⓖ Ⓗ Ⓙ	19 Ⓐ Ⓑ Ⓒ Ⓓ	26 Ⓕ Ⓖ Ⓗ Ⓙ	33 Ⓐ Ⓑ Ⓒ Ⓓ	40 Ⓕ Ⓖ Ⓗ Ⓙ
6 Ⓕ Ⓖ Ⓗ Ⓙ	13 Ⓐ Ⓑ Ⓒ Ⓓ	20 Ⓕ Ⓖ Ⓗ Ⓙ	27 Ⓐ Ⓑ Ⓒ Ⓓ	34 Ⓕ Ⓖ Ⓗ Ⓙ	
7 Ⓐ Ⓑ Ⓒ Ⓓ	14 Ⓕ Ⓖ Ⓗ Ⓙ	21 Ⓐ Ⓑ Ⓒ Ⓓ	28 Ⓕ Ⓖ Ⓗ Ⓙ	35 Ⓐ Ⓑ Ⓒ Ⓓ	

Practice Test 3

EXAMINEE STATEMENTS, CERTIFICATION, AND SIGNATURE

1. **Statements:** I understand that by registering for, launching, starting, or submitting answer documents for an ACT® test, I am agreeing to comply with and be bound by the *Terms and Conditions: Testing Rules and Policies for the ACT® Test* ("Terms").

   I UNDERSTAND AND AGREE THAT THE TERMS PERMIT ACT TO CANCEL MY SCORES IN CERTAIN CIRCUMSTANCES. THE TERMS ALSO LIMIT DAMAGES AVAILABLE TO ME AND REQUIRE ARBITRATION OF CERTAIN DISPUTES. BY AGREEING TO ARBITRATION, ACT AND I BOTH WAIVE THE RIGHT TO HAVE THOSE DISPUTES HEARD BY A JUDGE OR JURY.

   I understand that ACT owns the test questions and responses, and I will not share them with anyone by any form of communication before, during, or after the test administration. I understand that taking the test for someone else may violate the law and subject me to legal penalties.

   I consent to the collection and processing of personally identifying information I provide, and its subsequent use and disclosure, as described in the ACT Privacy Policy (www.act.org/privacy.html). I also permit ACT to transfer my personally identifying information to the United States, to ACT, or to a third-party service provider, where it will be subject to use and disclosure under the laws of the United States, including being accessible to law enforcement or national security authorities.

2. **Certification:** Copy the italicized certification below, then sign, date, and print your name in the spaces provided.

   *I agree to the **Statements** above and certify that I am the person whose information appears on this form.*

   _____

   _____

| Your Signature | Today's Date | Print Your Name |

 **Form 19MC5**
2023 | 2024

Directions

This booklet contains tests in English, mathematics, reading, and science. These tests measure skills and abilities highly related to high school course work and success in college. **Calculators may be used on the mathematics test only.**

The questions in each test are numbered, and the suggested answers for each question are lettered. On the answer document, the rows of ovals are numbered to match the questions, and the ovals in each row are lettered to correspond to the suggested answers.

For each question, first decide which answer is best. Next, locate on the answer document the row of ovals numbered the same as the question. Then, locate the oval in that row lettered the same as your answer. Finally, fill in the oval completely. Use a soft lead pencil and make your marks heavy and black. **Do not use ink or a mechanical pencil.**

Mark only one answer to each question. If you change your mind about an answer, erase your first mark thoroughly before marking your new answer. For each question, make certain that you mark in the row of ovals with the same number as the question.

Only responses marked on your answer document will be scored. Your score on each test will be based only on the number of questions you answer correctly during the time allowed for that test. You will **not** be penalized for guessing. **It is to your advantage to answer every question even if you must guess.**

You may work on each test **only** when the testing staff tells you to do so. If you finish a test before time is called for that test, you should use the time remaining to reconsider questions you are uncertain about in that test. You may **not** look back to a test on which time has already been called, and you may **not** go ahead to another test. To do so will disqualify you from the examination.

Lay your pencil down immediately when time is called at the end of each test. You may **not** for any reason fill in or alter ovals for a test after time is called for that test. To do so will disqualify you from the examination.

Do not fold or tear the pages of your test booklet.

**DO NOT OPEN THIS BOOKLET
UNTIL TOLD TO DO SO.**

The ONLY Official Prep Guide from the Makers of the ACT

Taking Additional Practice Tests

1 ■ ■ ■ ■ ■ ■ ■ ■ ■ 1

ENGLISH TEST
45 Minutes—75 Questions

DIRECTIONS: In the five passages that follow, certain words and phrases are underlined and numbered. In the right-hand column, you will find alternatives for the underlined part. In most cases, you are to choose the one that best expresses the idea, makes the statement appropriate for standard written English, or is worded most consistently with the style and tone of the passage as a whole. If you think the original version is best, choose "NO CHANGE." In some cases, you will find in the right-hand column a question about the underlined part. You are to choose the best answer to the question.

You will also find questions about a section of the passage, or about the passage as a whole. These questions do not refer to an underlined portion of the passage, but rather are identified by a number or numbers in a box.

For each question, choose the alternative you consider best and fill in the corresponding oval on your answer document. Read each passage through once before you begin to answer the questions that accompany it. For many of the questions, you must read several sentences beyond the question to determine the answer. Be sure that you have read far enough ahead each time you choose an alternative.

PASSAGE I

Ukulele Life

My older sister was a guitar buff <u>and my idol</u> when I
₁
was growing up. She would teach me songs on her acoustic guitar now and then after school and on long family road trips to the beach. In those moments, my sister and I were the closest we've ever been. And my guitar itself felt like, well, family.

When my sister left Chicago for college in California, I began carting my guitar <u>around everywhere:</u> to school,
₂

to work, to <u>friends houses.</u> Years later, my guitar
₃

accompanied me on business <u>trips. No matter where I was,</u>
₄
playing it made me feel a little bit closer to home.

1. If the writer were to delete the underlined portion, the paragraph would primarily lose:
   - **A.** an indication that the narrator learned to play guitar at a relatively young age.
   - **B.** an indication of why the narrator became interested in playing the guitar.
   - **C.** a detail that specifies how much older the sister is compared to the narrator.
   - **D.** a detail that reveals the amount of musical talent the narrator's sister had.

2. **F.** NO CHANGE
   G. around. Everywhere,
   H. around everywhere;
   J. around everywhere

3. **A.** NO CHANGE
   B. friend's house's.
   C. friends' houses.
   D. friend's houses.

4. **F.** NO CHANGE
   G. trips and no matter where I was
   H. trips. No matter where I was
   J. trips, no matter where I was,

GO ON TO THE NEXT PAGE.

1 ■ ■ ■ ■ ■ ■ ■ ■ 1

But one day, after landing in Honolulu, Hawaii,

for an extended trip, I couldn't locate my guitar on

the luggage carousel. Panicked, I <u>assailed airport</u>
                                        5

personnel, <u>who assured myself</u> that they would
              6

try to recover my beloved instrument. At that

<u>moment of my extended trip,</u> continuing the trip
           7

without it seemed impossible.

My worries began to dissipate, <u>otherwise,</u> as I
                                    8

walked out of the airport and <u>upon</u> the balmy Hawaiian
                                9

air. In front of me, a man was playing what looked like

a miniature guitar. Warm, mellow tones <u>accrued</u> from
                                          10

the instrument, complementing the lyrical rhythm of

the Hawaiian words he sang. It was a ukulele.

As soon as I could, I bought a ukulele of my own.

<u>I began to linger on</u> the beach, where several native
          11

Hawaiians often played. I watched them for hours, my

ukulele in my hands, and practiced. Unlike the guitar,

which has six strings, my ukulele had four; to make

the same chords with the uke, I had to learn completely

different finger positions. I also had trouble with dexterity

at first because the neck of the uke is much narrower

<u>then that of a guitar.</u> I had to retrain my fingers to make
          12

smaller movements in order to shape the chords.

5. Which choice best illustrates the fervor with which the narrator communicated with the airport personnel?
   A. NO CHANGE
   B. approached
   C. questioned
   D. contacted

6. F. NO CHANGE
   G. whom assured myself
   H. whom assured me
   J. who assured me

7. A. NO CHANGE
   B. moment, due to the fact that I was on an extended trip,
   C. very moment during my time in Honolulu,
   D. moment,

8. F. NO CHANGE
   G. therefore,
   H. though,
   J. instead,

9. A. NO CHANGE
   B. amid
   C. onto
   D. into

10. F. NO CHANGE
    G. distributed
    H. appeared
    J. issued

11. A. NO CHANGE
    B. Beginning to linger on
    C. Lingering on
    D. On

12. F. NO CHANGE
    G. than that of a guitar.
    H. than it.
    J. then it.

GO ON TO THE NEXT PAGE.

Taking Additional Practice Tests

When I wasn't working, I was on the

beach, losing myself in the bright notes of

the uke. Eventually, I began playing music
                                        ‾‾‾‾
                                         13

like "He'eia" as the locals.
              ‾‾
              14

And the sound of the ukulele is synonymous
‾‾
                    15
with the romance and beauty of Hawaii's beaches.
‾‾
                    15

13. Which choice best specifies the type of songs the narrator played on the ukulele?
- **A.** NO CHANGE
- **B.** Hawaiian classics
- **C.** tropical tunes
- **D.** things

14. **F.** NO CHANGE
- **G.** through
- **H.** with
- **J.** along

15. Which choice best concludes the essay by emphasizing the central point made in the first and second paragraphs?
- **A.** NO CHANGE
- **B.** And I couldn't think of a better way to spend my guitarless time in Honolulu.
- **C.** And although I was guitarless and far from family, I felt like I was home.
- **D.** And even though I was on a business trip, I didn't want to leave.

PASSAGE II

Hedy Lamarr, Across the Spectrum

In 1940, Hedy Lamarr was becoming a Hollywood

star, but she was bored. On set for only three months

of the year, she filled her spare time with an unusual

hobby: inventing. World War II was underway in

Europe, where Lamarr had grown up, and she hoped

to invent something to help the Allied cause. Because

Lamarr's former husband had often discussed his

work in munitions, the actress knew about weaponry.

GO ON TO THE NEXT PAGE.

1 ■ ■ ■ ■ ■ ■ ■ ■ 1

She had ideas of her own, including <u>an idea of hers</u>
                                              16
for a torpedo with a sophisticated radio-controlled

guidance system. ☐17☐ Lamarr knew that radio signals

on one frequency <u>is easy to jam</u> by anyone sending a
                        18

competing signal on the same <u>frequency. She envisioned a</u>
                                          19
system that used dozens of frequencies to transmit a

signal to guide torpedoes. To protect the signal further,

transmitters and receivers would jump from frequency

to frequency in a predetermined order that would seem

random to an outsider. Such a signal <u>like that would be</u>
                                              20
hard to detect and nearly impossible to disrupt.

    [1] In August 1940, Lamarr met composer George

Antheil, and the two began collaborating. [2] Antheil, who

had synchronized player pianos for his compositions, had

the mechanical knowledge that Lamarr needed to <u>instigate</u>
                                                        21
her idea. [3] Then in 1942, the inventors heard that the

Navy had rejected their idea. [4] They submitted the

"Secret Communication System" to the military in June

1941. [5] In the decades after the <u>war, however,</u> the US
                                          22
military discovered the value of Lamarr's idea, which

came to be called "spread spectrum," and used it in

guidance, radio, and navigation systems. ☐23☐

16. F. NO CHANGE
   G. one idea that she had
   H. her own idea
   J. one

17. At this point, the writer is considering dividing the
paragraph into two. Making this change would help
organize the essay by separating:
   A. an analysis of Lamarr's first invention from details
about another one she later developed.
   B. information about the origin of Lamarr's idea from
details about how the invention would work.
   C. an overview of Lamarr's film career from an
account of how she conceived of her invention.
   D. details about Lamarr's childhood from general
information about radio signals.

18. F. NO CHANGE
   G. has been easy to jam
   H. are easily jammed
   J. is easily jammed

19. A. NO CHANGE
   B. frequency she envisioned. A
   C. frequency, she envisioned a
   D. frequency she envisioned; a

20. F. NO CHANGE
   G. similar to that would be
   H. would be difficult and
   J. would be

21. A. NO CHANGE
   B. implement
   C. discharge
   D. uphold

22. F. NO CHANGE
   G. war; however,
   H. war, however
   J. war however

23. For the sake of logic and cohesion, Sentence 3 should
be placed:
   A. where it is now.
   B. before Sentence 1.
   C. after Sentence 4.
   D. after Sentence 5.

GO ON TO THE NEXT PAGE.

1 ■ ■ ■ ■ ■ ■ ■ ■ ■ **1**

In 1978, spread spectrum was declassified,

and it made a difference. Devices that operate
        ——————————
              24

wirelessly, cellular phones, wireless Internet networks,
————————————————————————
              25

the Global Positioning System—functioning because
                              —————————
                                  26

of Lamarr's idea. It wasn't until 1996 that Lamarr and
        ——
        27

Antheil, they were finally given credit for spread spectrum.
————————————————————
        28

However, they were awarded the Pioneer Award from the
————————
    29
Electronic Frontier Foundation. Upon hearing of her

award, Lamarr said, "It's about time."

24. Which choice most strongly and specifically empha-
    sizes that the declassification of spread spectrum was
    a turning point in the history of communication
    technology?
    F. NO CHANGE
    G. transformed the communication landscape.
    H. had an impact on communications.
    J. revolutionized things.

25. A. NO CHANGE
    B. wirelessly—cellular phones,
    C. wirelessly: cellular phones,
    D. wirelessly, cellular phones

26. F. NO CHANGE
    G. to function
    H. function
    J. DELETE the underlined portion.

27. A. NO CHANGE
    B. Such
    C. This
    D. That

28. F. NO CHANGE
    G. Antheil—both finally got
    H. Antheil finally to receive
    J. Antheil finally received

29. A. NO CHANGE
    B. Conversely, they
    C. Anyway, they
    D. They

Question 30 asks about the preceding passage
as a whole.

---

30. Suppose the writer's primary purpose had been to give
    an overview of the history of an important invention.
    Would this essay accomplish that purpose?
    F. Yes, because it recounts the story of Lamarr and
       Antheil's invention of spread spectrum and the
       invention's significance.
    G. Yes, because it shows how Lamarr and Antheil
       changed the course of World War II by inventing
       spread spectrum.
    H. No, because although it describes Lamarr and
       Antheil's invention, it does not establish the
       importance of spread spectrum.
    J. No, because it instead focuses on Lamarr, Antheil,
       and their collaborations in the film industry.

GO ON TO THE NEXT PAGE.

PASSAGE III

Climbing Mt. Windmill

[1]

They're some 45,000 electricity-generating
<u>   </u>
    31

wind turbines in the United States, and the task

of repairing and maintaining these huge machines

<u>have represented</u> a substantial undertaking. Ladders
    32

inside the towers simplify access to the generators

and controllers within the turbine housing. <u>In contrast,</u>
                                                  33

servicing the turbine <u>blades those long fiberglass</u>
                            34

<u>vanes that slice through the air,</u> is a serious challenge.
        34

[2]

[A] Rock climbers are comfortable in high places

and capable, equipped with rope and other simple gear,

of <u>scaling almost anything.</u> After completing specialized
        35

training, <u>rock climbers become ideal "rope technicians."</u>
                36

[3]

When the rope technicians arrive <u>across</u> a turbine,
                                       37

they first lock the blades into a "bunny ears" position, in

which two blades angle up and one blade points straight

down. The technicians climb the ladder inside the tower,

secure themselves with ropes and harnesses, open a hatch

in the turbine's housing, and rappel down the vertical

blade.

[4]

Certainly, turbine blades withstand severe stress.

The blades zip through the elements as fast as 200 miles

---

31. A. NO CHANGE
    B. There are
    C. Their is
    D. There's

32. F. NO CHANGE
    G. are representing
    H. represents
    J. represent

33. A. NO CHANGE
    B. Likewise,
    C. Instantly,
    D. First,

34. F. NO CHANGE
    G. blades—those long fiberglass vanes that slice through the air—
    H. blades—those long fiberglass vanes that slice through the air,
    J. blades, those long fiberglass vanes that slice through the air

35. A. NO CHANGE
    B. climbing nearly anything—something they're able to do.
    C. ascending just about anything by climbing it.
    D. using rope to climb almost anything.

36. F. NO CHANGE
    G. old skills and new knowledge turn rock climbers into ideal "rope technicians."
    H. new careers as "rope technicians" open up for rock climbers.
    J. ideal "rope technicians" can be made out of rock climbers.

37. A. NO CHANGE
    B. with
    C. via
    D. at

GO ON TO THE NEXT PAGE.

1 ■ ■ ■ ■ ■ ■ ■ ■ ■ 1

per hour, braving heat, hail, blizzards, and more. Yet

despite enduring such harsh conditions, most turbine

blades that rope technicians service only need a thorough

cleaning or other basic upkeep, such as a new coat of paint.

[B] Sometimes, the task can be more complicated: patching

fiberglass damage from a lightning strike, for example.

[5]

The largest wind turbine blades are
                                  38
over 270 feet long. Technicians work in
    38

pairs; while they don't climb in high winds,
    39

extreme temperatures, or precipitation. Whether there's
                                        40
lightning within thirty miles, the technicians stay on

the ground. [C] Precautions such as these—along with
                                   41

rigorous procedures and training, make the job quite safe.
                                  42
[6]

For many rock climbers, being a rope

technician is a dream job. [D] Fresh air, great vistas,

to practice climbing daily, and ample time off to scale
    43

actual rocks—it's not a typical job description, is it?
                           44

38. Given that all the choices are true, which one would provide the most effective introduction to the paragraph?
F. NO CHANGE
G. The number of wind turbine–related jobs has doubled in five years.
H. A typical wind turbine has about 8,000 parts.
J. Whatever the job, safety is the first priority.

39. A. NO CHANGE
B. pairs, and
C. pairs,
D. pairs

40. F. NO CHANGE
G. So that
H. Unless
J. If

41. A. NO CHANGE
B. these;
C. these,
D. these

42. F. NO CHANGE
G. is making
H. has made
J. makes

43. A. NO CHANGE
B. they practice climbing regularly,
C. while often practicing climbing,
D. plenty of climbing practice,

44. The writer wants to end this sentence by emphasizing that rock climbers in particular may find being a rope technician an appealing occupation. Which choice best accomplishes that goal?
F. NO CHANGE
G. what inspires rock climbers to reach such heights?
H. what more could a climber want?
J. ready to sign up yet?

GO ON TO THE NEXT PAGE.

Question 45 asks about the preceding passage as a whole.

45. The writer wants to add the following sentence to the essay:

> Enter rock climbers.

The sentence would most logically be placed at:

  A. Point A in Paragraph 2.
  B. Point B in Paragraph 4.
  C. Point C in Paragraph 5.
  D. Point D in Paragraph 6.

PASSAGE IV

> The following paragraphs may or may not be in the most logical order. Each paragraph is numbered in brackets, and question 59 will ask you to choose where Paragraph 3 should most logically be placed.

Christy's Constitution

[1]

From shoes to chandelier, *Scene at the Signing of the Constitution of the United States* blend accuracy with
₄₆

artistic license to achieve the artist's vision of an event
₄₇
that took place in Philadelphia's Independence Hall. The
₄₇
artist, Howard Chandler Christy, was born in 1873, long

after George Washington presided—over the momentous
₄₈

event that in 1787 served the final role of ending the
₄₉
Constitutional Convention.

46. F. NO CHANGE
  G. have blended
  H. are blending
  J. blends

47. Which choice best indicates where the painting is on display?
  A. NO CHANGE
  B. in a way that is not immediately apparent to all who see it on display.
  C. in one of the most famous paintings in Washington, DC.
  D. on a canvas that has been on display for many decades.

48. F. NO CHANGE
  G. presided,
  H. presided
  J. presided;

49. A. NO CHANGE
  B. ended in the conclusion of
  C. finished off
  D. concluded

GO ON TO THE NEXT PAGE.

1 ▪ ▪ ▪ ▪ ▪ ▪ ▪ ▪ ▪ 1

[2]

[1] The group portrait, as big as a billboard, hangs in the US Capitol building, where it was installed in 1940. [2] Christy's prior preparations in advance of the work
50
included a visit to Philadelphia to study how the light falls through the windows in Independence Hall. [3] Christy arranged to see the inkwells into which the
51
quills would have been dipped as the delegates prepared to make history. [4] He scoured countless drawings of period furniture and fabrics, noting color, texture, design.
52

[5] Hunting down portraits of the signers and scrutinized
53

them. 54

[3]

Such measures may seem standard in the making of historical paintings, but that is not the case. For example, in Emanuel Luetze's *Washington Crossing the Delaware*, the president strikes a noble pose on a boat. Experts now agree could not have been the vessel
55
that carried the revolutionary leader across the river. In another, painting of the signing of the US Constitution,
56
artist Barry Faulkner places the figures in a Roman ruin.

[4]

Accurate in many respects, Christy's painting also plays with the truth to suggest the grandeur of the moment. For instance, Washington benefits from more

50. F. NO CHANGE
G. preparation work leading up to
H. advance preparations preceding
J. preparations for

51. A. NO CHANGE
B. which
C. of
D. DELETE the underlined portion.

52. F. NO CHANGE
G. of which were noted
H. because they were noted
J. DELETE the underlined portion.

53. A. NO CHANGE
B. While hunting
C. As he hunted
D. He hunted

54. The writer wants to add the following statement to the paragraph:

> He deliberately timed his trip for September, the month in which the thirty-nine signers had put their names on the revered document.

This statement would most logically be placed after:

F. Sentence 1.
G. Sentence 2.
H. Sentence 3.
J. Sentence 4.

55. A. NO CHANGE
B. boat experts
C. boat; experts
D. boat, experts

56. F. NO CHANGE
G. another painting of the signing,
H. another painting of the signing
J. another painting, of the signing

GO ON TO THE NEXT PAGE.

than his share of natural light, which singles him out

in Christy's famous painting. Many of the assembled
57

57. Which choice both supports the claim the writer makes
    in the preceding sentence about the grandeur of the
    moment and best emphasizes that Christy deliberately
    presents Washington as having a special status among
    the signers?
    A. NO CHANGE
    B. as a hero among heroes.
    C. with visual effects.
    D. in the group.

men, luminaries as Benjamin Franklin and James Madison,
58
improbably stare the viewer squarely in the eye. Their

expressions suggest they are well aware of their own

importance but even more aware of the viewer's, almost

as if one more signature will give the document its full

meaning.

58. F. NO CHANGE
    G. including such luminaries as
    H. who are luminaries
    J. DELETE the underlined portion.

Questions 59 and 60 ask about the preceding passage as a whole.

---

59. For the sake of logic and cohesion, Paragraph 3 should
    be placed:
    A. where it is now.
    B. before Paragraph 1.
    C. after Paragraph 1.
    D. after Paragraph 4.

60. Suppose the writer's primary purpose had been to
    examine how a work of art changed the direction of an
    artist's career. Would this essay accomplish that
    purpose?
    F. Yes, because it indicates that Christy led a trend in
       striving for authenticity in historical paintings.
    G. Yes, because it reveals that a single painting put
       Christy in the national spotlight.
    H. No, because it focuses on Christy's approach to a
       particular painting but does not discuss the paint-
       ing's effect on Christy's career.
    J. No, because it indicates that Christy consistently
       focused on historical subject matter throughout his
       career.

PASSAGE V

The Artful Stitch of *Paj Ntaub*

She depicts flowers with layers of petals, intricate

spirals and rosettes, teardrops bending within circles, and

dizzying mazes of lines—embroidering them in vibrant
61
reds, blues, pinks, yellows, and greens on fabric of delicate

silk or cotton. Pang Xiong Sirirathasuk Sikoun is a master

of *paj ntaub*, or "flower cloth" embroidery, the most

difficult of the century's-oldest Hmong needlework arts.
62

61. Which choice best maintains the stylistic pattern of
    descriptions established earlier in the sentence?
    A. NO CHANGE
    B. something with a dizzying effect—
    C. mazes that she creates—
    D. so many lines—

62. F. NO CHANGE
    G. centuries-old
    H. centuries'-old
    J. century's-old

GO ON TO THE NEXT PAGE.

Taking Additional Practice Tests

1 ■ ■ ■ ■ ■ ■ ■ ■ ■ 1

Paj ntaub is increasingly made in lighter, softer shades

today. 63 She's been creating stitched textiles since she

was a young woman, and lived in northern Laos. For the
                    ——————
                      64

past several decades, she's been designing *paj ntaub* in

Philadelphia, Pennsylvania, where she also teaches her

craft.

    Flower cloth (commonly as a shirt, dress,
                   ————————————————————
                            65

coat, or collar) is made to be worn as clothing and,
——————————
    65

depending on the amount of needlework on the piece,

is designed either for everyday wear or for a special
——
66

occasion. With pattern names such as "elephant's foot"

and "snail house" and images of animals framed by

geometric designs, *paj ntaub* patterns are versatile.
                   ———————————————————————
                             67

What distinguishes *paj ntaub* from other Hmong

needlework arts is the artist's use of tiny, tight stitches,
                                        ———————————————————
                                               68

and several complex techniques. One technique is

reverse appliqué, in which shapes are cut out from,
        ———————————————
              69

rather than adding on top of, the embroidered fabric.
         ——————
           70

63. The writer is considering deleting the preceding sentence. Should the sentence be kept or deleted?

   A. Kept, because it compares Pang Xiong's embroidery style with that of modern *paj ntaub*.
   B. Kept, because it places the subject of the essay in a modern context.
   C. Deleted, because it detracts from the paragraph's focus on the various styles of ancient Hmong needlework arts.
   D. Deleted, because it adds a detail that is irrelevant to the paragraph's introduction of Pang Xiong's connection to *paj ntaub*.

64. **F.** NO CHANGE
   G. woman living
   H. woman, who lives
   J. woman, having lived

65. The best placement for the underlined portion would be:

   A. where it is now.
   B. after the word *made*.
   C. after the word *clothing*.
   D. after the word *needlework*.

66. **F.** NO CHANGE
   G. have been designed
   H. are designed
   J. design

67. Which choice most clearly builds on the information provided earlier in the sentence about a common theme in *paj ntaub* patterns and images?

   A. NO CHANGE
   B. only a master artist is able to create *paj ntaub* clothing for special occasions.
   C. *paj ntaub* patterns are extraordinarily colorful.
   D. *paj ntaub* celebrates the natural world.

68. **F.** NO CHANGE
   G. tiny tight, stitches
   H. tiny, tight stitches
   J. tiny tight stitches,

69. **A.** NO CHANGE
   B. appliqué which
   C. appliqué and
   D. appliqué,

70. **F.** NO CHANGE
   G. as an addition
   H. to add them
   J. added

GO ON TO THE NEXT PAGE.

Another is elaborate overstitching: thousands of layered stitches are applied to <u>its surface.</u>
₇₁

Pang Xiong regrets that most people she knows today wear only <u>regular</u> clothes. When she was growing
₇₂
up in Laos, she explains, she had few items of clothing, but each garment she owned was handcrafted *paj ntaub*.

<u>However, she</u> still wears flower cloth every day and
₇₃

would like to inspire <u>others to do so.</u> Pang Xiong
₇₄
teaches *paj ntaub* in art museums—including at the Smithsonian Institution, where some of her textiles are on permanent display—and in community settings around Philadelphia. 75 Pang Xiong is showing a new generation the joys of *paj ntaub* and beautiful handcrafted clothing.

71. **A.** NO CHANGE
    B. the surface of the fabric.
    C. the surface of it.
    D. their surface.

72. The writer is considering revising the underlined portion to the following:

    mass-produced

    Should the writer make this revision?

    F. Yes, because the revision creates a clearer contrast between the homogeneous styles of clothing that are popular today and the handcrafted *paj ntaub*.
    G. Yes, because the revision emphasizes Pang Xiong's desire for her handcrafted *paj ntaub* to be sold on a large scale in stores.
    H. No, because the original word reinforces the idea that although *paj ntaub* clothing can be used for everyday wear, it should be saved for special occasions.
    J. No, because the original word more specifically describes the type of clothing Pang Xiong disapproves of.

73. **A.** NO CHANGE
    B. For example, she
    C. Besides, she
    D. She

74. Which choice most clearly and concisely indicates that Pang Xiong wants other people to wear and appreciate handcrafted clothing?
    F. NO CHANGE
    G. people to also attempt that approach.
    H. people she knows.
    J. others.

75. Which of the following true statements, if added here, would best build on the ideas presented in this paragraph and connect to the final sentence of the essay?
    A. She loves when people, no matter what their ethnicity, wear traditional clothing every day.
    B. She often teaches *paj ntaub* to Hmong adults her age who want to learn new techniques.
    C. Recently, she worked with nine young Hmong women in a formal apprenticeship.
    D. One of her own favorite pieces tells the story of her family.

END OF TEST 1

STOP! DO NOT TURN THE PAGE UNTIL TOLD TO DO SO.

2 △ △ △ △ △ △ △ △ △ **2**

MATHEMATICS TEST
60 Minutes — 60 Questions

DIRECTIONS: Solve each problem, choose the correct answer, and then fill in the corresponding oval on your answer document.

Do not linger over problems that take too much time. Solve as many as you can; then return to the others in the time you have left for this test.

You are permitted to use a calculator on this test. You may use your calculator for any problems you choose, but some of the problems may best be done without using a calculator.

Note: Unless otherwise stated, all of the following should be assumed.

1. Illustrative figures are NOT necessarily drawn to scale.
2. Geometric figures lie in a plane.
3. The word *line* indicates a straight line.
4. The word *average* indicates arithmetic mean.

---

1. A marble will be randomly selected from a bag of solid-colored marbles. The probability of selecting a red marble is $\frac{5}{19}$. The probability of selecting a blue marble is $\frac{4}{19}$. What is the probability of selecting a red marble *or* a blue marble?

    A. $\frac{1}{19}$

    B. $\frac{9}{19}$

    C. $\frac{9}{38}$

    D. $\frac{20}{38}$

    E. $\frac{20}{361}$

DO YOUR FIGURING HERE.

2. The graph below shows the number of students who were present on Thursday from each of the 5 groups in Ms. Meagan's class. What is the probability that a student selected at random from the class on Thursday is in Group 4 ?

    F. $\frac{1}{28}$

    G. $\frac{1}{14}$

    H. $\frac{1}{5}$

    J. $\frac{1}{4}$

    K. $\frac{1}{2}$

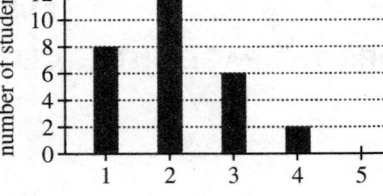

GO ON TO THE NEXT PAGE.

2 △ △ △ △ △ △ △ △ △ 2

3. Consider the equation $k = \frac{7}{5}j + 54$. For what value of j is the value of k equal to 40 ?

   A. -10

   B. $-\frac{98}{5}$

   C. $\frac{178}{7}$

   D. $\frac{200}{7}$

   E. 56

4. What is $|3 - x|$ when $x = 8$?
   F. -11
   G. -5
   H. 5
   J. 8
   K. 11

5. When Tyrese fell asleep one night, the temperature was 24°F. When Tyrese awoke the next morning, the temperature was −16°F. Letting + denote a rise in temperature and − denote a drop in temperature, what was the change in temperature from the time Tyrese fell asleep until the time he awoke?
   A. −40°F
   B. −8°F
   C. +4°F
   D. +8°F
   E. +40°F

6. Ming purchased a car that had a purchase price of $5,400, which included all other costs and tax. She paid $1,000 as a down payment and got a loan for the rest of the purchase price. Ming paid off the loan by making 28 payments of $200 each. The total of all her payments, including the down payment, was how much more than the car's purchase price?
   F. $ 200
   G. $1,200
   H. $4,400
   J. $5,600
   K. $6,600

7. Shown below is a regular hexagon inscribed in a circle whose radius is 4 inches. What is the perimeter, in inches, of the hexagon?

   A. 8π
   B. $12\sqrt{3}$
   C. 18
   D. 20
   E. 24

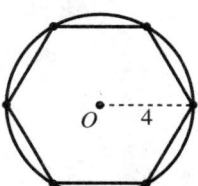

DO YOUR FIGURING HERE.

GO ON TO THE NEXT PAGE.

Taking Additional Practice Tests

2 △ △ △ △ △ △ △ △ △ **2**

8. The floor plan for an L-shaped storage building is shown below with distances marked in feet. What is the floor area of the building, in square feet?

(Note: Walls in this building meet only at right angles.)

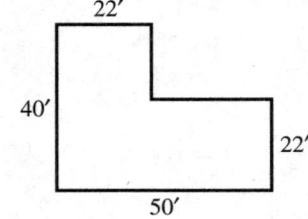

F. 190
G. 504
H. 1,232
J. 1,496
K. 1,980

DO YOUR FIGURING HERE.

9. Quadrilateral *ABCD* with vertices $A(-2,0)$, $B(0,4)$, $C(5,5)$, and $D(8,2)$ will be graphed in the standard (x,y) coordinate plane below.

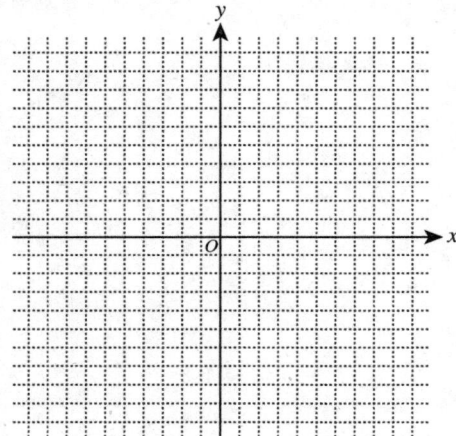

Which of the following is a type of quadrilateral determined by these vertices?

A. Kite
B. Parallelogram
C. Trapezoid
D. Rectangle
E. Square

10. Given that $f(x) = 3x + 7$ and $g(x) = \frac{x^2}{2}$, what is the value of $f\big(g(4)\big)$?

F. 8
G. 19
H. 31
J. 152
K. 180.5

GO ON TO THE NEXT PAGE.

2 △ △ △ △ △ △ △ △ △ 2

11. At her hot dog stand, Julie sells hot dogs for $2 each. Purchasing hot dogs and other supplies costs $200 per month. The solution of which of the following inequalities models the numbers of hot dogs, h, Julie can sell per month and make a profit?

A. $h - 200 > 0$
B. $h - 200 < 0$
C. $h + 200 > 0$
D. $2h - 200 < 0$
E. $2h - 200 > 0$

DO YOUR FIGURING HERE.

12. In the standard (x,y) coordinate plane, what is the slope of the line $3x + 8y = 5$?

F. -3

G. $-\dfrac{3}{8}$

H. $\dfrac{3}{5}$

J. 3

K. 5

13. Which of the following (x,y) pairs is the solution for the system of equations $x + 2y = 2$ and $-2x + y = 16$?

A. $(-6,4)$
B. $(-1,1.5)$
C. $(\ 1,0.5)$
D. $(\ 0,1)$
E. $(\ 2,0)$

14. On a map, $\dfrac{1}{4}$ inch represents 16 actual miles. Two towns that are $2\dfrac{3}{4}$ inches apart on this map are how many actual miles apart?

F. $\ \ 11$
G. $\ \ 16$
H. $\ \ 44$
J. $\ \ 64$
K. 176

15. Which of the following matrices is equal to $4\begin{bmatrix} -1 & 2 \\ 0 & -4 \end{bmatrix}$?

A. $\begin{bmatrix} -4 & -8 \end{bmatrix}$

B. $\begin{bmatrix} 4 \\ -16 \end{bmatrix}$

C. $\begin{bmatrix} 3 & 6 \\ 4 & 0 \end{bmatrix}$

D. $\begin{bmatrix} -\frac{1}{4} & \frac{1}{2} \\ 0 & -1 \end{bmatrix}$

E. $\begin{bmatrix} -4 & 8 \\ 0 & -16 \end{bmatrix}$

GO ON TO THE NEXT PAGE.

Taking Additional Practice Tests

The ONLY Official Prep Guide from the Makers of the ACT

2      **2**

16. What is the value of tan A in right triangle $\triangle ABC$ below?

DO YOUR FIGURING HERE.

F. $\frac{8}{17}$

G. $\frac{8}{15}$

H. $\frac{15}{17}$

J. $\frac{15}{8}$

K. $\frac{17}{8}$

17. Tina runs at a rate of 8 miles per hour. At that rate, how many miles will she run in 12 minutes?

A. $\frac{5}{8}$

B. $\frac{2}{3}$

C. $1\frac{1}{2}$

D. $1\frac{3}{5}$

E. 2

18. A function $f(x)$ is defined as $f(x) = -6x^2$. What is $f(-3)$?

F. −324
G. −54
H. 54
J. 108
K. 324

19. In the figure below, A is on $\overleftrightarrow{BE}$ and C is on $\overleftrightarrow{BD}$. What is the measure of $\angle ABC$?

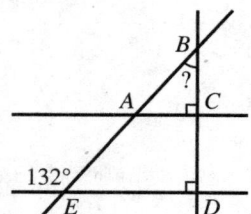

A. 24°
B. 42°
C. 45°
D. 48°
E. 66°

GO ON TO THE NEXT PAGE.

2 △ △ △ △ △ △ △ △ △ **2**

20. Marcos programs his calculator to evaluate a linear function, but he doesn't say what the function is. When 5 is entered, the calculator displays the value 2. When 15 is entered, the calculator displays the value 6. Which of the following expressions explains what the calculator will display when any number, n, is entered?

F. $\frac{2}{5}n$

G. $\frac{5}{2}n$

H. $n - 3$

J. $n - 9$

K. $\frac{5}{2}n - \frac{21}{2}$

21. On Friday, the temperature at 8:00 a.m. was 49°F and rose at a constant rate of $\frac{1}{2}$°F per hour until noon. A cold front passed through at noon, and the temperature then fell at a constant rate of 1°F per hour. The temperature first fell below 49°F between:

A. noon and 1 p.m.
B. 1 p.m. and 2 p.m.
C. 2 p.m. and 3 p.m.
D. 3 p.m. and 4 p.m.
E. 4 p.m. and 5 p.m.

22. Letter grades in Hugo's math class are based on the percent of the total possible points on 4 unit exams (each worth 100 points) and the final exam (worth 200 points) and are assigned according to the chart below.

Range	Course grade
At least 90%	A
80%–89%	B
70%–79%	C
60%–69%	D
Less than 60%	F

The number of points Hugo scored on the unit exams this term were 82, 88, 91, and 83. When course grades were posted, Hugo's course grade was listed as a B. Which of the following could NOT have been the number of points he scored on the final exam?

F. 136
G. 156
H. 166
J. 176
K. 196

GO ON TO THE NEXT PAGE.

2 △ △ △ △ △ △ △ △ △ 2

DO YOUR FIGURING HERE.

Use the following information to answer questions 23–25.

Halle is bowling a series of 3 games. She has bowled 2 of 3 games with scores of 148 and 176. The figure below is a top view of the bowling lane. The dimensions for the bowling lane are given in the figure. The *pin deck* is the rectangular area within the bowling lane where the 10 bowling pins are set up.

(Note: The figure is not drawn to scale.)

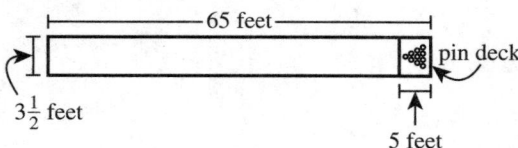

23. The diameter of each pin at its base is 2.25 in. When all of the pins are set up, which of the following values is closest to the area, in square inches, that is covered by the bases of the pins?

   A.   40
   B.   71
   C.   111
   D.   125
   E.   159

24. What is the ratio of the total area of the bowling lane to the area of the pin deck?

   F.   12:1
   G.   13:1
   H.   13:12
   J.   127:17
   K.   137:17

25. What score will Halle need to earn in her 3rd game to have an average score of 172 for the 3 games?

   A.   165
   B.   172
   C.   182
   D.   192
   E.   200

_____

26. The area of a rectangle is 300 square meters, and its length is 3 times its width. How many meters wide is the rectangle?

   F.   10
   G.   30
   H.   50
   J.   100
   K.   150

GO ON TO THE NEXT PAGE.

2 △ △ △ △ △ △ △ △ △ **2**

27. A parallelogram has a perimeter of 96 inches, and 1 of its sides measures 16 inches. If it can be determined, what are the lengths, in inches, of the other 3 sides?

A. 16, 16, 48
B. 16, 24, 24
C. 16, 32, 32
D. 16, 40, 40
E. Cannot be determined from the given information

28. Elmhurst Street is a two-way street. In each direction, it has one 12-foot-wide lane for car traffic, one 6-foot-wide bike lane, and one 8-foot-wide parking lane. How many feet wide is Elmhurst Street?

F. 26
G. 38
H. 52
J. 60
K. 80

29. At Central High School, 4 out of every 10 students ride the bus to and from school, and 3 out of every 8 who ride the bus are freshmen. If there are 2,500 students at Central, how many of the students are freshmen who ride the bus?

A. 375
B. 412
C. 428
D. 561
E. 705

30. If $90° < \theta < 180°$ and $\sin \theta = \frac{20}{29}$, then $\cos \theta = $?

F. $\frac{29}{20}$

G. $\frac{20}{21}$

H. $-\frac{21}{29}$

J. $-\frac{29}{21}$

K. $-\frac{29}{20}$

31. Given $f(x) = \frac{2}{x+1}$, what is(are) the real value(s) of t for which $f(t) = t$?

A. −1 only
B. 2 only
C. −2 and 1 only
D. −1 and 2 only
E. 1 and 2 only

DO YOUR FIGURING HERE.

Taking Additional Practice Tests

GO ON TO THE NEXT PAGE.

2   **2**

Use the following information to answer questions 32–35.

DO YOUR FIGURING HERE.

In the figure below, a highway rest area (at D) and radar stations (at A and B) lie on a level east-west line; A is 9,000 feet due west of D. An airplane (at C) is shown directly above the rest area, flying due west at a constant speed of 300 feet per second and at a constant altitude of 12,000 feet. The airplane is located at a straight-line distance of 15,000 feet from the radar station at A and 13,000 feet from the radar station at B.

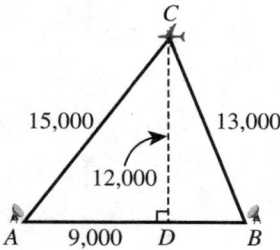

32. Which of the following values is closest to the distance, in feet, between the 2 radar stations?

F.   5,000
G.   10,000
H.   10,500
J.   14,000
K.   15,000

33. Let A, C, and D lie in the standard (x,y) coordinate plane such that A is at $(0,0)$ and D is at $(9,000, 0)$. Which of the following equations represents the line along which the airplane is flying?

A. $x = 9,000$
B. $x = 15,000$
C. $y = 12,000$
D. $y = 13,000$
E. $y = 15,000$

34. Which of the following values is closest to the number of seconds it will take for the airplane to fly from C to the point directly above the radar station at A ?

F.   17
G.   30
H.   40
J.   43
K.   50

GO ON TO THE NEXT PAGE.

2 △ △ △ △ △ △ △ △ △ **2**

35. When considering the changing triangle formed by A, B, and the moving airplane (C), which of the angles below increases in measure as the airplane flies due west beyond the point directly above A ?

    I. $\angle A$
    II. $\angle B$
    III. $\angle C$

  A. I only
  B. II only
  C. I and II only
  D. I and III only
  E. II and III only

DO YOUR FIGURING HERE.

36. Troy made a rectangular poster that is 4 feet long and 2 feet wide. The poster is too large to fit in the available display space, so Troy is going to make a new poster that will have an area that is 50% of the area of the original poster. The length of Troy's new poster will be $\frac{3}{4}$ the length of the original poster. How many feet wide will the new poster be?

  F. $\frac{3}{4}$

  G. $1\frac{1}{3}$

  H. $1\frac{1}{2}$

  J.   3

  K. 6

37. What is the solution set of the equation
$x + 6 = 2(x + 3) - x$?

  A. The empty set (no solution)
  B. {0}
  C. {2}
  D. {3}
  E. The set of all real numbers

38. Steve plans to use 28 feet of fencing to enclose a region of his yard for a pen for his pet rabbit. What is the area, in square feet, of the largest rectangular region Steve can enclose?

  F.   40
  G. 45
  H. 48
  J.   49
  K. 196

GO ON TO THE NEXT PAGE.

Taking Additional Practice Tests

2 △ △ △ △ △ △ △ △ △ **2**

39. There are exactly 5 people in a bookstore at 12:00 p.m. Each person earns an annual income that is between $30,000 and $35,000. No one enters or leaves the bookstore until 12:15 p.m., when a professional athlete with an annual income of more than $1,000,000 enters the bookstore and joins the other 5 people. The mean, median, range, and standard deviation of the annual incomes of the 5 people in the bookstore at 12:00 p.m. are calculated and compared to the same 4 statistics of the annual incomes of the 6 people in the bookstore at 12:15 p.m. If it can be determined, which of the 4 statistics changed the least?

- **A.** Range
- **B.** Mean
- **C.** Median
- **D.** Standard deviation
- **E.** Cannot be determined from the given information

40. Ana and Amy started a landscaping job together. When Ana stopped, she had completed $\frac{2}{5}$ of the job. When Amy stopped, she had completed $\frac{1}{3}$ of the job. Then Ruben completed the rest of the job in 2 hours. Assume that Ana, Amy, and Ruben all worked at the same rate. Which of the following values is closest to the number of hours it would have taken 1 of them to complete the entire job alone?

- **F.** 0.37
- **G.** 1.27
- **H.** 2.73
- **J.** 5.00
- **K.** 7.50

41. If a and b are positive real numbers, which of the following is equivalent to $\frac{\left(2a^{-1}\sqrt{b}\right)^4}{ab^{-3}}$?

- **A.** $8a^2b^4$

- **B.** $\dfrac{8b^6}{a^4}$

- **C.** $\dfrac{16b^5}{a^5}$

- **D.** $\dfrac{16b^4}{a^5}$

- **E.** $\dfrac{16b}{a^3}$

GO ON TO THE NEXT PAGE.

2 △ △ △ △ △ △ △ △ △ **2**

42. To become a contestant on a quiz show, a person must correctly order 4 rock stars by age, from youngest to oldest. The contestant knows which one is the oldest rock star, but randomly guesses at the order of the other 3 rock stars. What is the probability the contestant will get all 4 in the correct order?

DO YOUR FIGURING HERE.

   F. $\frac{1}{24}$

   G. $\frac{1}{6}$

   H. $\frac{1}{4}$

   J. $\frac{1}{3}$

   K. $\frac{1}{2}$

43. Which of the following expressions is equivalent to $\dfrac{\frac{x}{3}+\frac{1}{2}}{\frac{2}{3}-\frac{1}{4}}$?

   A. $\dfrac{-x-1}{5}$

   B. $\dfrac{2x+6}{5}$

   C. $\dfrac{4x+3}{5}$

   D. $\dfrac{4x+6}{5}$

   E. $4x+6$

44. An automobile license plate number issued by a certain state has 6 character positions. Each of the first 3 positions contains a single digit from 0 through 9. Each of the last 3 positions contains 1 of the 26 letters of the alphabet. Digits and letters of the alphabet can be repeated on a license plate. How many different such license plate numbers can be made?

   F.   36
   G.   46,656
   H.   1,000,000
   J. 12,812,904
   K. 17,576,000

GO ON TO THE NEXT PAGE.

△ △ △ △ △ △ △ △ △

45. The function $y = f(x)$ is graphed in the standard (x,y) coordinate plane below.

DO YOUR FIGURING HERE.

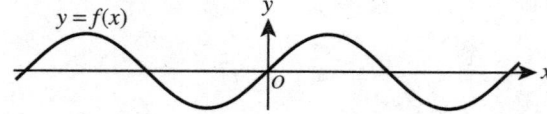

The points on the graph of the function $y = 3 + f(x - 1)$ can be obtained from the points on $y = f(x)$ by a shift of:

A. 1 unit to the right and 3 units up.
B. 1 unit to the right and 3 units down.
C. 3 units to the right and 1 unit up.
D. 3 units to the right and 1 unit down.
E. 3 units to the left and 1 unit down.

46. When $\log_5 x = -2$, what is x ?

F. -32

G. -25

H. -10

J. $\frac{1}{10}$

K. $\frac{1}{25}$

47. Which of the following lists those integer values of D for which the fraction $\frac{2}{D}$ lies between $\frac{1}{5}$ and $\frac{1}{3}$?

A. 4 only
B. 3, 4, and 5
C. 8 only
D. 7, 8, and 9
E. 16 only

48. For all real numbers a, b, and c such that $a > b$ and $c < 0$, which of the following inequalities *must* be true?

F. $\frac{a}{c} < \frac{b}{c}$

G. $\frac{a}{c} > \frac{b}{c}$

H. $ac > bc$

J. $a + c < b + c$

K. $a < b - c$

GO ON TO THE NEXT PAGE.

2 △ △ △ △ △ △ △ △ △ 2

49. The triangle shown below has side lengths 37, 38, and 39 inches. Which of the following expressions gives the measure of the largest angle of the triangle?

(Note: For every triangle with sides of length a, b, and c that are opposite $\angle A$, $\angle B$, and $\angle C$, respectively, $c^2 = a^2 + b^2 - 2ab \cos C$.)

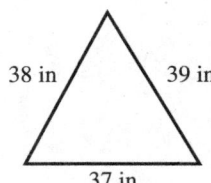

38 in   39 in

37 in

A. $\cos^{-1}\left(-\dfrac{37^2 - 38^2 - 39^2}{2(38)(39)}\right)$

B. $\cos^{-1}\left(-\dfrac{39^2 - 37^2 - 38^2}{2(37)(38)}\right)$

C. $\cos^{-1}\left(37^2 - 38^2 - 39^2 + 2(38)(39)\right)$

D. $\cos^{-1}\left(38^2 - 37^2 - 39^2 + 2(37)(39)\right)$

E. $\cos^{-1}\left(39^2 - 37^2 - 38^2 + 2(37)(38)\right)$

50. Pete has an average score of exactly x points on 4 equally weighted tests. How many points higher than x must Pete score on the 5th equally weighted test to raise his average score after the 5th test to $x + 2$ points?

F. 2
G. 4
H. 5
J. 8
K. 10

51. The intersection of lines l and m forms the 4 angles $\angle A$, $\angle B$, $\angle C$, and $\angle D$. The measure of $\angle B$ is $3\frac{1}{2}$ times the measure of $\angle A$. Which of the following values is closest to the measure of $\angle A$?

A. 20°
B. 26°
C. 35°
D. 40°
E. 51°

52. A sequence is defined for all positive integers by $s_n = 2s_{(n-1)} + n + 1$ and $s_1 = 3$. What is s_4 ?

F. 9
G. 18
H. 22
J. 49
K. 111

DO YOUR FIGURING HERE.

Taking Additional Practice Tests

GO ON TO THE NEXT PAGE.

2   **2**

53. If a is an integer less than -1, which of the following orders the expressions $|a|$, $-a^2$, and $-\frac{1}{a}$ from least value to greatest value?

A. $-\frac{1}{a} < -a^2 < |a|$

B. $-\frac{1}{a} < |a| < -a^2$

C. $|a| < -\frac{1}{a} < -a^2$

D. $-a^2 < |a| < -\frac{1}{a}$

E. $-a^2 < -\frac{1}{a} < |a|$

DO YOUR FIGURING HERE.

54. At the school carnival, Ann is playing a game involving a stack of 10 index cards. Each card has a single number written on it: 1 card has a 1, 2 cards have a 2, 3 cards have a 3, and 4 cards have a 4. Ann will choose 1 card at random, and she will be awarded the number of points equal to the number written on the card. Let the random variable X represent the number of points Ann receives on any 1 draw. What is the expected value of X ?

F. 0.4
G. 1
H. 2.5
J. 3
K. 4

55. Which of the following is equivalent to the sum of any 3 consecutive odd integers, x, y, and z, such that $x < y < z$?

A. $3z$

B. $3y$

C. $3x$

D. $3x + 2$

E. $\frac{x+y+z}{3}$

56. The mean of the set of 5 numbers $\{42, 3, 11, 27, x\}$ is 24, and the median of the set of 4 numbers $\{53, 8, 29, y\}$ is 38. If it can be determined, which of the following values is equal to $x - y$?

F. -38
G. -10
H. 10
J. 38
K. Cannot be determined from the given information

GO ON TO THE NEXT PAGE.

2 △ △ △ △ △ △ △ △ △ **2**

57. Consider all rectangles such that the rectangle's length is greater than the rectangle's width and the length and width are whole numbers of inches. Which of the following perimeters, in inches, is NOT possible for such a rectangle with an area of 144 square inches?

A. 48
B. 60
C. 80
D. 102
E. 148

58. The equation $(x - 7)^2 + (y - 8)^2 = 10$ is that of a circle that lies in the standard (x,y) coordinate plane. One endpoint of a diameter of the circle has y-coordinate 11. What is the y-coordinate of the other endpoint of that diameter?

F. 1
G. 3
H. 4
J. 5
K. 8

59. The plans for a diving pool call for a rectangular prism that has a length of 30 meters, a width of 25 meters, and a depth of 5 meters. If the plans are changed to increase both the length and the width of the pool by 10%, what will be the increase, to the nearest 1%, in the volume of the pool?

A. 10%
B. 17%
C. 20%
D. 21%
E. 33%

60. One solution of the equation $4x^3 - 2x^2 + x + 7 = 0$ is $x = -1$. Which of the following describes the other 2 solutions?

F. Both are negative real numbers.
G. One is a negative real number, and the other is a positive real number.
H. Both are positive real numbers.
J. One is a positive real number, and the other is a complex number that is not real.
K. Both are complex numbers that are not real.

END OF TEST 2

STOP! DO NOT TURN THE PAGE UNTIL TOLD TO DO SO.

DO NOT RETURN TO THE PREVIOUS TEST.

3

3

READING TEST
35 Minutes — 40 Questions

DIRECTIONS: There are several passages in this test. Each passage is accompanied by several questions. After reading a passage, choose the best answer to each question and fill in the corresponding oval on your answer document. You may refer to the passages as often as necessary.

Passage I

LITERARY NARRATIVE: This passage is adapted from the short story "Pride" by Alice Munro (©2011 by Alice Munro).

Oneida didn't go to school with the rest of us. She went to a girls' school, a private school. Even in the summers she was not around much. I believe the family had a place on Lake Simcoe.

5　Oneida was an unusual name. Her father, I believe, called her Ida. Ida's father ran the bank. Even in those days bankers came and went, I suppose to keep them from ever getting too cozy with the customers. But the Jantzens had been having their way in town for too long
10　for any regulations to matter, or that was how it seemed. Horace Jantzen had certainly the look of a man born to be in power. A heavy white beard and a ponderous expression.

In the hard times of the Thirties people were still
15　coming up with ideas. You can be sure, men were nursing a notion bound to make them a million dollars. A million dollars in those days was a million dollars.

It wasn't any railway bum, however, who got into the bank to talk to Horace Jantzen. Who knows if it was
20　a single person or a cohort. Maybe a stranger or some friends of friends. Well dressed and plausible looking, you may be sure. Horace set store by appearances. He wasn't a fool, though maybe not as quick as he should have been to smell a rat.

25　The idea was the resurrection of the steam-driven car, such as had been around at the turn of the century. Horace Jantzen may have had one himself and had a fondness for them. This new model would be an improved version, of course, and have the advantages of
30　being economical and not making a racket.

I'm not acquainted with the details, having been in high school at the time. But I can imagine the leak of talk and the scoffing and enthusiasm and the news getting through of some entrepreneurs from Toronto or
35　Windsor or Kitchener getting ready to set up locally. Some hotshots, people would say. And others would ask if they had the backing.

They did indeed, because the bank had put up the loan. It was Jantzen's decision and there was some con-
40　fusion that he had put in his own money. He may have done so, but he had also dipped improperly into bank funds, thinking no doubt that he could pay it back with nobody the wiser. Maybe the laws were not so tight then. There were actually men hired and the old Livery
45　Stable was cleared out to be their place of operations. And here my memory grows shaky, because I graduated from high school, and I had to think about earning a living if that was possible. I settled for bookkeeping, and that meant going out of town to apprentice to an
50　outfit in Goderich. By the time I got back home the steam-car operation was spoken of with scorn by the people who had been against it and not at all by those who had promoted it. The visitors to town who promoted it had disappeared.

55　The bank had lost a lot of money. There was talk not of cheating but of mismanagement. Somebody had to be punished. Any ordinary manager would have been out on his ear, but given that it was Horace Jantzen this was avoided. What happened to him was almost worse.
60　He was switched to the job of bank manager in the little village of Hawksburg, about six miles up the highway. Prior to this there had been no manager there at all, because they didn't need one. There had just been a head cashier and an underling cashier, both women.

65　Surely he could have refused, but pride, as it was thought, chose otherwise. Pride chose that he be driven every morning those six miles to sit behind a partial wall of cheap varnished boards, no proper office at all. There he sat and did nothing until it was time for him to
70　be driven home. The person who drove him was his daughter. Sometime in these years of driving she made the transition from Ida to Oneida. At last she had something to do.

If I picture Oneida and her father on these journeys
75　to and from Hawksburg, I see him riding in the back seat, and her in front, like a chauffeur. It may have been that he was too bulky to ride up beside her. I don't see Oneida looking downtrodden or unhappy at the arrangement, nor her father looking actually unhappy. Dignity
80　was what he had, and plenty of it. She had something different. When she went into a store or even walked on the street there seemed to be a little space cleared around her, made ready for whatever she might want or greetings she might spread. She seemed then a bit flus-
85　tered but gracious, ready to laugh a little at herself or the situation. Of course she had her good bones and

GO ON TO THE NEXT PAGE.

3 ▓▓▓▓▓▓▓▓▓▓▓▓▓▓▓▓▓▓▓▓▓▓▓ **3**

bright looks, all that fair dazzle of skin and hair. So it might seem strange that I could feel sorry for her, the way she was all on the surface of things, trusting.

1. Based on the passage, it could be assumed that the narrator gained the knowledge to tell this story about Jantzen by:

A. piecing the story together out of hearsay and his own recollections.
B. learning the details directly from Jantzen.
C. fabricating the entire story because it didn't really happen.
D. being a participant in the events as they unfolded.

2. In the context of the passage, which of the following statements most strongly foreshadows Jantzen's downfall?

F. "Ida's father ran the bank" (line 6).
G. "In the hard times of the Thirties people were still coming up with ideas" (lines 14–15).
H. "He wasn't a fool, though maybe not as quick as he should have been to smell a rat" (lines 23–24).
J. "Horace Jantzen may have had one himself and had a fondness for them" (lines 27–28).

3. The passage suggests that in considering who convinced Jantzen to invest in manufacturing steam-driven cars, most people in town:

A. could list everyone who was involved.
B. believed some were friends of friends while others were complete strangers.
C. figured it had been an old cohort of Jantzen's who had fallen on hard times.
D. indulged in speculation, but didn't know for sure who it had been.

4. Which of the following is true of people's behavior when the narrator returned to town after his apprenticeship?

  I. Visitors who promoted steam cars had left town.
  II. People in town blamed the loss of money on Jantzen having cheated.
  III. People in town who had favored the plan to bring back steam cars stopped speaking of the cars.
  IV. People who had been against the plan to bring back steam cars spoke of the cars scornfully.

F. I and II only
G. III and IV only
H. I, III, and IV only
J. II, III, and IV only

5. Which of the following best paraphrases the narrator's comments in lines 14–16?

A. People in their thirties had the best ideas for making money.
B. Because times were hard, people were trying to find new money-making schemes.
C. Men were making as much as a million dollars a year in the 1930s.
D. Everyone was sure that they should take their money-making plans to Jantzen.

6. As it is used in line 16, the word *nursing* most nearly means:

F. rearing.
G. educating.
H. healing.
J. fostering.

7. The narrator speculates that whoever convinced Jantzen to invest in a steam-driven car must have been:

A. well dressed; Jantzen would have been impressed by someone who looked affluent.
B. wealthy; otherwise, Jantzen wouldn't have risked loaning the money.
C. elderly; Jantzen would have trusted someone who could remember the original steam-driven cars.
D. intelligent; it would have taken someone clever to convince Jantzen to invest.

8. Based on the passage, it's most logical to conclude that the original steam-driven cars were:

F. expensive and noisy.
G. reliable and fast.
H. unattractive and impractical.
J. luxurious and durable.

9. According to the passage, the majority of the investment money to manufacture a steam-driven car came from:

A. some of Jantzen's wealthy friends.
B. Jantzen's entire life savings.
C. the bank Jantzen was managing.
D. entrepreneurs from Toronto, Windsor, or Kitchener.

10. The narrator states that people assumed it was pride that drove Jantzen to:

F. invest in steam-driven cars.
G. agree to manage the Hawksburg bank.
H. look miserable while Oneida drove him to work.
J. create a makeshift office out of varnished boards.

GO ON TO THE NEXT PAGE.

3 ███████████████████████████████████ **3**

Passage II

SOCIAL SCIENCE: Passage A is adapted from *Plastic: A Toxic Love Story* by Susan Freinkel (©2011 by Susan Freinkel). Passage B is adapted from *American Plastic: A Cultural History* by Jeffrey L. Meikle (©1995 by Jeffrey L. Meikle).

Passage A by Susan Freinkel

Designers were enthralled by the universe of possibility from plastics' earliest days. They loved the design freedom that synthetics offered and the spirit of modernity the materials embodied. To furniture
5   designer Paul T. Frankl, a material like Bakelite, the world's first synthetic plastic, spoke "in the vernacular of the twentieth century . . . the language of invention, of synthesis," and he urged his fellow designers to use their full imaginative powers to explore the new materi-
10 als' frank artificiality. As interpreted by Frankl and other designers working with Bakelite in the '30s and '40s, that was the language of streamlining, a lingo of curves and dashes and teardrop shapes that created a feeling of speed and motion in everyday objects.
15 Streamline a fountain pen and even that stolid item declared: we're hurtling toward the future here!

There was another reason designers embraced plastics. From the mid-twentieth century on, modern design has been guided by an egalitarian gospel, a
20 belief that good design needn't cost a lot of money, that even the most mundane items could be things of beauty. "Get the most of the best to the most for the least" was the way Ray and Charles Eames put it in their famous tongue-twisting credo. Plastics were the ideal medium
25 for that mission: malleable, relatively inexpensive, and made for mass manufacture.

Yet, as in any new relationship, there were risks. It was all too easy to exploit plastics' powers of mimicry to produce the kinds of imitations—pseudo-wood cabi-
30 nets and faux-leather recliners—that contributed to the growing reputation of plastic as an inferior material. Plastics' adaptability and glibness undermined their capacity to achieve "dignity" as legitimate materials worthy of being taken seriously, one critic wrote.

35 This impression was exacerbated by people's unfortunate experiences with plastics in the immediate postwar years. There were plastic plates that melted in hot water, plastic toys that cracked on Christmas morning, plastic raincoats that grew clammy and fell apart in
40 the rain. Polymer technology improved during the 1950s as manufacturers figured out how to make better plastics and, even more important, how to match the right polymer with the right application. But the damage to plastic's reputation had been done.

Passage B by Jeffrey L. Meikle

45 Worrying about the image of plastic made sense in 1945 when unfamiliar new materials confronted wary consumers. By the mid-1950s, however, no one was ignorant of plastic because it surrounded everyone.

Sidney Gross, who joined *Modern Plastics* in 1952 and
50 became editor in 1968, recalled that he had "agitated a lot" over the years to get SPI, the trade association for the plastics industry, to quit trying to convince people "that plastic is not bad." It was a waste of money because plastic's image—good or bad—did not really
55 matter. The key to plastic's success, as he saw it, was always "selling the manufacturer." Once plastic products filled the stores, people had no choice but to consume what they were offered. Most of the time, Gross maintained, after the industry had solved postwar qual-
60 ity problems, plastic objects did work better. Things made of plastic were better designed and lasted longer. People intuitively recognized that fact even if they retained an intellectual notion that plastic was bad or shoddy. In short, nothing succeeded like success.

65 Often plastic did offer a significant improvement on whatever it replaced. A sleepy householder had to watch only once in disbelief as a polyethylene juice pitcher bounced off the kitchen floor to begin accepting plastic in a practical way no matter how strong the con-
70 ceptual disdain for it. Even plastic toys, despite the brittle polystyrene items that broke on Christmas morning, proved superior in many ways. A toy soldier of molded polyethylene could not scratch the furniture as readily as an old-fashioned lead soldier. Most people who
75 expressed negative attitudes about plastic used it anyway without thinking about it, either because a particular use had proven itself or because an inexpensive trouble-free alternative no longer existed. As *House Beautiful* observed in 1955, "The news is not that plas-
80 tics exist, but [that] they have already been so assimilated into our lives." The average person was "conditioned to plastics." They had penetrated so far into the material fabric of everyday life that their presence could not be denied no matter how many people
85 considered them second-rate substitutes or a sad commentary on modern times.

11. In the context of Passage A, the author uses the description of a fountain pen (lines 15–16) most nearly to:

   A. lament the way that unique objects began to look identical after the advent of streamlining.

   B. critique designers for creating items that were beautiful rather than functional.

   C. illustrate how even everyday items could be designed to appear modern.

   D. exemplify the kind of item that remained largely unaffected by new design trends.

GO ON TO THE NEXT PAGE.

3 3

12. The main idea of the second paragraph (lines 17–26) is that plastics:

F. appealed to a prevailing philosophy of providing great design to many people for a low cost.

G. quickly became popular enough to inspire a number of famous credos and advertising slogans.

H. created a challenge for designers, who were not used to working with such a malleable material.

J. inspired an artistic movement whose members prized mundane objects rather than beautiful ones.

13. According to Passage A, one reason for designers' early interest in plastics was that:

A. the materials' ability to be freely shaped encouraged inventiveness.

B. consumers' demand for attractively designed items was high.

C. a person creating everyday items out of plastics was seen as a bold risk taker.

D. older materials like Bakelite were difficult to work with.

14. It can reasonably be inferred from Passage A that before the 1950s, plastics manufacturers had not yet figured out:

F. how to mold plastics to create the impression of streamlining.

G. which plastics were best suited to specific purposes.

H. whether consumers would buy everyday items made of plastics.

J. whether designers would embrace working with plastics.

15. In the context of Passage B, the statement "They had penetrated so far into the material fabric of everyday life" (lines 82–83) most nearly refers to the way that plastics came to be:

A. considered a symbol of increased consumerism.

B. preferred by most consumers to more conventional materials.

C. perceived as a threat to traditional ways of life.

D. pervasive to the extent that they were integral to people's routines.

16. In Passage B, the primary purpose of the details about the polyethylene juice pitcher (lines 66–70) is to:

F. describe an advertisement created by the plastic industry in an attempt to improve plastic's image.

G. show how people might be persuaded by plastic's durability despite disliking plastic in general.

H. demonstrate how dramatically plastic's quality improved between 1945 and the mid-1950s.

J. provide an example of the kinds of mishaps that biased people against plastic.

17. Passage B most nearly suggests that compared to toys made of traditional materials, toys made of plastic were often:

A. more flexible and more detailed.

B. less costly and sturdier.

C. less durable but also less destructive.

D. more popular with kids but less popular with parents.

18. To support their claims about the public's perception of plastics during the time periods discussed in the passages, both passage authors:

F. quote people who used or wrote about plastics.

G. analyze publications that promoted plastics.

H. define key concepts used to market plastics.

J. personify artwork or objects made of plastics.

19. Both passages suggest that one bias the public held in the postwar years was that items made of plastic were:

A. unattractive in design.

B. unnervingly artificial.

C. expensive novelties.

D. inferior substitutes.

20. Which of the following statements best compares the ways the authors of Passage A and Passage B use details about plastic toys on Christmas morning?

F. Passage A uses the toys as an example of good design, while Passage B uses the toys as proof that plastic items were superior to what they replaced.

G. Passage A uses the toys to illustrate plastic's popularity, while Passage B uses the toys to illustrate the lack of practical plastic goods.

H. Both passages use the toys to show the variety of plastic items produced during the postwar era.

J. Both passages use the toys as an example of early problems with plastic's quality.

GO ON TO THE NEXT PAGE.

3 ▬▬▬▬▬▬▬▬▬▬▬▬▬▬▬▬▬▬▬▬▬▬ 3

Passage III

HUMANITIES: This passage is adapted from the article "The Myth of Gabriel García Márquez: How the Colombian Writer Really Changed Literature" by Michael Wood (©2009 by Washington Post.Newsweek Interactive Co. LLC).

Many years later, and many times over, the writer Gabriel García Márquez was to remember the day he discovered how to set about writing his great novel. He was driving from Mexico City to Acapulco when the
5 illumination hit him. He turned the car around, went home, and locked himself away for 18 months. When he reappeared, he had the manuscript of *One Hundred Years of Solitude* in his hands.

When Gerald Martin, around the middle of his rich
10 and resourceful biography of García Márquez, starts to tell this story, the reader may be a little surprised, even disappointed. "He had not been driving long that day when . . . García Márquez, as if in a trance, turned the Opel around, and drove back in the direction of Mexico
15 City. And then . . ." Up to this point, Martin has not been challenging what he calls his subject's "mythomania"—how could he, since it's the basis of the writer's art and fame—but he has not been retelling the myths, either. He has been grounding them, laying out the
20 pieces of what became the puzzles. And that's what he's doing here, too.

After "and then," Martin writes in mock apology, "It seems a pity to intervene in the story at this point but the biographer feels constrained to point out that
25 there have been many versions of this story . . . and that the one just related cannot be true." The truth was no doubt less "miraculous," to use Martin's word. The writer probably continued to Acapulco. He didn't live in total seclusion for 18 months. And García Márquez
30 wasn't starting a new book; he was reviving an old one.

What García Márquez found was a way of telling it. He would combine, as he frequently said, the narrative tone of his grandmother with that of the author Franz Kafka. She told fantastic stories as if they were
35 true, because for her, they were true. Kafka told them that way because he was Kafka. After his moment of illumination García Márquez came more and more to look for (and often to find) the truth in the fantastic, to pursue whatever truth was lurking in the nonliteral
40 reading of literally presented events.

Just because the miracle didn't happen as the story says it did doesn't mean there wasn't a miracle. *One Hundred Years of Solitude* changed García Márquez's life entirely, and it changed literature. When he got into
45 the car to set out for Acapulco, he was a gifted and hardworking writer, certainly. When he got out of the car, he was on his way to the Nobel Prize, which he won in 1982.

García Márquez made many jokes about his fame
50 over the years. These jokes are witty and complicated acts of gratitude for a destiny the writer was sure could

have been quite different. One of his finest sentences, written in an article in 1983, concerns a dream of the life he might have led if he had stayed in his isolated
55 birthplace of Aracataca, Colombia. "I would not perhaps be the same person I am now but maybe I would have been something better: just a character in one of the novels I would never have written."

The term "mythomania" certainly covers García
60 Márquez's stories about his life and plenty of his journalism. But his fiction is different. It takes pieces of already thoroughly mythified reality—there is scarcely an extravagant incident in his novels and stories that doesn't have some sort of basis in specific, local fact or
65 legend—and finds the perfect, unforgettable literary home for them. But García Márquez neither copies nor further mythifies these facts and legends. He honors them, to borrow a well-placed word from Martin:

[O]ver the dark story of conquest and violence,
70   tragedy and failure, he laid the other side of the
    continent, the carnival spirit, the music and the
    art of the Latin American people, the ability to
    honor life even in its darkest corners.

To honor life, I take Martin as saying, is to cele-
75 brate dignity, courage, and style wherever they are found and in whatever forms they take. It is not to deny darkness or even to believe it has its compensations.

Martin's biography is itself rather a dark affair—appropriately, since he is telling the life of a man whose
80 autobiography is an elaborate historical myth. In García Márquez's own accounts, his life is both hard and magical. But it's never sad, and Martin evokes the sorrow that must lurk in such a life. There is perhaps a slight imbalance in Martin's insistence on the writer's sad-
85 ness, an excess of melancholy; but it's a good corrective to García Márquez's own joking cheerfulness and elaborate ironies, and we can return to the master if we get too depressed.

21. The primary function of the first paragraph is to:

A. correct misconceptions about how long it took García Márquez to write *One Hundred Years of Solitude*.

B. describe García Márquez's approach to writing novels.

C. relate a story about García Márquez that Martin discusses in his biography.

D. provide background information about García Márquez's childhood.

GO ON TO THE NEXT PAGE.

3   3

22. Based on the passage, which of the following best describes the passage author's opinion of García Márquez's writing?

    F. He considers García Márquez to be a gifted writer.

    G. He prefers García Márquez's journalism to García Márquez's novels.

    H. He thinks García Márquez's novels borrow too heavily from local facts and legends.

    J. He believes that García Márquez's writing contains excessive melancholy.

23. The "illumination" mentioned in lines 5 and 37 most nearly refers to:

    A. the realization García Márquez had concerning the approach he should take in writing *One Hundred Years of Solitude*.

    B. Martin's discovery that García Márquez modeled his writing after Franz Kafka's.

    C. the passage author's discovery that García Márquez based his stories on local facts and legends.

    D. the awareness by García Márquez of how miraculous it was that he completed *One Hundred Years of Solitude*.

24. The passage most strongly suggests that a reader might "be a little surprised, even disappointed" (lines 11–12) while reading Martin's book because Martin:

    F. is critical of García Márquez's preference for writing in seclusion.

    G. focuses on analyzing the novels of García Márquez rather than discussing his development as a writer.

    H. interrupts a familiar story about García Márquez to claim that it's not true.

    J. fails to adequately explain why García Márquez drove back to Mexico City.

25. As it is used in line 24, the word *constrained* most nearly means:

    A. restrained.

    B. compelled.

    C. coerced.

    D. limited.

26. According to García Márquez, his grandmother told fantastic stories as if they were true because she:

    F. was imitating Kafka.

    G. believed they were true.

    H. hoped to become a successful author.

    J. had learned the technique from García Márquez.

27. The passage indicates that the comments García Márquez makes about his fame demonstrate his:

    A. hope that his best work has yet to be written.

    B. concern that his accomplishments are distorted by others.

    C. gratitude that his life has unfolded the way it has.

    D. belief that he deserves more credit for his wit and the complexity of his writing.

28. According to García Márquez, he might have become "something better" (line 57) if he had:

    F. written *One Hundred Years of Solitude* sooner.

    G. completed his journey to Acapulco.

    H. taken his fame less seriously.

    J. stayed in Aracataca, Colombia.

29. The passage author indicates that Martin's biography helps balance García Márquez's:

    A. denial that fiction writing is worthy of merit.

    B. joking cheerfulness and elaborate ironies.

    C. belief that darkness has its compensations.

    D. refusal to write about life's tragedies.

30. As it is used in line 87, the word *master* refers to:

    F. the passage author.

    G. Martin.

    H. Kafka.

    J. García Márquez.

GO ON TO THE NEXT PAGE.

Taking Additional Practice Tests

3   **3**

Passage IV

NATURAL SCIENCE: This passage is adapted from the essay
"Our Place in the Universe" by Alan Lightman (©2012 by
Harper's Magazine Foundation).

One measure of the progress of human civilization
is the increasing scale of our maps. A clay tablet dating
from about the twenty-fifth century B.C. found near
what is now the Iraqi city of Kirkuk depicts a river
5 valley with a plot of land labeled as being 354 *iku*
(about thirty acres) in size. In the earliest recorded cosmologies, such as the Babylonian *Enuma Elish*, from
around 1500 B.C., the oceans, the continents, and the
heavens were considered finite, but there were no scien-
10 tific estimates of their dimensions. The early Greeks,
including Homer, viewed Earth as a circular plane with
the ocean enveloping it and Greece at the center, but
there was no understanding of scale. In the early sixth
century B.C., the Greek philosopher Anaximander,
15 whom historians consider the first mapmaker, and his
student Anaximenes proposed that the stars were
attached to a giant crystalline sphere. But again there
was no estimate of its size.

The first large object ever accurately measured
20 was Earth, accomplished in the third century B.C. by
Eratosthenes, a geographer who ran the Library of
Alexandria. From travelers, Eratosthenes had heard the
intriguing report that at noon on the summer solstice, in
the town of Syene, due south of Alexandria, the sun
25 casts no shadow at the bottom of a deep well. Evidently
the sun is directly overhead at that time and place.
(Before the invention of the clock, noon could be
defined at each place as the moment when the sun was
highest in the sky, whether that was exactly vertical or
30 not.) Eratosthenes knew that the sun was not overhead
at noon in Alexandria. In fact, it was tipped 7.2 degrees
from the vertical, or about one fiftieth of a circle—a
fact he could determine by measuring the length of the
shadow cast by a stick planted in the ground. That the
35 sun could be directly overhead in one place and not
another was due to the curvature of Earth. Eratosthenes
reasoned that if he knew the distance from Alexandria
to Syene, the full circumference of the planet must be
about fifty times that distance. Traders passing through
40 Alexandria told him that camels could make the trip to
Syene in about fifty days, and it was known that a
camel could cover one hundred stadia (almost eleven
and a half miles) in a day. So the ancient geographer
estimated that Syene and Alexandria were about
45 570 miles apart. Consequently, the complete circumference of Earth he figured to be about 50 × 570 miles, or
28,500 miles. This number was within 15 percent of the
modern measurement, amazingly accurate considering
the imprecision of using camels as odometers.

50   As ingenious as they were, the ancient Greeks
were not able to calculate the size of our solar system.
That discovery had to wait for the invention of the telescope, nearly two thousand years later. In 1672, the
French astronomer Jean Richer determined the distance
55 from Earth to Mars by measuring how much the position of the latter shifted against the background of stars

from two different observation points on Earth. The two
points were Paris and Cayenne, French Guiana. Using
the distance to Mars, astronomers were also able to
60 compute the distance from Earth to the sun, approximately 100 million miles.

A few years later, Isaac Newton managed to estimate the distance to the nearest stars. (Only someone as
accomplished as Newton could have been the first to
65 perform such a calculation and have it go almost unnoticed among his other achievements.) If one assumes
that the stars are similar objects to our sun, equal in
intrinsic luminosity, Newton asked, how far away
would our sun have to be in order to appear as faint as
70 nearby stars? Writing his computations in a spidery
script, with a quill dipped in the ink of oak galls,
Newton correctly concluded that the nearest stars are
about 100,000 times the distance from Earth to the sun,
about 10 trillion miles away. Newton's calculation is
75 contained in a short section of his *Principia* titled
simply "On the distance of the stars."

Newton's estimate of the distance to nearby stars
was larger than any distance imagined before in human
history. Even today, nothing in our experience allows us
80 to relate to it. The fastest most of us have traveled is
about 500 miles per hour, the cruising speed of a jet. If
we set out for the nearest star beyond our solar system
at that speed, it would take us about 5 million years to
reach our destination. If we traveled in the fastest
85 rocket ship ever manufactured on Earth, the trip would
last 100,000 years, at least a thousand human life spans.

31. The overall organization of the passage is best
described as a:

   A. chronological account of scientists' attempts to
      determine the distance of the stars from Earth.
   B. series of historical examples explaining how
      increasingly large distances were measured.
   C. step-by-step explanation of the calculations used
      to measure Earth's circumference.
   D. collection of anecdotes describing how maps of
      the universe have changed over time.

32. The main function of the first paragraph is to:

   F. list the distances and measurements that were
      known when Eratosthenes made his calculations.
   G. explain what led early geographers to conclude
      that Earth was curved.
   H. demonstrate how humans' sense of their surround-
      ings has expanded over time.
   J. summarize contributions the ancient Greeks made
      to astronomy.

GO ON TO THE NEXT PAGE.

3 ▬▬▬▬▬▬▬▬▬▬▬▬▬▬▬▬▬▬ 3

33. Based on the passage, one similarity among the ancient models of the universe described in lines 6–18 is that:

A. they were based on the assumption that the universe was infinite.

B. they provided no scientific estimates of the size or scale of the objects they identified.

C. their depictions of geographical features were surprisingly accurate according to modern maps.

D. the people who developed them positioned their homelands as the center of the universe.

34. The main idea of the last paragraph is that:

F. nothing in our experience allows us to relate to the distance from Earth to the nearest stars.

G. recent advancements in space travel make the distance from Earth to the nearest stars seem small.

H. the time it would take to travel the distance from Earth to the nearest stars has been calculated only recently.

J. the nearest stars are more distant from Earth than Newton predicted.

35. According to the passage, the early Greeks imagined Earth as a:

A. circular plane with the ocean enveloping it and Greece at the center.

B. giant crystalline sphere to which the stars were attached.

C. planet tilted 7.2 degrees from the vertical.

D. plot of land 354 *iku* in size.

36. Based on the passage, to calculate the distance between Syene and Alexandria, Eratosthenes required information about the:

F. curvature of Earth and the angle of the sun in each city.

G. number of miles in one hundred stadia and the complete circumference of Earth.

H. height of the sun at noon in each city and the length of shadows cast on the ground.

J. time it took camels to travel between the cities and the distance camels could cover in one day.

37. The passage indicates that astronomers could not calculate the distance from Earth to other points in the solar system until:

A. they had identified proper observation points.

B. they applied ancient Greek calculations.

C. the telescope was invented.

D. Earth and Mars aligned.

38. The passage suggests that compared to his other work, Newton's calculation of the distance to the nearest stars was:

F. more important.

G. more speculative.

H. less complete.

J. less acknowledged.

39. It can reasonably be inferred from the passage that the author includes the description of Newton's handwriting and writing tools (lines 70–74) primarily to:

A. highlight how advanced Newton's calculation was by contrasting it with Newton's old-fashioned writing method.

B. suggest one reason Newton's calculation took so long to decipher.

C. describe the artistic flourishes of the section of *Principia* in which Newton's calculation appears.

D. illustrate the number of mistakes Newton made before arriving at the correct calculation.

40. As it is used in line 82, the phrase *set out* most nearly means:

F. described a vision.

G. stated a purpose.

H. started a journey.

J. created an arrangement.

END OF TEST 3

STOP! DO NOT TURN THE PAGE UNTIL TOLD TO DO SO.

DO NOT RETURN TO A PREVIOUS TEST.

SCIENCE TEST

35 Minutes—40 Questions

DIRECTIONS: There are several passages in this test. Each passage is followed by several questions. After reading a passage, choose the best answer to each question and fill in the corresponding oval on your answer document. You may refer to the passages as often as necessary.

You are NOT permitted to use a calculator on this test.

Passage I

If a gum is added to water (such as the water in a food product), the *viscosity* (resistance to flow) of the resulting aqueous mixture changes. Table 1 shows, for each of 4 gums (Gums W, X, Y, and Z), the viscosity, in centipoise (cP), of a 1.0% by mass aqueous mixture of the gum at 3 temperatures and at 3 resting times. A *resting time* is a period of time an aqueous mixture of a gum sits at rest just after having been prepared.

Table 1				
Gum	Temperature (°C)	Viscosity (cP) of a 1.0% aqueous gum mixture at a resting time of:		
		30 min	75 min	120 min
W	25	4,826	8,300	11,288
	45	3,250	6,825	9,282
	65	2,549	3,849	5,158
X	25	2,562	4,058	5,534
	45	2,100	3,462	4,686
	65	1,640	2,509	3,387
Y	25	1,201	1,994	2,771
	45	781	1,639	2,279
	65	531	802	1,075
Z	25	1,064	1,879	2,668
	45	512	1,562	2,233
	65	384	626	864

Figure 1 shows, for a certain temperature and a certain resting time, how the viscosity of aqueous mixtures of each of the 4 gums varies with gum concentration in percent by mass.

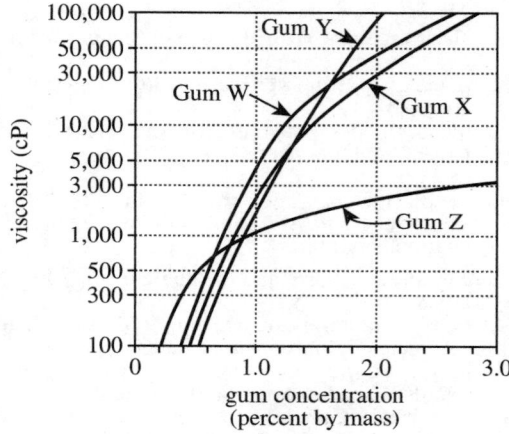

Figure 1

Table and figure adapted from G. O. Phillips and P. A. Williams, eds., *Handbook of Hydrocolloids*, 2nd ed. ©2009 by CRC Press and Woodhead Publishing, Ltd.

GO ON TO THE NEXT PAGE.

4 ○ ○ ○ ○ ○ ○ ○ ○ **4**

1. Based on Table 1, which of the following graphs best compares the viscosities of 1.0% aqueous mixtures of Gums W, X, Y, and Z at 45°C and a resting time of 75 min ?

A.
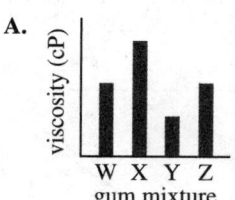

C.
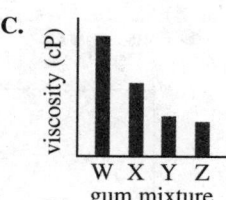

B.
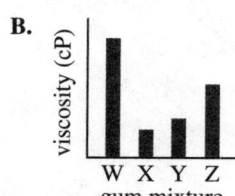

D.
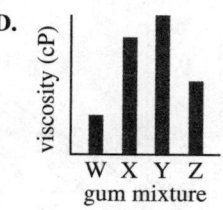

2. Based on Table 1, if a just-prepared 1.0% aqueous mixture of Gum Y is allowed to sit at rest for 100 min at 65°C, its viscosity will most likely be:

   F. less than 500 cP.
   G. between 500 cP and 800 cP.
   H. between 800 cP and 1,100 cP.
   J. greater than 1,100 cP.

3. Consider the viscosities shown in Figure 1 for a gum concentration of 2.0%. What is the order of the gums corresponding to those viscosities, from lowest viscosity to highest viscosity?

   A. Gum W, Gum Y, Gum X, Gum Z
   B. Gum W, Gum Z, Gum X, Gum Y
   C. Gum Z, Gum X, Gum W, Gum Y
   D. Gum Z, Gum Y, Gum W, Gum X

4. Under the conditions that are the basis for Figure 1, a 1.3% aqueous mixture of which gum has the highest viscosity?

   F. Gum W
   G. Gum X
   H. Gum Y
   J. Gum Z

5. Based on Table 1, a 1.0% aqueous mixture of Gum Z at 30°C and a resting time of 75 min would most likely have a viscosity closest to which of the following?

   A. 1,250 cP
   B. 1,750 cP
   C. 2,050 cP
   D. 2,350 cP

6. Under the conditions that are the basis for Figure 1, an aqueous mixture of which gum has a viscosity of 100,000 cP at a *lower* concentration than any of the other 3 gums?

   F. Gum W
   G. Gum X
   H. Gum Y
   J. Gum Z

GO ON TO THE NEXT PAGE.

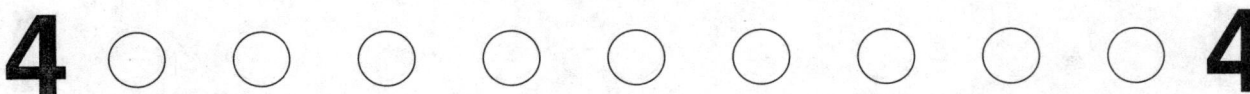

Passage II

Biodiesel (BD) is a renewable alternative to traditional petroleum diesel (PD). BD is typically prepared by reacting soybean oil with methanol in the presence of a catalyst, forming compounds called *fatty acid methyl esters* (FAMEs). In contrast, PD contains no FAMEs. The presence of FAMEs in BD causes BD to absorb infrared light differently than does PD. This difference allows pure BD, pure PD, and mixtures of BD and PD to be distinguished by analyzing the absorbance of infrared light.

Students performed 3 studies in which they determined the infrared absorbance characteristics of pure BD, pure PD, and mixtures of BD and PD.

Study 1

The students measured the absorbance, A, of a sample of pure BD and a sample of pure PD at *wavenumbers* from 600 cm^{-1} through $1{,}800 \text{ cm}^{-1}$. The wavenumber corresponding to a given wavelength is defined as $\frac{1}{\text{the wavelength}}$, where the wavelength is given in cm and the resulting wavenumber is given in cm^{-1}. They plotted the results for each sample (see Figure 1).

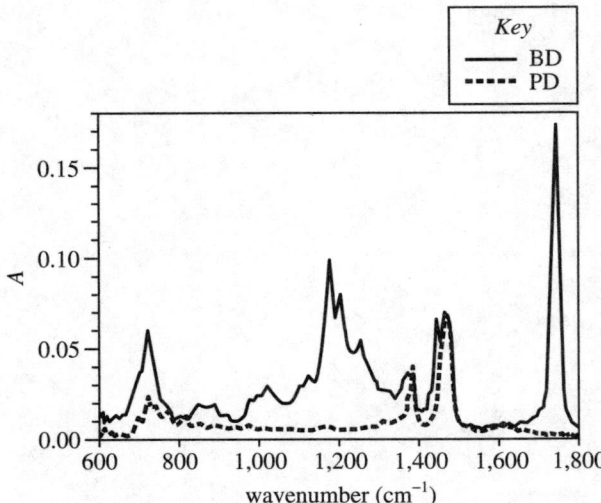

Figure 1

Study 2

The students prepared 7 different mixtures of BD and PD, each containing a different percent by volume of BD. Then, they measured A at $1{,}746 \text{ cm}^{-1}$ for a sample of each of the 7 mixtures, a sample of pure BD, and a sample of pure PD (see Figure 2).

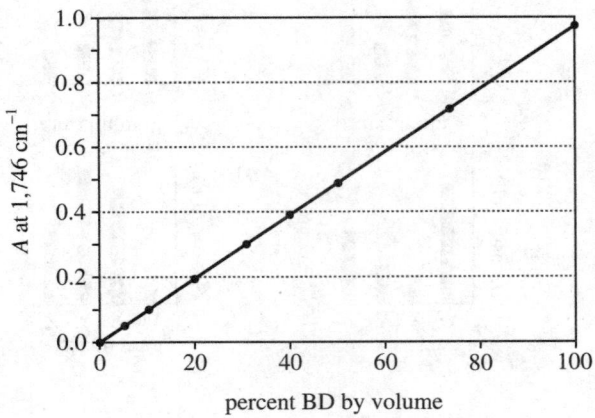

Figure 2

Figures 1 and 2 adapted from A. P. Ault and R. Pomery, "Quantitative Investigations of Biodiesel Fuel Using Infrared Spectroscopy: An Instrumental Analysis Experiment for Undergraduate Chemistry Students." ©2011 by Division of Chemical Education, Inc., American Chemical Society.

Study 3

The students obtained 4 different samples of commercial fuel blends of BD and PD (Samples W–Z). They measured A at $1{,}746 \text{ cm}^{-1}$ for each sample, and then used Figure 2 to calculate the percent BD by volume of each sample (see Table 1).

Table 1	
Sample	Percent BD by volume
W	4.0
X	6.0
Y	4.8
Z	4.7

Table 1 adapted from Z. V. Feng and J. T. Buchman, "Instrumental Analysis of Biodiesel Content in Commercial Diesel Blends: An Experiment for Undergraduate Analytical Chemistry." ©2012 by Division of Chemical Education, Inc., American Chemical Society.

GO ON TO THE NEXT PAGE.

7. If the students had tested a 60% BD by volume sample in Study 2, A at 1,746 cm^{-1} would most likely have been:

A. less than 0.45.
B. between 0.45 and 0.55.
C. between 0.55 and 0.65.
D. greater than 0.65.

8. In Study 2, among the samples tested, as the percent by volume of BD increased, A at 1,746 cm^{-1}:

F. increased only.
G. decreased only.
H. increased and then decreased.
J. decreased and then increased.

9. Based on the results of Study 2, which fuel sample in Study 3 most likely had the smallest A at 1,746 cm^{-1} ?

A. Sample W
B. Sample X
C. Sample Y
D. Sample Z

10. The production of BD as described in the passage is best represented by which of the following chemical equations?

F. FAMEs + catalyst → soybean oil + methanol
G. FAMEs + methanol → soybean oil + catalyst
H. Soybean oil + methanol $\xrightarrow{\text{catalyst}}$ FAMEs
J. Soybean oil + FAMEs $\xrightarrow{\text{catalyst}}$ methanol

11. Suppose that in Study 1 the students had measured the absorbance at wavenumbers from 600 cm^{-1} through only 1,600 cm^{-1} (instead of through 1,800 cm^{-1}). Based on Figure 1, would the students more likely have measured the absorbance in Study 2 at a wavenumber of 1,172 cm^{-1} or at a wavenumber of 1,464 cm^{-1} ?

A. A wavenumber of 1,172 cm^{-1}, because PD, but not BD, absorbs strongly at this wavenumber.
B. A wavenumber of 1,172 cm^{-1}, because BD, but not PD, absorbs strongly at this wavenumber.
C. A wavenumber of 1,464 cm^{-1}, because PD, but not BD, absorbs strongly at this wavenumber.
D. A wavenumber of 1,464 cm^{-1}, because BD, but not PD, absorbs strongly at this wavenumber.

12. Consider a sample that contains only FAMEs. Based on the results of Study 1, would the sample more strongly absorb light at a wavenumber of 900 cm^{-1} or light at a wavenumber of 1,250 cm^{-1} ?

F. A wavenumber of 900 cm^{-1}; PD contains FAMEs, and PD absorbed more strongly at 900 cm^{-1} than it did at 1,250 cm^{-1}.
G. A wavenumber of 900 cm^{-1}; BD contains FAMEs, and BD absorbed more strongly at 900 cm^{-1} than it did at 1,250 cm^{-1}.
H. A wavenumber of 1,250 cm^{-1}; PD contains FAMEs, and PD absorbed more strongly at 1,250 cm^{-1} than it did at 900 cm^{-1}.
J. A wavenumber of 1,250 cm^{-1}; BD contains FAMEs, and BD absorbed more strongly at 1,250 cm^{-1} than it did at 900 cm^{-1}.

13. Consider the percent BD by volume listed in Table 1 for Sample Y. A 10 liter (L) volume of Sample Y would contain approximately what volume of BD, in liters and in milliliters (mL) ?

	L	mL
A.	0.5	500
B.	0.5	5,000
C.	5	500
D.	5	5,000

GO ON TO THE NEXT PAGE.

4 ○ ○ ○ ○ ○ ○ ○ ○ ○ **4**

Passage III

Earth's gravitational field extends both above and below Earth's surface. In Figure 1, both the value of this field, g_E, and the average density, ρ, of matter within Earth are graphed versus distance, r, from Earth's center. In addition, Figure 1 identifies 5 regions, each of which is located either above or below Earth's surface.

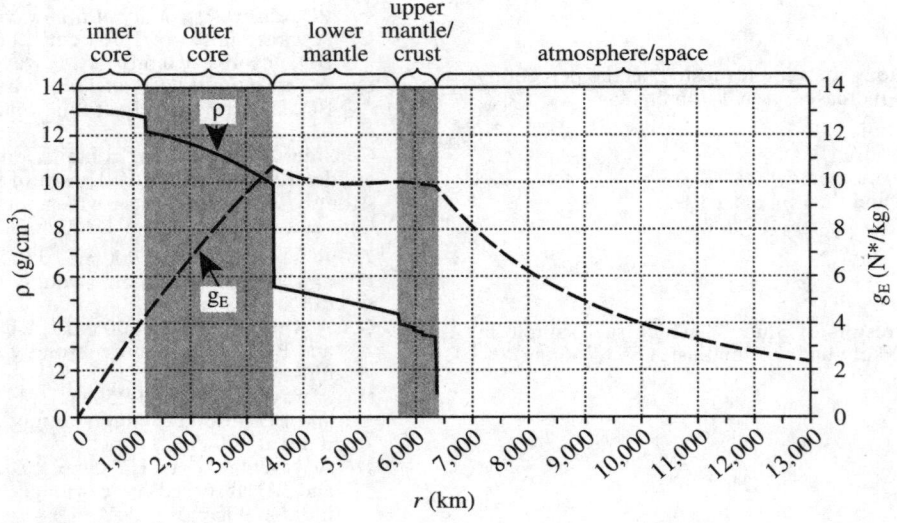

*newtons, a unit of force

Figure 1

Figure 2 shows the percent of Earth's mass located within a given distance r from Earth's center. For example, 10% of Earth's mass is located within 2,300 km of Earth's center, 20% of Earth's mass is located within 2,900 km of Earth's center, and so on.

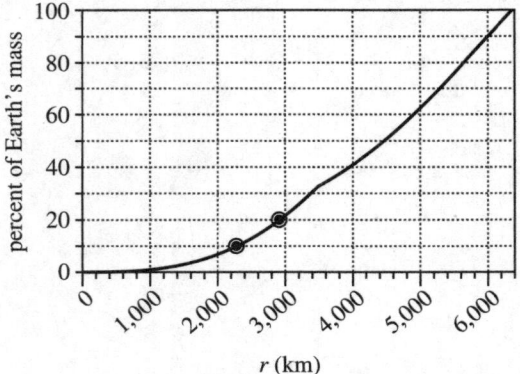

Figure 2

Figures adapted from A. M. Dziewonski and D. L. Anderson, "Preliminary Reference Earth Model." ©1981 by Elsevier B.V.

GO ON TO THE NEXT PAGE.

4 ◯ ◯ ◯ ◯ ◯ ◯ ◯ ◯ ◯ **4**

14. According to Figure 1, which 2 regions are most similar in thickness?

    F. The inner core and the outer core
    G. The inner core and the upper mantle/crust
    H. The outer core and the lower mantle
    J. The outer core and the upper mantle/crust

15. According to Figure 2, the innermost 30% of Earth's mass is located between $r = 0$ km and:

    A. $r = 3,400$ km.
    B. $r = 3,900$ km.
    C. $r = 4,500$ km.
    D. $r = 5,300$ km.

16. Figures 1 and 2 indicate that Earth's radius is approximately:

    F. 1,400 km.
    G. 3,500 km.
    H. 5,700 km.
    J. 6,400 km.

17. Based on Figure 1, the approximate value of Earth's gravitational field at $r = 14,000$ km is most likely:

    A. less than 0.5 N/kg.
    B. between 0.5 N/kg and 1.5 N/kg.
    C. between 1.5 N/kg and 2.5 N/kg.
    D. greater than 2.5 N/kg.

18. On average, Earth's crust is about 30 km thick. Based on Figure 2, the crust accounts for approximately what percent of Earth's mass?

    F. 1%
    G. 10%
    H. 90%
    J. 99%

19. Consider 2 hypothetical 1 kg rocks: one located at $r = 2,000$ km and the other located at $r = 4,000$ km. Based on Figure 1, which of these 2 rocks, if either, more likely weighs *less* ?

    A. The rock located at $r = 2,000$ km; the value of g_E is less at that location so the rock there has a smaller gravitational force exerted on it.
    B. The rock located at $r = 4,000$ km; the value of ρ is less at that location so the rock there has a smaller mass.
    C. Neither rock; the rocks have identical masses so they have the same weight.
    D. Neither rock; the value of g_E is the same for both rocks so they have the same weight.

GO ON TO THE NEXT PAGE.

4 ○ ○ ○ ○ ○ ○ ○ ○ ○ 4

Passage IV

Biological aging is the process by which the functions within an animal cell gradually decline, causing the cell to age. Four students each proposed an explanation for how this process occurs.

Student 1

Biological aging is caused solely by the *reactive oxygen species* (ROS) produced by cellular respiration. ROS are molecules that damage the proteins and lipids in a cell. A cell produces antioxidants, which eliminate ROS before they cause cell damage. However, the amount of antioxidants produced by a cell is always less than what is needed to eliminate all the ROS produced by that cell. Therefore, ROS damage accumulates in a cell, causing it to age.

Student 2

Biological aging is caused solely by the formation of *cross-links* (a type of chemical bond) between the proteins in a cell, causing these proteins to form clumps. These clumps accumulate in a cell, interfering with the cell's functions, causing it to age. Although ROS is damaging to proteins and lipids, this damage never occurs in a cell because the amount of antioxidants produced by a cell is always greater than what is needed to eliminate all the ROS produced by that cell.

Student 3

Biological aging is caused solely by the DNA damage that results from cell exposure to certain environmental agents. The extent of DNA damage caused by these agents eventually exceeds the cell's ability to repair this damage. Therefore, DNA damage accumulates in a cell, causing it to age. Although cells do produce ROS, ROS damage never accumulates in a cell. While cross-linked proteins do form clumps in a cell, these clumps never affect cell function.

Student 4

Biological aging is caused solely by the *lipofuscin* (a brown pigment made of oxidized lipids) produced by cellular respiration. Lipofuscin forms clumps that accumulate in a cell, interfering with the cell's functions, causing it to age. Although cells do produce ROS, ROS damage never accumulates in a cell. Because protein cross-links are short-lived, protein clumps never accumulate in a cell. The extent of DNA damage that occurs in a cell never exceeds the cell's ability to repair that damage.

20. Which of the students, if any, claimed that biological aging is caused by a substance produced by cellular respiration?

    F. Student 1 only
    G. Students 1 and 4 only
    H. Students 2 and 3 only
    J. None of the students

21. Suppose it were determined that the rate of biological aging in an animal cell is directly proportional to the number of chemical bonds formed between the proteins in that cell. This finding would be most consistent with the explanation given by:

    A. Student 1.
    B. Student 2.
    C. Student 3.
    D. Student 4.

22. Based on Student 2's explanation, the substances present in cells that are most directly involved with biological aging are composed of what type of subunits?

    F. Amino acids
    G. Fatty acids
    H. Monosaccharides
    J. Nucleotides

23. *Carnosine* is a substance that prevents protein cross-linking in animal cells. Which student would be most likely to predict that the average concentration of carnosine in the cells of young adults would be greater than the average concentration of carnosine in the cells of elderly adults?

    A. Student 1
    B. Student 2
    C. Student 3
    D. Student 4

24. Which of the students claimed that biological aging occurs because a substance accumulates into clumps that interfere with cellular function?

    F. Students 1 and 2 only
    G. Students 2 and 4 only
    H. Students 1, 3, and 4 only
    J. Students 1, 2, 3, and 4

GO ON TO THE NEXT PAGE.

4 ○ ○ ○ ○ ○ ○ ○ ○ **4**

25. Student 1's explanation would be most strongly supported if which of the following observations were made?

   A. Increasing the number of protein cross-links in animal cells increases the rate at which those cells age.

   B. Decreasing the number of protein cross-links in animal cells increases the rate at which those cells age.

   C. Increasing the antioxidant concentration in animal cells increases the rate at which those cells age.

   D. Decreasing the antioxidant concentration in animal cells increases the rate at which those cells age.

26. *Compound X* is a chemical that causes genetic mutations in human cells. Suppose it were determined that human neurons grown in the presence of Compound X age at the same rate as human neurons grown in the absence of Compound X. This finding would *weaken* the explanation(s) given by which of the students?

   F. Student 2 only

   G. Student 3 only

   H. Students 1 and 3 only

   J. Students 2 and 4 only

GO ON TO THE NEXT PAGE.

4   **4**

Passage V

In a lake, water *leaches* (dissolves out) soluble organic compounds from decaying tree leaves, producing *dissolved organic carbon* (DOC). DOC is subsequently removed from the water if it is *adsorbed* by (becomes adhered to the surface of) clay mineral particles that are suspended in the water. Three studies done at a lake examined DOC adsorption by 3 clay minerals—CM1, CM2, and CM3—found in the lake's sediment.

Green leaves were collected from 5 types of trees around the lake (maple, oak, pine, magnolia, and rhododendron). A 5 L volume of lake water was filtered to remove all solid particles. The following procedures were performed for each type of leaf: A 100 g sample of the leaves was mixed with a 1 L volume of the filtered lake water. The mixture was then placed in the dark for 10 weeks at 4°C while leaching occurred. At 10 weeks, the mixture was filtered to remove all solid particles. The resulting liquid (the *leachate*) was analyzed for DOC.

Study 1

The following procedures were performed for each leachate: A 100 mL volume of the leachate was mixed with 10 g of CM1. The mixture was stirred continuously for 2 hr, then filtered to remove all solid particles. The resulting liquid (the *filtrate*) was analyzed for DOC. The percent of the leachate DOC that had been adsorbed by CM1 was calculated (see Figure 1).

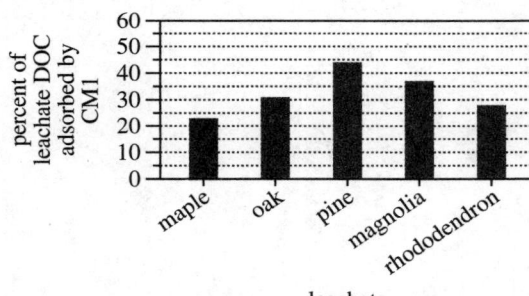

Figure 1

Study 2

Study 1 was repeated, substituting CM2 for CM1 (see Figure 2).

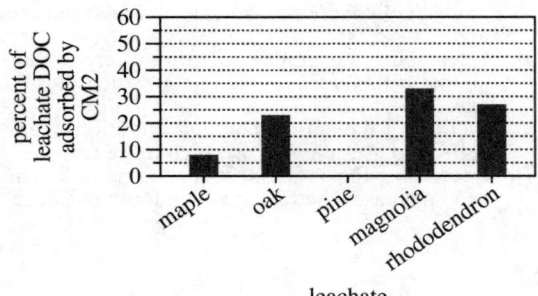

Figure 2

Study 3

Study 1 was repeated, substituting CM3 for CM1 (see Figure 3).

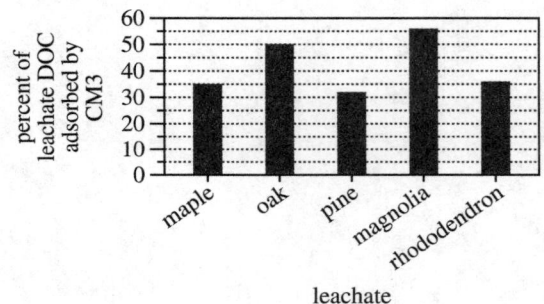

Figure 3

Figures and table adapted from Todd Tietjen, Anssi Vähätalo, and Robert Wetzel, "Effects of Clay Mineral Turbidity on Dissolved Organic Carbon and Bacterial Production." ©2005 by the Swiss Federal Institute for Environmental Science and Technology.

GO ON TO THE NEXT PAGE.

4 ○ ○ ○ ○ ○ ○ ○ ○ 4

27. According to the results of the studies, from which of the 5 leachates was the greatest percent of DOC adsorbed by CM1, CM2, and CM3, respectively?

	CM1	CM2	CM3
A.	maple	maple	rhododendron
B.	oak	pine	magnolia
C.	pine	magnolia	rhododendron
D.	pine	magnolia	magnolia

28. According to the results of Study 3, the percent of leachate DOC adsorbed by CM3, averaged across the 5 types of leaves, is closest to which of the following?

    F. 10%
    G. 20%
    H. 30%
    J. 40%

29. Is the statement "CM2 adsorbed a greater percent of the DOC in the maple leachate than did CM3" supported by the results of Studies 2 and 3 ?

    A. Yes; CM2 adsorbed 35% of the leachate DOC, whereas CM3 adsorbed 7%.
    B. Yes; CM2 adsorbed 55% of the leachate DOC, whereas CM3 adsorbed 17%.
    C. No; CM2 adsorbed 7% of the leachate DOC, whereas CM3 adsorbed 35%.
    D. No; CM2 adsorbed 17% of the leachate DOC, whereas CM3 adsorbed 55%.

30. What was the independent (manipulated) variable in each of the 3 studies and what was the independent variable across the 3 studies?

	in each study	across the studies
F.	type of lake water	type of clay mineral
G.	type of leaf leachate	type of clay mineral
H.	volume of leaf leachate	mass of clay mineral
J.	volume of filtrate	mass of leaves

31. According to the results of the studies, which of the 3 clay minerals, if any, reduced the DOC in the oak leachate by more than 50% ?

    A. CM1 only
    B. CM2 only
    C. CM1 and CM3 only
    D. None of the 3 clay minerals

32. Is a mixture of any one of the leachates and any one of the clay minerals properly considered a solution?

    F. Yes, because the clay mineral particles are dissolved in the leachate.
    G. Yes, because the clay mineral particles are not dissolved in the leachate.
    H. No, because the clay mineral particles are dissolved in the leachate.
    J. No, because the clay mineral particles are not dissolved in the leachate.

33. In lake water, DOC is broken down into simpler compounds by electromagnetic energy in the visible wavelength range. What action was taken in the studies to prevent this process from occurring?

    A. Each mixture of leaves and filtered lake water was placed in the dark.
    B. Each mixture of filtrate and clay mineral was placed in the dark.
    C. Each mixture of leaves and lake water was filtered.
    D. Each mixture of leachate and clay mineral was filtered.

Taking Additional Practice Tests

GO ON TO THE NEXT PAGE.

Passage VI

Plant roots can respond to a stimulus. Response to light is *phototropism*; response to gravity is *gravitropism*. Growth toward a stimulus is a *positive tropism*; growth away from a stimulus is a *negative tropism*.

For 2 experiments with *wild-type* (WT) and *mutant* (M) *Arabidopsis* seeds, nutrient agar was put into each of 8 petri dishes (PD1–PD8).

Experiment 1

Six WT *Arabidopsis* seeds were placed in each of PD1 and PD2. Six M *Arabidopsis* seeds were placed in each of PD3 and PD4. Then, PD1 and PD3 were placed in the dark for 70 hr, and PD2 and PD4 were exposed to light from above for 70 hr. Figure 1 shows the growth of the *hypocotyls* (seedling stems) above the surface of the nutrient agar and the growth of the *radicles* (seedling roots) below the surface of the nutrient agar in each dish at 70 hr.

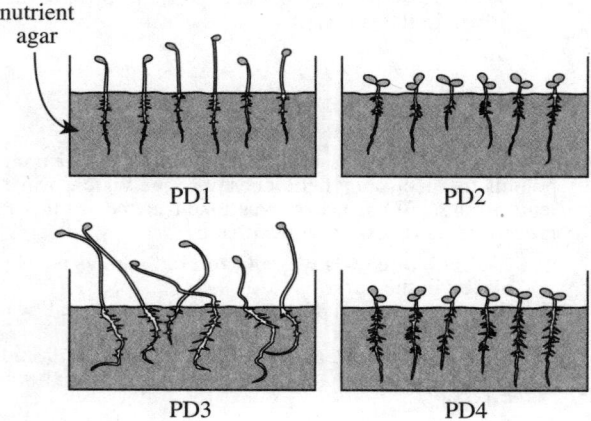

Figure 1

Experiment 2

Six WT *Arabidopsis* seeds were placed in each of PD5 and PD6. Six M *Arabidopsis* seeds were placed in each of PD7 and PD8. Then, PD5–PD8 were exposed to light from above for 70 hr. After 70 hr, each petri dish was turned 90° such that each dish was vertical and the seedlings in each dish were approximately horizontal (see Figure 2).

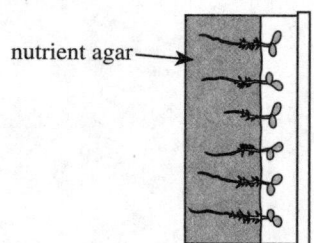

Figure 2

Then, PD5 and PD7 were exposed to light from above for 25 hr while PD6 and PD8 were exposed to light from below for 25 hr. At various times during the 25 hr, the downward curvature, in degrees (°), of the radicle (relative to its starting position) of each seedling in each dish was measured. The average downward curvature of the radicles in each dish at each measurement time is shown in Figure 3.

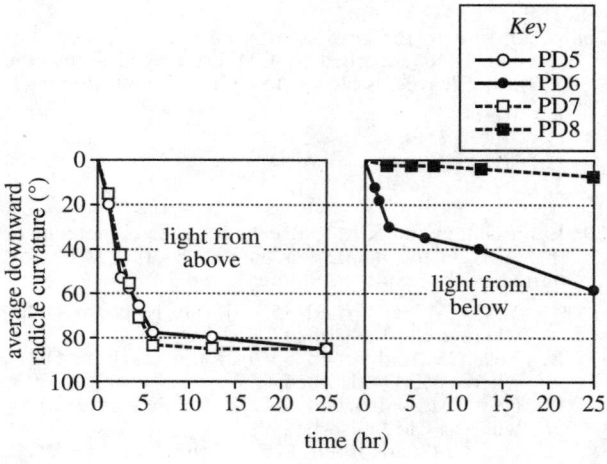

Figure 3

34. Which of the following figures best shows the orientation of PD5 before the petri dish was turned 90° ?

F.

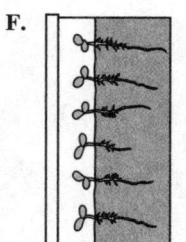

G.

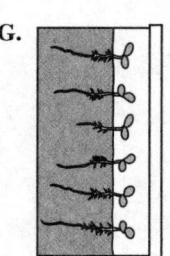

H.

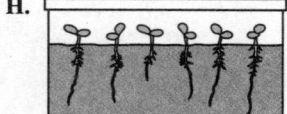

J.

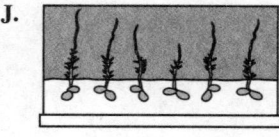

GO ON TO THE NEXT PAGE.

4 ◯ ◯ ◯ ◯ ◯ ◯ ◯ ◯ ◯ **4**

35. PD8 contained the same type of seeds, and was subject to the same growth conditions before being turned 90°, as which petri dish in Experiment 1 ?

A. PD1
B. PD2
C. PD3
D. PD4

36. Based on the results of Experiment 1, in the absence of light, did the radicles of the M *Arabidopsis* seedlings have the same response to gravity as did the radicles of the WT seedlings?

F. No; the variation in the orientation of the radicles in PD3 was greater than that of the radicles in PD1.
G. No; the variation in the orientation of the radicles in PD4 was greater than that of the radicles in PD2.
H. Yes; the variation in the orientation of the radicles in PD3 was the same as that of the radicles in PD1.
J. Yes; the variation in the orientation of the radicles in PD4 was the same as that of the radicles in PD2.

37. During the 25 hr in Experiment 2 that WT *Arabidopsis* seedlings were exposed to light from below, did the hypocotyls of the seedlings more likely exhibit positive phototropism or negative phototropism?

A. Positive, because seedling hypocotyls typically grow away from a light stimulus.
B. Positive, because seedling hypocotyls typically grow toward a light stimulus.
C. Negative, because seedling hypocotyls typically grow away from a light stimulus.
D. Negative, because seedling hypocotyls typically grow toward a light stimulus.

38. Based on the results shown in Figure 1 for PD2, is *Arabidopsis* a monocot or a dicot?

F. Monocot; seedlings have 1 cotyledon.
G. Monocot; seedlings have 2 cotyledons.
H. Dicot; seedlings have 1 cotyledon.
J. Dicot; seedlings have 2 cotyledons.

39. In Experiment 2, each petri dish had how many different orientations?

A. 1
B. 2
C. 3
D. 4

40. To evaluate the effect of light on the growth of WT *Arabidopsis* seedlings, the results for which 2 petri dishes in Experiment 1 should be compared?

F. PD1 and PD2
G. PD1 and PD3
H. PD2 and PD3
J. PD2 and PD4

END OF TEST 4

STOP! DO NOT RETURN TO ANY OTHER TEST.

Taking Additional Practice Tests

You may wish to photocopy these sample answer document pages to respond to the practice ACT Writing Test.

Please enter the information at the right before beginning the writing test.

Use a No. 2 pencil only. Do NOT use a mechanical pencil, ink, ballpoint, or felt-tip pen.

WRITING TEST BOOKLET NUMBER

Print your 9-digit **Booklet Number** in the boxes at the right.

WRITING TEST FORM

Print your 5-character **Test Form** in the boxes at the right and fill in the corresponding ovals.

Begin WRITING TEST here.

If you need more space, please continue on the following page.

1

WRITING TEST

_____

_____

_____

_____

_____

_____

_____

_____

_____

_____

_____

_____

_____

_____

_____

_____

_____

_____

_____

_____

_____

_____

_____

_____

_____

_____

_____

_____

_____

_____

_____

If you need more space, please continue on the following page.

2

WRITING TEST

_____

_____

_____

_____

_____

_____

_____

_____

_____

_____

_____

_____

_____

_____

_____

_____

_____

_____

_____

_____

_____

_____

_____

_____

_____

_____

_____

_____

_____

If you need more space, please continue on the following page.

3

WRITING TEST

STOP here with the writing test.

4

Practice Writing Test Prompt 3

Your Signature: _____
(Do not print.)

Print Your Name Here: _____

Your Date of Birth:

☐☐ – ☐☐ – ☐☐☐☐
Month   Day   Year

Form 19WT5

The ACT® WRITING TEST BOOKLET

You must take the multiple-choice tests before you take the writing test.

Directions

This is a test of your writing skills. You will have **forty** (40) minutes to read the prompt, plan your response, and write an essay in English. Before you begin working, read all material in this test booklet carefully to understand exactly what you are being asked to do.

You will write your essay on the lined pages in the **answer document** provided. Your writing on those pages will be scored. You may use the unlined pages in this test booklet to plan your essay. Your work on these pages will not be scored.

Your essay will be evaluated based on the evidence it provides of your ability to:

- clearly state your own perspective on a complex issue and analyze the relationship between your perspective and at least one other perspective
- develop and support your ideas with reasoning and examples
- organize your ideas clearly and logically
- communicate your ideas effectively in standard written English

Lay your pencil down immediately when time is called.

DO NOT OPEN THIS BOOKLET UNTIL TOLD TO DO SO.

 PO Box 168
Iowa City, IA 52243-0168

The ONLY Official Prep Guide from the Makers of the ACT

Winning

"It's not whether you win or lose, it's how you play the game." This popular expression, often repeated by coaches, parents, and competitors alike, encourages us to ignore victories and defeats and to focus instead on our effort. Yet we all know how good winning can feel. Not only does it offer a sense of pride and accomplishment, but we are often rewarded and praised for our victories in athletics, academics, the arts, and so on. Even when we've worked hard and performed well, there can be a sense of emptiness if our best efforts do not lead to a win. To what extent, then, is it true that effort in competition is more important than the final result? Given these contradictory views, it is worth considering the importance of winning.

Read and carefully consider these perspectives. Each suggests a particular way of thinking about the importance of winning.

Perspective One	Perspective Two	Perspective Three
People are programmed to compete. We can tell ourselves that effort is more important than the end result, but in truth, we are naturally inclined to strive for victory.	In any competition, victory depends on a number of factors outside our control—talent and luck, for example. Our effort is the only thing we *can* control and thus is more important than the final result.	An emphasis on winning teaches us to see others as enemies to defeat. As a result, our world becomes a more hostile, less cooperative place.

Essay Task

Write a unified, coherent essay about the importance of winning. In your essay, be sure to:

- clearly state your own perspective on the issue and analyze the relationship between your perspective and at least one other perspective
- develop and support your ideas with reasoning and examples
- organize your ideas clearly and logically
- communicate your ideas effectively in standard written English

Your perspective may be in full agreement with any of those given, in partial agreement, or completely different.

Planning Your Essay

Your work on these prewriting pages will not be scored.

Use the space below and on the back cover to generate ideas and plan your essay. You may wish to consider the following as you think critically about the task:

Strengths and weaknesses of different perspectives on the issue
- What insights do they offer, and what do they fail to consider?
- Why might they be persuasive to others, or why might they fail to persuade?

Your own knowledge, experience, and values
- What is your perspective on this issue, and what are its strengths and weaknesses?
- How will you support your perspective in your essay?

If you need more space to plan, please continue on the following page.

Planning Your Essay

Use this page to continue planning your essay. Your work on this page will not be scored.

Passage I

Question 1. The best answer is **B** because it correctly identifies the rhetorical impact of losing the phrase "and my idol." An idol is greatly admired, so it is logical to conclude that if the narrator idolized her sister—"a guitar buff"—she would want to learn to play the guitar, too.

The best answer is NOT:

A because it fails to correctly identify the rhetorical impact of the phrase "and my idol." This phrase indicates nothing about the narrator's age when she learned to play the guitar.

C because it fails to correctly identify the rhetorical impact of the phrase "and my idol." This phrase suggests nothing about the age difference between the narrator and her sister.

D because it fails to correctly identify the rhetorical impact of the phrase "and my idol." This phrase suggests nothing about degree of musical talent.

Question 2. The best answer is **F** because it provides the appropriate punctuation (a colon) to precede a list (the places the narrator took her guitar).

The best answer is NOT:

G because it introduces unnecessary punctuation that makes the narrator's point less clear and creates an ungrammatical sentence. Placing the period after the word *around* creates a vague statement that loses the emphatic point that the narrator carried the guitar around everywhere (not just around). In addition, the unnecessary punctuation creates an ungrammatical sentence (a fragment in this case) beginning with the word *Everywhere*.

H because it uses grammatically incorrect punctuation (a semicolon) to introduce a list.

J because it fails to provide any punctuation to precede the list. The statement ending with the word *everywhere* is a complete sentence that requires punctuation to precede the list.

Question 3. The best answer is **C** because it correctly distinguishes between possessives and plurals by using an apostrophe to form the plural possessive *friends'* and no apostrophe in the plural noun *houses*.

The best answer is NOT:

A because it incorrectly provides the plural noun *friends* where the plural possessive *friends'* is needed.

B because it incorrectly provides the singular possessive *friend's* where a plural is needed and incorrectly provides the singular possessive *house's* where the plural noun *houses* is needed.

D because it incorrectly provides the singular possessive *friend's*.

Question 4. The best answer is **F** because it provides the appropriate punctuation and capitalization for the two complete sentences and supplies the necessary comma after the introductory clause "No matter where I was" to avoid ambiguity in terms of whether the writer is saying "No matter where I was" or "No matter where I was playing."

The best answer is NOT:

G because it lacks a comma after the word *and*, creating a run-on sentence.

H because it lacks a comma after the word *was*, creating ambiguity in terms of whether the writer is saying "No matter where I was" or "No matter where I was playing."

J because it incorrectly uses commas to join two complete statements without any connector words.

Question 5. The best answer is **A** because it provides the most precise expression of the idea described in the stem. The word *assailed* best illustrates "the fervor with which the narrator communicated with the airport personnel" because it figuratively conveys the narrator's energy in the interaction.

The best answer is NOT:

B because it provides a word choice that fails to precisely describe the idea identified in the stem; the neutral word *approached* does not adequately illustrate fervor.

C because it provides a word choice that fails to precisely describe the idea identified in the stem; the neutral word *questioned* does not adequately illustrate fervor.

D because it provides a word choice that fails to precisely describe the idea identified in the stem; the neutral word *contacted* does not adequately illustrate fervor.

Question 6. The best answer is **J** because it provides the appropriate pronouns for this sentence. The subjective pronoun case *who* is needed here because the word *who* serves as the subject of the dependent clause, and the pronoun *me* is the object.

The best answer is NOT:

F because it inappropriately uses a reflexive pronoun. The object is not the same person as the subject, so the reflexive pronoun *myself* is grammatically incorrect.

G because it incorrectly provides the objective pronoun case *whom* where the subjective pronoun case is needed. In addition, the object is not the same person as the subject, so the reflexive pronoun *myself* is grammatically incorrect.

H because it incorrectly provides the objective pronoun case *whom* where the subjective pronoun case is needed.

Question 7. **The best answer is D** because it eliminates redundancy and unnecessary wordiness.

The best answer is NOT:

A because it fails to eliminate redundancy at the paragraph level; the idea that this is an extended trip is mentioned earlier in the paragraph.

B because it fails to eliminate wordiness and redundancy at the paragraph level; the phrase "due to the fact that I was on an extended trip" contains a redundant reference to the extended trip and lacks concision.

C because it fails to eliminate redundancy at the paragraph level; the idea that the narrator is in Hawaii is mentioned earlier in the paragraph.

Question 8. **The best answer is H** because it provides the most logical transition based on the surrounding context. The word *though* logically conveys the shift from the narrator feeling upset in the preceding paragraph to the narrator's worries dissipating.

The best answer is NOT:

F because it provides an illogical transition word; the word *otherwise* provides no logical meaning in this context.

G because it provides an illogical transition word; the word *therefore* suggests a cause-effect relationship between ideas that does not exist here.

J because it provides an illogical transition word; the word *instead* means "alternatively," which makes no sense in this context.

Question 9. **The best answer is D** because it provides the idiomatically correct preposition in context. The phrase "into the . . . air" is consistent with standard English usage.

The best answer is NOT:

A because it provides the preposition *upon*, which creates an idiomatically nonstandard expression.

B because it provides the preposition *amid*, which creates an idiomatically nonstandard expression.

C because it provides the preposition *onto*, which creates an idiomatically nonstandard expression.

Question 10. The best answer is **J** because it is the most precise word for the context. The word *issued* correctly and logically conveys the idea that the tones came from an instrument.

The best answer is NOT:

F because it supplies an imprecise word choice for the context; the word *accrued* conveys the idea of accumulating, which does not make sense for describing musical tones.

G because it supplies an imprecise word choice for the context; the word *distributed* conveys the idea of something being passed out or delivered, which does not make sense for describing musical tones.

H because it supplies an imprecise word choice for the context; the word *appeared* conveys the idea of something becoming visible, which does not make sense for describing musical tones.

Question 11. The best answer is **A** because it is a complete statement, preventing the introduction of a rhetorically ineffective fragment.

The best answer is NOT:

B because it creates a sentence fragment.

C because it creates a sentence fragment.

D because it creates a sentence fragment.

Question 12. The best answer is **G** because it uses the appropriate conjunction for indicating a comparison (the word *than*), and the phrase "that of a guitar" clearly indicates that the comparison is between the guitar and the ukulele.

The best answer is NOT:

F because it uses the adverb *then* instead of the conjunction *than*.

H because it contains the pronoun *it*, which has no clear antecedent here, making the sentence unclear in terms of what is being compared.

J because it incorrectly supplies the adverb *then* where the conjunction *than* is needed. In addition, it contains the pronoun *it*, which has no clear antecedent here, making the sentence unclear in terms of what is being compared.

Question 13. The best answer is **B** because it provides the most specific description of the music the narrator played, as defined in the stem.

The best answer is NOT:

A because it uses the general word *music*, which lacks the specificity of the term "Hawaiian classics."

C because it uses the general term "tropical tunes," which lacks the specificity of the term "Hawaiian classics."

D because it uses the general word *things*, which is too vague to have any specific meaning.

Question 14. The best answer is **H** because it provides the idiomatically correct preposition in context. The phrase "playing . . . with the locals" is clear and consistent with standard English usage.

The best answer is NOT:

F because it creates the phrase "playing . . . as the locals," which is unclear in meaning and is inconsistent with standard English usage.

G because it creates the phrase "playing . . . through the locals," which creates an illogical meaning and is inconsistent with standard English usage.

J because it creates the phrase "playing . . . along the locals," which is unclear in meaning and is inconsistent with standard English usage.

Question 15. The best answer is **C** because it best expresses the idea specified in the stem by referring to the narrator's closeness to her sister and love of playing the guitar. These are key points in the first two paragraphs.

The best answer is NOT:

A because it fails to fulfill the goal specified in the stem; neither the ukulele nor Hawaii is mentioned in the first two paragraphs.

B because it fails to fulfill the goal specified in the stem; the narrator's time in Hawaii is not discussed in the first two paragraphs.

D because it fails to fulfill the goal specified in the stem; the narrator's business trip is not the central focus of the first two paragraphs.

Passage II

Question 16. **The best answer is J** because it eliminates redundancy and unnecessary wordiness.

The best answer is NOT:

F because it fails to eliminate redundancy at the sentence level; the sentence already mentions that she had ideas.

G because it fails to eliminate redundancy at the sentence level; the sentence already mentions that she had ideas.

H because it fails to eliminate redundancy at the sentence level; the sentence already mentions that she had ideas, so we know the ideas were her own.

Question 17. **The best answer is B** because it provides the most accurate description of how the paragraph break would create two separate but cohesive paragraphs. The information that precedes this point focuses on why and how Lamarr came up with the idea for "a sophisticated radio-controlled guidance system." But the information that follows this point has a different focus; it explains how Lamarr's invention would work.

The best answer is NOT:

A because it provides an inaccurate description of the two paragraphs that would be created; it suggests that two inventions are discussed here when only one is mentioned.

C because it provides an inaccurate description of the essay's focus here; the section preceding this point in the essay does not provide an overview of Lamarr's film career.

D because it provides an inaccurate description of the two paragraphs that would be created; except for mentioning where she grew up, the section preceding this point in the essay does not include details about Lamarr's childhood, and the section that follows focuses on Lamarr's work in particular rather than on general information about radio signals.

Question 18. **The best answer is H** because it ensures correct subject-verb agreement. The plural verb form *are jammed* agrees with the plural subject *radio signals*.

The best answer is NOT:

F because it lacks subject-verb agreement; the singular verb form *is* does not agree with the plural subject *radio signals*.

G because it lacks subject-verb agreement; the singular verb form *has been* does not agree with the plural subject *radio signals*.

J because it lacks subject-verb agreement; the singular verb form *is jammed* does not agree with the plural subject *radio signals*.

Question 19. The best answer is **A** because it correctly separates two distinct statements into two sentences with correct punctuation.

The best answer is NOT:

B because it incorrectly places a period after the word *envisioned*, creating a sentence fragment beginning with the word *A*.

C because it incorrectly uses a comma to join two independent clauses.

D because it incorrectly places a semicolon after the word *envisioned*. A semicolon must be followed by an independent clause rather than a fragment.

Question 20. The best answer is **J** because it eliminates redundancy and unnecessary wordiness.

The best answer is NOT:

F because it fails to eliminate redundancy at the sentence level; the phrase "like that" is redundant because the word *such* is used earlier in the sentence.

G because it fails to eliminate redundancy at the sentence level; the phrase "similar to that" is redundant because the word *such* is used earlier in the sentence.

H because it fails to eliminate redundancy at the sentence level; the word *difficult* is redundant because the word *hard* is used later in the sentence.

Question 21. The best answer is **B** because it provides the most precise wording for the context; the word *implement* suggests putting something into action, which precisely describes what Lamarr was trying to do.

The best answer is NOT:

A because it is illogical in this context; the word *instigate* suggests provoking or inciting, which is not something one does to an idea.

C because it is illogical in this context; the word *discharge* suggests the idea of unloading something, which makes no sense in this context.

D because it is illogical in this context; the word *uphold* suggests supporting or defending something. Lamarr wanted to put her idea into practice; she did not need to defend it.

Question 22. The best answer is **F** because it provides appropriate and consistent punctuation (commas) to set off the nonessential element (the word *however*).

The best answer is NOT:

G because it fails to provide appropriate and consistent punctuation to set off the nonessential element by substituting a semicolon for the comma after the word *war*.

H because it fails to provide appropriate and consistent punctuation to set off the nonessential element by omitting the comma after the word *however*.

J because it lacks any punctuation to set off the nonessential element.

Question 23. The best answer is **C** because it is the most effective placement of the statement in terms of logic and cohesion. Placing Sentence 3 after Sentence 4 ensures that the paragraph discusses the events in chronological order.

The best answer is NOT:

A because it creates a sequence of events that is not chronological; the event in Sentence 3 occurs after the event in Sentence 4.

B because it creates a sequence of events that is not chronological; the event in Sentence 3 occurs after the event in Sentence 1.

D because it creates a sequence of events that is not chronological; the event in Sentence 3 occurs before the event in Sentence 5.

Question 24. The best answer is **G** because it best expresses the idea specified in the stem by strongly and specifically emphasizing that the declassification of spread spectrum was a turning point in the history of communication. The word *transformed* indicates a dramatic change in communications, and the phrase "communications landscape" indicates that the change affected many facets of communication.

The best answer is NOT:

F because it is a less effective choice based on the goal specified in the stem; the phrase "made a difference" is too general to suggest a turning point.

H because it is a less effective choice based on the goal specified in the stem; even though the phrase "had an impact on communications" suggests that the declassification of spread spectrum had a strong effect on communications, the phrase fails to clearly indicate a turning point in the history of communication technology.

J because it is a less effective choice based on the goal specified in the stem; the phrase "revolutionized things" is imprecise and unclear.

Question 25. **The best answer is B** because it provides the appropriate punctuation (an em dash) to set off the nonessential element (the phrase "cellular phones, wireless Internet networks, the Global Positioning System"). The em dash that precedes the nonessential element is consistent with the em dash that follows the nonessential element.

The best answer is NOT:

A because it fails to use appropriate and consistent punctuation to set off the nonessential element; a comma rather than an em dash precedes the nonessential element.

C because it fails to use appropriate and consistent punctuation to set off the nonessential element; a colon rather than an em dash precedes the nonessential element.

D because it fails to use appropriate and consistent punctuation to set off the nonessential element; a comma rather than an em dash precedes the nonessential element. In addition, it fails to include the comma after the word *phones* to appropriately separate items in a list.

Question 26. **The best answer is H** because it corrects the introduction of a rhetorically ineffective fragment by providing the appropriate verb form *function* to make this a complete sentence.

The best answer is NOT:

F because it creates a sentence fragment; it lacks a predicate.

G because it creates a sentence fragment; it lacks a predicate.

J because it creates a sentence fragment; it lacks a predicate.

Question 27. **The best answer is A** because it creates an expression consistent with standard English usage. The idiom "It wasn't until" is used to emphasize that a relatively lengthy period passed before Lamarr and Antheil were given credit for spread spectrum.

The best answer is NOT:

B because it is an idiomatically nonstandard and vague expression; the word *Such* has no clear antecedent.

C because it introduces a vague pronoun; the pronoun *This* has no clear antecedent.

D because it introduces a vague pronoun; the pronoun *That* has no clear antecedent.

Question 28. The best answer is **J** because it corrects the introduction of an error in coordination and subordination.

The best answer is NOT:

F because it contains an error in coordination created by adding a comma and the word *they* after the name *Antheil*, making the relationship between what comes before and after the comma unclear.

G because it contains an error in coordination created by adding an em dash and the word *both* after the name *Antheil*; the em dash serves no clear purpose here and therefore makes the relationship between what comes before and after the em dash unclear.

H because it contains an error in coordination. The compound subject *Lamarr and Antheil* is incorrectly followed by the infinitive verb form *to receive*, failing to provide a predicate for the sentence.

Question 29. The best answer is **D** because it eliminates the illogical and confusing transition word. The link between this sentence and the preceding one is obvious; no other transition is needed.

The best answer is NOT:

A because it provides an illogical transition word for the context; the word *However* suggests two opposing ideas, which is not the case here.

B because it provides an illogical transition word for the context; the word *Conversely* suggests two opposing ideas, which is not the case here.

C because it provides an unnecessary transition word for the context; there is no clear rhetorical purpose for the word *Anyway* in this context.

Question 30. The best answer is **F** because it offers a clear and convincing reason the essay accomplishes the purpose identified in the stem. This essay gives an overview of the history of Lamarr's invention. The essay begins with Lamarr's idea and then goes on to explain how the invention was developed and why it was important.

The best answer is NOT:

G because it identifies an incorrect reason the essay has accomplished the specified purpose; Lamarr and Antheil could not have changed the course of World War II with spread spectrum because, according to the essay, spread spectrum was not fully developed until after World War II.

H because it indicates that the essay hasn't accomplished the specified primary purpose when it has; the second half of the essay explains the importance of spread spectrum.

J because it indicates that the essay hasn't accomplished the specified primary purpose when it has and identifies a reason that does not accurately describe the essay; the essay gives very little attention to the film industry.

ENGLISH • PRACTICE TEST 3 • EXPLANATORY ANSWERS

Passage III

Question 31. The best answer is **B** because it properly distinguishes among pronouns, contractions, and possessives by providing the phrase "There are" to correctly set up the independent clause and agree with plural noun *turbines*.

The best answer is NOT:

A because it incorrectly provides the contraction *They're*, which means "They are." This phrase creates an ungrammatical sentence.

C because it incorrectly substitutes the possessive *Their*, creating an ungrammatical sentence.

D because it incorrectly substitutes the contraction *There's*, which means "There is." This phrase creates an ungrammatical sentence and fails to agree with the plural noun *turbines*.

Question 32. The best answer is **H** because it ensures correct subject-verb agreement. The subject of this part of the sentence is the singular word *task*. The singular verb form *represents* agrees with the singular subject *task*.

The best answer is NOT:

F because it lacks subject-verb agreement; the plural verb form *have represented* does not agree with the singular subject *task*.

G because it lacks subject-verb agreement; the plural verb form *are representing* does not agree with the singular subject *task*.

J because it lacks subject-verb agreement; the plural verb form *represent* does not agree with the singular subject *task*.

Question 33. The best answer is **A** because it correctly signals a contrast between this sentence and the preceding sentence. The idea that servicing the turbine blades "that slice through the air is a serious challenge" contrasts with the preceding idea that "ladders inside the tower simplify access to the generators and controllers."

The best answer is NOT:

B because it signals a similarity rather than a contrast between the ideas in these two sentences.

C because it signals a time marker that is illogical; there is nothing in the essay to suggest servicing the turbine blades happens instantly.

D because it incorrectly signals a transition to an order of steps.

Taking Additional Practice Tests

Question 34. The best answer is **G** because it provides appropriate and consistent punctuation (em dashes) before and after the nonessential element ("those long fiberglass vanes that slice through the air").

The best answer is NOT:

F because it lacks appropriate punctuation after the word *blades* to correctly set off the nonessential element.

H because it uses inconsistent punctuation (an em dash after the word *blades* and a comma after the word *air*) to set off the nonessential element.

J because it lacks appropriate punctuation after the word *air* to correctly set off the nonessential element.

Question 35. The best answer is **A** because it prevents the introduction of redundant or unnecessary wording.

The best answer is NOT:

B because it introduces redundancy at the sentence level; the phrase "something they're able to do" is redundant because the sentence already says "Rock climbers are . . . capable."

C because it contains an internal redundancy; ascending and climbing indicate the same action.

D because it introduces redundancy at the sentence level; the phrase "using rope" is redundant because the use of rope has already been mentioned in the sentence.

Question 36. The best answer is **F** because it prevents the introduction of a squinting modifier. It correctly places the subject ("rock climbers") after the comma so that the introductory clause "After completing specialized training" correctly modifies "rock climbers."

The best answer is NOT:

G because it creates a squinting modifier; it incorrectly makes "old skills and new knowledge" the subject, which suggests that "old skills and new knowledge" have completed specialized training.

H because it creates a squinting modifier; it incorrectly makes "new careers" the subject, which suggests that "new careers" have completed specialized training.

J because it shifts to the passive voice, making it unclear who has completed specialized training.

Question 37. The best answer is **D** because it correctly provides the appropriate preposition for the standard English phrase "arrive at."

The best answer is NOT:

A because it incorrectly provides the preposition *across*, which creates a nonstandard and illogical phrase; technicians could not arrive by being across the turbine.

B because it incorrectly substitutes the preposition *with*, which creates a nonstandard and illogical phrase; the word *with* suggests that the technicians already had the turbine with them when they arrived.

C because it incorrectly substitutes the preposition *via*, which creates a nonstandard and illogical phrase; the word *via* suggests that the technicians reached a new location by using a turbine.

Question 38. The best answer is **J** because it provides the most effective introduction to the paragraph. "Whatever the job, safety is the first priority" correctly introduces the main topic of the paragraph: safety.

The best answer is NOT:

F because it provides a detail (the length of the blades) that is not clearly connected to the main topic of the paragraph: safety.

G because it provides a detail (the rise in the number of turbine-related jobs) that is not clearly connected to the main topic of the paragraph: safety.

H because it provides a detail (the number of parts) that is not clearly connected to the main topic of the paragraph: safety.

Question 39. The best answer is **B** because it correctly punctuates two independent clauses with a comma and the word *and*.

The best answer is NOT:

A because it incorrectly uses a semicolon to separate an independent clause and a dependent clause.

C because it incorrectly uses a comma to join two independent clauses, which creates a run-on sentence.

D because it fails to provide any punctuation between two independent clauses.

Question 40. The best answer is **J** because it uses the most logical subordinate conjunction for the context. The word *If* correctly introduces a conditional clause that explains when technicians stay on the ground.

The best answer is NOT:

F because it provides an imprecise word choice; the word *Whether* incorrectly indicates that the sentence will present two options, which it does not do.

G because it provides an imprecise word choice; the phrase "So that" illogically suggests the intention of creating lightning.

H because it provides an imprecise word choice; the word *Unless* illogically suggests that the technicians do not stay on the ground when there's lightning, which contradicts the idea that the technicians take safety precautions.

Question 41. The best answer is **C** because it ensures appropriate and consistent punctuation (commas) before and after the nonessential element ("along with rigorous procedures and training").

The best answer is NOT:

A because it uses punctuation (an em dash) that is inconsistent with the punctuation used later in the sentence (a comma after the word *training*) to set off the nonessential element.

B because it substitutes punctuation (a semicolon) that is inconsistent with the punctuation used later in the sentence (a comma after the word *training*) to set off the nonessential element.

D because it lacks appropriate punctuation after the word *these* to correctly set off the nonessential element.

Question 42. The best answer is **F** because it ensures correct subject-verb agreement. The subject of the sentence is the plural word *Precautions*. The plural verb form *make* agrees with the plural subject *Precautions*.

The best answer is NOT:

G because it lacks subject-verb agreement; the singular verb form *is making* does not agree with the plural subject *Precautions*.

H because it lacks subject-verb agreement; the singular verb form *has made* does not agree with the plural subject *Precautions*.

J because it lacks subject-verb agreement; the singular verb form *makes* does not agree with the plural subject *Precautions*.

Question 43. The best answer is **D** because it corrects the introduction of an error in parallelism regarding the noun phrases. The noun phrase "plenty of climbing practice" correctly parallels the structure of the other noun phrases in the sentence ("fresh air," "great vistas," and "ample time off").

The best answer is NOT:

A because it disrupts the parallel structure by interrupting the series of noun phrases with the infinitive phrase "to practice climbing daily."

B because it disrupts the parallel structure by interrupting the series of noun phrases with the independent clause "they practice climbing regularly."

C because it disrupts the parallel structure by interrupting the series of noun phrases with the conditional phrase "while often practicing climbing."

Question 44. The best answer is **H** because it best expresses the idea specified in the stem that "rock climbers in particular may find being a rope technician an appealing occupation." The question "what more could a climber want?" suggests that the elements identified earlier in the sentence would appeal to rock climbers; rock climbers could want nothing more.

The best answer is NOT:

F because it is an ineffective choice based on the goal specified in the stem; it poses a question about the job of a rope technician in general rather than expressing the idea specified in the stem.

G because it is an ineffective choice based on the goal specified in the stem; it poses a question about rock climbers in general rather than expressing the idea specified in the stem.

J because it is an ineffective choice based on the goal specified in the stem; it poses a question directly to the reader (who may or may not be a rock climber) rather than expressing the idea specified in the stem.

Question 45. The best answer is **A** because the statement "Enter rock climbers" introduces rock climbers, the main subject of the essay. Point A correctly places this sentence where it would introduce rock climbers prior to any other reference to rock climbers in the essay.

The best answer is NOT:

B because it would interrupt the paragraph by reintroducing rock climbers. At this point in the essay, it is already clear that rope technicians are often rock climbers.

C because it would interrupt the paragraph by reintroducing rock climbers. At this point in the essay, it is already clear that rope technicians are often rock climbers.

D because it would interrupt the paragraph by reintroducing rock climbers. At this point in the essay, it is already clear that rope technicians are often rock climbers.

Passage IV

Question 46. **The best answer is J** because it ensures correct subject-verb agreement. The singular verb form *blends* agrees with the singular subject *Scene at the Signing of the Constitution of the United States* (the title of the painting).

The best answer is NOT:

F because it lacks subject-verb agreement; the plural verb form *blend* does not agree with the singular subject.

G because it lacks subject-verb agreement; the plural verb form *have blended* does not agree with the singular subject.

H because it lacks subject-verb agreement; the plural verb form *are blending* does not agree with the singular subject.

Question 47. **The best answer is C** because it provides the clearest and most specific information asked for in the stem by indicating where the painting is on display (Washington, DC).

The best answer is NOT:

A because it fails to indicate what the stem asks for; it gives the location of the event characterized in the painting rather than where the painting is on display.

B because it fails to indicate what the stem asks for; it mentions the experience of those who see the painting on display but gives no indication of the location.

D because it fails to indicate what the stem asks for; it mentions that the painting has been on display but gives no indication of the location.

Question 48. **The best answer is H** because it eliminates the unnecessary punctuation between the verb and the preposition.

The best answer is NOT:

F because it provides unnecessary punctuation; the em dash after the word *presided* creates an unclear sentence with an illogical interruption of the phrase "presided over."

G because it introduces unnecessary punctuation; the comma after the word *presided* creates an unclear sentence with an illogical interruption of the phrase "presided over."

J because it introduces unnecessary punctuation; the semicolon after the word *presided* creates an unclear sentence with an illogical interruption of the phrase "presided over." In addition, the phrase following the semicolon forms an incomplete statement.

Question 49. The best answer is **D** because it eliminates redundancy by providing the most precise and concise wording. In addition, it maintains a tone that is consistent with the rest of the essay.

> **The best answer is** NOT:
>
> **A** because it contains an internal redundancy; the phrase "final role" and the word *ending* mean the same thing.
>
> **B** because it contains an internal redundancy; the word *ended* and the phrase "in the conclusion of" mean the same thing.
>
> **C** because it provides a phrase that is imprecise in meaning and creates a tone that is too informal for the essay.

Question 50. The best answer is **J** because it eliminates redundancy by providing the most precise and concise wording.

> **The best answer is** NOT:
>
> **F** because it contains an internal redundancy; the word *prior* and the phrase "in advance of" mean the same thing.
>
> **G** because it contains an internal redundancy; the word *preparation* and the phrase "leading up to" mean the same thing.
>
> **H** because it contains an internal redundancy; the words *advance* and *preceding* mean the same thing.

Question 51. The best answer is **A** because it prevents the introduction of an error in subordination in the sentence structure. The phrase "into which" most clearly and correctly establishes that the quills would have been dipped into the inkwells.

> **The best answer is** NOT:
>
> **B** because it introduces an error in subordination; it inaccurately reads as though the inkwells are being dipped into something rather than the quills being dipped into the inkwells.
>
> **C** because it introduces an error in subordination; it creates a sentence with unclear meaning in terms of the relationship between or actions with the inkwells and quills.
>
> **D** because it introduces an error in subordination; it creates a sentence with unclear meaning in terms of the relationship between or actions with the inkwells and quills.

Question 52. The best answer is **F** because it prevents the introduction of an error in subordination in sentence structure. The sentence clearly and correctly establishes that Christy was "noting color, texture, design" while scouring countless drawings.

The best answer is NOT:

G because it introduces an error in subordination; it creates a sentence with unclear meaning in terms of what was noted and by whom.

H because it introduces an error in subordination; it creates a sentence with unclear meaning in terms of what was noted.

J because it introduces an error in subordination; it creates a sentence with unclear meaning in terms of the nature of the drawings Christy scoured.

Question 53. The best answer is **D** because it corrects the introduction of a rhetorically ineffective fragment. The phrase "He hunted" provides both the subject and verb for the sentence.

The best answer is NOT:

A because it creates a rhetorically ineffective sentence fragment.

B because it introduces a rhetorically ineffective sentence fragment.

C because it introduces a rhetorically ineffective sentence fragment.

Question 54. The best answer is **G** because it is the most effective placement of the sentence in terms of logic and cohesion. Sentence 2 informs the reader about Christy's trip "to Philadelphia to study how the light falls through the windows." The added sentence provides more information about the reason for the trip, logically following Sentence 2. Sentences 3 and 4 should follow the added sentence because Sentences 3 and 4 focus on more specific aspects of Christy's preparations for creating the painting.

The best answer is NOT:

F because it is an illogical placement of the sentence within the paragraph. The added sentence expands on why and when Christy traveled to Philadelphia, so it would be illogical to place it after Sentence 1, which gives information about where and when the painting was installed and precedes any reference to Christy's trip to Philadelphia. The references to "He" and "his trip" in the added sentence would have no clear meaning.

H because it is an illogical placement of the sentence within the paragraph. The added sentence expands on why and when Christy traveled to Philadelphia, so it would be illogical to place it after Sentence 3, which focuses more specifically on the inkwells and quills.

J because it is an illogical placement of the sentence within the paragraph. The added sentence expands on why and when Christy traveled to Philadelphia, so it would be illogical to place it after Sentence 4, which focuses more specifically on Christy's research involving drawings of period furniture and fabrics.

Question 55. The best answer is **B** because it correctly eliminates the punctuation separating the word *boat* from the description that tells us about that boat (one that "experts now agree could not have been the vessel that carried the revolutionary leader across the river").

The best answer is NOT:

A because it provides unnecessary punctuation; it incorrectly provides a period separating the word *boat* from the description that tells us about that boat and creates a rhetorically ineffective fragment starting with the word *Experts*.

C because it introduces unnecessary punctuation; it incorrectly provides a semicolon separating the word *boat* from the description that tells us about that boat. In addition, it incorrectly creates a fragment following the semicolon.

D because it introduces unnecessary punctuation; it incorrectly provides a comma separating the word *boat* from the description that tells us about that boat.

Question 56. The best answer is **H** because it correctly eliminates unnecessary punctuation in the phrase "another painting of the signing."

The best answer is NOT:

F because it provides unnecessary punctuation; the comma after the word *another* incorrectly sets off the phrase "painting of the signing of the US Constitution" as a nonessential element.

G because it provides unnecessary punctuation; the comma after the word *signing* incorrectly sets off the phrase "of the US Constitution" as a nonessential element.

J because it provides unnecessary punctuation; the comma after the word *painting* incorrectly sets off the phrase "of the signing of the US Constitution" as a nonessential element.

Question 57. The best answer is **B** because it best expresses the idea specified in the stem by supporting the claim about the grandeur of the moment and emphasizing that Christy gave Washington a special status. The phrase "a hero among heroes" emphasizes the grandeur by characterizing all the signers as heroic and singling out Washington's special status as the most heroic of the group.

The best answer is NOT:

A because it fails to express the idea specified in the stem; it references the fame of Christy's painting but says nothing about Washington's special status.

C because it fails to express the idea specified in the stem; it mentions that Christy used visual techniques to single Washington out, but it does nothing to support the claim about the grandeur of the moment.

D because it fails to express the idea specified in the stem; it mentions that Christy did single Washington out, but does nothing to support the claim about the grandeur of the moment.

Question 58. The best answer is **G** because it eliminates an error in subordination in the sentence structure. The correct sentence structure makes clear that Franklin and Madison are examples of the many luminaries depicted in the painting.

The best answer is NOT:

F because it contains an error in subordination; the faulty sentence structure makes it unclear whether Franklin and Madison are in the painting or are absent but are being compared to the figures who are in the painting.

H because it introduces an error in subordination; the faulty sentence structure illogically suggests that only Franklin and Madison are being referred to by the phrase "many of the assembled men."

J because it introduces an error in subordination; the faulty sentence structure illogically suggests that only Franklin and Madison are being referred to by the phrase "many of the assembled men."

Question 59. The best answer is **A** because it creates the most logical ordering of paragraphs within the essay. Paragraph 2 describes the measures Christy took to prepare for the work on his famous painting. Paragraph 3 then logically begins with the phrase "Such measures may seem standard," which directly refers to the measures described in Paragraph 2.

The best answer is NOT:

B because it creates an illogical ordering of the paragraphs within the essay; Paragraph 3 begins with "Such measures may seem standard," which would make no sense as the first paragraph of the essay. The reader would not know to whom or what the essay is referring.

C because it creates an illogical ordering of the paragraphs within the essay; Paragraph 3 begins with "Such measures may seem standard," which has no clear connection to Paragraph 1. Paragraph 1 introduces the painting rather than the measures Christy took to produce it.

D because it creates an illogical ordering of the paragraphs within the essay; Paragraph 3 begins with "Such measures may seem standard," which has no clear connection to Paragraph 4. Rather, Paragraph 4 logically follows Paragraph 3 because Paragraph 3 refers to a painting that is not historically accurate, and Paragraph 4 begins with the statement "Christy's painting also plays with the truth."

Question 60. The best answer is H because it offers a clear and convincing reason the essay does not accomplish the purpose identified in the stem. Rather than explaining how Christy's painting changes the direction of his career, the essay focuses on Christy's approach to creating *Scene at the Signing of the Constitution of the United States.*

The best answer is NOT:

F because it indicates that the essay has accomplished the primary purpose identified in the stem when it hasn't and gives an inaccurate description of the essay. The essay does not indicate that Christy's painting led a trend in historical art.

G because it indicates that the essay has accomplished the primary purpose identified in the stem when it hasn't and gives an inaccurate description of the essay. The essay does not discuss the impact of *Scene at the Signing of the Constitution of the United States* on Christy's career.

J because it fails to offer a clear and convincing reason the essay does not accomplish the purpose identified in the stem. The essay does not indicate or address Christy's subject matter throughout his career; it focuses on only one painting.

Passage V

Question 61. The best answer is A because it best maintains the stylistic pattern established earlier in the sentence. The phrase "dizzying mazes of lines" contains a detailed image that most closely matches the pattern of detailed images created by the adjectives and nouns in the phrases "layers of petals, intricate spirals and rosettes, teardrops bending within circles."

The best answer is NOT:

B because it fails to maintain the stylistic pattern; the phrase "something with a dizzying effect" is too vague to match the level of detail established in the preceding phrases in the series.

C because it fails to maintain the stylistic pattern; the phrase "mazes that she creates" disrupts the pattern because it has significantly less detail and specificity and reintroduces the subject.

D because it fails to maintain the stylistic pattern; the phrase "so many lines" disrupts the pattern because it has significantly less detail and specificity than preceding phrases in the series.

Question 62. **The best answer is G** because it correctly distinguishes between plurals and possessives. The term *centuries-old* is correctly written as a compound adjective (to convey that *paj ntaub* has been practiced for many centuries) rather than a possessive noun.

The best answer is NOT:

F because it inaccurately substitutes the singular possessive *century's* for the plural noun *centuries*. In addition, it substitutes the superlative *oldest* for the word *old* when there is no clear context to indicate a comparison with other forms of Hmong needlework.

H because it inaccurately substitutes the plural possessive *centuries'* for the plural noun *centuries*.

J because it inaccurately substitutes the singular possessive *century's* for the plural noun *centuries*.

Question 63. **The best answer is D** because it deletes irrelevant information. The first paragraph is mainly about Pang Xiong as a master of *paj ntaub*, but the sentence in question describes recent trends in *paj ntaub* in general. Details about recent trends in *paj ntaub* are irrelevant at this point in the essay.

The best answer is NOT:

A because it retains irrelevant information and inaccurately describes the relationship between the sentence in question and the surrounding text. The sentence in question offers no connection to Pang Xiong's embroidery style.

B because it retains irrelevant information and inaccurately describes the relationship between the sentence in question and the surrounding text. Pang Xiong's work with *paj ntaub* is the main subject of the essay. The sentence in question offers no connection to Pang Xiong, so its reference to recent trends fails to place the subject of the essay in a modern context.

C because it offers an incorrect reason to delete information and inaccurately describes the relationship between the sentence in question and the surrounding text. The paragraph focuses on Pang Xiong as a master of a single style of Hmong needlework: *paj ntaub*. The paragraph does not describe the various styles of ancient Hmong needlework arts.

Question 64. The best answer is **G** because it eliminates an error in coordination in sentence structure. The participial phrase "living in northern Laos" modifies the word *woman* and accurately explains that Pang Xiong lived in northern Laos when she was a young woman.

The best answer is NOT:

F because it creates an error in coordination; the comma after the word *woman* separates two coordinate elements, creating an ungrammatical sentence that is unclear in terms of the relationship between the details about when Pang Xiong was a young woman and when she lived in northern Laos.

H because it introduces an error in coordination; it creates an ungrammatical shift in verb tense that makes the meaning of the sentence unclear.

J because it introduces an error in coordination; it creates an ungrammatical sentence that is unclear in terms of the relationship between the detail about living in northern Laos and how long Pang Xiong has been creating stitched textiles.

Question 65. The best answer is **C** because it corrects the introduction of a misplaced modifier. The parenthetical phrase offers examples of types of clothing, so it would most logically be placed after the word *clothing* to modify it and offer clarification about how flower cloth is "worn as clothing."

The best answer is NOT:

A because it creates a misplaced modifier; the placement of the parenthetical phrase after the term "flower cloth" suggests that flower cloth is defined by the phrase "commonly as a shirt, dress, coat, or collar," which is inaccurate based on the information given in the essay.

B because it introduces a misplaced modifier; the placement of the parenthetical phrase after the word *made* suggests that the parenthetical phrase explains or defines how flower cloth is made, which it does not.

D because it introduces a misplaced modifier; the placement of the parenthetical phrase after the word *needlework* suggests that the parenthetical phrase explains or defines something about needlework, which it does not.

Question 66. The best answer is **F** because it ensures subject-verb agreement; the singular verb form *is designed* agrees with the singular subject *Flower cloth*.

The best answer is NOT:

G because it lacks subject-verb agreement; the plural verb form *have been designed* does not agree with the singular subject *Flower cloth*.

H because it lacks subject-verb agreement; the plural verb form *are designed* does not agree with the singular subject *Flower cloth*.

J because it lacks subject-verb agreement; the plural verb form *design* does not agree with the singular subject *Flower cloth*.

Question 67. The best answer is **D** because it best expresses the idea specified in the stem by building on the information provided earlier in the sentence about a common theme in *paj ntaub* patterns and images. The sentence refers to animals, which leads to a common theme of celebrating the natural world.

The best answer is NOT:

A because it fails to express the idea specified in the stem; the idea of versatile patterns is too vague and broad to build on the theme of animals or the natural word.

B because it fails to express the idea specified in the stem; the detail about master artists creating *paj ntaub* clothing for special occasions has no clear connection to the common animal patterns referred to earlier in the sentence.

C because it fails to express the idea specified in the stem; the idea that *paj ntaub* patterns are colorful has no clear connection to the common animal patterns referred to earlier in the sentence.

Question 68. The best answer is **H** because it correctly separates two coordinate adjectives (*tiny* and *tight*) with a comma while omitting unnecessary punctuation after the words *tight* (between the adjective and the noun) and *stitches* (clearly indicating that the artist makes use of two key features: "tiny, tight stitches" and "several complex techniques").

The best answer is NOT:

F because it contains unnecessary punctuation; the comma after the word *stitches* inappropriately separates the two features the artist makes use of: "tiny, tight stitches" and "several complex techniques."

G because it contains unnecessary punctuation; it inaccurately separates the adjective *tight* from the noun it needs to modify: *stitches*.

J because it both fails to include necessary punctuation and contains unnecessary punctuation; it fails to separate the two coordinate adjectives (*tight* and *tiny*) with a comma, and it places a comma after the word *stitches*, which inappropriately separates the two features the artist makes use of: "tiny, tight stitches" and "several complex techniques."

Question 69. The best answer is **A** because it prevents the introduction of an error in coordination and subordination in the sentence structure. The preposition *in* is needed before the relative pronoun *which* to indicate that what follows in the sentence describes "reverse appliqué."

The best answer is NOT:

B because it introduces an error in subordination; it creates an ungrammatical sentence with an unclear meaning in terms of the relationship between the term "reverse appliqué" and the information that follows.

C because it introduces an error in coordination; it creates both a run-on sentence and an unclear statement in terms of the relationship between the term "reverse appliqué" and the information about the shapes being cut out.

D because it introduces an error in coordination; the comma after the word *appliqué* inappropriately creates two complete statements joined by a comma. This introduces an ungrammatical and unclear statement in terms of the relationship between the term "reverse appliqué" and the information about the shapes being cut out.

Question 70. The best answer is **J** because it eliminates an error in parallelism in the sentence structure. It provides the appropriate passive voice form *added* to parallel the passive voice form *are cut*, which is used earlier in the sentence.

The best answer is NOT:

F because it contains an error in parallelism; it incorrectly uses the present participle *adding* rather than the passive voice form *added*.

G because it introduces an error in parallelism; it incorrectly uses the phrase "as an addition" rather than the passive voice form *added*.

H because it introduces an error in parallelism; it incorrectly uses the phrase "to add them" rather than the passive voice form *added*.

Question 71. The best answer is **B** because it corrects the use of a vague pronoun. The phrase "the surface of the fabric" clearly identifies where the stitches are layered: on the fabric.

The best answer is NOT:

A because it uses a vague pronoun; the possessive pronoun *its* has no clear antecedent, making it unclear which object's surface is being referred to.

C because it introduces a vague pronoun; the pronoun *it* has no clear antecedent, making it unclear which object's surface is being referred to.

D because it introduces a vague pronoun; the pronoun *their* has no clear antecedent, making it unclear which object's surface is being referred to.

Question 72. The best answer is **F** because it correctly identifies that the writer should make the revision and accurately states the rhetorical impact of doing so. The adjective *regular* is vague; the more specific adjective *mass-produced* creates a clearer contrast between the homogeneous styles of clothing that are popular today and handcrafted *paj ntaub*.

The best answer is NOT:

G because it inaccurately states the rhetorical impact of making the revision. Although the adjective *mass-produced* describes the clothing that Pang Xiong is not fond of, it does nothing to indicate how or where Pang Xiong wants her work sold.

H because it incorrectly indicates that the writer should not make the revision. In addition, it inaccurately states the rhetorical impact of the original word. The word *regular* applies to clothing most people wear today; it does not refer to *paj ntaub* clothing at all.

J because it incorrectly indicates that the writer should not make the revision. In addition, it inaccurately states the rhetorical impact of the original word. The adjective *mass-produced* is more specific than the vague adjective *regular*.

Question 73. The best answer is **D** because it accurately eliminates the use of unnecessary transition words. No transition word or phrase is needed to clarify the connection between the ideas in this sentence and the preceding one.

The best answer is NOT:

A because it provides a transition word that is illogical for the context; the word *However* suggests that this sentence will present a contrast to what came before, which is not the case here.

B because it introduces a transition word that is illogical for the context; the transition phrase "For example" suggests that the sentence will provide an example, which is not the case here.

C because it introduces a transition word that is illogical for the context; the word *Besides* fails to provide a logical transition from the discussion of Pang Xiong's clothing when she was young to the discussion of Pang Xiong's clothing today and how she would like to inspire others. It is unclear what the word *Besides* would mean in this context.

Question 74. **The best answer is F** because it provides the clearest and most precise wording based on the stem. The phrase "to do so" clearly refers to wearing flower cloth, which is precisely what Pang Xiong wants to inspire others to do. This wording best indicates that Pang Xiong wants others to share her appreciation of *paj ntaub* by wearing it.

The best answer is NOT:

G because it is unnecessarily wordy and imprecise. The phrase "attempt that approach" is less precise because it does not clearly refer to the specific action of wearing flower cloth.

H because it does not offer precise wording to indicate that Pang Xiong wants others to share her appreciation of *paj ntaub* by wearing it. It vaguely states that Pang Xiong wants to inspire people she knows, but it doesn't indicate what she wants to inspire them to do.

J because it does not offer precise wording to indicate that Pang Xiong wants others to share her appreciation of *paj ntaub* by wearing it. Instead, it vaguely indicates that she wants to inspire others in general.

Question 75. **The best answer is C** because it is the most effective sentence to connect the ideas in the paragraph based on the criteria in the stem. By explaining that Pang Xiong has recently worked with nine young Hmong women in a formal apprenticeship, the sentence builds on the ideas mentioned earlier in the paragraph: that Pang Xiong wants to inspire an appreciation of *paj ntaub* in others and teaches the skill. The sentence also connects to the final sentence of the essay because it refers to nine young Hmong apprentices who are examples of the "new generation" mentioned in the final sentence.

The best answer is NOT:

A because it offers little connection to ideas presented earlier in the paragraph and fails to connect to the final sentence in the essay; this sentence mentions Pang Xiong's appreciation of others wearing traditional clothing in general (not only *paj ntaub*) but offers no connection to her "showing a new generation the joys of *paj ntaub*."

B because it builds on one idea presented earlier in the paragraph (teaching) but fails to connect to the final sentence in the essay; this sentence focuses on Hmong adults who are Pang Xiong's age rather than on the "new generation" referred to in the final sentence.

D because it offers no connection to the ideas presented earlier in the paragraph or to the final sentence of the essay; this sentence refers to Pang Xiong's family's story, but her family is not discussed elsewhere in the paragraph.

MATHEMATICS • PRACTICE TEST 3 • EXPLANATORY ANSWERS

Question 1. The correct answer is B. The probability of selecting either a red marble or a blue marble is calculated by adding the probability of selecting a red marble and the probability of selecting a blue marble: $\frac{5}{19} + \frac{4}{19} = \frac{9}{19}$. If you chose **A**, you may have thought the probability is the positive difference between the probability of selecting a red marble and the probability of selecting a blue marble. If you chose **C**, you may have added the values in the numerator and the values in the denominator. If you chose **D**, you may have multiplied the numerators and added the denominators. If you chose **E**, you may have multiplied the probabilities.

Question 2. The correct answer is G. The graph shows that, of the students who were present on Thursday, 8 were in Group 1, 12 were in Group 2, 6 were in Group 3, 2 were in Group 4, and 0 were in Group 5. The probability that a student from Group 4 is selected at random from the class on Thursday can be calculated by taking the number of students present on Thursday who were in Group 4 and dividing it by the total number of students present on Thursday in the class: $\frac{2}{8+12+6+2+0} = \frac{2}{28} = \frac{1}{14}$. If you chose **F**, you may have incorrectly identified the number of students present on Thursday who were in Group 4 as 1 instead of 2. If you chose **H**, you may have found the probability of selecting Group 4 from the 5 groups. If you chose **J**, you may have found the probability of selecting Group 4 from the 4 nonempty groups. If you chose **K**, you may have found the probability of selecting 1 student from Group 4.

Question 3. The correct answer is A. To solve for the value of j given a value of k, substitute the value of k into the equation to get $40 = \frac{7}{5}j + 54$; subtract 54 from both sides of the equation, $40 - 54 = \frac{7}{5}j + 54 - 54$, to get $-14 = \frac{7}{5}j$; and multiply both sides of the equation by $\frac{5}{7}$, $\left(\frac{5}{7}\right)(-14) = \left(\frac{5}{7}\right)\left(\frac{7}{5}\right)j$, to get $-10 = j$. If you chose **B**, you may have multiplied by $\frac{7}{5}$ instead of its reciprocal: $\left(\frac{7}{5}\right)(-14) = \frac{-98}{5}$. If you chose **C**, you may have multiplied 40 by $\frac{5}{7}$ and then subtracted from 54: $54 - 40\left(\frac{5}{7}\right) = \frac{178}{7}$. If you chose **D**, you may have forgotten the 54 and solved $40 = \frac{7}{5}j$: $40\left(\frac{5}{7}\right) = \frac{200}{7}$. If you chose **E**, you may have forgotten the 54 and attempted to solve $40 = \frac{7}{5}j$ but multiplied by $\frac{7}{5}$ instead of its reciprocal: $40\left(\frac{7}{5}\right) = 56$.

Question 4. The correct answer is H. First, substitute the value of x into the expression: $|3 - 8|$. Next, subtract 8 from 3: $|3 - 8| = |-5|$. Finally, because the absolute value of a number is its distance from 0, and because distance is positive, the absolute value of −5 is 5. If you chose **F**, you may have thought the absolute value bars change the − sign to +, calculated 3 + 8, and then changed the sign of 11 to −11. If you chose **G**, you may have subtracted 8 from 3 but neglected to calculate the absolute value. If you chose **J**, you may have simply chosen the value of x. If you chose **K**, you may have thought the absolute value bars change the − sign to + and calculated 3 + 8.

Question 5. The correct answer is A. The change in temperature can be determined by subtracting the starting temperature from the ending temperature: $-16 - 24 = -40$. If you chose **B**, you may have added instead of subtracting, $-16 + 24$, and made the result negative because the temperature dropped. If you chose **D**, you may have added instead of subtracting: $-16 + 24$. If you chose **E**, you may have subtracted in the wrong order or considered the starting temperature to be $-16°F$ and the ending temperature to be $24°F$: $24 - (-16) = 40$.

Question 6. **The correct answer is G.** The amount of money Ming paid for the car after the $1,000 down payment and 28 payments of $200 each is $1,000 + 28(\$200) = \$6,600$. Because the car had a purchase price of $5,400, the total she paid was $1,200 more than the purchase price: $\$6,600 - \$5,400 = \$1,200$. If you chose **F**, you may have subtracted the purchase price of the car from only the total Ming paid in the 28 payments: $28(\$200) - \$5,400 = \$200$. If you chose **H**, you may have subtracted the down payment from the purchase price of the car: $\$5,400 - \$1,000 = \$4,400$. If you chose **J**, you may have calculated the total Ming paid in the 28 payments: $28(\$200) = \$5,600$. If you chose **K**, you may calculated the total Ming paid for the car and neglected to calculate how much more that was than the purchase price: $\$1,000 + 28(\$200) = \$6,600$.

Question 7. **The correct answer is E.** When a regular hexagon is inscribed in a circle, the radius of the circle is the same value as each side length of the hexagon because the diagonals of a hexagon form 6 congruent equilateral triangles. Because all the side lengths of a regular hexagon are the same and there are 6 sides in a hexagon, multiply the side length by 6 to find the perimeter: $4(6) = 24$. If you chose **A**, you may have calculated the circumference of the circle: $2(4)\pi = 8\pi$. If you chose **B**, you may have thought that diagonals of the hexagon form 6 congruent 30-60-90 triangles and used $\frac{4\sqrt{3}}{2}$ as a side length: $\left(\frac{4\sqrt{3}}{2}\right)(6) = 12\sqrt{3}$. If you chose **C**, you may have thought that the side lengths of the hexagon were each 1 less than the radius of the circle: $(4-1)(6) = 18$. If you chose **D**, you may have correctly determined that the side lengths were 4 but multiplied by 5 sides instead of 6: $4(5) = 20$.

Question 8. **The correct answer is J.** The L-shaped floor plan is a composite shape. Find the missing horizontal length by subtracting the given horizontal lengths: $50 - 22 = 28$. Find the missing vertical length by subtracting the given vertical lengths: $40 - 22 = 18$. One possible method to find the area of the composite shape is to find the area that remains when a 28-by-18 rectangle is subtracted from a 50-by-40 rectangle: $(50)(40) - (28)(18) = 2,000 - 504 = 1,496$. If you chose **F**, you may have thought both missing lengths were 28 and found the perimeter of the floor plan instead of the area: $22 + 28 + 28 + 22 + 50 + 40 = 190$. If you chose **G**, you may have calculated the area of the 28-by-18 rectangle that is not included in the floor plan: $28 \times 18 = 504$. If you chose **H**, you may have found a missing length to be 28 and thought the floor plan could be decomposed into two rectangles that are 22 by 28: $2(22)(28) = 1,232$. If you chose **K**, you may have calculated the sum of the area of a 22-by-50 rectangle and a 22-by-40 rectangle, which represents an overlap: $22(50) + 22(40) = 1,980$.

Question 9. **The correct answer is C.** To classify the type of quadrilateral determined by the vertices, calculate the slopes of the sides to figure out which, if any, sides are parallel. The slope of $\overline{AB}$ is $\frac{4-0}{0-(-2)} = \frac{4}{2} = 2$. The slope of $\overline{BC}$ is $\frac{5-4}{5-0} = \frac{1}{5}$. The slope of $\overline{CD}$ is $\frac{2-5}{8-5} = \frac{-3}{3} = -1$.

The slope of $\overline{DA}$ is $\frac{0-2}{-2-8} = \frac{-2}{-10} = \frac{1}{5}$. There are two sides with a slope of $\frac{1}{5}$, $\overline{BC}$ and $\overline{DA}$. Because $\overline{BC}$ and $\overline{DA}$ have the same slope, they are parallel. The other sides are not parallel to each other. A trapezoid has exactly one pair of parallel sides. Therefore, Quadrilateral $ABCD$ is a trapezoid. If you chose **A**, you may have thought the diagonals were perpendicular. If you chose **B**, **D**, or **E**, which are all parallelograms, you may have thought one pair of parallel sides was enough, or you may have miscalculated the slopes of the sides.

Question 10. The correct answer is H. Given that $f(x) = 3x + 7$ and $g(x) = \frac{x^2}{2}$, $f(g(x)) = 3\left(\frac{x^2}{2}\right) + 7$. For $x = 4$, $f(g(4)) = 3\left(\frac{4^2}{2}\right) + 7 = 3\left(\frac{16}{2}\right) + 7 = 3(8) + 7 = 24 + 7 = 31$. If you chose **F**, you may have calculated $g(4)$: $g(4) = \frac{4^2}{2} = 8$. If you chose **G**, you may have calculated $f(4)$: $f(4) = 3(4) + 7 = 19$. If you chose **J**, you may have calculated the product of $g(4)$ and $f(4)$: $\left(\frac{4^2}{2}\right)(3(4) + 7) = \left(\frac{16}{2}\right)(12 + 7) = (8)(19) = 152$. If you chose **K**, you may have calculated $g(f(4))$: $g(f(4)) = \frac{(3(4)+7)^2}{2} = \frac{(12+7)^2}{2} = \frac{(19)^2}{2} = \frac{361}{2} = 180.5$.

Question 11. The correct answer is E. Julie's profit is the product of the number of hot dogs she sells and the price she sells them for minus the cost of her supplies: $2h - 200$. In order for her to make a profit, that value must be greater than 0: $2h - 200 > 0$. If you chose **A**, you selected the inequality that models making a profit if each hot dog sells for $1 each. If you chose **B**, you selected the inequality that models making no profit if each hot dog sells for $1 each. If you chose **C**, you may have thought that the purchase of supplies increased the profit and selected the inequality that models a profit if each hot dog sells for $1 each. If you chose **D**, you selected the inequality that models the number of hot dogs Julie can sell that keeps her from making a profit.

Question 12. The correct answer is G. To determine the slope of the line $3x + 8y = 5$, rewrite the equation of the line to its slope-intercept form, $y = mx + b$, where m is the slope of the line and b is the y-intercept. Subtract $3x$ from both sides of the equation to get $8y = -3x + 5$, and then divide both sides of the equation by 8 to get $y = -\frac{3}{8}x + \frac{5}{8}$. Therefore, the slope is $-\frac{3}{8}$. If you chose **F**, you may have thought the slope was the coefficient of the x term when the equation was in this form: $8y = -3x + 5$. If you chose **H**, you may have thought the slope was the coefficient of the x term when you divided by 5: $3x + 8y = 5$, $\frac{3}{5}x + \frac{8}{5}y = \frac{5}{5}$. If you chose **J**, you may have thought the slope was the coefficient of the x term in the given form of the equation: $3x + 8y = 5$. If you chose **K**, you may have thought the slope was the constant in the given form of the equation: $3x + 8y = 5$.

Question 13. The correct answer is A. The solution to the system of equations is the (x, y) pair that satisfies both equations in the system. One way to solve this system is by substitution. Begin by solving one of the equations for one of its variables. Then, substitute the solution from this first step into the other equation. If you solve the first equation for x, you have $x+2y=2$, $x=2-2y$. Next, substitute this expression for x into the second equation to get $-2x+y=16 \Leftrightarrow -2(2-2y)+y=16$. Now, solve this new equation for y: $-2(2-2y)+y=16 \Leftrightarrow -4+4y+y=16 \Leftrightarrow -4+5y=16 \Leftrightarrow 5y=20 \Leftrightarrow y=4$. You can substitute this y-value into either equation to solve for the x value: $-2x+y=16 \Leftrightarrow -2x+4=16 \Leftrightarrow -2x=12 \Leftrightarrow x=-6$. Thus, the solution to the system is $(-6,4)$. If you chose **B**, you may have selected a value for x and used it to solve the first equation for y: $x=-1 \Rightarrow -1+2y=2 \Rightarrow 2y=3 \Rightarrow y=1.5$. If you chose **C**, you may have selected a value for x and used it to solve the first equation for y: $x=1 \Rightarrow 1+2y=2 \Rightarrow 2y=1 \Rightarrow y=0.5$. If you chose **D**, you may have selected a value for y and used it to solve the first equation for x: $y=1 \Rightarrow x+2(1)=2 \Rightarrow x=0$. If you chose **E**, you may have selected a value for y and used it to solve the first equation for x: $y=0 \Rightarrow x+2(0)=2 \Rightarrow x=2$.

Question 14. The correct answer is K. Convert the $2\frac{3}{4}$ inches on the map to the number of miles apart the towns are by multiplying $2\frac{3}{4}$ inches ($2\frac{3}{4}=\frac{11}{4}$) by 16 miles per $\frac{1}{4}$ of an inch. The inches cancel out, leaving the number of miles apart the towns are: $\frac{11}{4}$ in $\times \dfrac{16 \text{ miles}}{\frac{1}{4} \text{ in}}$ = 176 miles. If you chose **F**, you may have calculated $\dfrac{\frac{11}{4}}{\frac{1}{4}}=11$. If you chose **G**, you selected the number of miles that are represented by $\frac{1}{4}$ inch, not $2\frac{3}{4}$ inches. If you chose **H**, you may have calculated $\frac{11}{4}(16)=44$. If you chose **J**, you may have calculated $\frac{16}{\frac{1}{4}}=64$, which is how many miles are represented by 1 inch.

Question 15. The correct answer is E. To multiply a matrix by a scalar, you multiply each term in the matrix by the scalar: $4\begin{bmatrix} -1 & 2 \\ 0 & -4 \end{bmatrix}=\begin{bmatrix} 4(-1) & 4(2) \\ 4(0) & 4(-4) \end{bmatrix}=\begin{bmatrix} -4 & 8 \\ 0 & -16 \end{bmatrix}$. If you chose **A**, you may have been thinking of matrix multiplication and multiplied each term in the matrix by the scalar and then added the terms of each column: $\begin{bmatrix} 4(-1)+4(0) & 4(2)+4(-4) \end{bmatrix}=\begin{bmatrix} -4 & -8 \end{bmatrix}$. If you chose **B**, you may have multiplied each term in the matrix by the scalar and then added the terms of each row: $\begin{bmatrix} 4(-1)+4(2) \\ 4(0)+4(-4) \end{bmatrix}=\begin{bmatrix} 4 \\ -16 \end{bmatrix}$. If you chose **C**, you may have added the scalar to each term in the matrix: $\begin{bmatrix} 4+(-1) & 4+2 \\ 4+0 & 4+(-4) \end{bmatrix}=\begin{bmatrix} 3 & 6 \\ 4 & 0 \end{bmatrix}$. If you chose **D**, you may have divided each term in the matrix by the scalar: $\begin{bmatrix} \frac{-1}{4} & \frac{2}{4} \\ \frac{0}{4} & \frac{-4}{4} \end{bmatrix}=\begin{bmatrix} -\frac{1}{4} & \frac{1}{2} \\ 0 & -1 \end{bmatrix}$.

Question 16. The correct answer is J. The tangent of an angle in a right triangle is equal to the ratio of the length of the leg opposite that angle to the length of the leg adjacent to that angle: $\tan A = \frac{BC}{AC}=\frac{15}{8}$. If you chose **F**, you might have found $\cos A$. If you chose **G**, you may have found $\cot A$. If you chose **H**, you may have found $\sin A$. If you chose **K**, you may have found the reciprocal of $\cos A$, $\sec A$.

MATHEMATICS • PRACTICE TEST 3 • EXPLANATORY ANSWERS

Question 17. **The correct answer is D.** Observe that 8 miles per hour is equal to $\frac{8\text{ miles}}{60\text{ minutes}} = \frac{2}{15}$ miles per minute. Because distance is equal to the product of rate and time, it will take 12 minutes for Tina to run $\frac{2}{15}(12) = \frac{8}{5} = 1\frac{3}{5}$ miles. If you chose **A**, you may have divided the rate in minutes per mile by the time in minutes: $\frac{\left(\frac{60\text{ minutes}}{8\text{ miles}}\right)}{12\text{ minutes}} = \left(\frac{60\text{ minutes}}{8\text{ miles}}\right)\left(\frac{1}{12\text{ minutes}}\right) = \frac{3}{8}\left(\frac{1}{\text{mile}}\right)$. Notice that this is the reciprocal of the key. If you chose **B**, you may have divided the rate, in miles per hour, by the time, in minutes: $\frac{8}{12} = \frac{2}{3}$. If you chose **C**, you may have divided the time, in minutes, by the rate, in miles per hour: $\frac{12}{8} = \frac{3}{2}$.

Question 18. **The correct answer is G.** $f(-3) = -6(-3)^2 = -6(9) = -54$. If you chose **F**, you may have multiplied the 6 by -3 before squaring it: $-(6 \cdot -3)^2 = -324$. If you chose **H**, you may have squared 3 instead of -3: $-6\left(-(3)^2\right) = -6(-9) = 54$. If you chose **J**, you may have squared 6 instead of -3: $-6^2(-3) = 108$. If you chose **K**, you may have multiplied the -6 by -3 before squaring it: $(-6 \cdot -3)^2 = 324$.

Question 19. **The correct answer is B.** Because $\overleftrightarrow{BC}$ is perpendicular to both $\overleftrightarrow{AC}$ and $\overleftrightarrow{DE}$, $\overleftrightarrow{AC}$ is parallel to $\overleftrightarrow{DE}$. Because $\overleftrightarrow{AC}$ and $\overleftrightarrow{DE}$ are two parallel lines cut by transversal $\overleftrightarrow{BE}$, alternate interior angles are congruent. Thus, $m\angle CAE = 132°$. Angles $\angle CAE$ and $\angle BAC$ form a straight line; thus they are supplementary: $m\angle BAC = 180° - 132° = 48°$. Because $\angle BAC$ and $\angle ABC$ are the acute angles of right triangle $\triangle ABC$, they are complementary: $m\angle ABC = 90° - 48° = 42°$. If you chose **A**, you may have computed $90 - \frac{132}{2}$. If you chose **C**, you may have thought $\triangle ABC$ was isosceles and computed $\frac{90}{2}$. If you chose **D**, you may have found $m\angle BAC$ instead of $m\angle ABC$. If you chose **E**, you may have computed $\frac{132}{2}$.

Question 20. **The correct answer is F.** Because the function value at 5 is 2, and the function value at 15 is 6, the rate of change of the function is $\frac{6-2}{15-5} = \frac{4}{10} = \frac{2}{5}$. Because the function is linear, you can use the point-slope formula $y - y_1 = m(x - x_1)$ where m is the rate of change, x_1 is a specific input of the function, and y_1 is the respective output. Substituting $m = \frac{2}{5}$, $x_1 = 5$, and $y_1 = 2$ gives you the equation $y - 2 = \frac{2}{5}(x - 5) \rightarrow y = \frac{2}{5}x$. If you chose **B**, you may have switched the input and output values: $m = \frac{15-5}{6-2} = \frac{5}{2} \rightarrow y - 5 = \frac{5}{2}(x - 2) \rightarrow y = \frac{5}{2}x$. If you chose **C**, you may have selected an expression that was true for an input of 5 only: $n - 3 \rightarrow 5 - 3 = 2$. If you chose **D**, you may have selected the expression that was true for an input of 15 only: $n - 9 \rightarrow 15 - 9$. If you chose **E**, you may have selected an expression that was true for an input of 5 only: $\frac{5}{2}(n - 5) + 2 \rightarrow \frac{5}{2}(5 - 5) + 2 = 2$.

Question 21. **The correct answer is C.** The first table lists the temperatures at each hour between 8:00 a.m. and noon. The second table lists the temperatures at each hour between noon and 4:00 p.m. Because the temperature fell at a constant rate, it first fell below 49°F sometime between 2:00 p.m. and 3:00 pm.

Temperature rose $\frac{1}{2}$°F each hour		Temperature fell 1°F each hour	
Time	Temperature in °F	Time	Temperature in °F
8:00 a.m.	49°F	Noon	51°F
9:00 a.m.	$49\frac{1}{2}$°F	1:00 p.m.	50°F
10:00 a.m.	50°F	2:00 p.m.	49°F
11:00 a.m.	$50\frac{1}{2}$°F	3:00 p.m.	48°F
Noon	51°F	4:00 p.m.	47°F

If you chose **A**, you may have thought the temperature at noon was $49\frac{1}{2}$°F. If you chose **B**, you picked the option that would be true if the temperature had fallen at 2°F each hour. If you chose **D**, you did not consider non-integer degree values between 49°F and 48°F. If you chose **E**, you picked the option that would be true if the temperature had fallen at $\frac{1}{2}$°F each hour.

Question 22. The correct answer is K. The 4 unit exams and the final exam were worth a total of 600 points. The lowest number of points that earned a grade of B was 600(0.80) = 480 points. The lowest number of points that earned a grade of A was 600(0.90) = 540 points. Therefore, students with scores ranging from 480 points to 539 points earned a grade of B. On the 4 unit exams, Hugo earned a total of 82 + 88 + 91 + 83 = 344 points. Thus, his final exam score was between 480 – 344 = 136 points and 539 – 344 = 195 points. If you chose **F**, **G**, **H**, or **J**, you picked a score on the final exam that is in the range 136–195 and, thus, results in a grade of B.

Question 23. The correct answer is A. The base of each of the 10 bowling pins shown in the figure is represented by a circle. The area of a circle with radius r is πr^2. Therefore, when all of the pins are set up, the total area, in square inches, that is covered by the bases of the 10 pins is $10\cdot\pi\left(\frac{2.25}{2}\right)^2 \approx 39.8$ or 40 square inches. If you chose **B**, you may have chosen the value closest to 10 times the circumference (πd) of a single bowling pin: $10\cdot\pi(2.25) \approx 71$. If you chose **C**, you may have chosen the value closest to the sum of the area of 10 pins and 10 times the circumference of a single bowling pin: 40 + 71 = 111. If you chose **D**, you may have squared the number of pins and dropped the pi, $10^2\cdot\left(\frac{2.25}{2}\right)^2 \approx 127$, which is closest to 125. If you chose **E**, you may have used the diameter instead of the radius: $10\cdot\pi(2.25)^2 \approx 159$.

Question 24. The correct answer is G. In the figure, the bowling area and the pin deck are each in the shape of a rectangle. The area of a rectangle with length L and width W is LW. Therefore, the total area of the bowling lane is 65(3.5) = 227.5 square feet. Similarly, the area of the pin deck is 5(3.5) = 17.5 square feet. Therefore, the ratio of the total area of the bowling lane to the area of the pin deck is $\frac{227.5}{17.5} = \frac{13}{1} \Rightarrow$ 13:1. If you chose **F**, you may have chosen the ratio of the area of the non-pin deck bowling lane to the area of the pin deck: $\frac{(65-5)\cdot3.5}{5\cdot3.5} \Rightarrow \frac{60}{5} \Rightarrow$ 12:1. If you chose **H**, you may have chosen the ratio of the total area of the bowling lane to the area of the non-pin deck bowling lane: $\frac{65 \cdot 3.5}{(60-5) \cdot 3.5} \Rightarrow \frac{65}{60} \Rightarrow 13:12$. If you chose **J**, you may have chosen the ratio of the perimeter of the non-pin deck bowling lane to the perimeter of the pin deck: $\frac{2(65-5)+2(3.5)}{2(5)+2(3.5)} \Rightarrow \frac{127}{17} \Rightarrow 127:17$. If you chose **K**, you may have chosen the ratio of the total perimeter of the bowling lane to the perimeter of the pin deck: $\frac{2(65)+2(3.5)}{2(5)+2(3.5)} \Rightarrow \frac{137}{17} \Rightarrow 137:17$.

Question 25. The correct answer is D. Let x represent the score Halle needs to earn in her 3rd game. Then, to find this unknown score, solve the equation $\frac{148+176+x}{3} = 172$. First, add the numbers in the numerator of the fraction on the left side of the equation: $\frac{324+x}{3} = 172$. Next, multiply by 3 on both sides of the equation: $3\left(\frac{324+x}{3}\right) = 3(172) \Leftrightarrow 324 + x = 516$. Therefore, $x = 516 - 324 = 192$. So, Halle needs to earn 192 points in her 3rd game to have an average score of 172 points. If you chose **A**, you may have computed $\frac{148+176+172}{3} \approx 165$. If you chose **B**, you may have thought the unknown score was equal to the given average. If you chose **C**, you may have computed $2(172) - \frac{324}{2} = 182$. If you chose **E**, you picked the option that would earn Halle an average greater than 172, because $\frac{148+176+200}{3} \approx 175$.

Question 26. The correct answer is F. The area of a rectangle is equal to the product of its width and length: $A = WL$. You can call the unknown width x and the unknown length $3x$ because the length is 3 times the width. Then, $300 = x(3x)$. To solve for x, you divide both sides by 3 and then take the square root. 300 divided by 3 is 100. The positive square root of 100 is 10. So the width, x, is 10. If you chose **G**, you found the length instead of the width; you should have chosen the shorter of 10 and 30. If you chose **H**, you may have divided 300 by 3 to get 100 but then took half of 100 instead of taking the square root. If you chose **J**, you may have divided 300 by 3 and then stopped. If you chose **K**, you may have divided 300 by 3 to get 100, but then you took half of 100 to get 50 and then multiplied by 3 to get the length.

Question 27. The correct answer is C. Every parallelogram has 2 pairs of congruent sides. So if 1 of its sides measures 16, then another side must measure 16, and there must be 2 more sides of unknown length. Call that unknown length x. The perimeter is the sum of all the side lengths; we have $96 = 16 + 16 + x + x$, or $96 = 32 + 2x$. Subtract 32 and divide by 2, and you get $x = 32$. If you chose **A**, you may have solved $96 = 16 + 16 + 16 + x$, using 16 as 3 side lengths. If you chose **B**, you may have solved the equation $96 = 16 + 2(x + 16)$ for x. If you chose **D**, you may have solved the equation $96 = 16 + x + x$ for x.

Question 28. The correct answer is H. Each of two directions has three lanes. You can add the widths of the lanes, $12 + 6 + 8$, and then multiply by 2 to account for both directions: $2(12 + 6 + 8) = 52$. If you chose **F**, you may have forgotten to multiply by 2. If you chose **G**, you may have doubled the 12 but not the 6 or 8: $(12 + 12 + 6 + 8)$.

Question 29. The correct answer is A. If there are 2,500 students and 4 out of every 10 students ride the bus, then the number of students who ride the bus, x, can be found by solving $\frac{4}{10} = \frac{x}{2,500}$. The number of students who ride the bus is 1,000. If 3 out of every 8 who ride the bus are freshman, then the number of students who are freshman and ride the bus, y, can be found by solving $\frac{3}{8} = \frac{y}{1,000}$. Alternatively, you can find $\frac{3}{8}$ of $\frac{4}{10}$ of 2,500 by multiplying $\frac{3}{8} \cdot \frac{4}{10} \cdot 2,500 = 375$.

Question 30. The correct answer is H. Using the Pythagorean identity, $\sin^2\theta + \cos^2\theta = 1$, we have $\left(\frac{20}{29}\right)^2 + \cos^2\theta = 1$, which is equivalent to $\cos^2\theta = \frac{441}{841}$, which is equivalent to $\cos\theta = \pm\frac{21}{29}$. Because 90 degrees $< \cos\theta <$ 180 degrees, $\cos\theta$ must be negative. If you chose **F**, you may have found cosecant instead of cosine. If you chose **G**, you may have found tangent instead of cosine and forgot to consider the quadrant. If you chose **J**, you may have found secant instead of cosine. If you chose **K**, you may have found cosecant instead of cosine and changed the sign to negative.

Question 31. The correct answer is C. To find $f(t) = t$, solve the equation $t = \frac{2}{t+1}$ by multiplying both sides by $(t + 1)$. This gives you $t(t+1) = 2 \rightarrow t^2 + t - 2 = 0 \rightarrow (t+2)(t-1) = 0 \rightarrow t = -2$ or $t = 1$. Because the function $f(t) = \frac{2}{t+1}$ is undefined only when both -2 and 1 are values for which $f(t) = t$. If you chose **A**, you may have found the value for which $f(x)$ is undefined. If you chose **B** or **D**, you may have factored incorrectly: $(t-2)(t+1) = 0$. If you chose **E**, you may have incorrectly factored $t^2 + t - 2 = 0$ to be $(t-2)(t-1) = 0$.

Question 32. The correct answer is J. To find the distance between the 2 radar stations, you have to find AB in the given figure. Using the Pythagorean Theorem, $BD^2 + CD^2 = BC^2$; thus, $BD^2 + 12{,}000^2 = 13{,}000^2 \rightarrow BD = 5{,}000$. Alternatively, you could recognize that this triangle is similar to the triangle that represents the Pythagorean triple: 5-12-13. Because $BD = 5{,}000$ and $AD = 9{,}000$, $AB = 5{,}000 + 9{,}000 = 14{,}000$. If you chose **F**, you may have found BD instead of AB. If you chose **G**, you may have thought $BD = 13{,}000 - 12{,}000$ and then added $1{,}000 + 9{,}000$. If you chose **K**, you may have thought triangle $\triangle ABC$ was isosceles.

Question 33. The correct answer is C. Because the airplane is flying due west and point A is due west of point D, the airplane is flying on a path parallel to $\overrightarrow{AD}$. In the standard (x,y) coordinate plane, both A and D are on the x-axis, so the airplane is flying on a line parallel to the x-axis. Because the airplane is 12,000 feet above $D(9{,}000, 0)$, the airplane is currently at $(9{,}000, 12{,}000)$. The line that is parallel to the x-axis and goes through $(9{,}000, 12{,}000)$ is $y = 12{,}000$. If you chose **A**, you may have chosen the vertical line that goes through $(9{,}000, 12{,}000)$ instead of the horizontal line. If you chose **D**, you may have used the straight-line distance the plane was from B instead of the distance the plane was from $\overrightarrow{AD}$. If you chose **E**, you may have used the straight-line distance the plane was from A instead of the distance the plane was from $\overrightarrow{AD}$.

Question 34. The correct answer is G. Because the airplane is currently directly above D and flying on a path parallel to $\overrightarrow{AD}$ to get to a point directly above A, it will travel this distance: $AD = 9{,}000$ feet. Because the airplane is traveling at a rate of 300 feet per second, the time it will take the airplane is $\frac{9{,}000 \text{ feet}}{300 \text{ feet/sec}} = 30$ seconds. If you chose **F**, you may have confused Station B and Station A and divided 5,000 (the distance from D to B) by 300. If you chose **H**, you may have divided 12,000 by 300. If you chose **J**, you may have divided 13,000 by 300. If you chose **K**, you may have divided 15,000 by 300.

Question 35. The correct answer is A. When the airplane is directly above point A, it forms the right triangle $\triangle ABC$ shown in Figure 1. From question 32, you know that $AB = 14,000$. You also know that $m\angle A$ is 90°, and you can estimate that $m\angle B$ and $m\angle C$ are both between 40° and 50°. Figure 2 shows the new triangle at a certain point in time after the plane has flown due west. Notice that $\angle A$ in Figure 2 is larger than in Figure 1 and $\angle B$ and $\angle C$ are smaller than in Figure 1. You can estimate $m\angle A$ to be greater than 90° and both $m\angle B$ and $m\angle C$ to be less than 40°. This shows that $m\angle A$ is increasing, and $m\angle B$ and $m\angle C$ are decreasing. Therefore, "I only" is the correct answer.

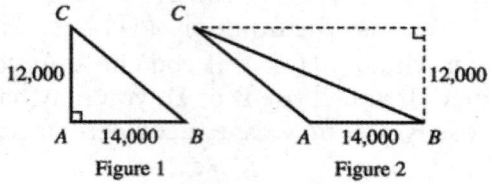

Figure 1   Figure 2

Question 36. The correct answer is G. The area of the original poster is $4(2) = 8$ square feet. The area of the new poster will be $0.5(8) = 4$ square feet. The length of the new poster will be $\frac{3}{4}(4) = 3$ feet. Therefore, the width of the new poster will be $\frac{\text{Area of the new poster}}{\text{Length of the new poster}} = \frac{4 \text{ square feet}}{3 \text{ feet}} = 1\frac{1}{3}$ feet. If you chose **F**, you may have chosen the given fraction or you may have found the reciprocal of the width of the new poster: $\frac{\text{Length of the new poster}}{\text{Area of the new poster}}$. If you chose **H**, you selected the value that is $\frac{3}{4}$ of the width of the original poster: $\frac{3}{4}(2)$. If you chose **J**, you selected the value that is $\frac{3}{4}$ of the area of the new poster: $\frac{3}{4}(4)$. If you chose **K**, you selected the value that is $\frac{3}{4}$ of the area of the original poster: $\frac{3}{4}(8)$.

Question 37. The correct answer is E. To find the solution set, simplify the right side of the equation. Multiply the 2 and the binomial $(x + 3)$ to get $x + 6 = 2x + 6 - x$. Next, combine like terms to get $x + 6 = x + 6$. Observe that the resulting equation will be true for any real number x. If you chose **A**, you may have multiplied the 2 by the first term in the binomial only and then solved: $x + 6 = 2x + 3 - x \Rightarrow x + 6 = x + 3 \Rightarrow 6 = 3$. If you chose **B**, **C**, or **D**, you may have verified that the given equation was satisfied with the value in the set.

Question 38. The correct answer is J. Let L be the length of the region. Let W be the width of the region. The perimeter, in feet, of the region will be $2L + 2W = 28$. To express the width W in terms of the length L, rewrite the equation as $2W = 28 - 2L$ or $W = 14 - L$. The area, in square feet, of the region is $A = LW$. Use the fact that $W = 14 - L$ to rewrite the area as $A = L(14 - L)$ or $A = 14L - L^2$. This quadratic equation represents a function of L where the maximum value occurs at the vertex. Thus, the maximum value occurs for $L = -\frac{14}{2(-1)} = 7$, and the maximum value is $A = 7(14 - 7) = 49$. So, the area of the largest rectangular region Steve can enclose is 49 square feet. If you chose **F**, you may have thought the dimensions 4 and 10 yield the greatest area. If you chose **G**, you may have thought the dimensions 5 and 9 yield the greatest area. If you chose **H**, you may have thought 6 and 8 yield the greatest area and didn't consider that a square is a rectangle. If you chose **K**, you may have mistaken the width as $28 - L$ and the area as $A = L(28 - L)$, which yields $L = 14$ and $W = 14$.

Question 39. The correct answer is C. The addition of the professional athlete's annual income will not change the median significantly. The median is calculated using the middle 1 or 2 values in a data set, written in numeric order, so it will not be influenced by an extreme outlier. The median annual income of the original group of 5 people is between $30,000 and $35,000 and so is the median annual income of the new group of 6 people. If you chose **A**, you picked a measure that is not resistant to outliers. Because the range is based on the minimum and maximum values in a data set, it will be influenced by the extreme outlier. The range of the annual income of the original group of 5 people is roughly $35,000 - $30,000 = $5,000, but the range of the annual income of the new group of 6 people is roughly $1,000,000 - $30,000 = $970,000. If you chose **B**, you picked a measure that is not resistant to outliers. The mean is calculated using every value in the data set. Thus, it will be influenced by the extreme outlier. If you chose **D**, you picked a measure that is not resistant to outliers. The standard deviation is roughly the typical distance that the values in a data set fall from the mean. In the original group of 5 people, all of the values are reasonably close to the mean, so the standard deviation is small. But because there is an outlier of $1,000,000 in the new group of 6 people, the typical distance of the values from the mean is much higher, so the standard deviation is much higher.

Question 40. The correct answer is K. Ana and Amy completed $\frac{2}{5} + \frac{1}{3} = \frac{6+5}{15} = \frac{11}{15}$ of the job. Ruben finished the remaining $1 - \frac{11}{15} = \frac{4}{15}$ of the job in 2 hours. Because all 3 worked at the same rate, each person completed $\frac{4/15}{2} = \frac{4}{30}$ of the job per hour. It follows that it would have taken 1 person, working alone, $\frac{1}{\frac{4}{30}} = \frac{30}{4} = 7.5$ hours to complete the entire job. If you chose **F**, you may have solved $\frac{2}{5}x + \frac{1}{3}x + 2x = 1$. If you chose **G**, you may have computed $2 - \frac{1}{3} - \frac{2}{5}$. If you chose **H**, you may have computed $\frac{2}{5} + \frac{1}{3} + 2$. If you chose **J**, you may have thought Ana worked 2 hours so you computed $\frac{2/5}{2} = \frac{2}{10} \Rightarrow \frac{1}{\frac{10}{2}} \Rightarrow \frac{10}{2}$.

Question 41. The correct answer is C. Applying the exponent of 4 to all factors in the numerator gives $\frac{16a^{-4}b^2}{ab^{-3}}$. Rewriting this expression gives $16a^{-5}b^5$, which is equivalent to $\frac{16b^5}{a^5}$. If you chose **B**, you may have multiplied the coefficient 2 by the exponent 4 and combined the exponents -1 and 4 to get $\frac{8a^{-3}b^3}{ab^{-3}}$. If you chose **D**, you may have mistaken the square root symbol for a 4th root. If you chose **E**, you may have ignored the square root symbol and thought $\frac{b^4}{b^{-3}}$ equals b^{4-3} and also thought $\frac{a^{-4}}{a^1}$ equals a^{-4+1}.

Question 42. The correct answer is G. The contestant knows the oldest, so the probability of getting the oldest correct is 1. The contestant guesses the 2nd oldest from the other 3 rock stars, so the probability of getting the 2nd oldest correct is $\frac{1}{3}$. Assuming the first 2 are correct, the probability of guessing the 3rd oldest is $\frac{1}{2}$, which leaves only 1 person for the 4th oldest. Multiplying these probabilities, $1 \cdot \frac{1}{3} \cdot \frac{1}{2} \cdot 1$, you get $\frac{1}{6}$. If you chose **F**, you may have thought the contestant guessed all 4 and multiplied $\frac{1}{4} \cdot \frac{1}{3} \cdot \frac{1}{2} \cdot 1$. If you chose **H**, you may have chosen the denominator 4 because there were 4 rock stars. If you chose **J**, you may have chosen the denominator 3 because there were 3 positions the contestant didn't know. If you chose **K**, you may have thought the contestant could be either correct or incorrect with equal probability.

Question 43. The correct answer is D. Here is one course of simplification.

Rewrite the given expression with two pairs of common denominators: $\dfrac{\frac{2x}{6} + \frac{3}{6}}{\frac{8}{12} - \frac{3}{12}}$

Combine fractions with like denominators: $\dfrac{\frac{2x+3}{6}}{\frac{5}{12}}$

Rewrite, using multiplication of the reciprocal: $\frac{2x+3}{6} \cdot \frac{12}{5}$

Reduce the 12 and 6 to 2 and 1: $\frac{2x+3}{1} \cdot \frac{2}{5}$

Multiply numerators, using distribution, and multiply denominators: $\frac{2 \cdot 2x + 2 \cdot 3}{5 \cdot 1}$

If you chose **A**, you may have neglected to get common denominators and added numerators and denominators to get $\dfrac{\frac{x+1}{5}}{\frac{1}{-1}}$. If you chose **B**, you may have neglected to distribute the factor 2 to the $2x$ in the last step. If you chose **C**, you may have neglected to distribute the factor 2 to the 3 in the last step. If you chose **E**, you may have thought that $\frac{2}{3} - \frac{1}{4}$ in the first step was $\frac{1}{12}$.

Question 44. The correct answer is K. The fundamental counting principle allows us to multiply the number of ways to fill each position to get the total number of unique strings of characters. There are 10 digits that could fill each of the first 3 positions and 26 letters that could fill each of the last 6 positions, so the number of license plates is $10 \cdot 10 \cdot 10 \cdot 26 \cdot 26 \cdot 26$. If you chose **F**, you may have added 10 and 26. If you chose **G**, you may have thought there were only 6 possible characters for each of the 6 positions. If you chose **H**, you may have thought that no letters and only digits were being used. If you chose **J**, you may have thought there were only 9 digits instead of 10.

Question 45. The correct answer is A. The function $y = 3 + f(x-1)$ is equivalent to $(y-3) = f(x-1)$. To turn $(y-3) = f(x-1)$ into $y = f(x)$, we'd have to add 1 to x and add 3 to y. So the graph of $(y-3) = f(x-1)$ will be shifted 1 unit to the right and 3 units up. For example, the point $(0,0)$ satisfies $y = f(x)$, and the point $(1,3)$ satisfies $(y-3) = f(x-1)$. If you chose **B**, you may have thought $y = 3 + f(x-1)$ was equivalent to $(y+3) = f(x-1)$. If you chose **C**, you may have confused the directions right and up. If you chose **D**, you may have thought the positive 3 and negative 1 meant there must be some shift in a positive direction (right) and some shift in a negative direction (down). If you chose **E**, you may have thought $y = 3 + f(x-1)$ was equivalent to $(y-3) = f(x-1)$ but then mixed up the x and y axes and didn't realize the shift on each axis should be in the positive direction.

Question 46. The correct answer is K. The logarithmic equation $\log_5 x = -2$ is equivalent to the exponential equation $5^{-2} = x$. Because $5^{-2} = \frac{1}{5^2}$, it follows that $x = \frac{1}{25}$. If you chose **F**, you might have thought the logarithmic equation $\log_5 x = -2$ was equivalent to the exponential equation $(-2)^5 = x$. If you chose **G**, you might have thought the logarithmic equation $\log_5 x = -2$ was equivalent to the exponential equation $-5^2 = x$. If you chose **H**, you might have thought the logarithmic equation $\log_5 x = -2$ was equivalent to the equation $-2(5) = x$. If you chose **J**, you might have thought $5^{-2} = \frac{1}{2(5)}$.

Question 47. The correct answer is D. The fraction $\frac{1}{5} = \frac{2}{10}$ and $\frac{1}{3} = \frac{2}{6}$. Because $\frac{2}{10} < \frac{2}{9} < \frac{2}{8} < \frac{2}{7} < \frac{2}{6}$, it follows that $\frac{2}{D}$ is between $\frac{1}{5}$ and $\frac{1}{3}$ for $D = 7, 8,$ and 9. If you chose **A**, you might have ignored the 2 in $\frac{2}{D}$. If you chose **B**, you might have ignored the 2 in $\frac{2}{D}$ and included the denominators of the given fractions as well as $\frac{1}{4}$. If you chose **C**, you might have known $\frac{1}{4}$ was between $\frac{1}{5}$ and $\frac{1}{3}$ and converted $\frac{1}{4}$ to $\frac{2}{8}$ but didn't consider other values for D. If you chose **E**, you might have added the denominators of $\frac{2}{10}$ and $\frac{2}{6}$.

Question 48. The correct answer is F. Whenever you multiply or divide both sides of an inequality by a negative number, you must reverse the inequality symbol. The inequality $a > b$ is equivalent to $\frac{a}{c} < \frac{b}{c}$. If you chose **G** or **H**, then you might not have realized that when you multiply or divide both sides of an inequality by a negative number, you must reverse the inequality symbol. Notice that the inequality $8 > 2$ is true, but both inequalities $\frac{8}{-2} > \frac{2}{-2}$ and $8(-2) > 2(-2)$ are false. If you chose **J**, you might not have remembered the additive property of inequality that says if $a > b$, then $a + c > b + c$. Thus, it is false that $a + c < b + c$. Adding or subtracting a negative number from both sides of the inequality does not require reversing the inequality symbol. If you chose **K**, you might not have realized that this inequality is not true for all values of a, b, and c. Notice that the inequality $8 > 2$, but $8 < 2 - (-1)$ is not true.

Question 49. The correct answer is B. Subtracting $a^2 + b^2$ from both sides of the equation $c^2 = a^2 + b^2 - 2ab\cos C$ gives $c^2 - a^2 - b^2 = -2ab\cos C$. Dividing that equation by $-2ab$ and then taking the inverse cosine of both sides gives $\cos^{-1}\left(-\frac{c^2 - a^2 - b^2}{2ab}\right) = C$. Let $\angle C$ be the largest angle in the triangle. Because the largest angle, C, is opposite the longest side, define $c = 39$. Plugging in the values $c = 39$, $a = 37$, and $b = 38$ gives the equation $\cos^{-1}\left(-\frac{39^2 - 37^2 - 38^2}{2(37)(38)}\right) = C$. If you chose **A**, you might have thought the largest angle was opposite the shortest side. If you chose **C**, **D**, or **E**, you might have added $2ab$ instead of dividing by $2ab$.

Question 50. The correct answer is K. If Pete's average score on 4 tests is x points, then the sum of his scores on those 4 tests is $4x$ points. Let y be Pete's score on the 5th test. His average score on all 5 tests is $\frac{4x + y}{5} = x + 2$. Multiplying both sides of this equation by 5 gives $4x + y = 5x + 10$. Subtracting $4x$ from both sides gives $y = x + 10$. His average score on the 5th test must be 10 greater than x. If you chose **F**, you might have thought the question

Taking Additional Practice Tests

asked how many points higher than x is $x + 2$. If you chose **G**, you might have thought that $x + 2$ was the average of 2 scores (old test and new test) instead of 5 scores. If you chose **H**, you might have chosen a number equal to the total number of tests. If you chose **J**, you might have multiplied the change in average, 2, by the number of tests already taken, 4.

Question 51. **The correct answer is D.** Two intersecting lines form pairs of adjacent angles, called *linear pairs,* which are supplementary. Also, two intersecting lines form pairs of congruent angles, called *vertical angles.* Because the measure of $\angle B$ is $3\frac{1}{2}$ times the measure of $\angle A$, the angles are not congruent angles. Therefore, $\angle B$ and $\angle A$ must be adjacent angles that form a linear pair, and so they are supplementary. Let x be the measure of $\angle A$ in degrees. Then, $x + 3.5x = 180$ and so $4.5x = 180 \Leftrightarrow x = 40$. Hence, the measure of $\angle A$ is $40°$. If you chose **A**, you may have thought the angles were complementary, $x + 3.5x = 90$. If you chose **B**, you may have computed $\frac{90}{3.5} \approx 26$. If you chose **E**, you may have computed $\frac{180}{3.5} \approx 51$.

Question 52. **The correct answer is J.** The sequence is defined recursively, so begin with the given initial value of $s_1 = 3$ and compute the values of s_2, s_3, and s_4. Each calculation is shown in the table.

n	$s_n = 2s_{(n-1)} + n + 1$
1	$s_1 = 3$
2	$s_2 = 2s_{(2-1)} + 2 + 1 = 2s_1 + 2 + 1 = 2(3) + 2 + 1 = 9$
3	$s_3 = 2s_{(3-1)} + 3 + 1 = 2s_2 + 3 + 1 = 2(9) + 3 + 1 = 22$
4	$s_4 = 2s_{(4-1)} + 4 + 1 = 2s_3 + 4 + 1 = 2(22) + 4 + 1 = 49$

If you chose **F**, you may have stopped at s_2. If you chose **G**, you may have multiplied 2 times the value of s_2. If you chose **H**, you may have stopped at s_3.

Question 53. **The correct answer is E.** If a is an integer less than -1, then $|a|$ is greater than 1. Also, if a is an integer less than -1, then a^2 is an integer greater than 1, and thus, $-a^2$ is an integer less than -1. Finally, if a is an integer less than -1, then $\frac{1}{a}$ is a negative number greater than -1, and thus, $-\frac{1}{a}$ is a positive number less than 1. So $-a^2 < -1 < -\frac{1}{a} < 1 < |a|$. Therefore, the expressions ordered from least to greatest are $-a^2 < -\frac{1}{a} < |a|$. If you chose **A** or **B**, you may not have noticed that $-\frac{1}{a}$ is a positive number and $-a^2$ is a negative number. If you chose **C**, you may have ordered the expressions from greatest to least. If you chose **D**, you may not have noticed that $-\frac{1}{a}$ is less than 1 and $|a|$ is greater than 1.

Question 54. **The correct answer is J.** First create the probability distribution for the random variable X. There are 10 equally likely outcomes in the sample space: 1, 2, 2, 3, 3, 3, 4, 4, 4, 4. Each value of X and its associated probability, $P(X)$, is listed in the table. The expected value of X, $E(X)$, is calculated by adding all $X \cdot P(X)$ products. Thus, $E(X) = \Sigma XP(X) = 1(0.1) + 2(0.2) + 3(0.3) + 4(0.4) = 3$. If you chose **F**, you may have divided the number of distinct cards by the total number of cards: $\frac{4}{10} = 0.4$. If you chose **G**, you may have chosen the sum of all the probabilities, $\Sigma P(X) = 1$. If you chose **H**, you may have found the mean of 1, 2, 3, and 4. If you chose **K**, you may have thought "expected value" meant the value of X that is associated with the greatest probability.

X	$P(X)$
1	$\frac{1}{10} = 0.1$
2	$\frac{2}{10} = 0.2$
3	$\frac{3}{10} = 0.3$
4	$\frac{4}{10} = 0.4$

Question 55. The correct answer is B. Define 3 consecutive odd integers x, y, and z such that $x < y < z$ with the expressions $x = 2n + 1$, $y = 2n + 3$, and $z = 2n + 5$ where n is an integer. The sum of x, y, and z is, therefore, $2n + 1 + 2n + 3 + 2n + 5 = 6n + 9 = 3(2n + 3) = 3y$. If you chose **A** or **C**, you may have chosen an expression that represents the sum if x, y, and z are the same number. If you chose **D**, you may have rewritten $x + y + z$ as $x + x + 2 + x + 2 + 2$ and then incorrectly simplified to $3x + 2$. If you chose **E**, you may have chosen the expression that represents the average of the 3 consecutive odd integers rather than the sum.

Question 56. The correct answer is G. Because the mean of the 5 numbers is 24, the sum of the 5 numbers must be 5(24). Solving $42 + 3 + 11 + 27 + x = 120$ gives $x = 37$. Because the median of the 4 numbers is 38, the arithmetic mean of the middle 2 numbers (2nd and 3rd greatest numbers) must be 38. One of the middle numbers must be 29 because 8 is less and 53 is greater. Solving $\frac{29+y}{2} = 38$ gives $y = 47$. Therefore, $x - y = 37 - 47$. If you chose **F**, you may have taken the additive inverse of the given median. If you chose **H**, you may have calculated $47 - 37$. If you chose **J**, you may have chosen the given median. If you chose **K**, you may have thought the value of y couldn't be determined because the order of the 4 numbers wasn't given.

Question 57. The correct answer is A. Let the length and width of such a rectangle be l inches and w inches. It is given that the area is 144 square inches, so $lw = 144$. If we assume **A** is true, the perimeter is 48 inches, and $l + w = 24$ inches. Solving the system $\begin{cases} lw=144 \\ l+w=24 \end{cases}$, we get only one solution: $l = w = 12$. But this doesn't meet the condition that the rectangle's length is greater than the width. Therefore, 48 inches cannot be the perimeter for such a rectangle. Alternatively, you can write all lw factor pairs of 144 (where $l \neq w$) and double each $l + w$ sum to get possible $2(l + w)$ perimeters. If you chose **B**, you didn't realize that $l = 24$ and $w = 6$ satisfy the conditions. If you chose **C**, you didn't realize that $l = 36$ and $w = 4$ satisfy the conditions. If you chose **D**, you didn't realize that $l = 48$ and $w = 3$ satisfy the conditions. If you chose **E**, you didn't realize that $l = 72$ and $w = 2$ satisfy the conditions.

Question 58. The correct answer is J. The y-coordinate of the center of the circle is 8. One endpoint of a diameter has a y-coordinate of 11, which is 3 greater than 8. So the other endpoint must have a y-coordinate that is 3 less than 8. If you chose **F**, you may have subtracted $11 - 10$. If you chose **G**, you may have used the x-coordinate of the center, 7, and subtracted the difference of 11 and 7 from 7; or you may have subtracted the y-coordinate of the center from 11. If you chose **H**, you may have subtracted the x-coordinate of the center from 11. If you chose **K**, you may have chosen the y-coordinate of the center.

Question 59. The correct answer is D. For any values of length, width, and depth, the volume reflecting the increase in length and width can be represented by $(1.1l)(1.1w)(d)$, which is equivalent to $1.21(lwd)$. The value 1.21 represents a 21% increase. If you chose **A**, you may have thought the percent increase in volume would equal the percent increase in length and width. If you chose **B**, you may have rounded the result of $\frac{1.21-1}{1.21}$ to the nearest 1%. If you chose **C**, you may have added 10% + 10%. If you chose **E**, you may have thought all three dimensions were increased by 10%.

Question 60. The correct answer is K. Because $x = -1$ is a solution, $x + 1$ is a linear factor. Dividing $4x^3 - 2x^2 + x + 7$ by $x + 1$ gives $4x^2 - 6x + 7$. The discriminant of the quadratic formula is $b^2 - 4ac$, which for $4x^2 - 6x + 7$ is equal to $(-6)^2 - 4(4)(7)$. If you chose **F**, you may have thought a negative discriminant meant the solutions are both negative.

Passage I

Question 1. The best answer is **A** because the narrator makes clear that he does not know or remember all the details of the story he relates about Jantzen. The narrator states, "I'm not acquainted with the details, having been in high school at the time. But I can imagine" (lines 31–32). Later, the narrator points out that his memory "grows shaky" (line 46) because he had graduated from high school and moved out of town. When the narrator returned, "the steam-car operation was spoken of with scorn by the people who had been against it" (lines 50–52), which suggests hearsay.

The best answer is NOT:

B because the passage does not mention the narrator ever having spoken with Jantzen. Instead, the narrator states that he was "not acquainted with the details" (line 31).

C because the passage does not indicate that the entire story is fabricated. The narrator frames the story as if it actually happened, providing details about Jantzen and enough information about the events to strongly suggest that the story did happen.

D because the passage makes clear that the narrator was not a participant in the events. "I'm not acquainted with the details. . . . But I can imagine" (lines 31–32).

Question 2. The best answer is **H** because the phrase "though maybe not as quick as he should have been to smell a rat" (lines 23–24) suggests that Jantzen was not sensitive to the possibility that someone might try to take advantage of him. For the narrator to bring up Jantzen's not being quick to "smell a rat" hints that Jantzen, ultimately, was tricked in some way.

The best answer is NOT:

F because, as it is presented in the passage, the fact that Jantzen ran the bank does not in itself foreshadow his downfall more strongly than response H does. This detail is used to help establish Jantzen's position.

G because the passage does not make a clear connection between people coming up with ideas in the Thirties and Jantzen's downfall. This detail provides context for the story rather than strongly foreshadowing Jantzen's downfall.

J because, though the passage mentions that Jantzen might have had a steam-driven car, and that he may have had a fondness for them, the detail does not provide foreshadowing. It suggests one reason Jantzen might have been interested in the idea to resurrect the steam-driven car.

Question 3. The best answer is **D** because the passage suggests that people in town didn't know who convinced Jantzen to invest in steam-driven cars. Lines 19–21: "Who knows if it was a single person or a cohort. Maybe a stranger or some friends of friends."

The best answer is NOT:

A because the passage does not indicate that the townspeople knew who was involved in the investment scheme. Instead, lines 19–21 suggest that they could only speculate about this.

B because although strangers and friends of friends are mentioned as people who hypothetically could have convinced Jantzen to invest (lines 20–21), their involvement is portrayed as speculation only. The suggestion is that the townspeople didn't know, not that some people believed it was strangers and others believed it was friends of friends.

C because although an undescribed cohort is mentioned as possibly convincing Jantzen to invest (line 20), any involvement is portrayed as speculation only.

Question 4. The best answer is **H** because the passage presents options I, III, and IV as being true of the townspeople's behavior, as conveyed in lines 50–54. "By the time I got back home the steam-car operation was spoken of with scorn by the people who had been against it and not at all by those who had promoted it. The visitors to town who promoted it had disappeared."

The best answer is NOT:

F because it includes option II, "People in town blamed the loss of money on Jantzen having cheated." This contradicts the point made in lines 55–56: "There was talk not of cheating but of mismanagement."

G because it does not include option I, "Visitors who promoted steam cars had left town," which is made clear in lines 53–54.

J because it includes option II, "People in town blamed the loss of money on Jantzen having cheated." This contradicts information provided in lines 55–56: "There was talk not of cheating but of mismanagement."

Question 5. The best answer is B because lines 14–16 state that times were hard in the Thirties and that people were coming up with ideas to make money. "In the hard times of the Thirties people were still coming up with ideas. You can be sure, men were nursing a notion bound to make them a million dollars." "In the hard times of the Thirties" indicates that times were hard. "Men were nursing a notion bound to make them a million dollars" indicates that people were trying to come up with money-making schemes.

The best answer is NOT:

A because lines 14–16 refer to the 1930s, not to people in their thirties. This is supported by the reference to "those days" in line 17.

C because the lines suggest that men wanted to make a million dollars ("nursing a notion bound to make them a million dollars"), not that they were actually making as much as a million dollars a year.

D because the lines do not indicate or suggest that people felt that they should take their money-making plans to Jantzen. The lines instead capture a general trend in the 1930s, according to the narrator.

Question 6. The best answer is J because *fostering*, a synonym for *nursing*, makes sense in the context of people coming up with new money-making schemes (lines 14–17). In this context, *fostering* means "to promote the growth and development of," which is similar to the meaning of *nursing* as the word is used in the sentence.

The best answer is NOT:

F because *rearing* is not a contextually appropriate synonym for *nursing* as the word is used in the sentence. "To rear" means to support until maturity, usually in the context of people or animals, or to erect by building, which does not make sense in context.

G because *educating* is not a contextually appropriate synonym for *nursing* as the word is used in the sentence. *Educating* usually refers to teaching or informing, which does not make sense in context.

H because *healing* is not a contextually appropriate synonym for *nursing* as the word is used in the sentence. *Healing* typically means *curing*, which does not make sense in context.

Taking Additional Practice Tests

Question 7. The best answer is **A** because as the narrator speculates about who might have convinced Jantzen to invest, he notes Jantzen's admiration of appearances. Lines 21–22: "Well dressed and plausible looking, you may be sure. Horace set store by appearances."

The best answer is NOT:

B because the narrator does not suggest that Jantzen would not have loaned money to someone who wasn't wealthy. The passage implies that the person would have been "well dressed and plausible looking," but the focus is on appearances, not wealth or risk.

C because the narrator does not mention age as a factor Jantzen would have considered, nor does the passage indicate that Jantzen would have trusted someone who had once owned a steam-driven car.

D because the narrator does not indicate the person who convinced Jantzen to invest needed to be intelligent. Instead, the narrator suggests Jantzen would have relied on appearances. "Well dressed and plausible looking, you may be sure. Horace set store by appearances" (lines 21–22). Jantzen himself may not have been "as quick as he should have been to smell a rat" (lines 23–24), which implies he may have been fooled rather easily.

Question 8. The best answer is **F** because the passage makes clear that the new version of the steam-driven car would be an improved version of earlier models. The passage states that the new model would be less expensive and quiet, which suggests that the earlier cars were expensive and noisy. "This new model would be an improved version, of course, and have the advantages of being economical and not making a racket" (lines 28–30).

The best answer is NOT:

G because there is no indication in the passage that the original steam-driven cars were reliable or fast.

H because the passage does not indicate that the original steam-driven cars were unattractive and impractical. Impracticality may be implied since economy is mentioned as a benefit of the new model, but attractiveness is never mentioned.

J because the passage does not indicate that the original steam-driven cars were luxurious or durable.

Question 9. The best answer is **C** because the passage makes clear in lines 38–39 that "the bank had put up the loan." It goes on: "It was Jantzen's decision and there was some confusion that he had put in his own money. He may have done so, but he had also dipped improperly into bank funds, thinking no doubt that he could pay it back with nobody the wiser" (lines 39–43).

The best answer is NOT:

A because the passage does not mention any involvement of "some of Jantzen's wealthy friends."

B because the passage states in lines 40–41 that Jantzen may have invested his own money but does not indicate that this definitely occurred or that it was his entire life savings. The passage bluntly states, however, that he did use bank funds. "But he had also dipped improperly into bank funds, thinking no doubt that he could pay it back with nobody the wiser" (lines 41–43).

D because the passage does not make clear that the entrepreneurs from Toronto, Windsor, or Kitchener referred to in lines 34–35 invested any money. The passage states that "others would ask if they [the entrepreneurs] had backing," and goes on to say that "they did indeed, because the bank had put up the loan" (lines 36–39).

Question 10. The best answer is **G** because lines 65–68 state that it was pride that led Jantzen to agree to take the job at the Hawksburg bank. "Surely he could have refused, but pride, as it was thought, chose otherwise. Pride chose that he be driven every morning those six miles to sit behind a partial wall of cheap varnished boards, no proper office at all."

The best answer is NOT:

F because pride is not presented as a possible reason for Jantzen's decision to invest in steam-driven cars. The narrator speculates that Jantzen may have been swayed by someone plausible looking and also suggests that Jantzen may have had a steam-driven car himself and may have "had a fondness for them" (lines 27–28).

H because the narrator makes it clear that Jantzen did not look unhappy when Oneida drove him to work. Lines 77–80: "I don't see Oneida looking downtrodden or unhappy at the arrangement, nor her father looking actually unhappy. Dignity was what he had, and plenty of it."

J because although the passage notes that Jantzen had to sit in an office made out of varnished boards, the passage does not indicate that Jantzen himself created the office.

Passage II

Question 11. The best answer is C because the paragraph in which the description of the fountain pen appears is about the ways in which plastic allowed designers to embrace "the spirit of modernity" (lines 3–4). In addition, the lines before the mention of the fountain pen suggest that everyday objects, when created out of plastic, could seem exciting. Lines 12–16: ". . . a lingo of curves and dashes and teardrop shapes that created a feeling of speed and motion in everyday objects. Streamline a fountain pen and even that stolid item declared: we're hurtling toward the future here!"

The best answer is NOT:

A because the passage does not mention plastic items looking identical as a result of being streamlined.

B because the passage does not indicate that designers were critiqued for creating items that were beautiful rather than functional.

D because it contradicts the suggestion in the passage that fountain pens were in fact changed by new design trends. Lines 15–16: "Streamline a fountain pen and even that stolid item declared: we're hurtling toward the future here!"

Question 12. The best answer is F because the paragraph notes that plastics allowed designers to create quality designs at lower prices. "There was another reason designers embraced plastics. From the mid-twentieth century on, modern design has been guided by an egalitarian gospel, a belief that good design needn't cost a lot of money" (lines 17–20).

The best answer is NOT:

G because the paragraph mentions only one slogan that was associated with plastics, and the slogan supports the main idea that plastics could be used to create appealing products at low prices.

H because the paragraph does not mention that plastics were challenging to work with.

J because the paragraph does not indicate that designers who embraced plastics prized the mundane over the beautiful. Rather, the idea was that mundane things could be made beautiful.

Question 13. The best answer is A because a number of points in the passage suggest that designers felt that plastics encouraged inventiveness. Lines 2–4: "They loved the design freedom that synthetics offered and the spirit of modernity the materials embodied." Lines 5–10: "Bakelite, the world's first synthetic plastic, spoke 'in the vernacular of the twentieth century . . . the language of invention, of synthesis,' and he [Frankl] urged his fellow designers to use their full imaginative powers to explore the new materials' frank artificiality."

The best answer is NOT:

B because the passage does not mention that consumers demanded attractively designed items.

C because the passage does not indicate that people who created items out of plastics were seen as risk takers.

D because the passage does not suggest or indicate that Bakelite was difficult to work with.

Question 14. The best answer is G because the passage lists a number of examples of items made from plastics that didn't work for the purposes for which they were made. The passage also states that during the 1950s, plastic technology improved, in turn improving the objects that were made from plastics. Lines 37–43: "There were plastic plates that melted in hot water, plastic toys that cracked on Christmas morning, plastic raincoats that grew clammy and fell apart in the rain. Polymer technology improved during the 1950s as manufacturers figured out how to make better plastics and, even more important, how to match the right polymer with the right application."

The best answer is NOT:

F because the passage notes that even in the 1930s and 1940s, plastics could be made to appear streamlined. Lines 10–12: "As interpreted by Frankl and other designers working with Bakelite in the '30s and '40s, that was the language of streamlining."

H because there is no indication that manufacturers had not figured out whether consumers would buy plastics. In fact, the examples listed in the last paragraph (plastic plates, plastic toys, plastic raincoats) suggest that consumers did buy everyday items made of plastics.

J because the first paragraph of the passage notes that designers loved to work with plastics. Lines 1–4: "Designers were enthralled by the universe of possibility from plastics' earliest days. They loved the design freedom that synthetics offered and the spirit of modernity the materials embodied."

Question 15. The best answer is **D** because the lines that come before this statement make it clear that plastics had become part of people's everyday routines. "As *House Beautiful* observed in 1955, 'The news is not that plastics exist, but [that] they have already been so assimilated into our lives.' The average person was 'conditioned to plastics'" (lines 78–82).

The best answer is NOT:

A because the passage does not mention that the production and use of plastics represented increased consumerism.

B because the passage does not indicate that people preferred to buy things made out of plastics over things made out of other materials. The passages stresses that consumers didn't really have a choice because plastic "surrounded everyone" (line 48). "Once plastic products filled the stores, people had no choice but to consume what they were offered" (lines 56–58). "The average person was 'conditioned to plastics'" (lines 81–82).

C because the passage does not indicate that people found plastics to be a threat to traditional ways of life.

Question 16. The best answer is **G** because the passage asserts that "a sleepy householder had to watch only once in disbelief as a polyethylene juice pitcher bounced off the kitchen floor to begin accepting plastic in a practical way no matter how strong the conceptual disdain for it" (lines 66–70). The juice pitcher provides a specific example of plastic's durability, which was enough to overcome "disdain" for the material.

The best answer is NOT:

F because the passage does not indicate that the juice pitcher was part of an advertisement.

H because the paragraph in which the quoted lines appear is not about how plastics improved, but rather about the effects of improvements. As noted in response G, the lines serve as an example of plastic's durability.

J because the lines show how plastic could win people over, not bias people against it. "A sleepy householder had to watch only once in disbelief as a polyethylene juice pitcher bounced off the kitchen floor to begin accepting plastic in a practical way no matter how strong the conceptual disdain for it" (lines 66–70).

Question 17. The best answer is C because the passage specifically describes toys that were made out of plastic as being both less durable and less destructive. Lines 70–74: "Even plastic toys, despite the brittle polystyrene items that broke on Christmas morning, proved superior in many ways. A toy soldier of molded polyethylene could not scratch the furniture as readily as an old-fashioned lead soldier."

The best answer is NOT:

A because the passage does not mention that plastic toys were more flexible and detailed.

B because the passage does not indicate that plastic toys were less costly, and, as noted in response C, they were often less sturdy than nonplastic toys. Lines 70–71: "Even plastic toys, despite the brittle polystyrene items that broke on Christmas morning."

D because the passage does not discuss the relative popularity of plastic toys among kids and parents.

Question 18. The best answer is F because both passages include quotations about plastics, either from designers who used plastics or from publications writing about plastics. Passage A: "To furniture designer Paul T. Frankl, a material like Bakelite, the world's first synthetic plastic, spoke 'in the vernacular of the twentieth century . . . the language of invention, of synthesis'" (lines 4–8). "Plastics' adaptability and glibness undermined their capacity to achieve 'dignity' as legitimate materials worthy of being taken seriously, one critic wrote" (lines 32–34). Passage B: "Sidney Gross, who joined *Modern Plastics* in 1952 and became editor in 1968, recalled that he had 'agitated a lot' over the years to get SPI, the trade association for the plastics industry, to quit trying to convince people 'that plastic is not bad'" (lines 49–53). "As *House Beautiful* observed in 1955, 'The news is not that plastics exist, but [that] they have already been so assimilated into our lives.' The average person was 'conditioned to plastics'" (lines 78–82).

The best answer is NOT:

G because although Passage B refers to *Modern Plastics* and *House Beautiful*, it does not analyze these publications or assert that they promoted plastics. Passage A does not mention publications that promoted plastics.

H because neither passage defines the key concepts that were used to market plastics.

J because neither passage personifies artwork or objects that were made of plastics.

Question 19. The best answer is **D** because both passages indicate that the public believed plastic was interior. Passage A, lines 30–31: "The growing reputation of plastic as an inferior material." Lines 35–40: "This impression was exacerbated by people's unfortunate experiences with plastics in the immediate postwar years. There were plastic plates that melted in hot water, plastic toys that cracked on Christmas morning, plastic raincoats that grew clammy and fell apart in the rain." In Passage B, lines 58–64 indicate that after the plastics industry solved postwar quality problems and plastics worked better, people still held on to the idea that plastic was inferior. "Things made of plastic were better designed and lasted longer. People intuitively recognized that fact even if they retained an intellectual notion that plastic was bad or shoddy."

The best answer is NOT:

A because there is no indication in either passage that people found plastics unattractive in design. In fact, Passage A suggests that items made from plastics could be beautiful. Lines 18–21: "From the mid-twentieth century on, modern design has been guided by an egalitarian gospel, a belief that good design needn't cost a lot of money, that even the most mundane items could be things of beauty." Passage B does not discuss plastics' aesthetic qualities.

B because although plastics' artificiality is mentioned in Passage A, it is not suggested that this is unnerving, but rather that it is something to be embraced. Lines 8–10: "He urged his fellow designers to use their full imaginative powers to explore the new materials' frank artificiality." Passage B does not discuss plastics' artificiality.

C because Passage A notes that plastics were relatively inexpensive. Lines 24–26: "Plastics were the ideal medium for that mission: malleable, relatively inexpensive, and made for mass manufacture." Passage B does not discuss the cost of plastics. Moreover, neither passage indicates that the public believed items made of plastics were "novelties."

Question 20. **The best answer is J** because both passages use toys as an example of problems with the quality of plastics. In Passage A, the example follows a paragraph that asserts plastic's reputation as an inferior material. Lines 35–40: "This impression [that plastics were inferior] was exacerbated by people's unfortunate experiences with plastics in the immediate postwar years. There were plastic plates that melted in hot water, plastic toys that cracked on Christmas morning, plastic raincoats that grew clammy and fell apart in the rain." The passage goes on to assert that technology improved during the 1950s, but "the damage to plastic's reputation had been done" (lines 43–44). In Passage B, toys also provide an example of a flaw. Lines 70–72: "Even plastic toys, despite the brittle polystyrene items that broke on Christmas morning, proved superior in many ways." In this case, despite the problem with quality ("brittle polystyrene items that broke on Christmas morning"), plastic could be superior in other ways ("not scratch the furniture").

The best answer is NOT:

F because although Passage B notes that plastic items could be superior to what they replaced ("Even plastic toys, despite the brittle polystyrene items that broke on Christmas morning, proved superior in many ways"), Passage A uses toys as an example of bad design, not good design. Lines 35–40: "This impression was exacerbated by people's unfortunate experiences with plastics in the immediate postwar years. There were plastic plates that melted in hot water, plastic toys that cracked on Christmas morning, plastic raincoats that grew clammy and fell apart in the rain."

G because Passage A does not mention that plastic toys were particularly popular, and the example of toys in Passage B is used to demonstrate both quality problems and plastics' superiority.

H because, in both passages, the example of toys is provided to show problems with plastics, not the variety of plastic items that were produced. Passage A: "This impression was exacerbated by people's unfortunate experiences with plastics in the immediate postwar years. There were . . . plastic toys that cracked on Christmas morning" (lines 35–39). Passage B: ". . . plastic toys, despite the brittle polyethylene items that broke on Christmas morning" (lines 70–71).

Passage III

Question 21. The best answer is C because the paragraph tells a story that is narrated in a biography of García Márquez. The author of the passage specifically notes this at the beginning of the second paragraph. "When Gerald Martin, around the middle of his rich and resourceful biography of García Márquez, starts to tell this story" (lines 9–11).

The best answer is NOT:

A because as noted in response C, the paragraph tells the story of García Márquez's writing the novel. The paragraph does not mention misconceptions about how long it took to write *One Hundred Years of Solitude*.

B because the paragraph describes only the circumstances surrounding García Márquez's writing one particular novel, not novels in general.

D because the paragraph does not discuss García Márquez's childhood at all.

Question 22. The best answer is F because the author of the passage specifically states that he believes García Márquez to be a gifted writer. Lines 44–46: "When he got into the car to set out for Acapulco, he was a gifted and hardworking writer, certainly."

The best answer is NOT:

G because although the passage mentions García Márquez's journalism, there is no mention in the passage that the author preferred his journalism to his novels.

H because although the author of the passage notes that García Márquez's novels borrow from local facts and legends, there is no indication that he thinks García Márquez does so too much. Lines 61–66: "It takes pieces of already thoroughly mythified reality—there is scarcely an extravagant incident in his novels and stories that doesn't have some sort of basis in specific, local fact or legend—and finds the perfect, unforgettable literary home for them."

J because the author of the passage refers to Martin's insistence on excessive melancholy, not García Márquez's. Lines 83–87: "There is perhaps a slight imbalance in Martin's insistence on the writer's sadness, an excess of melancholy; but it's a good corrective to García Márquez's own joking cheerfulness and elaborate ironies."

Question 23. The best answer is A because in the first paragraph of the passage, it is made clear that the "illumination" is referring to García Márquez's writing of the novel. "Many years later, and many times over, the writer Gabriel García Márquez was to remember the day he discovered how to set about writing his great novel. He was driving from Mexico City to Acapulco when the illumination hit him" (lines 1–5). When the word is used again in line 37, it is in reference to the story that is first told in the first paragraph.

The best answer is NOT:

B because the passage notes that García Márquez directly stated that he modeled an aspect of his writing after Kafka's, not that Martin discovered this. Lines 31–34: "What García Márquez found was a way of telling it. He would combine, as he frequently said, the narrative tone of his grandmother with that of the author Franz Kafka."

C because the reference to "illumination" occurs well before the passage author notes that García Márquez based his stories on local facts and legends, and also because the use of "illumination," as noted in response A, is in reference to García Márquez, not the passage's author.

D because there is no indication in the passage that García Márquez considered his completion of *One Hundred Years of Solitude* miraculous. As noted in response A, the use of "illumination" refers to García Márquez's discovery of "how to set about writing his great novel" (line 3).

Question 24. The best answer is H because Martin interrupts the story about García Márquez to claim that it is not true. Lines 9–12: "When Gerald Martin, around the middle of his rich and resourceful biography of García Márquez, starts to tell this story, the reader may be a little surprised, even disappointed." Lines 22–26: "After 'and then,' Martin writes in mock apology, 'It seems a pity to intervene in the story at this point but the biographer feels constrained to point out that there have been many versions of this story . . . and that the one just related cannot be true.'"

The best answer is NOT:

F because there is no indication in the passage that García Márquez preferred to write in seclusion.

G because the passage does not indicate that Martin's biography of García Márquez focuses on analyzing his novels rather than on discussing the author's development as a writer.

J because, as noted in response H, the disappointment the reader might feel is in reference to the story not being true, not to the lack of information about why García Márquez drove back to Mexico City. In addition, later in the passage Martin notes that García Márquez probably did not drive back to Mexico City. Lines 27–28: "The writer probably continued to Acapulco."

Question 25. The best answer is **B** because *compelled* means "urged forcefully or irresistibly," which makes it a contextually appropriate synonym of *constrained* here. Martin feels as if he must point out that the story cannot be true.

The best answer is NOT:

A because *restrain* means to hold back from, and the author is not holding back from pointing out that "there have been many versions of this story . . . and that the one just related cannot be true" (lines 25–26).

C because *coerced* implies being persuaded by outside forces, and there is no indication in the passage that Martin had to be persuaded by someone else to share the truth about García Márquez's story.

D because *limited* means confined or restricted, and there is no indication in the passage that Martin felt that his options were restricted.

Question 26. The best answer is **G** because the passage specifically notes that García Márquez's grandmother believed the stories she told were true. Lines 32–35: "He would combine, as he frequently said, the narrative tone of his grandmother with that of the author Franz Kafka. She told fantastic stories as if they were true, because for her, they were true."

The best answer is NOT:

F because the passage notes that García Márquez imitated Kafka, not that his grandmother did. Lines 32–34: "He would combine, as he frequently said, the narrative tone of his grandmother with that of the author Franz Kafka."

H because there is no indication in the passage that García Márquez's grandmother hoped to become a successful author.

J because the passage states that García Márquez learned from his grandmother, not that his grandmother learned from him. Lines 32–34: "He would combine, as he frequently said, the narrative tone of his grandmother with that of the author Franz Kafka."

Question 27. The best answer is **C** because the passage notes that García Márquez made jokes that indicated his gratitude for his life. "García Márquez made many jokes about his fame over the years. These jokes are witty and complicated acts of gratitude for a destiny the writer was sure could have been quite different" (lines 49–52).

The best answer is NOT:

A because there is no mention in the passage that García Márquez ever hoped that his best work had yet to be written.

B because there is no mention in the passage that García Márquez was ever concerned that his accomplishments had been distorted by others.

D because there is no mention in the passage that García Márquez ever believed that he deserved more credit for his wit and the complexity of his writing.

Question 28. The best answer is **J** because the passage cites a quotation by García Márquez that suggests he believed he might have been a better person if he had stayed in Aracataca. "One of his finest sentences, written in an article in 1983, concerns a dream of the life he might have led if he had stayed in his isolated birthplace of Aracataca, Colombia. 'I would not perhaps be the same person I am now but maybe I would have been something better: just a character in one of the novels I would never have written'" (lines 52–58).

The best answer is NOT:

F because there is no indication in the passage that García Márquez ever stated that he should have written *One Hundred Years of Solitude* sooner.

G because there is no indication in the passage that García Márquez ever stated that he wished he had completed his journey to Acapulco. In addition, the passage suggests that García Márquez did complete his journey. Lines 27–28: "The writer probably continued to Acapulco."

H because there is no indication in the passage that García Márquez ever wished he had taken his fame less seriously.

Question 29. The best answer is **B** because the passage author directly states that the biography helps balance García Márquez's joking cheerfulness and elaborate ironies. Lines 83–88: "There is perhaps a slight imbalance in Martin's insistence on the writer's sadness, an excess of melancholy; but it's a good corrective to García Márquez's own joking cheerfulness and elaborate ironies, and we can return to the master if we get too depressed."

The best answer is NOT:

A because, as noted in response B, the author directly states that the biography helps balance García Márquez's joking cheerfulness and elaborate ironies.

C because, as noted in response B, the author directly states that the biography helps balance García Márquez's joking cheerfulness and elaborate ironies.

D because, as noted in response B, the author directly states that the biography helps balance García Márquez's joking cheerfulness and elaborate ironies.

Question 30. The best answer is **J** because in this context, *master* refers to García Márquez, who is referenced earlier in the sentence. Lines 83–88: "There is perhaps a slight imbalance in Martin's insistence on the writer's sadness, an excess of melancholy; but it's a good corrective to García Márquez's own joking cheerfulness and elaborate ironies, and we can return to the master if we get too depressed." The passage author is asserting that we can return to the master himself, García Márquez, when Martin's biography seems too dark.

The best answer is NOT:

F because, as noted in response J, in this context, *master* refers to García Márquez, who is referenced earlier in the sentence. Lines 83–88: "There is perhaps a slight imbalance in Martin's insistence on the writer's sadness, an excess of melancholy; but it's a good corrective to García Márquez's own joking cheerfulness and elaborate ironies, and we can return to the master if we get too depressed." If the passage author were referring to himself here, it would not make sense in context.

G because, as noted in response J, in this context, *master* refers to García Márquez, who is referenced earlier in the sentence. Lines 83–88: "There is perhaps a slight imbalance in Martin's insistence on the writer's sadness, an excess of melancholy; but it's a good corrective to García Márquez's own joking cheerfulness and elaborate ironies, and we can return to the master if we get too depressed." García Márquez's joking cheerfulness is in contrast to Martin's melancholy.

H because, as noted in response J, in this context, *master* refers to García Márquez, who is referenced earlier in the sentence. Lines 83–88: "There is perhaps a slight imbalance in Martin's insistence on the writer's sadness, an excess of melancholy; but it's a good corrective to García Márquez's own joking cheerfulness and elaborate ironies, and we can return to the master if we get too depressed." The reference to Kafka comes much earlier in the passage, and therefore does not make sense in this context.

Passage IV

Question 31. The best answer is B because the passage explains how increasingly large distances were measured throughout history. The first sentence of the passage helps establish the overall organization: "One measure of the progress of human civilization is the increasing scale of our maps." What follows is a series of historical examples to illustrate this idea. The first paragraph describes a map from the twenty-fifth century B.C. showing a thirty-acre plot of land; the second paragraph describes Eratosthenes's process for measuring the circumference of Earth in the third century B.C.; the third paragraph describes Richer's measurement of the distance between Earth and Mars in 1672; the fourth paragraph describes Newton's measurement of the distance between Earth and the nearest stars. Each example is of an increasingly large distance.

The best answer is NOT:

A because the passage is about more than just attempts to determine the distance of stars from Earth. As noted in response B, the passage describes attempts to measure distance on Earth as well as distances from Earth to other objects in the universe.

C because although the passage does include an explanation of the calculations used by Eratosthenes to measure Earth's circumference, this is limited to one paragraph. It does not describe the passage as a whole.

D because "collection of anecdotes" doesn't capture how the passage moves through historical examples of increasingly large distances. Response B more accurately captures the passage's overall organization.

Question 32. The best answer is H because the paragraph presents examples of the ways in which humans' understanding of their surroundings expanded over time. The first sentence of the paragraph, "One measure of the progress of human civilization is the increasing scale of our maps" (lines 1–2), suggests that the paragraph will discuss this expansion. The paragraph begins with an example of a relatively small scale and proceeds with examples that show how this scale broadened.

The best answer is NOT:

F because the paragraph does not discuss Eratosthenes or the time period in which he made his calculations.

G because there is no discussion in the paragraph of early geographers concluding that Earth was curved.

J because although the paragraph acknowledges the ancient Greeks, it does not summarize all of their contributions to astronomy. Instead, the information is included to show how humans' understanding of their surroundings expanded over time, as noted in response H.

Question 33. The best answer is B because the passage notes that these models of the universe did not include size or scale of objects. Lines 6–10: "In the earliest recorded cosmologies, such as the Babylonian *Enuma Elish*, from around 1500 B.C., the oceans, the continents, and the heavens were considered finite, but there were no scientific estimates of their dimensions." Lines 10–13: "The early Greeks, including Homer, viewed Earth as a circular plane with the ocean enveloping it and Greece at the center, but there was no understanding of scale." Lines 13–18: "In the early sixth century B.C., the Greek philosopher Anaximander, whom historians consider the first mapmaker, and his student Anaximenes proposed that the stars were attached to a giant crystalline sphere. But again there was no estimate of its size."

The best answer is NOT:

A because the passage notes that in at least one of the models, the universe was considered finite. "In the earliest recorded cosmologies, such as the Babylonian *Enuma Elish*, from around 1500 B.C., the oceans, the continents, and the heavens were considered finite, but there were no scientific estimates of their dimensions" (lines 6–10).

C because there is no mention in these lines of any similarities between ancient models of the universe and modern maps.

D because only one of the examples of the ancient models of the universe is noted to have positioned the citizens' homelands at the center of the universe. "The early Greeks, including Homer, viewed Earth as a circular plane with the ocean enveloping it and Greece at the center, but there was no understanding of scale" (lines 10–13).

Question 34. The best answer is F because the passage notes that we do not have sufficient experience to relate to the distance from Earth to the nearest stars. "Newton's estimate of the distance to nearby stars was larger than any distance imagined before in human history. Even today, nothing in our experience allows us to relate to it" (lines 77–80). The examples that follow in the paragraph help illustrate this point.

The best answer is NOT:

G because it contradicts the paragraph's point that even advancements in space travel would not make the distance from Earth to the nearest stars seem small. In fact, the passage notes that "if we traveled in the fastest rocket ship ever manufactured on Earth, the trip would last 100,000 years, at least a thousand human life spans" (lines 84–86).

H because the last paragraph is not about when the distance was calculated. Rather, the paragraph is about how far this distance is—so far that nothing in our experience allows us to relate to it.

J because the paragraph does not indicate that Newton's estimate of the distance between Earth and the nearest stars was incorrect.

Question 35. The best answer is **A** according to lines 10–13: "The early Greeks, including Homer, viewed Earth as a circular plane with the ocean enveloping it and Greece at the center, but there was no understanding of scale."

The best answer is NOT:

B because it was Anaximander and Anaximenes who described Earth as a giant crystalline sphere with stars attached. "In the early sixth century B.C., the Greek philosopher Anaximander, whom historians consider the first mapmaker, and his student Anaximenes proposed that the stars were attached to a giant crystalline sphere" (lines 13–17).

C because the passage mentions 7.2 degrees in relation to Eratosthenes's work to calculate the circumference of Earth. "Eratosthenes knew that the sun was not overhead at noon in Alexandria. In fact, it was tipped 7.2 degrees from the vertical, or about one fiftieth of a circle" (lines 30–32).

D because the measurement of a plot of land 354 *iku* in size was recorded well before the time of the ancient Greeks. "A clay tablet dating from about the twenty-fifth century B.C. found near what is now the Iraqi city of Kirkuk depicts a river valley with a plot of land labeled as being 354 *iku* (about thirty acres) in size" (lines 2–6).

Question 36. The best answer is **J** because the passage states, "Eratosthenes reasoned that if he knew the distance from Alexandria to Syene, the full circumference of the planet must be about fifty times that distance. Traders passing through Alexandria told him that camels could make the trip to Syene in about fifty days, and it was known that a camel could cover one hundred stadia (almost eleven and a half miles) in a day" (lines 36–43). This information suggests that Eratosthenes needed to know the time it took camels to travel between the cities and how far they could travel in a day.

The best answer is NOT:

F because the passage notes that Eratosthenes used information about the curvature of Earth and the angle of the sun to calculate the circumference of Earth, not the distance between Syene and Alexandria.

G because the passage notes that Eratosthenes used his knowledge of the distance between Syene and Alexandria to calculate the circumference of Earth. Lines 36–39: "Eratosthenes reasoned that if he knew the distance from Alexandria to Syene, the full circumference of the planet must be about fifty times that distance." He could not know Earth's circumference until he knew the distance between these cities.

H because, as noted in response F, Eratosthenes used information about the height of the sun at noon in each city and the length of shadows cast on the ground to calculate the circumference of Earth, not to calculate the distance between Syene and Alexandria.

Question 37. The best answer is **C** because the passage suggests that the distance from Earth to other points in the solar system could not be calculated until the telescope was invented. "As ingenious as they were, the ancient Greeks were not able to calculate the size of our solar system. That discovery had to wait for the invention of the telescope, nearly two thousand years later" (lines 50–53).

The best answer is NOT:

A because there is no mention in the passage that astronomers needed to find proper observation points before they could determine the distance between Earth and other points in the solar system.

B because there is no mention in the passage of astronomers using ancient Greek calculations to determine the distance between Earth and other objects in the solar system.

D because there is no mention in the passage that Earth and Mars had to align for astronomers to calculate the distance from Earth to other points in the solar system.

Question 38. The best answer is **J** because the passage indicates that Newton's calculation of the distance to the nearest stars was less acknowledged than his other work. "Only someone as accomplished as Newton could have been the first to perform such a calculation and have it go almost unnoticed among his other achievements" (lines 63–66). "Almost unnoticed among his other achievements" suggests that this calculation was less acknowledged than other achievements.

The best answer is NOT:

F because the passage indicates that Newton's calculation was "almost unnoticed among his other achievements" (lines 65–66). This suggests that his other achievements were considered more important.

G because there's no indication in the passage that this work was speculative or that it was more speculative than Newton's other work.

H because there's no indication in the passage that this work was not complete or that it was less complete than Newton's other work.

Question 39. The best answer is **A** because the language used to describe how Newton wrote his calculation emphasizes the time period in which he worked and how old-fashioned his tools seemed, particularly in the context of describing an advanced, complicated calculation: "Writing his computations in a spidery script, with a quill dipped in the ink of oak galls" (lines 70–71). Newton was calculating the distance of stars ten trillion miles away while using a rudimentary writing tool.

The best answer is NOT:

B because there is no indication in the passage of how long Newton's calculation took, much less that it took a long time to decipher.

C because there is no description in the passage of the artistic flourishes in the section of Newton's *Principia* in which the calculation appears.

D because there is no mention in the passage of the mistakes Newton made when calculating the distance between Earth and the nearest stars.

Question 40. The best answer is **H** because the paragraph is about travel and distance. The lines before *set out* help make this clear. "The fastest most of us have traveled is about 500 miles per hour, the cruising speed of a jet. If we set out for the nearest star beyond our solar system at that speed, it would take us about 5 million years to reach our destination" (lines 80–84).

The best answer is NOT:

F because the sentence is about travel, not about a vision. "Described a vision" doesn't make sense in this context.

G because the sentence is about travel, not about stating a purpose. "Stated a purpose" doesn't make sense in this context.

J because the sentence is about travel, not about creating an arrangement. "Created an arrangement" doesn't make sense in this context.

Passage I

1. **The best answer is C.** According to Table 1, at 45°C after a 75 min resting time, a 1.0% aqueous mixture of Gum W has a viscosity of 6,825 cP, an aqueous mixture of Gum X has a viscosity of 3,462 cP, an aqueous mixture of Gum Y has a viscosity of 1,639 cP, and an aqueous mixture of Gum Z has a viscosity of 1,562 cP. The viscosity decreases from Gum W to X to Y to Z. **A, B,** and **D** are incorrect; these graphs do not show the correct trend of decreasing viscosity. **C** is correct.

2. **The best answer is H.** According to Table 1, for a given temperature, the viscosity of a gum mixture increased as the rest time increased. A 1.0% mixture of Gum Y at 65°C had a viscosity of 802 cP after a resting time of 75 min and a viscosity of 1,075 cP after a resting time of 102 min. One would predict that after a resting time of 100 min, the viscosity would most likely be between 802 cP and 1,075 cP. **F** and **G** are incorrect; the viscosity would be greater than 800 cP. **H** is correct. **J** is incorrect; the viscosity would be less than 1,100 cP.

3. **The best answer is C.** According to Figure 1, for a gum concentration of 2.0%, Gum Z had the lowest viscosity, followed by Gum X, then Gum W. Gum Y had the highest viscosity. **A** and **B** are incorrect; the 2.0% mixture of Gum Z had the lowest viscosity. **C** is correct. **D** is incorrect; the 2.0% mixture of Gum Y had the highest viscosity.

4. **The best answer is F.** According to Figure 1, a 1.3% aqueous mixture of Gum W had the highest viscosity, greater than 10,000 cP. **F** is correct. **G** is incorrect; the viscosity of a 1.3% aqueous mixture of Gum X was less than 10,000 cP. **H** is incorrect; the viscosity of a 1.3% aqueous mixture of Gum Y was less than 10,000 cP. **J** is incorrect; the viscosity of a 1.3% aqueous mixture of Gum Z was less than 10,000 cP.

5. **The best answer is B.** According to Table 1, the viscosity of the aqueous gum mixtures decreased as the temperature increased. A 1.0% aqueous mixture of Gum Z at 25°C and a resting time of 75 min had a viscosity of 1,879 cP, and a similar solution at 45°C had a viscosity of 1,562 cP. One would predict that a 1.0% aqueous mixture of Gum Z at 30°C and a resting time of 75 min would have a viscosity between 1,562 cP and 1,879 cP. **A** is incorrect; the viscosity would be greater than 1,562 cP. **B** is correct. **C** and **D** are incorrect; the viscosity would be less than 1,879 cP.

6. **The best answer is H.** According to Figure 1, Gum Y had a viscosity of 100,000 cP at a gum concentration of approximately 2.2%. Gums X and Y did not have a viscosity of 100,000 cP until their concentrations were greater than 2.5%. The viscosity of Gum Z did not reach 100,000 cP even at a gum concentration of 3.0%. Gum Y had a viscosity of 100,000 cP at a lower concentration than any of the other 3 gums. **F** is incorrect; Gum W had a viscosity of 100,000 cP at a concentration greater than 2.5%. **G** is incorrect; Gum X had a viscosity of 100,000 cP at a concentration greater than 2.5%. **H** is correct; Gum Y had a viscosity of 100,000 cP at a concentration of approximately 2.25%. **J** is incorrect; Gum Z did not have a viscosity of 100,000 cP at any concentration.

Passage II

7. **The best answer is C.** According to Figure 1, a 60% BD by volume sample would have an A of approximately 0.6 at 1,746 cm^{-1}. **A** and **B** are incorrect; A would be greater than 0.55. **C** is correct. **D** is incorrect; A would be less than 0.65.

8. **The best answer is F.** According to Figure 2, as the percent by volume of BD increased, A at 1,746 cm^{-1} also increased. **F** is correct. **G, H,** and **J** are incorrect; A increased only.

9. **The best answer is A.** According to Figure 2, as the percent BD by volume decreased, A at 1,746 cm^{-1} also decreased. The fuel sample in Study 3 with the smallest A would be that with the lowest percent BD by volume. Sample W had the lowest percent BD by volume. **A** is correct; the percent BD by volume for Sample W was 4.0%. **B** is incorrect; the percent BD by volume for Sample X was 6.0%. **C** is incorrect; the percent BD by volume for Sample Y was 4.8%. **D** is incorrect; the percent BD by volume for Sample Z was 4.7%.

10. **The best answer is H.** In order to answer this item, the examinee must know that a catalyst is not a reactant or a product and how to write a chemical equation. According to the passage, soybean oil and methanol react in the presence of a catalyst to form FAMEs. Soybean oil and methanol are the reactants, and FAMEs are the products. **F, G,** and **J** are incorrect; FAMEs should appear on the product side of the equation. **H** is correct.

11. **The best answer is B.** In order to gain useful information from the absorbance data for Study 2, the students had to measure the absorbance at a wavenumber at which either BD or PD, but not both, absorbed strongly. According to Figure 1, BD absorbed strongly at 1,172 cm^{-1} and PD did not, while both BD and PD absorbed at 1,464 cm^{-1}. The students would most likely have measured the absorbance in Study 2 at 1,172 cm^{-1}. **A** is incorrect; BD absorbed strongly at 1,172 cm^{-1}, and PD did not. **B** is correct. **C** and **D** are incorrect; a wavenumber of 1,172 cm^{-1} would have been a better choice.

12. **The best answer is J.** According to the passage, BD contained FAMEs and PD did not. Figure 1 shows that BD did not strongly absorb light at a wavenumber of 900 cm^{-1} but did absorb at 1,250 cm^{-1}. A sample that contained only FAMEs would show the same absorbance behavior. **F** and **G** are incorrect; the sample would more strongly absorb at a wavenumber of 1,250 cm^{-1}. **H** is incorrect; PD does not contain FAMEs. **J** is correct.

13. **The best answer is A.** In order to answer this item, the examinee must know that there are 1,000 mL in 1 L. According to Table 1, Sample Y is 4.8% BD by volume. A 10 L sample would therefore contain approximately 0.05×10 L = 0.5 L of BD, which is equal to $0.5 \text{ L} \times \frac{1000 \text{ mL}}{1 \text{ L}} = 500$ mL. **A** is correct. **B** is incorrect; 0.5 L = 500 mL. **C** and **D** are incorrect; the sample would contain 0.5 L of BD.

Passage III

14. **The best answer is H.** According to Figure 1, the inner core is approximately 1,200 km thick, the outer core is approximately 2,300 km thick, the lower mantle is approximately 2,200 km thick, and the upper mantle/crust is approximately 600 km thick. The outer core and lower mantle are most similar in thickness. **F, G,** and **J** are incorrect; the outer core and lower mantle are most similar, with thicknesses of approximately 2,300 km and 2,200 km, respectively. **H** is correct.

15. **The best answer is A.** Figure 2 shows that the innermost 30% of Earth's mass is located between $r = 0$ km and $r = 3,400$ km. **A** is correct. **B** is incorrect; just under 40% of Earth's mass is located between $r = 0$ km and $r = 3,900$ km. **C** is incorrect; approximately 50% of Earth's mass is located between $r = 0$ km and $r = 4,500$ km. **D** is incorrect; 70% of Earth's mass is located between $r = 0$ km and $r = 5,300$ km.

16. **The best answer is J.** According to Figure 1, the crust ends and the atmosphere begins at $r = 6,400$ km. Figure 2 shows that 100% of Earth's mass is located within 6,400 km of the center of Earth. From both figures, it can be concluded that Earth's radius is approximately 6,400 km. **F** is incorrect; 1,400 km is the radius of the inner core. **G** is incorrect; 3,500 km is the distance from the center of Earth to the edge of the outer core. **H** is incorrect; 5,700 km is the distance from the center of Earth to the edge of the lower mantle. **J** is correct; 6,400 km is the distance from the center of Earth to Earth's surface.

17. **The best answer is C.** According to Figure 2, throughout the atmosphere and into space, as the distance from the center of Earth increases, the strength of the gravitational field decreases. At $r = 13,000$ km, $g_E =$ approximately 2.4 N/kg. Based on the rate at which g_E was decreasing, at $r = 14,000$ km, g_E would most likely be close to 2.0 N/kg. **A** and **B** are incorrect; g_E would most likely be greater than 1.5 N/kg. **C** is correct. **D** is incorrect; g_E would most likely be less than 2.5 N/kg.

18. **The best answer is F.** According to Figure 2, the outermost 400 km contains 10% of Earth's mass. Earth's crust, the outermost 30 km, therefore contains much less than 10% of Earth's mass. **F** is correct. **G** is incorrect; the outermost 400 km contains 10% of Earth's mass. **H** is incorrect; the outermost 4,000 km contains 90% of Earth's mass. **J** is incorrect; 99% of Earth's mass in contained in the outermost 5,400 km.

19. **The best answer is A.** In order to answer this item, the examinee must know that weight is directly proportional to gravitational field strength. According to Figure 1, at $r = 2,000$ km, $g_E = 7$ N/kg, and at $r = 4,000$ km, $g_E = 10.2$ N/kg. Because the strength of the gravitational field is less at $r = 2,000$ km, the rock will weigh less at $r = 2,000$ km than at $r = 4,000$ km. **A** is correct. **B** is incorrect; the rock located at $r = 4,000$ km will weigh more. **C** is incorrect; because the rocks have identical masses, the rock in the stronger gravitational field will weigh more. **D** is incorrect; the value of g_E is not the same at both locations.

Passage IV

20. **The best answer is G.** According to the passage, Student 1 stated that biological aging is caused by ROS produced by cellular respiration. Student 4 stated that biological aging is caused by lipofuscin produced by cellular respiration. Neither Student 2 nor Student 3 claimed that the cause of biological aging is related to cellular respiration. **F** is incorrect; Student 4 also claimed that biological aging is caused by a substance produced by cellular respiration. **G** is correct; Students 1 and 4 claimed that biological aging is caused by a substance produced by cellular respiration. **H** is incorrect; Students 2 and 3 did not claim that the cause of biological aging is related to cellular respiration. **J** is incorrect; Students 1 and 4 made the claim about cellular respiration.

21. **The best answer is B.** Student 2 claimed that biological aging is caused by cross-links formed between proteins in the cell. Cross-links are a type of chemical bond. None of the other students' explanations involved the formation of chemical bonds between proteins. The finding would be most consistent with the explanation given by Student 2. **A** is incorrect; Student 1 claimed that biological aging is caused by ROS. **B** is correct. **C** is incorrect; Student 3 claimed that biological aging is caused by DNA damage and that cross-linked proteins do not affect cell function. **D** is incorrect; Student 4 claimed that biological aging is caused by lipofuscin and that cross-linked proteins do not accumulate in the cell.

22. **The best answer is F.** In order to answer this item, the examinee must know that proteins are composed of amino acids. Student 2 claimed that biological aging is caused by cross-linking between proteins. **F** is correct. **G** is incorrect; fatty acids are not found in proteins. **H** is incorrect; monosaccharides are not found in proteins. **J** is incorrect; nucleotides are found in DNA, not proteins.

23. **The best answer is B.** Student 2 claimed that the accumulation of protein clumps formed by cross-linking of the proteins causes biological aging. Student 2 would most likely predict that a substance that prevents cross-linking would be present in a greater concentration in the cells of young adults where less cross-linking is found. **A** is incorrect; Student 1 did not address cross-linking of proteins in their explanation. **B** is correct. **C** is incorrect; Student 3 claimed that cross-linked proteins do not affect cell function. **D** is incorrect; Student 4 claimed that protein clumps do not accumulate in the cell.

24. **The best answer is G.** According to the passage, Student 2 claimed that biological aging is due to protein cross-linking that forms clumps of protein. Student 4 claimed that biological aging is due to lipofuscin that forms clumps. **F** is incorrect; Student 1 claimed that biological aging is due to ROS that damage proteins and lipids in a cell. **G** is correct. **H** and **J** are incorrect; Student 1 claimed that biological aging is due to ROS that damage proteins and lipids in a cell, and Student 3 claimed that biological aging is due to DNA damage.

SCIENCE • PRACTICE TEST 3 • EXPLANATORY ANSWERS

25. **The best answer is D.** According to the passage, Student 1 claimed that biological aging is due to ROS that damage proteins and lipids in the cell. Antioxidants eliminate ROS before they cause damage; however, the cell does not produce enough antioxidants to eliminate all the ROS. **A** and **B** are incorrect; Student 1's explanation did not involve cross-linked proteins. **C** is incorrect; this observation would weaken Student 1's explanation. **D** is correct.

26. **The best answer is G.** In order to answer this item, the examinee must know that genetic mutations are caused by DNA damage. According to the passage, only Student 3 claimed that damage to the DNA is responsible for biological aging. The finding that a mutagen does not affect aging would weaken Student 3's explanation. **F** is incorrect; Student 2 claimed that biological aging is caused by cross-linked proteins, and the finding would not weaken their explanation. **G** is correct. **H** is incorrect; Student 1 claimed that biological aging is caused by ROS, and the finding would not weaken their explanation. **J** is incorrect; Student 2 claimed that biological aging is caused by cross-linked proteins, and Student 4 claimed that DNA damage is not a factor in biological aging. The finding would weaken neither Student 2's nor Student 4's explanation.

Passage V

27. **The best answer is D.** According to Figure 1, the greatest percent of DOC adsorbed by CM1 was adsorbed from the pine leachate. According to Figure 2, the greatest percent of DOC adsorbed by CM2 was adsorbed from the magnolia leachate. Figure 3 shows that the greatest percent of DOC adsorbed by CM3 was adsorbed from the magnolia leachate. **A** and **B** are incorrect; the greatest percent of DOC from the pine leachate was adsorbed by CM1. **C** is incorrect; the greatest percent of DOC from the magnolia leachate was adsorbed by CM3. **D** is correct.

28. **The best answer is J.** According to Figure 3, the percent of leachate DOC adsorbed by CM3 varied from 32% to 56%. The average was 42%, but one can estimate that it must have been between 30% and 56%. **F, G,** and **H** are incorrect; the average was greater than 30%. **J** is correct.

29. **The best answer is C.** According to Figure 2, CM2 adsorbed 7% of the DOC in the maple leachate. Figure 3 shows that CM3 adsorbed 35% of the DOC in the maple leachate. The results of Studies 2 and 3 do not support the statement. A greater percentage of DOC in the maple leachate was adsorbed by CM3 than by CM2. **A** and **B** are incorrect; the results do not support the statement. **C** is correct. **D** is incorrect; CM2 adsorbed 7% and CM3 adsorbed 35% of the DOC in the maple leachate.

30. **The best answer is G.** In each study, 5 different types of leaf leachate were used. Each study used 1 type of clay mineral, but a different type of clay mineral was used in each study. **F** is incorrect; the type of lake water used was the same in all studies. **G** is correct. **H** is incorrect; the volume of leaf leachate was the same in all studies. **J** is incorrect; the volume of filtrate was not varied in each study.

31. **The best answer is D.** According to Figure 1, CM1 reduced the DOC in the oak leachate by 31%. Figure 2 shows that CM2 reduced the DOC in the oak leachate by 23%, and Figure 3 shows that CM3 reduced the DOC in the oak leachate by 50%. None of the clay minerals reduced the DOC in the oak leachate by more than 50%. **A, B,** and **C** are incorrect; all clay minerals reduced the DOC in the oak leachate by 50% or less. **D** is correct.

32. **The best answer is J.** In order to answer this item, the examinee must be able to distinguish between a suspension and a solution. According to the passage, in each of the studies, the leachate was prepared by mixing filtered lake water with a sample of leaves. After time was allowed for leaching, the mixture was filtered to remove all solid particles. The leachate was then mixed with the clay mineral. After 2 hours of stirring, the mixture was filtered to remove all solid particles. The presence of solid particles in the mixture indicated that the mixture was a suspension and not a solution. **F** and **G** are incorrect; the mixture was not a solution. **H** is incorrect; the clay mineral particles were not dissolved in the leachate. **J** is correct.

33. **The best answer is A.** According to the passage, the leachate was prepared by allowing the mixture of lake water and leaves to sit for 10 weeks at 4°C in the dark. Keeping the mixture in the dark ensured that none of the DOC would be broken down by electromagnetic energy in the visible wavelength range (i.e., light). **A** is correct. **B** is incorrect; the filtrate and clay mineral were not placed in the dark. **C** is incorrect; filtering the mixture of leaves and lake water would not prevent the breakdown of DOC by visible light. **D** is incorrect; filtering the leachate and clay mineral would not prevent the breakdown of DOC by visible light.

Passage VI

34. **The best answer is H.** According to the passage, all eight Petri dishes were set up in the same way. PD5 was turned 90° so that the dish was vertical. **F** and **G** are incorrect; the Petri dishes shown are both in a vertical orientation, indicating that they have been turned and are not in their original orientation. **H** is correct. **J** is incorrect; the Petri dish would have to be right side up when the experiment was set up, and at no time was the dish inverted.

35. **The best answer is D.** According to Experiment 2, PD8 contained M *Arabidopsis* seeds and was exposed to light from above for 70 hr. **A** is incorrect; PD1 contained WT *Arabidopsis* seeds and was placed in the dark for 70 hr. **B** is incorrect; PD2 contained WT *Arabidopsis* seeds. **C** is incorrect; PD3 was placed in the dark for 70 hr. **D** is correct; PD4 contained M *Arabidopsis* seeds and was exposed to light from above for 70 hr.

36. **The best answer is F.** According to Experiment 1, PD1 contained WT *Arabidopsis* seeds and was placed in the dark. PD3 contained M *Arabidopsis* seeds and was placed in the dark. Figure 1 shows that the radicles in PD1 extended straight down, and the radicles in PD3 had more random growth. The radicles did not have the same response to gravity. **F** is correct. **G** is incorrect; PD2 and PD4 were exposed to light. **H** and **J** are incorrect; the radicles did not have the same response to gravity.

37. **The best answer is B.** In order to answer this item, the examinee must know that above-ground plant growth typically exhibits positive phototropism. **A** is incorrect; hypocotyls typically grow toward a light stimulus. **B** is correct. **C** and **D** are incorrect; the hypocotyls most likely exhibited positive phototropism.

38. **The best answer is J.** In order to answer this item, the examinee must know that cotyledons are embryonic leaves. Plants having embryos with one seed leaf are monocots. Plants having embryos with two seed leaves are dicots. Figure 2 shows that each seedling had 2 leaves, and therefore *Arabidopsis* is a dicot. **F** and **G** are incorrect; *Arabidopsis* is a dicot. **H** is incorrect; the seedlings had 2 cotyledons. **J** is correct.

39. **The best answer is B.** According to the passage, the Petri dishes were set up with the agar and seeds and were turned 90° after being exposed to light for 70 hr. The orientation of the Petri dishes was changed one time, and therefore each Petri dish had 2 different orientations. **A, C,** and **D** are incorrect; the Petri dishes had 2 different orientations. **B** is correct.

40. **The best answer is F.** In order to determine the effect of light on the growth of WT *Arabidopsis* seedlings, the results for the Petri dish with WT *Arabidopsis* placed in the dark (PD1) and the Petri dish with WT *Arabidopsis* exposed to light (PD2) should be compared. **F** is correct. **G** and **H** are incorrect; PD3 contained M *Arabidopsis* seeds. **J** is incorrect; PD4 contained M *Arabidopsis* seeds.

The ACT® *Sample Answer Document*

EXAMINEE STATEMENTS, CERTIFICATION, AND SIGNATURE

1. **Statements**: I understand that by registering for, launching, starting, or submitting answer documents for an ACT® test, I am agreeing to comply with and be bound by the *Terms and Conditions: Testing Rules and Policies for the ACT® Test* ("Terms").

   I UNDERSTAND AND AGREE THAT THE TERMS PERMIT ACT TO CANCEL MY SCORES IN CERTAIN CIRCUMSTANCES. THE TERMS ALSO LIMIT DAMAGES AVAILABLE TO ME AND REQUIRE ARBITRATION OF CERTAIN DISPUTES. BY AGREEING TO ARBITRATION, ACT AND I BOTH WAIVE THE RIGHT TO HAVE THOSE DISPUTES HEARD BY A JUDGE OR JURY.

   I understand that ACT owns the test questions and responses, and I will not share them with anyone by any form of communication before, during, or after the test administration. I understand that taking the test for someone else may violate the law and subject me to legal penalties. I consent to the collection and processing of personally identifying information I provide, and its subsequent use and disclosure, as described in the ACT Privacy Policy (www.act.org/privacy.html). I also permit ACT to transfer my personally identifying information to the United States, to ACT, or to a third-party service provider, where it will be subject to use and disclosure under the laws of the United States, including being accessible to law enforcement or national security authorities.

2. **Certification**: Copy the italicized certification below, then sign and date in the spaces provided.

   *I agree to the **Statements** above and certify that I am the person whose information appears on this form.*

   _____

   _____

   _____   _____
   Your Signature   Today's Date

Do NOT mark in this shaded area.

USE A NO. 2 PENCIL ONLY.
(Do NOT use a mechanical pencil, ink, ballpoint, correction fluid, or felt-tip pen.)

A NAME, MAILING ADDRESS, AND TELEPHONE
(Please print.)

Last Name   First Name   MI (Middle Initial)

House Number & Street (Apt. No.); or PO Box & No.; or RR & No.

City   State/Province   ZIP/Postal Code

Area Code   Number   Country

ACT, Inc.—Confidential Restricted when data present

ALL examinees must complete block A – please print.

Blocks B, C, and D are required for all examinees. Find the MATCHING INFORMATION on your ticket. Enter it EXACTLY the same way, even if any of the information is missing or incorrect. Fill in the corresponding ovals. If you do not complete these blocks to match your previous information EXACTLY, your scores will be **delayed up to 8 weeks**.

ACT®

PO BOX 168, IOWA CITY, IA 52243-0168

B MATCH NAME
(First 5 letters of last name)

C MATCH NUMBER

D DATE OF BIRTH

Month	Day	Year
○ January		
○ February		
○ March	① ①	① ①
○ April	② ②	② ②
○ May	③ ③	③ ③
○ June	④ ④	④ ④
○ July	⑤ ⑤	⑤ ⑤
○ August	⑥ ⑥	⑥ ⑥
○ September	⑦ ⑦	⑦ ⑦
○ October	⑧ ⑧	⑧ ⑧
○ November	⑨ ⑨	⑨ ⑨
○ December	⓪ ⓪	⓪ ⓪

01121523W   (A)203023-001:654321   ISD36401   Printed in the US.

Taking Additional Practice Tests

PAGE 2

Marking Directions: Mark only **one** oval for each question. Fill in response completely. Erase errors cleanly without smudging.

Correct mark: ○ ● ○ ○

Do NOT use these *incorrect* **or** *bad* **marks.**

Incorrect marks: ⊘ ⊗ ⊖ ⊝
Overlapping mark: ○ ⊙ ⬤⬤
Cross-out mark: ○ ⬤ ○ ○
Smudged erasure: ○ ○ ◍ ○
Mark is too light: ◍ ○ ○ ○

BOOKLET NUMBER

(grid of ovals numbered 1–0 in 9 columns)

Print your 5-character **Test Form** in the boxes at the right and fill in the corresponding ovals.

FORM

(grid showing 1 1 M C 1 / 2 2 ... with ovals numbered 1–0)

TEST 1: ENGLISH

1 Ⓐ Ⓑ Ⓒ Ⓓ	14 Ⓕ Ⓖ Ⓗ Ⓙ	27 Ⓐ Ⓑ Ⓒ Ⓓ	40 Ⓕ Ⓖ Ⓗ Ⓙ	53 Ⓐ Ⓑ Ⓒ Ⓓ	66 Ⓕ Ⓖ Ⓗ Ⓙ
2 Ⓕ Ⓖ Ⓗ Ⓙ	15 Ⓐ Ⓑ Ⓒ Ⓓ	28 Ⓕ Ⓖ Ⓗ Ⓙ	41 Ⓐ Ⓑ Ⓒ Ⓓ	54 Ⓕ Ⓖ Ⓗ Ⓙ	67 Ⓐ Ⓑ Ⓒ Ⓓ
3 Ⓐ Ⓑ Ⓒ Ⓓ	16 Ⓕ Ⓖ Ⓗ Ⓙ	29 Ⓐ Ⓑ Ⓒ Ⓓ	42 Ⓕ Ⓖ Ⓗ Ⓙ	55 Ⓐ Ⓑ Ⓒ Ⓓ	68 Ⓕ Ⓖ Ⓗ Ⓙ
4 Ⓕ Ⓖ Ⓗ Ⓙ	17 Ⓐ Ⓑ Ⓒ Ⓓ	30 Ⓕ Ⓖ Ⓗ Ⓙ	43 Ⓐ Ⓑ Ⓒ Ⓓ	56 Ⓕ Ⓖ Ⓗ Ⓙ	69 Ⓐ Ⓑ Ⓒ Ⓓ
5 Ⓐ Ⓑ Ⓒ Ⓓ	18 Ⓕ Ⓖ Ⓗ Ⓙ	31 Ⓐ Ⓑ Ⓒ Ⓓ	44 Ⓕ Ⓖ Ⓗ Ⓙ	57 Ⓐ Ⓑ Ⓒ Ⓓ	70 Ⓕ Ⓖ Ⓗ Ⓙ
6 Ⓕ Ⓖ Ⓗ Ⓙ	19 Ⓐ Ⓑ Ⓒ Ⓓ	32 Ⓕ Ⓖ Ⓗ Ⓙ	45 Ⓐ Ⓑ Ⓒ Ⓓ	58 Ⓕ Ⓖ Ⓗ Ⓙ	71 Ⓐ Ⓑ Ⓒ Ⓓ
7 Ⓐ Ⓑ Ⓒ Ⓓ	20 Ⓕ Ⓖ Ⓗ Ⓙ	33 Ⓐ Ⓑ Ⓒ Ⓓ	46 Ⓕ Ⓖ Ⓗ Ⓙ	59 Ⓐ Ⓑ Ⓒ Ⓓ	72 Ⓕ Ⓖ Ⓗ Ⓙ
8 Ⓕ Ⓖ Ⓗ Ⓙ	21 Ⓐ Ⓑ Ⓒ Ⓓ	34 Ⓕ Ⓖ Ⓗ Ⓙ	47 Ⓐ Ⓑ Ⓒ Ⓓ	60 Ⓕ Ⓖ Ⓗ Ⓙ	73 Ⓐ Ⓑ Ⓒ Ⓓ
9 Ⓐ Ⓑ Ⓒ Ⓓ	22 Ⓕ Ⓖ Ⓗ Ⓙ	35 Ⓐ Ⓑ Ⓒ Ⓓ	48 Ⓕ Ⓖ Ⓗ Ⓙ	61 Ⓐ Ⓑ Ⓒ Ⓓ	74 Ⓕ Ⓖ Ⓗ Ⓙ
10 Ⓕ Ⓖ Ⓗ Ⓙ	23 Ⓐ Ⓑ Ⓒ Ⓓ	36 Ⓕ Ⓖ Ⓗ Ⓙ	49 Ⓐ Ⓑ Ⓒ Ⓓ	62 Ⓕ Ⓖ Ⓗ Ⓙ	75 Ⓐ Ⓑ Ⓒ Ⓓ
11 Ⓐ Ⓑ Ⓒ Ⓓ	24 Ⓕ Ⓖ Ⓗ Ⓙ	37 Ⓐ Ⓑ Ⓒ Ⓓ	50 Ⓕ Ⓖ Ⓗ Ⓙ	63 Ⓐ Ⓑ Ⓒ Ⓓ	
12 Ⓕ Ⓖ Ⓗ Ⓙ	25 Ⓐ Ⓑ Ⓒ Ⓓ	38 Ⓕ Ⓖ Ⓗ Ⓙ	51 Ⓐ Ⓑ Ⓒ Ⓓ	64 Ⓕ Ⓖ Ⓗ Ⓙ	
13 Ⓐ Ⓑ Ⓒ Ⓓ	26 Ⓕ Ⓖ Ⓗ Ⓙ	39 Ⓐ Ⓑ Ⓒ Ⓓ	52 Ⓕ Ⓖ Ⓗ Ⓙ	65 Ⓐ Ⓑ Ⓒ Ⓓ	

TEST 2: MATHEMATICS

1 Ⓐ Ⓑ Ⓒ Ⓓ Ⓔ	11 Ⓐ Ⓑ Ⓒ Ⓓ Ⓔ	21 Ⓐ Ⓑ Ⓒ Ⓓ Ⓔ	31 Ⓐ Ⓑ Ⓒ Ⓓ Ⓔ	41 Ⓐ Ⓑ Ⓒ Ⓓ Ⓔ	51 Ⓐ Ⓑ Ⓒ Ⓓ Ⓔ
2 Ⓕ Ⓖ Ⓗ Ⓙ Ⓚ	12 Ⓕ Ⓖ Ⓗ Ⓙ Ⓚ	22 Ⓕ Ⓖ Ⓗ Ⓙ Ⓚ	32 Ⓕ Ⓖ Ⓗ Ⓙ Ⓚ	42 Ⓕ Ⓖ Ⓗ Ⓙ Ⓚ	52 Ⓕ Ⓖ Ⓗ Ⓙ Ⓚ
3 Ⓐ Ⓑ Ⓒ Ⓓ Ⓔ	13 Ⓐ Ⓑ Ⓒ Ⓓ Ⓔ	23 Ⓐ Ⓑ Ⓒ Ⓓ Ⓔ	33 Ⓐ Ⓑ Ⓒ Ⓓ Ⓔ	43 Ⓐ Ⓑ Ⓒ Ⓓ Ⓔ	53 Ⓐ Ⓑ Ⓒ Ⓓ Ⓔ
4 Ⓕ Ⓖ Ⓗ Ⓙ Ⓚ	14 Ⓕ Ⓖ Ⓗ Ⓙ Ⓚ	24 Ⓕ Ⓖ Ⓗ Ⓙ Ⓚ	34 Ⓕ Ⓖ Ⓗ Ⓙ Ⓚ	44 Ⓕ Ⓖ Ⓗ Ⓙ Ⓚ	54 Ⓕ Ⓖ Ⓗ Ⓙ Ⓚ
5 Ⓐ Ⓑ Ⓒ Ⓓ Ⓔ	15 Ⓐ Ⓑ Ⓒ Ⓓ Ⓔ	25 Ⓐ Ⓑ Ⓒ Ⓓ Ⓔ	35 Ⓐ Ⓑ Ⓒ Ⓓ Ⓔ	45 Ⓐ Ⓑ Ⓒ Ⓓ Ⓔ	55 Ⓐ Ⓑ Ⓒ Ⓓ Ⓔ
6 Ⓕ Ⓖ Ⓗ Ⓙ Ⓚ	16 Ⓕ Ⓖ Ⓗ Ⓙ Ⓚ	26 Ⓕ Ⓖ Ⓗ Ⓙ Ⓚ	36 Ⓕ Ⓖ Ⓗ Ⓙ Ⓚ	46 Ⓕ Ⓖ Ⓗ Ⓙ Ⓚ	56 Ⓕ Ⓖ Ⓗ Ⓙ Ⓚ
7 Ⓐ Ⓑ Ⓒ Ⓓ Ⓔ	17 Ⓐ Ⓑ Ⓒ Ⓓ Ⓔ	27 Ⓐ Ⓑ Ⓒ Ⓓ Ⓔ	37 Ⓐ Ⓑ Ⓒ Ⓓ Ⓔ	47 Ⓐ Ⓑ Ⓒ Ⓓ Ⓔ	57 Ⓐ Ⓑ Ⓒ Ⓓ Ⓔ
8 Ⓕ Ⓖ Ⓗ Ⓙ Ⓚ	18 Ⓕ Ⓖ Ⓗ Ⓙ Ⓚ	28 Ⓕ Ⓖ Ⓗ Ⓙ Ⓚ	38 Ⓕ Ⓖ Ⓗ Ⓙ Ⓚ	48 Ⓕ Ⓖ Ⓗ Ⓙ Ⓚ	58 Ⓕ Ⓖ Ⓗ Ⓙ Ⓚ
9 Ⓐ Ⓑ Ⓒ Ⓓ Ⓔ	19 Ⓐ Ⓑ Ⓒ Ⓓ Ⓔ	29 Ⓐ Ⓑ Ⓒ Ⓓ Ⓔ	39 Ⓐ Ⓑ Ⓒ Ⓓ Ⓔ	49 Ⓐ Ⓑ Ⓒ Ⓓ Ⓔ	59 Ⓐ Ⓑ Ⓒ Ⓓ Ⓔ
10 Ⓕ Ⓖ Ⓗ Ⓙ Ⓚ	20 Ⓕ Ⓖ Ⓗ Ⓙ Ⓚ	30 Ⓕ Ⓖ Ⓗ Ⓙ Ⓚ	40 Ⓕ Ⓖ Ⓗ Ⓙ Ⓚ	50 Ⓕ Ⓖ Ⓗ Ⓙ Ⓚ	60 Ⓕ Ⓖ Ⓗ Ⓙ Ⓚ

TEST 3: READING

1 Ⓐ Ⓑ Ⓒ Ⓓ	8 Ⓕ Ⓖ Ⓗ Ⓙ	15 Ⓐ Ⓑ Ⓒ Ⓓ	22 Ⓕ Ⓖ Ⓗ Ⓙ	29 Ⓐ Ⓑ Ⓒ Ⓓ	36 Ⓕ Ⓖ Ⓗ Ⓙ
2 Ⓕ Ⓖ Ⓗ Ⓙ	9 Ⓐ Ⓑ Ⓒ Ⓓ	16 Ⓕ Ⓖ Ⓗ Ⓙ	23 Ⓐ Ⓑ Ⓒ Ⓓ	30 Ⓕ Ⓖ Ⓗ Ⓙ	37 Ⓐ Ⓑ Ⓒ Ⓓ
3 Ⓐ Ⓑ Ⓒ Ⓓ	10 Ⓕ Ⓖ Ⓗ Ⓙ	17 Ⓐ Ⓑ Ⓒ Ⓓ	24 Ⓕ Ⓖ Ⓗ Ⓙ	31 Ⓐ Ⓑ Ⓒ Ⓓ	38 Ⓕ Ⓖ Ⓗ Ⓙ
4 Ⓕ Ⓖ Ⓗ Ⓙ	11 Ⓐ Ⓑ Ⓒ Ⓓ	18 Ⓕ Ⓖ Ⓗ Ⓙ	25 Ⓐ Ⓑ Ⓒ Ⓓ	32 Ⓕ Ⓖ Ⓗ Ⓙ	39 Ⓐ Ⓑ Ⓒ Ⓓ
5 Ⓐ Ⓑ Ⓒ Ⓓ	12 Ⓕ Ⓖ Ⓗ Ⓙ	19 Ⓐ Ⓑ Ⓒ Ⓓ	26 Ⓕ Ⓖ Ⓗ Ⓙ	33 Ⓐ Ⓑ Ⓒ Ⓓ	40 Ⓕ Ⓖ Ⓗ Ⓙ
6 Ⓕ Ⓖ Ⓗ Ⓙ	13 Ⓐ Ⓑ Ⓒ Ⓓ	20 Ⓕ Ⓖ Ⓗ Ⓙ	27 Ⓐ Ⓑ Ⓒ Ⓓ	34 Ⓕ Ⓖ Ⓗ Ⓙ	
7 Ⓐ Ⓑ Ⓒ Ⓓ	14 Ⓕ Ⓖ Ⓗ Ⓙ	21 Ⓐ Ⓑ Ⓒ Ⓓ	28 Ⓕ Ⓖ Ⓗ Ⓙ	35 Ⓐ Ⓑ Ⓒ Ⓓ	

TEST 4: SCIENCE

1 Ⓐ Ⓑ Ⓒ Ⓓ	8 Ⓕ Ⓖ Ⓗ Ⓙ	15 Ⓐ Ⓑ Ⓒ Ⓓ	22 Ⓕ Ⓖ Ⓗ Ⓙ	29 Ⓐ Ⓑ Ⓒ Ⓓ	36 Ⓕ Ⓖ Ⓗ Ⓙ
2 Ⓕ Ⓖ Ⓗ Ⓙ	9 Ⓐ Ⓑ Ⓒ Ⓓ	16 Ⓕ Ⓖ Ⓗ Ⓙ	23 Ⓐ Ⓑ Ⓒ Ⓓ	30 Ⓕ Ⓖ Ⓗ Ⓙ	37 Ⓐ Ⓑ Ⓒ Ⓓ
3 Ⓐ Ⓑ Ⓒ Ⓓ	10 Ⓕ Ⓖ Ⓗ Ⓙ	17 Ⓐ Ⓑ Ⓒ Ⓓ	24 Ⓕ Ⓖ Ⓗ Ⓙ	31 Ⓐ Ⓑ Ⓒ Ⓓ	38 Ⓕ Ⓖ Ⓗ Ⓙ
4 Ⓕ Ⓖ Ⓗ Ⓙ	11 Ⓐ Ⓑ Ⓒ Ⓓ	18 Ⓕ Ⓖ Ⓗ Ⓙ	25 Ⓐ Ⓑ Ⓒ Ⓓ	32 Ⓕ Ⓖ Ⓗ Ⓙ	39 Ⓐ Ⓑ Ⓒ Ⓓ
5 Ⓐ Ⓑ Ⓒ Ⓓ	12 Ⓕ Ⓖ Ⓗ Ⓙ	19 Ⓐ Ⓑ Ⓒ Ⓓ	26 Ⓕ Ⓖ Ⓗ Ⓙ	33 Ⓐ Ⓑ Ⓒ Ⓓ	40 Ⓕ Ⓖ Ⓗ Ⓙ
6 Ⓕ Ⓖ Ⓗ Ⓙ	13 Ⓐ Ⓑ Ⓒ Ⓓ	20 Ⓕ Ⓖ Ⓗ Ⓙ	27 Ⓐ Ⓑ Ⓒ Ⓓ	34 Ⓕ Ⓖ Ⓗ Ⓙ	
7 Ⓐ Ⓑ Ⓒ Ⓓ	14 Ⓕ Ⓖ Ⓗ Ⓙ	21 Ⓐ Ⓑ Ⓒ Ⓓ	28 Ⓕ Ⓖ Ⓗ Ⓙ	35 Ⓐ Ⓑ Ⓒ Ⓓ	

The ACT® *Sample Answer Document*

EXAMINEE STATEMENTS, CERTIFICATION, AND SIGNATURE

1. **Statements**: I understand that by registering for, launching, starting, or submitting answer documents for an ACT® test, I am agreeing to comply with and be bound by the *Terms and Conditions: Testing Rules and Policies for the ACT® Test* ("Terms").

I UNDERSTAND AND AGREE THAT THE TERMS PERMIT ACT TO CANCEL MY SCORES IN CERTAIN CIRCUMSTANCES. THE TERMS ALSO LIMIT DAMAGES AVAILABLE TO ME AND REQUIRE ARBITRATION OF CERTAIN DISPUTES. BY AGREEING TO ARBITRATION, ACT AND I BOTH WAIVE THE RIGHT TO HAVE THOSE DISPUTES HEARD BY A JUDGE OR JURY.

I understand that ACT owns the test questions and responses, and I will not share them with anyone by any form of communication before, during, or after the test administration. I understand that taking the test for someone else may violate the law and subject me to legal penalties. I consent to the collection and processing of personally identifying information I provide, and its subsequent use and disclosure, as described in the ACT Privacy Policy (www.act.org/privacy.html). I also permit ACT to transfer my personally identifying information to the United States, to ACT, or to a third-party service provider, where it will be subject to use and disclosure under the laws of the United States, including being accessible to law enforcement or national security authorities.

2. **Certification**: Copy the italicized certification below, then sign and date in the spaces provided.

I agree to the **Statements** *above and certify that I am the person whose information appears on this form.*

_____

_____

_____   _____

Your Signature   Today's Date

Do NOT mark in this shaded area.

USE A NO. 2 PENCIL ONLY.
(Do NOT use a mechanical pencil, ink, ballpoint, correction fluid, or felt-tip pen.)

A NAME, MAILING ADDRESS, AND TELEPHONE
(Please print.)

Last Name   First Name   MI (Middle Initial)

House Number & Street (Apt. No.); or PO Box & No.; or RR & No.

City   State/Province   ZIP/Postal Code

Area Code   Number   Country

ACT, Inc.—Confidential Restricted when data present

ALL examinees must complete block A – please print.

Blocks B, C, and D are required for all examinees. Find the MATCHING INFORMATION on your ticket. Enter it EXACTLY the same way, even if any of the information is missing or incorrect. Fill in the corresponding ovals. If you do not complete these blocks to match your previous information EXACTLY, your scores will be **delayed up to 8 weeks.**

ACT®
PO BOX 168, IOWA CITY, IA 52243-0168

B MATCH NAME
(First 5 letters of last name)

C MATCH NUMBER

D DATE OF BIRTH

Month	Day	Year
January		
February		
March		
April		
May		
June		
July		
August		
September		
October		
November		
December		

01121523W   (A)203023-001:654321   ISD36401   Printed in the US.

Taking Additional Practice Tests

PAGE 2

Marking Directions: Mark only **one** oval for each question. Fill in response completely. Erase errors cleanly without smudging.

Correct mark: ○ ● ○ ○

Do NOT use these *incorrect* or *bad* **marks.**

Incorrect marks: ○ ○ ○
Overlapping mark: ○ ○
Cross-out mark: ○ ○
Smudged erasure: ○ ○ ○
Mark is too light: ● ○ ○ ○

BOOKLET NUMBER

① ① ① ① ① ① ① ①
② ② ② ② ② ② ② ②
③ ③ ③ ③ ③ ③ ③ ③
④ ④ ④ ④ ④ ④ ④ ④
⑤ ⑤ ⑤ ⑤ ⑤ ⑤ ⑤ ⑤
⑥ ⑥ ⑥ ⑥ ⑥ ⑥ ⑥ ⑥
⑦ ⑦ ⑦ ⑦ ⑦ ⑦ ⑦ ⑦
⑧ ⑧ ⑧ ⑧ ⑧ ⑧ ⑧ ⑧
⑨ ⑨ ⑨ ⑨ ⑨ ⑨ ⑨ ⑨
⓪ ⓪ ⓪ ⓪ ⓪ ⓪ ⓪ ⓪

Print your 5-character **Test Form** in the boxes at the right <u>and</u> fill in the corresponding ovals.

FORM

① ① Ⓜ Ⓒ ①
② ②   ②
③   ③
④   ④
⑤   ⑤
⑥   ⑥
⑦   ⑦
⑧   ⑧
⑨   ⑨
⓪   ⓪

TEST 1: ENGLISH

1 Ⓐ Ⓑ Ⓒ Ⓓ   14 Ⓕ Ⓖ Ⓗ Ⓙ   27 Ⓐ Ⓑ Ⓒ Ⓓ   40 Ⓕ Ⓖ Ⓗ Ⓙ   53 Ⓐ Ⓑ Ⓒ Ⓓ   66 Ⓕ Ⓖ Ⓗ Ⓙ
2 Ⓕ Ⓖ Ⓗ Ⓙ   15 Ⓐ Ⓑ Ⓒ Ⓓ   28 Ⓕ Ⓖ Ⓗ Ⓙ   41 Ⓐ Ⓑ Ⓒ Ⓓ   54 Ⓕ Ⓖ Ⓗ Ⓙ   67 Ⓐ Ⓑ Ⓒ Ⓓ
3 Ⓐ Ⓑ Ⓒ Ⓓ   16 Ⓕ Ⓖ Ⓗ Ⓙ   29 Ⓐ Ⓑ Ⓒ Ⓓ   42 Ⓕ Ⓖ Ⓗ Ⓙ   55 Ⓐ Ⓑ Ⓒ Ⓓ   68 Ⓕ Ⓖ Ⓗ Ⓙ
4 Ⓕ Ⓖ Ⓗ Ⓙ   17 Ⓐ Ⓑ Ⓒ Ⓓ   30 Ⓕ Ⓖ Ⓗ Ⓙ   43 Ⓐ Ⓑ Ⓒ Ⓓ   56 Ⓕ Ⓖ Ⓗ Ⓙ   69 Ⓐ Ⓑ Ⓒ Ⓓ
5 Ⓐ Ⓑ Ⓒ Ⓓ   18 Ⓕ Ⓖ Ⓗ Ⓙ   31 Ⓐ Ⓑ Ⓒ Ⓓ   44 Ⓕ Ⓖ Ⓗ Ⓙ   57 Ⓐ Ⓑ Ⓒ Ⓓ   70 Ⓕ Ⓖ Ⓗ Ⓙ
6 Ⓕ Ⓖ Ⓗ Ⓙ   19 Ⓐ Ⓑ Ⓒ Ⓓ   32 Ⓕ Ⓖ Ⓗ Ⓙ   45 Ⓐ Ⓑ Ⓒ Ⓓ   58 Ⓕ Ⓖ Ⓗ Ⓙ   71 Ⓐ Ⓑ Ⓒ Ⓓ
7 Ⓐ Ⓑ Ⓒ Ⓓ   20 Ⓕ Ⓖ Ⓗ Ⓙ   33 Ⓐ Ⓑ Ⓒ Ⓓ   46 Ⓕ Ⓖ Ⓗ Ⓙ   59 Ⓐ Ⓑ Ⓒ Ⓓ   72 Ⓕ Ⓖ Ⓗ Ⓙ
8 Ⓕ Ⓖ Ⓗ Ⓙ   21 Ⓐ Ⓑ Ⓒ Ⓓ   34 Ⓕ Ⓖ Ⓗ Ⓙ   47 Ⓐ Ⓑ Ⓒ Ⓓ   60 Ⓕ Ⓖ Ⓗ Ⓙ   73 Ⓐ Ⓑ Ⓒ Ⓓ
9 Ⓐ Ⓑ Ⓒ Ⓓ   22 Ⓕ Ⓖ Ⓗ Ⓙ   35 Ⓐ Ⓑ Ⓒ Ⓓ   48 Ⓕ Ⓖ Ⓗ Ⓙ   61 Ⓐ Ⓑ Ⓒ Ⓓ   74 Ⓕ Ⓖ Ⓗ Ⓙ
10 Ⓕ Ⓖ Ⓗ Ⓙ   23 Ⓐ Ⓑ Ⓒ Ⓓ   36 Ⓕ Ⓖ Ⓗ Ⓙ   49 Ⓐ Ⓑ Ⓒ Ⓓ   62 Ⓕ Ⓖ Ⓗ Ⓙ   75 Ⓐ Ⓑ Ⓒ Ⓓ
11 Ⓐ Ⓑ Ⓒ Ⓓ   24 Ⓕ Ⓖ Ⓗ Ⓙ   37 Ⓐ Ⓑ Ⓒ Ⓓ   50 Ⓕ Ⓖ Ⓗ Ⓙ   63 Ⓐ Ⓑ Ⓒ Ⓓ
12 Ⓕ Ⓖ Ⓗ Ⓙ   25 Ⓐ Ⓑ Ⓒ Ⓓ   38 Ⓕ Ⓖ Ⓗ Ⓙ   51 Ⓐ Ⓑ Ⓒ Ⓓ   64 Ⓕ Ⓖ Ⓗ Ⓙ
13 Ⓐ Ⓑ Ⓒ Ⓓ   26 Ⓕ Ⓖ Ⓗ Ⓙ   39 Ⓐ Ⓑ Ⓒ Ⓓ   52 Ⓕ Ⓖ Ⓗ Ⓙ   65 Ⓐ Ⓑ Ⓒ Ⓓ

TEST 2: MATHEMATICS

1 Ⓐ Ⓑ Ⓒ Ⓓ Ⓔ   11 Ⓐ Ⓑ Ⓒ Ⓓ Ⓔ   21 Ⓐ Ⓑ Ⓒ Ⓓ Ⓔ   31 Ⓐ Ⓑ Ⓒ Ⓓ Ⓔ   41 Ⓐ Ⓑ Ⓒ Ⓓ Ⓔ   51 Ⓐ Ⓑ Ⓒ Ⓓ Ⓔ
2 Ⓕ Ⓖ Ⓗ Ⓙ Ⓚ   12 Ⓕ Ⓖ Ⓗ Ⓙ Ⓚ   22 Ⓕ Ⓖ Ⓗ Ⓙ Ⓚ   32 Ⓕ Ⓖ Ⓗ Ⓙ Ⓚ   42 Ⓕ Ⓖ Ⓗ Ⓙ Ⓚ   52 Ⓕ Ⓖ Ⓗ Ⓙ Ⓚ
3 Ⓐ Ⓑ Ⓒ Ⓓ Ⓔ   13 Ⓐ Ⓑ Ⓒ Ⓓ Ⓔ   23 Ⓐ Ⓑ Ⓒ Ⓓ Ⓔ   33 Ⓐ Ⓑ Ⓒ Ⓓ Ⓔ   43 Ⓐ Ⓑ Ⓒ Ⓓ Ⓔ   53 Ⓐ Ⓑ Ⓒ Ⓓ Ⓔ
4 Ⓕ Ⓖ Ⓗ Ⓙ Ⓚ   14 Ⓕ Ⓖ Ⓗ Ⓙ Ⓚ   24 Ⓕ Ⓖ Ⓗ Ⓙ Ⓚ   34 Ⓕ Ⓖ Ⓗ Ⓙ Ⓚ   44 Ⓕ Ⓖ Ⓗ Ⓙ Ⓚ   54 Ⓕ Ⓖ Ⓗ Ⓙ Ⓚ
5 Ⓐ Ⓑ Ⓒ Ⓓ Ⓔ   15 Ⓐ Ⓑ Ⓒ Ⓓ Ⓔ   25 Ⓐ Ⓑ Ⓒ Ⓓ Ⓔ   35 Ⓐ Ⓑ Ⓒ Ⓓ Ⓔ   45 Ⓐ Ⓑ Ⓒ Ⓓ Ⓔ   55 Ⓐ Ⓑ Ⓒ Ⓓ Ⓔ
6 Ⓕ Ⓖ Ⓗ Ⓙ Ⓚ   16 Ⓕ Ⓖ Ⓗ Ⓙ Ⓚ   26 Ⓕ Ⓖ Ⓗ Ⓙ Ⓚ   36 Ⓕ Ⓖ Ⓗ Ⓙ Ⓚ   46 Ⓕ Ⓖ Ⓗ Ⓙ Ⓚ   56 Ⓕ Ⓖ Ⓗ Ⓙ Ⓚ
7 Ⓐ Ⓑ Ⓒ Ⓓ Ⓔ   17 Ⓐ Ⓑ Ⓒ Ⓓ Ⓔ   27 Ⓐ Ⓑ Ⓒ Ⓓ Ⓔ   37 Ⓐ Ⓑ Ⓒ Ⓓ Ⓔ   47 Ⓐ Ⓑ Ⓒ Ⓓ Ⓔ   57 Ⓐ Ⓑ Ⓒ Ⓓ Ⓔ
8 Ⓕ Ⓖ Ⓗ Ⓙ Ⓚ   18 Ⓕ Ⓖ Ⓗ Ⓙ Ⓚ   28 Ⓕ Ⓖ Ⓗ Ⓙ Ⓚ   38 Ⓕ Ⓖ Ⓗ Ⓙ Ⓚ   48 Ⓕ Ⓖ Ⓗ Ⓙ Ⓚ   58 Ⓕ Ⓖ Ⓗ Ⓙ Ⓚ
9 Ⓐ Ⓑ Ⓒ Ⓓ Ⓔ   19 Ⓐ Ⓑ Ⓒ Ⓓ Ⓔ   29 Ⓐ Ⓑ Ⓒ Ⓓ Ⓔ   39 Ⓐ Ⓑ Ⓒ Ⓓ Ⓔ   49 Ⓐ Ⓑ Ⓒ Ⓓ Ⓔ   59 Ⓐ Ⓑ Ⓒ Ⓓ Ⓔ
10 Ⓕ Ⓖ Ⓗ Ⓙ Ⓚ   20 Ⓕ Ⓖ Ⓗ Ⓙ Ⓚ   30 Ⓕ Ⓖ Ⓗ Ⓙ Ⓚ   40 Ⓕ Ⓖ Ⓗ Ⓙ Ⓚ   50 Ⓕ Ⓖ Ⓗ Ⓙ Ⓚ   60 Ⓕ Ⓖ Ⓗ Ⓙ Ⓚ

TEST 3: READING

1 Ⓐ Ⓑ Ⓒ Ⓓ   8 Ⓕ Ⓖ Ⓗ Ⓙ   15 Ⓐ Ⓑ Ⓒ Ⓓ   22 Ⓕ Ⓖ Ⓗ Ⓙ   29 Ⓐ Ⓑ Ⓒ Ⓓ   36 Ⓕ Ⓖ Ⓗ Ⓙ
2 Ⓕ Ⓖ Ⓗ Ⓙ   9 Ⓐ Ⓑ Ⓒ Ⓓ   16 Ⓕ Ⓖ Ⓗ Ⓙ   23 Ⓐ Ⓑ Ⓒ Ⓓ   30 Ⓕ Ⓖ Ⓗ Ⓙ   37 Ⓐ Ⓑ Ⓒ Ⓓ
3 Ⓐ Ⓑ Ⓒ Ⓓ   10 Ⓕ Ⓖ Ⓗ Ⓙ   17 Ⓐ Ⓑ Ⓒ Ⓓ   24 Ⓕ Ⓖ Ⓗ Ⓙ   31 Ⓐ Ⓑ Ⓒ Ⓓ   38 Ⓕ Ⓖ Ⓗ Ⓙ
4 Ⓕ Ⓖ Ⓗ Ⓙ   11 Ⓐ Ⓑ Ⓒ Ⓓ   18 Ⓕ Ⓖ Ⓗ Ⓙ   25 Ⓐ Ⓑ Ⓒ Ⓓ   32 Ⓕ Ⓖ Ⓗ Ⓙ   39 Ⓐ Ⓑ Ⓒ Ⓓ
5 Ⓐ Ⓑ Ⓒ Ⓓ   12 Ⓕ Ⓖ Ⓗ Ⓙ   19 Ⓐ Ⓑ Ⓒ Ⓓ   26 Ⓕ Ⓖ Ⓗ Ⓙ   33 Ⓐ Ⓑ Ⓒ Ⓓ   40 Ⓕ Ⓖ Ⓗ Ⓙ
6 Ⓕ Ⓖ Ⓗ Ⓙ   13 Ⓐ Ⓑ Ⓒ Ⓓ   20 Ⓕ Ⓖ Ⓗ Ⓙ   27 Ⓐ Ⓑ Ⓒ Ⓓ   34 Ⓕ Ⓖ Ⓗ Ⓙ
7 Ⓐ Ⓑ Ⓒ Ⓓ   14 Ⓕ Ⓖ Ⓗ Ⓙ   21 Ⓐ Ⓑ Ⓒ Ⓓ   28 Ⓕ Ⓖ Ⓗ Ⓙ   35 Ⓐ Ⓑ Ⓒ Ⓓ

TEST 4: SCIENCE

1 Ⓐ Ⓑ Ⓒ Ⓓ   8 Ⓕ Ⓖ Ⓗ Ⓙ   15 Ⓐ Ⓑ Ⓒ Ⓓ   22 Ⓕ Ⓖ Ⓗ Ⓙ   29 Ⓐ Ⓑ Ⓒ Ⓓ   36 Ⓕ Ⓖ Ⓗ Ⓙ
2 Ⓕ Ⓖ Ⓗ Ⓙ   9 Ⓐ Ⓑ Ⓒ Ⓓ   16 Ⓕ Ⓖ Ⓗ Ⓙ   23 Ⓐ Ⓑ Ⓒ Ⓓ   30 Ⓕ Ⓖ Ⓗ Ⓙ   37 Ⓐ Ⓑ Ⓒ Ⓓ
3 Ⓐ Ⓑ Ⓒ Ⓓ   10 Ⓕ Ⓖ Ⓗ Ⓙ   17 Ⓐ Ⓑ Ⓒ Ⓓ   24 Ⓕ Ⓖ Ⓗ Ⓙ   31 Ⓐ Ⓑ Ⓒ Ⓓ   38 Ⓕ Ⓖ Ⓗ Ⓙ
4 Ⓕ Ⓖ Ⓗ Ⓙ   11 Ⓐ Ⓑ Ⓒ Ⓓ   18 Ⓕ Ⓖ Ⓗ Ⓙ   25 Ⓐ Ⓑ Ⓒ Ⓓ   32 Ⓕ Ⓖ Ⓗ Ⓙ   39 Ⓐ Ⓑ Ⓒ Ⓓ
5 Ⓐ Ⓑ Ⓒ Ⓓ   12 Ⓕ Ⓖ Ⓗ Ⓙ   19 Ⓐ Ⓑ Ⓒ Ⓓ   26 Ⓕ Ⓖ Ⓗ Ⓙ   33 Ⓐ Ⓑ Ⓒ Ⓓ   40 Ⓕ Ⓖ Ⓗ Ⓙ
6 Ⓕ Ⓖ Ⓗ Ⓙ   13 Ⓐ Ⓑ Ⓒ Ⓓ   20 Ⓕ Ⓖ Ⓗ Ⓙ   27 Ⓐ Ⓑ Ⓒ Ⓓ   34 Ⓕ Ⓖ Ⓗ Ⓙ
7 Ⓐ Ⓑ Ⓒ Ⓓ   14 Ⓕ Ⓖ Ⓗ Ⓙ   21 Ⓐ Ⓑ Ⓒ Ⓓ   28 Ⓕ Ⓖ Ⓗ Ⓙ   35 Ⓐ Ⓑ Ⓒ Ⓓ

Practice Test 4

EXAMINEE STATEMENTS, CERTIFICATION, AND SIGNATURE

1. **Statements:** I understand that by registering for, launching, starting, or submitting answer documents for an ACT® test, I am agreeing to comply with and be bound by the *Terms and Conditions: Testing Rules and Policies for the ACT® Test* ("Terms").

   I UNDERSTAND AND AGREE THAT THE TERMS PERMIT ACT TO CANCEL MY SCORES IN CERTAIN CIRCUMSTANCES. THE TERMS ALSO LIMIT DAMAGES AVAILABLE TO ME AND REQUIRE ARBITRATION OF CERTAIN DISPUTES. BY AGREEING TO ARBITRATION, ACT AND I BOTH WAIVE THE RIGHT TO HAVE THOSE DISPUTES HEARD BY A JUDGE OR JURY.

   I understand that ACT owns the test questions and responses, and I will not share them with anyone by any form of communication before, during, or after the test administration. I understand that taking the test for someone else may violate the law and subject me to legal penalties.

   I consent to the collection and processing of personally identifying information I provide, and its subsequent use and disclosure, as described in the ACT Privacy Policy (www.act.org/privacy.html). I also permit ACT to transfer my personally identifying information to the United States, to ACT, or to a third-party service provider, where it will be subject to use and disclosure under the laws of the United States, including being accessible to law enforcement or national security authorities.

2. **Certification:** Copy the italicized certification below, then sign, date, and print your name in the spaces provided.

   *I agree to the **Statements** above and certify that I am the person whose information appears on this form.*

_____

_____

Your Signature   Today's Date   Print Your Name

The **ACT**®   **Form 20MC6**
2023 | 2024

Directions

This booklet contains tests in English, mathematics, reading, and science. These tests measure skills and abilities highly related to high school course work and success in college. **Calculators may be used on the mathematics test only.**

The questions in each test are numbered, and the suggested answers for each question are lettered. On the answer document, the rows of ovals are numbered to match the questions, and the ovals in each row are lettered to correspond to the suggested answers.

For each question, first decide which answer is best. Next, locate on the answer document the row of ovals numbered the same as the question. Then, locate the oval in that row lettered the same as your answer. Finally, fill in the oval completely. Use a soft lead pencil and make your marks heavy and black. **Do not use ink or a mechanical pencil.**

Mark only one answer to each question. If you change your mind about an answer, erase your first mark thoroughly before marking your new answer. For each question, make certain that you mark in the row of ovals with the same number as the question.

Only responses marked on your answer document will be scored. Your score on each test will be based only on the number of questions you answer correctly during the time allowed for that test. You will **not** be penalized for guessing. **It is to your advantage to answer every question even if you must guess.**

You may work on each test **only** when the testing staff tells you to do so. If you finish a test before time is called for that test, you should use the time remaining to reconsider questions you are uncertain about in that test. You may **not** look back to a test on which time has already been called, and you may **not** go ahead to another test. To do so will disqualify you from the examination.

Lay your pencil down immediately when time is called at the end of each test. You may **not** for any reason fill in or alter ovals for a test after time is called for that test. To do so will disqualify you from the examination.

Do not fold or tear the pages of your test booklet.

DO NOT OPEN THIS BOOKLET
UNTIL TOLD TO DO SO.

The ONLY Official Prep Guide from the Makers of the ACT

1 ■ ■ ■ ■ ■ ■ ■ ■ ■ 1

ENGLISH TEST
45 Minutes—75 Questions

DIRECTIONS: In the five passages that follow, certain words and phrases are underlined and numbered. In the right-hand column, you will find alternatives for the underlined part. In most cases, you are to choose the one that best expresses the idea, makes the statement appropriate for standard written English, or is worded most consistently with the style and tone of the passage as a whole. If you think the original version is best, choose "NO CHANGE." In some cases, you will find in the right-hand column a question about the underlined part. You are to choose the best answer to the question.

You will also find questions about a section of the passage, or about the passage as a whole. These questions do not refer to an underlined portion of the passage, but rather are identified by a number or numbers in a box.

For each question, choose the alternative you consider best and fill in the corresponding oval on your answer document. Read each passage through once before you begin to answer the questions that accompany it. For many of the questions, you must read several sentences beyond the question to determine the answer. Be sure that you have read far enough ahead each time you choose an alternative.

PASSAGE I

From Salad to Symphony

[1]

Though they can often be seen lugging bags stuffed with fresh vegetables home from Beijing markets, brothers Nan Weidong and Nan Weiping are not chefs—they are musicians. [A] Their instruments of choice is considered
                                                                         1
rather unusual: a pan pipe fashioned from carrots, an ocarina created from a sweet potato, other brightly colored vegetables. Gourds,
                                        2

daikon radishes, and other vegetables, are used
                                    3
to round out the "orchestra."

[2]

From an early age, the Nan brothers, raised on a vegetable farm in China's Anhui province, who were
                                                    4
taught to play conventional musical instruments by their father, a music teacher. [B] The siblings' love of music and passion for performance led them to begin

1. **A.** NO CHANGE
   B. does seem
   C. are
   D. is

2. Which choice best maintains the pattern established in the sentence's two previous examples?
   F. NO CHANGE
   G. vegetable instruments of all shapes and sizes.
   H. a flute made from a bamboo shoot.
   J. a certain type of root vegetable.

3. **A.** NO CHANGE
   B. other; vegetables are used
   C. other vegetables are used,
   D. other vegetables are used

4. **F.** NO CHANGE
   G. were
   H. and were
   J. DELETE the underlined portion.

GO ON TO THE NEXT PAGE.

experimenting with vegetable musical instruments a

few years ago.

[3]

Working by hand while constructing their edible
5

instruments, the brothers manually bore holes into the

vegetables by using long metal drill bits, snacking on

discarded pieces as they work. [C] Weiping says that

to create a low pitch, which makes a deep hole.
6

Nonetheless, a high pitch requires a shallow hole.
7

Other factors, like, the diameter of the hole and
8

changes in air temperature and humidity, also

effects the sound quality.
9

[4]

[1] A newly picked vegetable that sits at the market

for even one day may lose much of its water content,

producing a pitch that is out of tune. [2] Because of this,
10

the brothers must carve a fresh set of instruments before

each performance. [3] Still, the most critical ingredient

in creating high-quality sound, Weidong says, is the
11

vegetables' high water content. ☐12

5. **A.** NO CHANGE
   B. Eating unused vegetable parts while they construct
   C. Using metal tools to construct
   D. To construct

6. **F.** NO CHANGE
   G. having made
   H. by making
   J. he makes

7. **A.** NO CHANGE
   B. Conversely,
   C. Otherwise,
   D. Even so,

8. **F.** NO CHANGE
   G. factors—like
   H. factors, like
   J. factors like

9. **A.** NO CHANGE
   B. affects
   C. affect
   D. effect

10. **F.** NO CHANGE
    G. such vegetables produce
    H. it will produce
    J. this produces

11. **A.** NO CHANGE
    B. sound, Weidong says
    C. sound Weidong says,
    D. sound Weidong says

12. Which sequence of sentences makes this paragraph most logical?
    F. NO CHANGE
    G. 1, 3, 2
    H. 2, 1, 3
    J. 3, 1, 2

Taking Additional Practice Tests

GO ON TO THE NEXT PAGE.

1 ■ ■ ■ ■ ■ ■ ■ ■ 1

[5]

While the brothers' musical repertoire is as varied
$\overline{\phantom{\text{13}}}$
                    13
as their instruments, ranging from traditional Chinese

flute music to modern pop songs. [D] They maintain that

different vegetables have different scales and are therefore

suited to different types of music. Since 2011, the Nan

brothers have performed regularly, playing a wide variety

of music on their edible instruments and bringing a whole

new meaning to the idea of playing with your food. [14]

13. **A.** NO CHANGE
    B. With the brothers' musical repertoire being
    C. Having the brothers' musical repertoire be
    D. The brothers' musical repertoire is

14. At this point, the writer is considering adding the following true statement:

    > Each pitch is tested and perfected with the help of an old electronic tuner.

    Should the writer make this addition here?

    F. Yes, because it supports the idea that the brothers exercise care and attention to detail as they craft their vegetable instruments.
    G. Yes, because it helps explain how vegetables can be turned into precise musical instruments.
    H. No, because it provides information about the process of creating instruments that is not relevant at this point in the essay.
    J. No, because it conflicts with the idea that the brothers have a strong musical background.

    Question 15 asks about the preceding passage as a whole.
    ---

15. The writer wants to add the following sentence to the essay:

    > As teenagers, they performed with a local theater company.

    The sentence would most logically be placed at:

    A. Point A in Paragraph 1.
    B. Point B in Paragraph 2.
    C. Point C in Paragraph 3.
    D. Point D in Paragraph 5.

PASSAGE II

Nature Meets Art

[1]

Located in Olympic Sculpture Park in Seattle,

artist Mark Dion's *Neukom Vivarium* has been called

a combination of art and ecology, sculpture and nature.

GO ON TO THE NEXT PAGE.

The installation contains a sixty-foot-long nurse log, it is
a slowly decaying piece of tree trunk that provides a home
and nutrients for young plants and supports a variety of
microbial life. [A] This single log offers visitors to the

urban park, a glimpse into the complicated cycle of life
unfolding in the forests outside the city.

[2]

Vivarium comes from the Latin word *vivus*, which
means "alive"—a fitting description for a piece of art that
exemplifies a thriving forest ecosystem. [B] Dion found
the log, part of a western hemlock lying in a Washington

forest, and, transporting it to the city along with some
of the soil, fungi, and plants that had surrounded the
tree. [C] Working with a team of scientists and
architects, Dion installed the log in a specially
constructed eighty-foot-long greenhouse. The
greenhouse is customized with magnifying glasses
and microscopes that disclose minute details of the
life supported by the log. Repeated visits to the

installation reveals the larger process of decay
and transformation.

[3]

In the wild, this complex, interconnected
system of life would have had no trouble sustaining
itself. In the city, however, maintaining the nurse log
requires a great number of energy and technology. [D]

16. F. NO CHANGE
 G. the term "nurse log" is defined as
 H. this type of log is
 J. DELETE the underlined portion.

17. A. NO CHANGE
 B. log, in addition to acting as a home and providing
  nutrients for young plants, offers visitors
 C. massive piece of tree (a sixty-foot log) offers
  visitors
 D. decaying nurse log offers visitors who come

18. F. NO CHANGE
 G. park a glimpse into the complicated cycle of life
 H. park a glimpse into the complicated cycle of life,
 J. park, a glimpse into the complicated cycle of life,

19. A. NO CHANGE
 B. laying within
 C. lying with
 D. laying in

20. F. NO CHANGE
 G. and, to transport
 H. and transported
 J. transported

21. A. NO CHANGE
 B. log, repeating
 C. log repeating
 D. log, repeated

22. F. NO CHANGE
 G. has revealed
 H. is revealing
 J. reveal

23. A. NO CHANGE
 B. a great amount in
 C. great amounts of
 D. great numbers in

GO ON TO THE NEXT PAGE.

1 ■ ■ ■ ■ ■ ■ ■ ■ **1**

Humidity is electronically monitored, the soil is

constantly replenished with nutrients, and sunlight is
<u>_____</u>
                          24

filtered through green-hued glass designed to mimic

the color of a forest canopy. [25]

[4]

    For Dion, the amount of work <u>in the middle</u>
                                        26
<u>of a busy city</u> required to sustain this ecosystem
      26

conveys an important message. <u>According with the</u>
                                         27
artist, the constant effort substitutes for what nature does

instinctively, which highlights the fact that "it's incredibly

difficult, expensive, and technological to approximate that

system." In other words, nature, once <u>destroyed is virtually</u>
                                                28
impossible to reconstruct.

24. **F.** NO CHANGE
    G. constantly provided with and restored by nutrients on a regular basis,
    H. often constantly replenished with healthful nutrients,
    J. constantly replenished with restorative nutrients regularly,

25. If the writer were to delete the preceding sentence, the paragraph would primarily lose a statement that:
    A. explains why good air quality and healthy soil are necessary to maintain nature-based exhibits.
    B. illustrates how much effort is required to ensure that the exhibit survives in an urban setting.
    C. describes how the greenhouse is more important to the installation than is the nurse log.
    D. emphasizes how difficult it was for Dion to build the greenhouse.

26. The best placement for the underlined portion would be:
    F. where it is now.
    G. before the word *the*.
    H. after the word *this*.
    J. after the word *ecosystem*.

27. **A.** NO CHANGE
    B. In accordance with
    C. In accord with
    D. According to

28. **F.** NO CHANGE
    G. destroyed, is virtually,
    H. destroyed, is virtually
    J. destroyed is virtually,

Questions 29 and 30 ask about the preceding passage as a whole.

---

29. The writer is considering adding the following parenthetical information to the essay:

    (The *Neukom* in the installation's title refers to the name of the work's patrons.)

    If the writer were to add this sentence, it would most logically be placed at:

    A. Point A in Paragraph 1.
    B. Point B in Paragraph 2.
    C. Point C in Paragraph 2.
    D. Point D in Paragraph 3.

30. Suppose the writer's primary purpose had been to describe how one artist uses a work of art to educate people about an issue the artist feels is important. Would this essay accomplish that purpose?

    F. Yes, because it describes how Dion saw that local forests were being destroyed and then decided to make a sculpture out of a fallen tree.
    G. Yes, because it describes Dion's nature-based installation and explains the message Dion hopes to convey through *Neukom Vivarium*.
    H. No, because it focuses on what Dion's installation looks like and how it contributes to the Olympic Sculpture Park.
    J. No, because it fails to indicate what *Neukom Vivarium*'s viewers actually learn from the installation.

GO ON TO THE NEXT PAGE.

1 ▪ ▪ ▪ ▪ ▪ ▪ ▪ ▪ ▪ ▪ **1**

PASSAGE III

Internet Gain: Andreessen's Mosaic

Before Mosaic—the web browser widely credited with popularizing the World Wide Web—was invented, the Internet wasn't user-friendly. Internet <u>navigation required</u> knowledge of specific typed commands; online documents, ₃₁ consisting almost entirely of text, were hard to locate and download. <u>Given these obstructive hindrances,</u> many ₃₂ people assumed the web would remain the domain of technology experts and never have mass appeal. Marc Andreessen believed the <u>opposite, everyone would</u> ₃₃

want the Internet. ☐ 34

As a student <u>worker, for the National Center for</u> ₃₅ <u>Supercomputing Applications, (NCSA)</u> at the University ₃₅

of Illinois, Andreessen <u>became enthralled</u> by the Internet. ₃₆ In 1992, he conceived of a browser that would simplify web navigation. Rather than typing specific commands, people would be able to access different web pages by clicking on icons. He showed his idea to fellow student Eric Bina, who helped refine the program. The two then worked with the NCSA to develop Mosaic, <u>which became</u> available in 1993. Free to anyone with ₃₇ an Internet connection, Mosaic quickly became popular.

31. A. NO CHANGE
   B. navigation, which required
   C. navigation that required
   D. navigation requiring

32. F. NO CHANGE
   G. What with the problematic issues,
   H. Because of these difficulties,
   J. Owing to the messiness,

33. A. NO CHANGE
   B. opposite; because
   C. opposite:
   D. opposite

34. Which of the following statements, if added here, would provide the best transition to the discussion of Andreessen's browser?
   F. He thought Internet speeds would eventually increase.
   G. The amount of information online was immense.
   H. Few people had Internet access at the time.
   J. People just needed the right tool.

35. A. NO CHANGE
   B. worker, for the National Center for Supercomputing Applications, (NCSA),
   C. worker for the National Center for Supercomputing Applications, (NCSA),
   D. worker for the National Center for Supercomputing Applications (NCSA)

36. Which choice most strongly conveys that Andreessen developed a strong affinity for the Internet?
   F. NO CHANGE
   G. first gained access to
   H. spent many hours on
   J. saw the utility of

37. A. NO CHANGE
   B. the NCSA made the program
   C. they made Mosaic
   D. it became

GO ON TO THE NEXT PAGE.

1 ▪ ▪ ▪ ▪ ▪ ▪ ▪ ▪ 1

Approximately 60,000 copies of the browser were
‾‾‾‾‾‾‾‾‾‾‾‾‾‾‾‾‾‾‾‾‾‾‾‾‾‾‾‾‾‾‾
                              38
downloaded in its first year.

Mosaic was soon not the first web browser, but
          ‾‾‾‾
          39
it surpassed all rivals. Unlike other browsers, Mosaic

was easy to install, and it worked on every operating

system. It was the first browser to display pictures

and text on the same page ⏐40⏐ . Featuring hyperlinks,

the user of the program was able to visit other web
‾‾‾‾‾‾‾‾‾‾‾‾‾‾‾‾‾‾‾‾‾‾‾‾‾‾‾‾‾‾‾‾‾
                    41
pages with one click. "With Mosaic," said one writer,

"the online world appears to be a vast, interconnected

universe of information." ⏐42⏐

Even though it gave way to other, more

sophisticated browsers within a few years, Mosaic

showed average users the significance of the Internet.

Comparatively, its simplicity encouraged people to
‾‾‾‾‾‾‾‾‾‾‾‾
    43
create and upload their own content. In the year

Mosaic was discharged, 623 websites existed.
              ‾‾‾‾‾‾‾‾‾‾
                44

38. **F.** NO CHANGE
    G. That year, approximately 60,000 copies of the browser
    H. Approximately 60,000 copies of the browser (Mosaic)
    J. Approximately, but not exactly, 60,000 copies of the browser

39. The best placement for the underlined portion would be:
    A. where it is now.
    B. after the word *Mosaic*.
    C. after the word *browser* (and before the comma).
    D. after the word *it*.

40. At this point, the writer is considering adding the following phrase (adjusting the punctuation as needed):

    adding much-needed visual appeal

    Should the writer make this addition?
    F. Yes, because it reveals that Mosaic was the first browser to display pictures alongside text.
    G. Yes, because it emphasizes that using Mosaic made web browsing more enjoyable.
    H. No, because it implies that the text-based documents on the Internet weren't useful.
    J. No, because it suggests that, initially, Mosaic was similar to other web browsers.

41. **A.** NO CHANGE
    B. the program's user was enabled
    C. the program enabled the user
    D. it was easy for the user

42. If the writer were to delete the preceding sentence, the essay would primarily lose a statement that:
    F. argues that, before Mosaic, few people searched the Internet for information.
    G. specifies some of the features that made Mosaic popular among its users.
    H. credits Mosaic with making the Internet feel more coherent to users.
    J. compares the designs of later web browsers to Mosaic's design.

43. **A.** NO CHANGE
    B. Moreover,
    C. Conversely,
    D. Instead,

44. **F.** NO CHANGE
    G. relinquished,
    H. released,
    J. emitted,

GO ON TO THE NEXT PAGE.

Four years later, there were more than 600,000.
                                        45

45. Given that all the choices are true, which one best concludes the essay by using specific information to complete the contrast begun in the previous sentence?

A. NO CHANGE
B. Mosaic's point-and-click interface revolutionized the way people used the Internet.
C. Andreessen would go on to develop another highly successful web browser.
D. Since then, the web has expanded at an exponential rate.

PASSAGE IV

A Poetic Olympics

[1]

During athletic festivals in ancient Greece, great poets were placed alongside champion athletes. This
                     46
has never been true of the modern Olympic Games. [A] The Olympic literary competition, reintroduced in 1912 in Stockholm and included in the Games for decades,

is poorly remembered and rarely missed. The only genuine
                    47

public excitement for even the very first modern, Olympic
                                    48
literary contest was focused on the scandal surrounding the winning poem. [B]

[2]

French aristocrat Baron Pierre de Coubertin, who in 1896 founded the modern Olympic Games, he insisted
                                              49
that talent in the fine arts was as important as skill in

athletics. After years of opposition from officials whom
                                              50
felt that the modern Games should focus solely on athletics, Coubertin implemented fine arts competitions, known as the Pentathlon of Muses, in 1912. [C]

46. Which choice most clearly emphasizes the overwhelmingly positive reception great poets enjoyed during athletic festivals in ancient Greece?

F. NO CHANGE
G. celebrated
H. accepted
J. liked

47. Given that all the choices are accurate, which one best connects this sentence to the information that follows in the next sentence?

A. NO CHANGE
B. was featured along with competitions in music composition, architecture, sculpture, and painting.
C. is sometimes commented upon when the Olympic Games are held today.
D. was an homage to the traditions of the people of ancient Greece.

48. F. NO CHANGE
G. very, first, modern Olympic
H. very first, modern Olympic,
J. very first modern Olympic

49. A. NO CHANGE
B. insistent in his belief
C. insisting
D. insisted

50. F. NO CHANGE
G. themselves whom
H. who
J. which

GO ON TO THE NEXT PAGE.

For the literary contest, it would submit an unpublished
51

work; Coubertin did not establish a length requirement.
52
After a long deliberation during the literary event's first

year; finally judges named duo George Hohrod and Martin
53
Eschbach as gold medalists for their poem "Ode to Sport."

[3]

The judges, so impressed by "Ode to Sport" that
54
they called it "the perfect poem," refused to award either

silver or bronze medals to any other literary competitors.

Weeks, after the Games had come to an end, the judges
55
attempted to contact Hohrod and Eschbach given that

the two had not come forward to receive their medals.

The judges discovered that neither author existed.
56

51. **A.** NO CHANGE
    B. competitors
    C. those
    D. they

52. Given that all the choices are accurate, which one provides information about the Olympic literary contest that is most clearly relevant at this point in the essay?
    F. NO CHANGE
    G. work. At the Olympic Games in Paris in 1924, a poem about fencing called "Sword Songs" was the winning piece.
    H. work, though critics mocked some of the limitations placed on writers.
    J. work, preferably a poem, that was "inspired by the idea of sport."

53. **A.** NO CHANGE
    B. year, judges
    C. year, then judges
    D. year. Judges

54. **F.** NO CHANGE
    G. judges, and having been
    H. judges had been
    J. judges were

55. **A.** NO CHANGE
    B. Weeks after the Games had come to an end,
    C. Weeks, after the Games had come to an end
    D. Weeks after the Games had come to an end

56. Given that all the choices are true, which one most effectively leads the reader from the information about Hohrod and Eschbach in the preceding sentence to the information about Coubertin in the next sentence?
    F. NO CHANGE
    G. After "Ode to Sport" won, Swedish art academies claimed that the contest, with its thematic focus on sport, lacked purpose.
    H. Submissions began to arrive in anticipation of the next Olympic literary competition.
    J. The judges had read the winning poem, "Ode to Sport," aloud to spectators.

GO ON TO THE NEXT PAGE.

A few years later, Coubertin admitted that he himself had submitted "the perfect poem" pseudonymously. [57]

[4]

The judges argued that they did not know that Coubertin had written "Ode to Sport." But once Coubertin's ruse was uncovered, distrust for the already unpopular competition expanded as a result—and the feeling endured. [D] The literary competition was dropped after the 1948 London Games. Many of the winning poems have since vanished, with only their titles remaining. Few literary historians think that much has been lost.

57. At this point, the writer is considering adding the following sentence:

> The founder of the modern Olympic Games, Coubertin was also the person who brought about the fine arts competitions.

Given that the information is true, should the writer make this addition here?

A. Yes, because it makes clear why Coubertin didn't include his real name on his poetry submission.
B. Yes, because it suggests that Coubertin knew that the poem he submitted was particularly well written.
C. No, because it repeats information about Coubertin that is provided earlier in the essay.
D. No, because it doesn't make clear whether Coubertin had discussed "Ode to Sport" with the judges of the literary competition.

58. F. NO CHANGE
G. increased even though dislike of it was not new—
H. grew—
J. blew up because of this unveiling—

Questions 59 and 60 ask about the preceding passage as a whole.

59. The writer is considering adding the following sentence to the essay:

> Over the years, the contest attracted many people who wanted to be poets but few talented poets, and even contest organizers began to doubt the quality of the submissions.

If the writer were to add this sentence, it would most logically be placed at:

A. Point A in Paragraph 1.
B. Point B in Paragraph 1.
C. Point C in Paragraph 2.
D. Point D in Paragraph 4.

60. Suppose the writer's primary purpose had been to explain a lesser-known aspect of a widely known event. Would this essay accomplish that purpose?

F. Yes, because it outlines Coubertin's most important accomplishments as the founder of the modern Olympic Games.
G. Yes, because it describes an element of the modern Olympic Games that was relatively short lived and is not very well remembered.
H. No, because it instead considers the merits of fine arts competitions being a part of popular athletic events.
J. No, because it instead discusses the poem "Ode to Sport" and explains why the poem influenced Coubertin to compete in literary competitions.

PASSAGE V

Capturing the Arctic

San Francisco native, Louise Arner Boyd, first saw the blue glaciers and glittering fjords

of the Arctic ice cap during a 1924 photography expedition to Spitsbergen, a Norwegian island.

61. A. NO CHANGE
B. native Louise Arner Boyd
C. native Louise Arner Boyd,
D. native, Louise Arner Boyd

62. F. NO CHANGE
G. cap, which she had never before seen,
H. cap—both glaciers and fjords—
J. cap initially

GO ON TO THE NEXT PAGE.

1 ▪ ▪ ▪ ▪ ▪ ▪ ▪ ▪ ▪ 1

In the United States, little was known about the Arctic: its
$\underset{63}{\text{}}$

nearly frozen seas, packed with icebergs, made boat travel
$\underset{64}{\text{}}$
to the area treacherous. But Boyd, an amateur naturalist
and practiced photographer, made exploring this wide,

frigid terrain her life's focus. She would lead seven Arctic
$\underset{65}{\text{}}$
expeditions, six by sea and one by air, mainly to the east
coast of Greenland.

   Boyd's first two Arctic trips, taken in a small ship
with a small crew, were designed for photographing the
magnificent glaciers. Soon her interest in the region
$\underset{66}{\text{}}$
expanded beyond capturing its beauty. She secured a
$\underset{66}{\text{}}$
larger, sturdier ship, the *Veslekari*, and invited several
scientists to travel with her. Over the course of three
1930s voyages, she led her team to the farthest

reaches of the Arctic, in 1938, the group anchored
$\underset{67}{\text{}}$

close south of the North Pole. Botanists gathered
$\underset{68}{\text{}}$

plant specimens from the tundra—paleogeologists
$\underset{69}{\text{}}$
studied the ancient ice fields, and hydrogeographers
searched for mountains on the ocean floor.

---

63. A. NO CHANGE
   B. their
   C. it's
   D. its'

64. If the writer were to delete the underlined portion (adjusting the punctuation as needed), the essay would primarily lose:
   F. an indication that the purpose of the 1924 photography expedition Boyd participated in was to photograph icebergs.
   G. an explanation of a technique used by seafarers to make traveling the dangerous seas near Spitsbergen safer.
   H. an example of a particular danger facing people who might have attempted to travel the Arctic by boat.
   J. a reason most seafaring boats in the 1920s weren't equipped to navigate around icebergs.

65. Given that all the choices are accurate, which one most strongly suggests that Boyd conceived of and managed the seven Arctic expeditions?
   A. NO CHANGE
   B. be a part of
   C. experience
   D. embark on

66. Given that all the choices are true, which one most effectively leads the reader from the first sentence of this paragraph to the information that follows in the next two sentences?
   F. NO CHANGE
   G. Boyd had the opportunity to present some of these early photographs to the king and queen of England.
   H. In 1960, Boyd became the first woman to be elected to the board of the American Geographical Society.
   J. On both journeys, the crew came ashore on a group of islands called Franz Josef Land.

67. A. NO CHANGE
   B. Arctic and
   C. Arctic;
   D. Arctic

68. F. NO CHANGE
   G. nearby
   H. about
   J. just

69. A. NO CHANGE
   B. tundra,
   C. tundra:
   D. tundra

GO ON TO THE NEXT PAGE.

1 ■ ■ ■ ■ ■ ■ ■ ■ **1**

Boyd took thousands of photographs. She worked with the best equipment available, including a tripod-mounted large-format camera that freed crisp,
70

high-resolution images of the landscape. She knew about
71
photogrammetry, the science of making 3-D measurements from photographic images, Boyd used precise methods to choose locations and camera positions for its shots. Her
72
well-executed photos, featured in her book *The Fiord*

Region of East Greenland, provided the basis for the first
73
accurate large-scale maps of the east coast of the country.

The polar expert's final Arctic journey in 1955 was
74
over the North Pole, in a chartered flight. Her aerial
74
photos document the trip. Today, scientists are exploring how Boyd's photographs and writing, along with her team's studies, might be used to monitor environmental change in the Arctic.

70. F. NO CHANGE
G. delivered
H. performed
J. disengaged

71. A. NO CHANGE
B. The advanced knowledge she had of
C. She had advanced knowledge of
D. Knowledgeable about

72. F. NO CHANGE
G. his or her
H. their
J. her

73. A. NO CHANGE
B. established the foundation that was the springboard to
C. gave support that assisted in the making of
D. lent themselves to the purpose of creating

74. Which choice provides the clearest indication that Boyd's chartered flight over the North Pole was her final Arctic journey ever, not only her final Arctic journey in the year 1955?
F. NO CHANGE
G. The polar expert's final Arctic journey in 1955 was a chartered flight over the North Pole.
H. A chartered flight over the North Pole in 1955 was the polar expert's final Arctic journey.
J. A chartered flight over the North Pole was the polar expert's final Arctic journey in 1955.

Question 75 asks about the preceding passage as a whole.

75. Suppose the writer's primary purpose had been to explain the way Boyd's photographs were used to make maps of the east coast of Greenland. Would this essay accomplish that purpose?
A. Yes, because the writer hints that because Boyd had studied photogrammetry, she deliberately created photographs that could be used to make maps.
B. Yes, because the writer makes clear that Boyd had photographed a region that, before her expeditions, had not been thoroughly documented.
C. No, because although the writer mentions that Boyd's photographs were used to make maps, the writer does not elaborate on how this was done.
D. No, because the writer instead focuses on describing how Boyd positioned her camera to create high-resolution images of glaciers.

END OF TEST 1

STOP! DO NOT TURN THE PAGE UNTIL TOLD TO DO SO.

2 △ △ △ △ △ △ △ △ △ 2

MATHEMATICS TEST
60 Minutes—60 Questions

DIRECTIONS: Solve each problem, choose the correct answer, and then fill in the corresponding oval on your answer document.

Do not linger over problems that take too much time. Solve as many as you can; then return to the others in the time you have left for this test.

You are permitted to use a calculator on this test. You may use your calculator for any problems you choose, but some of the problems may best be done without using a calculator.

Note: Unless otherwise stated, all of the following should be assumed.

1. Illustrative figures are NOT necessarily drawn to scale.
2. Geometric figures lie in a plane.
3. The word *line* indicates a straight line.
4. The word *average* indicates arithmetic mean.

---

1. Xuan sold 9 used books for $9.80 each. With the money from these sales, she bought 4 new books and had $37.80 left over. What was the average amount Xuan paid for each new book?

   A. $ 5.60
   B. $ 9.45
   C. $10.08
   D. $12.60
   E. $22.05

2. A point at $(-5,7)$ in the standard (x,y) coordinate plane is translated right 7 coordinate units and down 5 coordinate units. What are the coordinates of the point after the translation?

   F. $(-12,12)$
   G. $(\ 0,\ 0)$
   H. $(\ 2,\ 2)$
   J. $(\ 2,12)$
   K. $(\ 12,12)$

3. Shantiel left her home at 9:00 a.m. on Tuesday and traveled 648 miles. When she arrived at her destination it was 3:00 a.m. the next day. Given that her home and her destination are in the same time zone, which of the following is closest to her average speed, in miles per hour, for this trip?

   A. 72
   B. 54
   C. 36
   D. 31
   E. 18

DO YOUR FIGURING HERE.

GO ON TO THE NEXT PAGE.

2 △ △ △ △ △ △ △ △ △ **2**

DO YOUR FIGURING HERE.

4. The text message component of each of Juan's monthly phone bills consists of $10.00 for the first 300 text messages sent that month, plus $0.10 for each additional text message sent that month. On Juan's most recent phone bill he was charged a total of $16.50 for text messages. For how many text messages in total was Juan charged on this bill?

  F. 235
  G. 285
  H. 315
  J. 365
  K. 465

5. Which of the following matrices is equal to

$$\begin{bmatrix} 9 & 8 \\ -4 & 7 \end{bmatrix} + \begin{bmatrix} -6 & 6 \\ 5 & 4 \end{bmatrix} ?$$

  A. $\begin{bmatrix} 3 & 14 \\ 1 & 11 \end{bmatrix}$

  B. $\begin{bmatrix} 3 & 14 \\ 9 & 11 \end{bmatrix}$

  C. $\begin{bmatrix} 15 & 14 \\ 9 & 11 \end{bmatrix}$

  D. $\begin{bmatrix} 17 & 0 \\ 3 & 9 \end{bmatrix}$

  E. $\begin{bmatrix} -14 & 86 \\ 59 & 4 \end{bmatrix}$

6. A function, f, is defined by $f(x,y) = 3x^2 - 4y$. What is the value of $f(4,3)$?

  F. 11
  G. 24
  H. 36
  J. 65
  K. 132

7. A certain group consists of 5 children, 3 of whom are age 10 and 2 of whom are age 5. What is the mean age of the children in the group?

  A. 5
  B. 7
  C. 7.5
  D. 8
  E. 10

8. In the figure shown below, $\overline{AC} \parallel \overline{DE}$; $BD = AD$; D and E are on $\overline{AB}$ and $\overline{BC}$, respectively; $AC = 8$ feet; and the height of $\triangle ABC$ is 10 feet. What is DE, in feet?

  F. 2
  G. 3
  H. 4
  J. 5
  K. 6

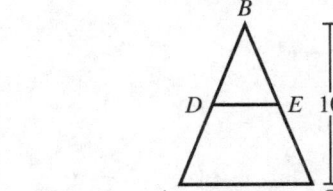

GO ON TO THE NEXT PAGE.

2 △ △ △ △ △ △ △ △ △ **2**

9. In a poll of 500 registered voters, 337 voters favored a proposal to increase funding for local schools. Suppose the poll is indicative of how the 22,000 registered voters will vote on the proposal. Which of the following values is closest to how many of the 22,000 registered voters will be expected to vote in favor of the proposal?

A. 13,200
B. 14,830
C. 21,840
D. 22,000
E. 32,640

10. Diego purchased a car that had a purchase price of $13,400, which included all other costs and tax. He paid $400 as a down payment and got a loan for the rest of the purchase price. Diego paid off the loan by making 48 payments of $300 each. The total of all his payments, including the down payment, was how much more than the car's purchase price?

F. $ 1,000
G. $ 1,400
H. $13,000
J. $14,400
K. $14,800

11. In the standard (x,y) coordinate plane, what is the slope of the line $4x + 7y = 9$?

A. $-\frac{4}{7}$

B. $\frac{4}{9}$

C. -4

D. 4

E. 9

12. In the figure below, $\overleftrightarrow{AD}$ intersects $\overleftrightarrow{BG}$ at C and is perpendicular to $\overleftrightarrow{DE}$. Line $\overleftrightarrow{DE}$ intersects $\overleftrightarrow{BG}$ at F. Given that the measure of $\angle EFG$ is 25°, what is the measure of $\angle BCD$?

F. 65°
G. 115°
H. 120°
J. 130°
K. 155°

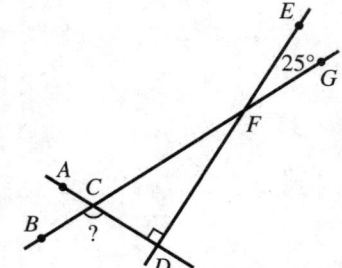

DO YOUR FIGURING HERE.

GO ON TO THE NEXT PAGE.

2 △ △ △ △ △ △ △ △ △ **2**

13. What is the sum of the 2 solutions of the equation $x^2 + x - 30 = 0$?

   A. −30
   B. −6
   C. −1
   D.   0
   E.   5

DO YOUR FIGURING HERE.

14. The volume of a sphere is $\frac{4\pi r^3}{3}$, where r is the radius of the sphere. What is the volume, in cubic yards, of a sphere with a *diameter* of 4 yards?

   F. $\frac{32}{3}\pi$

   G. $\frac{64}{3}\pi$

   H. 32π

   J. 48π

   K. $\frac{256}{3}\pi$

15. What is the smallest integer greater than $\sqrt{85}$?

   A.   5
   B.   9
   C. 10
   D. 12
   E. 43

16. The 3 statements below are true for the elements of sets A, B, C, and D.

     I. All elements of A are elements of B.
    II. All elements of C are elements of D.
   III. No elements of D are elements of B.

Which of the following statements *must* be true?

   F. All elements of A are elements of C.
   G. All elements of B are elements of D.
   H. All elements of C are elements of B.
   J. No elements of A are elements of B.
   K. No elements of A are elements of C.

17. In the standard (x,y) coordinate plane, the midpoint of $\overline{AB}$ is at $(2,1)$, and A is at $(8,10)$. What is the x-coordinate of B ?

   A. −4
   B. −6
   C. −8
   D.   3
   E.   5

GO ON TO THE NEXT PAGE.

2 △ △ △ △ △ △ △ △ △ **2**

18. Lena will pick 1 card at random from a pack of 25 baseball cards. Each card features the fielding position for 1 of 25 different baseball players. Each player in the pack has only 1 fielding position. The table below lists the frequency of fielding positions in the pack. What is the probability that the card Lena picks will feature an outfielder or a pitcher?

Fielding position	Frequency
Catcher	4
Infielder	6
Pitcher	8
Outfielder	7

F. 9%
G. 28%
H. 32%
J. 56%
K. 60%

19. According to a soil analysis, a certain lawn requires an application of 40.0 kg of nitrogen phosphate when the average temperature is 75.0°F. To avoid burning the grass, the required application amount decreases 1.2 kg for each 1.0°F that the average temperature is above 75.0°F. To the nearest 0.1 kg, what is the required application amount of nitrogen phosphate when the average temperature is 83.0°F ?

A. 30.4
B. 30.8
C. 33.3
D. 38.4
E. 38.8

20. In the figure below, all segments that meet do so at right angles. What is the area, in square units, of the shaded region?

F. $2\frac{1}{4}$

G. 3

H. $3\frac{1}{3}$

J. 4

K. 7

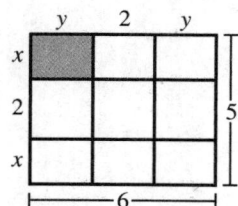

21. The perimeter of a certain scalene triangle is 100 inches. The side lengths of the triangle are represented by $5x$, $3x + 30$, and $2x + 10$, respectively. What is the length, in inches, of the longest side of the triangle?

A. 6
B. 22
C. 30
D. 48
E. 72

DO YOUR FIGURING HERE.

GO ON TO THE NEXT PAGE.

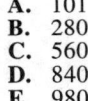

△ △ △ △ △ △ △ △ △ **2**

DO YOUR FIGURING HERE.

22. The mayor of Westbrook is deciding how to assign the 6 council members to the row of seats below.

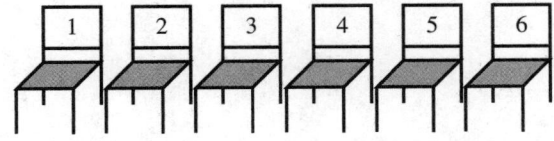

From how many different arrangements can she choose?

F. 21
G. 36
H. 64
J. 720
K. 6,000,000

23. The sum of 2 and 200% of 1 has the same value as which of the following calculations?

A. 100% of 2
B. 150% of 2
C. 300% of 2
D. 300% of 1
E. 400% of 1

24. The graph in the standard (x,y) coordinate plane below is represented by one of the following equations. Which equation?

F. $y = -\frac{3}{2}x + 2$

G. $y = -\frac{3}{2}x + 3$

H. $y = -\frac{2}{3}x + 2$

J. $y = -\frac{2}{3}x + 3$

K. $y = \frac{2}{3}x + 2$

25. Kamini is constructing the kite shown below. The kite includes 2 perpendicular supports, one of length 40 inches and the other of length 28 inches. The ends of the supports are connected with string to form a 4-sided figure that is symmetric with respect to the longer support. A layer of paper will cover the interior of the 4-sided figure. Which of the following is closest to the area, in square inches, that Kamini will cover with paper?

A. 101
B. 280
C. 560
D. 840
E. 980

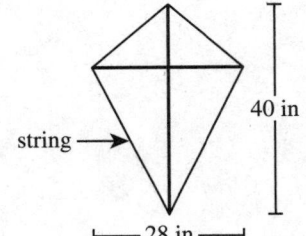

GO ON TO THE NEXT PAGE.

2   **2**

Use the following information to answer questions 26–29.

DO YOUR FIGURING HERE.

The top view and side view of a 40-foot-long swimming pool are shown in the figure below. All dimensions given are in feet.

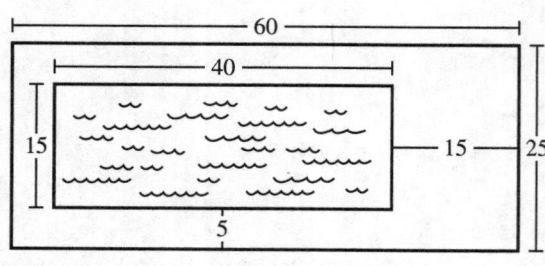

top view

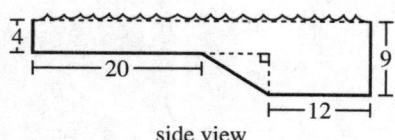

side view

The top view shows the top rectangular surface of the pool and the surrounding rectangular patio. All 4 walls of the pool are vertical and perpendicular to the top surface. The side view shows a cross section along the length of the pool. All cross sections parallel to the side view are congruent. The shallow end has a constant depth of 4 ft. The deep end has a constant depth of 9 ft. A rectangular surface connects the shallow and deep ends.

26. What is the area, in square feet, of the patio surrounding the pool?

    F.   500
    G.   600
    H.   900
    J. 1,100
    K. 1,350

27. Johann put up a fence along the outer edge of the patio. Given that the materials for the fence cost $12 per foot, what was the total cost of the materials for the fence?

    A. $1,020
    B. $1,320
    C. $1,800
    D. $2,040
    E. $3,360

GO ON TO THE NEXT PAGE.

2 △ △ △ △ △ △ △ △ △ **2**

28. A full lap is 2 times the length of the pool. Johann swam 5 full laps of the pool in $4\frac{1}{2}$ minutes. Which of the following values is closest to Johann's average swimming speed, in feet per minute?

   F.   35
   G.   45
   H.   60
   J.   90
   K. 120

DO YOUR FIGURING HERE.

29. The side view of the pool is placed in the standard (x,y) coordinate plane, keeping the same orientation and scale, such that both vertical segments showing depth are parallel to the y-axis. Which of the following values is closest to the slope of the line segment connecting the shallow end to the deep end?

   A. −0.44
   B. −0.63
   C. −0.75
   D. −1.33
   E. −1.60

30. A construction company builds 3 different models of houses (A, B, and C). They order all the bathtubs, shower stalls, and sinks for the houses from a certain manufacturer. Each model of house contains different numbers of these bathroom fixtures. The tables below give the number of each kind of these fixtures required for each model and the cost to the company, in dollars, of each type of fixture.

Fixture	Model		
	A	B	C
Bathtubs	1	1	2
Shower stalls	0	1	1
Sinks	1	2	4

Fixture	Cost
Bathtub	$250
Shower stall	$150
Sink	$120

The company plans to build 3 A's, 4 B's, and 6 C's. What will be the cost to the company of exactly enough of these bathroom fixtures to put the required number in all of these houses?

   F. $ 1,940
   G. $ 2,070
   H. $ 8,940
   J. $ 9,180
   K. $10,450

GO ON TO THE NEXT PAGE.

2   **2**

31. Shown below, a board 5 feet 6 inches long is cut into 2 equal parts. What is the length, to the nearest inch, of each part?

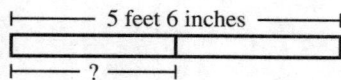

- **A.** 2 feet 5 inches
- **B.** 2 feet 8 inches
- **C.** 2 feet 9 inches
- **D.** 3 feet 0 inches
- **E.** 3 feet 5 inches

DO YOUR FIGURING HERE.

32. A company that builds bridges used a pile driver to drive a post into the ground. The post was driven 18 feet into the ground by the first hit of the pile driver. On each hit after the first hit, the post was driven into the ground an additional distance that was $\frac{2}{3}$ the distance the post was driven in the previous hit. After a total of 4 hits, the post was driven how many feet into the ground?

- **F.** $28\frac{8}{9}$
- **G.** 30
- **H.** $43\frac{1}{3}$
- **J.** 48
- **K.** 54

33. In the standard (x,y) coordinate plane, A' is the image resulting from the reflection of the point $A(2,-3)$ across the y-axis. What are the coordinates of A'?

- **A.** $(-3, 2)$
- **B.** $(-2,-3)$
- **C.** $(-2, 3)$
- **D.** $(2, 3)$
- **E.** $(3,-2)$

GO ON TO THE NEXT PAGE.

2 △ △ △ △ △ △ △ △ △ **2**

34. To increase the mean of 4 numbers by 3, by how much would the sum of the 4 numbers have to increase?

F. $\frac{3}{4}$

G. 1

H. $\frac{4}{3}$

J. 7

K. 12

DO YOUR FIGURING HERE.

35. Which of the following expressions is equivalent to $(3 + x)^{-100}$?

A. $-3^{100} - x^{100}$

B. $-300 - 100x$

C. $\frac{1}{3^{100}} + \frac{1}{x^{100}}$

D. $\frac{1}{(3x)^{100}}$

E. $\frac{1}{(3 + x)^{100}}$

36. Consider the graph of the equation $y = \frac{3x - 12}{2x - 6}$ in the standard (x,y) coordinate plane. Which of the following equations represents the *vertical* asymptote of the graph?

F. $x = 2$
G. $x = 3$
H. $x = 4$
J. $x = 6$
K. $x = 12$

37. For every pair of real numbers x and y such that $xy = 0$ and $\frac{x}{y} = 0$, which of the following statements is true?

A. $x = 0$ and $y = 0$
B. $x \neq 0$ and $y = 0$
C. $x = 0$ and $y \neq 0$
D. $x \neq 0$ and $y \neq 0$
E. None of the statements is true for every such pair of real numbers x and y.

GO ON TO THE NEXT PAGE.

2 △ △ △ △ △ △ △ △ △ 2

Use the following information to answer questions 38–40.

Walter recently vacationed in Paris. While there, he visited the Louvre, a famous art museum. Afterward, he took a 3.7-kilometer cab ride from the Louvre to the Eiffel Tower. A tour guide named Amélie informed him that 2.5 million rivets were used to build the tower, which stands 320 meters tall.

38. Walter's cab ride lasted 15 minutes. Which of the following values is closest to the average speed, in miles per hour, of the cab?

(Note: 1 mile ≈ 1.6 kilometers)

F.   9
G.   15
H.   21
J.   24
K.   35

39. When written in scientific notation, the number of rivets used to build the Eiffel Tower is equal to which of the following expressions?

A. 2.5×10^6
B. 2.5×10^7
C. 2.5×10^8
D. 25×10^6
E. 25×10^7

40. At a certain point, the angle of elevation formed by the level ground and the line from that point to the top of the Eiffel Tower is 70°. Which of the following expressions is equal to the distance, in meters, between that point and the center of the base of the tower?

F.   320 cos 70°

G.   320 sin 70°

H.   320 tan 70°

J. $\dfrac{320}{\sin 70°}$

K. $\dfrac{320}{\tan 70°}$

---

41. When the vector $a\mathbf{i} + 3\mathbf{j}$ is added to the vector $-2\mathbf{i} + b\mathbf{j}$, the sum is $6\mathbf{i} - 6\mathbf{j}$. What are the values of a and b ?

A. $a = -9$ and $b = 8$
B. $a = -8$ and $b = 9$
C. $a = -4$ and $b = 3$
D. $a = 4$ and $b = -3$
E. $a = 8$ and $b = -9$

GO ON TO THE NEXT PAGE.

2 △ △ △ △ △ △ △ △ △ **2**

42. Given $c = 10b^3 + 50$, which of the following is an expression for b in terms of c ?

F. $\left(\frac{c}{10} - 5\right)^{\frac{1}{3}}$

G. $\left(\frac{c}{10} + 5\right)^{\frac{1}{3}}$

H. $\frac{1}{10}(c - 50)^{\frac{1}{3}}$

J. $c^3 + 5$

K. $10c^3 + 50$

43. Given $f(x) = x^2 + 3x$ and $g(x) = x + 1$, what is $f(g(x))$?

A. $x^2 + 5x + 4$
B. $x^2 + 3x + 1$
C. $x^3 + 5x^2 + 4x$
D. $x^3 + 4x^2 + 3x$
E. $x^4 + 4x^3 + 3x^2$

44. The diameter of one circle is 12 inches long. The diameter of a second circle is 25% longer than the diameter of the first circle. To the nearest square inch, how much larger is the area of the second circle than the area of the first circle?

F.   7
G.   28
H.   44
J.   64
K. 254

45. What is the product of the mean and the median of the first 6 prime numbers?

(Note: 2 is the first prime number.)

A. 27
B. 37
C. 39
D. 41
E. 42

46. For all real values of x, which of the following equations is true?

F. $\sin(7x) + \cos(7x) = 7$
G. $\sin(7x) + \cos(7x) = 1$
H. $7\sin(7x) + 7\cos(7x) = 14$
J. $\sin^2(7x) + \cos^2(7x) = 7$
K. $\sin^2(7x) + \cos^2(7x) = 1$

DO YOUR FIGURING HERE.

Taking Additional Practice Tests

GO ON TO THE NEXT PAGE.

2   **2**

47. In the figure shown below, A, B, and D lie on a circle whose center is O, a diameter is $\overline{AB}$, $\overline{CD}$ is perpendicular to $\overline{AB}$ at C, the length of $\overline{AD}$ is 5 m, and the length of $\overline{BD}$ is 12 m. What is the length, in meters, of $\overline{CD}$?

DO YOUR FIGURING HERE.

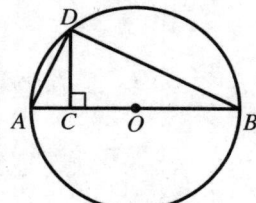

  A. $\dfrac{60}{13}$

  B. $\dfrac{65}{12}$

  C. 13

  D. $\dfrac{156}{5}$

  E. 60

48. If a and b are real numbers such that $a > 0$ and $b < 0$, then which of the following is equivalent to $|a| - |b|$?

  F. $|a - b|$
  G. $|a + b|$
  H. $|a| + |b|$
  J. $a - b$
  K. $a + b$

49. If $x < y$ and $y < 4$, then what is the greatest possible integer value of $x + y$?

  A. 0
  B. 3
  C. 4
  D. 7
  E. 8

50. Given that y varies directly as the *square* of x, if $y = 20$ when $x = 2$, what is y when $x = 3$?

  F. 75
  G. 45
  H. 30
  J. 21
  K. 15

GO ON TO THE NEXT PAGE.

2 △ △ △ △ △ △ △ △ △ **2**

51. Shown below in the standard (x,y) coordinate plane are 2 circles and 1 ellipse, each centered at $(0,0)$. The larger circle has equation $x^2 + y^2 = 25$ and intersects the ellipse at exactly 2 points, both on the x-axis. The smaller circle has equation $x^2 + y^2 = 4$ and intersects the ellipse at exactly 2 points, both on the y-axis. Which of the following equations represents the ellipse?

A. $\dfrac{x^2}{2} + \dfrac{y^2}{5} = 1$

B. $\dfrac{x^2}{4} + \dfrac{y^2}{25} = 1$

C. $\dfrac{x^2}{5} + \dfrac{y^2}{2} = 1$

D. $\dfrac{x^2}{25} + \dfrac{y^2}{4} = 1$

E. $\dfrac{x^2}{100} + \dfrac{y^2}{16} = 1$

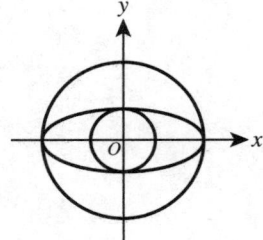

52. The mean of 5 integers is 52. The median of these 5 integers is 82. Three of the integers are 0, 12, and 82. Which of the following could be one of the other integers?

F.   52
G.   66
H.   84
J.   86
K. 105

53. An integer is *abundant* if its positive integer factors, excluding the integer itself, have a sum that is greater than the integer. How many of the integers 6, 8, 10, and 12 are abundant?

A. 0
B. 1
C. 2
D. 3
E. 4

54. Vanna walked at a rate of 2 miles per hour for 10 minutes and then walked at a rate of 3 miles per hour for 5 minutes. Which of the following gives the average rate, in miles per hour, at which she walked over this 15-minute period?

F. $\dfrac{1}{3}$

G. $\dfrac{7}{3}$

H. $\dfrac{7}{24}$

J. $\dfrac{7}{180}$

K. $\dfrac{35}{2}$

GO ON TO THE NEXT PAGE.

2 △ △ △ △ △ △ △ △ △ 2

55. The ratio of Alani's height to Baahir's height is 5:7. The ratio of Baahir's height to Connor's height is 4:3. What is the ratio of Alani's height to Connor's height?

A.   2:3
B.   8:11
C.   15:28
D.   20:21
E.   28:15

DO YOUR FIGURING HERE.

56. For all $x > 0$, which of the following expressions is NOT equivalent to $\sqrt{\sqrt[3]{x^2}}$?

F. $\sqrt[3]{x}$

G. $\sqrt[6]{x^2}$

H. $\sqrt[3]{\sqrt{x^2}}$

J. $x^{\frac{1}{3}}$

K. $x^{\frac{2}{3}}$

57. If the length of a rectangle is increased by 25% and the width is decreased by 10%, the area of the resulting rectangle is larger than the area of the original rectangle by what percent?

A.   2.5%
B.   12.5%
C.   15%
D.   22.5%
E.   35%

58. Five balls, numbered 1, 2, 3, 4, and 5, are placed in a bin. Two balls are drawn at random without replacement. What is the probability that the sum of the numbers on the balls drawn is 7 ?

F. $\frac{1}{5}$

G. $\frac{2}{5}$

H. $\frac{4}{5}$

J. $\frac{5}{9}$

K. $\frac{4}{25}$

GO ON TO THE NEXT PAGE.

2 △ △ △ △ △ △ △ △ △ **2**

59. Consider the family of functions $y = f(x) = \sin x + c$, where c is a real number. Which of the following number lines represents the graph of all and only the possible values of c for which the graph of y has no x-intercepts?

DO YOUR FIGURING HERE.

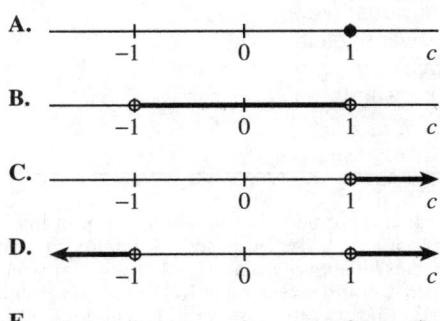

A.

B.

C.

D.

E.

60. Tameka calculates that she needs 360 square feet of new carpet. But the type of carpet that she wants is priced by the square *yard*. How many square yards of carpet does she need?

   F.   15
   G. 40
   H. 60
   J.   90
   K. 120

END OF TEST 2

STOP! DO NOT TURN THE PAGE UNTIL TOLD TO DO SO.

DO NOT RETURN TO THE PREVIOUS TEST.

Taking Additional Practice Tests

3 3

READING TEST
35 Minutes—40 Questions

DIRECTIONS: There are several passages in this test. Each passage is accompanied by several questions. After reading a passage, choose the best answer to each question and fill in the corresponding oval on your answer document. You may refer to the passages as often as necessary.

Passage I

LITERARY NARRATIVE: This passage is adapted from the novel *The Cat's Table* by Michael Ondaatje (©2011 by Michael Ondaatje).

The ship *Oronsay* is departing from Colombo, Ceylon (a city in what is today Sri Lanka), in the early 1950s.

Michael was eleven years old that night when, green as he could be about the world, he climbed aboard the first and only ship of his life. It felt as if a city had been added to the coast, better lit than any
5 town or village. He went up the gangplank, watching only the path of his feet—nothing ahead of him existed—and continued till he faced the dark harbour and sea. There were outlines of other ships farther out, beginning to turn on lights. He stood alone, smelling
10 everything, then came back through the noise and the crowd to the side that faced land. A yellow glow over the city. Already it felt there was a wall between him and what took place there. Stewards began handing out food and cordials. He ate several sandwiches, and after
15 that he made his way down to his cabin, undressed, and slipped into the narrow bunk. He'd never slept under a blanket before, save once in Nuwara Eliya. He was wide awake. The cabin was below the level of the waves, so there was no porthole. He found a switch
20 beside the bed and when he pressed it his head and pillow were suddenly lit by a cone of light.

He did not go back up on deck for a last look, or to wave at his relatives who had brought him to the harbour. He could hear singing and imagined the slow and
25 then eager parting of families taking place in the thrilling night air. I do not know, even now, why he chose this solitude. Had whoever brought him onto the *Oronsay* already left? In films people tear themselves away from one another weeping, and the ship separates
30 from land while the departed hold on to those disappearing faces until all distinction is lost.

I try to imagine who the boy on the ship was. Perhaps a sense of self is not even there in his nervous stillness in the narrow bunk, in this green grasshopper
35 or little cricket, as if he has been smuggled away accidentally, with no knowledge of the act, into the future.

* * *

What had there been before such a ship in my life? A dugout canoe on a river journey? A launch in Trincomalee harbour? There were always fishing boats on our
40 horizon. But I could never have imagined the grandeur of this castle that was to cross the sea. The longest journeys I had made were car rides to Nuwara Eliya and Horton Plains, or the train to Jaffna, which we boarded at seven a.m. and disembarked from in the late after-
45 noon. We made that journey with our egg sandwiches, a pack of cards, and a small Boy's Own adventure.

But now it had been arranged I would be travelling to England by ship, and that I would be making the journey alone. No mention was made that this might be
50 an unusual experience or that it could be exciting or dangerous, so I did not approach it with any joy or fear. I was not forewarned that the ship would have seven levels, hold more than six hundred people including a captain, nine cooks, engineers, a veterinarian, and that
55 it would contain a small jail and chlorinated pools that would actually sail with us over two oceans. The departure date was marked casually on the calendar by my aunt, who had notified the school that I would be leaving at the end of the term. The fact of my being at sea
60 for twenty-one days was spoken of as having not much significance, so I was surprised my relatives were even bothering to accompany me to the harbour. I had assumed I would be taking a bus by myself and then change onto another at Borella Junction.

65 There had been just one attempt to introduce me to the situation of the journey. A lady named Flavia Prins, whose husband knew my uncle, turned out to be making the same journey and was invited to tea one afternoon to meet with me. She would be travelling in First Class
70 but promised to keep an eye on me. I shook her hand carefully, as it was covered with rings and bangles, and she then turned away to continue the conversation I had interrupted. I spent most of the hour listening to a few uncles and counting how many of the trimmed sand-
75 wiches they ate.

On my last day, I found an empty school examination booklet, a pencil, a pencil sharpener, a traced map of the world, and put them into my small suitcase.

As I got into the car, it was explained to me that
80 after I'd crossed the Indian Ocean and the Arabian Sea and the Red Sea, and gone through the Suez Canal into

GO ON TO THE NEXT PAGE.

3 ▬▬▬▬▬▬▬▬▬▬▬▬▬▬▬▬▬▬▬▬▬▬▬ **3**

the Mediterranean, I would arrive one morning on a
small pier in England and my mother would meet me
there. It was not the magic or the scale of the journey
85 that was of concern to me, but that detail of how my
mother could know when exactly I would arrive in that
other country.

And if she would be there.

1. The passage can most reasonably be described as being
   divided into two sections that, taken together, explore:
   A. Michael's first week on the *Oronsay* as told from
      two perspectives, one being that of Michael's
      mother.
   B. elements of Michael's journey as told from two
      perspectives, one being that of Michael as a young
      boy.
   C. two outcomes of Michael's journey, both presented
      from the perspective of Michael as an adult.
   D. Michael's relationship with his family, presented
      from the perspective of two of Michael's relatives.

2. The description of the *Oronsay* as having seven levels,
   nine cooks, a veterinarian, a small jail, and chlorinated
   pools (lines 52–56) most strongly supports which of
   the following statements about the *Oronsay* or its
   passengers?
   F. "It felt as if a city had been added to the coast"
      (lines 3–4).
   G. "The cabin was below the level of the waves, so
      there was no porthole" (lines 18–19).
   H. "I do not know, even now, why he chose this soli-
      tude" (lines 26–27).
   J. "But now it had been arranged I would be travel-
      ling to England by ship" (lines 47–48).

3. As it is used in lines 65–66, the phrase "introduce me
   to the situation of the journey" most nearly means:
   A. list for the narrator the people he will likely meet
      on his trip.
   B. explain to the narrator what his mother knows
      about his trip.
   C. draw for the narrator a map of the exact route of
      his trip.
   D. prepare the narrator in general for the circum-
      stances of his trip.

4. Based on the passage, Michael's relatives arrange for
   and approach Michael's journey to England in a
   manner that can best be described as:
   F. fearful and tense.
   G. excited and frantic.
   H. meticulous and generous.
   J. understated and matter-of-fact.

5. The passage makes clear that once Michael boards the
   Oronsay, he feels that the city he is leaving has
   become:
   A. morally corrupt.
   B. physically shut off from him.
   C. aesthetically beautiful.
   D. figuratively lifted and carried with him.

6. The main point of the second paragraph (lines 22–31)
   is for the narrator to analyze the circumstance of:
   F. Michael's relatives leaving the harbor as soon as
      Michael had boarded the *Oronsay*.
   G. Michael enjoying listening to families singing but
      refusing to join in with them.
   H. Michael not returning to the deck to wave good-
      bye to his relatives.
   J. Michael's relatives weeping as the *Oronsay*
      departed.

7. The interaction between Michael and Flavia Prins that
   is described in the passage most strongly suggests that
   although Prins has promised to keep an eye on Michael
   during his journey, she is:
   A. fairly indifferent to him and not particularly
      focused on his well-being.
   B. likely going to retract her promise as a result of
      Michael's rude behavior during tea.
   C. planning to make sure someone else provides him
      with constant attention and care.
   D. intending to ignore him, if not make certain that
      his journey is difficult.

8. In the passage, Michael is metaphorically referred to
   as:
   F. a smuggler.
   G. rings and bangles.
   H. green grass.
   J. a little cricket.

9. The passage indicates that Michael's journey to Eng-
   land will require:
   A. relying on the expertise of a team of captains.
   B. disembarking the *Oronsay* midjourney.
   C. avoiding traveling on the Red Sea.
   D. spending twenty-one days at sea.

10. It can most reasonably be inferred from the passage
    that the narrator counts the sandwiches his uncles eat
    (lines 73–75) mainly because the narrator:
    F. wants to know how many sandwiches he will be
       given to eat once he boards the ship.
    G. hopes that his uncles like the sandwiches.
    H. feels bored as the adults converse.
    J. is nervous around his loud uncles.

GO ON TO THE NEXT PAGE.

3 ▬▬▬▬▬▬▬▬▬▬▬▬▬▬▬▬▬▬▬▬▬▬▬ **3**

Passage II

SOCIAL SCIENCE: Passage A is adapted from "The Unified Theory of Gumbo" by Lolis Eric Elie (©2012 by Smithsonian Institution). Passage B is adapted from "The Borscht Belt" by Julia Ioffe (©2012 by Condé Nast).

Passage A by Lolis Eric Elie

As the Cajun craze had its way with America in the 1980s, I began to hear tourists, visitors and transplants to New Orleans praising this or that gumbo for its thickness and darkness. This was strange to me.
5 Gumbo was supposed to be neither thick nor dark. Even more important, "dark" and "thick" were being used not as adjectives, but as achievements. It was as if making a dark gumbo was a culinary accomplishment on par with making a featherlight biscuit or a perfectly barbecued
10 beef brisket. Naturally, I viewed these developments with suspicion and my suspicion focused on the kitchen of Commander's Palace and its celebrated chef, Paul Prudhomme.

Prudhomme hails from Cajun Country, near
15 Opelousas, Louisiana. He refers to his cooking not so much as Cajun, but as "Louisiana cooking," and thus reflective of influences beyond his home parish. For years I blamed him for the destruction of the gumbo universe. Many of the chefs and cooks in New Orleans
20 restaurants learned under him or under his students. Many of these cooks were not from Louisiana, and thus had no homemade guide as to what good gumbo was supposed to be. As I saw it then, these were young, impressionable cooks who lacked the loving guidance
25 and discipline that only good home training can provide.

My reaction was admittedly nationalistic, since New Orleans is my nation. The Cajun incursion in and of itself didn't bother me. We are all enriched immea-
30 surably when we encounter other people, other languages, other traditions, other tastes. What bothered me was the tyrannical influence of the tourist trade. Tourist trap restaurants, shops, cooking classes, and at times it seemed the whole of the French Quarter, were given
35 over to providing visitors with what they expected to find. There was no regard for whether the offerings were authentic New Orleans food or culture. Suddenly andouille sausage became the local standard even though most New Orleanians had never heard of it.
40 Chicken and andouille gumbo suddenly was on menus all over town. This was the state of my city when I moved back here in 1995.

Passage B by Julia Ioffe

As a self-appointed guardian of authentic Russian fare, Maksim Syrnikov, who has spent the past two
45 decades studying traditional Russian cuisine, has a problem: Russians don't hold Russian food in particularly high esteem. When they eat out, they favor more exotic cuisines, like Italian or Japanese. The tendency to find foreign food more desirable is a prejudice that
50 goes back centuries—to a time when the Russian aristocracy spoke French, not Russian. Russian food is pooh-poohed as unhealthy and unsophisticated.

Among the many things that annoy Syrnikov is the fact that a good number of the despised Russian dishes
55 aren't even Russian. "I did an informal survey of eighteen- to twenty-five-year-olds in Moscow and St. Petersburg, and asked them, 'Name some traditional Russian dishes,'" Syrnikov told me. "What they named was horrible: borscht, which is Ukrainian, and potatoes,
60 which are an American plant. In the middle of the eighteenth century, there were *riots* because people didn't want to grow potatoes." He insists that real Russian food contained no potatoes, no tomatoes, few beets, and little meat. Instead, there were a lot of grains, fish, and
65 dairy, as well as honey, cucumbers, turnips, cabbage, apples, and the produce of Russia's vast forests—mushrooms and berries. Because of the climate, little of this was eaten fresh; it was salted, pickled, or dried for the long winter. Most of Russia ate this way until the twen-
70 tieth century.

By exploring the Russian food that existed before potatoes, Syrnikov hopes to help Russians reacquaint themselves with the country's agrarian roots, and to convince them that their national cuisine can be just as
75 flavorful as anything they might find in a sushi bar. He spends his time travelling through the countryside in search of old recipes, trying them himself, and blogging about his experiences. Often, he is brought in as a consultant on projects to make a restaurant authentically
80 Russian. Recently, he hatched a plan for a user-generated database of folk recipes. "My idea is to send out a call across all of Russia," he told me. "If you have a grandmother who makes *shanishki*"—disk-shaped pastries—"take a picture of them, write down the
85 recipe. To me, it's absolutely obvious that, if we don't wake up and find out from these old women and set it down on paper, in twenty years we won't have anyone to ask. Russian culture will lose a very significant part of itself."

11. The author of Passage A mentions "a featherlight biscuit" and "a perfectly barbecued beef brisket" (lines 9–10) primarily to:

   A. contrast their deliciousness with the inferior taste of a dark and thick gumbo.

   B. offer additional examples of New Orleans cuisine that was, in the author's view, being corrupted.

   C. illustrate the types of authentic New Orleans food that tourists used to gravitate toward.

   D. provide examples of what the author views as real culinary successes, in contrast to dark gumbo.

GO ON TO THE NEXT PAGE.

3 ▬▬▬▬▬▬▬▬▬▬▬▬▬▬▬▬▬▬▬▬ **3**

12. It can reasonably be inferred that the author of Passage A thinks that in comparison to authentic Cajun cuisine, Prudhomme's "Louisiana cooking":

   F. demands less creativity.
   G. requires more discipline.
   H. is much easier to master.
   J. reflects broader influences.

13. The author of Passage A most directly indicates that he originally attributed the ruin of the gumbo universe to which of the following?

   A. Tourists monopolizing New Orleans's entire French Quarter
   B. The Cajun craze that took hold of the United States in the 1980s
   C. The sudden prevalence of chicken and andouille gumbo in the 1990s
   D. The pervasive influence of Prudhomme on New Orleans restaurants

14. The author of Passage B most strongly indicates that Syrnikov believes Russians tend not to favor their national cuisine mainly because:

   F. they are embarrassed by their country's agrarian history and want to distance themselves from it.
   G. the prejudices held by Russia's ruling class long ago led to a ban on traditional Russian cuisine.
   H. they consider food from other countries to be more appealing and more refined.
   J. only old women know how to make traditional Russian dishes like *shanishki*.

15. The author of Passage B describes some of Syrnikov's common activities in lines 75–81 primarily to:

   A. suggest that Syrnikov feels overwhelmed by the scope and number of his projects.
   B. emphasize Syrnikov's dedication to helping Russians rediscover their true culinary roots.
   C. imply that Syrnikov plans to open his own authentic Russian restaurant after completing his research.
   D. downplay Syrnikov's lack of culinary training by focusing on his experience with traditional folk recipes.

16. According to Passage B, Syrnikov makes which of the following claims regarding potatoes?

   F. Potatoes were once a staple ingredient in traditional Russian cuisine.
   G. Potatoes were grown throughout Russia until the twentieth century.
   H. Potatoes were unpopular in eighteenth-century Russia.
   J. Potatoes actually originated in Ukraine, not in Russia.

17. As he is presented in Passage B, Syrnikov most clearly indicates that he believes failing to record traditional Russian folk recipes will:

   A. force Russian cuisine to reinvent itself.
   B. ruin his existing database of folk recipes.
   C. result in a significant loss of Russian culture.
   D. lead younger generations of Russians to learn folk recipes from their grandmothers.

18. Which of the following statements best captures a main difference in the focus of the two passages?

   F. Passage A focuses on the author's interactions with Prudhomme, while Passage B focuses on Syrnikov's frustration with the ignorance of the general Russian public.
   G. Passage A focuses on how the tourist trade affected New Orleans cuisine, while Passage B focuses on how communities are working together to preserve authentic Russian fare.
   H. Passage A focuses on the author's prejudice against food from non-Cajun cultures, while Passage B focuses on Syrnikov's attempt to spread awareness about what Russian cuisine truly is.
   J. Passage A focuses on the author's struggle with public perception of authentic New Orleans food, while Passage B focuses on Syrnikov's efforts to correct misconceptions about Russian cuisine.

19. With regard to their own region's authentic cuisine, both New Orleans transplants in Passage A and modern Russians in Passage B are characterized as being:

   A. perplexed.
   B. disdainful.
   C. misinformed.
   D. knowledgeable.

20. Both passages support the idea that learning how to cook traditional and authentic regional food is best accomplished by:

   F. gleaning knowledge from cooks native to the area.
   G. studying under professional chefs in a restaurant.
   H. traveling and learning about other cultures' foods.
   J. receiving hands-on training in a culinary school.

Taking Additional Practice Tests

GO ON TO THE NEXT PAGE.

3 ▬▬▬▬▬▬▬▬▬▬▬▬▬▬▬▬▬▬ 3

Passage III

HUMANITIES: This passage is adapted from the article "An Interview with C. E. Morgan" by Thomas Fabisiak (©2010 by University of North Carolina-Chapel Hill).

All the Living is C. E. Morgan's debut novel. Set in rural Kentucky in the 1980s, her novel follows a young couple's struggles as they take responsibility for a family farm.

Thomas Fabisiak: In what way does the fact that your descriptive work in *All the Living* focuses on landscape make it a political act?

C. E. Morgan: I think it's akin to the moral force that's
5 there in fiction in the presentation of character. Fiction asks us to bring sustained attention to the Other; when a reader chooses to continue reading a novel, regardless of the likability of a character, the sustained attention to that character has moral ramifications. Landscape writ-
10 ing—most especially when it's done at length and in a style that deviates from prose norms, so that its very presentation is interruptive or "estranging" as the formalists might have said—encourages the reader to stop, reread, listen, imagine, reconsider, admire, appreciate
15 with new eyes. The reader might complain that this kind of writing draws attention to itself, but this kind of writing doesn't merely draw attention to its own aesthetic strategies—it also draws attention to land. The land is imperiled; we know that. Land is always imper-
20 iled wherever the human puts his or her foot. The attention paid to landscape in a narrative is, I believe, attention that's paid to land itself, not just to marks on a page. Deep appreciation can result from an engagement with that kind of beauty, and that can manifest in
25 action. That is how it might be seen as a political act to do this kind of writing (particularly about a region, such as this one, rural Kentucky, that is continuously being ravaged by corporations that consumers unwittingly feed).

30 **Thomas Fabisiak:** In addition to landscape, though, *All the Living* also involves a sustained focus on work, and specifically on work on the land, farming, taking care of animals, etc. Together these suggest an overarching pastoral quality. Without wanting you to interpret *All*
35 *the Living* for readers, because you've told me that you hate imposing yourself into people's encounters with the book, I'm wondering if you could say something about your focus on work, and whether and to what extent it is related to the focus on landscape more gen-
40 erally. One thing that occurred to me repeatedly as I was reading the book was that, as a writer, you work very meticulously, and take "your work" as seriously, perhaps, as "the work" itself in the sense of the finished book, etc. Would I be wrong to think that there may be
45 a latent ethical, if not political, component to this aspect of your writing as well, both in your own commitment to hard work and in the ongoing presence of the theme of work in the novel?

C. E. Morgan: Well, while there are many novels I
50 admire that depict working-class labor (*Anna Karenina* and *In the Skin of the Lion* and *Germinal* are the first

that spring to mind), the presence of work—agrarian or domestic—in *All the Living* was not a self-conscious choice. For that matter, even though I conceptualize
55 landscape writing as overtly political, that doesn't mean I self-consciously insert it in a text where it doesn't belong. With *All the Living*, I don't feel I made choices in the first draft of the novel. It felt like the book just came, and it came with an inborn temperament, tenor,
60 and set of characters and concerns. I obeyed the book. Or perhaps, because a text is not a willful or sentient being (though it sometimes feels like it!), it might be more accurate to say I obeyed the hazy, deepest part of the brain, which bypasses the intellect as it constructs
65 meaning via image, myth, poetry: our essential languages.

For myself, though you're right that I work intensely on any project when I have one, I don't think of my writing as a job. I think of it as a vocation, and as such,
70 there's a huge gulf between what I do and capitalist notions of productivity, though the work is disseminated in the marketplace through a capitalist framework. I'm very wary of rigorous work ethic for the sake of rigorous work ethic—this idea that a writer should
75 produce a novel every year or two years, that they should be punching a clock somehow. A lot of people seem to buy into that; it's hard not to in this culture. But I don't want to produce just to produce. I don't want to write just to write, or publish just to get a pay-
80 check. I see no value in that. Frankly, the world doesn't need more books; it needs better books. Vocation is tied up with notions of service, and as an artist you serve people by giving them your best, the work you produce that you truly believe to be of value, not just what
85 you're capable of producing if you work ten hours a day every day for forty years.

21. The structure of the passage can best be described as an interview in which the interviewee:

   A. defends herself against harsh commentary by the interviewer.
   B. challenges the interviewer, urging him to ask her relevant questions.
   C. turns questions asked to her back to the interviewer, inviting a casual dialogue.
   D. responds to the interviewer's questions with involved, abstract answers.

22. In the passage, Morgan argues that, for the reader, landscape writing might feel particularly "interruptive or 'estranging'" (line 12) when it is presented:

   F. in an otherwise plot-driven novel.
   G. by an unskilled or inexperienced writer.
   H. at length and in an unconventional prose style.
   J. in the opening pages of a novel.

GO ON TO THE NEXT PAGE.

3 ▬▬▬▬▬▬▬▬▬▬▬▬▬▬▬▬▬▬▬▬▬▬ **3**

23. Based on the passage, how would Morgan respond to a reader's complaint that landscape writing "draws attention to itself" (line 16)?

   A. She would agree but claim that landscape writing also draws attention to land.
   B. She would agree but claim that if the writer had been focused, landscape writing should be engaging.
   C. She would disagree, arguing that landscape writing focuses solely on drawing attention to land.
   D. She would disagree, arguing that some readers are simply not willing to read landscape writing.

24. In the passage, Morgan most strongly suggests that a reader's attention to the land while reading a landscape narrative might lead the reader to:

   F. act to protect the land.
   G. forget that the land is in peril.
   H. misinterpret the writer's purpose.
   J. research the writer's academic background.

25. As it is used in line 22, the word *marks* most nearly refers to:

   A. creases and smudges.
   B. words and symbols.
   C. notches and ticks.
   D. lines and boundaries.

26. As it is used in line 24, the phrase "that kind of beauty" most specifically refers to the beauty of the:

   F. human being.
   G. intellect.
   H. political act.
   J. land.

27. The passage makes clear that, from a previous exchange with Morgan, Fabisiak knows that Morgan does not like to do which of the following?

   A. Interpret *All the Living* for her readers
   B. Tell her readers that, like the characters in *All the Living*, she lives in Kentucky
   C. Work ten hours a day every day
   D. Discuss which regions of the United States she plans to write about

28. The passage most strongly suggests that Morgan focuses on depicting which types of work in her novel *All the Living* ?

   F. Corporate or agrarian
   G. Agrarian or domestic
   H. Domestic or creative
   J. Creative or corporate

29. Morgan directly compares a writer being expected to produce a novel every year or two years to the act of having to:

   A. work overtime.
   B. assemble products in a factory.
   C. punch a clock.
   D. sell goods on commission.

30. In the passage, Morgan makes clear her perspective that an artist is serving people when that artist takes which of the following approaches to his or her work?

   F. Continually offering new work that the artist knows people will want to buy
   G. Regularly studying others' work and learning from it
   H. Creating and presenting work that the artist believes to be valuable
   J. Modifying the focus of the work when people's interest in it wanes

GO ON TO THE NEXT PAGE.

3   3

Passage IV

NATURAL SCIENCE: This passage is adapted from *Free Radicals* by Michael Brooks (©2011 by Michael Brooks).

As the twentieth century began, Robert Millikan was fast approaching forty. All around him, physics was at its most exhilarating, yet Millikan had done practically nothing. So he decided to measure *e*, the charge
5 on the electron.

Millikan's idea was simple. A droplet of water that had been given an electric charge would be attracted to a metal plate which carried an opposite charge. He arranged his apparatus so that the electrical attraction
10 pulled the droplet up, while gravity pulled it down. This gave him a way to measure *e*. First he would find the mass of the droplet. Then he would measure the voltage needed for the attraction to the metal plate to cancel out the downward pull of gravity. From those two pieces of
15 information he could get a measure of the charge on the droplet.

The experiment was far from simple to carry out, however. Finding that the water droplets tended to evaporate before any measurements could be made,
20 Millikan set to the task of trying the same trick with oil droplets.

In 1910, at the age of forty-two, he finally published a value for *e*. It was meant to be his career-defining publication. Eventually, it was—but Millikan
25 still had years of difficult and dirty work ahead of him.

The Austrian physicist Felix Ehrenhaft refuted Millikan's results with a similar set of experiments that seemed to show that electrical charge can be infinitely small. There is no fundamental, minimum unit of
30 charge, Ehrenhaft said; there is no 'electron'. The series of experiments the desperate Millikan then performed were to cast a lasting shadow over his scientific integrity.

According to biologist Richard Lewontin, Millikan
35 'went out of his way to hide the existence of inconvenient data'. David Goodstein, a physics professor, says Millikan 'certainly did not commit scientific fraud'. So where does the truth lie?

The debate hangs on a phrase in Millikan's 1913
40 paper refuting Ehrenhaft and showing that every measurement of electric charge gives a value of *e* or an integer multiple of *e*. In his 1913 paper, Millikan says that his data table '*contains a complete summary of the results obtained on all of the 58 different drops upon*
45 *which complete series of observations were made*'. The statement is written in italics, as if to give it special weight. The notebooks for the 1913 paper show that Millikan actually took data on 100 oil droplets. Did Millikan cherry-pick the data in order to confirm his
50 original result and crush Ehrenhaft underfoot?

He certainly had motive. In Millikan's 1910 paper he had made the 'mistake' of full disclosure with state-

ments such as, 'Although all of these observations gave values of *e* within 2 percent of the final mean, the
55 uncertainties of the observations were such that . . . I felt obliged to discard them'. This admirable honesty about the selection of data points had given Ehrenhaft ammunition that he used enthusiastically in his long feud with Millikan. Perhaps, with the italicised state-
60 ment, Millikan was making sure that he gave his foe no more.

That would certainly explain something that is otherwise inexplicable. Millikan aborted the experimental run on twenty-five of the droplets in the work
65 reported in the 1913 paper. According to Goodstein, Millikan preferred to use droplets that showed a change in charge, gaining or losing an electron (as he saw it) during the measurement. Millikan may also have judged some droplets to be too small or too large to
70 yield reliable data, Goodstein says. If they were too large, they would fall too rapidly to be reliably observed. Too small, and their fall (and thus the charge result) would be affected by random collisions with air molecules. Goodstein interprets the italicised statement
75 as an assertion that there were only fifty-eight 'complete enough' sets of data.

But Goodstein undoes his defence by stating that in order to make the 'too large' or 'too small' distinction, *all* the data would need to have been taken in the
80 first place.

Millikan certainly did not convince his peers straight away. The arguments with Ehrenhaft rumbled on long enough for Millikan's Nobel Prize to be delayed for three years—it eventually came in 1923.

85 But here's the point: Millikan was right about the electron and its charge. Few laboratories managed to replicate Ehrenhaft's results, but students now replicate Millikan's results all across the world. No one now believes that the fundamental unit of charge is anything
90 other than Millikan's *e*.

To get his Nobel Prize, Millikan had to play hard and fast with what we might call 'accepted practice'.

31. The main purpose of the passage is to use the example of Millikan to show:

A. how a theory becomes accepted.
B. that some well-accepted scientific ideas have a sullied past.
C. the challenges scientists faced in measuring *e*.
D. that some scientists get credit for work that is not their own.

GO ON TO THE NEXT PAGE.

3   3

32. Based on the passage, the debate between Millikan and Ehrenhaft is best described as:

    F. tense; their professional reputations were at stake.
    G. unprofessional; they sabotaged each other's experiments.
    H. collegial; each wanted to push the other to create a stronger theory.
    J. indirect; although their work intersected along some lines, they were primarily working in different fields.

33. The passage indicates that the debate regarding Millikan's integrity centers on:

    A. others' ability to replicate the results of Ehrenhaft's experiments more readily than those of Millikan's experiments.
    B. Millikan's decision to switch from using water droplets to oil droplets.
    C. certain statements Millikan made about the apparatus he used in his experiments.
    D. a discrepancy between data in Millikan's 1913 paper and information in his notebooks.

34. It can reasonably be inferred that the passage author considers Millikan's decision to offer full disclosure in his 1910 paper as:

    F. an understandable mistake that most scientists rightfully avoid.
    G. an admirable choice with an unfortunate consequence.
    H. a strategic decision that paid off in the end.
    J. a naive decision revealing desperation.

35. The passage indicates that in his experiment to measure e, Millikan switched from water to oil droplets because:

    A. other physicists had found that oil droplets were easier to work with.
    B. with oil he found it easier to form droplets with little variation in size.
    C. oil droplets allowed him to take accurate measurements more consistently.
    D. oil droplets could be reused for other experiments.

36. In the passage, the primary purpose of the ninth paragraph (lines 62–76) is to:

    F. present Goodstein's defense of Millikan's choices regarding the data reported in Millikan's 1913 paper.
    G. argue against Goodstein's interpretation of Millikan's motives.
    H. summarize the current prevailing view of Millikan's methods.
    J. offer an overview of Millikan's explanation of how he organized and presented his data.

37. The passage indicates that Ehrenhaft's experiments led him to make which of the following assertions in refuting the claims in Millikan's 1910 paper?

    A. There is no electron.
    B. Millikan's value for e is too low.
    C. Millikan failed to take prevailing scientific theories into account.
    D. The value of e varies with the substance one is measuring.

38. Based on the passage, the author's assertion that Millikan's experiments "were to cast a lasting shadow over his scientific integrity" (lines 32–33) is best described as:

    F. an opinion based on casual assumptions about scientists working in the early 1900s.
    G. an opinion based on the passage author's efforts to imagine himself in Millikan's position.
    H. a reasoned judgment based on consideration of the debate sparked by these experiments.
    J. a fact that Millikan clearly explains in his notebooks.

39. The passage author references Lewontin and Goodstein in the sixth paragraph (lines 34–38) primarily in order to:

    A. identify two leading arguments about Millikan's methodology.
    B. explain how a scientist's background might influence his or her opinion of Millikan's findings.
    C. emphasize that current experiments on the electron contradict Millikan's findings.
    D. highlight the difficulty Millikan's contemporaries had in replicating Millikan's experiments.

40. As it is used in line 39, the phrase *hangs on* most nearly means:

    F. continues.
    G. depends on.
    H. sticks with.
    J. blames on.

END OF TEST 3

STOP! DO NOT TURN THE PAGE UNTIL TOLD TO DO SO.

DO NOT RETURN TO A PREVIOUS TEST.

SCIENCE TEST

35 Minutes—40 Questions

DIRECTIONS: There are several passages in this test. Each passage is followed by several questions. After reading a passage, choose the best answer to each question and fill in the corresponding oval on your answer document. You may refer to the passages as often as necessary.

You are NOT permitted to use a calculator on this test.

Passage I

Table 1 lists the name, chemical formula, *molecular mass* (the mass of 1 molecule in atomic mass units, amu), and BP (the boiling point at 1 atmosphere of pressure) of various compounds. The first compound listed is composed of the elements carbon (C) and hydrogen (H). Each of the other compounds is composed of C, H, and either fluorine (F), chlorine (Cl), bromine (Br), or iodine (I). The elements F, Cl, Br, and I belong to the *halogen* family.

Table 1			
Name	Chemical formula	Molecular mass (amu)	BP (°C)
Methane	CH_4	16	−162
Fluoromethane	CH_3F	34	−78
Difluoromethane	CH_2F_2	52	−52
Trifluoromethane	CHF_3	70	−82
Chloromethane	CH_3Cl	51	−24
Dichloromethane	CH_2Cl_2	85	40
Trichloromethane	$CHCl_3$	119	61
Bromomethane	CH_3Br	95	4
Dibromomethane	CH_2Br_2	174	97
Tribromomethane	$CHBr_3$	253	149
Iodomethane	CH_3I	142	42
Diiodomethane	CH_2I_2	268	182
Triiodomethane	CHI_3	394	218

Table 1 adapted from W. M. Haynes, ed., *CRC Handbook of Chemistry and Physics on CD-ROM*, Version 2011. ©2011 by CRC Press, LLC.

Figure 1 shows a plot of BP versus molecular mass for 3 groups of compounds (Groups 1–3). Each compound in each group is composed of C and 1 or more halogens.

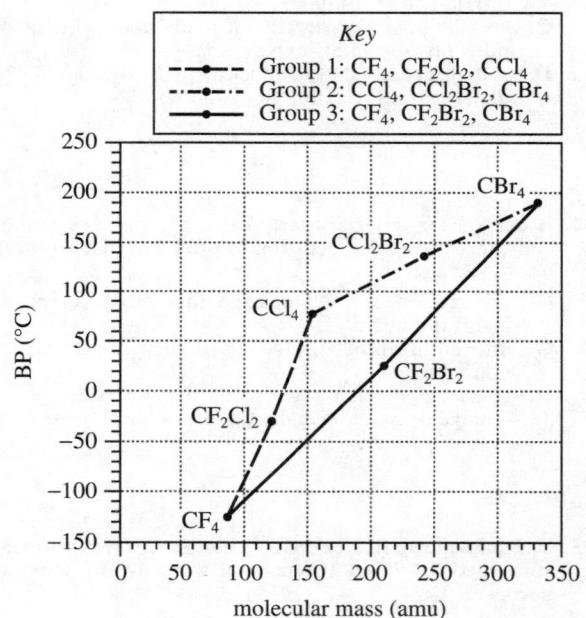

Key
- - - ● - - - Group 1: CF_4, CF_2Cl_2, CCl_4
- · - ● - · - Group 2: CCl_4, CCl_2Br_2, CBr_4
———●——— Group 3: CF_4, CF_2Br_2, CBr_4

Figure 1

Figure 1 adapted from Michael Laing, "Boiling Points of the Family of Small Molecules, $CH_wF_xCl_yBr_z$: How Are They Related to Molecular Mass?" ©2001 by Division of Chemical Education, Inc., American Chemical Society.

GO ON TO THE NEXT PAGE.

4 ○ ○ ○ ○ ○ ○ ○ ○ ○ **4**

1. The compound represented in Figure 1 that has a BP of −30°C has a molecular mass of about:

   A.   90 amu.
   B. 120 amu.
   C. 150 amu.
   D. 210 amu.

2. According to Figure 1, of the following compounds, which one has the highest BP ?

   F. CF_4
   G. CF_2Cl_2
   H. CF_2Br_2
   J. CCl_4

3. According to Table 1, the relationship between molecular mass and BP among the compounds $CHCl_3$, $CHBr_3$, and CHI_3 is best represented by which of the following graphs?

   A.
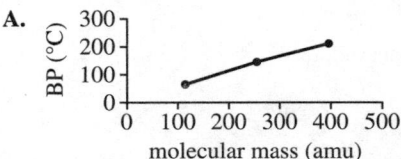

   B.
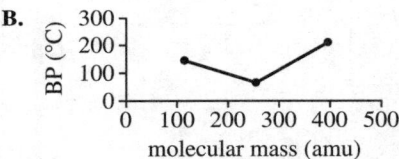

   C.
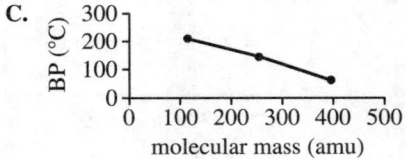

   D.
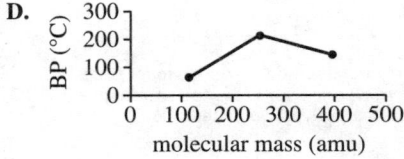

4. At 1 atmosphere of pressure, the temperature at which CH_2I_2 boils is how much greater than the temperature at which CH_4 boils?

   F. 162°C
   G. 268°C
   H. 344°C
   J. 430°C

5. According to Table 1 and Figure 1, the molecular mass of CF_4 is closest to the molecular mass of which of the following compounds?

   A. Dichloromethane
   B. Trichloromethane
   C. Iodomethane
   D. Dibromomethane

6. The *atomic mass* (the mass of 1 atom, in amu) of C is 12 amu. Based on the molecular mass of CBr_4 shown in Figure 1, the atomic mass of Br is closest to which of the following?

   F. 20 amu
   G. 35 amu
   H. 80 amu
   J. 127 amu

GO ON TO THE NEXT PAGE.

4 ○ ○ ○ ○ ○ ○ ○ ○ ○ **4**

Passage II

Urushiols are the oils in poison ivy that cause allergic reactions in humans. The higher the *U:S ratio*—the ratio of unsaturated (U) urushiols to saturated (S) urushiols—the more severe the reaction.

From 1999 to 2004, poison ivy plants (PIPs) were grown in 2 identical outdoor plots under identical conditions except for the atmospheric CO_2 concentration.

Figure 1 shows, for each plot, the yearly dry biomass per plant. Figure 2 shows the yearly percent of original PIPs surviving in each plot. Figure 3 shows, for each plot in 2004, the percent of U urushiols per plant, the percent of S urushiols per plant, and the U:S ratio per plant.

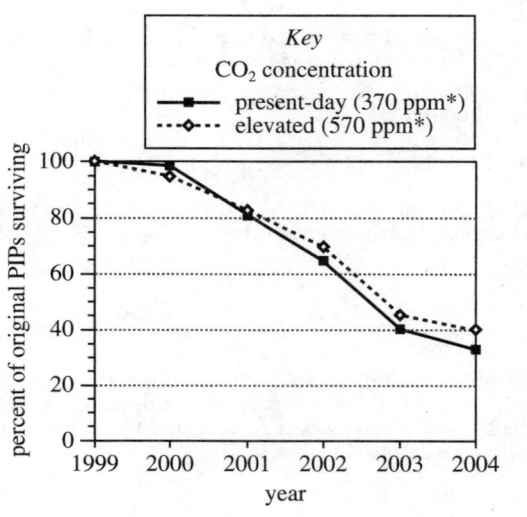

*ppm = parts per million

Figure 2

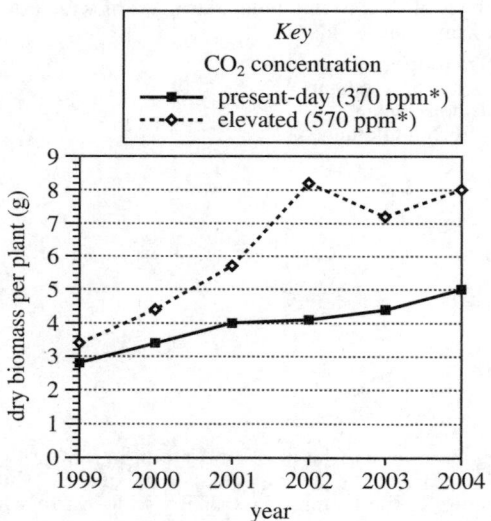

*ppm = parts per million

Figure 1

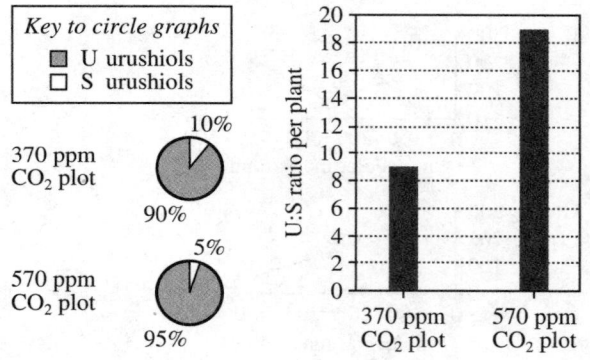

Figure 3

Figures adapted from "Biomass and Toxicity Responses of Poison Ivy (*Toxicodendron radicans*) to Elevated Atmospheric CO_2." ©2006 by the National Academy of Sciences.

GO ON TO THE NEXT PAGE.

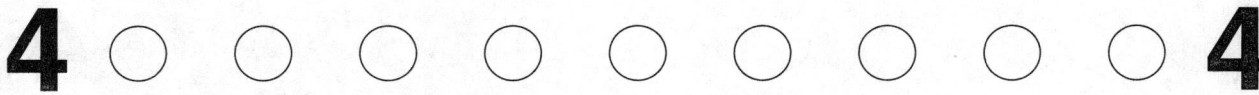

4 ○ ○ ○ ○ ○ ○ ○ ○ ○ **4**

7. According to Figure 3, for the present-day CO_2 concentration plot, the percent of U urushiols per plant in 2004 was:

   A. 10%.
   B. 20%.
   C. 50%.
   D. 90%.

8. According to Figure 2, which plot had the higher percent of original PIPs surviving at the end of the study?

   F. The present-day CO_2 plot, by a difference of 1%
   G. The present-day CO_2 plot, by a difference of 7%
   H. The elevated CO_2 plot, by a difference of 1%
   J. The elevated CO_2 plot, by a difference of 7%

9. Based on the passage, which of the factors listed below was(were) the same for the 2 plots?

      I. Atmospheric CO_2 concentration in each plot
     II. Soil type in each plot
    III. Amount of water applied to each plot

   A. I only
   B. I and II only
   C. II and III only
   D. I, II, and III

10. According to Figure 1, from 1999 to 2004, how did the dry biomasses per plant for the 2 plots compare? The dry biomass per plant grown in a CO_2 concentration of 370 ppm was:

    F. always the same as the dry biomass per plant grown in a CO_2 concentration of 570 ppm.
    G. always greater than the dry biomass per plant grown in a CO_2 concentration of 570 ppm.
    H. always less than the dry biomass per plant grown in a CO_2 concentration of 570 ppm.
    J. in some years greater than, but in other years less than, the dry biomass per plant grown in a CO_2 concentration of 570 ppm.

11. Based on Figure 2, what percent of PIPs grown in the plot with a CO_2 concentration of 370 ppm had *died* by the year 2003 ?

    A. 40%
    B. 45%
    C. 55%
    D. 60%

12. According to Figure 3, which plot produced a higher percent of S urushiols per plant?

    F. The present-day CO_2 concentration plot; 10% of the urushiols produced per plant were saturated.
    G. The present-day CO_2 concentration plot; 90% of the urushiols produced per plant were saturated.
    H. The elevated CO_2 concentration plot; 5% of the urushiols produced per plant were saturated.
    J. The elevated CO_2 concentration plot; 95% of the urushiols produced per plant were saturated.

GO ON TO THE NEXT PAGE.

4 ○ ○ ○ ○ ○ ○ ○ ○ ○ 4

Passage III

When the ozone (O_3) in air is mixed with an acidic solution of iodide ion (I^-), the O_3 reacts to form triiodide ion (I_3^-), O_2, and H_2O.

$$O_3 + 3I^- + 2H^+ \rightarrow I_3^- + O_2 + H_2O$$

Students performed an experiment to determine the concentration of O_3 in samples of air. Figure 1 shows the relationship between the concentration of I_3^-, in μmol/L, and the concentration of O_3, in parts per billion (ppb), under the conditions of the experiment.

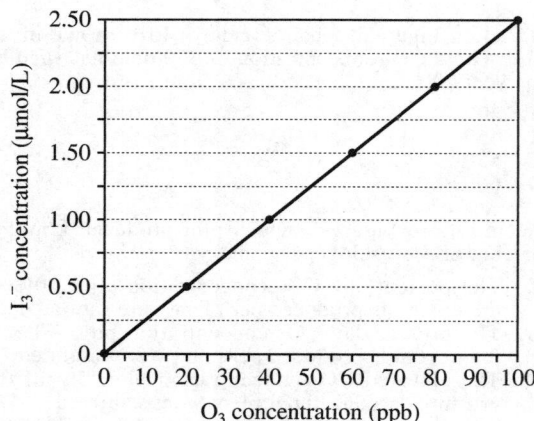

Figure 1

Experiment

At each of 4 outdoor sites, the students assembled the apparatus shown in Figure 2. First, they attached a long piece of tubing to a stand so that one end of the tubing was 1.5 m above the ground. Then, they placed the other end of the tubing into one hole of a 2-holed stopper. Next, they placed one end of a shorter piece of tubing into the second hole of the 2-holed stopper and attached the other end of the shorter tubing to a vacuum pump.

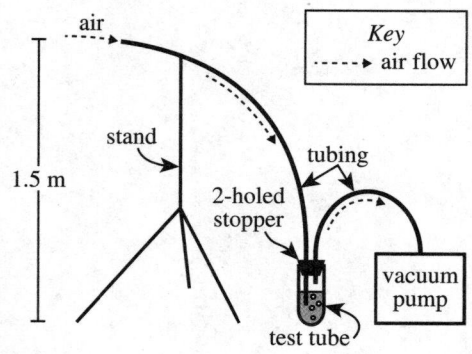

Figure 2

At each site, the students performed the following 2 steps every half hour from 12:30 p.m. to 5:30 p.m. on a particular day:

1. A 10.0 mL volume of an aqueous acidic solution having a 10 mg/mL concentration of I^- was placed into a clean, empty test tube that was then sealed with the 2-holed stopper.

2. The vacuum pump was turned on for 25 min to collect an air sample. Then, the pump was turned off and the concentration of I_3^-, in micromoles/liter (μmol/L), in the solution was measured.

The results are shown in Figure 3.

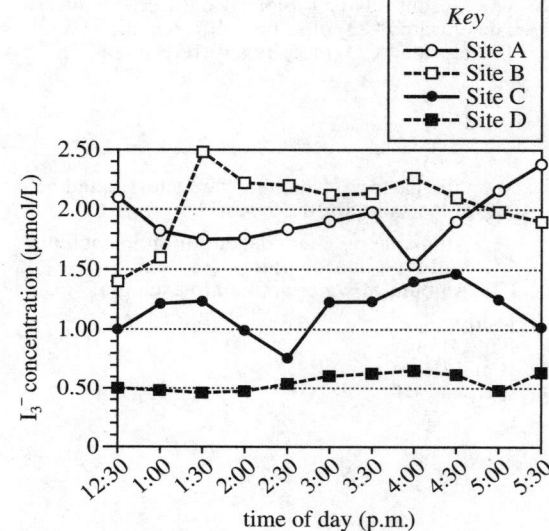

Figure 3

Figures adapted from J. V. Seeley et al., "A Simple Method for Measuring Ground-Level Ozone in the Atmosphere." ©2005 by the Division of Chemical Education, Inc., American Chemical Society.

13. Based on Figures 1 and 3, the air sample collected at which of the following combinations of time and location had the *lowest* O_3 concentration?

	time	location
A.	2:30 p.m.	Site B
B.	2:30 p.m.	Site C
C.	4:00 p.m.	Site B
D.	4:00 p.m.	Site C

GO ON TO THE NEXT PAGE.

4 ○ ○ ○ ○ ○ ○ ○ ○ **4**

14. Consider the air samples that were collected at the 4 sites at 2:00 p.m. Based on Figures 1 and 3, what is the order of those samples from lowest O_3 concentration to highest O_3 concentration?

   F. Site A, Site B, Site C, Site D
   G. Site C, Site B, Site A, Site D
   H. Site D, Site C, Site A, Site B
   J. Site D, Site A, Site C, Site B

15. Based on Figures 1 and 3, which site had the highest overall average O_3 concentration across all the air samples?

   A. Site A
   B. Site B
   C. Site C
   D. Site D

16. Based on Figures 1 and 3, the O_3 concentration at 5:00 p.m. at Site B was approximately how many times as great as the O_3 concentration at 2:00 p.m. at Site C ?

   F. 0.5
   G. 2
   H. 3
   J. 4

17. At Site A, was the O_3 concentration highest at 4:00 p.m. or at 5:30 p.m. ?

   A. 4:00 p.m.; the I_3^- concentration was highest at 4:00 p.m., and the higher the I_3^- concentration, the higher the O_3 concentration.
   B. 4:00 p.m.; the I_3^- concentration was lowest at 4:00 p.m., and the lower the I_3^- concentration, the higher the O_3 concentration.
   C. 5:30 p.m.; the I_3^- concentration was highest at 5:30 p.m., and the higher the I_3^- concentration, the higher the O_3 concentration.
   D. 5:30 p.m.; the I_3^- concentration was lowest at 5:30 p.m., and the lower the I_3^- concentration, the higher the O_3 concentration.

18. When a vacuum pump was operating during Step 2, it drew air through the solution in the test tube. Assuming that the pump drew air at a rate of 200 mL/min, how many milliliters of air were drawn through the solution in the test tube each time Step 2 was performed?

   F. 200 mL
   G. 550 mL
   H. 2,500 mL
   J. 5,000 mL

19. Suppose that the actual O_3 concentration at 12:30 p.m. at Site C was 43 ppb. Based on Figures 1 and 3, which of the following expressions would give the percent error for the value of the O_3 concentration that was determined at 12:30 p.m. at Site C ?

   A. $\dfrac{|40\ \text{ppb} - 43\ \text{ppb}|}{43\ \text{ppb}} \times 100\%$

   B. $\dfrac{|40\ \text{ppb} - 43\ \text{ppb}|}{40\ \text{ppb}} \times 100\%$

   C. $\dfrac{|100\ \text{ppb} - 43\ \text{ppb}|}{43\ \text{ppb}} \times 100\%$

   D. $\dfrac{|100\ \text{ppb} - 43\ \text{ppb}|}{40\ \text{ppb}} \times 100\%$

Taking Additional Practice Tests

GO ON TO THE NEXT PAGE.

4 ◯ ◯ ◯ ◯ ◯ ◯ ◯ ◯ ◯ 4

Passage IV

When waves of laser light pass through a narrow slit and onto a screen, they form a pattern of light and dark bands on the screen, as shown in Figure 1.

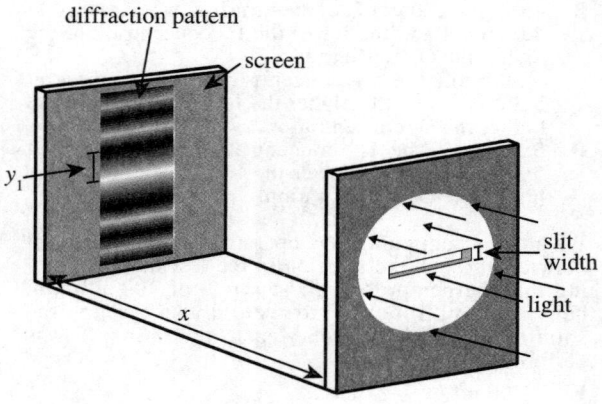

Figure 1

Figure 1 adapted from Francis Sears and Mark Zemanski, *College Physics*. ©1960 by Addison Wesley Publishing Co., Inc.

This phenomenon is called *diffraction*, and the pattern is called a *diffraction pattern*.

In each of the following studies of diffraction, students directed laser light through a slit, forming a diffraction pattern on a screen. They measured y_1, the distance from the center of the brightest band in the pattern to the center of one of the 2 adjacent dark bands. In each study, x was the distance between the slit and the screen.

Study 1

In Trials 1–4, the slit width was varied, the wavelength of the laser light was fixed, and x was 6.00 m. The results are shown in Table 1.

	Table 1	
Trial	Slit width (mm)	y_1 (mm)
1	0.12	30.0
2	0.24	15.0
3	0.36	10.0
4	0.48	7.5

Study 2

In Trials 5–8, the slit width was 0.24 mm, the wavelength (color) of the laser light was varied, and x was 6.00 m. The results are shown in Table 2.

	Table 2	
Trial	Wavelength (nm)	y_1 (mm)
5	400 (violet)	10.0
6	500 (green)	12.5
7	600 (yellow)	15.0
8	700 (red)	17.5

Study 3

In Trials 9–12, the slit width was 0.24 mm, the wavelength was the same as in Study 1, and x was varied. The results are shown in Table 3.

	Table 3	
Trial	x (m)	y_1 (mm)
9	3.00	7.5
10	6.00	15.0
11	9.00	22.5
12	12.00	30.0

20. In Study 2, y_1 would most likely have been less than 10.0 mm if the students had used a laser emitting light having which of the following wavelengths?

    F. 300 nm
    G. 500 nm
    H. 700 nm
    J. 900 nm

GO ON TO THE NEXT PAGE.

4   **4**

21. For fixed values of wavelength and slit width, which of the following graphs best represents the relationship between y_1 and x ?

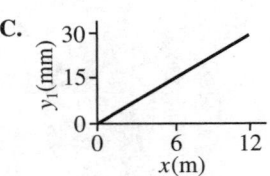

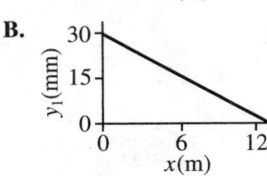

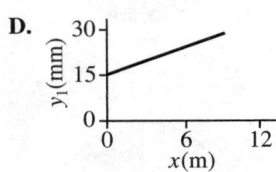

22. Suppose that the procedure performed in Trial 2 was repeated, except that x was 9.00 m. Based on the results of Studies 1 and 3, would y_1 more likely have been greater than 15.0 mm or less than 15.0 mm ?

F. Greater, because y_1 increased as x increased.
G. Greater, because y_1 increased as x decreased.
H. Less, because y_1 decreased as x increased.
J. Less, because y_1 decreased as x decreased.

23. During the 3 studies, the students did NOT examine the relationship between y_1 and the:

A. width of the slit.
B. wavelength of laser light.
C. distance between the slit and the screen.
D. distance between the slit and the laser.

24. As the wavelength of light increases, the energy of a *photon* (particle of light) decreases. In which of the following trials of Study 2 was the energy of a photon greatest?

F. Trial 5
G. Trial 6
H. Trial 7
J. Trial 8

25. For fixed values of wavelength and x, when the slit width was doubled, the distance from the center of the brightest band in the pattern to the center of one of the 2 adjacent dark bands:

A. was doubled.
B. was halved.
C. remained unchanged.
D. varied with no general trend.

26. What is the result of Trial 7 expressed in *meters* (m) ?

F. 0.00150 m
G. 0.0150 m
H. 0.150 m
J. 1.50 m

GO ON TO THE NEXT PAGE.

4 ○ ○ ○ ○ ○ ○ ○ ○ ○ 4

Passage V

Unlike most volcanoes, *hot spot volcanoes* (HSVs) develop far from tectonic plate boundaries. Two scientists discuss the origin and properties of HSVs.

Scientist 1

In the mantle beneath an HSV, at depths between 200 km and 400 km, hot magma rises toward Earth's surface in one large column called a *mantle plume*. The ascending magma causes earthquakes and creates networks of large fractures in crustal rocks. Propagation of these fracture networks enables magma to reach the surface more easily, which is why the frequency of eruptions at an HSV typically increases over time. Magma that does not breach Earth's surface will cool and eventually sink back down into the mantle.

HSVs erupt iron-rich lavas that are chemically similar to mantle rocks. Olivine and pyroxenes are the most abundant minerals in mantle rocks and in the lavas erupted at HSVs. The lavas at HSVs also retain a lot of water from the mantle. By weight, water vapor accounts for 75% of the total gas output at HSVs, while CO_2 accounts for only 10%–15%. All other gases combined never account for more than 10%–15% of the total gas output. Kilauea Caldera, in Hawaii, erupts this way.

Scientist 2

In certain places near the top of the mantle, at depths of less than 100 km, a high concentration of dissolved CO_2 allows mantle rocks to melt at lower temperatures than they normally would. This is how the magma that fuels an HSV forms. The magma then rises toward Earth's surface in small isolated bodies that melt through the entire thickness of the crust, sometimes causing small fractures (less than 1 km long) in crustal rocks. Each eruption at an HSV depletes some of the excess CO_2, which is why eruption frequency at an HSV will typically slow down over time.

HSVs erupt lavas in which feldspar is the most abundant mineral. These aluminum-rich lavas contain much less water than most mantle rocks. By weight, CO_2 and water vapor each account for 45% of the total gas output at HSVs. Carbon monoxide (CO) accounts for 6% of the total gas output, and all other gases combined account for only 4%. Mt. Erebus, in Antarctica, erupts this way.

27. Which of the following pie charts is most consistent with Scientist 2's description of the total gas output at HSVs ?

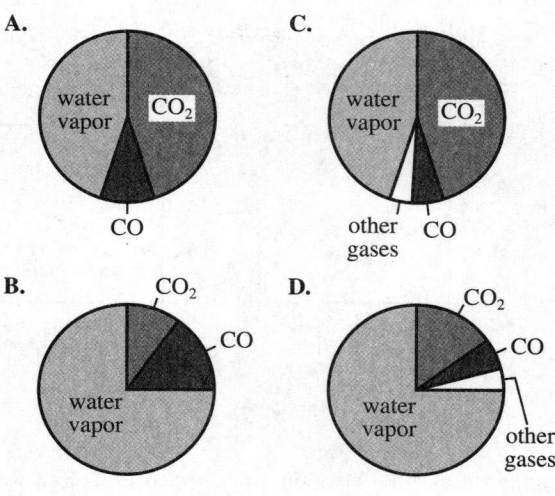

28. Which of the scientists, if either, state(s) that ascending magma causes earthquakes?

F. Scientist 1 only
G. Scientist 2 only
H. Both Scientist 1 and Scientist 2
J. Neither Scientist 1 nor Scientist 2

29. *Basalt* is a volcanic rock that contains abundant iron and is less than 10% feldspar by volume. In contrast, the volcanic rock *phonolite* is mostly feldspar by volume. Based on the passage, which of these 2 types of rock would each scientist more likely expect to see at an HSV ?

	Scientist 1	Scientist 2
A.	basalt	basalt
B.	basalt	phonolite
C.	phonolite	basalt
D.	phonolite	phonolite

GO ON TO THE NEXT PAGE.

4 ○ ○ ○ ○ ○ ○ ○ ○ ○ **4**

30. Suppose it were discovered that older HSVs erupt more frequently than younger HSVs. This discovery would better support the viewpoint of which scientist?

F. Scientist 1; Scientist 1 claims that eruption frequency decreases over time.
G. Scientist 1; Scientist 1 claims that eruption frequency increases over time.
H. Scientist 2; Scientist 2 claims that eruption frequency decreases over time.
J. Scientist 2; Scientist 2 claims that eruption frequency increases over time.

31. The *lithosphere* is a zone of Earth's interior that extends from the surface to a maximum depth of approximately 200 km. Which of the scientists, if either, discuss(es) a process that may extend *beneath* the lithosphere?

A. Scientist 1 only
B. Scientist 2 only
C. Both Scientist 1 and Scientist 2
D. Neither Scientist 1 nor Scientist 2

32. Suppose that another scientist claims that most mantle rocks contain water. Which of the scientists, if either, would be likely to agree with this claim?

F. Scientist 1 only
G. Scientist 2 only
H. Both Scientist 1 and Scientist 2
J. Neither Scientist 1 nor Scientist 2

33. A material that lowers the melting point of rocks is called a *flux*. The melting of rocks due to the presence of a flux is called *flux melting*. Flux melting is a feature of which scientist's discussion, and based on that scientist's discussion, what material is acting as the flux?

A. Scientist 1; iron
B. Scientist 2; iron
C. Scientist 1; CO_2
D. Scientist 2; CO_2

GO ON TO THE NEXT PAGE.

4 ◯ ◯ ◯ ◯ ◯ ◯ ◯ ◯ ◯ **4**

Passage VI

Gene expression in eukaryotes is controlled by *regulatory DNA sequences* (RSs). RSs determine whether, for a particular type of cell, the expression of a gene is turned on or turned off.

Figure 1 shows the coding region of Gene X and shows 3 RSs (RS1–RS3) that are thought to be associated with Gene X. Figure 1 also shows the known expression pattern of Gene X across 6 types of mammalian cells (cell types A–F).

Scientists did 2 experiments to study how RS1, RS2, and RS3 control the expression of Gene X in each of cell types A–F. In each experiment, they prepared *GFP reporter genes*. GFP is a protein that emits green light when viewed with a certain microscope. Reporter genes are DNA molecules that contain RSs of interest and the coding region for an easily detectable protein.

Experiment 1

GFP reporter genes that contained RS1–RS3 and the coding region for GFP were prepared (see Figure 2). The reporter genes were then *transfected* (delivered) into cells of each of cell types A–F. Then, 48 hr after transfection, the cells were viewed with the microscope to determine if the GFP reporter genes were expressed. Figure 2 also shows the expression pattern of the GFP reporter gene across cell types A–F.

Experiment 2

Experiment 1 was repeated except that 5 types of GFP reporter genes were prepared. Each type of reporter gene contained either 0, 1, or 2 of the RSs and the coding region for GFP (see Figure 3). Figure 3 also shows the expression patterns of the 5 types of GFP reporter genes across cell types A–F.

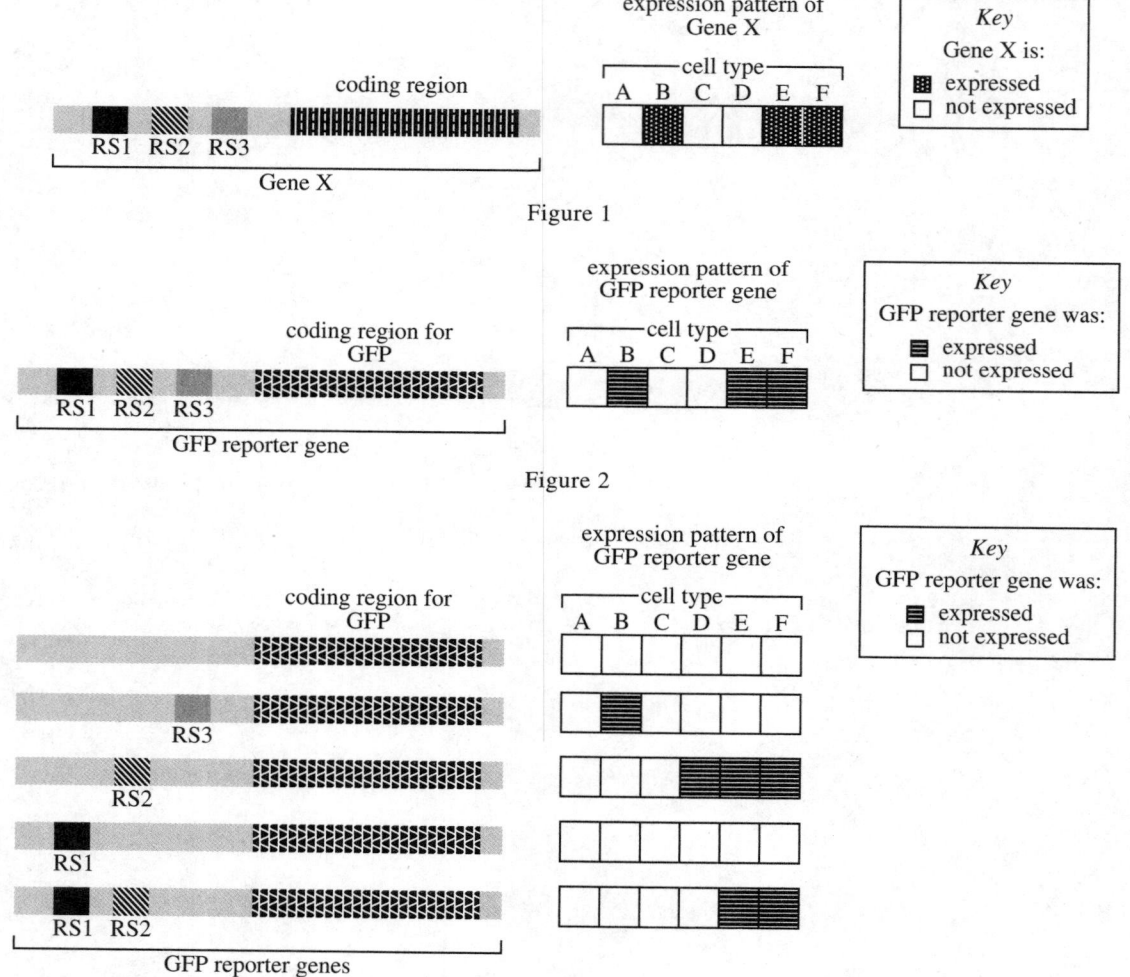

Figure 1

Figure 2

Figure 3

GO ON TO THE NEXT PAGE.

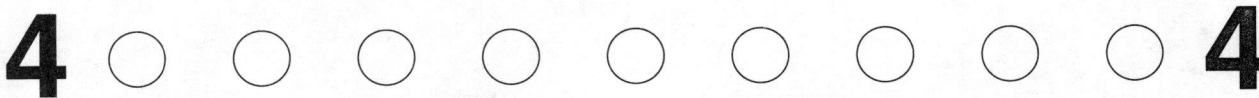

Figures adapted from Bruce Alberts et al., *Molecular Biology of the Cell*, 5th ed. ©2008 by Bruce Alberts, Alexander Johnson, Julian Lewis, Martin Raff, Keith Roberts, and Peter Walter.

34. Based on the results of Experiment 2, RS2 turns on the expression of the GFP reporter gene in which of the cell types?

F. Cell type B only
G. Cell types E and F only
H. Cell types A, B, and C only
J. Cell types D, E, and F only

35. According to the results of Experiments 1 and 2, when the cells were viewed with the microscope, green light was NEVER observed for which of the cell types?

A. Cell type A only
B. Cell type C only
C. Cell types A and C only
D. Cell types A, C, and D only

36. The gene that codes for the enzyme β-*galactosidase* is a common reporter gene. Consider the combination of RSs in the reporter gene shown below.

coding region for
β-galactosidase

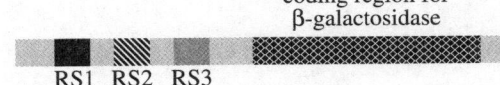

RS1 RS2 RS3

Which of the following patterns of β-galactosidase enzymatic activity would most likely result from transfecting the cells of cell types A–F with the above reporter gene?

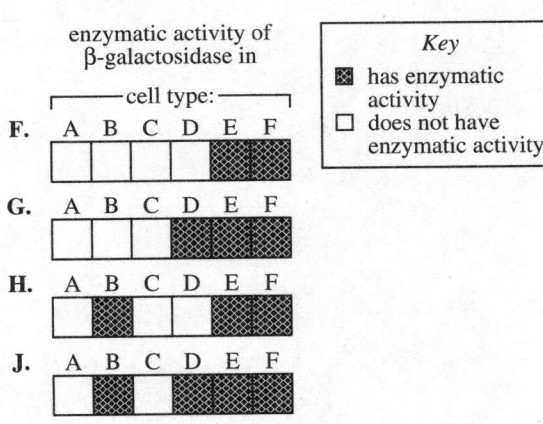

enzymatic activity of
β-galactosidase in

Key
⊠ has enzymatic activity
☐ does not have enzymatic activity

37. Based on the results of Experiment 2, the expression of the GFP reporter genes in cell type F was turned on by which of the 3 RSs ?

A. RS1 only
B. RS2 only
C. RS3 only
D. RS1 and RS2 only

38. What is the most likely reason that reporter genes were used in Experiments 1 and 2 ?

F. The protein product of Gene X could be more easily observed than could the protein product of the reporter genes.
G. The protein product of the reporter genes could be more easily observed than could the protein product of Gene X.
H. RS1–RS3 cannot control the expression of Gene X in the cell types studied.
J. RS1–RS3 cannot control the expression of the reporter genes in the cell types studied.

39. Consider the expression pattern of the GFP reporter gene in Experiment 2 that contained only RS1 and RS2. What is the most likely reason that the GFP reporter gene was NOT expressed in cell type D ? In cell type D, gene expression was turned:

A. on by RS1.
B. on by RS2.
C. off by RS1.
D. off by RS2.

40. Do the results of Experiments 1 and 2 indicate that the expression of Gene X is controlled by each of RS1–RS3 ?

F. No; only 1 of the 3 RSs appeared to affect the expression of the GFP reporter gene in all of the cell types.
G. No; only 2 of the 3 RSs appeared to affect the expression of the GFP reporter gene in all of the cell types.
H. Yes; each of the 3 RSs appeared to affect the expression of the GFP reporter gene in all of the cell types.
J. Yes; each of the 3 RSs appeared to affect the expression of the GFP reporter gene in at least 1, but not all, of the cell types.

END OF TEST 4

STOP! DO NOT RETURN TO ANY OTHER TEST.

You may wish to photocopy these sample answer document pages to respond to the practice ACT Writing Test.

Please enter the information at the right before beginning the writing test.

Use a No. 2 pencil only. Do NOT use a mechanical pencil, ink, ballpoint, or felt-tip pen.

WRITING TEST BOOKLET NUMBER

Print your 9-digit **Booklet Number** in the boxes at the right.

WRITING TEST FORM

Print your 5-character **Test Form** in the boxes at the right and fill in the corresponding ovals.

Begin WRITING TEST here.

_____

_____

_____

_____

_____

_____

_____

_____

_____

_____

_____

_____

_____

_____

_____

_____

_____

_____

_____

_____

_____

_____

_____

If you need more space, please continue on the following page.

1

The ONLY Official Prep Guide from the Makers of the ACT

WRITING TEST

_____
_____
_____
_____
_____
_____
_____
_____
_____
_____
_____
_____
_____
_____
_____
_____
_____
_____
_____
_____
_____
_____
_____
_____
_____
_____

If you need more space, please continue on the following page.

2

WRITING TEST

_____
_____
_____
_____
_____
_____
_____
_____
_____
_____
_____
_____
_____
_____
_____
_____
_____
_____
_____
_____
_____
_____
_____
_____
_____
_____
_____
_____
_____

If you need more space, please continue on the following page.

3

WRITING TEST

_____

_____

_____

_____

_____

_____

_____

_____

_____

_____

_____

_____

_____

_____

_____

_____

_____

_____

_____

_____

_____

_____

_____

_____

_____

_____

STOP here with the writing test.

4

Practice Writing Test Prompt 4

Your Signature: _____
(Do not print.)

Print Your Name Here: _____

Your Date of Birth:

| | | – | | | – | | | | |
Month   Day   Year

Form 20WT6

The **ACT**® WRITING TEST BOOKLET

You must take the multiple-choice tests before you take the writing test.

Directions

This is a test of your writing skills. You will have **forty** (40) minutes to read the prompt, plan your response, and write an essay in English. Before you begin working, read all material in this test booklet carefully to understand exactly what you are being asked to do.

You will write your essay on the lined pages in the **answer document** provided. Your writing on those pages will be scored. You may use the unlined pages in this test booklet to plan your essay. Your work on these pages will not be scored.

Your essay will be evaluated based on the evidence it provides of your ability to:

- clearly state your own perspective on a complex issue and analyze the relationship between your perspective and at least one other perspective
- develop and support your ideas with reasoning and examples
- organize your ideas clearly and logically
- communicate your ideas effectively in standard written English

Lay your pencil down immediately when time is called.

DO NOT OPEN THIS BOOKLET UNTIL TOLD TO DO SO.

PO Box 168
Iowa City, IA 52243-0168

The ONLY Official Prep Guide from the Makers of the ACT

Motivation and Reward

From good grades in school to praise from a coach to monetary bonuses at work, rewards are commonly used as tools of motivation. People are often willing, or even eager, to work longer or harder when they know that better performance may earn them a reward. But while rewards may encourage desirable behavior, they can come with drawbacks as well. Prizes and incentives can distract people from the meaning and value of their work, and external sources of motivation can interfere with the ability to motivate oneself. Is it wise, then, to use rewards as a tool of motivation?

Read and carefully consider these perspectives. Each suggests a particular way of thinking about the question above.

Perspective One	Perspective Two	Perspective Three
There are many things in life that we will never be rewarded for doing but must do anyway. If we come to expect a prize for everything, we will be ill prepared for this unpleasant reality.	The promise of a reward can bring out the best in us. Incentives give us a clear target to work toward and a reason to push beyond the limits of what we think we are capable of achieving.	Rewards teach us that things are not worth doing if they do not promise us recognition or compensation. We learn to value the potential reward instead of the activity and thus fail to develop any real interests or passions.

Essay Task

Write a unified, coherent essay in which you address the question of whether it is wise to use rewards as a tool of motivation. In your essay, be sure to:

- clearly state your own perspective and analyze the relationship between your perspective and at least one other perspective
- develop and support your ideas with reasoning and examples
- organize your ideas clearly and logically
- communicate your ideas effectively in standard written English

Your perspective may be in full agreement with any of those given, in partial agreement, or completely different.

Planning Your Essay

Your work on these prewriting pages will not be scored.

Use the space below and on the back cover to generate ideas and plan your essay. You may wish to consider the following as you think critically about the task:

Strengths and weaknesses of different perspectives on the issue
- What insights do they offer, and what do they fail to consider?
- Why might they be persuasive to others, or why might they fail to persuade?

Your own knowledge, experience, and values
- What is your perspective on this issue, and what are its strengths and weaknesses?
- How will you support your perspective in your essay?

If you need more space to plan, please continue on the following page.

Planning Your Essay

Use this page to continue planning your essay. Your work on this page will not be scored.

ENGLISH • PRACTICE TEST 4 • EXPLANATORY ANSWERS

Passage I

Question 1. The best answer is **C** because it ensures correct subject-verb agreement. The plural verb *are* agrees with the plural subject *instruments*.

The best answer is NOT:

A because it lacks subject-verb agreement; the singular verb *is considered* does not agree with the plural subject *instruments*.

B because it lacks subject-verb agreement; the singular verb *does seem* does not agree with the plural subject *instruments*.

D because it lacks subject-verb agreement; the singular verb *is* does not agree with the plural subject *instruments*.

Question 2. The best answer is **H** because it best maintains the pattern established in the sentence's two previous examples. The first two examples follow a specific pattern of introducing the instrument and then describing what it was made from. The phrase "a flute made from a bamboo shoot" precisely follows this pattern.

The best answer is NOT:

F because it fails to maintain the pattern; the phrase "other brightly colored vegetables" does not introduce an instrument followed by what it was made from.

G because it fails to maintain the pattern; the phrase "vegetable instruments of all shapes and sizes" does not introduce an instrument followed by what it was made from.

J because it fails to maintain the pattern; the phrase "a certain type of root vegetable" does not introduce an instrument followed by what it was made from.

Question 3. The best answer is **D** because it eliminates unnecessary punctuation between the last item in the list that comprises the compound subject ("Gourds, daikon radishes, and other vegetables") and the verb *are used*.

The best answer is NOT:

A because it provides unnecessary punctuation (a comma) that incorrectly separates the last part of the compound subject from the verb.

B because it provides unnecessary punctuation (a semicolon) that incorrectly separates the modifier (*other*) from the word it modifies (*vegetables*).

C because it provides unnecessary punctuation (a comma) that incorrectly sets off the final phrase of the sentence ("to round out the orchestra") as a nonessential element. This phrase is essential because it explains what the vegetables are used for.

Question 4. The best answer is **G** because it correctly provides the main verb *were* to create a grammatically correct sentence that clearly conveys how the brothers learned to play instruments.

The best answer is NOT:

F because it incorrectly provides the modifying phrase "who were" where a main verb is needed. This creates a sentence fragment.

H because it incorrectly includes the word *and* before the main verb *were*, which could be used only if the sentence had set up two things the brothers did (lived on a farm and were taught, for example). That is not the case here.

J because it incorrectly omits the main verb *were*. This creates a sentence fragment.

Question 5. The best answer is **D** because it eliminates redundancy and unnecessary wordiness.

The best answer is NOT:

A because it introduces redundancy at the sentence level; the word *manually* (used later in the sentence) clearly conveys that the work was done by hand, making the phrase "Working by hand" redundant.

B because it introduces redundancy at the sentence level; the end of the sentence makes clear that the brothers consume discarded pieces of vegetables as they work, so the phrase "Eating unused vegetable parts" is redundant.

C because it introduces redundancy at the sentence level; the sentence later says the brothers use "metal drill bits," so the phrase "Using metal tools" is redundant.

Question 6. The best answer is **J** because it correctly provides the subject *he* and verb *makes* in the second half of the sentence to clearly explain how Weiping creates a low pitch.

The best answer is NOT:

F because it omits the subject *he* in the second half of the sentence and uses the modifying phrase "which makes" where a main verb is needed. This creates a sentence fragment with no clear meaning.

G because it omits the subject *he* in the second half of the sentence and uses the phrase "having made" where a main verb is needed. This creates a sentence fragment with no clear meaning.

H because it omits the subject *he* in the second half of the sentence and uses the phrase "by making" where a main verb is needed. This creates a sentence fragment with no clear meaning.

Question 7. The best answer is **B** because it provides the most logical transition based on the surrounding context. The preceding sentence explains how Weiping creates a low pitch. What follows presents a contrast because it explains how Weiping creates a high pitch. The word *Conversely* most clearly and logically sets up the contrast between these two ideas.

The best answer is NOT:

A because it provides an illogical transition based on the surrounding context. The word *Nonetheless* suggests that what follows explains that even though one condition exists (the need to create a deep hole for a low pitch), another condition could still exist. The word *Nonetheless* also suggests that the coexistence of these two conditions might be surprising or unexpected. That is not the case here. Rather, it makes sense that if a deep hole makes a low sound, then a shallow hole would make a higher sound.

C because it provides an illogical transition based on the surrounding context. The word *Otherwise* suggests that what follows describes what will happen if the first condition (creating a deep hole) is not met. That is not the case here.

D because it provides an illogical transition based on the surrounding context. The phrase "Even so" suggests that what follows explains that even though one condition exists (the need to create a deep hole for a low pitch), another condition could still exist. This phrase also suggests that the coexistence of these two conditions might be surprising or unexpected. That is not the case here. Rather, it makes sense that if a deep hole makes a low sound, then a shallow hole would make a higher sound.

Question 8. The best answer is **H** because it uses punctuation consistent with what appears later in the sentence (a comma) to correctly set off a nonessential element. The comma after the word *factors* correctly sets off the phrase "like the diameter of the hole and changes in air temperature and humidity" as a nonessential element. This is extra information without which the sentence would still be grammatically correct and logical.

The best answer is NOT:

F because it incorrectly places commas before and after the word *like*, suggesting that the word *like* is the nonessential element. This creates an ungrammatical and unclear sentence.

G because it uses punctuation (an em dash) that is inconsistent with what appears later in the sentence (a comma) to set off the nonessential element. A nonessential element must be set off with consistent punctuation (pairs of commas, em dashes, or parentheses).

J because it incorrectly omits the punctuation necessary to set off the nonessential element.

Question 9. The best answer is **C** because it ensures correct subject-verb agreement; the plural verb *affect* agrees with the plural subject *factors*. In addition, it correctly distinguishes between the words *affect* and *effect*; the transitive verb *affect* is correct for this context because it clearly conveys that other factors cause an impact on the sound quality.

The best answer is NOT:

A because it fails to correctly distinguish between the words *affect* and *effect*; the word *effects* is incorrect in this context because it would illogically suggest that the factors listed produce the sound quality rather than having an impact on the sound quality. In addition, it lacks subject-verb agreement, using a singular verb where a plural verb is needed to agree with the plural subject *factors*.

B because it lacks subject-verb agreement; the singular verb *affects* does not agree with the plural subject *factors*.

D because it fails to correctly distinguish between the words *affect* and *effect*; the word *effect* is incorrect for this context because it would illogically suggest that the factors listed produce the sound quality rather than having an impact on the sound quality.

Question 10. The best answer is **F** because it correctly provides the participle *producing* to establish the second part of the sentence as a participial phrase describing how the loss of water affects the pitch.

The best answer is NOT:

G because it replaces the participle with a subject ("such vegetables") and verb (*produce*), making the second part of the sentence an independent clause. This results in two independent clauses joined only by a comma, which is grammatically incorrect.

H because it replaces the participle with a subject (*it*) and verb (*will produce*), making the second part of the sentence an independent clause. This results in two independent clauses joined only by a comma, which is grammatically incorrect.

J because it replaces the participle with a subject (*this*) and verb (*produces*), making the second part of the sentence an independent clause. This results in two independent clauses joined only by a comma, which is grammatically incorrect.

Question 11. The best answer is **A** because it correctly uses consistent punctuation (commas) to set off the nonessential element. The phrase "Weidong says" is a clarifying detail that is not essential to the sentence and is therefore set off with commas after the words *sound* and *says*.

The best answer is NOT:

B because it omits the second comma (after the word *says*) and therefore fails to correctly set off the nonessential element.

C because it omits the first comma (after the word *sound*) and therefore fails to correctly set off the nonessential element.

D because it omits the commas after the words *sound* and *says* and therefore fails to correctly set off the nonessential element.

Question 12. The best answer is **J** because it puts the sentences in a sequence that makes the paragraph most logical. The word *Still* at the beginning of Sentence 3 creates the most logical connection to the end of the preceding paragraph by indicating that even though there are many factors that affect sound, water content is the most crucial. Sentence 1 logically follows Sentence 3 because it explains how quickly water content (the most crucial ingredient) is lost. Sentence 2 begins with the phrase "Because of this," which indicates a causal relationship. This sentence most logically follows Sentence 1 because the fact that the vegetables lose water content quickly most logically explains why the brothers must carve fresh instruments before each performance.

The best answer is NOT:

F because it offers an illogical sequence of sentences in the paragraph. Sentence 1 offers no clear relationship to the information given at the end of the third paragraph. In addition, Sentence 3 should not follow Sentence 2 because the word *Still* at the beginning of Sentence 3 offers no clear relationship to Sentence 2. It is illogical to say that even though fresh instruments must be carved before each performance, water is the most crucial ingredient.

G because it offers an illogical sequence of sentences in the paragraph. Sentence 1 offers no clear relationship to the information given at the end of the third paragraph. In addition, Sentence 3 should not follow Sentence 1 because the word *Still* at the beginning of Sentence 3 offers no clear relationship to Sentence 1. It is illogical to say that even though picked vegetables lose water quickly, water is the most crucial ingredient.

H because it offers an illogical sequence of sentences in the paragraph. Sentence 1 explains why the brothers must carve fresh instruments before each show (discussed in Sentence 2). Placing Sentence 2 before Sentence 1 would eliminate the necessary causal relationship between these two sentences. In addition, Sentence 3 should not follow Sentence 1 because the word *Still* at the beginning of Sentence 3 offers no clear relationship to Sentence 1. It is illogical to say that even though picked vegetables lose water quickly, water is the most crucial ingredient.

Question 13. The best answer is **D** because it correctly provides the subject ("The brothers' musical repertoire") and the main verb *is* to create the main clause "The brothers' musical repertoire is as varied as their instruments." The second half of the sentence is correctly set up as a participial phrase describing the variation in the brothers' repertoire.

The best answer is NOT:

A because it creates a sentence fragment by providing an introductory dependent clause ("While the brothers' musical repertoire is as varied as their instruments") where a main clause is needed.

B because it creates a sentence fragment by providing an introductory phrase ("With the brothers' musical repertoire being as varied as their instruments") where a main clause is needed.

C because it creates a sentence fragment by providing an introductory phrase ("Having the brothers' musical repertoire be as varied as their instruments") where a main clause is needed.

Question 14. The best answer is **H** because it provides a clear and convincing reason the sentence should not be added; the fact that each pitch is tested and perfected with an old tuner is not relevant to the concluding paragraph's more general discussion of the Nan brothers' performances and range of instruments.

The best answer is NOT:

F because it fails to provide a clear and convincing reason the sentence should be added. Even if the idea that the brothers test and perfect each pitch somewhat suggests the care and attention to detail with which the brothers craft their instruments, this point is not relevant to the concluding paragraph's more general discussion of the Nan brothers' performances and range of instruments.

G because it fails to provide a clear and convincing reason the sentence should be added. Even if the idea that the brothers test and perfect each pitch somewhat hints that the vegetables can be made into precise instruments, this point is not relevant to the concluding paragraph's more general discussion of the Nan brothers' performances and range of instruments.

J because it fails to provide a clear and convincing reason the sentence should not be added. The statement about how pitches are tested in no way conflicts with the idea that the brothers have a strong musical background. Rather, the statement should not be added because it is irrelevant to the concluding paragraph's more general discussion of the Nan brothers' performances and range of instruments.

Question 15. The best answer is B because it is the most effective placement of the sentence in terms of logic and cohesion. The statement about the brothers performing with a local theater company logically fits at Point B because it explains their connection to theater immediately before the paragraph references their "passion for performance."

The best answer is NOT:

A because it would interrupt the general description of the brothers' work using vegetables to craft instruments. The fact that they performed with a local theater company has no clear relationship to the discussion of their work at this point in the essay.

C because it would interrupt the discussion of how the brothers create their instruments. The fact that they performed with a local theater company has no clear relationship to how they make their instruments.

D because it would interrupt the discussion of the range of instruments and the repertoire. The fact that the Nan brothers performed with a local theater company has no clear relationship to the discussion at this point in the essay.

Passage II

Question 16. The best answer is J because it creates a grammatically correct and complete sentence by omitting the repetition of the subject (*it*) and a second main verb *is*. Deleting the phrase "it is" correctly allows for the second half of the sentence to work as an appositive that explains what a nurse log is.

The best answer is NOT:

F because it adds a subject (*it*) and verb (*is*), establishing the second part of the sentence as an independent clause. This creates a run-on sentence by incorrectly joining two independent clauses using a comma without a coordinating conjunction.

G because it adds a subject ("the term 'nurse log'") and verb (*is defined*), establishing the second part of the sentence as an independent clause. This creates a run-on sentence by incorrectly joining two independent clauses using a comma without a coordinating conjunction.

H because it adds a subject ("this type of log") and verb (*is*), establishing the second part of the sentence as an independent clause. This creates a run-on sentence by incorrectly joining two independent clauses using a comma without a coordinating conjunction.

Question 17. **The best answer is A** because it does not introduce redundancy or unnecessary wordiness.

The best answer is NOT:

B because it introduces redundancy at the paragraph level; the phrase "in addition to acting as a home and providing nutrients for young plants" is redundant because this point is made clear in the preceding sentence.

C because it introduces redundancy at the paragraph level; the parenthetical noting the size of the log is redundant because this detail is made clear in the preceding sentence.

D because it introduces redundancy at the paragraph level; because the preceding sentence clearly describes the log as decaying, it is redundant to include that point again.

Question 18. **The best answer is G** because it eliminates unnecessary punctuation that incorrectly separates the park's visitors from what they saw.

The best answer is NOT:

F because it provides unnecessary punctuation; the comma after the word *park* incorrectly separates the visitors (the indirect object) from what they are offered ("a glimpse into the complicated cycle of life").

H because it provides unnecessary punctuation; the comma after the word *life* incorrectly separates the modifier ("unfolding in the forests outside the city") from what it modifies ("the complicated cycle of life").

J because it provides unnecessary punctuation. The commas after the words *park* and *life* incorrectly set off the direct object phrase that explains what visitors are offered ("a glimpse into the complicated cycle of life"). This creates an ungrammatical and illogical sentence.

Question 19. **The best answer is A** because it correctly distinguishes between the frequently confused words *lying* and *laying* and applies the idiomatically correct preposition *in* for the context. The word *lying* correctly indicates that the log itself is on the forest floor.

The best answer is NOT:

B because it fails to properly distinguish between the words *lying* and *laying*. The phrase "laying within" illogically suggests that the log is laying something else down inside the forest.

C because it provides the preposition *with*, which creates a nonstandard expression.

D because it fails to properly distinguish between the words *lying* and *laying*; the word *laying* illogically suggests that the log is laying something else down. In addition, it provides the preposition *in*, which creates a nonstandard expression.

Question 20. The best answer is **H** because it prevents an error in parallelism between the two parts of the sentence; the past tense *transported* correctly parallels the past tense *found* used previously in the sentence. In addition, the phrase "and transported" correctly provides the word *and* to indicate that Dion carried out two actions: he found the log and transported it.

The best answer is NOT:

F because it contains an error in parallelism; it uses the participle *transporting* where the finite verb *transported* is needed to parallel the previous finite verb *found*. In addition, it incorrectly places a comma after the word *and*, causing the phrase "transporting it to the city along with some of the soil" to look as if it is set off as a nonessential element.

G because it introduces an error in parallelism by using the infinitive *to transport* where the finite verb *transported* is needed to parallel the previous finite verb *found*. In addition, it incorrectly places a comma after the word *and*, causing the phrase "to transport it to the city along with some of the soil" to look as if it is set off as a nonessential element.

J because it introduces an error in coordination; omitting the conjunction *and* makes it look like the sentence is setting up a list indicating that Dion carried out at least three actions (found the log, transported the log, and did something else), but this is not the case.

Question 21. The best answer is **A** because it prevents the creation of a run-on sentence by establishing two complete sentences separated by a period.

The best answer is NOT:

B because it creates a run-on sentence by incorrectly joining two complete sentences using a comma without a coordinating conjunction.

C because it creates a run-on sentence by incorrectly joining two complete sentences without any punctuation or coordinating conjunction.

D because it creates a run-on sentence by incorrectly joining two complete sentences using a comma without a coordinating conjunction.

Question 22. The best answer is **J** because it ensures correct subject-verb agreement. The plural verb *reveal* agrees with the plural subject *visits*.

The best answer is NOT:

F because it lacks subject-verb agreement; the singular verb *reveals* does not agree with the plural subject *visits*.

G because it lacks subject-verb agreement; the singular verb *has revealed* does not agree with the plural subject *visits*.

H because it lacks subject-verb agreement; the singular verb *is revealing* does not agree with the plural subject *visits*.

Question 23. The best answer is **C** because it correctly distinguishes between the frequently confused words *number* and *amount*; the nouns *energy* and *technology* are both noncountable and therefore require the word *amount*. It correctly uses the plural noun *amounts* because there are two things needed for maintaining the nurse log: energy and technology. Finally, it correctly uses the preposition *of* to create an expression consistent with standard English usage.

The best answer is NOT:

A because it fails to correctly distinguish between the words *number* and *amount*, creating an expression that is inconsistent with standard English usage.

B because it uses the singular word *amount* where a plural is needed, and it incorrectly applies the preposition *in* where the word *of* is needed to create an expression consistent with standard English usage.

D because it fails to correctly distinguish between the words *numbers* and *amounts*, and it incorrectly applies the preposition *in* where the word *of* is needed to create an expression consistent with standard English usage.

Question 24. The best answer is **F** because it does not introduce redundancy or unnecessary wordiness.

The best answer is NOT:

G because it contains an internal redundancy; in this context, the word *constantly* and the phrase "on a regular basis" convey the same meaning.

H because it contains an internal redundancy; nutrients are healthy, so it is redundant to add the adjective *healthful*.

J because it contains an internal redundancy; in this context, the words *constantly* and *regularly* convey the same meaning.

Question 25. **The best answer is B** because it correctly identifies the rhetorical impact of losing the preceding sentence. The preceding sentence offers three examples (monitored humidity, soil replenishment, and filtered sunlight) to illustrate the level of effort required to maintain the nurse log in the city.

The best answer is NOT:

A because it incorrectly identifies the rhetorical impact of losing the preceding sentence. The preceding sentence refers to the necessity of monitoring humidity and replenishing soil, but it does not explain why this is "necessary to maintain nature-based exhibits" in general. It is solely focused on this particular nurse log.

C because it incorrectly identifies the rhetorical impact of losing the preceding sentence. Although the greenhouse houses the nurse log and allows for the maintenance of the nurse log in the city environment, the preceding sentence does not compare the importance of the greenhouse and nurse log in any way.

D because it incorrectly identifies the rhetorical impact of losing the preceding sentence. The preceding sentence describes some of the difficulties of maintaining the nurse log in a city environment, but it does not discuss anything in connection to "how difficult it was for Dion to build the greenhouse."

Question 26. **The best answer is J** because it corrects a misplaced modifier. Placing the modifying phrase "in the middle of a busy city" after the word *ecosystem* clearly and logically explains that the ecosystem was in the middle of the city.

The best answer is NOT:

F because it contains a misplaced modifier. Placing the modifying phrase after the word *work* suggests an illogical causal relationship by indicating that the required work conveyed an important message because it took place in the middle of the city.

G because it introduces a misplaced modifier. Placing the modifying phrase after the word *the* creates an ungrammatical and illogical sentence suggesting that the required work conveyed an important message because it took place in the middle of the city.

H because it introduces a misplaced modifier. Placing the modifying phrase after the word *this* creates an ungrammatical sentence. The modifying phrase must follow the noun it is meant to modify.

Question 27. The best answer is **D** because it correctly distinguishes between the phrases "In accordance with" and "According to" to provide the phrase that is most contextually appropriate. The phrase "According to" accurately conveys that the sentence is explaining the artist's perspective. In addition, the phrase supplies the idiomatically correct preposition *to*.

The best answer is NOT:

A because it provides the idiomatically incorrect preposition *with* where the preposition *to* is needed.

B because it fails to correctly distinguish between the phrases "According to" and "In accordance with." The phrase "In accordance with" incorrectly signals a sense of agreement between two parties rather than indicating that what follows conveys the artist's perspective.

C because it provides a phrase that does not make sense in context. The phrase "In accord with" incorrectly signals a sense of collaboration and agreement between two parties rather than indicating that what follows conveys the artist's perspective.

Question 28. The best answer is **H** because it uses consistent punctuation (commas) to correctly set off a nonessential element. The phrase "once destroyed" is not essential to the sentence and is therefore set off with commas after the words *nature* and *destroyed*.

The best answer is NOT:

F because it fails to provide the necessary punctuation to set off the nonessential element ("once destroyed").

G because although it correctly sets off the nonessential element ("once destroyed"), it incorrectly places a comma after the word *virtually*, which incorrectly separates the modifier (*virtually*) from the word it modifies (*impossible*).

J because it fails to provide the necessary punctuation to set off the nonessential element ("once destroyed") and incorrectly places a comma after the word *virtually*, which incorrectly separates the modifier (*virtually*) from the word it modifies (*impossible*).

Question 29. **The best answer is B** because the parenthetical explains the origin of part of the installation's title. Paragraph 2 begins by explaining the meaning of the word *Vivarium* in the installation's title. The parenthetical explaining the other half of the title (*Neukom*) would most logically be placed at Point B, which appears right after the explanation of *Vivarium*.

The best answer is NOT:

A because the parenthetical does not describe anything specific about the installation or what a nurse log is, which is the focus of the discussion at Point A.

C because the parenthetical does not describe anything in relation to Dion's process of finding the log or creating the installation, which is the focus of the discussion at Point C.

D because the parenthetical does not describe anything in relation to the work required to maintain the nurse log in the city, which is the focus of the discussion at Point D.

Question 30. **The best answer is G** because it offers a clear and convincing reason the essay accomplishes the purpose identified in the stem. The essay "describes Dion's nature-based installation" in the first three paragraphs and then explains his purpose in conveying to others the importance of sustaining ecosystems.

The best answer is NOT:

F because it fails to provide a clear and convincing reason the essay accomplishes the purpose identified in the stem. It provides a version of how Dion's installation came about that differs from the essay and does not address the message Dion hopes to share in order to educate others.

H because it fails to provide a clear and convincing reason the essay has not accomplished the purpose identified in the stem. It inaccurately asserts that the essay focuses on the appearance of the installation specifically in relation to Olympic Sculpture Park. The essay focuses much more on Dion's message and how the installation conveys that message than it does on the installation's appearance.

J because it fails to provide a clear and convincing reason the essay has not accomplished the purpose identified in the stem. The last paragraph of the essay does address what viewers learn from the installation.

ENGLISH • PRACTICE TEST 4 • EXPLANATORY ANSWERS

Passage III

Question 31. The best answer is **A** because it prevents the introduction of an error in coordination between the two parts of the sentence; the use of a semicolon after the word *commands* demands that the first part of the sentence be an independent clause. The phrase "Internet navigation required" provides the subject ("Internet navigation") and verb (*required*) needed to correctly establish the first part of the sentence as an independent clause.

The best answer is NOT:

B because it introduces an error in coordination between the two parts of the sentence; the modifying phrase "which required" replaces the main verb *required*. This makes the first part of the sentence a sentence fragment. A sentence fragment cannot be joined to an independent clause by a semicolon.

C because it introduces an error in coordination between the two parts of the sentence; the modifying phrase "that required" replaces the main verb *required*. This makes the first part of the sentence a sentence fragment. A sentence fragment cannot be joined to an independent clause by a semicolon.

D because it introduces an error in coordination between the two parts of the sentence; the modifying participle *requiring* replaces the main verb *required*. This makes the first part of the sentence a sentence fragment. A sentence fragment cannot be joined to an independent clause by a semicolon.

Question 32. The best answer is **H** because it offers phrasing that is both stylistically and tonally consistent with the essay as a whole.

The best answer is NOT:

F because it fails to match the established style. The phrasing of "obstructive hindrances" sounds too formal and contains an internal redundancy; hindrances are obstructive by nature, so it is unnecessary to include the adjective at all.

G because it fails to match the established style; the phrase "What with the problematic issues" is too informal for the style and tone of the essay.

J because it fails to match the established style; the phrase "Owing to the messiness" is too informal for the style and tone of the essay.

Question 33. The best answer is C because it provides the correct punctuation (a colon) to join two independent clauses such that the second clause explains or expands on the first clause. In this case, the idea that Andreessen believed everyone would want the Internet further explains what the writer means by the statement "Marc Andreessen believed the opposite."

The best answer is NOT:

A because it incorrectly joins two independent clauses using a comma without a coordinating conjunction, which creates a run-on sentence.

B because it incorrectly uses a semicolon to join the independent clause ("Marc Andreessen believed the opposite") and the dependent clause ("because everyone would want the Internet"). A semicolon can only be used to join two independent clauses.

D because it fails to provide any punctuation to join the two independent clauses, which creates a run-on sentence.

Question 34. The best answer is J because it provides the best transition to the discussion of Andreessen's browser. The paragraph that follows describes what Andreessen created: a tool for using the Internet. The sentence "People just needed the right tool" would therefore provide the most effective transition from the discussion of why the Internet wasn't user-friendly to the discussion of the tool Andreessen created to help solve that problem.

The best answer is NOT:

F because it fails to provide a logical transition to the discussion of Andreessen's browser. The statement about Andreessen's belief that Internet speeds would increase does not clearly connect to the development of Mosaic.

G because it fails to provide a logical transition to the discussion of Andreessen's browser. The statement about the amount of information online does not clearly connect to the development of Mosaic.

H because it fails to provide a logical transition to the discussion of Andreessen's browser. The statement about the limited number of people who had Internet access does not clearly connect to the development of Mosaic.

Question 35. **The best answer is D** because it correctly eliminates the unnecessary punctuation in the phrase "As a student worker for the National Center for Supercomputing Applications (NCSA) at the University of Illinois." The abbreviation *NCSA* should be separated from the center's full name only by parentheses, and no punctuation should separate the noun phrase "As a student worker" from the prepositional phrase explaining who or what the student worked for.

The best answer is NOT:

A because it incorrectly sets off the prepositional phrase "for the National Center for Supercomputing Applications" with commas. In addition, it incorrectly places a comma between the full name of the center and the parenthetical abbreviation for it.

B because it incorrectly sets off the prepositional phrase "for the National Center for Supercomputing Applications" with commas. In addition, the phrase incorrectly sets off the abbreviation with commas when the abbreviation is already enclosed by parentheses.

C because it incorrectly sets off the abbreviation with commas when the abbreviation is already enclosed by parentheses.

Question 36. **The best answer is F** because it best expresses the idea specified in the stem. The phrase "became enthralled" indicates that Andreessen was so drawn to the Internet that he was captivated by the it and therefore "most strongly conveys that Andreessen developed a strong affinity for the Internet."

The best answer is NOT:

G because it fails to express the idea specified in the stem. Pointing out that Andreessen "first gained access to" the Internet at NCSA does not convey any sense that Andreessen developed an affinity for the Internet.

H because it is a less effective choice for expressing the idea specified in the stem. Although some sense of affinity could be suggested by the idea that Andreessen "spent many hours" on the Internet, it is unclear if this was by choice or necessity. In addition, there is no indication of Andreessen developing an affinity for the Internet.

J because it fails to express the idea specified in the stem. The fact that Andreessen "saw the utility of" the Internet does little to convey any sense of Andreessen developing an affinity for it.

Question 37. The best answer is **A** because it prevents the creation of a run-on sentence. The dependent clause "which became available in 1993" follows the independent clause and is properly set off as a nonessential element that describes a detail about Mosaic.

The best answer is NOT:

B because it creates a run-on sentence by incorrectly joining two independent clauses ("The two then worked with the NCSA to develop Mosaic" and "the NCSA made the program available in 1993") using a comma without a coordinating conjunction.

C because it creates a run-on sentence by incorrectly joining two independent clauses ("The two then worked with the NCSA to develop Mosaic" and "they made Mosaic available in 1993") using a comma without a coordinating conjunction.

D because it creates a run-on sentence by incorrectly joining two independent clauses ("The two then worked with the NCSA to develop Mosaic" and "it became available in 1993") using a comma without a coordinating conjunction.

Question 38. The best answer is **F** because it does not introduce redundancy or unnecessary wordiness.

The best answer is NOT:

G because it introduces redundancy at the sentence level. The sentence specifies that the 60,000 copies were downloaded in Mosaic's first year, so it is redundant to include the phrase "That year" at the beginning of the sentence.

H because it introduces redundancy at the paragraph level. The paragraph already clearly identifies Mosaic as the program that could be downloaded; it is unnecessary to add a parenthetical to the last sentence of the paragraph to clarify which program is being discussed.

J because it contains an internal redundancy; the word *Approximately* means the same thing as the phrase "but not exactly."

Question 39. The best answer is D because it correctly places the modifying adverb *soon* after the word *it*; in this location, the adverb *soon* modifies the verb *surpassed* in the second independent clause to create a grammatically correct statement with the most logical meaning in context.

The best answer is NOT:

A because it contains a misplaced modifier. Placing the adverb *soon* after the word *was* creates a statement that illogically suggests Mosaic was the first web browser but then lost that status. This is impossible. When a new browser is invented, it does not replace others as the first browser.

B because it introduces a misplaced modifier. Placing the adverb *soon* after the word *Mosaic* creates a statement that illogically suggests Mosaic was the first web browser but then lost that status. This is impossible. When a new browser is invented, it does not replace others as the first browser.

C because it introduces a misplaced modifier. Placing the adverb *soon* after the word *browser* creates a statement that illogically suggests Mosaic was the first web browser but then lost that status. This is impossible. When a new browser is invented, it does not replace others as the first browser.

Question 40. The best answer is G because it correctly indicates that the phrase should be added and accurately identifies the rhetorical impact of making that addition. The phrase "adding much-needed visual appeal" helps emphasize the impact of displaying pictures and text on the same page: it made browsing more enjoyable.

The best answer is NOT:

F because although it correctly indicates that the phrase should be added, it fails to accurately identify the rhetorical impact of making that addition. The sentence does not need the added phrase to reveal that Mosaic was the first browser to display pictures alongside text; the sentence makes that point clear without the addition of the phrase.

H because it incorrectly indicates that the phrase should not be added and inaccurately describes the rhetorical impact of the phrase. The suggested phrase points out the visual appeal of adding pictures; this does not indicate that text-based documents therefore weren't useful.

J because it incorrectly indicates that the phrase should not be added and inaccurately describes the rhetorical impact of the phrase. The suggested phrase points out the visual appeal of adding pictures; it does not indicate that Mosaic was like other browsers initially and later added visuals.

Question 41. **The best answer is C** because it creates a sentence structure wherein the correct subject ("the program") immediately follows the modifying phrase ("featuring hyperlinks"). This structure clearly and logically indicates that the program featured hyperlinks.

The best answer is NOT:

A because it creates an illogical sentence; it establishes "the user" as the subject, which illogically suggests that the user featured hyperlinks.

B because it creates an illogical sentence; it establishes "the program's user" as the subject, which illogically suggests that the user featured hyperlinks.

D because it creates a dangling modifier; this structure fails to establish a clear and logical relationship between the modifying phrase "featuring hyperlinks" and the rest of the sentence. What exactly featured hyperlinks remains unclear.

Question 42. **The best answer is H** because it correctly identifies the rhetorical impact of losing the preceding sentence. The quotation in the preceding sentence specifically credits Mosaic with making the Internet seem "interconnected" or "coherent."

The best answer is NOT:

F because it fails to properly identify the rhetorical impact of losing the preceding sentence. The quotation in the preceding sentence makes no mention of what people did before Mosaic was invented.

G because it fails to properly identify the rhetorical impact of losing the preceding sentence. The quotation in the preceding sentence does not reference specific features that made Mosaic popular.

J because it fails to properly identify the rhetorical impact of losing the preceding sentence. The quotation in the preceding sentence does not compare Mosaic to, or even mention, the designs of later web browsers.

Question 43. The best answer is **B** because it provides the most logical transition based on the surrounding context. The word *Moreover* creates the most logical transition because the text that follows the transition word expands upon the idea in the preceding sentence about Mosaic's effect on average users.

The best answer is NOT:

A because it provides an illogical transition based on the surrounding context. The word *Comparatively* suggests that what follows presents a comparison to what came before, which is not the case here.

C because it provides an illogical transition based on the surrounding context. The word *Conversely* suggests that what follows presents a contrast to what came before, which is not the case here.

D because it provides an illogical transition based on the surrounding context. The word *Instead* suggests that what follows offers information about what Mosaic could do in place of what was described in the preceding sentence, but that is not the case here.

Question 44. The best answer is **H** because it provides the most precise word choice for the context. The word *released* precisely conveys the idea that Mosaic was made available to the public.

The best answer is NOT:

F because it supplies an imprecise word choice for the context; the word *discharged* illogically suggests that the browser was let go from a position or duty.

G because it supplies an imprecise word choice for the context; the word *relinquished* illogically suggests that the browser was given up.

J because it supplies an imprecise word choice for the context; the word *emitted* illogically suggests that the browser was given off (like heat or light) from something.

Question 45. The best answer is **A** because it provides the most effective conclusion based on the criterion in the stem. The "contrast begun in the previous sentence" refers to the fact that there were 623 websites when Mosaic was released. The specific detail about the existence of more than 600,000 sites four years later provides the most direct contrast by highlighting the difference in the number of sites.

The best answer is NOT:

B because it fails to provide an effective conclusion based on the criterion in the stem. Mosaic's point-and-click interface offers no direct relationship to the number of websites in existence when Mosaic was released.

C because it fails to provide an effective conclusion based on the criterion in the stem. The fact that Andreessen would go on to develop another browser offers no direct relationship to the number of websites in existence when Mosaic was released.

D because it fails to provide an effective conclusion based on the criterion in the stem. Although the sentence highlights the expansion of the Internet, this general assertion offers no direct contrast to the specific number of websites in existence when Mosaic was released.

Passage IV

Question 46. The best answer is **G** because it best expresses the idea specified in the stem. The word *celebrated* best expresses an "overwhelmingly positive reception."

The best answer is NOT:

F because it is a less effective choice relative to the goal specified in the stem. In context, the idea that "poets were placed alongside champion athletes" hints at the idea that the poets were honored just as much as champion athletes. However, the word *placed* is much weaker than the word *celebrated* in expressing an "overwhelmingly positive reception."

H because it fails to express the idea specified in the stem. The word *accepted* can be understood as a neutral idea, or it can even convey a sense of reticence, as if the poets were only reluctantly accepted. Neither of these meanings expresses an "overwhelmingly positive reception."

J because it is a less effective choice relative to the goal specified in the stem. The word *liked* conveys that the poets were appreciated, but it is less effective than the word *celebrated* in conveying the sense of an "overwhelmingly positive reception."

Question 47. The best answer is A because it most effectively connects this sentence to the information in the next sentence. The sentence that follows highlights the scandal as evoking the only public excitement for the literary competition. The phrase "is poorly remembered and rarely missed" provides the most effective connection because it establishes that there has been little appreciation for the literary competition.

The best answer is NOT:

B because it fails to provide a logical connection to the next sentence. The detail about other competitions offers no direct connection to the next sentence, which specifically highlights the scandal as evoking the only public excitement relating to the literary competition.

C because it fails to provide a logical connection to the next sentence. The fact that the literary competition is sometimes commented upon today offers no direct connection to the next sentence, which specifically highlights the scandal as evoking the only public excitement relating to the literary competition.

D because it fails to provide a logical connection to the next sentence. The fact that the literary competition was an homage to the traditions of ancient Greece offers no direct connection to the next sentence, which specifically highlights the scandal as evoking the only public excitement relating to the literary competition.

Question 48. The best answer is J because it eliminates unnecessary punctuation in the modifying phrase that describes which literary contest is being discussed: "the very first modern Olympic literary contest."

The best answer is NOT:

F because it provides unnecessary punctuation by incorrectly placing a comma after the word *modern*; the word *modern* directly modifies "Olympic literary contest" and therefore cannot be separated from that phrase by any punctuation.

G because it provides unnecessary punctuation by incorrectly placing commas after the words *very* and *first*. The word *very* is an intensifier that modifies the word *first*, so these two words cannot be separated by any punctuation. The word *first* modifies the phrase "modern Olympic literary contest" and therefore cannot be separated from that phrase by any punctuation.

H because it provides unnecessary punctuation by incorrectly placing a comma after the words *first* and *Olympic*. The word *first* modifies the phrase "modern Olympic literary contest" and therefore cannot be separated from that phrase by any punctuation. The word *Olympic* modifies "literary contest" and therefore cannot be separated from that phrase by any punctuation.

Question 49. The best answer is D because it correctly omits the repetition of the subject (*he*) while maintaining the main verb *insisted*; this correctly creates a complete sentence.

The best answer is NOT:

A because it incorrectly repeats the subject; the subject ("French aristocrat Baron Pierre de Coubertin") is already stated in the first part of the sentence, so the subject *he* should not be used in the second part of the sentence.

B because it omits the main verb *insisted*, using instead the modifying phrase "insistent in his belief." This creates a sentence fragment that seems to have one long, modified subject but no predicate.

C because it omits the main verb *insisted*, using instead the modifier *insisting*. This creates a sentence fragment that seems to have one long, modified subject but no predicate.

Question 50. The best answer is H because it provides the appropriate pronoun for this sentence. The subjective pronoun *who* is needed because it is the subject of the verb *felt* (creating the phrase "who felt"). This construction clearly indicates that what follows helps describe the officials' perspective on the modern Olympic Games.

The best answer is NOT:

F because it incorrectly provides the objective pronoun *whom* when the subjective pronoun is needed.

G because it incorrectly provides the objective pronoun *whom* when the subjective pronoun is needed. In addition, it unnecessarily includes the reflexive pronoun *themselves*, which does not contribute to the meaning of the sentence.

J because it incorrectly provides the word *which*; the word *who* is needed because the sentence refers to people.

Question 51. The best answer is B because it corrects the use of a vague pronoun. The word *competitors* clearly indicates who would submit the work for the contest.

The best answer is NOT:

A because it uses a vague pronoun; the antecedent for the word *it* would seem to be the Pentathlon of Muses, which is illogical in this context. The Pentathlon cannot submit work.

C because it introduces a vague pronoun; the pronoun *those* has no clear antecedent, making it unclear who would submit the work for the contest.

D because it introduces a vague pronoun; the pronoun *they* has no clear antecedent because the competitors or authors have not been mentioned yet. Therefore, who would submit work for the contest remains unclear.

Question 52. **The best answer is J** because it provides the most relevant detail about the Olympic literary contest at this point in the essay. The detail that submissions should be in the form of a poem "inspired by the idea of sport" directly connects to the paragraph's introduction of the literary contest; it provides basic information about what kinds of writing should be submitted.

The best answer is NOT:

F because it provides a vague detail about Coubertin not having established a length requirement; this is only loosely related to the basic introduction of the literary contest. The detail about the preference for submissions to be poems inspired by sports is much more relevant to the basic introduction of the contest.

G because it provides a detail that is unrelated to the basic introduction of the literary contest. The title of the piece that won twelve years later (in 1924) is irrelevant to the discussion of the basic requirements and establishment of the literary contest in its first modern Olympics.

H because it provides a vague detail that is irrelevant to the basic introduction of the literary contest. There is little information about the "limitations placed on writers" in this paragraph, so the point about critics mocking such limitations has no direct relationship to the discussion at this point in the essay.

Question 53. **The best answer is B** because it correctly places a comma after the word *year* to separate the introductory phrase ("After a long deliberation during the literary event's first year") from the rest of the sentence. This creates a grammatically correct and clear statement about the judges' actions.

The best answer is NOT:

A because it incorrectly uses a semicolon to separate the introductory phrase from the main clause, creating an ungrammatical sentence.

C because it incorrectly joins the introductory phrase to the main clause with a comma and the word *then*. In addition, the word *then* repeats the idea conveyed by the word *after* at the beginning of the sentence. This creates an ungrammatical and unclear sentence.

D because it incorrectly uses a period to separate the introductory phrase from the main clause. The phrase "After a long deliberation during the literary event's first year" is a sentence fragment.

Question 54. The best answer is **F** because it correctly provides a subject (*judges*) to clearly indicate who refused to award the medals. In addition, it includes a comma after the word *judges*, which correctly sets off the phrase "so impressed by 'Ode to Sport' that they called it 'the perfect poem'" as a nonessential element.

The best answer is NOT:

G because it creates an error in coordination between the nonessential element and the rest of the sentence. The word *and* creates an unclear and ungrammatical relationship between the main clause ("The judges refused to award either silver or bronze medals to any other literary competitors") and the nonessential element ("so impressed by 'Ode to Sport' that they called it 'the perfect poem'"). The word *and* incorrectly seems to set up the nonessential element as an addition to another nonessential element, which it is not.

H because it creates an error in coordination between the two parts of the sentence. The sentence already has the main verb *refused* to describe what the judges did; adding a second main verb (*had been*) creates an unclear and ungrammatical sentence.

J because it creates an error in coordination between the two parts of the sentence. The sentence already has the main verb *refused* to describe what the judges did; adding a second main verb (*were*) creates an unclear and ungrammatical sentence.

Question 55. The best answer is **B** because it omits the comma after *Weeks* to ensure that the phrase "after the Games had come to an end" is not set off in the sentence. The phrase "after the Games had come to an end" is essential information that modifies the word *Weeks*. Omitting the comma creates a grammatical sentence that clearly explains when the judges attempted to contact Hohrod and Eschbach.

The best answer is NOT:

A because it incorrectly places commas after the words *Weeks* and *end*, which incorrectly indicates that the phrase "after the Games had come to an end" is a nonessential element.

C because it incorrectly places a comma after the word *Weeks*, which creates an ungrammatical and unclear sentence. Setting off the word *Weeks* makes the sentence confusing because the word *Weeks* has no clear relationship to the rest of the sentence.

D because it incorrectly omits the comma that should follow the introductory phrase "Weeks after the Games had come to an end."

Question 56. **The best answer is F** because it most effectively leads the reader from the preceding information about Hohrod and Eschbach to the information that follows about Coubertin. The preceding sentence explains that the judges were unsuccessful in reaching Hohrod and Eschbach, and the sentence that follows explains that Coubertin admitted to being the real author. The sentence explaining the judges' discovery that Hohrod and Eschbach did not exist provides a clear and logical connection between these events.

The best answer is NOT:

G because it fails to provide an effective connection between the preceding information about Hohrod and Eschbach and the information that follows about Coubertin. The Swedish art academies' claims about the competition have no relationship to the sequence of events that occurred between "Ode to Sport" winning and Coubertin admitting that he was the author.

H because it fails to provide an effective connection between the preceding information about Hohrod and Eschbach and the information that follows about Coubertin. The arrival of submissions for the following year's competition has no relationship to the sequence of events that occurred between "Ode to Sport" winning and Coubertin admitting that he was the author.

J because it fails to provide an effective connection between the preceding information about Hohrod and Eschbach and the information that follows about Coubertin. The fact that the judges had read "Ode to Sport" aloud has no relationship to the sequence of events that occurred between "Ode to Sport" winning and Coubertin admitting that he was the author.

Question 57. **The best answer is C** because it accurately explains that adding the sentence would repeat information provided earlier in the essay. The sentence includes two details: Coubertin founded the modern Olympic Games and established the fine arts competition. These details are introduced in the second paragraph of the essay.

The best answer is NOT:

A because it fails to identify the fact that the sentence contains information that is already given in the essay. The idea that Coubertin did not include his real name because he was involved in establishing the competition is not a valid reason for adding redundant information.

B because it fails to identify the fact that the sentence contains information that is already given in the essay. In addition, it inaccurately describes the proposed addition; the sentence does not at all suggest that Coubertin knew his poem was well written.

D because it inaccurately describes why the sentence should not be added. Although it is true that the sentence does not make clear whether Coubertin discussed the poem with the judges, the primary reason the sentence should not be added is that it would introduce redundancy.

Question 58. The best answer is H because it eliminates redundancy and unnecessary wordiness.

The best answer is NOT:

F because it introduces redundancy at the sentence level; the causal relationship is established by the introductory phrase "once Coubertin's ruse was uncovered," so it is redundant to add "as a result."

G because it introduces redundancy at the sentence level; the sentence establishes that the contest was "already unpopular," so it is redundant to add "even though dislike of it was not new."

J because it introduces redundancy at the sentence level; the causal relationship is established by the introductory phrase "once Coubertin's ruse was uncovered," so it is redundant to add "because of this unveiling."

Question 59. The best answer is D because it is the most effective placement of the statement in terms of logic and cohesion. The sentence explains the growing distrust of the competition, even among its organizers. This point would logically follow the sentence explaining that distrust of the competition grew after Coubertin's ruse was uncovered. In addition, it would logically precede the sentence explaining when the competition was finally dropped from the Olympic Games.

The best answer is NOT:

A because it would interrupt the paragraph by introducing information about the growing distrust of the competition in the middle of offering more general information about the competition and the surrounding scandal.

B because it would interrupt the transition between the first two paragraphs. The first paragraph ends with the introduction of the scandal surrounding the first modern Olympic literary contest, and the second paragraph begins the story of how that contest began and how the scandal erupted. It would be illogical to interrupt that transition with a point about the growing distrust of the competition.

C because it would interrupt the discussion of how the competition worked in the modern Olympic Games. The statement about the growing distrust of the competition has no clear relationship to the basic description of how the competition worked.

Question 60. The best answer is G because it offers a clear and convincing reason the essay accomplishes the purpose identified in the stem: it accurately explains that the essay is describing the Pentathlon of Muses, "an element of the modern Olympic Games that was relatively short lived and is not very well remembered."

The best answer is NOT:

F because it fails to offer a clear and convincing reason the essay accomplishes the purpose identified in the stem. It inaccurately describes the essay; rather than outlining "Coubertin's most important accomplishments as the founder of the modern Olympic Games," the essay focuses on Coubertin's role in one small piece of the modern Olympic Games—the Pentathlon of Muses.

H because it indicates the essay hasn't accomplished the specified primary purpose when it has. In doing so, it inaccurately asserts that the essay "considers the merits of fine arts competitions being a part of popular athletic events." The essay does not do this. Rather, it focuses specifically on the lesser-known history of the Pentathlon of Muses.

J because it indicates the essay hasn't accomplished the specified primary purpose when it has. In doing so, it inaccurately asserts that the essay discusses Coubertin's poem "and explains why the poem influenced Coubertin to compete in literary competitions." The essay does not do this. Rather, it focuses specifically on the relatively unknown history of the Pentathlon of Muses.

Passage V

Question 61. The best answer is B because it omits the commas to ensure that the essential element ("Louise Arner Boyd") is not set off in the sentence.

The best answer is NOT:

A because it incorrectly places commas before and after the name "Louise Arner Boyd," which sets off the name as a nonessential element. In addition, the comma after the word *native* separates the modifying phrase "San Francisco native" from the subject it modifies, "Louise Arner Boyd." The comma after the name *Boyd* separates the subject from the verb.

C because it incorrectly places a comma after the name *Boyd*, which separates the subject from the verb.

D because it incorrectly places a comma after the word *native*, which separates the modifying phrase "San Francisco native" from the subject it modifies, "Louise Arner Boyd."

Question 62. The best answer is **F** because it does not introduce redundancy or unnecessary wordiness.

The best answer is NOT:

G because it introduces redundancy at the sentence level. The sentence already tells us that Boyd first saw the Arctic glaciers and fjords in 1924, so it is redundant to add the phrase "which she had never before seen."

H because it introduces redundancy at the sentence level. The sentence already tells us that Boyd saw Arctic glaciers and fjords, so it is redundant to add the phrase "both glaciers and fjords."

J because it introduces redundancy at the sentence level. The sentence already tells us that Boyd first saw the Arctic glaciers and fjords in 1924. The word *initially* simply repeats the idea that this was the first time she saw the glaciers and fjords.

Question 63. The best answer is **A** because it correctly distinguishes between plural and singular possessives and contractions by using the word *its* to indicate a singular possessive referring to the Arctic.

The best answer is NOT:

B because it incorrectly uses the plural possessive *their* to refer to the singular subject *the Arctic*.

C because it incorrectly uses the contraction *it's* (meaning "it is") where the singular possessive (*its*) is needed.

D because it incorrectly uses the nonword *its'*, which appears to be a singular possessive form of *its* that erroneously includes an apostrophe. The possessive *its* never has an apostrophe.

Question 64. **The best answer is H** because it correctly identifies the primary rhetorical impact of losing the phrase "packed with icebergs." The next part of the sentence states that travel by boat was treacherous; the phrase "packed with icebergs" offers one example of a particular danger that creates this condition.

The best answer is NOT:

F because it incorrectly identifies the primary rhetorical purpose of the phrase "packed with icebergs." This phrase offers no indication of the purpose of the 1924 expedition Boyd participated in. Rather, it describes a particular danger for boat travel in the Arctic in general.

G because it incorrectly identifies the primary rhetorical purpose of the phrase "packed with icebergs." This phrase does not serve as an explanation of techniques for making travel safer on the seas near Spitsbergen. Rather, it describes one particular danger for boat travel in the Arctic in general.

J because it incorrectly identifies the primary rhetorical purpose of the phrase "packed with icebergs." This phrase offers no indication of why boats were not equipped to navigate around icebergs. It simply notes one particular danger of boat travel in the Arctic in general.

Question 65. **The best answer is A** because it best expresses the idea specified in the stem that "Boyd conceived of and managed the seven Arctic expeditions." The word *lead* most strongly conveys the leadership role Boyd took in planning and managing these expeditions.

The best answer is NOT:

B because it is an ineffective choice based on the goal specified in the stem; the phrase "be a part of" indicates that Boyd was a participant, but it fails to convey that she "conceived of and managed" the expeditions.

C because it is an ineffective choice based on the goal specified in the stem; the word *experience* indicates that Boyd was a participant, but it fails to convey that she "conceived of and managed" the expeditions.

D because it is an ineffective choice based on the goal specified in the stem; the phrase "embark on" indicates that Boyd went on the expeditions, but it fails to convey that she "conceived of and managed" the expeditions.

Question 66. The best answer is **F** because it most effectively leads the reader from the first sentence of the paragraph to the information in the next two sentences. The statement about Boyd's expanding interest provides a smooth link that explains the shift from Boyd's focus during her first two Arctic trips (photographing the Arctic's glaciers) to the broader goals of her later voyages (carrying out a range of scientific studies).

The best answer is NOT:

G because it provides an illogical transition to the two sentences that follow, which describe the larger ship and the broader focus of the voyages. Boyd's opportunity to share her early photographs with the king and queen of England is not related to the later voyages and therefore fails to lead the reader from the first sentence to the two sentences that follow.

H because it provides an illogical transition to the two sentences that follow, which describe the larger ship and the broader focus of the voyages. The fact that Boyd was "the first woman to be elected to the board of the American Geographical Society" is not related to the later voyages and therefore fails to lead the reader from the first sentence to the two sentences that follow.

J because it provides a weak transition to the two sentences that follow, which describe the larger ship and the broader focus of the voyages. The fact that the first two voyages landed "on a group of islands called Franz Josef Land" is not related to the later voyages and therefore fails to lead the reader from the first sentence to the two sentences that follow.

Question 67. The best answer is **C** because it correctly joins two closely related independent clauses with a semicolon.

The best answer is NOT:

A because it incorrectly uses a comma to join two independent clauses, which creates a run-on sentence.

B because it uses only the word *and* to join two independent clauses, which creates a run-on sentence. The coordinating conjunction *and* requires a comma in order to correctly join two independent clauses.

D because it incorrectly uses a comma to join two independent clauses, which creates a run-on sentence.

Question 68. **The best answer is J** because it creates an expression consistent with standard English usage to indicate that the location is close to, but south of, the North Pole.

The best answer is NOT:

F because it creates a nonstandard expression that is unclear in meaning. The phrase "close south" does not clearly explain the location in relation to the North Pole.

G because it creates a nonstandard expression that is unclear in meaning. The phrase "anchored nearby south of the North Pole" suggests that a place has already been mentioned, and the group anchored nearby. However, no such place is mentioned in the essay.

H because it creates a nonstandard expression that only vaguely indicates the location in relation to the North Pole.

Question 69. **The best answer is B** because it correctly uses commas to separate items in a series. The sentence lists three teams of scientists and what they did. The comma after the word *tundra* correctly separates the first item in this list ("Botanists gathered plant specimens from the tundra") from the second item in the list ("paleogeologists studied the ancient ice fields").

The best answer is NOT:

A because it uses inconsistent punctuation to separate items in a list. The em dash after the word *tundra* is inconsistent with the comma used later in the sentence and creates an unclear and ungrammatical relationship between the first and second items in the list.

C because it uses inconsistent punctuation to separate items in a list. The colon after the word *tundra* is inconsistent with the comma used later in the sentence and creates an unclear and ungrammatical relationship between the first and second items in the list.

D because it incorrectly omits punctuation between items in a list, creating an unclear and ungrammatical relationship between the first and second items in the list.

Question 70. The best answer is **G** because it provides the most precise word choice for the context. The word *delivered* correctly and logically conveys that the camera produced (or delivered) high-quality photos.

The best answer is NOT:

F because it supplies an imprecise word choice for the context; the word *freed* illogically suggests that the landscape images were trapped and then set free by the camera.

H because it supplies an imprecise word choice for the context; the word *performed* illogically suggests that the camera carried out images, which does not make sense in this context.

J because it supplies an imprecise word choice for the context; the word *disengaged* illogically suggests that the images were trapped and then separated or released from the camera.

Question 71. The best answer is **D** because it corrects the run-on by replacing the phrase "She knew about" with the phrase "knowledgeable about." This creates a clear causal relationship between the two parts of the sentence, communicating that because Boyd was knowledgeable about photogrammetry, she was able to use very precise methods to set up her shots.

The best answer is NOT:

A because it creates a run-on sentence by joining two independent clauses ("She knew about photogrammetry" and the clause beginning "Boyd used precise methods") using a comma without a coordinating conjunction.

B because it creates an ungrammatical sentence; the noun phrase ("The advanced knowledge she had of photogrammetry") does not convey a clear relationship to the main clause about Boyd using precise methods to set up her shots.

C because it creates a run-on sentence by joining two independent clauses ("She had advanced knowledge of photogrammetry" and the clause beginning "Boyd used precise methods") using a comma without a coordinating conjunction.

Taking Additional Practice Tests

Question 72. **The best answer is J** because it ensures correct agreement between the singular feminine pronoun *her* and the singular feminine antecedent *Boyd*, making clear that the shots in question are Boyd's.

The best answer is NOT:

F because it lacks agreement between the pronoun *its* and the antecedent *Boyd*. Because *Boyd* is the antecedent, a singular feminine pronoun is needed.

G because it lacks agreement between the pronoun phrase "his or her" and the antecedent *Boyd*. Because *Boyd* is the antecedent, a singular feminine pronoun is needed.

H because it lacks agreement between the plural pronoun *their* and the singular antecedent *Boyd*. By this point in the essay, Boyd has been identified as a woman by the use of the word *she*. Therefore, the singular feminine pronoun *her* is needed for agreement.

Question 73. **The best answer is A** because it does not introduce redundancy or unnecessary wordiness.

The best answer is NOT:

B because it contains an internal redundancy; a foundation provides the basis for later ideas and work, just as a springboard leads to later ideas and work. In this context, the words *foundation* and *springboard* indicate the same thing.

C because it contains an internal redundancy; giving support conveys the idea of providing assistance, so it is redundant to say that something "gave support that assisted."

D because it introduces unnecessary wordiness. The phrase "lent themselves" creates unnecessary agency on the part of the photos; it suggests that the photos might have chosen to help create the first accurate large-scale maps of the area. In addition, the phrase "the purpose of" is unnecessary; it adds words that do not contribute to the overall meaning or clarify any particular point.

Question 74. The best answer is **H** because it best expresses the idea specified in the stem. When the phrase "in 1955" immediately follows the phrase "A chartered flight over the North Pole," the sentence can then go on to explain that this particular Arctic journey was Boyd's last.

The best answer is NOT:

F because it fails to express the idea specified in the stem. Because the phrase "in 1955" immediately follows the phrase "final Arctic journey," it indicates that this might have been Boyd's final Arctic journey for the year 1955. However, it remains unclear if she made any Arctic journeys in later years.

G because it fails to express the idea specified in the stem. Because the phrase "in 1955" immediately follows the phrase "final Arctic journey," it indicates that this might have been Boyd's final Arctic journey for the year 1955. However, it remains unclear if she made any Arctic journeys in later years.

J because it fails to express the idea specified in the stem. Because the phrase "in 1955" immediately follows the phrase "final Arctic journey," it indicates that this might have been Boyd's final Arctic journey for the year 1955. However, it remains unclear if she made any Arctic journeys in later years.

Question 75. The best answer is **C** because it offers a clear and convincing reason the essay does not accomplish the purpose identified in the stem. The essay only briefly mentions that Boyd's photographs provided the basis for the first large-scale maps of the east coast of Greenland. The essay never expands on that point to explain how this was done.

The best answer is NOT:

A because it indicates the essay has accomplished the specified primary purpose when it hasn't. Suggesting that the essay hints at a particular point does not describe the essay's primary purpose. In addition, the essay never fully addresses how Boyd's photographs provided the basis for the first large-scale maps of the east coast of Greenland.

B because it indicates the essay has accomplished the specified primary purpose when it hasn't. Explaining that Boyd had been the first to photograph this region thoroughly does not explain how her photographs were later used to make maps of the east coast of Greenland.

D because it offers an inaccurate description of the essay and therefore fails to explain why the essay does not accomplish the purpose specified in the stem. Although the essay mentions that Boyd positioned her camera to create high-resolution images, it does not focus on this point. In addition, focusing on how Boyd positioned her camera would still fail to explain how Boyd's photographs were used to make maps of the east coast of Greenland.

Question 1. The correct answer is D. The average amount Xuan paid for each new book is given by $\frac{9(\$9.80) - \$37.80}{4} = \$12.60$. Multiply to find the amount from the sales, subtract to find the total amount spent on the new books, and divide to find the average spent per new book. If you answered **A**, you may have divided by 9 instead of 4: $\frac{9(\$9.80) - \$37.80}{9} = \$5.60$. If you answered **B**, you may have divided the leftover dollar amount by 4: $\frac{\$37.80}{4} = \$9.45$. If you answered **C**, you may have divided by the difference of 9 and 4: $\frac{9(\$9.80) - \$37.80}{9 - 4} = \$10.08$. If you answered **E**, you may have forgotten to subtract before dividing: $\frac{9(\$9.80)}{4} = \$22.05$.

Question 2. The correct answer is H. The coordinates of the point after the translation are given by $(-5 + 7, 7 - 5)$, which is $(2,2)$ because translating right 7 coordinate units corresponds to adding 7 to the x-coordinate, and translating down 5 coordinate units corresponds to subtracting 5 from the y-coordinate. If you answered **F**, you may have subtracted instead of adding and added instead of subtracting: $(-5 - 7, 7 + 5)$. If you answered **G**, you may have switched the 7 and 5: $(-5 + 5, 7 - 7)$. If you answered **J**, you may have added for both coordinates instead of subtracting for the downward translation: $(-5 + 7, 7 + 5)$. If you answered **K**, you may have added 5 and 7 for both coordinates: $(5 + 7, 7 + 5)$.

Question 3. The correct answer is C. Shantiel's average speed, in miles per hour, is given by $\frac{648}{24 - (9 - 3)} = 36$. Divide the number of miles traveled by the elapsed time. To find the elapsed time, you could realize that 9 a.m. the next day would be 24 hours after the time she left, and 3 a.m. the next day is 6 hours before 9 a.m. the next day. If you answered **A**, you may have divided by 9 instead of 18: $\frac{648}{9} = 72$. If you answered **B**, you may have thought the elapsed time was 12 instead of 18: $\frac{648}{9 + 3} = 54$. If you answered **D**, you may have thought the elapsed time was 21 instead of 18: $\frac{648}{9 + 12} \approx 31$. If you answered **E**, you may have found the elapsed time only: $24 - (9 - 3) = 18$.

Question 4. The correct answer is J. The total number of text messages for which Juan was charged on this bill is given by $300 + \frac{\$16.50 - \$10.00}{\$0.10} = 365$. The bill was greater than $10.00, so Juan sent at least 300 text messages. To find how many more than 300, subtract $10.00 from the total charge of $16.50 to find that he was charged $6.50 more than the initial $10.00, and then divide the difference by the $0.10 charge per text message beyond the first 300. If you answered **F**, you may have subtracted from instead of adding to the first 300 messages: $300 - \frac{\$16.50 - \$10.00}{\$0.10} = 235$. If you answered **G**, you may have subtracted from instead of adding to the first 300 messages, forgotten to subtract the initial $10.00 from the $16.50, and divided by $1.10 instead of $0.10: $300 - \frac{\$16.50}{\$1.10} = 285$. If you answered **H**, you may have forgotten to subtract the initial $10.00 from the $16.50 and then divided by $1.10 instead of $0.10: $300 + \frac{\$16.50}{\$1.10} = 315$. If you answered **K**, you may have forgotten to subtract the initial $10.00 from the $16.50: $300 + \frac{\$16.50}{\$0.10} = 465$.

Question 5. The correct answer is A. The sum of the matrices is given by $\begin{bmatrix} 9+(-6) & 8+6 \\ -4+5 & 7+4 \end{bmatrix}$. Add all pairs of corresponding entries. If you answered **B**, you may have disregarded the negative in the first matrix: $\begin{bmatrix} 9+(-6) & 8+6 \\ 4+5 & 7+4 \end{bmatrix}$. If you answered **C**, you may have disregarded both negatives: $\begin{bmatrix} 9+6 & 8+6 \\ 4+5 & 7+4 \end{bmatrix}$. If you answered **D**, you may have added elements within each matrix instead of the corresponding elements: $\begin{bmatrix} 9+8 & -6+6 \\ -4+7 & 5+4 \end{bmatrix}$. If you answered **E**, you may have multiplied the matrices instead of adding: $\begin{bmatrix} 9(-6)+8(5) & 9(6)+8(4) \\ -4(-6)+7(5) & -4(6)+7(4) \end{bmatrix}$.

Question 6. The correct answer is H. The value of $f(4,3)$ is given by $3(4)^2 - 4(3) = 3(16) - 4(3) = 48 - 12 = 36$, which is found by substituting x and y with 4 and 3, respectively, and then squaring, multiplying, and subtracting. If you answered **F**, you may have mixed up the values substituted for x and y: $3(3)^2 - 4(4) = 3(9) - 4(4) = 27 - 16 = 11$. If you answered **G**, you may have squared the 3 instead of the 4 in the first term: $3^2(4) - 4(3) = 9(4) - 4(3) = 36 - 12 = 24$. If you answered **J**, you may have mixed up the values substituted for x and y and multiplied before squaring: $(3(3))^2 - 4(4) = 9^2 - 16 = 81 - 16 = 65$. If you answered **K**, you may have multiplied before squaring: $(3(4))^2 - 4(3) = 12^2 - 12 = 144 - 12 = 132$.

Question 7. The correct answer is D. The mean age is given by $\frac{3(10) + 2(5)}{5} = 8$. If you answered **A**, you may have found the mean of the four numbers given in the first sentence after "5 children": $\frac{3 + 10 + 2 + 5}{4} = 5$. If you answered **B**, you may have mixed up the number of children at each age: $\frac{2(10) + 3(5)}{5} = 7$. If you answered **C**, you may have found the mean of the two unique ages: $\frac{10 + 5}{2} = 7.5$. If you answered **E**, you found the mode, the most frequently occurring age: 10.

Question 8. The correct answer is H. The value DE, in feet, is 4. Because $\overline{AC} \parallel \overline{DE}$, by corresponding angles, we have $\angle A \cong \angle BDE$. We know $\angle B \cong \angle B$, and so by the angle-angle postulate, we know $\triangle ABC \sim \triangle DBE$. Because $BD = AD$, we know $BD = \frac{1}{2}BA$. Therefore, $DE = \frac{1}{2}AC = \frac{1}{2}(8) = 4$. If you answered **F**, you may have subtracted 8 from 10: $10 - 8 = 2$. If you answered **G**, you may have subtracted half of 10 from 8: $8 - \frac{10}{2} = 3$. If you answered **J**, you may have taken half of 10 instead of half of 8: $\frac{10}{2} = 5$.

Question 9. The correct answer is B. The number expected to vote in favor of the proposal is given by the solution to the proportion $\frac{337}{500} = \frac{x}{22,000}$; $500x = 337(22,000)$; $x = \frac{337(22,000)}{500} = 14,828$. If you answered **A**, you may have rounded $\frac{337}{500}$ to $\frac{3}{5}$ and solved the proportion $\frac{3}{5} = \frac{x}{22,000}$. If you answered **C**, you may have subtracted the difference of 500 and

337 from 22,000: $22,000-(500-337)=21,837$. If you answered **D**, you chose the total number of registered voters. If you answered **E**, you may have solved a different proportion: $\frac{337}{500}=\frac{22,000}{x}$.

Question 10. The correct answer is G. The difference between the total of all Diego's payments and the car's purchase price is given by $\$400+48(\$300)-\$13,400=\$1,400$. To the down payment, add the product of 48 payments and the amount per payment, and then subtract the purchase price. If you answered **F**, you may have forgotten to add the down payment: $48(\$300)-\$13,400=\$1,000$. If you answered **H**, you may have subtracted the down payment from the purchase price, disregarding the monthly payments: $\$13,400-\$400=\$13,000$. If you answered **J**, you found the amount made in monthly payments: $48(\$300)=\$14,400$. If you answered **K**, you didn't subtract the purchase price $\$400+48(\$300)+\$14,800$.

Question 11. The correct answer is A. Rearrange the given equation into slope-intercept form, $y=mx+b$, where m is the slope. $4x+7y=9 \rightarrow 7y=-4x+9 \rightarrow y=-\frac{4}{7}x+\frac{9}{7}$. In this equation, $m=-\frac{4}{7}$. If you chose **B**, you may have divided the whole equation by 9 first and interpreted the coefficient of x as the slope before rearranging the rest of the equation into slope-intercept form. If you chose **C**, you may not have divided the rearranged equation by 7 before interpreting the coefficient of x as the slope. If you chose **D**, you may have interpreted the given coefficient of x as the slope without rearranging the equation. If you chose **E**, you may have interpreted the right side of the equation as the slope.

Question 12. The correct answer is G. Because $\angle BCD$ is supplementary to $\angle DCF$, $m\angle BCD+m\angle DCF=180°$. To find $m\angle DCF$, use the angle sum of ΔDCF, $m\angle CFD+m\angle FDC+m\angle DCF=180°$. Notice that $m\angle CFD=m\angle GFE=25°$ because they are vertical angles. Because $\angle FDC$ is a right angle, the angle sum is $25°+90°+m\angle DCF=180° \rightarrow m\angle DCF=180°-(25°+90°)=65°$. Substituting $m\angle DCF=65°$ into the first equation, $m\angle BCD+m\angle DCF=180°$, results in $m\angle BCD+65°=180° \rightarrow m\angle BCD=115°$. If you chose **F**, you may have found $m\angle DCF$ and not used its supplementary relationship with $\angle BCD$. If you chose **H** or **J**, you may have tried to estimate the measure from the figure. If you chose **K**, you may have tried to use $m\angle GFE=25°$ as a supplementary angle to $\angle BCD$.

Question 13. The correct answer is C. Factoring the polynomial in the given equation results in $(x+6)(x-5)=0$. The solutions of this equation are the values of x that make the equation true. Because the left side of the equation is a product of two factors, it is sufficient for either factor to be zero, meaning $(x+6)=0$ and $(x-5)=0$. The solutions to these two equations are –6 and 5. The sum of these two solutions is $-6+5=-1$. If you chose **A**, you may have thought that the coefficient –30 was a solution to the equation. If you chose **B** or **E**, you may have tried substituting –6 or 5 and found that this made the given equation true. If you chose **D**, you may have thought that the right side of the given equation was the solution.

MATHEMATICS • PRACTICE TEST 4 • EXPLANATORY ANSWERS

Question 14. The correct answer is F. The radius of the sphere is half the diameter, so $r = 2$ yards. Substituting this into the given volume formula results in $\frac{4\pi(2)^3}{3} = \frac{4(8)\pi}{3} = \frac{32}{3}\pi$ cubic yards. If you chose **G**, you may have computed $\frac{4^3\pi}{3}$. If you chose **H**, you may have forgotten to include the denominator of the given formula in your answer. If you chose **J**, you may have multiplied the diameter by 3 and forgotten to include the denominator of the given formula. If you chose **K**, you may have substituted the diameter instead of the radius.

Question 15. The correct answer is C. Estimate $\sqrt{85}$ by using the known values of perfect squares $9 = \sqrt{81}$ and $10 = \sqrt{100}$. Because $9 = \sqrt{81} < \sqrt{85} < \sqrt{100} = 10$, you can conclude that $9 < \sqrt{85} < 10$, which means that 10 is the smallest integer greater than $\sqrt{85}$ because there are no integers between 9 and 10. If you chose **A**, you may have thought you were looking for the smallest digit in the number 85. If you chose **B**, you may have found that $\sqrt{85} \approx 9.2195$ and rounded down. If you chose **D**, you may have checked that 12 was larger than $\sqrt{85}$ and may not have looked for a smaller integer. If you chose **E**, you may have thought that the square root meant to divide by 2.

Question 16. The correct answer is K. The relationships in the three statements can be represented as shown in this figure.

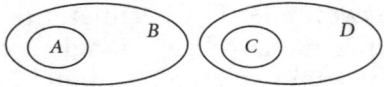

Because no elements of D are elements of B, $D \cap B = \varnothing$, it must follow that no elements of A are elements of C, $C \cap A = \varnothing$, because A and C are entirely contained in B and D, respectively, $A \subset B$ and $C \subset D$. **F** cannot be true because no elements of A are elements of C. **G** cannot be true because no elements of D are elements of B. **H** cannot be true because B and D have no common elements, and any element of C is an element of D. **J** cannot be true because all elements of A are elements of B.

Question 17. The correct answer is A. The midpoint $(2,1)$ must also be the midpoint of the x- and y-component distances of the length of $\overline{AB}$. Because the x-distance from point A to $(2,1)$ is $8 - 2 = 6$, point B must be 6 units from $(2,1)$ in the x-direction, which is $2 - 6 = -4$. If you chose **B**, you may have found the change in the x-coordinate from $(2,1)$ to point A. If you chose **C**, you may have found the y-coordinate of point B. If you chose **D**, you may have found half the x-distance from point A to $(2,1)$. If you chose **E**, you may have found the x-coordinate of the midpoint of $(2,1)$ and point A.

Question 18. The correct answer is K. The total number of either pitcher or outfielder cards is $8 + 7 = 15$. The probability of finding one of these 15 cards in one pick is the fraction of desired outcomes over all possible outcomes, $\frac{15}{25} = 60\%$. If you chose **F**, you may have found the probability of each desired outcome, multiplied them, and rounded to the nearest percentage. If you chose **G**, you may have found the probability of picking an outfielder only. If you chose **H**, you may have found the probability of picking a pitcher only. If you chose **J**, you may have found the probability of picking an infielder or a pitcher.

Question 19. The correct answer is A. Let the change in mass of nitrogen phosphate used be y and the change in the average temperature be x. Then x and y are in a proportional relationship where $y = -1.2x$. For the given change of $83.0°F - 75.0°F = 8.0°F$, $y = -1.2(8.0) = -9.6$ kg. Because this is a change from a starting mass of 40.0 kg, the required application amount is $40.0 - 9.6 = 30.4$ kg. If you chose **B**, you may have added 1.2 and 8.0 to find the change in mass. If you chose **C**, you may have divided 40 by 1.2. If you chose **D**, you may have subtracted the change in temperature from the mass before multiplying by 1.2. If you chose **E**, you may have found the required application amount for a change of only $1°F$.

Question 20. The correct answer is G. The area of the shaded region is xy. From the figure, create the equations $6 = y + 2 + y$ and $5 = x + 2 + x$, which follow from the equivalent side lengths of the rectangle. Solve each of these equations: $6 = y + 2 + y \rightarrow 2y = 6 - 2 \rightarrow y = 2$ and $5 = x + 2 + x \rightarrow 2x = 5 - 2 \rightarrow x = \frac{3}{2}$. Then the shaded area $xy = \left(\frac{3}{2}\right)2 = 3$ square units. If you chose **F**, you may have found the value of x and squared it. If you chose **H**, you may have assumed all the regions were equal in area and divided 30 by 9. If you chose **J**, you may have assumed all the regions were equal in area and that the whole figure was a square with a side length of 6 units. If you chose **K**, you may have found $2(x + y)$ instead of xy.

Question 21. The correct answer is D. The perimeter of the scalene triangle given is 100 inches. We also know that the perimeter of the triangle is the sum of the lengths of its sides. For this triangle, that means the triangle has a perimeter of $5x + (3x + 30) + (2x + 10) = 10x + 40$. Therefore, $10x + 40$ must equal 100 inches because both values are the perimeter of this triangle. Thus, $10x = 60$ and $x = 6$. Because the sides of this triangle are $5x$, $3x + 30$, and $2x + 10$, we know that the side lengths are $5(6) = 30$, $3(6) + 30 = 48$, and $2(6) + 10 = 22$. Because 48 is the largest among 30, 48, and 22, we know that the longest side of this triangle is 48 inches. If you chose **A**, you may have thought the longest side of the triangle was the value of x. If you chose **B**, you may have thought the longest side was the side of length $2x + 10$. If you chose **C**, you may have thought the longest side was the side of length $5x$.

Question 22. The correct answer is J. Because each council member gets a seat, there are 6 members that could be in Seat 1. Because someone is already in Seat 1, there are 5 options for Seat 2. Because someone is already in Seats 1 and 2, there are 4 options for Seat 3. Similarly, there are 3 options for Seat 4, 2 options for Seat 5, and 1 option for Seat 6. Thus, the number of different arrangements is $6(5)(4)(3)(2)(1) = 720$. If you chose **F**, you may have added $6 + 5 + 4 + 3 + 2 + 1 = 21$ instead of multiplying. If you chose **G**, you may have multiplied the number of council members by the number of seats available. If you chose **H**, you may have taken $\frac{6^6}{6!}$ and rounded to the nearest integer. If you chose **K**, you may have taken 6 council members and added a 0 in front of it for each seat available.

Question 23. The correct answer is E. 200% of 1 is 2(1) = 2. The sum of 2 and 200% of 1 is equivalent to 2 + 2 = 4. 400% of 1 is 4(1) = 4. If you chose **A**, you may have thought that 100% of 2, which equals 2, equals 4. If you chose **B**, you may have thought that 150% of 2, which equals 3, equals 4. If you chose **C**, you may have thought that 300% of 2, which equals 6, equals 4. If you chose **D**, you may have thought that 300% of 1, which equals 3, equals 4.

Question 24. The correct answer is H. Given two points of a line, (x_1, y_1) and (x_2, y_2), the slope of the line is given by $\frac{y_2 - y_1}{x_2 - x_1}$. For this line, the points given are $(0, 2)$ and $(3, 0)$. So, the slope of the line is $\frac{0-2}{3-0} = \frac{-2}{3} = -\frac{2}{3}$. The y-intercept of this line is $(0, 2)$. The slope-intercept form of a line is given by $y = mx + b$ where m is the slope and b is the y-value of the y-intercept. Therefore, the slope-intercept form of this line is $y = -\frac{2}{3}x + 2$. If you chose **F**, you may have thought that the slope of a line is given by $\frac{x_2 - x_1}{y_2 - y_1}$. If you chose **G**, you may have thought that the slope of a line is given by $\frac{x_2 - x_1}{y_2 - y_1}$ and that b is the x-value of the x-intercept. If you chose **J**, you may have thought that b is the x-value of the x-intercept. If you chose **K**, you may have thought that the slope of a line is given by $-\frac{y_2 - y_1}{x_2 - x_1}$.

Question 25. The correct answer is C. The area of a kite is given by $\frac{1}{2}$ multiplied by its length multiplied by its width. So, for this kite, the area is given by $\frac{1}{2}(40)(28) = 560$. If you chose **A**, you may have thought the area is given by $2(40) + 2(28) - 5(7)$. If you chose **B**, you may have thought the area is given by $\frac{1}{4}$ multiplied by its length multiplied by its width. If you chose **D**, you may have thought the area is given by $\frac{3}{4}$ multiplied its length multiplied by its width. If you chose **E**, you may have thought the area was given by $\frac{7}{8}(40)(28)$.

Question 26. The correct answer is H. The surface area, including the top of the pool, is $60(25) = 1,500$. The area of the surface of the pool is $15(40) = 600$. Therefore, the area of the patio surrounding the pool is $1,500 - 600 = 900$ square feet. If you chose **F**, you may have calculated the area by $(60 - 40)25$. If you chose **G**, you may have calculated the surface of the pool. If you chose **J**, you may have calculated the area by $25(60) - 40(5)(2)$. If you chose **K**, you may have calculated the area by $25(60) - 15\left(\frac{40}{4}\right)$.

Question 27. The correct answer is D. The cost of the materials is the cost per foot multiplied by the number of feet. Because the number of feet is the perimeter of the outer edge of the patio, the number of feet is $2(60) + 2(25) = 170$. Therefore, the cost is $\$12(170) = \$2,040$. If you chose **A**, you may have calculated the perimeter as $60 + 25 = 85$. If you chose **B**, you may have calculated the perimeter of the pool instead of the perimeter of the outside of the patio, $2(40) + 2(15) = 110$. If you chose **C**, you may have calculated the perimeter as $6(25)$. If you chose **E**, you may have calculated the cost of a fence around the perimeter of the pool and the cost of a fence around the outside of the patio and added them together.

Question 28. The correct answer is J. Johann's average speed can be calculated by dividing the total distance over the total time. The total distance is given by 5(2)(40) = 400. Therefore, the average speed is given by $\frac{400}{4.5} \approx 89$. If you chose **F**, you may have calculated the total distance by $5\left(\frac{1}{2}\right)(60)$. If you chose **G**, you may have calculated the total distance by 5(40). If you chose **H**, you may have calculated the total distance by 5(60). If you chose **K**, you may have calculated the total distance by 5(2)(60).

Question 29. The correct answer is B. The slope can be found as rise over run. The rise can be calculated by 4-9. The run can be calculated by 40-20-12. Therefore, the slope is $-\frac{5}{8} = -0.625$. If you chose **A**, you may have calculated $-\frac{4}{9}$. If you chose **C**, you may have calculated $-\frac{9}{12}$. If you chose **D**, you may have calculated $-\frac{12}{9}$. If you chose **E**, you may have calculated $-\frac{8}{5}$.

Question 30. The correct answer is K. The company will order 3(1) + 4(1) + 6(2) = 19 bathtubs, 3(0) + 4(1) + 6(1) = 10 shower stalls, and 3(1) + 4(2) + 6(4) = 35 sinks. This will cost 19($250) + 10($150) + 35($120) = $10,450. If you chose **F**, you may have calculated the number of bathtubs as 1 + 0 + 1, the number of shower stalls as 1 + 1 + 2, and the number of sinks as 2 + 1 + 4. If you chose **G**, you may have calculated the number of bathtubs as 1 + 1 + 2, the number of shower stalls as 0 + 1 + 1, and the number of sinks as 1 + 2 + 4, gotten a total of $2,140, and decided that this was close enough to $2,070. If you chose **H**, you may have calculated the number of bathtubs as 3(1 + 0 + 1), the number of shower stalls as 4(1 + 1 + 2), and the number of sinks as 6(2 + 1 + 4). If you chose **J**, you may have calculated the number of bathtubs as 3(1) + 4(0) + 6(1), the number of shower stalls as 3(1) + 4(1) + 6(2), and the number of sinks as 3(2) + 4(1) + 6(4).

Question 31. The correct answer is C. To calculate half the length, exchange 1 foot for 12 inches. Thus, 5 feet 6 inches is the same as 4 feet 18 inches. Then divide each number by 2, resulting in 2 feet 9 inches. If you answered **A**, you may have dropped the original 6 inches, converted 1 foot to 10 inches, and divided 4 feet 10 inches by 2. If you answered **B**, you may have converted 1 foot to 10 inches and divided 4 feet 16 inches by 2. If you answered **D**, you may have rounded up to the next foot to 6 feet and divided it by 2. If you answered **E**, you may have added 1 to the number of feet and subtracted 1 from the number of inches; then you may have divided the number of feet by 2 and left the number of inches as is, resulting in 3 feet 5 inches.

Question 32. The correct answer is H. The total number of feet is the sum of the first four drives: $\left(18 + 18 \times \frac{2}{3} + 12 \times \frac{2}{3} + 8 \times \frac{2}{3} = 43\frac{1}{3}\right)$. If you answered **F**, you may have added $12 + 8 + 5\frac{1}{3} + 3\frac{5}{9}$. If you answered **G**, you may have added only the first two heights: 18 + 12. If you answered **J**, you may have added 18 + 12 + 18. If you answered **K**, you may have multiplied 18 × 3.

Question 33. **The correct answer is B.** To reflect a point across the y-axis, multiply its x-coordinate by -1 and do not change its y-coordinate. So $(2, -3)$ becomes $(2 \times -1, 3)$, or $(-2, 3)$. If you answered **A**, you may have interchanged the coordinates. If you answered **C**, you may have multiplied both coordinates by -1. If you answered **D**, you may have multiplied the y-coordinate by -1. If you answered **E**, you may have interchanged the coordinates and then multiplied them both by -1.

Question 34. **The correct answer is K.** The mean is the sum of the four numbers divided by 4: $\frac{a+b+c+d}{4} = mean$. Adding 3 to both sides yields $\frac{a+b+c+d}{4} + 3 = mean + 3$. It follows that $\frac{a+b+c+d}{4} + 3 = \frac{a+b+c+d+x}{4} = mean + 3$ where x is the addition to the four numbers that results in the new mean. Now $\frac{a+b+c+d}{4} + 3 = \frac{a+b+c+d}{4} + \frac{12}{4} = \frac{a+b+c+d+12}{4}$, so $x = 12$. If you answered **F**, you may have divided the increase in the mean by the four numbers. If you answered **G**, you may have subtracted the increase in the mean from the four numbers. If you answered **H**, you may have divided the four numbers by the increase in the mean. If you answered **J**, you may have added the increase in the mean and the four numbers.

Question 35. **The correct answer is E.** Using laws of exponents, the expression is equivalent to $(3+x)^{100 \times (-1)} = [(3+x)^{100}]^{-1} = \frac{1}{(3+x)^{100}}$. If you answered **A**, you may have distributed the -1 to each term and then distributed the 100 as the exponent of each term: $-1(3^{100} + x^{100})$. If you answered **B**, you may have multiplied each term by the exponent: $-100(3+x)$. If you answered **C**, you may have used the equivalent expression $\frac{1}{(3+x)^{100}}$ and then distributed the exponent to each term. If you answered **D**, you may have used the equivalent expression $\frac{1}{(3+x)^{100}}$ and then thought $3 + x = 3x$.

Question 36. **The correct answer is G.** To find a vertical asymptote, set the denominator equal to 0, $2x - 6 = 0$, and solve for x. One method for solving is to first divide both sides by 2, $x - 3 = 0$, so $x = 3$. If you answered **F**, you may have divided the constant term in the numerator by the constant term in the denominator. If you answered **H**, you may have set the numerator equal to 0, $3x - 12 = 0$, and divided each side by 3, $x - 4 = 0$, so $x = 4$. If you answered **J**, you may have set the denominator equal to 0, $2x - 6 = 0$, and then divided only the x term by 2, $x - 6 = 0$, so $x = 6$. If you answered **K**, you may have set the numerator equal to 0, $3x - 12 = 0$, and divided only the x term by 3, $x - 12 = 0$, so $x = 12$.

Question 37. The correct answer is C. The equation $xy = 0$ and the zero-product rule require that either x or y is equal to 0 or that both x and y are equal to 0. The second equation $\frac{x}{y} = 0$ requires that x is equal to 0 and y is not equal to 0. Combining the requirements of these two equations, it follows that both $x = 0$ and $y \neq 0$ must be true. If you answered **A**, you may have considered only the first equation and misinterpreted the zero-product rule as stating that the value of both variables must be 0. If you answered **B**, you may have considered the second equation but switched the restrictions and thought $x \neq 0$ and $y = 0$. If you answered **D**, you may have considered the second equation but thought both the numerator and the denominator must not be 0. If you answered **E**, you may have tried to list all the restrictions together and obtained y may be 0 or y may not be 0, which is not an answer choice.

Question 38. The correct answer is F. To convert $\frac{3.7 \ km}{15 \ min}$ to $\frac{miles}{hour}$, it is necessary to multiply $\frac{3.7 \ km}{15 \ min} \times \frac{60 \ min}{1 \ hour} \times \frac{1 \ mile}{1.6 \ km} \approx 9.25$ miles per hour. If you answered **G**, you may have multiplied $\frac{3.7 \ km}{15 \ min} \times \frac{60 \ min}{1 \ hour}$. If you answered **H**, you may have calculated $\frac{60 \ min}{15 \ min}(3.7 + 1.6)$. If you answered **J**, you may have multiplied $\frac{3.7 \ km}{15 \ min} \times \frac{60 \ min}{1 \ hour} \times 1.6$. If you answered **K**, you may have calculated $\frac{3.7(15)}{1.6}$.

Question 39. The correct answer is A. One million can be written as $1,000,000 = 10^6$, so 2.5 million can be written as 2.5×10^6. If you answered **B**, you may have thought that because 1 million has 7 digits, the exponent is 7. If you answered **C**, you probably thought there are 7 digits in a million and then added 1 digit to the left in 2.5, resulting in 8 for the exponent. If you answered **D**, you may have dropped the decimal in 2.5 and used the exponent of 10 for 1 million. If you answered **E**, you may have dropped the decimal point and thought the exponent for 1 million is 7.

Question 40. The correct answer is K. Let x be the distance along the level ground between the point adjacent to the 70° angle and the center of the base of the tower. Then, by the definition of tangent, $\tan 70° = \frac{320}{x}$ or $= \frac{320}{\tan 70°}$. If you answered **F**, you may have used the equation $\cos 70° = \frac{x}{320}$. If you answered **G**, you may have used the equation $\sin 70° = \frac{x}{320}$. If you answered **H**, you may have used the equation $\tan 70° = \frac{x}{320}$. If you answered **J**, you may have used the equation $\sin 70° = \frac{320}{x}$.

Question 41. The correct answer is E. Adding the vectors and setting that sum equal to $6\mathbf{i} - 6\mathbf{j}$ results in $(a\mathbf{i} + 3\mathbf{j}) + (-2\mathbf{i} + b\mathbf{j}) = (6\mathbf{i} - 6\mathbf{j})$. Equating the coefficients on each side for $\mathbf{i}$ and $\mathbf{j}$ separately results in $a - 2 = 6$ or $a = 8$ and $3 + b = -6$ or $b = -9$. If you answered **A**, you may have solved the equations correctly but set the variables equal to the other variable's value. If you answered **B**, you may have solved the correct equations but used the wrong sign in the resulting values. If you answered **C**, you may have solved $a - 2 = -6$ and $3 + b = 6$. If you answered **D**, you may have solved $a + 2 = 6$ and $3 - b = 6$.

Question 42. The correct answer is F. Subtracting 50 from both sides results in $c-50=10b^3$. Dividing by 10 on both sides results in $\frac{c}{10} - 5 = b^3$. Taking the third root of both sides and swapping the two expressions results in $b = \left(\frac{c}{10} - 5\right)^{\frac{1}{3}}$. If you answered **G**, you may have put the 50 on the left side without changing the sign and then divided and took the third root as shown. If you answered **H**, you may have subtracted the 50 and divided by 10, but when taking the third root was done, the third root of the $\frac{1}{10}$ was not done. If you answered **J**, you may have divided only the 50 and the 10 by 10, resulting in $c = b^3 + 5$, then added the 5 on the left side of the equation and subtracted it from the left, and then switched the exponent from b to c, resulting in $c^3 + 5 = b$. If you answered **K**, you may have switched the b and c.

Question 43. The correct answer is A. Substituting $x + 1$ for x in $f(x)$ results in $(x+1)^2 + 3(x+1) = x^2 + 2x + 1 + 3x + 3$ or $x^2 + 5x + 4$. If you answered **B**, you may have substituted $x^2 + 3x$ in $g(x)$, resulting in $(x^2 + 3x) + 1$ or $x^2 + 3x + 1$. If you answered **C**, you may have substituted $x(x+1)^2 + 3x(x+1) = x^3 + 2x^2 + x + 3x^2 + 3x = x^3 + 25 + 4x$. If you answered **D**, you may have substituted $x^2(x+1) + 3x(x+1) = x^3 + x^2 + 3x^2 + 3x = x^3 + 4x^2 + 3x$. If you answered **E**, you may have substituted $x^3(x+1) + 3x^2(x+1) = x^4 + x^3 + 3x^3 + 3x^2 = x^4 + 4x^3 + 3x^2$.

Question 44. The correct answer is J. The diameter of the second circle is found by multiplying 12 by 1.25, resulting in 15. Dividing the diameters by 2 to get the radius of each results in 6 and 7.5. Using the area of a circle with radius r formula πr^2 results in the areas of the two circles being 36π and 56.25π. The difference in the areas is 20.25π, or about 64. If you answered **F**, you may have substituted the difference between the radii into the area formula, resulting in 2.25π, or about 7. If you answered **G**, you may have substituted the difference in the diameters into the area formula, resulting in 9π, or about 28. If you answered **H**, you may have found 25% of the area of the second circle, $0.25 \times \pi(7.5)^2$, or about 44. If you answered **K**, you may have substituted the diameters in for the radii in the area formula, resulting in 144π and 225π. The difference is 81π, or about 254.

Question 45. The correct answer is D. The first six prime numbers are 2, 3, 5, 7, 11, and 13. The median is the average of the middle two numbers 5 and 7, which is 6. The mean is the sum of the numbers, 41, divided by the number of terms, 6, which is 6.83. The product of 6 and 6.83 is 41. If you answered **A**, you may have used the numbers 2, 3, 4, 5, 6, and 7. The median is 4.5, and you multiplied by the number of items, resulting in 27. If you answered **B**, you may have used the numbers 2, 3, 5, 7, 9, and 11. The median is 6 and the mean is $\frac{37}{6}$. The product of the mean and the median is 37. If you answered **C**, you may have used the numbers 2, 4, 6, 7, 9, and 11. The median is the average of 6 and 7, or 6.5. Multiplying by the number of items results in 39. If you answered **E**, you may have used the first six even numbers 2, 4, 6, 8, 10, and 12. The median is 7 and the mean is 6. The product of 7 and 6 is 42.

Question 46. **The correct answer is K.** By the Pythagorean identity, $\sin^2(7x)+\cos^2(7x)=1$ is true for all real values of x. If you chose **F**, you determined that for all real values of x, $\sin(7x) + \cos(7x) = 7$ even though $\sin(7(0)) + \cos(7(0)) = 0 + 1 = 1$. If you chose **G**, you determined that for all real values of x, $\sin(7x) + \cos(7x) = 7$ even though $\sin(7\pi)+\cos(7\pi)=0+(-1)=-1$. If you chose **H**, you determined that for all real values of x, $7\sin(7x) + \cos(7x) = 14$ even though $7\sin(7(0)) + 7\cos(7(0)) = 7(0) + 7(1) = 7$. If you chose **J**, you determined that for all real values of x, $\sin^2(7x)+\cos^2(7x)=7$ even though $\sin(7(0)) * \sin(7(0)) + \cos(7(0)) * \cos(7(0)) = 0(0) + 1(1) = 1$.

Question 47. **The correct answer is A.** Because $\overline{AB}$ is a diameter, $\angle ADB$ is a right angle. Therefore, $\overline{AB}$ is a hypotenuse of $\triangle ADB$ and, by the Pythagorean theorem, has a length of $\sqrt{5^2+12^2} =13$ meters. Because the measure of angle DAC is congruent to the measure of angle DAB, and angle ADB and angle DCA are both right angles, then triangle ACD and triangle DBC are similar triangles. Therefore, $\frac{CD}{AD} = \frac{BD}{AB}$, which is equivalent to $\frac{CD}{5} = \frac{12}{13}$. Therefore, $CD = \frac{60}{13}$. If you chose **B**, you may have computed $\frac{(AB)(AD)}{BD}$. If you chose **C**, you may have computed AB. If you chose **D**, you may have computed $\frac{(AB)(BD)}{AD}$. If you chose **E**, you may have computed $(BD)(AD)$.

Question 48. **The correct answer is K.** Because $a > 0$, $|a| = a$. Because $b < 0$, $|b| = -b$. Therefore, $|a| - |b| = a + b$. If you chose **F**, you determined for all positive a and negative b that $|a| - |b| = |a - b|$ even though $|1| - |-1| = 0 \neq 2 = |1 - (-1)|$. If you chose **G**, you determined for all positive a and negative b that $|a| - |b| = |a + b|$ even though $|1| - |-2| = 3 \neq 1 = |1 + (-2)|$. If you chose **H**, you determined for all positive a and negative b that $|a| - |b| = |a| + |b|$ even though $|1| - |1| = 0 \neq 2 = |1| + |1|$. If you chose **J**, you determined for all positive a and negative b that $|1| - |-1| = 0 \neq 2 = 1 - (-1)$.

Question 49. **The correct answer is D.** Because $x < y < 4$ is the only restriction on x and y, it is possible for $x = 3.4$ and $y = 3.6$. Then $x + y = 3.4 + 3.6 = 7$. We also know that $x + y < y + y < 4 + 4 = 8$. So, the greatest possible integer value of $x + y$ is 7. If you chose **A**, you may have determined that $x + y$ could not be positive. If you chose **B**, you may have thought that 3 was the biggest integer that $x + y$ could be. If you chose **C**, you may have thought that 4 was the biggest integer that y could be. If you chose **E**, you may have thought **x** and **y** could each be 4.

Question 50. **The correct answer is G.** Because y varies directly as the square of x, then $y = kx^2$ for some constant k. Because $y = 20$ when $x = 2$, $20 = k(2^2)$, which means that $k = 5$. So, when $x = 3$, $y = 5(3^2) = 45$. If you chose **F**, you may have calculated $3(20 + 2 + 3)$. If you chose **H**, you may have used the equation $y = kx$ instead of the equation $y = kx^2$. If you chose **J**, you may have used the equation $y = k + x$ instead of the equation $y = kx^2$. If you chose **K**, you may have used the equation $y = k - x^2$ instead of the equation $y = kx^2$.

Question 51. The correct answer is D. The general equation for an ellipse centered at $(0, 0)$ is $\frac{x^2}{a^2} + \frac{y^2}{b^2} = 1$ where a is the length of the semimajor (horizontal) axis and b is the length of the semiminor (vertical) axis. The values for a and b can be found by checking the intersection points of the ellipse with each circle. Because the general equation of a circle with radius r centered at $(0, 0)$ is $x^2 + y^2 = r^2$, the larger circle has a radius of $\sqrt{25} = 5$ and the smaller circle has a radius of $\sqrt{4} = 2$. This means that the ellipse must intersect with these circles at key points of $(5, 0)$ and $(0, 2)$, corresponding with semimajor and semiminor axes lengths of $a = 5$ and $b = 2$, respectively. Using these as the parameters in the general ellipse equation results in $\frac{x^2}{25} + \frac{y^2}{4} = 1$. If you chose **A** or **B**, you may have used the wrong parameters for the semiminor and semimajor axes. If you chose **C**, you may have not squared the denominators. If you chose **E**, you may have thought a factor of 4 was necessary to include in the denominator.

Question 52. The correct answer is H. Let the two unknown integers be x and y. Because the median of the set is 82, conclude that $x \geq 82$ and $y \geq 82$ because $0 < 82$ and $12 < 82$. Then the set of integers is $\{0, 12, 82, x, y\}$. Write an equation to represent the mean: $\frac{0+12+82+x+y}{5} = 52$. Solve for $x + y$: $\frac{0+12+82+x+y}{5} = 52 \rightarrow 94 + x + y = 260 \rightarrow x + y = 166$. Combine with one of the inequalities to eliminate one variable: $x + 82 \leq x + y = 166 \rightarrow x + 82 \leq 166 \rightarrow x \leq 84$. The same can be done for y. Now there is both a lower and upper limit on the values of x and y, meaning that both values are between 82 and 84, inclusive. The only choice that fits these limits is **H**. If you chose **F** or **G**, you may not have considered that these values would change the median to something other than 82. If you chose **J** or **K**, you may not have considered that these values would change either the mean or the median.

Question 53. The correct answer is B. By the given definition, the integer 6 has factors of 1, 2, and 3 with a sum of $1 + 2 + 3 = 6$. The integer 8 has factors of 1, 2, and 4 with a sum of $1 + 2 + 4 = 7$. The integer 10 has factors of 1, 2, and 5 with a sum of $1 + 2 + 5 = 8$. The integer 12 has factors of 1, 2, 3, 4, and 6 with a sum of $1 + 2 + 3 + 4 + 6 = 16$. The only one of these integers that fits the given criteria of a factor sum greater than the integer itself is 12 because $16 > 12$.

Question 54. The correct answer is G. Vanna walked 2 miles per hour for $\frac{10}{60}$ of an hour and covered a distance of $2 \frac{\text{mile}}{\text{hour}} \times \frac{10}{60} \text{ hour} = \frac{1}{3} \text{ mile}$. Similarly, after her speed increased, she walked $3 \frac{\text{mile}}{\text{hour}} \times \frac{5}{60} \text{ hour} = \frac{1}{4} \text{ mile}$. This is a total of $\frac{1}{3} \text{ mile} + \frac{1}{4} \text{ mile} = \frac{4}{12} \text{ mile} + \frac{3}{12} \text{ mile} = \frac{7}{12} \text{ mile}$. Because she covered this distance in 15 minutes, her average rate over the whole distance is $\frac{\frac{7}{12} \text{ mile}}{\frac{15}{60} \text{ hour}} = \frac{7}{12} \times \frac{60 \text{ mile}}{15 \text{ hour}} = \frac{7 \text{ mile}}{3 \text{ hour}}$.

If you chose **F**, you may have only found the average rate for the first part of Vanna's walk. If you chose **H**, you may have added denominators when adding fractions. If you chose **J**, you may have divided by an extra factor of 60. If you chose **K**, you may have divided the sum of the rates by 2 instead of weighting the average rate by the time spent on each part of the walk.

Question 55. The correct answer is D. Let Alani's height be x. Then Baahir's height is $\frac{7}{5}x$ and Connor's height is $\frac{3}{4}\left(\frac{7}{5}x\right)=\frac{21}{20}x$. Dividing Alani's height by Connor's height to find the ratio results in $\frac{x}{\frac{21}{20}x}=\frac{20}{21}$. If you chose **A** or **B**, you may have subtracted or added the corresponding parts of each ratio. If you chose **C** or **E**, you may have multiplied the two given ratios.

Question 56. The correct answer is K. A square root is equivalent to a $\frac{1}{2}$ power. A cube root is equivalent to a $\frac{1}{3}$ power. Nesting a $\frac{1}{2}$ power and a $\frac{1}{3}$ power gives a $\frac{1}{6}$ power ($\frac{1}{2}\cdot\frac{1}{3}=\frac{1}{6}$). The base of the power is x^2, so we have $(x^2)^{\frac{1}{6}}=x^{2\left(\frac{1}{6}\right)}=x^{\frac{1}{3}}$. **F**, **G**, **H**, and **J** are all equivalent to $x^{\frac{1}{3}}$. Clearly, **K** is not equivalent to $x^{\frac{1}{3}}$; it is equivalent to $\left(x^{\frac{1}{3}}\right)^2$.

Question 57. The correct answer is B. Let l be the length and w be the width of the original rectangle. The area of the original rectangle is lw. Increasing something by 25% is equivalent to multiplying by $1 + 0.25$. Decreasing something by 10% is equivalent to multiplying by $1 - 0.10$. Therefore, $1.25l$ and $0.9w$ are the length and width, respectively, of the resulting rectangle. The area of the resulting rectangle is $(1.25l)(0.9w) = 1.125lw$. Multiplying by 1.125 is equivalent to increasing by 12.5%. If you answered **A**, you may have multiplied 25% and 10%. If you answered **C**, you may have subtracted 10% from 25%. If you answered **D**, you may have multiplied 25% and 100% – 10%. If you answered **E**, you may have added 25% and 10%.

Question 58. The correct answer is F. A sum of 7 can be obtained with 2 and 5, 5 and 2, 3 and 4, or 4 and 3. The probability of a 2 and a 5 is $\frac{1}{5}\times\left(\frac{1}{4}\right)=\frac{1}{20}$ because 1 of the 5 balls is a 2, and 1 of the 4 remaining balls is a 5. Similarly, the probability of a 5 and a 2 is $\frac{1}{20}$, the probability of a 3 and a 4 is $\frac{1}{20}$, and the probability of a 5 and a 2 is $\frac{1}{20}$. Adding the probabilities of each of these 4 ways to obtain a sum of 7 gives $4\left(\frac{1}{20}\right)=\frac{1}{5}$. If you answered **G**, you may have used 2, the number of balls selected, divided by 5, the total number of balls. If you answered **H**, you may have used 4, the number of balls that could be drawn first, to obtain a sum of 7 (2 or 3 or 4 or 5) divided by 5, the total number of balls. If you answered **J**, you may have used $\frac{4}{5}$ for the probability that the first selection could make a sum of 7 (as in **H**), used $\frac{1}{4}$ for the probability that the second selection would be the 1 ball out of the remaining 4 balls to complete the sum of 7, and then incorrectly added $\frac{4}{5}$ and $\frac{1}{4}$ instead of multiplying them $\left(\frac{4}{5}+\frac{1}{4}=\frac{4+1}{5+4}=\frac{5}{9}\right)$. If you answered **K**, you may have thought the probability for each of the 4 ways to obtain a sum of 7 is $\frac{1}{5}\left(\frac{1}{5}\right)=\frac{1}{25}$.

Question 59. The correct answer is D. A function whose graph has no x-intercepts has either a minimum value greater than 0 or a maximum value less than 0. The function $y = \sin x$ has a minimum value of -1. In order to shift the graph vertically enough so that the minimum value is greater than 0, you'd have to add a value greater than 1: $c > 1$. The function $y = \sin x$ has a maximum value of 1. In order to shift the graph vertically enough so that the maximum value is less than 0, you'd have to add a value less than -1: $c < -1$. If you answered **A**, you may have simply looked for the amplitude of $y = \sin x$. If you answered **B**, you may have found the correct bound values for c but got the shading wrong. If you answered **C**, you may have considered only shifting the graph up so the minimum value was greater than 0 but not considered shifting the graph down so the maximum value is less than 0. If you answered **E**, you may have thought that the minimum or maximum value could be 0.

Question 60. The correct answer is G. There are 3 feet in 1 yard, so there are $3^2 = 9$ square feet in 1 square yard. Divide the number of square feet needed by 9 to get the number of square yards needed: $360 \div 9 = 40$. If you answered **F**, you may have divided by $12(2) = 24$ instead of $3^2 = 9$. If you answered **H**, you may have divided by $3(2) = 6$ instead of $3^2 = 9$. If you answered **J**, you may have divided by $2^2 = 4$ instead of $3^2 = 9$. If you answered **K**, you may have divided by 3 instead of 9.

Passage I

Question 1. The best answer is B because although the narrator of the first section is never explicitly identified, it is clear that the narrator of the second section is Michael as a young boy. We know this from the first line of the second section: "What had there been before such a ship in my life?" (line 37), which makes it clear that the narrator of the second section is the same eleven-year-old boy described in the previous section. It is also correct to state that both perspectives describe "elements of Michael's journey," as the first section describes Michael's first experience on the ship, and the second section describes his attitude toward the journey on the day of his departure and the days leading up to his departure, both of which can be reasonably described as elements of Michael's "journey."

The best answer is NOT:

A because neither section describes Michael's first week on the *Oronsay*. The first section describes a portion of Michael's first day on the *Oronsay*, and the second section describes Michael's experiences leading up to his trip on the *Oronsay*. Also, there is no evidence to suggest that either section is being told from the perspective of Michael's mother.

C because neither section provides information about the outcomes of Michael's journey. Instead, both sections describe events that took place before the *Oronsay* left the harbor.

D because there is no evidence to suggest that either section is told from the perspective of one of Michael's relatives. Also, there is clear evidence throughout the passage that the second section is told from Michael's point of view, as indicated by the first line of the second section: "What had there been before such a ship in my life?" (line 37).

Question 2. The best answer is F because the description in lines 52–56 of the numerous amenities aboard the *Oronsay* suggests that the ship has many of the services that a city might have, which supports Michael's comparison of the ship to a city in lines 3–4.

The best answer is NOT:

G because the description of the amenities aboard the *Oronsay* does not support the fact that Michael's particular cabin was below the waves or lacked a porthole. The description of Michael's cabin is unrelated to the number of amenities aboard the ship.

H because the description of the amenities aboard the *Oronsay* does not support the fact that Michael chose to stay in his cabin instead of going back up for "a last look, or to wave at his relatives" (lines 22–23), which is what this statement about solitude is referring to. Michael's decision to choose solitude belowdecks instead of waving goodbye to his family is unrelated to the number of amenities aboard the ship.

J because the description of the amenities aboard the *Oronsay* does not support the fact that Michael's relatives decided to send him to England by ship. Lines 47–48 describe why Michael is on the *Oronsay*, but they do not indicate the size, scale, or complexity of the ship. There is no indication that the ship's amenities factored into the decision to send Michael to England by ship.

Question 3. **The best answer is D** because Michael indicates that his relatives did not provide much information to prepare him for his journey. "No mention was made that this might be an unusual experience or that it could be exciting or dangerous" (lines 49–51). "I was not forewarned that the ship would have seven levels" (lines 52–53). "The departure date was marked casually on the calendar. . . . The fact of my being at sea for twenty-one days was spoken of as having not much significance" (lines 56–61). Instead, "there had been just one attempt to introduce me to the situation of the journey" (lines 65–66). Flavia, who would be traveling on the same ship, was invited to tea by Michael's family; she then told Michael that "she would be travelling in First Class but promised to keep an eye on me" (lines 69–70). In doing so, she is giving Michael a small amount of information about the circumstances of his trip.

The best answer is NOT:

A because there is no evidence that Flavia lists anybody that Michael might meet on the ship. Instead, she simply tells Michael that she will be keeping an eye on him (line 70).

B because Michael's mother is never mentioned in his conversation with Flavia (lines 69–73). For this statement to be true, it would have been necessary for Flavia to explain to Michael what his mother knows about his trip, which she never does.

C because there is no evidence to suggest that Flavia or anyone else drew a map of the route for Michael.

Question 4. The best answer is J because the narrator's relatives do not seem to approach Michael's impending departure with any strong emotions at all: "No mention was made that this might be an unusual experience or that it could be exciting or dangerous, so I did not approach it with any joy or fear" (lines 49–51). Michael also describes his relatives as marking his departure date "casually" on the calendar (line 57) and claims that his journey "was spoken of as having not much significance" (lines 60–61). All of these details suggest that his relatives were understated and matter-of-fact about Michael's journey.

The best answer is NOT:

F because there is no evidence to suggest that Michael's relatives expressed fear in relation to his journey. Michael claims that "no mention was made that this might be an unusual experience or that it could be exciting or dangerous, so I did not approach it with any joy or fear" (lines 49–51). This suggests that his relatives were neither fearful nor tense about the journey.

G because there is no evidence to suggest that Michael's relatives expressed excitement or seemed frantic prior to his departure. Michael's departure date was marked casually on the calendar, and Michael notes that "the fact of my being at sea for twenty-one days was spoken of as having not much significance" (lines 59–61). This suggests that his relatives did not view the experience as worthy of excitement.

H because there is no evidence to suggest that Michael's relatives' actions were either meticulous or generous. They made little effort to prepare him for the details of his trip: "I was not forewarned that the ship would have seven levels, hold more than six hundred people including a captain, nine cooks, engineers, a veterinarian, and that it would contain a small jail and chlorinated pools that would actually sail with us over two oceans" (lines 52–56). The narrator also expresses surprise that his relatives accompanied him at all (lines 61–62). These details do not characterize the relatives as either "generous" or "meticulous."

Question 5. **The best answer is B** because the passage states that once Michael is on the ship, "already it felt there was a wall between him and what took place there" (lines 12–13). This suggests that Michael feels physically separated from the city on boarding the ship.

The best answer is NOT:

A because there is no evidence to suggest that Michael sees the city as morally corrupt. In fact, there is no point in the passage where he remarks on the moral character of the city in any way.

C because there is no evidence to suggest that Michael sees the city as aesthetically beautiful. The passage states that there is a "yellow glow over the city" (lines 11–12), but there is no indication that Michael finds this glow beautiful. In fact, there is no point in the passage where Michael remarks on the beauty of the city in any way.

D because there is no evidence to suggest that Michael feels he is taking the city with him. Instead, the line "already it felt there was a wall between him and what took place there" (lines 12–13) suggests that Michael feels separated from the city after boarding the ship.

Question 6. **The best answer is H** because the main point of the second paragraph is for the narrator to analyze why Michael did not return to the deck to wave goodbye to his relatives. The narrator states "I do not know, even now, why he chose this solitude" (lines 26–27) and then proposes a potential reason for Michael's behavior, asking "Had whoever brought him onto the *Oronsay* already left?" (lines 27–28). The narrator also compares Michael's behavior to how people generally react to such departures in films (lines 28–31). At each of these points, the narrator is trying to understand and contextualize Michael's decision to stay in his cabin.

The best answer is NOT:

F because the passage never states that Michael's relatives left the harbor as soon as Michael boarded the *Oronsay*. The narrator instead wonders whether they had already left by the time Michael was on the ship: "Had whoever brought him onto the *Oronsay* already left?" (lines 27–28).

G because the narrator does not state that Michael enjoyed the singing. The narrator describes Michael listening to the singing and imagining the parting of families, but he never discusses whether or not Michael enjoyed the singing: "He could hear singing and imagined the slow and then eager parting of families taking place in the thrilling night air" (lines 24–26).

J because there is no evidence to suggest that Michael's relatives were weeping as the *Oronsay* departed. In fact, the narrator wonders whether his relatives had already left (lines 27–28), and the actual whereabouts or reactions of Michael's relatives are left ambiguous.

Question 7. The best answer is **A** because Flavia interacts with Michael very minimally, and she resumes her other conversation as soon as the interaction is over. "She then turned away to continue the conversation I had interrupted" (lines 72–73). It can also be inferred that Flavia does not interact with Michael again after this brief exchange, as Michael claims that he "spent most of the hour listening to a few uncles and counting how many of the trimmed sandwiches they ate" (lines 73–75), which also suggests a certain degree of indifference toward Michael on the part of Flavia.

The best answer is NOT:

B because there is no evidence that Flavia viewed Michael's behavior as rude. Though Michael does characterize his interaction with her as an interruption (line 73), it can be inferred that Flavia was invited to tea specifically to meet with Michael: "A lady named Flavia Prins, whose husband knew my uncle, turned out to be making the same journey and was invited to tea one afternoon to meet with me" (lines 66–69). Because their meeting was the stated purpose of the tea, it is not reasonable to assume that Flavia viewed Michael's brief interaction with her as rude, even if she expressed indifference toward him, and there is no evidence to suggest that she plans to retract her promise.

C because there is no evidence that Flavia was planning to find someone else to care for Michael. Instead, she claims that she will keep an eye on him and makes no mention of anyone else: "She would be travelling in First Class but promised to keep an eye on me" (lines 69–70).

D because although it could reasonably be inferred that Flavia intends to ignore Michael, there is no evidence to suggest that she plans to make his life difficult. Instead, she simply promises to keep an eye on him (line 70) before resuming her previous conversation, which suggests that she is indifferent to Michael and will likely do little to make his life either better or worse.

Question 8. The best answer is **J** because the narrator compares Michael to a "little cricket" (line 35) when imagining him in his narrow bunk.

The best answer is NOT:

F because although the narrator describes Michael as having been "smuggled away" (line 35), the narrator never refers to him as a "smuggler." In this metaphor, Michael is the thing being smuggled, not the smuggler.

G because the narrator never describes Michael as "rings and bangles." Instead, this is how Michael describes Flavia's jewelry: "I shook her hand carefully, as it was covered with rings and bangles" (lines 70–71).

H because the narrator never refers to Michael as green grass. Instead, he refers to him as a "green grasshopper" (line 34).

Question 9. **The best answer is D** because Michael mentions that he will spend twenty-one days at sea when speaking about his journey: "The fact of my being at sea for twenty-one days was spoken of as having not much significance" (lines 59–61).

The best answer is NOT:

A because the passage never states that Michael will have to rely on the expertise of a team of captains at any point. In fact, Michael only mentions the existence of one captain when he states that the ship will hold "more than six hundred people including a captain" (lines 53–54).

B because there is no evidence to suggest that Michael will disembark midjourney. The passage states that Michael will "arrive one morning on a small pier in England" (lines 82–83), but there is no mention of this arrival coming in the middle of the ship's journey.

C because the passage instead states that Michael's journey will take him across the Red Sea. "After I'd crossed the Indian Ocean and the Arabian Sea and the Red Sea . . . I would arrive one morning on a small pier in England" (lines 80–83).

Question 10. **The best answer is H** because Michael is largely ignored by the adults after his brief interaction with Flavia, and the fact that he does not recount anything else about the adults' conversations and busies himself with the mundane task of counting sandwiches suggests that he does not find their conversations to be interesting or relevant.

The best answer is NOT:

F because there is no evidence to suggest that Michael believes the number of sandwiches his uncles eat is in any way related to the number of sandwiches that he will receive on the trip. In fact, there is no evidence to suggest that Michael knew there would be sandwiches aboard the *Oronsay*, as the tea scene takes place before he boards the ship.

G because there is no evidence to suggest that Michael is concerned with whether or not his uncles are enjoying the sandwiches. Instead, he is simply listening to the uncles and counting the sandwiches (lines 73–75).

J because there is no evidence to suggest that Michael feels nervous around his uncles, nor that he believes his uncles to be loud. Instead, he simply states that he spent the hour listening to his uncles (lines 73–75).

Passage II

Question 11. The best answer is D because the author of Passage A views dark gumbo as a poor execution of gumbo and is using the biscuit and brisket to illustrate real culinary achievements. In the first paragraph of Passage A, the author laments the fact that he has heard people praising gumbo for its thickness and darkness. "This was strange to me. Gumbo was supposed to be neither thick nor dark" (lines 4–5). He goes on to note, "Even more important, 'dark' and 'thick' were being used not as adjectives, but as achievements. It was as if making a dark gumbo was a culinary accomplishment on par with making a featherlight biscuit or a perfectly barbecued beef brisket" (lines 5–10). Here the biscuit and brisket are being held up as accomplishments, examples of foods the author views as real culinary successes. The author is suggesting that dark gumbo is not actually "on par with" a featherlight biscuit or perfectly barbecued beef brisket.

The best answer is NOT:

A because the author does not discuss taste in this paragraph or in the passage as a whole. Rather, the focus is on the preparation of and ingredients in gumbo. The primary function of these examples is to point out that dark gumbo is not a culinary achievement.

B because the author does not indicate that featherlight biscuits and perfectly barbecued beef brisket are specific to New Orleans cuisine. Nor does the author suggest that these foods have been corrupted; rather, they are held up as a standard of culinary achievement.

C because neither featherlight biscuits nor perfectly barbecued beef brisket are identified as being authentic New Orleans food. Moreover, the only New Orleans food that is discussed as being appealing to tourists is gumbo. Lines 2–4: "I began to hear tourists, visitors and transplants to New Orleans praising this or that gumbo for its thickness and darkness."

Question 12. The best answer is J because the author directly states that though Prudhomme "hails from Cajun Country" (line 14), his "Louisiana cooking" has been influenced by Louisiana more broadly. Lines 15–17: "He refers to his cooking not so much as Cajun, but as 'Louisiana cooking,' and thus reflective of influences beyond his home parish."

The best answer is NOT:

F because there is no indication in the passage that Prudhomme's Louisiana cooking demands less creativity than Cajun cuisine. The author is concerned with authenticity, not creativity.

G because there is no indication in the passage that Prudhomme's Louisiana cooking requires more discipline than Cajun cuisine. In fact, the author claims that chefs trained under Prudhomme "lacked the loving guidance and discipline that only good home training can provide" (lines 24–26).

H because there is no indication in the passage that the author believes Prudhomme's Louisiana cooking is much easier to master than Cajun cuisine. The author does note that a lack of discipline has contributed to Prudhomme's influence, but that lack of discipline is relative to "good home training" in terms of what good gumbo is supposed to be. It is not a comment on the actual difficulty in mastering either of these styles.

Question 13. The best answer is D because the author directly states that he blamed Prudhomme for the ruin of the gumbo universe. Lines 17–19: "For years I blamed him [Prudhomme] for the destruction of the gumbo universe." Because many of the chefs and cooks in New Orleans were trained by Prudhomme or his students, and many were not from Louisiana, "they had no homemade guide as to what good gumbo was supposed to be" (lines 22–23).

The best answer is NOT:

A because the influence of tourists is treated as part of the problem but not the direct cause. The author notes that he is bothered by "the tyrannical influence of the tourist trade" (line 32) and that "the whole of the French Quarter" at times seemed to cater to what tourists "expected to find" (lines 34–36). Tourists expected to find these dishes because many of the chefs and cooks in New Orleans were not actually from New Orleans and had learned under Prudhomme or his students. Moreover, Prudhomme is blamed directly in lines 17–19: "For years I blamed him [Prudhomme] for the destruction of the gumbo universe."

B because the author directly states, "The Cajun incursion in and of itself didn't bother me" (lines 28–29).

C because there is no indication in the passage that a sudden prevalence of chicken and andouille gumbo resulted in the ruin of the gumbo universe. Chicken and andouille gumbo is mentioned as being "on menus all over town" (lines 40–41) in 1995, after Prudhomme's influence had taken hold.

Question 14. The best answer is **H** because the author of Passage B states that Syrnikov has a problem: "Russians don't hold Russian food in particularly high esteem. When they eat out, they favor more exotic cuisines, like Italian or Japanese. The tendency to find foreign food more desirable is a prejudice that goes back centuries—to a time when the Russian aristocracy spoke French, not Russian. Russian food is pooh-poohed as unhealthy and unsophisticated" (lines 46–52).

The best answer is NOT:

F because there is no indication in the passage that Syrnikov believes Russians are embarrassed by their country's agrarian history and want to distance themselves from it. Rather, Syrnikov believes that Russians have simply lost touch with their agrarian roots.

G because there is no indication in the passage that the prejudices held by Russia's ruling class led to an actual ban on Russian cuisine. The passage notes only that the tendency to find foreign food more desirable is a prejudice that dates back to a time when the Russian aristocracy spoke French, not Russian.

J because although Syrnikov asserts that people need to start writing down traditional recipes from "old women" in Russia, this is presented as a way to preserve a significant part of Russian culture rather than a reason for Russians not favoring their national cuisine overall.

Question 15. The best answer is **B** because the paragraph begins with an assertion that Syrnikov hopes to reacquaint Russians with their agrarian roots and to convince them that their national cuisine can be just as good as other cuisines. What follows in lines 75–81 is a list of ways Syrnikov is hoping to educate people. Traveling the countryside, trying the recipes he finds, blogging, consulting, and planning a user-generated database for recipes show his dedication to helping Russians find their true culinary roots.

The best answer is NOT:

A because there is no suggestion in the passage that Syrnikov is overwhelmed by the scope and number of his projects.

C because there is no indication in the passage that Syrnikov plans to open his own authentic restaurant. He has consulted "on projects to make a restaurant authentically Russian" (lines 79–80), but the passage does not suggest a goal to open his own restaurant.

D because the passage does not suggest that Syrnikov lacks culinary training.

Question 16. The best answer is **H** because Syrnikov is quoted as stating the following: "In the middle of the eighteenth century, there were *riots* because people didn't want to grow potatoes" (lines 60–62).

The best answer is NOT:

F because Syrnikov states that potatoes are actually an American plant. "He insists that real Russian food contained no potatoes" (lines 62–63).

G because Syrnikov states that potatoes were an American plant and not part of real Russian food. "Instead, there were lots of grains, fish, and dairy, as well as honey, cucumbers, turnips, cabbage, apples, and the produce of Russia's vast forests….Most of Russia ate this way until the twentieth century" (lines 64–70).

J because Syrnikov states that potatoes are an American plant, not a Ukrainian plant. "What they named was horrible: borscht, which is Ukrainian, and potatoes, which are an American plant" (lines 58–60).

Question 17. The best answer is **C** because in lines 85–89, Syrnikov is quoted as saying, in reference to writing down recipes held by grandmothers across Russia, "To me, it's absolutely obvious that, if we don't wake up and find out from these old women and set it down on paper, in twenty years we won't have anyone to ask. Russian culture will lose a very significant part of itself."

The best answer is NOT:

A because Syrnikov believes that if the traditional Russian cuisine is not recorded, it will be lost, and "Russian culture will lose a very significant part of itself" (lines 88–89). He does not connect that loss of identity with Russian cuisine needing to reinvent itself.

B because there is no mention in Passage B of an existing database of folk recipes. Instead, Syrnikov's plan is to use these folk recipes to build a database.

D because Syrnikov believes the opposite will happen. If the recipes are not recorded, then future generations will not be able to learn them.

Question 18. The best answer is **J** because the author of Passage A clearly struggles with the public's misperception of authentic New Orleans food, while Passage B outlines Syrnikov's efforts to correct misconceptions about Russian cuisine. In Passage A, the author is concerned that Prudhomme's influence and the tourist trade have resulted in inauthentic New Orleans food. "There was no regard for whether the offerings were authentic New Orleans food or culture" (lines 36–37). In Passage B, Syrnikov is presented as believing that many Russians don't actually know what foods are traditional Russian dishes: "Among the many things that annoy Syrnikov is the fact that a good number of the despised Russian dishes aren't even Russian" (lines 53–55). Syrnikov "hopes to help Russians reacquaint themselves with the country's agrarian roots, and to convince them that their national cuisine can be just as flavorful as anything they might find in a sushi bar" (lines 72–75).

The best answer is NOT:

F because there is no indication in Passage A that the author and Prudhomme have actually interacted. Moreover, although Passage B does present Syrnikov as being annoyed that the Russian public is ignorant about true Russian cuisine, this is not the primary focus of the passage. Rather, the focus is on Syrnikov's efforts to correct these misconceptions.

G because Passage B is not concerned with how communities are working together to preserve Russian cuisine. Rather, Passage B describes Syrnikov's efforts to educate the Russian people about true Russian cuisine.

H because there is no indication in Passage A that the author is prejudiced against non-Cajun food. The author states that "the Cajun incursion in and of itself didn't bother me. We are all enriched immeasurably when we encounter other people" (lines 28–30).

Question 19. **The best answer is C** because both New Orleans transplants and modern Russians are presented as being misinformed about their authentic cuisines. In Passage A, the author notes that New Orleans transplants were praising gumbo for its thickness and darkness, but real gumbo "was supposed to be neither thick nor dark" (line 5). In Passage B, lines 55–60 detail a survey Syrnikov conducted with residents of Moscow and St. Petersburg, in which they were asked to name traditional Russian dishes. "What they named was horrible: borscht, which is Ukrainian, and potatoes, which are an American plant" (lines 58–60).

The best answer is NOT:

A because there is no indication in either passage that New Orleans transplants or modern Russians are perplexed. They do not display confusion about their region's authentic cuisine; rather, they are simply misinformed.

B because New Orleans transplants are not presented as disdainful in Passage A. Instead, they praise "this or that gumbo for its thickness and darkness" (lines 3–4). But in praising this gumbo, they are not disdainful of what the passage author regards as real gumbo; they are simply misinformed. In Passage B, modern Russians are presented as being disdainful of some dishes that they believe are traditional Russian dishes, but Syrnikov points out that many of these dishes aren't actually authentic Russian cuisine.

D because neither passage presents New Orleans transplants or modern Russians as knowledgeable. They are presented as the opposite. In Passage A, the author notes that New Orleans transplants praise "this or that gumbo for its thickness and darkness" (lines 3–4), but gumbo "was supposed to be neither thick nor dark" (line 5). In Passage B, modern Russians are presented as being disdainful of some dishes that they believe are traditional Russian dishes, but Syrnikov points out that many of these dishes aren't actually authentic Russian cuisine. "Among the many things that annoy Syrnikov is the fact that a good number of the despised Russian dishes aren't even Russian" (lines 53–55).

Question 20. The best answer is **F** because in Passage A, the author says the following about many of the cooks in New Orleans: "Many of these cooks were not from Louisiana, and thus had no homemade guide as to what good gumbo was supposed to be. As I saw it then, these were young, impressionable cooks who lacked the loving guidance and discipline that only good home training can provide" (lines 21–26). In Passage B, Syrnikov outlines a goal to create a database of Russian folk recipes by sending out "a call across all of Russia" (line 82) to connect with the women holding these recipes. "If we don't wake up and find out from these old women and set it down on paper, in twenty years we won't have anyone to ask. Russian culture will lose a very significant part of itself" (lines 85–89).

The best answer is NOT:

G because neither passage supports the idea that cooking authentic food is best accomplished by studying under chefs. In Passage A, the author asserts that studying under Prudhomme contributed to the problem of inauthentic gumbo: "Many of the chefs and cooks in New Orleans restaurants learned under him or under his students. Many of these cooks were not from Louisiana, and thus had no homemade guide as to what good gumbo was supposed to be" (lines 19–23). In Passage B, no mention is made of studying under chefs in restaurants. Instead, Syrnikov indicates that authentic Russian cuisine must be preserved by gathering folk recipes from "old women" across Russia.

H because neither passage presents evidence that the best way to learn how to cook traditional or authentic food is by learning about other cultures' foods. Instead, both assert that the best way to learn is from cooks native to the area. In Passage A, the author notes that New Orleans cooks need "the loving guidance and discipline that only good home training can provide" (lines 24–26). Although the author of Passage A also states that "we are all enriched immeasurably when we encounter other people, other languages, other traditions, other tastes" (lines 29–31), this is not said in relation to learning how to cook authentic New Orleans food. Passage B notes that Syrnikov travels the Russian countryside in search of traditional recipes, but he is doing this to learn about food specific to Russian culture.

J because neither passage discusses a need to be trained in a culinary school. Rather, both passages assert that traditional or authentic cuisine can best be learned from home cooks.

Passage III

Question 21. The best answer is D because the interviewee, Morgan, does respond to the questions of the interviewer, Fabisiak, with in-depth, involved, and somewhat philosophical answers. For example, when the interviewer asks Morgan about her focus on work and to what extent it's related to a focus on landscape more generally, Morgan does not provide a short or simple answer. She begins by responding to the question as it relates to *All the Living*, insisting that the presence of work in *All the Living* was not a "self-conscious choice" (lines 53–54), before moving into a discussion about how this particular book was written and then ruminating on her writing process in general. She goes into detail when describing how *All the Living* was written: "I don't feel I made choices in the first draft of the novel. . . . I obeyed the book" (lines 57–60). In the same level of detail, she describes her feelings about writing as a vocation, arriving at this conclusion: "Frankly, the world doesn't need more books; it needs better books. Vocation is tied up with notions of service, and as an artist you serve people by giving them your best, the work you produce that you truly believe to be of value" (lines 80–84).

The best answer is NOT:

A because the interviewer does not offer harsh commentary that requires Morgan to defend herself. The interviewer simply asks questions about Morgan's writing, which she responds to with in-depth, thoughtful answers.

B because at no point in the interview does Morgan urge the interviewer to ask her more relevant questions.

C because, although there is an element of dialogue to the interview, Morgan does not turn any of the questions back to the interviewer.

Question 22. The best answer is H because Morgan directly states in lines 9–15, "Landscape writing—most especially when it's done at length and in a style that deviates from prose norms, so that its very presentation is interruptive or 'estranging' as the formalists might have said—encourages the reader to stop, reread, listen, imagine, reconsider, admire, appreciate with new eyes."

The best answer is NOT:

F because Morgan makes no mention of plot when discussing how landscape writing might feel "interruptive or 'estranging.'"

G because Morgan makes no mention of the skill of the writer when discussing how landscape writing might feel "interruptive or 'estranging.'"

J because Morgan makes no mention of the opening pages of a novel when discussing how landscape writing might feel "interruptive or 'estranging.'"

716 The Official ACT Prep Guide

Question 23. The best answer is **A** because Morgan agrees that landscape writing draws attention to itself but notes that it also draws attention to the land. She states, "The reader might complain that this kind of writing draws attention to itself, but this kind of writing doesn't merely draw attention to its own aesthetic strategies—it also draws attention to land" (lines 15–18).

The best answer is NOT:

B because Morgan does not discuss the focus of the writer in terms of landscape writing calling attention to itself.

C because Morgan asserts that landscape writing does draw attention to itself but also draws attention to land: "this kind of writing doesn't merely draw attention to its own aesthetic strategies—it also draws attention to land" (lines 16–18).

D because Morgan never indicates that some readers are unwilling to read landscape writing.

Question 24. The best answer is **F** because Morgan suggests that appreciation for the land can result in action. In lines 18–20, she states, "The land is imperiled; we know that. Land is always imperiled wherever the human puts his or her foot." She goes on to argue that attention paid to the land in a narrative can lead to an appreciation of the land, which can then lead to action: "Deep appreciation can result from an engagement with that kind of beauty, and that can manifest in action. That is how it might be seen as a political act to do this kind of writing (particularly about a region, such as this one, rural Kentucky, that is continuously being ravaged by corporations that consumers unwittingly feed)" (lines 23–29).

The best answer is NOT:

G because Morgan does not suggest that a reader's attention to the land will lead the reader to forget that the land is in peril. She suggests the opposite, that "attention paid to landscape in a narrative is . . . attention that's paid to land itself" and that "deep appreciation can result from an engagement with that kind of beauty, and that can manifest in action" (lines 20–25).

H because there is no indication in the passage that Morgan believes a reader's attention to the land will lead the reader to misinterpret the writer's purpose.

J because there is no indication in the passage that Morgan believes a reader's attention to the land will lead the reader to research a writer's academic background.

Question 25. The best answer is **B** because Morgan asserts that landscape writing doesn't just draw attention to the words on the page ("marks"), it also draws attention to the land itself. "This kind of writing doesn't merely draw attention to its own aesthetic strategies—it also draws attention to land" (lines 16–18). Readers will not just be focused on the physical marks on the page ("words and symbols") but on the land being described itself.

The best answer is NOT:

A because "creases and smudges" would not capture Morgan's intent, which is to assert that landscape writing doesn't just draw attention to the writing ("marks on a page") but also to the land. "Creases and smudges" would not make sense in this context.

C because "notches and ticks" would not capture Morgan's intent, which is to assert that landscape writing doesn't just draw attention to the writing ("marks on a page") but also to the land. "Notches and ticks" would not make sense in this context.

D because "lines and boundaries" would not capture Morgan's intent, which is to assert that landscape writing doesn't just draw attention to the writing ("marks on a page") but also to the land. "Lines and boundaries" would not make sense in this context.

Question 26. The best answer is **J** because at this point in the passage, Morgan is discussing attention paid to landscape in a narrative and the affect it can have on readers. She asserts that "attention paid to landscape in a narrative is . . . attention that's paid to land itself" (lines 20–22). She goes on to claim that "deep appreciation" for the land can result from an engagement "with that kind of beauty" (lines 23–24)—the beauty of the land being described in the narrative.

The best answer is NOT:

F because Morgan is not discussing humans in her work. She is focused on landscape writing.

G because Morgan is not discussing intellect at this point. She is describing how landscape writing can lead to a deep appreciation for the land on the part of the reader.

H because at this point Morgan is commenting on the land itself, not on a political act. She is noting that appreciation for the land (a result of attention paid to the landscape in a narrative) can result from an engagement with the land's beauty. She goes on to note that this is why landscape writing can be seen as a political act, but she is not specifically referring to a political act when she says "deep appreciation can result from an engagement with that kind of beauty" (lines 23–24). That "deep appreciation" of and "engagement with" refers to the land.

Question 27. The best answer is **A** because Fabisiak prefaces a question about Morgan's focus on work with the following: "Without wanting you to interpret *All the Living* for readers, because you've told me that you hate imposing yourself into people's encounters with the book" (lines 34–37). It is clear from this statement that Fabisiak has learned this from Morgan herself ("you've told me").

The best answer is NOT:

B because there is no indication in the passage that Morgan does not like to tell her readers that she lives in Kentucky.

C because although Fabisiak notes that Morgan takes work seriously and acknowledges a "commitment to hard work" (lines 46–47), there is no indication that Fabisiak knows Morgan doesn't like to work ten hours every day. In the interview, Morgan notes that "as an artist you serve people by giving them your best . . . not just what you're capable of producing if you work ten hours a day every day for forty years" (lines 82–86), but there is no indication that Fabisiak and Morgan have discussed ten-hour days before this interview.

D because there is no indication in the passage that Morgan does not like to discuss which regions of the United States she plans to write about.

Question 28. The best answer is **G** because Morgan states that "the presence of work—agrarian or domestic—in *All the Living* was not a self-conscious choice" (lines 52–54). This suggests that the book depicts both agrarian and domestic work.

The best answer is NOT:

F because although corporations are mentioned in the passage, Morgan does not indicate that there is anything in her book that discusses corporate work. Corporations are mentioned by Morgan in the context of how they harm the land in rural Kentucky: "continuously being ravaged by corporations that consumers unwittingly feed" (lines 27–29).

H because creative work is not mentioned or suggested as a focus of *All the Living*.

J because neither creative nor corporate work are mentioned or suggested as a focus of *All the Living*.

Question 29. The best answer is **C** because in lines 74–76, Morgan states that "this idea that a writer should produce a novel every year or two years, that they should be punching a clock somehow" is something that she's wary of. In this statement, she is comparing producing a novel every year or two to punching a clock—to "rigorous work ethic for the sake of rigorous work ethic" (lines 73–74).

The best answer is NOT:

A because Morgan does not directly compare being expected to produce a novel every one or two years to working overtime.

B because Morgan neither mentions the assembly of products in a factory nor compares it to the expectation to produce a novel every one or two years.

D because Morgan does not compare being expected to produce a novel every one or two years to selling goods on commission.

Question 30. The best answer is **H** because Morgan states that "as an artist you serve people by giving them your best, the work you produce that you truly believe to be of value" (lines 82–84).

The best answer is NOT:

F because Morgan does not believe that artists should continually offer new work that they know people will buy. She says, "I don't want to produce just to produce. I don't want to write just to write, or publish just to get a paycheck. I see no value in that" (lines 78–80).

G because Morgan does not mention that an artist is serving other people by studying others' work and learning from it. Rather, she believes that "as an artist you serve people by giving them your best" (lines 82–83).

J because Morgan never mentions that a writer should modify the focus of their work when people lose interest.

Passage IV

Question 31. The best answer is B because the main purpose of the passage is to discuss how the scientific theory of *e*, which is now well accepted, had a controversial past. After introducing Millikan's initial discovery of *e*, the passage states that "Millikan still had years of difficult and dirty work ahead of him" (lines 24–25). From this point, the passage primarily focuses on the feud between Millikan and Ehrenhaft, and how Millikan's attempts to prove his theory correct would "cast a lasting shadow over his scientific integrity" (lines 32–33), as he was accused of cherry-picking data (line 49) and hiding data that he considered inconvenient (lines 35–36). The passage also states that Millikan "did not convince his peers straight away" (lines 81–82) and that the arguments between him and Ehrenhaft delayed Millikan's Nobel Prize for three years (lines 82–84), concluding with the claim that "to get his Nobel Prize, Millikan had to play hard and fast with what we might call 'accepted practice'" (lines 91–92). Because the focus of the passage is on the controversial past of a well-accepted theory, it is reasonable to conclude that the passage's main purpose was to use Millikan's theory of *e* as an example of a well-accepted scientific idea that has a "sullied past."

The best answer is NOT:

A because the main focus of the passage is on the controversy surrounding the existence of *e*, not on the process by which theories become accepted. Although the passage states that Millikan "did not convince his peers straight away" (lines 81–82), it does not discuss how he did come to convince his peers, and although it says that his Nobel Prize was "delayed for three years" (line 84), it does not explain how he gained enough acceptance to receive the prize in 1923. If anything, the passage focuses on the ways in which Millikan's theory was initially not accepted, despite the fact that he was correct. And the passage never suggests that the process by which Millikan's theory was accepted is representative of the process in general.

C because although the passage does mention some challenges Millikan faced when measuring *e*, these challenges are discussed in the context of Millikan's selective use of data and the way in which Millikan's use of data "cast a lasting shadow over his scientific integrity" (lines 32–33). Also, although Millikan's scientific work was likely quite challenging and rigorous, the passage does not focus on characterizing it as such. When describing Millikan's process in the second paragraph, the passage begins by stating "Millikan's idea was simple" (line 6), followed by a relatively straightforward description of Millikan's experiment. The passage does later state that "the experiment was far from simple to carry out" (line 17), as the water droplets "tended to evaporate before any measurements could be made" (lines 18–19), but the passage then immediately describes Millikan's solution—"trying the same trick with oil droplets" (lines 20–21)—and, in the very next sentence, describes Millikan publishing his findings (lines 22–23). After this point, the passage focuses almost entirely on the controversy surrounding Millikan's 1913 paper and discusses any difficulties he faced only in the context of this controversy. For all of these reasons, it is not accurate to say that the main focus of the passage was to describe the difficulties scientists faced in measuring *e*.

D because at no point does the passage claim that Millikan received credit for work that was not his own. Although the passage states that Millikan "had to play hard and fast with what we might call 'accepted practice'" (lines 91–92) in order to get his Nobel Prize, this is in reference to Millikan potentially cherry-picking data (line 49) and hiding data that he considered inconvenient (lines 35–36), not to Millikan receiving credit for another scientist's work. Also, there is no evidence to suggest that any scientist other than Millikan received credit for Millikan's work, because he was eventually awarded a Nobel Prize in 1923 (line 84).

Question 32. The best answer is F because both Ehrenhaft's and Millikan's reputations were at stake, and they both went to great lengths to protect their reputations. The author characterizes both scientists as highly emotionally invested in proving their theories right. After Ehrenhaft first published a refutation of Millikan's results, the passage states that "the series of experiments the desperate Millikan then performed were to cast a lasting shadow over his scientific integrity" (lines 30–33). The characterization of Millikan as "desperate" suggests that Ehrenhaft's refutation of Millikan's paper inspired an emotional response in Millikan, and the fact that Millikan's subsequent experiments "cast a lasting shadow over his scientific integrity" (lines 32–33) demonstrates that Millikan's reputation relied heavily on the success and reliability of his findings and publications. Also, the passage states that Millikan's admirable honesty in his initial paper gave Ehrenhaft "ammunition that he used enthusiastically in his long feud with Millikan" (lines 58–59). The use of the word *enthusiastically* suggests that Ehrenhaft, like Millikan, was emotionally invested in proving his own theory correct. Due to the high emotional investment on the part of both parties, coupled with the public nature of their "long feud," it is reasonable to describe their relationship as "tense" and to claim that both of their reputations were at stake.

The best answer is NOT:

G because there is no evidence to suggest that either Millikan or Ehrenhaft sabotaged one another's experiments in any way. Instead, each one performed their own experiments to refute the claim of the other. The passage states that "Ehrenhaft refuted Millikan's results with a similar set of experiments" (lines 26–27), and Millikan responded by publishing a paper "refuting Ehrenhaft and showing that every measurement of electric charge gives a value of e or an integer multiple of e" (lines 40–42).

H because there is no evidence to suggest that Millikan and Ehrenhaft wanted to push each other to create a stronger theory, nor is it accurate to describe their relationship as collegial. Instead, the passage describes Millikan as wanting to "crush Ehrenhaft underfoot" (line 50) and states that Ehrenhaft used Millikan's "admirable honesty" surrounding his selection of data points as "ammunition" in their "long feud" (lines 56–59).

J because the passage specifically states that Millikan and Ehrenhaft were working on the exact same question in the field of physics—the value and existence of e—and as a result, it is not accurate to claim that Millikan and Ehrenhaft were "primarily working in different fields."

Question 33. The best answer is D because the debate surrounding Millikan's experiments was centered on a discrepancy between a statement in Millikan's paper and a statement found in Millikan's notebooks. In his paper, Millikan wrote that his data table contained "*a complete summary of the results obtained on all of the 58 different drops upon which complete series of observations were made*" (lines 43–45). The use of the phrase "the results obtained on all of the 58 different drops" gives the impression that Millikan used only fifty-eight drops in his experiment and that all of these drops were included in the paper. However, the passage states that "the notebooks for the 1913 paper show that Millikan actually took data on 100 oil droplets" (lines 47–48). This suggests that Millikan did not include all the data from his experiments in the paper and that he in fact omitted data from forty-two drops, leading others to question whether or not Millikan had decided to "cherry-pick the data in order to confirm his original result" (lines 49–50).

The best answer is NOT:

A because the passage actually indicates the opposite, claiming that "few laboratories managed to replicate Ehrenhaft's results" (lines 86–87), but "students now replicate Millikan's results all across the world" (lines 87–88).

B because at no point does the passage suggest that Millikan's decision to switch to oil droplets was controversial. The passage only notes that Millikan switched to oil droplets because water droplets evaporated "before any measurements could be made" (line 19).

C because at no point does the passage suggest that the apparatus Millikan used to conduct his experiments was controversial.

Question 34. The best answer is G because the author describes Millikan's decision as honest and admirable: "This admirable honesty about the selection of data points had given Ehrenhaft ammunition that he used enthusiastically in his long feud with Millikan" (lines 56–59). This suggests that the author finds Millikan's initial honesty to be admirable, though he acknowledges that Ehrenhaft used Millikan's admirable honesty about his less-than-perfect data to refute Millikan's findings and claim that Millikan's data were inaccurate. The author believes that it was Ehrenhaft's refutation that led Millikan to hide data in his subsequent experiment, which then led to the "lasting shadow over his scientific integrity" (lines 32–33) that would haunt Millikan for years and delay his Nobel Prize. Therefore, it is reasonable to say that the author believes that Millikan's "admirable honesty" had unfortunate consequences.

The best answer is NOT:

F because there is no indication in the passage that the author views Millikan's decision as a mistake that "most scientists rightfully avoid." Though the author does note that Millikan made the "mistake of full disclosure" (line 52), this disclosure is described as "admirable honesty" (line 56), which suggests that the author views Millikan's decision to disclose his data as an honorable decision. Because of this, it doesn't make sense to say that the author views Millikan's full disclosure as a practice that other scientists "rightfully avoid." Rather, the author seems to feel that Millikan's full disclosure in his initial experiment was an admirable decision.

H because Millikan's decision was at no point described as strategic. Moreover, it was Millikan's full disclosure that gave Ehrenhaft the "ammunition" (line 58) he needed to question Millikan's results in the first place, which in turn led to Millikan concealing data in his 1913 paper, a decision that would cast a shadow over his scientific integrity (lines 32–33). Instead of characterizing Millikan's full disclosure as a strategic decision, the author describes it as "admirable honesty" (line 56).

J because although it might be reasonable to characterize Millikan's full disclosure as naive, at no point does the author characterize his decision as desperate. Instead, the author describes Millikan's response to Ehrenhaft's refutation as "desperate" (line 31) and claims that this desperation caused Millikan to conceal data in his 1913 paper. The author describes Millikan's full disclosure in his 1910 paper as "admirable honesty" (line 56).

Question 35. The best answer is **C** because the passage states that Millikan used oil droplets because he had a difficult time measuring water droplets before they evaporated: "Finding that water droplets tended to evaporate before any measurements could be made, Millikan set to the task of trying the same trick with oil droplets" (lines 18–21).

The best answer is NOT:

A because at no point does the passage state that other physicists used oil droplets. Rather, the passage states that Millikan used oil droplets because he found that water droplets evaporated too quickly and were therefore difficult to measure (lines 18–21).

B because although the passage states that Millikan may have "judged some droplets to be too small or too large to yield reliable data" (lines 69–70), the passage at this point is discussing only oil droplets, and the passage never states that oil droplets form more consistently sized droplets than water droplets. Rather, the passage states that Millikan used oil droplets because he found that water droplets evaporated too quickly and were therefore difficult to measure (lines 18–21).

D because at no point does the passage mention that Millikan reused either oil or water droplets for any of his experiments. Rather, the passage states that Millikan used oil droplets because he found that water droplets evaporated too quickly and were therefore difficult to measure (lines 18–21).

Question 36. The best answer is **F** because the primary purpose of this paragraph is to present Goodstein's justification for why Millikan only included data from fifty-eight of the one hundred water droplets in his paper. Goodstein argues that Millikan may have excluded certain data points that were either too large or too small to yield reliable data (lines 68–70), because droplets that were too small could not be reliably measured due to random collisions with air particles (lines 72–74), and droplets that were too big would fall too fast, making them difficult to reliably measure (lines 70–72). Goodstein then argues that Millikan could have potentially viewed the fifty-eight drops as the only samples that were "complete enough" (lines 75–76) to be included in the paper, which would justify Millikan's claim that his data table contained "*a complete summary of the results obtained on all of the 58 different drops upon which complete series of observations were made*" (lines 43–45). Because the author spends the entire paragraph describing Goodstein's defense of Millikan, it is reasonable to conclude that the main purpose of the paragraph is to present Goodstein's defense of Millikan.

The best answer is NOT:

G because the author does not argue against Goodstein's interpretations of Millikan's motives at any point during this particular paragraph. Instead, he describes Goodstein's rationale for Millikan's exclusion of data points that were too large or too small (lines 68–74) and ends by offering Goodstein's conclusion that Millikan could have viewed the fifty-eight drops as the only samples that were "complete enough" (lines 75–76) to be included in the paper. In the subsequent paragraph, the author describes the manner in which "Goodstein undoes his defence" (line 77) of Millikan, but the author does not mention this at any point during the ninth paragraph (lines 62–76).

H because the author does not describe Millikan's methods in much detail during this paragraph. Instead, he describes Goodstein's rationale for excluding data points that were too large or too small (lines 68–74) and ends by offering Goodstein's conclusion that Millikan could have viewed the fifty-eight drops as the only samples that were "complete enough" (lines 75–76) to be included in the paper. So, although the author does mention Millikan's methods, it is only in the context of Goodstein's defense of Millikan's decision to only include fifty-eight drops in his data set. The author also does not mention any perspective on Millikan's methods aside from Goldstein's during this paragraph.

J because the author only briefly describes how Millikan's data are represented, and this is only in the context of Goodstein's defense of Millikan's decision to only include fifty-eight drops in his data set. Furthermore, the paragraph does not include Millikan's explanation for any of his methods; it instead includes an explanation from Goldstein justifying the way in which Millikan presented his data.

Question 37. The best answer is **A** because according to the passage, Ehrenhaft claimed that there is no fundamental minimum unit of charge and therefore no electron: "There is no fundamental, minimum unit of charge, Ehrenhaft said; there is no 'electron'" (lines 29–30).

The best answer is NOT:

B because at no point does the passage state that Ehrenhaft believed that Millikan's value for e was too low. Instead, the passage states that Ehrenhaft's experiments "seemed to show that electrical charge can be infinitely small" (lines 28–29), that "there is no fundamental, minimum unit of charge" (lines 29–30), and that "there is no 'electron'" (line 30).

C because at no point does the passage state that Ehrenhaft accused Millikan of failing to take prevailing scientific theories into account. To refute Millikan, Ehrenhaft instead conducted a "similar set of experiments that seemed to show that electrical charge can be infinitely small" (lines 27–29). This led Ehrenhaft to conclude that "there is no 'electron'" (line 30), and he reached this conclusion based on his own attempts to replicate Millikan's experiments, not on prevailing scientific theories.

D because at no point does the passage state that Ehrenhaft believed that the value of e varies based on the substance one is measuring. Instead, Ehrenhaft concluded that "there is no fundamental, minimum unit of charge" and that "there is no 'electron'" (lines 29–30).

Question 38. The best answer is **H** because although the assertion that Millikan's experiments "cast a lasting shadow over his scientific integrity" (lines 32–33) is an inherently subjective judgment, it is fair to characterize it as a "reasoned" judgment, as the author offers a great deal of evidence to support this statement. He quotes the biologist Richard Lewontin, who accused Millikan of going "out of his way to hide the existence of inconvenient data" (lines 35–36), and then references David Goodstein, who stated that Millikan "certainly did not commit scientific fraud" (line 37). Although Goodstein disagrees with Lewontin, it is clear that Goodstein is arguing against the viewpoint that Millikan committed scientific fraud, which suggests that the belief that Millikan committed fraud is not uncommon. Furthermore, the passage claims that Millikan was unable to convince his peers straight away (lines 81–82), as evidenced by the fact that Millikan's Nobel Prize was delayed for three years (lines 83–84). Therefore, it is accurate to describe the author's statement as a reasoned judgment, considering the evidence he provides for the controversy surrounding Millikan's 1913 paper.

The best answer is NOT:

F because it is not accurate to describe the author's statement as being based on "casual assumptions about scientists working in the early 1900s." Instead, the author provides detailed evidence to support his statement. He quotes Richard Lewontin, a scientist who believes that Millikan deliberately hid the existence of inconvenient data (lines 35–36), as well as scientist David Goodstein, who claimed that Millikan "certainly did not commit scientific fraud" (line 37). This quote suggests that Goodstein is arguing against others who do believe that Millikan committed scientific fraud, which suggests that this view is not uncommon. Furthermore, the author claims that Millikan was unable to convince his peers straight away (lines 81–82), and, as evidence, he states that Millikan's Nobel Prize was delayed for three years as a result of his peers' distrust (lines 82–84). Because the author provides evidence to support his assertion, including quotations from other scientists, it is not reasonable to characterize this statement as a "casual assumption."

G because at no point does the author attempt to imagine himself in Millikan's position. In fact, the author does not mention himself directly at any point during the passage. Therefore, it is not reasonable to conclude that the author was attempting to imagine himself in Millikan's position.

J because the author mentions Millikan's notebooks only briefly, claiming that Millikan's notebooks show that he "actually took data on 100 oil droplets" (line 48), and the notebooks are not mentioned at any other point.

Question 39. **The best answer is A** because the paragraph describes the two prevailing arguments about Millikan's methodologies by offering two conflicting viewpoints. The biologist Richard Lewontin accuses Millikan of going "out of his way to hide the existence of inconvenient data" (lines 35–36), which suggests that Lewontin believes that Millikan did commit a certain degree of scientific fraud. However, David Goodstein states that Millikan "certainly did not commit scientific fraud" (line 37). By offering quotations from these two scientists, the author provides two conflicting viewpoints on the same topic: one stating that Millikan did commit fraud and the other stating that he did not. By providing two contrasting quotes from two other scientists, and by ending the paragraph with the question, "So where does the truth lie?" (lines 37–38), the author introduces the reader to the two prevailing opinions surrounding the ethics of Millikan's methodologies.

The best answer is NOT:

B because the author does not discuss the background of either Lewontin or Goodstein in great detail. Although he does state that Lewontin is a biologist and that Goodstein is a physics professor, he does not try to analyze how either individual's scientific background may have influenced his opinions about Millikan. Instead, he simply provides quotations from both scientists demonstrating their contrasting opinions, poses the question, "So where does the truth lie?" (lines 37–38), and then moves on to his own analysis of Millikan's methodologies without mentioning either scientist's background again.

C because the author does not discuss any experiments that refute Millikan's findings in this paragraph. Instead, he provides two quotations from two different scientists discussing the legitimacy of Millikan's methodologies. In fact, at no point during the passage does the author state that current experiments refute Millikan's results. Instead, the passage states that "students now replicate Millikan's results all across the world" (lines 87–88), which suggests that the opposite is true: modern experiments confirm Millikan's results.

D because the author does not discuss any attempts to replicate Millikan's experiments in this paragraph. Instead, the author provides two quotations from two different scientists discussing the legitimacy of Millikan's methodologies. In fact, at no point during the passage does the author state Millikan's contemporaries had difficulties replicating his findings.

Question 40. **The best answer is G** because the passage states that "the debate hangs on a phrase in Millikan's 1913 paper" (lines 39–40), meaning that the debate depends on the existence of Millikan's claim that his data table contained "*a complete summary of the results obtained on all of the 58 different drops upon which complete series of observations were made*" (lines 43–45). The debate centers entirely on this phrase and the discrepancies between this phrase and Millikan's notebooks: without the existence of this phrase, the debate surrounding Millikan's academic integrity would not exist. Therefore, it makes sense to say that the debate "depends on" a phrase in Millikan's 1913 paper.

The best answer is NOT:

F because it does not make sense to say that the debate "continues a phrase in Millikan's 1913 paper." This would suggest that the existence of the phrase is somehow being "continued" by the debate surrounding it, which is illogical.

H because it does not make sense to say that the debate "sticks with a phrase in Millikan's 1913 paper," because the phrase "sticks with" colloquially refers to a decision to endure an activity or to stay alongside a person, and this would suggest that the debate is somehow "enduring" or "remaining with" the phrase in Millikan's 1913 paper, which is illogical.

J because it doesn't make sense to say that the debate "blames on a phrase in Millikan's 1913 paper." Although it would make sense to say that the debate "is blamed on a phrase in Millikan's 1913 paper," the phrase "the debate blames on" doesn't make sense, because it's not clear what or who is being blamed, and what for, which makes this statement illogical.

Passage I

1. **The best answer is B.** According to Figure 1, CF_2Cl_2 has a boiling point of −30°C and a molecular mass of 130 amu. **A** is incorrect; CF_4, with a boiling point of −125°C, has a molecular mass of 90 amu. **B** is correct. **C** is incorrect; CCl_4, with a boiling point of 80°C, has a molecular mass of 150 amu. **D** is incorrect; CF_2Br_2, with a boiling point of 25°C, has a molecular mass of 210 amu.

2. **The best answer is J.** In Figure 1 BP is shown on the y-axis. The higher the position of a point on the graph relative to the y-axis, the greater the boiling point. Of the compounds listed in the answers, CCl_4 has the highest BP, approximately 75°C. **F** is incorrect; CF_4 has a boiling point of −125°C. **G** is incorrect; CF_2Cl_2 has a boiling point of −30°C. **H** is incorrect; CF_2Br_2 has a boiling point of 25°C. **J** is correct.

3. **The best answer is A.** Table 1 shows that of the three compounds listed, both the molecular mass and the BP of $CHCl_3$ are the lowest and those of CHI_3 are the highest. As the molecular mass increases, the BP increases. **A** is correct; this graph shows BP increasing as molecular mass increases. **B** is incorrect; this graph shows BP decreasing and then increasing as molecular mass increases. **C** is incorrect; this graph shows BP decreasing as molecular mass increases. **D** is incorrect; this graph shows BP increasing and then decreasing as molecular mass increases.

4. **The best answer is H.** According to Table 1, at 1 atmosphere of pressure, CH_2I_2 has a BP of 182°C and CH_4 has a BP of −162°C. The BP of CH_2I_2 is 344°C greater than the BP of CH_4 (182 − (−162) = 344). **F, G,** and **J** are incorrect; the difference is 344°C. **H** is correct.

5. **The best answer is A.** According to Figure 1, the molecular mass of CF_4 is approximately 90 amu. Of the compounds listed in the answers, the molecular mass of dichloromethane—85 amu—is closest to that of CF_4. **A** is correct. **B** is incorrect; the molecular mass of trichloromethane is 119 amu. **C** is incorrect; the molecular mass of iodomethane is 142 amu. **D** is incorrect; the molecular mass of dibromomethane is 174 amu.

6. **The best answer is H.** In order to answer this item, the examinee must understand how to interpret chemical formulas. CBr_4 contains 1 carbon atom and 4 bromine atoms. According to Figure 1, CBr_4 has a molecular mass of 330 amu. If C has a mass of 12 amu, then the mass of the 4 Br is 318 (330 − 12 = 318). The mass of 1 Br is 79.5 amu (318 ÷ 4 = 79.5). **F, G,** and **J** are incorrect; the atomic mass of Br is closest to 80 amu. **H** is correct.

Passage II

7. **The best answer is D.** According to the passage, the present-day CO_2 concentration was 370 ppm. Figure 3 shows that the percentage of U urushiols per plant in 2004 in the 370 ppm CO_2 plot was 90%. **A, B,** and **C** are incorrect; the percentage of U urushiols per plant was 90%. **D** is correct.

8. **The best answer is J.** Figure 2 shows that at the end of the study, in 2004, 40% of the original PIPs in the elevated CO_2 concentration plot survived and approximately 33% of the PIPs in the present-day CO_2 concentration plot survived. **F** and **G** are incorrect; the elevated CO_2 plot had the higher percentage of original PIPs surviving. **H** is incorrect; the difference was 7%. **J** is correct.

9. **The best answer is C.** According to the passage, the conditions in both plots were identical except for the CO_2 concentration. **A, B,** and **D** are incorrect; the CO_2 concentrations were not the same. **C** is correct.

10. **The best answer is H.** According to Figure 1, at all times the dry biomass per plant was greater for the elevated CO_2 concentration plot than for the present-day CO_2 concentration plot. **F, G,** and **J** are incorrect; the dry biomass per plant was always greater for the elevated CO_2 concentration plot. **H** is correct.

11. **The best answer is D.** According to Figure 2, in 2003, 40% of the original PIPs survived in the plot with a CO_2 concentration of 370 ppm, and therefore 60% of the original PIPs had died. **A, B,** and **C** are incorrect; 60% of the original PIPs had died. **D** is correct.

12. **The best answer is F.** Figure 3 shows that the present-day CO_2 concentration plot had 10% S urushiols per plant, and the elevated CO_2 concentration plot had 5% S urushiols per plant. The present-day CO_2 concentration plot had a higher percentage of S urushiols per plant. **F** is correct. **G** is incorrect; 10% of the urushiols were saturated. **H** and **J** are incorrect; a greater percentage was produced in the present-day CO_2 concentration plot.

SCIENCE • PRACTICE TEST 4 • EXPLANATORY ANSWERS

Passage III

13. **The best answer is B.** According to Figure 1, as the I_3^- concentration increases, the O_3 concentration also increases. Figure 3 shows that at both 2:30 p.m. and 4:00 p.m., the I_3^- concentration at Site C was lower than that at Site B. The I_3^- concentration at Site C at 2:30 p.m. was approximately 0.3 ppm, and the I_3^- concentration at Site C at 4:00 p.m. was approximately 1.4 ppm. The I_3^- concentration, and therefore the O_3 concentration, was lowest at Site C at 2:30 p.m. **A, C,** and **D** are incorrect; the O_3 was lowest at Site C at 2:30 p.m. **B** is correct.

14. **The best answer is H.** According to Figure 1, as the I_3^- concentration increases, the O_3 concentration also increases. Figure 3 shows that at 2:00 p.m., Site D had the lowest I_3^- concentration, and therefore O_3 concentration, followed by Site C and then Site A, and Site B had the highest I_3^- concentration. **F, G,** and **J** are incorrect; the correct order from lowest O_3 concentration to highest is Site D, Site C, Site A, Site B. **H** is correct.

15. **The best answer is B.** According to Figure 1, as the I_3^- concentration increases, the O_3 concentration also increases. Figure 3 shows that the highest I_3^- concentration, and therefore the highest O_3 concentration, was measured at Site B at 1:30 p.m. **A, C,** and **D** are incorrect; the highest I_3^- concentration, and therefore the highest O_3 concentration, was measured at Site B. **B** is correct.

16. **The best answer is G.** Figure 3 shows that at 5:00 p.m. the I_3^- concentration at Site B was 2.00 μmol/L and the I_3^- concentration at Site C at 2:00 p.m. was 1.00 μmol/L. According to Figure 1, this corresponds to an O_3 concentration of 80 ppb for Site B and 40 ppb for Site C. The O_3 concentration at Site B at 5:00 p.m. was two times greater than the O_3 concentration at Site C at 2:00 p.m. **F, H,** and **J** are incorrect; the O_3 concentration was two times greater at 5:00 p.m. at Site B than at 2:00 p.m. at Site C. **G** is correct.

17. **The best answer is C.** According to Figure 1, as the I_3^- concentration increased, the O_3 concentration also increased. Figure 3 shows that the I_3^- concentration was greater at 5:30 p.m. at Site A than at 4:00 p.m. Because the O_3 concentration increased as the I_3^- concentration increased, the O_3 concentration was also greater at 5:30 p.m. at Site A than at 4:00 p.m. **A** and **B** are incorrect; the O_3 concentration was greater at 5:30 p.m. **C** is correct. **D** is incorrect; the higher the I_3^- concentration, the higher the O_3 concentration.

18. **The best answer is J.** In order to answer this item, the examinee must understand proportional reasoning involving units of measure. According to the passage, in Step 2 the vacuum pump was turned on for 25 min. If the pump drew in air at a rate of 200 mL/min, then the volume of air drawn through the test tube each time Step 2 was performed is equal to $\frac{200 \text{ mL}}{1 \text{ min}} \times 25 \text{ min} = 5{,}000 \text{ mL}$. **F** is incorrect; 200 mL would be drawn through the test tube if the pump ran for 1 minute. **G** is incorrect; 550 mL would be drawn through the test tube if the pump ran for 2.75 min. **H** is incorrect; 2,500 mL would be drawn through the test tube if the pump ran for 12.5 min. **J** is correct; 5,000 mL would be drawn through the test tube if the pump ran for 25 min.

19. **The best answer is A.** In order to answer this item, the examinee must know the mathematical definition of percent error. According to Figure 3, at 12:30 p.m. at Site C, the measured, or experimental, value for the I_3^- concentration was 1.00 μmol/L. Figure 1 shows that an I_3^- concentration of 1.00 μmol/L corresponds to an O_3 concentration of 40 ppb. The percent error can be calculated as follows: $\left| \frac{\text{experimental value} - \text{actual value}}{\text{actual value}} \right| \times 100\% = \left| \frac{40 \text{ ppb} - 43 \text{ ppb}}{43 \text{ ppb}} \right| \times 100\%$. **A** is correct. **B** is incorrect; the divisor should be the actual value of 43 ppb. **C** and **D** are incorrect; the experimental value is 40 ppb.

Passage IV

20. **The best answer is F.** According to the results of Study 2, as the wavelength decreased, y_1 also decreased. At a wavelength of 400 nm, $y_1 = 10.0$ mm. A value of y_1 less than 10.0 mm would most likely be obtained at a wavelength shorter than 400 nm. **F** is correct. **G** is incorrect; when the wavelength was 500 nm, $y_1 = 12.5$ mm. **H** is incorrect; when the wavelength was 700 nm, $y_1 = 17.5$ mm. **J** is incorrect; at a wavelength of 900 mm, y_1 would most likely be greater than 17.5 mm.

21. **The best answer is C.** In Study 3, slit width and wavelength were fixed while x was varied. The results shown in Table 3 indicate that y_1 increased as x increased. **A** and **B** are incorrect; both graphs show y_1 decreasing as x increases. **C** is correct. **D** is incorrect; according to Table 3, when $x = 3.00$ m, $y_1 = 7.5$ mm. The graph shown in **D** does not show this data point.

22. **The best answer is F.** According to the passage, $x = 6.00$ m in Trial 2. Table 1 shows that for Trial 2, $y_1 = 15.0$ mm. The results of Study 3 in Table 3 show that as x increased, y_1 also increased. One would predict that repeating Trial 2 with $x = 9.00$ m would result in a value of y_1 greater than 15.0 mm. (This is confirmed by noting that Trial 11 is the same as Trial 2 with $x = 9.00$ m and $y_1 = 22.5$ mm.) **F** is correct. **G** is incorrect; y_1 increased and x increased. **H** and **J** are incorrect; y_1 would be greater than 15.0 mm.

23. **The best answer is D. A** is incorrect; the width of the slit was varied in Study 1. **B** is incorrect; the wavelength of the laser light was varied in Study 2. **C** is incorrect; the distance between the slit and the screen was varied in Study 3. **D** is correct; the distance between the slit and the laser was not varied in any of the studies.

24. **The best answer is F.** According to Table 2, the wavelength was shortest in Trial 5 (400 nm), and therefore the energy of the photons was greatest in Study 5. **F** is correct. **G** is incorrect; the wavelength of light used in Trial 6 was 500 nm, a longer wavelength than that used in Trial 5. **H** is incorrect; the wavelength of light used in Trial 7 was 600 nm, a longer wavelength than that used in Trial 5. **J** is incorrect; the wavelength of light used in Trial 8 was 700 nm, a longer wavelength than that used in Trial 5.

25. **The best answer is B.** According to Table 1, when the slit width was doubled from 0.12 mm to 0.24 mm, the distance between the bands (y_1) decreased from 30.0 mm to 15.0 mm. As the slit width doubled, y_1 was halved. **A** is incorrect; y_1 was cut in half. **B** is correct. **C** is incorrect; y_1 decreased. **D** is incorrect; y_1 consistently decreased by one-half. As slit width increased further, from 0.24 mm to 0.48 mm, y_1 decreased from 15.0 mm to 7.5 mm.

26. **The best answer is G.** In order to answer this item, the examinee must know that 1 m = 1,000 mm. According to Table 2, in Trial 7 $y_1 = 15.0$ mm. In meters this is equal to 0.015 m. **F, H,** and **J** are incorrect; 15.0 mm is equal to 0.015 m. **G** is correct.

Passage V

27. **The best answer is C.** According to Scientist 2, CO_2 and water vapor each account for 45% of the total gas output. CO accounts for 6%, and the remaining 4% is all other gases combined. **A** is incorrect; this pie chart does not include the other gases. **B** is incorrect; this pie chart indicates that 75% of the output is water vapor. **C** is correct; this pie chart correctly illustrates the percentage of each gas in the output. **D** is incorrect; this pie chart indicates that 75% of the output is water vapor.

28. **The best answer is F.** According to Scientist 1, ascending magma causes earthquakes. Scientist 2 states that magma rises toward Earth's surface and sometimes causes small fractures, but Scientist 2 does not state that the rising magma causes earthquakes. **F** is correct. **G, H,** and **J** are incorrect; Scientist 1 states that ascending magma causes earthquakes.

29. **The best answer is B.** According to the passage, Scientist 1 claims that the iron-rich lava and mantle rocks at HSVs are abundant in olivine and pyroxenes. Because feldspar is not abundant, it is most likely that Scientist 1 would expect basalt to be found at an HSV. Scientist 2 claims that feldspar is the most abundant mineral. It is most likely that Scientist 2 would expect phonolite to be found at an HSV. **A** is incorrect; because phonolite is rich in feldspar, Scientist 2 would expect phonolite to be found at an HSV. **B** is correct. **C** and **D** are incorrect; because phonolite is rich in feldspar, Scientist 1 would not expect phonolite to be found at an HSV.

30. **The best answer is G.** According to Scientist 1, the frequency of eruptions increases over time, but Scientist 2 claims that the eruption frequency will slow down over time. The discovery that older HSVs erupt more frequently than younger HSVs would best support the viewpoint of Scientist 1. **F** is incorrect; Scientist 1 claims that eruption frequency increases over time. **G** is correct. **H** and **J** are incorrect; the discovery would best support Scientist 1.

31. **The best answer is A.** Scientist 1 claims that mantle plumes exist at depths between 200 km and 400 km. Scientist 2 refers to the magma found at depths of less than 100 km. Only Scientist 1 discusses a process that may extend beneath the lithosphere (a depth below 200 km). **A** is correct. **B, C,** and **D** are incorrect; only Scientist 1 discusses a process that occurs beneath the lithosphere.

32. **The best answer is H.** Scientist 1 claims that the lavas at HSVs retain a lot of water from the mantle, but Scientist 2 claims that the lavas contain much less water than most mantle rocks. Assuming that not all the water was lost as water vapor, both scientists would most likely agree that the mantle rocks contained some water. **F, G,** and **J** are incorrect; both scientists would most likely agree that the rocks contained some water. **H** is correct.

33. **The best answer is D.** Scientist 2 states that a high concentration of dissolved CO_2 allows mantle rocks to melt at lower temperatures than they normally would. In this case, CO_2 is acting as a flux. **A** is incorrect; only Scientist 2's discussion includes flux melting. **B** is incorrect; CO_2 is the flux. **C** is incorrect; only Scientist 2's discussion includes flux melting. **D** is correct.

Passage VI

34. **The best answer is J.** According to Figure 3, when the GFP reporter gene was prepared with only RS2, the GFP reporter gene was expressed in cell types D, E, and F. **F, G,** and **H** are incorrect; the GFP reporter gene was expressed in cell types D, E, and F only. **J** is correct.

35. **The best answer is C.** According to the passage, GFP emits a green light when viewed with a certain microscope. In Experiment 1, GFP was not expressed in cell types A, C, and D. In Experiment 2, GFP was not expressed in cell types A or C. Throughout both experiments GFP was not expressed in cell types A or C, and therefore green light was not observed for cell types A or C. **A** and **B** are incorrect; green light was not observed for cell types A and C. **C** is correct. **D** is incorrect; because GFP was expressed in cell type D when the reporter gene contained only RS2 and the coding region, green light was observed for cell type D.

36. **The best answer is H.** According to Figure 2, when GFP reporter genes containing RS1–RS3 and the coding region for GFP were prepared and transfected into cells, the GFP reporter gene was expressed in cell types B, E, and F. If the reporter gene containing RS1–RS3 and the coding region for β-galactosidase was transfected into cell types A–F, then one would predict that cell types B, E, and F would show enzymatic activity. **F, G,** and **J** are incorrect; RS1–RS3 appear to be responsible for turning on gene expression in cell types B, E, and F, and therefore one would expect cell types B, E, and F to have enzymatic activity. **H** is correct.

37. **The best answer is B.** According to Figure 3, the GFP reporter gene was expressed in cell type F when the gene contained RS2 and when the gene contained RS1 and RS2, but the GFP reporter gene was not expressed in cell type F when the gene contained only RS1, indicating that the expression was turned on by RS2. **A** is incorrect; the GFP reporter gene was not expressed when only RS1 was present. **B** is correct; the GFP reporter gene was expressed when only RS2 was present. **C** is incorrect; the GFP reporter gene was not expressed when only RS3 was present. **D** is incorrect; the GFP reporter gene was expressed when only RS2 was present.

38. **The best answer is G.** According to the passage, reporter genes code for easily detectable proteins. Studying the reporter genes would make it much easier to determine the influence of the RSs. **F** is incorrect; it is most likely that the protein product of the reporter gene was more easily observed than the protein product of Gene X. **G** is correct. **H** is incorrect; the passage states that the three RSs were thought to be associated with Gene X. **J** is incorrect; the studies show that the three RSs did control the expression of the reporter genes.

39. **The best answer is C.** According to Figure 3, gene expression in cell type D was turned on when RS2 was used alone. Because gene expression in cell type D was turned off when RS1 and RS2 were both used, it can be concluded that RS1 turns off gene expression in cell type D. **A** is incorrect; gene expression is not turned on by RS1 in any cell type studied. **B** is incorrect; gene expression is turned on by RS2 in cell type D, but this does not explain why gene expression was turned off in cell type D when RS1 and RS2 were combined. **C** is correct. **D** is incorrect; gene expression is not turned off by RS2.

40. **The best answer is J.** According to Figures 2 and 3, RS1 appears to turn off GFP reporter gene expression in cell type D; RS2 appears to turn on expression in cell types D, E, and F; and RS3 appears to turn on gene expression in cell type B. All three RSs appear to control the expression of GFP reporter genes in one or more cell types. If the three RSs have the same control over the expression of Gene X, then the results indicate that the expression of Gene X is controlled by each RS in at least one cell type. **F** and **G** are incorrect; all three RSs do appear to control the expression of Gene X. **H** is incorrect; none of the RSs appears to affect expression in all the cell types. **J** is correct.

The ACT® *Sample Answer Document*

EXAMINEE STATEMENTS, CERTIFICATION, AND SIGNATURE

1. **Statements**: I understand that by registering for, launching, starting, or submitting answer documents for an ACT® test, I am agreeing to comply with and be bound by the *Terms and Conditions: Testing Rules and Policies for the ACT® Test* ("Terms").

I UNDERSTAND AND AGREE THAT THE TERMS PERMIT ACT TO CANCEL MY SCORES IN CERTAIN CIRCUMSTANCES. THE TERMS ALSO LIMIT DAMAGES AVAILABLE TO ME AND REQUIRE ARBITRATION OF CERTAIN DISPUTES. BY AGREEING TO ARBITRATION, ACT AND I BOTH WAIVE THE RIGHT TO HAVE THOSE DISPUTES HEARD BY A JUDGE OR JURY.

I understand that ACT owns the test questions and responses, and I will not share them with anyone by any form of communication before, during, or after the test administration. I understand that taking the test for someone else may violate the law and subject me to legal penalties. I consent to the collection and processing of personally identifying information I provide, and its subsequent use and disclosure, as described in the ACT Privacy Policy (www.act.org/privacy.html). I also permit ACT to transfer my personally identifying information to the United States, to ACT, or to a third-party service provider, where it will be subject to use and disclosure under the laws of the United States, including being accessible to law enforcement or national security authorities.

2. **Certification**: Copy the italicized certification below, then sign and date in the spaces provided.

*I agree to the **Statements** above and certify that I am the person whose information appears on this form.*

_____

_____

_____   _____
Your Signature   Today's Date

Do NOT mark in this shaded area.

USE A NO. 2 PENCIL ONLY.
(Do NOT use a mechanical pencil, ink, ballpoint, correction fluid, or felt-tip pen.)

A NAME, MAILING ADDRESS, AND TELEPHONE
(Please print.)

Last Name   First Name   MI (Middle Initial)

House Number & Street (Apt. No.); or PO Box & No.; or RR & No.

City   State/Province   ZIP/Postal Code

Area Code   Number   Country

ACT, Inc.—**Confidential Restricted when data present**

ALL examinees must complete block A – please print.

Blocks B, C, and D are required for all examinees. Find the MATCHING INFORMATION on your ticket. Enter it EXACTLY the same way, even if any of the information is missing or incorrect. Fill in the corresponding ovals. If you do not complete these blocks to match your previous information EXACTLY, your scores will be **delayed up to 8 weeks**.

ACT®

PO BOX 168, IOWA CITY, IA 52243-0168

01121523W   (A)203023-001:654321   ISD36401   Printed in the US.

B MATCH NAME (First 5 letters of last name)

C MATCH NUMBER

D DATE OF BIRTH

Month	Day	Year
January		
February		
March		
April		
May		
June		
July		
August		
September		
October		
November		
December		

Taking Additional Practice Tests

The ONLY Official Prep Guide from the Makers of the ACT

PAGE 2

Marking Directions: Mark only **one** oval for each question. Fill in response completely. Erase errors cleanly without smudging.

Correct mark: ⚪ ⚫ ⚪ ⚪

Do **NOT** use these *incorrect* or *bad* marks.

Incorrect marks: ⊘ ⊗ ⬤ ⊖
Overlapping mark: ⊘
Cross-out mark: ⊘
Smudged erasure: ⚪ ⚪ ⚪ ⚪
Mark is too light: ⚪ ⚪ ⚪ ⚪

BOOKLET NUMBER

① ① ① ① ① ① ① ① ①
② ② ② ② ② ② ② ② ②
③ ③ ③ ③ ③ ③ ③ ③ ③
④ ④ ④ ④ ④ ④ ④ ④ ④
⑤ ⑤ ⑤ ⑤ ⑤ ⑤ ⑤ ⑤ ⑤
⑥ ⑥ ⑥ ⑥ ⑥ ⑥ ⑥ ⑥ ⑥
⑦ ⑦ ⑦ ⑦ ⑦ ⑦ ⑦ ⑦ ⑦
⑧ ⑧ ⑧ ⑧ ⑧ ⑧ ⑧ ⑧ ⑧
⑨ ⑨ ⑨ ⑨ ⑨ ⑨ ⑨ ⑨ ⑨
⓪ ⓪ ⓪ ⓪ ⓪ ⓪ ⓪ ⓪ ⓪

Print your 5-character **Test Form** in the boxes at the right <u>and</u> fill in the corresponding ovals.

FORM

① ① Ⓜ Ⓒ ①
② ②   ②
③   ③
④   ④
⑤   ⑤
⑥   ⑥
⑦   ⑦
⑧   ⑧
⑨   ⑨
⓪   ⓪

TEST 1: ENGLISH

1 Ⓐ Ⓑ Ⓒ Ⓓ	14 Ⓕ Ⓖ Ⓗ Ⓙ	27 Ⓐ Ⓑ Ⓒ Ⓓ	40 Ⓕ Ⓖ Ⓗ Ⓙ	53 Ⓐ Ⓑ Ⓒ Ⓓ	66 Ⓕ Ⓖ Ⓗ Ⓙ
2 Ⓕ Ⓖ Ⓗ Ⓙ	15 Ⓐ Ⓑ Ⓒ Ⓓ	28 Ⓕ Ⓖ Ⓗ Ⓙ	41 Ⓐ Ⓑ Ⓒ Ⓓ	54 Ⓕ Ⓖ Ⓗ Ⓙ	67 Ⓐ Ⓑ Ⓒ Ⓓ
3 Ⓐ Ⓑ Ⓒ Ⓓ	16 Ⓕ Ⓖ Ⓗ Ⓙ	29 Ⓐ Ⓑ Ⓒ Ⓓ	42 Ⓕ Ⓖ Ⓗ Ⓙ	55 Ⓐ Ⓑ Ⓒ Ⓓ	68 Ⓕ Ⓖ Ⓗ Ⓙ
4 Ⓕ Ⓖ Ⓗ Ⓙ	17 Ⓐ Ⓑ Ⓒ Ⓓ	30 Ⓕ Ⓖ Ⓗ Ⓙ	43 Ⓐ Ⓑ Ⓒ Ⓓ	56 Ⓕ Ⓖ Ⓗ Ⓙ	69 Ⓐ Ⓑ Ⓒ Ⓓ
5 Ⓐ Ⓑ Ⓒ Ⓓ	18 Ⓕ Ⓖ Ⓗ Ⓙ	31 Ⓐ Ⓑ Ⓒ Ⓓ	44 Ⓕ Ⓖ Ⓗ Ⓙ	57 Ⓐ Ⓑ Ⓒ Ⓓ	70 Ⓕ Ⓖ Ⓗ Ⓙ
6 Ⓕ Ⓖ Ⓗ Ⓙ	19 Ⓐ Ⓑ Ⓒ Ⓓ	32 Ⓕ Ⓖ Ⓗ Ⓙ	45 Ⓐ Ⓑ Ⓒ Ⓓ	58 Ⓕ Ⓖ Ⓗ Ⓙ	71 Ⓐ Ⓑ Ⓒ Ⓓ
7 Ⓐ Ⓑ Ⓒ Ⓓ	20 Ⓕ Ⓖ Ⓗ Ⓙ	33 Ⓐ Ⓑ Ⓒ Ⓓ	46 Ⓕ Ⓖ Ⓗ Ⓙ	59 Ⓐ Ⓑ Ⓒ Ⓓ	72 Ⓕ Ⓖ Ⓗ Ⓙ
8 Ⓕ Ⓖ Ⓗ Ⓙ	21 Ⓐ Ⓑ Ⓒ Ⓓ	34 Ⓕ Ⓖ Ⓗ Ⓙ	47 Ⓐ Ⓑ Ⓒ Ⓓ	60 Ⓕ Ⓖ Ⓗ Ⓙ	73 Ⓐ Ⓑ Ⓒ Ⓓ
9 Ⓐ Ⓑ Ⓒ Ⓓ	22 Ⓕ Ⓖ Ⓗ Ⓙ	35 Ⓐ Ⓑ Ⓒ Ⓓ	48 Ⓕ Ⓖ Ⓗ Ⓙ	61 Ⓐ Ⓑ Ⓒ Ⓓ	74 Ⓕ Ⓖ Ⓗ Ⓙ
10 Ⓕ Ⓖ Ⓗ Ⓙ	23 Ⓐ Ⓑ Ⓒ Ⓓ	36 Ⓕ Ⓖ Ⓗ Ⓙ	49 Ⓐ Ⓑ Ⓒ Ⓓ	62 Ⓕ Ⓖ Ⓗ Ⓙ	75 Ⓐ Ⓑ Ⓒ Ⓓ
11 Ⓐ Ⓑ Ⓒ Ⓓ	24 Ⓕ Ⓖ Ⓗ Ⓙ	37 Ⓐ Ⓑ Ⓒ Ⓓ	50 Ⓕ Ⓖ Ⓗ Ⓙ	63 Ⓐ Ⓑ Ⓒ Ⓓ	
12 Ⓕ Ⓖ Ⓗ Ⓙ	25 Ⓐ Ⓑ Ⓒ Ⓓ	38 Ⓕ Ⓖ Ⓗ Ⓙ	51 Ⓐ Ⓑ Ⓒ Ⓓ	64 Ⓕ Ⓖ Ⓗ Ⓙ	
13 Ⓐ Ⓑ Ⓒ Ⓓ	26 Ⓕ Ⓖ Ⓗ Ⓙ	39 Ⓐ Ⓑ Ⓒ Ⓓ	52 Ⓕ Ⓖ Ⓗ Ⓙ	65 Ⓐ Ⓑ Ⓒ Ⓓ	

TEST 2: MATHEMATICS

1 Ⓐ Ⓑ Ⓒ Ⓓ Ⓔ	11 Ⓐ Ⓑ Ⓒ Ⓓ Ⓔ	21 Ⓐ Ⓑ Ⓒ Ⓓ Ⓔ	31 Ⓐ Ⓑ Ⓒ Ⓓ Ⓔ	41 Ⓐ Ⓑ Ⓒ Ⓓ Ⓔ	51 Ⓐ Ⓑ Ⓒ Ⓓ Ⓔ
2 Ⓕ Ⓖ Ⓗ Ⓙ Ⓚ	12 Ⓕ Ⓖ Ⓗ Ⓙ Ⓚ	22 Ⓕ Ⓖ Ⓗ Ⓙ Ⓚ	32 Ⓕ Ⓖ Ⓗ Ⓙ Ⓚ	42 Ⓕ Ⓖ Ⓗ Ⓙ Ⓚ	52 Ⓕ Ⓖ Ⓗ Ⓙ Ⓚ
3 Ⓐ Ⓑ Ⓒ Ⓓ Ⓔ	13 Ⓐ Ⓑ Ⓒ Ⓓ Ⓔ	23 Ⓐ Ⓑ Ⓒ Ⓓ Ⓔ	33 Ⓐ Ⓑ Ⓒ Ⓓ Ⓔ	43 Ⓐ Ⓑ Ⓒ Ⓓ Ⓔ	53 Ⓐ Ⓑ Ⓒ Ⓓ Ⓔ
4 Ⓕ Ⓖ Ⓗ Ⓙ Ⓚ	14 Ⓕ Ⓖ Ⓗ Ⓙ Ⓚ	24 Ⓕ Ⓖ Ⓗ Ⓙ Ⓚ	34 Ⓕ Ⓖ Ⓗ Ⓙ Ⓚ	44 Ⓕ Ⓖ Ⓗ Ⓙ Ⓚ	54 Ⓕ Ⓖ Ⓗ Ⓙ Ⓚ
5 Ⓐ Ⓑ Ⓒ Ⓓ Ⓔ	15 Ⓐ Ⓑ Ⓒ Ⓓ Ⓔ	25 Ⓐ Ⓑ Ⓒ Ⓓ Ⓔ	35 Ⓐ Ⓑ Ⓒ Ⓓ Ⓔ	45 Ⓐ Ⓑ Ⓒ Ⓓ Ⓔ	55 Ⓐ Ⓑ Ⓒ Ⓓ Ⓔ
6 Ⓕ Ⓖ Ⓗ Ⓙ Ⓚ	16 Ⓕ Ⓖ Ⓗ Ⓙ Ⓚ	26 Ⓕ Ⓖ Ⓗ Ⓙ Ⓚ	36 Ⓕ Ⓖ Ⓗ Ⓙ Ⓚ	46 Ⓕ Ⓖ Ⓗ Ⓙ Ⓚ	56 Ⓕ Ⓖ Ⓗ Ⓙ Ⓚ
7 Ⓐ Ⓑ Ⓒ Ⓓ Ⓔ	17 Ⓐ Ⓑ Ⓒ Ⓓ Ⓔ	27 Ⓐ Ⓑ Ⓒ Ⓓ Ⓔ	37 Ⓐ Ⓑ Ⓒ Ⓓ Ⓔ	47 Ⓐ Ⓑ Ⓒ Ⓓ Ⓔ	57 Ⓐ Ⓑ Ⓒ Ⓓ Ⓔ
8 Ⓕ Ⓖ Ⓗ Ⓙ Ⓚ	18 Ⓕ Ⓖ Ⓗ Ⓙ Ⓚ	28 Ⓕ Ⓖ Ⓗ Ⓙ Ⓚ	38 Ⓕ Ⓖ Ⓗ Ⓙ Ⓚ	48 Ⓕ Ⓖ Ⓗ Ⓙ Ⓚ	58 Ⓕ Ⓖ Ⓗ Ⓙ Ⓚ
9 Ⓐ Ⓑ Ⓒ Ⓓ Ⓔ	19 Ⓐ Ⓑ Ⓒ Ⓓ Ⓔ	29 Ⓐ Ⓑ Ⓒ Ⓓ Ⓔ	39 Ⓐ Ⓑ Ⓒ Ⓓ Ⓔ	49 Ⓐ Ⓑ Ⓒ Ⓓ Ⓔ	59 Ⓐ Ⓑ Ⓒ Ⓓ Ⓔ
10 Ⓕ Ⓖ Ⓗ Ⓙ Ⓚ	20 Ⓕ Ⓖ Ⓗ Ⓙ Ⓚ	30 Ⓕ Ⓖ Ⓗ Ⓙ Ⓚ	40 Ⓕ Ⓖ Ⓗ Ⓙ Ⓚ	50 Ⓕ Ⓖ Ⓗ Ⓙ Ⓚ	60 Ⓕ Ⓖ Ⓗ Ⓙ Ⓚ

TEST 3: READING

1 Ⓐ Ⓑ Ⓒ Ⓓ	8 Ⓕ Ⓖ Ⓗ Ⓙ	15 Ⓐ Ⓑ Ⓒ Ⓓ	22 Ⓕ Ⓖ Ⓗ Ⓙ	29 Ⓐ Ⓑ Ⓒ Ⓓ	36 Ⓕ Ⓖ Ⓗ Ⓙ
2 Ⓕ Ⓖ Ⓗ Ⓙ	9 Ⓐ Ⓑ Ⓒ Ⓓ	16 Ⓕ Ⓖ Ⓗ Ⓙ	23 Ⓐ Ⓑ Ⓒ Ⓓ	30 Ⓕ Ⓖ Ⓗ Ⓙ	37 Ⓐ Ⓑ Ⓒ Ⓓ
3 Ⓐ Ⓑ Ⓒ Ⓓ	10 Ⓕ Ⓖ Ⓗ Ⓙ	17 Ⓐ Ⓑ Ⓒ Ⓓ	24 Ⓕ Ⓖ Ⓗ Ⓙ	31 Ⓐ Ⓑ Ⓒ Ⓓ	38 Ⓕ Ⓖ Ⓗ Ⓙ
4 Ⓕ Ⓖ Ⓗ Ⓙ	11 Ⓐ Ⓑ Ⓒ Ⓓ	18 Ⓕ Ⓖ Ⓗ Ⓙ	25 Ⓐ Ⓑ Ⓒ Ⓓ	32 Ⓕ Ⓖ Ⓗ Ⓙ	39 Ⓐ Ⓑ Ⓒ Ⓓ
5 Ⓐ Ⓑ Ⓒ Ⓓ	12 Ⓕ Ⓖ Ⓗ Ⓙ	19 Ⓐ Ⓑ Ⓒ Ⓓ	26 Ⓕ Ⓖ Ⓗ Ⓙ	33 Ⓐ Ⓑ Ⓒ Ⓓ	40 Ⓕ Ⓖ Ⓗ Ⓙ
6 Ⓕ Ⓖ Ⓗ Ⓙ	13 Ⓐ Ⓑ Ⓒ Ⓓ	20 Ⓕ Ⓖ Ⓗ Ⓙ	27 Ⓐ Ⓑ Ⓒ Ⓓ	34 Ⓕ Ⓖ Ⓗ Ⓙ	
7 Ⓐ Ⓑ Ⓒ Ⓓ	14 Ⓕ Ⓖ Ⓗ Ⓙ	21 Ⓐ Ⓑ Ⓒ Ⓓ	28 Ⓕ Ⓖ Ⓗ Ⓙ	35 Ⓐ Ⓑ Ⓒ Ⓓ	

TEST 4: SCIENCE

1 Ⓐ Ⓑ Ⓒ Ⓓ	8 Ⓕ Ⓖ Ⓗ Ⓙ	15 Ⓐ Ⓑ Ⓒ Ⓓ	22 Ⓕ Ⓖ Ⓗ Ⓙ	29 Ⓐ Ⓑ Ⓒ Ⓓ	36 Ⓕ Ⓖ Ⓗ Ⓙ
2 Ⓕ Ⓖ Ⓗ Ⓙ	9 Ⓐ Ⓑ Ⓒ Ⓓ	16 Ⓕ Ⓖ Ⓗ Ⓙ	23 Ⓐ Ⓑ Ⓒ Ⓓ	30 Ⓕ Ⓖ Ⓗ Ⓙ	37 Ⓐ Ⓑ Ⓒ Ⓓ
3 Ⓐ Ⓑ Ⓒ Ⓓ	10 Ⓕ Ⓖ Ⓗ Ⓙ	17 Ⓐ Ⓑ Ⓒ Ⓓ	24 Ⓕ Ⓖ Ⓗ Ⓙ	31 Ⓐ Ⓑ Ⓒ Ⓓ	38 Ⓕ Ⓖ Ⓗ Ⓙ
4 Ⓕ Ⓖ Ⓗ Ⓙ	11 Ⓐ Ⓑ Ⓒ Ⓓ	18 Ⓕ Ⓖ Ⓗ Ⓙ	25 Ⓐ Ⓑ Ⓒ Ⓓ	32 Ⓕ Ⓖ Ⓗ Ⓙ	39 Ⓐ Ⓑ Ⓒ Ⓓ
5 Ⓐ Ⓑ Ⓒ Ⓓ	12 Ⓕ Ⓖ Ⓗ Ⓙ	19 Ⓐ Ⓑ Ⓒ Ⓓ	26 Ⓕ Ⓖ Ⓗ Ⓙ	33 Ⓐ Ⓑ Ⓒ Ⓓ	40 Ⓕ Ⓖ Ⓗ Ⓙ
6 Ⓕ Ⓖ Ⓗ Ⓙ	13 Ⓐ Ⓑ Ⓒ Ⓓ	20 Ⓕ Ⓖ Ⓗ Ⓙ	27 Ⓐ Ⓑ Ⓒ Ⓓ	34 Ⓕ Ⓖ Ⓗ Ⓙ	
7 Ⓐ Ⓑ Ⓒ Ⓓ	14 Ⓕ Ⓖ Ⓗ Ⓙ	21 Ⓐ Ⓑ Ⓒ Ⓓ	28 Ⓕ Ⓖ Ⓗ Ⓙ	35 Ⓐ Ⓑ Ⓒ Ⓓ	

The ACT® *Sample Answer Document*

EXAMINEE STATEMENTS, CERTIFICATION, AND SIGNATURE

1. **Statements**: I understand that by registering for, launching, starting, or submitting answer documents for an ACT® test, I am agreeing to comply with and be bound by the *Terms and Conditions: Testing Rules and Policies for the ACT® Test* ("Terms").

   I UNDERSTAND AND AGREE THAT THE TERMS PERMIT ACT TO CANCEL MY SCORES IN CERTAIN CIRCUMSTANCES. THE TERMS ALSO LIMIT DAMAGES AVAILABLE TO ME AND REQUIRE ARBITRATION OF CERTAIN DISPUTES. BY AGREEING TO ARBITRATION, ACT AND I BOTH WAIVE THE RIGHT TO HAVE THOSE DISPUTES HEARD BY A JUDGE OR JURY.

   I understand that ACT owns the test questions and responses, and I will not share them with anyone by any form of communication before, during, or after the test administration. I understand that taking the test for someone else may violate the law and subject me to legal penalties. I consent to the collection and processing of personally identifying information I provide, and its subsequent use and disclosure, as described in the ACT Privacy Policy (www.act.org/privacy.html). I also permit ACT to transfer my personally identifying information to the United States, to ACT, or to a third-party service provider, where it will be subject to use and disclosure under the laws of the United States, including being accessible to law enforcement or national security authorities.

2. **Certification**: Copy the italicized certification below, then sign and date in the spaces provided.

*I agree to the **Statements** above and certify that I am the person whose information appears on this form.*

_____

_____

_____   _____
Your Signature   Today's Date

Do NOT mark in this shaded area.

USE A NO. 2 PENCIL ONLY.
(Do NOT use a mechanical pencil, ink, ballpoint, correction fluid, or felt-tip pen.)

A
NAME, MAILING ADDRESS, AND TELEPHONE
(Please print.)

Last Name   First Name   MI (Middle Initial)

House Number & Street (Apt. No.); or PO Box & No.; or RR & No.

City   State/Province   ZIP/Postal Code

Area Code   Number   Country

ACT, Inc.—Confidential Restricted when data present

ALL examinees must complete block A – please print.

Blocks B, C, and D are required for all examinees. Find the MATCHING INFORMATION on your ticket. Enter it EXACTLY the same way, even if any of the information is missing or incorrect. Fill in the corresponding ovals. If you do not complete these blocks to match your previous information EXACTLY, your scores will be **delayed up to 8 weeks.**

ACT®
PO BOX 168, IOWA CITY, IA 52243-0168

B MATCH NAME
(First 5 letters of last name)

C MATCH NUMBER

D DATE OF BIRTH

Month	Day	Year
○ January		
○ February		
○ March		
○ April		
○ May		
○ June		
○ July		
○ August		
○ September		
○ October		
○ November		
○ December		

01121523W   (A)203023-001:654321   ISD36401   Printed in the US.

PAGE 2

Marking Directions: Mark only **one** oval for each question. Fill in response completely. Erase errors cleanly without smudging.

Correct mark: ○ ● ○ ○

Do NOT use these *incorrect* or *bad* marks.

Incorrect marks: ⊘ ⊗ ⊖ ⊙
Overlapping mark: ○ ○ ◖◗ ○
Cross-out mark: ○ ◉ ○ ○
Smudged erasure: ○ ○ ◌ ○
Mark is too light: ◌ ○ ○ ○

BOOKLET NUMBER

(grid of ovals numbered 1–0 in ten columns)

Print your 5-character **Test Form** in the boxes at the right and fill in the corresponding ovals.

FORM

(grid of ovals: ① ① Ⓜ Ⓒ ①, ② ②, ③, ④, ⑤, ⑥, ⑦, ⑧, ⑨, ⑩)

TEST 1: ENGLISH

1 Ⓐ Ⓑ Ⓒ Ⓓ	14 Ⓕ Ⓖ Ⓗ Ⓙ	27 Ⓐ Ⓑ Ⓒ Ⓓ	40 Ⓕ Ⓖ Ⓗ Ⓙ	53 Ⓐ Ⓑ Ⓒ Ⓓ	66 Ⓕ Ⓖ Ⓗ Ⓙ
2 Ⓕ Ⓖ Ⓗ Ⓙ	15 Ⓐ Ⓑ Ⓒ Ⓓ	28 Ⓕ Ⓖ Ⓗ Ⓙ	41 Ⓐ Ⓑ Ⓒ Ⓓ	54 Ⓕ Ⓖ Ⓗ Ⓙ	67 Ⓐ Ⓑ Ⓒ Ⓓ
3 Ⓐ Ⓑ Ⓒ Ⓓ	16 Ⓕ Ⓖ Ⓗ Ⓙ	29 Ⓐ Ⓑ Ⓒ Ⓓ	42 Ⓕ Ⓖ Ⓗ Ⓙ	55 Ⓐ Ⓑ Ⓒ Ⓓ	68 Ⓕ Ⓖ Ⓗ Ⓙ
4 Ⓕ Ⓖ Ⓗ Ⓙ	17 Ⓐ Ⓑ Ⓒ Ⓓ	30 Ⓕ Ⓖ Ⓗ Ⓙ	43 Ⓐ Ⓑ Ⓒ Ⓓ	56 Ⓕ Ⓖ Ⓗ Ⓙ	69 Ⓐ Ⓑ Ⓒ Ⓓ
5 Ⓐ Ⓑ Ⓒ Ⓓ	18 Ⓕ Ⓖ Ⓗ Ⓙ	31 Ⓐ Ⓑ Ⓒ Ⓓ	44 Ⓕ Ⓖ Ⓗ Ⓙ	57 Ⓐ Ⓑ Ⓒ Ⓓ	70 Ⓕ Ⓖ Ⓗ Ⓙ
6 Ⓕ Ⓖ Ⓗ Ⓙ	19 Ⓐ Ⓑ Ⓒ Ⓓ	32 Ⓕ Ⓖ Ⓗ Ⓙ	45 Ⓐ Ⓑ Ⓒ Ⓓ	58 Ⓕ Ⓖ Ⓗ Ⓙ	71 Ⓐ Ⓑ Ⓒ Ⓓ
7 Ⓐ Ⓑ Ⓒ Ⓓ	20 Ⓕ Ⓖ Ⓗ Ⓙ	33 Ⓐ Ⓑ Ⓒ Ⓓ	46 Ⓕ Ⓖ Ⓗ Ⓙ	59 Ⓐ Ⓑ Ⓒ Ⓓ	72 Ⓕ Ⓖ Ⓗ Ⓙ
8 Ⓕ Ⓖ Ⓗ Ⓙ	21 Ⓐ Ⓑ Ⓒ Ⓓ	34 Ⓕ Ⓖ Ⓗ Ⓙ	47 Ⓐ Ⓑ Ⓒ Ⓓ	60 Ⓕ Ⓖ Ⓗ Ⓙ	73 Ⓐ Ⓑ Ⓒ Ⓓ
9 Ⓐ Ⓑ Ⓒ Ⓓ	22 Ⓕ Ⓖ Ⓗ Ⓙ	35 Ⓐ Ⓑ Ⓒ Ⓓ	48 Ⓕ Ⓖ Ⓗ Ⓙ	61 Ⓐ Ⓑ Ⓒ Ⓓ	74 Ⓕ Ⓖ Ⓗ Ⓙ
10 Ⓕ Ⓖ Ⓗ Ⓙ	23 Ⓐ Ⓑ Ⓒ Ⓓ	36 Ⓕ Ⓖ Ⓗ Ⓙ	49 Ⓐ Ⓑ Ⓒ Ⓓ	62 Ⓕ Ⓖ Ⓗ Ⓙ	75 Ⓐ Ⓑ Ⓒ Ⓓ
11 Ⓐ Ⓑ Ⓒ Ⓓ	24 Ⓕ Ⓖ Ⓗ Ⓙ	37 Ⓐ Ⓑ Ⓒ Ⓓ	50 Ⓕ Ⓖ Ⓗ Ⓙ	63 Ⓐ Ⓑ Ⓒ Ⓓ	
12 Ⓕ Ⓖ Ⓗ Ⓙ	25 Ⓐ Ⓑ Ⓒ Ⓓ	38 Ⓕ Ⓖ Ⓗ Ⓙ	51 Ⓐ Ⓑ Ⓒ Ⓓ	64 Ⓕ Ⓖ Ⓗ Ⓙ	
13 Ⓐ Ⓑ Ⓒ Ⓓ	26 Ⓕ Ⓖ Ⓗ Ⓙ	39 Ⓐ Ⓑ Ⓒ Ⓓ	52 Ⓕ Ⓖ Ⓗ Ⓙ	65 Ⓐ Ⓑ Ⓒ Ⓓ	

TEST 2: MATHEMATICS

1 Ⓐ Ⓑ Ⓒ Ⓓ Ⓔ	11 Ⓐ Ⓑ Ⓒ Ⓓ Ⓔ	21 Ⓐ Ⓑ Ⓒ Ⓓ Ⓔ	31 Ⓐ Ⓑ Ⓒ Ⓓ Ⓔ	41 Ⓐ Ⓑ Ⓒ Ⓓ Ⓔ	51 Ⓐ Ⓑ Ⓒ Ⓓ Ⓔ
2 Ⓕ Ⓖ Ⓗ Ⓙ Ⓚ	12 Ⓕ Ⓖ Ⓗ Ⓙ Ⓚ	22 Ⓕ Ⓖ Ⓗ Ⓙ Ⓚ	32 Ⓕ Ⓖ Ⓗ Ⓙ Ⓚ	42 Ⓕ Ⓖ Ⓗ Ⓙ Ⓚ	52 Ⓕ Ⓖ Ⓗ Ⓙ Ⓚ
3 Ⓐ Ⓑ Ⓒ Ⓓ Ⓔ	13 Ⓐ Ⓑ Ⓒ Ⓓ Ⓔ	23 Ⓐ Ⓑ Ⓒ Ⓓ Ⓔ	33 Ⓐ Ⓑ Ⓒ Ⓓ Ⓔ	43 Ⓐ Ⓑ Ⓒ Ⓓ Ⓔ	53 Ⓐ Ⓑ Ⓒ Ⓓ Ⓔ
4 Ⓕ Ⓖ Ⓗ Ⓙ Ⓚ	14 Ⓕ Ⓖ Ⓗ Ⓙ Ⓚ	24 Ⓕ Ⓖ Ⓗ Ⓙ Ⓚ	34 Ⓕ Ⓖ Ⓗ Ⓙ Ⓚ	44 Ⓕ Ⓖ Ⓗ Ⓙ Ⓚ	54 Ⓕ Ⓖ Ⓗ Ⓙ Ⓚ
5 Ⓐ Ⓑ Ⓒ Ⓓ Ⓔ	15 Ⓐ Ⓑ Ⓒ Ⓓ Ⓔ	25 Ⓐ Ⓑ Ⓒ Ⓓ Ⓔ	35 Ⓐ Ⓑ Ⓒ Ⓓ Ⓔ	45 Ⓐ Ⓑ Ⓒ Ⓓ Ⓔ	55 Ⓐ Ⓑ Ⓒ Ⓓ Ⓔ
6 Ⓕ Ⓖ Ⓗ Ⓙ Ⓚ	16 Ⓕ Ⓖ Ⓗ Ⓙ Ⓚ	26 Ⓕ Ⓖ Ⓗ Ⓙ Ⓚ	36 Ⓕ Ⓖ Ⓗ Ⓙ Ⓚ	46 Ⓕ Ⓖ Ⓗ Ⓙ Ⓚ	56 Ⓕ Ⓖ Ⓗ Ⓙ Ⓚ
7 Ⓐ Ⓑ Ⓒ Ⓓ Ⓔ	17 Ⓐ Ⓑ Ⓒ Ⓓ Ⓔ	27 Ⓐ Ⓑ Ⓒ Ⓓ Ⓔ	37 Ⓐ Ⓑ Ⓒ Ⓓ Ⓔ	47 Ⓐ Ⓑ Ⓒ Ⓓ Ⓔ	57 Ⓐ Ⓑ Ⓒ Ⓓ Ⓔ
8 Ⓕ Ⓖ Ⓗ Ⓙ Ⓚ	18 Ⓕ Ⓖ Ⓗ Ⓙ Ⓚ	28 Ⓕ Ⓖ Ⓗ Ⓙ Ⓚ	38 Ⓕ Ⓖ Ⓗ Ⓙ Ⓚ	48 Ⓕ Ⓖ Ⓗ Ⓙ Ⓚ	58 Ⓕ Ⓖ Ⓗ Ⓙ Ⓚ
9 Ⓐ Ⓑ Ⓒ Ⓓ Ⓔ	19 Ⓐ Ⓑ Ⓒ Ⓓ Ⓔ	29 Ⓐ Ⓑ Ⓒ Ⓓ Ⓔ	39 Ⓐ Ⓑ Ⓒ Ⓓ Ⓔ	49 Ⓐ Ⓑ Ⓒ Ⓓ Ⓔ	59 Ⓐ Ⓑ Ⓒ Ⓓ Ⓔ
10 Ⓕ Ⓖ Ⓗ Ⓙ Ⓚ	20 Ⓕ Ⓖ Ⓗ Ⓙ Ⓚ	30 Ⓕ Ⓖ Ⓗ Ⓙ Ⓚ	40 Ⓕ Ⓖ Ⓗ Ⓙ Ⓚ	50 Ⓕ Ⓖ Ⓗ Ⓙ Ⓚ	60 Ⓕ Ⓖ Ⓗ Ⓙ Ⓚ

TEST 3: READING

1 Ⓐ Ⓑ Ⓒ Ⓓ	8 Ⓕ Ⓖ Ⓗ Ⓙ	15 Ⓐ Ⓑ Ⓒ Ⓓ	22 Ⓕ Ⓖ Ⓗ Ⓙ	29 Ⓐ Ⓑ Ⓒ Ⓓ	36 Ⓕ Ⓖ Ⓗ Ⓙ
2 Ⓕ Ⓖ Ⓗ Ⓙ	9 Ⓐ Ⓑ Ⓒ Ⓓ	16 Ⓕ Ⓖ Ⓗ Ⓙ	23 Ⓐ Ⓑ Ⓒ Ⓓ	30 Ⓕ Ⓖ Ⓗ Ⓙ	37 Ⓐ Ⓑ Ⓒ Ⓓ
3 Ⓐ Ⓑ Ⓒ Ⓓ	10 Ⓕ Ⓖ Ⓗ Ⓙ	17 Ⓐ Ⓑ Ⓒ Ⓓ	24 Ⓕ Ⓖ Ⓗ Ⓙ	31 Ⓐ Ⓑ Ⓒ Ⓓ	38 Ⓕ Ⓖ Ⓗ Ⓙ
4 Ⓕ Ⓖ Ⓗ Ⓙ	11 Ⓐ Ⓑ Ⓒ Ⓓ	18 Ⓕ Ⓖ Ⓗ Ⓙ	25 Ⓐ Ⓑ Ⓒ Ⓓ	32 Ⓕ Ⓖ Ⓗ Ⓙ	39 Ⓐ Ⓑ Ⓒ Ⓓ
5 Ⓐ Ⓑ Ⓒ Ⓓ	12 Ⓕ Ⓖ Ⓗ Ⓙ	19 Ⓐ Ⓑ Ⓒ Ⓓ	26 Ⓕ Ⓖ Ⓗ Ⓙ	33 Ⓐ Ⓑ Ⓒ Ⓓ	40 Ⓕ Ⓖ Ⓗ Ⓙ
6 Ⓕ Ⓖ Ⓗ Ⓙ	13 Ⓐ Ⓑ Ⓒ Ⓓ	20 Ⓕ Ⓖ Ⓗ Ⓙ	27 Ⓐ Ⓑ Ⓒ Ⓓ	34 Ⓕ Ⓖ Ⓗ Ⓙ	
7 Ⓐ Ⓑ Ⓒ Ⓓ	14 Ⓕ Ⓖ Ⓗ Ⓙ	21 Ⓐ Ⓑ Ⓒ Ⓓ	28 Ⓕ Ⓖ Ⓗ Ⓙ	35 Ⓐ Ⓑ Ⓒ Ⓓ	

TEST 4: SCIENCE

1 Ⓐ Ⓑ Ⓒ Ⓓ	8 Ⓕ Ⓖ Ⓗ Ⓙ	15 Ⓐ Ⓑ Ⓒ Ⓓ	22 Ⓕ Ⓖ Ⓗ Ⓙ	29 Ⓐ Ⓑ Ⓒ Ⓓ	36 Ⓕ Ⓖ Ⓗ Ⓙ
2 Ⓕ Ⓖ Ⓗ Ⓙ	9 Ⓐ Ⓑ Ⓒ Ⓓ	16 Ⓕ Ⓖ Ⓗ Ⓙ	23 Ⓐ Ⓑ Ⓒ Ⓓ	30 Ⓕ Ⓖ Ⓗ Ⓙ	37 Ⓐ Ⓑ Ⓒ Ⓓ
3 Ⓐ Ⓑ Ⓒ Ⓓ	10 Ⓕ Ⓖ Ⓗ Ⓙ	17 Ⓐ Ⓑ Ⓒ Ⓓ	24 Ⓕ Ⓖ Ⓗ Ⓙ	31 Ⓐ Ⓑ Ⓒ Ⓓ	38 Ⓕ Ⓖ Ⓗ Ⓙ
4 Ⓕ Ⓖ Ⓗ Ⓙ	11 Ⓐ Ⓑ Ⓒ Ⓓ	18 Ⓕ Ⓖ Ⓗ Ⓙ	25 Ⓐ Ⓑ Ⓒ Ⓓ	32 Ⓕ Ⓖ Ⓗ Ⓙ	39 Ⓐ Ⓑ Ⓒ Ⓓ
5 Ⓐ Ⓑ Ⓒ Ⓓ	12 Ⓕ Ⓖ Ⓗ Ⓙ	19 Ⓐ Ⓑ Ⓒ Ⓓ	26 Ⓕ Ⓖ Ⓗ Ⓙ	33 Ⓐ Ⓑ Ⓒ Ⓓ	40 Ⓕ Ⓖ Ⓗ Ⓙ
6 Ⓕ Ⓖ Ⓗ Ⓙ	13 Ⓐ Ⓑ Ⓒ Ⓓ	20 Ⓕ Ⓖ Ⓗ Ⓙ	27 Ⓐ Ⓑ Ⓒ Ⓓ	34 Ⓕ Ⓖ Ⓗ Ⓙ	
7 Ⓐ Ⓑ Ⓒ Ⓓ	14 Ⓕ Ⓖ Ⓗ Ⓙ	21 Ⓐ Ⓑ Ⓒ Ⓓ	28 Ⓕ Ⓖ Ⓗ Ⓙ	35 Ⓐ Ⓑ Ⓒ Ⓓ	

Practice Test 5

EXAMINEE STATEMENTS, CERTIFICATION, AND SIGNATURE

1. **Statements:** I understand that by registering for, launching, starting, or submitting answer documents for an ACT® test, I am agreeing to comply with and be bound by the *Terms and Conditions: Testing Rules and Policies for the ACT® Test* ("Terms").

   I UNDERSTAND AND AGREE THAT THE TERMS PERMIT ACT TO CANCEL MY SCORES IN CERTAIN CIRCUMSTANCES. THE TERMS ALSO LIMIT DAMAGES AVAILABLE TO ME AND REQUIRE ARBITRATION OF CERTAIN DISPUTES. BY AGREEING TO ARBITRATION, ACT AND I BOTH WAIVE THE RIGHT TO HAVE THOSE DISPUTES HEARD BY A JUDGE OR JURY.

   I understand that ACT owns the test questions and responses, and I will not share them with anyone by any form of communication before, during, or after the test administration. I understand that taking the test for someone else may violate the law and subject me to legal penalties.

   I consent to the collection and processing of personally identifying information I provide, and its subsequent use and disclosure, as described in the ACT Privacy Policy (www.act.org/privacy.html). I also permit ACT to transfer my personally identifying information to the United States, to ACT, or to a third-party service provider, where it will be subject to use and disclosure under the laws of the United States, including being accessible to law enforcement or national security authorities.

2. **Certification:** Copy the italicized certification below, then sign, date, and print your name in the spaces provided.

   *I agree to the **Statements** above and certify that I am the person whose information appears on this form.*

_____

_____

| Your Signature | Today's Date | Print Your Name |

The ACT® Form 21MC8
2023 | 2024

Directions

This booklet contains tests in English, mathematics, reading, and science. These tests measure skills and abilities highly related to high school course work and success in college. **Calculators may be used on the mathematics test only.**

The questions in each test are numbered, and the suggested answers for each question are lettered. On the answer document, the rows of ovals are numbered to match the questions, and the ovals in each row are lettered to correspond to the suggested answers.

For each question, first decide which answer is best. Next, locate on the answer document the row of ovals numbered the same as the question. Then, locate the oval in that row lettered the same as your answer. Finally, fill in the oval completely. Use a soft lead pencil and make your marks heavy and black. **Do not use ink or a mechanical pencil.**

Mark only one answer to each question. If you change your mind about an answer, erase your first mark thoroughly before marking your new answer. For each question, make certain that you mark in the row of ovals with the same number as the question.

Only responses marked on your answer document will be scored. Your score on each test will be based only on the number of questions you answer correctly during the time allowed for that test. You will **not** be penalized for guessing. **It is to your advantage to answer every question even if you must guess.**

You may work on each test **only** when the testing staff tells you to do so. If you finish a test before time is called for that test, you should use the time remaining to reconsider questions you are uncertain about in that test. You may **not** look back to a test on which time has already been called, and you may **not** go ahead to another test. To do so will disqualify you from the examination.

Lay your pencil down immediately when time is called at the end of each test. You may **not** for any reason fill in or alter ovals for a test after time is called for that test. To do so will disqualify you from the examination.

Do not fold or tear the pages of your test booklet.

DO NOT OPEN THIS BOOKLET
UNTIL TOLD TO DO SO.

The ONLY Official Prep Guide from the Makers of the ACT

1 ■ ■ ■ ■ ■ ■ ■ 1

ENGLISH TEST

45 Minutes—75 Questions

DIRECTIONS: In the five passages that follow, certain words and phrases are underlined and numbered. In the right-hand column, you will find alternatives for the underlined part. In most cases, you are to choose the one that best expresses the idea, makes the statement appropriate for standard written English, or is worded most consistently with the style and tone of the passage as a whole. If you think the original version is best, choose "NO CHANGE." In some cases, you will find in the right-hand column a question about the underlined part. You are to choose the best answer to the question.

You will also find questions about a section of the passage, or about the passage as a whole. These questions do not refer to an underlined portion of the passage, but rather are identified by a number or numbers in a box.

For each question, choose the alternative you consider best and fill in the corresponding oval on your answer document. Read each passage through once before you begin to answer the questions that accompany it. For many of the questions, you must read several sentences beyond the question to determine the answer. Be sure that you have read far enough ahead each time you choose an alternative.

PASSAGE I

A Mouthful of Music

Mouth music is the name given in English to the many ways <u>by</u> imitating the sounds of musical instruments with
1
the human voice. Forms of mouth music are performed

around the world, but the genre <u>being</u> particularly popular
2
in England, Ireland, and Scotland. In this Celtic region, *lilting* and *jigging* are two of the lively names used to refer to this musical form.

Celtic mouth music exists to accompany dancing, so the rhythms and sounds are <u>first-class and the words take a back seat.</u>
3
Instead of using traditional lyrics, singers often

produce nonsense <u>syllables, called vocables to</u>
4
represent specific instrumental sounds, such as those of bagpipes or violins. The results are songs that rarely make literal sense but nevertheless flow in a way <u>easier</u> to dance to.
5

1. **A.** NO CHANGE
   B. with
   C. of
   D. at

2. **F.** NO CHANGE
   G. was being
   H. is
   J. DELETE the underlined portion.

3. **A.** NO CHANGE
   B. more important than the lyrics.
   C. a bigger deal than the words.
   D. way more vital than verse.

4. **F.** NO CHANGE
   G. syllables called vocables,
   H. syllables, called vocables,
   J. syllables called, vocables,

5. **A.** NO CHANGE
   B. easily
   C. that is easy
   D. DELETE the underlined portion.

GO ON TO THE NEXT PAGE.

One Scottish form of mouth music, *puirt-a-beul*, is performed entirely in the Gaelic language and accompanies traditional dance steps. The often tongue-twisting lyrics
6
require much practice to perfect. The greater challenge for

many puirt-a-beul singers, though, is learning when to
7
breathe. A poorly timed breath might break a song's

flow, interrupting the steady beat it relies on to help
8
time their steps.

9 Instruments were prohibitively expensive and

thus scarce in isolated Scottish villages in order to fill
10
the void, mouth music emerged and provided residents

with the music they wanted for dancing. Additionally,

puirt-a-beul gave anyone whomever didn't read music
11
a way to learn and pass on traditional songs.

The continuing popularity of Celtic

mouth music is testament to the vitality of them.
12
In the 1990s, groups like Mouth Music from Scotland

and The Cranberries from Ireland rose to fame,

exposing with audiences Celtic mouth music worldwide.
13

6. If the writer were to delete the underlined portion, the sentence would primarily lose:

F. a description that emphasizes the difficulty of puirt-a-beul.

G. information about writing lyrics for puirt-a-beul music.

H. an indication of how often puirt-a-beul is performed in the Celtic culture.

J. an example of a training exercise puirt-a-beul singers use to practice lyrics.

7. A. NO CHANGE
B. at the same time,
C. this time,
D. still,

8. F. NO CHANGE
G. dancers rely
H. they rely
J. relied

9. Given that all the following statements are true, which one, if added here, would most effectively introduce the subject of the paragraph?

A. Puirt-a-beul was most likely invented out of necessity.

B. Mouth music singers must have a good sense of rhythm.

C. Celtic mouth music, including puirt-a-beul, has influenced jazz scat singing.

D. Another form of mouth music that originated in Scotland is the waulking song.

10. F. NO CHANGE
G. villages and in
H. villages. In
J. villages, in

11. A. NO CHANGE
B. which
C. whom
D. who

12. F. NO CHANGE
G. this musical form.
H. itself.
J. one.

13. A. NO CHANGE
B. exposing audiences worldwide to Celtic mouth music.
C. for audiences worldwide exposing Celtic mouth music.
D. worldwide exposing Celtic mouth music to audiences.

GO ON TO THE NEXT PAGE.

Taking Additional Practice Tests

1 ■ ■ ■ ■ ■ ■ ■ ■ **1**

The bands' celebrity <u>continually survives</u> as they
14

<u>combine traditional mouth music with modern rhythms.</u>
15

14. **F.** NO CHANGE
    G. still remains and carries on
    H. stays sticking around
    J. endures

15. Given that all the choices are accurate, which one most effectively expresses the idea that the bands incorporate both classic Celtic music and current influences into their music?

    A. NO CHANGE
    B. continue to produce new music and release new albums.
    C. put on concerts around the world.
    D. sing and dance on stage.

PASSAGE II

Making the Desert Bloom

More than two thousand years ago, a people the
<u>Romans, called the Garamantes,</u> created a complex
16
civilization in one of the world's driest places—the Sahara
Desert. Beginning around 500 BCE, they built towns and
villages, <u>cloth was manufactured there</u> and jewelry, and
17
traded throughout North Africa and the Mediterranean.
They also grew a variety of crops, including wheat,
dates, palms, grapes, figs, and melons. ⬚18

The survival of their civilization depended on
hundreds of miles of underground tunnels. These tunnels
carried water to desert settlements from an aquifer, an
underground water source, <u>in the distant mountains.</u>
19

The water ran through sloping, <u>hand-dug</u> tunnels
20
called foggaras, which could be as deep as one hundred
thirty feet below ground. These tunnels were connected
to the surface by ventilation shafts every thirty feet or so.

16. **F.** NO CHANGE
    G. Romans called the Garamantes,
    H. Romans called: the Garamantes
    J. Romans called the Garamantes

17. **A.** NO CHANGE
    B. the manufacture of cloth took place
    C. manufactured cloth
    D. cloth

18. If the writer were to delete the preceding sentence, the paragraph would primarily lose a concluding statement that:

    F. suggests the Garamantes were successful farmers in that they grew a variety of crops.
    G. summarizes the information presented about the Garamantes.
    H. indicates the products that the Garamantes exported to Rome.
    J. takes the focus off the Garamantes and places it on the products they imported.

19. Which choice provides new information to the essay?

    A. NO CHANGE
    B. upon which they depended.
    C. used by the Garamantes.
    D. a key to their survival.

20. Which choice best indicates the method used to build the tunnels?

    F. NO CHANGE
    G. underground
    H. dimly lit
    J. desert

GO ON TO THE NEXT PAGE.

When the tunnels reached a town or field, the water flowed
into <u>more easy</u> accessible surface canals or reservoirs.
₂₁

<u>Having left no clues, archaeologists</u> don't know how
₂₂
the Garamantes learned to build foggaras. Other such
tunnels exist in Iran, Algeria, Tunisia, and elsewhere.

Because the canals were underground, the water they
carried stayed clean and didn't evaporate. And because the
water came from an aquifer rather <u>then from its</u> rainfall,
₂₃
the supply was unaffected by drought. The Garamantes

<u>could of relied</u> on a constant supply of water for drinking,
₂₄

washing, and irrigation. <u>Moreover,</u> the cold, damp air of
₂₅
the foggaras lowered the temperature inside the homes
that were built over them, resulting in an ancient form
of air-conditioning.

The Garamantes <u>who</u> thrived until about 500 CE,
₂₆
when some archaeologists believe they began to deplete

the aquifer. <u>As</u> the foggaras supplied less and less water,
₂₇

the Garamantes' population <u>declined, their</u> civilization
₂₈
eventually collapsed. However, at least six hundred of
the ancient foggaras survive. The stone mounds that mark
their ventilation shafts are still visible in what is now
southwestern Libya, <u>where they can be seen even now.</u>
₂₉

21. A. NO CHANGE
    B. more easily
    C. easier and
    D. easy and

22. F. NO CHANGE
    G. A genuine puzzle to scientists, archaeologists
    H. Giving no indication, archaeologists
    J. Archaeologists

23. A. NO CHANGE
    B. than from
    C. then
    D. by

24. F. NO CHANGE
    G. had to of relied
    H. could rely
    J. relies

25. A. NO CHANGE
    B. Nevertheless,
    C. In contrast,
    D. Even so,

26. F. NO CHANGE
    G. many of whom
    H. having
    J. DELETE the underlined portion.

27. A. NO CHANGE
    B. As to when
    C. Whereas
    D. Though

28. F. NO CHANGE
    G. declined the Garamantes'
    H. declined. Their
    J. declined their

29. A. NO CHANGE
    B. a place where visitors can see these amazing signs
       of an ancient civilization.
    C. the location that continues to present visitors with
       a view of these remnants of a time gone by.
    D. DELETE the underlined portion and end the sen-
       tence with a period.

GO ON TO THE NEXT PAGE.

Taking Additional Practice Tests

1 ■ ■ ■ ■ ■ ■ ■ ■ ■ 1

> Question 30 asks about the preceding passage as a whole.

30. Suppose the writer's primary purpose had been to present information about a civilization's efforts to overcome a natural obstacle in order to survive. Would this essay accomplish that purpose?
   - F. Yes, because it explains that the Garamantes traded throughout North Africa and the Mediterranean.
   - G. Yes, because it describes the Garamantes' method of bringing water to an otherwise dry area, allowing the Garamantes to thrive there.
   - H. No, because the foggaras were not naturally occurring tunnels.
   - J. No, because the foggaras ultimately led to the downfall of the Garamantes' civilization.

PASSAGE III

Neutrinos on Ice

At the IceCube Neutrino Observatory in Antarctica, eighty-six cables descend 2,500 meters <u>down</u> into the
₃₁
glacial terrain. Each cable is equipped with sixty digital

optical modules <u>(DOMs), which, are programmed,</u> to
₃₂
detect a faint blue flash known as Cherenkov radiation.

This <u>radiation:</u> a veritable shock wave of photonic
₃₃
energy—is emitted when subatomic particles called

neutrinos collide with electrons in the molecules of ice.

Although there are countless neutrinos in the

universe <u>(fifty trillion neutrinos pass through your body</u>
₃₄
<u>every second)</u>, actually detecting them is a formidable
₃₄
task. Neutrinos carry no electrical charge, are practically

weightless, and travel at nearly the speed of light.

Neutrinos are rarely affected by matter or electromagnetic

fields. <u>For this purpose,</u> many neutrinos have been
₃₅
traveling through space unimpeded for billions

of years.

31. A. NO CHANGE
   B. down below
   C. downwards
   D. DELETE the underlined portion.

32. F. NO CHANGE
   G. (DOMs), which are programmed
   H. (DOMs): which are programmed
   J. (DOMs); which are programmed

33. A. NO CHANGE
   B. radiation—
   C. radiation;
   D. radiation

34. If the writer were to delete the underlined portion (adjusting the punctuation as needed), the essay would primarily lose information that:
   F. specifies why neutrinos are practically weightless.
   G. explains how neutrinos pass through matter.
   H. indicates why there are so many neutrinos.
   J. emphasizes how numerous neutrinos are.

35. A. NO CHANGE
   B. In contrast,
   C. Besides,
   D. In fact,

GO ON TO THE NEXT PAGE.

On some occasions however; neutrinos do collide
36

with other particles. 37 Scientists specifically selected

the site of the IceCube Neutrino Observatory to facilitate
38

the detection of such a collision. Not only is the Antarctic

subterranean ice exceptionally clear, it is also less

pressurized due to it's subzero altitude. These factors
39

increase the chance of DOMs detecting the blue flash

that signifies a neutrino collision. Once this detection

occurs, data is gathered and transferred to laboratories

at the University of Wisconsin. Here, the origin of each

of these neutrinos is determined by analyzing the direction
40

and intensity of the flash.

Determining neutrinos' origins could provide
41

scientists with new insights into the universe. For instance,
41

some neutrinos are produced during supernovae (the

collapsing of stars). The origins of these neutrinos could
42

36. F. NO CHANGE
G. occasions, however,
H. occasions, however;
J. occasions, however

37. At this point, the writer is considering adding the following true sentence:

> In 1956, during the Cowan-Reines neutrino experiment, a neutrino was detected for the first time.

Should the writer make this addition?

A. Yes, because the information is relevant to the history of neutrino detection outlined in the paragraph.
B. Yes, because the information indicates that subzero altitude is essential to the detection of neutrinos.
C. No, because the information is unrelated to the discussion of why scientists selected the location of the IceCube Neutrino Observatory.
D. No, because the information is unrelated to why the detection of neutrinos is facilitated by zero-gravity conditions.

38. F. NO CHANGE
G. Observatory, and to
H. Observatory. To
J. Observatory; to

39. A. NO CHANGE
B. their
C. its
D. its'

40. F. NO CHANGE
G. have been
H. are being
J. are

41. Which of the following true sentences best introduces the main idea of the paragraph?

A. NO CHANGE
B. For decades, scientists have been trying to learn more about gamma rays through the study of supernovae.
C. Recently, at IceCube, scientists discovered two neutrinos, which they now refer to as Bert and Ernie.
D. Neutrinos can now be created in laboratories, using a particle accelerator called a Super Proton Synchrotron.

42. F. NO CHANGE
G. stars) and the
H. stars), the
J. stars) the

GO ON TO THE NEXT PAGE.

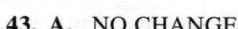

1 ■ ■ ■ ■ ■ ■ ■ ■ ■ **1**

give us opulent information about how, when, and why
43
stars collapse. Scientists are optimistic that the neutrinos

detected at IceCube could lead to new ways of looking

at our galaxy—and galaxies beyond.
44

43. **A.** NO CHANGE
B. invaluable
C. upscale
D. lavish

44. The writer wants to emphasize that information gar-
nered from the detected neutrinos at IceCube could
have dramatic effects on how scientists study the universe. Which choice best accomplishes that goal?

F. NO CHANGE
G. phenomena that have puzzled scientists over the
last decade.
H. common occurrences in space.
J. the world around us.

Question 45 asks about the preceding passage
as a whole.

---

45. Suppose the writer's primary purpose had been to outline a scientific theory concerning the origins of a particle in nature. Would this essay accomplish that goal?

A. Yes, because it explains how scientists are discovering new reasons why neutrinos emit a blue flash
known as Cherenkov radiation.
B. Yes, because it summarizes how DOMs at the
IceCube Neutrino Observatory track neutrinos to
their origins despite neutrinos' numerous collisions with matter and electromagnetic forces.
C. No, because it describes instead how neutrinos are
detected at an observatory and how these detec-
tions could benefit future scientific research.
D. No, because it details instead how new research on
neutrinos could potentially contradict a commonly
held theory about supernovae.

PASSAGE IV

Clinton Hill's Found Artist

[1]

At the Urban Vintage, my favorite café here in

Clinton Hill, Brooklyn, I found a table by the window

and checked the day's news on my laptop. On the

New York Times home page, I noticed an article about

Rafael Leonardo Black, a 64-year-old Clinton Hill

artist who had just been discovered. [A]
46

46. **F.** NO CHANGE
G. of whom
H. which
J. whom

GO ON TO THE NEXT PAGE.

[2]

Black, a native of Aruba, has been creating art in his
New York City studio apartment for over three decades.
Until recently, few people had seen his work. I wondered
why—and learned he simply never cared to share it. Black
has worked as a typist, a salesperson, and a receptionist.
He never expected (or tried) to make a living as an artist.
However, in May of 2013, art dealer Francis Naumann,
directed to Black's art by one of Black's longtime friends,
displayed sixteen of the artist's drawings in a solo show.

Within days, ten of Black's pieces sold for, prices ranging
from $16,000 to $28,000. [B]

[3]

Black draws collages in black No. 2
pencil on white board and they're packed with

depictions, in the form of drawings, of ancient myths,
historical events, and popular culture. I found a collage
titled *Seven Lamps* in a quick search online. [C] It
features a representation of a British psychedelic poster,
a portrayal of Danish surrealist painter, Wilhelm Freddie,
at work, and a tiny figure of Los Angeles architect Simon
Rodia. The images are stacked, forming a surreal tower.

47. **A.** NO CHANGE
B. originally from Aruba, for more than half his life
C. living in Clinton Hill but a native of Aruba,
D. a newly found artist originally from Aruba,

48. Given that all the choices are accurate, which one provides the best transition to the information in the following sentence?
F. NO CHANGE
G. was taking down an artist's long-running exhibition at his Manhattan gallery.
H. became aware that Black had never shown his drawings, formally or otherwise.
J. recognized that no one in the New York City art world had heard of Black.

49. **A.** NO CHANGE
B. sold—for
C. sold; for
D. sold for:

50. **F.** NO CHANGE
G. board. They're
H. board, they're
J. board they're

51. **A.** NO CHANGE
B. black pencil drawings that depict
C. drawings that create collages of
D. depictions of

52. **F.** NO CHANGE
G. painter Wilhelm Freddie,
H. painter, Wilhelm Freddie
J. painter Wilhelm Freddie

GO ON TO THE NEXT PAGE.

1 ■ ■ ■ ■ ■ ■ ■ ■ ■ 1

I wasn't sure how the drawings in *Seven Lamps*—so

detailed that I could see the folds in Rodia's clothing—fit
$\overline{53}$

together logically, but I liked that there was so much for
$\overline{54}$

me to puzzle over. Maybe this complexity
$\overline{54}$

in May helps explain why Black's work created such a stir.
$\overline{55}$

[4]

I read that Black observes the sudden interest
$\overline{56}$

in his drawings. [D] He says he's always been an artist,

regardless of who knew it. Given that I know the city, I'll
$\overline{57}$

keep checking the *Times* for word of his next show. When

I walk home from the Urban Vintage, its décor often being
$\overline{58}$

updated with restored antiques and vintage housewares, I
$\overline{58}$

wonder if I'll pass the brownstone building where, Black,
$\overline{59}$

creates his fascinating, newly found art.

---

53. **A.** NO CHANGE
  B. has fit
  C. is fit
  D. fits

54. If the writer were to delete the underlined portion (adjusting the punctuation as needed), the essay would primarily lose a:
  F. claim arguing that the reason Naumann chose to show Black's art is that the art offers so much for a viewer to reflect upon and analyze.
  G. detail indicating that the narrator appreciated Black's collage even though he or she might not have understood its overall intent.
  H. comment suggesting that though the narrator enjoys only some of Black's art, he or she is glad that Black has been discovered.
  J. statement revealing the narrator's belief that the best modern art is understood only by the artist who created it.

55. The best placement for the underlined portion would be:
  A. where it is now.
  B. after the word *Maybe*.
  C. after the word *explain*.
  D. after the word *stir* (and before the period).

56. The writer wants to clearly establish that the newspaper article claims Black is unmoved by the sudden interest in his art. Which choice best accomplishes that goal?
  F. NO CHANGE
  G. is nearly a celebrity in Clinton Hill due to
  H. has benefited financially from
  J. gives little thought to

57. Which choice provides the most effective transition from the preceding sentence to this sentence?
  A. NO CHANGE
  B. Since I'm knowledgeable about art and books,
  C. Now that I know about him,
  D. Knowing that I like news,

58. **F.** NO CHANGE
  G. Vintage, easily carrying my lightweight laptop in my old, navy blue messenger bag,
  H. Vintage this evening—I can't be late to meet a friend exactly at eight—
  J. Vintage tonight,

59. **A.** NO CHANGE
  B. building where Black
  C. building, where Black
  D. building: where Black

GO ON TO THE NEXT PAGE.

Question 60 asks about the preceding passage as a whole.

60. The writer is considering adding the following sentence to the essay:

> Fortunately, the web page included a key that identified the people, places, and events—most of which I had never even heard of—that Black portrays in this piece.

If the writer were to add this sentence, it would most logically be placed at:

F. Point A in Paragraph 1.
G. Point B in Paragraph 2.
H. Point C in Paragraph 3.
J. Point D in Paragraph 4.

PASSAGE V

Cher Ami, Pigeon Hero

Pigeons have a fairly poor reputation. In many

urban areas, they are considered little more than,
61

"rats with wings," blamed for spreading disease and
62

despoiling statues. For example, one species, the homing
63

pigeon, which is among the best navigators of the natural
64

world. There navigational ability has earned the homely
65
pigeon an undeniable place in history.

61. A. NO CHANGE
B. than—
C. than;
D. than

62. F. NO CHANGE
G. wings" and they are blamed
H. wings," they are blamed
J. wings." Blamed

63. A. NO CHANGE
B. Similarly,
C. However,
D. Thus,

64. F. NO CHANGE
G. pigeon that
H. pigeon,
J. pigeon

65. A. NO CHANGE
B. They're
C. It's
D. Its

GO ON TO THE NEXT PAGE.

Former modern technologies like the radio or
$\underline{\hspace{1cm}}$
           66
telephone, commanders on the battlefield often faced

challenges in communicating, depending on their location.
                                 $\overline{\hspace{3cm}}$
                                          67
One solution was to use homing pigeons to carry messages

from the front lines back to headquarters. The pigeon was

a particularly good soldier in such endeavors: It flew fast.

It flew high. And it always quickly returned and came back
                            $\overline{\hspace{4cm}}$
                                        68
to its home roost.

The most famous avian war hero is perhaps Cher Ami,

whose name means *dear friend*. One of six hundred birds

used by the US Army Signal Corps in France during

World War I, all twelve of Cher Ami's missions were
               $\overline{\hspace{4cm}}$
                          69
deemed successful. His last was instrumental in saving
$\overline{\hspace{3cm}}$
        69
hundreds of lives.

Near Verdun, France, the 77th Infantry Division

became separated from US forces. The men were

surrounded by German troops and were rapidly running

out of rations. They were separated from other US forces.
              $\overline{\hspace{5cm}}$
                          70

They had but one link to headquarters homing pigeons.
                        $\overline{\hspace{2cm}}$
                                71

It was becoming clear that the Americans were unaware
$\overline{\hspace{2cm}}$
        72
of the 77th's whereabouts, the situation grew dire.

66. **F.** NO CHANGE
    G. Before
    H. Earlier
    J. Prior

67. The writer is considering revising the underlined portion to the following:

    especially across long distances and difficult terrain.

    Should the writer make this revision?

    A. Yes, because it offers a better indication of the circumstances that made communication difficult.
    B. Yes, because it more clearly identifies the locations of and distances between troops.
    C. No, because it adds information that is irrelevant to the paragraph's discussion of pigeons.
    D. No, because it suggests that homing pigeons are unnecessary today.

68. **F.** NO CHANGE
    G. speedily returned, coming home
    H. returned home
    J. returned

69. **A.** NO CHANGE
    B. the twelve missions Cher Ami flew were successful.
    C. successful missions by Cher Ami numbered twelve.
    D. Cher Ami flew twelve successful missions.

70. **F.** NO CHANGE
    G. German troops were all around them.
    H. They would soon be out of rations.
    J. DELETE the underlined portion.

71. **A.** NO CHANGE
    B. headquarters:
    C. headquarters;
    D. headquarters,

72. **F.** NO CHANGE
    G. Having become
    H. As it became
    J. It became

GO ON TO THE NEXT PAGE.

Major Whittlesey wrote a note about the 77th's location, placed it in a canister attached to the pigeon's leg, and watched as the bird flew out in the midst of battle. Despite being wounded in flight, Cher Ami managed to deliver the message to headquarters; the unit known as "the Lost Battalion" would be rescued.

News reports around the world touted the bird's heroism. The French military awarded Cher Ami a <u>medal, the</u> War Cross. Although one might question
—73—

the extent <u>in</u> which Cher Ami understood his mission,
—74—

his story <u>proves that pigeons are unique.</u>
—75—

73. **A.** NO CHANGE
    B. medal, it was the
    C. medal, that was
    D. medal. The

74. **F.** NO CHANGE
    G. of
    H. to
    J. DELETE the underlined portion.

75. Which choice best concludes the sentence and essay by connecting Cher Ami's story to a specific idea raised in the first paragraph of the essay?
    A. NO CHANGE
    B. is testimony to the homing pigeon's navigational skill and instinct.
    C. has made people reconsider the definition of heroism.
    D. suggests that even birds can be brave.

END OF TEST 1

STOP! DO NOT TURN THE PAGE UNTIL TOLD TO DO SO.

Taking Additional Practice Tests

2 △ △ △ △ △ △ △ △ △ 2

MATHEMATICS TEST
60 Minutes—60 Questions

DIRECTIONS: Solve each problem, choose the correct answer, and then fill in the corresponding oval on your answer document.

Do not linger over problems that take too much time. Solve as many as you can; then return to the others in the time you have left for this test.

You are permitted to use a calculator on this test. You may use your calculator for any problems you choose, but some of the problems may best be done without using a calculator.

Note: Unless otherwise stated, all of the following should be assumed.

1. Illustrative figures are NOT necessarily drawn to scale.
2. Geometric figures lie in a plane.
3. The word *line* indicates a straight line.
4. The word *average* indicates arithmetic mean.

---

1. The parallelogram below has consecutive angles with measures $x°$ and $25°$. What is the value of x ?

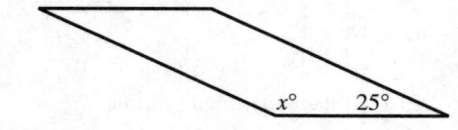

A. 100
B. 115
C. 130
D. 140
E. 155

DO YOUR FIGURING HERE.

2. A retail sales associate's daily commission during 1 week was $30 on Monday and Tuesday and $70 on Wednesday, Thursday, and Friday. What was the associate's average daily commission for these 5 days?

F. $50
G. $51
H. $54
J. $55
K. $56

3. What is the greatest common factor of 45, 50, and 84 ?

A. 0
B. 1
C. 2
D. 3
E. 5

4. For what value of x is the equation $2(x - 12) + x = 36$ true?

F. 4
G. 8
H. 16
J. 20
K. 30

GO ON TO THE NEXT PAGE.

2 △ △ △ △ △ △ △ △ △ 2

5. A bag contains exactly 22 solid-colored buttons: 4 red, 6 blue, and 12 white. What is the probability of randomly selecting 1 button that is NOT white?

A. $\frac{5}{11}$

B. $\frac{5}{6}$

C. $\frac{2}{3}$

D. $\frac{1}{22}$

E. $\frac{1}{10}$

6. On a map, $\frac{1}{2}$ inch represents 12 actual miles. Two towns that are 5 inches apart on this map are how many actual miles apart?

F. 120
G. 60
H. 30
J. 24
K. 12

7. Caden had exactly 45 plants to sell. After Day 1 of his sale, he had exactly 42 plants left. After Day 2, Caden had exactly 39 plants left. After Day 3, he has exactly 36 plants left. Assuming Caden will continue to sell plants at that daily rate, how many of these plants will he have left at the end of Day 6 ?

A. 33
B. 27
C. 24
D. 6
E. 3

8. An on-demand movie service charges $5 per month, plus $2 for each movie rented. Which of the following equations models the relationship between M, the number of movies rented per month, and T, the total monthly cost, in dollars, for the service?

F. $M = 5 + 2T$
G. $M = 2 + 5T$
H. $T = 5 + 2M$
J. $T = 2 + 5M$
K. $T = (5 + 2)M$

9. What are the solutions to the quadratic equation $(2x + 5)(3x - 4) = 0$?

A. -5 and 4

B. $-\frac{5}{2}$ and $-\frac{4}{3}$

C. $-\frac{5}{2}$ and $\frac{4}{3}$

D. $\frac{5}{2}$ and $-\frac{4}{3}$

E. $\frac{5}{2}$ and $\frac{4}{3}$

GO ON TO THE NEXT PAGE.

2 △ △ △ △ △ △ △ △ △ **2**

DO YOUR FIGURING HERE.

10. An 8-inch-by-6-inch rectangle is cut along a diagonal to form 2 triangles. What is the area, in square inches, of each triangle?

 F.   7
 G. 12
 H. 14
 J. 24
 K. 48

11. In a class of tenth graders, no student participated in more than 1 of the following extracurricular activities: $\frac{2}{3}$ the class played in the band; $\frac{1}{6}$ sang in the chorus; $\frac{1}{10}$ played football; and $\frac{1}{60}$ played basketball. What fraction of the class did not participate in any 1 of these 4 activities?

 A.   0

 B. $\frac{1}{5,400}$

 C. $\frac{1}{20}$

 D. $\frac{74}{79}$

 E. $\frac{57}{60}$

12. What is the smallest integer greater than $\sqrt{61}$?

 F.   4
 G.   7
 H.   8
 J.   10
 K.   31

13. In $\triangle ABC$ shown below, $\sin C = \frac{2}{3}$ and the length of $\overline{AB}$ is 6 inches. What is the length, in inches, of $\overline{AC}$?

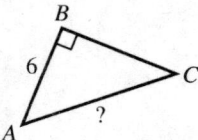

 A. $\sqrt{5}$
 B. $\sqrt{13}$
 C.   4
 D.   5
 E.   9

GO ON TO THE NEXT PAGE.

2 △ △ △ △ △ △ △ △ △ **2**

14. The table below shows the first 5 terms of an arithmetic sequence. Which of the following is a general expression for the *n*th term?

Term position (*n*)	*n*th term
1	1
2	5
3	9
4	13
5	17

F. $2n - 1$
G. $3n - 2$
H. $4n - 3$
J. $5n - 4$
K. $6n - 5$

15. What is the perimeter, in feet, of the figure shown below?

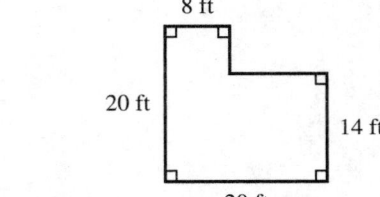

A. 60
B. 62
C. 70
D. 80
E. 84

16. Manuel estimates that $\frac{2}{3}$ of a pizza is left. Stephen estimates that $\frac{3}{4}$ is left. They are going to compromise for a joint estimate by using the number halfway between their 2 estimates. What is their joint estimate?

F. $\frac{17}{24}$

G. $\frac{5}{12}$

H. $\frac{5}{8}$

J. $\frac{5}{7}$

K. $\frac{1}{2}$

17. So far this basketball season, Sherita made 46 of her first 60 free throws, giving her a free-throw average of about 76.7%. What is the minimum number of free throws she would need to make from now on in order to have a free-throw average of at least 80% ?

A. 2
B. 3
C. 10
D. 14
E. 20

DO YOUR FIGURING HERE.

GO ON TO THE NEXT PAGE.

2 △ △ △ △ △ △ △ △ △ **2**

18. Two functions are defined as $f(x) = 2x - 1$ and $g(x) = x^2 + 1$. Which of the following expressions represents $f(g(x))$?

F. $x^2 + 2x$

G. $2x^2 + 1$

H. $2x^2 + 2$

J. $4x^2$

K. $4x^2 - 4x + 2$

19. Data Set A consists of the 8 numbers listed below. Data Set B consists of the 8 numbers in A and a 9th number, which is greater than 90. How will the mean and the median of B compare to the mean and the median of A ?

$$62, 76, 76, 80, 82, 87, 94, 96$$

A. The mean and the median of B will each be greater than the mean and the median of A.

B. The mean and the median of B will each be less than the mean and the median of A.

C. The mean and the median of B will each be the same as the mean and the median of A.

D. The mean of B will be the same as the mean of A, and the median of B will be greater than the median of A.

E. The mean of B will be greater than the mean of A, and the median of B will be the same as the median of A.

20. A truck traveling at 35 mph has a leaky radiator that is losing 4 fluid ounces per minute. How many *miles* will the truck travel before the radiator, which held 480 fluid ounces when it began to leak, is empty?

F.   13.7

G. 17.5

H. 35.0

J.   70.0

K. 120.0

21. In the standard (x,y) coordinate plane, what is the midpoint of the line segment that has endpoints $(-5,8)$ and $(3,-1)$?

A. $(-2, -9)$

B. $\left(-1, \dfrac{7}{2}\right)$

C. $\left(\dfrac{3}{2}, 1\right)$

D. $\left(4, -\dfrac{9}{2}\right)$

E. $(8, -9)$

DO YOUR FIGURING HERE.

GO ON TO THE NEXT PAGE.

2 △ △ △ △ △ △ △ △ △ **2**

22. The ordered pairs (x,y) in one of the following tables belong to a linear function. Which one?

DO YOUR FIGURING HERE.

F.

x	y
0	1
1	0
2	1
3	0

J.

x	y
0	0
1	1
2	0
3	1

G.

x	y
0	2
1	1
2	1
3	0

K.

x	y
0	0
1	1
2	4
3	9

H.

x	y
0	3
1	2
2	1
3	0

23. In $\triangle ABC$ shown below, $m\angle A = x°$, $m\angle B = (2x)°$, $m\angle C = (3x)°$, $AB = c$ inches, $AC = b$ inches, and $BC = a$ inches. Which of the following inequalities correctly relates the side lengths of $\triangle ABC$?

(Note: $m\angle A$ denotes the measure of $\angle A$, and AB denotes the length of $\overline{AB}$. The triangle is NOT drawn to scale.)

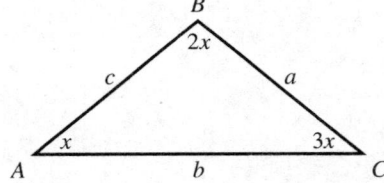

A. $a < b < c$
B. $a < c < b$
C. $b < a < c$
D. $c < a < b$
E. $c < b < a$

24. What is the slope of the line that passes through $(1,5)$ and $(17,7)$ in the standard (x,y) coordinate plane?

F. $\frac{1}{8}$

G. $\frac{2}{3}$

H. $\frac{3}{2}$

J. $\frac{5}{2}$

K. 8

GO ON TO THE NEXT PAGE.

Taking Additional Practice Tests

2 △ △ △ △ △ △ △ △ △ **2**

25. The perimeter of a particular rectangle is 36 centimeters. The longer sides of the rectangle are each 2 centimeters longer than each of the shorter sides of the rectangle. What is the length, in centimeters, of one of the longer sides of this rectangle?

   A. 8
   B. 9
   C. 10
   D. 18
   E. 32

DO YOUR FIGURING HERE.

Use the following information to answer questions 26–28.

Winter Fun Ski Resort sells only 2 types of tickets—adult and student. On Monday, the resort sold 200 tickets, 1 ticket to each skier. Of those tickets, 25 were sold to first-time skiers. When Alyssa skis the resort's main run, her elevation, E feet, at any point on the run is modeled by the equation $E = \dfrac{300{,}000}{t + 100}$ where t is the number of seconds after she begins skiing at the start of the main run.

26. The resort collected a total of $6,000 in ticket sales on Monday. The price of an adult ticket is $50 and the price of a student ticket is $25. How many adult and student tickets were sold on Monday?

	adult	student
F.	40	160
G.	80	120
H.	100	100
J.	120	80
K.	160	40

27. On Monday, the resort sold 1 ticket to each of the 8 members of the Herzog family. Assume this family is a representative sample of all of the skiers at the resort on Monday. How many of the 8 members of the Herzog family are NOT first-time skiers?

   A. 1
   B. 2
   C. 4
   D. 6
   E. 7

28. What is Alyssa's elevation, in feet, at the start of the main run?

   F.   30
   G.   300
   H.   3,000
   J. 30,000
   K. 300,000

GO ON TO THE NEXT PAGE.

2 △ △ △ △ △ △ △ △ △ **2**

29. One side of square *ABCD* has a length of 18 meters. A certain rectangle whose area is equal to the area of *ABCD* has a width of 6 meters. What is the length, in meters, of the certain rectangle?

DO YOUR FIGURING HERE.

- A. 18
- B. 24
- C. 27
- D. 30
- E. 54

30. The 2×2 matrices *A* and *B* below are related to matrix *C* by the equation $C = 2A - 3B$. What is matrix *C* ?

$$A = \begin{bmatrix} 3 & 5 \\ -2 & 1 \end{bmatrix} \quad B = \begin{bmatrix} -4 & 5 \\ 2 & 1 \end{bmatrix}$$

- F. $\begin{bmatrix} 18 & -5 \\ -10 & -1 \end{bmatrix}$
- G. $\begin{bmatrix} 13 & -10 \\ -8 & -2 \end{bmatrix}$
- H. $\begin{bmatrix} 10 & 5 \\ -6 & 1 \end{bmatrix}$
- J. $\begin{bmatrix} 6 & -1 \\ -5 & -1 \end{bmatrix}$
- K. $\begin{bmatrix} -6 & 25 \\ 2 & 5 \end{bmatrix}$

31. Jen is doing an experiment to determine whether a high-protein food affects the ability of white mice to find their way through a maze. The mice in the experimental group were given the high-protein food; the mice in the control group were given regular food. Jen then timed the mice as they found their way through the maze. The table below shows the results.

Mouse number	Experimental group	Control group
1	1 min 46 sec	2 min 13 sec
2	2 min 2 sec	1 min 49 sec
3	2 min 20 sec	2 min 28 sec
4	1 min 51 sec	2 min 7 sec
5	1 min 41 sec	1 min 58 sec

The average time the mice in the experimental group took to find their way through the maze was how many seconds less than the average time taken by the mice in the control group?

- A. 8
- B. 11
- C. 13
- D. 16
- E. 19

GO ON TO THE NEXT PAGE.

2   **2**

32. In the United States, phone numbers begin with a 3-digit area code. Now, there are restrictions on some of the digits, but in the future, as more and more area codes are needed, the restrictions may need to be lifted. If, and when, there are no restrictions and each of the 3 digits can be any integer from 0 through 9, how many area codes will be possible?

F.   27
G.   30
H.   720
J.   729
K.   1,000

DO YOUR FIGURING HERE.

33. The function $y = 2\sin(8\pi x)$ is graphed in the standard (x,y) coordinate plane below. How many x-intercepts does the graph of this function have on the interval $0 < x < 1$?

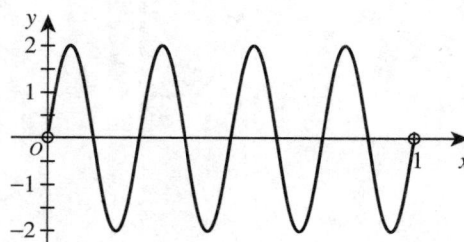

A.   2
B.   4
C.   7
D.   8
E.   9

34. If both x and $\left(\dfrac{x}{3} + \dfrac{x}{7} + \dfrac{x}{9}\right)$ are positive integers, what is the least possible value of x?

F.   21
G.   27
H.   36
J.   63
K.   189

GO ON TO THE NEXT PAGE.

2 △ △ △ △ △ △ △ △ △ 2

Use the following information to answer questions 35–38.

DO YOUR FIGURING HERE.

In parallelogram *ABCD* shown below, the diagonals intersect at *E*, $m\angle BDC = 42°$, $m\angle BDA = 71°$, and $AB = \left(\frac{2}{3}n - 5\right)$ inches.

(Note: The figure is NOT drawn to scale; $m\angle PQR$ denotes the measure of $\angle PQR$.)

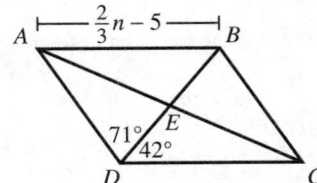

35. What is $m\angle BAD$?
- **A.** 23°
- **B.** 42°
- **C.** 48°
- **D.** 67°
- **E.** 71°

36. Given that $DC = \left(\frac{1}{3}n + 7\right)$ inches, what is the value of *n* ?
- **F.** 2
- **G.** 4
- **H.** 6
- **J.** 12
- **K.** 36

37. Suppose *A* and *C* are located at (2,10) and (30,3), respectively, in the standard (*x*,*y*) coordinate plane. What are the coordinates of *E* ?
- **A.** $\left(-\frac{7}{2}, 14\right)$
- **B.** $\left(\frac{13}{2}, 16\right)$
- **C.** $\left(14, -\frac{7}{2}\right)$
- **D.** $\left(14, \frac{7}{2}\right)$
- **E.** $\left(16, \frac{13}{2}\right)$

38. Which of the following triangles is congruent to $\triangle ABE$?
- **F.** $\triangle ADC$
- **G.** $\triangle AED$
- **H.** $\triangle BCE$
- **J.** $\triangle BCD$
- **K.** $\triangle CDE$

GO ON TO THE NEXT PAGE.

2 △   △   △   △   △   △   △   △   △ **2**

39. Which of the following expressions is equal to $(a + \sqrt{b})(a - 2\sqrt{b})$ for all positive real numbers a and b ?

A. $a^2 - 3a\sqrt{b}$

B. $a^2 - a\sqrt{b} - 2b$

C. $a^2 - a\sqrt{b} - 2\sqrt{2b}$

D. $a^2 - 3a\sqrt{b} - 2b$

E. $a^2 + 3a\sqrt{b} - 2b$

40. The track for a model railroad display is set up as 2 circles that are tangent to one another and have diameters of 30 feet and 50 feet, respectively, as shown below. The engine of the train travels at a constant rate of 75 feet per minute. To the nearest minute, how many minutes does the engine take to go in a figure 8 pattern around the entire track exactly 1 time?

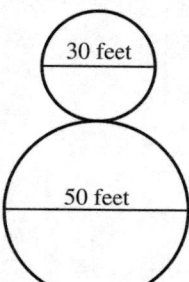

F. 1

G. 2

H. 3

J. 4

K. 7

41. $\left(\dfrac{4}{5}\right)^{-\frac{3}{2}} = ?$

A. $\dfrac{5}{2}$

B. $\dfrac{5\sqrt{5}}{8}$

C. $\dfrac{4\sqrt{2}}{5}$

D. $\dfrac{\sqrt{5}}{2}$

E. $-\dfrac{6}{5}$

42. What is the value of the positive real number x such that $\log_x\left(\dfrac{1}{25}\right) = -2$?

F. 5

G. 50

H. $\dfrac{1}{50}$

J. $\dfrac{1}{5}$

K. $\dfrac{25}{2}$

DO YOUR FIGURING HERE.

GO ON TO THE NEXT PAGE.

2 △ △ △ △ △ △ △ △ △ 2

43. The points $(-4,-5)$, $(0,-3)$, and $(6,0)$ lie on a line in the standard (x,y) coordinate plane. Which of the following points also lies on that line?

  A. $(-3,-4)$
  B. $(-1,-4)$
  C. $(1,-2)$
  D. $(4,-1)$
  E. $(9, 1)$

44. Rya and Sampath start running laps from the same starting line at the same time and in the same direction on a certain indoor track. Rya completes one lap in 16 seconds, and Sampath completes the same lap in 28 seconds. Both continue running at their same respective rates and in the same direction for 10 minutes. What is the fewest number of seconds after starting that Rya and Sampath will again be at their starting line at the same time?

  F. 88
  G. 112
  H. 120
  J. 220
  K. 448

45. The CFO of Math King Enterprises estimates that if the company sets a price of c cents for each unit of their new product, then the weekly profit from selling the product will be modeled by $p(c) = 1{,}600c - 4c^2$, where $0 \le c \le 400$. According to this model, for which of the following values of c will the weekly profit for this product be the largest?

  A. 20
  B. 40
  C. 100
  D. 200
  E. 400

46. Given consecutive positive integers a, b, c, and d such that $a < b < c < d$, which of the following expressions has the greatest value?

  F. $\dfrac{a}{b}$

  G. $\dfrac{b}{c}$

  H. $\dfrac{c}{d}$

  J. $\dfrac{a+b}{b+c}$

  K. $\dfrac{b+c}{c+d}$

47. The ratio of the perimeters of two squares is 2:3. If the area of the larger square is 324 square feet, what is the length, in feet, of the side of the smaller square?

  A. 12
  B. 18
  C. 24
  D. 27
  E. 36

DO YOUR FIGURING HERE.

GO ON TO THE NEXT PAGE.

2 △ △ △ △ △ △ △ △ △ 2

48. What is the set of all integer solutions for the inequality $-1 \leq x - \sqrt{5} < 4$?

F. {3, 4, 5}

G. {2, 3, 4, 5, 6}

H. {2, 3, 4, 5}

J. {1, 2, 3, 4, 5, 6}

K. {1, 2, 3, 4, 5}

49. Wind blowing against a flat surface exerts a maximum force equal to kSv^2, where S is the area of the surface, v is the wind's velocity, and k is a constant. If a 40 mile-per-hour (mph) wind can exert a maximum force of 50 pounds on a 1-square-foot flat surface, what is the maximum force, in pounds, that an 80 mph wind can exert on a 2-square-foot flat surface?

A. 100

B. 128

C. 200

D. 400

E. 1,600

50. Roger will pour concrete to make a sidewalk with the dimensions, in feet, shown in the figure below. He will pour the concrete to a depth of 4 *inches*. One bag of concrete mix makes 0.6 cubic feet of concrete. What is the least whole number of bags of concrete mix that Roger needs in order to make the sidewalk?

F. 16
G. 44
H. 50
J. 58
K. 67

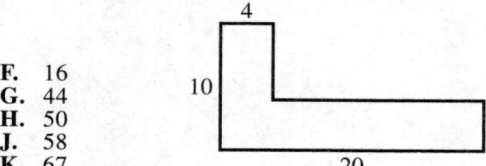

51. Radius $\overline{OA}$ of the circle shown below is perpendicular to $\overline{AP}$. The circle intersects $\overline{OP}$ at B. The length of $\overline{AP}$ is 12 centimeters, and the measure of $\angle APO$ is 20°. Which of the following values is closest to the length, in centimeters, of $\overline{BP}$?

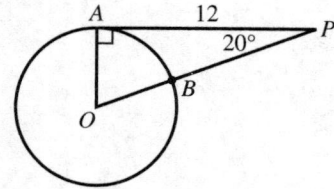

(Note: sin 20° ≈ 0.342, cos 20° ≈ 0.940, and tan 20° ≈ 0.364)

A. 2.1

B. 4.4

C. 6.9

D. 7.6

E. 8.4

DO YOUR FIGURING HERE.

GO ON TO THE NEXT PAGE.

2 △ △ △ △ △ △ △ △ △ **2**

52. The average of 10 test scores is x. When the highest score and lowest score are removed from the 10 scores, the average is y. Which of the following is an expression for the average of the highest score and lowest score?

F. $10x - 8y$

G. $\dfrac{x+y}{2}$

H. $\dfrac{10x + 8y}{2}$

J. $\dfrac{10x - 8y}{2}$

K. $\dfrac{10x + 8y}{18}$

DO YOUR FIGURING HERE.

53. Which of the following is the solution set of $27^{n^2} = 9^{5n-4}$?

A. $\left\{-4, \dfrac{2}{3}\right\}$

B. $\left\{-1, \dfrac{8}{3}\right\}$

C. $\left\{-\dfrac{2}{3}, 4\right\}$

D. $\{1, 4\}$

E. $\left\{\dfrac{4}{3}, 2\right\}$

54. Each face of 2 cubes with faces numbered from 1 through 6 has a $\dfrac{1}{6}$ chance of landing up when the 2 cubes are tossed. What is the probability that the sum of the numbers on the faces landing up will be less than 6 ?

F. $\dfrac{5}{36}$

G. $\dfrac{5}{18}$

H. $\dfrac{5}{13}$

J. $\dfrac{5}{12}$

K. $\dfrac{13}{36}$

GO ON TO THE NEXT PAGE.

2 △ △ △ △ △ △ △ △ △ **2**

55. At 2:00 p.m., Louisa leaves Kansas City in her car traveling east on I-70 toward St. Louis at an average speed of 68 mph. At precisely the same time, Antonio leaves St. Louis in his car traveling west on I-70 toward Kansas City at an average speed of 57 mph. The driving distance from St. Louis to Kansas City is 240 miles. At what time, to the nearest minute, will they drive past each other on I-70 ?

   A. 3:46 p.m.
   B. 3:50 p.m.
   C. 3:53 p.m.
   D. 3:55 p.m.
   E. 4:06 p.m.

56. There are 10 points in a plane, and no 3 of the points are collinear. These 10 points, taken 2 points at a time, determine how many distinct lines?

   F. 10
   G. 20
   H. 35
   J. 45
   K. 90

57. The expression $n!$ (read as *n factorial*) is defined as the product of all positive integers up to and including n, whenever n is a positive integer. For example, $4! = 1 \cdot 2 \cdot 3 \cdot 4$. Whenever n is a positive integer, which of the following is equivalent to $\frac{(n+1)!6!}{n!3!}$?

   A. $120(n + 1)$

   B. 120

   C. 2

   D. $\frac{2(n+1)}{n}$

   E. $\frac{(6n+6)!}{(3n)!}$

58. Which of the following *must* be true for each set of 4 consecutive positive integers?

   I. At least 1 of the 4 integers is prime.
   II. At least 2 of the 4 integers have a common prime factor.
   III. At least 1 of the 4 integers is a factor of at least 1 of the 3 other integers.

   F. I only
   G. II only
   H. I and III only
   J. II and III only
   K. I, II, and III

DO YOUR FIGURING HERE.

GO ON TO THE NEXT PAGE.

2 △ △ △ △ △ △ △ △ △ **2**

59. When $(x + 1)^4$ is expanded and like terms are combined, what is the coefficient of x^2 ?

A. 0
B. 1
C. 2
D. 4
E. 6

DO YOUR FIGURING HERE.

60. A hill makes an angle of 20° with the horizontal, $\overrightarrow{AD}$, as shown below. A taut guy wire, $\overline{AB}$, extends from the base of the hill, point A, to point B on a vertical pole. Point B is 25 ft directly above where the pole is inserted into the ground at point C. Given that the length of $\overline{AC}$ is 60 ft, which of the following expressions represents the length, in feet, of the guy wire?

(Note: For a triangle with sides of length a, b, and c that are opposite angles $\angle A$, $\angle B$, and $\angle C$, respectively, $\dfrac{\sin \angle A}{a} = \dfrac{\sin \angle B}{b} = \dfrac{\sin \angle C}{c}$ and $c^2 = a^2 + b^2 - 2ab \cos \angle C$.)

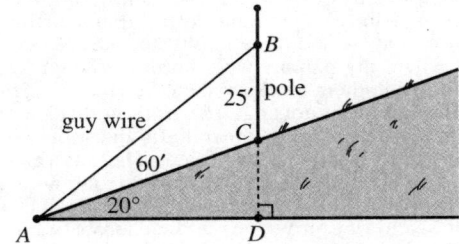

F. $\dfrac{25 \sin 60°}{\sin 20°}$

G. $\dfrac{25 \sin 70°}{\sin 20°}$

H. $\dfrac{25 \sin 110°}{\sin 20°}$

J. $\sqrt{60^2 + 25^2 - 2(60)(25) \cos 70°}$

K. $\sqrt{60^2 + 25^2 - 2(60)(25) \cos 110°}$

END OF TEST 2

STOP! DO NOT TURN THE PAGE UNTIL TOLD TO DO SO.

DO NOT RETURN TO THE PREVIOUS TEST.

Taking Additional Practice Tests

3   3

READING TEST
35 Minutes—40 Questions

DIRECTIONS: There are several passages in this test. Each passage is accompanied by several questions. After reading a passage, choose the best answer to each question and fill in the corresponding oval on your answer document. You may refer to the passages as often as necessary.

Passage I

LITERARY NARRATIVE: Passage A is adapted from the essay "Touring Home" by Susan Power (©1996 by Susan Power). Passage B is adapted from the memoir *Beyond the Narrow Gate: The Journey of Four Chinese Women from the Middle Kingdom to Middle America* by Leslie Chang (©1999 by Leslie Chang).

Passage A by Susan Power

My mother tells me stories every day: while she cleans, while she cooks, on our way to the library, standing in the checkout line at the supermarket. I like to share her stories with other people and chatter away
5 when I am able to command adult attention.

"She left the reservation when she was sixteen years old," I tell my audience. Sixteen sounds very old to me, but I always state the number because it seems integral to my recitation. "She had never been on a train
10 before or used a telephone. She left Standing Rock to take a job in Chicago so she could help out the family during the War. She was so petrified of the new surroundings, she stayed in her seat all the way from McLaughlin, South Dakota, to Chicago, Illinois, and
15 didn't move once."

I usually laugh after saying this because I cannot imagine my mother being afraid of anything. She is so tall, a true Dakota woman; she rises against the sun like a skyscraper, and when I draw her picture in my note-
20 book, she takes up the entire page. She talks politics and attends sit-ins and says what's on her mind.

I am her small shadow and witness. I am the timid daughter who can rage only on paper.

We don't have much money, but Mom takes me
25 from one end of the city to the other, on foot, on buses. I will grow up believing that Chicago belongs to me, because it was given to me by my mother.

Some days we haunt the Art Institute, and my mother pauses before a Picasso. "He did this during his
30 blue period," she tells me.

I squint at the blue man holding a blue guitar. "Was he very sad?" I ask.

"Yes, I think he was." My mother takes my hand and looks away from the painting. I can see a story
35 developing behind her eyes, and I tug on her arm to release the words. She will tell me why Picasso was blue, what his thoughts were as he painted this canvas. She relates anecdotes I will never find in books, never see footnoted in a biography of the master artist. I don't
40 even bother to check these references because I like my mother's version best.

Passage B by Leslie Chang

Water belongs to everyone and to no one. For this reason, I have always had a particular affinity for it, which may strike some as mysterious. Westerners ask
45 me where my parents were born, as though the answer will enable them to glean some knowledge. The answer is Beijing and Luoyang. The truth is that this response signifies nothing. The meaningful question would be to ask where my ancestors lived. The answer to that is
50 inland. My father's people came from Wuhan, birthplace of the Chinese republic and the capital of Hubei, that sweltering province sandwiched between Sichuan and Anhui. My mother's father was from Inner Mongolia, land of desert and grassy plains.

55 Yet water calls to me. I remain convinced that I would find peace if I could only have a house by the ocean. I insisted on being married near the sea. This bond, I know, comes from my mother.

She longs for a view more than anything else.
60 Once, staying at a hotel in San Francisco, she insisted on seeing three different rooms before she found one with which she was satisfied. It was on a floor so high it made me dizzy, with a corner window overlooking the bay. Even so, my mother spent most of her time on
65 the bridge linking the elevator bank to our wing. The bridge consisted almost entirely of windows. It offered a view in either direction that was brilliant and blinding. If there had been a chair, she could have sat forever, letting the gold sun and blue sea overwhelm her
70 through the glass.

My mother may have descended from inland people, but they were also nomads. Her father once rode his horse practically the length of China, from Inner Mongolia to Guangzhou, a distance of some
75 twelve hundred miles. My mother could only become a

GO ON TO THE NEXT PAGE.

3 ▬▬▬▬▬▬▬▬▬▬▬▬▬▬▬▬▬▬▬▬▬▬ **3**

nomad herself—forever moving, changing and going, yet always retaining some essential part of her being, recognizable and intact in spite of all the places she has been. In this, she is like water, not dead water but fear-
80 somely alive. When she gazes out on its shimmering expanse, she sees her own reflection. When I gaze out, I see her, my mother, always pulling away, returning and pulling away again. I drink from her, and she slips between my fingertips. She has borne me all this way. I
85 cannot decide whether I want her to stay or go. When she is here, I wish she would leave. When she is gone, I wish she would return. She pulls away again, a force as elemental as the ebbing tide. I remain a child on the shore, eagerly collecting the sea glass and driftwood
90 she has left behind.

Questions 1–3 ask about Passage A.

1. In Passage A, the narrator directly compares her mother to a:

   A. Picasso painting.
   B. shadow and witness.
   C. story behind someone's eyes.
   D. skyscraper against the sun.

2. The narrator of Passage A most strongly suggests that the reason she began to believe Chicago belongs to her is that she:

   F. could eventually take several different routes to travel from one end of the city to the other without getting lost.
   G. had watched her mother directly influence the politics of the city.
   H. felt she could move about the city almost unseen, like a small shadow.
   J. initially explored the city with her mother as her affirming guide, so her connection to the city seemed familial.

3. It can most reasonably be inferred from Passage A that the narrator doesn't bother to verify that her mother's ideas about Picasso and his work are accurate primarily because the narrator:

   A. doesn't know which references would be best for her to consult.
   B. is confident that what her mother says about the artist is accurate and feels that checking references would be a waste of time.
   C. doesn't care whether her mother is accurate given how much the narrator likes what her mother says about the artist.
   D. wants to hold to her own ideas about the artist, regardless of what her mother says about him.

Questions 4–7 ask about Passage B.

4. In Passage B, the narrator most strongly suggests that she believes her answer to which of the following questions does not provide significant information about her background?

   F. How is your mother like your other ancestors?
   G. Where did your ancestors live?
   H. Where were your parents born?
   J. Why does water call to you?

5. As they are used in Passage B, the word *blinding* (line 68) and the word *overwhelm* (line 69) both have a connotation that most strongly suggests a feeling of:

   A. fright.
   B. awe.
   C. regret.
   D. quietness.

6. In line 79, the word *dead* is most nearly used to describe water that is:

   F. colorless.
   G. obsolete.
   H. stagnant.
   J. frozen.

7. The last sentence of Passage B can best be described as a:

   A. metaphor for the narrator's feelings as her mother goes away from her.
   B. memory of childhood and of her mother that the narrator holds dear.
   C. literal explanation of the way the narrator reacts to her mother's actions.
   D. reference to a set of objects that the narrator as a child often found on the shore.

Questions 8–10 ask about both passages.

8. Which of the following actions do the narrators of both passages closely connect with their mothers?

   F. Traveling and moving
   G. Exploring Chicago streets
   H. Speaking openly and boldly
   J. Staying at hotels in cities

9. The narrator of Passage B would be more likely than the narrator of Passage A to describe her relationship with her mother as being marked by:

   A. moments of lively conversation and pure joy.
   B. years of fierce competition and debate.
   C. displays of physical affection and warmth.
   D. feelings of distance and tension.

GO ON TO THE NEXT PAGE.

3 ⬛⬛⬛⬛⬛⬛⬛⬛⬛⬛⬛⬛⬛⬛⬛⬛ **3**

10. In both Passage A and Passage B, the narrator of the passage shares information about her mother's:

F. personal history.
G. physical appearance.
H. academic interests.
J. relationship to the narrator's father.

Passage II

SOCIAL SCIENCE: This passage is adapted from *The Frozen-Water Trade: A True Story* by Gavin Weightman (©2003 by Gavin Weightman).

When the first comprehensive report on the ice industry of the United States was commissioned in 1879 as part of a national census, it was estimated that about eight million tons were harvested annually,
5 though the business was so extensive and production so poorly documented that this was, at best, a well-informed guess. The figures were put together by one Henry Hall, who signed himself "special agent" and gave an account of the great growth of the industry in
10 the preceding ten years. Of the eight million tons of ice harvested, about five million reached the consumer—the rest melted during shipment and storage. By far the biggest market was in New York, and none of its ice was manufactured artificially: it was all cut in winter
15 and stored in hundreds of timber warehouses that lined the lakes and rivers and had a capacity of up to fifty thousand tons each. Between New York and Albany, 150 miles up the Hudson River, there were 135 icehouses, but even this was not enough to supply the
20 metropolis, which relied heavily on imports. In fact, in the year of the great ice census, New York and Philadelphia suffered one of their recurrent ice "famines," when unseasonably warm weather destroyed the harvest on the Hudson and local lakes, and the price of ice rose
25 from $4 to $5 a ton. That year the ice was fifteen to twenty inches thick in Maine, a top-quality crop, and it could be shipped down to New York at an estimated cost of $1.50 a ton. This produced a frenzy of harvesting on the Kennebec, Penobscot, and Sheepscot Rivers,
30 and two thousand cargoes of ice packed in hay and sawdust were shipped south to New York, Philadelphia, and other more southern cities, where they were sold for a total of around $1.5 million.

Though the demand for ice rose annually, the New
35 York suppliers did not explore the use of artificial refrigeration. Instead, they began to buy up sections of the Kennebec River shoreline and to erect great wooden warehouses there, transforming the landscape of the river for many miles. It was the same farther inland,
40 where ice companies bought up shoreline along the lakes and put up storehouses to supply the meat industry of Chicago and the brewers of Milwaukee, as well as millions of domestic consumers.

The first real crisis in the natural-ice trade was
45 caused not by competition from artificial manufacture, but by pollution. As the cities grew, they encroached on the rivers and lakes from which the ice was cut, and soon there were health scares. This produced a search for cleaner supplies away from towns, and stimulated
50 the search for a means of manufacturing ice with pure water. The realization that the bacteria that cause diseases such as typhoid were not killed off in frozen water added to the urgency of finding safer forms of refrigeration.

55 The natural-ice trade began to decline from the early decades of the twentieth century, though in more remote areas of North America where electric power was not available but lake ice was abundant in winter, it survived as late as the 1950s. As ice harvesting died
60 out, the evidence of its former vast scale rapidly disappeared. There was no alternative use for the great icehouses, many of which simply burned down, often set alight by a spark from a steam train—they were surprisingly flammable, as most were made of wood and kept
65 as dry as possible to better preserve the blocks of ice they housed. But the majority were demolished or simply rotted away.

Over a wide area of the northern states, young diving enthusiasts with no knowledge of the former ice
70 trade still emerge from lakes and rivers clutching an impressive variety of odd implements—plows and chisels and scrapers that fell through the ice during the harvesting. One or two museums keep small displays of these tools, and collectors have preserved manufactur-
75 ers' catalogs that proudly present their versions of the ice plow, the ice saw, the grapple, the Jack grapple, the breaking-off bar, the caulk bar, the packing chisel, the house bar, the fork bar, the float hook, the line marker, and many other specialist implements the use
80 of which has long been forgotten.

The inner-city icehouses have also gone, and the ice wagon and the iceman are rapidly fading memories. All that is left in America of this once-great industry is the water itself, which provided a continuously renew-
85 able supply of ice each winter. There are few memorials on the banks of the rivers and lakes that once produced such a vital crop.

11. Which of the following events referred to in the passage occurred last chronologically?

A. The first comprehensive report on the ice industry of the United States was commissioned.
B. Divers emerged from lakes and rivers clutching ice industry implements.
C. Two thousand cargoes of ice were sold for around $1.5 million.
D. The price of ice rose from $4 to $5 a ton.

GO ON TO THE NEXT PAGE.

3   **3**

12. The passage states that, in terms of the natural-ice industry, the decade from 1869 to 1879 was characterized by:

  F. significant growth.
  G. damaging publicity.
  H. high shipping prices.
  J. mildly declining demand.

13. As it is used in lines 19–20, the phrase *the metropolis* most likely refers to:

  A. Albany.
  B. New York City.
  C. Philadelphia.
  D. the average US city of the 1870s.

14. Based on the passage, the 1879 Maine ice that was fifteen to twenty inches thick can best be described as:

  F. a top-quality crop that was shipped to New York City, Philadelphia, and destinations further south.
  G. sufficient for local demand but not a solution to the problem of the ice "famine" in the South.
  H. typical of Maine crops of ice until the ice "famine" struck.
  J. remarkable but surpassed in size and quality by crops the following year.

15. The main idea of the fourth paragraph (lines 55–67) is that:

  A. the natural-ice industry declined over several decades, leaving few traces of its magnitude.
  B. the arrival of the steam train signaled the demise of ice harvesting.
  C. icehouses were extremely flammable and therefore few remain.
  D. in the 1950s, the natural-ice industry experienced a short-lived revival.

16. The author most clearly indicates that the contents of the manufacturers' catalogs referred to in the fifth paragraph (lines 68–80) typify the natural-ice industry's:

  F. rapid response to market changes.
  G. ability to erect icehouses quickly.
  H. wide array of tools.
  J. simple work.

17. On which of the following points does the author contradict himself elsewhere in the passage?

  A. "Of the eight million tons of ice harvested, about five million reached the consumer" (lines 10–11).
  B. "The New York suppliers did not explore the use of artificial refrigeration" (lines 34–36).
  C. "There was no alternative use for the great icehouses" (lines 61–62).
  D. "All that is left in America of this once-great industry is the water itself" (lines 83–84).

18. According to the passage, in the time period referred to in the first paragraph, how much of New York City's ice was made artificially?

  F. The vast majority
  G. About half
  H. About ten percent
  J. None

19. The passage states that for shipping purposes, natural ice was sometimes packed in:

  A. refrigerated boxcars.
  B. waterproof tarps.
  C. sawdust and hay.
  D. paper and cloth.

20. The passage indicates that the first real crisis in the natural-ice industry can be attributed to:

  F. the Great Depression.
  G. weather pattern changes.
  H. the advent of refrigeration.
  J. polluted water.

GO ON TO THE NEXT PAGE.

3

3

Passage III

HUMANITIES: This passage is adapted from the article "Read My Lips" by Chiara Barzini (©2012 by the Harper's Magazine Foundation).

In the passage, *dubbing* primarily refers to providing a film with a new sound track, especially dialogue, in a different language.

Filmmakers have debated the respective merits of subtitles and dubbing since the earliest sound films. In "The Impossible Life of Clark Costa," published in 1940 in the film journal *Cinema*, director Michelangelo
5 Antonioni wrote that Romolo Costa, the person who dubbed all of actor Clark Gable's performances, was a "hybrid individual born out of a chemical combination." This "half Clark, half Costa" was unbearable to Antonioni, who considered dubbing to be a mere
10 "acoustic surrogate" of acting. To him, dubbing compromised the intention of the director, leading to an artificial product that lacked artistic unity. Director Pier Paolo Pasolini, who called both dubbing and subtitles "evils," said that, between the two, dubbing was the less
15 harmful, since it allowed you to see the picture in full. Director Jean Renoir called dubbing a "monstrosity, a challenge to human and divine laws."

Director Federico Fellini didn't agree with any of them. Dubbing was an extension of his shoots, a tech-
20 nique he would use to retouch and rewrite. He mercilessly dubbed over his actors, changing dialogue in postproduction, sometimes having worked without a script. (He reportedly instructed his actors to count aloud in front of the camera so that he could insert new
25 dialogue afterward.) Renato Cortesi, a veteran Fellini dubber, told me that, during the filming of *Amarcord* (1973), he witnessed Fellini ask an old Neapolitan lady to tell him a sad story. Over footage of this woman recounting a tragic tale about her grandson, Fellini
30 added a new sound track about war and hunger recorded by an actor from Emilia-Romagna, combining the vivid expressiveness of the South with his favorite northern accent.

If you visit a dubbing studio, the over-the-top zest
35 of the actors is evident in everything from their melodramatic speech to their movements; standing in front of the microphone, they coil and twitch. I asked Cortesi whether this was a consequence of having to focus one's lifelong talent into the few centimeters between
40 mouth and microphone, a kind of bodily rebellion to the condition of being heard but not seen, and he laughed. "Of course it isn't easy to spend a life in the darkness, but this is hardly the reason why they twitch and turn! Dubbers are used to reciting while trying to re-create
45 the bodily sensations of what they see on the screen before them. If there is running in the film, they will run on their feet. The moving," he explained, "is the result of re-creating large movements in small spaces."

There are still few options for those seeking to
50 watch subtitled, original-language films at a movie house in Italy. The Metropolitan cinema on Via del Corso closed recently after a long battle involving intel-

lectuals, show-business people, and American and British expats in Rome, to be replaced with a clothing
55 store. Italians remain hooked on dubbing—perhaps because of simple affection. Familiar voices yield emotional attachment.

Francesco Vairano, a dubber and dubbing director known for adapting foreign films considered to be
60 "undubbable," such as the French box office hit *Bienvenue chez les Ch'tis* ("Welcome to the Sticks," 2008), which relies on linguistic misunderstandings for much of its comedy, explained that actors become just as attached to their parts as audiences do. Vairano has
65 been one of the few directors to break the habit of matching the same Italian dubber to a foreign actor for all his films, preferring instead to select the dubber according to the requirements of the role, and, he admits, he was hated by all the prima donna dubbers for
70 this. "If you take that actor away from them," he told me, "they will insult you."

In 2007, I met dubber Luca Ward, who provided the voice of the narrator for a romantic comedy I co-wrote, *Scusa ma Ti Chiamo Amore* ("Sorry but I Love
75 You"). What I didn't then know was that everyone Ward met wanted him to recite actor Samuel L. Jackson's Ezekiel 25:17 passage from the film *Pulp Fiction*, and that I should consider it an honor that he would offer a performance to a stranger. When he finally did recite
80 the monologue, it was astonishing, every dramatic pause carefully timed and every word perfectly enunciated. I understood that, if anybody took Samuel L. Jackson away from Ward, it would have meant taking away a part of his soul; he was, as Antonioni would say,
85 half Ward, half Jackson. Leaving the day's recording session, Ward told me he was off to have dinner with actress Meg Ryan, before raising an eyebrow and clarifying, "With Meg Ryan's *dubber* . . . I am having dinner with Meg Ryan's voice."

21. The last sentence of the passage primarily serves to illustrate the passage author's central claim that:

   A. a dubber wants others in the film industry to respect the actor he or she usually dubs.
   B. the work of Ryan's dubber is as effective as that of Jackson's dubber.
   C. a dubber begins to seem almost like a hybrid of him- or herself and the actor he or she dubs.
   D. Ward is unlike most dubbers in that he prefers to dub many different actors.

22. It can reasonably be inferred from the passage that regarding whether dubbing is useful or valuable, Vairano would most strongly sympathize with the views of:

   F. Antonioni.
   G. Fellini.
   H. Pasolini.
   J. Renoir.

GO ON TO THE NEXT PAGE.

3 ━━━━━━━━━━━━━━━━━━━━━━━━━━━━━━ **3**

23. The main function of the second paragraph (lines 18–33) is for the passage author to present:

   A. her own ideas as an example of a contemporary perspective on the merits of dubbing.
   B. a perspective on dubbing that bluntly counters those outlined in the first paragraph.
   C. Fellini's personal, direct response to Renoir's criticism of his work.
   D. a claim, centered on Fellini's work, that strengthens the argument she makes in the first paragraph.

24. The anecdote about Fellini's footage of a woman recounting a tragic tale (lines 25–33) primarily serves to:

   F. explain why Fellini preferred to feature voices with northern accents in his films.
   G. provide a famous example of Fellini closely following scripted dialogue.
   H. illustrate the extent to which dubbing was a part of Fellini's craft.
   J. show why Fellini preferred his actors to follow a script rather than tell their own stories.

25. As Cortesi is presented in the passage, does he agree with the passage author's assumptions about the reason for dubbers' "over-the-top zest" (line 34)?

   A. Yes, and he thinks that she should visit his dubbing studio to see how he works.
   B. Yes, and he suggests that the reason is the dubber's condition of being heard but not seen.
   C. No, and he gruffly makes clear his belief that she does not at all understand a dubber's work.
   D. No, and he corrects her misinterpretation with an explanation of his own.

26. It can most reasonably be inferred from the passage that the Metropolitan cinema on Via del Corso was known for showing films that had been:

   F. dubbed only.
   G. subtitled only.
   H. both dubbed and subtitled.
   J. neither dubbed nor subtitled.

27. The passage most strongly suggests that at movie houses in Italy today, compared to subtitled, original-language films, dubbed films can be found:

   A. much more easily.
   B. about as easily.
   C. slightly less easily.
   D. much less easily.

28. The passage indicates that a foreign film with which of the following characteristics is particularly difficult to dub?

   F. Linguistic misunderstanding that creates comedy
   G. Dramatic action that advances plot
   H. Reverse chronology that provides context
   J. Extensive monologues that further characterization

29. According to the passage, the work of dubbing director Vairano differs from that of most other Italian directors in that Vairano:

   A. focuses on dubbing French films into Italian.
   B. does not necessarily match the same Italian dubber to the same foreign actor for all his films.
   C. works mostly with "prima donna" dubbers.
   D. does not believe that dialogue should be rewritten during a dubbing session.

30. As it is used in lines 16–17, the phrase *a challenge to* most nearly means:

   F. an assault on.
   G. a declaration of.
   H. a question for.
   J. an offer to.

GO ON TO THE NEXT PAGE.

3 ▬▬▬▬▬▬▬▬▬▬▬▬▬▬▬▬▬▬▬▬ **3**

Passage IV

NATURAL SCIENCE: This passage is adapted from the essay
"Making Stuff: From Bacon to Bakelite" by Philip Ball (©2010
by Philip Ball).

During the Industrial Revolution, the high price of
steel meant that many large engineering projects were
carried out that used instead cast iron, which is brittle
and prone to failure. This was why Henry Bessemer's
5 new process for making steel was greeted with jubilation: the details, announced at a meeting of the British
Association in 1856, were published in full in *The
Times*. Bessemer himself was lauded not just as an
engineer but as a scientist, being elected a Fellow of the
10 Royal Society in 1879.

Bessemer's process controlled the amount of
carbon mixed with iron to make steel. That the proportion of carbon governs the hardness was first noted in
1774 by the Swedish metallurgist Torbern Bergmann,
15 who was by any standards a scientist, teaching chemistry, physics and mathematics at Uppsala. Bergmann
made an extensive study of the propensity of different
chemical elements to combine with one another—a
property known as elective affinity, central to the
20 eighteenth-century notion of chemical reactivity. He
was a mentor and sponsor of Carl Wilhelm Scheele, the
greatest Swedish chemist of the age and co-discoverer
of oxygen.

Oxygen, as a component of air, was the key to the
25 Bessemer process. It offered a way of removing impurities from pig iron and adjusting its carbon content
during conversion to steel. A blast of air through the
molten metal turned impurities such as silicon into light
silica slag (a collection of compounds removed from
30 metal in the smelting process), and removed carbon in
the form of volatile carbon dioxide. Pig iron contains as
much as 4 per cent carbon; steels have only around
0.3–2 per cent. Meanwhile, the heat produced in these
reactions with oxygen kept the iron molten without the
35 need for extra fuel.

It was long known that steel can be improved with
a spice of other elements. A dash of the metal manganese helps to remove oxygen and sulphur from the
iron, and most of the manganese currently produced
40 globally is used for this purpose. Manganese also
makes steel stronger, while nickel and chromium
improve its hardness. And chromium is the key additive
in stainless steel—in a proportion of more than about
11 per cent, it makes the metal rust-resistant. Most
45 modern steels are therefore alloys blended to give the
desired properties.

But is this science? Some of the early innovations
in steel alloys were chance discoveries, often due to
impurities incorporated by accident. In this respect,
50 metallurgy has long retained the air of an artisan craft,
akin to the trial-and-error explorations of dyers, glass-
makers and potters. But the reason for this empiricism
is not that the science of metallurgy is trivial; it
is because it is so difficult. According to Rodney

55 Cotterill, a remarkable British physicist whose expertise stretched from the sciences of materials to that of
the brain, 'metallurgy is one of our most ancient arts,
but is often referred to as one of the youngest sciences'.

One of the principal difficulties in understanding
60 the behaviour of materials such as steel is that this
depends on its structure over a wide range of length
scales, from the packing of individual atoms to the size
and shape of grains micrometres or even millimetres in
size. Science has trouble dealing with such a span of
65 scales. One might regard this difficulty as akin to that
in the social sciences, where social behaviour is governed by how individuals behave but also how we interact on the scale of families and neighbourhoods, within
entire cities, and at a national level. (That's why the
70 social sciences are arguably among the hardest of sciences too.)

The mechanical properties of metals depend on
how flaws in the crystal structure, called defects, move
and interact. These defects are produced by almost
75 inevitable imperfections in the regular stacking of
atoms in the crystalline material. The most common
type of stacking fault is called a dislocation. Metals
bend, rather than shattering like porcelain, because dislocations can shift around and accommodate the defor-
80 mation. But if dislocations accumulate and get
entangled, restricting their ability to move, the metal
becomes brittle. This is what happens after repeated
deformation, causing the cracking known as metal
fatigue. Dislocations can also get trapped at the bound-
85 aries between the fine, microscopic grains that divide a
metal into mosaics of crystallites. The arrest of dislocations at grain edges means that metals may be made
harder by reducing the size of their grains, a useful
trick for modifying their mechanical behaviour.

31. The main purpose of the passage is to:
   A. explain in detail the various experiments Bessemer
      conducted in order to develop a better steel.
   B. provide an overview of some of the scientific prin-
      ciples that apply to the creation and behavior of
      steel.
   C. describe some of the philosophical questions con-
      cerning metallurgy.
   D. illustrate the differences between pig iron and cast
      iron.

32. The author most likely includes details about the initial
    response to Bessemer's new steel-making process in
    order to:
   F. emphasize that Bessemer's new process was a sig-
      nificant achievement for industry.
   G. provide support for the author's opinion that
      Bessemer's new process was prone to failure.
   H. describe Bessemer's qualifications as an engineer.
   J. provide specific examples of the criticism that
      Bessemer's new process received.

GO ON TO THE NEXT PAGE.

3 ▬▬▬▬▬▬▬▬▬▬▬▬▬▬▬▬▬▬▬▬ **3**

33. It can reasonably be inferred that the author includes the information that Bergmann was a mentor and sponsor of Scheele's mainly to:

A. introduce the fact that Bergmann was a teacher as well as a scientist.
B. suggest that Bergmann was a more successful scientist than Scheele was.
C. give an example of the eighteenth-century notion of scientific communities.
D. reinforce Bergmann's credibility as a scientist.

34. According to the passage, which of the following conversions is a direct result of adding oxygen to molten pig iron?

F. Light silica slag is converted into carbon dioxide.
G. Carbon dioxide is converted into carbon.
H. Silicon is converted into light silica slag.
J. Impurities in the metal are converted into silicon.

35. In the context of the passage, the main effect of the word "spice" (line 37) is to emphasize that:

A. elements must be gradually mixed into steel in order to produce the desired effect.
B. adding certain elements to steel can enrich the steel's quality.
C. manganese, chromium, and nickel are used sparingly in steel because of their expense.
D. blending elements is a trial-and-error process that has not yet yielded positive results.

36. Based on the passage, with which of the following statements would the author most likely agree?

F. Metallurgy is not an art because it requires too much scientific knowledge.
G. Metallurgy is too difficult to be considered a science.
H. Metallurgy is a science as well as an art.
J. Metallurgy is a trivial science.

37. The passage most strongly suggests that the study of the behavior of materials and the study of the social sciences are similar because they:

A. require analyses that span a wide range of scales.
B. are based on trial-and-error experimentation.
C. involve examination of the size and shape of individual atoms.
D. produce results that must be interpreted by both scientists and artists.

38. The main idea of the last paragraph is that:

F. defects in the crystal structure of a metal determine that metal's mechanical properties.
G. dislocations are the most common type of stacking fault in a metal.
H. the mechanical behavior of a metal can be modified by increasing the size of a metal's grains.
J. microscopic grains divide a metal into mosaics of crystallites.

39. As it is used in line 56, the word *stretched* most nearly means:

A. strained.
B. exaggerated.
C. extended.
D. amplified.

40. According to the passage, reducing the size of a metal's grains can make the metal:

F. more rust-resistant.
G. more brittle.
H. finer.
J. harder.

END OF TEST 3

STOP! DO NOT TURN THE PAGE UNTIL TOLD TO DO SO.

DO NOT RETURN TO A PREVIOUS TEST.

Taking Additional Practice Tests

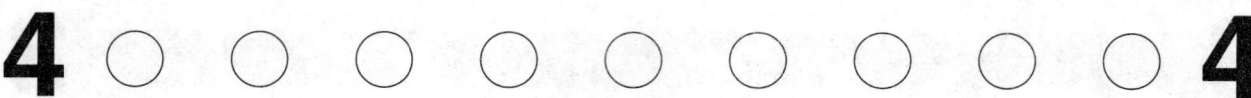

SCIENCE TEST

35 Minutes—40 Questions

DIRECTIONS: There are several passages in this test. Each passage is followed by several questions. After reading a passage, choose the best answer to each question and fill in the corresponding oval on your answer document. You may refer to the passages as often as necessary.

You are NOT permitted to use a calculator on this test.

Passage I

The termite *Reticulitermes flavipes* consumes wood and bark. A study examined whether the consumption of wood or bark mulch by *R. flavipes* varies with the type of mulch or the age of the mulch. Separate portions of each of 5 types of mulch were aged (allowed to decay) for 1, 24, and 48 weeks. Then, 2 g of each type of 1-week-old mulch were put into a box, 2 g of each type of 24-week-old mulch were put into a second box, and 2 g of each type of 48-week-old mulch were put into a third box. Next, 1 g of *R. flavipes* was added to each box. After 15 days, the mass of mulch consumed, in milligrams (mg), was determined for each type and age of mulch (see figure).

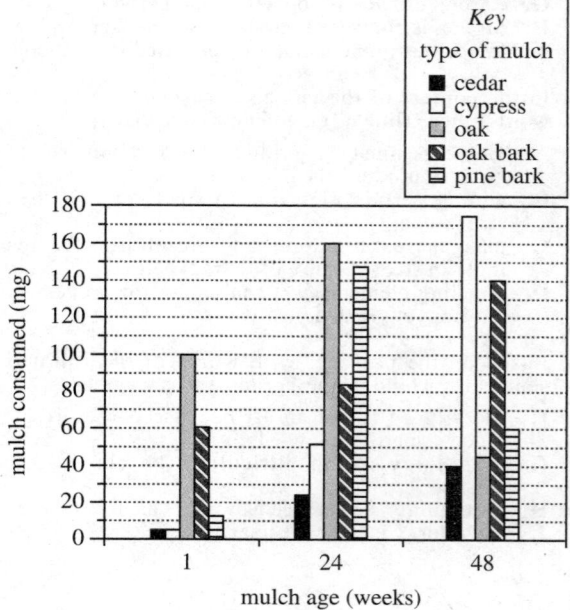

Figure adapted from O. P. Pinzon, R. M. Houseman, and C. J. Starbuck, "Feeding, Weight Change, Survival, and Aggregation of *Reticulitermes flavipes* (Kollar) (Isoptera: Rhinotermitidae) in Seven Varieties of Differentially-Aged Mulch." ©2006 by the Horticultural Research Institute.

GO ON TO THE NEXT PAGE.

4 ○ ○ ○ ○ ○ ○ ○ ○ **4**

1. Of the following combinations of type of mulch and mulch age, which combination resulted in the greatest mass of mulch consumed by *R. flavipes* ?

	type of mulch	mulch age
A.	oak	24 weeks
B.	pine bark	24 weeks
C.	oak	48 weeks
D.	pine bark	48 weeks

2. Which of the following statements about the effect of mulch age on the consumption of mulch by *R. flavipes* is consistent with the figure? As mulch age increased from 1 week through 48 weeks, the mass of mulch consumed by *R. flavipes*:

F. decreased for all 5 types of mulch.
G. increased for all 5 types of mulch.
H. initially decreased for all 5 types of mulch, but then increased for some of the 5 types of mulch.
J. initially increased for all 5 types of mulch, but then decreased for some of the 5 types of mulch.

3. Based on the passage, would *R. flavipes* be classified as an autotroph or as a detritivore, and why?

A. Autotroph, because *R. flavipes* produces its own energy without consuming organic material.
B. Autotroph, because *R. flavipes* obtains its energy by consuming decaying organic material.
C. Detritivore, because *R. flavipes* produces its own energy without consuming organic material.
D. Detritivore, because *R. flavipes* obtains its energy by consuming decaying organic material.

4. Based on the passage, is the primary food source of *R. flavipes* more likely cellulose or cholesterol?

F. Cellulose; *R. flavipes* consumes the cell membranes of animal cells, and the cell membranes of animal cells contain cellulose.
G. Cellulose; *R. flavipes* consumes the cell walls of plant cells, and the cell walls of plant cells consist primarily of cellulose.
H. Cholesterol; *R. flavipes* consumes the cell membranes of animal cells, and the cell membranes of animal cells contain cholesterol.
J. Cholesterol; *R. flavipes* consumes the cell walls of plant cells, and the cell walls of plant cells consist primarily of cholesterol.

5. Which of the following statements comparing the consumption by *R. flavipes* of 1-week-old oak mulch, 24-week-old oak mulch, and 48-week-old oak mulch is supported by the figure?

A. More 1-week-old mulch was consumed than 24-week-old mulch, and more 24-week-old mulch was consumed than 48-week-old mulch.
B. Less 1-week-old mulch was consumed than 24-week-old mulch, and less 24-week-old mulch was consumed than 48-week-old mulch.
C. More 1-week-old mulch was consumed than 24-week-old mulch, and less 24-week-old mulch was consumed than 48-week-old mulch.
D. Less 1-week-old mulch was consumed than 24-week-old mulch, and more 24-week-old mulch was consumed than 48-week-old mulch.

6. What mass, in *grams* (NOT milligrams), of the 48-week-old oak bark mulch was consumed by *R. flavipes* ?

F. 0.06 g
G. 0.14 g
H. 0.6 g
J. 1.4 g

GO ON TO THE NEXT PAGE.

4   **4**

Passage II

Samples of Species C bacteria must often be transported from the areas in which they are collected. During transport, the samples are typically packed in ice to keep them alive. However, ice is not always available where the samples are collected.

Scientists studied how *lyophilization* (a freeze-drying process that doesn't require ice) followed by incubation affects the survival of 2 strains (Strain E and Strain V2) of Species C bacteria.

Experiment 1

The scientists placed a 100 μL (1 μL = 10^{-3} mL) sample of a nutrient medium containing 4×10^6 Strain E elementary bodies into each of 8 sterile test tubes. An *elementary body* is the infective form of Species C. The sample in each of the tubes was then lyophilized, and each tube was sealed. Two of the tubes were incubated at 4°C, 2 were incubated at 20°C, 2 were incubated at 30°C, and 2 were incubated at 37°C.

One week after the start of incubation, the *percent survival* (the percent of the elementary bodies that survived) was determined for the sample in 1 of the 2 tubes at each temperature. Then, 1 month after the start of incubation, the percent survival was determined for the sample in the remaining tube at each temperature. The results are shown in Table 1.

Table 1			
Strain	Incubation temperature (°C)	Percent (%) survival at:	
		1 week	1 month
E	4	52	51
	20	69	42
	30	5	4
	37	0	0

Experiment 2

The scientists repeated Experiment 1, except with Strain V2 instead of Strain E. The results are shown in Table 2.

Table 2			
Strain	Incubation temperature (°C)	Percent (%) survival at:	
		1 week	1 month
V2	4	59	6
	20	29	4
	30	2	2
	37	0	0

Tables adapted from Adrian Eley et al., "Effect of Storage Temperature on Survival of *Chlamydia trachomatis* after Lyophilization." ©2006 by American Society for Microbiology.

GO ON TO THE NEXT PAGE.

4 ○ ○ ○ ○ ○ ○ ○ ○ **4**

7. Which of the following statements describes a difference between Experiment 1 and Experiment 2 ?

   A. A different incubation temperature was tested in Experiment 1 than in Experiment 2.
   B. A different strain of Species C was tested in Experiment 1 than in Experiment 2.
   C. Samples in Experiment 1 were lyophilized before being transported, whereas samples in Experiment 2 were transported on ice.
   D. Samples in Experiment 1 were incubated for 1 week before being transported, whereas samples in Experiment 2 were incubated for 1 month before being transported.

8. Suppose that in Experiment 2 the scientists had determined the percent survival for a sample incubated at 25°C for 1 week. The percent survival of the Strain V2 elementary bodies in the sample would most likely have been:

   F. 0%.
   G. between 2% and 29%.
   H. between 29% and 59%.
   J. greater than 59%.

9. At which 2 temperatures was the percent survival of Strain V2 elementary bodies less for the longer incubation time than for the shorter incubation time?

   A. 4°C and 20°C
   B. 4°C and 37°C
   C. 20°C and 30°C
   D. 20°C and 37°C

10. Which of the following questions was NOT addressed by the experiments?

   F. Does incubation time affect the percent survival of Strain E and Strain V2 elementary bodies after lyophilization?
   G. Does temperature affect the percent survival of Strain E and Strain V2 elementary bodies after lyophilization?
   H. Does the number of Strain E or Strain V2 elementary bodies present in a sample before lyophilization affect their percent survival?
   J. Do Strain E elementary bodies have a greater percent survival than Strain V2 elementary bodies after lyophilization and incubation?

11. One week after the start of incubation, which of the 4 samples of Strain V2 elementary bodies would have been *least* likely to infect another organism that came into contact with the samples?

   A. The sample that had been incubated at 4°C
   B. The sample that had been incubated at 10°C
   C. The sample that had been incubated at 20°C
   D. The sample that had been incubated at 37°C

12. Suppose that a scientist wants to transport a lyophilized sample of Strain E elementary bodies. Based on the results of Experiment 1, which of the following combinations of temperature and transportation time would most likely ensure the greatest percent survival of the elementary bodies?

   F. 4°C and 1 week
   G. 4°C and 1 month
   H. 20°C and 1 week
   J. 20°C and 1 month

13. Consider the rating system in the table below for the percent survival of elementary bodies after lyophilization.

Rating	Percent survival
Excellent	> 90%
Good	≥ 30% and ≤ 90%
Poor	< 30%

   Based on this table, what is the total number of tubes in Experiment 1 that contained samples having a poor percent survival?

   A. 2
   B. 4
   C. 6
   D. 8

Taking Additional Practice Tests

GO ON TO THE NEXT PAGE.

Passage III

When an object is submerged in a fluid, the object displaces a volume of fluid equal to the object's submerged volume. The fluid exerts an upward *buoyant force* on the object that is equal in magnitude to the weight of the displaced fluid. The object floats if the buoyant force equals the object's weight.

A group of students conducted 2 studies on buoyant forces using 3 fluids—water, Fluid A, and Fluid B—having densities of 1.0 g/cm^3, 1.25 g/cm^3, and 1.50 g/cm^3, respectively.

Study 1

The students placed a 10 cm long cylinder in a container of water and measured the length of the portion of the cylinder that was submerged. They then repeated this procedure with a container of Fluid A and a container of Fluid B (see Figure 1).

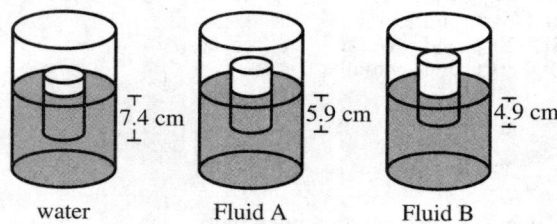

water   Fluid A   Fluid B

Figure 1

Study 2

The students placed a stone—either Stone X, Stone Y, or Stone Z—in a net that was tied to a spring balance. They recorded the force measured by the balance as the stone's weight, *W*. They then submerged the stone in water and again recorded the force measured by the balance (see Figure 2).

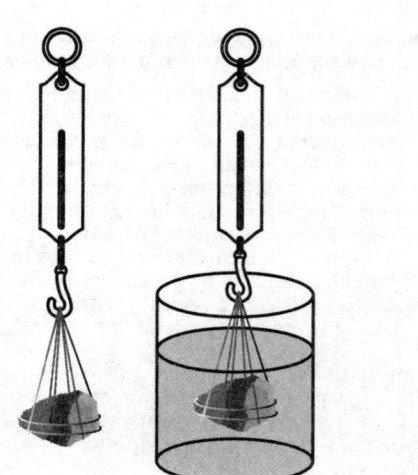

Figure 2

The students calculated the buoyant force on the stone in water as *W* minus the force that was measured when the stone was submerged. They repeated this procedure to test all 3 stones in all 3 fluids. Table 1 lists each stone's volume, in cm^3, and *W*, in newtons (N), as well as the buoyant force, in N, on each stone in the fluid.

Table 1					
Stone	Volume (cm^3)	W (N)	Buoyant force (N) in:		
			water	Fluid A	Fluid B
X	48	1.50	0.47	0.59	0.70
Y	96	1.50	0.94	1.18	1.41
Z	96	3.00	0.94	1.18	1.41

GO ON TO THE NEXT PAGE.

14. Based on the results of Study 2, as the density of the fluid in which Stone X was submerged increased, the buoyant force on Stone X:

   F. decreased only.
   G. increased only.
   H. decreased and then increased.
   J. varied with no general trend.

15. Based on the results of Study 2, for Stone Y, what was the difference between the buoyant force in Fluid A and the buoyant force in Fluid B ?

   A. 0.11 N
   B. 0.23 N
   C. 0.47 N
   D. 0.71 N

16. Suppose the students decide to study whether a cylinder's volume determines the submerged length of the cylinder in a given fluid. Which of the following procedural changes should the students make to Study 1 ? The students should test:

   F. a single cylinder with multiple fluids; the fluids should each have the same density as the cylinder.
   G. a single cylinder with multiple fluids; the fluids should have different densities.
   H. multiple cylinders with a single fluid; the cylinders should have different volumes but the same density.
   J. multiple cylinders with a single fluid; the cylinders should have different weights but the same volume.

17. In Study 1, did the cylinder displace a greater volume of water or a greater volume of Fluid A ?

   A. Water, because the cylinder's submerged length was greater in water than in Fluid A.
   B. Water, because the cylinder's submerged length was greater in Fluid A than in water.
   C. Fluid A, because the cylinder's submerged length was greater in water than in Fluid A.
   D. Fluid A, because the cylinder's submerged length was greater in Fluid A than in water.

18. Suppose that in Study 1 the students had placed the cylinder in a container of fluid having a density of 1.60 g/cm^3. The submerged length of the cylinder would most likely have been:

   F. less than 4.9 cm.
   G. between 4.9 cm and 5.9 cm.
   H. between 5.9 cm and 7.4 cm.
   J. greater than 7.4 cm.

19. Suppose that in Study 2 the students had tested a stone having the same weight as Stone Z but a larger volume than Stone Z. Which of the following statements about the buoyant force on this submerged stone would be correct? The buoyant force on this stone in:

   A. water would have been less than 0.94 N.
   B. Fluid A would have been less than 1.18 N.
   C. Fluid B would have been greater than 1.41 N.
   D. water would have been greater than the buoyant force on this stone in Fluid A.

20. Assume that Atlantic Ocean water has a density of 1.01 g/cm^3 and that Pacific Ocean water has a density of 1.03 g/cm^3. Based on the results of Study 1, in which ocean would a given iceberg more likely have the greater submerged volume?

   F. The Atlantic Ocean, because the results of Study 1 indicate that submerged volume increases as fluid density decreases.
   G. The Atlantic Ocean, because the results of Study 1 indicate that submerged volume decreases as fluid density decreases.
   H. The Pacific Ocean, because the results of Study 1 indicate that submerged volume increases as fluid density decreases.
   J. The Pacific Ocean, because the results of Study 1 indicate that submerged volume decreases as fluid density decreases.

GO ON TO THE NEXT PAGE.

Taking Additional Practice Tests

4 ○ ○ ○ ○ ○ ○ ○ ○ **4**

Passage IV

Chemical reactions that release heat are *exothermic* reactions. The amount of heat released depends on the number of moles of reactants consumed in the reaction. A *mole* of any substance is 6×10^{23} molecules or formula units of the substance.

When sodium hypochlorite (NaClO) and sodium iodide (NaI) are dissolved in acidic H_2O, an exothermic reaction occurs:

$$NaClO + NaI \rightarrow products + heat$$

Students did an experiment to study this reaction.

Experiment

In each of 8 trials, the students performed Steps 1–5:

1. A known volume of a 0.2 mole/L aqueous NaClO solution was poured into a foam coffee cup. A lid was placed on the cup.

2. A thermometer was placed into the solution through a hole in the lid. The solution's initial temperature, T_i, of 22.0°C was recorded.

3. The lid was lifted, and a known volume of a 0.2 mole/L aqueous NaI solution, also at a T_i of 22.0°C, was poured into the cup. The lid was put back on the cup, and the solution was swirled.

4. The solution's final (maximum) temperature, T_f, was measured.

5. The change in temperature, ΔT, was calculated:

$$\Delta T = T_f - T_i$$

The data for each trial are shown in Table 1.

	Table 1			
Trial	Volume of NaClO solution (mL)	Volume of NaI solution (mL)	T_f (°C)	ΔT (°C)
1	0	100	22.0	0.0
2	25	75	25.5	3.5
3	50	50	29.0	7.0
4	70	30	31.7	9.7
5	75	25	32.5	10.5
6	80	20	30.6	8.6
7	90	10	26.2	4.2
8	100	0	22.0	0.0

The students plotted ΔT versus the volume of NaClO solution for each trial (see Figure 1).

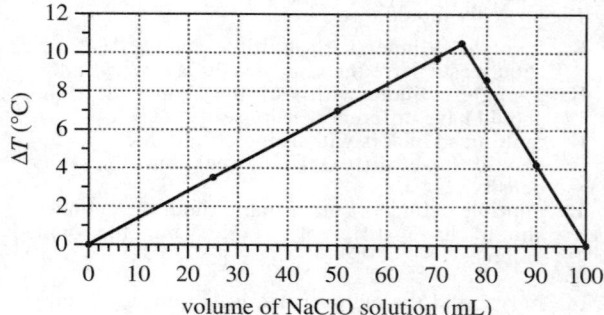

Figure 1

Table and figure adapted from M. Jerome Bigelow, "Thermochemistry of Hypochlorite Oxidations." ©1969 by Division of Chemical Education, Inc., American Chemical Society.

Then they identified the trial for which ΔT had its greatest value. The ratio of the volume of the NaClO solution to the volume of the NaI solution for this trial is the *mole ratio* for the reaction.

GO ON TO THE NEXT PAGE.

4 ○ ○ ○ ○ ○ ○ ○ ○ **4**

21. If a trial had been performed with 60 mL of NaClO solution and 40 mL of NaI solution, T_f would most likely have been:

   A. less than 25.5°C.
   B. between 25.5°C and 29.0°C.
   C. between 29.0°C and 31.7°C.
   D. greater than 31.7°C.

22. Before the experiment, a student predicted that ΔT for Trial 2 would be greater than ΔT for Trial 6. Do the results shown in Table 1 support this prediction?

   F. No; ΔT for Trial 2 was 5.1°C less than ΔT for Trial 6.
   G. No; ΔT for Trial 2 was 8.6°C less than ΔT for Trial 6.
   H. Yes; ΔT for Trial 2 was 5.1°C greater than ΔT for Trial 6.
   J. Yes; ΔT for Trial 2 was 8.6°C greater than ΔT for Trial 6.

23. In each trial, the *total* volume of solution poured into the cup was:

   A.   25 mL.
   B.   50 mL.
   C.   75 mL.
   D. 100 mL.

24. Consider the trial for which the volume of NaClO was 4 times as great as the volume of NaI. For this trial, T_f was:

   F. 25.5°C.
   G. 26.2°C.
   H. 30.6°C.
   J. 32.5°C.

25. Suppose a trial had been performed with 20 mL of NaClO solution and 80 mL of NaI solution. Based on Figure 1, ΔT for this new trial would most likely have been closest to which of the following?

   A. 1°C
   B. 3°C
   C. 5°C
   D. 7°C

26. Which of the following statements best explains why ΔT was 0.0°C for Trial 8 ? The volume of solution added was 0 mL for one of the:

   F. products, NaClO, so no reaction had occurred.
   G. products, NaI, so no reaction had occurred.
   H. reactants, NaClO, so no reaction had occurred.
   J. reactants, NaI, so no reaction had occurred.

27. Suppose that the reaction studied had been *endothermic*. As the endothermic reaction progressed, would the solution temperature more likely have decreased or increased?

   A. Decreased, because the reaction would have released heat.
   B. Decreased, because the reaction would have absorbed heat.
   C. Increased, because the reaction would have released heat.
   D. Increased, because the reaction would have absorbed heat.

GO ON TO THE NEXT PAGE.

4 ○ ○ ○ ○ ○ ○ ○ ○ **4**

Passage V

When rocks are melted at very high temperatures beneath Earth's surface, *magma* (molten rock) is formed. The gases CO_2 and H_2O can dissolve in magma. Figure 1 shows, for 4 different magmas (leucitite, basanite, rhyolite, and tholeiitic basalt), how the solubility of CO_2 in the magma at 1,150°C varies with pressure (in megapascals, MPa).

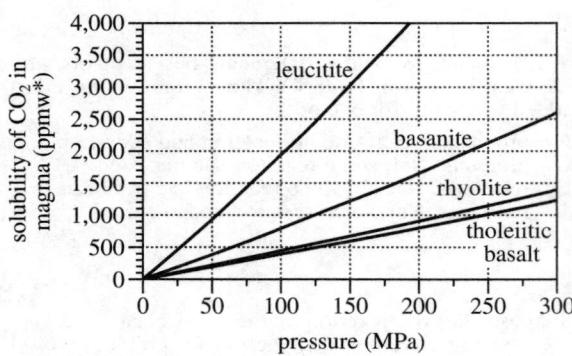

*parts per million by weight

Figure 1

Figure 2 shows, at 3 different pressures, how the solubility of CO_2 in rhyolite magma varies with temperature.

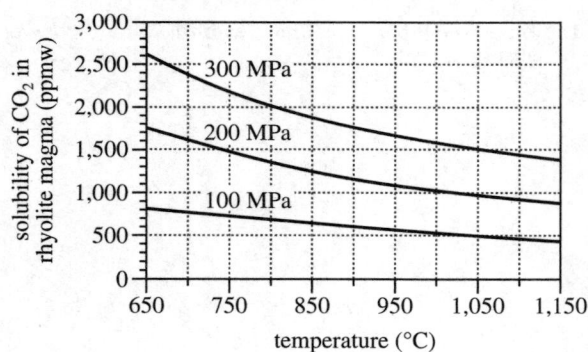

Figure 2

Figure 2 adapted from Robert A. Fogel and Malcolm J. Rutherford, "The Solubility of Carbon Dioxide in Rhyolitic Melts: A Quantitative FTIR Study." ©1990 by the Mineralogical Society of America.

Figure 3 shows, at 4 different pressures, how the solubility of CO_2 in rhyolite magma at 750°C varies with the weight percent of H_2O in the magma.

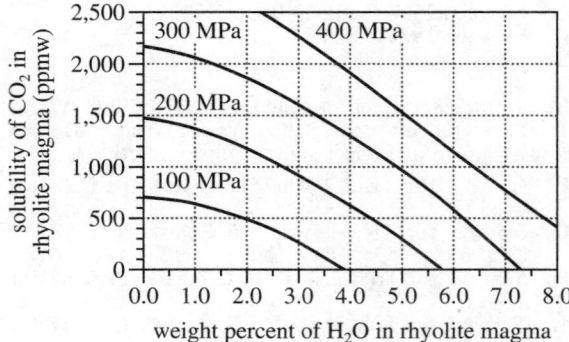

Figure 3

Figures 1 and 3 adapted from Jacob B. Lowenstern, "Carbon Dioxide in Magmas and Implications for Hydrothermal Systems." ©2001 by Springer-Verlag.

28. According to Figure 2, at 300 MPa, the solubility of CO_2 in rhyolite magma is closest to 2,000 ppmw at which of the following temperatures?

   F. 700°C
   G. 750°C
   H. 800°C
   J. 850°C

29. Based on Figure 3, at 750°C and 350 MPa, rhyolite magma having a solubility of CO_2 equal to 1,250 ppmw would most likely have a weight percent of H_2O that is:

   A. less than 2.0%.
   B. between 2.0% and 4.0%.
   C. between 4.0% and 6.0%.
   D. greater than 6.0%.

GO ON TO THE NEXT PAGE.

4 ○ ○ ○ ○ ○ ○ ○ ○ **4**

30. According to Figure 1, at 1,150°C, the solubility of CO_2 in basanite magma and the solubility of CO_2 in tholeiitic basalt magma are closest in value at which of the following pairs of pressures?

	basanite magma	tholeiitic basalt magma
F.	50 MPa	200 MPa
G.	50 MPa	250 MPa
H.	125 MPa	200 MPa
J.	125 MPa	250 MPa

31. Based on Figure 1, at 1,150°C and 150 MPa, the solubility of CO_2 in leucitite magma is approximately how much greater than or less than the solubility of CO_2 in rhyolite magma?

A. 1,750 ppmw greater
B. 2,300 ppmw greater
C. 1,750 ppmw less
D. 2,300 ppmw less

32. According to Figure 2, increasing the temperature from 650°C to 1,150°C has the *lesser* effect on the solubility of CO_2 in rhyolite magma at which pressure, 100 MPa or 300 MPa ?

F. 100 MPa; the solubility of CO_2 decreases by about 400 ppmw.
G. 100 MPa; the solubility of CO_2 decreases by about 1,300 ppmw.
H. 300 MPa; the solubility of CO_2 decreases by about 400 ppmw.
J. 300 MPa; the solubility of CO_2 decreases by about 1,300 ppmw.

33. Consider the solubility of CO_2 in rhyolite magma at 750°C and 200 MPa, as shown in Figure 2. According to Figure 3, this rhyolite magma has a weight percent of H_2O closest to which of the following?

A. 0.0%
B. 2.0%
C. 4.0%
D. 6.0%

GO ON TO THE NEXT PAGE.

4 ◯ ◯ ◯ ◯ ◯ ◯ ◯ ◯ 4

Passage VI

When viewed from Earth, the other planets in the solar system usually appear to move *prograde* (eastward relative to the stars). Occasionally, however, each planet appears to briefly move *retrograde* (westward relative to the stars). For example, Figure 1 shows Mars's position relative to the stars on 9 dates between July 24, 2005, and February 26, 2006.

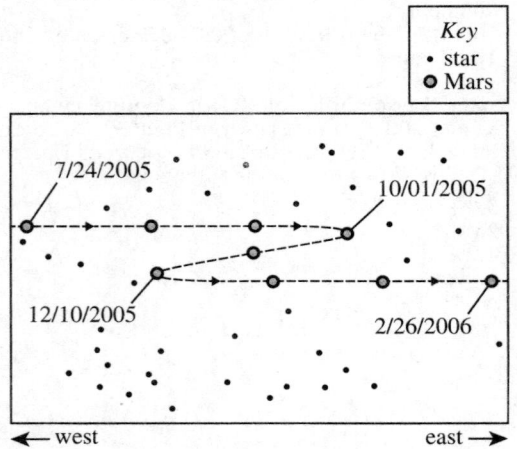

Key
• star
⊙ Mars

7/24/2005   10/01/2005

12/10/2005   2/26/2006

← west   east →

Figure 1

Two hypotheses were proposed to explain why the planets occasionally appear to move retrograde.

Hypothesis 1

Earth is the solar system's central body, and the other bodies move around Earth in looped orbits. Each body (except Earth) has 2 circles associated with it: a *deferent* and an *epicycle*. Both circles rotate counterclockwise, and their combined motions result in a body following a looped orbit. In Figure 2, the left panel shows Mars's deferent and epicycle, and the right panel shows Mars's orbit.

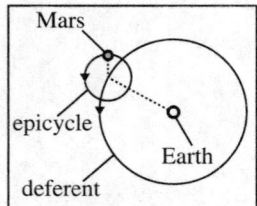
Mars
epicycle
Earth
deferent

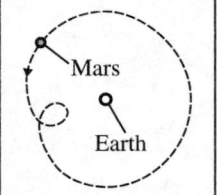
Mars
Earth

Figure 2

As a body passes through a loop, the body's motion changes from prograde to retrograde and back. The larger a body's deferent, the more loops in the body's orbit, and the more often that body passes through a loop.

Hypothesis 2

The Sun is the solar system's central body, and the planets move counterclockwise around the Sun in elliptical orbits. The larger a planet's orbit, the more time the planet takes to complete a revolution around the Sun. As a result, the line of sight from Earth to a given planet drifts over time. Figure 3 shows the orbits of Earth and Mars, and the positions of Earth and Mars, on each of the 4 dates labeled in Figure 1. For each date, the line of sight from Earth to Mars is projected onto a view of the sky.

There are 2 rules for apparent retrograde motion:

• A planet with an orbit larger than Earth's appears to move retrograde whenever Earth passes between the Sun and that planet. The larger that planet's orbit, the more often a pass occurs.

• A planet with an orbit smaller than Earth's appears to move retrograde whenever that planet passes between the Sun and Earth. The *smaller* that planet's orbit, the more often a pass occurs.

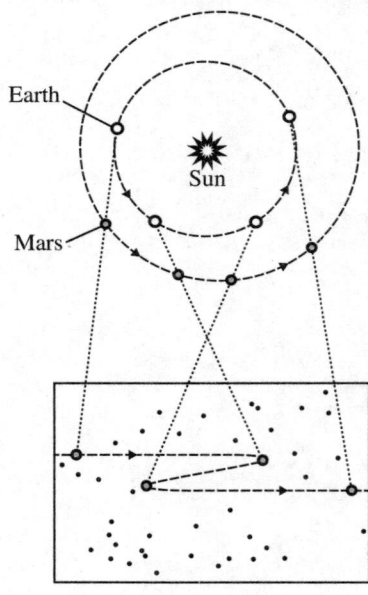
Earth
Sun
Mars

Figure 3

GO ON TO THE NEXT PAGE.

4 ◯ ◯ ◯ ◯ ◯ ◯ ◯ ◯ **4**

34. Which of the following statements best describes a primary difference between the two hypotheses? Hypothesis 1 claims that all planets follow:

F. looped orbits around Earth, whereas Hypothesis 2 claims that all planets follow elliptical orbits around the Sun.

G. looped orbits around Earth, whereas Hypothesis 2 claims that all planets follow elliptical orbits around Earth.

H. elliptical orbits around the Sun, whereas Hypothesis 2 claims that all planets follow looped orbits around the Sun.

J. elliptical orbits around the Sun, whereas Hypothesis 2 claims that all planets follow looped orbits around Earth.

35. Assume that Figures 2 and 3 are drawn to scale. Which of the figures, if either, implies that the distance between Earth and Mars varies with time?

A. Figure 2 only
B. Figure 3 only
C. Both Figure 2 and Figure 3
D. Neither Figure 2 nor Figure 3

36. Consider both the interval of time represented in Figures 1 and 3 and the reason that, according to Hypothesis 2, the line of sight from Earth to Mars drifts over time. Is the top portion of Figure 3 consistent with that reason?

F. Yes; Earth is shown as having the smaller orbit and as having completed a greater percentage of its revolution around the Sun than is Mars.

G. Yes; Earth is shown as having the larger orbit and as having completed a greater percentage of its revolution around the Sun than is Mars.

H. No; Earth is shown as having the smaller orbit and as having completed a greater percentage of its revolution around the Sun than is Mars.

J. No; Earth is shown as having the larger orbit and as having completed a greater percentage of its revolution around the Sun than is Mars.

37. Based on Figure 1, as viewed from Earth, for approximately how many days between July 2005 and February 2006 did Mars move retrograde?

A. 30
B. 70
C. 150
D. 220

38. A supporter of Hypothesis 1 and a supporter of Hypothesis 2 would both be likely to agree with which of the following statements? When viewed from Earth, if a planet appears to be moving prograde, that planet is actually moving:

F. clockwise around Earth.
G. clockwise around the central body in the solar system.
H. counterclockwise around the Sun.
J. counterclockwise around the central body in the solar system.

39. Based on Figures 1 and 3, if Hypothesis 2 is correct, which of the following figures most likely shows the positions of Earth and Mars on November 7, 2005 ?

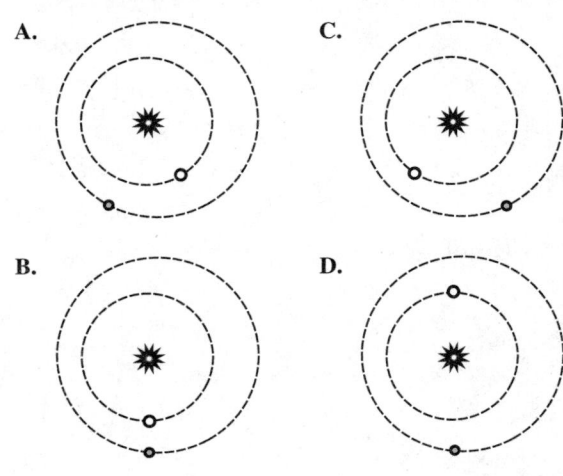

A.   C.

B.   D.

40. Can Hypothesis 2 explain why Venus occasionally appears to move retrograde?

F. Yes; Hypothesis 2 accounts for the motion of planets that are closer to the Sun than Earth is.
G. Yes; Hypothesis 2 accounts for the motion of planets that are farther from the Sun than Earth is.
H. No; Hypothesis 2 does not account for the motion of planets that are closer to the Sun than Earth is.
J. No; Hypothesis 2 does not account for the motion of planets that are farther from the Sun than Earth is.

END OF TEST 4

STOP! DO NOT RETURN TO ANY OTHER TEST.

Taking Additional Practice Tests

You may wish to photocopy these sample answer document pages to respond to the practice ACT Writing Test.

Please enter the information at the right before beginning the writing test.

Use a No. 2 pencil only. Do NOT use a mechanical pencil, ink, ballpoint, or felt-tip pen.

WRITING TEST BOOKLET NUMBER

Print your 9-digit **Booklet Number** in the boxes at the right.

WRITING TEST FORM

Print your 5-character **Test Form** in the boxes at the right and fill in the corresponding ovals.

Begin WRITING TEST here.

If you need more space, please continue on the following page.

1

WRITING TEST

_____
_____
_____
_____
_____
_____
_____
_____
_____
_____
_____
_____
_____
_____
_____
_____
_____
_____
_____
_____
_____
_____
_____
_____
_____
_____

If you need more space, please continue on the following page.

2

WRITING TEST

_____
_____
_____
_____
_____
_____
_____
_____
_____
_____
_____
_____
_____
_____
_____
_____
_____
_____
_____
_____
_____
_____
_____
_____
_____
_____
_____
_____
_____

If you need more space, please continue on the following page.

3

WRITING TEST

_____

_____

_____

_____

_____

_____

_____

_____

_____

_____

_____

_____

_____

_____

_____

_____

_____

_____

_____

_____

_____

_____

_____

_____

_____

_____

_____

STOP here with the writing test.

4

Practice Writing Test Prompt 5

Your Signature: _____
(Do not print.)

Print Your Name Here: _____

Your Date of Birth:

☐☐ –	☐☐ –	☐☐☐☐	
Month	Day	Year	

Form 21WT8

The **ACT®** WRITING TEST BOOKLET

You must take the multiple-choice tests before you take the writing test.

Directions

This is a test of your writing skills. You will have **forty** (40) minutes to read the prompt, plan your response, and write an essay in English. Before you begin working, read all material in this test booklet carefully to understand exactly what you are being asked to do.

You will write your essay on the lined pages in the **answer document** provided. Your writing on those pages will be scored. You may use the unlined pages in this test booklet to plan your essay. Your work on these pages will not be scored.

Your essay will be evaluated based on the evidence it provides of your ability to:

- clearly state your own perspective on a complex issue and analyze the relationship between your perspective and at least one other perspective
- develop and support your ideas with reasoning and examples
- organize your ideas clearly and logically
- communicate your ideas effectively in standard written English

Lay your pencil down immediately when time is called.

DO NOT OPEN THIS BOOKLET UNTIL TOLD TO DO SO.

PO Box 168
Iowa City, IA 52243-0168

The ONLY Official Prep Guide from the Makers of the ACT

Digital Disconnect

Some people purposely avoid digital tools and technology because they value a "disconnected" lifestyle. These people may choose not to carry cell phones, have internet service at home, or participate in social media. But digital tools and technologies are a part of almost every aspect of modern life. Banking, shopping, schoolwork, and all forms of business communication become more dependent on digital connections each year. Is it wise, then, to avoid the digital world?

Read and carefully consider these perspectives. Each suggests a particular way of thinking about the question above.

Perspective One	Perspective Two	Perspective Three
Most digital tools and technology make life easier. Avoiding those things is foolish because it often means making a simple task harder for ourselves.	Some things can't be done digitally: experiencing nature, exercising, and spending time with other people. We should avoid the digital world more often so we don't neglect these important parts of life.	Avoiding the digital world is the same as isolating yourself from society. It is unwise and possibly even unhealthy to stay away from digital tools and technologies.

Essay Task

Write a unified, coherent essay in which you address the question of whether it is wise to avoid the digital world. In your essay, be sure to:

- clearly state your own perspective and analyze the relationship between your perspective and at least one other perspective
- develop and support your ideas with reasoning and examples
- organize your ideas clearly and logically
- communicate your ideas effectively in standard written English

Your perspective may be in full agreement with any of those given, in partial agreement, or completely different.

Planning Your Essay

Your work on these prewriting pages will not be scored.

Use the space below and on the back cover to generate ideas and plan your essay. You may wish to consider the following as you think critically about the task:

Strengths and weaknesses of different perspectives on the issue
- What insights do they offer, and what do they fail to consider?
- Why might they be persuasive to others, or why might they fail to persuade?

Your own knowledge, experience, and values
- What is your perspective on this issue, and what are its strengths and weaknesses?
- How will you support your perspective in your essay?

If you need more space to plan, please continue on the following page.

Planning Your Essay

Use this page to continue planning your essay. Your work on this page will not be scored.

ENGLISH • PRACTICE TEST 5 • EXPLANATORY ANSWERS

Passage I

Question 1. The best answer is **C** because it is the only option that provides a preposition that fits the context of the sentence and creates a standard English idiom ("ways of imitating").

The best answer is NOT:

A because the phrase "ways by imitating" is not idiomatically sound.

B because the phrase "ways with imitating" is not idiomatically sound.

D because the phrase "ways at imitating" is not idiomatically sound.

Question 2. The best answer is **H** because it provides the appropriate verb form and verb tense (*is*) for the second independent clause in this sentence.

The best answer is NOT:

F because the participle *being* leaves the second independent clause without a predicate.

G because the verb "was being" creates an illogical shift in verb tense. The first clause of the sentence uses present tense, so the second clause should also use present tense.

J because a deletion would leave the second independent clause without a predicate.

Question 3. The best answer is **B** because it maintains the style and tone of the essay.

The best answer is NOT:

A because the phrase "take a back seat" strays from the more formal style of this essay.

C because the phrase "a bigger deal" strays from the more formal style of this essay.

D because the phrase "way more vital" is too colloquial for the style and tone of this essay.

Question 4. The best answer is **H** because it provides the appropriate punctuation (commas) to set off the nonessential element "called vocables."

The best answer is NOT:

F because it is missing the second comma to set off the nonessential element.

G because it is missing the first comma to set off the nonessential element.

J because the comma after *called* is misplaced; it should be after *syllables* to set off the nonessential element.

Question 5. **The best answer is** C because it creates a sentence that is structurally sound and has proper subordination.

The best answer is NOT:

A because the word *easier* is a comparative adjective, but the sentence makes no comparison. In addition, it creates an awkward, unclear sentence.

B because the word *easily* is an adverb, but there is no word for the adverb to modify. It also creates an awkward, unclear sentence.

D because the phrase "flow in a way to dance to" creates an awkward, unclear sentence.

Question 6. **The best answer is** F because the phrase "often tongue-twisting," which describes the lyrics of puirt-abeul, suggests a sequence of words or sounds that are difficult to pronounce.

The best answer is NOT:

G because "tongue-twisting" is not related to writing lyrics; the phrase describes words or sounds that are difficult to pronounce.

H because "often" refers to the frequency with which the puirt-a-beul lyrics are "tongue-twisting," not the frequency with which puirt-a-beul is performed.

J because there is no mention of any training exercises for puirt-a-beul.

Question 7. **The best answer is** A because it provides the most logical transitional word to connect this sentence with the preceding one. The word *though* is used to indicate a statement that contrasts with something that has been said previously. In this paragraph, the idea that the "lyrics require much practice to perfect" is contrasted with the idea that "learning when to breathe" is the "greater challenge."

The best answer is NOT:

B because the transitional phrase "at the same time" inaccurately suggests that the "greater challenge" is happening simultaneously with the requirement for "much practice to perfect."

C because it inaccurately suggests that the "greater challenge" of "learning when to breathe" is a one-time occurrence.

D because the word *still* does not link this sentence with the preceding one in a logical way.

Question 8. The best answer is **G** because it clarifies that it is the dancers who are relying on "the steady beat," and it avoids using a pronoun with an unclear referent.

The best answer is NOT:

F because the pronoun *it* has no clear referent.

H because the pronoun *they* has no clear referent.

J because it leaves the pronoun *their*, which appears later in the sentence, with no clear referent.

Question 9. The best answer is **A** because it is the only option that introduces the discussion that puirt-a-beul was invented out of necessity, which is the main focus of the paragraph.

The best answer is NOT:

B because the main focus of the paragraph is why puirt-a-beul was invented, not how mouth music singers must have good rhythm.

C because the main focus of the paragraph is why puirt-a-beul was invented, not how it has influenced jazz scat singing.

D because the main focus of the paragraph is why puirt-a-beul was invented, not where another form of mouth music originated.

Question 10. The best answer is **H** because it is the only option that has correct sentence structure. It creates two complete sentences using a period to separate two independent clauses.

The best answer is NOT:

F because it creates a run-on sentence.

G because it creates a run-on sentence.

J because it creates a comma splice.

Question 11. The best answer is D because it uses the appropriate pronoun case. The nominative pronoun *who* is used to introduce a clause about a person, and in this instance, the person is *anyone*.

The best answer is NOT:

A because the pronoun *whomever* is the objective case, and the sentence requires a subjective pronoun because of the verb "didn't read."

B because the pronoun *which* is used for things, not people.

C because the pronoun *whom* is the objective case, and the sentence requires a nominative case.

Question 12. The best answer is G because it clarifies that "this musical form" is referring to the popularity of Celtic mouth music, and it avoids using a pronoun with an unclear referent.

The best answer is NOT:

F because the pronoun *them* has no referent.

H because the reflexive pronoun *itself* has no clear antecedent.

J because there is no referent for the word *one*.

Question 13. The best answer is B because it creates a logical sentence with all modifiers correctly placed.

The best answer is NOT:

A because it creates an awkward sentence structure that lacks clarity. In addition, the phrase "exposing with audiences" is not a standard English idiom.

C because it creates a sentence that is both unclear and nonsensical.

D because the word *worldwide* is misplaced; it should be placed after *audiences*.

Question 14. The best answer is J because it provides the clearest, most concise wording for this sentence and avoids redundancy.

The best answer is NOT:

F because it is redundant; the adverb *continually* is unnecessary because the word *survives* already suggests a continuation.

G because it is redundant; "still remains" and "carries on" mean the same thing.

H because it is redundant and awkward; *stays* and "sticking around" mean the same thing.

Question 15. The best answer is **A** because the phrase "traditional mouth music with modern rhythms" in the underlined portion indicates that the bands incorporate "classic Celtic music and current influences" into their music.

> The best answer is NOT:
>
> **B** because it lacks any reference to the bands' incorporating classic Celtic music.
>
> **C** because it lacks any reference to the bands' incorporating classic Celtic music or current influences.
>
> **D** because singing and dancing on stage is unrelated to how the bands incorporate classic Celtic music and current influences.

Passage II

Question 16. The best answer is **J** because it is the only option that does not add unnecessary and confusing punctuation.

> The best answer is NOT:
>
> **F** because the phrase "called the Garamantes" is an essential element that should not be separated from the rest of the clause.
>
> **G** because the phrase beginning with the word *created* is essential and should not be separated from the rest of the clause.
>
> **H** because the colon after the word *called* is incorrect as it breaks up the complete subject in this sentence.

Question 17. The best answer is **C** because it is the only option that provides parallel verb structure.

> The best answer is NOT:
>
> **A** because it shifts to passive voice; the other verbs are in active voice.
>
> **B** because it shifts to passive voice; the other verbs are in active voice.
>
> **D** because it does not include a verb and so is not parallel with the other elements.

Question 18. The best answer is **F** because the preceding sentence lists the variety of crops the Garamantes grew, which clearly implies that they were successful farmers.

The best answer is NOT:

G because the concluding statement does not summarize previous information. It provides new information about farming.

H because the concluding statement includes no information about where or even if the crops were exported.

J because the concluding statement includes no information about the Garamantes importing crops.

Question 19. The best answer is **A** because it is the only choice that adds new information. This is the first reference to "distant mountains," the source of the underground water.

The best answer is NOT:

B because it is redundant; the preceding sentence notes that the civilization depended on the underground tunnels.

C because it is redundant; the preceding paragraph already established that the essay is about the Garamantes.

D because it is redundant; the preceding sentence notes that the civilization depended on the underground tunnels.

Question 20. The best answer is **F** because it is the only option that indicates the method for building the tunnels.

The best answer is NOT:

G because the word *underground* does not indicate the method for building the tunnels.

H because the phrase "dimly lit" does not indicate the method for building the tunnels.

J because the word *desert* does not indicate the method for building the tunnels.

Question 21. The best answer is **B** because the comparative adverb "more easily" appropriately modifies the adjective *accessible*. It also indicates a comparison between the accessibility of the water before and after the tunnels reached a town or field.

The best answer is NOT:

A because the phrase "more easy" is not a correct comparative adverbial form.

C because the comparative adjective *easier* illogically modifies the nouns *canals* and *reservoirs*.

D because the phrase "easy and" is an imprecise and unclear description.

Question 22. The best answer is **J** because it is the only option that does not create a misplaced or dangling modifier.

The best answer is NOT:

F because the introductory phrase inaccurately modifies the archaeologists as if they were the ones who "left no clues."

G because the introductory phrase inaccurately modifies the archaeologists as though they were a "genuine puzzle."

H because the introductory phrase inaccurately modifies the archaeologists as though they were the ones who gave "no indication."

Question 23. The best answer is **B** because the word *than* is the correct word to use in this context; it is a conjunction used to make a comparison, which this sentence does. It also creates a standard English idiom.

The best answer is NOT:

A because the word *then* is not the correct word to use in this context; the phrase "rather then" is not a standard English idiom.

C because the word *then* is not the correct word to use in this context; the phrase "rather then" is not a standard English idiom.

D because the word *by* is not the correct word to use in this context; the phrase "rather by" is not a standard English idiom.

Question 24. The best answer is H because it is the only option that uses the appropriate verb form. The water from the aquifer meant that the Garamantes "could rely" on "a constant supply of water."

The best answer is NOT:

F because it is not a proper verb form.

G because it is not a proper verb form.

J because the singular verb form *relies* does not agree with its plural subject *Garamantes*.

Question 25. The best answer is A because it provides the most logical transitional word to connect this sentence with the preceding one. The word *Moreover* means *furthermore*, and this sentence provides further information about the benefits of the underground canals.

The best answer is NOT:

B because the transitional word *Nevertheless* suggests contrasting ideas, but the information in this sentence does not contrast with the idea in the preceding sentence.

C because the transitional phrase "In contrast" suggests contrasting ideas, but the information in this sentence does not contrast with the idea in the preceding sentence.

D because the transitional phrase "Even so" suggests contrasting ideas, but the information in this sentence does not contrast with the idea in the preceding sentence.

Question 26. The best answer is J because deleting the underlined portion is the only option that has correct sentence structure. It creates a complete sentence with a clear subject and predicate.

The best answer is NOT:

F because it creates a sentence fragment.

G because it creates a sentence fragment.

H because it creates a sentence fragment.

Question 27. The best answer is **A** because it provides the most logical subordinating conjunction to introduce the dependent clause in this sentence. The conjunction *As* is used to indicate that something happens during the time when something else is taking place.

The best answer is NOT:

B because the phrase "As to when" is unclear and unnecessarily wordy.

C because the word *Whereas* indicates contrast or comparison; this sentence is making a connection, not a comparison.

D because the word *Though* results in an illogical statement.

Question 28. The best answer is **H** because it is the only option that has correct sentence structure. It creates two complete sentences using a period to separate two independent clauses.

The best answer is NOT:

F because it creates a comma splice.

G because it creates a run-on sentence.

J because it creates a run-on sentence.

Question 29. The best answer is **D** because deleting the underlined portion avoids redundancy with information elsewhere in the paragraph.

The best answer is NOT:

A because it is redundant; preceding information notes that the ancient shafts are visible.

B because it is redundant and wordy; preceding information notes that the ancient shafts are visible.

C because it is redundant and wordy; preceding information notes that the ancient shafts are visible.

Question 30. The best answer is **G** because this option clearly indicates why the essay does fulfill the writer's primary purpose. The main focus of the essay is describing how the Garamantes were able to meet their need for water in a dry area.

The best answer is NOT:

F because trade is only mentioned briefly in the first paragraph, and it has nothing to do with overcoming a natural obstacle.

H because the fact that the foggaras were not naturally occurring does support the primary purpose of explaining how the Garamantes overcame a natural obstacle.

J because the lack of water, not the foggaras, led to the Garamantes' downfall; in fact, the foggaras aided the Garamantes by moving the water from the mountains to their settlements.

Passage III

Question 31. The best answer is **D** because deleting the underlined portion avoids redundancy with information elsewhere in the paragraph.

The best answer is NOT:

A because it is redundant; *down* and *descend* provide the same information.

B because it is redundant; "down below" and *descend* provide the same information.

C because it is redundant; *downwards* and *descend* provide the same information.

Question 32. The best answer is **G** because it provides the appropriate punctuation for this sentence. A comma is needed after *(DOMs)* to separate the two clauses in this sentence.

The best answer is NOT:

F because the verb "are programmed" is essential and should not be set off with commas.

H because a colon should not be used to separate an independent clause from a relative clause.

J because the semicolon creates a sentence fragment.

Question 33. The best answer is **B** because it provides the appropriate punctuation (a dash) to set off the nonessential element and also because the element ends with a dash.

The best answer is NOT:

A because a colon is not used to introduce a nonessential element.

C because a semicolon is not used to introduce a nonessential element.

D because the lack of punctuation creates a confusing sentence. The nonessential element "a veritable shock wave of photonic energy" should be set off with dashes.

Question 34. The best answer is **J** because the phrase "fifty trillion neutrinos" in the underlined portion is an enormous number meant to emphasize how numerous neutrinos are.

The best answer is NOT:

F because even though the underlined portion implies that neutrinos have little weight, it does not specify why this is so.

G because the underlined portion notes that neutrinos pass through a body; it does not explain how this happens.

H because the underlined portion notes that there are "fifty trillion neutrinos," but it does not explain why this number is so high.

Question 35. The best answer is **D** because it provides the most logical transition to connect this sentence with the preceding one. The phrase "In fact" is used to emphasize the assertion that "Neutrinos are rarely affected by matter or electromagnetic fields."

The best answer is NOT:

A because the transitional phrase "For this purpose" does not logically link the idea in this sentence with the idea in the preceding one.

B because the transitional phrase "In contrast" suggests two opposing ideas, which does not characterize the ideas in these two sentences.

C because the transitional word *Besides* means "in addition to," but the idea in the second sentence emphasizes what is asserted in the first sentence; it does not add another assertion.

Question 36. The best answer is **G** because it provides the appropriate punctuation (commas) to set off the nonessential element *however*.

The best answer is NOT:

F because it is missing the first comma to set off the nonessential element, and the semicolon creates a sentence fragment.

H because the semicolon creates a sentence fragment.

J because it is missing the second comma to set off the nonessential element.

Question 37. The best answer is **C** because it clearly explains why the new sentence should not be added. The information in the first two sentences about neutrinos colliding and the selection of the site to detect those collisions would be interrupted by irrelevant information on a completely different topic.

The best answer is NOT:

A because the suggested revision is not relevant to the discussion of colliding neutrinos.

B because the suggested revision says nothing about subzero altitude.

D because zero-gravity conditions are mentioned later in the paragraph; therefore, this is not a logical reason for not adding the sentence.

Question 38. The best answer is **F** because it is the only option that has correct sentence structure.

The best answer is NOT:

G because it creates an awkward sentence with faulty coordination.

H because it creates a sentence fragment.

J because it creates a sentence fragment.

Question 39. The best answer is **C** because it provides the appropriate singular possessive pronoun for this sentence. The singular *its* refers to the singular noun *ice* that appears earlier in the sentence.

The best answer is NOT:

A because it is a contraction, not a singular possessive pronoun.

B because it is a plural possessive pronoun, not a singular possessive pronoun.

D because it is not a correct form of possessive pronoun.

Question 40. The best answer is F because it is the only option that has appropriate subject-verb agreement. The singular verb *is* agrees with its singular subject *origin*.

The best answer is NOT:

G because it does not agree with the singular subject *origin*.

H because it does not agree with the singular subject *origin*.

J because it does not agree with the singular subject *origin*.

Question 41. The best answer is A because it is the only option that introduces the discussion of the origins of neutrinos, which is the main focus of the paragraph.

The best answer is NOT:

B because the main focus of the paragraph is the origins of neutrinos, not scientists learning more about gamma rays.

C because the main focus of the paragraph is the origins of neutrinos, not the discovery of the specific neutrinos Bert and Ernie.

D because the main focus of the paragraph is the origins of neutrinos, not the particle accelerator.

Question 42. The best answer is F because it is the only option that has correct sentence structure. It creates two complete sentences using a period to separate two independent clauses.

The best answer is NOT:

G because it creates a run-on sentence.

H because it creates a comma splice.

J because it creates a run-on sentence.

Question 43. The best answer is B because it provides the most precise wording for this sentence. The word *invaluable* means "extremely useful" and accurately describes the information that could be obtained by learning more about the origins of neutrinos.

The best answer is NOT:

A because it means "luxurious or lavish," which is not contextually appropriate.

C because it means "high-priced or posh," which is not contextually appropriate.

D because it means *opulent*, which is not contextually appropriate.

Question 44. The best answer is **F** because it is the only option that emphasizes how information gleaned from neutrinos could have dramatic effects on how scientists study the universe.

The best answer is NOT:

G because it does not indicate how information gained from neutrinos could impact scientists' study of the universe.

H because it does not indicate how information gained from neutrinos could impact scientists' study of the universe.

J because it does not indicate how information gained from neutrinos could impact scientists' study of the universe.

Question 45. The best answer is **C** because this option clearly indicates why the essay does not meet the writer's primary purpose. The main focus of the essay is on how scientists at the IceCube Neutrino Observatory detect neutrinos and how this could benefit future research; it does not outline any scientific theory.

The best answer is NOT:

A because Cherenkov radiation is mentioned only briefly in the first paragraph; it is not the main focus of the essay.

B because DOMs are mentioned only briefly in the first paragraph; they are not the main focus of the essay.

D because the essay suggests that research on neutrinos could lead to new discoveries; it does not suggest that this research might contradict any other theories.

Passage IV

Question 46. The best answer is **F** because it uses the appropriate pronoun case. The nominative pronoun *who* is used to introduce a clause about a person, and in this instance, the person is "Rafael Leonardo Black."

The best answer is NOT:

G because "of whom" is a genitive form of the relative pronoun *whom*, which is the wrong pronoun case for this sentence.

H because the pronoun *which* is used for things, not people.

J because *whom* is the objective pronoun case, which is the wrong pronoun case for this sentence.

Question 47. The best answer is **A** because it provides the clearest, most concise wording and avoids redundancy.

The best answer is NOT:

B because it is redundant; if Black, who is 64, has been creating art "for over three decades," he has been doing so for more than half his life.

C because it is redundant; the preceding paragraph notes that Black lives in Clinton Hill.

D because it is redundant; the preceding paragraph notes that Black had recently been discovered.

Question 48. The best answer is **F** because information about Naumann's decision to display Black's drawings is the best transition to the fact that "ten of Black's pieces sold."

The best answer is NOT:

G because information about how "ten of Black's pieces sold" within days makes no sense if it is not preceded by information about where and how they sold.

H because information about how "ten of Black's pieces sold" within days makes no sense if it is not preceded by information about where and how they sold.

J because information about how "ten of Black's pieces sold" within days makes no sense if it is not preceded by information about where and how they sold.

Question 49. The best answer is **B** because it provides the most appropriate punctuation to set off the prepositional phrase in this sentence; the dash is used to emphasize the prices buyers paid for Black's work.

The best answer is NOT:

A because the comma after the word *for* incorrectly interrupts the prepositional phrase.

C because a semicolon should not separate an independent clause from a prepositional phrase.

D because the colon after the word *for* incorrectly interrupts the prepositional phrase.

Question 50. The best answer is **G** because it is the only option that has correct sentence structure. It creates two complete sentences using a period to separate two independent clauses.

The best answer is NOT:

F because it creates a run-on sentence.

H because it creates a comma splice.

J because it creates a run-on sentence.

Question 51. The best answer is **D** because it provides the clearest, most concise wording for this sentence and avoids redundancy.

The best answer is NOT:

A because it is redundant; *depictions* and *drawings* mean the same thing.

B because it is redundant; preceding information notes that the drawings were done in pencil.

C because it is redundant; preceding information notes that the drawings are collages.

Question 52. The best answer is **J** because the name "Wilhelm Freddie" is an essential element and should not be set off in the sentence.

The best answer is NOT:

F because the commas are incorrect; "Wilhelm Freddie" is essential and should not be set off with commas.

G because it adds an incorrect comma after *Freddie*.

H because it adds an incorrect comma after *painter*.

Question 53. The best answer is **A** because it is the only option that has appropriate subject-verb agreement. The plural verb *fit* agrees with its plural subject *drawings*.

The best answer is NOT:

B because it does not agree with the plural subject *drawings*.

C because it does not agree with the plural subject *drawings*.

D because it does not agree with the plural subject *drawings*.

Question 54. The best answer is **G** because the underlined portion states that the narrator liked how much there was to puzzle over, which indicates the narrator's appreciation as well as suggests that the narrator did not understand the overall intent of the collage.

The best answer is NOT:

F because the underlined portion does not make an argument or discuss Naumann in any way.

H because the underlined portion in no way refers to Black being discovered as an artist.

J because the underlined portion reveals the narrator's thoughts about one collage; it does not discuss modern art in general.

Question 55. The best answer is **D** because the best placement for the phrase "in May" is at the end of the sentence, since Black's work created "a stir" in May.

The best answer is NOT:

A because the phrase "this complexity in May" illogically reads as though Black's work was complex only in May.

B because the phrase "Maybe in May this complexity helps explain" illogically reads as though the complexity in Black's work can be explained only in May.

C because the phrase "Maybe this complexity helps explain in May" illogically reads as though the complexity in Black's work can be explained only in May.

Question 56. The best answer is **J** because it is the only option that establishes that Black is *unmoved* by the interest in his art.

The best answer is NOT:

F because the word *observes* does not indicate Black was unmoved by the sudden interest in his art as clearly as **J** does.

G because it describes Black's celebrity status rather than indicating his response to the sudden interest in his art.

H because it describes the financial benefits to Black rather than indicating his response to the sudden interest in his art.

Question 57. The best answer is **C** because it provides the most logical transition between the two sentences. Black wasn't well known, but now that the narrator knows who Black is, he or she will be on the lookout for Black's next show.

The best answer is NOT:

A because the narrator's knowledge of the city has no relationship to his or her desire to go to Black's next show.

B because information about the narrator's knowledge of art and books is not relevant to the discussion of Black's anonymity in the preceding sentence.

D because the narrator's interest in news has no relationship to his or her interest in going to Black's next art show.

Question 58. The best answer is J because it does not add irrelevant information to the sentence or essay.

The best answer is NOT:

F because information about the Urban Vintage's décor is not relevant to the essay's focus on Black and his work.

G because information about the narrator's laptop is not relevant to the essay's focus on Black and his work.

H because information about the narrator's meeting with a friend is not relevant to the essay's focus on Black and his work.

Question 59. The best answer is B because it is the only option that does not add unnecessary and confusing punctuation.

The best answer is NOT:

A because *Black* is an essential element that should not be separated from the rest of the clause.

C because the clause beginning with the word *where* is essential and should not be separated from the rest of the sentence.

D because the clause beginning with the word *where* is essential and should not be separated from the rest of the sentence.

Question 60. The best answer is H because Point C in Paragraph 3 is the only logical place to add information that refers to Black's collage *Seven Lamps*. In the new sentence, the phrase "in this piece" clearly refers to the only piece specifically mentioned by name: *Seven Lamps*.

The best answer is NOT:

F because the proposed sentence refers to a specific work Black created, and no specific work is introduced until Paragraph 3. Therefore, this placement is illogical.

G because the proposed sentence refers to a specific work Black created, and no specific work is introduced until Paragraph 3. Therefore, this placement is illogical.

J because the proposed sentence would have no clear referent at Point D, and it would interrupt the flow of the narrative in Paragraph 4.

Passage V

Question 61. **The best answer is D** because it is the only option that does not add unnecessary and confusing punctuation.

> **The best answer is** NOT:
>
> **A** because the phrase beginning after the word *than* is essential and should not be separated from the rest of the clause.
>
> **B** because there is no pause in thought after the word *than*, so the dash is unnecessary.
>
> **C** because the semicolon after the word *than* is incorrect as it creates two sentence fragments.

Question 62. **The best answer is F** because it is the only option that has correct sentence structure. It uses a comma to set off the nonessential element that starts with the word *blamed*.

> **The best answer is** NOT:
>
> **G** because it creates a run-on sentence.
>
> **H** because it creates a comma splice.
>
> **J** because it creates a sentence fragment.

Question 63. **The best answer is C** because it provides the most logical transition to connect this sentence with the preceding one. The word *However* signals two opposing ideas, which is accurate here. Pigeons are first described as nuisances, but one species of pigeon is not a nuisance. Rather, it is a great navigator.

> **The best answer is** NOT:
>
> **A** because the transitional phrase "For example" should logically be followed by an example of a disease-spreading pigeon, but it is followed by an example of a valued pigeon.
>
> **B** because the transitional word *Similarly* signals two ideas that are essentially the same, which does not occur in the two linked sentences.
>
> **D** because the transitional word *Thus* signals a cause-effect relationship between ideas, which is not the case here.

Question 64. The best answer is **H** because it provides the appropriate punctuation (a comma) to set off the appositive ("the homing pigeon").

The best answer is NOT:

F because it creates a sentence fragment.

G because it creates a sentence fragment.

J because the comma after *pigeon* is missing, resulting in an incorrectly subordinated sentence.

Question 65. The best answer is **D** because it provides the appropriate possessive pronoun for this sentence. The singular *Its* refers to the singular noun *pigeon* that appears later in the sentence.

The best answer is NOT:

A because it is an adverb, not a possessive pronoun.

B because it is a contraction, not a possessive pronoun.

C because it is a contraction, not a possessive pronoun.

Question 66. The best answer is **G** because it provides the most logical subordinating conjunction to introduce the dependent clause in this sentence. The conjunction *Before* means "during the period of time preceding a particular event."

The best answer is NOT:

F because it is not a subordinating conjunction and so is imprecise in the context.

H because it is not a subordinating conjunction and so is imprecise in the context.

J because it is not a subordinating conjunction and so is imprecise in the context.

Question 67. The best answer is **A** because it provides the best explanation of the specific communication challenges the battlefield commanders faced.

The best answer is NOT:

B because the suggested revision does not clearly identify specific locations or distances.

C because the suggested revision is relevant to the discussion of "challenges in communication."

D because the suggested revision says nothing about pigeons today.

Question 68. The best answer is **J** because it provides the clearest, most concise wording for this sentence and avoids redundancy.

The best answer is NOT:

F because it is redundant; *returned* and "came back" mean the same thing.

G because it is redundant; "coming home" and "to its home roost" mean the same thing.

H because it is redundant; "returned home" and "to its home roost" mean the same thing.

Question 69. The best answer is **D** because it correctly places the modifiers in the sentence. The introductory phrase refers to a bird that was one of six hundred used in World War I, so the noun immediately after that phrase must be *Cher Ami*, the bird to which the phrase refers.

The best answer is NOT:

A because the introductory phrase should modify *Cher Ami*, not Cher Ami's twelve missions.

B because the introductory phrase should modify *Cher Ami*, not Cher Ami's twelve missions.

C because the introductory phrase should modify *Cher Ami*, not Cher Ami's twelve missions.

Question 70. The best answer is **J** because deleting the underlined portion avoids redundancy with information elsewhere in the paragraph.

The best answer is NOT:

F because it repeats information that is already given in the first sentence of the paragraph.

G because it repeats information that is already given in the second sentence of the paragraph.

H because it repeats information that is already given in the second sentence of the paragraph.

Question 71. The best answer is **B** because it provides the appropriate punctuation for this sentence. A colon is needed here because the sentence describes one link to headquarters and is followed by a phrase emphasizing what that link is. This construction calls for punctuation that shows the sharp break in the sentence.

The best answer is NOT:

A because the colon needed to separate the independent clause from the phrase that follows it is missing.

C because a semicolon should not be used to separate an independent clause from a phrase.

D because a comma is not the appropriate punctuation to separate the independent clause from the phrase that follows it. The phrase "homing pigeons" does not rename or describe the noun *headquarters* that it directly follows.

Question 72. The best answer is **H** because it is the only option that has correct sentence structure. It uses a subordinating conjunction (*As*) to introduce the introductory dependent clause, which prevents the sentence from being a comma splice.

The best answer is NOT:

F because it creates a comma splice.

G because it creates a dangling modifier. The notion that the situation became clear that the Americans were unaware of the 77th's whereabouts is nonsensical.

J because it creates a comma splice.

Question 73. The best answer is **A** because it is the only option that has correct sentence structure. It uses a comma to separate the appositive phrase "the War Cross" from the rest of the sentence. The phrase "the War Cross" directly describes the noun preceding it (*medal*).

The best answer is NOT:

B because it creates a comma splice.

C because it creates a comma splice.

D because it creates a sentence fragment.

Question 74. The best answer is **H** because the expression "extent to which" is a standard English idiom. This expression is used to discuss how true a statement might be. In this case, the sentence poses the question: To what degree did Cher Ami understand what he was doing?

The best answer is NOT:

F because the phrase "extent in which" is not a standard English idiom and does not fit the context.

G because the phrase "extent of which" is not a standard English idiom.

J because the phrase "extent which" is not a standard English idiom.

Question 75. The best answer is **B** because it is the only option that clearly refers to an idea expressed in the first paragraph. The last two sentences in the first paragraph say that homing pigeons are "among the best navigators of the natural world" and have an extraordinary "navigational ability." This option connects the idea of navigational skill with Cher Ami's missions.

The best answer is NOT:

A because it is too vague to specifically connect to any of the information in the first paragraph.

C because the first paragraph never discusses heroism.

D because it is too vague to specifically connect to any of the information in the first paragraph.

Question 1. The correct answer is E. A parallelogram consists of 2 pairs of parallel lines. Any 2 consecutive angles in the parallelogram are supplementary. Since the angle that measures $x°$ and the angle that measures $25°$ are adjacent, these 2 angles are supplementary, and therefore $x° + 25° = 180°$. Solving this equation by subtracting $25°$ from each side shows us that $x = 155°$. If you chose **A**, you may have multiplied $25°$ by 4 to get x. If you chose **B**, you may have thought the 2 angles were complementary and then added $25°$ to each side instead of subtracting. If you chose **C**, you may have subtracted $25°$ from $180°$ twice instead of once. If you chose **D**, you may have added $25°$ twice to $90°$ to get x.

Question 2. The correct answer is H. The retail associate's commission was $30 on Monday, $30 on Tuesday, $70 on Wednesday, $70 on Thursday, and $70 on Friday. In order to find the total commission the associate made for these 5 days, we add these 5 values together to get $30 + $30 + $70 + $70 + $70 = $270. In order to find the average daily commission for these 5 days, we divide the total commission by the number of days, 5. Therefore, the associate's average daily commission is $\frac{\$270}{5} = \$54$. If you chose **F**, you may have found the average of $30 and $70. If you chose **G**, you may have found the average of $30 and $70 and then added $1. If you chose **J**, you may have found $54 and then added $1. If you chose **K**, you may have found $54 and then added $2.

Question 3. The correct answer is B. Since $45 = 3^2 \cdot 5$, the factors of 45 are 1, 3, 5, 9, 15, and 45. Since $50 = 2 \cdot 5^2$, the factors of 50 are 1, 2, 5, 10, 25, and 50. Since $84 = 2^2 \cdot 3 \cdot 7$, the factors of 84 are 1, 2, 3, 4, 6, 7, 12, 14, 21, 28, 42, and 84. So, 45, 50, and 84 share only the common factor 1. Therefore, the greatest common factor of 45, 50, and 84 is 1. If you chose **A**, you may have thought 45, 50, and 84 had no common factor. If you chose **C**, you may have considered the greatest common factor of only 50 and 84. If you chose **D**, you may have considered the greatest common factor of only 45 and 84. If you chose **E**, you may have considered the greatest common factor of only 45 and 50.

Question 4. The correct answer is J. To solve the equation $2(x - 12) + x = 36$, we must isolate x. First, we use the distributive property to obtain the equivalent equation $2x - 2 \cdot 12 + x = 36$. Then we multiply 2 by 12 to obtain the equivalent equation $2x - 24 + x = 36$. Then we add 24 to both sides to obtain the equivalent equation $2x + x = 36 + 24$. Adding like terms together on both sides gives us the equivalent equation $3x = 60$. Then we divide both sides by 3 to get $x = 20$. If you chose **F**, you may have subtracted 24 from one side and added 24 to the other side instead of adding 24 to both sides. If you chose **G**, you may have distributed the 2 only to the x and then added 12 to one side and subtracted it from the other side instead of adding 12 to both sides. If you chose **H**, you may have distributed 2 to only the first term. If you chose **K**, you may have ignored the second x in the original equation and solved the equation $2(x - 12) = 36$.

MATHEMATICS • PRACTICE TEST 5 • EXPLANATORY ANSWERS

Question 5. The correct answer is A. There are 12 white buttons and 22 total buttons. Thus there are $22 - 12 = 10$ buttons that are not white. The probability of selecting 1 button that is not white is the fraction in which the numerator is the number of buttons that are not white and the denominator is the total number of buttons. Therefore, the probability of selecting 1 button that is not white is $\frac{10}{22} = \frac{5}{11}$. If you chose **B**, you may have added the number of red buttons to the number of blue buttons and divided by the number of white buttons. If you chose **C**, you may have divided the number of non-white colors by the number of colors. If you chose **D**, you may have divided 1 by the total number of buttons. If you chose **E**, you may have divided 1 by the number of buttons that are not white.

Question 6. The correct answer is F. Since $\frac{1}{2}$ inch represents 12 miles, and 5 is $\frac{5}{\frac{1}{2}} = 10$ times as long as $\frac{1}{2}$, 5 inches represents $10(12) = 120$ miles. If you chose **G**, you may have multiplied 12 by 5. If you chose **H**, you may have multiplied 12 by 5 by $\frac{1}{2}$. If you chose **J**, you may have multiplied 12 by 2. If you chose **K**, you may have decided that all distances are represented by 12 miles.

Question 7. The correct answer is B. Since Caden started with 45 plants and had 42 plants at the end of day 1, he sold $45 - 42 = 3$ plants on day 1. Since Caden had 42 plants at the end of day 1 and 39 plants at the end of day 2, he sold $42 - 39 = 3$ plants on day 2. Since Caden had 39 plants at the end of day 2 and 36 plants at the end of day 3, he sold $39 - 36 = 3$ plants on day 3. At the end of day 6, Caden will have sold plants for 6 days. Since Caden sells 3 plants per day, he will have sold $3 \cdot 6 = 18$ plants. Since he started with 45 plants, he will have $45 - 18 = 27$ plants left. If you chose **A**, you may have chosen the number of plants left at the end of day 4. If you chose **C**, you may have chosen the number of plants left at the end of day 7. If you chose **D**, you may have chosen the day. If you chose **E**, you may have chosen the number of plants sold each day.

Question 8. The correct answer is H. Since T represents the monthly cost, and the monthly cost is \$5 plus \$2 per movie rented, the relationship can be modeled by $T = 5 + 2M$. If you chose **F**, you may have switched the meanings of T and M. If you chose **G**, you may have switched the meanings of T and M and thought the cost was \$2 per month and \$5 per movie rented. If you chose **J**, you may have thought the cost was \$2 per month and \$5 per movie rented. If you chose **K**, you may have thought you had to pay the monthly cost every time a movie was rented instead of just once a month.

Question 9. The correct answer is C. We know that $(2x + 5)(3x - 4) = 0$. According to the Zero Factor Theorem, this is only true if $2x + 5 = 0$ or $3x - 4 = 0$. If we solve both of these equations, we find that the 2 solutions to the original equation are $x = -\frac{5}{2}$ and $x = \frac{4}{3}$. If you chose **A**, you may have taken the opposite of the constants in the original equation. If you chose **B**, **D**, or **E**, you may have solved the 2 equations incorrectly.

Question 10. **The correct answer is J.** The area of a rectangle can be found by multiplying its length and width. Therefore, the area of this rectangle is $8 \cdot 6 = 48$ square inches. Since each triangle is half the area of the rectangle, the area of each triangle must be $48 \cdot \frac{1}{2} = 24$ square inches. If you chose **F**, you may have taken the average of the 2 lengths. If you chose **G**, you may have multiplied 24 square inches by $\frac{1}{2}$. If you chose **H**, you may have added the 2 lengths. If you chose **K**, you may have multiplied the 2 lengths.

Question 11. **The correct answer is C.** Each fraction represents a portion of the class that participated in band, chorus, football, or basketball. The sum of these fractions represents the portion of the entire class that participated in some extracurricular activity. No student participated in more than 1 activity, so there is no overlap; in other words, none of the students who played in the band also sang in the chorus, etc. To add these fractions, express them as equivalent fractions with common denominators: $\left(\frac{2}{3}\right)\left(\frac{20}{20}\right) + \left(\frac{1}{6}\right)\left(\frac{10}{10}\right) + \left(\frac{1}{10}\right)\left(\frac{6}{6}\right) + \frac{1}{60} = \frac{40}{60} + \frac{10}{60} + \frac{6}{60} + \frac{1}{60} = \frac{57}{60}$. The item asks for the fraction of the class who did NOT participate in any of the 4 activities, so subtract $\frac{57}{60}$ from 1 to get a difference of $\frac{3}{60}$. An equivalent form of $\frac{3}{60}$ is $\frac{3 \div 3}{60 \div 3} = \frac{1}{20}$. If you chose **A**, you may have interpreted "no student participated in more than 1 of the following extracurricular activities" in the first sentence to mean that 0 students participated in the activities. If you chose **B**, you multiplied all the numerators, multiplied all the denominators, and then simplified the fraction: $\frac{(2)(1)(1)(1)}{(3)(6)(10)(60)} = \frac{2}{10,800} = \frac{2 \div 2}{10,800 \div 2} = \frac{1}{5,400}$. If you chose **D**, you added all the numerators and all the denominators $\left(\frac{2+1+1+1}{3+6+10+60}\right)$, and then you subtracted that sum from 1 to get $\frac{74}{79}$. If you chose **E**, you chose the total fraction of students who participated in any of the 4 activities.

Question 12. **The correct answer is H.** The set of integers consists of 0, the counting numbers $\{1, 2, 3, \ldots\}$, and the opposite of the counting numbers $\{\ldots, -3, -2, -1\}$. The value of 1^2 is $(1)(1)$, which is 1; the value of 2^2 is $(2)(2)$, which is 4; and so on, as shown in the table:

Number, n	n^2	Value of n^2
3	3^2	9
4	4^2	16
5	5^2	25
6	6^2	36
7	7^2	49
8	8^2	64
9	9^2	81
10	10^2	100

The square root of 9, or $\sqrt{9}$, is 3 because $3^2 = 9$; the square root of 16, or $\sqrt{16}$, is 4 because $4^2 = 16$; and so on. The value 61 is between 49 (which is 7^2) and 64 (which is 8^2). Another way to express this is $49 < 61 < 64$. If we take the square root of each value, the inequality remains true: $\sqrt{49} < \sqrt{61} < \sqrt{64}$. Further simplifying, we can write $7 < \sqrt{61} < 8$. The inequality shows that the next greatest integer than $\sqrt{61}$ is 8. If you chose **F**, you may have used a calculator to evaluate $\sqrt{61}$, divided that number by 2, and then rounded to the nearest integer. If you chose **G**, you chose the greatest integer less than $\sqrt{61}$. If you chose **J**, you may have used a calculator to evaluate $\sqrt{61}$ and rounded to the nearest 10. If you chose **K**, you may have divided 61 by 2 instead of finding the square root of 61. When 61 is divided by 2, the quotient is 30.5, which rounds to 31.

Question 13. The correct answer is E. The sine ratio of a nonright angle of a right triangle is the ratio of the length of the side opposite the angle to the length of the hypotenuse of the triangle, or $\frac{\text{opposite}}{\text{hypotenuse}}$. The length of the side opposite angle C is given (6 inches), and the length of the hypotenuse of the right triangle is unknown. The sine ratio at C is also given $\left(\frac{2}{3}\right)$. Let x be the length of the hypotenuse, and use the proportion $\frac{2}{3} = \frac{6}{x}$ to solve for x. Cross multiplying gives us $2x = (3)(6)$, or equivalently $2x = 18$. Divide both sides of the equation by 2 to find the value of x: $\frac{2x}{2} = \frac{18}{2}$, or $x = 9$. If you chose **A**, you found the square root of the difference of 3^2 and 2^2. If you chose **B**, you found the square root of the sum of 3^2 and 2^2. If you chose **C**, you found $\frac{2}{3}$ of 6. If you chose **D**, you found the difference of 3^2 and 2^2.

Question 14. The correct answer is H. In an arithmetic sequence, the difference between any two consecutive terms is constant. This is called the common difference. Here, the common difference between any two consecutive terms is 4: $17 - 13 = 4$; $13 - 9 = 4$; $9 - 5 = 4$; and $5 - 1 = 4$. In the general expression, the common difference is the coefficient of n, where n is the term position. This is because every time n increases by 1, the nth term increases by 4. So, the general expression must include $4n$. To find the constant in the expression, find the nth term for term position $n = 0$. The nth term for term position 1 is 1. To find the nth term for term position 0, subtract the common difference, 4, from 1: $1 - 4 = -3$. The constant in the expression is -3. So, the general expression is $4n - 3$. If you chose **F**, **G**, **J**, or **K**, you chose an expression that works only for the first pair of numbers in the table.

Question 15. The correct answer is D. The perimeter of any polygon is the sum of the lengths of the polygon's sides. If we extend the sides measuring 14 feet and 8 feet, a square can be formed as shown in the following diagram. This is because there are right angles present at the corners and two consecutive sides are congruent.

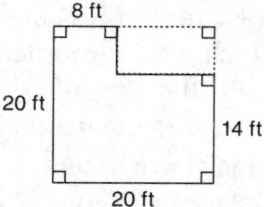

Squares have 4 congruent sides. So, we know that $14 + ? = 20$ in the following diagram.

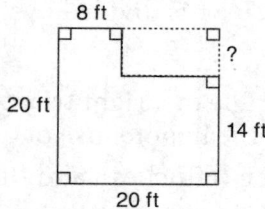

Since $14 + 6 = 20$, the unknown length is 6 feet. Note that this is the same length as the unknown vertical side of the polygon because the dotted figure in the following diagram is a rectangle (there are 4 right angles).

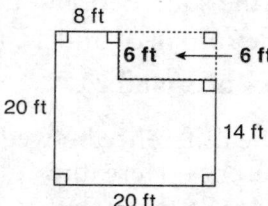

To find the unknown horizontal side of the polygon, we can use the same logic.

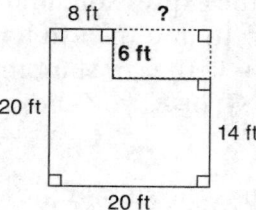

Because squares have 4 congruent sides, it is true that $8 + ? = 20$. Since $8 + 12 = 20$, the unknown length is 12 feet.

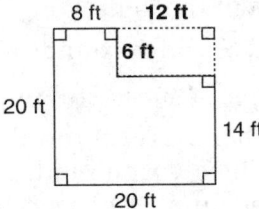

This is the same length as the unknown horizontal side of the polygon.

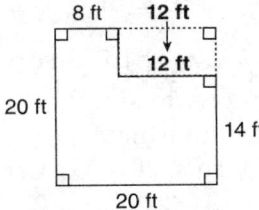

Now we have all the lengths of the sides of the polygon. To find the perimeter, add the lengths: $8 + 6 + 12 + 14 + 20 + 20 = 80$ feet. If you chose **A**, you multiplied 20 feet by 3. If you chose **B**, you added only the measurements shown on the figure. If you chose **C**, you left out the unknown side length of the top horizontal side. If you chose **E**, you may have assumed that the unknown side lengths were 8 feet and 14 feet, making the perimeter $20 + 20 + 14 + 14 + 8 + 8$.

Question 16. The correct answer is F. To find the number halfway between $\frac{2}{3}$ and $\frac{3}{4}$, find the average of the two numbers. Add the numbers by expressing them as equivalent fractions with common denominators: $\left(\frac{2}{3}\right)\left(\frac{4}{4}\right) + \left(\frac{3}{4}\right)\left(\frac{3}{3}\right) = \frac{8}{12} + \frac{9}{12} = \frac{17}{12}$. Then, divide the sum by 2: $\frac{17}{12} \div 2 = \left(\frac{17}{12}\right)\left(\frac{1}{2}\right) = \frac{17}{24}$. If you chose **G**, you added the numerators of the fractions and multiplied the denominators of the fractions: $\frac{2+3}{(3)(4)} = \frac{5}{12}$. If you chose **H**, you may have correctly expressed the fractions as equivalent fractions with common denominators but found the sum of the numerators to be 15 instead of 17. If you chose **J**, you added the fractions by adding the numerators and denominators: $\frac{2+3}{3+4} = \frac{5}{7}$. If you chose **K**, you may have multiplied the given fractions: $\frac{(2)(3)}{(3)(4)} = \frac{6}{12} = \frac{6 \div 6}{12 \div 6} = \frac{1}{2}$.

Question 17. **The correct answer is C.** So far, Sherita has made $\frac{46}{60}$ of her free throws—the numerator is the number of successful free throws, and the denominator is the total number of attempts at free throws. This free-throw average is rounded to 76.7% in the item. We can verify this by dividing 46 by 60 and noting that the quotient $\frac{46}{60} = 0.7\overline{6}$, which rounds to 76.7%. (Note that $x\% = \frac{x}{100}$). Now, Sherita is going to make more attempts at successful free throws to increase her free-throw average. Let x be the minimum number of free throws Sherita must make from now on to have a free-throw average of 80%. Since x is the additional number of successful free throws, x is added to both the numerator (the number of successful free throws) and the denominator (the total number of attempts at free throws): $\frac{46+x}{60+x}$. She wants a free-throw average of at least 80%, which can be expressed as $\frac{46+x}{60+x} \geq 0.8$, or $\frac{46+x}{60+x} \geq \frac{8}{10}$. Since we want the minimum and not a range, we can use the equality $\frac{46+x}{60+x} = \frac{8}{10}$. To solve for x, first cross multiply: $8(60+x) = 10(46+x)$. Use the distributive property to simplify: $480 + 8x = 460 + 10x$. Use the addition property of equality as the first step to isolate x: $480 + (-460) + 8x + (-8x) = 460 + (-460) + 10x + (-8x)$. Then combine like terms: $20 = 2x$. Use the multiplication property of equality to further isolate x: $\left(\frac{1}{2}\right)(20) = \left(\frac{1}{2}\right)(2x)$. Then multiply: $10 = x$. If you chose **A**, you may have set up an equation equivalent to $\frac{x}{60} = 0.8$ and then solved for x by cross multiplying: $x = (60)(0.8) = 48$. You then subtracted 46 from 48. If you chose **B**, you may have found a decimal approximation for $\frac{46}{60} \approx 0.77$ and multiplied by 100: $(0.77)(100) = 77$. You then subtracted that from 80. If you chose **D**, you subtracted 46 from 60. If you chose **E**, you subtracted 60 from 80.

Question 18. **The correct answer is G.** Substitute the expression equal to $g(x)$ for the x in the expression for $f(x)$: $2(x^2 + 1) - 1$. Then, use the distributive property to simplify: $(2)(x^2) + (2)(1) - 1 = 2x^2 + 2 - 1$. Finally, combine like terms: $2x^2 + 1$. If you chose **F**, you added the expressions equal to $f(x)$ and $g(x)$. If you chose **H**, you substituted the expression equal to $g(x)$ for the x in the expression for $f(x)$ but did not subtract 1. If you chose **J**, you may have substituted only the $2x$ from $f(x)$ into the x in $g(x)$ and then added the constants from $f(x)$ and $g(x)$: $(2x)^2 + 1 - 1$. You then multiplied and combined like terms to simplify to get $4x^2 + 0$. If you chose **K**, you found $g(f(x))$.

Question 19. The correct answer is A. The mean of a set of data is the sum of all the data points divided by the number of data points in the set. Data Set A has 8 numbers, so divide the sum of the numbers by 8 to find the mean: $\frac{62+76+76+80+82+87+94+96}{8}=81.625$. Data Set B has 9 numbers: all the numbers of Data Set A and an additional number that is greater than 90. Assume the 9th number is 90. Then the mean of Data Set B would be $\frac{62+76+76+80+82+87+94+96+90}{9}=82.\overline{5}$, which is greater than the mean of Data Set A, 81.625. With a 9th number greater than 90, the mean of Data Set B would be greater than $82.\overline{5}$. (If the 9th number were 91, the mean would be $82.\overline{6}$; if the 9th number were 92, the mean would be $82.\overline{7}$, etc.) Therefore, the mean of Data Set B is greater than the mean of Data Set A. When a data set has an even number of data points, the median is the average of the middle two data points after the data points are in order (ascending or descending). The median of Data Set A is $\frac{80+82}{2}=81$. When a data set has an odd number of data points, the median is the middle number after the data points are in order (ascending or descending). Data Set B has an odd number of data points: the 8 numbers in Data Set A and an additional 9th number greater than 90. The 9th number could be in three different positions among the 8 Data Set A numbers in order. Let X represent the 9th number:

Position 1: 62, 76, 76, 80, 82, 87, X, 94, 96

Position 2: 62, 76, 76, 80, 82, 87, 94, X, 96

Position 3: 62, 76, 76, 80, 82, 87, 94, 96, X

Whatever position the 9th number is in, 82 is the median because it is the 5th (the middle) of 9 numbers in order. Since 82 is greater than 81, the median of Data Set B is greater than the median of Data Set A. If you chose **B**, you may have confused Data Set A for Data Set B, reversing the relationships between the means and medians of both sets. If you chose **C**, you may have assumed that since the 9th number was the last number added to the data set, it doesn't change the mean or median of the set. If you chose **D**, you may have noticed that adding a number greater than 90 would change the median from 81 to 82, but you may have used the logic described for choice **C** for the mean. If you chose **E**, you may have noticed that adding a number greater than 90 would change the mean from 81.625 to a value greater than $82.\overline{5}$, but you may have used the logic described for choice **C** for the median.

Question 20. The correct answer is J. Since the truck is losing 4 fluid ounces of radiator fluid per minute and there are 60 minutes in 1 hour, the truck will lose $(60)(4)=240$ fluid ounces per hour. The truck's radiator holds 480 fluid ounces, so it will take $480\div240=2$ hours for the tank to be empty. The truck is traveling at 35 miles per hour, so in 2 hours it will have traveled $(35)(2)=70$ miles. If you chose **F**, you may have divided 480 by 35. If you chose **G**, you may have divided the speed of the truck by 2. If you chose **H**, you may have selected the speed of the truck. If you chose **K**, you may have divided 480 by 4.

Question 21. The correct answer is B. The midpoint of a line segment that has end points at (x_1, y_1) and (x_2, y_2) is $\left(\frac{x_1+x_2}{2}, \frac{y_1+y_2}{2}\right)$. The midpoint of this segment is thus $\left(\frac{3+(-5)}{2}, \frac{-1+8}{2}\right) = \left(-1, \frac{7}{2}\right)$. If you chose **A**, you may have subtracted the y_2 value in the formula instead of adding, then forgotten to divide by 2: $(3-5, -1-8) = (-2, -9)$. If you chose **C**, you may have mixed up x_1 and y_2 in the formula: $\left(\frac{8+(-5)}{2}, \frac{-1+3}{2}\right) = \left(\frac{3}{2}, 1\right)$. If you chose **D**, you may have subtracted the x_2 and y_2 values in the formula instead of adding: $\left(\frac{3-(-5)}{2}, \frac{-1-8}{2}\right) = \left(4, -\frac{9}{2}\right)$. If you chose **E**, you may have subtracted the x_2 and y_2 values in the formula instead of adding, then forgotten to divide by 2: $(3-(-5), -1-8) = (8, -9)$.

Question 22. The correct answer is H. A linear function has a constant rate of change, $\frac{y_2-y_1}{x_2-x_1}$, for all points (x_1, y_1) and (x_2, y_2). Because **H** is the only choice where the rate of change is constant for all the given points, it must be the linear function. Notice $\frac{2-3}{1-0} = \frac{1-2}{2-1} = \frac{0-1}{3-2} = -1$, so -1 is the constant rate of change. If you chose **F**, you may not have realized that because $\frac{0-1}{1-0} \neq \frac{1-0}{2-1}$, the function is not linear. If you chose **G**, you may not have realized that because $\frac{1-2}{1-0} \neq \frac{1-1}{2-1}$, the function is not linear. If you chose **J**, you may not have realized that because $\frac{1-0}{1-0} \neq \frac{0-1}{2-1}$, the function is not linear. If you chose **K**, you may not have realized that because $\frac{1-0}{1-0} \neq \frac{4-1}{2-1}$, the function is not linear.

Question 23. The correct answer is A. The longest side of a triangle is opposite the largest angle, and the shortest side of a triangle is opposite the smallest angle. Since $x < 2x < 3x$, $m\angle A < m\angle B < m\angle C$. Since the side lengths of the sides opposite $\angle A$, $\angle B$, and $\angle C$ are a inches, b inches, and c inches, respectively, $a < b < c$. If you chose **B**, you may have correctly realized that a was shortest but incorrectly ordered b and c. If you chose **C**, you may have correctly realized that c was longest but incorrectly ordered b and a. If you chose **D**, you may have known that $a < b$ but incorrectly thought that c was shortest instead of longest. If you chose **E**, you may have ordered the side lengths from longest to shortest instead of shortest to longest.

Question 24. The correct answer is F. The slope of a line through points (x_1, y_1) and (x_2, y_2) is $m = \frac{y_2-y_1}{x_2-x_1}$. The slope of this line is thus $m = \frac{7-5}{17-1} = \frac{2}{16} = \frac{1}{8}$. If you chose **G**, you may have added the values in the formula instead of subtracting: $\frac{7+5}{17+1} = \frac{12}{18} = \frac{2}{3}$. If you chose **H**, you may have added the values in the formula instead of subtracting and mixed up the numerator and denominator: $\frac{17+1}{7+5} = \frac{18}{12} = \frac{3}{2}$. If you chose **J**, you may have mixed up the values in the formula: $\frac{x_2-y_2}{y_1-x_1} = \frac{17-7}{5-1} = \frac{10}{4} = \frac{5}{2}$. If you chose **K**, you may have mixed up the numerator and denominator: $\frac{17-1}{7-5} = \frac{16}{2} = 8$.

Question 25. The correct answer is C. Let the length of the shorter side of the rectangle be x centimeters. The longer side is then $(x+2)$ centimeters. The perimeter of the rectangle is then $(2x+2(x+2))$ centimeters. Solving the equation below tells us that the length of the shorter side of the triangle is 8 centimeters and that of the longer side is $(8+2)=10$ centimeters.

$$2x+2(x+2)=36$$
$$2x+2x+4=36$$
$$4x+4=36$$
$$4x=32$$
$$x=8$$

If you chose **A**, you may have found the length of the shorter side instead of the longer side. If you chose **B**, you may have thought the rectangle was a square and thus the length of all sides was equal to $\frac{36}{4}=9$ centimeters. If you chose **D**, you may have divided the 2 numbers given in the stem: $\frac{36}{2}=18$. If you chose **E**, you may have forgotten to divide by 4 in the equation above and thought that because $4x=32$, the length of the longer side was 32 centimeters.

Question 26. The correct answer is F. Let a be the number of adult tickets sold. Since 200 total tickets were sold, the number of student tickets sold is $200-a$. Since the price of an adult ticket is $50 and a student ticket is $25, the total collected from adult and student tickets is $(50a+25(200-a))$ dollars. Solving the equation below tells us that 40 adult tickets were sold and $200-40=160$ student tickets were sold.

$$50a+25(200-a)=6,000$$
$$50a+5,000-25a=6,000$$
$$25a+5,000=6,000$$
$$25a=1,000$$
$$a=40$$

If you selected **G**, you may have thought that 80 adult tickets were sold and found the number of student tickets based on this. If you selected **H**, you may have thought that the number of adult tickets and student tickets must be equal. If you selected **J**, you may have thought that 80 student tickets were sold and found the number of adult tickets based on this. If you selected **K**, you may have mixed up the number of adult tickets sold with the number of student tickets sold.

Question 27. The correct answer is E. 25 out of 200 tickets were sold to first-time skiers. Since $\frac{25}{200}=\frac{1}{8}$, 1 out of the 8 members of the Herzog family is a first-time skier, and the other 7 are not first-time skiers. If you selected **A**, you may have found the number who were first-time skiers instead of the number who were not first-time skiers. If you selected **B**, **C**, or **D**, you may not have known to first set up the proportion $\frac{25}{200}=\frac{x}{8}$ to find the number of family

834 **The Official ACT Prep Guide**

members who were first-time skiers, then to find $8 - x$ to calculate the number who were not first-time skiers. You may have guessed a reasonable number of family members.

Question 28. The correct answer is H. Alyssa's elevation in feet is $E = \frac{300,000}{t+100}$. Since t is the number of seconds after she begins skiing, $t = 0$ corresponds to the start of the main run. The corresponding E value is 3,000: $E = \frac{300,000}{0+100} = 3,000$. If you selected **F**, you may have divided 300,000 by 10,000 instead of 100. If you selected **G**, you may have divided 300,000 by 1,000 instead of 100. If you selected **J**, you may have divided 300,000 by 10. If you selected **K**, you may have divided 300,000 by 1 instead of dividing by 100.

Question 29. The correct answer is E. The area of square $ABCD$ is $18^2 = 324$ square meters. Since the width of the rectangle is 6 meters and the area is 324 square meters, the length is found by solving the equation $l(6) = 324$. The length is thus $l = \frac{324}{6} = 54$ meters. If you selected **A**, you may have thought that the length of the rectangle must be equal to the length of $ABCD$. If you selected **B**, you may have added the length of the square to the width of the rectangle: $18 + 6 = 24$. If you selected **C**, you may have divided the area by 2(6) instead of 6: $l = \frac{324}{2(6)} = 27$. If you selected **D**, you may have confused area with perimeter and thought that the perimeter of $ABCD$ was equal to the perimeter of the rectangle: $2l + 2(6) = 4(18) \rightarrow l = 30$.

Question 30. The correct answer is F. You get $C = \begin{bmatrix} 18 & -5 \\ -10 & -1 \end{bmatrix}$ by performing the steps below.

Step 1. Plug the matrices into the equation: $C = 2\begin{bmatrix} 3 & 5 \\ -2 & 1 \end{bmatrix} - 3\begin{bmatrix} -4 & 5 \\ 2 & 1 \end{bmatrix}$

Step 2. Multiply by the scalars: $C = \begin{bmatrix} 6 & 10 \\ -4 & 2 \end{bmatrix} - \begin{bmatrix} -12 & 15 \\ 6 & 3 \end{bmatrix}$

Step 3. Subtract: $C = \begin{bmatrix} 6-(-12) & 10-15 \\ -4-6 & 2-3 \end{bmatrix} = \begin{bmatrix} 18 & -5 \\ -10 & -1 \end{bmatrix}$

If you selected **G**, you may have found $3A - B$ for the first-column entries, then found $A - 3B$ for the second-column entries: $\begin{bmatrix} 3(3)+4 & 5-3(5) \\ 3(-2)-2 & 1-3(1) \end{bmatrix}$. If you selected **H**, you may not have multiplied matrix B by 3 and instead found $2A - B$. If you selected **J**, you may have added 2 to the elements in matrix A and added 3 to the elements in matrix B instead of multiplying them by the scalars. You then subtracted the matrices: $\begin{bmatrix} 2+3 & 2+5 \\ 2-2 & 2+1 \end{bmatrix} - \begin{bmatrix} 3-4 & 3+5 \\ 3+2 & 3+1 \end{bmatrix} = \begin{bmatrix} 5-(-1) & 7-8 \\ 0-5 & 3-4 \end{bmatrix}$. If you selected **K**, you may have found $2A + 3B$ instead of $2A - 3B$.

Question 31. The correct answer is B. First, add up the total times for each group. The total time for the experimental group is 9 min 40 sec or $9 \text{ min} \times \frac{60 \text{ sec}}{1 \text{ min}} + 40 \text{ sec} = 580 \text{ sec}$. The average time for the experimental group is $580 \div 5 = 116$ sec per mouse. The total time for the control group is 10 min 35 sec or $10 \text{ min} \times \frac{60 \text{ sec}}{1 \text{ min}} + 35 \text{ sec} = 635 \text{ sec}$. The average time for the control group is $635 \div 5 = 127$ sec per mouse. Next, find the difference in the two averages: $127 - 116 = 11$ sec. If you chose **A**, you may have found the difference in the times for the middle mouse (Mouse 3). If you chose **C**, you may have treated the minutes and seconds separately, subtracted those amounts, and then divided by the number of mice. The total minutes for each group would be 7 and 8. $8 - 7 = 1$ min. The total seconds for each group would be 160 and 155. $160 - 155 = 5$ sec. 1 min is 60 sec, and $60 + 5 = 65$ sec. Then you may have divided: $60 \div 5 = 13$ sec. If you chose **D**, you may have found the difference in the median times for the 2 groups. If you chose **E**, you may have made 10 min 35 sec into 9 min 135 sec for the control group. Then the difference between the groups would be 95 sec, and $95 \div 5 = 19$ sec.

Question 32. The correct answer is K. Each of the 3 digits has 10 possible integer choices, 0 through 9. In order to find the number of combinations, multiply by the number of possible values for each digit: $10 \times 10 \times 10 = 1,000$. If you chose **F**, you may have thought there were only 9 possible integers and that you should add: $9 + 9 + 9 = 27$. If you chose **G**, you may have added: $10 + 10 + 10 = 30$. If you chose **H**, you may have decreased the possible values for each successive digit: $10 \times 9 \times 8 = 720$. If you chose **J**, you may have used only 9 possible integers instead of 10: $9 \times 9 \times 9 = 729$.

Question 33. The correct answer is C. An x-intercept is where the graph crosses the x-axis or where $y = 0$. The number of x-intercepts on the interval may be found by counting them on the graph. Another method is to find them algebraically by solving $2 \sin(8\pi x) = 0 \rightarrow \sin(8\pi x) = 0$. Sine functions are cyclic and are equal to zero whenever you take the sine of πk such that k is an integer. Solve $8\pi x = \pi k \rightarrow x = \frac{k}{8}$. Recall that $0 < x < 1$, so the only values of k that satisfy $x = \frac{k}{8}$ and the domain restriction are $\frac{1}{8}, \frac{2}{8}, \frac{3}{8}, \frac{4}{8}, \frac{5}{8}, \frac{6}{8}$, and $\frac{7}{8}$. If you chose **A**, you may have counted the number of endpoints only. If you chose **B**, you may have calculated $\frac{8\pi}{2\pi}$. If you chose **D**, you may have calculated $2\left(\frac{8\pi}{2\pi}\right)$. If you chose **E**, you may have calculated $2\left(\frac{8\pi}{2\pi}\right) + 1$.

Question 34. The correct answer is J. First, find a least common denominator of $\frac{x}{3} + \frac{x}{7} + \frac{x}{9}$, which is $3 \times 3 \times 7$ or 63. So $\frac{x}{3} + \frac{x}{7} + \frac{x}{9} = \frac{21x}{63} + \frac{9x}{63} + \frac{7x}{63} = \frac{37x}{63}$. In order for $\frac{37x}{63}$ to be an integer, $37x$ must be divisible by 63, and since 37 is prime, the smallest positive integer value of x that will allow for that is $x = 63$. If you chose **F**, you may have used 3(7) as the least common multiple (LCM). If you chose **G**, you may have used 3(9) as the LCM. If you chose **H**, you may have used 4(9) as the LCM. If you chose **K**, you may have used 3(7)(9) as the LCM.

Question 35. **The correct answer is D.** In parallelograms, adjacent angles are supplementary. Therefore, $m\angle BAD + m\angle ADC = 180$, so $m\angle BAD = 180° - (71° + 42°) = 67°$. If you chose **A**, you may have computed $(71° + 42°) - 90°$. If you chose **B**, you may have thought that $\angle BDC$ and $\angle BAD$ were the same angle measure. If you chose **C**, you may have computed $90° - 42°$. If you chose **E**, you may have thought that $\angle ABD$ and $\angle BAD$ were the same angle measure.

Question 36. **The correct answer is K.** In parallelograms, opposite sides are equal in length. Therefore, $AB = DC$, so $\frac{2}{3}n - 5 = \frac{1}{3}n + 7 \rightarrow \frac{1}{3}n = 12 \rightarrow n = 36$. If you chose **F**, you may have computed $\frac{2}{3}n - 5 = \frac{1}{3}n + 7 \rightarrow \frac{3}{3}n = 2$. If you chose **G**, you may have computed $\frac{2}{3}n - 5 = \frac{1}{3}n + 7 \rightarrow n = \frac{12}{3}$. If you chose **H**, you may have computed $\frac{2}{3}n - 5 = \frac{1}{3}n + 7 \rightarrow \frac{1}{3}n = 2$. If you chose **J**, you may have computed $\frac{2}{3}n - 5 = \frac{1}{3}n + 7 \rightarrow \frac{3}{3}n = 12$.

Question 37. **The correct answer is E.** In parallelograms, the diagonals bisect each other, so E is the midpoint of segment $\overline{AC}$. The coordinates for E are found using the midpoint formula: $\left(\frac{x_1 + x_2}{2}, \frac{y_1 + y_2}{2}\right) \rightarrow \left(\frac{30 + 2}{2}, \frac{10 + 3}{2}\right) \rightarrow \left(\frac{32}{2}, \frac{13}{2}\right) \rightarrow \left(16, \frac{13}{2}\right)$. If you chose **A**, **B**, **C**, or **D** you may have misremembered the midpoint formula. You may have computed $\left(\frac{3 - 10}{2}, \frac{30 - 2}{2}\right)$, $\left(\frac{10 + 3}{2}, \frac{30 + 2}{2}\right)$, $\left(\frac{30 - 2}{2}, \frac{3 - 10}{2}\right)$, or $\left(\frac{30 - 2}{2}, \frac{10 - 3}{2}\right)$ for **A**, **B**, **C**, or **D**, respectively.

Question 38. **The correct answer is K.** In the parallelogram, $\angle EDC \cong \angle EBA$ because alternate interior angles of parallel lines are congruent; $AB = CD$ because opposite sides of a parallelogram are equal; and $\angle DCE \cong \angle BAE$ because alternate interior angles are congruent. Therefore, $\triangle ABE \cong \triangle CDE$ by angle-side-angle (ASA). Similar proofs by side-angle-side (SAS) or side-side-side (SSS) would yield the same result. If you chose **F**, **G**, **H**, or **J**, you may have mistaken which sides and angles are congruent.

Question 39. **The correct answer is B.** First, multiply the terms using the distributive property, which is sometimes called FOIL, for binomials: $a^2 - 2a\sqrt{b} + a\sqrt{b} - 2(\sqrt{b})^2$. Then combine the like terms: $a^2 - a\sqrt{b} - 2(\sqrt{b})^2$. Next, simplify the power and root term: $a^2 - a\sqrt{b} - 2b$. If you chose **A**, you may have computed $a^2 + a\sqrt{b} - 2a\sqrt{b} - 2a\sqrt{b}$. If you chose **C**, you may have computed $a^2 + a\sqrt{b} - 2a\sqrt{b} - 2(\sqrt{2b})$. If you chose **D**, you may have computed $a^2 - a\sqrt{b} - 2a\sqrt{b} - 2(\sqrt{b})^2$. If you chose **E**, you may have computed $a^2 + a\sqrt{b} + 2a\sqrt{b} - 2(\sqrt{b})^2$.

Question 40. **The correct answer is H.** First, find the distance the engine will travel around both circles. The circumference of a circle is $C = 2\pi r$. The total distance is $2\pi\left(\frac{30}{2}\right) + 2\pi\left(\frac{50}{2}\right) = 80\pi$. Next, divide the distance by the rate: $\frac{80\pi}{75} \approx 3.4$. If you chose **F**, you may have computed $\frac{30 + 50}{75}$. If you chose **G**, you may have computed $\frac{\frac{30 + 50}{2}\pi}{75}$. If you chose **J**, you might have rounded up or estimated incorrectly. If you chose **K**, you may have computed $\frac{2\pi(30 + 50)}{75}$.

Question 41. The correct answer is B. To simplify an expression with a negative fractional exponent, apply the positive of the exponent to the reciprocal of the base of the expression. Thus, $\left(\frac{4}{5}\right)^{-\frac{3}{2}} = \left(\frac{5}{4}\right)^{\frac{3}{2}}$. To simplify an expression with a fractional exponent, use the exponent rule $x^{\frac{m}{n}} = \sqrt[n]{x^m}$. Therefore, $\left(\frac{5}{4}\right)^{\frac{3}{2}} = \sqrt[2]{\left(\frac{5}{4}\right)^3} = \sqrt{\frac{125}{64}} = \frac{\sqrt{125}}{\sqrt{64}} = \frac{\sqrt{25 \cdot 5}}{8}$. If you chose **A**, you picked the value equal to $\frac{4^{\frac{1}{2}}}{5^{-1}} = \frac{5}{4^{-\frac{1}{2}}}$. If you chose **C**, you picked the value equal to $\left(\frac{4}{5}\right)\left(\sqrt{2}\right)$. If you chose **D**, you picked the value equal to $\left(\frac{4}{5}\right)^{-\frac{1}{2}} = \left(\frac{5}{4}\right)^{\frac{1}{2}} = \sqrt{\frac{5}{4}}$. If you chose **E**, you picked the value equal to $\left(\frac{4}{5}\right)\left(-\frac{3}{2}\right)$.

Question 42. The correct answer is F. The logarithmic equation $\log_x\left(\frac{1}{25}\right) = -2$ is equivalent to the exponential equation $x^{-2} = \frac{1}{25}$. Because $x^{-2} = \frac{1}{x^2}$ and $\frac{1}{25} = \frac{1}{5^2}$, it follows that $x = 5$. If you chose **G**, you may have thought $x^{-2} = \frac{2}{x}$, so that $\frac{2}{x} = \frac{1}{25}$. If you chose **H**, you may have thought the logarithmic equation $\log_x\left(\frac{1}{25}\right) = -2$ was equivalent to the equation $2x = \frac{1}{25}$. If you chose **J**, you may have thought the logarithmic equation $\log_x\left(\frac{1}{25}\right) = -2$ was equivalent to the equation $x^2 = \frac{1}{25}$. If you chose **K**, you may have thought $x^{-2} = \frac{1}{2x}$, so that $\frac{1}{2x} = \frac{1}{25}$.

Question 43. The correct answer is D. The line has an x-intercept at $(6, 0)$ and a y-intercept at $(0, -3)$. The slope of the line passing through these intercepts is equal to $\frac{-3-0}{0-6} = \frac{-3}{-6} = \frac{1}{2}$. Thus, the equation of the line in slope-intercept form is given by $y = \frac{1}{2}x - 3$. The only point in the options given that satisfies this equation is $(4, -1)$. If you chose **A**, you may have added 1 to each of the coordinates of the point $(-4, -5)$. If you chose **B**, you may have subtracted 1 from each of the coordinates of the point $(0, -3)$. If you chose **C**, you may have added 1 to each of the coordinates of the point $(0, -3)$. If you chose **E**, you picked the point that satisfies the equation $y = \frac{1}{3}x - 2$.

Question 44. The correct answer is G. After the runners have started, the shortest length of time it will take for them to again be at their starting line at the same time is equal to the least common multiple of 16 seconds and 28 seconds. The prime factorizations of 16 and 28 are $16 = 2 \cdot 2 \cdot 2 \cdot 2 = 2^4$ and $28 = 2 \times 2 \times 7 = 2^2 \times 7$. So, the least common multiple of 16 and 28 is $2^4 \cdot 7 = 112$. If you chose **F**, you picked the value that is 2 times the sum of 16 and 28: $2(16 + 28)$. If you chose **H**, you picked the value that is 10 times the difference of 28 and 16: $10(28 - 16)$. If you chose **J**, you picked the value that is 5 times the sum of 16 and 28: $5(16 + 28)$. If you chose **K**, you picked the value that is the product of 16 and 28: $16 \cdot 28$.

MATHEMATICS • PRACTICE TEST 5 • EXPLANATORY ANSWERS

Question 45. **The correct answer is D**. The profit function $p(c)=1{,}600c-4c^2$ where $0\le c\le 400$ is quadratic and attains its maximum value at the vertex of the function. Thus, the value of c for which the weekly profit will be the largest is $c=-\frac{b}{2a}=-\frac{1{,}600}{2(-4)}=200$. If you chose **A**, you picked the value equivalent to $\sqrt{\frac{1{,}600}{4}}$. If you chose **B**, you picked the value equivalent to $\sqrt{1{,}600}$. If you chose **C**, you picked the value equivalent to $\frac{1{,}600}{4^2}$. If you chose **E**, you picked the largest value of c.

Question 46. **The correct answer is H**. Since a, b, c, and d are consecutive positive integers such that $a<b<c<d$, it follows that $\frac{a}{b}<\frac{b}{c}<\frac{c}{d}$. Now consider the inequality $\frac{a}{b}+1<\frac{b}{c}+1$. Combining the fractions gives $\frac{a}{b}+\frac{b}{b}<\frac{b}{c}+\frac{c}{c}$, or $\frac{a+b}{b}<\frac{b+c}{c}$. Multiplying both sides of this new inequality by $\frac{b}{b+c}$ gives $\frac{a+b}{b+c}<\frac{b}{c}$. Note that $\frac{a+b}{b+c}<\frac{b}{c}<\frac{c}{d}$. Similarly, $\frac{b}{c}+1<\frac{c}{d}+1=\frac{b+c}{c}<\frac{c+d}{d}$, and $\frac{b+c}{c+d}<\frac{c}{d}$. Therefore, $\frac{c}{d}$ has the greatest value. If you chose **F**, **G**, **J**, or **K**, then a counterexample would be $a=1$, $b=2$, $c=3$, and $d=4$. So, $\frac{1}{2}<\frac{3}{4}$, which disproves **F**; $\frac{2}{3}<\frac{3}{4}$, which disproves **G**; $\frac{1+2}{2+3}=\frac{3}{5}<\frac{3}{4}$, which disproves **J**; and $\frac{2+3}{3+4}=\frac{5}{7}\approx 0.7<\frac{3}{4}$, which disproves **K**.

Question 47. **The correct answer is A**. The area of the larger square is 324 square feet, so the length, in feet, of the side of the larger square is $\sqrt{324}=18$ feet. The ratio of the perimeters of the two squares is $2:3$, so the ratio of the side lengths of the two squares is $x:18$, where x is the length, in feet, of the smaller square. It follows that $\frac{2}{3}=\frac{x}{18}$; $3x=2(18)$; $3x=36$; $x=12$. If you chose **B**, you picked the value that is the length of the larger square. If you chose **C**, you picked the value that is twice the length of the smaller square. If you chose **D**, you may have solved the equation $\frac{2}{3}=\frac{18}{x}$. If you chose **E**, you may have solved the equation $\frac{2}{18}=\frac{x}{324}$.

Question 48. **The correct answer is G**. Consider the inequality $-1\le x-\sqrt{5}<4$. Adding $\sqrt{5}$ to all three parts of the inequality gives $-1+\sqrt{5}\le x<4+\sqrt{5}$. Now, since $4<5<9$, it follows that $\sqrt{4}<\sqrt{5}<\sqrt{9}$, or $2<\sqrt{5}<3$. Therefore, $-1+2<-1+\sqrt{5}<-1+3$, or $1<-1+\sqrt{5}<2$. Similarly, $4+2<4+\sqrt{5}<4+3$, or $6<4+\sqrt{5}<7$. Therefore, the set of all integers that satisfy the inequality is $\{2, 3, 4, 5, 6\}$. If you chose **F**, you may have used $<$ on both ends of the inequality, replaced $\sqrt{5}$ with 3 on the lower bound of the inequality, and replaced $\sqrt{5}$ with 2 on the upper bound of the inequality: $2=-1+3<x<4+2=6$. If you chose **H**, you may have worked similarly to **F** but used $\le$ on the left side of the inequality: $2\le x<6$. If you chose **J**, you may have used a lower bound of $0<-1+\sqrt{5}<x$ and an upper bound of $x<4+\sqrt{5}<7$. If you chose **K**, you may have replaced $\sqrt{5}$ with 2 in the inequality: $1=-1+2\le x<4+2=6$.

Question 49. The correct answer is D. For the 40-mph wind, $kSv^2 = k(1)(40^2) = 50$, so $k = \frac{50}{1,600} = \frac{1}{32}$. It follows that for the 80-mph wind, $\frac{1}{32}(2)(80^2) = 400$. If you chose **A**, you may have computed the force the 40-mph wind exerts on a 2-square-foot flat surface: $\frac{1}{32}(2)(40^2) = 100$. If you chose **B**, you picked the value that is equivalent to $\frac{80^2}{50} = \frac{6,400}{50}$. If you chose **C**, you may have computed the force the 80-mph wind exerts on a 1-square-foot flat surface: $\frac{1}{32}(1)(80^2) = 200$. If you chose **E**, you picked the value that is equivalent to $\frac{80^2}{2^2} = \frac{6,400}{4}$.

Question 50. The correct answer is J. The area of the sidewalk will be $20(10) - 6(16) = 200 - 96 = 104$ square feet. The volume of concrete needed to make the sidewalk is $104 \cdot \left(4 \text{ in} \cdot \frac{1 \text{ ft}}{12 \text{ in}}\right) = \frac{104}{3}$ cubic feet. The number of bags of concrete needed to make the sidewalk is $\frac{104}{3} \div 0.6 = \frac{104}{1.8} \approx 57.8$, or 58 whole bags. If you chose **F**, you may have computed the volume of the sidewalk as $104 \div 4 = 26$ and the number of bags as $26 \cdot 0.6 = 15.6$, or 16.

If you chose **G**, you may have computed the volume of the sidewalk as 26 as in **F** and the number of bags as $26 \div 0.6 \approx 43.3$, or 44. If you chose **H**, you may have computed the area of the sidewalk as $4(10) + 4(20) = 40 + 80 = 120$ square feet, the volume as $120 \cdot \left(\frac{1 \text{ ft}}{4 \text{ in}}\right) = 30$ cubic feet, and the number of bags as $30 \div 0.6 = 50$. If you chose **K**, you may have computed the area of the sidewalk as 120 as in **H**, the volume as $120 \cdot \left(4 \text{ in} \cdot \frac{1 \text{ ft}}{12 \text{ in}}\right) = 40$ cubic feet, and the number of bags as $40 \div 0.6 \approx 66.7$, or 67.

Question 51. The correct answer is E. Let r be the radius of the circle. Since $\triangle OAP$ is a right triangle, then $\tan 20° = \frac{r}{12}$ and so $r = 12 \tan 20° \approx 4.368$ given the approximation in the item. Let x be the length of BP in centimeters. Again, since $\triangle OAP$ is a right triangle, we can apply the Pythagorean theorem $r^2 = 12^2 + (r+x)^2$, which we can rewrite as $x^2 + 2(4.368)x - 144 = 0$ and solve using the quadratic equation and we get $x \approx \frac{-8.736 \pm \sqrt{8.736^2 - 4(1)(-144)}}{2} \approx 8.402$ or -17.138. The positive value is the only one that makes sense. If you chose **A**, you may have used $\cos 20° = \frac{12}{r+x}$ and incorrectly thought $r = x$, thus concluding $x = \frac{12}{2 \cos 20°} \approx 2.1$. If you chose **B**, you may have found the length of the radius and assumed that was the length of the desired segment. If you chose **C**, you may have assumed $r = x$ and solved the equation $x^2 + 144 = (2x)^2$. If you chose **D**, you may have correctly determined the length of the radius and then subtracted that from the given length of segment $\overline{AP}$.

Question 52. The correct answer is J. The average of the 10 scores is x, and so the total sum is $10x$. Let h = highest score and l = lowest score; then $y = \frac{10x - (h+l)}{8}$. Thus $h + l = 10x - 8y$, so the average of the highest and lowest score is $\frac{h+l}{2} = \frac{10x - 8y}{2}$. If you chose **F**, you may have correctly found the sum of the highest and lowest value but did not average the two. If you chose **G**, you may have found the average of the two given averages x and y. If you chose **H**, you may have incorrectly changed a sign when solving for the sum of the highest and lowest values, $y = \frac{10x - (h+l)}{8} \rightarrow h + l = 10x + 8y$. If you chose **K**, you may have found the average of the original 10 test scores plus the list of 8 test scores after removing the highest and lowest scores.

Question 53. The correct answer is E. Both sides of the equation can be written as a power of 3, as follows $3^{3n^2} = 3^{2(5n-4)}$. Since both sides of the equation have the same base, then their exponents must be equal. Hence, we need to solve $3n^2 = 10n - 8$, or $3n^2 - 10n + 8 = 0$. Factoring this quadratic equation gives $(3n - 4)(n - 2) = 0$, so our solutions are $n = \left\{\frac{4}{3}, 2\right\}$. If you chose **A**, you may have correctly determined equivalent exponents, but incorrectly factored the quadratic equation $3n^2 - 10n + 8$ as $(3n - 2)(n + 4)$. If you chose **B**, you may have determined the common base of 3, but rewritten the original equation as $3^{3n^2} = 3^{5n+8}$ and solved the quadratic equation $3n^2 - 5n - 8 = 0$. If you chose **C**, you may have correctly determined equivalent exponents, but changed a sign in the quadratic equation required to solve, so you solved $3n^2 - 10n - 8 = 0$. If you chose **D**, you may have set the exponents equal to each other and solved the quadratic equation $n^2 - 5n + 4 = 0$.

Question 54. The correct answer is G. There are 36 possible outcomes from rolling 2 dice and recording the numbers that land face up: $\{(1,1),(1,2),(1,3),(1,4),\ldots,(6,6)\}$. Adding the 2 numbers gives the following list: $\{2, 3, 4, 5, 6, 7, 3, 4, 5, 6, 7, 8, 4, 5, 6, 7, 8, 9, 5, 6, 7, 8, 9, 10, 6, 7, 8, 9, 10, 11, 7, 8, 9, 10, 11, 12\}$. The number of outcomes less than 6 is 10. Thus, the probability is $\frac{10}{36} = \frac{5}{18}$. If you chose **K**, you may have miscounted the number of outcomes less than 6 to be 13, but correctly determined the number of possible outcomes of 36 and got $\frac{13}{36}$. If you chose **J**, you may have counted the number of outcomes less than or equal to 6, which is 15, and divided by the total number of outcomes for the 2 dice. If you chose **H**, you may have miscounted the total number of possible outcomes as 39 and counted the total number of outcomes less than or equal to 6 to get a probability of $\frac{15}{39} = \frac{5}{13}$. If you chose **F**, you may have counted the number of possibilities for a single roll less than 6 and divided by the total number of outcomes for the 2 dice.

Question 55. The correct answer is D. Let t be the amount of time, in hours, both drivers have been traveling. Louisa has driven $68t$ miles and Antonio has driven $57t$ miles. At the time they pass each other, they will have driven a combined 240 miles, that is, $68t + 57t = 240$. The solution for t in this equation is 1.92, which is approximately 1 hour 55.2 minutes, since $0.92 \text{ hr} \cdot \frac{60 \text{ min}}{1 \text{ hr}} = 55.2$ min. Thus, they pass each other at approximately $3:55$ p.m. If you chose **A**, you may have used 68 mph for both drivers, then solved $68t + 68t = 240$. If you chose

B, you may have found the average of the rates 68 mph and 57 mph, which is 62.5, and then divided 240 by 62.5, which gives 3.84 hours, which would convert to approximately 3 hours 50 minutes, and ignored the start time of 2:00 p.m. If you chose **C**, you may have calculated the time using 70 instead of 68—that is, you may have solved the equation $70t + 57t = 240$ or divided 240 by 68 to get approximately 3.529, which incorrectly thinks is 3 hours 53 minutes or 3:53 p.m. If you chose **E**, you may have used 57 mph for both drivers, then solved $57t + 57t = 240$.

Question 56. The correct answer is J. Selecting every possible pair of points from among 10 points is by definition the combination of 10 things taken 2 at a time, $\binom{10}{2} = \frac{10!}{(10-2)!2!} = \frac{10 \cdot 9 \cdot 8!}{8!2!} = \frac{10 \cdot 9}{2} = 45$. If you chose **F**, you may have thought 10 points would give 10 lines. If you chose **G**, you may have thought 10 points taken 2 at a time is $10 \cdot 2$. If you chose **H**, you may not have been sure how to count the number of lines and so you may have computed $\frac{10(10-3)}{2}$. If you chose **K**, you may have counted each line twice by counting 10 choices for the 1st point and 9 choices for the 2nd point, without accounting for the fact that switching points will give the same line.

Question 57. The correct answer is A. Using the given definition, manipulate the fraction to get an equivalent expression $\frac{(n+1)!6!}{n!3!} = \frac{(n+1)n!6 \cdot 5 \cdot 4 \cdot 3!}{n!3!} = (n+1)6 \cdot 5 \cdot 4 = 120(n+1)$. If you chose **B**, you may have calculated $\frac{6!}{3!}$ and ignored n. If you chose **C**, you may have calculated $\frac{6}{3}$ and ignored n and the factorials. If you chose **D**, you may have ignored the factorials and simplified. If you chose **E**, you may have thought that multiplication and the factorial operation can switch order, that is, $n!m! = (nm)!$.

Question 58. The correct answer is G. Consider 4 consecutive positive integers: n, $n+1$, $n+2$, $n+3$. It is not necessary that at least 1 is prime, for example, $n = 24$. Thus, statement I may not be true. In any sequence of 4 consecutive positive integers, exactly 2 are even and thus divisible by the prime number 2; thus, II must always be true. Last, III is not necessarily true. Consider $n = 24$ again: Among 24, 25, 26, and 27, none is a factor of any other number in the list. If you chose **F**, you may have thought that at least 1 of the 4 integers is prime, since it is true for all $n < 24$. If you chose **H**, you may not have realized that any list of 4 consecutive positive integers must contain 2 even numbers. Also, you may have thought at least 1 is prime and that at least 1 of the integers is a factor of another since it is true for $n = 1, 2,$ or 3. If you chose **J**, you may have observed that I is not always true and II is always true, but you incorrectly interpreted III. If you chose **K**, you may have thought all 3 options are always true.

Question 59. **The correct answer is E.** The expanded form of $(x+1)^4$ is as follows: $(x+1)(x+1)(x+1)(x+1) = x^4 + 4x^3 + 6x^2 + 4x + 1$. The coefficient of x^2 is 6. If you chose **A**, you may have thought the expansion of $(x+1)^4$ is $x^4 + 1$, and so there is no x^2 term. If you chose **B**, you may have thought the expansion of $(x+1)^4$ is $x^4 + x^3 + x^2 + x + 1$, and so the coefficient of interest is 1. If you chose **C**, you may have thought the expansion of $(x+1)^4$ is $x^4 + 2x^3 + 4x^2 + 2x + 1$, and so the coefficient of interest is 4. If you chose **D**, you may have thought the expansion of $(x+1)^4$ is $x^4 + 4x^3 + 4x^2 + 4x + 1$, and so the coefficient of interest is 4.

Question 60. **The correct answer is K.** From the diagram, $\triangle ADC$ is a right triangle. So $m\angle ACD = 90° - 20° = 70°$. By the property of supplementary angles, $m\angle ACB = 180° - 70° = 110°$. In $\triangle ACB$, two sides and the included angle are known, so the law of cosines will give the measure of the remaining side. Let g = length of guy wire. Thus, $g^2 = 60^2 + 25^2 - 2(60)(25)\cos 110°$. Taking the square root of both sides gives the desired result. If you chose **F**, you may have incorrectly assumed $m\angle BAC = 20°$ and $m\angle ACB = 60°$, then calculated the length of the guy wire using the law of sines, $\frac{\sin 60°}{g} = \frac{\sin 20°}{25}$. If you chose **G**, you may have incorrectly assumed $m\angle BAC = 20°$ and $m\angle ACB = 70°$, then calculated the length of the guy wire using the law of sines, $\frac{\sin 70°}{g} = \frac{\sin 20°}{25}$. If you chose **H**, you may have correctly determined $m\angle ACB$ but incorrectly thought $m\angle BAC = 20°$ and then correctly applied the law of sines, $\frac{\sin 110°}{g} = \frac{\sin 20°}{25}$. If you chose **J**, you may have incorrectly thought that $m\angle ACB = 90° - 20° = 70°$, and then correctly used the law of cosines, $g^2 = 60^2 + 25^2 - 2(60)(25)\cos 70°$.

Passage I

Question 1. The best answer is D because the narrator states that her mother "rises against the sun like a skyscraper" (lines 18–19).

The best answer is NOT:

A because although the narrator and her mother view a Picasso painting (lines 28–29), the narrator does not compare her mother to a Picasso painting.

B because when the narrator refers to shadow and witness, she is talking about herself, not her mother. Line 22: "I am her small shadow and witness."

C because "a story developing behind her eyes" (lines 34–35) is the narrator's description of something she sees in her mother rather than a comparison between her mother and something else.

Question 2. The best answer is J because after explaining that her mother took her all around Chicago, the narrator states that the city "was given to me by my mother" (line 27).

The best answer is NOT:

F because although the narrator describes traveling "from one end of the city to the other" (line 25), she does not mention her ability to do so without getting lost.

G because although the narrator notes that her mother talks about politics (lines 20–21), she does not indicate that her mother influenced city politics.

H because although the narrator refers to herself as a small shadow (line 22), she does so in the context of describing herself in relation to her mother, not in the context of her relationship to Chicago.

Question 3. The best answer is C because the narrator explains that the reason she doesn't verify her mother's ideas about Picasso is that "I like my mother's version best" (lines 40–41).

The best answer is NOT:

A because there is no indication in the passage that the narrator doesn't know which references to check; she indicates that the reason she doesn't check them is that she prefers her mother's anecdotes to others she might find (lines 40–41).

B because the narrator does not indicate that she believes her mother's anecdotes are accurate; she simply prefers them (lines 40–41).

D because it contradicts the narrator's statement that "I like my mother's version best" (lines 40–41).

Question 4. The best answer is H because the narrator states that the answer to the question of where her parents were born "signifies nothing" (line 48) in regard to understanding the narrator and her family.

The best answer is NOT:

F because the narrator makes no reference to questions regarding how her mother may have been like the narrator's other ancestors.

G because the narrator states that "the meaningful question would be to ask where my ancestors lived" (lines 48–49).

J because the answer to the question would provide significant information about the narrator's background. She notes that her connection to water "comes from my mother" (line 58).

Question 5. The best answer is B because in the context of the passage, "blinding" (line 68) and "overwhelm" (line 69) serve to illustrate the sense of reverence the narrator's mother feels for the power and beauty of the sea as she observes it.

The best answer is NOT:

A because there is no indication in the passage that the narrator's mother felt fright in response to watching the sea; rather, it was an experience she sought out. Line 59: "She longs for a view more than anything else."

C because there is no indication in the passage that the narrator's mother felt regret in response to watching the sea; rather, she was drawn to the sea and went to great lengths to acquire a good view of it (lines 59–62).

D because there is no indication in the passage that the narrator's mother experienced quietness in response to watching the sea; rather, the narrator's use of "blinding" (line 68) and "overwhelm" (line 69) suggest a dramatic and thrilling experience.

Question 6. The best answer is **H** because the comparison of the narrator's mother to water follows from the description of the mother as a nomad or one who, while able to keep a part of herself the same, is constantly moving and changing. According to the narrator, her mother is "forever moving, changing and going, yet always retaining some essential part of her being, recognizable and intact in spite of all the places she has been. In this, she is like water, not dead water but fearsomely alive" (lines 76–80). In this context, "dead" (line 79) refers to stagnant water, or water that doesn't move and sustain life.

The best answer is NOT:

F because the narrator's description of her mother, which is illustrated by the contrast between water that is dead and water that is alive, is evocative of movement and change, not color (lines 76–80).

G because the word "obsolete" does not relate to the contrast being made in the passage between movement and the lack of movement.

J because while "frozen" can suggest a lack of movement, "stagnant" creates a better contrast with water that is "alive." In the context of water, "stagnant" suggests a lack of movement, to the point of being unhealthy and unable to sustain life, while "frozen" simply suggests a different state.

Question 7. The best answer is **A** because the last sentence of the passage is part of the narrator's metaphor likening her mother to water (lines 81–90). In the sentence, the narrator depicts herself as a child collecting sea glass and driftwood, or what her mother leaves behind when she goes away.

The best answer is NOT:

B because the narrator does not make any reference to memory; the child in the sentence represents the narrator at the time she is writing, as an adult.

C because the sentence is not a literal explanation of what the narrator is doing but rather a metaphorical description of how she reacts when her mother goes away.

D because the sentence is not a literal description of what the narrator found as a child but rather a metaphorical description of how she reacts when her mother goes away.

Question 8. The best answer is F because traveling and moving are referenced in both passages. Passage A, lines 24–25: "We don't have much money, but Mom takes me from one end of the city to the other, on foot, on buses." Passage B, lines 75–79: "My mother could only become a nomad herself—forever moving, changing and going, yet always retaining some essential part of her being, recognizable and intact in spite of all the places she has been."

The best answer is NOT:

G because Chicago is referenced in Passage A (line 11 and line 26) but not in Passage B.

H because speaking openly and boldly is referenced in Passage A (lines 20–21) but not in Passage B.

J because staying at a hotel is referenced in Passage B (lines 60–62) but not in Passage A.

Question 9. The best answer is D because in Passage B, the narrator uses language that evokes distance and tension to describe the conflicted feelings she has about her mother. Lines 81–87: "When I gaze out, I see her, my mother, always pulling away, returning and pulling away again. I drink from her, and she slips between my fingertips. She has borne me all this way. I cannot decide whether I want her to stay or go. When she is here, I wish she would leave. When she is gone, I wish she would return."

The best answer is NOT:

A because there is no reference in either passage to lively conversation or joy experienced by the narrators. There are no examples of conversation in Passage B, and those referenced in Passage A are one-sided or brief. Lines 32–33: "'Was he very sad?' I ask. 'Yes, I think he was.'"

B because there is no reference in either passage to fierce competition or debate between the narrator and her mother.

C because there is no reference in either passage to physical affection or warmth from the narrator's mother.

Question 10. The best answer is **F** because both passages include information about the narrators' mothers' lives. Passage A, lines 9–15: "She had never been on a train before or used a telephone. She left Standing Rock to take a job in Chicago so she could help out the family during the War. She was so petrified of the new surroundings, she stayed in her seat all the way from McLaughlin, South Dakota, to Chicago, Illinois, and didn't move once." Passage B, lines 44–47: "Westerners ask me where my parents were born, as though the answer will enable them to glean some knowledge. The answer is Beijing and Luoyang." Passage B, lines 53–54: "My mother's father was from Inner Mongolia, land of desert and grassy plains."

The best answer is NOT:

G because although in Passage A the narrator describes her mother's height (lines 17–20), in Passage B, the narrator does not describe her mother's physical appearance at all.

H because there is no mention in either passage of the narrator's mother's academic interests.

J because while in Passage B the narrator describes where her father was from (lines 50–53), there is no mention in Passage A of the narrator's father at all, and there is no mention in either passage of the relationship between the narrator's mother and father.

Passage II

Question 11. The best answer is **B** because the passage states that young diving enthusiasts "still emerge" with implements "of the former ice trade" (lines 68–71), which indicates that the action continues in the present day, long after the ice trade's end.

The best answer is NOT:

A because the passage states that the "first comprehensive report on the ice industry of the United States was commissioned in 1879" (lines 1–3).

C because the passage indicates that this sale took place "in the year of the great ice census" (line 21), which was commissioned in 1879 (lines 1–3).

D because the passage indicates that this was the price of ice "in the year of the great ice census" (line 21), which was commissioned in 1879 (lines 1–3).

Question 12. The best answer is **F** because the passage states that the 1879 national census reported "an account of the great growth of the [ice] industry in the preceding ten years" (lines 9–10).

The best answer is NOT:

G because there is no indication in the passage that damaging publicity affected the natural-ice industry in this period.

H because although the passage mentions an estimated shipping cost of $1.50 per ton (line 28) the passage does not indicate whether this was considered a high price.

J because although the passage notes the decline of the natural-ice industry, it states that the decline began in "the early decades of the twentieth century" (lines 55–56).

Question 13. The best answer is **B** because the passage states that New York was "by far the biggest market" (lines 12–13), and it can reasonably be inferred that New York was the metropolis subsequently described as being supplied by imports and icehouses (lines 18–20).

The best answer is NOT:

A because although the passage states that there were 135 icehouses between New York and Albany (lines 17–18), the passage does not indicate that Albany was a large ice market.

C because although the passage mentions the city of Philadelphia, it is in reference to the city's ice shortage after "unseasonably warm weather" (line 23).

D because the passage does not mention or generalize about average US cities of the 1870s.

Question 14. The best answer is **F** because the passage describes the fifteen-to-twenty-inch ice in Maine as "a top-quality crop" (line 26) and states that two thousand cargoes of this ice "were shipped south to New York, Philadelphia, and other more southern cities" (lines 31–32).

The best answer is NOT:

G because the passage indicates that the ice was shipped south to various locations rather than remaining in Maine to meet local demand.

H because the passage does not indicate that the ice "famine" negatively affected the 1879 Maine ice crop.

J because although the passage states that "the demand for ice rose annually" (line 34), it does not indicate that the size or quality of the ice changed in the subsequent year.

Question 15. The best answer is **A** because the paragraph states that the "natural-ice trade began to decline from the early decades of the twentieth century" (lines 55–56) and claims that much of the "evidence of its former vast scale rapidly disappeared" (lines 60–61) with the loss of the icehouses.

The best answer is NOT:

B because although the paragraph mentions that sparks from steam trains occasionally caused icehouses to burn down (lines 62–63), it does not suggest that the steam train signaled the demise of ice harvesting.

C because although the paragraph notes that icehouses easily caught fire (lines 62–65), this is a subordinate detail in the paragraph rather than the main idea.

D because although the paragraph states that the natural-ice industry survived into the late 1950s in remote areas (lines 56–59), this is not characterized as a short-lived revival of the industry.

Question 16. The best answer is **H** because the fifth paragraph describes the "impressive variety of odd implements" (lines 70–71) found in waters formerly utilized by the ice industry. The range of "many other specialist implements" (line 79) found in industry catalogs supports the inference that these were typical ice industry tools.

The best answer is NOT:

F because the paragraph does not refer to the natural-ice industry's ability to respond rapidly to market changes.

G because the paragraph does not refer to the natural-ice industry's ability to erect icehouses quickly.

J because the paragraph does not indicate that ice harvesting was simple work.

Question 17. The best answer is **D** because the passage indicates that artifacts of the natural-ice industry remain, stating that divers "still emerge from lakes and rivers clutching an impressive variety of odd implements—plows and chisels and scrapers that fell through the ice during the harvesting" (lines 69–73). The passage also notes that "one or two museums keep small displays of these tools" (lines 73–74) and that "collectors have preserved manufacturers' catalogs" (lines 74–75).

The best answer is NOT:

A because the author does not contradict this statement elsewhere in the passage.

B because the author does not contradict this statement elsewhere in the passage.

C because the author does not contradict the statement elsewhere in the passage.

Question 18. The best answer is **J** because the passage states that "the biggest market was in New York, and none of its ice was manufactured artificially" (lines 12–14).

The best answer is NOT:

F because the passage states that "none of its ice was manufactured artificially" (lines 13–14).

G because the passage states that "none of its ice was manufactured artificially" (lines 13–14).

H because the passage states that "none of its ice was manufactured artificially" (lines 13–14).

Question 19. The best answer is **C** because the passage states that the ice harvested in Maine was "packed in hay and sawdust" (lines 30–31) to be shipped south.

The best answer is NOT:

A because the passage does not indicate that natural ice was shipped in refrigerated boxcars.

B because the passage does not indicate that natural ice was shipped in waterproof tarps.

D because the passage does not indicate that natural ice was shipped in paper and cloth.

Question 20. The best answer is **J** because the passage states that "The first real crisis in the natural-ice trade was caused not by competition from artificial manufacture, but by pollution" (lines 44–46).

The best answer is NOT:

F because the passage does not refer to the impact of the Great Depression on the natural-ice industry.

G because the passage does not state that weather pattern changes caused the first crisis in the natural-ice industry.

H because although the passage mentions artificial refrigeration (lines 35–36), it does not claim that artificial refrigeration caused the first crisis in the natural-ice industry.

READING • PRACTICE TEST 5 • EXPLANATORY ANSWERS

Passage III

Question 21. **The best answer is C** because the passage explores the claim that dubbing is a hybrid form that incorporates the artistry of both the actor and dubber, beginning with Antonioni's description of Romolo Costa as "a hybrid individual born out of a chemical combination" (lines 7–8). The hybrid identities of dubbers are indicated in Vairano's account of how some dubbers were associated with particular actors. The passage describes that dubber Luca Ward considers himself "half Ward, half [Samuel L.] Jackson" (line 85). Ward conflates the identities of Meg Ryan and her dubber (lines 86–89), further emphasizing the idea of hybridity between the dubber and actor.

The best answer is NOT:

A because the passage does not describe how dubbers want to be regarded by actors.

B because the passage does not compare the work of these two dubbers.

D because although the passage indicates that Ward's approach differs from other dubbers' (lines 64–68), this is a detail from the passage, not the central claim.

Question 22. **The best answer is G** because the comparison to Fellini accurately reflects Variano's point of view that dubbing can be useful. The passage describes how dubbing was part of Fellini's creative process. Lines 19–20: "Dubbing was an extension of his shoots, a technique he would use to retouch and rewrite." The passage describes how Vairano selects dubbers according to who would perform best in the particular role, which is similar to how Fellini used dubbing creatively.

The best answer is NOT:

F because the passage notes that Antonioni disapproved of dubbing. "This 'half Clark, half Costa' was unbearable to Antonioni, who considered dubbing to be a mere 'acoustic surrogate' of acting" (lines 8–10).

H because the passage notes that Pasolini also disapproved of dubbing. "Director Pier Paolo Pasolini, who called both dubbing and subtitles 'evils'" (lines 13–14).

J because the passage notes that Renoir also disapproved of dubbing. "Director Jean Renoir called dubbing a 'monstrosity, a challenge to human and divine laws'" (lines 16–17).

Question 23. The best answer is **B** because the second paragraph describes Fellini's extensive use of dubbing. The first paragraph of the passage recounts the perspectives of directors critical of dubbing. Lines 18–20: "Director Frederico Fellini didn't agree with any of them. Dubbing was an extension of his shoots, a technique he would use to retouch and rewrite."

The best answer is NOT:

A because the paragraph does not relate the author's perspective on dubbing.

C because although the passage notes that Renoir was critical of dubbing, his comments are about dubbing in general, not in reference to Fellini's work. Lines 16–17: "Director Jean Renoir called dubbing a 'monstrosity, a challenge to human and divine laws.'"

D because the paragraph's focus on Fellini does not function to support an argument made in the first paragraph. The first paragraph presents perspectives of directors who were against the use of dubbing; this paragraph presents an opposing perspective. Lines 18–19: "Director Frederico Fellini didn't agree with any of them."

Question 24. The best answer is **H** because the anecdote mainly provides an example of how dubbing was an integral part of Fellini's creative process.

The best answer is NOT:

F because although the passage mentions that Fellini favored the northern accent (lines 32–33), this is a detail from the anecdote rather than its main function.

G because the anecdote is unclear about whether Fellini followed a scripted dialogue in this instance. The passage notes that Fellini did not always follow a script. Lines 20–23: "He mercilessly dubbed over his actors, changing dialogue in postproduction, sometimes having worked without a script."

J because the passage notes that Fellini did not always follow a script. Lines 20–23: "He mercilessly dubbed over his actors, changing dialogue in postproduction, sometimes having worked without a script."

Question 25. The best answer is **D** because the passage makes clear that Cortesi disagrees with the author's assumptions, offering his own explanation. Lines 44–46: "Dubbers are used to reciting while trying to re-create the bodily sensations of what they see on the screen before them."

The best answer is NOT:

A because the passage indicates that Cortesi disagrees with the author (lines 37–43).

B because the passage indicates that Cortesi disagrees with the author (lines 37–43).

C because although the passage indicates that Cortesi disagrees with the author (lines 37–43), Cortesi's response is not characterized as gruff.

Question 26. The best answer is **G** because the details in the passage suggest that the Metropolitan cinema was a place to watch subtitled films. "There are still few options for those seeking to watch subtitled, original-language films at a movie house in Italy. The Metropolitan cinema on Via del Corso closed recently after a long battle" (lines 51–52).

The best answer is NOT:

F because the passage does not indicate that the Metropolitan cinema was a place to watch dubbed films.

H because the details in the passage suggest that the Metropolitan cinema was a place to watch subtitled films only.

J because the details in the passage suggest that the Metropolitan cinema was a place to watch subtitled films.

Question 27. The best answer is **A** because the passage most strongly suggests that the Italian preference for dubbing correlates to finding dubbed films much more easily than subtitled films. The passage asserts that "Italians remain hooked on dubbing" (line 55), and the last two paragraphs of the passage describe a thriving dubbing industry. The passage describes the options for watching a subtitled film as "few" (line 49).

The best answer is NOT:

B because the passage notes there are "few options" (line 49) for watching subtitled films in Italy, but dubbed films remain popular (line 55).

C because the passage notes there are "few options" (line 49) for watching subtitled films in Italy, but dubbed films remain popular (line 55).

D because the passage notes there are "few options" (line 49) for watching subtitled films in Italy, but dubbed films remain popular (line 55).

Question 28. The best answer is **F** because in the passage, the film *Bienvenue chez le Ch'tis* is provided as an example of a film considered undubbable due to its comedic reliance on linguistic misunderstanding. Lines 60–63: "Francesco Vairano, a dubber and dubbing director known for adapting foreign films considered to be 'undubbable,' such as the French box office hit *Bienvenue chez le Ch'tis* ('Welcome to the Sticks,' 2008), which relies on linguistic misunderstandings for much of its comedy."

The best answer is NOT:

G because there is no mention in the passage of dramatic action that advances the plot.

H because there is no mention in the passage of reverse chronology that provides context.

J because there is no mention in the passage of extensive monologues that provide further characterization.

Question 29. The best answer is **B** because the passage explains that Vairano uses different dubbers with different actors. Lines 64–67: "Vairano has been one of the few directors to break the habit of matching the same Italian dubber to a foreign actor for all his films."

The best answer is NOT:

A because although the passage identifies one French film that Vairano dubbed (lines 60–61), it does not say that dubbing French films is Vairano's focus.

C because the passage does not indicate that Vairano mostly worked with "prima donna" dubbers and even notes that Vairano "was hated by all the prima donna dubbers" (line 69).

D because there is no indication in the passage of whether Vairona thinks dialogue should be rewritten during dubbing.

Question 30. The best answer is **F** because "assault" is a synonym of "challenge." The negative connotation of the word "assault" is consistent with the negative connotation of the word "monstrosity" (line 16) in the same sentence. "An assault on" can be substituted for the phrase "a challenge to" without changing the meaning of the sentence.

The best answer is NOT:

G because "a declaration of" has a different meaning than "a challenge to," and it would not make sense in the context of the sentence.

H because although "question" can be a synonym for "challenge," the phrase "a question for human and divine laws" would not be contextually appropriate in this sentence.

J because "an offer to" and "a challenge to" have different meanings, and it would not make sense in the context of the sentence.

Passage IV

Question 31. The best answer is **B** because the passage focuses on presenting information about various scientific aspects of the creation and behavior of steel.

The best answer is NOT:

A because although the passage discusses Bessemer's process for improving steel, it does not discuss the various experiments Bessemer conducted to develop the process.

C because although the fifth paragraph (lines 47–58) addresses philosophical questions about metallurgy, these questions function as subordinate details that contribute to the main focus of the passage.

D because although both cast iron and pig iron are mentioned in the passage, they are not directly compared, and an illustration of their differences is not a central element of the passage.

Question 32. The best answer is F because the description of the initial response to Bessemer's process helps the author establish its success and impact in the manufacturing industry. Lines 1–6: "During the Industrial Revolution, the high price of steel meant that many large engineering projects were carried out that used instead cast iron, which is brittle and prone to failure. This was why Henry Bessemer's new process for making steel was greeted with jubilation."

The best answer is NOT:

G because the author does not assert an opinion that Bessemer's process was prone to failure.

H because although the author states that Bessemer was lauded as an engineer (lines 8–9), the description of the initial response to Bessemer's process does not relate directly to his qualifications as an engineer.

J because the author does not provide specific examples of criticism that Bessemer's new process received.

Question 33. The best answer is D because the author includes a number of details that help establish Bergmann's credibility. His mentorship and sponsorship of Scheele, described as a great scientist, is one of these details. Lines 20–23: "He was a mentor and sponsor of Carl Wilhelm Scheele, the greatest Swedish chemist of the age and co-discoverer of oxygen."

The best answer is NOT:

A because although the information suggests that Bergmann was a teacher as well as a scientist, that point alone does not have a clear function in the context of the passage.

B because no comparison of Bergmann and Scheele is made in the passage.

C because there is no support in the passage indicating that the information serves to provide an example of eighteenth-century scientific communities.

Question 34. The best answer is **H** because the passage directly states that adding oxygen to molten pig iron results in silicon being converted into light silica slag. Lines 24–29: "Oxygen, as a component of air, was the key to the Bessemer process. It offered a way of removing impurities from pig iron and adjusting its carbon content during conversion to steel. A blast of air through the molten metal turned impurities such as silicon into light silica slag."

The best answer is NOT:

F because although the passage mentions light silica slag as a by-product of the Bessemer process (lines 28–29), it does not indicate that the slag is converted to carbon dioxide.

G because the passage indicates that carbon is released from pig iron in the form of volatile carbon dioxide (lines 30–31), not that carbon dioxide is converted into carbon.

J because the passage indicates that silicon is one of the impurities that are converted by the process and does not indicate that impurities are converted into silicon. Lines 27–29: "A blast of air through the molten metal turned impurities such as silicon into light silica slag."

Question 35. The best answer is **B** because, in the context of the passage, the word "spice" (line 37), in conjunction with the word "dash" in the following sentence, is used to suggest something added to enhance something else, which is a main focus of the discussion of steel in the fourth paragraph (lines 36–46). Lines 36–37: "It was long known that steel can be improved with a spice of other elements. A dash of the metal manganese helps."

The best answer is NOT:

A because there is no indication in the passage that elements need to be added to steel gradually to produce the desired effect.

C because there is no indication in the passage that manganese, chromium, and nickel are expensive.

D because the positive results of blending elements are discussed in the fourth paragraph (lines 36–46). The passage indicates that adding a specific proportion of chromium (lines 42–44) makes steel rust-resistant, which contradicts the idea that blending elements has not yet yielded positive results.

Question 36. The best answer is **H** because although the author indicates that there have been questions raised about whether metallurgy is a science or an art, he suggests his view that it is both. Lines 49–54: "In this respect, metallurgy has long retained the air of an artisan craft…it is because it is so difficult." He includes a quote from a well-respected physicist to support his view. Lines 54–58: "According to Rodney Cotterill, a remarkable British physicist whose expertise stretched from the sciences of materials to that of the brain, 'metallurgy is one of our most ancient arts, but is often referred to as one of the youngest sciences.'"

The best answer is NOT:

F because it contradicts the idea that metallurgy is both an art and a science, which the author puts forth in the fifth paragraph (lines 47–58).

G because although the author states that metallurgy is difficult, he does not do so to suggest that this is the reason why metallurgy is not considered a science. Lines 52–54: "But the reason for this empiricism is not that the science of metallurgy is trivial; it is because it is so difficult."

J because it directly contradicts a statement by the author. Lines 52–54: "But the reason for this empiricism is not that the science of metallurgy is trivial; it is because it is so difficult."

Question 37. The best answer is **A** because in comparing the behavior of materials to the study of the social sciences, the passage suggests that both require the study of a wide range of scales. Lines 64–69: "Science has trouble dealing with such a span of scales. One might regard this difficulty as akin to that in the social sciences, where social behaviour is governed by how individuals behave but also how we interact on the scale of families and neighborhoods, within entire cities, and at a national level."

The best answer is NOT:

B because the passage does not suggest that the study of the social sciences is based on trial-and-error experimentation.

C because the passage explains that the study of the social sciences involves the study of people (lines 67–69). The passage does not suggest that the study of social sciences involves the examination of individual atoms.

D because the passage does not indicate that either field of study produces results that must be interpreted by both scientist and artists.

Question 38. The best answer is **F** because the paragraph as a whole describes the way various defects in the crystal structure of a metal influence its behavior, as introduced in the first sentence of the paragraph. Lines 72–74: "The mechanical properties of metals depend on how flaws in the crystal structure, called defects, move and interact."

The best answer is NOT:

G because although the paragraph notes dislocations as the most common fault (line 77), this is a subordinate detail in the paragraph rather than the main idea.

H because the paragraph does not describe how increasing a metal's grain size would modify its behavior.

J because although the paragraph mentions that grains may divide into crystallite mosaics (lines 85–86), this is a subordinate detail in the paragraph rather than the main idea.

Question 39. The best answer is **C** because "stretched" can mean "extended," and this meaning is contextually appropriate in the description of the wide range of Cotterill's expertise. Lines 54–57: "According to Rodney Cotterill, a remarkable British physicist whose expertise stretched from the sciences of materials to that of the brain."

The best answer is NOT:

A because although "stretched" can mean "strained," it is not contextually appropriate to say that "Cotterill's expertise strained from the sciences of materials to that of the brain."

B because although "stretched" can mean "exaggerated," it is not contextually appropriate to say that "Cotterill's expertise exaggerated from the sciences of materials to that of the brain."

D because although "stretched" can mean "amplified," it is not contextually appropriate to say that "Cotterill's expertise amplified from the sciences of materials to that of the brain."

Question 40. The best answer is J because the passage directly states that reducing the size of a metal's grains can make the metal harder. Lines 86–89: "The arrest of dislocations at grain edges means that metals may be made harder by reducing the size of their grains, a useful trick for modifying their mechanical behaviour."

The best answer is NOT:

F because the passage does not state that reducing the size of a metal's grains can make the metal more rust-resistant.

G because the passage does not state that reducing the size of a metal's grains can make the metal more brittle.

H because the passage does not state that reducing the size of a metal's grain can make the metal finer.

Passage I

Question 1. The best answer is A. According to the figure, 160 mg of 24-week-old oak mulch was consumed, 148 mg of 24-week-old pine bark mulch was consumed, 45 mg of 48-week-old oak mulch was consumed, and 60 mg of 48-week-old pine bark was consumed. The greatest mass consumed was of 24-week-old oak mulch. **A** is correct. **B, C,** and **D** are incorrect; 160 mg of 24-week-old oak mulch was consumed, which is more than any other combination of mulch and mulch age listed.

Question 2. The best answer is J. According to the figure, as mulch age increased, the consumption of cedar, cypress, and oak bar mulches increased. As mulch age increased, the consumption of oak and pine bark mulches increased and then decreased. **F** is incorrect; the mass of mulch consumed did not decrease for any of the types of mulches. **G** is incorrect; the mass of mulch consumed increased for only 3 types of mulches. **H** is incorrect; the mass of mulch consumed did not initially decrease for any of the types of mulches. **J** is correct.

Question 3. The best answer is D. In order to answer this item, the examinee must know that detritivores, and not autotrophs, obtain energy by consuming dead and decaying plant matter. According to the passage, the mulch was allowed to decay before consumption by the termites. The termites consumed decaying plant matter and are therefore detritivores. **A** and **B** are incorrect; the termites are not autotrophs. **C** is incorrect; the termites consumed decaying organic material. **D** is correct.

Question 4. The best answer is G. In order to answer this item, the examinee must know that cell walls are composed primarily of cellulose. Because the termites consume mulch, they are consuming a considerable amount of cellulose. **F** is incorrect; the termites are not consuming animal cells. **G** is correct. **H** is incorrect; the termites are not consuming animal cells. **J** is incorrect; the cell walls of the plant cells are composed primarily of cellulose, not cholesterol.

Question 5. The best answer is D. According to the figure, 100 mg of 1-week-old oak mulch was consumed, 160 mg of 24-week-old oak mulch was consumed, and approximately 45 mg of 48-week-old oak mulch was consumed. **A** is incorrect; more 24-week-old mulch was consumed than 1-week-old mulch. **B** is incorrect; more 24-week-old mulch was consumed than 48-week-old mulch. **C** is incorrect; less 1-week-old mulch was consumed than 24-week-old mulch. **D** is correct.

Question 6. The best answer is G. In order to answer this item, the examinee must know that 1 g = 1,000 mg. According to the figure, 140 mg of 48-week-old oak bark mulch was consumed.

$$140 \text{ mg} \times \frac{1 \text{ g}}{1,000 \text{ mg}} = 0.14 \text{ g}$$

F, H, and **J** are incorrect; 0.14 g of 48-week-old oak bar mulch was consumed. **G** is correct.

Passage II

Question 7. The best answer is B. According to the passage, Experiment 2 followed the same procedure as Experiment 1 except a different strain of Species C was used. **A** is incorrect; the same incubation temperatures were tested in both experiments. **B** is correct. **C** is incorrect; samples from both experiments were lyophilized, and none was transported on ice. **D** is incorrect; the incubation times were the same for both experiments.

Question 8. The best answer is G. According to Table 2, as the incubation temperature increased, the percent survival at 1 week decreased. At an incubation temperature of 20°C, Strain V2 had a 29% survival rate at 1 week, and at an incubation temperature of 30°C, Strain V2 had a 2% survival rate at 1 week. One would predict that at an incubation temperature of 25°C, Strain V2 would have a percent survival at 1 week between 2% and 29%. **F** is incorrect; the survival rate would be greater than 2%. **G** is correct. **H** and **J** are incorrect; the survival rate would be less than 29%.

Question 9. The best answer is A. According to Table 2, for Strain V2, the percent survival was less for the longer incubation time at temperatures of 4°C and 20°C. The percent survival was the same for both incubation times at temperatures of 30°C and 37°C. **A** is correct. **B**, **C**, and **D** are incorrect; the percent survival was the same for both incubation times at temperatures of 30°C and 37°C.

Question 10. The best answer is H. According to the passage, Strain E was studied in Experiment 1, and Strain V2 was studied in Experiment 2. The bacteria were lyophilized in both experiments. The incubation time and temperature were varied in both experiments, and the percent survival was determined. **F** is incorrect; the incubation time was varied in both experiments. **G** is incorrect; the temperature was varied in both experiments. **H** is correct. **J** is incorrect; two different strains were studied in the experiments.

Question 11. The best answer is D. According to Table 2, after 1 week, the sample incubated at 37°C had a 0% survival rate and therefore would not have been able to infect another organism. **A** is incorrect; the sample incubated at 4°C had a 59% survival rate. **B** is incorrect; the sample incubated at 20°C had a 29% survival rate. **C** is incorrect; the sample incubated at 30°C had a 2% survival rate. **D** is correct.

Question 12. The best answer is H. According to Table 1, the sample incubated at 20°C for 1 week had the highest percent survival (69%). **F** is incorrect; the sample incubated at 4°C for 1 week had a survival rate of 52%. **G** is incorrect; the sample incubated at 4°C for 1 month had a survival rate of 51%. **H** is correct. **J** is incorrect; the sample incubated at 20°C for 1 month had a survival rate of 42%.

Question 13. The best answer is B. According to Table 1, the two samples incubated at 30°C and the two samples incubated at 37°C all had percent survival rates less than 30%. The percent survival rates for the samples incubated at 4°C and 20°C were all greater than 30%. **A**, **C**, and **D** are incorrect; 4 samples had percent survival rates less than 30%. **B** is correct.

Passage III

Question 14. The best answer is G. According to the passage, of the fluids studied, water was the least dense and Fluid B was the most dense. Table 1 shows that the buoyant force on Stone X was greatest in Fluid B and lowest in water. The buoyant force on Stone X increased as the density of the fluid in which it was submerged increased. **F** is incorrect; the buoyant force increased. **G** is correct. **H** is incorrect; the buoyant force increased only. **J** is incorrect; there was a trend: the buoyant force increased.

Question 15. The best answer is B. According to Table 1, the buoyant force for Stone Y was 1.18 N in Fluid A and 1.41 N in Fluid B. The difference was 1.41 N − 1.18 N = 0.23 N. **A, C,** and **D** are incorrect; the difference was 0.23 N. **B** is correct.

Question 16. The best answer is H. In order to determine the effect of the cylinder's volume on the submerged length of the cylinder, the students must vary the cylinder's volume and measure the submerged length. **F** and **G** are incorrect; the students must use multiple cylinders with different volumes. **H** is correct. **J** is incorrect; the cylinders must have different volumes.

Question 17. The best answer is A. Based on Figure 1, as the length of the portion of the cylinder that was submerged increased, the amount of water that was displaced also increased. Figure 1 also shows that the submerged length was greatest when the cylinder was placed in water, and therefore the amount of fluid that was displaced was greatest in water. **A** is correct. **B** is incorrect; the submerged length was greater in water than in Fluid A. **C** and **D** are incorrect; a greater volume of water was displaced than Fluid A.

Question 18. The best answer is F. According to Study 1, as the density of the fluid increased, the submerged length of the cylinder decreased. The density of Fluid B was 1.50 g/cm^3, and the submerged length of the cylinder in Fluid B was 4.9 cm. One would predict that if the cylinder had been placed in a container of fluid having a density of 1.60 g/cm^3, the submerged length of the cylinder would have been less than 4.9 cm. **F** is correct. **G, H,** and **J** are incorrect; the submerged length would most likely have been less than 4.9 cm.

Question 19. The best answer is C. A stone with a volume larger than that of Stone Z would displace more water than did Stone Z. According to the passage, the buoyant force exerted on the submerged stone is equal in magnitude to the weight of the displaced fluid. Because more fluid would be displaced, the buoyant force on the new stone would be greater than the buoyant force on Stone Z. **A** is incorrect; in water, the buoyant force on Stone Z was 0.94 N. The buoyant force on the larger stone would be greater than 0.94 N. **B** is incorrect; in Fluid A, the buoyant force on Stone Z was 1.18 N. The buoyant force on the larger stone would be greater than 1.18 N. **C** is correct. **D** is incorrect; because water is less dense than Fluid A, the weight of the displaced water (and therefore the buoyant force in water) would be less than the weight of displaced Fluid A (and therefore the buoyant force in Fluid A).

Question 20. The best answer is F. According to the passage and Figure 1, the submerged length increased as density decreased. It follows that the iceberg would have the greatest submerged volume in the less dense Atlantic Ocean. **F** is correct. **G** is incorrect; submerged volume increased as fluid density decreased. **H** and **J** are incorrect; the iceberg would most likely have the greatest submerged volume in the Atlantic Ocean.

Passage IV

Question 21. The best answer is C. According to Table 1, the total volume of solution in each trial was 100 mL. As the volume of NaClO solution increased from 0 mL to 75 mL, T_f increased. When 50 mL of NaClO solution and 50 mL of NaI solution were used, T_f = 29.0°C, and when 70 mL of NaClO solution and 30 mL of NaI solution were used, T_f = 31.7°C. One would predict that repeating the experiment with 60 mL of NaClO solution and 40 mL of NaI solution would cause T_f to be between 29.0°C and 31.7°C. **A** and **B** are incorrect; T_f would be greater than 29.0°C. **C** is correct. **D** is incorrect; T_f would be less than 31.7°C.

Question 22. The best answer is F. According to Table 1, ΔT = 3.5°C for Trial 2, and ΔT = 8.6°C for Trial 6. ΔT was 5.1°C less for Trial 2 than Trial 6. The results do not support the student's prediction. **F** is correct. **G** is incorrect; ΔT = 8.6°C for Trial 6, so the difference between Trials 2 and 6 was 5.1°C. **H** and **J** are incorrect; the results do not support the prediction. ΔT for Trial 2 was less than ΔT for Trial 6.

Question 23. The best answer is D. According to Table 1, for each trial, the sum of the volume of NaClO solution and the volume of NaI solution was equal to 100 mL. **A**, **B**, and **C** are incorrect; the total volume of solution used was 100 mL. **D** is correct.

Question 24. The best answer is H. According to Table 1, 80 mL of NaClO and 20 mL of NaI were used in Trial 6 (80 mL = 4 × 20 mL), and T_f = 30.6°C. **F**, **G**, and **J** are incorrect; T_f = 30.6°C in Trial 6 when the volume of NaClO (80 mL) was 4 times as great as the volume of NaI (20 mL). **H** is correct.

Question 25. The best answer is B. According to Figure 1, when 20 mL of NaClO solution was used, ΔT was just under 3°C. **A**, **C**, and **D** are incorrect; Figure 1 shows that ΔT is closest to 3°C. **B** is correct.

Question 26. The best answer is J. In order to answer this item, the examinee must understand how to read chemical equations. Table 1 shows that in Trial 8, 0 mL of NaI was added. According to the equation shown in the passage, NaI is a reactant in the chemical reaction. Without both reactants present, the reaction will not proceed and no heat will be generated, resulting in ΔT = 0°C. **F** and **G** are incorrect; 0 mL of NaI was added, and NaI is a reactant. **H** is incorrect; 100 mL of NaClO was used. **J** is correct.

Question 27. **The best answer is** B. In order to answer this item, the examinee must know that heat is absorbed during an endothermic reaction. If the reaction had been endothermic, then the reaction would have absorbed heat from the surroundings, and the temperature of the solution would have decreased. **A** is incorrect; as stated in the passage, heat is released in an exothermic reaction. **B** is correct. **C** and **D** are incorrect; the solution temperature increases when the reaction is exothermic, as is illustrated in the results of the experiment.

Passage V

Question 28. **The best answer is** H. According to Figure 2, at 300 MPa, the solubility of CO_2 in rhyolite magma is 2,000 ppmw at 800°C. **F** is incorrect; the solubility is approximately 2,350 ppmw at 700°C. **G** is incorrect; the solubility is approximately 2,200 ppmw at 750°C. **H** is correct. **J** is incorrect; the solubility is approximately 1,850 ppmw at 850°C.

Question 29. **The best answer is** C. According to Figure 3, at 750°C for a given solubility of CO_2 in rhyolite magma, the pressure increased as the weight percent of H_2O in the magma increased. When the solubility of CO_2 in rhyolite magma was 1,250 ppmw and the pressure was 300 MPa, the weight percent of H_2O in the magma was approximately 4.3%, and when the pressure was 400 MPa, the weight percent of H_2O in the magma was approximately 5.7%. One would predict that at 750°C and 350 MPa, rhyolite magma having a solubility of CO_2 equal to 1,250 ppmw would have a weight percent of H_2O between 4.3% and 5.7%. **A** and **B** are incorrect; the weight percent of H_2O in the magma would be greater than 4.0%. **C** is correct. **D** is incorrect; the weight percent of H_2O would be less than 6%.

Question 30. **The best answer is** J. According to Figure 1, at 1,150°C and 50 MPa, the solubility of CO_2 in basanite magma was 300 ppmw, and at 1,150°C and 125 MPa, the solubility was 1,000 ppmw. At 1,150°C and 200 MPa, the solubility of CO_2 in tholeiitic basalt magma was 700 ppmw, and at 1,150°C and 250 MPa, the solubility of CO_2 was 1,000 ppmw. The CO_2 solubilities were closest in value when basanite magma was at 125 MPa and tholeiitic basalt magma was at 250 MPa. **F**, **G**, and **H** are incorrect; the CO_2 solubilities for both types of magmas were 1,000 ppmw at 125 MPa for basanite magma and 250 MPa for tholeiitic basalt magma. **J** is correct.

Question 31. **The best answer is** B. According to Figure 1, at 1,150°C and 150 MPa, the solubility of CO_2 in leucite magma was 3,000 ppmw, and the solubility of CO_2 in rhyolite magma was 700 ppmw. The solubility in leucite magma was 2,300 ppmw greater. **A** is incorrect; the solubility is 2,300 ppmw greater in leucite magma. **B** is correct. **C** and **D** are incorrect; the solubility was greater in leucite magma than in rhyolite magma.

Question 32. The best answer is F. According to Figure 2, as the temperature increased from 650°C to 1,150°C, the solubility of CO_2 in rhyolite magma at 100 MPa decreased from 800 ppmw to 400 ppmw, and the solubility at 300 MPa decreased from 2,600 ppmw to 1,300 ppmw. Increasing the temperature had a lesser effect on the solubility of CO_2 at 100 MPa. **F** is correct. **G** is incorrect; the solubility decreased by only 400 ppmw, from 800 ppmw to 400 ppmw. **H** and **J** are incorrect; a greater effect was seen at 300 MPa.

Question 33. The best answer is A. According to Figure 2, at 750°C and 200 MPa, the solubility of CO_2 in rhyolite magma is 1,500 ppmw. Figure 3 shows that at 200 MPa and a CO_2 solubility of 1,500 ppmw, rhyolite magma contains 0% H_2O. **A** is correct. **B** is incorrect; rhyolite magma with 2% H_2O has a CO_2 solubility of 1,250 ppmw at 200 MPa. **C** is incorrect; rhyolite magma with 4% H_2O has a CO_2 solubility of 700 ppmw at 200 MPa. **D** is incorrect; CO_2 is insoluble in rhyolite magma with 6% H_2O at 200 MPa.

Passage VI

Question 34. The best answer is F. According to Hypothesis 1, Earth is the solar system's central body, and other bodies move around Earth in looped orbits. Hypothesis 2 states that the Sun is the solar system's central body, and the planets move around the Sun in elliptical orbits. **F** is correct. **G** is incorrect; Hypothesis 2 claims that the planets follow elliptical orbits around the Sun, not Earth. **H** and **J** are incorrect; Hypothesis 1 claims that the planets follow looped orbits.

Question 35. The best answer is C. According to Figure 2, as Mars loops, the distance between Earth and Mars varies. Figure 3 shows that as Earth and Mars orbit the Sun, the distance between them varies. This is fairly obvious, as they are relatively near one another on 10/01/2005 and 12/10/2005 and farther apart on 7/24/2005 and 2/26/2006. **A**, **B**, and **D** are incorrect; both Figures 2 and 3 imply that the distance between Earth and Mars varies. **C** is correct.

Question 36. The best answer is F. The top portion of Figure 3 is consistent with Hypothesis 2, showing that over time, Earth will move a greater percentage of its smaller orbit than will Mars. **F** is correct. **G** is incorrect; Earth is shown as having a smaller orbit. **H** and **J** are incorrect; the top portion is consistent with the reasoning presented in Hypothesis 2.

Question 37. The best answer is B. According to the passage, Mars appears to move retrograde when it is moving westward relative to the stars. Figure 1 shows that Mars is moving westward, and therefore retrograde, between 10/01/2005 and 12/10/2005, a period of 70 days. **A**, **C**, and **D** are incorrect; Mars is retrograde for 70 days. **B** is correct.

Question 38. The best answer is J. Figure 2 shows that Mars's deferent is a counterclockwise circle around Earth, the central body of the solar system according to Hypothesis 1. Figure 3 shows that Mars moves in a counterclockwise circle around the Sun, the central body of the solar system according to Hypothesis 2. F and G are incorrect; according to the hypotheses, Mars moves in a counterclockwise direction around the central body of the solar system. H is incorrect; Hypothesis 1 states that Mars orbits Earth. J is correct.

Question 39. The best answer is B. According to Figure 1, the first position shown on Figure 3 corresponds to 7/24/2005, the second corresponds to 10/01/2005, and the third corresponds to 12/10/2005. On November 7, 2005, the positions of Earth and Mars would be between those found on 10/01/2005 and 12/10/2005. These positions are best illustrated by B. A is incorrect; this figure illustrates the positions of Mars in October and Earth in December. B is correct. C is incorrect; this figure illustrates the positions of Earth in October and Mars in December. D is incorrect; this figure illustrates the likely positions of Earth and Mars around April or May.

Question 40. The best answer is F. In order to answer this item, the examinee must know that Venus is closer to the Sun than is Earth. The second rule for apparent retrograde motion in Hypothesis 2 explains retrograde motion observed in a planet with an orbit smaller than Earth's. F is correct. G is incorrect; Venus is closer to the Sun than is Earth. H and J are incorrect; Hypothesis 2 does explain why Venus occasionally appears to move retrograde.

The ACT® *Sample Answer Document*

EXAMINEE STATEMENTS, CERTIFICATION, AND SIGNATURE

1. **Statements**: I understand that by registering for, launching, starting, or submitting answer documents for an ACT® test, I am agreeing to comply with and be bound by the *Terms and Conditions: Testing Rules and Policies for the ACT® Test* ("Terms").

   I UNDERSTAND AND AGREE THAT THE TERMS PERMIT ACT TO CANCEL MY SCORES IN CERTAIN CIRCUMSTANCES. THE TERMS ALSO LIMIT DAMAGES AVAILABLE TO ME AND REQUIRE ARBITRATION OF CERTAIN DISPUTES. BY AGREEING TO ARBITRATION, ACT AND I BOTH WAIVE THE RIGHT TO HAVE THOSE DISPUTES HEARD BY A JUDGE OR JURY.

   I understand that ACT owns the test questions and responses, and I will not share them with anyone by any form of communication before, during, or after the test administration. I understand that taking the test for someone else may violate the law and subject me to legal penalties. I consent to the collection and processing of personally identifying information I provide, and its subsequent use and disclosure, as described in the ACT Privacy Policy (www.act.org/privacy.html). I also permit ACT to transfer my personally identifying information to the United States, to ACT, or to a third-party service provider, where it will be subject to use and disclosure under the laws of the United States, including being accessible to law enforcement or national security authorities.

2. **Certification**: Copy the italicized certification below, then sign and date in the spaces provided.

   *I agree to the **Statements** above and certify that I am the person whose information appears on this form.*

   _____

   _____

   _____   _____
   Your Signature   Today's Date

⬤ Do NOT mark in this shaded area.

USE A NO. 2 PENCIL ONLY.
(Do NOT use a mechanical pencil, ink, ballpoint, correction fluid, or felt-tip pen.)

A NAME, MAILING ADDRESS, AND TELEPHONE (Please print.)

Last Name   First Name   MI (Middle Initial)

House Number & Street (Apt. No.); or PO Box & No.; or RR & No.

City   State/Province   ZIP/Postal Code

Area Code   Number   Country

ACT, Inc.—Confidential Restricted when data present

ALL examinees must complete block A – please print.

Blocks B, C, and D are required for all examinees. Find the MATCHING INFORMATION on your ticket. Enter it EXACTLY the same way, even if any of the information is missing or incorrect. Fill in the corresponding ovals. If you do not complete these blocks to match your previous information EXACTLY, your scores will be **delayed up to 8 weeks**.

ACT®

PO BOX 168, IOWA CITY, IA 52243-0168

B MATCH NAME (First 5 letters of last name)

Ⓐ Ⓐ Ⓐ Ⓐ Ⓐ
Ⓑ Ⓑ Ⓑ Ⓑ Ⓑ
Ⓒ Ⓒ Ⓒ Ⓒ Ⓒ
Ⓓ Ⓓ Ⓓ Ⓓ Ⓓ
Ⓔ Ⓔ Ⓔ Ⓔ Ⓔ
Ⓕ Ⓕ Ⓕ Ⓕ Ⓕ
Ⓖ Ⓖ Ⓖ Ⓖ Ⓖ
Ⓗ Ⓗ Ⓗ Ⓗ Ⓗ
Ⓘ Ⓘ Ⓘ Ⓘ Ⓘ
Ⓙ Ⓙ Ⓙ Ⓙ Ⓙ
Ⓚ Ⓚ Ⓚ Ⓚ Ⓚ
Ⓛ Ⓛ Ⓛ Ⓛ Ⓛ
Ⓜ Ⓜ Ⓜ Ⓜ Ⓜ
Ⓝ Ⓝ Ⓝ Ⓝ Ⓝ
Ⓞ Ⓞ Ⓞ Ⓞ Ⓞ
Ⓟ Ⓟ Ⓟ Ⓟ Ⓟ
Ⓠ Ⓠ Ⓠ Ⓠ Ⓠ
Ⓡ Ⓡ Ⓡ Ⓡ Ⓡ
Ⓢ Ⓢ Ⓢ Ⓢ Ⓢ
Ⓣ Ⓣ Ⓣ Ⓣ Ⓣ
Ⓤ Ⓤ Ⓤ Ⓤ Ⓤ
Ⓥ Ⓥ Ⓥ Ⓥ Ⓥ
Ⓦ Ⓦ Ⓦ Ⓦ Ⓦ
Ⓧ Ⓧ Ⓧ Ⓧ Ⓧ
Ⓨ Ⓨ Ⓨ Ⓨ Ⓨ
Ⓩ Ⓩ Ⓩ Ⓩ Ⓩ

C MATCH NUMBER

① ① ① ①   ① ① ① ① ①
② ② ② ②   ② ② ② ② ②
③ ③ ③ ③   ③ ③ ③ ③ ③
④ ④ ④ ④   ④ ④ ④ ④ ④
⑤ ⑤ ⑤ ⑤   ⑤ ⑤ ⑤ ⑤ ⑤
⑥ ⑥ ⑥ ⑥   ⑥ ⑥ ⑥ ⑥ ⑥
⑦ ⑦ ⑦ ⑦   ⑦ ⑦ ⑦ ⑦ ⑦
⑧ ⑧ ⑧ ⑧   ⑧ ⑧ ⑧ ⑧ ⑧
⑨ ⑨ ⑨ ⑨   ⑨ ⑨ ⑨ ⑨ ⑨
⓪ ⓪ ⓪ ⓪   ⓪ ⓪ ⓪ ⓪ ⓪

D DATE OF BIRTH

Month	Day	Year
○ January		
○ February		
○ March	① ①	① ①
○ April	② ②	② ②
○ May	③ ③	③ ③
○ June	④	④ ④
○ July	⑤	⑤ ⑤
○ August	⑥	⑥ ⑥
○ September	⑦	⑦ ⑦
○ October	⑧	⑧ ⑧
○ November	⑨	⑨ ⑨
○ December	⓪	⓪ ⓪

Taking Additional Practice Tests

PAGE 2

Marking Directions: Mark only **one** oval for each question. Fill in response completely. Erase errors cleanly without smudging.

Correct mark: ○ ● ○ ○

- -

Do NOT use these *incorrect* or *bad* **marks.**

Incorrect marks: ⊘ ⊗ ⊜ ⊝
Overlapping mark: ○ ○ ⊙⊕
Cross-out mark: ○ ⊗ ○
Smudged erasure: ○ ○ ◐
Mark is too light: ◐ ○ ○ ○

BOOKLET NUMBER

①	①	①	①	①	①	①	①	①
②	②	②	②	②	②	②	②	②
③	③	③	③	③	③	③	③	③
④	④	④	④	④	④	④	④	④
⑤	⑤	⑤	⑤	⑤	⑤	⑤	⑤	⑤
⑥	⑥	⑥	⑥	⑥	⑥	⑥	⑥	⑥
⑦	⑦	⑦	⑦	⑦	⑦	⑦	⑦	⑦
⑧	⑧	⑧	⑧	⑧	⑧	⑧	⑧	⑧
⑨	⑨	⑨	⑨	⑨	⑨	⑨	⑨	⑨
⓪	⓪	⓪	⓪	⓪	⓪	⓪	⓪	⓪

Print your 5-character **Test Form** in the boxes at the right <u>and</u> fill in the corresponding ovals.

FORM

①	①	Ⓜ	Ⓒ	①
②	②			②
	③			③
	④			④
	⑤			⑤
	⑥			⑥
	⑦			⑦
	⑧			⑧
	⑨			⑨
	⓪			⓪

TEST 1: ENGLISH

1 Ⓐ Ⓑ Ⓒ Ⓓ	14 Ⓕ Ⓖ Ⓗ Ⓙ	27 Ⓐ Ⓑ Ⓒ Ⓓ	40 Ⓕ Ⓖ Ⓗ Ⓙ	53 Ⓐ Ⓑ Ⓒ Ⓓ	66 Ⓕ Ⓖ Ⓗ Ⓙ
2 Ⓕ Ⓖ Ⓗ Ⓙ	15 Ⓐ Ⓑ Ⓒ Ⓓ	28 Ⓕ Ⓖ Ⓗ Ⓙ	41 Ⓐ Ⓑ Ⓒ Ⓓ	54 Ⓕ Ⓖ Ⓗ Ⓙ	67 Ⓐ Ⓑ Ⓒ Ⓓ
3 Ⓐ Ⓑ Ⓒ Ⓓ	16 Ⓕ Ⓖ Ⓗ Ⓙ	29 Ⓐ Ⓑ Ⓒ Ⓓ	42 Ⓕ Ⓖ Ⓗ Ⓙ	55 Ⓐ Ⓑ Ⓒ Ⓓ	68 Ⓕ Ⓖ Ⓗ Ⓙ
4 Ⓕ Ⓖ Ⓗ Ⓙ	17 Ⓐ Ⓑ Ⓒ Ⓓ	30 Ⓕ Ⓖ Ⓗ Ⓙ	43 Ⓐ Ⓑ Ⓒ Ⓓ	56 Ⓕ Ⓖ Ⓗ Ⓙ	69 Ⓐ Ⓑ Ⓒ Ⓓ
5 Ⓐ Ⓑ Ⓒ Ⓓ	18 Ⓕ Ⓖ Ⓗ Ⓙ	31 Ⓐ Ⓑ Ⓒ Ⓓ	44 Ⓕ Ⓖ Ⓗ Ⓙ	57 Ⓐ Ⓑ Ⓒ Ⓓ	70 Ⓕ Ⓖ Ⓗ Ⓙ
6 Ⓕ Ⓖ Ⓗ Ⓙ	19 Ⓐ Ⓑ Ⓒ Ⓓ	32 Ⓕ Ⓖ Ⓗ Ⓙ	45 Ⓐ Ⓑ Ⓒ Ⓓ	58 Ⓕ Ⓖ Ⓗ Ⓙ	71 Ⓐ Ⓑ Ⓒ Ⓓ
7 Ⓐ Ⓑ Ⓒ Ⓓ	20 Ⓕ Ⓖ Ⓗ Ⓙ	33 Ⓐ Ⓑ Ⓒ Ⓓ	46 Ⓕ Ⓖ Ⓗ Ⓙ	59 Ⓐ Ⓑ Ⓒ Ⓓ	72 Ⓕ Ⓖ Ⓗ Ⓙ
8 Ⓕ Ⓖ Ⓗ Ⓙ	21 Ⓐ Ⓑ Ⓒ Ⓓ	34 Ⓕ Ⓖ Ⓗ Ⓙ	47 Ⓐ Ⓑ Ⓒ Ⓓ	60 Ⓕ Ⓖ Ⓗ Ⓙ	73 Ⓐ Ⓑ Ⓒ Ⓓ
9 Ⓐ Ⓑ Ⓒ Ⓓ	22 Ⓕ Ⓖ Ⓗ Ⓙ	35 Ⓐ Ⓑ Ⓒ Ⓓ	48 Ⓕ Ⓖ Ⓗ Ⓙ	61 Ⓐ Ⓑ Ⓒ Ⓓ	74 Ⓕ Ⓖ Ⓗ Ⓙ
10 Ⓕ Ⓖ Ⓗ Ⓙ	23 Ⓐ Ⓑ Ⓒ Ⓓ	36 Ⓕ Ⓖ Ⓗ Ⓙ	49 Ⓐ Ⓑ Ⓒ Ⓓ	62 Ⓕ Ⓖ Ⓗ Ⓙ	75 Ⓐ Ⓑ Ⓒ Ⓓ
11 Ⓐ Ⓑ Ⓒ Ⓓ	24 Ⓕ Ⓖ Ⓗ Ⓙ	37 Ⓐ Ⓑ Ⓒ Ⓓ	50 Ⓕ Ⓖ Ⓗ Ⓙ	63 Ⓐ Ⓑ Ⓒ Ⓓ	
12 Ⓕ Ⓖ Ⓗ Ⓙ	25 Ⓐ Ⓑ Ⓒ Ⓓ	38 Ⓕ Ⓖ Ⓗ Ⓙ	51 Ⓐ Ⓑ Ⓒ Ⓓ	64 Ⓕ Ⓖ Ⓗ Ⓙ	
13 Ⓐ Ⓑ Ⓒ Ⓓ	26 Ⓕ Ⓖ Ⓗ Ⓙ	39 Ⓐ Ⓑ Ⓒ Ⓓ	52 Ⓕ Ⓖ Ⓗ Ⓙ	65 Ⓐ Ⓑ Ⓒ Ⓓ	

TEST 2: MATHEMATICS

1 Ⓐ Ⓑ Ⓒ Ⓓ Ⓔ	11 Ⓐ Ⓑ Ⓒ Ⓓ Ⓔ	21 Ⓐ Ⓑ Ⓒ Ⓓ Ⓔ	31 Ⓐ Ⓑ Ⓒ Ⓓ Ⓔ	41 Ⓐ Ⓑ Ⓒ Ⓓ Ⓔ	51 Ⓐ Ⓑ Ⓒ Ⓓ Ⓔ
2 Ⓕ Ⓖ Ⓗ Ⓙ Ⓚ	12 Ⓕ Ⓖ Ⓗ Ⓙ Ⓚ	22 Ⓕ Ⓖ Ⓗ Ⓙ Ⓚ	32 Ⓕ Ⓖ Ⓗ Ⓙ Ⓚ	42 Ⓕ Ⓖ Ⓗ Ⓙ Ⓚ	52 Ⓕ Ⓖ Ⓗ Ⓙ Ⓚ
3 Ⓐ Ⓑ Ⓒ Ⓓ Ⓔ	13 Ⓐ Ⓑ Ⓒ Ⓓ Ⓔ	23 Ⓐ Ⓑ Ⓒ Ⓓ Ⓔ	33 Ⓐ Ⓑ Ⓒ Ⓓ Ⓔ	43 Ⓐ Ⓑ Ⓒ Ⓓ Ⓔ	53 Ⓐ Ⓑ Ⓒ Ⓓ Ⓔ
4 Ⓕ Ⓖ Ⓗ Ⓙ Ⓚ	14 Ⓕ Ⓖ Ⓗ Ⓙ Ⓚ	24 Ⓕ Ⓖ Ⓗ Ⓙ Ⓚ	34 Ⓕ Ⓖ Ⓗ Ⓙ Ⓚ	44 Ⓕ Ⓖ Ⓗ Ⓙ Ⓚ	54 Ⓕ Ⓖ Ⓗ Ⓙ Ⓚ
5 Ⓐ Ⓑ Ⓒ Ⓓ Ⓔ	15 Ⓐ Ⓑ Ⓒ Ⓓ Ⓔ	25 Ⓐ Ⓑ Ⓒ Ⓓ Ⓔ	35 Ⓐ Ⓑ Ⓒ Ⓓ Ⓔ	45 Ⓐ Ⓑ Ⓒ Ⓓ Ⓔ	55 Ⓐ Ⓑ Ⓒ Ⓓ Ⓔ
6 Ⓕ Ⓖ Ⓗ Ⓙ Ⓚ	16 Ⓕ Ⓖ Ⓗ Ⓙ Ⓚ	26 Ⓕ Ⓖ Ⓗ Ⓙ Ⓚ	36 Ⓕ Ⓖ Ⓗ Ⓙ Ⓚ	46 Ⓕ Ⓖ Ⓗ Ⓙ Ⓚ	56 Ⓕ Ⓖ Ⓗ Ⓙ Ⓚ
7 Ⓐ Ⓑ Ⓒ Ⓓ Ⓔ	17 Ⓐ Ⓑ Ⓒ Ⓓ Ⓔ	27 Ⓐ Ⓑ Ⓒ Ⓓ Ⓔ	37 Ⓐ Ⓑ Ⓒ Ⓓ Ⓔ	47 Ⓐ Ⓑ Ⓒ Ⓓ Ⓔ	57 Ⓐ Ⓑ Ⓒ Ⓓ Ⓔ
8 Ⓕ Ⓖ Ⓗ Ⓙ Ⓚ	18 Ⓕ Ⓖ Ⓗ Ⓙ Ⓚ	28 Ⓕ Ⓖ Ⓗ Ⓙ Ⓚ	38 Ⓕ Ⓖ Ⓗ Ⓙ Ⓚ	48 Ⓕ Ⓖ Ⓗ Ⓙ Ⓚ	58 Ⓕ Ⓖ Ⓗ Ⓙ Ⓚ
9 Ⓐ Ⓑ Ⓒ Ⓓ Ⓔ	19 Ⓐ Ⓑ Ⓒ Ⓓ Ⓔ	29 Ⓐ Ⓑ Ⓒ Ⓓ Ⓔ	39 Ⓐ Ⓑ Ⓒ Ⓓ Ⓔ	49 Ⓐ Ⓑ Ⓒ Ⓓ Ⓔ	59 Ⓐ Ⓑ Ⓒ Ⓓ Ⓔ
10 Ⓕ Ⓖ Ⓗ Ⓙ Ⓚ	20 Ⓕ Ⓖ Ⓗ Ⓙ Ⓚ	30 Ⓕ Ⓖ Ⓗ Ⓙ Ⓚ	40 Ⓕ Ⓖ Ⓗ Ⓙ Ⓚ	50 Ⓕ Ⓖ Ⓗ Ⓙ Ⓚ	60 Ⓕ Ⓖ Ⓗ Ⓙ Ⓚ

TEST 3: READING

1 Ⓐ Ⓑ Ⓒ Ⓓ	8 Ⓕ Ⓖ Ⓗ Ⓙ	15 Ⓐ Ⓑ Ⓒ Ⓓ	22 Ⓕ Ⓖ Ⓗ Ⓙ	29 Ⓐ Ⓑ Ⓒ Ⓓ	36 Ⓕ Ⓖ Ⓗ Ⓙ
2 Ⓕ Ⓖ Ⓗ Ⓙ	9 Ⓐ Ⓑ Ⓒ Ⓓ	16 Ⓕ Ⓖ Ⓗ Ⓙ	23 Ⓐ Ⓑ Ⓒ Ⓓ	30 Ⓕ Ⓖ Ⓗ Ⓙ	37 Ⓐ Ⓑ Ⓒ Ⓓ
3 Ⓐ Ⓑ Ⓒ Ⓓ	10 Ⓕ Ⓖ Ⓗ Ⓙ	17 Ⓐ Ⓑ Ⓒ Ⓓ	24 Ⓕ Ⓖ Ⓗ Ⓙ	31 Ⓐ Ⓑ Ⓒ Ⓓ	38 Ⓕ Ⓖ Ⓗ Ⓙ
4 Ⓕ Ⓖ Ⓗ Ⓙ	11 Ⓐ Ⓑ Ⓒ Ⓓ	18 Ⓕ Ⓖ Ⓗ Ⓙ	25 Ⓐ Ⓑ Ⓒ Ⓓ	32 Ⓕ Ⓖ Ⓗ Ⓙ	39 Ⓐ Ⓑ Ⓒ Ⓓ
5 Ⓐ Ⓑ Ⓒ Ⓓ	12 Ⓕ Ⓖ Ⓗ Ⓙ	19 Ⓐ Ⓑ Ⓒ Ⓓ	26 Ⓕ Ⓖ Ⓗ Ⓙ	33 Ⓐ Ⓑ Ⓒ Ⓓ	40 Ⓕ Ⓖ Ⓗ Ⓙ
6 Ⓕ Ⓖ Ⓗ Ⓙ	13 Ⓐ Ⓑ Ⓒ Ⓓ	20 Ⓕ Ⓖ Ⓗ Ⓙ	27 Ⓐ Ⓑ Ⓒ Ⓓ	34 Ⓕ Ⓖ Ⓗ Ⓙ	
7 Ⓐ Ⓑ Ⓒ Ⓓ	14 Ⓕ Ⓖ Ⓗ Ⓙ	21 Ⓐ Ⓑ Ⓒ Ⓓ	28 Ⓕ Ⓖ Ⓗ Ⓙ	35 Ⓐ Ⓑ Ⓒ Ⓓ	

TEST 4: SCIENCE

1 Ⓐ Ⓑ Ⓒ Ⓓ	8 Ⓕ Ⓖ Ⓗ Ⓙ	15 Ⓐ Ⓑ Ⓒ Ⓓ	22 Ⓕ Ⓖ Ⓗ Ⓙ	29 Ⓐ Ⓑ Ⓒ Ⓓ	36 Ⓕ Ⓖ Ⓗ Ⓙ
2 Ⓕ Ⓖ Ⓗ Ⓙ	9 Ⓐ Ⓑ Ⓒ Ⓓ	16 Ⓕ Ⓖ Ⓗ Ⓙ	23 Ⓐ Ⓑ Ⓒ Ⓓ	30 Ⓕ Ⓖ Ⓗ Ⓙ	37 Ⓐ Ⓑ Ⓒ Ⓓ
3 Ⓐ Ⓑ Ⓒ Ⓓ	10 Ⓕ Ⓖ Ⓗ Ⓙ	17 Ⓐ Ⓑ Ⓒ Ⓓ	24 Ⓕ Ⓖ Ⓗ Ⓙ	31 Ⓐ Ⓑ Ⓒ Ⓓ	38 Ⓕ Ⓖ Ⓗ Ⓙ
4 Ⓕ Ⓖ Ⓗ Ⓙ	11 Ⓐ Ⓑ Ⓒ Ⓓ	18 Ⓕ Ⓖ Ⓗ Ⓙ	25 Ⓐ Ⓑ Ⓒ Ⓓ	32 Ⓕ Ⓖ Ⓗ Ⓙ	39 Ⓐ Ⓑ Ⓒ Ⓓ
5 Ⓐ Ⓑ Ⓒ Ⓓ	12 Ⓕ Ⓖ Ⓗ Ⓙ	19 Ⓐ Ⓑ Ⓒ Ⓓ	26 Ⓕ Ⓖ Ⓗ Ⓙ	33 Ⓐ Ⓑ Ⓒ Ⓓ	40 Ⓕ Ⓖ Ⓗ Ⓙ
6 Ⓕ Ⓖ Ⓗ Ⓙ	13 Ⓐ Ⓑ Ⓒ Ⓓ	20 Ⓕ Ⓖ Ⓗ Ⓙ	27 Ⓐ Ⓑ Ⓒ Ⓓ	34 Ⓕ Ⓖ Ⓗ Ⓙ	
7 Ⓐ Ⓑ Ⓒ Ⓓ	14 Ⓕ Ⓖ Ⓗ Ⓙ	21 Ⓐ Ⓑ Ⓒ Ⓓ	28 Ⓕ Ⓖ Ⓗ Ⓙ	35 Ⓐ Ⓑ Ⓒ Ⓓ	

The ACT® *Sample Answer Document*

EXAMINEE STATEMENTS, CERTIFICATION, AND SIGNATURE

1. Statements: I understand that by registering for, launching, starting, or submitting answer documents for an ACT® test, I am agreeing to comply with and be bound by the *Terms and Conditions: Testing Rules and Policies for the ACT® Test* ("Terms").

I UNDERSTAND AND AGREE THAT THE TERMS PERMIT ACT TO CANCEL MY SCORES IN CERTAIN CIRCUMSTANCES. THE TERMS ALSO LIMIT DAMAGES AVAILABLE TO ME AND REQUIRE ARBITRATION OF CERTAIN DISPUTES. BY AGREEING TO ARBITRATION, ACT AND I BOTH WAIVE THE RIGHT TO HAVE THOSE DISPUTES HEARD BY A JUDGE OR JURY.

I understand that ACT owns the test questions and responses, and I will not share them with anyone by any form of communication before, during, or after the test administration. I understand that taking the test for someone else may violate the law and subject me to legal penalties. I consent to the collection and processing of personally identifying information I provide, and its subsequent use and disclosure, as described in the ACT Privacy Policy (www.act.org/privacy.html). I also permit ACT to transfer my personally identifying information to the United States, to ACT, or to a third-party service provider, where it will be subject to use and disclosure under the laws of the United States, including being accessible to law enforcement or national security authorities.

2. Certification: Copy the italicized certification below, then sign and date in the spaces provided.

*I agree to the **Statements** above and certify that I am the person whose information appears on this form.*

_____

_____

_____   _____
Your Signature   Today's Date

[●] **Do NOT mark in this shaded area.**

USE A NO. 2 PENCIL ONLY.
(Do NOT use a mechanical pencil, ink, ballpoint, correction fluid, or felt-tip pen.)

A   NAME, MAILING ADDRESS, AND TELEPHONE
(Please print.)

Last Name   First Name   MI (Middle Initial)

House Number & Street (Apt. No.); or PO Box & No.; or RR & No.

City   State/Province   ZIP/Postal Code

Area Code   Number   Country

ACT, Inc.—Confidential Restricted when data present

ALL examinees must complete block A – please print.

Blocks B, C, and D are required for all examinees. Find the MATCHING INFORMATION on your ticket. Enter it EXACTLY the same way, even if any of the information is missing or incorrect. Fill in the corresponding ovals. If you do not complete these blocks to match your previous information EXACTLY, your scores will be **delayed up to 8 weeks**.

ACT®

PO BOX 168, IOWA CITY, IA 52243-0168

B   MATCH NAME
(First 5 letters of last name)

(ovals A–Z, O for each of 5 letters)

C   MATCH NUMBER

(ovals 1–9, 0)

D   DATE OF BIRTH

Month	Day	Year
January		
February		
March	1 1	1 1
April	2 2	2 2
May	3 3	3 3
June	4 4	4
July	5 5	5
August	6 6	6
September	7 7	7
October	8 8	8
November	9	9
December	0 0	0 0

01121523W   (A)203023-001:654321   ISD36401   Printed in the US.

PAGE 2

Marking Directions: Mark only **one** oval for each question. Fill in response completely. Erase errors cleanly without smudging.

Correct mark: ○ ● ○ ○

- -

Do NOT use these *incorrect* **or** *bad* **marks.**

Incorrect marks: ⊘ ⊗ ⊖ ⊙
Overlapping mark: ○○●○
Cross-out mark: ○⊗○○
Smudged erasure: ○○◐○
Mark is too light: ◐○○○

BOOKLET NUMBER

① ① ① ① ① ① ① ① ①
② ② ② ② ② ② ② ② ②
③ ③ ③ ③ ③ ③ ③ ③ ③
④ ④ ④ ④ ④ ④ ④ ④ ④
⑤ ⑤ ⑤ ⑤ ⑤ ⑤ ⑤ ⑤ ⑤
⑥ ⑥ ⑥ ⑥ ⑥ ⑥ ⑥ ⑥ ⑥
⑦ ⑦ ⑦ ⑦ ⑦ ⑦ ⑦ ⑦ ⑦
⑧ ⑧ ⑧ ⑧ ⑧ ⑧ ⑧ ⑧ ⑧
⑨ ⑨ ⑨ ⑨ ⑨ ⑨ ⑨ ⑨ ⑨
⓪ ⓪ ⓪ ⓪ ⓪ ⓪ ⓪ ⓪ ⓪

Print your 5-character **Test Form** in the boxes at the right and fill in the corresponding ovals.

FORM

① ① Ⓜ Ⓒ ①
② ② ②
③ ③
④ ④
⑤ ⑤
⑥ ⑥
⑦ ⑦
⑧ ⑧
⑨ ⑨
⓪ ⓪

TEST 1: ENGLISH

1 Ⓐ Ⓑ Ⓒ Ⓓ	14 Ⓕ Ⓖ Ⓗ Ⓙ	27 Ⓐ Ⓑ Ⓒ Ⓓ	40 Ⓕ Ⓖ Ⓗ Ⓙ	53 Ⓐ Ⓑ Ⓒ Ⓓ	66 Ⓕ Ⓖ Ⓗ Ⓙ
2 Ⓕ Ⓖ Ⓗ Ⓙ	15 Ⓐ Ⓑ Ⓒ Ⓓ	28 Ⓕ Ⓖ Ⓗ Ⓙ	41 Ⓐ Ⓑ Ⓒ Ⓓ	54 Ⓕ Ⓖ Ⓗ Ⓙ	67 Ⓐ Ⓑ Ⓒ Ⓓ
3 Ⓐ Ⓑ Ⓒ Ⓓ	16 Ⓕ Ⓖ Ⓗ Ⓙ	29 Ⓐ Ⓑ Ⓒ Ⓓ	42 Ⓕ Ⓖ Ⓗ Ⓙ	55 Ⓐ Ⓑ Ⓒ Ⓓ	68 Ⓕ Ⓖ Ⓗ Ⓙ
4 Ⓕ Ⓖ Ⓗ Ⓙ	17 Ⓐ Ⓑ Ⓒ Ⓓ	30 Ⓕ Ⓖ Ⓗ Ⓙ	43 Ⓐ Ⓑ Ⓒ Ⓓ	56 Ⓕ Ⓖ Ⓗ Ⓙ	69 Ⓐ Ⓑ Ⓒ Ⓓ
5 Ⓐ Ⓑ Ⓒ Ⓓ	18 Ⓕ Ⓖ Ⓗ Ⓙ	31 Ⓐ Ⓑ Ⓒ Ⓓ	44 Ⓕ Ⓖ Ⓗ Ⓙ	57 Ⓐ Ⓑ Ⓒ Ⓓ	70 Ⓕ Ⓖ Ⓗ Ⓙ
6 Ⓕ Ⓖ Ⓗ Ⓙ	19 Ⓐ Ⓑ Ⓒ Ⓓ	32 Ⓕ Ⓖ Ⓗ Ⓙ	45 Ⓐ Ⓑ Ⓒ Ⓓ	58 Ⓕ Ⓖ Ⓗ Ⓙ	71 Ⓐ Ⓑ Ⓒ Ⓓ
7 Ⓐ Ⓑ Ⓒ Ⓓ	20 Ⓕ Ⓖ Ⓗ Ⓙ	33 Ⓐ Ⓑ Ⓒ Ⓓ	46 Ⓕ Ⓖ Ⓗ Ⓙ	59 Ⓐ Ⓑ Ⓒ Ⓓ	72 Ⓕ Ⓖ Ⓗ Ⓙ
8 Ⓕ Ⓖ Ⓗ Ⓙ	21 Ⓐ Ⓑ Ⓒ Ⓓ	34 Ⓕ Ⓖ Ⓗ Ⓙ	47 Ⓐ Ⓑ Ⓒ Ⓓ	60 Ⓕ Ⓖ Ⓗ Ⓙ	73 Ⓐ Ⓑ Ⓒ Ⓓ
9 Ⓐ Ⓑ Ⓒ Ⓓ	22 Ⓕ Ⓖ Ⓗ Ⓙ	35 Ⓐ Ⓑ Ⓒ Ⓓ	48 Ⓕ Ⓖ Ⓗ Ⓙ	61 Ⓐ Ⓑ Ⓒ Ⓓ	74 Ⓕ Ⓖ Ⓗ Ⓙ
10 Ⓕ Ⓖ Ⓗ Ⓙ	23 Ⓐ Ⓑ Ⓒ Ⓓ	36 Ⓕ Ⓖ Ⓗ Ⓙ	49 Ⓐ Ⓑ Ⓒ Ⓓ	62 Ⓕ Ⓖ Ⓗ Ⓙ	75 Ⓐ Ⓑ Ⓒ Ⓓ
11 Ⓐ Ⓑ Ⓒ Ⓓ	24 Ⓕ Ⓖ Ⓗ Ⓙ	37 Ⓐ Ⓑ Ⓒ Ⓓ	50 Ⓕ Ⓖ Ⓗ Ⓙ	63 Ⓐ Ⓑ Ⓒ Ⓓ	
12 Ⓕ Ⓖ Ⓗ Ⓙ	25 Ⓐ Ⓑ Ⓒ Ⓓ	38 Ⓕ Ⓖ Ⓗ Ⓙ	51 Ⓐ Ⓑ Ⓒ Ⓓ	64 Ⓕ Ⓖ Ⓗ Ⓙ	
13 Ⓐ Ⓑ Ⓒ Ⓓ	26 Ⓕ Ⓖ Ⓗ Ⓙ	39 Ⓐ Ⓑ Ⓒ Ⓓ	52 Ⓕ Ⓖ Ⓗ Ⓙ	65 Ⓐ Ⓑ Ⓒ Ⓓ	

TEST 2: MATHEMATICS

1 Ⓐ Ⓑ Ⓒ Ⓓ Ⓔ	11 Ⓐ Ⓑ Ⓒ Ⓓ Ⓔ	21 Ⓐ Ⓑ Ⓒ Ⓓ Ⓔ	31 Ⓐ Ⓑ Ⓒ Ⓓ Ⓔ	41 Ⓐ Ⓑ Ⓒ Ⓓ Ⓔ	51 Ⓐ Ⓑ Ⓒ Ⓓ Ⓔ
2 Ⓕ Ⓖ Ⓗ Ⓙ Ⓚ	12 Ⓕ Ⓖ Ⓗ Ⓙ Ⓚ	22 Ⓕ Ⓖ Ⓗ Ⓙ Ⓚ	32 Ⓕ Ⓖ Ⓗ Ⓙ Ⓚ	42 Ⓕ Ⓖ Ⓗ Ⓙ Ⓚ	52 Ⓕ Ⓖ Ⓗ Ⓙ Ⓚ
3 Ⓐ Ⓑ Ⓒ Ⓓ Ⓔ	13 Ⓐ Ⓑ Ⓒ Ⓓ Ⓔ	23 Ⓐ Ⓑ Ⓒ Ⓓ Ⓔ	33 Ⓐ Ⓑ Ⓒ Ⓓ Ⓔ	43 Ⓐ Ⓑ Ⓒ Ⓓ Ⓔ	53 Ⓐ Ⓑ Ⓒ Ⓓ Ⓔ
4 Ⓕ Ⓖ Ⓗ Ⓙ Ⓚ	14 Ⓕ Ⓖ Ⓗ Ⓙ Ⓚ	24 Ⓕ Ⓖ Ⓗ Ⓙ Ⓚ	34 Ⓕ Ⓖ Ⓗ Ⓙ Ⓚ	44 Ⓕ Ⓖ Ⓗ Ⓙ Ⓚ	54 Ⓕ Ⓖ Ⓗ Ⓙ Ⓚ
5 Ⓐ Ⓑ Ⓒ Ⓓ Ⓔ	15 Ⓐ Ⓑ Ⓒ Ⓓ Ⓔ	25 Ⓐ Ⓑ Ⓒ Ⓓ Ⓔ	35 Ⓐ Ⓑ Ⓒ Ⓓ Ⓔ	45 Ⓐ Ⓑ Ⓒ Ⓓ Ⓔ	55 Ⓐ Ⓑ Ⓒ Ⓓ Ⓔ
6 Ⓕ Ⓖ Ⓗ Ⓙ Ⓚ	16 Ⓕ Ⓖ Ⓗ Ⓙ Ⓚ	26 Ⓕ Ⓖ Ⓗ Ⓙ Ⓚ	36 Ⓕ Ⓖ Ⓗ Ⓙ Ⓚ	46 Ⓕ Ⓖ Ⓗ Ⓙ Ⓚ	56 Ⓕ Ⓖ Ⓗ Ⓙ Ⓚ
7 Ⓐ Ⓑ Ⓒ Ⓓ Ⓔ	17 Ⓐ Ⓑ Ⓒ Ⓓ Ⓔ	27 Ⓐ Ⓑ Ⓒ Ⓓ Ⓔ	37 Ⓐ Ⓑ Ⓒ Ⓓ Ⓔ	47 Ⓐ Ⓑ Ⓒ Ⓓ Ⓔ	57 Ⓐ Ⓑ Ⓒ Ⓓ Ⓔ
8 Ⓕ Ⓖ Ⓗ Ⓙ Ⓚ	18 Ⓕ Ⓖ Ⓗ Ⓙ Ⓚ	28 Ⓕ Ⓖ Ⓗ Ⓙ Ⓚ	38 Ⓕ Ⓖ Ⓗ Ⓙ Ⓚ	48 Ⓕ Ⓖ Ⓗ Ⓙ Ⓚ	58 Ⓕ Ⓖ Ⓗ Ⓙ Ⓚ
9 Ⓐ Ⓑ Ⓒ Ⓓ Ⓔ	19 Ⓐ Ⓑ Ⓒ Ⓓ Ⓔ	29 Ⓐ Ⓑ Ⓒ Ⓓ Ⓔ	39 Ⓐ Ⓑ Ⓒ Ⓓ Ⓔ	49 Ⓐ Ⓑ Ⓒ Ⓓ Ⓔ	59 Ⓐ Ⓑ Ⓒ Ⓓ Ⓔ
10 Ⓕ Ⓖ Ⓗ Ⓙ Ⓚ	20 Ⓕ Ⓖ Ⓗ Ⓙ Ⓚ	30 Ⓕ Ⓖ Ⓗ Ⓙ Ⓚ	40 Ⓕ Ⓖ Ⓗ Ⓙ Ⓚ	50 Ⓕ Ⓖ Ⓗ Ⓙ Ⓚ	60 Ⓕ Ⓖ Ⓗ Ⓙ Ⓚ

TEST 3: READING

1 Ⓐ Ⓑ Ⓒ Ⓓ	8 Ⓕ Ⓖ Ⓗ Ⓙ	15 Ⓐ Ⓑ Ⓒ Ⓓ	22 Ⓕ Ⓖ Ⓗ Ⓙ	29 Ⓐ Ⓑ Ⓒ Ⓓ	36 Ⓕ Ⓖ Ⓗ Ⓙ
2 Ⓕ Ⓖ Ⓗ Ⓙ	9 Ⓐ Ⓑ Ⓒ Ⓓ	16 Ⓕ Ⓖ Ⓗ Ⓙ	23 Ⓐ Ⓑ Ⓒ Ⓓ	30 Ⓕ Ⓖ Ⓗ Ⓙ	37 Ⓐ Ⓑ Ⓒ Ⓓ
3 Ⓐ Ⓑ Ⓒ Ⓓ	10 Ⓕ Ⓖ Ⓗ Ⓙ	17 Ⓐ Ⓑ Ⓒ Ⓓ	24 Ⓕ Ⓖ Ⓗ Ⓙ	31 Ⓐ Ⓑ Ⓒ Ⓓ	38 Ⓕ Ⓖ Ⓗ Ⓙ
4 Ⓕ Ⓖ Ⓗ Ⓙ	11 Ⓐ Ⓑ Ⓒ Ⓓ	18 Ⓕ Ⓖ Ⓗ Ⓙ	25 Ⓐ Ⓑ Ⓒ Ⓓ	32 Ⓕ Ⓖ Ⓗ Ⓙ	39 Ⓐ Ⓑ Ⓒ Ⓓ
5 Ⓐ Ⓑ Ⓒ Ⓓ	12 Ⓕ Ⓖ Ⓗ Ⓙ	19 Ⓐ Ⓑ Ⓒ Ⓓ	26 Ⓕ Ⓖ Ⓗ Ⓙ	33 Ⓐ Ⓑ Ⓒ Ⓓ	40 Ⓕ Ⓖ Ⓗ Ⓙ
6 Ⓕ Ⓖ Ⓗ Ⓙ	13 Ⓐ Ⓑ Ⓒ Ⓓ	20 Ⓕ Ⓖ Ⓗ Ⓙ	27 Ⓐ Ⓑ Ⓒ Ⓓ	34 Ⓕ Ⓖ Ⓗ Ⓙ	
7 Ⓐ Ⓑ Ⓒ Ⓓ	14 Ⓕ Ⓖ Ⓗ Ⓙ	21 Ⓐ Ⓑ Ⓒ Ⓓ	28 Ⓕ Ⓖ Ⓗ Ⓙ	35 Ⓐ Ⓑ Ⓒ Ⓓ	

TEST 4: SCIENCE

1 Ⓐ Ⓑ Ⓒ Ⓓ	8 Ⓕ Ⓖ Ⓗ Ⓙ	15 Ⓐ Ⓑ Ⓒ Ⓓ	22 Ⓕ Ⓖ Ⓗ Ⓙ	29 Ⓐ Ⓑ Ⓒ Ⓓ	36 Ⓕ Ⓖ Ⓗ Ⓙ
2 Ⓕ Ⓖ Ⓗ Ⓙ	9 Ⓐ Ⓑ Ⓒ Ⓓ	16 Ⓕ Ⓖ Ⓗ Ⓙ	23 Ⓐ Ⓑ Ⓒ Ⓓ	30 Ⓕ Ⓖ Ⓗ Ⓙ	37 Ⓐ Ⓑ Ⓒ Ⓓ
3 Ⓐ Ⓑ Ⓒ Ⓓ	10 Ⓕ Ⓖ Ⓗ Ⓙ	17 Ⓐ Ⓑ Ⓒ Ⓓ	24 Ⓕ Ⓖ Ⓗ Ⓙ	31 Ⓐ Ⓑ Ⓒ Ⓓ	38 Ⓕ Ⓖ Ⓗ Ⓙ
4 Ⓕ Ⓖ Ⓗ Ⓙ	11 Ⓐ Ⓑ Ⓒ Ⓓ	18 Ⓕ Ⓖ Ⓗ Ⓙ	25 Ⓐ Ⓑ Ⓒ Ⓓ	32 Ⓕ Ⓖ Ⓗ Ⓙ	39 Ⓐ Ⓑ Ⓒ Ⓓ
5 Ⓐ Ⓑ Ⓒ Ⓓ	12 Ⓕ Ⓖ Ⓗ Ⓙ	19 Ⓐ Ⓑ Ⓒ Ⓓ	26 Ⓕ Ⓖ Ⓗ Ⓙ	33 Ⓐ Ⓑ Ⓒ Ⓓ	40 Ⓕ Ⓖ Ⓗ Ⓙ
6 Ⓕ Ⓖ Ⓗ Ⓙ	13 Ⓐ Ⓑ Ⓒ Ⓓ	20 Ⓕ Ⓖ Ⓗ Ⓙ	27 Ⓐ Ⓑ Ⓒ Ⓓ	34 Ⓕ Ⓖ Ⓗ Ⓙ	
7 Ⓐ Ⓑ Ⓒ Ⓓ	14 Ⓕ Ⓖ Ⓗ Ⓙ	21 Ⓐ Ⓑ Ⓒ Ⓓ	28 Ⓕ Ⓖ Ⓗ Ⓙ	35 Ⓐ Ⓑ Ⓒ Ⓓ	

Practice Test 6

EXAMINEE STATEMENTS, CERTIFICATION, AND SIGNATURE

1. **Statements:** I understand that by registering for, launching, starting, or submitting answer documents for an ACT® test, I am agreeing to comply with and be bound by the *Terms and Conditions: Testing Rules and Policies for the ACT® Test* ("Terms").

   I UNDERSTAND AND AGREE THAT THE TERMS PERMIT ACT TO CANCEL MY SCORES IN CERTAIN CIRCUMSTANCES. THE TERMS ALSO LIMIT DAMAGES AVAILABLE TO ME AND REQUIRE ARBITRATION OF CERTAIN DISPUTES. BY AGREEING TO ARBITRATION, ACT AND I BOTH WAIVE THE RIGHT TO HAVE THOSE DISPUTES HEARD BY A JUDGE OR JURY.

   I understand that ACT owns the test questions and responses, and I will not share them with anyone by any form of communication before, during, or after the test administration. I understand that taking the test for someone else may violate the law and subject me to legal penalties.

   I consent to the collection and processing of personally identifying information I provide, and its subsequent use and disclosure, as described in the ACT Privacy Policy (www.act.org/privacy.html). I also permit ACT to transfer my personally identifying information to the United States, to ACT, or to a third-party service provider, where it will be subject to use and disclosure under the laws of the United States, including being accessible to law enforcement or national security authorities.

2. **Certification:** Copy the italicized certification below, then sign, date, and print your name in the spaces provided.

   *I agree to the **Statements** above and certify that I am the person whose information appears on this form.*

_____

_____

 Your Signature _____ Today's Date _____ Print Your Name

 The **ACT**®   **Form 22MC9**
2023 | 2024

Taking Additional Practice Tests

Directions

This booklet contains tests in English, mathematics, reading, and science. These tests measure skills and abilities highly related to high school course work and success in college. **Calculators may be used on the mathematics test only.**

The questions in each test are numbered, and the suggested answers for each question are lettered. On the answer document, the rows of ovals are numbered to match the questions, and the ovals in each row are lettered to correspond to the suggested answers.

For each question, first decide which answer is best. Next, locate on the answer document the row of ovals numbered the same as the question. Then, locate the oval in that row lettered the same as your answer. Finally, fill in the oval completely. Use a soft lead pencil and make your marks heavy and black. **Do not use ink or a mechanical pencil.**

Mark only one answer to each question. If you change your mind about an answer, erase your first mark thoroughly before marking your new answer. For each question, make certain that you mark in the row of ovals with the same number as the question.

Only responses marked on your answer document will be scored. Your score on each test will be based only on the number of questions you answer correctly during the time allowed for that test. You will **not** be penalized for guessing. **It is to your advantage to answer every question even if you must guess.**

You may work on each test **only** when the testing staff tells you to do so. If you finish a test before time is called for that test, you should use the time remaining to reconsider questions you are uncertain about in that test. You may **not** look back to a test on which time has already been called, and you may **not** go ahead to another test. To do so will disqualify you from the examination.

Lay your pencil down immediately when time is called at the end of each test. You may **not** for any reason fill in or alter ovals for a test after time is called for that test. To do so will disqualify you from the examination.

Do not fold or tear the pages of your test booklet.

DO NOT OPEN THIS BOOKLET
UNTIL TOLD TO DO SO.

1 ▪ ▪ ▪ ▪ ▪ ▪ ▪ ▪ ▪ 1

ENGLISH TEST
45 Minutes—75 Questions

DIRECTIONS: In the five passages that follow, certain words and phrases are underlined and numbered. In the right-hand column, you will find alternatives for the underlined part. In most cases, you are to choose the one that best expresses the idea, makes the statement appropriate for standard written English, or is worded most consistently with the style and tone of the passage as a whole. If you think the original version is best, choose "NO CHANGE." In some cases, you will find in the right-hand column a question about the underlined part. You are to choose the best answer to the question.

You will also find questions about a section of the passage, or about the passage as a whole. These questions do not refer to an underlined portion of the passage, but rather are identified by a number or numbers in a box.

For each question, choose the alternative you consider best and fill in the corresponding oval on your answer document. Read each passage through once before you begin to answer the questions that accompany it. For many of the questions, you must read several sentences beyond the question to determine the answer. Be sure that you have read far enough ahead each time you choose an alternative.

PASSAGE I

Double the Manta Rays

There are thousands of new animal species identified
      1
each year, the vast majority are small or geographically

isolated. So as graduate student Andrea Marshall studied

manta rays, which are neither small nor isolated, she didn't

expect to identify a new species. Mantas, which are
                                      2
plankton-eating relatives of stingrays that look like pairs

of enormous black wings—up to twenty-five feet wide—
                             3
flying slowly through the water. Encompassing wide

swaths of both temperate and tropical oceans, the manta's

range abuts every continent but Antarctica.

During Marshall's research off the coast of

Mozambique, she observed intriguing physical

variations, in the mantas she swam amongst.
      4

1. **A.** NO CHANGE
   B. Scientists say thousands of new animal species are
   C. Of the thousands of new animal species
   D. Thousands of new animal species are

2. **F.** NO CHANGE
   G. Mantas are
   H. Mantas,
   J. DELETE the underlined portion (adjusting the capitalization as needed).

3. **A.** NO CHANGE
   B. wings: up to twenty-five feet wide—
   C. wings, up to twenty-five feet wide—
   D. wings, up to twenty-five feet wide:

4. **F.** NO CHANGE
   G. variations—in the mantas
   H. variations, in the mantas,
   J. variations in the mantas

GO ON TO THE NEXT PAGE.

Her beachside lodgings in Mozambique now

house the Marine Megafauna Research Center.
_____5

She began to suspect that the one recognized

species of manta might in fact be two species.

[1] To investigate, Marshall began collecting data.
[2] Other data required a closer look. [3] The skin of all

mantas, for example, is embedded with tiny, toothlike
_____6

"denticles." [4] Marshall found that denticles on some

mantas were randomly spaced and occasionally

overlapped, whereas denticles on other mantas were

evenly spaced and never overlapped. [5] Another discovery

was: that some mantas had egg-shaped masses at the base
_____7

of their tail fins. [6] Each mass contained a bony spine

about an inch long—the vestige of a stinging barb from

the manta's ancestors. 8

In 2009, Marshall announced, with
_____9

two other scientists, that indeed there
_____9

is two manta species. The reef manta,
__
10

Manta alfredi, is the smaller and more

common of the two. Thriving in shallow water,

it kind of sticks around one area. In contrast, the
_____11

giant manta, *Manta birostris*, favors deep water

and migrates thousands of miles a year.

5. The writer is considering deleting the underlined sentence. Should the writer make this deletion?
   A. Yes, because the sentence interrupts the account of how Marshall came to investigate the possibility that there were two manta ray species.
   B. Yes, because the sentence fails to clarify why Marshall did her research in Mozambique.
   C. No, because the sentence explains how Marshall created a large scientific institution even though she started as a lone researcher.
   D. No, because the sentence clarifies Marshall's role at the Marine Megafauna Center.

6. F. NO CHANGE
   G. happen to be
   H. were
   J. are

7. A. NO CHANGE
   B. was, that,
   C. was that
   D. was, that

8. The writer wants to add the following sentence to this paragraph:
   > Some of the data were basic, such as manta coloration and size.

   The sentence would most logically be placed:
   F. after Sentence 1.
   G. after Sentence 2.
   H. after Sentence 3.
   J. after Sentence 4.

9. Which choice best conveys that Marshall's announcement was backed by scientific data?
   A. NO CHANGE
   B. surprised many scientists by announcing
   C. had the evidence to announce
   D. at long last announced

10. F. NO CHANGE
    G. exists
    H. was
    J. are

11. A. NO CHANGE
    B. rarely ventures far from its home territory.
    C. doesn't delight in slogging long distances.
    D. loves hanging around its neighborhood.

GO ON TO THE NEXT PAGE.

The fact that such large animals went undifferentiated
<u>that</u>
12

highlights how little scientists know for so long about
<u>highlights how little scientists know for so long about</u>
13

these gentle giants. At the moment, manta ray populations
<u>At the moment, manta ray populations</u>
14
face an array of threats worldwide.
<u>face an array of threats worldwide.</u>
14

12. F. NO CHANGE
   G. whether
   H. which
   J. how

13. A. NO CHANGE
   B. for so long highlights how little scientists know
   C. highlights for so long how little scientists know
   D. highlights how for so long little scientists know

14. Which of the following true statements best concludes this paragraph and the essay by suggesting that the scientific study of manta rays will continue?
   F. NO CHANGE
   G. A 2009 documentary film about Dr. Marshall related the story of her manta-species discovery.
   H. Dr. Marshall once described the manta ray as "like the largest, most beautiful underwater bird."
   J. Fortunately, mantas have a devoted and expert researcher in Dr. Marshall.

Question 15 asks about the preceding passage as a whole.

---

15. Suppose that the writer's purpose had been to survey the scientific community's response to the identification of the two manta species. Would this essay accomplish that purpose?
   A. Yes, because it explains that the scientific community enthusiastically accepted the identification of the two manta species.
   B. Yes, because it relates that Marshall's research was thorough and well documented.
   C. No, because it presents only one scientist's response to the identification of the two manta species.
   D. No, because it focuses on how Marshall's research led to the discovery of the two manta species.

PASSAGE II

Origins of Aspirin

When a plant is attacked by bacteria, fungi, or insects, it produces chemicals, called salicylates, that help the plant produce enzymes or toxins capable of destroying the plant's attackers. Salicylates may also play a role in the plant's ability to regulate its <u>temperature; in effect, helping</u>
16
the plant tolerate heat and cold. Humans have used the

salicylic acids found in <u>plants, particularly in the bark</u>
17
<u>of the willow tree,</u> to fight disease and to reduce fevers.
17

16. F. NO CHANGE
   G. temperature, helping
   H. temperature, this helps
   J. temperature. As a result, helping

17. A. NO CHANGE
   B. plants—particularly in the bark—of the willow tree,
   C. plants; particularly in the bark of the willow tree,
   D. plants particularly, in the bark of the willow tree,

GO ON TO THE NEXT PAGE.

The first known references to willow bark's medicinal use date from ancient Egypt and Sumeria. On a Sumerian stone tablet from 3000 BCE, <u>lists willow among</u> dozens of plants used to treat illnesses. An Egyptian papyrus from **18**

<u>approximately about</u> 1534 BCE refers to willow's use as **19** an all-purpose medicine.

<u>Though willow trees are often found near water</u> **20** <u>and have become religious symbols in many cultures,</u> **20** its medicinal use gradually fell out of favor in Europe.

Apothecaries increasingly <u>preferred</u> the imported bark of **21** South American cinchona trees as a fever reducer, even though willow grew abundantly throughout Europe.

<u>The high cost of importing</u> **22**

cinchona <u>bark however, was</u> expensive. **23**

<u>Consequently,</u> in the mid-1700s, English minister **24**

Edward Stone <u>had began</u> to seek a substitute. He **25** noted that the bitter taste of willow bark was reminiscent of the bitter taste of cinchona bark.

18. F. NO CHANGE
   G. willow is listed among
   H. willow is listed on
   J. lists willow on

19. A. NO CHANGE
   B. an estimation of
   C. in the region of
   D. about

20. Given that all the choices are true, which one would provide the most logical transition to the new subject of this paragraph?
   F. NO CHANGE
   G. While the use of willow bark remained a commonplace method to reduce aches, pains, and fevers around the world,
   H. Though the ancient Egyptian physician Imhotep was worshipped as a god of healing and thought to have used willow bark,
   J. Despite the fact that possible side effects to using willow bark could sometimes include stomach aches and dizziness,

21. A. NO CHANGE
   B. would of preferred
   C. will prefer
   D. prefer

22. F. NO CHANGE
   G. Importing the high price tag of
   H. The high importation cost of
   J. Importing

23. A. NO CHANGE
   B. bark; however,
   C. bark, however,
   D. bark, however

24. F. NO CHANGE
   G. Nevertheless,
   H. Furthermore,
   J. Likewise,

25. A. NO CHANGE
   B. would have began
   C. begun
   D. began

GO ON TO THE NEXT PAGE.

1 ■ ■ ■ ■ ■ ■ ■ ■ ■ ■ 1

Known also for his interest in astronomy, Stone
                                    26

pulverized some willow bark and adds its powder
                                    27

to a liquid. He administered the medicine to people
                          28

suffering from fevers, he then noted that it worked.
                  29
      As the field of medicine evolved, so did the use of

willow bark. Searching for a way to make the salicylic

acid in willow bark less abrasive to the stomach, in 1853

French chemist Charles von Gerhardt created a synthetic

version. Decades later, German chemist Felix Hoffmann

combined synthetic salicylic acid with acetic acid,

inventing a consumer-friendly powdered formula that

would come to be known as aspirin.

26. Given that all the choices are accurate, which one provides the most logical transition from the preceding sentence?
   F. NO CHANGE
   G. Assuming diseases and their cures derive from the same environments,
   H. Believing that the two plants must share similar qualities,
   J. Living on the outskirts of the town of Chipping Norton,

27. A. NO CHANGE
    B. then added it's
    C. added its
    D. adds it's

28. Which choice best emphasizes the experimental nature of the liquid Stone created?
    F. NO CHANGE
    G. He tested his new concoction on
    H. The liquid was given to benefit
    J. He decided to give the drink to

29. A. NO CHANGE
    B. fevers, he was elated to find that
    C. fevers which
    D. fevers. It

┌───┐
│ Question 30 asks about the preceding passage │
│ as a whole.   │
└───┘

30. Suppose the writer's primary purpose had been to outline the development of a common medicine. Would this essay accomplish that purpose?
   F. Yes, because the essay describes how Egyptians used to administer willow bark and how this process evolved from ancient Sumerian practices.
   G. Yes, because the essay documents the historical use of willow bark as a medicine and traces its gradual refinement into modern aspirin.
   H. No, because the essay primarily explains the function of salicylates in willow bark and how aspirin affects the human body.
   J. No, because the essay primarily compares the use of willow bark to the use of cinchona bark in eighteenth-century European medicine.

GO ON TO THE NEXT PAGE.

PASSAGE III

Good Vibrations

In his studio in Dusseldorf, Germany,

paint is what photographer Martin Klimas
   _____
                    31
carefully pours onto a rubber membrane placed
_____
   31
on top of an audio speaker. The paint collects in

a puddle of colors; rich oranges and powder blues,
             _____
                              32
hot pinks and electric yellows. Klimas attaches his

camera to a tripod and positions the camera so it is
             _____
                33

level with the paint puddle. He then sets a sound
_____
  34
trigger (a device that automatically snaps a photo

when a given sound level is reached) on his camera.

Finally, he inserts Daft Punk's *Homework* CD into a

stereo, cranks up the volume to ten, and pushes Play.
        _____
                     35

The result is what Klimas calls a "sonic sculpture."

The vibrations produced by Daft Punk's dance anthem

"Around the World" has caused the paint to rise and
                   _____
                      36
fall, to string and swirl, to splatter and stretch. It is

this image that Klimas's camera captures—sound
_____
                 37
visually rendered by the effects of the vibrations

on the paint. Although Klimas's photographs only

capture an instant of the paint erupting in arcs of color,

each of the photographs is unique to a given song.

31. A. NO CHANGE
   B. there is paint carefully being poured by photographer Martin Klimas
   C. paint is carefully poured by Martin Klimas, a photographer,
   D. photographer Martin Klimas carefully pours paint

32. F. NO CHANGE
   G. colors: rich oranges and powder blues,
   H. colors: rich oranges; and powder blues
   J. colors; rich oranges and powder blues;

33. Which of the following alternatives to the underlined portion would NOT be acceptable?
   A. tripod, and he
   B. tripod and he
   C. tripod. He
   D. tripod; he

34. F. NO CHANGE
   G. eye-to-eye with
   H. the same as
   J. equal to

35. Which choice provides the most dramatic description of Klimas's action?
   A. NO CHANGE
   B. turns the volume knob a bit higher,
   C. increases the volume of the output,
   D. adjusts the speaker's output level,

36. F. NO CHANGE
   G. cause
   H. is causing
   J. causes

37. A. NO CHANGE
   B. pic, frozen in time's embrace that Klimas's camera has snapped—
   C. picture that Klimas's photographic paraphernalia has managed to catch—
   D. snapshot that Klimas's photographic machine snares—

GO ON TO THE NEXT PAGE.

1 ■ ■ ■ ■ ■ ■ ■ ■ ■ **1**

"I leave the creation of the picture to the sound itself,"
                                                    38
Klimas says.

Klimas's idea for his sonic sculptures were sparked
                                            39

by the experiments, of Swiss scientist, Hans Jenny. In the
        40

1960s, Jenny's study on the effects of sound vibrations
        41
on various materials. For example, Jenny discovered that

low sonic tones caused powdery substances to form into

uniform lines, while deeper tones caused the same powder

to form into more nuanced patterns. [42] Klimas relies

on similar principles, only with a more compelling

component: music. Klimas has photographed sonic

sculptures of classical music by Wagner and Bach;

jazz by Miles Davis, Charlie Parker, and John Coltrane;

and psychedelic rock by Pink Floyd and Jimi Hendrix.

While he acknowledges that all forms of music

can generate sonic sculptures. Klimas says, "I
                        43
typically select something dynamic and percussive."

That would certainly impress Jenny. After all, to create
        44
his art, Klimas needs his paint to get up and dance.

38. Which of the following quotations from Klimas provides the most relevant information at this point in the essay?
F. NO CHANGE
G. "The most annoying thing was cleaning up the set thoroughly after every single shot,"
H. "In general, I use normal photographic equipment and common music stuff,"
J. "The shooting is mostly about repeating the process again and again,"

39. **A.** NO CHANGE
B. have been
C. was
D. are

40. **F.** NO CHANGE
G. experiments, of Swiss scientist
H. experiments of Swiss, scientist
J. experiments of Swiss scientist

41. **A.** NO CHANGE
B. while Jenny studied
C. Jenny, to study
D. Jenny studied

42. At this point, the writer is considering dividing the paragraph into two. Should the writer begin or not begin a new paragraph here, and why?
F. Begin a new paragraph because the essay shifts here from an explanation of the harmonics of music to a discussion of Klimas's taste in music.
G. Begin a new paragraph because the essay shifts here from a discussion of Jenny's experiments to a discussion of the music Klimas uses for his artwork.
H. DO NOT begin a new paragraph because doing so would interrupt the analysis of Jenny's experiments.
J. DO NOT begin a new paragraph because doing so would interrupt a description of Klimas's scientific background.

43. **A.** NO CHANGE
B. sculptures, and
C. sculptures,
D. sculptures;

44. Which sentence most effectively leads the reader from the Klimas quotation to the concluding sentence of the essay?
F. NO CHANGE
G. That's simply a matter of taste.
H. That seems unwise.
J. That makes sense.

GO ON TO THE NEXT PAGE.

Question 45 asks about the preceding passage as a whole.

45. Suppose the writer's primary purpose had been to document the process of an artist. Would this essay accomplish that purpose?

    A. Yes, because the essay focuses on how Jenny used an artistic process similar to Klimas's process.

    B. Yes, because the essay describes how Klimas photographs the effects of vibrations created by music on paint.

    C. No, because the essay focuses on the cultural significance of Klimas's artwork.

    D. No, because the essay provides a general overview of how Jenny's experiments have inspired visual artists like Klimas.

PASSAGE IV

Building and Rebuilding "the King of Roads"

[1]

Separating Oregon from Washington, the Columbia River Gorge is eighty-five miles of flowing water, there are tree-covered bluffs, and roaring waterfalls.
46

These striking features daunted would-be road builders
47
until 1913. That year, Samuel Hill and Samuel Lancaster, a businessman and an engineer, respectively, began constructing a road through the gorge to connect the towns along the river. [A] Their design went beyond practicalities it showcased the scenic grandeur of the
48

gorge where the Columbia River is located.
49

46. **F.** NO CHANGE
    G. tree-covered bluffs flank the river,
    H. featuring tree-covered bluffs,
    J. tree-covered bluffs,

47. Which choice most clearly indicates that the features of the Columbia River Gorge intimidated road builders and kept them from constructing the highway?

    A. NO CHANGE
    B. posed problems for
    C. slowed potential
    D. challenged

48. **F.** NO CHANGE
    G. practicalities: and
    H. practicalities:
    J. practicalities,

49. **A.** NO CHANGE
    B. gorge, which is over eighty miles long.
    C. gorge and its scenery.
    D. gorge.

GO ON TO THE NEXT PAGE.

Taking Additional Practice Tests

1 ■ ■ ■ ■ ■ ■ ■ ■ ■ 1

[2]

Featuring seven viaducts and eighteen bridges, the
Columbia River Highway was a marvel. [B] Roadside
overlooks with benches <u>for sitting by the road</u> offered
₅₀

travelers the chance to take <u>in</u> a view of the river or
₅₁
a waterfall. Guardrails made of local rock lined the

route and blurred the distinction between <u>that and</u>
₅₂

environment. [C] Engineers created ☐53 openings in

the side of one <u>tunnel; enabling</u> motorists surrounded by
₅₄
rock to glimpse the river below. Completed in 1922, the

highway earned the local nickname "the King of Roads."

[3]

Impressive as it was, the highway was soon outmoded
because of increased traffic and larger vehicles. <u>In time,</u>
₅₅
Oregon built a new road along the Columbia, much of

the highway was destroyed to make room; other stretches

were abandoned. By 1954, only the western third of the

<u>original road was still in use,</u> mainly by tourists seeking
₅₆
waterfalls. [D]

---

50. F. NO CHANGE
   G. alongside the road
   H. for travelers
   J. DELETE the underlined portion.

51. A. NO CHANGE
   B. up
   C. on
   D. DELETE the underlined portion.

52. F. NO CHANGE
   G. this and the
   H. road and
   J. it and it's

53. At this point, the writer is considering adding the following accurate phrase:

   an unprecedented five

   Should the writer make this addition here?

   A. Yes, because it adds a detail that highlights the impressive design of the highway.
   B. Yes, because it hints at how the engineers were able to make openings in the tunnel.
   C. No, because it provides information that is unrelated to the sentence.
   D. No, because it suggests that creating intricate tunnels was easy for road engineers.

54. F. NO CHANGE
   G. tunnel; an achievement that enabled
   H. tunnel, this enabled
   J. tunnel, enabling

55. A. NO CHANGE
   B. When
   C. Soon
   D. DELETE the underlined portion.

56. F. NO CHANGE
   G. road that first existed continued in a functional capacity,
   H. highway that was completed in 1922 continued to be utilized,
   J. original highway was still being utilized by the driving populace,

GO ON TO THE NEXT PAGE.

[4]

In the 1980s, however, local people's interest in the original highway abounded. In 1981, the National Park
<u>57</u>
Service offered suggestions for restoring parts of the road and repurposing unused sections of it as a trail. Since then, crumbling stone guardrails along the roadside have been repaired. Damaged bridges and viaducts have been rebuilt. <u>Tunnels, now empty and strong, had</u>
<u>58</u>
<u>rubble removed from them.</u> Today, hikers and bikers
<u>58</u>
on the Historic Columbia River Highway Trail experience

a site that became a National Historic Landmark in 2000.
<u>59</u>

57. Which choice most clearly conveys that people's interest in the original Columbia River Highway was not a new phenomenon?
  A. NO CHANGE
  B. took hold.
  C. rekindled.
  D. set in.

58. Which choice most closely maintains the sentence pattern the writer has established in the previous two sentences?
  F. NO CHANGE
  G. Rubble-filled tunnels have been emptied and strengthened.
  H. The tunnels have had the rubble removed from them, and people have strengthened them.
  J. Once filled with rubble, tunnels have been emptied and strengthened.

59. Given that all the choices are accurate, which one best concludes the essay by referring back to the first paragraph?
  A. NO CHANGE
  B. the gorge on sections of the road where it wasn't feasible to restore motor vehicle traffic.
  C. the splendor of the highway that Hill and Lancaster envisioned over one hundred years ago.
  D. a beautiful path that has become a popular tourist destination.

Question 60 asks about the preceding passage as a whole.

60. The writer wants to add the following sentence to the essay:

  The rest of the highway fell into disrepair.

The sentence would most logically be placed at:
  F. Point A in Paragraph 1.
  G. Point B in Paragraph 2.
  H. Point C in Paragraph 2.
  J. Point D in Paragraph 3.

GO ON TO THE NEXT PAGE.

Taking Additional Practice Tests

1 ■ ■ ■ ■ ■ ■ ■ ■ ■ 1

Selling Hip-Hop

One night in the late seventies,

at a popular club in New York City,

singer and music producer Sylvia Robinson had
                   61

a revelation. At the time, hip-hop subculture—based

on the graffiti, breakdancing, deejaying, and rapping

art forms—were emerging as a phenomenon. Robinson
               62

watched as DJ Lovebug Starski spun records for the

crowd and rapped over the instrumental breaks in the

music. Every time the DJ chanted, "Throw your hands

in the air," everyone obeyed. Robinson could hear the
                        63

enthusiasm shared between the hip-hop performer and

his audience. She knew she had to capture that excitement

on record.

Robinson wasted no time in recruiting three aspiring

rappers: Big Bank Hank, Master Gee, and Wonder Mike—
 64

to record on her label as the Sugarhill Gang. [65] Wanting

to re-create the feel-good vibe of the music she'd heard,

an upbeat disco record provided the background that
                                    66

the rappers rhymed over. The resulting track, "Rapper's
 66

Delight," sold fourteen million copies; Robinson had

produced the first rap record to break into the charts.

61. A. NO CHANGE
   B. singer, and music producer, Sylvia Robinson,
   C. singer and music producer, Sylvia Robinson,
   D. singer, and music producer Sylvia Robinson

62. F. NO CHANGE
   G. have emerged
   H. was emerging
   J. are emerging

63. A. NO CHANGE
   B. obeyed by throwing their hands in the air.
   C. heeded the DJ's call and obeyed him.
   D. did what he said and obeyed.

64. F. NO CHANGE
   G. rappers—
   H. rappers;
   J. rappers,

65. At this point, the writer is considering adding the following true statement:

   Robinson and her husband would go on to form other record labels as well.

   Should the writer make this addition here?

   A. Yes, because it suggests that the Sugarhill Gang was able to choose where they wanted to record "Rapper's Delight."
   B. Yes, because it helps explain why Big Bank Hank, Master Gee, and Wonder Mike decided to record with Robinson.
   C. No, because it interrupts the paragraph's discussion of how "Rapper's Delight" was created.
   D. No, because it fails to specify the time period in which Robinson and her husband started their labels.

66. F. NO CHANGE
   G. an upbeat disco record provided by Robinson was rhymed over by the rappers.
   H. rhymes were created by the rappers over an upbeat disco record.
   J. Robinson had the rappers rhyme over an upbeat disco record.

GO ON TO THE NEXT PAGE.

Nevertheless, Robinson's musical
67

instincts, and business savvy had served her well
68
with the Sugarhill Gang. However, there was more to

hip-hop music than party-ready club anthems. She hoped
69
to capitalize on her success by expanding the genre,

Robinson signed Grandmaster Flash and the Furious Five,

a group that already had a following, to her label.

Robinson allowed the group to record a track that
70
studio musician Edward Fletcher had written. The track,

titled "The Message," encountered new commercial
71
hip-hop ground by addressing harsh realities of inner-city

life. It was a far cry from the more digestible singles the

group had previously released because the rappers were
72
hesitant to record it. But Robinson believed it was a

surefire hit. In the opposite fashion, Fletcher and
73
Melle Mel (one of the Furious Five) recorded the

track, which became the group's biggest hit.

Its socially conscious rhymes helped usher in a
74

new generation of artists and secured Robinson's
75
legacy in the landscape of commercial hip-hop.

67. A. NO CHANGE
  B. On the other hand,
  C. As a result,
  D. DELETE the underlined portion.

68. F. NO CHANGE
  G. instincts, and, business savvy
  H. instincts and business savvy
  J. instincts and business savvy,

69. A. NO CHANGE
  B. She was hoping
  C. The hope was
  D. Hoping

70. Which choice most effectively indicates that Robinson had to convince Grandmaster Flash and the Furious Five to record "The Message"?
  F. NO CHANGE
  G. persuaded
  H. helped
  J. asked

71. A. NO CHANGE
  B. protected
  C. covered
  D. filled

72. F. NO CHANGE
  G. released although
  H. released, so
  J. released, for

73. A. NO CHANGE
  B. first place,
  C. same way,
  D. end,

74. F. NO CHANGE
  G. Its socially conscience
  H. It's socially conscious
  J. It's socially conscience

75. Which of the following alternatives to the underlined portion would NOT be acceptable?
  A. artists, and it secured
  B. artists and securing
  C. artists and secure
  D. artists, securing

END OF TEST 1

STOP! DO NOT TURN THE PAGE UNTIL TOLD TO DO SO.

Taking Additional Practice Tests

2 △ △ △ △ △ △ △ △ △ 2

MATHEMATICS TEST
60 Minutes—60 Questions

DIRECTIONS: Solve each problem, choose the correct answer, and then fill in the corresponding oval on your answer document.

Do not linger over problems that take too much time. Solve as many as you can; then return to the others in the time you have left for this test.

You are permitted to use a calculator on this test. You may use your calculator for any problems you choose, but some of the problems may best be done without using a calculator.

Note: Unless otherwise stated, all of the following should be assumed.

1. Illustrative figures are NOT necessarily drawn to scale.
2. Geometric figures lie in a plane.
3. The word *line* indicates a straight line.
4. The word *average* indicates arithmetic mean.

---

1. A function, f, is defined by $f(x,y) = 3x^2 - 4y$. What is the value of $f(3,2)$?

   A. 0
   B. 10
   C. 19
   D. 24
   E. 28

2. In the figure below, $\angle BAC$ measures $35°$, $\angle ABC$ measures $95°$, and points B, C, and D are collinear. What is the measure of $\angle ACD$?

   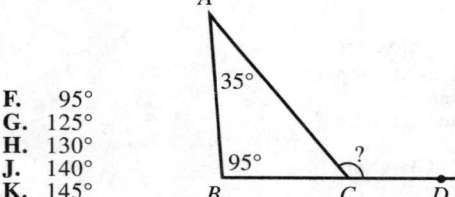

   F.   95°
   G. 125°
   H. 130°
   J. 140°
   K. 145°

3. For all nonzero values of x and y, which of the following expressions is equivalent to $-\dfrac{36x^4y^3}{4xy}$?

   A. $-40x^3y^2$
   B. $-32x^3y^2$
   C. $-9x^5y^4$
   D. $-9x^4y^3$
   E. $-9x^3y^2$

4. At a certain airline company, the cost to transfer mileage points from one person's account to another person's account is $0.75 for every 100 mileage points transferred plus a onetime $20 processing fee. What is the cost to transfer 7,000 mileage points from one account to another at that airline company?

   F. $25.25
   G. $67.50
   H. $72.50
   J. $75.00
   K. $95.00

DO YOUR FIGURING HERE.

GO ON TO THE NEXT PAGE.

2 △ △ △ △ △ △ △ △ △ **2**

5. For $x = -5$, what is the value of $4x^2 - 11x$?
   A. -155
   B. -84
   C. -45
   D. 84
   E. 155

6. Taho earns his regular pay of \$11 per hour for up to 40 hours of work per week. For each hour over 40 hours of work per week, Taho earns $1\frac{1}{2}$ times his regular pay. How much does Taho earn in a week in which he works 50 hours?

   F. \$550
   G. \$605
   H. \$625
   J. \$750
   K. \$825

7. A science class has 8 juniors and 4 seniors. The teacher will randomly select 2 students, one at a time, to represent the class in a committee at the school. Given that the first student selected is a junior, what is the probability that the second student selected will be a senior?

   A. $\frac{1}{11}$

   B. $\frac{1}{4}$

   C. $\frac{3}{11}$

   D. $\frac{1}{3}$

   E. $\frac{4}{11}$

8. When Tyrone fell asleep one night, the temperature was 24°F. When Tyrone awoke the next morning, the temperature was −12°F. Letting + denote a rise in temperature and − denote a drop in temperature, what was the change in temperature from the time Tyrone fell asleep until the time he awoke?

   F. −36°F
   G. −12°F
   H. +6°F
   J. +12°F
   K. +36°F

9. The total cost of renting a car is \$35.00 for each day the car is rented plus 42.5¢ for each mile the car is driven. What is the total cost of renting the car for 6 days and driving 350 miles?

   (Note: No sales tax is involved.)

   A. \$ 154.75
   B. \$ 224.88
   C. \$ 358.75
   D. \$ 420.00
   E. \$1,697.50

DO YOUR FIGURING HERE.

Taking Additional Practice Tests

GO ON TO THE NEXT PAGE.

2   **2**

10. In the standard (x,y) coordinate plane, what is the slope of the line through $(-6,4)$ and $(1,3)$?

DO YOUR FIGURING HERE.

F. $-\dfrac{7}{5}$

G. $-\dfrac{1}{5}$

H. $-\dfrac{1}{7}$

J. $\dfrac{1}{7}$

K. $\dfrac{1}{5}$

11. One morning at a coffee shop, each customer ordered either decaf or regular coffee, and each ordered it either with milk or without milk. The number of customers who ordered each type of coffee with or without milk is listed in the table below.

Order	Decaf	Regular	Total
With milk	12	8	20
Without milk	6	10	16
Total	18	18	36

A customer will be randomly selected from all 36 customers for a prize. What is the probability that the selected customer will have ordered a regular coffee without milk?

A. $\dfrac{1}{6}$

B. $\dfrac{5}{18}$

C. $\dfrac{5}{13}$

D. $\dfrac{1}{2}$

E. $\dfrac{5}{8}$

12. Which of the following inequalities describes the solution set for $3x - 5 < 2x + 1$?

F. $x < -4$

G. $x > -\dfrac{4}{5}$

H. $x < \dfrac{6}{5}$

J. $x < 6$

K. $x > 6$

13. Which of the following expressions is equivalent to $4(x + 2) + 3(2x - 1)$?

A. $3x + 8$
B. $5(2x + 1)$
C. $10(x + 1)$
D. $10x + 11$
E. $15x$

GO ON TO THE NEXT PAGE.

2   **2**

14. What is 4% of 1.36×10^4 ?

    F.   340
    G.   544
    H.   3,400
    J.   5,440
    K. 54,400

DO YOUR FIGURING HERE.

15. What is the least common denominator of the fractions

$\frac{4}{35}$, $\frac{1}{77}$, and $\frac{3}{22}$?

    A.   110
    B.   770
    C.   2,695
    D.   8,470
    E. 59,290

16. The point (3,27) is labeled on the graph of $f(x) = x^3$ in the standard (x,y) coordinate plane below. The graph of $f(x)$ will be translated 3 coordinate units to the left. Which of the following points will be on the image of the graph after the translation?

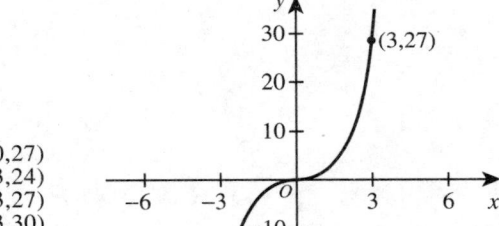

    F. (0,27)
    G. (3,24)
    H. (3,27)
    J. (3,30)
    K. (6,27)

17. In the standard (x,y) coordinate plane, what is the midpoint of the line segment that has endpoints (−6,9) and (2,5) ?

    A. (−4,−4)

    B. (−2, 7)

    C. $\left(\frac{3}{2}, \frac{7}{2} \right)$

    D. (4,−2)

    E. (8,−4)

18. What value of x satisfies the equation $\frac{x^2 + 2x}{x + 2} = 2$?

    F. −4
    G. −3
    H. −2
    J.   1
    K.   2

GO ON TO THE NEXT PAGE.

2 △ △ △ △ △ △ △ △ △ **2**

Use the following information to answer
questions 19–21.

A large theater complex surveyed 5,000 adults. The results
of the survey are shown in the tables below.

Age groups	Number
21–30	2,750
31–40	1,225
41–50	625
51 or older	400

Moviegoer category	Number
Very often	830
Often	1,650
Sometimes	2,320
Rarely	200

Tickets are $9.50 for all regular showings and $7.00 for
matinees.

19. Based on the survey results, what was the average
number of moviegoers for each of the 4 categories?

A.   610
B. 1,060
C. 1,240
D. 1,250
E. 1,985

20. Suppose all the adults surveyed happened to attend
1 movie each in one particular week. The total amount
spent on tickets by those surveyed in that week was
$44,000.00. How many adults attended matinees that
week?

F.   500
G. 1,400
H. 2,500
J. 3,600
K. 4,500

GO ON TO THE NEXT PAGE.

2 △ △ △ △ △ △ △ △ △ **2**

21. One of the following circle graphs represents the proportion by age group of the adults surveyed. Which one?

A.
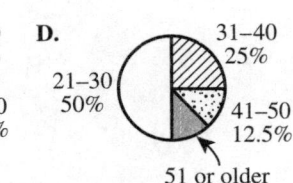
31–40
24.5%
21–30
55%
41–50
12.5%
51 or older
8%

D.
31–40
25%
21–30
50%
41–50
12.5%
51 or older
12.5%

B.
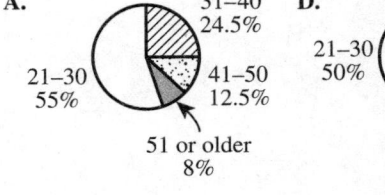
31–40
35%
21–30
45%
41–50
15%
51 or older
5%

E.
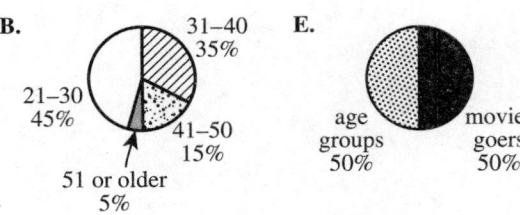
age groups
50%
movie-goers
50%

C.
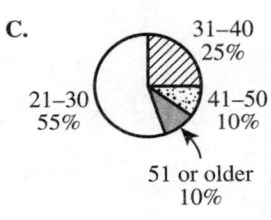
31–40
25%
21–30
55%
41–50
10%
51 or older
10%

---

22. In the figure shown below, all angles are right angles, and the side lengths given are in centimeters. What is the area, in square centimeters, of the figure?

F. 42
G. 75
H. 93
J. 99
K. 117

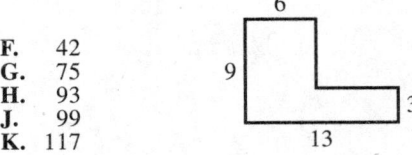
6
9
13
3

23. In the figure below, E is on $\overline{CA}$, and the measures of $\angle BED$ and $\angle AEB$ are 90° and 145°, respectively. If it can be determined, what is the measure of $\angle CED$?

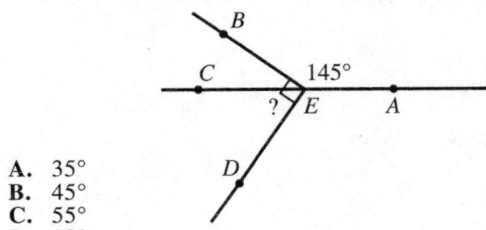
B
C
145°
?
E
A
D

A. 35°
B. 45°
C. 55°
D. 80°
E. Cannot be determined from the given information

GO ON TO THE NEXT PAGE.

DO YOUR FIGURING HERE.

24. In the standard (x,y) coordinate plane, the graph of the function $y = 5\sin(x) - 7$ undergoes a single translation such that the equation of its image is $y = 5\sin(x) - 14$. Which of the following describes this translation?

F. Up 7 coordinate units
G. Down 7 coordinate units
H. Left 7 coordinate units
J. Right 7 coordinate units
K. Right 14 coordinate units

25. What is the value of $\left(9^{\frac{1}{2}} + 16^{\frac{1}{2}}\right)^2$?

A.   7
B.   25
C.   49
D. 337
E. 625

26. A right triangle is shown in the figure below. What is the value of $\sin\theta$?

F. $\dfrac{5}{13}$

G. $\dfrac{5}{12}$

H. $\dfrac{12}{13}$

J. $\dfrac{13}{12}$

K. $\dfrac{13}{5}$

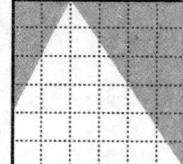

27. A 6-inch-by-6-inch square grid shown below is divided into 36 squares, each with a side length of 1 inch. Each vertex of the 2 shaded triangles lies at an intersection of 2 grid lines. What fractional part of the 6-inch-by-6-inch square is shaded?

A. $\dfrac{2}{3}$

B. $\dfrac{4}{5}$

C. $\dfrac{4}{9}$

D. $\dfrac{5}{9}$

E. $\dfrac{8}{9}$

28. All the values in the equation below are exact. What value of c makes the equation true?

$$(4.25 \times 10^{2c+4})(6 \times 10^7) = 255$$

F. -7
G. -6.5
H. -5
J. -4.5
K. -4

GO ON TO THE NEXT PAGE.

2   **2**

29. Which of the following inequalities is true for all positive integers m ?

   A. $m \le \dfrac{1}{m}$

   B. $m \le \sqrt{m}$

   C. $m \ge m^2$

   D. $m \le m + 1$

   E. $m \ge \sqrt{m + 1}$

DO YOUR FIGURING HERE.

30. A formula for the volume, V, of a right circular cylinder is $V = \pi r^2 h$, where r is the radius and h is the height. The cylindrical tank shown below has radius 5 meters and height 3 meters and is filled with water.

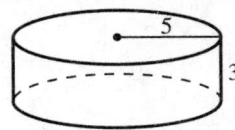

Given that the weight of 1 cubic meter of water is approximately 2,205 pounds, the weight, in pounds, of the water in the tank is:

   F. less than 200,000.
   G. between 200,000 and 300,000.
   H. between 300,000 and 500,000.
   J. between 500,000 and 1,000,000.
   K. more than 1,000,000.

31. Graphed in the standard (x,y) coordinate plane below is a right triangle with vertices $(0,0)$, $(-40,0)$, and $(0,30)$. What is the length, in coordinate units, of the hypotenuse of the triangle?

   A. 30
   B. 35
   C. 40
   D. 50
   E. 70

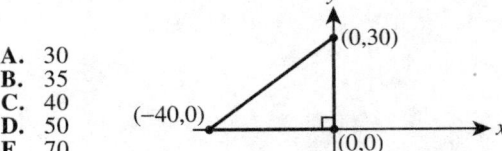

32. Every graph in one of the following categories has a vertical line of symmetry regardless of how it is oriented in the standard (x,y) coordinate plane. Which one?

   F. Circles
   G. Squares
   H. Ellipses
   J. Triangles
   K. Rectangles

GO ON TO THE NEXT PAGE.

Taking Additional Practice Tests

2 △ △ △ △ △ △ △ △ △ 2

33. In the standard (x,y) coordinate plane, the graph of $y = 30(x + 17)^2 - 42$ is a parabola. What are the coordinates of the vertex of the parabola?

    A. $(-30, -42)$
    B. $(-17, -42)$
    C. $(\ 17, -42)$
    D. $(\ 17,\ 42)$
    E. $(\ 30,\ 42)$

DO YOUR FIGURING HERE.

34. One side of square $ABCD$ has a length of 15 meters. A certain rectangle whose area is equal to the area of $ABCD$ has a width of 10 meters. What is the length, in meters, of the rectangle?

    F. 15
    G. 20
    H. 22.5
    J. 25
    K. 37.5

35. The average weight of 10 boys is 77.0 pounds. If the youngest boy is excluded, the average weight of the 9 remaining boys is 78.0 pounds. What is the weight, in pounds, of the youngest boy?

    A. 62
    B. 68
    C. 70
    D. 78
    E. 87

36. The total amount of a certain substance present in a laboratory experiment is given by the formula $A = A_0\left(2^{\frac{h}{5}}\right)$, where A is the total amount of the substance h hours after an initial amount (A_0) of the substance began accumulating. Which of the following expressions gives the number of hours it will take an initial amount of 10 grams of this substance to accumulate to 100 grams?

    F.   5
    G. 25
    H. $\log_2(50)$
    J. $5\log_2(10)$
    K. $5\log_{20}(100)$

GO ON TO THE NEXT PAGE.

2 △ △ △ △ △ △ △ △ △ **2**

37. For all values of x greater than 3, which of the following
    expressions is equivalent to $\dfrac{x^2 - x - 6}{x^2 - 9}$?

    A. $\dfrac{-x - 6}{-9}$

    B. $\dfrac{x - 2}{x - 3}$

    C. $\dfrac{x - 2}{x + 3}$

    D. $\dfrac{x + 2}{x - 3}$

    E. $\dfrac{x + 2}{x + 3}$

DO YOUR FIGURING HERE.

38. Shown below, a board 9 feet 4 inches long is cut into
    2 equal parts. What is the length, to the nearest inch, of
    each part?

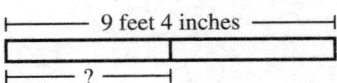

    F. 4 feet 5 inches
    G. 4 feet 7 inches
    H. 4 feet 8 inches
    J. 5 feet 4 inches
    K. 5 feet 5 inches

39. If the positive integers x and y are relatively prime (their
    greatest common factor is 1) and $\dfrac{1}{2} + \dfrac{1}{3} \cdot \dfrac{1}{4} \div \dfrac{1}{5} = \dfrac{x}{y}$,
    then $x + y = $?

    A. 23
    B. 25
    C. 49
    D. 91
    E. 132

40. What is the 358th digit after the decimal point in the
    repeating decimal $0.\overline{3178}$?

    F. 0
    G. 3
    H. 1
    J. 7
    K. 8

41. To promote a new brand of shoes, a shoe store will run
    a promotion using a jar containing 3 red balls marked
    "10% off," 2 white balls marked "30% off," and
    1 green ball marked "60% off." Each customer will
    randomly select 1 ball from the jar to determine the
    discount that the customer will receive on any single
    pair of the new brand of shoes. Given that the new
    brand of shoes regularly costs $60 per pair, what is the
    average discount amount, in dollars, that the store can
    expect to give each customer due to this promotion?

    A. $ 6
    B. $10
    C. $15
    D. $20
    E. $25

GO ON TO THE NEXT PAGE.

Taking Additional Practice Tests

2   **2**

> Use the following information to answer questions 42–44.

DO YOUR FIGURING HERE.

A 500-square-mile national park in Kenya has large and small protected animals. The number of *large* protected animals at the beginning of 2014 is given in the table below.

Large animal	Number
Elephant	600
Rhinoceros	100
Lion	200
Leopard	300
Zebra	400
Giraffe	800
Total	2,400

At the beginning of 2014, the number of *all* protected animals in the park was 10,000. Zoologists predict that for each year from 2015 to 2019, the total number of protected animals in the park at the beginning of the year will be 2% more than the number of protected animals in the park at the beginning of the previous year.

42. At the beginning of 2014, the number of lions in the park was p percent of the total number of *large* animals. Which of the following is closest to the value of p ?

F.　2
G.　8
H.　9
J.　11
K.　12

43. In this park, the average number of gallons of water consumed per day by each elephant, lion, and giraffe is 50, 5, and 10, respectively. Which of the following matrix products yields the average total number of gallons of water consumed per day by all the elephants, lions, and giraffes in the park?

A.　$\begin{bmatrix} 600 & 200 & 800 \end{bmatrix} \begin{bmatrix} 50 \\ 5 \\ 10 \end{bmatrix}$

B.　$\begin{bmatrix} 600 & 800 & 200 \end{bmatrix} \begin{bmatrix} 50 \\ 5 \\ 10 \end{bmatrix}$

C.　$\begin{bmatrix} 600 \\ 200 \\ 800 \end{bmatrix} \begin{bmatrix} 50 & 5 & 10 \end{bmatrix}$

D.　$\begin{bmatrix} 600 \\ 800 \\ 200 \end{bmatrix} \begin{bmatrix} 50 & 5 & 10 \end{bmatrix}$

E.　$\begin{bmatrix} 600 \\ 800 \\ 200 \end{bmatrix} \begin{bmatrix} 50 \\ 5 \\ 10 \end{bmatrix}$

GO ON TO THE NEXT PAGE.

2 △ △ △ △ △ △ △ △ △ **2**

44. Let t be a positive integer less than 6. Based on the zoologists' prediction, which of the following expressions represents the number of protected animals in the park t years after the beginning of 2014 ?

F. $10,000 + 0.02t$

G. $10,000 + 0.2t$

H. $10,000(1 + 0.02^t)$

J. $10,000(1 + 0.02)^t$

K. $10,000(1 + 0.2)^t$

DO YOUR FIGURING HERE.

45. Anela and Jacob plan to attend a concert in Brady. Anela will drive 375 km to Brady at a constant speed of 75 km/hr, stopping one time for a 30-minute break. Jacob will start 600 km from Brady and will drive at a constant speed of 90 km/hr for 2 hours. He will take a 1-hour break and then drive to Brady at a constant speed of 70 km/hr. To the nearest 0.1 hour, Jacob must leave how much earlier than Anela in order for them to arrive in Brady at the same time?

A. 2.2
B. 2.5
C. 3.1
D. 3.5
E. 4.0

46. Which of the following is equal to $\frac{3x + 5}{2x} - \frac{7x - 3}{2x}$, for all $x \neq 0$?

F. $-4x + 8$

G. $-4x + 2$

H. $-2x + 1$

J. $\frac{-2x + 4}{x}$

K. 2

47. A rectangular stage is 90 feet long and 30 feet wide. What is the area, in square *yards*, of this stage?

A. $30\sqrt{3}$
B. 300
C. 675
D. 900
E. 2,700

GO ON TO THE NEXT PAGE.

2       **2**

48. A rectangle, with its vertex coordinates labeled, is graphed in the standard (x,y) coordinate plane below. A *lattice point* is a point with coordinates that are both integers. A lattice point inside but NOT on the rectangle will be chosen at random. What is the probability that the sum of the x-coordinate and the y-coordinate of the chosen lattice point will be odd?

DO YOUR FIGURING HERE.

F. $\dfrac{1}{5}$

G. $\dfrac{2}{5}$

H. $\dfrac{7}{15}$

J. $\dfrac{17}{35}$

K. $\dfrac{1}{2}$

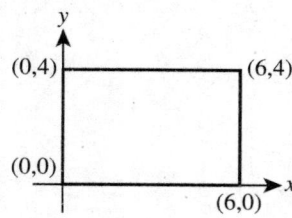

49. The nth term of an arithmetic progression is given by the formula $a_n = a_1 + (n-1)d$, where d is the common difference and a_1 is the first term. If the third term of an arithmetic progression is $\dfrac{5}{2}$ and the sixth term is $\dfrac{1}{4}$, what is the seventh term?

A. $-\dfrac{1}{2}$

B. 0

C. $\dfrac{1}{2}$

D. $\dfrac{3}{4}$

E. 1

50. The probability of Jamie being chosen to bat first in the lineup for his baseball team is $\dfrac{1}{9}$. What are the odds in favor of Jamie being chosen to bat first?

(Note: The *odds* in favor of an event are defined as the ratio of the probability that the event will happen to the probability that the event will NOT happen.)

F. $\dfrac{1}{8}$

G. $\dfrac{1}{9}$

H. $\dfrac{1}{10}$

J. $\dfrac{8}{1}$

K. $\dfrac{9}{1}$

GO ON TO THE NEXT PAGE.

2 △ △ △ △ △ △ △ △ △ **2**

51. A 120-liter solution that is 5% salt is mixed with an 80-liter solution that is 15% salt. The combined solution is what percent salt?

   A. 8%
   B. 9%
   C. 10%
   D. 11%
   E. 12%

52. A 50-foot-long rectangular swimming pool with vertical sides is 3 feet deep at the shallow end and 10 feet deep at the deep end. The bottom of the pool slopes downward at a constant angle from horizontal along the length of the pool. Which of the following expressions gives this constant angle?

(Note: For $-\frac{\pi}{2} < x < \frac{\pi}{2}$, $y = \tan x$ if and only if $x = \tan^{-1} y$.)

   F. $\tan^{-1}\left(\frac{7}{50}\right)$

   G. $\tan^{-1}\left(\frac{13}{50}\right)$

   H. $\tan^{-1}\left(\frac{7}{10}\right)$

   J. $\tan^{-1}\left(\frac{50}{13}\right)$

   K. $\tan^{-1}\left(\frac{50}{7}\right)$

53. A hyperbola that has vertices (1,2) and (3,2) and that passes through the origin is shown below in the standard (x,y) coordinate plane. The hyperbola has which of the following equations?

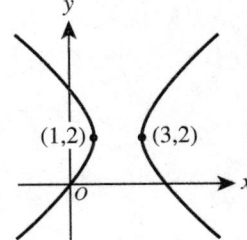

   A. $\dfrac{(x-2)^2}{1} - \dfrac{3(y-2)^2}{4} = 1$

   B. $\dfrac{(x-2)^2}{1} - \dfrac{4(y-2)^2}{3} = 1$

   C. $\dfrac{(x+2)^2}{1} - \dfrac{3(y+2)^2}{4} = 1$

   D. $\dfrac{(x-2)^2}{1} + \dfrac{3(y-2)^2}{4} = 1$

   E. $\dfrac{(x+2)^2}{1} + \dfrac{4(y+2)^2}{3} = 1$

GO ON TO THE NEXT PAGE.

2 △ △ △ △ △ △ △ △ △ **2**

54. As shown below, Alli walked her dog 250 feet due east from the entrance of a dog park to a trash can and then walked 700 feet in a straight line 25° north of east to a bench. Which of the following expressions is equal to the distance, in feet, between the entrance and the bench?

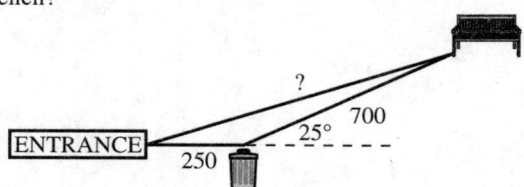

F. $\dfrac{950}{\cos 25°}$

G. $\dfrac{250}{\cos 25°} + 700$

H. $\dfrac{250}{\sin 155°} + 700$

J. $\sqrt{700^2 + 250^2 - 2(700)(250)\cos 25°}$

K. $\sqrt{700^2 + 250^2 - 2(700)(250)\cos 155°}$

55. For real numbers a, b, and c such that $a > b > c$ and $b > 0$, which of the statements below is(are) *always* true?

  I. $|a| > |b|$
  II. $|a| > |c|$
  III. $|b| > |c|$

A. I only
B. II only
C. I and II only
D. II and III only
E. I, II, and III

56. Kenji and Mary are members of a school committee that will be meeting this afternoon. The 6 members of the committee will be seated randomly around a circular table. What is the probability that Kenji and Mary will NOT sit next to each other at the meeting?

F. $\dfrac{1}{5}$

G. $\dfrac{1}{3}$

H. $\dfrac{2}{5}$

J. $\dfrac{3}{5}$

K. $\dfrac{4}{5}$

57. The digit in the ones place of 2^{88} is 6. What is the digit in the ones place of 2^{90} ?

A. 0
B. 2
C. 4
D. 6
E. 8

GO ON TO THE NEXT PAGE.

2 △ △ △ △ △ △ △ △ △ **2**

58. Which of the following expressions represents the area, in square coordinate units, of △RST shown in the standard (x,y) coordinate plane below?

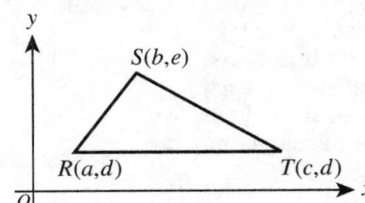

DO YOUR FIGURING HERE.

F. $\frac{1}{2}(c-a)(e-d)$

G. $\frac{1}{2}c(e-b)$

H. $\frac{1}{2}e(c-a)$

J. $\frac{1}{2}((e-d)^2+(b-a)^2)((e-d)^2+(b-c)^2)$

K. $\frac{1}{2}\left(\sqrt{(e-d)^2+(b-a)^2}\right)\left(\sqrt{(e-d)^2+(b-c)^2}\right)$

59. In the complex numbers, where $i^2=-1$, what complex number x is a solution to the equation $x(2+3i)=1$?

A. $\frac{2}{13}-\frac{3}{13}i$

B. $\frac{2}{5}+\frac{3}{5}i$

C. 1

D. -1

E. $-\frac{i}{13}$

60. The rectangular container shown below has a small compartment for water created by a rectangular dividing wall of negligible width. One face of the dividing wall, shown shaded, has an area of 39 square inches. What is the volume, in cubic inches, of the larger compartment?

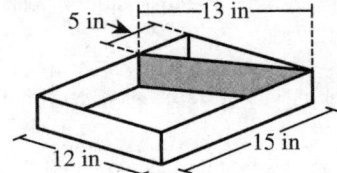

F. 180
G. 195
H. 390
J. 450
K. 540

END OF TEST 2

STOP! DO NOT TURN THE PAGE UNTIL TOLD TO DO SO.

DO NOT RETURN TO THE PREVIOUS TEST.

3 ████████████████████████████████ **3**

READING TEST

35 Minutes—40 Questions

DIRECTIONS: There are several passages in this test. Each passage is accompanied by several questions. After reading a passage, choose the best answer to each question and fill in the corresponding oval on your answer document. You may refer to the passages as often as necessary.

Passage I

LITERARY NARRATIVE: This passage is adapted from the novel *Love Marriage* by V. V. Ganeshananthan (©2008 by Vasugi Ganeshananthan).

He met her, my mother, in New York City, and the Heart said plaintively: *Thump thump thump.* That was not the sound of illness. Theirs was an auspicious meeting, although no one had troubled to check the align-
5 ment of the stars; the young woman was twenty-seven—old for a prospective bride?—but she did not look it. She had a generous face, he said to himself.

He liked her glossy sheaf of dark hair, her sparse
10 brows, her pronounced chin, her full lower lip. She smiled with her mouth closed because she did not like her teeth. He could already see within the structure of her face how she would become thinner, that her bones would give her older face a certain elegance, a chiseled
15 and austere severity. He liked her precision in even the smallest of tasks, like arranging hibiscus in a vase. Her reserve, her inability to say anything truly personal in public. He thought she might be full of secrets and wanted to know them. She never raised her voice, but
20 she did not speak softly. *How are you? That's a beautiful sari. How are the children? I like this rice.* She liked her food steaming and spicy, as he did. She made her own clothes, staying up late into the night, her foot on the pedal of a sewing machine that had belonged to her
25 mother and had crossed the ocean with her. Her hemlines suited both the times and her young pale slimness, which reminded him of a flowering tree by his home in Jaffna. He never caught her admitting she was wrong; her words clambered around that impossibility, but so
30 sheepishly that he found it endearing. In a noisy room he learned to tell the clear bell sound of her bangles apart from the rest.

Suddenly, he was no longer thinking about widows or about repeating his own father's collapse. It was as
35 though an invisible conductor was directing the pulling of strings to draw them together. Whether it was Murali who managed to get introduced to Vani or the other way around, no one else really remembers. And they will never admit which one of them was responsible. And
40 yet, it was this simple: a friend of his noticed that they were staying near each other. Perhaps Murali could give

Vani a ride home? Yes, yes, two heads nodded. They left the party they were at too quickly to say all their good-byes. After the door closed behind them the space
45 where they had been was filled with the laughter of friends.

He took her home. She boarded with a family in Brooklyn. During the car ride they were silent. It was a strange and comfortable silence for two people who had
50 waited for so long to be alone. The thrum of the motor was loud because the car was old. When they turned around the corner he pulled over and turned the engine off and there was a quiet as loud as the motor had been. He walked her to her door and she thanked him. She did
55 not ask him in for a cup of coffee; it was not her house. But it was out of his way and both of them knew it. She forgot that she did not like her teeth and bared them at him. Her smile, for once, was not self-conscious. She watched him drive away, waving from the window.

60 The Sri Lankan elders of New York City were all too eager to play parents to the couple. She was Proper: smart and polite and a good cook and lovely. Vani had a job, and more important than any of these things, she had grace, which was something that could not be
65 taught. Murali, of course, was the Beloved Parentless Boy; their favorite bachelor-doctor whom they took into their homes and bosoms and tried to smother with welcome and curry. Occasions were arranged; even the very rooms seemed to conspire to make the two end up
70 next to each other. And then one day something was suggested by one of those elders. And somehow the pair of them were *talking* about it. To each other. Directly.

Which was a faux pas. But neither of them
75 minded.

Oceans away, families exploded. True to form, his family's discord faded quickly. But her family almost did not consent: afraid of the Improper, they questioned his intentions, his failure to observe certain formalities,
80 his ancestry, his habits and his character. He heard about what they had said and turned to her, his eyes full of questions.

They may not know these things about you, she said, but I do.

GO ON TO THE NEXT PAGE.

3 ░░░░░░░░░░░░░░░░░░░░░░░░░░░░ **3**

85   Are you sure? he asked her. The unsaid: they may not forgive you for this.

    Positive, she answered. Countries away, Vani's brother crashed into Murali's brother's house, yelling: *Who* is this doctor who wants to marry my *sister? Who*
90 is this doctor who is *in love with my sister?*

    The nerve of Murali, they thought. In Love? These were not words they were used to saying.

1. The third paragraph (lines 33–46) marks a shift from the second paragraph's focus on Murali's impressions of Vani to the rest of the passage's focus on:

  A. Murali's life as a married man.
  B. Murali's concerns about marriage.
  C. Murali and Vani's courtship and its effects on others.
  D. Murali's characteristics and his family conflicts.

2. Details in the second paragraph (lines 9–32) primarily characterize Vani as:

  F. reserved but self-assured.
  G. severe and impolite.
  H. intelligent and apologetic.
  J. beautiful but unkempt.

3. Which of the following events mentioned in the passage occurred first chronologically?

  A. The elders organized occasions in which Vani and Murali would be together.
  B. A friend suggested that Murali drive Vani home.
  C. Vani smiled at Murali without thinking about her teeth.
  D. Vani's brother burst into Murali's brother's home.

4. As it is presented in the passage, the italicized portion "*How are you? That's a beautiful sari. How are the children? I like this rice*" (lines 20–21) most likely indicates:

  F. the types of pleasantries that Murali would prepare in his head before meeting someone new.
  G. parts of a conversation between Murali and Vani when they were first introduced.
  H. comments typical of the kind that Vani would make when in public.
  J. secret thoughts that Murali imagined Vani to be thinking.

5. According to the passage, one similarity between Murali and Vani is that both:

  A. enjoyed eating spicy food.
  B. were born in New York City.
  C. had a passion for cooking.
  D. worked at a medical clinic.

6. In the context of the passage, the statement "And they will never admit which one of them was responsible" (lines 38–39) most strongly suggests that:

  F. neither Murali nor Vani remembers who first sought to be introduced to the other.
  G. each of Murali and Vani's friends claims to have been the one who introduced the two of them.
  H. Murali initiated contact with Vani, though he would stubbornly deny that he did so.
  J. both Murali and Vani refuse to confess to initiating their introduction to each other.

7. In the passage, the narrator makes clear that Vani didn't ask Murali in for coffee because Vani:

  A. felt extremely self-conscious in Murali's presence.
  B. did not want to invite Murali into someone else's house.
  C. assumed that Murali wanted to get home at a reasonable hour.
  D. did not want to further burden Murali with her requests.

8. The passage indicates that the description of Vani in lines 61–65 most closely reflects the perspective of:

  F. Murali.
  G. Vani's family in Sri Lanka.
  H. Murali's friends in New York City.
  J. the Sri Lankan elders in New York City.

9. It can reasonably be inferred from the passage that, by traditional standards, the Sri Lankan community would have considered Murali and Vani's direct discussion of marriage to be:

  A. proper.
  B. sensible.
  C. superficial.
  D. unconventional.

10. As it is used in line 79, the word *observe* most nearly means:

  F. study.
  G. follow.
  H. express.
  J. perceive.

Taking Additional Practice Tests

GO ON TO THE NEXT PAGE.

3   3

Passage II

SOCIAL SCIENCE: Passage A is adapted from the article "Our Vanishing Night" by Verlyn Klinkenborg (©2008 by National Geographic Society, Inc.). Passage B is adapted from the book *The End of Night: Searching for Natural Darkness in an Age of Artificial Light* by Paul Bogard (©2013 by Paul Bogard).

Passage A by Verlyn Klinkenborg

For most of human history, the phrase "light pollu-tion" would have made no sense. Imagine walking toward London on a moonlit night around 1800, when it was Earth's most populous city. Nearly a million people
5 lived there, making do, as they always had, with can-dles and rushlights and torches and lanterns. Only a few houses were lit by gas, and there would be no public gaslights in the streets or squares for another seven years. From a few miles away, you would have been as
10 likely to *smell* London as to see its dim collective glow.

Now most of humanity lives under intersecting domes of reflected, refracted light, of scattering rays from overlit cities and suburbs, from light-flooded highways and factories. Nearly all of nighttime Europe
15 is a nebula of light, as is most of the United States and all of Japan. In the south Atlantic the glow from a single fishing fleet—squid fishermen luring their prey with metal halide lamps—can be seen from space, burn-ing brighter, in fact, than Buenos Aires or Rio de
20 Janeiro.

In most cities the sky looks as though it has been emptied of stars, leaving behind a vacant haze that mir-rors our fear of the dark. We've grown so used to this pervasive orange haze that the original glory of an unlit
25 night—dark enough for the planet Venus to throw shad-ows on Earth—is wholly beyond our experience. And yet above the city's pale ceiling lies the rest of the uni-verse, utterly undiminished by the light we waste—a bright shoal of stars and planets and galaxies, shining in
30 seemingly infinite darkness.

We've lit up the night as if it were an unoccupied country, when nothing could be further from the truth. Among mammals alone, the number of nocturnal species is astonishing. Light is a powerful biological
35 force, and on many species it acts as a magnet, a process being studied by researchers such as Travis Longcore and Catherine Rich. The effect is so powerful that scientists speak of songbirds and seabirds being "captured" by searchlights on land or by the light from
40 gas flares on marine oil platforms, circling and circling in the thousands.

Passage B by Paul Bogard

Unless Vincent Van Gogh's *The Starry Night* from 1889 is traveling as part of an exhibition, it hangs at home on its wall at the Museum of Modern Art
45 (MoMA) in Manhattan as fifty million people pass by every year. On a Saturday morning I stand near Van Gogh's scene of stars and moon and sleeping town, talking with its guardian for the day, Joseph, as he

repeats, "No flash, no flash," "Two feet away," and
50 "Too close, too close" again and again as people from around the world crowd near. "What's the appeal of this painting?" I ask. "It's beautiful," he says. "What more can you say than that?"

You could rightly leave it at that. But I love the
55 story this painting tells, of a small dark town, a few yellow-orange gaslights in house windows, under a giant swirling and waving blue-green sky. This is a painting of our world from before night had been pushed back to the forest and the seas, from back when
60 sleepy towns slept without streetlights. People are too quick, I think, to imagine the story of this painting—and especially this sky—is simply that of "a werewolf of energy," as Joachim Pissarro, curator at the MoMA exhibition Van Gogh and the Colors of the Night, would
65 tell me. While Van Gogh certainly had his troubles, this painting looks as it does in part because it's of a time that no longer exists, a time when the night sky would have looked a lot more like this. Does Van Gogh use his imagination? Of course, but this is an imagined sky
70 inspired by a real sky of a kind few of the fifty million MoMA visitors have ever seen. It's an imagined sky inspired by the real sky over a town much darker than the towns we live in today. So a painting of a night imagined? Sure. But unreal?

75 In our age, yes. But Van Gogh lived in a time before electric light. In a letter from the summer of 1888, he described what he'd seen while walking a southern French beach:

The deep blue sky was flecked with clouds of a
80 blue deeper than the fundamental blue of intense cobalt, and others of a clearer blue, like the blue whiteness of the Milky Way. In the blue depth the stars were sparkling, greenish, yellow, white, pink, more brilliant, more
85 sparkling gemlike than at home—even in Paris: opals you might call them, emeralds, lapis lazuli, rubies, sapphires.

It's remarkable to modern eyes, first of all, that Van Gogh would reference the stars over Paris—no one
90 has seen a sky remotely close to this over Paris for at least fifty years. But stars of different colors? It's true.

Questions 11–13 ask about Passage A.

---

11. The main idea of the first paragraph of Passage A is that:

A. before electricity, it was difficult to travel to London at night.
B. gas lighting existed long before it was widely used.
C. light pollution is a relatively recent phenomenon in human history.
D. because of its large population, London has had light pollution for centuries.

GO ON TO THE NEXT PAGE.

3 3

12. In the third paragraph of Passage A (lines 21–30), the author makes a contrast between the:
   F. hazy night sky over cities today and the bright stars and planets that exist above it.
   G. gray night sky over cities and the various colors of the stars.
   H. brightness of the planet Venus on an unlit night and the comparative dimness of the stars.
   J. appreciation that people once had for stars and the apathy that is pervasive today.

13. It can reasonably be inferred from Passage A that an animal "captured" by light is most nearly one that:
   A. has lost the ability to search for food in dark areas.
   B. is irresistibly drawn to artificial light at night.
   C. is confined to limited dark areas at night.
   D. has lost its natural habitat to urban expansion.

Questions 14–17 ask about Passage B.

14. Compared to what Joseph appreciates about *The Starry Night*, the author of Passage B is more appreciative of the:
   F. painting's vivid colors.
   G. beauty of the painting.
   H. story the painting tells.
   J. technique used in the painting.

15. The main purpose of the first paragraph of Passage B (lines 42–53) is to introduce the passage by:
   A. describing *The Starry Night* and providing an idea of the painting's popularity.
   B. conveying the passage author's excitement when he first saw *The Starry Night*.
   C. showing examples of people's expectations about *The Starry Night* and their reactions to it.
   D. establishing when and why Van Gogh painted *The Starry Night*.

16. Based on Passage B, which of the following statements best summarizes the passage author's point about Van Gogh's use of imagination while painting *The Starry Night* ?
   F. Van Gogh had to rely heavily on his imagination because he usually painted during the daytime.
   G. Van Gogh's work is almost entirely imagined because the painting's stars have colors that are unlike actual stars.
   H. Van Gogh used his imagination in part, but his painting was also inspired by the real night sky he observed.
   J. Van Gogh barely used his imagination at all; he tried to depict the vivid night sky exactly as it was.

17. As it is used in line 90, the phrase *remotely close to* most nearly means:
   A. exactly similar to.
   B. anything like.
   C. anywhere nearby.
   D. somewhat adjacent to.

Questions 18–20 ask about both passages.

18. Which of the following statements best captures the main difference in the information presented in the two passages?
   F. Passage A summarizes the process by which light at night became common, whereas Passage B explores one person's reaction to Van Gogh's *The Starry Night*.
   G. Passage A offers suggestions for restoring darkness to today's night, whereas Passage B compares the night skies of several Van Gogh paintings.
   H. Passage A discusses the problems of today's bright night sky, whereas Passage B explains how people in Van Gogh's time used light at night.
   J. Passage A gives an overview of the issue of light at night, whereas Passage B examines the matter of light at night through a discussion of Van Gogh's *The Starry Night*.

19. One similarity between the passages is that, in order to make a point about light at night, both authors discuss:
   A. how dark large cities once were.
   B. the opinions of scientific researchers.
   C. well-known works of art.
   D. personal memories of when night was darker.

20. Compared to Passage B, Passage A offers more information about the:
   F. effects lighting up the night sky can have on animals.
   G. colorful appearance stars had prior to electric lights.
   H. interaction between nature and the imagination.
   J. places where night's original darkness remains.

GO ON TO THE NEXT PAGE.

3 ▬▬▬▬▬▬▬▬▬▬▬▬▬▬▬▬▬▬▬▬ **3**

Passage III

HUMANITIES: This passage is adapted from the essay "On Places, Photographs, and Memory" by Chris Engman (©2012 by Chris Engman).

Recently I visited a place that I knew intimately in childhood, a waterfall with cliffs on both sides and a pool of cold water below. We used to jump from those cliffs despite our parents' concerns. I loved this place,
5 and revisiting it I am amazed by all that I can remember. Bends in trails, sap stains on bark, crooks in branches, the intricate web of root structures, the shape of trees—all are startlingly unchanged and I remember them precisely. A small tree is in the middle of the trail.
10 I put my hand on it for support and drops of moisture fall on my back from above, and I realize: I have done this before. I remember the sensation precisely, the sound of rustling leaves above, the freshness of the smell, the temperature of the droplets, the mixture of
15 apprehension and pleasure. Standing on a rock ledge getting ready to jump, I reach for a handhold so I can lean over the edge and prepare myself for what I am about to do. The shape of the rock where my hand touches it is known to me: I have performed this ritual.

20 Places hold memories better than people and better than photographs. Family, or people from our past who may remind us of events in our lives and with whom we may reminisce, are themselves constantly changing, as is their version of events. Conversations with others
25 about shared experiences of the past can seem to augment memory but quite often, more often than we probably realize, they operate in the opposite way: they alter or even replace our own memories with those of another. Whatever the event, one's memory of it is
30 inevitably altered through conversation; recalling the same event at a later date, it becomes difficult or impossible to distinguish an original memory from the altered version that emerged.

Photographs act on us in a similar fashion. What-
35 ever their apparent precision or correctness, photographs inaccurately reflect experience from the start. They convert the three dimensions of space into two and eliminate the third spatial dimension and time. Also sacrificed are smell, touch, sound, and context. In a
40 word, a photograph is an abstraction of experience. Yet we take them compulsively. We fill scrapbooks and hard drives with family outings, vacations, ballgames— Scotty in front of Niagara Falls, Dad and Grandma smiling in front of the famous restaurant—in the hope
45 of freezing time, making experience tangible for future reference, preserving memory. I do it, too. But it is well to realize that photographs do not preserve memory, they replace memory. Just as photographs are an abstraction of experience, they are even more so an
50 abstraction of memory—a dangerously compelling abstraction. Memories are fragile and impressionable. They cannot hold up against the seemingly irrefutable factuality of a photograph. It isn't that what is in a photograph is false: a photograph's version of events did
55 happen, what is in a picture did indeed pass before the

lens. The problem is that photographs only tell such a small part of any story. And while they may be technically correct, nonetheless they deceive. Does a smile in a photograph mean that a person is happy? Or does it
60 mean that a photographer prodded, "look up and smile"? Was the fish I caught really bigger than my uncle's, or did I cleverly, intentionally hold mine closer to the lens? Photographs deceive in another respect. Whatever the event one wishes to preserve, snapshots
65 are most commonly a break from that event. The moment that a photograph is taken is experienced as a moment taking a photograph, not as a moment engaged in the activity implied by the resulting image. Time taken to make photographs is time subtracted from the
70 experience of the thing being photographed. What photographs most accurately record, ultimately, is nothing more than the act of photography, itself.

To be sure, photographs can form a record of our lives that has value, and I cherish my old snapshots as
75 much as the next person. But as image-makers and consumers, which all of us are these days, there is also value to be had in a recognition of the limits of photography to the facility of memory—in an understanding of what images can and cannot offer us in this regard.
80 Moreover it is precisely the deceitfulness of photography as it pertains to memory that gives the medium its unique platform to address the nature of memory itself: its malleability, its unreliability, its elusiveness. It seems to me that no conversation or photograph can
85 make memory so vivid or recognizable, so physically palpable, as the return to a place.

21. The passage as a whole can best be described as:
   A. a summary of a childhood incident followed by reflections on how the memory of that incident has changed.
   B. a description of an experience followed by consideration of a topic raised by that experience.
   C. an account of the author's lifelong interest in a hobby.
   D. an explanation of why the author's opinions on a topic have changed.

22. Which of the following statements best represents the passage's central claim?
   F. The accuracy of most memories is improved by viewing photographs related to the memories.
   G. Revisiting a place evokes clearer and more accurate memories than conversations or photographs.
   H. The truth represented by a photograph is only as accurate as your memory of the event in the photograph.
   J. Memories are sustained over time only through a combination of conversations, photographs, and visits to places.

GO ON TO THE NEXT PAGE.

3

3

23. The author's tone when recounting his visit to the waterfall can best be described as:

A. joking.
B. gloomy.
C. pleading.
D. reverent.

24. The main idea of the second paragraph (lines 20–33) is that:

F. over time, some memories fade.
G. frequently, reminiscing with other people changes one's memories.
H. reminiscing with other people helps preserve one's memories.
J. family members better evoke one's memories than nonfamily members.

25. When the author states "What photographs most accurately record, ultimately, is nothing more than the act of photography, itself" (lines 70–72), he most nearly means that:

A. the quality of a photograph reflects the skill of the photographer.
B. when viewing a photograph, people forget that the photographer is an unseen participant in the scene.
C. photographs by nature are records of brief moments.
D. photographs tend to depict people stopping an activity and posing for the photographer.

26. It can most reasonably be inferred that immediately after the events described in the first paragraph, the author:

F. hikes back down the cliffs.
G. sits on the rock ledge.
H. jumps into the water below.
J. takes a photograph of the scene.

27. Which of the following details does the author use to support his claim that photographs don't accurately reflect experiences?

A. Photographs are usually only taken by adults.
B. People take photographs without considering the best way to photograph an event.
C. Photographs don't record the passage of time.
D. The human eye can discern more detail than a photograph can capture.

28. The information between the dashes in lines 43–44 primarily serves to:

F. highlight the difference between trivial pictures and meaningful pictures.
G. exemplify the kind of commonplace pictures that people take.
H. point out the usefulness of photographs in capturing moments in our lives.
J. list events from the author's life that he wishes he had pictures of.

29. The phrase "seemingly irrefutable factuality" (lines 52–53) mainly serves to emphasize that photographs:

A. convey an impression of objective truth.
B. help clarify the events being photographed.
C. record details that can't be proven.
D. imply a story beyond what they actually depict.

30. As it is used in line 82, the word *nature* most nearly means:

F. temperament.
G. essence.
H. scenery.
J. environment.

GO ON TO THE NEXT PAGE.

3   3

Passage IV

NATURAL SCIENCE: This passage is adapted from the article "Reinventing the Leaf" by Antonio Regalado (©2010 by Scientific American, a division of Nature America, Inc.).

Nathan S. Lewis has been giving a lecture on the energy crisis that is both terrifying and exhilarating. To avoid potentially debilitating global warming, the chemist says civilization must be able to generate more
5 than 10 trillion watts of clean, carbon-free energy by 2050. That level is three times the U.S.'s average energy demand of 3.2 trillion watts.

Before Lewis's crowds get too depressed, he tells them there is one source of salvation: the sun pours
10 more energy onto the earth every hour than humankind uses in a year. But to be saved, humankind needs a radical breakthrough in solar-fuel technology: artificial leaves that will capture solar rays and churn out chemical fuel on the spot, much as plants do. We can burn the
15 fuel, as we do oil or natural gas, to power cars, create heat or generate electricity, and we can store the fuel for use when the sun is down.

Lewis's lab is one of several that are crafting prototype leaves, not much larger than computer chips,
20 designed to produce hydrogen fuel from water, rather than the glucose fuel that natural leaves create. Unlike fossil fuels, hydrogen burns clean. Other researchers are working on competing ideas for capturing the sun's energy, such as algae that has been genetically altered
25 to pump out biofuels, or on new biological organisms engineered to excrete oil. All these approaches are intended to turn sunlight into chemical energy that can be stored, shipped and easily consumed. Lewis argues, however, that the man-made leaf option is the most
30 likely to scale up to the industrial levels needed to power civilization.

Although a few lab prototypes have produced small amounts of direct solar fuel—or electrofuel, as the chemicals are sometimes called—the technology
35 has to be improved so the fuel can be manufactured on a massive scale, very inexpensively. To power the U.S., Lewis estimates the country would need to manufacture thin, flexible solar-fuel films, instead of discrete chip-like devices, that roll off high-speed production lines
40 the way newsprint does. The films would have to be as cheap as wall-to-wall carpeting and eventually cover an area the size of South Carolina.

Far from being a wild dream, direct solar-fuel technology has been advancing in fits and starts ever
45 since President Jimmy Carter's push for alternative energy sources during the 1970s oil shocks. Now, with a new energy and climate crunch looming, solar fuel is suddenly gaining attention.

In photosynthesis, green leaves use the energy in
50 sunlight to rearrange the chemical bonds of water and carbon dioxide, producing and storing fuel in the form

of sugars. "We want to make something as close to a leaf as possible," Lewis says, meaning devices that work as simply, albeit producing a different chemical
55 output. The artificial leaf Lewis is designing requires two principal elements: a collector that converts solar energy (photons) into electrical energy (electrons) and an electrolyzer that uses the electron energy to split water into oxygen and hydrogen. A catalyst—a chemi-
60 cal or metal—is added to help achieve the splitting. Existing photovoltaic cells already create electricity from sunlight, and electrolyzers are used in various commercial processes, so the trick is marrying the two into cheap, efficient solar films.

65 Bulky prototypes have been developed just to demonstrate how the marriage would work. Engineers at a Japanese automaker, for example, have built a box that stands taller than a refrigerator and is covered with photovoltaic cells. An electrolyzer, inside, uses the
70 solar electricity to break water molecules. The box releases the resulting oxygen to the ambient air and compresses and stores the remaining hydrogen, which the automaker would like to use to recharge fuel-cell cars.

75 In principle, the scheme could solve global warming: only sunlight and water are needed to create energy, the by-product is oxygen, and the exhaust from burning the hydrogen later in a fuel cell is water. The problem is that commercial solar cells contain expen-
80 sive silicon crystals. And electrolyzers are packed with platinum, to date the best material for catalyzing the water-splitting reaction, but it costs $1,500 an ounce.

Lewis calculates that to meet global energy demand, future solar-fuel devices would have to cost
85 less than $1 per square foot of sun-collecting surface and be able to convert 10 percent of that light energy into chemical fuel. Fundamentally new, massively scalable technology such as films or carpets made from inexpensive materials are needed.

31. The main function of the seventh and eighth paragraphs (lines 65–82) is to:
   A. suggest that solar technology has advanced but still faces problems that prevent it from being a viable power source on a large scale.
   B. introduce the information that under specific laboratory conditions electrolyzers can be used to release energy from water molecules.
   C. establish that the United States and Japan are collaborating on research on new energy sources.
   D. question whether the auto industry will be a leader in the race to develop new sources of energy.

GO ON TO THE NEXT PAGE.

3 ▬▬▬▬▬▬▬▬▬▬▬▬▬▬▬▬▬▬▬▬▬▬ **3**

32. Based on the passage, whose opinion is it that there is a need for "more than 10 trillion watts of clean, carbon-free energy by 2050" (lines 4–6)?

   F. Researchers in South Carolina who are developing a form of artificial algae
   G. An unidentified chemist whom Lewis challenges in his lectures
   H. Lewis as expressed in lectures he gives on the subject of world energy needs
   J. The author before attending a lecture by Lewis that changed the author's mind

33. Based on the passage, what is the relationship between the "radical breakthrough" referred to in line 12 and the capabilities described in lines 14–17?

   A. Both were made possible as a result of Lewis's work in his lab.
   B. Both serve as examples for Lewis of the energy industry's misguided focus on consumption.
   C. The breakthrough will make the capabilities possible.
   D. The breakthrough has been made based on the capabilities.

34. According to the passage, one challenge facing Lewis in developing his energy solution is the:

   F. high price of the silicon crystals and platinum that are integral to the process.
   G. lack of technology to split water into hydrogen and oxygen.
   H. diminishing availability of federal funding for his research.
   J. public's reluctance to embrace new technology.

35. According to Lewis, compared to the amount of energy the sun pours onto the earth in one hour, what amount of energy does humankind use in one year?

   A. A smaller amount
   B. The same amount
   C. Twice the amount
   D. Ten times the amount

36. According to the passage, what size are the prototype leaves being developed in Lewis's lab?

   F. About the size of a human hand
   G. About the size of a maple leaf
   H. Not much larger than a carpet square
   J. Not much larger than a computer chip

37. As it is used in line 25, the phrase *pump out* most nearly means:

   A. remove.
   B. drain.
   C. produce.
   D. siphon.

38. According to the passage, what physical form does Lewis imagine his artificial leaves will ideally take?

   F. Chiplike devices
   G. Thin, flexible films
   H. Rigid miniature solar panels
   J. Refrigerated photovoltaic cells

39. The passage states that the two principal elements of Lewis's artificial leaf technology are:

   A. a fuel cell and ambient air.
   B. solar electricity and a catalyst.
   C. platinum and silicon.
   D. a collector and an electrolyzer.

40. According to the passage, what is one outcome of the process of burning hydrogen in a fuel cell?

   F. The electron energy splits silicon crystals.
   G. The hydrogen bonds with oxygen.
   H. The fuel cell's lining deteriorates.
   J. The exhaust produced is water.

END OF TEST 3

STOP! DO NOT TURN THE PAGE UNTIL TOLD TO DO SO.

DO NOT RETURN TO A PREVIOUS TEST.

Taking Additional Practice Tests

SCIENCE TEST

35 Minutes—40 Questions

DIRECTIONS: There are several passages in this test. Each passage is followed by several questions. After reading a passage, choose the best answer to each question and fill in the corresponding oval on your answer document. You may refer to the passages as often as necessary.

You are NOT permitted to use a calculator on this test.

Passage I

The *molar volume* of a gas is the volume occupied by 1 mole (mol; 6×10^{23} atoms or molecules) of that gas at a given pressure and temperature.

Table 1 shows how the molar volume, in L, of each of 6 gases—helium (He), neon (Ne), argon (Ar), hydrogen (H_2), nitrogen (N_2), and oxygen (O_2)—varies with pressure, in atmospheres (atm), at a temperature of 273 kelvins (K).

Table 1						
Pressure (atm)	Molar volume (L) at 273 K of:					
	He	Ne	Ar	H_2	N_2	O_2
0.500	44.825	44.810	44.774	44.818	44.781	44.773
1.00	22.424	22.409	22.374	22.417	22.380	22.372
5.00	4.503	4.488	4.453	4.496	4.459	4.451
10.0	2.262	2.248	2.213	2.256	2.219	2.211
50.0	0.471	0.456	0.421	0.465	0.430	0.420
100.0	0.247	0.233	0.200	0.242	0.210	0.198

Table 2 shows how the molar volume of each of the 6 gases varies with temperature at a pressure of 1.00 atm.

Table 2						
Temperature (K)	Molar volume (L) at 1.00 atm of:					
	He	Ne	Ar	H_2	N_2	O_2
223	18.321	18.304	18.257	18.312	18.263	18.256
323	26.504	26.513	26.486	26.521	26.492	26.485
373	30.670	30.617	30.595	30.625	30.601	30.594
573	47.041	47.031	47.022	47.040	47.028	47.021
773	63.453	63.443	63.440	63.452	63.446	63.440

GO ON TO THE NEXT PAGE.

1. Based on Table 1, for H_2 at 273 K, the absolute value of the difference between the molar volume at 5.00 atm and the molar volume at 10.0 atm is approximately:

   A. 1.8 L.
   B. 2.2 L.
   C. 4.0 L.
   D. 5.0 L.

2. Consider the molar volumes of He, Ar, H_2, and N_2 listed in Table 2 at 323 K. What is the order of these gases from the gas having the smallest molar volume to the gas having the largest molar volume?

   F. Ar, He, N_2, H_2
   G. Ar, N_2, He, H_2
   H. H_2, He, N_2, Ar
   J. H_2, N_2, He, Ar

3. Based on Tables 1 and 2, at any given temperature and pressure, the molar volume of which other gas is most similar to the molar volume of O_2 ?

   A. He
   B. Ar
   C. H_2
   D. N_2

4. An *ideal gas* has a molar volume of 63.429 L at 1.00 atm and 773 K. At 1.00 atm and 773 K, how many of the gases listed in Table 2 have a *smaller* molar volume than that of an ideal gas?

   F. 0
   G. 2
   H. 4
   J. 6

5. In a gas sample, collisions between gas particles are common. The average time a gas particle spends between one collision and the next is called the *mean free time*. In general, mean free time decreases as a sample's volume decreases. Based on Table 1, the mean free time would be *least* for a 1 mol sample of which gas at which pressure?

   A. He at 0.500 atm
   B. O_2 at 0.500 atm
   C. He at 100.0 atm
   D. O_2 at 100.0 atm

6. Consider 2 separate 1 mol samples of O_2, each at a pressure of 1 atm. One sample has a volume of about 18 L, and the other has a volume of about 63 L. Based on Table 2, the average kinetic energy of the O_2 molecules is more likely greater in which sample?

   F. The 18 L sample, because it's at the lower temperature.
   G. The 18 L sample, because it's at the higher temperature.
   H. The 63 L sample, because it's at the lower temperature.
   J. The 63 L sample, because it's at the higher temperature.

GO ON TO THE NEXT PAGE.

4 ◯ ◯ ◯ ◯ ◯ ◯ ◯ ◯ **4**

Passage II

Scientists conducted 3 experiments to study the transfer of bacteria from one surface to another by 2 species of flies: *Musca domestica* and *Sarcophaga carnaria*.

Experiment 1

A group of 10 *M. domestica* was tested using this procedure:

1. Each fly was placed in a separate enclosure containing *Escherichia coli* (a type of bacteria) and allowed to walk on the *E. coli* for 5 min.

2. Each fly was then immediately placed in a separate petri dish containing sterile nutrient agar. Five minutes later, the flies were removed from the dishes.

3. The dishes were incubated at 37°C for 24 hr so that each *E. coli* cell on the dish divided to form a separate colony, and then the number of *E. coli* colonies on each dish was counted.

4. The average number of colonies per dish was calculated.

This procedure was also used to test a group of 10 *S. carnaria*. The results are shown in Figure 1.

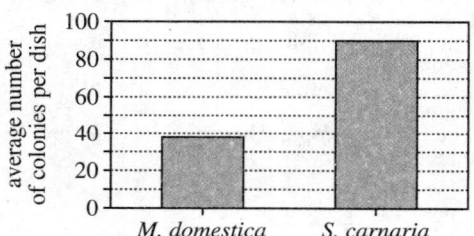

Figure 1

Experiment 2

The procedure from Experiment 1 was repeated with each of 3 groups of 10 *S. carnaria* except that the flies in each group were allowed to walk on the *E. coli* for a different period of time—5 min, 30 min, or 60 min—before each fly was placed in a separate petri dish containing nutrient agar. The results are shown in Figure 2.

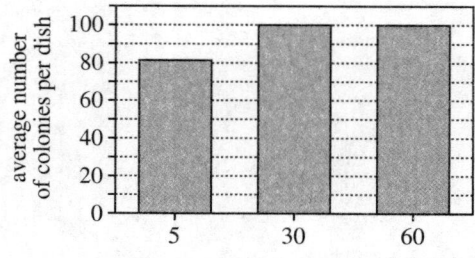

Figure 2

Experiment 3

The procedure from Experiment 1 was repeated with each of 3 groups of 10 *S. carnaria* except that, after Step 1, the flies in each group were allowed a different period of time—0 min, 30 min, or 60 min—to clean themselves before each fly was placed in a separate petri dish containing sterile nutrient agar. The results are shown in Figure 3.

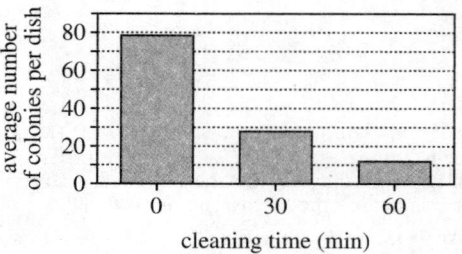

Figure 3

Figures adapted from Julie J. Shaffer, Kasey Jo Warner, and W. Wyatt Hoback, "Filthy Flies? Experiments to Test Flies as Vectors of Bacterial Disease." ©2007 by National Association of Biology Teachers.

7. As the amount of cleaning time increased, the average number of colonies per dish:

   A. increased only.
   B. decreased only.
   C. increased and then decreased.
   D. decreased and then increased.

8. What was the total number of flies tested in Experiment 3 ?

   F.   5
   G. 10
   H. 24
   J. 30

9. A scientist claimed that some species of flies spread bacterial diseases. Are the results of Experiment 1 consistent with this claim?

   A. Yes; based on Figure 1, the flies transferred bacteria from one surface to another.
   B. Yes; based on Figure 1, *M. domestica* transferred bacteria to *S. carnaria*.
   C. No; based on Figure 1, the flies did not transfer bacteria from one surface to another.
   D. No; based on Figure 1, *M. domestica* did not transfer bacteria to *S. carnaria*.

GO ON TO THE NEXT PAGE.

4 ○ ○ ○ ○ ○ ○ ○ ○ **4**

10. In the experiments, why was it necessary for the nutrient agar in the petri dishes to be sterile until the flies were placed in the dishes?

F. To ensure that any colonies that formed came from bacteria present in the nutrient agar before the flies were placed in the dishes

G. To ensure that any colonies that formed came from bacteria transferred to the nutrient agar by the flies

H. To ensure that the nutrient agar contained all the nutrients necessary for the flies to reproduce

J. To ensure that the nutrient agar contained all the nutrients necessary for the bacteria to reproduce

11. A student claimed that Species X flies would transfer more *E. coli* cells to a petri dish containing nutrient agar than would either *M. domestica* or *S. carnaria*. Which of the following experiments would best test the student's claim?

A. Repeat Experiment 1 except include a group of 10 Species X flies.

B. Repeat Experiment 1 except with a different species of bacteria.

C. Repeat Experiment 2 except include a group of 10 Species X flies.

D. Repeat Experiment 2 except with a different species of bacteria.

12. Which of the following statements gives the most likely hypothesis for Experiment 3 ?

F. *S. carnaria* remove bacteria when they clean themselves.

G. The longer *S. carnaria* are exposed to bacteria, the more bacteria they transfer between surfaces.

H. *M. domestica* transfer more bacteria between surfaces than do *S. carnaria*.

J. *M. domestica* are better at removing bacteria during cleaning than are *S. carnaria*.

13. Which of the following is the most likely reason that the average number of colonies per dish for *S. carnaria* shown in Figure 1 was different from the average number of colonies per dish for the flies that spent 5 min walking on the *E. coli* in Experiment 2 ?

A. By chance, the *M. domestica* in Experiment 2 transferred, on average, fewer *E. coli* than did the *S. carnaria* in Experiment 1.

B. By chance, the *S. carnaria* in Experiment 2 transferred, on average, fewer *E. coli* than did the *S. carnaria* in Experiment 1.

C. The *M. domestica* in Experiment 2 walked on the *E. coli* for a shorter period of time than did the *S. carnaria* in Experiment 1.

D. The *S. carnaria* in Experiment 2 walked on the *E. coli* for a shorter period of time than did the *S. carnaria* in Experiment 1.

GO ON TO THE NEXT PAGE.

4 ◯ ◯ ◯ ◯ ◯ ◯ ◯ ◯ ◯ **4**

Passage III

Forest fires require oxygen (O_2) to burn. Figure 1 shows the number of *paleowildfires* (large forest fires known from the rock record) for each 10-million-year interval of the *Mesozoic era* (250–65 million years ago, mya). Figure 1 also shows a model of the percent O_2 by volume (%O_2) in Earth's atmosphere from 250 mya to 70 mya.

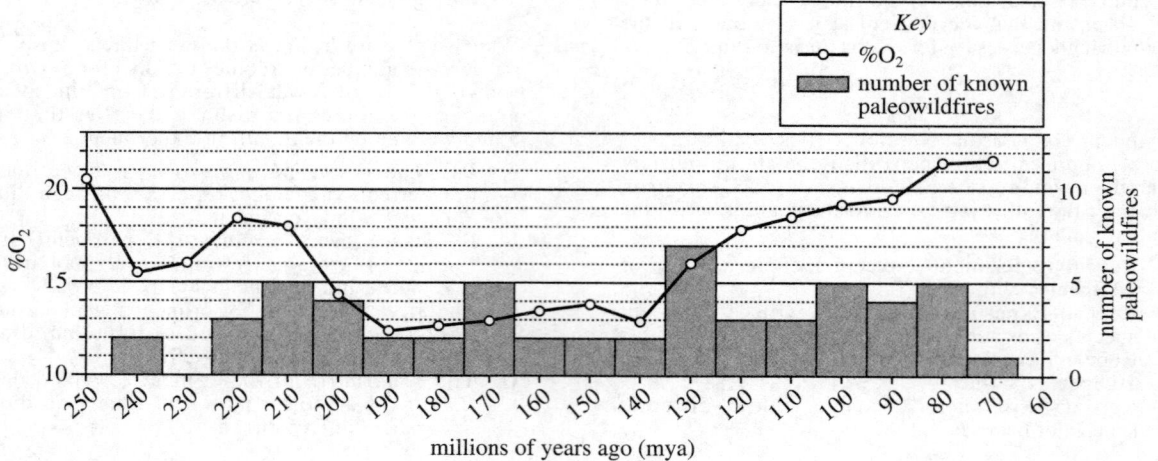

Figure 1

To study how %O_2 affects burning, scientists attempted to ignite 7 samples of each of 4 different materials, 1 sample at a time, in a chamber. For each set of samples of the same material, the initial %O_2 in the chamber ranged from 12% to 18%. Figure 2 shows, for each sample that ignited, the duration of the sample's flame.

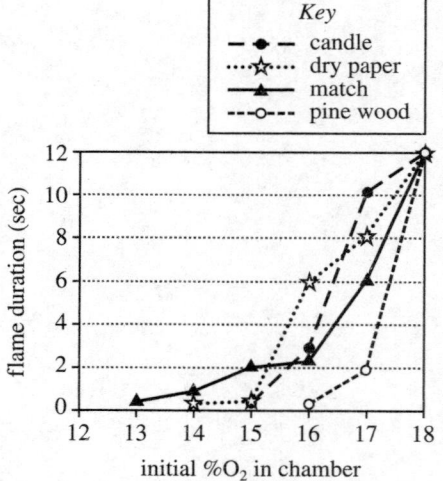

Note: At an initial %O_2 of 18, all samples burned to ash in 12 seconds.

Figure 2

Figures adapted from C. M. Belcher and J. C. McElwain, "Limits for Combustion in Low O_2 Redefine Paleoatmospheric Predictions for the Mesozoic." ©2008 by American Association for the Advancement of Science.

GO ON TO THE NEXT PAGE.

14. The %O_2 in Earth's atmosphere today is about 21. According to Figure 1, at which of the following times during the Mesozoic era was the %O_2 in Earth's atmosphere closest to the %O_2 in Earth's atmosphere today?

   F. 250 mya
   G. 200 mya
   H. 150 mya
   J. 100 mya

15. According to Figure 2, at an initial %O_2 of 17, approximately how many seconds greater was the flame duration for dry paper than the flame duration for pine wood?

   A. 2
   B. 4
   C. 6
   D. 8

16. A scientist claimed that paleowildfires could only have occurred when the %O_2 was higher than 15. For which of the following time intervals during the Mesozoic era are the data in Figure 1 *inconsistent* with this claim?

   F. 250–230 mya
   G. 180–160 mya
   H. 120–100 mya
   J. 90–70 mya

17. According to Figure 2, what is the order of the 4 materials tested, from the material that required the highest initial %O_2 to ignite to the material that required the lowest initial %O_2 to ignite?

   A. Match, pine wood, dry paper, candle
   B. Match, dry paper, pine wood, candle
   C. Pine wood, candle, dry paper, match
   D. Pine wood, dry paper, candle, match

18. According to Figure 1, how many paleowildfires are known from the rock record between 95 mya and 85 mya ?

   F. 4
   G. 9
   H. 14
   J. 19

19. According to Figure 2, at an initial %O_2 of 16, which of the 4 materials sustained a flame the longest?

   A. Candle
   B. Dry paper
   C. Match
   D. Pine wood

GO ON TO THE NEXT PAGE.

4 ◯ ◯ ◯ ◯ ◯ ◯ ◯ ◯ **4**

Passage IV

Four students observed that in a population of land plants, Population A, a plant could have a green stem or a purple stem. Each student proposed an explanation for this observation.

Student 1

All plants in Population A produce the green pigment chlorophyll. If a plant receives 8 hr or more of sunlight each day, it also produces a purple pigment, causing its stem to be purple. If a plant receives less than 8 hr of sunlight each day, it does not produce this purple pigment, so its stem is green. All plants in Population A are genetically identical, so they all have the ability to produce both pigments.

Student 2

All plants in Population A produce the green pigment chlorophyll. If a plant receives too little *phosphorus* (a nutrient), it also produces a purple pigment, causing its stem to be purple. If a plant receives enough phosphorus, it does not produce this purple pigment, so its stem is green. All plants in Population A are genetically identical, so they all have the ability to produce both pigments. The amount of sunlight received by a plant does not affect stem color.

Student 3

All plants in Population A produce the green pigment chlorophyll. The production of purple pigment is determined by Gene Q, which has 2 alleles (Q and q) and 3 possible genotypes (QQ, Qq, and qq). A plant with either the Gene Q genotype QQ or the Gene Q genotype Qq produces the purple pigment, causing its stem to be purple. A plant with the Gene Q genotype qq does not produce this purple pigment, so its stem is green. The amount of sunlight or nutrients received by a plant does not affect stem color.

Student 4

All plants in Population A produce the green pigment chlorophyll. The production of purple pigment is determined by Gene Q, which has 2 alleles (Q and q) and 3 possible genotypes (QQ, Qq, and qq). A plant with the Gene Q genotype qq produces the purple pigment, causing its stem to be purple. A plant with either the Gene Q genotype QQ or the Gene Q genotype Qq does not produce this purple pigment, so its stem is green. The amount of sunlight or nutrients received by a plant does not affect stem color.

20. Which student would be the most likely to agree that the soil in which a Population A plant is grown will influence its stem color?
    - **F.** Student 1
    - **G.** Student 2
    - **H.** Student 3
    - **J.** Student 4

21. Suppose it were found that the presence of the purple pigment in some plant tissues protects those tissues from being damaged by sunlight. Would this finding better support the explanation of Student 1 or the explanation of Student 2 ?
    - **A.** Student 1, because Student 1 indicated that the plants receiving the most sunlight will have purple stems.
    - **B.** Student 1, because Student 1 indicated that the plants receiving the most sunlight will have green stems.
    - **C.** Student 2, because Student 2 indicated that the plants receiving the most sunlight will have purple stems.
    - **D.** Student 2, because Student 2 indicated that the plants receiving the most sunlight will have green stems.

22. All 4 of the students' explanations are consistent with which of the following statements? In Population A:
    - **F.** both green-stemmed plants and purple-stemmed plants produce a pigment that can be used for photosynthesis.
    - **G.** only green-stemmed plants produce a pigment that can be used for photosynthesis.
    - **H.** only purple-stemmed plants produce a pigment that can be used for photosynthesis.
    - **J.** neither green-stemmed plants nor purple-stemmed plants produce a pigment that can be used for photosynthesis.

GO ON TO THE NEXT PAGE.

23. Which of the students, if any, would be likely to agree that providing a purple-stemmed plant from Population A with additional sunlight will cause its stem to become green?

  A. Student 1 only
  B. Students 1 and 3 only
  C. Students 3 and 4 only
  D. None of the students

24. Suppose 2 of the purple-stemmed plants in the population were crossed and 52 purple-stemmed and 15 green-stemmed offspring were produced. If all the parents and offspring in the cross were grown under the same conditions, these results would best support the explanation of which student?

  F. Student 1
  G. Student 2
  H. Student 3
  J. Student 4

25. Based on Student 4's explanation, if a purple-stemmed plant and a green-stemmed plant from Population A are crossed and they produce both purple-stemmed offspring and green-stemmed offspring, the Gene Q genotype of the parent with the:

  A. purple stem must be QQ.
  B. purple stem must be Qq.
  C. green stem must be QQ.
  D. green stem must be Qq.

26. Which of the students would be likely to agree that a plant receiving 9 hr of sunlight each day could have either a purple stem or a green stem?

  F. Student 1 only
  G. Student 2 only
  H. Students 3 and 4 only
  J. Students 2, 3, and 4 only

GO ON TO THE NEXT PAGE.

4 ○ ○ ○ ○ ○ ○ ○ ○ **4**

Passage V

Liquid H_2O can be broken down into hydrogen gas (H_2) and oxygen gas (O_2) by *electrolysis* according to the following chemical equation:

$$2H_2O \rightarrow 2H_2 + O_2$$

A scientist performed an experiment to study the electrolysis of H_2O using electricity generated from sunlight.

Experiment

Steps 1–5 were performed daily for 12 months:

1. A tank fitted with 2 electrodes—an *anode* (where O_2 would be produced) and a *cathode* (where H_2 would be produced)—was assembled. Each electrode was suspended in an inverted plastic tube, and each tube was marked to allow gas volume to be measured.

2. Four liters (4.0 L) of a 25% by mass aqueous solution of sodium hydroxide (NaOH) was added to the tank. As a result, the tubes were completely filled with the solution.

3. At 8:00 a.m., a rectangular solar cell was attached to the electrodes and placed next to a particular south-facing window for 8 hr. (Figure 1 shows the apparatus at the initiation of electrolysis.)

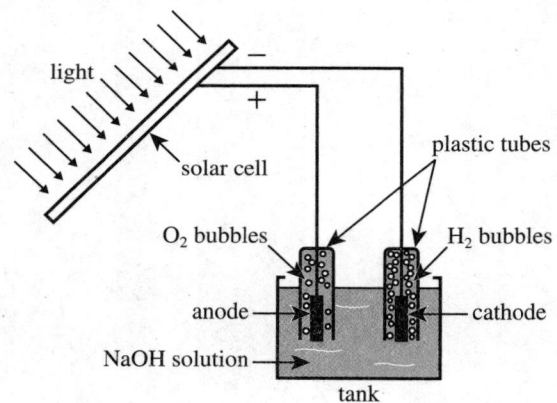

Figure 1

4. Eight hours later, the solar cell was detached from the electrodes, and the amount of H_2 that had been produced was measured.

5. The tank, tubes, and electrodes were cleaned and dried for reuse.

Figure 2 shows the total volume of H_2 produced (in L) in each month of the experiment. Table 1 shows the average *solar irradiance* (power per unit area), in watts per square meter (W/m^2), at the location of the solar cell during each month of the experiment.

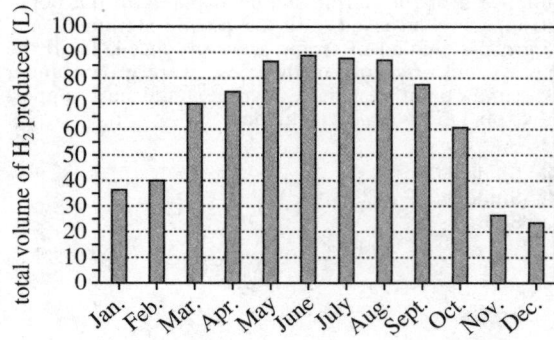

Figure 2

Table 1	
Month	Average solar irradiance (W/m^2)
January	77.8
February	106.4
March	153.8
April	170.7
May	197.5
June	213.1
July	206.4
August	198.7
September	183.1
October	137.1
November	59.9
December	52.3

Figures and table adapted from Sergii Bespalko, "Hydrogen Production by Water Electrochemical Photolysis Using PV-Module." ©2011 by Sergii Bespalko.

GO ON TO THE NEXT PAGE.

27. Based on Figure 2 and Table 1, during the month in which a total of 70 L of H_2 was produced, the average solar irradiance was:

    A. 77.8 W/m^2.
    B. 153.8 W/m^2.
    C. 197.5 W/m^2.
    D. 206.4 W/m^2.

28. Based on the description of the experiment, at 4:00 p.m. on each day, did the scientist measure the amount of gas produced at the anode or the cathode?

    F. The anode, because the anode is where H_2 was produced.
    G. The anode, because the anode is where O_2 was produced.
    H. The cathode, because the cathode is where H_2 was produced.
    J. The cathode, because the cathode is where O_2 was produced.

29. Consider the percent by mass of NaOH in the solution added to the tank in Step 2. Approximately what mass of NaOH was in 200 g of this solution?

    A. 25 g
    B. 50 g
    C. 200 g
    D. 225 g

30. Based on the chemical equation and Figure 2, approximately how many liters of O_2 (NOT H_2) were produced in February?

    F. 20 L
    G. 40 L
    H. 80 L
    J. 100 L

31. Based on the description of the experiment, in the month of June how many total liters of NaOH solution were added to the tank?

    A. 4.0 L, because Step 2 was performed once in June, on June 1.
    B. 8.0 L, because Step 2 was performed twice in June, once on June 1 and once on June 30.
    C. 120 L, because Step 2 was performed 30 times in June, once each day.
    D. 240 L, because Step 2 was performed 60 times in June, twice each day.

32. Based on Table 1, on May 11, was the solar irradiance of the solar cell less than, equal to, or greater than 197.5 W/m^2 ?

    F. Less
    G. Equal
    H. Greater
    J. Cannot be determined from the given information

33. Suppose the experiment was repeated, except that the scientist added only pure liquid H_2O to the tank in Step 2. Based on the description of the experiment, would this change have more likely resulted in more H_2 being produced or less H_2 being produced?

    A. More H_2; pure liquid H_2O has more ions and thus higher electrical conductivity than does an aqueous NaOH solution.
    B. More H_2; pure liquid H_2O has fewer ions and thus lower electrical conductivity than does an aqueous NaOH solution.
    C. Less H_2; pure liquid H_2O has more ions and thus higher electrical conductivity than does an aqueous NaOH solution.
    D. Less H_2; pure liquid H_2O has fewer ions and thus lower electrical conductivity than does an aqueous NaOH solution.

GO ON TO THE NEXT PAGE.

Taking Additional Practice Tests

4   **4**

Passage VI

A *standing wave* on a taut string is a wave that appears to vibrate without traveling along the string. Such waves are called the string's *harmonics*. Each harmonic has a characteristic number of *nodes*: locations between the ends of the string that do not move (the ends of the string do not count as nodes). Figure 1 illustrates a harmonic and also the apparatus that a student used to perform 2 experiments on standing waves.

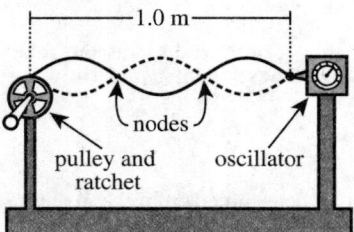

Note: Figure not drawn to scale.

Figure 1

A string having a mass per unit length of μ was attached on one end to an *oscillator* (a motor that vibrates) and on the other end to a pulley and ratchet. The student could select the frequency, *f* (the number of cycles per second), of the oscillator's vibration. By cranking the ratchet, the student could vary the force of tension, *T*, in the string.

Experiment 1

With 0.10 newtons (N) of tension in String X (μ = 0.02 g/cm), the student varied *f*. She noted that standing waves occurred only at certain values of *f*. The student sketched the first 5 harmonics and recorded *f* (in hertz, Hz) for each. She repeated this procedure for String Y (μ = 0.08 g/cm) and for String Z (μ = 0.16 g/cm). See Table 1.

Table 1		f (Hz) for String:		
Harmonic	Sketch	X	Y	Z
1st		11.2	5.59	3.95
2nd		22.4	11.2	7.91
3rd		33.5	16.8	11.9
4th		44.7	22.4	15.8
5th		55.9	28.0	19.8

Experiment 2

Beginning again with String X, the student set the oscillator to vibrate at $f = 25.0$ Hz. She then varied *T*, and noted that standing waves occurred only at certain values of *T*. The student recorded *T* for the first 5 harmonics. She repeated this procedure for Strings Y and Z. See Table 2.

Table 2			
	T (N) in String:		
Harmonic	X	Y	Z
1st	0.50	2.00	4.00
2nd	0.13	0.50	1.00
3rd	0.06	0.22	0.44
4th	0.03	0.13	0.25
5th	0.02	0.08	0.16

GO ON TO THE NEXT PAGE.

34. Based on the sketches made in Experiment 1, the string shown in Figure 1 is vibrating in which harmonic?

F. 1st
G. 2nd
H. 3rd
J. 4th

35. In a new trial, the student made the following sketch of a standing wave on String Z.

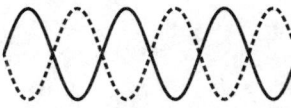

Based on the results of Experiments 1 and 2, this standing wave occurred at which approximate values of f and T ?

A. $f = 0.10$ Hz and $T = 0.11$ N
B. $f = 0.10$ Hz and $T = 23.7$ N
C. $f = 25.0$ Hz and $T = 0.11$ N
D. $f = 25.0$ Hz and $T = 23.7$ N

36. A piece of String Y that is 1 cm in length would have the same mass as a piece of:

F. String X that is 1 cm in length.
G. String X that is 4 cm in length.
H. String Z that is 1 cm in length.
J. String Z that is 4 cm in length.

37. The student reported the data in Table 1 with how many *significant digits* ?

A. Some data were reported with 1 significant digit, and some were reported with 2 significant digits.
B. Some data were reported with 2 significant digits, and some were reported with 3 significant digits.
C. All data were reported with 2 significant digits.
D. All data were reported with 3 significant digits.

38. For a string at constant tension, let f_n represent the frequency of the nth harmonic (f_1 is the frequency of the 1st harmonic, f_2 is the frequency of the 2nd harmonic, f_3 is the frequency of the 3rd harmonic, and so on). Which of the following equations for f_n is consistent with the results of Experiment 1 for String X ?

F. $f_n = n + f_1$
G. $f_n = n - f_1$
H. $f_n = n \times f_1$
J. $f_n = n \div f_1$

39. Suppose that a string having a mass per unit length of 0.32 g/cm had been tested in Experiment 2. The 4th harmonic of this string would most likely have occurred at a tension:

A. less than 0.03 N.
B. between 0.03 N and 0.13 N.
C. between 0.13 N and 0.25 N.
D. greater than 0.25 N.

40. Based on the results of Experiments 1 and 2, for a given harmonic, as μ increased, did f increase or decrease, and did T increase or decrease?

	f	T
F.	increased	increased
G.	increased	decreased
H.	decreased	increased
J.	decreased	decreased

END OF TEST 4

STOP! DO NOT RETURN TO ANY OTHER TEST.

Taking Additional Practice Tests

You may wish to photocopy these sample answer document pages to respond to the practice ACT Writing Test.

Please enter the information at the right before beginning the writing test.

Use a No. 2 pencil only. Do NOT use a mechanical pencil, ink, ballpoint, or felt-tip pen.

WRITING TEST BOOKLET NUMBER

Print your 9-digit **Booklet Number** in the boxes at the right.

WRITING TEST FORM

Print your 5-character **Test Form** in the boxes at the right and fill in the corresponding ovals.

Begin WRITING TEST here.

If you need more space, please continue on the following page.

1

WRITING TEST

_____
_____
_____
_____
_____
_____
_____
_____
_____
_____
_____
_____
_____
_____
_____
_____
_____
_____
_____
_____
_____
_____
_____
_____
_____
_____
_____

2

If you need more space, please continue on the following page.

WRITING TEST

_____

_____

_____

_____

_____

_____

_____

_____

_____

_____

_____

_____

_____

_____

_____

_____

_____

_____

_____

_____

_____

_____

_____

_____

_____

_____

_____

_____

If you need more space, please continue on the following page.

3

The ONLY Official Prep Guide from the Makers of the ACT

WRITING TEST

_____
_____
_____
_____
_____
_____
_____
_____
_____
_____
_____
_____
_____
_____
_____
_____
_____
_____
_____
_____
_____
_____
_____
_____
_____
_____
_____
_____
_____
_____

STOP here with the writing test.

4

Practice Writing Test Prompt 6

Your Signature: _____
(Do not print.)

Print Your Name Here: _____

Your Date of Birth:

☐	☐	–	☐	☐	–	☐ ☐ ☐ ☐
Month			Day			Year

Form 22WT9

The ACT® WRITING TEST BOOKLET

You must take the multiple-choice tests before you take the writing test.

Directions

This is a test of your writing skills. You will have **forty** (40) minutes to read the prompt, plan your response, and write an essay in English. Before you begin working, read all material in this test booklet carefully to understand exactly what you are being asked to do.

You will write your essay on the lined pages in the **answer document** provided. Your writing on those pages will be scored. You may use the unlined pages in this test booklet to plan your essay. Your work on these pages will not be scored.

Your essay will be evaluated based on the evidence it provides of your ability to:

- clearly state your own perspective on a complex issue and analyze the relationship between your perspective and at least one other perspective
- develop and support your ideas with reasoning and examples
- organize your ideas clearly and logically
- communicate your ideas effectively in standard written English

Lay your pencil down immediately when time is called.

DO NOT OPEN THIS BOOKLET UNTIL TOLD TO DO SO.

PO Box 168
Iowa City, IA 52243-0168

The ONLY Official Prep Guide from the Makers of the ACT

Taking Additional Practice Tests

Field Trips

In elementary school, class trips to visit museums, science laboratories, zoos, and historical sites are relatively common. Such field trips can provide unique educational opportunities and connect what is learned in the classroom to the world beyond school. But field trips are not as common in the high school setting. Most classes tend to be limited to the school grounds—in a classroom or computer lab. Given the benefits they provide, should field trips be a standard part of the high school experience?

Read and carefully consider these perspectives. Each suggests a particular way of thinking about the question above.

Perspective One	Perspective Two	Perspective Three
Confining students to the classroom stifles their academic development. Field trips encourage motivation and interest among students, which enhances their learning.	High school students require structure and discipline, which are not available in a field trip setting. Students treat it as an opportunity to socialize rather than a chance to learn.	Field trips cost money, and many school budgets are strained. A high school's limited resources should be spent at the school.

Essay Task

Write a unified, coherent essay in which you address the question of whether field trips should be a standard part of the high school experience. In your essay, be sure to:

- clearly state your own perspective and analyze the relationship between your perspective and at least one other perspective
- develop and support your ideas with reasoning and examples
- organize your ideas clearly and logically
- communicate your ideas effectively in standard written English

Your perspective may be in full agreement with any of those given, in partial agreement, or completely different.

Planning Your Essay

Your work on these prewriting pages will not be scored.

Use the space below and on the back cover to generate ideas and plan your essay. You may wish to consider the following as you think critically about the task:

Strengths and weaknesses of different perspectives on the issue
- What insights do they offer, and what do they fail to consider?
- Why might they be persuasive to others, or why might they fail to persuade?

Your own knowledge, experience, and values
- What is your perspective on this issue, and what are its strengths and weaknesses?
- How will you support your perspective in your essay?

If you need more space to plan, please continue on the following page.

Planning Your Essay

Use this page to continue planning your essay. Your work on this page will not be scored.

Passage I

Question 1. The best answer is **C** because it is the only option that has correct sentence structure. It uses a preposition to begin an introductory dependent clause that links to an independent clause, which creates a complete sentence.

> The best answer is NOT:
>
> **A** because it creates two independent clauses that are separated by a comma, which creates a run-on sentence.
>
> **B** because it creates two independent clauses that are separated by a comma, which creates a run-on sentence.
>
> **D** because it creates two independent clauses that are separated by a comma, which creates a run-on sentence.

Question 2. The best answer is **G** because it is the only option that has correct sentence structure. It creates a complete sentence with a main subject and main verb.

> The best answer is NOT:
>
> **F** because it adds the relative pronoun *which* before the verb, resulting in a sentence fragment.
>
> **H** because it creates a long clause that is a sentence fragment.
>
> **J** because, like H, it creates a long clause that is a sentence fragment.

Question 3. The best answer is **A** because it provides the appropriate punctuation (dashes) to set off the nonessential element "up to twenty-five feet wide."

> The best answer is NOT:
>
> **B** because a colon is not used to introduce a nonessential element.
>
> **C** because the punctuation used to set off a nonessential element must match; since the nonessential element ends with a dash, it cannot be set off with a comma at the beginning.
>
> **D** because a colon is not used to complete a nonessential element.

Question 4. **The best answer is J** because it does not include any unnecessary punctuation.

The best answer is NOT:

F because it has an unnecessary comma after *variations*.

G because it has an unnecessary dash after *variations*.

H because it has two unnecessary commas that incorrectly set off "in the mantas" from the rest of the sentence.

Question 5. **The best answer is A** because it clearly explains why the sentence should be deleted. The information about Marshall's beachside lodgings in Mozambique is not relevant to the paragraph's discussion of how Marshall came to investigate the possibility that there were two manta ray species.

The best answer is NOT:

B because the information about why Marshall did her research in Mozambique is not relevant to the discussion of how Marshall came to investigate the possibility that there were two manta ray species.

C because the sentence refers to Marshall's beachside lodgings in Mozambique, which are not related to how Marshall, who started as a lone researcher, ended up creating a large scientific institution.

D because the sentence refers to Marshall's beachside lodgings in Mozambique, which are not related to Marshall's role at the Marine Megafauna Center.

Question 6. **The best answer is F** because it is the only option with correct subject-verb agreement. The singular subject *skin* must have a singular verb.

The best answer is NOT:

G because *happen* is a plural verb, and the subject of the sentence is singular.

H because *were* is a plural verb, and the subject of the sentence is singular.

J because *are* is a plural verb, and the subject of the sentence is singular.

Question 7. **The best answer is C** because it does not include any unnecessary punctuation.

The best answer is NOT:

A because it has an unnecessary colon after the word *was*.

B because it has two unnecessary commas that incorrectly set off the word *that* from the rest of the sentence.

D because it has an unnecessary comma after the word *was*.

Question 8. The best answer is **F** because after Sentence 1 is the only logical place to add information that refers to the basic data Marshall began collecting.

The best answer is NOT:

G because Sentence 2 begins with "Other data," which refers back to the phrase "Some of the data" in the new sentence, so it would be illogical to place the new sentence after Sentence 2.

H because to place the sentence after Sentence 3 would interrupt the discussion of the manta denticles.

J because to place the sentence after Sentence 4 would interrupt the introduction of another discovery Marshall made in regard to the mantas.

Question 9. The best answer is **C** because it best expresses the idea specified in the stem. The word choice in this option (*evidence*) best conveys that the announcement was backed by scientific data.

The best answer is NOT:

A because the wording doesn't clearly indicate that the announcement was backed by scientific data.

B because the wording doesn't clearly indicate that the announcement was backed by scientific data.

D because the wording doesn't clearly indicate that the announcement was backed by scientific data.

Question 10. The best answer is **J** because it is the only option with correct subject-verb agreement. The plural subject "two manta species" must have a plural verb.

The best answer is NOT:

F because *is* is a singular verb, and the subject of the sentence is plural.

G because *exists* is a singular verb, and the subject of the sentence is plural.

H because *was* is a singular verb, and the subject of the sentence is plural.

Question 11. The best answer is **B** because it maintains the overall style and tone of the essay. The language here is neither overly informal nor too formal.

The best answer is NOT:

A because the wording is too informal compared to the rest of the essay.

C because the wording introduces a tone that is not consistent with the rest of the essay.

D because the wording is too informal compared to the rest of the essay.

Question 12. The best answer is **F** because it creates a sentence that is structurally sound and has proper subordination.

The best answer is NOT:

G because *whether* is not the correct subordinating conjunction to use in this context and creates an illogical sentence.

H because *which* is not the correct subordinating conjunction to use in this context and creates an illogical sentence.

J because *how* is not the correct subordinating conjunction to use in this context and creates an illogical sentence.

Question 13. The best answer is **B** because it creates a logical sentence with correctly placed modifiers. The phrase "for so long" refers to the amount of time large animals went *undifferentiated* and so is correctly placed after that word.

The best answer is NOT:

A because the phrase "for so long" is incorrectly placed so that it appears to modify *know*, creating an illogical sentence.

C because the phrase "for so long" is incorrectly placed so that it appears to modify *highlights*, creating an illogical sentence.

D because the phrase "for so long" is incorrectly placed so that it appears to modify *how*, creating an illogical sentence.

Question 14. The best answer is **J** because it is the only option that clearly supports the suggestion that the scientific study of manta rays will continue: it is because Dr. Marshall, an expert researcher, is so devoted to manta rays.

The best answer is NOT:

F because the fact that the current manta ray population faces an array of threats across the world does not support the suggestion that the scientific study of manta rays will continue.

G because the fact that a documentary film about Dr. Marshall was released in 2009 does not support the suggestion that the scientific study of manta rays will continue.

H because the fact that Dr. Marshall once described the manta ray as a large and beautiful underwater bird does not support the suggestion that the scientific study of manta rays will continue.

Question 15. The best answer is **D** because this option clearly indicates why the essay does not meet the writer's primary purpose. The main focus of the essay is on how Marshall's research led to the discovery of the two manta species; it is not about surveying the scientific community's response to the identification of the two species.

The best answer is NOT:

A because the fact that the scientific community accepted the identification of the two species is not the main focus of the essay.

B because the fact that Marshall's research was thorough and well documented is not the main focus of the essay.

C because the essay does not present any scientific responses to Marshall's identification of the two species.

Passage II

Question 16. The best answer is **G** because it is the only option that has correct sentence structure. It correctly uses a comma to connect the independent clause to the participial phrase.

The best answer is NOT:

F because it inserts a semicolon after *temperature*, which creates a sentence fragment because what comes after the semicolon is a participial phrase.

H because the comma after *temperature* is separating two independent clauses, which creates a run-on sentence.

J because it inserts a period after *temperature*, which creates a sentence fragment because what comes after the period is a participial phrase.

Question 17. The best answer is **A** because it provides the appropriate punctuation (commas) to set off the adverbial phrase "particularly in the bark of the willow tree."

The best answer is NOT:

B because it contains misplaced and inconsistent punctuation, creating an unclear sentence. The second dash after *bark* interrupts the adverbial phrase. In addition, an adverbial phrase should be set off by the same punctuation on both sides, either commas or dashes, but not both.

C because a colon is not used to introduce an adverbial phrase.

D because it contains misplaced punctuation, creating an unclear sentence. The first comma should precede, not follow, the word *particularly*.

Question 18. The best answer is **G** because it creates a sentence that is structurally sound; it has a subject and uses the correct preposition.

The best answer is NOT:

F because it has no subject.

H because *on* is not the right preposition to show the relationship between willow and the other plants.

J because it has no subject.

Question 19. The best answer is **D** because it provides the clearest, most concise wording.

The best answer is NOT:

A because it is redundant; *approximately* and *about* essentially have the same meaning.

B because "an estimation of" is both wordy and awkward.

C because "in the region of" is both wordy and vague.

Question 20. The best answer is **G** because it is the only option that provides a logical transition to the information presented in the paragraph it introduces.

The best answer is NOT:

F because the information in this clause does not logically connect to the information in the rest of the paragraph.

H because the information in this clause does not logically connect to the information in the rest of the paragraph.

J because the information in this clause does not logically connect to the information in the rest of the paragraph.

Question 21. The best answer is **A** because it is the only option that has consistent verb tense. The verb *preferred* should match the tense in the rest of the paragraph.

The best answer is NOT:

B because "would of" is an incorrect verb form of "would have," which creates a sentence that is both unclear and lacks consistent verb tense.

C because the verb "will prefer" creates a sentence that lacks consistent verb tense.

D because the verb *prefer* creates a sentence that lacks consistent verb tense.

Question 22. The best answer is **J** because it provides the clearest, most concise wording.

The best answer is NOT:

F because it is redundant; "high cost" and *expensive* essentially have the same meaning.

G because it is redundant; "high price tag" and *expensive* essentially have the same meaning, and the phrasing is wordy and awkward.

H because it is redundant; "high importation cost of" and *expensive* essentially have the same meaning, and the phrasing is wordy and awkward.

Question 23. The best answer is **C** because it provides the appropriate punctuation (commas) to set off the conjunctive adverb *however*.

The best answer is NOT:

A because it lacks a comma before *however*.

B because a colon creates a sentence fragment.

D because it lacks a comma after *however*.

Question 24. The best answer is **F** because it provides the most logical transition word to connect this sentence with the preceding one. The word *consequently* provides a resolution to the earlier word *however* in the previous sentence, helping to explain the pivot away from cinchona bark to willow bark.

The best answer is NOT:

G because the word *nevertheless* is illogical in relation to the previous sentence.

H because the word *furthermore* is illogical in relation to the previous sentence.

J because the word *likewise* is illogical in relation to the previous sentence.

Question 25. The best answer is **D** because the word *began*, the simple past tense, is the correct form of the verb as is it used in this sentence.

> **The best answer is** NOT:
>
> **A** because the past tense is appropriate here, not the past perfect. Additionally, the past-perfect tense is "had begun," not "had began."
>
> **B** because the past tense is appropriate here, not the past-perfect subjunctive mood. Additionally, the past-perfect subjunctive mood is "would have begun," not "would have began."
>
> **C** because *began* is the correct form of the past tense, not *begun*.

Question 26. The best answer is **H** because it is the only option that provides a logical transition from the information presented in the previous sentence.

> **The best answer is** NOT:
>
> **F** because this phrase is illogical in relation to the previous sentence and what follows in this sentence.
>
> **G** because this phrase is illogical in relation to the previous sentence and what follows in this sentence.
>
> **J** because this phrase is illogical in relation to the previous sentence and what follows in this sentence.

Question 27. The best answer is **C** because it is the only choice that uses the correct verb tense and the correct form of the possessive pronoun *its*.

> **The best answer is** NOT:
>
> **A** because *adds* is the incorrect tense of the verb as it is used in this sentence.
>
> **B** because *it's* is the incorrect form of the possessive pronoun.
>
> **D** because *adds* is the incorrect tense of the verb as its used in this sentence, and *it's* is the incorrect form of the possessive pronoun.

Question 28. The best answer is **G** because it best expresses the idea specified in the stem. *Tested* emphasizes that the medicine was experimental in nature.

> **The best answer is NOT:**
>
> **F** because the wording doesn't clearly indicate that the medicine was experimental in nature.
>
> **H** because the wording doesn't clearly indicate that the medicine was experimental in nature.
>
> **J** because the wording doesn't clearly indicate that the medicine was experimental in nature.

Question 29. The best answer is **D** because it is the only option that has correct sentence structure. It creates two independent sentences.

> **The best answer is NOT:**
>
> **A** because it creates two independent clauses that are separated by a comma, which creates a run-on sentence.
>
> **B** because it creates two independent clauses that are separated by a comma, which creates a run-on sentence.
>
> **C** because a comma is needed before a nonrestrictive relative clause introduced by *which*.

Question 30. The best answer is **G** because this option clearly indicates why the essay does fulfill the writer's primary purpose. The essay outlines the development of a common medicine by documenting the historical use of willow bark as a medicine and tracing its gradual refinement into modern aspirin.

> **The best answer is NOT:**
>
> **F** because the essay does not focus on how the Egyptians and Sumerians administered willow bark.
>
> **H** because the essay does not focus on the function of salicylates and how aspirin affects the human body.
>
> **J** because the essay does not focus on comparing the use of willow bark to that of cinchona bark in the eighteenth century.

Passage III

Question 31. The best answer is D because it is the only option that has correct sentence structure. It correctly places "painter Martin Klimas" immediately after the introductory phrase "in his studio in Dusseldorf, Germany," which correctly modifies the word *his*.

The best answer is NOT:

A because it introduces a dangling modifier. The logical referent for *his* is Klimas, not the paint.

B because it introduces a dangling modifier. The independent clause begins with "there is," which leaves no logical subject for *his* to modify.

C because, like A and B, it introduces a dangling modifier. The logical referent for *his* is Klimas, not the paint.

Question 32. The best answer is G because it provides appropriate punctuation (a colon) to set off examples of the information that precedes the colon. The sentence refers to the paint that collects in a "puddle of colors" and is followed by a list of those colors. G also includes a comma to separate the two pairs of hues in the sentence.

The best answer is NOT:

F because a semicolon should not be used to introduce a list.

H because a semicolon should not be used to separate items in a list where commas can be used instead. It also omits a comma after *blues*.

J because a semicolon should not be used to introduce a list or to separate items in a list where commas can be used instead.

Question 33. The best answer is B because it includes two independent clauses that are joined only by *and*, which results in a run-on sentence.

The best answer is NOT:

A because it correctly inserts a comma and the conjunction *and* between the two independent clauses.

C because it correctly ends the first independent clause with a period and begins the second one with a capital letter.

D because it correctly uses a semicolon to join two closely related independent clauses.

Question 34. The best answer is F because "level with" is precise and appropriately conveys how the camera is positioned relative to the paint puddle.

> **The best answer is NOT:**
>
> **G** because the phrase "eye-to-eye with" isn't appropriate in this context, as neither the camera nor the puddle has eyes.
>
> **H** because "the same as" falsely equates the camera to the paint puddle. They are different things.
>
> **J** because the phrase "equal to" indicates that the camera and the paint puddle are somehow equal, which doesn't make sense.

Question 35. The best answer is A because it best expresses the idea specified in the stem. The word choice in this option is the most dramatic, which is what the question asks for. *Crank* indicates an aggressive movement, and *ten* is often the highest level that volume can be turned to.

> **The best answer is NOT:**
>
> **B** because the wording isn't as dramatic as the wording in A. "A bit higher" is a small increase.
>
> **C** because the wording isn't as dramatic as the wording in A. "Increases the volume of the output" is straightforward and undramatic.
>
> **D** because the wording isn't as dramatic as the wording in A. "Adjusts the speaker's output level" is straightforward and undramatic.

Question 36. The best answer is G because it is the only option with correct subject-verb agreement. The plural subject *vibrations* must have a plural verb.

> **The best answer is NOT:**
>
> **F** because "has caused" is a singular verb, and the subject of the sentence is plural.
>
> **H** because "is causing" is a singular verb, and the subject of the sentence is plural.
>
> **J** because *causes* is a singular verb, and the subject of the sentence is plural.

Question 37. The best answer is **A** because it maintains the overall style and tone of the essay. The language here is neither overly informal nor too formal.

The best answer is NOT:

B because the phrase "frozen in time's embrace" is too flowery compared with the rest of the essay, and the words *pic* and *snapped* are too casual.

C because the wording is too informal compared with the rest of the essay.

D because the wording is too informal compared with the rest of the essay.

Question 38. The best answer is **F** because at this point, the writer is discussing how Klimas's photos are unique to each song. The quotation about letting the sound of the music create the picture is therefore the most relevant.

The best answer is NOT:

G because this quotation is about how annoying it was to clean up after each shot, which is not relevant at this point in the essay.

H because a quotation about using normal photographic equipment and common music is less relevant at this point than the quotation in F is.

J because this quotation is about the repetitive nature of the process, which is less relevant at this point than the quotation in F is.

Question 39. The best answer is **C** because it is the only option with correct subject-verb agreement. The singular subject *idea* must have a singular verb.

The best answer is NOT:

A because *were* is a plural verb, and the subject of the sentence is singular.

B because "have been" is a plural verb, and the subject of the sentence is singular.

D because *are* is a plural verb, and the subject of the sentence is singular.

Question 40. The best answer is **J** because it does not include any unnecessary punctuation.

The best answer is NOT:

F because it has two unnecessary commas that incorrectly set off "of Swiss scientist" from the rest of the sentence.

G because it has an unnecessary comma after *experiments*.

H because it has an unnecessary comma after *Swiss*.

Question 41. The best answer is **D** because it is the only option that has correct sentence structure. It creates a complete sentence with a main subject and main verb.

The best answer is NOT:

A because it creates a long phrase that is a sentence fragment. The phrase has no verb.

B because it adds the subordinating conjunction *while* before the subject and verb, resulting in a long dependent clause that is a sentence fragment.

C because, like A, it creates a long phrase that is a sentence fragment. The phrase has no verb.

Question 42. The best answer is **G** because the essay does shift at this point from information about Jenny's experiments to the music Klimas uses in his work. Dividing the paragraph at this point makes sense.

The best answer is NOT:

F because even though it makes sense to divide the paragraph, the essay is not discussing harmonics or Klimas's taste in music at this point.

H because dividing the paragraph here would not interrupt an analysis of Jenny's experiments, as those are not being analyzed at this point in the essay.

J because dividing the paragraph here would not interrupt a description of Klimas's scientific background, as that is not discussed in the essay.

Question 43. The best answer is **C** because it is the only option that has correct sentence structure. It correctly uses a comma to connect the introductory dependent clause to the independent clause of the sentence.

The best answer is NOT:

A because it inserts a period after *sculptures*, which creates a sentence fragment because what comes before the period is a dependent clause.

B because it adds the conjunction *and* between the dependent clause and independent clause of the sentence, which results in incorrect subordination.

D because it inserts a semicolon after *sculptures*, which creates a sentence fragment because what comes before the semicolon is a dependent clause.

Question 44. **The best answer is J** because this sentence links the idea of using dynamic and percussive music to the idea that Klimas needs the paint to "get up and dance."

The best answer is NOT:

F because a sentence speculating that such music would impress Jenny is not an effective transition here.

G because a sentence stating that Klimas's music selection is a matter of taste is not an effective transition here.

H because a sentence saying that dynamic and percussive music is an unwise choice is illogical and is not an effective transition here.

Question 45. **The best answer is B** because this option clearly indicates why the essay does fulfill the writer's primary purpose. The essay explains how Klimas creates his art by photographing the effects of music on paint.

The best answer is NOT:

A because the essay does not focus on the artistic process that Jenny used.

C because the essay does not focus on the cultural significance of Klimas's photos.

D because the essay does not give an overview of how Jenny's experiments have inspired other artists.

Passage IV

Question 46. **The best answer is J** because it creates a sentence that is structurally sound and is parallel in grammatical structure to the surrounding phrases.

The best answer is NOT:

F because the clause "there are tree-covered bluffs" disrupts the parallel structure of the series phrases.

G because the clause "tree-covered bluffs flank the river" disrupts the parallel structure of the series of phrases.

H because the phrase "featuring tree-covered bluffs" disrupts the parallel structure of the series of phrases.

Question 47. The best answer is **A** because it best expresses the idea specified in the stem. The phrase "daunted would-be" best indicates that the builders who intended to construct the highway were intimidated by the features of the gorge.

The best answer is NOT:

B because the wording doesn't clearly indicate that the builders who intended to construct the highway were intimidated by the features of the gorge.

C because the wording doesn't clearly indicate that the builders who intended to construct the highway were intimidated by the features of the gorge.

D because the wording doesn't clearly indicate that the builders who intended to construct the highway were intimidated by the features of the gorge.

Question 48. The best answer is **H** because it provides appropriate punctuation (a colon) to connect two independent clauses and indicate the relationship between them. In this sentence, the information in the second clause ("showcased the scenic grandeur") illustrates and expands upon information in the first clause ("design went beyond practicalities").

The best answer is NOT:

F because no punctuation between two independent clauses creates a run-on sentence.

G because the coordinating conjunction *and* is not used with a colon to join two independent clauses.

J because a comma between two independent clauses creates a run-on sentence.

Question 49. The best answer is **D** because it provides the clearest, most concise wording.

The best answer is NOT:

A because it is redundant; "Columbia River" is referenced earlier in the paragraph.

B because it is redundant; the length of the gorge is referenced earlier in the paragraph.

C because it is redundant and wordy; the gorge's scenery is referenced earlier in the sentence.

Question 50. The best answer is J because deleting the underlined portion provides the clearest, most concise wording.

The best answer is NOT:

F because it is redundant and wordy; the location of the benches is referenced earlier in the sentence, and benches are typically for sitting.

G because it is redundant and wordy; the location of the benches is referenced earlier in the sentence.

H because it is redundant; that the benches were for travelers' use is referenced later in the sentence.

Question 51. The best answer is A because it is the only option that creates a standard English idiom ("take in a view").

The best answer is NOT:

B because the phrase "take up a view" is not idiomatic standard English.

C because the phrase "take on a view" is not idiomatic standard English.

D because the phrase "take a view" is not idiomatic standard English.

Question 52. The best answer is H because it is the only option that is clear. The word *road* clearly indicates that the distinction that was blurred was between "road and environment," which prevents ambiguity regarding what the writer is referring to at this point in the sentence.

The best answer is NOT:

F because the pronoun *that* is ambiguous, lacking a clear antecedent.

G because the pronoun *this* is ambiguous, lacking a clear antecedent.

J because the pronoun *it* is ambiguous, lacking a clear antecedent. In addition, the word *it's* is the incorrect form of the possessive pronoun.

Question 53. The best answer is **A** because it clearly explains why the phrase should be added to the sentence. The detail helps develop and support the overarching idea in the paragraph that the design of the Columbia River Highway was impressive, with five tunnels previously being unheard of in such a design.

The best answer is NOT:

B because the phrase, though it should be added, does not imply how the engineers were able to make openings in the tunnel.

C because the phrase, which should be added, makes clear that there were several openings in the side of one tunnel; this relates to information in the sentence about motorists' ability to glimpse the river below.

D because the phrase, which should be added, does not suggest that creating intricate tunnels was easy for engineers.

Question 54. The best answer is **J** because it is the only option that has correct sentence structure. It creates a grammatically correct sentence by using a comma to separate an independent clause from a participial phrase.

The best answer is NOT:

F because it inserts a semicolon after *tunnel*, which creates a sentence fragment because what follows the semicolon is a participial phrase.

G because, like F, it inserts a semicolon after *tunnel*, which creates a sentence fragment because what follows the semicolon is a participial phrase.

H because the comma after *tunnel* is separating two independent clauses, which creates a run-on sentence.

Question 55. The best answer is **B** because it is the only option that has correct sentence structure. It uses a subordinating conjunction to begin the introductory dependent clause that links to an independent clause, which creates a complete sentence.

The best answer is NOT:

A because it creates a run-on sentence. "In time" is a prepositional phrase, not a subordinating conjunction. "In time, Oregon built a new road along the Columbia" is an independent clause.

C because it creates a run-on sentence. The word *soon* is an adverb, not a subordinating conjunction. "Soon Oregon built a new road along the Columbia" is an independent clause.

D because it creates a run-on sentence. "Oregon built a new road along the Columbia" is an independent clause.

Question 56. The best answer is **F** because it maintains the overall style and tone of the essay.

The best answer is NOT:

G because the wording introduces a wordy, pretentious tone that is not consistent with the rest of the essay.

H because the wording introduces an elevated, formal tone that is not consistent with the rest of the essay. In addition, the phrase "was completed in 1922" is redundant with information presented in the previous paragraph.

J because the wording introduces an elevated, formal tone that is not consistent with the rest of the essay.

Question 57. The best answer is **C** because it best expresses the idea specified in the stem. The word *rekindled* clearly conveys that people's interest in the Columbia River Highway in the 1980s was a renewal of earlier interest in the original highway.

The best answer is NOT:

A because the wording doesn't clearly convey that people's interest in the Columbia River Highway in the 1980s was a renewal of earlier interest in the original highway.

B because the wording doesn't clearly convey that people's interest in the Columbia River Highway in the 1980s was a renewal of earlier interest in the original highway.

D because the wording doesn't clearly convey that people's interest in the Columbia River Highway in the 1980s was a renewal of earlier interest in the original highway.

Question 58. The best answer is **G** because it maintains the sentence pattern the writer has established in the previous two sentences by using simple sentence structure, passive voice, present-perfect tense, and similar ordering of words and phrases. This approach creates a sense of repetition and emphasis for stylistic effect.

The best answer is NOT:

F because it does not maintain the sentence pattern the writer has established in the previous two sentences.

H because it does not maintain the sentence pattern the writer has established in the previous two sentences.

J because it does not maintain the sentence pattern the writer has established in the previous two sentences.

Question 59. The best answer is **C** because it is the only option that clearly refers back to information in the first paragraph, which mentions that Hill and Lancaster began constructing the road in 1913 and that their design showcased the splendor of the gorge.

The best answer is NOT:

A because the first paragraph does not state that the site became a National Historic Landmark in 2000.

B because the first paragraph does not discuss uses for sections of the road where it was not feasible to restore motor traffic.

D because the idea that the Historic Columbia River Highway Trail has become a popular tourist destination is not referred to in the first paragraph.

Question 60. The best answer is **J** because Point D in Paragraph 3 is the most logical place to add information about the eventual disrepair of what remained of the original Columbia River Highway. Paragraph 3 as a whole focuses on the highway's decrease in use and resulting decline, so a sentence about the highway's condition fits logically at Point D and helps the overall understanding of the paragraph.

The best answer is NOT:

F because placing the sentence at Point A would interrupt the discussion of Hill and Lancaster's role in the design and construction of the original Columbia River Highway.

G because placing the sentence at Point B would interrupt the introduction of the discussion of particular design features of the original Columbia River Highway.

H because placing the sentence at Point C would interrupt the list of design features of the original Columbia River Highway.

Passage V

Question 61. The best answer is **A** because the name "Sylvia Robinson" is an essential element and should not be set off in the sentence.

The best answer is NOT:

B because "Sylvia Robinson" is an essential element and should not be set off with commas.

C because "Sylvia Robinson" is an essential element and should not be set off with commas.

D because it adds a comma after *singer*, which is incorrect.

Question 62. The best answer is **H** because it is the only option with correct subject-verb agreement. The singular subject *subculture* must have a singular verb.

The best answer is NOT:

F because *were* is a plural verb, and the subject of the sentence is singular.

G because *have* is a plural verb, and the subject of the sentence is singular.

J because *are* is a plural verb, and the subject of the sentence is singular.

Question 63. The best answer is **A** because it provides the clearest, most concise wording.

The best answer is NOT:

B because it is redundant; the sentence already indicates the action people were taking when they obeyed the directive from the DJ.

C because it is redundant; "heeded the DJ's call" and "obeyed him" are redundant phrases.

D because it is redundant; "did what he said" is redundant with *obeyed*.

Question 64. The best answer is **G** because it provides the appropriate punctuation (a dash) to set off the nonessential element "Big Bank Hank, Master Gee, and Wonder Mike" and also because the element ends with a dash.

The best answer is NOT:

F because a colon is not used to introduce a nonessential element.

H because a semicolon is not used to introduce a nonessential element.

J because the punctuation used to set off a nonessential element must match; since the nonessential element ends with a dash, it cannot be set off with a comma at the beginning.

Question 65. The best answer is **C** because it clearly explains why the new sentence should not be added. The information about Robinson and her husband forming other record labels is not relevant to the paragraph's discussion of how "Rapper's Delight" was created.

The best answer is NOT:

A because the suggested addition refers to the future labels Robinson would form, which logically would have no bearing on where the Sugarhill Gang would choose to record at the time being referenced.

B because the suggested addition refers to the future labels Robinson would form, and since the three rappers had already signed with Robinson at the time being referenced, it would be illogical to say Robinson's future labels had any effect on why they decided to record with her.

D because the time period in which Robinson and her husband started other record labels is not relevant to the paragraph's discussion of how "Rapper's Delight" was created.

Question 66. The best answer is **J** because it is the only option that has correct sentence structure. The introductory phrase correctly modifies *Robinson*, because Robinson wanted to "re-create the feel-good vibe of the music."

The best answer is NOT:

F because the introductory phrase incorrectly modifies "an upbeat disco record" as if the record were "wanting to re-create the feel-good vibe of the music."

G because the introductory phrase incorrectly modifies "an upbeat disco record" as if the record were "wanting to re-create the feel-good vibe of the music."

H because the introductory phrase incorrectly modifies *rhymes* as if the rhymes were "wanting to re-create the feel-good vibe of the music."

Question 67. The best answer is **D** because no transition word or phrase is necessary at this point.

The best answer is NOT:

A because the word *Nevertheless* suggests that the idea in this sentence is in opposition with the idea in the preceding sentence, which is incorrect.

B because the phrase "On the other hand" suggests that the idea in this sentence is in opposition with the idea in the preceding sentence, which is incorrect.

C because the phrase "As a result" indicates that Robinson's instincts having served her well was directly caused by her producing a successful rap record, which is illogical.

Question 68. The best answer is **H** because it does not include any unnecessary punctuation.

The best answer is NOT:

F because it has an unnecessary comma after *instincts*.

G because it has two unnecessary commas that incorrectly set off the word *and* from the rest of the sentence.

J because it has an unnecessary comma after *savvy*.

Question 69. The best answer is **D** because it is the only option that has correct sentence structure. It uses a gerund to begin the introductory dependent clause that links to an independent clause, which creates a complete sentence.

The best answer is NOT:

A because it creates two independent clauses that are separated by a comma, which creates a run-on sentence.

B because it creates two independent clauses that are separated by a comma, which creates a run-on sentence.

C because it creates two independent clauses that are separated by a comma, which creates a run-on sentence.

Question 70. The best answer is **G** because it best expresses the idea specified in the stem. The word option in this choice (*persuaded*) most effectively indicates that Robinson had to be convincing.

The best answer is NOT:

F because the wording doesn't effectively indicate that Robinson had to be convincing.

H because the wording doesn't effectively indicate that Robinson had to be convincing.

J because the wording doesn't effectively indicate that Robinson had to be convincing.

Question 71. The best answer is C because it is the only option that creates a standard English idiom ("covered new ground").

The best answer is NOT:

A because the phrase "encountered new ground" is not an idiomatically sound expression in standard English.

B because the phrase "protected new ground" is not an idiomatically sound expression in standard English.

D because the phrase "filled new ground" is not an idiomatically sound expression in standard English.

Question 72. The best answer is H because it provides the most logical conjunction to connect the ideas presented in this sentence. The song's focus was weightier and very different from other singles the group had released, and this caused them to be hesitant to record it.

The best answer is NOT:

F because the subordinating conjunction *because* is not logical in context; the song wasn't different than previous singles because of the rappers' hesitancy to record it.

G because the subordinating conjunction *although* is not logical in context; the song wasn't different than previous singles in spite of the rappers' hesitancy to record it.

J because the coordinating conjunction *for* is not logical in context; the song wasn't different than previous singles because of the rappers' hesitancy to record it.

Question 73. The best answer is D because it provides the most logical transitional phrase in context. The preceding sentences describe the tension between Robinson's determination to record "The Message" and the group's hesitancy to record it. But eventually, or "in the end," two group members recorded the song, and it became a success.

The best answer is NOT:

A because the phrase "in the opposite fashion" signals that what follows in the sentence presents a contrast to the idea in the preceding sentences, which is incorrect.

B because the phrase "in the first place" is illogical when the sentence is in fact describing the outcome of the situation described in the preceding sentences.

C because the phrase "in the same way" indicates that what follows in the sentence is similar to the idea described in the preceding sentences, which is incorrect.

Question 74. The best answer is **F** because the possessive adjective *Its* and the adjective *conscious* are the correct words to use in this context.

The best answer is NOT:

G because the noun *conscience* is incorrect in this context. It should be the adjective *conscious*.

H because the contraction *It's* is incorrect in this context. It should be the possessive adjective *its*.

J because the noun *conscience* and the contraction *It's* are both incorrect in this context.

Question 75. The best answer is **B** because it fails to correctly subordinate the sentence's second clause; it incorrectly uses a coordinating conjunction (*and*) to connect an independent clause and a dependent clause.

The best answer is NOT:

A because it creates an acceptable sentence construction in that it uses a coordinating conjunction and a comma to connect two independent clauses.

C because it creates an acceptable sentence construction in that it uses *and* to connect two parallel verb phrases.

D because it creates an acceptable sentence construction in that it uses a comma and a gerund to connect an independent clause and a dependent clause.

Question 1. The correct answer is **C**. Substitute 3 for x and 2 for y to get $3(3^2) - 4(2) = 3(9) - 8 = 27 - 8$, or 19. If you answered **A**, you may have substituted 2 for x and 3 for y to get $3(2^2) - 4(3) = 3(4) - 12 = 12 - 12$, or 0. If you answered **B**, you may have substituted 3 for x and 2 for y and multiplied the exponent to get $3(3)(2) - 4(2) = 3(6) - 8 = 18 - 8$, or 10. If you answered **D**, you may have substituted 2 for x and 3 for y, and then squared the product of 2 and 3 before applying the exponent to get $[3(2)]^2 - 4(3) = (6^2) - 12 = 36 - 12$, or 24. If you answered **E**, you may have substituted 2 for x and 2 for y, and then squared the product of 2 and 3 before applying the exponent to get $[3(2)]^2 - 4(2) = (6^2) - 8 = 36 - 8$, or 28.

Question 2. The correct answer is **H**. Use the exterior angle theorem to determine that the measure of $\angle ACD$ is the sum of the measures of the interior angles $\angle BAC$ and $\angle ABC$ or $35° + 95° = 130°$. If you answered **F**, you may have thought $\angle ABC$ and $\angle ACD$ have the same measure. If you answered **G**, you may have added $35° + 90° = 125°$. If you answered **J**, you may have added $90° + (180° - 35° - 95°) = 90° + 50° = 140°$. If you answered **K**, you may have subtracted the measure of $\angle BAC$ from $180°$ to get $180° - 35°$, or $145°$.

Question 3. The correct answer is **E**. First, divide the constants to get $-\frac{36}{4}$ or -9, and then apply the exponent rule for division to get $x^{4-1}y^{3-1}$, or $x^3 y^2$. By combining the constant and the variable expression, the fraction is equivalent to $-9x^3 y^2$. If you answered **A**, you may have added the constants, $-(36 + 4) = -40$, and correctly applied the exponent rule for division to get $-40x^3 y^2$. If you answered **B**, you may have subtracted the constants, $-(36 - 4) = -32$ and correctly applied the exponent rule for division to get $-32x^3 y^2$. If you answered **C**, you may have correctly calculated the constant as -9, and then, you may have incorrectly applied the exponent rule for division and added exponents to get $x^{4+1}y^{3+1}$, or $x^5 y^4$, thus obtaining $-9x^5 y^4$. If you answered **D**, you may have correctly calculated the constant as -9, and then, you may have thought the exponents in the denominator of the fraction were both 0 and applied the exponent rule for division to get $x^{4-0}y^{3-0}$, or $x^4 y^3$, thus obtaining $-9x^4 y^3$.

Question 4. The correct answer is **H**. Find how many batches of 100 mileage points are in 7,000, $\frac{7,000}{100} = 70$, multiply that by 0.75, $70[\$0.75] = \$52.50$, and then add 20.00 to get 72.50. If you answered **F**, you may have incorrectly found $\frac{7,000}{100}$ as 7, multiplied the 7 by 0.75 to get 5.25, and then added 20.00 to get 25.25. If you answered **G**, you may have found how many batches of 100 mileage points were in 7,000, $\frac{7,000}{100} = 70$, added 70 and 20 to get 90, and then multiplied 90 by 0.75 to get 67.50. If you answered **J**, you may have multiplied 0.75 by 100 to get 75.00. If you answered **K**, you may have multiplied 0.75 by 100 to get 75.00 and then added 20.00 to get 95.00.

Question 5. **The correct answer is E.** Substitute -5 for x to get $4(-5)^2 - 11(-5) = 4(25) + 55 = 100 + 55 = 155$. If you answered **A**, you may have correctly substituted but then simplified as $-100 - 55$ to get -155. If you answered **B**, you may have correctly substituted $4(-5)^2 - 11(-5)$ but then simplified as $-100 + 11 + 5$ to get -84. If you answered **C**, you may have correctly substituted but then simplified as $-100 + 55$ to get -45. If you answered **D**, you may have correctly substituted but then simplified as $100 - 11 - 5$ to get 84.

Question 6. **The correct answer is G.** Set up an expression that represents the sum of regular pay and overtime pay, with one addend for the regular hourly rate and one addend for the over-40-hours rate, $11(40) + 11(1.5)(50 - 40)$, to get $440 + 165$, or $605. If you answered **F**, you may have multiplied the regular hour rate by the total number of hours, $11(50)$, to get $550. If you answered **H**, you may have multiplied the total number of hours by the sum of 11 and 1.5 to get $50(12.5)$, or $625. If you answered **J**, you may have used 10 instead of 11 for the regular hourly rate and then multiplied the total number of hours by the over-40-hours rate to get $10(1.5)(50)$, or $750. If you answered **K**, you may have multiplied the over-40-hour rate by the total number of hours, $11(1.5)(50)$, to get $825.

Question 7. **The correct answer is E.** Since a junior has already been chosen that leaves 11 students—4 seniors and 7 juniors. The probability of choosing a senior is the number of seniors divided by the total number of students left, or $\frac{4}{11}$. If you answered **A**, you may have thought the probability was the number of students you were picking divided by the total number of students left, or $\frac{1}{11}$. If you answered **B**, you may have thought the probability was how many students were being picked over the number of seniors, or $\frac{1}{4}$. If you answered **C**, you thought the first student picked was a senior, resulting in 3 seniors and 11 total students, or a probability of $\frac{3}{11}$. If you answered **D**, you may have thought the first student picked was a senior and the probability was how many students were being picked over the number of seniors left, or $\frac{1}{3}$.

Question 8. **The correct answer is F.** The change in temperature is equal to the ending temperature minus the beginning temperature, $-12 - 24$ or $-36°F$. If you answered **G**, you may have added the 2 temperatures and attached a negative sign since the temperature decreased to get $-(24 - 12)$ or $-12°F$. If you answered **H**, you may have added the 2 temperatures and divided by 2 to get $\frac{-12 + 24}{2}$ or $+6°F$. If you answered **J**, you may have added the 2 temperatures to get $-12 + 24$ or $+12°F$. If you answered **K**, you may have subtracted the ending temperature from the beginning temperature to get $24 - (-12)$ or $+36°F$.

Question 9. **The correct answer is C.** The total cost of the car rental is equal to the sum of the total daily rental fee (the product of the number of days rented and the daily rental fee) and the total mileage fee (the product of the number of miles the car is driven and the per-mile fee), $6(35) + 350(0.425) = 210 + 158.75$, or $358.75. If you answered **A**, you may have added 6 to the product of the number of miles the car is driven and the per-mile fee to get $6 + 350(0.425) = 6 + 148.75$, or $154.75. If you answered **B**, you may have multiplied 35 by the sum of 6 and 0.425 to get $35(6 + 0.425)$, or $224.88. If you answered **D**, you may have found twice the product of 6 and 35 to get $2(6)(35.00)$, or $420.00. If you answered **E**, you may have found the total cost of the car rental using 4.25 for the per-mile fee to get $6(35) + 350(4.25) = 210 + 1{,}487.50$, or $1,697.50.

Question 10. **The correct answer is H.** The slope is defined as $\frac{y_1 - y_2}{x_1 - x_2}$. For these 2 points, it is $\frac{4-3}{-6-1}$, or $-\frac{1}{7}$. If you answered **F**, you may have added instead of subtracted to get $\frac{4+3}{-6+1}$, or $-\frac{7}{5}$. If you answered **G**, you may have subtracted the y terms and added the x terms to get $\frac{4-3}{-6+1}$, or $-\frac{1}{5}$. If you answered **J**, you may have subtracted the y terms in one order and the x terms in the opposite order to get $\frac{4-3}{1-(-6)}$, or $\frac{1}{7}$. If you answered **K**, you may have subtracted the y terms and added the x terms to get $\frac{3-4}{1-6}$, or $\frac{1}{5}$.

Question 11. **The correct answer is B.** To find the probability of the selected customer having ordered regular coffee without milk, first find the number in the cell where the "Regular" column and the "Without milk" row meet. Then place that number over the total number of customers to get $\frac{10}{36}$, or $\frac{5}{18}$. If you answered **A**, you may have found the cell where the "Decaf" column and the "Without milk" row meet and then put that number over the total number of customers to get $\frac{6}{36}$, or $\frac{1}{6}$. If you answered **C**, you may have found the cell where the "Regular" column and the "Without milk" row meet; you then put that number over the customer total minus that number to get $\frac{10}{36-10} = \frac{10}{26}$, or $\frac{5}{13}$. If you answered **D**, you may have found the cell where the "Regular" column and the "Total" row meet and then put that number over the total number of customers to get $\frac{18}{36}$, or $\frac{1}{2}$. If you answered **E**, you may have found the cell where the "Regular" column and the "Without milk" row meet and then found the cell where the "Total" column and the "Without milk" row meet. You then put the first number over the second to get $\frac{10}{16}$, or $\frac{5}{8}$.

Question 12. **The correct answer is J.** To solve the inequality, you subtract $2x$ and add 5 to both sides to get $3x - 2x < 1 + 5$, or $x < 6$. If you answered **F**, you may have subtracted $2x$ and added -5 to get $3x - 2x < 1 - 5$, or $x < -4$. If you answered **G**, you may have added $2x$ and -5 to get $3x + 2x < 1 - 5$, or $5x < -4$, or $x > -\frac{4}{5}$. If you answered **H**, you may have added $2x$ and 5 to get $3x + 2x < 1 + 5$, or $5x < 6$, or $x < \frac{6}{5}$. If you answered **K**, you may have subtracted $2x$ and added 5 and then switched the inequality sign to get $3x - 2x > 1 + 5$, or $x > 6$.

Question 13. The correct answer is B. To simplify the expression, you distribute the multiplication inside the parentheses to get $4x+8+6x-3$, or $10x+5$, which factors to $5(2x+1)$. If you answered **A**, you may have added all the terms to get $4+x+2+3+2x-1$, or $3x+8$. If you answered **C**, you may have distributed and added all the expressions to get $4x+8+6x+3$, or $10x+11$, and then you factored incorrectly to get $10(x+11-10)$ or $10(x+1)$. If you answered **D**, you may have distributed and added all the expressions to get $4x+8+6x+3$, or $10x+11$. If you answered **E**, you may have combined the expressions in the parentheses and then multiplied to get $4(3x)+3(x)$, or $15x$.

Question 14. The correct answer is G. Convert the percentage to a decimal and the scientific notation to standard form, and then multiply $0.04(13,600)$ to get 544. If you answered **F**, you may have divided by 4 to get $\frac{1.36}{4}$, or 0.34; decreased the exponent by 1; and then multiplied the exponential part to get $0.34(1,000)$, or 340. If you answered **H**, you may have divided by 0.4 to get $\frac{1.36}{0.4}$, or 3.4; decreased the exponent by 1; and then multiplied to get $3.4(1,000)$, or 3,400. If you answered **J**, you may have multiplied by 0.4 to get $0.4(13,600)$, or 5,440. If you answered **K**, you may have converted to standard form and then multiplied by 4 to get $4(13,600)$, or 54,400.

Question 15. The correct answer is B. Factor the denominators as $5(7)$, $7(11)$, and $2(11)$. Accounting for duplicates, you get $(5)(7)(11)(2)$, or 770. If you answered **A**, you may have multiplied to get $5(11)(2)$, or 110. If you answered **C**, you may have multiplied to get $35(77)$, or 2,695. If you answered **D**, you may have missed the duplicate 7 after you factored the denominators as $5(7)$, $7(11)$, and $2(11)$; you then multiplied to get $35(11)(22)$, or 8,470. If you answered **E**, you may have multiplied all 3 denominators to get $35(77)(22)$, or 59,290.

Question 16. The correct answer is F. A move 3 coordinate units to the left means you subtract 3 from the x-coordinate to get $(3-3, 27)$, or $(0, 27)$. If you answered **G**, you may have subtracted 3 from the y-coordinate to get $(3, 27-3)$, or $(3, 24)$. If you answered **H**, you may have thought that a translation does not change a graph, so $(3, 27)$ would still be on the graph. If you answered **J**, you may have added 3 to the y-coordinate to get $(3, 27+3)$, or $(3, 30)$. If you answered **K**, you may have added 3 to the x-coordinate to get $(3+3, 27)$, or $(6, 27)$.

Question 17. The correct answer is B. To find the midpoint, you average the x-coordinates and the y-coordinates to get $\left(\frac{-6+2}{2}, \frac{9+5}{2}\right)$, or $(-2, 7)$. If you answered **A**, you may have subtracted the first point's coordinates from the second point's coordinates but thought that a negative number, when subtracted, is still negative, yielding $(2-6, 5-9)$, or $(-4, -4)$. If you answered **C**, you may have added the coordinates of each point and divided by 2 to get $\left(\frac{-6+9}{2}, \frac{2+5}{2}\right)$, or $\left(\frac{3}{2}, \frac{7}{2}\right)$. If you answered **D**, you may have subtracted the first point's coordinates from the second point's coordinates and divided by 2 to get $\left(\frac{2-(-6)}{2}, \frac{5-9}{2}\right)$, or $(4, -2)$. If you answered **E**, you may have subtracted the first point's coordinates from the second point's coordinates to get $(2-(-6), 5-9)$, or $(8, -4)$.

Question 18. The correct answer is K. You simplified the fraction on the left to x, so you got $\frac{x(x+2)}{x+2} = 2$, or $x = 2$. If you answered **F**, you may have multiplied wrong to get $x^2 + 2x = x + 4$ and then subtracted wrong to get $x^2 + 3x - 4 = 0$. Then you factored the left side as $(x+4)(x-1) = 0$. Setting the factor equal to 0 and solving, you got $x = -4$. If you answered **G**, you may have rewritten the equation as $x + x + 2 + 2 + 2 = 0$ to get $2x + 6 = 0$, or $x = -3$. If you answered **H**, you may have set the denominator equal to 0 to get $x + 2 = 0$, or $x = -2$. If you answered **J**, you may have rewritten the left side as $\frac{x^2}{x} + \frac{2x}{2} = x + x = 2x$. Then, you set that side equal to the right side to get $2x = 2$, or $x = 1$.

Question 19. The correct answer is D. The total number of moviegoers surveyed is 5,000. To find the average, you need to divide 5,000 by the number of categories, 4, to get 1,250 moviegoers. If you answered **A**, you may have mistakenly and incorrectly added the numbers in the top 2 rows in the table to get $830 + 1,650 \rightarrow 2,440$, then divided by 4 to get $\frac{2,440}{4}$, or 610 moviegoers. If you answered **B**, you may have found the difference between the greatest and least numbers in the table and divided by 2 to get $\frac{2,320-200}{2}$, or 1,060 moviegoers. If you answered **C**, you may have mistakenly calculated the average of the 4 numbers as $\frac{4,960}{4}$, or 1,240 movie goers. If you answered **E**, you may have averaged the 2 greatest numbers in the table to get $\frac{2,320+1,650}{2}$, or 1,985 moviegoers.

Question 20. The correct answer is G. Let m be the number of matinee moviegoers. Set up the equation by multiplying the number of moviegoers by the cost per type of movie attendance to get $7m + 9.50(5,000 - m) = 44,000 \rightarrow 7m + 47,500 - 9.50m = 44,000 \rightarrow -2.5m = -3,500$, or $m = 1,400$ moviegoers. If you answered **F**, you may have set up the equation $7m + 9.50(5,000 - m) = 44,000 \rightarrow 7m + 47,500 = 44,000 \rightarrow 7m = 3,500$ to get $m = 500$ moviegoers. If you answered **H**, you may have divided 5,000 by 2 (the number of different prices) to get 2,500 moviegoers. If you answered **J**, you may have set up the equation $9.50m + 7(5,000 - m) = 44,000 \rightarrow 9.50m + 35,000 - 7m = 44,000 \rightarrow 2.5m = 9,000$ to get $m = 3,600$ moviegoers. If you answered **K**, you may have set up the equation $7m + 9.50(5,000 - m) = 44,000 \rightarrow 7m + 47,500 = 44,000 \rightarrow 7m = 3,500$ to get $m = 500$. Then you subtracted $5,000 - 500$ to get 4,500 moviegoers.

Question 21. The correct answer is A. You divided each age group number by 5,000 and then multiplied by 100 to get $\frac{2,750}{5,000}(100) = 55\%$, $\frac{1,225}{5,000}(100) = 24.5\%$, $\frac{625}{5,000}(100) = 12.5\%$, and $\frac{400}{5,000}(100) = 8\%$. These match the percentages in **A**. If you answered **B**, you may have estimated the percentages. If you answered **C**, you may have calculated the percentage for 21–30 and then rounded the other 3 percentages to the nearest 5%. If you answered **D**, you may have estimated the percentages. If you answered **E**, you may have tried to have the circle graph represent both tables.

Question 22. **The correct answer is G.** You can decompose the composite figure into 2 rectangles. If you extend the vertical line segment on the right of the 6-centimeter side, you have a 6 by 9 rectangle and a 3 by 7 rectangle (see Figure 1). The 7-centimeter side is found by calculating 13 − 6 = 7. The area of the 6 by 9 rectangle is 54 square centimeters, and the area of the 3 by 7 rectangle is 21 square centimeters. The total area is then 75 square centimeters, because 54 + 21 = 75. Alternatively, you could have found the area of the larger 9 by 13 rectangle and then subtracted the area of a 6 by 7 rectangle (see Figure 2). The 6-centimeter side of the rectangle shown shaded is found by calculating 9 − 3 = 6. The total area is then 75 square centimeters, because 9(13) − 6(7) = 75. If you selected **F**, you may have reasoned that the composite figure was a 9 by 13 rectangle with a 6 by 7 rectangle removed and found the area of the removed rectangle instead of the composite rectangle. If you selected **H**, you may have added the areas of a 6 by 9 rectangle and a 13 by 3 rectangle, not accounting for the overlap: 54 + 39 = 93. If you selected **J**, you may have estimated that the area of the composite figure was the same as that of a rectangle with width 9 centimeters and length 11 centimeters: 9(11) = 99. If you selected **K**, you may have found the area of a 9 by 13 rectangle, not accounting for the removed 6 by 7 rectangle: 9(13) = 117.

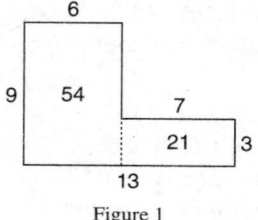

Figure 1

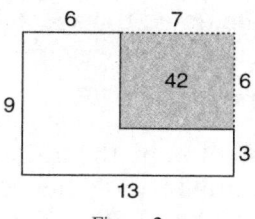

Figure 2

Question 23. **The correct answer is C.** Because $\angle BEC$ and $\angle AEB$ form a line, $m\angle BEC + m\angle AEB = 180°$. Solving for $m\angle BEC$ gives us that $m\angle BEC = (180 - 145)° = 35°$. By angle addition $m\angle BEC + m\angle CED = m\angle BED$. After substitution of known angles, we have $35 + m\angle CED = 90°$. Solving for $m\angle CED$ results in $m\angle CED = (90 - 35)° = 55°$. If you selected **A**, you may have found $m\angle BEC$ instead of $m\angle CED$. If you selected **B**, you may have incorrectly thought that $\overline{EC}$ bisected $\angle BED$, then calculated $m\angle CED = \left(\frac{90}{2}\right)°$. If you selected **D**, you may have known the angle appeared to be between 45° and 90° based on the diagram but may not have known how to calculate it exactly. If you selected **E**, you may have thought that the item didn't give you enough information to answer the question.

Question 24. **The correct answer is G.** Let $f(x) = 5\sin(x) - 7$. Since $5\sin(x) - 14 = 5\sin(x) - 7 - 7$, we can write the image of $f(x)$ after the transformation to be $f(x) - 7$. This is a translation of down 7 coordinate units. If you selected **F**, you may have confused $y - 7 = f(x)$ with $y = f(x) - 7$. If you selected **H**, you may have confused the negative direction on the x-axis with the negative direction on the y-axis. If you selected **J**, you may have confused $y = f(x - 7)$ with $y = f(x) - 7$. If you selected **K**, you may not have compared the subtracted 14 and the subtracted 7 and confused $y = f(x - 14)$ with $y = f(x) - 14$.

Question 25. The correct answer is **C**. Because $9^{\frac{1}{2}} = \sqrt{9} = 3$ and $16^{\frac{1}{2}} = \sqrt{16} = 4$, $\left(9^{\frac{1}{2}} + 16^{\frac{1}{2}} \right)^2 = (3+4)^2 = 7^2 = 49$. If you selected **A**, you may have found $9^{\frac{1}{2}} + 16^{\frac{1}{2}} = 7$ correctly but not squared the result. If you selected **B**, you may have you may have added the bases to get $\left((9+16)^{\frac{1}{2}} \right)^2$ and then simplified $\left(\sqrt{25} \right)^2$. If you selected **D**, you may have incorrectly simplified $\left(9^{\frac{1}{2}} + 16^{\frac{1}{2}} \right)^2$ to be $9^2 + 16^2$ and then calculated $9^2 + 16^2 = 81 + 256$. If you selected **E**, you may have incorrectly simplified $\left(9^{\frac{1}{2}} + 16^{\frac{1}{2}} \right)^2 = (9+16)^2$, then calculated 25^2.

Question 26. The correct answer is **F**. The sine of an angle in a right triangle is the ratio of the length of the side opposite that angle to the length of the hypotenuse of the triangle. To find the sine, we need to calculate the length of the side opposite the angle using the Pythagorean theorem, $a^2 + b^2 = c^2$. For the given triangle, $a^2 + 12^2 = 13^2$ so $a = \sqrt{13^2 - 12^2} = 5$. The length of the side opposite angle θ is 5 inches. Therefore, the sine of θ is $\frac{5}{13}$. If you selected **G**, you may have found $\tan \theta$, the ratio of the lengths of the opposite and adjacent sides. If you selected **H**, you may have found $\cos \theta$, the ratio of the length of the adjacent side to the length of the hypotenuse. If you selected **J**, you may have found $\sec \theta$, the ratio of the length of the hypotenuse to the length of the adjacent side. If you selected **K**, you may have found $\csc \theta$, the ratio of the length of the hypotenuse to the length of the opposite side.

Question 27. The correct answer is **C**. The shaded region is made up of 2 triangles. The smaller triangle has a base of 2 inches and a height of 4 inches. The larger triangle has a base of 4 inches and a height of 6 inches. Therefore, the total number of shaded square inches is $\frac{1}{2}(2)(4) + \frac{1}{2}(4)(6) = 4 + 12 = 16$. The shaded area is 16 square inches, and the total area is 36 square inches. The fractional part that is shaded is then $\frac{16}{36} = \frac{4}{9}$. If you selected **A**, you may have thought that both shaded triangles had an area of 12 square inches: $\frac{12+12}{36} = \frac{2}{3}$. If you selected **B**, you may have divided the area of the shaded region by the area of the unshaded region instead of the total area: $\frac{16}{36-16} = \frac{4}{5}$. If you selected **D**, you may have found the fractional part of the square that is unshaded instead of shaded: $\frac{36-16}{36} = \frac{5}{9}$. If you selected **E**, you may have not multiplied by $\frac{1}{2}$ when finding the area of the shaded triangles: $\frac{2(4)+4(6)}{36} = \frac{8+24}{36} = \frac{8}{9}$.

Question 28. **The correct answer is H.** By the communitive property of multiplication, $(4.25 \times 10^{2c+4})(6 \times 10^7) = 4.25 \times 6 \times 10^{2c+4} \times 10^7$. Because $4.25 \times 6 = 25.5$ and $10^{2c+4} \times 10^7 = 10^{2c+4+7}$, $(4.25 \times 10^{2c+4})(6 \times 10^7) = 25.5 \times 10^{2c+11}$. Because $25.5 \times 10^1 = 255$, we know that $2c + 11 = 1 \rightarrow 2c = -10 \rightarrow c = -5$. If you selected **F**, you may have incorrectly thought that $25.5 \times 10^{-3} = 255$ and then found the solution to $2c + 11 = -3$. If you selected **G**, you may have incorrectly thought that $25.5 \times 10^{-2} = 255$ and then found the solution to $2c + 11 = -2$. If you selected **J**, you may have incorrectly thought that $25.5 \times 10^2 = 255$ and then found the solution to $2c + 11 = 2$. If you selected **K**, you may have incorrectly thought that $25.5 \times 10^3 = 255$ and then found the solution to $2c + 11 = 3$.

Question 29. **The correct answer is D.** The value of $m + 1$ **is always 1 more than** m, thus $m + 1$ **is always greater than** m. If you selected one of the other choices, you may not have been able to produce a counter example. We know that $m \le \frac{1}{m}$ (choice **A**) is false because $2 > \frac{1}{2}$. We know that $m \le \sqrt{m}$ (choice **B**) is false because $4 > \sqrt{4} = 2$. We know that $m \ge m^2$ (choice **C**) is false because $3 < 3^2 = 9$. We know that $m \ge \sqrt{m+1}$ (choice **E**) is false because $1 < \sqrt{1+1} = \sqrt{2}$.

Question 30. **The correct answer is J.** The volume of the cylinder is $\pi r^2 h = \pi(5^2)3 = 75\pi$ cubic meters. Since each cubic meter is 2,205 pounds, using the approximation $\pi \approx 3.14$, the total weight is $75\pi(2,205) \approx 519,278$ pounds, which is between 500,000 pounds and 1,000,000 pounds. If you selected **F**, you may have not multiplied by pi when calculating the volume and found the total weight as $75(2,205) = 165,375$ pounds. If you selected **G**, you may have incorrectly calculated $\pi(5^2)3 \rightarrow \pi(5)(2)(3) = 30\pi$ cubic meters as the volume, then found the weight as $30\pi(2,205) \approx 207,711$ pounds. If you selected **H**, you may have mixed up the radius and the height of the cylinder and thought the volume was $\pi(3^2)5 = 45\pi$ cubic meters. You may then have calculated the weight as $45\pi(2,205) \approx 311,567$ pounds. If you selected **K**, you may have incorrectly calculated $\pi(5^2)3 \rightarrow \pi(5 \times 3)^2 = 225\pi$ cubic meters as the volume, then found the weight as $225\pi(2,205) \approx 1,557,833$ pounds.

Question 31. **The correct answer is D.** The length of the horizontal leg is 40 coordinate units, found by subtracting $0 - (-40)$. The length of the vertical leg is 30 coordinate units, found by subtracting $30 - 0$. To find the length of a hypotenuse, c, when you know the lengths of 2 legs, a and b, use the Pythagorean theorem: $c^2 = a^2 + b^2$. So $c^2 = 40^2 + 30^2$ and $c = \sqrt{1,600 + 900}$, which simplifies to $c = 50$. If you chose **A**, you may have found the length of the vertical leg. If you chose **B**, you may have found the mean of both leg lengths: $\frac{40+30}{2}$. If you chose **C**, you may have found the length of the horizontal leg. If you chose **E**, you may have found the sum of the leg lengths: $40 + 30$.

Question 32. The correct answer is F. Every circle has a vertical line of symmetry about its center (among infinitely many lines of symmetry). Any rotation of a circle about its center maps the circle onto itself. So, no matter where and how you draw a circle, it has a vertical line of symmetry. We can eliminate choices **G**, **H**, **J**, and **K** with counterexamples. This graphic gives all the lines of symmetry for a square, an ellipse, an equilateral triangle, and a rectangle. In the top row, they are oriented so 1 line of symmetry is vertical. In the bottom row, they are oriented so they do not have a vertical line of symmetry.

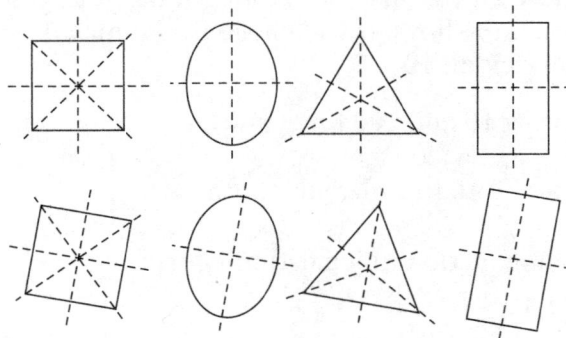

If you chose **G**, you may have done so because every square has 4 lines of symmetry, so 4 different orientations would result in a vertical line of symmetry; however, you didn't consider the orientations that do not result in a vertical line of symmetry. If you chose **H**, **J**, or **K**, you may have done so because ellipses, triangles, and rectangles are often drawn with vertical lines of symmetry, and you didn't consider counterexamples such as those shown in the bottom row of the graphic.

Question 33. The correct answer is B. The equation of this parabola is *almost* given in vertex form. Vertex form of a parabola is $y = a(x - h)^2 + k$, where (h,k) is the vertex of the parabola. The given equation is equivalent to $y = 30(x - (-17))^2 + (-42)$, which means $h = -17$ and $k = -42$. Therefore, the vertex is given by $(-17, -42)$. If you chose **A**, $(-a,k)$, you may have thought the x-coordinate of the vertex is equal to the opposite of a, the coefficient of the squared term. If you chose **C**, $(-h,k)$, you may have forgotten that h, the x-coordinate of the vertex, is *subtracted* from x, so you forgot to divide 17 by -1. If you chose **D**, $(-h,-k)$, you may have divided -42 by -1 instead of dividing 17 by -1. If you chose **E**, $(a,-k)$, you may have used a instead of h and $-k$ instead of k.

Question 34. The correct answer is H. First, find the area of square *ABCD*. For any square, all sides are congruent, so the length and width of square *ABCD* are both 15 meters. The area of any square or rectangle is the product of its length and width, so the area of square *ABCD* is $15(15) = 225$ square meters. We are told that the area of the rectangle is equal to the area of the square, so it is also 225 square meters. We divide the area of the rectangle by its width, 10 meters, to get $225 \div 10 = 22.5$ meters.

If you chose **F**, you may have assumed the length of the rectangle was equal to the length of the square. If you chose **G**, you may have thought the perimeters, not the areas, of the square and rectangle were equal: $2(15 + 15) = 2(10 + 20)$. If you chose **J**, you may have found the sum of the given lengths: $15 + 10$. If you chose **K**, you may have found the product of the given lengths and then divided by 4: $\frac{15 \cdot 10}{4} = 37.5$.

Question 35. **The correct answer is B.** Because the average of the 10 weights is 77 pounds, the total of the 10 weights is $77(10) = 770$ pounds. The average of the weights of the 9 oldest boys is 78 pounds, so the total of those 9 weights is $78(9) = 702$ pounds. The difference in totals gives the weight, in pounds, of the youngest boy: $770 - 702 = 68$.

If you chose **A**, you may have thought the youngest boy was the lightest of the group and chosen the least option among the choices. If you chose **C**, you may have estimated well but not known how to find the exact value. If you chose **D**, you may have thought the youngest boy weighed the same as the average of the 9 remaining boys. If you chose **E**, you may have added the total number of boys and their average weight: $10 + 77$.

Question 36. **The correct answer is J.** Substituting 10 and 100 for A and A_0, we have $100 = 10\left(2^{\frac{h}{5}}\right)$. To solve for h, first divide both sides by 10 to isolate the power: $10 = \left(2^{\frac{h}{5}}\right)$. Rewrite this exponential equation as an equivalent equation in logarithmic form: $\log_2 10 = \frac{h}{5}$. Finally, multiply both sides by 5: $5 \log_2 10 = h$.

If you chose **F**, you may have rewritten $100 = 10\left(2^{\frac{h}{5}}\right)$ by taking 10^2 first, resulting in $100 = 100^{\frac{h}{5}}$ and then solved correctly for h from this incorrect equation. If you chose **G**, you may have rewritten $100 = 10\left(2^{\frac{h}{5}}\right)$ as if the exponent were a factor, resulting in $100 = (10)(2)\left(\frac{h}{5}\right)$ and then solved correctly for h from this incorrect equation. If you chose **H**, you may have thought the product of 5 and $\log_2 10$ was $\log_2 50$. If you chose **K**, you may have multiplied the 10 and 2 on the right before rewriting the equation in logarithmic form: $100 = 20^{\frac{h}{5}} \rightarrow \log_{20} 100 = \frac{h}{5}$; you then solved correctly for h from this incorrect equation.

Question 37. **The correct answer is E.** Both the numerator and the denominator of the given fraction can be factored into 2 binomials: $\frac{(x-3)(x+2)}{(x-3)(x+3)}$. The identical binomials $(x - 3)$ cancel, leaving $\frac{x+2}{x+3}$. If you chose **A**, you may have thought you could cancel the identical terms x^2, even though they aren't factors. If you chose **B**, you may have factored incorrectly: $\frac{(x+3)(x-2)}{(x+3)(x-3)}$. If you chose **C**, you may have factored incorrectly: $\frac{(x+3)(x-2)}{(x+3)(x+3)}$. If you chose **D**, you may have factored incorrectly: $\frac{(x+3)(x+2)}{(x+3)(x-3)}$.

Question 38. **The correct answer is H.** We must find half of 9 feet 4 inches. To do this, we can find half of 9 feet, find half of 4 inches, and then add the results. Half of 9 feet is 4.5 feet, which is equivalent to 4 feet 6 inches (because there are 12 inches in 1 foot). Half of 4 inches is 2 inches. Now we can add 4 feet 6 inches plus 2 inches to get 4 feet 8 inches. Alternatively, we can convert 9 feet 4 inches to 112 inches. This comes from (9 feet)(12 inches per foot) + (4 inches). We divide 112 inches by 2 to get 56 inches and then convert 56 inches by finding how many whole groups of 12 inches go into 56 inches. There are 4 groups of 12 inches plus 8 inches left over. That is 4 feet 8 inches.

If you chose **F**, you may have taken half of 9 feet, which is 4.5 feet, and thought it was equivalent to 4 feet 5 inches. If you chose **G**, you may have thought 4.5 feet (half of 9 feet) was equivalent to 4 feet 5 inches and then added the 2 inches (half of 4 inches) to get 4 feet 7 inches. If you chose **J**, you may have converted 9 feet to 108 inches, divided 108 by 2, and then thought 54 inches was 5 feet 4 inches.

Question 39. **The correct answer is A.** Order of operations instructs us to perform the multiplication and division before the addition. Also, dividing by $\frac{1}{5}$ is equivalent to multiplying by 5. After multiplying $\frac{1}{3}$ and $\frac{1}{4}$ and 5, we have $\frac{1}{2} + \frac{5}{12} = \frac{x}{y}$. Because $\frac{1}{2}$ is equal to $\frac{6}{12}$, we have $\frac{11}{12} = \frac{x}{y}$. Because 11 and 12 are relatively prime, $x = 11$ and $y = 12$. Therefore, $x + y = 23$. If you chose **B**, you may have added $\frac{1}{2} + \frac{1}{3}$ to get $\frac{5}{6}$ before multiplying: $\frac{5}{6} \cdot \frac{1}{4} \cdot \frac{5}{1} = \frac{25}{24}$; you then chose the numerator of the result, $x = 25$. If you chose **C**, you may have added $\frac{1}{2} + \frac{1}{3}$ to get $\frac{5}{6}$ before multiplying: $\frac{5}{6} \cdot \frac{1}{4} \cdot \frac{5}{1} = \frac{25}{24}$; you then added $x + y$: 25 + 24 = 49. If you chose **D**, you may have multiplied by $\frac{1}{5}$ instead of multiplying by its reciprocal: $\frac{1}{2} + \frac{1}{60} = \frac{31}{60}$; you then added $x + y$: 31 + 60 = 91. If you chose **E**, you may have correctly solved for x and y but found the product xy instead of the sum $x + y$: 11(12) = 132.

Question 40. **The correct answer is H.** First, note that there are 4 repeating digits. This means than the 5th, 9th, 13th, etc., digits after the decimal point will be the same as the 1st digit after the decimal point, which is 3. In other words, any digit in a position corresponding to 1 mod 4 (has a remainder of 1 when divided by 4) will be 3. Similarly, any digit in a position corresponding to 2 mod 4 will be 1 (the 2nd digit). When we divide 358 by 4, we have a remainder of 2. Therefore, the 358th digit after the decimal point will be the same as the 2nd digit after the decimal point. This digit is 1.

If you chose **F**, you may have assumed the decimal terminated before position 358. If you chose **G**, you may have divided 358 by 5 instead of 4 (because there are 5 digits shown in the decimal, counting the 0) and chosen the remainder of that division. If you chose **J**, you may have divided 358 by 5 instead of 4 (because there are 5 digits shown in the decimal, counting the 0), and because the remainder of that division is 3, you chose the 3rd digit after the decimal point. If you chose **K**, you may have thought the digit must occur in both the given repeating decimal and 358.

Question 41. The correct answer is C. To answer this question, calculate the expected value of a random variable. The random variable is the discount amount per customer, measured in dollars. The value of the random variable depends on the color of the ball selected: $\$60 \cdot 0.10 = \$6$ for red, $\$60 \cdot 0.30 = \$18$ for white, and $\$60 \cdot 0.60 = \$36$ for green.

To calculate the expected value, multiply each of the possible values by its probability of occurring (the fraction of all balls that are a certain color), and then add the products. There is a $\frac{3}{6}$ probability of a red selection (a \$6 discount), a $\frac{2}{6}$ probability of a white selection (an \$18 discount), and a $\frac{1}{6}$ probability of a green selection (a \$36 discount). So, the expected value is $\$6 \cdot \frac{3}{6} + \$18 \cdot \frac{2}{6} + \$36 \cdot \frac{1}{6} = \$15$.

If you chose **A**, you likely multiplied the shoe price by the discount percentage for the color of the ball most likely to be selected ($\$60 \cdot 0.10$). If you chose **B**, you likely divided the sum of the 3 possible discount amounts by the number of balls in the jar: $\frac{\$6 + \$18 + \$36}{6}$. If you chose **D**, you likely found the average of the 3 possible discount amounts: $\frac{\$6 + \$18 + \$36}{3}$. If you chose **E**, you likely multiplied the discount percentage by \$100 instead of \$60 when finding the 3 possible discount amounts ($\$10 \cdot \frac{3}{6} + \$30 \cdot \frac{2}{6} + \$60 \cdot \frac{1}{6}$).

Question 42. The correct answer is G. To find p, the percentage of large animals that were lions, first divide the number of lions by the total number of animals. Then multiply that result by 100 to convert the decimal into a percentage: $\left(\frac{200}{2,400} \cdot 100\right)\% = 8\frac{1}{3}\%$, which rounds down to 8%. So, the choice that is closest to the value of p is 8.

If you chose **F**, you likely found the percentage of all animals that were lions: $\left(\frac{200}{10,000} \cdot 100\right)\%$. If you chose **H**, you may have rounded $8\frac{1}{3}$ up to 9. If you chose **J**, you may have found the ratio of animals that are NOT lions to animals that are lions: $\frac{2,400 - 200}{200}$. If you chose **K**, you likely divided the number of large animals by the number of lions: $\frac{2,400}{200}$.

Question 43. **The correct answer is A.** Only **A** and **B** are possible answers, since they are the only matrix products that result in a 1-by-1 matrix that represents the average daily total number of gallons of water consumed by all elephants, lions, and giraffes. The order of the entries in each matrix in **A** confirms that it is the correct choice. Since the left-to-right order of entries in the left matrix is the number of elephants (600), lions (200), and giraffes (800), the top-to-bottom order of entries in the right matrix must be the gallons of water for elephants (50), lions (5), and giraffes (10).

If you chose **B**, you likely didn't notice that the left-to-right order of entries in the left matrix (elephants, giraffes, lions) failed to correspond the top-to-bottom order of entries in the right matrix (elephants, lions, giraffes). If the entries in the left and right matrices are not ordered consistently, the value of the entry in the 1-by-1 matrix product will be incorrect. If you chose **C** or **D**, you did not recognize that a 3-by-1 matrix multiplied by a 1-by-3 matrix results in a 3-by-3 matrix, not a 1-by-1 matrix. If you chose **E**, you likely forgot that a 3-by-1 matrix cannot be multiplied by a 3-by-1 matrix. For matrices X and Y, the product XY exists only if the number of columns of X equal the number of rows of Y.

Question 44. **The correct answer is J.** Populations that grow by a fixed percentage each year for t years can be modeled with an exponential expression of the form $a(1+b)^t$, where a is the starting size of the population and b is the annual growth rate of the population. The growth rate should be rewritten as a decimal or fraction if it is given as a percentage. In this situation, $a = 10,000$ and $b = 2\% = 0.02$. So, the number of protected park animals t years after the beginning of 2014 is $10,000(1+0.02)^t$.

If you chose **F** or **G**, you likely didn't realize that linear expressions (expressions of the form $a+bt$) do not model populations that grow in the way described. Choice **G** also shows an incorrect conversion of a percentage to a decimal ($0.2 = 0.20 = 20\%$). If you chose **H**, you may not have realized that $(1+b^t)$ is not equivalent to $(1+b)^t$. The location of the right parenthesis matters! If you chose **K**, you likely made the same incorrect percentage-to-decimal conversion mentioned for **G**.

Question 45. **The correct answer is D.** Anela will arrive in 5.5 hours. To see why, add her driving time of 5 hours $\left(\frac{375 \text{ km}}{75 \text{ km/hr}}\right)$ to her break time of 0.5 hour (30 minutes is half an hour). As for Jacob, before his break he will drive 180 kilometers: $\frac{90 \text{ km}}{\text{hr}} \cdot 2$ hr. This leaves him with 420 kilometers left to drive: 600 − 180. It will take him 6 hours to drive that distance: $\frac{420 \text{ km}}{70 \text{ km/hr}}$. Adding his driving times to his break time shows that Jacob will arrive in 9 hours: 2 + 1 + 6. So, Anela and Jacob will arrive at the same time if Jacob leaves 3.5 hours earlier than Anela: 9 − 5.5.

If you chose **A**, you likely divided Jacob's starting distance from Brady by his speed before the break $\left(\frac{600 \text{ km}}{90 \text{ km/hr}}\right)$, added his break time (6.7 + 1 = 7.7), then subtracted from that Anela's total travel time: 7.7 − 5.5. If you chose **B**, you likely forgot to add Jacob's break time to his travel time: 8 − 5.5. If you chose **C**, you likely divided Jacob's starting distance from Brady by his speed after the break $\left(\frac{600 \text{ km}}{70 \text{ km/hr}}\right.$, or about 8.6 hours$\left.\right)$, and subtracted from that Anela's total travel time: 8.6 − 5.5. If you chose **E**, you likely forgot to add Anela's break time to her driving time, and so subtracted only 5 hours from Jacob's arrival time: 9 − 5.

Question 46. **The correct answer is J.** Rational expressions with the same denominator are subtracted the same way as fractions with the same denominator. The numerator of the result is the difference of the 2 numerators, while the denominator of the result is identical to the common denominator. The result is $\frac{(3x+5)-(7x-3)}{2x} = \frac{3x+5-7x+3}{2x} = \frac{-4x+8}{2x}$. The two terms in the numerator have a common factor of 2, meaning the result can be rewritten as $\frac{2(-2x+4)}{2x}$. The common factors of 2 can be canceled. So, the result is $\frac{-2x+4}{x}$.

If you chose **F**, you likely found the difference of the numerators ($-4x+8$) but thought the denominators cancel, since they are identical. If you chose **G**, you likely subtracted 3 instead of −3 when finding the difference of the numerators ($3x+5-7x-3=-4x+2$), and thought the denominators cancel. If you chose **H**, your work may have looked like this: $\frac{3x+5-7x-3}{2x} = \frac{-4x+2}{2x} = \frac{2(-2x+1)}{2x} = -2x+1$. This work reflects 2 errors: the subtraction error mentioned for **G**, and the deletion of x in the denominator when the common factor of 2 is canceled. If you chose **K**, you likely canceled the variables in each fraction and evaluated the resulting expression: $\frac{3+5}{2} - \frac{7-3}{2} = 4 - 2 = 2$.

Question 47. The correct answer is **B**. To find the area of the rectangular stage in square yards, first convert its length and width from feet to yards. Since there are 3 feet per yard, the stage is 30 yards long ($90 \div 3$) and 10 yards wide ($30 \div 3$). The area of a rectangle is its length times its width. So, the area of the stage is 30 yards $\cdot$ 10 yards $= 300$ square yards.

If you chose **A**, you likely calculated the area in square feet and then found its square root since the unit of measure is a square unit: $\sqrt{90 \cdot 30}$. If you chose **C**, you likely divided the area in square feet by the number of sides of the stage: $\frac{90 \cdot 30}{4}$. If you chose **D**, you likely divided the area in square feet by the number of feet in 1 yard to convert square feet into square yards: $\frac{90 \cdot 30}{3}$. If you chose **E**, you likely calculated the area in square feet, not square yards: $90 \cdot 30$.

Question 48. The correct answer is **H**. There are 15 lattice points inside the rectangle: (1,1), (1,2), (1,3), (2,1), (2,2), (2,3), (3,1), (3,2), (3,3), (4,1), (4,2), (4,3), (5,1), (5,2), (5,3). Seven of those lattice points have coordinates whose sum is odd: (1,2), (2,1), (2,3), (3,2), (4,1), (4,3), (5,2). So, the probability that the chosen lattice point will have coordinates with an odd-numbered sum is $\frac{7}{15}$.

If you chose **F**, you likely divided the number of lattice points randomly chosen (1) by the number of different odd x-coordinates and y-coordinates ($x = 1, 3, 5$ and $y = 1, 3$) of lattice points inside the rectangle. If you chose **G**, you likely counted only 6 of the 7 lattice points inside the rectangle with an odd-numbered sum: $\frac{6}{15}$. If you chose **J**, you likely divided the number of lattice points on and inside the rectangle with an odd-numbered sum (17) by the number of lattice points on and inside the rectangle (35). If you chose **K**, you likely thought that since an integer is either odd or even, then half the lattice points would have odd-numbered sums, and half the lattice points would have even-numbered sums.

Question 49. The correct answer is **A**. One method for finding the answer starts with solving the system of equations $\begin{array}{l} \frac{5}{2} = a_1 + 2d \\ \frac{1}{4} = a_1 + 5d \end{array}$. The top equation is the given formula rewritten to describe the third term, while the bottom equation describes the sixth term. Subtracting the bottom equation from the top equation gives $\frac{9}{4} = -3d$, or $d = -\frac{3}{4}$. Adding the common difference of $-\frac{3}{4}$ to the sixth term results in the seventh term. So, the seventh term is $\frac{1}{4} + \left(-\frac{3}{4}\right) = -\frac{1}{2}$.

If you chose **B**, you may have noticed that the progression decreases from the third term and the sixth term. Since **A** and **B** are the only choices less than the sixth term, you may have incorrectly guessed which of them was correct. If you chose **C**, you likely subtracted the sixth term from the opposite of d: $\frac{3}{4} - \frac{1}{4}$. If you chose **D**, you likely selected the fraction that resembled the common difference, though it is missing the negative sign. If you chose **E**, you likely omitted the negative sign on d when adding the common difference to the sixth term: $\frac{1}{4} + \frac{3}{4}$.

Question 50. The correct answer is F. The event for which you need to find the odds in favor is "Jamie will be chosen to bat first." The probability that Jamie will be chosen is $\frac{1}{9}$. The probability that Jamie will NOT be chosen is $1-\frac{1}{9}=\frac{8}{9}$. So, the odds in favor of Jamie being chosen to bat first is $\frac{1/9}{8/9}=\frac{1}{8}$.

If you chose **G**, you may have thought the probability of Jamie being chosen was equal to the odds in favor of Jamie being chosen. If you chose **H**, you likely found the probability of Jamie NOT being chosen to be $1+\frac{1}{9}=\frac{10}{9}$ and built the odds ratio with that value: $\frac{1/9}{10/9}$. If you chose **J**, you likely found the odds against Jamie being chosen: $\frac{8/9}{1/9}$. If you chose **K**, you may have thought odds in favor was the reciprocal of the probability of Jamie being chosen.

Question 51. The correct answer is B. Find the total amount of salt by adding 5% of 120 liters and 15% of 80 liters: $0.05(120) + 0.15(80) = 6 + 12 = 18$. Divide the 18 liters of salt by the 200-liter total: $18/200 = 0.09$. Finally, convert 0.09 to a percentage. If you chose **A**, you may have reasoned correctly that because there is more of the 5% solution than the 15% solution, the combined solution must be less than 10% salt (the average of 5% and 15%), but you were not able to find the exact percentage. If you chose **C**, you may have found the average of the given percentages: $\frac{5\%+15\%}{2}$. If you chose **E**, you may have found the average of the salt amounts from the original solutions: $\frac{6+18}{2}$.

Question 52. The correct answer is F. Draw a trapezoid to represent a cross section of the pool: vertical bases of 3 feet and 10 feet representing the shallow end and deep end of the pool, extend down from a 50-foot horizontal representing the length of the pool. The sloped bottom side of the trapezoid represents the sloped bottom of the pool. Find the point where the sloped bottom meets the 3-foot vertical base and label it X. Beginning at X, draw a 50-foot horizontal line segment through the trapezoid to the 10-foot base to form a right triangle. The acute angle X is opposite the side of length 7 feet (from $10 - 3$) and is adjacent to the side of length 50 feet. Therefore, $\tan X = \frac{7}{50}$. To solve for X, take the inverse tangent of both sides of the equation.

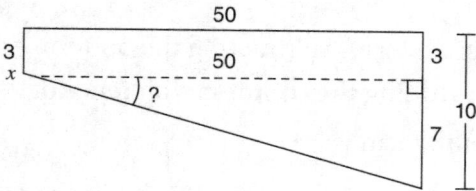

If you chose **G**, you may have added 10 feet and 3 feet instead of subtracting them. If you chose **H**, you may have made a ratio of the difference in depths to the greater depth: $\frac{10-3}{10}$. If you chose **J**, you may have added 10 feet and 3 feet instead of subtracting them *and* thought the tangent ratio is the adjacent side over the opposite side instead of the opposite side over the adjacent side. If you chose **K**, you may have thought the tangent ratio is the adjacent side over the opposite side instead of the opposite side over the adjacent side.

Question 53. **The correct answer is A.** The standard form of a hyperbola is $\frac{(x-h)^2}{a^2} - \frac{(y-k)^2}{b^2} = 1$, where the center of the hyperbola is (h,k). The center of the given hyperbola is $(2,2)$, so our answer should look like $\frac{(x-2)^2}{a^2} - \frac{(y-2)^2}{b^2} = 1$. So, among the answer choices, only **A** and **B** are possible. Rewrite **A** and **B** in standard form as $\frac{(x-2)^2}{1^2} - \frac{(y-2)^2}{\left(\sqrt{\frac{4}{3}}\right)^2} = 1$ and $\frac{(x-2)^2}{1^2} - \frac{(y-2)^2}{\left(\sqrt{\frac{3}{4}}\right)^2} = 1$,

respectively. Recall that the asymptotes of a hyperbola are lines that intersect at the center, forming an X shape, and that the branches of the hyperbola approach but do not intersect. The slope of the asymptote with positive slope is given by $\frac{b}{a}$. If you draw the asymptote with positive slope, you will realize it must be greater than 1. Therefore, $b > a$. For the equations in both **A** and **B**, the value of a is 1, so we want the equation where $b > 1$. This is true only of the equation in answer choice **A**. If you chose **B**, you may have forgotten to move the coefficients of the 2nd fraction's numerator to the denominator. If you chose **C**, you may have forgotten that h and k are subtracted from x and y. If you chose **D**, you may have forgotten that the 2nd fraction in standard form is subtracted instead of added. If you chose **E**, you may have made the 3 errors described in **B**, **C**, and **D**.

Question 54. **The correct answer is K.** Note that we are asked to find the length of the side opposite the obtuse angle of the triangle. The obtuse angle forms a linear pair with the 25° angle, so the measure of the obtuse angle must be 180° – 25° = 155°. To find the 3rd side length of a triangle when we know the opposite angle measure and the other 2 side lengths, we can use the law of cosines: $c^2 = a^2 + b^2 - 2(a)(b)\cos C$. Substitute 700 for a, 250 for b, and 155° for C to get $c^2 = 700^2 + 250^2 - 2(700)(250)\cos 155°$. Finally, take the square root of both sides to isolate c, the unknown side length. If you chose **F**, you may have added the given side lengths and used the given angle. If you chose **G**, you may have just chosen an expression that uses the given side lengths and angle measure. If you chose **H**, you may have found the relevant obtuse angle, but you didn't know how to proceed. If you chose **J**, you may have known to use the law of cosines, but you used the given 25° instead of the relevant interior angle measure of 155°.

Question 55. **The correct answer is A.** Because $b > 0$, b is positive. Because $a > b$, a is also positive. For any positive number, the absolute value of the number is equal to the number. Therefore, the first numbered inequality, $|a| > |b|$, is always true. We know that c is less than b, so c could be positive or negative. A counterexample shows that neither of the last 2 inequalities is always true: consider $a = 5$, $b = 3$, and $c = –7$. Then $|a| = 5$, $|b| = 3$, and $|c| = 7$, in which case $|c|$ is greater than both $|a|$ and $|b|$. Thus, **B**, **C**, and **D** are not always true. If you chose **E**, you may have ignored the absolute value bars in the given numbered inequalities.

Question 56. The correct answer is J. The committee is made up of Kenji, Mary, and 4 others. Imagine that Mary is seated. Someone will be randomly seated to her right. The probability that the person seated to Mary's right is not Kenji is $\frac{4}{5}$ because 4 of the 5 people not seated yet are not Kenji. Now imagine that someone who is not Kenji is seated to Mary's right, and someone will now be randomly seated to Mary's left. The probability that the person seated to Mary's left is not Kenji is $\frac{3}{4}$ because 3 of the 4 people not seated yet are not Kenji. Recall $P(A \text{ and } B) = P(A) \cdot P(B|A)$; the probability that events A and B occur is equal to the probability of A times the probability of B given that A has occurred. Therefore, we find the product of $\frac{4}{5}$ and $\frac{3}{4}$. Alternately, we can find the probability of the complement, that Kenji and Mary are seated next to each other and subtract that probability from 1. Imagine that Mary is seated. There are 5 positions in which Kenji can sit, 2 of which are next to Mary. So the probability that Kenji is seated next to Mary is $\frac{2}{5}$. Therefore, the probability that Kenji is not seated next to Mary is $1 - \frac{2}{5}$. If you chose **F**, you may have considered Mary seated and made a fraction of 1 person (Kenji) over the total number of people who are not yet seated. If you chose **G**, you may have made a fraction of 2 people (Kenji and Mary) over the total number of people. If you chose **H**, you may have found the probability that Kenji and Mary are seated next to each other, but you did not subtract from 1. If you chose **K**, you may have thought that the probability that Kenji is seated next to Mary is $\frac{1}{5}$. You then subtracted $\frac{1}{5}$ from 1.

Question 57. The correct answer is C. Note that 2^{90} is the product of 2^{88} and 2^2. That means that we can multiply 2^{88} by 4 to get 2^{90}. We know that 2^{88} has a 6 in the ones place. When we multiply the 6 in the ones place by 4, we get 24, which will result in a 4 in the ones place. If you chose **A**, you may have thought that you could add (instead of multiplying) 4 to 2^{88} to get 2^{90}. Adding 4 to 6 gives 10, which results in a 0 in the ones place. If you chose **B**, **D**, or **E**, you may have chosen one of the other possible digits that could be in the ones place of a power of 2.

Question 58. The correct answer is F. The area of a triangle with base b and height h is given by $\frac{1}{2}bh$. Recall that b and h must be perpendicular. The bottom side of the given triangle is horizontal because the endpoints both have a y-coordinate of d. Consider this side to be the base of the triangle, b, and find the length of this base by subtracting the x-coordinates: $c - a$. Now imagine the altitude of the triangle drawn from the point (b,e) down to our base at the point (b,d). The altitude would be vertical, making the x-coordinates of the endpoints both b. To find the altitude's length or height, h, subtract the y-coordinates: $e - d$. In the expression $\frac{1}{2}bh$, substitute $(c - a)$ for b and $(e - d)$ for h. If you chose **H**, you may have used just e for the height instead of $e - d$. If you chose **J**, you may have assumed sides $\overline{RS}$ and $\overline{ST}$ were perpendicular and tried to use the distance formula to represent their lengths, but you forgot to take the square root of the sums of the squares. If you chose **K**, you may have assumed sides $\overline{RS}$ and $\overline{ST}$ were perpendicular and used the distance formula to represent their lengths.

Question 59. The correct answer is A. To solve for x, divide both sides of the equation by $(2 + 3i)$. This gives the solution $\frac{1}{2+3i}$. To find which of the given answer choices is equivalent to our solution, multiply the numerator and denominator of our fraction by $2 - 3i$, the conjugate of the denominator: $\frac{1(2-3i)}{(2+3i)(2-3i)}$. Distribute to get $\frac{2-3i}{4-6i+6i-9i^2}$, and simplify the denominator: $\frac{2-3i}{13}$. Finally, decompose the fraction into addends using the numerator addends. If you chose **B**, you may have simplified $\frac{2-3i}{4-6i+6i-9i^2}$ as $\frac{-2-3i}{4-9}$ instead of $\frac{2-3i}{4+9}$. If you chose **C**, you may have thought the number to the right of the equal sign of the given equation was the solution. If you chose **D**, you may have thought $i = -1$ and simplified $\frac{1}{2+3i}$ as $\frac{1}{2-3}$. If you chose **E**, you may have evaluated correctly until $\frac{2-3i}{13}$ but then thought this was equivalent to $\frac{(2-3)i}{13}$.

Question 60. The correct answer is J. The shaded rectangular face of the dividing wall has an area of 39 square inches. Divide 39 square inches by the 13-inch length to find that the height of the dividing wall and container must be 3 inches. The base of the larger compartment is a trapezoid with parallel bases of 15 inches and 10 inches (from 15 − 5). The height of the trapezoid is 12 inches. The area of a trapezoid is given by $\frac{1}{2}(b_1 + b_2)h$. Substituting correctly gives $\frac{1}{2}(15+10)12$, which is equal to 150. The area of the trapezoidal base of the larger compartment is 150 square inches. Finally, multiply the area of the base times the height of 3 inches to get a volume of 450 cubic inches.

If you chose **F**, you may have tried to find the volume of the smaller triangular compartment, multiplying side lengths of 5 inches and 12 inches to get 60 square inches $\left(\text{forgetting to multiply by }\frac{1}{2}\right)$ and then multiplying by the 3-inch height. If you chose **G**, you may have multiplied 15 times 13. If you chose **H**, you may have thought you could find the area of the trapezoidal base of the larger compartment by multiplying the 13-inch side length by the 10-inch side length to get 130 square inches, and then you multiplied by the 3-inch height. If you chose **K**, you may have found the volume of the entire container: (15)(12)(3).

Passage I

Question 1. **The best answer is C** because the paragraphs that follow describe Murali and Vani's growing closeness with each other as they become a "couple" (line 61). The passage implies that the two were "talking" (line 72) about their future plans for marriage. Lines 76–92 recount the negative reactions of their respective families.

The best answer is NOT:

A because the passage does not depict a time in which Murali is yet married.

B because although the passage alludes to Murali's previously "thinking about widows or about repeating his own father's collapse" (lines 33–34), nowhere does the passage indicate that Murali has specific reservations about marriage.

D because although Murali is indirectly characterized in the narration, this is not the main focus of the paragraphs that follow. Murali's family conflicts are not specifically characterized in the passage.

Question 2. **The best answer is F** because the paragraph describes Vani's "reserve" (line 17). The passage also notes that "she did not speak softly" (Line 20), denoting her certainty about speaking and indicating that her reserve was not caused by a lack of confidence. The description of Vani sewing her own clothes (lines 22–25) suggests a determined self-reliance.

The best answer is NOT:

G because although Murali anticipates that Vani's face may take on an "austere severity" (line 15) when older, her manner is not described as being harsh or severe. Nowhere does the paragraph indicate that Vani is impolite.

H because the paragraph does not directly characterize Vani's intelligence, nor does it describe Vani as apologetic. The paragraph notes her avoidance of "admitting she was wrong" (line 28), which suggests that Vani may be unlikely to be especially apologetic.

J because although the paragraph describes qualities Murali admires, no specific claims are made about Vani's beauty. There is no support in the passage for the idea that Vani's appearance was unkempt. Murali notes Vani's "precision in even the smallest of tasks" (lines 15–16), which may extend to indicate precision in her personal style, as well.

Question 3. The best answer is **B** because, in recounting who "was responsible" (line 39) for the introduction, the paragraph indicates that the friend's suggestion that Murali drive Vani home provided the introduction that drew the two together.

The best answer is NOT:

A because the elders were "eager to play parents" (line 61) only after Murali and Vani were known as a "couple" (line 61).

C because Vani smiled with her teeth (lines 57–59) after she'd exited Murali's car at the conclusion of the drive to her home.

D because Vani's brother burst into Murali's brother's home after learning that Murali wanted to marry his sister (lines 87–89).

Question 4. The best answer is **H** because the quoted dialogue immediately follows the description of Vani's manner of speaking (lines 19–20), and the italicized portion serves to exemplify her calmly confident speech in public.

The best answer is NOT:

F because the passage does not provide any information that suggests Murali rehearses comments to himself in advance of speaking with someone previously unknown to him.

G because as the passage indicates, before Murali drove Vani home, the two had admired each other but hadn't yet been introduced (lines 34–39). During the car ride home, which served as their introduction to each other, "they were silent" (line 48).

J because although Murali thought Vani "might be full of secrets and wanted to know them" (lines 19–20), he does not speculate about what those secrets are.

Question 5. The best answer is **A** because as the passage states, Vani "liked her food steaming and spicy" (lines 21–22), as Murali did.

The best answer is NOT:

B because although the passage states that Vani and Murali met in New York City (line 1), it does not indicate that they were born there.

C because the passage doesn't indicate if either Vani or Murali had a passion for cooking.

D because although the passage states that "Vani had a job" (lines 62–63), it does not indicate where she worked. The passage describes Murali as a "bachelor-doctor" (line 66) but does not specifically indicate his place of work.

Question 6. The best answer is **J** because, as the passage indicates in lines 34–42, neither Murali nor Vani initiated direct contact with the other, and therefore neither of them would falsely claim or "admit" (line 39) responsibility.

The best answer is NOT:

F because the passage does not indicate that either Murali or Vani have forgotten, but rather that "no one else" (line 38) other than Murali and Vani remembers.

G because the passage doesn't indicate that a friend claims responsibility; aside from Murali and Vani, "no one else really remembers" (line 38).

H because Murali did not initiate contact with Vani, but rather, as the passage relates in lines 39–42, Murali and Vani had their first direct contact after a friend suggested that Murali could give Vani a ride home.

Question 7. The best answer is **B** because as the passage states, Vani "did not ask him in for a cup of coffee; it was not her house" (lines 54–55).

The best answer is NOT:

A because the silence of their ride home is described as "comfortable" (line 49), and there is no evidence to suggest Vani was self-conscious or uncomfortable.

C because the passage does not indicate at what time Vani and Murali left the party or whether it was late.

D because as the passage states, Murali gave Vani a ride home in response to a friend's suggestion (lines 41–42), rather than from a request from Vani.

Question 8. The best answer is **J** because the description of Vani serves to illustrate why the elders may have been "eager to play parents to the couple" (lines 60–61).

The best answer is NOT:

F because although Murali admired Vani, he was drawn by specific traits outlined in the second paragraph (lines 9–32), rather than the more generic virtues of being polite or being a good cook (line 62).

G because although the passage describes Vani's family's negative reaction to news of Murali's interest in Vani (lines 76–82), the passage does not indicate how the family regards Vani herself.

H because the passage's indication that a friend of Murali's suggested Murali could give Vani a ride home (lines 41–42) is the passage's only reference to a New York friend of Murali.

Question 9. The best answer is **D** because it can be inferred from the passage (lines 71–73) that Vani and Murali are "directly" (line 73) discussing plans to marry, which is confirmed by the passage's description of Vani's brother's angry reaction after learning of "this doctor who wants to marry" (line 89) his sister. Vani's family almost doesn't agree to the marriage because of their discomfort with Murali's "failure to observe certain formalities" (line 79). The passage indicates that it was unusual for a couple to discuss romantic feelings, that "these were not words they were used to saying" (lines 91–92).

The best answer is NOT:

A because as the passage states, Vani's family found their discussion "improper" (line 78).

B because there is no support in the passage for the idea that their direct discussion of marriage was considered sensible by the Sri Lankan community.

C because as the passage states, "oceans away, families exploded" (line 76) with shock and anger at the news, which suggests they understood the serious, committed intent of Vani and Murali's discussions.

Question 10. The best answer is **G** because "follow" is a synonym of "observe" in the context of adhering to certain traditions and practices. In this usage, the passage describes the family's perception that Murali has failed to follow the rules required by "certain formalities" (line 79).

The best answer is NOT:

F because although "study" can be a synonym for "observe," the passage describes that the family is disappointed by Murali's failure to act in a traditional way (lines 77–80), rather than by a failure to study certain traditions.

H because "express" and "observe" have different meanings, and "express" would not make sense in the context of the passage.

J because although "perceive" can be a synonym for "observe," the passage describes that the family is disappointed by Murali's failure to act in a traditional way (lines 77–80), rather than by a failure of his perception.

976 The Official ACT Prep Guide

Passage II

Question 11. The best answer is C because the first paragraph of Passage A states that "for most of human history, the phrase 'light pollution' would have made no sense" (lines 1–2). The details that follow describing the darkness of London, "Earth's most populous city" (line 4) in 1800, support this idea that light pollution created by artificial light is a relatively recent phenomenon.

The best answer is NOT:

A because although the paragraph relates the invitation to "imagine walking toward London on a moonlit night" (lines 2–3), it does not include a specific claim about travel difficulty, nor does it include a claim about the impact of electricity.

B because although the paragraph mentions the use of gas lighting (lines 6–9), these details serve to further emphasize how dark London was in 1800.

D because although the paragraph describes London as "Earth's most populous city" (line 4) in 1800, the darkness of such a populous city further illustrates the overall lack of light pollution.

Question 12. The best answer is F because the third paragraph of Passage A begins by stating that "in most cities the sky looks as though it has been emptied of stars, leaving behind a vacant haze" (lines 21–22). The third paragraph of Passage A concludes by describing the universe above "the city's pale ceiling" (line 27) as "a bright shoal of stars and planets and galaxies, shining in seemingly infinite darkness" (lines 28–30).

The best answer is NOT:

G because the paragraph does not describe the colors of stars.

H because although the paragraph refers to the planet Venus in lines 25–26, this reference serves to illustrate the darkness of the sky, and no comparison of the brightness of Venus to that of the stars is made.

J because although the paragraph states that people have "grown so used to this pervasive orange haze" (lines 23–24), it does not mention people's lost appreciation for stars or a pervasive apathy for stars today.

Question 13. The best answer is B because Passage A describes light as "a powerful biological force" (lines 34–35) that can act "as a magnet" (line 35). Passage A gives the example of songbirds and seabirds "circling and circling in the thousands" (lines 40–41) as a result of being drawn by the artificial light emitted by searchlights and gas flares.

> **The best answer is NOT:**
>
> **A** because Passage A does not refer to any animal's food-searching abilities, nor does it indicate that darkness would diminish those abilities.
>
> **C** because Passage A states that light "is a powerful biological force" (lines 34–35) that can act "as a magnet" (line 35) that draws animals. It does not indicate whether light levels drive animals to dark areas.
>
> **D** because Passage A does not refer to the natural habitats of animals or to urban expansion.

Question 14. The best answer is H because the author of Passage B states: "I love the story this painting tells, of a small dark town, a few yellow-orange gaslights in house windows, under a giant swirling and waving blue-green sky" (lines 54–57). In contrast, Joseph doesn't mention the story of the painting. "It's beautiful" (line 52), Joseph states, adding, "What more can you say than that?" (lines 52–53).

> **The best answer is NOT:**
>
> **F** because although the author of Passage B notes the "yellow-orange" (line 56) and "blue-green" (line 57) colors in the painting, the author focuses in greater detail on "the story this painting tells" (lines 54–55).
>
> **G** because Passage B indicates in lines 52–54 that both the author and Joseph admire the painting's beauty.
>
> **J** because Passage B does not include any information about the technique Van Gogh used to paint *The Starry Night*.

Question 15. The best answer is A because the first paragraph of Passage B describes *The Starry Night* as a "scene of stars and moon and sleeping town" (line 47). In addition, the first paragraph indicates the painting's popularity, noting that "fifty million people pass by every year" (lines 45–46).

> **The best answer is NOT:**
>
> **B** because the paragraph does not establish that the author of Passage B is seeing *The Starry Night* for the first time.
>
> **C** because the paragraph does not provide examples of people's expectations about *The Starry Night*.
>
> **D** because the paragraph does not establish why Van Gogh painted *The Starry Night*.

Taking Additional Practice Tests

Question 16. The best answer is **H** because the author of Passage B states, "Does Van Gogh use his imagination? Of course, but this is an imagined sky inspired by a real sky" (lines 68–70). The excerpt from Van Gogh's letter in lines 79–87 then describes the bright and colorful night sky that he observed in 1888.

The best answer is NOT:

F because Passage B does not establish the time of day in which Van Gogh painted.

G because the excerpt from Van Gogh's 1888 letter establishes that the artist witnessed a night sky with such vibrant colors that he compared the stars to jewels: "opals you might call them, emeralds, lapis lazuli, rubies, sapphires" (lines 86–87).

J because the author of Passage B argues that Van Gogh did use his imagination to paint *The Starry Night*, stating, "Does Van Gogh use his imagination? Of course, but this is an imagined sky inspired by a real sky" (lines 68–70).

Question 17. The best answer is **B** because in Passage B, Van Gogh's description of the stars as "more brilliant, more sparkling gemlike than at home—even in Paris" (lines 84–85) indicates that the stars over Paris would have been quite bright even in that "time before electric light" (lines 75–76). That this brightness would be "remarkable to modern eyes" (line 88) helps establish that in recent times, the night sky in Paris is much duller. Therefore, no one has recently seen "anything like" the night sky over Paris mentioned in Van Gogh's letter.

The best answer is NOT:

A because Passage B establishes a stark contrast between the two night skies in Paris rather than a strong similarity between them.

C because Passage B does not establish a spatial relationship between the two night skies in Paris.

D because Passage B does not establish a spatial relationship between the two night skies in Paris.

Question 18. The best answer is **J** because Passage A explores the issue of light at night, noting how "most of humanity" (line 11) lives beneath artificial light, positing that "in most cities the sky looks as though it has been emptied of stars" (lines 21–22) and that "we've lit up the night as if it were an unoccupied country" (lines 31–32). Passage B presents the issue of light at night by discussing the depiction of the night sky in Van Gogh's *The Starry Night*, describing it as "a painting of our world from before night had been pushed back to the forest and the seas, from back when sleepy towns slept without streetlights" (lines 57–60).

The best answer is NOT:

F because Passage A does not present a summary of the circumstances that led to light being common at night.

G because Passage A does not offer suggestions for restoring darkness to today's night. Additionally, Passage B provides information only about Van Gogh's *The Starry Night*.

H because Passage B does not provide an explanation for how people in Van Gogh's time used light at night.

Question 19. The best answer is **A** because the first paragraph of Passage A discusses the darkness of night in London in 1800. From the references to the bright stars of Paris in lines 83–91 of Passage B, it can be inferred that the night sky over the city of Paris was dark during Van Gogh's lifetime.

The best answer is NOT:

B because neither of the passage authors discuss the opinions of scientific researchers.

C because the author of Passage A does not discuss any well-known works of art.

D because neither of the passage authors discuss personal memories of when night was darker.

Question 20. The best answer is **F** because the last paragraph of Passage A describes the effects of artificial light on animals in lines 33–41, whereas Passage B does not mention animals at all.

The best answer is NOT:

G because in lines 79–91, Passage B provides information on the colorful appearance of stars prior to electric lights, whereas Passage A does not refer to star color at all.

H because Passage B makes the argument that Van Gogh's *The Starry Night* is both a reflection of nature and a work of imagination in lines 68–73, whereas Passage A does not refer to the imagination at all.

J because Passage B refers to night having "been pushed back to the forest and the seas" (lines 58–59), places where night's original darkness remains.

Passage III

Question 21. The best answer is B because the passage begins in lines 1–19 by recounting the author's experience returning to a once-familiar place and experiencing memories. This first paragraph provides an example of how "places hold memories" (line 20). The author proceeds to consider how personal memories can be affected by photographs and other factors.

The best answer is NOT:

A because although the passage alludes to a childhood experience in lines 3–4, the passage does not describe a specific incident.

C because although the author self-identifies as belonging to the "image-makers and consumers" (lines 75–76), the passage does not relate a specific narrative of the author's lifelong hobby of photography.

D because the passage does not indicate that the author's opinions on a topic have changed.

Question 22. The best answer is G because the author claims that "places hold memories better than people and better than photographs" (lines 20–21). Lines 24–29 describe how conversations may alter or replace memories, and the passage continues by exploring how "photographs do not preserve memory" (line 47) but instead "replace memory" (line 48).

The best answer is NOT:

F because the author claims in lines 24–29 that conversations may alter or replace memories and states that "photographs inaccurately reflect experience from the start" (lines 35–36).

H because the passage makes no claim that a person's memory of an event has any effect on the truth of a photograph depicting that event.

J because the passage does not establish that conversation, photographs, and visits to places are the exclusive sustainers of memories.

Question 23. The best answer is D because the author states, "I loved this place" (line 4) and describes himself as "amazed" (line 5). The reference to "this ritual" (line 19) also suggests an earnest seriousness.

The best answer is NOT:

A because the author's tone is sincere, rather than joking, in recounting how the place remains "startlingly unchanged" (line 8).

B because the waterfall reminds the author of positive childhood memories, and he describes his "mixture of apprehension and pleasure" (line 15).

C because the author does not make a request.

Question 24. The best answer is **G** because the details in the second paragraph support the claim that conversations about shared memories may "alter or even replace our own memories with those of another" (lines 27–28).

The best answer is NOT:

F because instead of focusing on the loss of the memory, the second paragraph focuses on how memories may be changed as a result of interactions with others.

H because in lines 27–28, reminiscing is portrayed as an activity that alters or replaces memories, rather than preserving them.

J because although the second paragraph identifies both "family" (line 21) and "people from our past who may remind us of events in our lives and with whom we may reminisce" (lines 21–23), it makes no distinction between how well family members or non-family members evoke memories.

Question 25. The best answer is **D** because the prior sentence describes how "snapshots are most commonly a break from the event" (lines 64–65), in which people pause to allow a photo to be taken. The moment captured in the photograph, therefore, "is experienced as a moment taking a photograph" (lines 66–67) rather than a moment in the experience being documented.

The best answer is NOT:

A because the quotation focuses on the act of photography itself, rather than the skill of the photographer.

B because the author's description of a photograph being taken in lines 64–70 focuses on the experience of being photographed and does not focus on the photographer as a participant in the action.

C because the author questions the degree to which photographs can be considered accurate records of experience, noting that "photographs only tell such a small part of any story" (lines 56–57) and that "they deceive" (line 58).

Question 26. The best answer is **H** because in the first paragraph the author states that he was "getting ready to jump" (line 16), leaning over the edge of the cliff to "prepare myself for what I am about to do" (lines 17–18). He describes the action he is about to take as "this ritual" (line 19), suggesting the repetition of the childhood action of when the author "used to jump from those cliffs" (lines 3–4).

The best answer is NOT:

F because the first paragraph does not mention the possibility of hiking back down, and the author instead describes "getting ready to jump" (line 16) from the cliff.

G because the first paragraph does not mention the possibility of sitting, and the author instead describes "getting ready to jump" (line 16) from the cliff.

J because the first paragraph does not indicate whether the author was in possession of a camera or intended to take a photograph.

Question 27. The best answer is **C** because in the third paragraph the author states that "photographs inaccurately reflect experience" (lines 35–36), partly as a result of "elimin[ating] . . . time" (line 38).

The best answer is NOT:

A because the author makes no reference to the age of people taking photographs.

B because although the author provides examples in lines 42–44 of different events a photograph might depict, the author does not indicate that there is a best way to photograph an event.

D because the author does not make a comparison between the ability of the human eye to capture detail and that of a photograph.

Question 28. The best answer is **G** because the information helps illuminate what kinds of experiences people try to capture in photographs, providing specific examples of the "family outings" and "vacations" mentioned in line 42.

The best answer is NOT:

F because the author makes no distinction between trivial and meaningful pictures, but instead uses these examples to support the claim that photographs are taken "in the hope of freezing time" (lines 44–45).

H because although the details in lines 43–44 are used as examples, they are utilized to support the claim that photographs are taken "in the hope of freezing time" (lines 44–45).

J because although the author states that "we fill scrapbooks and hard drives" (lines 41–42), the context makes clear that he means "we" in the collective sense, referring to people in general, rather than to himself, specifically. The author's statement, "I do it, too" (line 46) helps clarify that he was not referring specifically to himself in his use of the word "we" in line 41.

Question 29. The best answer is **A** because "objective truth" has a similar meaning as "irrefutable factuality" (lines 52–53) and "seemingly" (line 52) suggests something that appears to be true but isn't necessarily so—something that "conveys an impression." Further clarity is provided by the statement that "a photograph's version of events did happen" (lines 54–55) but only tells a "small part of any story" (line 57).

The best answer is NOT:

B because the author argues that "photographs are an abstraction of experience" (lines 48–49) and "an abstraction of memory" (lines 49–50), which, it can be inferred, would serve to make events less clear.

C because although the passage states that "a photograph's version of events did happen" (line 54–55), lines 56–58 state that the image can be deceptive by telling only a small part of the story.

D because the author claims that photographic depictions "only tell such a small part of any story" (lines 56–57) and "deceive" (line 58), rather than imply a story beyond the actual depiction.

Question 30. The best answer is G because "essence" is a synonym of "nature" in the context of the author's defining key qualities of memory in lines 82–83.

The best answer is NOT:

F because although "temperament" can be a synonym for "nature," the word is usually used to describe the mood or behavior of a living entity, making this a contextually inappropriate choice to modify "memory" in lines 82–83.

H because although "scenery" may sometimes be used to refer to natural surroundings or landscapes, the word would not make sense in the context of defining the key qualities or "nature" of memory in lines 82–83.

J because although "scenery" may sometimes be used to refer to natural settings, the word would not make sense in the context of defining the key qualities or "nature" of memory in lines 82–83.

Passage IV

Question 31. The best answer is A because lines 65–78 describe how a certain type of solar technology that uses electrolyzers demonstrates that the technology could work, "in principle" (line 75). The passage notes, however, that the models are "bulky" (line 65), and key components such as silicon crystals (line 80) and platinum (lines 81–82) are too expensive for use in large-scale implementation.

The best answer is NOT:

B because although the seventh paragraph states that an electrolyzer "uses the solar electricity to break water molecules" (lines 69–70), this detail is given in support of the paragraph's overall explanation of the technology.

C because although the seventh and eighth paragraphs (lines 65–82) describe a prototype made by a Japanese automaker, they do not indicate that the United States and Japan are working collaboratively on research.

D because although the seventh and eighth paragraphs (lines 65–82) describe a prototype made by a Japanese automaker, they do not question any aspect of the auto industry.

Question 32. The best answer is **H** because Nathan S. Lewis is identified as the speaker "giving a lecture" (line 1), and lines 4–6 present a paraphrase of the lecture's key claim.

The best answer is NOT:

F because although the passage mentions that "other researchers" (line 22) are researching uses of algae, this is given as an example of alternate research approaches, and the researchers' location is not given.

G because the passage attributes the claim in lines 4–6 to "the chemist" (lines 3–4) that is giving the lecture. Nathan S. Lewis was introduced in the preceding sentence (lines 1–2) as the speaker giving the lecture.

J because the passage author prefaces the claim in lines 4–6 with "the chemist says" (lines 3–4), indicating that what follows is the opinion of "the chemist," Nathan S. Lewis, and not the opinion of the author.

Question 33. The best answer is **C** because the passage states that "humankind needs a radical breakthrough in solar fuel technology" (lines 11–12), indicating that a technological breakthrough is necessary but has not yet occurred. The passage then indicates that such a breakthrough would involve using solar technology to "create heat or generate electricity" (lines 14–16) and "store the fuel for use when the sun is down" (lines 16–17).

The best answer is NOT:

A because the passage states that "humankind needs a radical breakthrough in solar fuel technology" (lines 11–12), indicating that a technological breakthrough has not yet occurred. The description of Lewis's research that follows in lines 18–22 suggests early progress toward the goal of "artificial leaves" (lines 13–14), but this work is too preliminary to have a broad impact.

B because the passage does not indicate that Lewis believes that either the breakthrough or the capabilities are misguided. The passage does not refer to the energy industry having a focus on consumption.

D because the passage states that "humankind needs a radical breakthrough in solar fuel technology" (lines 11–12), indicating that the breakthrough has not yet occurred. In addition, the passage suggests that the capabilities described in lines 14–17 will be the result of the radical breakthrough, not the cause.

Taking Additional Practice Tests

Question 34. The best answer is **F** because the passage states that "commercial solar cells contain expensive silicon crystals" (lines 79–80) and that platinum is "to date the best material for catalyzing the water-splitting reaction, but it costs $1,500 an ounce" (lines 81–82). The passage goes on to explain that, according to Lewis, "future solar-fuel devices would have to cost less than $1 per square foot of sun-collecting surface" (lines 84–85), suggesting that cheaper materials will be needed to implement solar technology on a large scale.

The best answer is NOT:

G because the passage relates that a device called an "electrolyzer" (line 58) can "split water into oxygen and hydrogen" (lines 58–59). The passage then goes on to explain that "electrolyzers are used in various commercial processes" (lines 62–63), indicating that a device capable of splitting water into hydrogen and oxygen already exists.

H because the passage does not refer to federal funding research for solar technology research, nor does it specifically indicate that Lewis lacks the federal funding necessary for his research.

J because the passage does not indicate that the public is reluctant to embrace new technology. Rather, it claims that "with a new energy and climate crunch looming, solar fuel is suddenly gaining attention" (lines 47–48).

Question 35. The best answer is **A** because, as the passage indicates in a paraphrase of Lewis's lectures, he tells his crowds that "the sun pours more energy onto the earth every hour than humankind uses in a year" (lines 9–11).

The best answer is NOT:

B because, as the passage indicates in a paraphrase of Lewis's lectures, he tells his crowds that "the sun pours more energy onto the earth every hour than humankind uses in a year" (lines 9–11).

C because, as the passage indicates in a paraphrase of Lewis's lectures, he tells his crowds that "the sun pours more energy onto the earth every hour than humankind uses in a year" (lines 9–11).

D because, as the passage indicates in a paraphrase of Lewis's lectures, he tells his crowds that "the sun pours more energy onto the earth every hour than humankind uses in a year" (lines 9–11).

Question 36. The best answer is **J** because the passage states that Lewis's lab is crafting prototype leaves that are "not much larger than computer chips" (line 19).

The best answer is NOT:

F because the passage does not compare the size of Lewis's prototype leaves to that of a human hand. Rather, the passage states that Lewis's lab is crafting prototype leaves that are "not much larger than computer chips" (line 19).

G because although the passage describes Lewis's solar technology as "artificial leaves" (lines 13–14), the passage goes on to explain that the prototype leaves crafted at Lewis's lab are "not much larger than computer chips" (line 19).

H because although the passage refers to films as "cheap as wall-to-wall carpeting" (line 41), the passage does not compare the size of Lewis's prototype leaves to that of a carpet square. Rather, the passage states that Lewis's lab is crafting prototype leaves that are "not much larger than computer chips" (line 19).

Question 37. The best answer is **C** because lines 24–26 describe projects that seek to "capture solar rays and churn out chemical fuel" (lines 13–14) and "turn sunlight into chemical energy that can be stored" (lines 27–28). In this context, when the passage states that the algae "has been genetically altered to pump out biofuels" (lines 24–25), it can be inferred that to "pump out" means "to produce."

The best answer is NOT:

A because when the passage states that the algae "has been genetically altered to pump out biofuels" (lines 24–25), it can be inferred that the goal is for the algae to produce, rather than to remove, fuel to use as an energy source.

B because when the passage states that the algae "has been genetically altered to pump out biofuels" (lines 24–25), it can be inferred that the goal is for the algae to produce, rather than to drain or diminish, fuel to use as an energy source.

D because when the passage states that the algae "has been genetically altered to pump out biofuels" (lines 24–25), it can be inferred that the goal is for the algae to produce, rather than to siphon or drain away, fuel to use as an energy source.

Question 38. The best answer is **G** because the passage states that Lewis estimates the need to "manufacture thin, flexible solar-fuel films" (lines 37–38) that would "roll off high-speed production lines the way newsprint does" (lines 39– 40).

The best answer is NOT:

F because, although the passage describes Lewis's initial prototypes as "not much larger than computer chips" (line 19), it paraphrases Lewis's prediction of the need for "thin, flexible solar-fuel films, instead of discrete chip-like devices" (lines 38–39).

H because the passage does not indicate that Lewis imagines small, rigid solar panels as the ideal, but rather "thin, flexible solar-fuel films" (line 38).

J because, although the passage does describe a Japanese prototype that is "taller than a refrigerator and is covered with photovoltaic cells" (lines 68–69), the passage does not relate this research to Lewis's ideals for energy innovation. Instead, the passage states that Lewis argues that "the man-made leaf option is most likely" (line 29) to provide a large-scale solar energy solution, which he imagines as being manufactured as "thin, flexible solar-fuel films" (line 38).

Question 39. The best answer is **D** because the passage states that Lewis's artificial leaf technology "requires two principal elements: a collector that converts solar energy (photons) into electrical energy (electrons) and an electrolyzer" (lines 55–59).

The best answer is NOT:

A because the passage does not indicate that either ambient air or fuel cells are the principal elements of Lewis's artificial leaves. Rather, the passage explains that the principal elements of Lewis's leaves are a collector and an electrolyzer (lines 55–59).

B because, while the passage indicates that a catalyst is needed to help an electrolyzer split oxygen and hydrogen (lines 59–60) and explains that an electrolyzer uses solar electricity to break water molecules (line 70), it does not indicate that these are the principal elements of Lewis's artificial leaves. Rather, the passage explains that the principal elements of Lewis's leaves are a collector and an electrolyzer (lines 55–59).

C because, while the passage does indicate that commercial solar cells contain silicon crystals (lines 79–80), and that electrolyzers contain platinum (lines 80–81), it does not indicate that these are the principal elements of Lewis's artificial leaves. Rather, the passage explains that the principal elements of Lewis's leaves are a collector and an electrolyzer (lines 55–59).

Question 40. **The best answer is J** because the passage states that "the exhaust from burning the hydrogen later in a fuel cell is water" (lines 77–78).

The best answer is NOT:

F because the passage does not claim that burning hydrogen in a fuel cell creates electron energy that splits silicon crystals. Instead, the passage states that "the exhaust from burning the hydrogen later in a fuel cell is water" (lines 77–78).

G because the passage does not claim that burning hydrogen in a fuel cell causes the hydrogen to bond with oxygen. Instead, the passage states that "the exhaust from burning the hydrogen later in a fuel cell is water" (lines 77–78).

H because the passage does not claim that burning hydrogen in a fuel cell causes the fuel cell's lining to deteriorate. Instead, the passage states that "the exhaust from burning the hydrogen later in a fuel cell is water" (lines 77–78).

Passage I

Question 1. The best answer is B. According to Table 1, at 273 K, the molar volume of H_2 at 5.00 atm is 4.496 L, and the molar volume of H_2 at 10.0 atm is 2.256 L. The absolute value of the difference between the two molar volumes is 2.240 L. **A, C,** and **D** are incorrect; the difference is closest to 2.2 L. **B** is correct.

Question 2. The best answer is G. According to Table 2, at 323 K, the molar volume of Ar was the smallest at 26.486 L, followed by N_2 with a molar volume of 26.492 L, then He with a molar volume of 26.504 L, and finally H_2 with the largest molar volume of 26.521 L. **F** is incorrect; the molar volume of He is greater than the molar volume of N_2. **G** is correct. **H** and **J** are incorrect; Ar has the smallest molar volume, and H_2 has the greatest molar volume.

Question 3. The best answer is B. In both Table 1 and Table 2, at any given temperature and pressure, the greatest difference between the molar volume of O_2 and the molar volume of Ar is 0.002 L. This is the smallest difference observed and makes the molar volume of O_2 most similar to the molar volume of Ar. **A** is incorrect; the molar volumes of O_2 and He differ by approximately 0.05 L. **B** is correct. **C** is incorrect; the molar volumes of O_2 and H_2 differ by a minimum of 0.012 L. **D** is incorrect; the molar volumes of O_2 and N_2 differ by a minimum of 0.006 L.

Question 4. The best answer is F. According to Table 2, at 1.00 atm and 773 K, the molar volumes of the gases range from 63.440 L to 63.453 L; none of these values are smaller than the molar volume of an ideal gas. **F** is correct. **G, H,** and **J** are incorrect; none of the gases listed in Table 2 have a molar volume less than the molar volume of an ideal gas.

Question 5. The best answer is D. Because the mean free time decreases as a sample's volume decreases, the mean free time would be least for a 1 mol sample of the gas with the smallest molar volume. According to Table 1, O_2 at 100.0 atm has a molar volume of 0.198 L. This is the smallest molar volume listed in Table 1. **A** is incorrect; He at 0.500 atm has a molar volume of 44.825 L, which is not the smallest of the gases listed. **B** is incorrect; O_2 at 0.500 atm has a molar volume of 44.773 L, which is not the smallest of the gases listed. **C** is incorrect; He at 100.0 atm has a molar volume of 0.247 L, which is not the smallest of the gases listed. **D** is correct; O_2 at 100.0 atm has the smallest molar volume of the gases listed and will therefore have the least mean free time.

Question 6. The best answer is J. In order to answer this item, the examinee must know that the average kinetic energy of the molecules in a sample of O_2 increases as the temperature increases. Based on Table 2, a 1 mol sample of O_2 with a volume of 18 L has a temperature of approximately 223 K, and a 1 mol sample of O_2 with a volume of 63 L has a temperature of approximately 773 K. The sample with the volume of 63 L has a higher temperature, and therefore the average kinetic energy of the molecules in this sample is greater. **F** and **G** are incorrect; the molecules in the sample with a volume of 63 L are more likely to have a greater average kinetic energy. **H** is incorrect; the average kinetic energy of the molecules in the 63 L sample is more likely greater because it is at the higher temperature not the lower temperature. **J** is correct.

Passage II

Question 7. The best answer is **B**. According to Figure 3, as cleaning time increased from 0 minutes to 30 minutes and then to 60 minutes, the corresponding average number of colonies per dish went from 79 to 29 and then to 12. **A** is incorrect; the trend consistently decreases not increases with increasing cleaning time. **B** is correct. **C** and **D** are incorrect; the average number of colonies trend did not start in one direction and then change to the opposite direction.

Question 8. The best answer is **J**. The description of Experiment 3 states that 3 groups of 10 *S. carnaria* flies were used. **F**, **G**, and **H** are incorrect; 5, 10, and 24 flies are less than the actual number of flies used in Experiment 3. **J** is correct; there were a total of 30 flies used in Experiment 3.

Question 9. The best answer is **A**. The first paragraph states that the experiments were conducted to study the transfer of bacteria from one surface to another by flies. It is true that the bacteria being transferred could be disease-causing and be spread by the flies after walking in the enclosure containing *E. coli*. **A** is correct; Figure 1 shows that after the flies walked in an enclosure containing *E. coli* and were then placed on the sterile nutrient agar, bacteria were cultured from the nutrient agar plates. **B** is incorrect; the 2 species of flies were examined in separate procedures. There was no interaction between the 2 species in the experiments, and Figure 1 does not show the results of such an interaction. **C** is incorrect; Figure 1 shows that both species of flies transferred *E. coli* from the enclosure to the nutrient agar. **D** is incorrect; the experiments did not mix flies of the 2 species and did not study whether one species of fly transferred bacteria to the other species, and Figure 1 does not show the results of such an interaction.

Question 10. The best answer is **G**. The experiments were done to determine if flies transferred bacteria from one surface to another. To ensure the flies were the only source of the bacteria colonies that grew on the nutrient agar, the agar had to be sterilized before the flies and any bacteria they carried were placed on the agar. **F** is incorrect; the agar was sterilized to be sure all bacteria on the agar were killed before the flies were placed in the dishes. **G** is correct. **H** is incorrect; the agar was not a food source for the flies, and sterilizing the agar would have done nothing to ensure that it had nutrients even if it were a food source. **J** is incorrect; the nutrient agar already contained the necessary nutrients for bacteria growth. The sterilization process kills any bacteria on the agar; it does not affect the bacteria nutrients that were already there.

Question 11. The best answer is A. To see if the new species (Species X) transferred more bacteria than either of the 2 species in the experiments, Species X flies would have to be subjected to the same procedures as the other 2 species. **A** is correct; only Experiment 1 used both original species of flies. Adding a group of Species X flies to that experiment would allow a comparison of the number of colonies transferred by each of the 3 species. These data would allow the student's claim to be evaluated. **B** is incorrect; just changing the kind of bacteria in Experiment 1 would still include only the original 2 species of flies; no Species X flies would be included. There would be no data for Species X that could be used to evaluate the claim. **C** is incorrect; Experiment 2 included only 1 of the 2 original species of flies. To evaluate the claim, data for all 3 species would need to be collected. The design of Experiment 2 would not provide those data. **D** is incorrect; just changing the kind of bacteria in Experiment 2 would still include only 1 of the original 2 species of flies; in addition, no Species X flies would be included. Data for all 3 species would need to be collected to evaluate the claim.

Question 12. The best answer is F. In Experiment 3, *S. carnaria* flies were allowed to walk in an enclosure containing *E. coli* and then allowed various lengths of time to clean themselves before being placed on nutrient agar. Figure 3 shows that the longer the time to clean, the fewer bacteria colonies were produced on the agar. **F** is correct; this experiment tested whether cleaning time affected the average number of colonies per dish, and the results indicate that the flies removed bacteria as they cleaned themselves. **G** is incorrect; Experiment 3 used the procedures from Experiment 1, where the flies were allowed to walk in the *E. coli* enclosure for exactly 5 minutes. Since exposure time was held constant, this experiment would not be able to test a hypothesis about the effect of varying exposure time. **H** and **J** are incorrect; Experiment 3 used only *S. carnaria* flies. Without the second species of fly included, Experiment 3 cannot test whether one species transferred more bacteria or removed bacteria better than the other species.

Question 13. The best answer is B. Figure 1 shows that the average number of colonies per dish for *S. carnaria* that had walked in the enclosure for 5 min was about 90. Figure 2 shows that the average number of colonies per dish for *S. carnaria* that had walked in the enclosure for 5 minutes, the same length of time as in Experiment 1, was about 82. Even though the conditions were the same (same species, same walking time), it would be common for the results to be different by chance. **A** is incorrect; the question asks why the results for *S. carnaria* were different in Experiment 1 and Experiment 2 even though the species of fly and the walk time were the same. The number of *E. coli* colonies transferred by the other species of fly would not explain the difference between the *S. carnaria* results since the *M. domestica* flies were tested separately. **B** is correct. **C** is incorrect; the question asks why the results for *S. carnaria* were different in Experiment 1 and Experiment 2 even though the species of fly and the walk time were the same. The number of *E. coli* colonies transferred by the other species of fly would not explain the difference between the *S. carnaria* results since the *M. domestica* flies were tested separately. **D** is incorrect; the *S. carnaria* data from Experiment 1 and the specified *S. carnaria* data from Experiment 2 were both for a walk time of 5 min. Since the walk times were the same, that could not be an explanation for the difference in the number of colonies.

Passage III

Question 14. The best answer is F. Figure 1 displays a plot line representing the %O_2 in Earth's atmosphere from 250 mya to 64 mya. The single data point along that line that is closest to 21% is at the x-axis value of 250 mya (a value of approximately 20.5%). **F** is correct. **G** is incorrect. The %O_2 value at 200 mya is approximately 14.5%, much less than 21%. **H** is incorrect. The %O_2 value at 150 mya is approximately 13.9%, much less than 21%. **J** is incorrect. The %O_2 value at 100 mya is approximately 19.1%, less than 21% and not as close to 21% as the data point at 250 mya.

Question 15. The best answer is C. Figure 2 shows that at an initial %O_2 of 17%, the flame duration for dry paper is approximately 8 sec and the flame duration for pine wood is approximately 2 sec. The difference is closest to 6 sec. **A** and **B** are incorrect. The values 2 sec and 4 sec are less than the actual difference of 6 sec. **C** is correct. **D** is incorrect. The value of 8 sec is greater than the actual difference of approximately 6 sec.

Question 16. The best answer is G. In Figure 1, there are 7 time periods, covering 200 mya–140 mya, in which paleowildfires occurred, but the %O_2 values were all less than 15%. Any interval within that range would have data that are inconsistent with the claim. **F** is incorrect. 250 mya–230 mya had paleowildfires, but the %O_2 was greater than 15%. Those data are consistent, not inconsistent, with the claim. **G** is correct. **H** and **J** are incorrect. Both 120 mya–100 mya and 90 mya–70 mya had paleowildfires, but the %O_2 was greater than 15%. Those data are consistent, not inconsistent, with the claim.

Question 17. The best answer is C. Figure 2 shows that the lowest initial %O_2 values at which each of the materials ignited are 13% for the match, 14% for the dry paper, 15% for the candle, and 16% for the pine wood. The order of the materials from highest initial %O_2 to ignite to lowest initial %O_2 to ignite is pine wood, candle, dry paper, and match. **A** and **B** are incorrect. Match would be last in the order, as it had the lowest initial %O_2 to ignite. **C** is correct. **D** is incorrect. Candle should come before dry paper in the order since the candle had a higher initial %O_2 to ignite than did the dry paper.

Question 18. The best answer is F. Figure 1 shows bars representing the number of paleowildfires for each of a number of time periods, each covering a 10 million year interval, starting 5 million years before the labeled year and ending 5 million years after the labeled year (e.g., the bar labeled 140 mya represents the period 145 mya–135 mya). The question asks about the data for 95 mya–85 mya, which corresponds to the bar labeled 90 mya. That bar shows there were 4 paleowildfires over that time interval. **F** is correct. **G**, **H**, and **J** are incorrect. The values 9, 14, and 19 are too high.

Question 19. The best answer is B. Figure 2 shows that at an initial %O_2 of 16%, the pine wood had a flame duration of approximately 0.1 sec, the match had a flame duration of approximately 2.2 sec, the candle had a flame duration of approximately 3 sec, and the dry paper had a flame duration of approximately 6 sec. **A** is incorrect. The dry paper had the longest flame duration. **B** is correct. **C** and **D** are incorrect. The dry paper had the longest flame duration.

Passage IV

Question 20. The best answer is G. In order to answer this item, the examinee must know that plants take up nutrients from the soil. Student 2 claimed that the amount of phosphorous (a nutrient) that a plant receives determines its stem color. It follows that Student 2 would be the most likely to agree that the soil in which a Population A plant is grown will influence its stem color. **F** is incorrect; Student 1 did not indicate that the stem color depended on the amount of nutrients that a plant receives. **G** is correct. **H** and **J** are incorrect; both Student 3 and Student 4 stated that the amount of nutrients received by a plant does not affect stem color.

Question 21. The best answer is A. Student 1 claimed that plants receiving 8 hr or more of sunlight each day had purple stems, which is consistent with the finding that the presence of the purple pigment in plant tissues protects the tissues from being damaged by sunlight. Student 2 claimed that the amount of sunlight a plant receives does not affect the stem color; this is not consistent with the finding. **A** is correct. **B** is incorrect; Student 1 indicated that plants receiving the most sunlight will have purple stems, not green stems. **C** and **D** are incorrect; the finding better supports the explanation of Student 1.

Question 22. The best answer is F. In order to answer this item, the examinee must know that the green pigment, chlorophyll, can be used for photosynthesis. All 4 of the students stated that all plants in Population A produce the green pigment chlorophyll. The explanations of all 4 students are therefore consistent with the statement that both green-stemmed and purple-stemmed plants produce a pigment that can be used for photosynthesis. **F** is correct. **G**, **H**, and **J** are incorrect; all 4 students stated that all the plants in Population A produce a pigment that can be used for photosynthesis.

Question 23. The best answer is D. Only Student 1 claimed that sunlight affects the plants' stem color; however, Student 1 stated that if a plant receives 8 hr or more of sunlight each day, then it produces the purple pigment and its stem will be purple. Student 1 would therefore not agree that providing a purple-stemmed plant with additional sunlight will change the stem color to green. Students 2, 3, and 4 would not be likely to agree that sunlight would affect the stems' color in any way. **A**, **B**, and **C** are incorrect; none of the students would be likely to agree that providing a purple-stemmed plant with additional sunlight will cause its stem to become green. **D** is correct.

Question 24. The best answer is H. In order to answer this item, the examinee must know how to work a genetic cross. According to Student 3's explanation, a plant with either the Gene Q genotype Qq or the Gene Q genotype QQ will produce the purple pigment, and therefore will have a purple stem. A plant with the Gene Q genotype qq will produce the green pigment, and therefore will have a green stem. If the 2 purple-stemmed plants that were crossed had the Qq genotype, then their offspring would be approximately 25% green-stemmed with the qq genotype, and approximately 75% purple-stemmed with either the QQ genotype or the Qq genotype. **F** is incorrect; based on Student 1's explanation, because the stem color depends on exposure to sunlight, plants grown under the same conditions would have the same stem color. **G** is incorrect; based on Student 2's explanation, because the stem color depends on the amount of phosphorous received by the plants, plants grown under the same conditions would have the same stem color. **H** is correct. **J** is incorrect; Student 4 claimed that purple-stemmed plants have the Gene Q genotype qq, and therefore all the offspring of 2 purple-stemmed plants would have purple stems.

Question 25. The best answer is D. In order to answer this item, the examinee must know how to work a genetic cross. Student 4 claimed that purple-stemmed plants have the Gene Q genotype qq and green-stemmed plants have either the Gene Q genotype Qq or QQ. A cross between a plant with the qq genotype (a purple-stemmed plant) and the Qq genotype (a green-stemmed plant) would produce some green-stemmed offspring with the Qq genotype and some purple-stemmed offspring with the qq genotype. **A** and **B** are incorrect; based on Student 4's explanation, the Gene Q genotype of the purple-stemmed parent must be qq. **C** is incorrect; a cross between a purple-stemmed plant with the qq genotype and a green-stemmed plant with the QQ genotype would produce only green-stemmed offspring with the Qq genotype. **D** is correct.

Question 26. The best answer is J. Student 1 claimed that plants that receive sunlight for 8 hr or more each day have a purple stem. All plants that receive 9 hr of sunlight per day would therefore have a purple stem, and none would have a green stem. Student 2, Student 3, and Student 4 all agreed that the amount of sunlight received by a plant does not affect the stem color, and therefore a plant receiving 9 hr of sunlight could have either a purple stem or a green stem. **F** is incorrect; Student 1 would not agree with the statement. **G** is incorrect; while Student 2 likely would agree, Students 3 and 4 would also agree with the statement. **H** is incorrect; while Students 3 and 4 likely would agree, Student 2 would also agree with the statement. **J** is correct; Students 2, 3, and 4 would all agree that a plant receiving 9 hr of sunlight each day could have either a purple stem or a green stem.

Passage V

Question 27. The best answer is B. According to Figure 2, March was the month in which a total of 70 L of H_2 was produced. According to Table 1, the average solar irradiance in the month of March was 153.8 W/m². **A** is incorrect; 77.8 W/m² was the average solar irradiance in January, not March. **B** is correct; in the month of March, when 70 L of H_2 was produced, the solar irradiance was 153.88 W/m². **C** is incorrect; 197.5 W/m² was the average solar irradiance in May, not March. **D** is incorrect; 206.4 W/m² was the average solar irradiance in July, not March.

Question 28. **The best answer is H.** According to Figure 1, O_2 is produced at the anode and H_2 is produced at the cathode during electrolysis. According to Step 3 of the experiment, electrolysis was initiated at 8:00 a.m. Then, eight hours later (at 4:00 p.m.), in Step 4, the amount of H_2 that had been produced was measured. **F** is incorrect; H_2 was not produced at the anode. **G** is incorrect; the amount of O_2 gas was not measured each day. **H** is correct; at 4:00 p.m. each day, the amount of H_2 gas was measured at the cathode. **J** is incorrect; O_2 gas was not produced at the cathode and was not measured each day.

Question 29. **The best answer is B.** According to the passage, a 25% by mass aqueous solution of NaOH was added to the tank in Step 2 of the experiment. In 200 g of this solution, 25% of the mass would be NaOH: 25% × 200 g = 50 g. **A** is incorrect; 25 g is 12.5% of 200 g. **B** is correct; 200 g of the solution would contain 50 g of NaOH. **C** is incorrect; 200 g of an aqueous solution of NaOH cannot contain 200 g of NaOH because that would not be a solution, it would be pure NaOH. **D** is incorrect; the mass of NaOH in the 200 g of solution cannot exceed the total mass of the solution.

Question 30. **The best answer is F.** In order to answer this item, the examinee must know that, for balanced chemical equations involving gases, the coefficients may be interpreted in terms of gas volumes. The balanced equation for the electrolysis reaction is $2H_2O \rightarrow 2H_2 + O_2$. So, for every 2 L of H_2 gas produced, 1 L of O_2 gas will be produced. According to Figure 2, 40 L of H_2 gas was produced in February. Therefore, the number of liters of O_2 produced was (40 L)/2 = 20 L. **F** is correct. **G** is incorrect; 40 L of H_2 were produced in February, and only half that amount of O_2 would have been produced. **H** is incorrect; this is twice the amount of H_2 that was produced, and according to the chemical equation only half as much O_2 would be produced. **J** is incorrect; the largest volume of H_2 produced in a month during the experiment was less than 90 L, so 100 L of O_2 could not have been produced in February since only half as much O_2 as H_2 could be produced each month.

Question 31. **The best answer is C.** According to the description of the experiment, Steps 1-5 were performed daily. Step 2 states that 4.0 L of NaOH solution were added to the tank. There are 30 days in June, so 30 days × $4.0 \frac{L}{day}$ = 120 L of NaOH solution were added in June. **A**, **B**, and **D** are incorrect; Step 2 was performed once daily for 30 days in June.

Question 32. **The best answer is J.** Table 1 gives the value of the average solar irradiance for each month, with no data provided for May 11 or any other individual day. **F**, **G**, and **H** are incorrect; 197.5 W/m^2 was the average solar irradiance for May, but without any data for May 11, there is no way to know whether the solar irradiance was less than, equal to, or greater than the average value. **J** is correct; with data given in Table 1 only for the average solar irradiance for May, the solar irradiance for May 11 cannot be determined from the given information.

Question 33. The best answer is D. In order to answer this item, the examinee must know that an aqueous NaOH solution has more ions than pure liquid H_2O, and that solutions with more ions have higher electrical conductivity. Since the H_2 gas is produced by the electrolysis of H_2O, the higher the conductivity the more H_2 produced. **A** is incorrect; pure liquid H_2O does not contain more ions than aqueous NaOH solution and does not have higher conductivity. **B** is incorrect; while pure liquid H_2O does have fewer ions and thus lower electrical conductivity than aqueous NaOH, that would result in less H_2, not more. **C** is incorrect; pure liquid H_2O would produce less H_2 because it has fewer ions, not more ions, than aqueous NaOH and thus has a lower electrical conductivity. **D** is correct; pure liquid H_2O has fewer ions and lower conductivity than aqueous NaOH and would produce less H_2 during electrolysis.

Passage VI

Question 34. The best answer is H. Figure 1 shows a vibrating string with 2 nodes, which matches the sketch in Table 1 for the 3rd harmonic. **F** is incorrect; the sketch in Table 1 for the 1st harmonic shows 0 nodes, and Figure 1 shows a string with 2 nodes. **G** is incorrect; the sketch in Table 1 for the 2nd harmonic shows 1 node, and Figure 1 shows a string with 2 nodes. **H** is correct; Figure 1 and the sketch in Table 1 for the 3rd harmonic both show a string with 2 nodes. **J** is incorrect; the sketch in Table 1 for the 4th harmonic shows 3 nodes, and Figure 1 shows a string with 2 nodes.

Question 35. The best answer is C. The sketch made in the new trial shows the vibrating string with 5 nodes. Based on the sketches shown in Table 1, the number of nodes on a vibrating string is always one more than the number of the harmonic. There are 4 nodes shown for the 5th harmonic, so a string having 5 nodes must correspond to the 6th harmonic. According to the results of Experiment 1 for String Z, as the number of the harmonic increases, the frequency increases by about 4 Hz. So, the frequency of the 6th harmonic should be greater than 19.8 Hz, or approximately 19.8 Hz + 4 Hz = 23.8 Hz. According to the results of Experiment 2, as the number of the harmonic increases, the tension, T, decreases. For String Z, the tension required for the 5th harmonic was 0.16 N, so the tension for the 6th harmonic should be less. **A** is incorrect; f should be greater than 19.8 Hz. **B** is incorrect; f should be greater than 19.8 Hz, and T should be less than 0.16 N. **C** is correct; 25.0 Hz is greater than 19.8 Hz, and 0.11 N is less than 0.16 N. **D** is incorrect; T should be less than 0.16 N.

Question 36. The best answer is G. For String Y, $\mu = 0.08$ g/cm. The mass of a piece of string is equal to its length multiplied by μ, so a piece of String Y that is 1 cm in length will have a mass of 1 cm $\times$ 0.08 $\frac{g}{cm}$ For String X, $\mu = 0.02$ g/cm, and for String Z, $\mu = 0.16$ g/cm. So, for a piece of String X to have the same mass as the piece of String Y, it would have to be 4 times as long, and for a piece of String Z to have the same mass it would have to be half the length. **F** and **H** are incorrect; String X and String Z have different values of μ than String Y, so 1 cm lengths of those strings would not have the same mass as a 1 cm length of String Y. **G** is correct; since String X has a value of μ that is ¼ the value of μ for String Y, a piece of String X that is 4 times as long (4 cm) will have the same mass as a 1 cm piece of String Y. **J** is incorrect; String Z has a greater value of μ than String Y, so a length greater than 1 cm would not have the same mass.

Question 37. The best answer is D. The rules for counting significant digits are as follows: 1) All non-zero digits are significant. 2) All zeros between non-zero digits are significant. 3) Zeros that appear after the decimal point are significant if they follow a non-zero digit. The number 1,250 contains 3 significant digits (1, 2, and 5; the zero is not significant), the number 125.0 contains 4 significant digits (1, 2, 5, and the 0 following the decimal point which occurs after 3 non-zero digits), the number 12.5 has 3 significant figures (1, 2, and 5 are all significant digits), and the number 0.00125 contains 3 significant digits (the 3 zeros that occur before the non-zero digits are not significant, but 1, 2, and 5 are significant). **A, B**, and **C** are all incorrect; the data in Table 1 were all reported with 3 significant digits. **D** is correct.

Question 38. The best answer is H. For String X, Table 1 lists 11.2 Hz as the frequency for the 1st harmonic (f_1). For String X, the frequency for the 2nd harmonic (n = 2) was 22.4 Hz (exactly twice f_1), and for the 3rd harmonic (n = 3) was 33.5 (approximately 3 times f_1). The rest of the data for String X follows the same pattern, indicating that the equation $f_n = n \times f_1$ is most consistent with the results of Experiment 1 for String X. **F** is incorrect; for the 2nd harmonic, the equation $f_n = n + f_1$ yields $f_n = 2 + 11.2 = 13.2$ Hz, which does not match the 2nd harmonic frequency (22.4 Hz) given in Table 1. **G** is incorrect; for the 2nd harmonic, the equation $f_n = n - f_1$ yields $f_n = 2 - 11.2 = -9.2$ Hz, and negative frequencies do not exist. This also does not match the 2nd harmonic frequency (22.4 Hz) given in Table 1. **H** is correct. **J** is incorrect; for the 2nd harmonic, the equation $f_n = n \div f_1$ yields $f_n = 2 \div 11.2 = 0.179$ Hz, which does not match the 2nd harmonic frequency (22.4 Hz) given in Table 1.

Question 39. The best answer is D. According to the description of the experiments, for String X, μ = 0.02 g/cm; for String Y, μ = 0.08 g/cm; and for String Z, μ = 0.16 g/cm. Table 2 shows that as μ increased from string to string, the tension increased, with String Z requiring a tension of 0.25 N for the 4th harmonic. A string with a mass per unit length, μ, of 0.32 g/cm would require a tension greater than 0.25 N. **A, B**, and **C** are incorrect; the indicated tensions are lower than 0.25 N, so they would not be great enough. **D** is correct; the tension required for the 4th harmonic of the new string would be greater than 0.25 N.

Question 40. The best answer is H. According to the description of the experiments, μ increased from String X to String Y, to String Z. Considering the results of Experiment 1 for the 3rd harmonic, f decreased from string to string, going from 33.5 Hz for String X, to 16.8 Hz for String Y, to 11.9 Hz for String Z. The results of Experiment 2 show that the tension, T, for the 3rd harmonic increased from string to string, going from 0.06 N for String X to 0.22 N for String Y, and 0.44 N for String Z. **F** is incorrect; f decreased as μ increased. **G** is incorrect; f decreased, and T increased as μ increased. **H** is correct. **J** is incorrect; T increased as μ increased.

Chapter 11: Scoring the Additional Practice Tests

After taking any of the ACT practice tests in Chapter 10, you are ready to score the test to see how you did. In this chapter, you learn how to determine your raw score, convert raw scores to scale scores, compute your Composite score, determine your estimated percentile ranks for each of your scale scores, and score your practice writing test essay.

Did you know? Practice tests taken on the online platform are scored automatically, allowing you to review your performance and see important areas to focus on right away.

Assuming you already scored practice test 1 (see chapter 3), you should be familiar with the scoring procedures.

When scoring each practice test and reviewing your scores, remember that your scores on the practice tests are only estimates of the scores that you will obtain on the ACT. If your score isn't as high as you expected, the cause could be related to any number of factors. Maybe you need to review important content and skills.

Maybe you should work a little faster, or more slowly and carefully, when taking the test. Perhaps you simply weren't doing your best work on the test. Or maybe you need to take more challenging courses to be better prepared. Keep in mind that a test score is just one indicator of your level of academic knowledge and skills. You know your own strengths and weaknesses better than anyone else, so keep them in mind as you evaluate your performance.

Scoring Your Practice Tests

For the multiple-choice tests (English, mathematics, reading, and science), the number of questions you answer correctly is called a *raw* score. To figure out your raw scores for the practice tests in this book count the number of correct answers for each test using the scoring keys provided in the following sections. Then you can convert your raw scores into *scale* scores. Scale scores are the scores that ACT reports to students, high schools, colleges, and scholarship agencies. Raw scores are converted to a common scale score to enhance score interpretation and allow comparability across different forms. After you've converted your raw scores for the practice tests to scale scores, you'll want to convert your scale scores to percentile ranks. Percentile ranks, which are explained in the following pages, are useful for interpreting your scores relative to the scores of others who have taken the ACT.

If you took the optional practice writing test, use the analytic rubric in chapter 3 (pages 109–110) to evaluate your essay and estimate your writing test score. Being objective about one's own work is difficult, and you have not had the extensive training provided to actual readers of the ACT writing test. However, it is to your advantage to read your own writing critically. Becoming your own editor helps you grow as a writer and as a reader, so it makes sense for you to evaluate your own practice essay. That having been said, it may also be helpful for you to give your practice essay to another reader to get another perspective: perhaps that of a classmate, a parent, or an English teacher, for example. To rate your essay, you and your reader should be familiar with the analytic rubric in chapter 3 and the sample essays and scoring explanations in chapter 9, and then assign your practice essay a score of 1 (low) through 6 (high) in each of the four writing domains (Ideas and Analysis, Development and Support, Organization, and Language Use and Conventions).

Your writing test should be based on two ratings, so you may either multiply your own rating times two, or sum your rating and another reader's rating to calculate your domain scores (2–12 for each domain). Your writing test score is the average of your domain scores and will be in a range of 2–12.

Scoring Practice Test 2

Scoring the Multiple-Choice Tests

To score each of your multiple-choice practice tests, starting with the English test, follow these six steps:

STEP 1. Write a "1" in the blank for each question that you answered correctly. An example is provided in the following box:

	Key		Your answer was
1.	A	–	Incorrect
2.	J	1	Correct
3.	B	1	Correct
4.	G	–	Incorrect

English ▪ Scoring Key ▪ Practice Test 2

	Key				Key				Key	
1.	A	_____		26.	J	_____		51.	A	_____
2.	G	_____		27.	A	_____		52.	G	_____
3.	C	_____		28.	F	_____		53.	A	_____
4.	G	_____		29.	C	_____		54.	J	_____
5.	D	_____		30.	H	_____		55.	D	_____
6.	G	_____		31.	D	_____		56.	F	_____
7.	B	_____		32.	F	_____		57.	D	_____
8.	J	_____		33.	C	_____		58.	G	_____
9.	B	_____		34.	H	_____		59.	B	_____
10.	F	_____		35.	C	_____		60.	G	_____
11.	D	_____		36.	J	_____		61.	D	_____
12.	F	_____		37.	D	_____		62.	H	_____
13.	B	_____		38.	F	_____		63.	C	_____
14.	F	_____		39.	D	_____		64.	G	_____
15.	A	_____		40.	J	_____		65.	C	_____
16.	F	_____		41.	B	_____		66.	J	_____
17.	C	_____		42.	F	_____		67.	A	_____
18.	G	_____		43.	C	_____		68.	F	_____
19.	A	_____		44.	G	_____		69.	B	_____
20.	H	_____		45.	C	_____		70.	G	_____
21.	C	_____		46.	J	_____		71.	B	_____
22.	H	_____		47.	C	_____		72.	H	_____
23.	A	_____		48.	H	_____		73.	C	_____
24.	H	_____		49.	C	_____		74.	J	_____
25.	D	_____		50.	J	_____		75.	B	_____

STEP 2. Add the numbers you entered in step 1 and write this total in the following shaded box. This is your raw score.

> **Number Correct (Raw Score) for:**
>
> **English Test (75 questions)**   _____

STEP 3. Repeat steps 1 and 2 for the ACT mathematics, reading, and science tests using the scoring keys on the following pages.

Mathematics ■ Scoring Key ■ Practice Test 2

	Key			Key			Key	
1.	C	_____	21.	D	_____	41.	A	_____
2.	J	_____	22.	G	_____	42.	G	_____
3.	E	_____	23.	C	_____	43.	D	_____
4.	F	_____	24.	H	_____	44.	G	_____
5.	C	_____	25.	E	_____	45.	D	_____
6.	G	_____	26.	G	_____	46.	G	_____
7.	B	_____	27.	E	_____	47.	E	_____
8.	H	_____	28.	F	_____	48.	H	_____
9.	C	_____	29.	D	_____	49.	D	_____
10.	G	_____	30.	H	_____	50.	J	_____
11.	C	_____	31.	A	_____	51.	E	_____
12.	G	_____	32.	J	_____	52.	F	_____
13.	D	_____	33.	A	_____	53.	B	_____
14.	G	_____	34.	K	_____	54.	F	_____
15.	D	_____	35.	B	_____	55.	E	_____
16.	H	_____	36.	F	_____	56.	K	_____
17.	A	_____	37.	E	_____	57.	A	_____
18.	J	_____	38.	K	_____	58.	F	_____
19.	C	_____	39.	D	_____	59.	D	_____
20.	H	_____	40.	H	_____	60.	K	_____

> **Number Correct (Raw Score) for:**
>
> **Math Test (60 questions)**   _____

Reading ■ Scoring Key ■ Practice Test 2

	Key			Key			Key	
1.	B		15.	C		29.	D	
2.	H		16.	H		30.	J	
3.	D		17.	A		31.	B	
4.	F		18.	J		32.	H	
5.	B		19.	A		33.	B	
6.	F		20.	J		34.	G	
7.	C		21.	B		35.	C	
8.	J		22.	G		36.	F	
9.	D		23.	D		37.	D	
10.	F		24.	G		38.	F	
11.	D		25.	C		39.	B	
12.	F		26.	H		40.	J	
13.	D		27.	A				
14.	G		28.	G				

Number Correct (Raw Score) for:

Reading Test (40 questions) _____

Science ■ Scoring Key ■ Practice Test 2

	Key			Key			Key	
1.	A		15.	A		29.	A	
2.	H		16.	F		30.	J	
3.	C		17.	D		31.	B	
4.	J		18.	G		32.	J	
5.	A		19.	C		33.	D	
6.	J		20.	G		34.	G	
7.	D		21.	B		35.	D	
8.	F		22.	F		36.	G	
9.	D		23.	B		37.	C	
10.	H		24.	H		38.	F	
11.	B		25.	C		39.	C	
12.	J		26.	G		40.	H	
13.	C		27.	D				
14.	J		28.	F				

Number Correct (Raw Score) for:

Science Test (40 questions) _____

Taking Additional Practice Tests

STEP 4. On each of the four tests, the total number of correct responses yields a raw score. Use the conversion table on the following page to convert your raw scores to scale scores. For each of the four tests, locate and circle your raw score or the range of raw scores that includes it in the conversion table. Then, read across to either outside column of the table and circle the scale score that corresponds to that raw score. As you determine your scale scores, enter them in the blanks provided below. The highest possible scale score for each test is 36. The lowest possible scale score for any of the four tests is 1.

	Your Scale Scores
English	_____
Mathematics	_____
Reading	_____
Science	_____
Sum of Scores	_____

STEP 5. Compute your Composite score by averaging the four scale scores. To do this, add your four scale scores and divide the sum by 4. If the resulting number ends in a fraction, round it off to the nearest whole number. (Round down any fraction less than one-half; round up any fraction that is one-half or more.) Enter this number in the appropriate blank below. This is your Composite score. The highest possible Composite score is 36. The lowest possible Composite score is 1.

	Your Scale Scores
English	_____
Mathematics	_____
Reading	_____
Science	_____
Sum of Scores	_____
Composite Score (sum ÷ 4)	_____

Scale Score Conversion Table: Practice Test 2

Scale Score	Raw Score				Scale Score
	English	Mathematics	Reading	Science	
36	73–75	59–60	40	39–40	36
35	71–72	57–58	39	38	35
34	69–70	55–56	37–38	37	34
33	68	54	36	–	33
32	67	53	35	36	32
31	66	52	34	35	31
30	65	50–51	33	34	30
29	64	48–49	32	33	29
28	63	46–47	31	32	28
27	61–62	42–45	30	31	27
26	59–60	40–41	29	30	26
25	57–58	37–39	28	28–29	25
24	54–56	35–36	27	27	24
23	51–53	32–34	25–26	25–26	23
22	48–50	31	23–24	23–24	22
21	45–47	29–30	22	22	21
20	42–44	27–28	21	20–21	20
19	40–41	25–26	19–20	19	19
18	38–39	23–24	18	17–18	18
17	36–37	20–22	17	16	17
16	33–35	16–19	15–16	14–15	16
15	30–32	13–15	14	13	15
14	27–29	10–12	12–13	11–12	14
13	25–26	8–9	11	10	13
12	23–24	6–7	10	9	12
11	20–22	5	8–9	8	11
10	18–19	4	7	7	10
9	15–17	–	6	6	9
8	13–14	3	5	5	8
7	11–12	–	4	4	7
6	8–10	2	–	3	6
5	7	–	3	2	5
4	5–6	1	2	–	4
3	3–4	–	–	1	3
2	2	–	1	–	2
1	0–1	0	0	0	1

STEP 6. Use the table on the following page to determine your estimated percentile ranks (percent at or below) for each of your scale scores. In the far left column of the table, circle your scale score for the English test (from the preceding page). Then read across to the percentile rank column for that test; circle or put a checkmark beside the corresponding percentile rank. Use the same procedure for the other three tests (from the preceding page). Using the right-hand column of scale scores for your science test and Composite scores may be easier. As you mark your percentile ranks, enter them in the blanks provided. You may also find it helpful to compare your performance with the national mean (average) score for each of the four tests and the Composite as shown at the bottom of the table.

Taking Additional Practice Tests

National Norms for ACT Test Scores
Reported During the 2022–2023 Reporting Year

Score	English	Math	Reading	Science	Composite	STEM	Score
36	100	100	100	100	100	100	36
35	99	99	98	99	99	99	35
34	96	99	96	98	99	99	34
33	94	98	94	97	98	98	33
32	93	97	91	96	96	97	32
31	91	96	89	95	95	96	31
30	90	95	87	93	93	94	30
29	89	93	84	92	91	93	29
28	87	91	82	90	89	90	28
27	85	89	80	88	86	88	27
26	83	85	77	86	83	85	26
25	81	81	75	83	80	81	25
24	77	77	72	78	76	77	24
23	73	73	68	72	72	72	23
22	68	68	63	65	67	68	22
21	64	65	57	60	62	63	21
20	58	62	52	54	56	57	20
19	52	58	46	48	50	51	19
18	48	53	41	41	45	45	18
17	44	47	36	34	38	37	17
16	40	38	32	28	32	29	16
15	35	25	27	22	26	21	15
14	29	14	23	17	19	13	14
13	23	6	17	12	13	7	13
12	19	2	12	8	7	3	12
11	14	1	7	5	2	1	11
10	9	1	3	3	1	1	10
9	4	1	2	1	1	1	9
8	2	1	1	1	1	1	8
7	1	1	1	1	1	1	7
6	1	1	1	1	1	1	6
5	1	1	1	1	1	1	5
4	1	1	1	1	1	1	4
3	1	1	1	1	1	1	3
2	1	1	1	1	1	1	2
1	1	1	1	1	1	1	1
Mean:	19.5	19.9	20.9	20.3	20.3	20.3	
SD:	7.2	5.7	7.1	5.9	6.0	5.5	

Note: These ranks are reported as "US Rank" on ACT score reports during the 2022–2023 reporting year (September 2022 through August 2023). The ranks are based on ACT-tested high school graduates of 2020, 2021, and 2022 (n=4,315,490).

Scoring Your Practice Writing Test 2 Essay

To score your practice writing test essay, follow these steps:

STEP 1. Use the guidelines from the writing test analytic rubric in chapter 3 (pages 109–110) to score your essay. Because many essays do not fit the exact description at each score point, read each description and try to determine which paragraph in the rubric best describes most of the characteristics of your essay.

STEP 2. Because your writing test domain scores are the sum of two readers' ratings of your essay, multiply your own 1–6 rating from step 1 by 2. Or, have both you and someone else read and score your practice essay, add those ratings together, and record the total in the Domain Score column in step 3.

STEP 3. Enter your writing test domain scores in the following box:

		Domain Score
Ideas and Analysis	_____ x 2 =	_____
Development and Support	_____ x 2 =	_____
Organization	_____ x 2 =	_____
Language Use and Convention	_____ x 2 =	_____

STEP 4. Enter the sum of the second-column scores here _____.

STEP 5. Divide sum by 4[†] (range 2–12). This is your Writing Subject score.

[†]Round value to the nearest whole number. Round down any fraction less than one-half; round up any fraction that is one-half or more.

STEP 6. Use the table below to determine your estimated percentile rank (percent at or below) for your writing subject score.

National Norms for ACT Writing Scores
Reported During the 2022–2023 Reporting Year

Score	ACT Score National Ranks	
	ELA	Writing
36	100	
35	99	
34	99	
33	99	
32	99	
31	97	
30	95	
29	93	
28	91	
27	88	
26	86	
25	83	
24	80	
23	76	
22	72	
21	67	
20	62	
19	57	
18	52	
17	46	
16	40	
15	34	
14	28	
13	22	
12	17	100
11	12	99
10	8	99
9	5	96
8	3	91
7	1	69
6	1	56
5	1	31
4	1	17
3	1	6
2	1	2
1	1	
Mean:	**18.8**	**6.3**
SD:	**6.3**	**1.8**

Note: These ranks are reported as "US Rank" on ACT score reports during the 2022–2023 reporting year (September 2022 through August 2023). The ranks are based on ACT-tested high school graduates of 2020, 2021, and 2022 who took the ACT Writing test (n=1,475,833).

Scoring Practice Test 3

Scoring the Multiple-Choice Tests

To score your multiple-choice practice tests, starting with the English test, follow these six steps:

STEP 1. Write a "1" in the blank for each question that you answered correctly. An example is provided in the following box:

	Key		Your answer was
1.	A	–	Incorrect
2.	J	1	Correct
3.	B	1	Correct
4.	G	–	Incorrect

English ■ Scoring Key ■ Practice Test 3

	Key			Key			Key	
1.	B		26.	H		51.	A	
2.	F		27.	A		52.	F	
3.	C		28.	J		53.	D	
4.	F		29.	D		54.	G	
5.	A		30.	F		55.	B	
6.	J		31.	B		56.	H	
7.	D		32.	H		57.	B	
8.	H		33.	A		58.	G	
9.	D		34.	G		59.	A	
10.	J		35.	A		60.	H	
11.	A		36.	F		61.	A	
12.	G		37.	D		62.	G	
13.	B		38.	J		63.	D	
14.	H		39.	B		64.	G	
15.	C		40.	J		65.	C	
16.	J		41.	C		66.	F	
17.	B		42.	F		67.	D	
18.	H		43.	D		68.	H	
19.	A		44.	H		69.	A	
20.	J		45.	A		70.	J	
21.	B		46.	J		71.	B	
22.	F		47.	C		72.	F	
23.	C		48.	H		73.	D	
24.	G		49.	D		74.	F	
25.	B		50.	J		75.	C	

STEP 2. Add the numbers you entered in step 1 and write this total in the following shaded box. This is your raw score.

Number Correct (Raw Score) for:

English Test (75 questions) _____

STEP 3. Repeat steps 1 and 2 for the ACT mathematics, reading, and science tests using the scoring keys on the following pages.

Mathematics ■ Scoring Key ■ Practice Test 3

	Key			Key			Key	
1.	B	____	21.	C	____	41.	C	____
2.	G	____	22.	K	____	42.	G	____
3.	A	____	23.	A	____	43.	D	____
4.	H	____	24.	G	____	44.	K	____
5.	A	____	25.	D	____	45.	A	____
6.	G	____	26.	F	____	46.	K	____
7.	E	____	27.	C	____	47.	D	____
8.	J	____	28.	H	____	48.	F	____
9.	C	____	29.	A	____	49.	B	____
10.	H	____	30.	H	____	50.	K	____
11.	E	____	31.	C	____	51.	D	____
12.	G	____	32.	J	____	52.	J	____
13.	A	____	33.	C	____	53.	E	____
14.	K	____	34.	G	____	54.	J	____
15.	E	____	35.	A	____	55.	B	____
16.	J	____	36.	G	____	56.	G	____
17.	D	____	37.	E	____	57.	A	____
18.	G	____	38.	J	____	58.	J	____
19.	B	____	39.	C	____	59.	D	____
20.	F	____	40.	K	____	60.	K	____

Number Correct (Raw Score) for:

Mathematics Test (60 questions) _____

Reading ■ Scoring Key ■ Practice Test 3

	Key	
1.	A	_____
2.	H	_____
3.	D	_____
4.	H	_____
5.	B	_____
6.	J	_____
7.	A	_____
8.	F	_____
9.	C	_____
10.	G	_____
11.	C	_____
12.	F	_____
13.	A	_____
14.	G	_____

	Key	
15.	D	_____
16.	G	_____
17.	C	_____
18.	F	_____
19.	D	_____
20.	J	_____
21.	C	_____
22.	F	_____
23.	A	_____
24.	H	_____
25.	B	_____
26.	G	_____
27.	C	_____
28.	J	_____

	Key	
29.	B	_____
30.	J	_____
31.	B	_____
32.	H	_____
33.	B	_____
34.	F	_____
35.	A	_____
36.	J	_____
37.	C	_____
38.	J	_____
39.	A	_____
40.	H	_____

Number Correct (Raw Score) for:

Reading Test (40 questions)   _____

Science ■ Scoring Key ■ Practice Test 3

	Key	
1.	C	_____
2.	H	_____
3.	C	_____
4.	F	_____
5.	B	_____
6.	H	_____
7.	C	_____
8.	F	_____
9.	A	_____
10.	H	_____
11.	B	_____
12.	J	_____
13.	A	_____
14.	H	_____

	Key	
15.	A	_____
16.	J	_____
17.	C	_____
18.	F	_____
19.	A	_____
20.	G	_____
21.	B	_____
22.	F	_____
23.	B	_____
24.	G	_____
25.	D	_____
26.	G	_____
27.	D	_____
28.	J	_____

	Key	
29.	C	_____
30.	G	_____
31.	D	_____
32.	J	_____
33.	A	_____
34.	H	_____
35.	D	_____
36.	F	_____
37.	B	_____
38.	J	_____
39.	B	_____
40.	F	_____

Number Correct (Raw Score) for:

Science Test (40 questions)   _____

STEP 4. On each of the four tests, the total number of correct responses yields a raw score. Use the conversion table on the following page to convert your raw scores to scale scores. For each of the four tests, locate and circle your raw score or the range of raw scores that includes it in the conversion table. Then, read across to either outside column of the table and circle the scale score that corresponds to that raw score. As you determine your scale scores, enter them in the blanks provided below. The highest possible scale score for each test is 36. The lowest possible scale score for any of the four tests is 1.

	Your Scale Scores
English	_____
Mathematics	_____
Reading	_____
Science	_____
Sum of Scores	_____

STEP 5. Compute your Composite score by averaging the four scale scores. To do this, add your four scale scores and divide the sum by 4. If the resulting number ends in a fraction, round it off to the nearest whole number. (Round down any fraction less than one-half; round up any fraction that is one-half or more.) Enter this number in the appropriate blank below. This is your Composite score. The highest possible Composite score is 36. The lowest possible Composite score is 1.

	Your Scale Scores
English	_____
Mathematics	_____
Reading	_____
Science	_____
Sum of Scores	_____
Composite Score (sum ÷ 4)	_____

Scale Score Conversion Table: Practice Test 3

Scale Score	Raw Score				Scale Score
	English	Mathematics	Reading	Science	
36	73–75	59–60	39–40	39–40	36
35	71–72	56–58	38	38	35
34	70	54–55	37	37	34
33	69	53	36	36	33
32	68	52	34–35	35	32
31	67	50–51	33	34	31
30	66	49	32	–	30
29	65	47–48	31	33	29
28	64	44–46	30	32	28
27	62–63	42–43	29	31	27
26	61	39–41	28	30	26
25	58–60	37–38	27	28–29	25
24	55–57	35–36	26	27	24
23	52–54	33–34	24–25	25–26	23
22	50–51	31–32	23	24	22
21	47–49	30	21–22	22–23	21
20	44–46	28–29	20	21	20
19	42–43	26–27	19	19–20	19
18	40–41	24–25	17–18	18	18
17	38–39	20–23	16	16–17	17
16	35–37	17–19	15	15	16
15	32–34	13–16	13–14	13–14	15
14	29–31	10–12	12	12	14
13	26–28	8–9	11	10–11	13
12	24–25	6–7	9–10	9	12
11	21–23	5	8	8	11
10	17–20	4	7	7	10
9	15–16	–	6	6	9
8	13–14	3	5	5	8
7	10–12	–	4	4	7
6	8–9	2	–	3	6
5	6–7	–	3	–	5
4	5	1	2	2	4
3	3–4	–	–	1	3
2	2	–	1	–	2
1	0–1	0	0	0	1

STEP 6. Use the table on the following page to determine your estimated percentile ranks (percent at or below) for each of your scale scores. In the far left column of the table, circle your scale score for the English test (from the preceding page). Then read across to the percentile rank column for that test; circle or put a checkmark beside the corresponding percentile rank. Use the same procedure for the other four tests (from the preceding page). Using the right-hand column of scale scores for your science test and Composite scores may be easier. As you mark your percentile ranks, enter them in the blanks provided. You may also find it helpful to compare your performance with the national mean (average) score for each of the five tests and the Composite as shown at the bottom of the table.

Taking Additional Practice Tests

National Norms for ACT Test Scores
Reported During the 2022–2023 Reporting Year

Score	English	Math	Reading	Science	Composite	STEM	Score
36	100	100	100	100	100	100	36
35	99	99	98	99	99	99	35
34	96	99	96	98	99	99	34
33	94	98	94	97	98	98	33
32	93	97	91	96	96	97	32
31	91	96	89	95	95	96	31
30	90	95	87	93	93	94	30
29	89	93	84	92	91	93	29
28	87	91	82	90	89	90	28
27	85	89	80	88	86	88	27
26	83	85	77	86	83	85	26
25	81	81	75	83	80	81	25
24	77	77	72	78	76	77	24
23	73	73	68	72	72	72	23
22	68	68	63	65	67	68	22
21	64	65	57	60	62	63	21
20	58	62	52	54	56	57	20
19	52	58	46	48	50	51	19
18	48	53	41	41	45	45	18
17	44	47	36	34	38	37	17
16	40	38	32	28	32	29	16
15	35	25	27	22	26	21	15
14	29	14	23	17	19	13	14
13	23	6	17	12	13	7	13
12	19	2	12	8	7	3	12
11	14	1	7	5	2	1	11
10	9	1	3	3	1	1	10
9	4	1	2	1	1	1	9
8	2	1	1	1	1	1	8
7	1	1	1	1	1	1	7
6	1	1	1	1	1	1	6
5	1	1	1	1	1	1	5
4	1	1	1	1	1	1	4
3	1	1	1	1	1	1	3
2	1	1	1	1	1	1	2
1	1	1	1	1	1	1	1
Mean:	19.5	19.9	20.9	20.3	20.3	20.3	
SD:	7.2	5.7	7.1	5.9	6.0	5.5	

Note: These ranks are reported as "US Rank" on ACT score reports during the 2022–2023 reporting year (September 2022 through August 2023). The ranks are based on ACT-tested high school graduates of 2020, 2021, and 2022 (n=4,315,490).

Scoring Your Practice Writing Test 3 Essay

To score your practice writing test essay, follow these steps:

STEP 1. Use the guidelines from the writing test analytic rubric in chapter 3 (pages 109–110) to score your essay. Because many essays do not fit the exact description at each score point, read each description and try to determine which paragraph in the rubric best describes most of the characteristics of your essay.

STEP 2. Because your writing test domain scores are the sum of two readers' ratings of your essay, multiply your own 1–6 rating from step 1 by 2. Or, have both you and someone else read and score your practice essay, add those ratings together, and record the total in the Domain Score column in step 3.

STEP 3. Enter your writing test domain scores in the following box:

			Domain Score
Ideas and Analysis	_____	x 2 =	_____
Development and Support	_____	x 2 =	_____
Organization	_____	x 2 =	_____
Language Use and Convention	_____	x 2 =	_____

STEP 4. Enter the sum of the second-column scores here _____.

STEP 5. Divide sum by 4[†] (range 2–12). This is your Writing Subject score.

[†]Round value to the nearest whole number. Round down any fraction less than one-half; round up any fraction that is one-half or more.

STEP 6. Use the table below to determine your estimated percentile rank (percent at or below) for your writing subject score.

National Norms for ACT Writing Scores
Reported During the 2022–2023 Reporting Year

Score	ACT Score National Ranks	
	ELA	Writing
36	100	
35	99	
34	99	
33	99	
32	99	
31	97	
30	95	
29	93	
28	91	
27	88	
26	86	
25	83	
24	80	
23	76	
22	72	
21	67	
20	62	
19	57	
18	52	
17	46	
16	40	
15	34	
14	28	
13	22	
12	17	100
11	12	99
10	8	99
9	5	96
8	3	91
7	1	69
6	1	56
5	1	31
4	1	17
3	1	6
2	1	2
1	1	
Mean:	18.8	6.3
SD:	6.3	1.8

Note: These ranks are reported as "US Rank" on ACT score reports during the 2022–2023 reporting year (September 2022 through August 2023). The ranks are based on ACT-tested high school graduates of 2020, 2021, and 2022 who took the ACT Writing test (n=1,475,833).

Scoring Practice Test 4

Scoring the Multiple-Choice Tests

To score each of your multiple-choice practice tests, starting with the English test, follow these steps:

STEP 1. Write a "1" in the blank for each question that you answered correctly. An example is provided in the following box:

	Key		Your answer was
1.	A	___	Incorrect
2.	J	1	Correct
3.	B	1	Correct
4.	G	___	Incorrect

English ▪ Scoring Key ▪ Practice Test 4

	Key			Key			Key	
1.	C	_____	26.	J	_____	51.	B	_____
2.	H	_____	27.	D	_____	52.	J	_____
3.	D	_____	28.	H	_____	53.	B	_____
4.	G	_____	29.	B	_____	54.	F	_____
5.	D	_____	30.	G	_____	55.	B	_____
6.	J	_____	31.	A	_____	56.	F	_____
7.	B	_____	32.	H	_____	57.	C	_____
8.	H	_____	33.	C	_____	58.	H	_____
9.	C	_____	34.	J	_____	59.	D	_____
10.	F	_____	35.	D	_____	60.	G	_____
11.	A	_____	36.	F	_____	61.	B	_____
12.	J	_____	37.	A	_____	62.	F	_____
13.	D	_____	38.	F	_____	63.	A	_____
14.	H	_____	39.	D	_____	64.	H	_____
15.	B	_____	40.	G	_____	65.	A	_____
16.	J	_____	41.	C	_____	66.	F	_____
17.	A	_____	42.	H	_____	67.	C	_____
18.	G	_____	43.	B	_____	68.	J	_____
19.	A	_____	44.	H	_____	69.	B	_____
20.	H	_____	45.	A	_____	70.	G	_____
21.	A	_____	46.	G	_____	71.	D	_____
22.	J	_____	47.	A	_____	72.	J	_____
23.	C	_____	48.	J	_____	73.	A	_____
24.	F	_____	49.	D	_____	74.	H	_____
25.	B	_____	50.	H	_____	75.	C	_____

STEP 2. Add the numbers you entered in step 1 and write this total in the following shaded box. This is your raw score.

> **Number Correct (Raw Score) for:**
>
> **English test (75 questions)** _____

STEP 3. Repeat steps 1 and 2 for the ACT mathematics, reading, and science tests using the scoring keys on the following pages.

Mathematics ■ Scoring Key ■ Practice Test 4

	Key			Key			Key	
1.	D	_____	21.	D	_____	41.	E	_____
2.	H	_____	22.	J	_____	42.	F	_____
3.	C	_____	23.	E	_____	43.	A	_____
4.	J	_____	24.	H	_____	44.	J	_____
5.	A	_____	25.	C	_____	45.	D	_____
6.	H	_____	26.	H	_____	46.	K	_____
7.	D	_____	27.	D	_____	47.	A	_____
8.	H	_____	28.	J	_____	48.	K	_____
9.	B	_____	29.	B	_____	49.	D	_____
10.	G	_____	30.	K	_____	50.	G	_____
11.	A	_____	31.	C	_____	51.	D	_____
12.	G	_____	32.	H	_____	52.	H	_____
13.	C	_____	33.	B	_____	53.	B	_____
14.	F	_____	34.	K	_____	54.	G	_____
15.	C	_____	35.	E	_____	55.	D	_____
16.	K	_____	36.	G	_____	56.	K	_____
17.	A	_____	37.	C	_____	57.	B	_____
18.	K	_____	38.	F	_____	58.	F	_____
19.	A	_____	39.	A	_____	59.	D	_____
20.	G	_____	40.	K	_____	60.	G	_____

> **Number Correct (Raw Score) for:**
>
> **Math test (60 questions)** _____

Reading ■ Scoring Key ■ Practice Test 4

	Key	
1.	B	_____
2.	F	_____
3.	D	_____
4.	J	_____
5.	B	_____
6.	H	_____
7.	A	_____
8.	J	_____
9.	D	_____
10.	H	_____
11.	D	_____
12.	J	_____
13.	D	_____
14.	H	_____

	Key	
15.	B	_____
16.	H	_____
17.	C	_____
18.	J	_____
19.	C	_____
20.	F	_____
21.	D	_____
22.	H	_____
23.	A	_____
24.	F	_____
25.	B	_____
26.	J	_____
27.	A	_____
28.	G	_____

	Key	
29.	C	_____
30.	H	_____
31.	B	_____
32.	F	_____
33.	D	_____
34.	G	_____
35.	C	_____
36.	F	_____
37.	A	_____
38.	H	_____
39.	A	_____
40.	G	_____

Number Correct (Raw Score) for:

Reading test (40 questions)   _____

Science ■ Scoring Key ■ Practice Test 4

	Key	
1.	B	_____
2.	J	_____
3.	A	_____
4.	H	_____
5.	A	_____
6.	H	_____
7.	D	_____
8.	J	_____
9.	C	_____
10.	H	_____
11.	D	_____
12.	F	_____
13.	B	_____
14.	H	_____

	Key	
15.	B	_____
16.	G	_____
17.	C	_____
18.	J	_____
19.	A	_____
20.	F	_____
21.	C	_____
22.	F	_____
23.	D	_____
24.	F	_____
25.	B	_____
26.	G	_____
27.	C	_____
28.	F	_____

	Key	
29.	B	_____
30.	G	_____
31.	A	_____
32.	H	_____
33.	D	_____
34.	J	_____
35.	C	_____
36.	H	_____
37.	B	_____
38.	G	_____
39.	C	_____
40.	J	_____

Number Correct (Raw Score) for:

Science test (40 questions)   _____

STEP 4. On each of the four tests, the total number of correct responses yields a raw score. Use the conversion table on the following page to convert your raw scores to scale scores. For each of the four tests, locate and circle your raw score or the range of raw scores that includes it in the conversion table. Then, read across to either outside column of the table and circle the scale score that corresponds to that raw score. As you determine your scale scores, enter them in the blanks provided below. The highest possible scale score for each test is 36. The lowest possible scale score for any of the four tests is 1.

	Your Scale Scores
English	_____
Mathematics	_____
Reading	_____
Science	_____
Sum of Scores	_____

STEP 5. Compute your Composite score by averaging the four scale scores. To do this, add your four scale scores and divide the sum by 4. If the resulting number ends in a fraction, round it off to the nearest whole number. (Round down any fraction less than one-half; round up any fraction that is one-half or more.) Enter this number in the appropriate blank below. This is your Composite score. The highest possible Composite score is 36. The lowest possible Composite score is 1.

	Your Scale Scores
English	_____
Mathematics	_____
Reading	_____
Science	_____
Sum of Scores	_____
Composite Score (sum ÷ 4)	_____

Scale Score Conversion Table:
Practice Test 4

Scale Score	Raw Score				Scale Score
	English	Mathematics	Reading	Science	
36	73–75	59–60	40	39–40	36
35	71–72	57–58	38–39	38	35
34	69–70	56	37	37	34
33	68	54–55	36	36	33
32	67	53	35	35	32
31	66	52	34	34	31
30	65	50–51	33	33	30
29	64	48–49	32	32	29
28	63	45–47	31	31	28
27	61–62	42–44	30	30	27
26	60	39–41	29	29	26
25	57–59	36–38	28	27–28	25
24	55–56	34–35	27	25–26	24
23	52–54	32–33	26	24	23
22	49–51	30–31	24–25	22–23	22
21	46–48	29	23	20–21	21
20	43–45	27–28	21–22	19	20
19	41–42	24–26	20	17–18	19
18	40	22–23	19	16	18
17	37–39	19–21	17–18	14–15	17
16	34–36	15–18	16	13	16
15	30–33	12–14	14–15	12	15
14	27–29	9–11	13	10–11	14
13	25–26	7–8	11–12	9	13
12	23–24	6	9–10	8	12
11	20–22	5	8	7	11
10	17–19	4	7	6	10
9	14–16	3	6	5	9
8	12–13	–	5	4	8
7	10–11	2	4	–	7
6	8–9	–	–	3	6
5	6–7	–	3	2	5
4	5	1	2	–	4
3	3–4	–	–	1	3
2	2	–	1	–	2
1	0–1	0	0	0	1

STEP 6. Use the table on the following page to determine your estimated percentile ranks (percent at or below) for each of your scale scores. In the far left column of the table, circle your scale score for the English test (from the preceding page). Then read across to the percentile rank column for that test; circle or put a checkmark beside the corresponding percentile rank. Use the same procedure for the other three tests (from the preceding page). Using the right-hand column of scale scores for your science test and Composite scores may be easier. As you mark your percentile ranks, enter them in the blanks provided. You may also find it helpful to compare your performance with the national mean (average) score for each of the four tests and the Composite as shown at the bottom of the table.

Taking Additional Practice Tests

National Norms for ACT Test Scores
Reported During the 2022–2023 Reporting Year

Score	English	Math	Reading	Science	Composite	STEM	Score
36	100	100	100	100	100	100	36
35	99	99	98	99	99	99	35
34	96	99	96	98	99	99	34
33	94	98	94	97	98	98	33
32	93	97	91	96	96	97	32
31	91	96	89	95	95	96	31
30	90	95	87	93	93	94	30
29	89	93	84	92	91	93	29
28	87	91	82	90	89	90	28
27	85	89	80	88	86	88	27
26	83	85	77	86	83	85	26
25	81	81	75	83	80	81	25
24	77	77	72	78	76	77	24
23	73	73	68	72	72	72	23
22	68	68	63	65	67	68	22
21	64	65	57	60	62	63	21
20	58	62	52	54	56	57	20
19	52	58	46	48	50	51	19
18	48	53	41	41	45	45	18
17	44	47	36	34	38	37	17
16	40	38	32	28	32	29	16
15	35	25	27	22	26	21	15
14	29	14	23	17	19	13	14
13	23	6	17	12	13	7	13
12	19	2	12	8	7	3	12
11	14	1	7	5	2	1	11
10	9	1	3	3	1	1	10
9	4	1	2	1	1	1	9
8	2	1	1	1	1	1	8
7	1	1	1	1	1	1	7
6	1	1	1	1	1	1	6
5	1	1	1	1	1	1	5
4	1	1	1	1	1	1	4
3	1	1	1	1	1	1	3
2	1	1	1	1	1	1	2
1	1	1	1	1	1	1	1
Mean:	19.5	19.9	20.9	20.3	20.3	20.3	
SD:	7.2	5.7	7.1	5.9	6.0	5.5	

Note: These ranks are reported as "US Rank" on ACT score reports during the 2022–2023 reporting year (September 2022 through August 2023). The ranks are based on ACT-tested high school graduates of 2020, 2021, and 2022 (n=4,315,490).

Scoring Your Practice Writing Test 4 Essay

To score your practice writing test essay, follow these steps:

STEP 1. Use the guidelines from the writing test analytic rubric in chapter 3 (pages 109–110) to score your essay. Because many essays do not fit the exact description at each score point, read each description and try to determine which paragraph in the rubric best describes most of the characteristics of your essay.

STEP 2. Because your writing test domain scores are the sum of two readers' ratings of your essay, multiply your own 1–6 rating from step 1 by 2. Or, have both you and someone else read and score your practice essay, add those ratings together, and record the total in the Domain Score column in step 3.

STEP 3. Enter your writing test domain scores in the following box.

			Domain Score
Ideas and Analysis	_____	× 2 =	_____
Development and Support	_____	× 2 =	_____
Organization	_____	× 2 =	_____
Language Use and Conventions	_____	× 2 =	_____

STEP 4. Enter the sum of the second-column scores here _____.

STEP 5. Divide sum by 4[†] (range 2–12). This is your Writing Subject score.

[†]Round value to the nearest whole number. Round down any fraction less than one-half; round up any fraction that is one-half or more.

STEP 6. Use the table below to determine your estimated percentile rank (percent at or below) for your writing subject score.

National Norms for ACT Writing Scores
Reported During the 2022–2023 Reporting Year

Score	ACT Score National Ranks	
	ELA	Writing
36	100	
35	99	
34	99	
33	99	
32	99	
31	97	
30	95	
29	93	
28	91	
27	88	
26	86	
25	83	
24	80	
23	76	
22	72	
21	67	
20	62	
19	57	
18	52	
17	46	
16	40	
15	34	
14	28	
13	22	
12	17	100
11	12	99
10	8	99
9	5	96
8	3	91
7	1	69
6	1	56
5	1	31
4	1	17
3	1	6
2	1	2
1	1	
Mean:	18.8	6.3
SD:	6.3	1.8

Note: These ranks are reported as "US Rank" on ACT score reports during the 2022–2023 reporting year (September 2022 through August 2023). The ranks are based on ACT-tested high school graduates of 2020, 2021, and 2022 who took the ACT Writing test (n=1,475,833).

Scoring Practice Test 5

Scoring Your Multiple-Choice Practice Tests

To score your multiple-choice practice tests, follow these eight steps:

STEP 1. Write a "1" in the blank for each English test question that you answered correctly. An example is provided in the box below:

	Key		Your answer was
1.	A		Incorrect
2.	J	1	Correct
3.	B	1	Correct
4.	G		Incorrect

English ■ Scoring Key ■ Practice Test 5

	Key			Key			Key	
1.	C	_____	26.	J	_____	51.	D	_____
2.	H	_____	27.	A	_____	52.	J	_____
3.	B	_____	28.	H	_____	53.	A	_____
4.	H	_____	29.	D	_____	54.	G	_____
5.	C	_____	30.	G	_____	55.	D	_____
6.	F	_____	31.	D	_____	56.	J	_____
7.	A	_____	32.	G	_____	57.	C	_____
8.	G	_____	33.	B	_____	58.	J	_____
9.	A	_____	34.	J	_____	59.	B	_____
10.	H	_____	35.	D	_____	60.	H	_____
11.	D	_____	36.	G	_____	61.	D	_____
12.	G	_____	37.	C	_____	62.	F	_____
13.	B	_____	38.	F	_____	63.	C	_____
14.	J	_____	39.	C	_____	64.	H	_____
15.	A	_____	40.	F	_____	65.	D	_____
16.	J	_____	41.	A	_____	66.	G	_____
17.	C	_____	42.	F	_____	67.	A	_____
18.	F	_____	43.	B	_____	68.	J	_____
19.	A	_____	44.	F	_____	69.	D	_____
20.	F	_____	45.	C	_____	70.	J	_____
21.	B	_____	46.	F	_____	71.	B	_____
22.	J	_____	47.	A	_____	72.	H	_____
23.	B	_____	48.	F	_____	73.	A	_____
24.	H	_____	49.	B	_____	74.	H	_____
25.	A	_____	50.	G	_____	75.	B	_____

STEP 2. Add the numbers you entered in step 1 and write this total in the following shaded box. This is your raw score.

> **Number Correct (Raw Score) for:**
>
> **Total Number Correct for English Test (75 questions)**   _____

STEP 3. Repeat Steps 1 and 2 for the ACT mathematics, reading, and science tests using the scoring keys on the following pages.

Mathematics ■ Scoring Key ■ Practice Test 5

	Key			Key			Key	
1.	E	_____	21.	B	_____	41.	B	_____
2.	H	_____	22.	H	_____	42.	F	_____
3.	B	_____	23.	A	_____	43.	D	_____
4.	J	_____	24.	F	_____	44.	G	_____
5.	A	_____	25.	C	_____	45.	D	_____
6.	F	_____	26.	F	_____	46.	H	_____
7.	B	_____	27.	E	_____	47.	A	_____
8.	H	_____	28.	H	_____	48.	G	_____
9.	C	_____	29.	E	_____	49.	D	_____
10.	J	_____	30.	F	_____	50.	J	_____
11.	C	_____	31.	B	_____	51.	E	_____
12.	H	_____	32.	K	_____	52.	J	_____
13.	E	_____	33.	C	_____	53.	E	_____
14.	H	_____	34.	J	_____	54.	G	_____
15.	D	_____	35.	D	_____	55.	D	_____
16.	F	_____	36.	K	_____	56.	J	_____
17.	C	_____	37.	E	_____	57.	A	_____
18.	G	_____	38.	K	_____	58.	G	_____
19.	A	_____	39.	B	_____	59.	E	_____
20.	J	_____	40.	H	_____	60.	K	_____

> **Number Correct (Raw Score) for:**
>
> **Total Number Correct for Math Test (60 questions)**   _____

Reading ■ Scoring Key ■ Practice Test 5

	Key			Key			Key	
1.	D	____	15.	A	____	29.	B	____
2.	J	____	16.	H	____	30.	F	____
3.	C	____	17.	D	____	31.	B	____
4.	H	____	18.	J	____	32.	F	____
5.	B	____	19.	C	____	33.	D	____
6.	H	____	20.	J	____	34.	H	____
7.	A	____	21.	C	____	35.	B	____
8.	F	____	22.	G	____	36.	H	____
9.	D	____	23.	B	____	37.	A	____
10.	F	____	24.	H	____	38.	F	____
11.	B	____	25.	D	____	39.	C	____
12.	F	____	26.	G	____	40.	J	____
13.	B	____	27.	A	____			
14.	F	____	28.	F	____			

Number Correct (Raw Score) for:

Total Number Correct for Reading Test (40 questions) _____

Science ■ Scoring Key ■ Practice Test 5

	Key			Key			Key	
1.	A	____	15.	B	____	29.	C	____
2.	J	____	16.	H	____	30.	J	____
3.	D	____	17.	A	____	31.	B	____
4.	G	____	18.	F	____	32.	F	____
5.	D	____	19.	C	____	33.	A	____
6.	G	____	20.	F	____	34.	F	____
7.	B	____	21.	C	____	35.	C	____
8.	G	____	22.	F	____	36.	F	____
9.	A	____	23.	D	____	37.	B	____
10.	H	____	24.	H	____	38.	J	____
11.	D	____	25.	B	____	39.	B	____
12.	H	____	26.	J	____	40.	F	____
13.	B	____	27.	B	____			
14.	G	____	28.	H	____			

Number Correct (Raw Score) for:

Total Number Correct for Science Test (40 questions) _____

STEP 4. On each of the four tests, the total number of correct responses yields a raw score. Use the conversion table on the following page to convert your raw scores to scale scores. For each of the four tests, locate and circle your raw score or the range of raw scores that includes it in the conversion table. Then, read across to either outside column of the table and circle the scale score that corresponds to that raw score. As you determine your scale scores, enter them in the blanks provided below. The highest possible scale score for each test is 36. The lowest possible scale score for any of the four tests is 1.

	Your Scale Scores
English	_____
Mathematics	_____
Reading	_____
Science	_____
Sum of Scores	_____

STEP 5. Compute your Composite score by averaging the four scale scores. To do this, add your four scale scores and divide the sum by 4. If the resulting number ends in a fraction, round it off to the nearest whole number. (Round down any fraction less than one-half; round up any fraction that is one-half or more.) Enter this number in the appropriate blank below. This is your Composite score. The highest possible Composite score is 36. The lowest possible Composite score is 1.

	Your Scale Scores
English	_____
Mathematics	_____
Reading	_____
Science	_____
Sum of Scores	_____
Composite Score (sum ÷ 4)	_____

Scale Score Conversion Table:
Practice Test 5

Scale Score	Raw Score				Scale Score
	English	Mathematics	Reading	Science	
36	73–75	58–60	39–40	39–40	36
35	70–72	56–57	38	38	35
34	69	54–55	37	–	34
33	68	52–53	36	37	33
32	67	51	35	36	32
31	66	50	–	–	31
30	65	48–49	34	35	30
29	64	46–47	33	34	29
28	62–63	44–45	32	33	28
27	61	41–43	31	32	27
26	59–60	38–40	30	31	26
25	57–58	36–37	29	29–30	25
24	54–56	34–35	28	27–28	24
23	51–53	32–33	26–27	25–26	23
22	49–50	30–31	25	23–24	22
21	46–48	29	24	21–22	21
20	43–45	28	22–23	19–20	20
19	41–42	26–27	21	18	19
18	40	24–25	20	16–17	18
17	38–39	21–23	18–19	14–15	17
16	35–37	18–20	17	13	16
15	31–34	14–17	15–16	12	15
14	29–30	11–13	14	10–11	14
13	27–28	9–10	12–13	9	13
12	24–26	7–8	11	8	12
11	21–23	6	9–10	7	11
10	18–20	5	8	6	10
9	16–17	4	7	5	9
8	13–15	3	6	4	8
7	11–12	–	5	–	7
6	9–10	2	4	3	6
5	7–8	–	3	2	5
4	5–6	1	–	–	4
3	4	–	2	1	3
2	2–3	–	1	–	2
1	0–1	0	0	0	1

STEP 6. Use the table on the following page to determine your estimated percentile ranks (percent at or below) for each of your scale scores. In the far left column of the table, circle your scale score for the English test (from the preceding page). Then read across to the percentile rank column for that test; circle or put a checkmark beside the corresponding percentile rank. Use the same procedure for the other three tests (from the preceding page). Using the right-hand column of scale scores for your science test and Composite scores may be easier. As you mark your percentile ranks, enter them in the blanks provided. You may also find it helpful to compare your performance with the national mean (average) score for each of the four tests and the Composite as shown at the bottom of the table.

Taking Additional Practice Tests

National Norms for ACT Test Scores
Reported During the 2022–2023 Reporting Year

Score	English	Math	Reading	Science	Composite	STEM	Score
36	100	100	100	100	100	100	36
35	99	99	98	99	99	99	35
34	96	99	96	98	99	99	34
33	94	98	94	97	98	98	33
32	93	97	91	96	96	97	32
31	91	96	89	95	95	96	31
30	90	95	87	93	93	94	30
29	89	93	84	92	91	93	29
28	87	91	82	90	89	90	28
27	85	89	80	88	86	88	27
26	83	85	77	86	83	85	26
25	81	81	75	83	80	81	25
24	77	77	72	78	76	77	24
23	73	73	68	72	72	72	23
22	68	68	63	65	67	68	22
21	64	65	57	60	62	63	21
20	58	62	52	54	56	57	20
19	52	58	46	48	50	51	19
18	48	53	41	41	45	45	18
17	44	47	36	34	38	37	17
16	40	38	32	28	32	29	16
15	35	25	27	22	26	21	15
14	29	14	23	17	19	13	14
13	23	6	17	12	13	7	13
12	19	2	12	8	7	3	12
11	14	1	7	5	2	1	11
10	9	1	3	3	1	1	10
9	4	1	2	1	1	1	9
8	2	1	1	1	1	1	8
7	1	1	1	1	1	1	7
6	1	1	1	1	1	1	6
5	1	1	1	1	1	1	5
4	1	1	1	1	1	1	4
3	1	1	1	1	1	1	3
2	1	1	1	1	1	1	2
1	1	1	1	1	1	1	1
Mean:	19.5	19.9	20.9	20.3	20.3	20.3	
SD:	7.2	5.7	7.1	5.9	6.0	5.5	

Note: These ranks are reported as "US Rank" on ACT score reports during the 2022–2023 reporting year (September 2022 through August 2023). The ranks are based on ACT-tested high school graduates of 2020, 2021, and 2022 (n=4,315,490).

Scoring Your Practice Writing Test 5 Essay

To score your practice writing test essay, follow these steps:

STEP 1. Use the guidelines from the writing test analytic rubric in chapter 3 (pages 109–110) to score your essay. Because many essays do not fit the exact description at each score point, read each description and try to determine which paragraph in the rubric best describes most of the characteristics of your essay.

STEP 2. Because your writing test domain scores are the sum of two readers' ratings of your essay, multiply your own 1–6 rating from step 1 by 2. Or, have both you and someone else read and score your practice essay, add those ratings together, and record the total in the Domain Score column in step 3.

STEP 3. Enter your writing test domain scores in the following box.

			Domain Score
Ideas and Analysis	_____	× 2 =	_____
Development and Support	_____	× 2 =	_____
Organization	_____	× 2 =	_____
Language Use and Conventions	_____	× 2 =	_____

STEP 4. Enter the sum of the second-column scores here _____.

STEP 5. Divide sum by 4† (range 2–12). This is your Writing test score.

†Round value to the nearest whole number. Round down any fraction less than one-half; round up any fraction that is one-half or more.

STEP 6. Use the table below to determine your estimated percentile rank (percent at or below) for your Writing test score.

National Norms for ACT Writing Scores
Reported During the 2022–2023 Reporting Year

Score	ACT Score National Ranks	
	ELA	**Writing**
36	100	
35	99	
34	99	
33	99	
32	99	
31	97	
30	95	
29	93	
28	91	
27	88	
26	86	
25	83	
24	80	
23	76	
22	72	
21	67	
20	62	
19	57	
18	52	
17	46	
16	40	
15	34	
14	28	
13	22	
12	17	100
11	12	99
10	8	99
9	5	96
8	3	91
7	1	69
6	1	56
5	1	31
4	1	17
3	1	6
2	1	2
1	1	
Mean:	18.8	6.3
SD:	6.3	1.8

Note: These ranks are reported as "US Rank" on ACT score reports during the 2022–2023 reporting year (September 2022 through August 2023). The ranks are based on ACT-tested high school graduates of 2020, 2021, and 2022 who took the ACT Writing test (n=1,475,833).

Scoring Practice Test 6

Scoring Your Multiple-Choice Practice Tests

To score your multiple-choice practice tests, follow these eight steps:

STEP 1. Write a "1" in the blank for each English test question that you answered correctly. An example is provided in the box below:

	Key		Your answer was
1.	A		Incorrect
2.	J	1	Correct
3.	B	1	Correct
4.	G		Incorrect

English ▪ Scoring Key ▪ Practice Test 6

	Key			Key			Key	
1.	C		26.	H		51.	A	
2.	G		27.	C		52.	H	
3.	A		28.	G		53.	A	
4.	J		29.	D		54.	J	
5.	A		30.	G		55.	B	
6.	F		31.	D		56.	F	
7.	C		32.	G		57.	C	
8.	F		33.	B		58.	G	
9.	C		34.	F		59.	C	
10.	J		35.	A		60.	J	
11.	B		36.	G		61.	A	
12.	F		37.	A		62.	H	
13.	B		38.	F		63.	A	
14.	J		39.	C		64.	G	
15.	D		40.	J		65.	C	
16.	G		41.	D		66.	J	
17.	A		42.	G		67.	D	
18.	G		43.	C		68.	H	
19.	D		44.	J		69.	D	
20.	G		45.	B		70.	G	
21.	A		46.	J		71.	C	
22.	J		47.	A		72.	H	
23.	C		48.	H		73.	D	
24.	F		49.	D		74.	F	
25.	D		50.	J		75.	B	

Taking Additional Practice Tests

STEP 2. Compute your total number correct for the English test by adding the numbers you entered in Step 1. Write this total in the blank in the shaded box below. This is your raw score.

Number Correct (Raw Score) for:

Total Number Correct for English Test (75 questions)   _____

STEP 3. Repeat Steps 1 and 2 for the ACT mathematics, reading, and science tests using the scoring keys on this page and the following page,

Mathematics ■ Scoring Key ■ Practice Test 6

	Key			Key			Key	
1.	C	_____	21.	A	_____	41.	C	_____
2.	H	_____	22.	G	_____	42.	G	_____
3.	E	_____	23.	C	_____	43.	A	_____
4.	H	_____	24.	G	_____	44.	J	_____
5.	E	_____	25.	C	_____	45.	D	_____
6.	G	_____	26.	F	_____	46.	J	_____
7.	E	_____	27.	C	_____	47.	B	_____
8.	F	_____	28.	H	_____	48.	H	_____
9.	C	_____	29.	D	_____	49.	A	_____
10.	H	_____	30.	J	_____	50.	F	_____
11.	B	_____	31.	D	_____	51.	B	_____
12.	J	_____	32.	F	_____	52.	F	_____
13.	B	_____	33.	B	_____	53.	A	_____
14.	G	_____	34.	H	_____	54.	K	_____
15.	B	_____	35.	B	_____	55.	A	_____
16.	F	_____	36.	J	_____	56.	J	_____
17.	B	_____	37.	E	_____	57.	C	_____
18.	K	_____	38.	H	_____	58.	F	_____
19.	D	_____	39.	A	_____	59.	A	_____
20.	G	_____	40.	H	_____	60.	J	_____

Number Correct (Raw Score) for:

Total Number Correct for Math Test (60 questions)   _____

Reading ■ Scoring Key ■ Practice Test 6

	Key			Key			Key	
1.	C	_____	15.	A	_____	29.	A	_____
2.	F	_____	16.	H	_____	30.	G	_____
3.	B	_____	17.	B	_____	31.	A	_____
4.	H	_____	18.	J	_____	32.	H	_____
5.	A	_____	19.	A	_____	33.	C	_____
6.	J	_____	20.	F	_____	34.	F	_____
7.	B	_____	21.	B	_____	35.	A	_____
8.	J	_____	22.	G	_____	36.	J	_____
9.	D	_____	23.	D	_____	37.	C	_____
10.	G	_____	24.	G	_____	38.	G	_____
11.	C	_____	25.	D	_____	39.	D	_____
12.	F	_____	26.	H	_____	40.	J	_____
13.	B	_____	27.	C	_____			
14.	H	_____	28.	G	_____			

Number Correct (Raw Score) for:

Total Number Correct for Reading Test (40 questions) _____

Science ■ Scoring Key ■ Practice Test 6

	Key			Key			Key	
1.	B	_____	15.	C	_____	29.	B	_____
2.	G	_____	16.	G	_____	30.	F	_____
3.	B	_____	17.	C	_____	31.	C	_____
4.	F	_____	18.	F	_____	32.	J	_____
5.	D	_____	19.	B	_____	33.	D	_____
6.	J	_____	20.	G	_____	34.	H	_____
7.	B	_____	21.	A	_____	35.	C	_____
8.	J	_____	22.	F	_____	36.	G	_____
9.	A	_____	23.	D	_____	37.	D	_____
10.	G	_____	24.	H	_____	38.	H	_____
11.	A	_____	25.	D	_____	39.	D	_____
12.	F	_____	26.	J	_____	40.	H	_____
13.	B	_____	27.	B	_____			
14.	F	_____	28.	H	_____			

Number Correct (Raw Score) for:

Total Number Correct for Science Test (40 questions) _____

Taking Additional Practice Tests

STEP 4. On each of the four tests, the total number of correct responses yields a raw score. Use the conversion table on the following page to convert your raw scores to scale scores. For each of the four tests, locate and circle your raw score or the range of raw scores that includes it in the conversion table. Then, read across to either outside column of the table and circle the scale score that corresponds to that raw score. As you determine your scale scores, enter them in the blanks provided below. The highest possible scale score for each test is 36. The lowest possible scale score for any of the four tests is 1.

	Your Scale Scores
English	_____
Mathematics	_____
Reading	_____
Science	_____
Sum of Scores	_____

STEP 5. Compute your Composite score by averaging the four scale scores. To do this, add your four scale scores and divide the sum by 4. If the resulting number ends in a fraction, round it off to the nearest whole number. (Round down any fraction less than one-half; round up any fraction that is one-half or more.) Enter this number in the appropriate blank below. This is your Composite score. The highest possible Composite score is 36. The lowest possible Composite score is 1.

	Your Scale Scores
English	_____
Mathematics	_____
Reading	_____
Science	_____
Sum of Scores	_____
Composite Score (sum ÷ 4)	_____

Scale Score Conversion Table: Practice Test 6

Scale Score	Raw Score				Scale Score
	English	**Mathematics**	**Reading**	**Science**	
36	73–75	58–60	39–40	39–40	36
35	69–72	55–57	38	38	35
34	68	54	37	37	34
33	67	52–53	36	36	33
32	65–66	51	35	35	32
31	64	50	34	34	31
30	63	48–49	33	33	30
29	62	46–47	–	32	29
28	60–61	44–45	32	31	28
27	59	42–43	31	30	27
26	57–58	40–41	30	29	26
25	55–56	38–39	29	27–28	25
24	52–54	36–37	28	25–26	24
23	49–51	34–35	26–27	23–24	23
22	46–48	32–33	25	22	22
21	43–45	31	23–24	20–21	21
20	40–42	29–30	22	19	20
19	38–39	27–28	20–21	17–18	19
18	37	25–26	19	16	18
17	35–36	22–24	17–18	14–15	17
16	32–34	18–21	16	12–13	16
15	29–31	15–17	14–15	11	15
14	27–28	11–14	13	10	14
13	25–26	9–10	11–12	9	13
12	23–24	7–8	9–10	8	12
11	20–22	6	8	7	11
10	17–19	5	7	6	10
9	15–16	4	6	5	9
8	12–14	–	5	4	8
7	10–11	3	4	–	7
6	8–9	2	–	3	6
5	6–7	–	3	2	5
4	5	1	2	–	4
3	3–4	–	–	1	3
2	2	–	1	–	2
1	0–1	0	0	0	1

STEP 6. Use the table on the following page to determine your estimated percentile ranks (percent at or below) for each of your scale scores. In the far left column of the table, circle your scale score for the English test (from the preceding page). Then read across to the percentile rank column for that test; circle or put a checkmark beside the corresponding percentile rank. Use the same procedure for the other three tests (from the preceding page). Using the right-hand column of scale scores for your science test and Composite scores may be easier. As you mark your percentile ranks, enter them in the blanks provided. You may also find it helpful to compare your performance with the national mean (average) score for each of the four tests and the Composite as shown at the bottom of the table.

National Norms for ACT Test Scores
Reported During the 2022–2023 Reporting Year

Score	English	Math	Reading	Science	Composite	STEM	Score
36	100	100	100	100	100	100	36
35	99	99	98	99	99	99	35
34	96	99	96	98	99	99	34
33	94	98	94	97	98	98	33
32	93	97	91	96	96	97	32
31	91	96	89	95	95	96	31
30	90	95	87	93	93	94	30
29	89	93	84	92	91	93	29
28	87	91	82	90	89	90	28
27	85	89	80	88	86	88	27
26	83	85	77	86	83	85	26
25	81	81	75	83	80	81	25
24	77	77	72	78	76	77	24
23	73	73	68	72	72	72	23
22	68	68	63	65	67	68	22
21	64	65	57	60	62	63	21
20	58	62	52	54	56	57	20
19	52	58	46	48	50	51	19
18	48	53	41	41	45	45	18
17	44	47	36	34	38	37	17
16	40	38	32	28	32	29	16
15	35	25	27	22	26	21	15
14	29	14	23	17	19	13	14
13	23	6	17	12	13	7	13
12	19	2	12	8	7	3	12
11	14	1	7	5	2	1	11
10	9	1	3	3	1	1	10
9	4	1	2	1	1	1	9
8	2	1	1	1	1	1	8
7	1	1	1	1	1	1	7
6	1	1	1	1	1	1	6
5	1	1	1	1	1	1	5
4	1	1	1	1	1	1	4
3	1	1	1	1	1	1	3
2	1	1	1	1	1	1	2
1	1	1	1	1	1	1	1
Mean:	19.5	19.9	20.9	20.3	20.3	20.3	
SD:	7.2	5.7	7.1	5.9	6.0	5.5	

Note: These ranks are reported as "US Rank" on ACT score reports during the 2022–2023 reporting year (September 2022 through August 2023). The ranks are based on ACT-tested high school graduates of 2020, 2021, and 2022 (n=4,315,490).

Scoring Your Practice Writing Test 6 Essay

To score your practice writing test essay, follow these steps:

STEP 1. Use the guidelines from the writing test analytic rubric in chapter 3 (pages 109–110) to score your essay. Because many essays do not fit the exact description at each score point, read each description and try to determine which paragraph in the rubric best describes most of the characteristics of your essay.

STEP 2. Because your writing test domain scores are the sum of two readers' ratings of your essay, multiply your own 1–6 rating from step 1 by 2. Or, have both you and someone else read and score your practice essay, add those ratings together, and record the total in the Domain Score column in step 3.

STEP 3. Enter your writing test domain scores in the following box:

			Domain Score
Ideas and Analysis	_____	x 2 =	_____
Development and Support	_____	x 2 =	_____
Organization	_____	x 2 =	_____
Language Use and Conventions	_____	x 2 =	_____

STEP 4. Enter the sum of the second-column scores here _____.

STEP 5. Divide sum by 4[†] (range 2–12). This is your Writing Subject score.

[†]Round value to the nearest whole number. Round down any fraction less than one-half; round up any fraction that is one-half or more.

STEP 6. Use the table below to determine your estimated percentile rank (percent at or below) for your Writing test score.

National Norms for ACT Writing Scores
Reported During the 2022–2023 Reporting Year

Score	ACT Score National Ranks	
	ELA	Writing
36	100	
35	99	
34	99	
33	99	
32	99	
31	97	
30	95	
29	93	
28	91	
27	88	
26	86	
25	83	
24	80	
23	76	
22	72	
21	67	
20	62	
19	57	
18	52	
17	46	
16	40	
15	34	
14	28	
13	22	
12	17	100
11	12	99
10	8	99
9	5	96
8	3	91
7	1	69
6	1	56
5	1	31
4	1	17
3	1	6
2	1	2
1	1	
Mean:	18.8	6.3
SD:	6.3	1.8

Note: These ranks are reported as "US Rank" on ACT score reports during the 2022–2023 reporting year (September 2022 through August 2023). The ranks are based on ACT-tested high school graduates of 2020, 2021, and 2022 who took the ACT Writing test (n=1,475,833).

12

Chapter 12: Interpreting Your ACT Test Scores and Ranks

After taking any test, students are eager to see how they've done. Assuming you took and scored ACT practice test 1 in chapter 3 or took other practice tests in chapter 10 and scored them in chapter 11, you have a great deal of information to consider when determining how well you did.

- **Raw scores:** ACT does not provide raw scores, but you have raw scores for the practice tests in this book.

- **Scale scores** are the scores that ACT reports to students, high schools, colleges, and scholarship agencies.

- **Composite score** is a scale score that reflects your overall performance on *all* of the multiple choice tests—English, math, reading, and science.

- **Ranks** indicate the approximate percentage of ACT-tested students who scored at or below each of your scores; for example, if your mathematics rank is 85%, then you scored as well as or better than 85% of the other students who took the mathematics test.

If you take the ACT you receive the *ACT Student Report*, which includes scale scores, the Composite score, and the rank for each score. You can visit www.act.org to view samples of this report as well as the High School and College reports.

ANN C TAYLOR (ACT ID: 201293212)
(061-450)
TEST DATE: APRIL 2021

The**ACT**®

Student Report

21	19	18	19	24	23	8	24
COMPOSITE	MATH	SCIENCE	STEM	ENGLISH	READING	WRITING	ELA

Your Score
Score
Score Range

Your STEM (Science, Technology, Engineering, and Math) score represents your overall performance on the science and math tests.

Your ELA (English Language Arts) score represents your overall performance on the English, reading, and writing tests.

The writing test scores range from 2-12.

ACT College Readiness Benchmarks

Readiness Benchmark
If your score is at or above the Benchmark, you have at least a 50% chance of obtaining a B or higher or about a 75% chance of obtaining a C or higher in specific first-year college courses in the corresponding subject area. There is currently no Benchmark for writing.

Your Score Range
Test scores are estimates of your educational development. Think of your true achievement on this test as being within a range that extends about one standard error of measurement, or about 1 point for the Composite and writing scores, and 2 points for STEM, ELA, and the other test scores, above and below your score.

US & State Rank
Your ranks tell you the approximate percentages of recent high school graduates in the US and your state who took the ACT® test and received scores that are the same as or lower than your scores. For example, a rank of 56 for your Composite score means 56% of students earned that Composite score or below.

US Rank

Composite	59%	
Math	54%	
Science	39%	
STEM	48%	
English	75%	
Reading	66%	
Writing	90%	
ELA	77%	

0   50%   100%

State Rank

Composite	36%	
Math	32%	
Science	19%	
STEM	26%	
English	57%	
Reading	48%	
Writing	72%	
ELA	43%	

0   50%   100%

Detailed Results

MATH   19

			ACT Readiness Range
Preparing for Higher Math	15 of 35	43%	
• Number & Quantity	3 of 5	60%	✓
• Algebra	4 of 8	50%	
• Functions	2 of 8	25%	
• Geometry	4 of 8	50%	
• Statistics & Probability	2 of 6	33%	
Integrating Essential Skills	11 of 25	44%	
Modeling	12 of 21	57%	

SCIENCE   18

Interpretation of Data	10 of 18	56%	
Scientific Investigation	2 of 10	20%	
Evaluation of Models, Inferences & Experimental Results	4 of 12	33%	

ENGLISH   24

			ACT Readiness Range
Production of Writing	17 of 23	74%	✓
Knowledge of Language	10 of 12	83%	✓
Conventions of Standard English	29 of 40	73%	✓

READING   23

Key Ideas & Details	17 of 24	71%	✓
Craft & Structure	5 of 10	50%	
Integration of Knowledge & Ideas	5 of 6	83%	✓
Understanding Complex Texts			

Below   Proficient   Above

Understanding Complex Texts: This indicator lets you know if you are understanding the central meaning of complex texts at a level that is needed to succeed in college courses with high reading demand.

WRITING   8

Ideas & Analysis	8
Development & Support	8
Organization	9
Language Use & Conventions	8

If you took the writing test, your essay was scored on a scale of 1 to 6 by two raters in each of the four writing domains. These domains represent essential skills and abilities that are necessary to meet the writing demands of college and career. Your domain scores, ranging from 2 to 12, are a sum of the two raters' scores. Your writing score is the average of your four domain scores rounded to the nearest whole number. To learn more about your writing score, visit **www.act.org/the-act/writing-scores**.

ACT Composite Score: ACT Math, Science, English, and Reading test scores and the Composite score range from 1 to 36. For each test, we converted your number of correct answers into a score within that range. Your Composite score is the average of your scores on the four subjects rounded to the nearest whole number. If you left any test completely blank, that score is reported as two dashes and no Composite score is computed.

ACT Readiness Range: This range shows where a student who has met the ACT College Readiness Benchmark on this subject test would typically perform.

Dashes (-) indicate information was not provided or could not be calculated.

In this chapter, we explain how to interpret your scores and use them as a tool to help inform your education and career decisions. We encourage you to look at your ACT test scores and ranks with additional information to help guide your future education and career planning.

Understanding Your ACT Test Results

Your scores, Composite score, and ranks provide a good indication of how well you did on the test, but you can interpret these scores on a deeper level to find out more about how well prepared you are to tackle a certain course of studies or pursue a specific career. In the following sections, we help you put your scores and ranks in perspective to make them more meaningful and relevant to your education and career planning.

How ACT Scores Your Multiple-Choice Tests

ACT scores the multiple-choice tests the same way you scored your ACT practice tests in chapters 3 and 11. The first step is to do exactly what you did for your practice tests: count the number of questions you answered correctly to determine your raw score. No points are deducted for incorrect answers.

The raw score is converted to a scale score to enhance score interpretation and allow comparability across different forms. Scale scores range from 1 (low) to 36 (high) for each of the four individual tests and for the Composite score, which is the average of the four test scores.

How ACT Scores Your Writing Test

Two trained readers score each writing test based on the analytic rubric presented on pages 109–110. Each reader scores your essay on a scale from 1 (low) to 6 (high) on each domain. If their scores differ by more than 1 point on any of the four domains, a third reader scores your essay to resolve the discrepancy. This method is designed to be as impartial as possible. The writing score is calculated from your domain scores and is reported on a 2-to-12 scale.

Recognizing That Test Scores Are Estimates of Educational Achievement

No test, including the ACT, is an exact measure of your educational achievement. We estimate the amount of imprecision using the "standard error of measurement." On the ACT, the standard error of measurement (SEM) is 2 points for each of the multiple-choice tests, 1 point for the writing test, and 1 point for the Composite score.

Because no test score is an exact measure of your achievement, think of each of your ACT scores as a range of scores rather than as a precise number. The SEM can be used to estimate ranges for your scores. To do this, just add the SEM to, and subtract it from, each of your scores. For example, if your score on the English test is 22, your true achievement is likely in the score range of 20 to 24 (22 plus or minus 2 points). Beginning with the September 2020 national test date, students who have taken the ACT test more than once will have a Superscore calculated on their behalf by ACT. Superscoring allows students to utilize their highest individual section scores across all of their test events for ACT to calculate the best possible Composite score. Students will have the option to send an individual full battery Composite score or a Superscore to colleges or scholarship agencies.

Using Ranks to Interpret Your Scores

The US and state ranks for a score tell you how your scores compare to those earned by recent high school graduates who took the ACT. The numbers indicate the cumulative percent of students who scored at or below a given score. For example, if your rank is 63%, then 63% of recent high school graduates who took the ACT scored at or below your score.

Comparing Your Test Scores to Each Other

Another way to interpret your ACT test scores is by comparing them to each other using the ranks. You may find it interesting, for example, to compare your ranks for the science and mathematics tests to your ranks for the reading and English tests. Perhaps you felt more comfortable and successful in some subject areas than in others. Making comparisons among your ACT test ranks can be especially helpful as you make decisions about the courses you will take in high school and college. A high rank in a particular area indicates that you compare well to other ACT test-takers in that subject. A low rank may indicate that you need to develop your skills more in that area.

Keep in mind, however, that scale scores from the different individual tests can't be directly compared to each other. Scoring 23 on the ACT English and mathematics tests, for example, doesn't necessarily mean that your levels of skill and knowledge in English are the same as they are in mathematics. The percentile ranks corresponding to the scores—not the scores themselves—are probably best for making comparisons among subject areas.

Comparing Your Scores and Ranks to Your High School Grades

After you take the ACT and receive your student report, compare your scores and ranks to your high school grades. Are your highest grades and highest ACT test scores and ranks in the same content areas? If so, you might want to consider college majors that would draw on your areas of greatest strength or seek to improve your knowledge and skills in weaker subject areas. However, if your grades and scores differ significantly, talk with your counselor about possible reasons for the differences.

Comparing Your Scores to Those of Enrolled First-Year College Students

Another way to understand your ACT test scores and ranks is by comparing them to those of students enrolled at colleges or universities you're interested in attending. This information can be very useful as you make decisions about applying for college. Keep in mind that admissions offices use a number of measures—including high school grades, recommendations, and extracurricular activities—to determine how students are likely to perform at their schools. Still, knowing that your ACT test scores are similar to those of students already enrolled at a college or university you're considering may make you more confident in applying for admission there.

Using ACT College and Career Readiness Standards to Help You Understand Your ACT Scores

After you calculate your scores, you may wonder what your test scores mean regarding how well you are prepared to tackle college-level courses. In other words, what do your test scores tell you about your knowledge and skills in English, math, reading, and science? One way to understand this is to consider your scores from the perspective of what students who have that score are likely to know and be able to do. ACT developed the College and Career Readiness Standards to tell you exactly that.

What Are the ACT College and Career Readiness Standards?

The ACT College and Career Readiness Standards are sets of statements that describe what students are *likely* to know and be able to do in each content area based on their scores on each of the tests (English, mathematics, reading, science, and writing). The statements serve as score descriptors and reflect a progression of skills and knowledge in a particular content area. The College and Career Readiness Standards are reported in terms of score range, so that the statements describe the knowledge and skills that students *typically* demonstrate who score in these different ranges on the multiple-choice tests: 13–15, 16–19, 20–23, 24–27, 28–32, 33–36. A score of 1–12 indicates the student is most likely beginning to develop the knowledge and skills described in the 13–15 score range for that particular test. All the College and Career Readiness Standards are cumulative, meaning that students typically can also demonstrate the skills and knowledge described in the score ranges below the range in which they scored.

How Can the ACT College and Career Readiness Standards Help You?

The purpose of the ACT College and Career Readiness Standards is to help you and others better understand what your ACT scores indicate about the knowledge and skills you likely have and what areas might need further development for you to be better prepared for college.

Because the ACT College and Career Readiness Standards provide statements that describe what you are *likely* to know and be able to do, you can use that information to help zero in on what specific steps you should take to further develop your college readiness. If, for example, you scored in the 16–19 range on the English test, you might infer that you likely have the skills and knowledge described in the 13–15 and in the 16–19 range. You might choose to take a closer look at the standards in the 20–23 and higher score ranges to see what courses to take, or what instruction you might need, to develop those particular areas in order to be better prepared for college. In other words, you can use the ACT College and Career Readiness Standards to help you select courses and instruction that will focus on preparing you for college.

Taking Additional Practice Tests

ACT College Readiness Benchmarks

ACT has identified the minimum score needed on each ACT test to indicate a 50% chance of obtaining a B or higher or about a 75% chance of obtaining a C or higher in the corresponding first-year college course. Your score report will have a visual representation of where you scored compared to the ACT College Readiness Benchmark.

ACT Test	ACT Benchmark Score	College Course
English	18	English Composition
Mathematics	22	Algebra
Reading	22	Social Sciences/Humanities
Science	23	Biology

To increase your college readiness, consider taking additional rigorous course work before you enter college. When you meet with your academic advisor to plan your first-year college courses, select courses that are appropriate for your academic background and reflect your planned curriculum.

Planning Your Education and Career

The *ACT Student Report* includes a College and Career Planning section that helps you explore college majors and occupations, consider your options, and develop plans. The information in this section is all about you. Majors and occupations you may want to explore have been listed here, because they are related to the interests you expressed or occupations you said you were considering.

Seeking Additional Information and Guidance

Your *ACT Student Report* will provide additional information to help you understand your ACT test results and use them to make important decisions about college and to explore possible future careers.

As you approach decisions about college and careers, be sure to take advantage of all the assistance you can find. Talk to your parents, counselors, and teachers; visit your local library; and talk directly to personnel at colleges in which you're interested. The more you can find out about all the educational options available to you and the level of your academic skills and knowledge (using such information as your ACT test results), the better prepared you'll be to make informed college and career choices.

ACT College and Career Readiness Standards—English

These standards describe what students who score in specific score ranges on the English test are likely to know and be able to do.

- Students who score in the 1–12 range are most likely beginning to develop the knowledge and skills assessed in the other ranges.

- The ACT College Readiness Benchmark for English is 18. Students who achieve this score on the ACT English test have a 50% likelihood of achieving a B or better in a first-year English composition course at a typical college. The knowledge and skills highly likely to be demonstrated by students who meet the benchmark are shaded.

Score Range	Production of Writing: Topic Development in Terms of Purpose and Focus (TOD)
13–15	TOD 201. Delete material because it is obviously irrelevant in terms of the topic of the essay
16–19	TOD 301. Delete material because it is obviously irrelevant in terms of the focus of the essay TOD 302. Identify the purpose of a word or phrase when the purpose is simple (e.g., identifying a person, defining a basic term, using common descriptive adjectives) TOD 303. Determine whether a simple essay has met a straightforward goal
20–23	TOD 401. Determine relevance of material in terms of the focus of the essay TOD 402. Identify the purpose of a word or phrase when the purpose is straightforward (e.g., describing a person, giving examples) TOD 403. Use a word, phrase, or sentence to accomplish a straightforward purpose (e.g., conveying a feeling or attitude)
24–27	TOD 501. Determine relevance of material in terms of the focus of the paragraph TOD 502. Identify the purpose of a word, phrase, or sentence when the purpose is fairly straightforward (e.g., identifying traits, giving reasons, explaining motivations) TOD 503. Determine whether an essay has met a specified goal TOD 504. Use a word, phrase, or sentence to accomplish a fairly straightforward purpose (e.g., sharpening an essay's focus, illustrating a given statement)

18

(continued)

Taking Additional Practice Tests

Score Range	Production of Writing: Topic Development in Terms of Purpose and Focus (TOD) *(continued)*
28–32	TOD 601. Determine relevance when considering material that is plausible but potentially irrelevant at a given point in the essay
	TOD 602. Identify the purpose of a word, phrase, or sentence when the purpose is subtle (e.g., supporting a later point, establishing tone) or when the best decision is to delete the text in question
	TOD 603. Use a word, phrase, or sentence to accomplish a subtle purpose (e.g., adding emphasis or supporting detail, expressing meaning through connotation)
33–36	TOD 701. Identify the purpose of a word, phrase, or sentence when the purpose is complex (e.g., anticipating a reader's need for background information) or requires a thorough understanding of the paragraph and essay
	TOD 702. Determine whether a complex essay has met a specified goal
	TOD 703. Use a word, phrase, or sentence to accomplish a complex purpose, often in terms of the focus of the essay

Score Range	Production of Writing: Organization, Unity, and Cohesion (ORG)
13–15	ORG 201. Determine the need for transition words or phrases to establish time relationships in simple narrative essays (e.g., *then*, *this time*)
16–19	ORG 301. Determine the most logical place for a sentence in a paragraph
	ORG 302. Provide a simple conclusion to a paragraph or essay (e.g., expressing one of the essay's main ideas)
20–23	ORG 401. Determine the need for transition words or phrases to establish straightforward logical relationships (e.g., *first*, *afterward*, *in response*)
	ORG 402. Determine the most logical place for a sentence in a straightforward essay
	ORG 403. Provide an introduction to a straightforward paragraph
	ORG 404. Provide a straightforward conclusion to a paragraph or essay (e.g., summarizing an essay's main idea or ideas)
	ORG 405. Rearrange the sentences in a straightforward paragraph for the sake of logic

18

Score Range	Production of Writing: Organization, Unity, and Cohesion (ORG) (continued)
24–27	**ORG 501.** Determine the need for transition words or phrases to establish subtle logical relationships within and between sentences (e.g., *therefore*, *however*, *in addition*)
	ORG 502. Provide a fairly straightforward introduction or conclusion to or transition within a paragraph or essay (e.g., supporting or emphasizing an essay's main idea)
	ORG 503. Rearrange the sentences in a fairly straightforward paragraph for the sake of logic
	ORG 504. Determine the best place to divide a paragraph to meet a particular rhetorical goal
	ORG 505. Rearrange the paragraphs in an essay for the sake of logic
28–32	**ORG 601.** Determine the need for transition words or phrases to establish subtle logical relationships within and between paragraphs
	ORG 602. Determine the most logical place for a sentence in a fairly complex essay
	ORG 603. Provide a subtle introduction or conclusion to or transition within a paragraph or essay (e.g., echoing an essay's theme or restating the main argument)
	ORG 604. Rearrange the sentences in a fairly complex paragraph for the sake of logic and coherence
33–36	**ORG 701.** Determine the need for transition words or phrases, basing decisions on a thorough understanding of the paragraph and essay
	ORG 702. Provide a sophisticated introduction or conclusion to or transition within a paragraph or essay, basing decisions on a thorough understanding of the paragraph and essay (e.g., linking the conclusion to one of the essay's main images)

Score Range	Knowledge of Language (KLA)
13–15	KLA 201. Revise vague, clumsy, and confusing writing that creates obvious logic problems
16–19	KLA 301. Delete obviously redundant and wordy material
	KLA 302. Revise expressions that deviate markedly from the style and tone of the essay
20–23	KLA 401. Delete redundant and wordy material when the problem is contained within a single phrase (e.g., "alarmingly startled," "started by reaching the point of beginning")
	KLA 402. Revise expressions that deviate from the style and tone of the essay
	KLA 403. Determine the need for conjunctions to create straightforward logical links between clauses
	KLA 404. Use the word or phrase most appropriate in terms of the content of the sentence when the vocabulary is relatively common
24–27	KLA 501. Revise vague, clumsy, and confusing writing
	KLA 502. Delete redundant and wordy material when the meaning of the entire sentence must be considered
	KLA 503. Revise expressions that deviate in subtle ways from the style and tone of the essay
	KLA 504. Determine the need for conjunctions to create logical links between clauses
	KLA 505. Use the word or phrase most appropriate in terms of the content of the sentence when the vocabulary is uncommon
28–32	KLA 601. Revise vague, clumsy, and confusing writing involving sophisticated language
	KLA 602. Delete redundant and wordy material that involves fairly sophisticated language (e.g., "the outlook of an aesthetic viewpoint") or that sounds acceptable as conversational English
	KLA 603. Determine the need for conjunctions to create subtle logical links between clauses
	KLA 604. Use the word or phrase most appropriate in terms of the content of the sentence when the vocabulary is fairly sophisticated
33–36	KLA 701. Delete redundant and wordy material that involves sophisticated language or complex concepts or where the material is redundant in terms of the paragraph or essay as a whole
	KLA 702. Use the word or phrase most appropriate in terms of the content of the sentence when the vocabulary is sophisticated

18

Score Range	Conventions of Standard English: Sentence Structure and Formation (SST)
13–15	SST 201. Determine the need for punctuation or conjunctions to join simple clauses SST 202. Recognize and correct inappropriate shifts in verb tense between simple clauses in a sentence or between simple adjoining sentences
16–19	SST 301. Determine the need for punctuation or conjunctions to correct awkward-sounding fragments and fused sentences as well as obviously faulty subordination and coordination of clauses SST 302. Recognize and correct inappropriate shifts in verb tense and voice when the meaning of the entire sentence must be considered
20–23	SST 401. Recognize and correct marked disturbances in sentence structure (e.g., faulty placement of adjectives, participial phrase fragments, missing or incorrect relative pronouns, dangling or misplaced modifiers, lack of parallelism within a simple series of verbs)
24–27	SST 501. Recognize and correct disturbances in sentence structure (e.g., faulty placement of phrases, faulty coordination and subordination of clauses, lack of parallelism within a simple series of phrases) SST 502. Maintain consistent and logical verb tense and pronoun person on the basis of the preceding clause or sentence
28–32	SST 601. Recognize and correct subtle disturbances in sentence structure (e.g., danglers where the intended meaning is clear but the sentence is ungrammatical, faulty subordination and coordination of clauses in long or involved sentences) SST 602. Maintain consistent and logical verb tense and voice and pronoun person on the basis of the paragraph or essay as a whole
33–36	SST 701. Recognize and correct very subtle disturbances in sentence structure (e.g., weak conjunctions between independent clauses, run-ons that would be acceptable in conversational English, lack of parallelism within a complex series of phrases or clauses)

18

Taking Additional Practice Tests

Score Range	Conventions of Standard English: Usage Conventions (USG)
13–15	USG 201. Form the past tense and past participle of irregular but commonly used verbs
	USG 202. Form comparative and superlative adjectives
16–19	USG 301. Determine whether an adjective form or an adverb form is called for in a given situation
	USG 302. Ensure straightforward subject-verb agreement
	USG 303. Ensure straightforward pronoun-antecedent agreement
	USG 304. Use idiomatically appropriate prepositions in simple contexts
	USG 305. Use the appropriate word in frequently confused pairs (e.g., *there* and *their*, *past* and *passed*, *led* and *lead*)
20–23	USG 401. Use the correct comparative or superlative adjective or adverb form depending on context (e.g., "He is the oldest of my three brothers")
	USG 402. Ensure subject-verb agreement when there is some text between the subject and verb
	USG 403. Use idiomatically appropriate prepositions, especially in combination with verbs (e.g., *long for*, *appeal to*)
	USG 404. Recognize and correct expressions that deviate from idiomatic English
24–27	USG 501. Form simple and compound verb tenses, both regular and irregular, including forming verbs by using *have* rather than *of* (e.g., "would have gone," not "would of gone")
	USG 502. Ensure pronoun-antecedent agreement when the pronoun and antecedent occur in separate clauses or sentences
	USG 503. Recognize and correct vague and ambiguous pronouns
28–32	USG 601. Ensure subject-verb agreement in some challenging situations (e.g., when the subject-verb order is inverted or when the subject is an indefinite pronoun)
	USG 602. Correctly use reflexive pronouns, the possessive pronouns *its* and *your*, and the relative pronouns *who* and *whom*
	USG 603. Use the appropriate word in less-common confused pairs (e.g., *allude* and *elude*)
33–36	USG 701. Ensure subject-verb agreement when a phrase or clause between the subject and verb suggests a different number for the verb
	USG 702. Use idiomatically and contextually appropriate prepositions in combination with verbs in situations involving sophisticated language or complex concepts

18

Score Range	Conventions of Standard English: Punctuation Conventions (PUN)
13–15	PUN 201. Delete commas that create basic sense problems (e.g., between verb and direct object)
16–19	PUN 301. Delete commas that markedly disturb sentence flow (e.g., between modifier and modified element) PUN 302. Use appropriate punctuation in straightforward situations (e.g., simple items in a series)
20–23	PUN 401. Delete commas when an incorrect understanding of the sentence suggests a pause that should be punctuated (e.g., between verb and direct object clause) PUN 402. Delete apostrophes used incorrectly to form plural nouns PUN 403. Use commas to avoid obvious ambiguity (e.g., to set off a long introductory element from the rest of the sentence when a misreading is possible) PUN 404. Use commas to set off simple parenthetical elements
24–27	PUN 501. Delete commas in long or involved sentences when an incorrect understanding of the sentence suggests a pause that should be punctuated (e.g., between the elements of a compound subject or compound verb joined by *and*) PUN 502. Recognize and correct inappropriate uses of colons and semicolons PUN 503. Use punctuation to set off complex parenthetical elements PUN 504. Use apostrophes to form simple possessive nouns
28–32	PUN 601. Use commas to avoid ambiguity when the syntax or language is sophisticated (e.g., to set off a complex series of items) PUN 602. Use punctuation to set off a nonessential/nonrestrictive appositive or clause PUN 603. Use apostrophes to form possessives, including irregular plural nouns PUN 604. Use a semicolon to link closely related independent clauses
33–36	PUN 701. Delete punctuation around essential/restrictive appositives or clauses PUN 702. Use a colon to introduce an example or an elaboration

18

Taking Additional Practice Tests

ACT College and Career Readiness Standards—Mathematics

These standards describe what students who score in specific score ranges on the mathematics test are likely to know and be able to do.

- Students who score in the 1–12 range are most likely beginning to develop the knowledge and skills assessed in the other ranges.

- The ACT College Readiness Benchmark for mathematics is 22. Students who achieve this score on the ACT mathematics test have a 50% likelihood of achieving a B or better in a first-year college algebra course at a typical college. The knowledge and skills highly likely to be demonstrated by students who meet the benchmark are shaded.

Score Range	Number and Quantity (N)
13–15	N 201. Perform one-operation computation with whole numbers and decimals
	N 202. Recognize equivalent fractions and fractions in lowest terms
	N 203. Locate positive rational numbers (expressed as whole numbers, fractions, decimals, and mixed numbers) on the number line
16–19	N 301. Recognize one-digit factors of a number
	N 302. Identify a digit's place value
	N 303. Locate rational numbers on the number line
	Note: A matrix as a representation of data is treated here as a basic table.
20–23	N 401. Exhibit knowledge of elementary number concepts such as rounding, the ordering of decimals, pattern identification, primes, and greatest common factor
	N 402. Write positive powers of 10 by using exponents
	N 403. Comprehend the concept of length on the number line, and find the distance between two points
	N 404. Understand absolute value in terms of distance
	N 405. Find the distance in the coordinate plane between two points with the same x-coordinate or y-coordinate
	N 406. Add two matrices that have whole number entries
24–27	N 501. Order fractions
	N 502. Find and use the least common multiple
	N 503. Work with numerical factors
	N 504. Exhibit some knowledge of the complex numbers
	N 505. Add and subtract matrices that have integer entries

22

Score Range	Number and Quantity (N) *(continued)*
28–32	N 601. Apply number properties involving prime factorization
	N 602. Apply number properties involving even/odd numbers and factors/multiples
	N 603. Apply number properties involving positive/negative numbers
	N 604. Apply the facts that π is irrational and that the square root of an integer is rational only if that integer is a perfect square
	N 605. Apply properties of rational exponents
	N 606. Multiply two complex numbers
	N 607. Use relations involving addition, subtraction, and scalar multiplication of vectors and of matrices
33–36	N 701. Analyze and draw conclusions based on number concepts
	N 702. Apply properties of rational numbers and the rational number system
	N 703. Apply properties of real numbers and the real number system, including properties of irrational numbers
	N 704. Apply properties of complex numbers and the complex number system
	N 705. Multiply matrices
	N 706. Apply properties of matrices and properties of matrices as a number system

Because algebra and functions are closely connected, some standards apply to both categories.

Score Range	Algebra (A)	Functions (F)
13–15	AF 201. Solve problems in one or two steps using whole numbers and using decimals in the context of money	
	A 201. Exhibit knowledge of basic expressions (e.g., identify an expression for a total as $b + g$) A 202. Solve equations in the form $x + a = b$, where a and b are whole numbers or decimals	F 201. Extend a given pattern by a few terms for patterns that have a constant increase or decrease between terms
16–19	AF 301. Solve routine one-step arithmetic problems using positive rational numbers, such as single-step percent	
	AF 302. Solve some routine two-step arithmetic problems	
	AF 303. Relate a graph to a situation described qualitatively in terms of familiar properties such as before and after, increasing and decreasing, higher and lower	
	AF 304. Apply a definition of an operation for whole numbers (e.g., $a \bullet b = 3a - b$)	

(continued)

(continued)

Score Range	Algebra (A)	Functions (F)
	A 301. Substitute whole numbers for unknown quantities to evaluate expressions A 302. Solve one-step equations to get integer or decimal answers A 303. Combine like terms (e.g., $2x + 5x$)	F 301. Extend a given pattern by a few terms for patterns that have a constant factor between terms
20–23	AF 401. Solve routine two-step or three-step arithmetic problems involving concepts such as rate and proportion, tax added, percentage off, and estimating by using a given average value in place of actual values AF 402. Perform straightforward word-to-symbol translations AF 403. Relate a graph to a situation described in terms of a starting value and an additional amount per unit (e.g., unit cost, weekly growth)	
	A 401. Evaluate algebraic expressions by substituting integers for unknown quantities A 402. Add and subtract simple algebraic expressions A 403. Solve routine first-degree equations A 404. Multiply two binomials A 405. Match simple inequalities with their graphs on the number line (e.g., $x > -3$) A 406. Exhibit knowledge of slope	F 401. Evaluate linear and quadratic functions, expressed in function notation, at integer values
24–27	AF 501. Solve multistep arithmetic problems that involve planning or converting common derived units of measure (e.g., feet per second to miles per hour) AF 502. Build functions and write expressions, equations, or inequalities with a single variable for common pre-algebra settings (e.g., rate and distance problems and problems that can be solved by using proportions) AF 503. Match linear equations with their graphs in the coordinate plane	

22

Score Range	Algebra (A)	Functions (F)
	A 501. Recognize that when numerical quantities are reported in real-world contexts, the numbers are often rounded	F 501. Evaluate polynomial functions, expressed in function notation, at integer values
	A 502. Solve real-world problems by using first-degree equations	F 502. Find the next term in a sequence described recursively
	A 503. Solve first-degree inequalities when the method does not involve reversing the inequality sign	F 503. Build functions and use quantitative information to identify graphs for relations that are proportional or linear
	A 504. Match compound inequalities with their graphs on the number line (e.g., $-10.5 < x < 20.3$)	F 504. Attend to the difference between a function modeling a situation and the reality of the situation
	A 505. Add, subtract, and multiply polynomials	F 505. Understand the concept of a function as having a well-defined output value at each valid input value
	A 506. Identify solutions to simple quadratic equations	F 506. Understand the concept of domain and range in terms of valid input and output, and in terms of function graphs
	A 507. Solve quadratic equations in the form $(x + a)(x + b) = 0$, where a and b are numbers or variables	F 507. Interpret statements that use function notation in terms of their context
	A 508. Factor simple quadratics (e.g., the difference of squares and perfect square trinomials)	F 508. Find the domain of polynomial functions and rational functions
	A 509. Work with squares and square roots of numbers	F 509. Find the range of polynomial functions
	A 510. Work with cubes and cube roots of numbers	F 510. Find where a rational function's graph has a vertical asymptote
	A 511. Work with scientific notation	F 511. Use function notation for simple functions of two variables
	A 512. Work problems involving positive integer exponents	
	A 513. Determine when an expression is undefined	
	A 514. Determine the slope of a line from an equation	

(*continued*)

*(**continued**)*

Score Range	Algebra (A)	Functions (F)
28–32	AF 601. Solve word problems containing several rates, proportions, or percentages AF 602. Build functions and write expressions, equations, and inequalities for common algebra settings (e.g., distance to a point on a curve and profit for variable cost and demand) AF 603. Interpret and use information from graphs in the coordinate plane AF 604. Given an equation or function, find an equation or function whose graph is a translation by a specified amount up or down	
	A 601. Manipulate expressions and equations A 602. Solve linear inequalities when the method involves reversing the inequality sign A 603. Match linear inequalities with their graphs on the number line A 604. Solve systems of two linear equations A 605. Solve quadratic equations A 606. Solve absolute value equations	F 601. Relate a graph to a situation described qualitatively in terms of faster change or slower change F 602. Build functions for relations that are inversely proportional F 603. Find a recursive expression for the general term in a sequence described recursively F 604. Evaluate composite functions at integer values
33–36	AF 701. Solve complex arithmetic problems involving percent of increase or decrease or requiring integration of several concepts (e.g., using several ratios, comparing percentages, or comparing averages) AF 702. Build functions and write expressions, equations, and inequalities when the process requires planning and/or strategic manipulation AF 703. Analyze and draw conclusions based on properties of algebra and/or functions AF 704. Analyze and draw conclusions based on information from graphs in the coordinate plane AF 705. Identify characteristics of graphs based on a set of conditions or on a general equation such as $y = ax^2 + c$ AF 706. Given an equation or function, find an equation or function whose graph is a translation by specified amounts in the horizontal and vertical directions	

Score Range	Algebra (A)	Functions (F)
	A 701. Solve simple absolute value inequalities	F 701. Compare actual values and the values of a modeling function to judge model fit and compare models
	A 702. Match simple quadratic inequalities with their graphs on the number line	F 702. Build functions for relations that are exponential
	A 703. Apply the remainder theorem for polynomials, that $P(a)$ is the remainder when $P(x)$ is divided by $(x - a)$	F 703. Exhibit knowledge of geometric sequences
		F 704. Exhibit knowledge of unit circle trigonometry
		F 705. Match graphs of basic trigonometric functions with their equations
		F 706. Use trigonometric concepts and basic identities to solve problems
		F 707. Exhibit knowledge of logarithms
		F 708. Write an expression for the composite of two simple functions

Score Range	Geometry (G)
13–15	G 201. Estimate the length of a line segment based on other lengths in a geometric figure
	G 202. Calculate the length of a line segment based on the lengths of other line segments that go in the same direction (e.g., overlapping line segments and parallel sides of polygons with only right angles)
	G 203. Perform common conversions of money and of length, weight, mass, and time within a measurement system (e.g., dollars to dimes, inches to feet, and hours to minutes)
16–19	G 301. Exhibit some knowledge of the angles associated with parallel lines
	G 302. Compute the perimeter of polygons when all side lengths are given
	G 303. Compute the area of rectangles when whole number dimensions are given
	G 304. Locate points in the first quadrant

(continued)

Taking Additional Practice Tests

Score Range	Geometry (G) (*continued*)
20–23	G 401. Use properties of parallel lines to find the measure of an angle
	G 402. Exhibit knowledge of basic angle properties and special sums of angle measures (e.g., 90°, 180°, and 360°)
	G 403. Compute the area and perimeter of triangles and rectangles in simple problems
	G 404. Find the length of the hypotenuse of a right triangle when only very simple computation is involved (e.g., 3–4–5 and 6–8–10 triangles)
	G 405. Use geometric formulas when all necessary information is given
	G 406. Locate points in the coordinate plane
	G 407. Translate points up, down, left, and right in the coordinate plane
24–27	G 501. Use several angle properties to find an unknown angle measure
	G 502. Count the number of lines of symmetry of a geometric figure
	G 503. Use symmetry of isosceles triangles to find unknown side lengths or angle measures
	G 504. Recognize that real-world measurements are typically imprecise and that an appropriate level of precision is related to the measuring device and procedure
	G 505. Compute the perimeter of simple composite geometric figures with unknown side lengths
	G 506. Compute the area of triangles and rectangles when one or more additional simple steps are required
	G 507. Compute the area and circumference of circles after identifying necessary information
	G 508. Given the length of two sides of a right triangle, find the third when the lengths are Pythagorean triples
	G 509. Express the sine, cosine, and tangent of an angle in a right triangle as a ratio of given side lengths
	G 510. Determine the slope of a line from points or a graph
	G 511. Find the midpoint of a line segment
	G 512. Find the coordinates of a point rotated 180° around a given center point

Score Range	Geometry (G) (*continued*)
28–32	G 601. Use relationships involving area, perimeter, and volume of geometric figures to compute another measure (e.g., surface area for a cube of a given volume and simple geometric probability)
	G 602. Use the Pythagorean theorem
	G 603. Apply properties of 30°–60°–90°, 45°–45°–90°, similar, and congruent triangles
	G 604. Apply basic trigonometric ratios to solve right-triangle problems
	G 605. Use the distance formula
	G 606. Use properties of parallel and perpendicular lines to determine an equation of a line or coordinates of a point
	G 607. Find the coordinates of a point reflected across a vertical or horizontal line or across $y = x$
	G 608. Find the coordinates of a point rotated 90° about the origin
	G 609. Recognize special characteristics of parabolas and circles (e.g., the vertex of a parabola and the center or radius of a circle)
33–36	G 701. Use relationships among angles, arcs, and distances in a circle
	G 702. Compute the area of composite geometric figures when planning and/or visualization is required
	G 703. Use scale factors to determine the magnitude of a size change
	G 704. Analyze and draw conclusions based on a set of conditions
	G 705. Solve multistep geometry problems that involve integrating concepts, planning, and/or visualization

Score Range	Statistics and Probability (S)
13–15	S 201. Calculate the average of a list of positive whole numbers
	S 202. Extract one relevant number from a basic table or chart, and use it in a single computation
16–19	S 301. Calculate the average of a list of numbers
	S 302. Calculate the average given the number of data values and the sum of the data values
	S 303. Read basic tables and charts
	S 304. Extract relevant data from a basic table or chart and use the data in a computation
	S 305. Use the relationship between the probability of an event and the probability of its complement

(*continued*)

Taking Additional Practice Tests

Score Range	Statistics and Probability (S) (*continued*)
20–23	S 401. Calculate the missing data value given the average and all data values but one S 402. Translate from one representation of data to another (e.g., a bar graph to a circle graph) S 403. Determine the probability of a simple event S 404. Describe events as combinations of other events (e.g., using *and*, *or*, and *not*) S 405. Exhibit knowledge of simple counting techniques
24–27	S 501. Calculate the average given the frequency counts of all the data values S 502. Manipulate data from tables and charts S 503. Compute straightforward probabilities for common situations S 504. Use Venn diagrams in counting S 505. Recognize that when data summaries are reported in the real world, results are often rounded and must be interpreted as having appropriate precision S 506. Recognize that when a statistical model is used, model values typically differ from actual values
28–32	S 601. Calculate or use a weighted average S 602. Interpret and use information from tables and charts, including two-way frequency tables S 603. Apply counting techniques S 604. Compute a probability when the event and/or sample space are not given or obvious S 605. Recognize the concepts of conditional and joint probability expressed in real-world contexts S 606. Recognize the concept of independence expressed in real-world contexts
33–36	S 701. Distinguish among mean, median, and mode for a list of numbers S 702. Analyze and draw conclusions based on information from tables and charts, including two-way frequency tables S 703. Understand the role of randomization in surveys, experiments, and observational studies S 704. Exhibit knowledge of conditional and joint probability S 705. Recognize that part of the power of statistical modeling comes from looking at regularity in the differences between actual values and model values

22

ACT College and Career Readiness Standards—Reading

These standards describe what students who score in specific score ranges on the reading test are likely to know and be able to do.

- Students who score in the 1–12 range are most likely beginning to develop the knowledge and skills assessed in the other ranges.

- The ACT College Readiness Benchmark for reading is 22. Students who achieve this score on the ACT reading test have a 50% likelihood of achieving a B or better in a first-year social science course at a typical college. The knowledge and skills highly likely to be demonstrated by students who meet the benchmark are shaded.

Score Range	Key Ideas and Details: Close Reading (CLR)
13–15	CLR 201. Locate basic facts (e.g., names, dates, events) clearly stated in a passage CLR 202. Draw simple logical conclusions about the main characters in somewhat challenging literary narratives
16–19	CLR 301. Locate simple details at the sentence and paragraph level in somewhat challenging passages CLR 302. Draw simple logical conclusions in somewhat challenging passages
20–23	CLR 401. Locate important details in somewhat challenging passages CLR 402. Draw logical conclusions in somewhat challenging passages CLR 403. Draw simple logical conclusions in more challenging passages CLR 404. Paraphrase some statements as they are used in somewhat challenging passages
24–27	CLR 501. Locate and interpret minor or subtly stated details in somewhat challenging passages CLR 502. Locate important details in more challenging passages CLR 503. Draw subtle logical conclusions in somewhat challenging passages CLR 504. Draw logical conclusions in more challenging passages CLR 505. Paraphrase virtually any statement as it is used in somewhat challenging passages CLR 506. Paraphrase some statements as they are used in more challenging passages

22

(continued)

Taking Additional Practice Tests

Score Range	Key Ideas and Details: Close Reading (CLR) (*continued*)
28–32	CLR 601. Locate and interpret minor or subtly stated details in more challenging passages CLR 602. Locate important details in complex passages CLR 603. Draw subtle logical conclusions in more challenging passages CLR 604. Draw simple logical conclusions in complex passages CLR 605. Paraphrase virtually any statement as it is used in more challenging passages
33–36	CLR 701. Locate and interpret minor or subtly stated details in complex passages CLR 702. Locate important details in highly complex passages CLR 703. Draw logical conclusions in complex passages CLR 704. Draw simple logical conclusions in highly complex passages CLR 705. Draw complex or subtle logical conclusions, often by synthesizing information from different portions of the passage CLR 706. Paraphrase statements as they are used in complex passages

Score Range	Key Ideas and Details: Central Ideas, Themes, and Summaries (IDT)
13–15	IDT 201. Identify the topic of passages and distinguish the topic from the central idea or theme
16–19	IDT 301. Identify a clear central idea in straightforward paragraphs in somewhat challenging literary narratives
20–23	IDT 401. Infer a central idea in straightforward paragraphs in somewhat challenging literary narratives IDT 402. Identify a clear central idea or theme in somewhat challenging passages or their paragraphs IDT 403. Summarize key supporting ideas and details in somewhat challenging passages
24–27	IDT 501. Infer a central idea or theme in somewhat challenging passages or their paragraphs IDT 502. Identify a clear central idea or theme in more challenging passages or their paragraphs IDT 503. Summarize key supporting ideas and details in more challenging passages

22

Score Range	Key Ideas and Details: Central Ideas, Themes, and Summaries (IDT) (*continued*)
28–32	IDT 601. Infer a central idea or theme in more challenging passages or their paragraphs
	IDT 602. Summarize key supporting ideas and details in complex passages
33–36	IDT 701. Identify or infer a central idea or theme in complex passages or their paragraphs
	IDT 702. Summarize key supporting ideas and details in highly complex passages

Score Range	Key Ideas and Details: Relationships (REL)
13–15	REL 201. Determine when (e.g., *first*, *last*, *before*, *after*) an event occurs in somewhat challenging passages
	REL 202. Identify simple cause-effect relationships within a single sentence in a passage
16–19	REL 301. Identify clear comparative relationships between main characters in somewhat challenging literary narratives
	REL 302. Identify simple cause-effect relationships within a single paragraph in somewhat challenging literary narratives
20–23	REL 401. Order simple sequences of events in somewhat challenging literary narratives
	REL 402. Identify clear comparative relationships in somewhat challenging passages
	REL 403. Identify clear cause-effect relationships in somewhat challenging passages
24–27	REL 501. Order sequences of events in somewhat challenging passages
	REL 502. Understand implied or subtly stated comparative relationships in somewhat challenging passages
	REL 503. Identify clear comparative relationships in more challenging passages
	REL 504. Understand implied or subtly stated cause-effect relationships in somewhat challenging passages
	REL 505. Identify clear cause-effect relationships in more challenging passages

22

(*continued*)

Taking Additional Practice Tests

Score Range	Key Ideas and Details: Relationships (REL) (*continued*)
28–32	REL 601. Order sequences of events in more challenging passages
	REL 602. Understand implied or subtly stated comparative relationships in more challenging passages
	REL 603. Identify clear comparative relationships in complex passages
	REL 604. Understand implied or subtly stated cause-effect relationships in more challenging passages
	REL 605. Identify clear cause-effect relationships in complex passages
33–36	REL 701. Order sequences of events in complex passages
	REL 702. Understand implied or subtly stated comparative relationships in complex passages
	REL 703. Identify clear comparative relationships in highly complex passages
	REL 704. Understand implied or subtly stated cause-effect relationships in complex passages
	REL 705. Identify clear cause-effect relationships in highly complex passages

Score Range	Craft and Structure: Word Meanings and Word Choice (WME)
13–15	WME 201. Understand the implication of a familiar word or phrase and of simple descriptive language
16–19	WME 301. Analyze how the choice of a specific word or phrase shapes meaning or tone in somewhat challenging passages when the effect is simple
	WME 302. Interpret basic figurative language as it is used in a passage
20–23	WME 401. Analyze how the choice of a specific word or phrase shapes meaning or tone in somewhat challenging passages
	WME 402. Interpret most words and phrases as they are used in somewhat challenging passages, including determining technical, connotative, and figurative meanings

22

Score Range	Craft and Structure: Word Meanings and Word Choice (WME) (continued)
24–27	WME 501. Analyze how the choice of a specific word or phrase shapes meaning or tone in somewhat challenging passages when the effect is subtle
	WME 502. Analyze how the choice of a specific word or phrase shapes meaning or tone in more challenging passages
	WME 503. Interpret virtually any word or phrase as it is used in somewhat challenging passages, including determining technical, connotative, and figurative meanings
	WME 504. Interpret most words and phrases as they are used in more challenging passages, including determining technical, connotative, and figurative meanings
28–32	WME 601. Analyze how the choice of a specific word or phrase shapes meaning or tone in complex passages
	WME 602. Interpret virtually any word or phrase as it is used in more challenging passages, including determining technical, connotative, and figurative meanings
	WME 603. Interpret words and phrases in a passage that makes consistent use of figurative, general academic, domain-specific, or otherwise difficult language
33–36	WME 701. Analyze how the choice of a specific word or phrase shapes meaning or tone in passages when the effect is subtle or complex
	WME 702. Interpret words and phrases as they are used in complex passages, including determining technical, connotative, and figurative meanings
	WME 703. Interpret words and phrases in a passage that makes extensive use of figurative, general academic, domain-specific, or otherwise difficult language

Score Range	Craft and Structure: Text Structure (TST)
13–15	TST 201. Analyze how one or more sentences in passages relate to the whole passage when the function is stated or clearly indicated
16–19	TST 301. Analyze how one or more sentences in somewhat challenging passages relate to the whole passage when the function is simple
	TST 302. Identify a clear function of straightforward paragraphs in somewhat challenging literary narratives

(continued)

Taking Additional Practice Tests

Score Range	Craft and Structure: Text Structure (TST) (continued)
20–23	TST 401. Analyze how one or more sentences in somewhat challenging passages relate to the whole passage TST 402. Infer the function of straightforward paragraphs in somewhat challenging literary narratives TST 403. Identify a clear function of paragraphs in somewhat challenging passages TST 404. Analyze the overall structure of somewhat challenging passages
24–27	TST 501. Analyze how one or more sentences in somewhat challenging passages relate to the whole passage when the function is subtle TST 502. Analyze how one or more sentences in more challenging passages relate to the whole passage TST 503. Infer the function of paragraphs in somewhat challenging passages TST 504. Identify a clear function of paragraphs in more challenging passages TST 505. Analyze the overall structure of more challenging passages
28–32	TST 601. Analyze how one or more sentences in complex passages relate to the whole passage TST 602. Infer the function of paragraphs in more challenging passages TST 603. Analyze the overall structure of complex passages
33–36	TST 701. Analyze how one or more sentences in passages relate to the whole passage when the function is subtle or complex TST 702. Identify or infer the function of paragraphs in complex passages TST 703. Analyze the overall structure of highly complex passages

Score Range	Craft and Structure: Purpose and Point of View (PPV)
13–15	PPV 201. Recognize a clear intent of an author or narrator in somewhat challenging literary narratives
16–19	PPV 301. Recognize a clear intent of an author or narrator in somewhat challenging passages
20–23	PPV 401. Identify a clear purpose of somewhat challenging passages and how that purpose shapes content and style PPV 402. Understand point of view in somewhat challenging passages

Score Range	Craft and Structure: Purpose and Point of View (PPV) (*continued*)
24–27	PPV 501. Infer a purpose in somewhat challenging passages and how that purpose shapes content and style
	PPV 502. Identify a clear purpose of more challenging passages and how that purpose shapes content and style
	PPV 503. Understand point of view in more challenging passages
28–32	PPV 601. Infer a purpose in more challenging passages and how that purpose shapes content and style
	PPV 602. Understand point of view in complex passages
33–36	PPV 701. Identify or infer a purpose in complex passages and how that purpose shapes content and style
	PPV 702. Understand point of view in highly complex passages

Score Range	Integration of Knowledge and Ideas: Arguments (ARG)
13–15	ARG 201. Analyze how one or more sentences in passages offer reasons for or support a claim when the relationship is clearly indicated
16–19	ARG 301. Analyze how one or more sentences in somewhat challenging passages offer reasons for or support a claim when the relationship is simple
20–23	ARG 401. Analyze how one or more sentences in somewhat challenging passages offer reasons for or support a claim
	ARG 402. Identify a clear central claim in somewhat challenging passages
24–27	ARG 501. Analyze how one or more sentences in more challenging passages offer reasons for or support a claim
	ARG 502. Infer a central claim in somewhat challenging passages
	ARG 503. Identify a clear central claim in more challenging passages
28–32	ARG 601. Analyze how one or more sentences in complex passages offer reasons for or support a claim
	ARG 602. Infer a central claim in more challenging passages
33–36	ARG 701. Analyze how one or more sentences in passages offer reasons for or support a claim when the relationship is subtle or complex
	ARG 702. Identify or infer a central claim in complex passages
	ARG 703. Identify a clear central claim in highly complex passages

22

Taking Additional Practice Tests

Score Range	Integration of Knowledge and Ideas: Multiple Texts (SYN)
13–15	SYN 201. Make simple comparisons between two passages
16–19	SYN 301. Make straightforward comparisons between two passages
20–23	SYN 401. Draw logical conclusions using information from two literary narratives
24–27	SYN 501. Draw logical conclusions using information from two informational texts
28–32	SYN 601. Draw logical conclusions using information from multiple portions of two literary narratives
33–36	SYN 701. Draw logical conclusions using information from multiple portions of two informational texts

Text Complexity Rubric—Reading

This rubric describes reading passages for ACT® Aspire® Grade 8, ACT® Aspire® Early High School, and the ACT.

Literary Narratives: Stories and Literary Nonfiction

	Somewhat Challenging Literary Narratives	More Challenging Literary Narratives	Complex Literary Narratives	Highly Complex Literary Narratives
Purpose/Levels of Meaning	• Have a largely straightforward purpose (chiefly literary nonfiction) • Contain literal and inferential levels of meaning (chiefly stories)	• Have a largely straightforward to somewhat complex purpose (chiefly literary nonfiction) • Contain literal, inferential, and interpretive levels of meaning (chiefly stories)	• Have a somewhat complex to complex purpose; apparent purpose may differ from real purpose (chiefly literary nonfiction) • Contain literal, inferential, and interpretive levels of meaning (chiefly stories)	• Have a complex purpose; apparent purpose may differ from real purpose (chiefly literary nonfiction) • Contain literal, inferential, and interpretive levels of meaning (chiefly stories)

	Somewhat Challenging Literary Narratives	More Challenging Literary Narratives	Complex Literary Narratives	Highly Complex Literary Narratives
Structure	• Use a mostly straightforward structure and a wide range of transitions (chiefly literary nonfiction) • Offer insights into people, situations, and events (e.g., motives) • May contain subplots, flashbacks, and flash-forwards (chiefly stories) • Explore largely straightforward conflicts that may be internal or external (chiefly stories) • May have multiple narrators, with switches clearly signaled; main characters exhibit growth and change (chiefly stories)	• Use a somewhat complex structure and a full range of transitions (chiefly literary nonfiction) • Offer deep insights into people, situations, and events (e.g., motives in conflict) • May contain numerous subplots, flashbacks, and flash-forwards as well as parallel and nonlinear plots; may lack clear resolution (chiefly stories) • Explore subtle conflicts that may be internal or external (chiefly stories) • May have multiple narrators; main characters are well rounded (chiefly stories)	• Use a complex structure (chiefly literary nonfiction) • Offer sophisticated and profound insights into people, situations, and events (e.g., philosophical commentary) • May contain numerous subplots, flashbacks, and flash-forwards as well as parallel and nonlinear plots; may lack clear resolution (chiefly stories) • Explore complex conflicts that are largely internal and lack an obvious or easy resolution (e.g., moral dilemmas) (chiefly stories) • May have multiple and/or unreliable narrator(s); main characters are well rounded (chiefly stories)	• Use a highly complex structure (chiefly literary nonfiction) • Offer sophisticated and profound insights into people, situations, and events (e.g., philosophical commentary) • Contain plots that are intricate, nonlinear, and/or difficult to discern; may lack resolution or may not be plot driven (chiefly stories) • Explore complex conflicts that are largely internal and lack an obvious or easy resolution (e.g., moral dilemmas) (chiefly stories) • May have multiple and/or unreliable narrator(s); main characters are well rounded (chiefly stories)

(continued)

Taking Additional Practice Tests

(continued)

	Somewhat Challenging Literary Narratives	More Challenging Literary Narratives	Complex Literary Narratives	Highly Complex Literary Narratives
Language	• Use some uncommon words and phrases (e.g., general academic [tier 2] words, archaic words, dialect) • Use varied sentence structures significantly more or less formal than in everyday language • Use some somewhat challenging nonliteral and figurative language and literary devices (e.g., symbols, irony) • Observe language conventions (e.g., standard paragraph breaks) (chiefly stories)	• Use some uncommon words and phrases (e.g., general academic [tier 2] words, archaic words, dialect) • Use varied, often complex, and formal sentence structures, with texts from earlier time periods containing structures uncommon in more modern reading • Consistently use somewhat challenging nonliteral and figurative language and literary devices (e.g., symbols, irony) • Largely observe language conventions, with some unconventional elements possible (e.g., dialogue marked with dashes) (chiefly stories)	• Consistently use uncommon words and phrases (e.g., general academic [tier 2] words, archaic words, dialect) • Use varied, often complex, and formal sentence structures, with texts from earlier time periods containing structures uncommon in more modern reading • Consistently use challenging nonliteral and figurative language and literary devices (e.g., extended metaphors, satire, parody) • May use unconventional language structures (e.g., stream-of-consciousness)	• Extensively use uncommon words and phrases (e.g., general academic [tier 2] words, archaic words, dialect) • Use varied, often complex, and formal sentence structures, with texts from earlier time periods containing structures uncommon in more modern reading • Extensively use challenging nonliteral and figurative language and literary devices (e.g., extended metaphors, satire, parody) • Use unconventional language structures (e.g., stream-of-consciousness)

	Somewhat Challenging Literary Narratives	More Challenging Literary Narratives	Complex Literary Narratives	Highly Complex Literary Narratives
Abstractness (chiefly literary nonfiction)	• Depict some abstract ideas and concepts that may be important to understanding the text	• Depict several abstract ideas and concepts that are essential to understanding the text	• Depict numerous abstract ideas and concepts that are essential to understanding the text	• Depict numerous abstract ideas and concepts that are essential to understanding the text
Density (chiefly literary nonfiction)	• Have moderate information/ concept density	• Have moderately high information/ concept density	• Have high information/ concept density	• Have very high information/ concept density
Knowledge Demands: Textual Analysis, Life Experiences, Cultural and Literary Knowledge	• Assume readers can read on literal and inferential levels • Assume readers can handle somewhat challenging themes and subject matter with some maturity and objectivity • Assume readers can relate to experiences outside of their own • Call on cultural or literary knowledge to some extent	• Assume readers can read on literal, inferential, and interpretive levels • Assume readers can handle somewhat challenging themes and subject matter with some maturity and objectivity • Assume readers can relate to experiences distinctly different from their own	• Assume readers can read on literal, inferential, and interpretive levels • Assume readers can handle challenging themes and subject matter with maturity and objectivity • Assume readers can relate to experiences distinctly different from their own • Call on cultural or literary knowledge to some extent	• Assume readers can read on literal, inferential, and interpretive levels • Assume readers can handle complex themes and subject matter with maturity and objectivity • Assume readers can relate to experiences distinctly different from their own • Require cultural or literary knowledge for full comprehension

(continued)

Taking Additional Practice Tests

(continued)

	Somewhat Challenging Literary Narratives	More Challenging Literary Narratives	Complex Literary Narratives	Highly Complex Literary Narratives
	• Have low intertextuality (i.e., make no/few or unimportant connections to other texts); drawing connections between texts at the level of theme may enhance understanding and appreciation	• Call on cultural or literary knowledge to some extent • Have moderate intertextuality (i.e., make some important connections to other texts); drawing connections between texts may enhance understanding and appreciation	• Have moderate intertextuality (i.e., make some important connections to other texts); drawing connections between texts may enhance understanding and appreciation	• Have high intertextuality (i.e., make many important connections to other texts); drawing connections between texts is essential for full understanding and appreciation

Informational Texts: Social Science, Humanities, and Natural Science

	Somewhat Challenging Informational Texts	More Challenging Informational Texts	Complex Informational Texts	Highly Complex Informational Texts
Purpose	• Have a largely straightforward purpose	• Have a largely straightforward to somewhat complex purpose	• Have a somewhat complex to complex purpose; apparent purpose may differ from real purpose	• Have a complex purpose; apparent purpose may differ from real purpose

	Somewhat Challenging Informational Texts	More Challenging Informational Texts	Complex Informational Texts	Highly Complex Informational Texts
Structure	• Use a mostly straightforward structure and a wide range of transitions • Exhibit norms and conventions of a general discipline (e.g., natural science)	• Use a somewhat complex structure and a full range of transitions • Exhibit norms and conventions of a general discipline (e.g., natural science	• Use a complex structure • Exhibit norms and conventions of a general discipline (e.g., natural science)	• Use a highly complex and possibly highly formalized structure (e.g., journal article) • Exhibit norms and conventions of a specific discipline (e.g., biology)
Language	• Use some general academic [tier 2] and domain-specific [tier 3] words and phrases • Use varied and some long and complicated sentence structures	• Consistently use general academic [tier 2] and domain-specific [tier 3] words and phrases • Use varied and often complex sentence structures, with consistent use of long and complicated structures	• Consistently use general academic [tier 2] and domain-specific [tier 3] words and phrases • Use varied and often complex sentence structures, with consistent use of long and complicated structures	• Extensively use general academic [tier 2] and domain-specific [tier 3] words and phrases • Use varied and often complex sentence structures, with consistent use of long and complicated structures
Abstractness	• Depict some abstract ideas and concepts that may be important to understanding the text	• Depict several abstract ideas and concepts that are essential to understanding the text	• Depict numerous abstract ideas and concepts that are essential to understanding the text	• Depict numerous abstract ideas and concepts that are essential to understanding the text
Density	• Have moderate information/concept density	• Have moderately high information/concept density	• Have high information/concept density	• Have very high information/concept density

(continued)

(continued)

	Somewhat Challenging Informational Texts	More Challenging Informational Texts	Complex Informational Texts	Highly Complex Informational Texts
Knowledge Demands: Textual Analysis, Life Experiences, Content and Discipline Knowledge	• Assume readers can read on literal and inferential levels • Assume readers can handle somewhat challenging subject matter, including perspectives, values, and ideas unlike their own, with some maturity and objectivity • Assume readers have everyday knowledge and some broad content knowledge, with texts at the high end of the range assuming some content knowledge • Have low intertextuality (i.e., make no/few or unimportant connections to other texts); drawing connections between texts at the level of general concept may enhance understanding	• Assume readers can read on literal, inferential, and evaluative levels • Assume readers can handle somewhat challenging subject matter, including perspectives, values, and ideas unlike their own, with some maturity and objectivity • Assume readers have some content knowledge, with texts at the high end of the range assuming some discipline-specific content knowledge • Have moderate intertextuality (i.e., make some important connections to other texts); drawing connections between texts may enhance understanding	• Assume readers can read on literal, inferential, and evaluative levels • Assume readers can handle challenging subject matter, including perspectives, values, and ideas in opposition to their own, with maturity and objectivity • Assume readers have some discipline-specific content knowledge • Have moderate intertextuality (i.e., make some important connections to other texts); drawing connections between texts may enhance understanding	• Assume readers can read on literal, inferential, and evaluative levels • Assume readers can handle complex subject matter, including perspectives, values, and ideas in opposition to their own, with maturity and objectivity • Assume readers have extensive discipline-specific content knowledge, often in specialized subjects or areas • Have high intertextuality (i.e., make many important connections to other texts); drawing connections between texts is essential for full understanding

ACT College and Career Readiness Standards—Science

These standards describe what students who score in specific score ranges on the science test are likely to know and be able to do.

- Students who score in the 1–12 range are most likely beginning to develop the knowledge and skills assessed in the other ranges.

- The ACT College Readiness Benchmark for science is 23. Students who achieve this score on the ACT science test have a 50% likelihood of achieving a B or better in a first-year biology course at a typical college. The knowledge and skills highly likely to be demonstrated by students who meet the benchmark are shaded.

Score Range	Interpretation of Data (IOD)
13–15	IOD 201. Select one piece of data from a simple data presentation (e.g., a simple food web diagram)
	IOD 202. Identify basic features of a table, graph, or diagram (e.g., units of measurement)
	IOD 203. Find basic information in text that describes a simple data presentation
16–19	IOD 301. Select two or more pieces of data from a simple data presentation
	IOD 302. Understand basic scientific terminology
	IOD 303. Find basic information in text that describes a complex data presentation
	IOD 304. Determine how the values of variables change as the value of another variable changes in a simple data presentation
20–23	IOD 401. Select data from a complex data presentation (e.g., a phase diagram)
	IOD 402. Compare or combine data from a simple data presentation (e.g., order or sum data from a table)
	IOD 403. Translate information into a table, graph, or diagram
	IOD 404. Perform a simple interpolation or simple extrapolation using data in a table or graph
24–27	IOD 501. Compare or combine data from two or more simple data presentations (e.g., categorize data from a table using a scale from another table)
	IOD 502. Compare or combine data from a complex data presentation
	IOD 503. Determine how the values of variables change as the value of another variable changes in a complex data presentation
	IOD 504. Determine and/or use a simple (e.g., linear) mathematical relationship that exists between data
	IOD 505. Analyze presented information when given new, simple information

23

(*continued*)

Taking Additional Practice Tests

Score Range	Interpretation of Data (IOD) (*continued*)
28–32	IOD 601. Compare or combine data from a simple data presentation with data from a complex data presentation
	IOD 602. Determine and/or use a complex (e.g., nonlinear) mathematical relationship that exists between data
	IOD 603. Perform a complex interpolation or complex extrapolation using data in a table or graph
33–36	IOD 701. Compare or combine data from two or more complex data presentations
	IOD 702. Analyze presented information when given new, complex information

Score Range	Scientific Investigation (SIN)
13–15	SIN 201. Find basic information in text that describes a simple experiment
	SIN 202. Understand the tools and functions of tools used in a simple experiment
16–19	SIN 301. Understand the methods used in a simple experiment
	SIN 302. Understand the tools and functions of tools used in a complex experiment
	SIN 303. Find basic information in text that describes a complex experiment
20–23	SIN 401. Understand a simple experimental design
	SIN 402. Understand the methods used in a complex experiment
	SIN 403. Identify a control in an experiment
	SIN 404. Identify similarities and differences between experiments
	SIN 405. Determine which experiments used a given tool, method, or aspect of design
24–27	SIN 501. Understand a complex experimental design
	SIN 502. Predict the results of an additional trial or measurement in an experiment
	SIN 503. Determine the experimental conditions that would produce specified results
28–32	SIN 601. Determine the hypothesis for an experiment
	SIN 602. Determine an alternate method for testing a hypothesis
33–36	SIN 701. Understand precision and accuracy issues
	SIN 702. Predict the effects of modifying the design or methods of an experiment
	SIN 703. Determine which additional trial or experiment could be performed to enhance or evaluate experimental results

23

Score Range	Evaluation of Models, Inferences, and Experimental Results (EMI)
13–15	**EMI 201.** Find basic information in a model (conceptual)
16–19	**EMI 301.** Identify implications in a model
	EMI 302. Determine which models present certain basic information
20–23	**EMI 401.** Determine which simple hypothesis, prediction, or conclusion is, or is not, consistent with a data presentation, model, or piece of information in text
	EMI 402. Identify key assumptions in a model
	EMI 403. Determine which models imply certain information
	EMI 404. Identify similarities and differences between models
24–27	**EMI 501.** Determine which simple hypothesis, prediction, or conclusion is, or is not, consistent with two or more data presentations, models, and/or pieces of information in text
	EMI 502. Determine whether presented information, or new information, supports or contradicts a simple hypothesis or conclusion, and why
	EMI 503. Identify the strengths and weaknesses of models
	EMI 504. Determine which models are supported or weakened by new information
	EMI 505. Determine which experimental results or models support or contradict a hypothesis, prediction, or conclusion
28–32	**EMI 601.** Determine which complex hypothesis, prediction, or conclusion is, or is not, consistent with a data presentation, model, or piece of information in text
	EMI 602. Determine whether presented information, or new information, supports or weakens a model, and why
	EMI 603. Use new information to make a prediction based on a model
33–36	**EMI 701.** Determine which complex hypothesis, prediction, or conclusion is, or is not, consistent with two or more data presentations, models, and/or pieces of information in text
	EMI 702. Determine whether presented information, or new information, supports or contradicts a complex hypothesis or conclusion, and why

23

Taking Additional Practice Tests

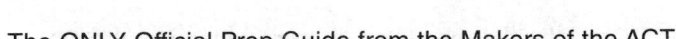

ACT College and Career Readiness Standards for science are measured in rich and authentic contexts based on science content that students encounter in science courses. This content includes the following:

Life Science/Biology

- Animal behavior
- Animal development and growth
- Body systems
- Cell structure and processes
- Ecology

- Evolution
- Genetics
- Homeostasis
- Life cycles
- Molecular basis of heredity

- Origin of life
- Photosynthesis
- Plant development, growth, structure
- Populations
- Taxonomy

Physical Science/Chemistry, Physics

- Atomic structure
- Chemical bonding, equations, nomenclature, reactions
- Electrical circuits
- Elements, compounds, mixtures
- Force and motions

- Gravitation
- Heat and work
- Kinetic and potential energy
- Magnetism
- Momentum

- The periodic table
- Properties of solutions
- Sound and light
- States, classes, and properties of matter
- Waves

Earth and Space Science

- Earthquakes and volcanoes
- Earth's atmosphere
- Earth's resources
- Fossils and geological time
- Geochemical cycles

- Groundwater
- Lakes, rivers, oceans
- Mass movements
- Plate tectonics
- Rocks, minerals

- Solar system
- Stars, galaxies, and the universe
- Water cycle
- Weather and climate
- Weathering and erosion

ACT College & Career Readiness Standards
▶ WRITING

These Standards describe what students who score in specific score ranges on the writing section of the ACT® college readiness assessment are likely to know and be able to do.

SCORE RANGE	Ideas and Analysis (I&A)
3–4	**I&A 201.** Understanding the task and writing with purpose A score in this range indicates that the writer is able to: — Generate a thesis that is unclear or not entirely related to the given issue — Respond weakly to other perspectives on the issue **I&A 202.** Analyzing critical elements of an issue and differing perspectives on it A score in this range indicates that the writer is able to: — Provide analysis that is incomplete or largely irrelevant
5–6	**I&A 301.** Understanding the task and writing with purpose A score in this range indicates that the writer is able to: — Generate a somewhat clear thesis that establishes a perspective on a contemporary issue — Respond to other perspectives on the issue **I&A 302.** Analyzing critical elements of an issue and differing perspectives on it A score in this range indicates that the writer is able to: — Establish a limited or tangential context for analysis — Provide analysis that is simplistic or somewhat unclear
7–8	**I&A 401.** Understanding the task and writing with purpose A score in this range indicates that the writer is able to: — Generate a clear thesis that establishes a perspective on a contemporary issue — Engage with other perspectives on the issue **I&A 402.** Analyzing critical elements of an issue and differing perspectives on it A score in this range indicates that the writer is able to: — Establish and employ a relevant context for analysis — Recognize implications, complexities and tensions, and/or underlying values and assumptions
9–10	**I&A 501.** Understanding the task and writing with purpose A score in this range indicates that the writer is able to: — Generate a precise thesis that establishes a perspective on a contemporary issue — Engage productively with other perspectives on the issue **I&A 502.** Analyzing critical elements of an issue and differing perspectives on it A score in this range indicates that the writer is able to: — Establish and employ a thoughtful context for analysis — Address implications, complexities and tensions, and/or underlying values and assumptions
11–12	**I&A 601.** Understanding the task and writing with purpose A score in this range indicates that the writer is able to: — Generate a nuanced, precise thesis that establishes a perspective on a contemporary issue — Engage critically with other perspectives on the issue **I&A 602.** Analyzing critical elements of an issue and differing perspectives on it A score in this range indicates that the writer is able to: — Establish and employ an insightful context for analysis — Examine implications, complexities and tensions, and/or underlying values and assumptions

Scores below 3 do not permit useful generalizations about students' writing abilities.

Taking Additional Practice Tests

ACT College & Career Readiness Standards

▸ WRITING

SCORE RANGE	Development and Support (D&S)
3–4	**D&S 201.** Building and strengthening the argument A score in this range indicates that the writer is able to: — Arrive at a weak understanding of the issue and differing perspectives on it through inadequate reasoning and examples — Offer a rationale that fails to clarify the argument — Provide elaboration of ideas and analysis that is illogical, disjointed, or circular
5–6	**D&S 301.** Building and strengthening the argument A score in this range indicates that the writer is able to: — Make use of mostly relevant reasoning and examples to support the thesis and arrive at a general or simplistic understanding of the issue — Offer a rationale that largely clarifies the argument — Provide elaboration of ideas and analysis that is somewhat repetitive or imprecise
7–8	**D&S 401.** Building and strengthening the argument A score in this range indicates that the writer is able to: — Make use of clear reasoning and examples to arrive at an understanding of the issue and differing perspectives on it — Adequately convey reasons why the argument is worth considering — Extend ideas and analysis by considering factors that complicate the writer's own perspective — Anticipate objections by qualifying the argument
9–10	**D&S 501.** Building and strengthening the argument A score in this range indicates that the writer is able to: — Make purposeful use of reasoning and examples to support the thesis and arrive at a deeper understanding of the issue — Capably convey reasons why the argument is worth considering — Enrich ideas and analysis by considering factors that complicate the writer's own perspective — Anticipate objections by qualifying the argument
11–12	**D&S 601.** Building and strengthening the argument A score in this range indicates that the writer is able to: — Make skillful use of reasoning and examples to broaden the context for analysis, support the thesis, and arrive at deeper insight into the issue — Effectively convey reasons why the argument is worth considering — Enrich and strengthen ideas and analysis by considering factors that complicate the writer's own perspective — Anticipate objections by qualifying the argument

Scores below 3 do not permit useful generalizations about students' writing abilities.

The ONLY Official Prep Guide from the Makers of the ACT

ACT College & Career Readiness Standards
▸ WRITING

SCORE RANGE	Organization (ORG)
3–4	**ORG 201. Grouping and connecting ideas** A score in this range indicates that the writer is able to: — Group ideas with little consistency or clarity — Use misleading and poorly formed transitions **ORG 202. Employing an organizational strategy** A score in this range indicates that the writer is able to: — Provide a minimal organizational structure in which some ideas are grouped locally
5–6	**ORG 301. Grouping and connecting ideas** A score in this range indicates that the writer is able to: — Group most ideas logically — Use transitions between and within paragraphs to clarify some relationships among ideas **ORG 302. Employing an organizational strategy** A score in this range indicates that the writer is able to: — Provide a basic organizational structure are grouped locally
7–8	**ORG 401. Grouping and connecting ideas** A score in this range indicates that the writer is able to: — Group and sequence ideas logically — Use transitions between and within paragraphs to clarify relationships among ideas **ORG 402. Employing an organizational strategy** A score in this range indicates that the writer is able to: — Make use of an emergent controlling idea or purpose to shape the argument
9–10	**ORG 501. Grouping and connecting ideas** A score in this range indicates that the writer is able to: — Group and sequence ideas logically to increase the effectiveness of the argument — Use transitions between and within paragraphs to consistently clarify relationships among ideas **ORG 502. Employing an organizational strategy** A score in this range indicates that the writer is able to: — Make use of a controlling idea or purpose to unify the argument
11–12	**ORG 601. Grouping and connecting ideas** A score in this range indicates that the writer is able to: — Group and sequence ideas logically, creating a progression that increases the effectiveness of the argument — Use transitions between and within paragraphs to strengthen the relationships among ideas **ORG 602. Employing an organizational strategy** A score in this range indicates that the writer is able to: — Make use of a controlling idea or purpose to unify and focus the argument

Scores below 3 do not permit useful generalizations about students' writing abilities.

Taking Additional Practice Tests

3

The ONLY Official Prep Guide from the Makers of the ACT

ACT College & Career Readiness Standards
▸ WRITING

SCORE RANGE	Language Use and Conventions (L&C)
3–4	**L&C 201. Using language to enhance meaning** A score in this range indicates that the writer is able to: — Make word choices that are rudimentary and frequently imprecise — Make stylistic choices, including voice, tone, and diction, that are inconsistent and are not always appropriate for the given writing purpose and topic **L&C 202. Applying the conventions of standard written English** A score in this range indicates that the writer is able to: — Compose sentences that sometimes have clear structures — Produce writing that has distracting errors in grammar, usage, and mechanics and only sometimes conveys meaning clearly
5–6	**L&C 301. Using language to enhance meaning** A score in this range indicates that the writer is able to: — Make word choices that are general and occasionally imprecise — Make stylistic choices, including voice, tone, and diction, that are not always appropriate for the given writing purpose and topic **L&C 302. Applying the conventions of standard written English** A score in this range indicates that the writer is able to: — Compose sentences that usually have clear structures but show little variety — Produce writing that has distracting errors in grammar, usage, and mechanics but, in most instances, conveys meaning clearly
7–8	**L&C 401. Using language to enhance meaning** A score in this range indicates that the writer is able to: — Make adequate word choices that convey the argument with clarity — Make stylistic choices, including voice, tone, and diction, that are appropriate for the given writing purpose and topic **L&C 402. Applying the conventions of standard written English** A score in this range indicates that the writer is able to: — Compose sentences with clear and occasionally varied structures — Produce writing that has errors in grammar, usage, and mechanics but conveys meaning clearly
9–10	**L&C 501. Using language to enhance meaning** A score in this range indicates that the writer is able to: — Make precise word choices that work in service of the argument — Make stylistic choices, including voice, tone, and diction, that are effective for the given writing purpose and topic **L&C 502. Applying the conventions of standard written English** A score in this range indicates that the writer is able to: — Compose sentences with clear and often varied structures — Produce writing that has only minor errors in grammar, usage, and mechanics
11–12	**L&C 601. Using language to enhance meaning** A score in this range indicates that the writer is able to: — Make skillful and precise word choices that enhance the argument — Make stylistic choices, including voice, tone, and diction, that are strategic and effective for the given writing purpose and topic **L&C 602. Applying the conventions of standard written English** A score in this range indicates that the writer is able to: — Compose sentences with clear and consistently varied structures — Produce writing that is free of all but a few minor errors in grammar, usage, and mechanics

> Scores below 3 do not permit useful generalizations about students' writing abilities.

4

5

Part Five:
Moving Forward to Test Day

In This Part

Even when you are fully prepared, mentally and physically, to take the ACT, you may need additional guidance to handle the logistics of arriving at the test center on time and with the necessary items. This part helps you avoid any unpleasant surprises on test day that might cause confusion and anxiety, which could negatively affect your performance. Specifically, in this part, you learn how to do the following:

Register for a convenient test date and test center in plenty of time to have your scores reported to the colleges and scholarship agencies of your choice by their deadlines.

Map a route and choose a means of travel that ensure you arrive at the test center on time.

Dress for comfort to ensure that you are not too hot or too cold when taking the test.

Pack everything you need for test day, so you are admitted to the testing room and have the items you need to take the test.

Find out what to expect at the test center in terms of check-in procedures, rules, and maintaining your composure and energy.

Obtain additional information you may need, including how to void your test on test day, retake the test, and gather additional information.

13

Chapter 13: Registering, Planning, and Packing for Test Day

When you feel ready to take the actual ACT, the time has come to register, plan, and pack for the upcoming day. Your goal is to avoid any unpleasant surprises on test day, such as getting lost on the way to the test center, showing up without a valid ID, or wearing the wrong clothing and being physically uncomfortable during the entire test. Such surprises distract you from what should be your sole focus on test day—doing your very best on the test.

In this chapter, we help you register for the ACT, avoid the most common pitfalls that test-takers encounter leading up to test day, offer guidance on how to dress and what to pack for test day, explain what you can expect at the test center, and give you a heads up about posttest concerns, such as voiding your test on test day, retaking the test, and reporting your scores.

National Testing Program Versus State and District Testing

ACT makes the test available via national testing centers and through certain school districts or states. Registration for and administration of the test varies accordingly. For example, if your district or state offers the test, you do not need to register for that test. Instead, your district or state registers for the test and chooses a school day on which to administer it. If you want to take the test at a national test center on a Saturday, you will need to register yourself for that test. Check with your counselor to find out whether your school offers the ACT or whether you must register individually to take the ACT at a national testing center.

Registering for the ACT

If your district or state offers the ACT for your grade level test, you can skip ahead to the section "Planning and Packing for Test Day." Your district or state will take the first two registration steps for you:

- Selects a test date (typically a school day)

- Chooses whether students will take the ACT with or without the writing test

Note: If you have a diagnosed disability or are an English language learner, and have documentation of receiving an accommodation or support in school, you *may* be eligible to take the ACT with that accommodation or support. Work with your school counselor or accommodations coordinator to determine if they have submitted the required documentation.

If your school does not offer the ACT, you must register for it through the ACT national testing program. In the following sections, we lead you through the process of choosing a national test date and test option (ACT with or without the writing test) and registering for the test. We also address special circumstances that could affect your registration.

Selecting a National Testing Date and Location

Prior to registering for the ACT through the ACT national testing program, choose the date on which you want to take the test. When choosing a date, consider the following:

- Available test dates and test centers near you

- College and scholarship application deadlines

- Where you stand in your high school coursework

- Whether you may want to take the ACT more than once

Let's look at each of these considerations in turn.

Checking Available Test Dates and Test Centers

The ACT is offered nationally and internationally several times a year. However, it's not offered at every test center on each test date. If you need to take the ACT on a day other than Saturday (for religious reasons), you'll want to be especially attentive in selecting a test date when a test center near you is open on a non-Saturday date.

One of the first things you should find out, then, is where and when the ACT is being offered in your area. A quick and easy way to access available test dates and find test centers is to visit ACT's website at www.actstudent.org. Search for **test dates and deadlines** to find test dates and registration deadlines. You can also look at nearby ACT test centers by searching for **ACT test centers**.

Note: You may *not* receive scores from more than one test taken on a scheduled national or international test date *and* one of the alternate test dates associated with that date. For example, suppose you take the test on Saturday *and* then again on the non-Saturday date associated with that Saturday. We will report only the scores from the first test. The second set of scores will be cancelled without refund.

Considering College and Scholarship Application Deadlines

Colleges and scholarship agencies may require that ACT test scores be submitted sometime during your junior year of high school. Find out what these deadlines are and then make absolutely sure that you take the test early enough to ensure that the colleges and scholarship agencies you're applying to receive your ACT test scores by those deadlines.

Score reports are usually ready about 2 to 8 weeks after the test date. To be on the safe side, consider taking your ACT at least 10 weeks prior to the earliest deadline.

You may not be certain yet which school or program you'll decide on. That's okay. Just be sure you're doing everything, including taking the ACT, early enough to keep all options open.

Gauging Where You Stand in Your High School Coursework and Whether You May Want to Take the ACT More Than Once

Another consideration in deciding when to take the ACT is where you stand in your high school coursework. If you're in a college-prep program and taking a lot of courses in English, mathematics, and science in your sophomore and junior years, taking the ACT in your junior year, while those subjects are still fresh in your memory, is probably best.

Perhaps you'll decide to take the ACT more than once, in hopes of improving your score. In that case, it's better to take the exam early in the spring of your junior year to allow time for a second try. If you find you're studying a significant amount of material covered on the ACT during your senior year, you may plan on retaking the ACT in your senior year, based on the reasonable assumption that your scores will reflect your improved knowledge and skills.

Taking the ACT in your junior year has several advantages:

- You probably will have completed much of the coursework corresponding to the material covered on the ACT.

- You will have your ACT scores and other information in time to help make decisions about your final year of high school coursework. (For example, you may decide to take additional classes in an area in which your test score was lower than you wanted it to be.)

- Colleges will know of your interest and have your scores in time to contact you during the summer before your senior year, when many of them like to send information about admissions, scholarships, advanced placement, and special programs to prospective students.

- You'll have your ACT scores and information from colleges in time to make decisions about visiting campuses or contacting schools.

- You'll have the opportunity to take the ACT again if you feel your scores don't accurately reflect your achievement.

Selecting a Test Option

When you register, you must choose one of two test options—the ACT (which includes the four multiple-choice tests: English, mathematics, reading, and science), or the ACT with the optional writing test (which includes the four multiple-choice tests plus a 40-minute writing test). Taking the writing test does not affect your composite score.

Not all institutions require the ACT writing test. Check directly with the institutions you are considering to find out their requirements, or ask your high school counselor which test option you should take.

Registering

The fastest and easiest way to register to take the ACT through its national testing program is online at www.actstudent.org. When you register on the web, you will know immediately if your preferred test center has space for you, and you can print your admission ticket. Read all the information on your admission ticket carefully to make sure it is correct.

You are guaranteed a seat and test booklet at a test center only if you register by the deadline for a test date. If you miss the late registration deadline, you can try to test as a "standby" examinee. Testing as a standby costs more and does not guarantee you a seat or test booklet. If you decide to take your chance as a standby, be sure to follow the instructions for standby testing on the ACT website. You must bring acceptable identification to be admitted. Standby examinees will be admitted only after all registered students have been seated for their test option.

However you register, you are encouraged to create your free ACT web account. You can use your ACT web account to do several things:

- View your scores and score report on the web at no charge.

- Send your scores to additional colleges.

- Receive email updates from ACT about changes to your registration.

- Make changes to your student profile.

- Print your admission ticket.

Registering under Special Circumstances

See the website or our online registration brochure for instructions if special circumstances apply to you—for example, if your religious beliefs prevent you from taking the exam on Saturday and no test centers in your area offer non-Saturday test dates or if you have a diagnosed disability or are an English language learner and require accommodations or supports.

If you have a diagnosed disability, or are an English language learner, and have documentation of receiving an accommodation or support in school, you *may* be eligible to take the ACT with that accommodation or support. Details about the procedures for applying to test with accommodations and supports are provided on the ACT website.

Planning and Packing for Test Day

At least one week before your scheduled test date, start planning and packing for test day. You need to know where you're going, how you're getting there, how much time the trip will take you, how to dress, and what to pack. In the following sections, we help you plan and pack for test day.

Getting to the Test Center

If your school is administering the ACT on a school day, you simply need to arrive at your school at the start of the school day. Testing will be the first activity of the day.

Under no circumstances will you be admitted to the test after the test booklets have been distributed, so be sure to arrive on time.

If you registered to take the test through the ACT national testing program, you'll be asked to report to the test center by 8:00 a.m. on your test date. Under no circumstances will you be admitted after the test booklets have been distributed, so be sure to arrive on time by 8:00 a.m.

You may need to walk a few blocks to get to the test center or drive several hours, perhaps to an unfamiliar city. Whatever your situation, be certain to allow plenty of time. We recommend that you plan to arrive 15 to 30 minutes early just in case you experience an unexpected delay.

Moving Forward to Test Day

Test centers vary considerably. You may be taking the ACT in your own high school, at a local community college, or in a large building on a nearby university campus. Your surroundings may be quite familiar or they may be new. If they're new, allow yourself a few extra minutes to get acclimated. Then try to forget about your surroundings so that you can concentrate on the test.

To ensure that you arrive on time, map your route to the test center and choose a means of travel—car, train, bus, taxi, bicycle, carpool with a friend . . . whatever works best for you.

One week prior to test day, travel to the testing center using the selected means of travel. By doing a test run on the same day and at the same time (but a week early), you gain a better sense of what traffic will be like, what your parking options will be, whether the buses are running during those times, and so on.

Dressing for Test Day

The night before the test, set out the clothes you want to wear. Dress in layers so that you can adjust to the temperature in your testing room.

Keep in mind that you're going to be sitting in the same place for more than three hours. Wearing something you're especially comfortable in may make you better able to relax and concentrate on the test. For many people, what they're wearing can make a difference in how they feel about themselves. Picking something you like and feel good wearing may boost your confidence.

Packing for Test Day: What to Bring

Bring with you only what you'll need that morning, because other materials will be in your way and may be prohibited in the test room. Be sure to bring these:

- **Your paper admission ticket** (if you are taking the test on a national or international ACT test date). Failure to bring your admission ticket will delay your scores. If your district or state is administering the test, you will not receive (or need) an admission ticket.

- **Acceptable photo identification.** Examples of acceptable identification include current identification issued by your city/state/federal government or school, on which both your name and current photograph appear (for example, driver's license or passport). Without acceptable identification, you will not be allowed to take the test. (See www.actstudent.org for details on what constitutes acceptable and unacceptable identification.)

- Several sharpened **soft-lead No. 2 pencils with good erasers** (no mechanical pencils or ink pens). Test the erasers to make sure they erase cleanly without leaving any residue.

- **A watch *without* an alarm function** to pace yourself. If your watch has an alarm function and the alarm goes off, it will disturb the other students, you will be dismissed, and your answer document will not be scored. Although the test supervisor will announce when 5 minutes remain on each test, not all test rooms have wall clocks for pacing yourself in the meantime.

- **A permitted calculator** if you wish to use one *on the mathematics test only* (for a list of permitted and prohibited calculators, visit www.actstudent.org). You are solely responsible for knowing whether a particular calculator is permitted.

- **A snack and a drink** to consume outside the test room only during the break.

Obtaining Additional Test Details

On certain national test dates, if you test at a national test center, you may request and pay for a copy of the multiple-choice test questions used to determine your scores, a list of your answers, and the answer key. If you take the writing test, you will also receive a copy of the writing prompt, scoring guidelines, and the scores assigned to your essay. You'll also get information about requesting a photocopy of your answer document for an additional fee. These services are not offered for all test dates, so if you're interested in receiving any of these services, you'll need to check the dates on ACT's website (www.actstudent.org) to be sure you're choosing a test date on which the desired service is available.

At the Test Center

Knowing ahead of time what to expect at the test center can alleviate any anxiety you may feel, ensure that you do everything ACT requires in terms of checking in and obeying the rules, and help you maintain your composure. In the following sections, we describe the check-in procedure, present the rules, encourage you to communicate with the testing staff (if necessary), and provide tips on maintaining your composure and energy level.

Checking In

The way **check-in procedures** are handled may vary from location to location. You may find that all students are met at a central location and directed from there to different classrooms. Signs may be posted, telling you that everyone whose last name falls between certain letters should report directly to a particular room. However this part of the check-in is handled at your location, you can anticipate that certain check-in procedures will be performed, including verification of your identity.

In the room you'll be directed to a seat by a member of the testing staff. If you are left-handed, let the testing staff know so that an appropriate desk or table may be made available to you.

Moving Forward to Test Day

Following the Rules

The below text was pulled from the Terms and Conditions: Testing Rules and Policies for the ACT® Test at the time of publishing.

The following behaviors are prohibited. You may be dismissed and/or your test may not be scored, at ACT's sole discretion, if you are found:

- Filling in or altering responses to any multiple-choice questions or continuing to write or alter the essay after time has been called. This means that you cannot make any changes to a test section outside of the designated time for that section, even to fix a stray mark or accidental keystroke.

- Looking back at a test section on which time has already been called.

- Looking ahead in the test.

- Looking at another person's test or answers.

- Giving or receiving assistance by any means.

- Discussing or sharing test questions, answers, or test form identification numbers at any time, including during test administration, during breaks, or after the test.

- Attempting to photograph, copy, or memorize test-related information or remove test materials, including questions or answers, from the test room in any way or at any time.

- Disclosing test questions or answers, in whole or in part, in any way or at any time, including through social media.

- Using a prohibited calculator (www.act.org/calculator-policy.html).

- Using a calculator on any test section other than mathematics.

- Sharing a calculator with another person.

- Wearing a watch during test administration. All watches must be removed and placed face up on the desk.

- Using a watch with recording, internet, communication, or calculator capabilities (e.g., a smart watch or fitness band).

- Accessing any electronic device other than an approved calculator or watch. **All** other electronic devices, including cell phones and other wearable devices, must be powered off and stored out of sight from the time you are admitted to your testing room until you are dismissed at the end of the test.

- Using highlighter pens, colored pens or pencils, notes, dictionaries, or other aids.

- Using scratch paper. **

- Not following instructions or abiding by the rules of the test center.

- Not following the rules of the test administration.

- Exhibiting confrontational, threatening, or unruly behavior.

- Violating any laws. If ACT suspects you have engaged in criminal activities in connection with a test, such activities may be reported to law enforcement agencies.

- Allowing an alarm on a personal item to sound in the test room or creating any other disturbance.

** If you are taking the ACT online, some use of ACT-provided scratch paper or dry erase surface may be permitted; all such use must be in accordance with ACT policies and procedures.

ACT may restrict the items you bring into the test center. All items brought into the test center, such as hats, purses, backpacks, cell phones, calculators, watches, and other electronic devices, may be searched at the discretion of ACT and its testing staff. Searches may include the use of tools, such as handheld metal detectors, that detect prohibited devices. ACT and its testing staff may confiscate and retain for a reasonable period of time any item suspected of having been used, or capable of being used, in violation of these prohibited behaviors. ACT may also provide such items to and permit searches by third parties in connection with an investigation conducted by ACT or others. ACT and its testing staff shall not be responsible for lost, stolen, or damaged items that you bring to a test center. Your test center may also have additional procedures with which you must comply.

Dismissal for Prohibited Behavior

Examinees who are dismissed because of prohibited behavior forfeit their registration for that test date. There are no options for refunds or appeals in situations involving prohibited behavior.

Eating, drinking, and the use of tobacco are not allowed in the test room. You may bring a snack to eat or drink before the test or during the break, but any food or beverage you bring must be put away during testing and must be consumed outside the test room.

Communicating with the Testing Staff

Although you are required to work silently during the test, you may need to communicate with the testing staff under certain circumstances, such as the following:

- **If you have problems with the testing environment, let the testing staff know immediately.** Possible problems include being seated below, over, or next to a heating or cooling vent that is making you too warm or too cold; having a defective chair or desk; poor lighting that makes reading difficult; or excessive noise.

- **If any aspect of the test-taking procedure is not perfectly clear to you, request clarification.** Testing staff will be available throughout the exam. In fact, they'll be moving quietly around the room while you're working. If you have a question about the administration of the test (not about any of the test questions), raise your hand and quietly ask for information.

Moving Forward to Test Day

- **If you need to use the restroom, ask.** Bathroom breaks are permitted during the test or between tests, but you're not allowed to make up the lost time.

- **If you become ill during the test, you may turn in your test materials and leave, if necessary.** Let the testing staff know that you are ill and whether you wish to have your answer document scored. One caution: Once you leave the test center, you won't be allowed to return and continue—so be sure that leaving is what you want to do. You might try closing your eyes or putting your head on the desk for a minute first; then if you feel better, you'll be able to continue.

Maintaining Your Composure and Energy

While you're waiting for the test to begin, you may find yourself getting anxious or jittery. That's perfectly normal. Most of us get nervous in new situations. People handle this nervousness in different ways.

Some people find it helpful to practice **mental and physical relaxation techniques.** If this appeals to you, try alternately flexing and relaxing your muscles, beginning at your toes and moving up through your shoulders, neck, and arms. Meanwhile, imagine yourself in a quiet, peaceful place: at the beach, in the mountains, or just in your favorite lounge chair. Breathe deeply and evenly.

Other people like to **redirect that nervous energy** and turn it to their advantage. For them, concentrating on the task at hand and shutting everything else out of their minds is the most helpful strategy. If this is your style, you may even want to close your eyes and imagine yourself already working on the exam, thinking about how it will feel to move confidently and smoothly through the tests.

If you have the chance, try out the two approaches on some classroom tests and see which one works better for you. The important thing is to keep the ACT in perspective. Try not to let it become larger than life. Remember, it's just one part of a long academic and professional career. If you begin to feel tired during the test, check your posture to make sure you're sitting up straight. Getting enough air in your lungs is difficult when you're slouching. You'll stay more alert and confident if your brain receives a steady supply of oxygen.

You might want to practice those relaxation techniques again, too, because tension contributes to fatigue. As you start a new test, you might find it helpful to stretch your neck and shoulder muscles, rotate your shoulders, stretch back in your chair and take some long, deep breaths.

You can expect a short break (approximately 10 to 15 minutes) after the second test. During this break, it's a good idea to stand up, walk around a little, stretch, and relax. You may wish to get a drink, have a snack, or use the restroom. Keep in mind, though, that you still have work ahead of you that requires concentrated effort. Eat lightly and return to the room quickly. The third test will start promptly, and you'll need to be back at your desk and ready to go on time.

Voiding Your Answer Documents on Test Day

If you have to leave before completing all tests, you must decide whether you want your answer document scored and then inform your supervisor if you do *not* want your answer document scored; otherwise, your answer document will be scored.

Once you break the seal on your multiple-choice test booklet, you cannot request a test date change. If you do not complete all your tests and want to test again, you will have to pay the full fee for your test option again. If you want to take the ACT again, see www.actstudent.org for your options. Once you begin filling out your answer document, you cannot change from one test option to another.

Testing More Than Once

If you think you can improve your scores, you can retake the ACT. ACT may limit the number of times you take the ACT. The current retest limit can be found at www.actstudent.org. Many students take the test twice, once as a junior and again as a senior. Of the students who took the ACT more than once:

- 56% increased their Composite score

- 20% had no change in their Composite score

- 24% decreased their Composite score

You determine which set of scores are sent to colleges or scholarship programs. ACT will release only the scores from the test date (month and year) and test location (e.g., national or state) you designate. This protects you and ensures that you direct the reporting of your scores.

Our mission is helping people achieve education and workplace success. Thank you for allowing ACT to be a part of your journey and good luck on test day.

Moving Forward to Test Day

NOTES

NOTES

NOTES

NOTES

NOTES

NOTES

NOTES